CORPORATE STRATEGY

Ex umbris et imaginibus in veritatem.
From shadows and imagination to the truth.

JOHN HENRY NEWMAN

CORPORATE STRATEGY

Richard Lynch

Associate Senior Lecturer
Middlesex University and the University of East London
Visiting Lecturer at City University, London
Managing Director of Aldersgate Consultancy Limited

FINANCIAL TIMES
PITMAN PUBLISHING

FINANCIAL TIMES

MANAGEMENT

LONDON · SAN FRANCISCO
KUALA LUMPUR · JOHANNESBURG

Financial Times Management delivers the knowledge,
skills and understanding that enable students,
managers and organisations to achieve their ambitions,
whatever their needs, wherever they are.

London Office:
128 Long Acre, London WC2E 9AN
Tel: +44 (0)171 447 2000
Fax: +44 (0)171 240 5771
Website: www.ftmanagement.com

A Division of Financial Times Professional Limited

First published in Great Britain in 1997

ISBN 0 273 60753 7

British Library Cataloguing in Publication Data
A CIP catalogue record for this book can be obtained from the British Library

10 9 8 7 6 5 4 3

Typeset by Pantek Arts, Maidstone, Kent.
Printed in Singapore through Addison Wesley Longman China Limited

The Publishers' policy is to use paper manufactured from sustainable forests.

ABBREVIATED CONTENTS

List of case studies *xiii*

About this book *xv*

Acknowledgements *xviii*

How to use this book *xx*

Plan of the book *xxii*

Part 1
INTRODUCTION *1*

1   Corporate strategy *4*

2   A review of theory and practice *37*

Part 2
ANALYSIS OF THE ENVIRONMENT *83*

3   Analysing the environment *86*

4   Analysing the market *122*

5   Analysing competitors *161*

6   Analysing customers *193*

Part 3
ANALYSIS OF RESOURCES *229*

7   Analysing resources *232*

8   Analysing human resources *270*

9   Analysing financial resources *307*

10   Analysing operations *348*

Part 4
THE PURPOSE OF THE ORGANISATION *385*

11   Background issues *388*

12   Mission and objectives *422*

Part 5
DEVELOPING THE STRATEGY *455*

13   Resource-based strategic options *458*

14   Market-based strategic options *483*

15   Strategy evaluation and selection – 1 *515*

16   Strategy evaluation and selection – 2 *545*

17   Finding the strategic route forward *582*

18   Strategy, structure and style *620*

Part 6
THE IMPLEMENTATION PROCESS *659*

19   Resource allocation, strategic planning and control *662*

20   Organisational structure and people issues *701*

21   Managing strategic change *734*

22   Building a cohesive corporate strategy *775*

Glossary *803*

Name index *813*

Subject index *817*

CONTENTS

List of case studies *xiii*
About this book *xv*
Acknowledgements *xviii*
How to use this book *xx*
Plan of the book *xxii*

Part 1
INTRODUCTION *1*

1 CORPORATE STRATEGY *4*
   Introduction 5
   Minicase 6
1.1 What is corporate strategy? *7*
1.2 Why is corporate strategy important? *15*
1.3 Core areas of corporate strategy *17*
1.4 Process, content and context *20*
1.5 Process: linking the three core areas *22*
1.6 Strategy development in public and
     non-profit organisations *27*
1.7 International dimensions in corporate
     strategy *28*
   Key reading 32
   Summary 33
   Questions 34
   Strategic project 35
   Further reading 35
   References 35

2 A REVIEW OF THEORY AND PRACTICE *37*
   Introduction 38
   Minicase 38
2.1 Historical foundations of strategy *39*
2.2 Prescriptive corporate strategy in practice *44*
2.3 Emergent corporate strategy in practice *52*
2.4 Prescriptive theories of corporate strategy *58*
2.5 Emergent theories of corporate strategy *65*
   Key reading 73
   Summary 75
   Questions 76
   Strategic project 77
   Further reading 78
   References 78

Part 2
ANALYSIS OF THE
ENVIRONMENT *83*

3 ANALYSING THE ENVIRONMENT *86*
   Introduction 87
   Minicase 88
3.1 Exploring the environment *90*
3.2 Consideration of the strategic
     environment *91*
3.3 Analysing the general environment *94*
3.4 Key factors for success in an industry *100*
3.5 Analysing the industry environment *101*
3.6 Analysing the competitive environment *108*
3.7 Analysing the customer and market
     segmentation *114*
3.8 Conclusions *116*
   Key reading 118
   Summary 119
   Questions 119
   Strategic project 120
   Further reading 120
   References 121

4 ANALYSING THE MARKET *122*
   Introduction 123
   Minicase 124
4.1 The rate of growth in the market place *125*
4.2 The role of government *133*
4.3 The opportunities for global market
     development *141*
   Key reading 156
   Summary 157
   Questions 158
   Strategic project 159
   Further reading 159
   References 160

CONTENTS

5   ANALYSING COMPETITORS 161
     Introduction 162
     Minicase 163
5.1 Sustainable competitive advantage 165
5.2 The intensity of competition in an
     industry 169
5.3 Aggressive competitive strategies 174
5.4 Strategic groups within an industry 179
5.5 Individual competitor analysis 181
5.6 Distributor analysis 183
5.7 International competition 186
     Key reading 188
     Summary 189
     Questions 190
     Strategic project 191
     Further reading 191
     References 191

6   ANALYSING CUSTOMERS 193
     Introduction 194
     Minicase 195
6.1 Customers and corporate strategy 196
6.2 Analysing customers 199
6.3 Communicating with customers and
     stakeholders 207
6.4 Strategic pricing and value for money 212
6.5 Customer/competitor matrix 217
6.6 International customer considerations 219
     Key reading 223
     Summary 225
     Questions 225
     Strategic project 226
     Further reading 227
     References 227

Part 3
ANALYSIS OF RESOURCES 229

7   ANALYSING RESOURCES 232
     Introduction 233
     Minicase 234
7.1 Prescriptive and emergent approaches to
     resource issues 235
7.2 Key factors for success in an industry 236
7.3 Resource analysis and adding value 243
7.4 Adding competitive value: the value chain and
     the value system 246
7.5 Cost reduction 252
7.6 Core resources, skills and competences 256

7.7 The SWOT analysis 262
     Key reading 265
     Summary 267
     Questions 267
     Strategic project 268
     Further reading 268
     References 269

8   ANALYSING HUMAN RESOURCES 270
     Introduction 271
     Minicase 272
8.1 Human resource analysis and corporate
     strategy 274
8.2 Human resource audit 276
8.3 Analysis of organisational culture 278
8.4 Analysis of strategic change in
     organisations 288
8.5 Analysis of politics, power and strategic
     change 293
8.6 International cultural perspectives 296
     Key reading 302
     Summary 303
     Questions 304
     Strategic project 304
     Further reading 305
     References 305

9   ANALYSING FINANCIAL RESOURCES 307
     Introduction 308
     Minicase 309
9.1 Analysing the sources of finance 312
9.2 Cost of funds and the optimal
     capital structure 320
9.3 Financial appraisal of strategy 327
9.4 Relationship between financial and corporate
     objectives 333
9.5 International aspects of financial
     resources 336
     Key reading 339
     Summary 340
     Questions 341
     Strategic project 342
     Further reading 342
     Appendix I: Heineken NV – extract from
        consolidated accounts 343
     Appendix II: Checklist of the main financial
        ratios 345
     References 346

10   ANALYSING OPERATIONS RESOURCES *348*
      Introduction 349
      Minicase 350
10.1 Operations and corporate strategy *351*
10.2 Analysis of the operations environment *352*
10.3 The role of operations in adding value and achieving sustainable competitive advantage *360*
10.4 Operations and technology strategy *366*
10.5 Service operations strategy *376*
      Key reading 380
      Summary 381
      Questions 382
      Strategic project 383
      Further reading 383
      References 383

Part 4
THE PURPOSE OF THE
ORGANISATION *385*

11   BACKGROUND ISSUES *388*
      Introduction 389
      Minicase 390
11.1 Developing a strategic vision for the future *392*
11.2 Using technology to develop competitive advantage *394*
11.3 Innovation and corporate strategy *402*
11.4 Quality and corporate strategy *411*
11.5 Competitive advantage and the purpose of the organisation *415*
      Key reading 416
      Summary 417
      Questions 418
      Strategic project 419
      Further reading 419
      References 419

12   MISSION AND OBJECTIVES *422*
      Introduction 423
      Minicase 424
12.1 Developing the mission and objectives *425*
12.2 Stakeholder analysis *427*
12.3 Company culture and mission *431*
12.4 Leadership and mission *432*
12.5 Business ethics in corporate strategy *435*
12.6 Developing the mission statement *438*
12.7 Developing the objectives *442*

12.8 Corporate, functional and business objectives *444*
12.9 Emergent strategy perspectives *446*
12.10 Shareholder and stakeholder power around the world *447*
      Key reading 450
      Summary 450
      Questions 452
      Strategic project 452
      Further reading 452
      References 453

Part 5
DEVELOPING THE STRATEGY *455*

13   RESOURCE-BASED STRATEGIC OPTIONS *458*
      Introduction 459
      Minicase 460
13.1 Prioritising strategic options *461*
13.2 Resource options based on value added and competitive advantage *463*
13.3 Resource-based options and constraints *469*
13.4 Resource options in some special types of organisation *475*
      Summary 479
      Questions 480
      Strategic project 481
      Further reading 481
      References 482

14   MARKET-BASED STRATEGIC OPTIONS *483*
      Introduction 484
      Minicase 485
14.1 Generic strategies *486*
14.2 Market Options Matrix *498*
14.3 Expansion Method Matrix *503*
      Summary 511
      Questions 512
      Strategic project 513
      Further reading 513
      References 513

15   STRATEGY EVALUATION AND SELECTION – 1 *515*
      Introduction 516
      Minicase 518
15.1 Evaluation criteria for strategy options *519*
15.2 Prioritising criteria *525*

15.3 Making an initial selection of the
     best option *529*
15.4 Exploring the initial evaluation in
     more depth *532*
     Summary 541
     Questions 542
     Strategic project 543
     Further reading 543
     References 544

16   STRATEGY EVALUATION AND
     SELECTION – 2 *545*
     Introduction 546
     Minicase 547
16.1 Applying business judgements and
     guidelines *548*
16.2 Empirical evidence of successful strategies *555*
16.3 Feasibility issues *561*
16.4 Business risk *564*
16.5 Stakeholder interests *567*
16.6 International corporate strategy selection *568*
     Summary 577
     Questions 578
     Strategic project 579
     Further reading 579
     Appendix: Calculation for Case study 16.2 580
     References 580

17   FINDING THE STRATEGIC ROUTE
     FORWARD *582*
     Introduction 583
     Minicase 584
17.1 Problems with the prescriptive strategic
     model *585*
17.2 The survival-based strategic route forward *593*
17.3 The uncertainty-based strategic route
     forward *597*
17.4 The negotiation-based strategic route
     forward *601*
17.5 The learning-based strategic route forward *606*
17.6 International considerations *609*
     Summary 615
     Questions 616
     Strategic project 617
     Further reading 617
     References 617

18   STRATEGY, STRUCTURE AND STYLE *620*
     Introduction 621
     Minicase 622

18.1 The basic relationship between strategy and
     structure *624*
18.2 Strategy before structure: Chandler's
     contribution *626*
18.3 Strategy before structure: Williamson's
     contribution *627*
18.4 Implications of designing structures to fit
     strategy *629*
18.5 Criticisms: strategy and structure are
     inter-linked *635*
18.6 The links between strategy and structure and
     the concept of strategic fit *642*
18.7 The choice of management style and
     culture *648*
     Summary 653
     Questions 655
     Strategic project 655
     Further reading 656
     References 656

Part 6
THE IMPLEMENTATION PROCESS *659*

19   RESOURCE ALLOCATION, STRATEGIC
     PLANNING AND CONTROL *662*
     Introduction 663
     Minicase 665
19.1 The implementation process *666*
19.2 Relationship between implementation and
     the strategy development process *670*
19.3 Objectives, task setting and communication
     processes *676*
19.4 Resource allocation *680*
19.5 Strategic planning *684*
19.6 Information, monitoring and control *691*
19.7 Implementation of international strategy *694*
     Key reading 696
     Summary 697
     Questions 698
     Strategic project 699
     Further reading 699
     References 699

20   ORGANISATIONAL STRUCTURE AND
     PEOPLE ISSUES *701*
     Introduction 702
     Minicase 703
20.1 Building the organisation's structure *704*
20.2 Types of organisational structure *707*

20.3 Organisational structures for innovation *714*

20.4 Building the most appropriate organisation structure *717*

20.5 Motivation and staffing in strategy implementation *721*

20.6 Strategy and structure in international organisations *722*

Key reading 729

Summary 730

Questions 731

Strategic project 732

Further reading 732

References 732

21 MANAGING STRATEGIC CHANGE *734*

Introduction 735

Minicase 736

21.1 The basic concept of strategic change *737*

21.2 Analysing the causes of strategic change *741*

21.3 Prescriptive approaches to managing strategic change *744*

21.4 Emergent approaches to managing change *750*

21.5 Developing a strategic change programme *756*

21.6 Culture, style and change *762*

21.7 International issues in managing strategic change *763*

Key reading 768

Summary 770

Questions 772

Strategic project 772

Further reading 772

References 773

22 BUILDING A COHESIVE CORPORATE STRATEGY *775*

Introduction 776

Minicase 777

22.1 Combining the elements of corporate strategy: the 'Seven S Framework' *778*

22.2 Implementation tasks in corporate strategy *786*

22.3 Longer-term strategy issues *790*

22.4 Conclusion: prescriptive and emergent strategies *793*

Key reading 797

Summary 799

Questions 800

Strategic project 800

Further reading 800

References 800

Glossary *803*

Name index *813*

Subject index *817*

LIST OF CASE STUDIES

Chapter 1
Minicase: Corporate strategy at Hewlett-Packard 6
1.1 Corporate profit disaster at IBM 12
1.2 Electrolux plans for growth 29

Chapter 2
Minicase: Attacking a dominant competitor: a joint venture strategy by Nestlé and General Mills 38
2.1 Prescriptive strategic planning at Spillers plc 49
2.2 Prescriptive strategy at Otto Versand 51
2.3 Emergent strategy at Spillers Baking 56
2.4 Dalgety corporate strategy continues 70
2.5 Strategy at Saes Getters 72

Chapter 3
Minicase: Usinor–Sacilor copes with a difficult environment 88
3.1 Steeled for global action 97
3.2 Benefon keeps in touch 117

Chapter 4
Minicase: Stora expands through acquisition and internal growth 124
4.1 Different strategies in the ice cream market 128
4.2 Coping with politics after apartheid 140
4.3 Corporate strategy in the world paper and pulp industry 151

Chapter 5
Minicase: Unilever ice cream defends its European market share 163
5.1 The fragmented European footwear market 171
5.2 Monopoly in Europe's national telecommunications companies 172
5.3 Oligopoly in European grocery retailing 173
5.4 Mars ice cream: distribution strategy problems 185
5.5 Nestlé attacking through acquisition and branding 187

Chapter 6
Minicase: Estimating demand for the Airbus SuperJumbo 195
6.1 Two ways of segmenting the European ice cream market 203
6.2 Different communications approaches at Häagen-Dazs and Boeing 210
6.3 Boeing's customer and competitor strategies for its new airliner, the Boeing 777 220

Chapter 7
Minicase: Utilising resources as Glaxo Wellcome Pharmaceuticals 234
7.1 How three European companies attempt to utilise their resources 240
7.2 Nolan Helmets 264

Chapter 8
Minicase: Barons swept out of fiefdoms at Royal Dutch/Shell 272
8.1 Culture, crisis and power at British Petroleum 286
8.2 Industry groups in Japan, Korea, Hong Kong and Italy 298
8.3 How Rank Xerox shifted its strategy and changed its organisation 300

Chapter 9
Minicase: Global expansion: brewing at Heineken NV 309
9.1 The financing of brewers' growth 316
9.2 Interbrew: the Stella Artois strategy 326
9.3 SCA's financial objectives 332
9.4 Financing growth at MorphoSys 338

Chapter 10
Minicase: Kvaerner's strategy to improve productivity at Govan Shipyard 350
10.1 Toyota: taking out costs and adding value 357
10.2 Cutting costs and increasing customer satisfaction at SKF 364
10.3 ISS cleans up against its European competitors 375

Chapter 11
Minicase: Imperfect vision at Daimler–Benz *390*
11.1   Motorola provides a competitive advantage *394*
11.2   Innovation at Corning *400*
11.3   How Perrier Water lost its sparkle and its independence *409*

Chapter 12
Minicase: The Ford Motor Company objective – to develop a global organisation *424*
12.1   Mission and objectives at Business in the Community *437*
12.2   Pink Elephant Company *449*

Chapter 13
Minicase: Hachette Media rescued, but what was the strategic logic? *460*
13.1   News Corporation builds a global television network – 1 *466*
13.2   Developing resource options at Eastman Kodak *478*

Chapter 14
Minicase: Market opportunities at Muzak Europe *485*
14.1   Two examples of generic strategy options analysis: the European ice cream industry and the global TV industry in the mid-1990s *491*
14.2   News Corporation builds a global television network – 2 *495*
14.3   Strategic choice at British Aerospace *508*

Chapter 15
Minicase: Eurofreeze evaluates its strategy options – 1 *518*
15.1   Eurofreeze evaluates its strategy options – 2 *524*
15.2   European expansion in the central heating market *538*

Chapter 16
Minicase: Swatch to the rescue *547*
16.1   Strategy transformation at Nokia *560*
16.2   Eurofreeze evaluates its strategy options – 3 *572*

Chapter 17
Minicase: How Honda came to dominate two major motorcycle markets *584*
17.1   Developing strategy in European telecommunications service companies *590*
17.2   European mobile telephones and Hutchison Mobilfunk *600*
17.3   Strategic choice at MCI *612*

Chapter 18
Minicase: How Sony moved out across Asia *622*
18.1   How General Motors organised its future *632*
18.2   ABB empowers its managers *650*

Chapter 19
Minicase: Implementing an unpopular strategy at Air France *665*
19.1   Strategic planning at Canon with a co-operative corporate style *673*
19.2   Informal strategic controls at Nestlé *682*
19.3   Financial planning at Hanson plc *694*

Chapter 20
Minicase: Organising for survival at Rolls-Royce Motors *703*
20.1   Organisation structure at Telepizza *713*
20.2   How Ford Motors went global *725*

Chapter 21
Minicase: Strategic change at Hoesch *736*
21.1   Owens-Corning reveals its strategies for change *743*
21.2   United Biscuits pulls out of the USA *748*
21.3   Culture and change at merchant bankers, S G Warburg *766*

Chapter 22
Minicase: The strategy implications of creating Novartis *777*
22.1   Long-term purpose at TomTec Imaging Systems *790*
22.2   A fundamental shift in strategy at Hanson plc *796*

ABOUT THIS BOOK

This book explores the fundamental decisions that need to be made about the future of organisations and how such matters are identified, evaluated and implemented. Its underlying theme is the need to consider not only the *rational approach* to strategic decision making but also the *creative aspects* of such decisions.

Objectives

The purpose of the book is to provide a clear, well structured and interesting treatment of corporate strategy, covering organisations in both the private and public sectors. The text has been specially designed in a modular format to provide both a summary of the main areas and a more detailed treatment for those wishing to explore issues in more depth.

More specifically, the objectives are:

- *To provide a comprehensive coverage of the main study areas in corporate strategy.* For example, the different functional areas of the organisation and important subject areas such as innovation and technology strategy are all explored.

- *To present the practical issues and problems of corporate strategy, so that the compromises and constraints of real organisations are considered.* Each chapter contains case studies which both illustrate the principles and raise subjects for group and class discussion.

- *To assist organisations to add value to their assets through the development of successful corporate strategy.* The search for best practice in the context of the organisation's competences and constraints is a constant theme.

- *To explore both the rational and the creative approaches to the development of corporate strategy.* This text takes the view that the classical approaches to rational corporate strategy development need to be complemented by the more recent ideas based on *crafting* strategy development.

- *To stimulate critical appraisal of the major theories, particularly with regard to their practical application in organisations.* Many of the leading conceptual approaches are first described and then subjected to critical comment. The aim is to encourage the reader to think carefully about such matters.

- *To outline the international implications of the corporate strategic process.* Many of the cases have an international dimension and most chapters have a separate section exploring international issues.

Who should use this book?

The book is intended to provide an introduction to corporate strategy for the many students in this area.

- *Undergraduate students* on Business Studies, modular and other courses will find the subject matter sufficiently structured to provide a route through the subject. No prior knowledge is assumed.

- *MBA students* will find the practical discussions and theoretical background useful. They will also be able to relate these to their own experience.

- *Postgraduate students* on other specialist taught masters' programmes will find that the extensive coverage of theories and, at times, critical comments, together with the background reading, provide a useful input to their thinking.

In addition, the book will also appeal to practising middle and senior managers involved in the development of corporate strategy. The cases and checklists, the structured approach and the comprehensive nature of the text will provide a useful compendium for practical application.

Distinctive features

Two-model structure For some years, there has been disagreement on the approach to be adopted in studying corporate strategy. The *rational* model – strategy options, selection and implementation – has been criticised by those favouring an approach based on the more *creative* aspects of strategy development. Given the lack of agreement between the approaches, *both* models are used throughout this book. They are *both* treated as contributing to the development of optimal corporate strategy: two sides of the same strategic coin.

Modular structure The subject can be treated in depth by taking each chapter in sequence. Alternatively, the book has been designed to be used as a complete course through the study of selected chapters only. The aim has been to make the subject more accessible at first reading to those requiring such an approach. The precise structure is explained in the section on 'How to use this book'.

Clear chapter structure Each chapter follows the same format: learning outcomes; short introduction; short opening case study; two longer case studies linked to the theory points in the text; regular summaries of key strategic principles; a key reading, if relevant; chapter summary; review and discussion questions; recommended further reading; a specific project; detailed notes and references. There is also a glossary of terms at the end of the book as an aid to comprehension.

Focussed case material There are over 80 cases in this book. Each case has been written or adapted to explore strategy issues relevant to its location in the text. Unlike most strategy texts, there are no integrative cases, which are readily available elsewhere. The cases have been especially designed for the larger class sizes and shorter discussion sessions now prevalent in many institutions, so they are shorter and directed at the issues raised in the chapter.

Key strategic principles and chapter summaries To aid learning and comprehension, frequent summaries are given of the main learning points under the heading of *key strategic principles*. In addition, at the end of each chapter there is an integrated summary of the areas explored.

International coverage There is extensive coverage of international strategic issues throughout the book. For ease of teaching and learning, the international theory has generally been placed towards the end of each chapter, but cases and examples are threaded through the text.

Selected further readings Every chapter (except those in Part 5) ends with a selected key reading to present another viewpoint or link strategy to another discipline. In addition, each chapter has a list of recommended further readings of items related to the chapter. The purpose is to allow the student to explore the subject matter further and act as a basis for projects, assignments and dissertations.

Strategic project Each chapter ends with a suggestion for a strategic project. It is based on a theme developed in the chapter and includes a comment on a current strategic issue. The projects are supported by further information available on the Internet.

  A key feature of the text is the selection of extracts from the *Financial Times*. These extracts are the copyright of the *Financial Times*, which has kindly given permission to reproduce them in this book.

Lecturer's Guide This is available to those lecturers adopting this textbook. It includes short commentaries on each chapter and comments on the cases, together with OHP masters.

Internet Further support material is available on the Financial Times Management Website at http://www.ftmanagement.com and this will be updated on a regular basis.

About the author

Richard Lynch studied at UMIST, Leeds University and the London Business School. He then spent over twenty years in business with well-known companies such as J Walter Thompson, Kraft Jacobs Suchard and Dalgety Spillers in positions in marketing and corporate strategy. During the early 1980s, he was a director of two public companies before setting up his own consultancy company specialising in European and international strategy. In the 1990s he has become increasingly involved in Higher Education. He has written four previous books on international marketing and strategy.

ACKNOWLEDGEMENTS

During the writing of this book, the text has benefited enormously from a panel of reviewers set up by Pitman Publishing. They are: Drs Robert Bood, Vakgroep Bedrijfseconomie, Faculty of Economics, Gronigen University; Stuart Bowie, Bristol Business School, University of the West of England; Ms Maria Brouwer, Department of Economics, Amsterdam University; Bruce Lloyd, Head of Strategy, Business School, South Bank University; Professor Bente R Lowendahl, Department of Strategy and Business History, Norwegian School of Management, Sandvika; Richard Morland, Senior Lecturer in Management, Department of Business Management, Brighton University; Dr Martyn Pitt, School of Management, Bath University; Professor Louis Printz, Department of Organisation and Management, Aarhus School of Business, Denmark; Professor Dr Jacob de Smit, Faculteit der Bedrijtskunde, Erasmus University, Rotterdam; and Bill Ramsay, Associate Fellow, Templeton College, Oxford.

In addition, others have also made a significant contribution: Dr Richard Gregson and Richard Cawley, European Business School, London; Professor Colin Haslam, Royal Holloway College, University of London; Dr Carol Vielba and Dr David Edelshain, City University Business School, London; Adrian Haberberg, University of Westminster, London; Dr Kazem Chaharbaghi, University of East London; Laurie Mullins, University of Portsmouth; and Val Lencioni and Dr Dennis Barker, Middlesex University Business School. I am also grateful to Middlesex University for a part-time sabbatical to write sections of the text.

Since becoming involved in higher education, I have lectured at universities in South East England, Singapore and elsewhere. The concepts and cases have benefited from the comments, challenges and contributions of many students over this time period and I am grateful to them all.

To provide real-life examples, I have been able to draw upon material provided by a number of organisations. In particular, I would like to thank Electrolux AB, Stora AB, Ford Motor Company, SKF AB and Business in the Community, London. I am also grateful to the *Financial Times* for permission to adapt a number of articles as case studies for use in the book. Numerous other authors and organisations have also given permission for extracts from their work to be used: these are acknowledged appropriately in the text.

Note that Chapter 16 presents a case study of two companies, Eurofreeze and Refrigor. These are wholly fictional names developed for the purposes of the case study. No link is intended with any real company that might be trading under these or similar names in frozen food or other products. As explained in the case, the data is derived from several real cases and has been disguised to protect confidentiality.

This book would never have happened without the major support and encouragement of the editorial team at Financial Times Management. Their professionalism, experience and knowledge have been invaluable. My thanks go to Catriona King in the very early days and, more recently, to the invaluable Stuart Hay, together with Simon Lake and Mark Allin. Elizabeth Tarrant has worked magnificently on the editorial process, Colin Reed has produced an excellent design and Helen Beltran has notably improved the text. Finally, Penelope Woolf has provided the bedrock of guidance and support on which all else has rested. My thanks to them all.

This book has a history stretching back over a number of years, including the author's experience in nearly thirty years as a line manager and consultant in industry. To all my many colleagues over the years, I offer my grateful thanks for all the lessons learnt.

Note: Every effort has been made to trace and acknowledge ownership of copyright. The publishers will be glad to hear from any copyright holders whom it has not been possible to contact.

HOW TO USE THIS BOOK

Corporate strategy is all-embracing and covers every aspect of the organisation, so its study can be both lengthy and time consuming. This book has been written to guide the reader through from its early stages of development. It can therefore be read from cover to cover; alternatively, it may be more useful to begin by concentrating on certain *key chapters*, which will provide an overview of the process and show the linkages that exist between the different areas. The areas can then be covered in more depth, if required, by reading the *related chapters*.

Key chapters	Related chapters
Part 1	
Chapter 1	Chapter 2
Part 2	
Chapter 3	Chapters 4, 5 and 6
Part 3	
Chapter 7	Chapters 8, 9 and 10
Part 4	
Chapters 11 and 12	None: both important
Part 5	
Chapters 13, 14, 15 and 17	Chapters 16 and 18
Part 6	
Chapters 19 and 21	Chapters 20 and 22

The key chapters might form the basis of a twelve-week modular course. The longer text including the related chapters might form the basis of a two-seminar programme.

Corporate strategy is complicated because there is no final agreement on what exactly should be included in the topic. There are two main strategic approaches worth mastering before venturing too far into the text. They are summarised in chapter 1 – the *prescriptive* and the *emergent* strategic approaches. Since these approaches are discussed extensively later in the book, they should be studied in Chapter 1 before moving on to other chapters. If you have trouble understanding these two elements, then you might also like to consult the early part of Chapter 2, which investigates them in more detail.

Each chapter then follows the same basic format:

● *Learning outcomes and introduction*. This summarises the main areas to be covered in the chapter and is useful as a summary of what to expect from the chapter.

- *Opening minicase.* This is designed to highlight a key strategy issue in the chapter and to provide an example that will then be explored in the text. It is therefore worth reading and using the case questions to ensure that you have understood the basics of the case. You can return to it once you have read the chapter.

- *Key strategic principles.* Each chapter then explores aspects of the subject and summarises them. These can be used to test your understanding of the text and also for revision purposes later.

- *Comment.* After the outline of a major strategic theory, there may be a section with this heading to explain some of the theoretical or practical difficulties associated with that topic. The opinions contained in such a section are deliberately designed to be controversial. The section is meant to make you think about the topic. If you agree with everything I have written, then I have failed!

- *Later case studies.* These are designed to provide further examples and raise additional strategic issues. It is worth exploring the questions.

- *End of chapter questions.* Some are designed to test your understanding of the material in the chapter. Others are present as possible essay topics and require you to undertake some research using the references and reading from the chapter. Some questions have been developed to encourage you to relate the chapter to your own experience: student societies and outside organisations to which you belong can all be considered using the chapter concepts. You may also be able to relate the chapter to your own work experience or to those of other members of your family or friends. All these will provide valuable insights and help you explore the concepts and reality of corporate strategy.

- *Strategic project.* Each chapter ends with a suggested topic that could form the basis of further research. There is data on the Internet to assist the process and your lecturer or tutor will be provided with details on how to access this.

- *Further reading.* This is designed to help when it comes to essay topics and dissertations. This section tries to keep to references in the major journals and books in order to make the process as accessible as possible.

PLAN OF THE BOOK

PART 1 – INTRODUCTION	
Chapter 1 Corporate strategy	Chapter 2 A review of theory and practice

PART 2 – ANALYSIS OF THE ENVIRONMENT			
Chapter 3 Analysing the environment	Chapter 4 Analysing the market	Chapter 5 Analysing competitors	Chapter 6 Analysing customers

PART 3 – ANALYSIS OF RESOURCES			
Chapter 7 Analysing resources	Chapter 8 Analysing human resources	Chapter 9 Analysing financial resources	Chapter 10 Analysing operations resources

PART 4 – THE PURPOSE OF THE ORGANISATION	
Chapter 11 Background issues	Chapter 12 Mission and objectives

PART 5 – DEVELOPING THE STRATEGY			
Chapter 13 Resource-based strategic options	Chapter 14 Market-based strategic options	Chapter 15 Strategy evaluation and selection – 1	Chapter 16 Strategy evaluation and selection – 2
Chapter 17 Finding the strategic route forward		Chapter 18 Strategy, structure and style	

PART 6 – THE IMPLEMENTATION PROCESS			
Chapter 19 Resource allocation, strategic planning and control	Chapter 20 Organisational structure and people issues	Chapter 21 Managing strategic change	Chapter 22 Building a cohesive corporate strategy

INTRODUCTION

This part of the book introduces the concept of corporate strategy. Chapter 1 explains the importance of the subject and its role in the development of the organisation. The two main approaches to corporate strategy are outlined and explored. Chapter 2 gives a fuller review of how corporate strategy has evolved and discusses in greater depth the two main approaches in its development.

PART 1

INTRODUCTION

- The *prescriptive* strategic process

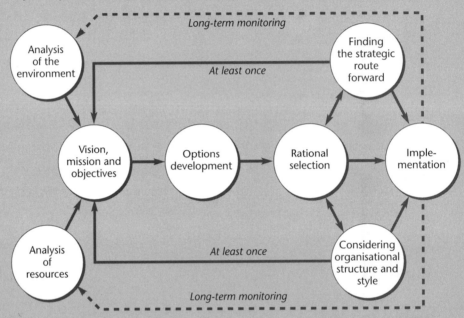

- The *emergent* strategic process

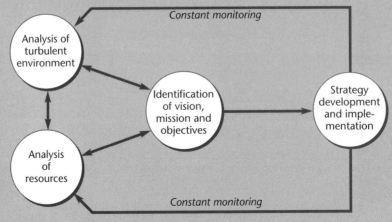

Chapter 1
CORPORATE STRATEGY

- *What is corporate strategy and why is it important?*
- *What are the core areas of corporate strategy and how do they link together?*
- *To what extent is corporate strategy different in public and non-profit organisations?*
- *What are the international dimensions of corporate strategy?*

Chapter 2
A REVIEW OF THEORY AND PRACTICE

- *How have current ideas on corporate strategy evolved?*
- *What are the main approaches to corporate strategy?*
- *What are the main prescriptive and emergent theories of strategy?*
- *How does the theory of corporate strategy relate to corporate practice?*

1

Corporate strategy

When you have worked through this chapter, you will be able to:

- define corporate strategy and explain its five special elements;

- outline the main reasons for the importance of corporate strategy;

- explain the core areas of corporate strategy and how they link together;

- distinguish between process, content and context of a corporate strategy;

- describe the extent to which corporate strategy is different in public and non-profit organisations;

- explain the difference between national and international corporate strategy.

INTRODUCTION

Corporate strategy is concerned with an organisation's basic direction for the future: its purpose, its ambitions, its resources and how it interacts with the world in which it operates.

Every aspect of the organisation plays a role in this strategy – its people, its finances, its production methods and its environment (including its customers). In this introductory chapter we examine how these broad areas need to be structured and developed if the organisation is to continue to operate effectively.

Corporate strategy is complicated by the fact that there is considerable disagreement between researchers on the subject and how its elements are linked together. There are two main routes and these are examined in this chapter: the prescriptive process and the emergent process. As a result, two models have been developed to explain the subject. These are shown in the opening diagram to this part of the book (*see* p 2).

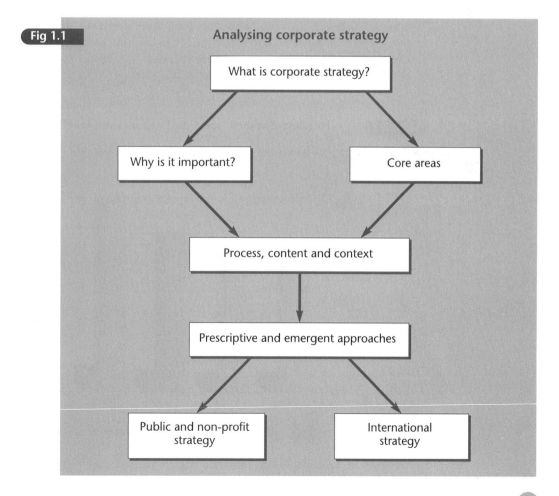

Fig 1.1

Analysing corporate strategy

- What is corporate strategy?
  - Why is it important?
  - Core areas
- Process, content and context
- Prescriptive and emergent approaches
  - Public and non-profit strategy
  - International strategy

MINICASE

Corporate strategy at Hewlett-Packard

When David Packard died in 1996, he left the bulk of the stake in the company he had founded with his partner, Bill Hewlett, to a charitable foundation. It was worth US$4.4 billion. Yet the two had set out 57 years earlier with only modest ambitions and no strategy for building a world company.

In 1939 Hewlett and Packard started their company with US$538 cash in a rented garage in Palo Alto, California. By 1996 the company employed 100 000 people in 120 countries and had annual sales of US$31 billion (*see* Fig 1.2). It made computers, printers and a wide range of electronic equipment for use in industry, medicine and science.

The company strategy has always emphasised excellence and innovation, and yet over the years there has been no grand vision of technological breakthrough nor any desire to take great risks. Describing the early days, Hewlett explained with a grin: 'Professors of management are devastated when I say we were successful because we had no plans. We just took on odd jobs.'

Without any doubt, the two partners had some early luck. Their company became an early leader in pocket calculators. They had been doubtful about the product's success but invested because they estimated that they only needed 10 000 unit sales to break even. They went on to sell 100 000 in the first year.

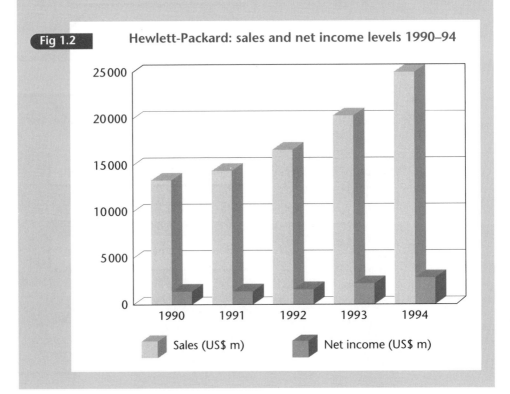

Fig 1.2 Hewlett-Packard: sales and net income levels 1990–94

Hewlett was over-simplifying, however, when he said that they had no plans. There were some sound corporate strategies.

- Over the years, the company has built market dominance in computer printers, specialist applications in science and medicine, and a range of joint ventures and alliances with others in the industry. In 1996, for example, the company signed a new alliance with Netscape Communications, the leading software developer for the Internet, to develop the technology and marketing further.

- Just as importantly, the company has developed its strategy *The HP Way* – an informal and open management style, introduced early on and still practised today. A further informal element was added – *MBWA: Management by Walking Around* – which involved literally wandering casually around anywhere in the operation.

- Profit was not seen as the sole objective. From the early days, employee share options were regularly given to employees.

The whole corporate strategy has been imitated by other high-tech companies and has significantly influenced the development of corporate strategy elsewhere.

CASE QUESTIONS

1 *How important to corporate strategy is profit or a similar quantified objective?*

2 *To what extent does management style also matter? Are these compatible?*

1.1 WHAT IS CORPORATE STRATEGY?

1.1.1 The essence of corporate strategy

Corporate strategy can be described as an organisation's *sense of purpose*. During its early years, Hewlett-Packard's sense of purpose was to provide work for the two partners and their immediate employees. In later years, the purpose changed as the company grew larger and developed. The purpose became a broader concept that included dividends to shareholders and service to a wide range of customers. This sense of purpose is essential to corporate strategy.

Commentators such as Ansoff [2] and Drucker[3] clearly refer to this aspect of strategy: mapping out the future directions that need to be adopted against the resources possessed by the organisation.

Purpose alone, however, is not strategy. *Plans* or *actions* need to be developed to put the purpose into practice. Thus at Hewlett-Packard, these included the production of the early personal calculators and, later, the investment in the Internet, both of which fulfilled the purpose of delivering profits to the company. Hewlett-Packard's plans also included the management style of the company.

This book tackles the way that the purpose and the plans or actions of an organisation are developed, the various methods of implementing the plans and how they change over time.

This sense of *purpose* and its associated *actions* can be seen in the following definition of corporate strategy:

> Corporate strategy is the pattern of major objectives, purposes or goals and essential policies or plans for achieving those goals, stated in such a way as to define what business the company is in or is to be in and the kind of company it is or is to be.[4]

However, it has to be said that there is no universal definition of strategy. For example, some writers include the *purpose* of the organisation as part of strategy, while others make firm distinctions between the purpose and the *actions* that then carry out this purpose. For reasons of simplicity, the above definition, which includes both purpose and actions, has been used.[5]

Examining the actions further, every organisation has to manage its strategies in three main areas:

● the organisation's internal *resources*;

● the external *environment* within which the organisation operates;

● the organisation's ability to *add value* to what it does.

Corporate strategy can be seen as the linking process between the management of the organisation's internal resources and its external relationships with its customers, suppliers, competitors and the economic and social environment in which it exists.

The organisation develops these relationships from its abilities and resources. Hence, the organisation uses its history, skills, resources, knowledge and various concepts to explore its future actions. Figure 1.3 shows some examples of this process.

Resources strategy The *resources* of an organisation include its human resource skills, the investment and the capital in every part of the organisation. Organisations need to develop

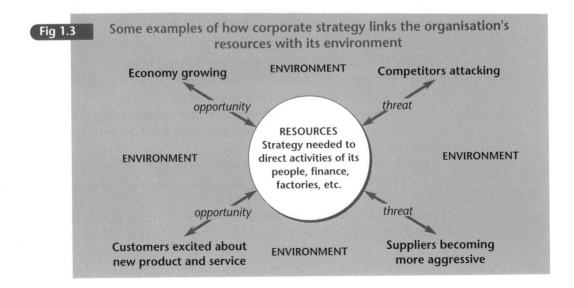

Fig 1.3 Some examples of how corporate strategy links the organisation's resources with its environment

corporate strategies to optimise the use of these resources. In particular, it is essential to investigate the *distinctive* capabilities that will allow the organisation to survive and prosper against competition. For example, Hewlett-Packard had distinctive capabilities in the production of computer printers and their associated software that set the standard for the industry. It had also invested heavily in branding its products and distribution systems. All these were part of its resources.

Environmental strategy

In this context *environment* encompasses every aspect external to the organisation itself: not only the economic and political circumstances, which may vary widely around the world, but also competitors, customers and suppliers, who may vary in being aggressive to a greater or lesser degree. Organisations therefore need to develop corporate strategies that are best suited to their strengths and weaknesses in relation to the environment in which they operate. For example, Hewlett-Packard faced a highly competitive environment for its printers in relation to Japanese companies such as Canon and OKI. In addition, the company had to cope with changing levels of economic growth in many markets around the world, which influenced the decisions of its customers to purchase new printers.

Some commentators, such as Ohmae,[6] suggest that a corporate strategy is really only needed when an organisation faces competitors: no competitive threat means no need for strategy. This is a rather narrow view of strategy and its environment: even a monopoly without competitors could need a strategy to defend its position. With a general move to privatise nationalised monopolies around the world, corporate strategy may be required for this reason alone. Equally, charitable foundations compete for funds from donors and sometimes for the volunteers that make the wheels turn. A corporate strategy is no less relevant in this context.

Other commentators, such as Mintzberg,[7] have suggested that the environment is so uncertain, particularly at a global level, that it may be impossible to *plan* a long-term corporate strategy. This may need to be *crafted*, i.e. built up gradually through a learning process involving experimentation. The organisation may be seeking to add value by operating effectively, but the ever-changing environment offers little or no possibility for the management to plan in advance. Examples of such environmental changes include:

● major technological change, such as the Internet;
● unexpected actions by government, such as a major crisis.

Such commentators argue that unpredictable environments make the task of devising a realistic corporate strategy more than mere planning. Strategies have to be devised to cope with such difficulties.

Adding value

There is a need to explore further the purpose of corporate strategy beyond the requirements of environmental change and management of resources. In essence, the need is to *add value* to what supplies are brought into the organisation. To ensure its long-term survival, an organisation must take the supplies it brings in, add value to these through its operations and then deliver its output to the customer (*see* Chapter 7).

Hewlett-Packard takes the supplies it buys in – such as components, energy, skills and capital equipment – and then uses its own resources and expertise to create a product from these supplies – such as a computer or a printer – that has a value which is higher than the combined value of all the supplies which have been used to make the product. It adds value and then passes the product on to its customers.

The purpose of corporate strategy is to bring about the conditions under which the organisation is able to create this vital additional value and to pass it on to its customers. Corporate strategy must also ensure that the organisation adapts to changing circumstances so that it can continue to add value in the future. The ways in which value can be added and enhanced are crucial to corporate strategy.

This added value will be distributed to the *stakeholders* in the organisation:

- *the shareholders*, who own the company and receive dividends on their shares;
- *the employees*, who receive some of the added value through their pay;
- *the management*, who receive added value through their pay and privileges;
- *the government*, who receive part of the added value in the form of taxes.

(An extended view of stakeholders to include all those who come into contact with the organisation, such as suppliers and customers, is explored in Chapter 12.)

The task of corporate strategy is to *create* a distinctive way ahead for an organisation, using whatever skills and resources it has, against the background of the environment and its constraints. In this context, *create* is used to describe the corporate strategy process: there are no easy solutions or simple answers in this subject area.

Corporate strategy is an inexact science. No single strategy will apply in all cases. While most would like to build on their skills, organisations will be influenced by their past experiences and culture, and constrained by their background, resources and their environment (just as we are in our own individual lives).

Nevertheless, corporate strategy is not without logic, or the application of scientific method and the use of evidence. At the end of the process, however, there is a place for the application of *business judgement*, as in our example, where Hewlett-Packard took a business judgement to go ahead in producing its early design of hand calculators because the break-even was acceptable.

In conclusion, it should be noted that there are writers who use terms other than corporate strategy to define strategy development: strategic management, business policy, competitive strategy, and so on. *Corporate strategy* is used here because it embraces every *type* of organisation – large and small; public, non-profit and privately-owned – and it is the most general expression of the *various levels* of strategy, including all the many lower levels within an organisation.

1.1.2 Key elements of strategic decisions

There are five key elements of strategic decisions that are related primarily to the organisation's ability to compete in the market place. To illustrate these elements, examples are given from the fast-moving global telecommunications market:

1 *Sustainable* Change that can be maintained over time. For the long-term survival of the organisation, it is important that the strategy is sustainable. There would be little point in France Telecom or Deutsche Telekom entering into new global alliances with the US company Sprint if the joint deal only lasted for a year. The partners are expecting to invest US$4 billion over the next five years.[8]

2 *Distinctive* Different from competitors, possibly involving innovation. A sustainable strategy is more likely if the strategy is distinctive from actual or potential competitors. One of the strategic problems with the telecommunications companies above is that it is not entirely clear how distinctive the new joint company, Atlas, will actually be. Nevertheless, corporate strategy concentrates on finding and exploiting such distinctions: ultimately, it is the organisation itself that must be distinctive. One major way of seeking distinctive solutions is to explore *innovative* ways forward – a constant theme of this book.

3 *Offer competitive advantage* Not only distinctive, but a real advantage that will allow the organisation to grow. Corporate strategy usually takes place in a competitive environment. Even monopolistic government organisations need to compete for funds with rival government bodies. In the global telecommunications market of the late 1990s, there is now a competitive mixture of government organisations and private companies. The new Atlas company will compete against several other major international joint ventures that are now being organised: for example, British Telecom and the US company, MCI, are investing around US$5.3 billion in their own joint company, called Concert.[9]

4 *Exploit linkages between the organisation and its environment* Links that cannot easily be duplicated and will contribute to superior performance. The strategy has to exploit the many linkages that exist between the organisation and its environment: suppliers, customers, competitors and often the government itself. Such linkages may be contractual and formal, or they may be vague and informal (just because they are not legally binding does not mean they have little importance). The most significant matching may be an informal arrangement that adds real and long-term benefit to both parties to the process. In the case of the telecommunications companies above, the large sums being invested certainly needed a formal agreement to secure the relationships. The linkages with governments and administrations of trading blocks such as the European Commission of the European Union (EU) are also vital to success: at the time of writing, the US government authorities and the European Commission have cleared the BT/MCI deal for operation in the USA and Europe, but the FT/DT/Sprint deal was still facing major hurdles. The US government said that the French and German telecommunications markets were not completely open for US companies to enter and, therefore, they saw no reason why they should be given access to the USA – an example of the type of matching that is needed in corporate strategy.

5 *Vision* The ability to move the organisation forward in a significant way beyond the current environment. This is likely to involve innovative strategies. In the fast-changing telecommunications scene, it is vital to have a vision of the future. This may involve the environment but is mainly for the organisation itself: knowing where BT or MCI might fit into a new global order in five or ten years will provide the picture that will challenge and direct decisions over the intervening period. It is highly likely to involve *innovative* solutions to the strategic problems facing the industry.

In the final analysis, corporate strategy is concerned with delivering long-term *added value* to the organisation.

To illustrate the importance of considering *all* these elements, we can take the case of a government-owned company, Telecom Italia. It was among the smaller companies wishing to develop its presence in the global telecommunications market in the early 1990s. In 1994 it announced that only a few companies would still manage to operate at a global level after the year 2000; Telecom Italia would do its utmost to be one of them.[10] Such a company would have to address the following questions. Where is our distinctiveness? Where is our competitive advantage? What linkages can we offer our international rivals? Merely expressing the wish to develop a strategy is unlikely to prove successful in itself. No doubt Telecom Italia had further ideas that it was not making public at that stage.

The key reading at the end of this chapter, taken from the work of Professor John Kay, further explores some essential aspects of corporate strategy.

Key strategic principles

- Corporate strategy is the pattern of major objectives, purposes or goals and the essential policies or plans for achieving those goals.

- Strategy is developed by a consideration of the resources of the organisation in relation to its environment, the prime purpose being to add value. The added value is then distributed among the stakeholders.

- There are five key elements of strategy, principally related to the need to offer advantages over competitors: sustainability; distinctiveness; competitive advantage; the exploitation of linkages between the organisation and its environment; and vision. Several of these elements may well involve innovative solutions to strategic issues.

CASE STUDY 1.1

Corporate profit disaster at IBM

During the period 1991 to 1993, the world's largest computer company, IBM, suffered a net loss of almost US$16 billion (half the total GDP of the Republic of Ireland) – one of the worst corporate profit disasters ever seen. Yet IBM was a highly respected company with a dominant market share, excellent employee policies, reliable products (if not the most innovative), close relationships with national governments, responsible local and national community policies, sound finances and extensive modern plant investment around the world. IBM's problem was essentially a failure in corporate strategy. (See Fig 1.4.)

The early days

During the 1970s and 1980s, IBM became the first-choice computer company for many of the world's leading companies; it had a remarkable global market share – approaching 60 per cent. It constructed its computers to its own proprietary standards so that they were incompatible with other computers. It offered large, fast and reliable machines that undertook tasks never before operated by machinery: accounting, invoicing and payroll. These major computational tasks were undertaken on large stand-alone machines in special air-conditioned rooms: these were called mainframe computers. Even though the capital costs of such machines were high – for example, over £1 million for a medium-sized machine – IBM customers still made substantial savings in numbers employed, reliability and speed of processing.

Above all, choosing IBM meant that risk was low for customers: 'No one ever got fired for buying IBM'. Hence, IBM dominated the market and earned around 60 per cent of its profits from its mainframe machines.

Over the years, much of IBM's smaller computer product range became so integrated around the world that IBM had no real idea of the profitability of individual parts: for example, it was not until 1993 that IBM took the first steps to separate out its AS/400 Division of mid-range computers. It needed a major change in corporate culture to achieve this, along with totally new control and reporting systems. By 1994, IBM was so pleased with its success on the AS/400 range that it was extending the process to other product ranges around the world.

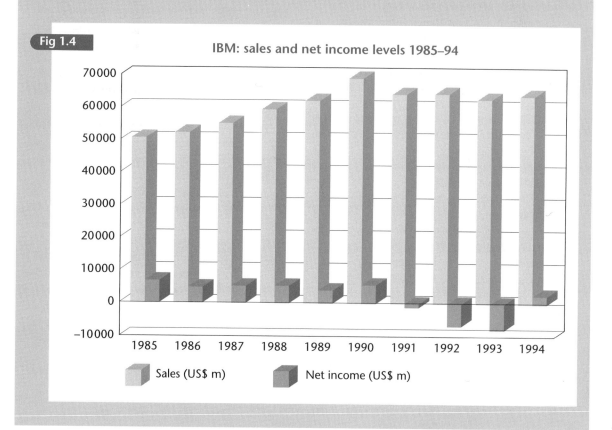

Fig 1.4

IBM: sales and net income levels 1985–94

Sales (US$ m) Net income (US$ m)

CASE STUDY 1.1 continued

In keeping with a large company, IBM had a policy of always maintaining shareholder dividends. Moreover, it had strong staff development and personnel procedures. For example, it was proud that it never made its employees compulsorily redundant. Reflecting its dominance of global computer markets, its culture was relaxed and supremely confident of its abilities and resources.

Development of the PC market

During the late 1970s and early 1980s, a separate parallel development occurred in global computer markets: small, personal computers with names like Osborne, Commodore and Sinclair were developed. Some of these were particularly user-friendly (for example, Apple Computers). By contrast in the early years, IBM preferred to maintain a lofty technical distance. It also took the view that the market was small and personal computers would never handle the mainframe problems. Some of these small machines were built around common computer chips and software. Although they did not have the capacity to handle any of the large computational problems of computer mainframes, the personal computer market was growing fast – over 100 per cent per annum in some years. In the late 1970s, IBM saw this and decided to launch its own small machine onto the market.

Because IBM's existing company structure was so large, slow and integrated, it chose to set up a totally new subsidiary to manufacture and market its first personal computer (PC). Moreover, it did not use its proprietary semiconductor chips and operating software but acquired them respectively from the large chip manufacturer, Intel (US), and from a small software company called Microsoft (US). IBM encouraged Intel and Microsoft to develop their standard products further and took the view that it was doing these companies and the PC customer a favour by making its designs standard around the world. Indeed, IBM was rather proud of establishing the global benchmark in this small specialist market sector as well as the much larger mainframe market. The claim 'IBM-compatible' became a common standard for most PCs, except Apple.

Technological advance

Throughout this period, the state of the world's economies had really very little influence on these developments. Computer markets were genuinely driven by innovation, new ideas and change to the extent that these over-rode problems in individual national economies.

Competitors found the IBM-compatible standardisation was helpful in expanding the market. However, sales also continued to grow because of technological advances, aggressive marketing and the emergence of low-cost producer countries such as Taiwan and Singapore. In addition, innovative companies such as Sun Microsystems found ways to enhance the power of the small PC – the workstation and computer networking were established. Computer chips had become more powerful and software more sophisticated. By the mid-1980s, PCs started to undertake the tasks formerly done by the smaller mainframe machines. By the mid-1990s, the same performance as the medium-sized mainframe could be obtained from a computer costing £20 000.

Marketing and service innovation

During the 1980s, PCs also became more reliable so that IBM's reputation for quality and reliability became less important. This also meant that PCs could be sold, installed and repaired without the expensive and vast IBM service organisation. Indeed, they could even be sold by mail order with technical support from dedicated technical operators – Dell Computers were innovators here. Such companies had even lower costs than IBM's suppliers, fewer overheads than the large IBM organisation and the same quality. Because of their smaller size, they were also able to respond more quickly to market changes.

IBM and other computer companies continued to spend funds branding their products. However, their suppliers also began to spend significant sums.

Impact on the existing computer companies and their suppliers

By the early 1990s, IBM's dominance was fading. It should be said that other computer companies such as Olivetti (Italy), DEC (US) and Bull (France) were also hit even harder than IBM. They all scrambled to find new strategies. Even in the late 1990s, many were still in trouble.

At the same time, the profit records of the two IBM suppliers mentioned above made interesting reading. Intel and Microsoft had used the earnings generated from IBM and from other sources to invest in proprietary technology – for example, the

Intel 'Pentium' microchip launched in 1993 and Microsoft's 'Windows' launched in the late 1980s and destined to dominate global software markets. Both supplier companies spent large sums of marketing funds on branding their products.

CASE QUESTIONS

1 *What was the strategic significance of IBM's decision to obtain supplies of computer chips and software from other manufacturers rather than make them itself?*

2 *How big a part did the change in computer technology play in IBM's problems? Could this have been predicted by IBM? What is the significance of your answer for corporate strategy?*

3 *How important was the decision of IBM's suppliers to spend marketing funds on branding their products? What strategic significance does this have for the late 1990s in computer markets?*

4 *Can you think of any reason why companies like Hewlett-Packard could continue to make adequate profits during this period?*

5 *Use the five key elements of strategy to evaluate IBM's corporate strategy. What conclusions do you draw for these and added value?*

Table 1.1

Comparative performance: IBM, Intel and Microsoft (US$ millions)

	1993	1992	1991
IBM			
Revenue	62 716	64 523	64 766
Net operating (loss) before changes in accounting principles	(7 987)	(6 865)	(598)
Intel			
Revenue	8 782	5 844	4 779
Net operating profit	3 392	1 490	1 080
Microsoft			
Revenue	3 753	2 759	1 843
Net operating profit	1 326	996	650

1.2 WHY IS CORPORATE STRATEGY IMPORTANT?

Corporate strategy is important because it deals with the major, fundamental issues that affect the future of organisations.[12] When an organisation makes major errors in corporate strategy, it will suffer the consequences, possibly risking its own survival. When the organisation develops its strategy well, it reaps the benefits. For example, there was a situation in the mid-1990s when IBM itself was threatened with collapse. Equally, the Hewlett-Packard case shows that a company that develops a viable corporate strategy is able to prosper. The two cases are used to provide some indications of the nature of corporate strategy and why it is important.

1 *Corporate strategy involves the entire organisation.* It covers all areas and functions of the business. It borrows best practice from each part and combines these, thus creating more than just the sum. IBM had some success but was slow and bureaucratic in involving the whole organisation in its strategic decisions. The Hewlett-Packard style was more informal, immediate and flexible in its approach to involving everyone in the organisation.

2 *Corporate strategy is likely to concern itself with the survival of the business as a minimum objective and the creation of value added as a maximum objective.* In earlier years, both IBM and Hewlett-Packard were concerned with generating wealth which would be shared among workers, senior management, shareholders and the national governments of the countries in which they made sales.

3 *Corporate strategy covers the range and depth of the organisation's activities.* By 1993, IBM had to consider the possibility of divesting some of its activities which had become over-extended (and, in practice, this is what it proceeded to do). Hewlett-Packard was able to continue investing and broadening its areas of activities through new links, such as the Internet.

4 *Corporate strategy directs the changing and evolving relationship of the organisation with its environment.* At the root of many of the problems of IBM was its rapidly changing environment; H-P was able to cope better.

5 *Corporate strategy is central to the development of distinctiveness.* By 1990, IBM was offering nothing that was sufficiently different from its competitors. Indeed, it was marketing products that were essentially the same but at a higher price than its competitors, justifying this on the basis of its reputation alone. By comparison, some of Hewlett-Packard's products had superior performance and attractive prices. It is not enough in strategy to be 'good'; it is vital to be better than competitors.

6 *Corporate strategy development is crucial to adding value,* rather than sales, profitability, market share, earnings per share or other indicators. IBM lost value over the years 1991–93. Hewlett-Packard consistently added value to its operations during these years.

In conclusion, it is evident with hindsight that IBM made a number of strategic mistakes. Most commentators would argue that this can be used to demonstrate the importance of corporate strategy.[13] This approach, although adopted in this book, is not without its pitfalls, the obvious one being that strategy may only become clear after it has been completed. Wisdom *after* the event is easy; wisdom *before* the event is essential if strategy is to be successful.

Even successful companies will have strategic problems that are difficult to resolve. Corporate strategy may involve conflicting and ambiguous outcomes. For example, Hewlett-Packard's corporate strategy drive for increased market share might conflict with its need to provide a dividend for its shareholders. Unlike many functional business problems where there are simple measures of success – did we achieve our brand share, our production target, our staff turnover reduction? – corporate strategy deals in 'complexity, ambiguity and fundamental issues that cannot be easily summarised'.[14] Some commentators argue that strategy is so complex that it cannot be usefully developed and is therefore of limited value.[15] These are important comments that will be explored further.

Key strategic principles

- Corporate strategy is important because it deals with the fundamental issues that affect the future of organisations.

- Corporate strategy integrates the various functional areas of the organisation and involves its survival and development. It concerns the whole range and depth of the organisation's activities, including its relationships with the environment. It seeks to develop distinctiveness and add value.

- Corporate strategy also deals in complexity, ambiguity and fundamental issues that cannot be easily summarised.

1.3 CORE AREAS OF CORPORATE STRATEGY

The three core areas of corporate strategy are:

1 *Strategic analysis*. The organisation, its mission and objectives have to be examined and analysed. Corporate strategy provides value for the people involved in the organisation – its *stakeholders* – but it is often the senior managers who develop the view of the organisation's overall objectives in the broadest possible terms. They conduct an examination of the *objectives* and the organisation's *relationship with its environment*. They will also analyse the *resources* of the organisation.

2 *Strategy development*. The strategy options have to be developed and then selected. To be successful, the strategy is likely to be built on the particular skills of the organisation and the special relationships that it has or can develop with those outside – suppliers, customers, distributors and government. For many organisations, this will mean developing advantages over competitors that are sustainable over time. There are usually many options available and one or more will have to be selected.

3 *Strategy implementation*. The selected options now have to be implemented. There may be major difficulties in terms of motivation, power relationships, government negotiations, company acquisitions and many other matters. A strategy that cannot be implemented is not worth the paper it is written on.

If a viable corporate strategy is to be developed, each of these three areas should be explored carefully. For the purpose of clarity, it is useful to separate the corporate strategy process into three core areas, as we have done above. It would be wrong, however, to think of the three core areas as being strictly sequential. While it is not possible to implement something that does not exist, many organisations will have some existing relationships with customers and suppliers that are well developed, and others that have not yet started. Even small, new companies rarely start with nothing; there is usually some basic set of skills or business idea. Imposing an artificial sequence on this process would be counterproductive.

In practice, the three core areas are interlocking and overlapping: for example, an objective may prove unrealistic once implemented and may therefore need to be modified (*see* Fig 1.5).

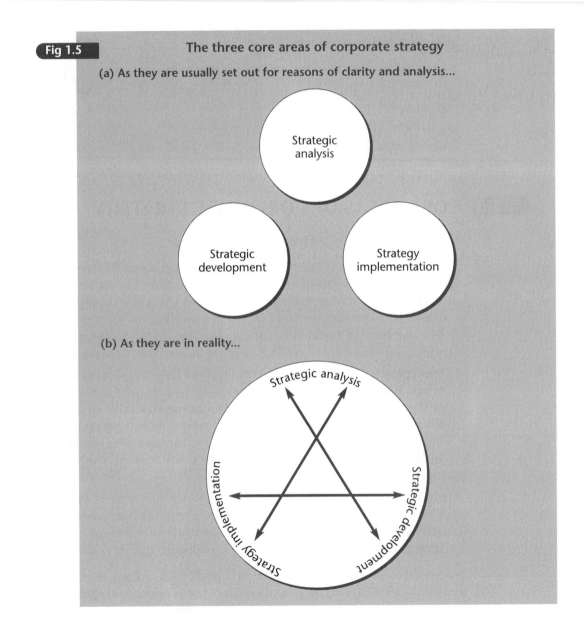

Fig 1.5 **The three core areas of corporate strategy**

(a) As they are usually set out for reasons of clarity and analysis...

Strategic analysis

Strategic development

Strategy implementation

(b) As they are in reality...

Strategic analysis

Strategy implementation

Strategic development

Table 1.2

Definition of terms used in the three core areas of strategy[16]

	Definition	Personal career example
Mission statement	Defines the business that the organisation is in against the values and expectations of the stakeholders.	To become a leading European industrialist.
Objectives (or goals)	State more precisely what is to be achieved and when the results are to be accomplished. Often quantified. (Note that there is no statement of how the results are to be attained.)	To achieve a directorship on the main board of a significant company by the age of 42.
Strategies	The pattern or plan that integrates an organisation's major goals or policies and action sequences into a cohesive whole. Usually deals with the *general principles* for achieving the objectives: why the organisation has chosen this particular route.	1 To obtain an MBA from a leading European business school. 2 To move into a leading consultancy company as a stepping stone to corporate HQ. 3 To obtain a key functional directorship by the age of 35 in the chosen company.
Plans (or programmes)	The *specific* actions that then follow from the strategies. They specify the step-by-step sequence of actions to achieve the major objectives.	1 To obtain a first class honours degree this year. 2 To take the next two years working in a merchant bank for commercial experience. 3 To identify three top business schools by December two years from now. 4 To make application to these schools by January of the following year.
Controls	The process of monitoring the proposed plans as they proceed and adjusting where necessary. There may well be some modification of the strategies as they proceed.	Marriage and children mean some compromise on the first two years above. Adjust plans back by three years.
Reward	The result of the successful strategy, adding value to the organisation and to the individual.	High salary and career satisfaction.

Table 1.2 lists some of the working definitions used in the three core areas of corporate strategy, some of which will already be familiar to you. To clarify the distinction between the terms, the table also includes the example of an ambitious young manager, showing his/her strategy for career progression. However, the example in Table 1.2 highlights two important qualifications to the three core areas:

● the influence of judgement and values;

● the high level of speculation involved in major assumptions.

The importance of *judgement and values* in arriving at the mission and objectives shows that corporate strategy is not a precise science. For example, in the hypothetical career example in Table 1.2, the person has a clear view on what is important in life if their ambitions are to be achieved; some people would not share these ambitious values. We examine the role of value judgements further in Chapter 12.

Moreover, corporate strategy may be *highly speculative and involve major assumptions* as it attempts to forecast the future of the organisation. For example, many of the later stages of the career progression in Table 1.2 involve some very difficult projections – on marriage, family and health, for example – that may well not be achieved. Indeed, given such uncertainties, it is difficult to see the example as anything more than an idealised series of wish-statements. In the same way, in the case of corporate strategy, there may be a largely false and perhaps unrealistic sense of direction.

Some books and research papers on corporate strategy do not recognise this problem and may be guilty of implying that corporate strategy has certainties about the future that it does not possess in reality[17]. This does not mean we should not explore the future directions of corporate strategy, just that we should be cautious about their meaning.

Key strategic principles

● The three core areas of corporate strategy are: strategic analysis; strategic development; and strategy implementation.

● There are two important qualifications to the three core areas. Judgement and values play an important role in determining the objectives and choice. Moreover, some elements are highly speculative and may involve major assumptions.

● There is considerable overlap between the three core areas, which are separated out for reasons of clarity but, in practice, may operate concurrently.

1.4 PROCESS, CONTENT AND CONTEXT

Recent research[18] has shown that in most situations corporate strategy is not simply a matter of taking a strategic decision and then implementing it. It often takes a considerable time to make the decision itself and then another delay before it comes into effect. The reason is that *people* are involved – managers, employees, suppliers and customers, for example. Any of these people may choose to apply their own business judgement to the chosen corporate strategy. They may influence both the initial decision and the subsequent actions that will implement it.

For this reason, an important distinction needs to be drawn in strategy development between *process*, *content* and *context*. Every strategic decision involves these three elements, which must be considered separately, as well as together.

Every strategic decision involves:

- *Context* – the environment within which the strategy operates and is developed. In the IBM case during the 1980s the context was the fast-changing technological development in personal computers.

- *Content* – the main actions of the proposed strategy. The content of the IBM strategy was the decision to launch the new PC and its subsequent performance in the market place.

- *Process* – how the actions link together or interact with each other as the strategy unfolds against what may be a changing environment. The process in the IBM case was the delay in launching the new product, the slow reaction to competitive actions and the interaction between the various parts of the company as it attempted to respond to competitor actions.

These three elements are the axes of the same three-dimensional cube of corporate strategy decision making (*see* Fig 1.6).

In most corporate strategy situations, the *context* and *content* are reasonably clear. It is the way in which strategy is developed and enacted – the *process* that causes the problems. Processes need investigation and are vague and quixotic because they involve people.

The difficulty is compounded by the problem that, during the implementation period, the process can influence the initial strategic decision. For example, as the process unfolded at IBM, competitive actions forced the organisation to make cutbacks that were not originally identified as part of the strategic content.

At various points throughout this book, the distinction between process, content and context will be useful in clarifying relationships.

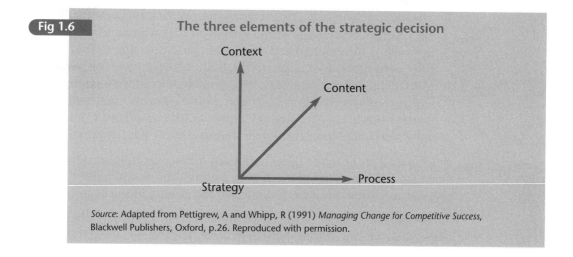

Fig 1.6

The three elements of the strategic decision

Context

Content

Strategy

Process

Source: Adapted from Pettigrew, A and Whipp, R (1991) *Managing Change for Competitive Success,* Blackwell Publishers, Oxford, p.26. Reproduced with permission.

> ### Key strategic principles
>
> - In corporate strategy development, it is necessary to distinguish between three elements: context, content and process.
>
> - In most corporate strategy situations, the context and content are reasonably clear; it is the process that causes the problem because process may influence the way that people in the organisation develop and implement strategy.
>
> - Process is the way actions link together or interact with each other as the strategy unfolds in the environment, which may itself be changing.

1.5 PROCESS: LINKING THE THREE CORE AREAS

1.5.1 Two different approaches to the process

Until now corporate strategy has been presented as a unified, cohesive subject. It is important at this point to explain and explore a fundamental disagreement which exists among commentators over the way that corporate strategy may be developed. Differing views on the content, process and nature of corporate strategy have arisen because of the breadth and complexity of the subject. For the present, the overall distinctions can be summarised as representing two main approaches to corporate strategy development:

1 *The prescriptive approach* Some commentators have judged corporate strategy to be essentially a linear and rational process, starting with where-we-are-now and then developing new strategies for the future (*see* Jauch and Glueck,[19] and Argenti[20]). A prescriptive corporate strategy is one whose *objective* has been defined in advance and whose *main elements* have been developed before the strategy commences.

2 *The emergent approach* Other commentators take the view that corporate strategy emerges, adapting to human needs and continuing to develop over time. It is evolving, incremental and continuous, and therefore cannot be easily or usefully summarised in a plan which then requires to be implemented (*see* Mintzberg,[21] Cyert and March[22]). Emergent corporate strategy is a strategy whose *final objective* is unclear and whose *elements* are developed during the course of its life, as the strategy proceeds. The theorists of this approach often argue that long-term prescriptive strategies are of limited value.

In Chapter 2 we examine these important differences in more detail. There are, for example, differences in approach even amongst those who judge that the process is rational and linear. Mintzberg[23] captured the essence of the distinction:

> 'The popular view sees the strategist as a planner or as a visionary; someone sitting on a pedestal dictating brilliant strategies for everyone else to implement. While recognising

the importance of thinking ahead and especially of the need for creative vision in this pedantic world, I wish to propose an additional view of the strategist – as a pattern recogniser, a learner if you will – who manages a process in which strategies (and visions) can emerge as well as be deliberately conceived.'

It should be noted here that Mintzberg sees merit in *both* approaches. (Both approaches can make a contribution and are not mutually exclusive. In many respects, they can be said to be like the human brain which has both a rational left side and an emotional right side. Both sides are needed for the brain to function properly.[24]) It can be argued that the same is true in corporate strategy. Reference is therefore made to both the prescriptive and emergent approaches throughout this book.

1.5.2 Impact on the three core areas

1 *The prescriptive approach* takes the view that the three core areas – strategic analysis, strategic development and strategy implementation – are linked together sequentially. Thus it is possible to use the analysis area to develop a strategy which is then implemented. The corporate strategy is *prescribed* in advance (*see* Fig 1.7 (a)).

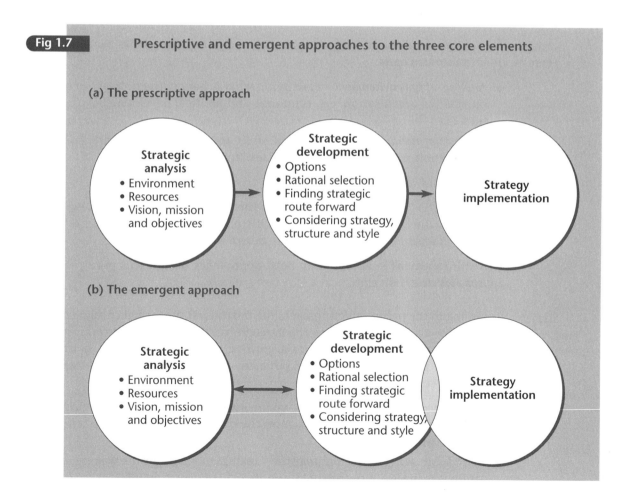

Fig 1.7 **Prescriptive and emergent approaches to the three core elements**

(a) The prescriptive approach

Strategic analysis
- Environment
- Resources
- Vision, mission and objectives

Strategic development
- Options
- Rational selection
- Finding strategic route forward
- Considering strategy, structure and style

Strategy implementation

(b) The emergent approach

Strategic analysis
- Environment
- Resources
- Vision, mission and objectives

Strategic development
- Options
- Rational selection
- Finding strategic route forward
- Considering strategy, structure and style

Strategy implementation

2   *The emergent approach* takes the view that the three core areas are essentially inter-related. However, it is usual to regard the analysis area as being distinctive and in advance of the other two elements. Because corporate strategy is then developed by an experimental process that involves trial and error, it is not appropriate to make a clear distinction between the strategy development and implementation phases: they are closely linked, one responding to the results obtained by the other. These relationships are shown in Fig 1.7 (b).

1.5.3   Developing models of corporate strategy

Based on the two approaches, it is possible to develop models to aid in understanding the way that corporate strategy operates. These models are explained here and will then be used throughout this book to structure our examination of corporate strategy.

The whole process is shown in Fig 1.8. By matching the numbers in the following sections with the numbers on the prescriptive model in Fig 1.8 overleaf, you will be able to follow the corporate strategy process and appreciate the differences between the two main approaches. Note that no numbers appear on the emergent model because its essence is that the process can occur in any order and elements can be inter-related.

Strategic analysis   The analytical phase of both the *prescriptive* and the *emergent* approach can be divided into two parts:

- *Analysis of the environment* – examining what is happening or likely to happen outside the organisation, e.g. economic and political developments, competition. **(1)**
- *Analysis of resources* – exploring the skills and resources available inside the organisation, e.g. human resources, plant, finance. **(2)**

These are followed by a third element:

- *Identification of vision, mission and objectives* – developing and reviewing the strategic direction and the more specific objectives, e.g. the maximisation of profit or return on capital, or in some cases a social service. **(3)**

This third element is accepted by both approaches but, at this point, the two approaches clearly diverge.

Strategy prescriptive approach   According to the prescriptive approach, the next step is the formal consideration of the options available to achieve the agreed objectives. **(4)** This is followed by a rational selection from the options according to identified criteria, in order to arrive at the prescriptive strategy. **(5)** In most cases, this choice is then subject to two further considerations:

- *Finding the strategic route forward* – taking into account new and emerging information to see how it might impact on the choice, with some adjustment being made if necessary. **(6)**
- *Considering strategy, structure and style* – taking into account the way the organisation is managed and structured, and its style of operation. **(7)**

Fig 1.8

The prescriptive and emergent strategic processes

(a) The prescriptive strategic process

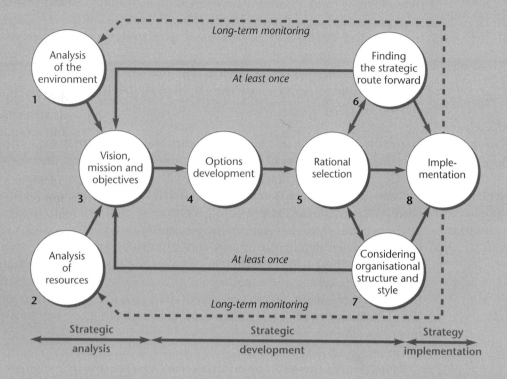

(b) The emergent strategic process

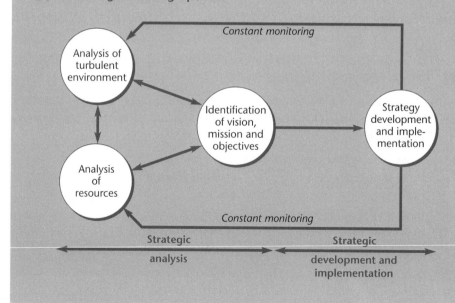

These may all need to be considered before a final decision is made on which strategy to pursue. It will usually be essential at this point to reconsider the impact of these choices on the basic mission and objectives of the organisation. This is because the strategic choice may have some implications for the mission and objectives, possibly even altering them. For example, it may turn out that the chosen strategy does not meet the objectives; either the strategy or the objectives will need to be changed. Once the strategy has been agreed, it is then implemented. **(8)**

In Fig 1.8(a) the steps in this process can be followed. It should be emphasised, however, that this diagram represents only one description of the approach; there are many different approaches, with strategists unable to agree on the definitive prescriptive route.

Strategy development and implementation – the emergent approach

Essentially, this takes a much more experimental view of the strategy choice and its implementation. It seeks to learn by trial, experimentation and discussion as strategies are developed. There is no final, agreed strategy but rather a series of experimental approaches that are considered by those involved and then developed further. Strategies emerge during a process of crafting and testing.

There is therefore no clear distinction in the emergent approach between the two stages of developing the strategy and its implementation.

Moreover, there is no need to identify a separate stage of discussion involving the leadership, culture and organisation, since all these will occur inevitably during the strategy development and implementation phase. Importantly, there is then a strong link back to the earlier analytical phase, enabling changes in the environment and resources to be reflected quickly in the adaptive, learning strategy. This is shown in Fig 1.8 (b).

By definition, there can be no single view of a process that emerges within an organisation – each one will be different. Figure 1.8 (b) serves to indicate the circulatory nature of the decision-making process according to this approach. There is no definitive emergent route.

Key strategic principles

- There are two main approaches to corporate strategy development: the *prescriptive* approach and the *emergent* approach. Each complements the other, and both are relevant to the strategy process.

- The *prescriptive* approach takes the view that the three core elements are linked together sequentially. The *emergent* approach regards the three core areas as being essentially inter-related.

- The two approaches can be used to develop models for the corporate strategy process. However, it should be recognised that every model is a compromise and may not reflect all the circumstances that exist in reality.

1.6 STRATEGY DEVELOPMENT IN PUBLIC AND NON-PROFIT ORGANISATIONS

1.6.1 Public organisations

In many countries across Europe, the public sector forms the major part of industrial and commercial activity, e.g. the telecommunications companies in Spain and Italy, although some of these are now being privatised.[25] Since such companies often compete internationally with the private sector, many of the same strategy considerations apply to public and to private organisations. The major difference has been the lack in government-owned institutions of the objective to deliver a profit. The European Commission has now taken the view that state subsidies may not be compatible with the Treaty of Rome, and public organisations have come under increasing pressure to apply commercial criteria.[26] In Europe, there are many organisations in the public sector, ranging from electricity supply in some countries to public health bodies in others. Their individual requirements for strategy development will depend on their precise nature. Certainly those that are being privatised will need to consider this area.

Outside Western Europe, many key industries remain in public ownership. However, the trend in most parts of the world is now towards privatising large public companies in the utilities and telecommunications sectors. The arguments in favour of the change of ownership are set out in the *World Bank Report 1994*.[27] The principal impact of privatisation on strategy will depend on the form that privatisation takes. Some companies may still remain monopolies even though they are in the private sector.

The main considerations regarding corporate strategy in public organisations include:

- *Policy and politics.* Some European countries and Asian countries, such as India and China, are committed to the view that public companies are there to provide a public service. Strategy is therefore directed towards achieving this aim. The political policy of the government will guide strategic development.

- *Monopoly suppliers.* Public authorities are often monopoly suppliers of a service. While they may be under pressure to operate efficiently (however that is defined), they may be unable to spend any surplus profits they generate. Moreover, they will be subject to changes in government policy direction and will lack the consistency of private organisations as a result. The lack of choice for customers will mean the suppliers are not really subject to the market pressures that affect business strategy in the private sector.

- *Bureaucracy and slower rate of change.* Being part of the public sector may affect the management style and values of managers and the workforce, leading specifically to greater bureaucracy and a slower rate of response to outside pressures.

- *Battle for resources from government.* Much of the real strategy in the public sector across Europe is fought over the allocation of resources from central government. Increases in annual budget allocations or cutbacks in funds affect fundamentally the service and level of investment in physical assets available to the public. There is no reason why such considerations should not be subject to strategic scrutiny, but the nature of the evidence and logic may be different.

1.6.2 Non-profit organisations

Both public and private organisations operate in this area: charities, churches, even some educational institutions, for example. Non-profit organisations are usually founded for reasons other than commercial considerations: for example, bird and animal welfare, disease research, international rescue, poverty alleviation. For these reasons, corporate strategy must first recognise and reflect the values held by such organisations.[28] It also needs to understand the voluntary nature of much of this activity and the varied sources of funds often available.

All of these considerations will have a profound effect on corporate strategy. Decision making may be slower and more uncertain. There may be more lobbying of funding bodies over individual decisions. There may be several conflicting objectives that make strategy difficult to develop. The style and expectations of the organisation need to be built into the strategy process.

Key strategic principles

- Public organisations are unlikely to have a profit objective. Strategy is therefore governed by broader public policy issues such as politics, monopoly supply, bureaucracy and the battle for resources from the government to fund the activities of the organisation.

- Strategy in non-profit organisations needs to reflect the values held by the institutions concerned. Decision making may be slower and more complex.

- Within the constraints outlined above, the basic strategic principles can then be applied.

1.7 INTERNATIONAL DIMENSIONS IN CORPORATE STRATEGY

While the principles of corporate strategy can be applied across the world, the international dimensions of strategy do introduce some specific and important considerations.[29]

- *International economies and their impact on trading between nations.* The completion of the Uruguay Round of the General Agreement on Tariffs and Trade in 1994, the enlargement of the European Union and the formation of the North American Free Trade Association in 1994 are all examples of such developments. All may provide opportunities and pose threats for company corporate strategy.

- *International finance, currency and tax.* For example, adverse currency movements could alone severely curtail gains to be made from other aspects of corporate strategy.

- *Economies of scale and production.* Coupled with the lower wage costs available in some countries, these have had a powerful impact on aspects of corporate strategy.

● *Differing cultures, beliefs and management styles around the world.* These are major factors that must form an important part of corporate strategy for international companies. Major strategic problems have arisen where international companies have considered these vital topics too late in the strategy process.

This is not a comprehensive list of major topics, but it does illustrate the specific impact on corporate strategy. International corporate strategy issues follow on naturally from such topics and will be explored later in this book. These include the corporate strategy aspects of:

● global branding;
● product quality;
● worldwide production and sourcing of products;
● international motivation and reward of employees;
● the balance to be adopted between the national autonomy of companies and the benefits to be gained by operating globally.

Key strategic principles

● The international dimensions of corporate strategy make its development more complicated.

● Among the topics that need careful consideration are: international economies and their impact on world trade, international finance, economies of scale derived from global production, differing cultures and beliefs.

CASE STUDY 1.2

Electrolux plans for growth

Electrolux is one of the world's leading producers of domestic and commercial electrical appliances, such as vacuum cleaners, washing machines, refrigerators and microwave ovens. Sales in 1993 were nearly US$13 billion, making it the largest such producer in Europe. Its international headquarters is in Sweden but it has around 40 factories in Europe and the USA. (See Fig 1.9.)

The company grew rapidly by the acquisition of a number of national domestic appliance companies in a number of European, North American and Asian countries over the period 1970 to 1990. As a consequence, Electrolux bought some companies that had strong and proud national traditions in manufacturing and marketing such products and some well-known brand names. In order to gain the benefits of the larger scale of operation, the company dropped some of the brand names over the years, but it kept others for products that were essentially made to more standardised international designs. Methods of using domestic appliances vary around the world, however, and so Electrolux was unable totally to standardise its products. For example, in some European countries, such as Italy, washing machine customers load their clothing from the top; in others, such as the UK, the majority of customers prefer side-loading machines.

CASE STUDY 1.2 continued

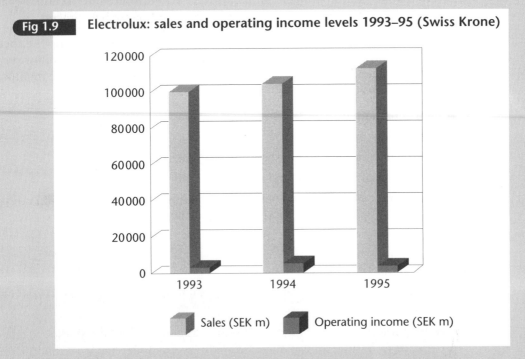

Fig 1.9 Electrolux: sales and operating income levels 1993–95 (Swiss Krone)

In the following extract from the company's Annual Report and Accounts for 1993, Electrolux outlines the corporate strategy it has followed for over twenty years.

Our mission and strategy

The Electrolux Group's operations shall be devoted mainly to household goods for indoor and outdoor use, along with the corresponding products for commercial users. On the basis of attractive products and rational operations, we aim to achieve a level of profitability that gives our shareholders good growth in net worth and dividends.

Our strategy has involved acquisitions and subsequent restructuring in order to obtain market positions and sales volumes in our core areas that would create a framework for long-term competitive strength. Our primary goal has been to maintain a position of leadership in our major geographical markets. In the light of greater internationalisation of products and markets, we aim today at long-term synergy effects on a global level for such activities as product development, purchasing and production of components, and marketing.

For the most part, we have reached our goals in terms of market positions. We are now the largest or the second largest on the world market in product areas that account for about 75 per cent of Group sales.

The implications of strategy

However, our strategy of acquisitions has involved comprehensive restructuring as well as extensive investment in new facilities and new generations of products. These resource-intensive changes were implemented during a recession, when demand was weak in several of our major markets. This has led to unsatisfactory profitability in recent years. We are now focussing primarily on:

● continuing the restructuring process and increasing internal efficiency;

● strengthening our core areas and streamlining the Group's structure;

● intensifying activities in new markets in Eastern Europe and Asia.

Over the last few years, we have gradually reduced cost levels as well as capital tied up in operations. Our Group-wide action program has been successful, but there is still room for improvement. We have continued to improve our production structure following the major investments of the latter part of the 1980s, which included the construction or renovation of five large plants for white goods [refrigerators, ovens, etc]. Over the last few years, we closed a number of smaller units which were not expected to be competitive in the long term, and this enabled an improvement in productivity. Our goal is an annual productivity increase of 4 to 5 per cent.

In terms of tied-up capital, we have been particularly successful in reducing inventories. After elimination of exchange-rate effects, inventories in 1993 were reduced to 16.1 per cent of sales and accounts receivable to 17.8 per cent. Our goal remains to reduce both inventories and accounts receivable to 15 per cent of sales. With the present volume of operations, this would free additional capital corresponding to SEK 3.5 billion annually.

Investment in new products

As part of the development of operations subsequent to acquisitions, we have made extensive investments in new products. The good sales growth reported in such areas as forestry and garden equipment, car safety equipment and compressors is traceable largely to this commitment. However, we must further intensify the rate of product renewal in order to achieve greater organic growth during the 1990s. In white goods, we have developed four new, well differentiated product ranges for the European market in recent years, the last of which was launched in 1993. A framework has thus been created for a more consistent positioning of our brands in specific European segments. A completely new product range for the Frigidaire brand was also launched in the US during the year. We are now in a phase of intensified commitment to marketing.

We have also allocated considerable resources in our various operations for development of more environmentally friendly products, for which sales are growing steadily. Our goal is to be leader in terms of improved environmental compatibility.

Opportunities for expansion

Since June 1992, we have been co-operating with AEG Hausegeräte, the white goods company within AEG of Germany, on product development and production of new items. Electrolux has a 20 per cent shareholding in the company. Early in December 1993, the Board of AEG offered us the opportunity to acquire all outstanding shares in their white goods subsidiary, including the purchase of the AEG brand name for white goods, floor-care products and other household appliances. This acquisition would give us a complete operation in Europe in terms of both geography and product range. The reason is that the company's sales are focused on central Europe, while Electrolux is particularly strong in northern and southern Europe. With AEG, we would have a market share equivalent to that of the leading producer, Bosch-Siemens. Germany is the largest white-goods market in Europe in both value and volume, and is the market driver for product development. A possible acquisition of AEG would be subject to approval under the EU Merger Control Regulation.

The political changes of recent years have created conditions for a truly global presence. Opportunities for expansion are being enhanced through the opening of new markets such as Eastern Europe, China and India, the creation of free-trade zones in various parts of the world and of course through GATT. Our goal is to double sales in Eastern Europe (currently SEK 2.2 billion) and in Asia (currently SEK 4.5 billion) over the next five years. Growth will be achieved gradually through the establishment of wholly or partly owned companies, since opportunities for acquisitions in these markets are limited.

Conclusion

It is difficult to evaluate the market situation in Europe for 1994. However, we do not expect any significant improvement over 1993. On the other hand, the economic recovery in the US is expected to continue and should involve increased demand in most areas.

Our view of the Group's long-term prospects has not changed. Our goal continues to be a return on equity of 15 per cent after tax over the course of the business cycle. Since the Group's potential for expansion is estimated at 5 to 10 per cent annually, achieving our goal will also involve a gradual strengthening of our equity/assets ratio.

CASE QUESTIONS

1 How would you summarise the company's mission and objectives? Where do garden equipment and forestry fit into this picture?

2 What strategies has it followed to achieve these? With what results?

3 Thinking back to your knowledge of the various functional areas of a business (marketing, finance, etc.), what in your opinion would have been the main problems that the company faced over the period? To what extent do you judge that they should form part of the formal corporate strategy of the company? Why?

4 Are there any areas of the Electrolux strategy that are perhaps not fully covered in the 1993 Report that you would consider to be important?

KEY READING

Successful corporate strategy[30]

In this extract from his book, Foundations of Corporate Success, *Professor John Kay explains the basic nature of corporate strategy and the strategies employed by successful companies.*

The subject of strategy analyses the firm's relationships with its environment, and a business strategy is a scheme for handling these relationships. Such a scheme may be articulated, or implicit, pre-programmed, or emergent. A strategy is a sequence of united events which amounts to a coherent pattern of business behaviour. All firms are part of a rich network of relationships. They must deal with customers and suppliers, with competitors and potential competitors. For many firms, the relationship with the government is also critical to their strategy. The government may buy the firm's products or regulate many of its activities.

These relationships may be *classical* and *contractual* – elaborately articulated in legal documents – or they may be *informal* and *relational*, and enforced primarily by the need the parties have to go on doing business with each other. They are designed to secure outcomes in which all parties win, because in commerce, as in life, relationships are rarely of the type in which one party gains what the other loses. They are designed to deal with the problems of co-operation, of co-ordination, and of differentiation. The unique structure of these relationships, their architecture, is the source of some firms' competitive advantage [*see* Chapter 6 of this book].

If the subject of business strategy focuses on the relationship between the firm and its environment, there are many key management issues which it does not address. Strategy is not principally concerned with employee motivation, or with finance, or with accounting, or with production scheduling and inventory control, although these may influence the firm's strategy and be influenced by it. In the last two decades, the pretensions and prestige of the subject of strategy have been such that strategists have stressed not only the central importance of the issues with which they deal but also the relevance of strategy to all aspects of business behaviour. For the same reasons, every-one involved in business – from the personnel manager to the public relations consultant – has asserted a right to contribute to the strategy process.

But strategy is not simply another word for important. There are many aspects to good management, and to say that strategy and operations management are distinct facets of it is not to disparage either. Yet there is a difference between strategy and these other elements of management practice which illuminates the nature of strategy itself and may partly explain its supposed primacy. In most industries, there are many firms which have their finance and accounting right, their human relations right, their information technology adapted to their needs. For one firm to succeed in these areas does not damage the others. In implementing finance and accounting, human relations, and information technology, it is right and normal, to look to the best practice in other firms.

But strategy is not like that. Honda and BMW did not establish their market positions by methods which built on the best practice of their competitors. For both companies, attempts to match their rivals' strategies failed. BMW's bubble cars were not as well regarded as Innocenti's, and its limousines were inferior to those of Mercedes. Honda was able to sell powerful motor bikes in the US only after its success with quite different products had destroyed its competitors' finances and established its own reputation. Successful strategy is rarely copycat strategy. It is based on doing well what rivals cannot do or cannot do readily, not what they can do or are already doing.

Source: Kay, J (1993) *Foundations of Corporate Success.* Reproduced by permission of Oxford University Press.

SUMMARY

● In this chapter, we have explored the nature of corporate strategy – linking process between the organisation and its environment – which focuses particularly on competitive advantage, the distinctive capabilities of the organisation and the need to be innovative. Adding value is of particular importance to most organisations, though for non-profit and government organisations this is not necessarily the case.

● Corporate strategy is important because it deals with the major, fundamental issues that affect the future of the organisation. It integrates the functional areas of the organisation, covering the range and depth of its activities.

● There are three core areas of corporate strategy: strategic analysis; strategic development; and strategy implementation. Although the three core areas are often presented as being strictly sequential, they interlock and overlap in practice. There are two important qualifications to the three core areas: the use of judgement and values to derive the strategy and the need to make highly speculative assessments about the future. Unless handled carefully, these may give a false sense of direction about the future.

● In developing corporate strategy, there is a need to distinguish between process, content and context. Process is the method by which the strategies are derived;

content is the strategic decisions then made; context is the environment within which the organisation operates and develops its strategies. Process is usually the area that causes the most problems because it is difficult to measure precisely.

● There is a fundamental disagreement between strategists regarding how corporate strategy can be developed. There are two basic routes: the *prescriptive approach* and the *emergent approach*. The prescriptive approach takes the view that the three core areas are linked together sequentially; the emergent approach regards the three core areas as being inter-related. The two approaches have some common elements in the early stages: analysis and the development of a mission for the organisation. Beyond this, they go their separate ways and lead to two different models for the corporate strategy process.

● In public sector, government-owned organisations, the strategy is usually governed by broader public policy concerns, rather than profits. In non-profit institutions, strategy needs to reflect the values of the particular organisation; the basic strategic principles can then be applied.

● In international terms, the development of corporate strategy is more complex for a number of reasons, including the impact on trade between nations, financial issues, economies of scale in global production and differing cultures and beliefs. All these make international corporate strategy more difficult to develop.

QUESTIONS

1 Examine the IBM case again and consider what alternative strategies you would have adopted, if you had been in charge. What do you still admire most about the company? As a work assignment, why not investigate the strategies IBM has adopted to overcome its problems? Since 1993, IBM has appointed a new chief executive, made major redundancies among the workforce, acquired new companies such as the computer software company, Lotus, and demerged part of its business. You might also examine the fortunes of the suppliers mentioned in the case.

2 As a work assignment, analyse the activities of Hewlett-Packard. Investigate in particular how it has managed to stay ahead of its competitors. Compare your answer with the five key elements of strategic decisions in Section 1.1.3.

3 In the key reading, Professor Kay makes the comment that motivation of employees is not really part of corporate strategy. Do you agree with this? Give reasons for your views.

4 Take the three core areas of corporate strategy and apply them to a decision with which you have recently been involved. For example, it might be the organisation of a student activity or the purchase of a major item of equipment. Did you analyse the facts, consider the options and make a selection? Does this description over-simplify the process because, for example, it was necessary to persuade others to spend some money?

5 To what extent do you agree with Professor Mintzberg's description of strategies emerging rather than being prescribed in advance? If you agree with his description,

what evidence do you have to support your view? If you disagree, then explain the basis of your rejection.

6 With the three core areas of corporate strategy in mind, identify how the strategy development process might vary for the following types of business: a global company such as IBM; a public service company such as a water provider (which might also be a monopoly); a non-profit organisation such as a student union or society.

7 If corporate strategy is so uncertain and has such a strong element of judgement, is there any point in its formal analysis? What arguments does the chapter use to justify such a process? Using your own value judgement, do you find them convincing?

STRATEGIC PROJECT

Corporate strategy in the computer industry

The cases in the chapter have examined aspects of corporate strategy in the global computer industry. You might like to pick up the challenge of investigating this further. For example, you could explore other companies, perhaps Apple Computers which has been in need of a new strategy for several years. You could explore the new links that are developing between telecommunications and the computer industry, especially for their innovative implications.

FURTHER READING

Professor Kay's book *Foundations of Corporate Success* (Oxford University Press, 1993) is an excellent introduction to the nature of corporate strategy; read the early chapters. In addition, the well-known book of readings and cases by Professors Mintzberg and Quinn, *The Strategy Process* (Prentice Hall, 1991), has an excellent selection of material on the nature of corporate strategy; read Chapter 1 in particular. The article by Professor Mintzberg on 'Crafting Strategy' in the *Harvard Business Review* (July–Aug 1987) is also strongly recommended.

REFERENCES

1 Case compiled by the author from the following published sources: Packard, D (1995) *The HP Way: How Bill Hewlett and I built our company. Hewlett-Packard Annual Report and Accounts* 1994, *Financial Times*, 21 Jan 1994, p24; 13 June 1994, p27; 28 Sept 1994, p33; 28 Mar 1996; 15 May 1996, p27.
2 Ansoff, I (1969) *Corporate Strategy*, Penguin, Harmondsworth, Ch 1.
3 Drucker, P (1961) *The Practice of Management*, Mercury, London, Ch 6.
4 Andrews, K (1971) *The Concept of Corporate Strategy*, Irwin, Homewood, Ill, p28.
5 Further definitions are discussed in Quinn, J B (1980) *Strategies for Change: Logical Incrementalism*, Irwin, Homewood, Ill, Ch 1.
6 Ohmae, K (1982) *The Mind of the Strategist*, Penguin, Harmondsworth, p36.
7 Mintzberg, H (1987) 'Crafting Strategy', *Harvard Business Review*, July–Aug.

8 Dickson, M (1994) 'We're trying to connect you', *Financial Times*, 16 June, p21.

9 Adonis, A (1994) 'US authorities clear BT and MCI alliance', *Financial Times*, 16 June, p24.

10 Hill, A (1994) 'Telecom Italia has hopes of being a world leader', *Financial Times*, 20 May, p23.

11 Case compiled by the author from the following published sources: Heller, R (1994) *The Fate of IBM*, Warner Books, London (easy-to-read and accurate). Carroll , P (1993) *The Unmaking of IBM,* Crown (rather one-sided). *Financial Times*: 7 Aug 1990, p14; 5 June 1991, article by Alan Cane; 8 Nov 1991, article by Alan Cane and Louise Kehoe; 5 May 1993, p17; 29 July 1993, p17; 14 Mar 1994, p17; 26 Mar 1994, p8; 28 Mar 1994, p15. *Economist*: 16 Jan 1993, p23. *Business Age*: April 1994, p 76. Note that this case simplifies the IBM story by emphasising the PC aspects. There are further parts to the story that can be read in the references above.

12 There is some disagreement regarding this statement (explored further in Chapter 2). For now, it is appropriate to note that according to J B Quinn, one of the distinguished writers and thinkers in the strategy field, strategic decisions are those that determine the overall direction of an enterprise and its ultimate viability in the light of the predictable, the unpredictable and the unknowable changes that may occur in its most important environments. Quinn, J B (1980) *Strategies for Change: Logical Incrementalism,* Irwin.

13 Porter, M E (1985) *Competitive Advantage*, Free Press, Boston, MA, argues vigorously for learning lessons from the mistakes of others, e.g. Ch 6, 'Competitor selection'.

14 Mintzberg, H and Quinn, J B (1991) *The Strategy Process,* 2nd edn, Prentice Hall, Upper Saddle River, NJ, Introduction.

15 Cyert, R M and March, J (1963) *A Behaviorial Theory of the Firm*, Prentice Hall, Upper Saddle River, NJ.

16 Partly adapted from Quinn, J B (1991) *Strategies for Change*, Ch 1, and Mintzberg, H and Quinn, J B (1991) *The Strategy Process*, Prentice Hall, Upper Saddle River, NJ.

17 For example, Gilmore, F F and Brandenburg, R G (1962) 'Anatomy of Corporate Planning', *Harvard Business Review*, 40, Nov–Dec, p61.

18 *See* for example, Pettigrew, A and Whipp, R (1991) *Managing Change for Competitive Success*, Blackwell, Oxford. See also Mintzberg, H (1987) Ibid.

19 Jauch, L R and Glueck, W (1988) *Business Policy and Strategic Management*, McGraw-Hill, NY.

20 Argenti, J (1965) *Corporate Planning*, Allen and Unwin, London.

21 Mintzberg, H (1987) 'Crafting Strategy', *Harvard Business Review*, July–Aug, p65.

22 Cyert, R M and March, J (1963) *A Behavioural Theory of the Firm*, Prentice Hall, Upper Saddle River, NJ.

23 Mintzberg, H (1987) Ibid.

24 This analogy was inspired by Professor Mintzberg's brief comment in his article: Mintzberg, H (1994) 'The Fall and Rise of Strategic Planning', *Harvard Business Review*, Jan–Feb, p114.

25 *See* Lynch, R (1994) *European Business Strategies,* 2nd edn, Kogan Page, London, pp203–5, for details of likely privatisation candidates and timing in telecommunications.

26 *See* Lynch, R (1992) *European Marketing*, Kogan Page, London, p173, for examples.

27 International Bank for Reconstruction and Development (1994) *World Development Report 1994*, Oxford University Press, New York. The report surveys this area in thoughtful detail.

28 Whelan, T L and Hunger, J D (1991) *Strategic Management*, 2nd edn, Addison-Wesley, Ch 11.

29 Ellis, J and Williams, D (1995) *International Business Strategy*, Pitman Publishing, London, Ch 1.

30 Kay, J (1993) *Foundations of Corporate Success*, Oxford University Press, Oxford.

2

A review of theory and practice

When you have worked through this chapter, you will be able to:

- outline the political and economic background to the development of corporate strategy in the twentieth century;

- describe and evaluate prescriptive strategic practice;

- describe and evaluate emergent strategic practice;

- identify the main theories associated with prescriptive corporate strategy;

- identify the main theories associated with emergent corporate strategy.

◖ INTRODUCTION

This chapter provides an overview of corporate strategy theories and practice. Each of the main theories is explored in further detail in later chapters, so it is possible to skip this chapter now and read it later, but you will miss the opportunity to gain an overview of the general theoretical structure of corporate strategy.

To provide a more substantial foundation for corporate strategy development, the prescriptive and emergent approaches of Chapter 1 deserve further exploration. They will benefit from being set against the background of the twentieth-century political and economic developments that prompted and shaped them.

Even within each route, prescriptive or emergent, there is substantial disagreement among strategists about how corporate strategy can and should be developed. Both routes contain many different interpretations and theories. If the dynamics are to be fully understood, it is important that some of these differences are explored.

MINICASE

Attacking a dominant competitor: a joint venture strategy by Nestlé and General Mills

Kelloggs (US) dominates the world's ready-to-eat breakfast cereal market. In 1989, Nestlé (Switzerland) and General Mills (US) agreed a joint venture to attack the market. The objectives of the new company were to achieve by the year 2000 global sales of US$1 billion and, within this figure, to take a 20 per cent share of the European market. This case examines the corporate strategy developed by their new joint company, Cereal Partners (CP).

Background

With a 38 per cent market share, Kelloggs is the breakfast cereal market leader in the USA – a market worth US$9 billion at retail selling prices. General Mills has built up its market share to around 22 per cent through a series of product launches over a period of 15 years. The market is growing around 1 per cent each year.

Outside the USA, the global market is worth around US$5 to 7 billion. It is growing in many countries by around 10 per cent each year. However, this is from a base of much smaller consumption per head than in the US. The only exception is the UK where people eat more breakfast cereals per head than in the US. Kelloggs has over 50 per cent market share of the non-US market. It has pursued a vigorous strategy of international market launches for over 40 years in many markets and over 70 years in the UK. Up to 1990, no other company had a significant share internationally.

Development of Cereal Partners

After several abortive attempts to develop internationally by itself, General Mills (GM) approached Nestlé about a joint venture in 1989. (A joint venture is a separate company with each parent holding an equal share and contributing according to its resources and skills; the joint venture then has its own management and can develop its own strategy within limits set by the parents.) Nestlé had also been attempting to launch its own breakfast cereal range without much success. Both companies were attracted by the high value added in this branded, heavily advertised consumer market.

GM's proposal to Nestlé was to develop a new 50/50 joint company. GM would contribute its products, technology and manufacturing expertise – for example, it made 'Golden Grahams' and 'Cheerios' in the USA. Nestlé would give its brand name, several under-utilised factories and its major strengths in global marketing and distribution – for example, it made 'Nescafé' coffee products. Both parties found the deal so attractive that they agreed it in only three weeks. It operates outside the USA and Canada, where GM retains its operations.

Over the next six years, CP was launched in 40 countries around the world. Products such as 'Golden Grahams', 'Cheerios' and 'Fibre 1' have appeared on grocery supermarket shelves. CP has used a mixture of launch strategies, depending on the market circumstances: acquisitions were used in the UK and Poland, new product launches in the rest of Europe, south and central America and South Africa, and existing Nestlé cereal products were taken over in South-East Asia. To keep Kelloggs guessing about its next market moves and to satisfy local taste variations, CP has also varied the product range launched in each country. By 1995, the company was half way towards reaching its targets: US$500 million sales worldwide and around 10 per cent of the European market. Its operations were into profit in a number of European countries.

CASE QUESTION

Using the description of prescriptive and emergent strategies from Chapter 1 (and Chapter 2 if you need it), decide the following: was CP pursuing a prescriptive strategy, an emergent strategy, or both?

2.1 HISTORICAL FOUNDATIONS OF STRATEGY

In Chapter 1, we saw that corporate strategy relates the activities of the organisation to the environment in which it operates. As a result of increasing wealth, changes in industrialisation, shifts in the power balance between nations and many other factors, this environment is constantly changing. Corporate strategy and the prevailing logic supporting it will, by definition, change as the environment surrounding the organisation changes. Before we examine the theories surrounding corporate strategy, it is therefore appropriate to explore those theories in a historical context.

Until the late nineteenth century, organisations which were not owned by the nation state were too small to be considered as corporations. Small artisan factories driven by crafts may have needed strategies to survive and prosper against competitors, but formal corporate strategy did not exist. Table 2.1 shows how matters have developed since that time.

Table 2.1

The development of corporate strategy in the twentieth century, showing important environmental influences

Period	Environment	Strategy and management developments
1900–1910	• Colonial wars • Global trading of commodities	• Beginnings of examination of the management task, e.g. F W Taylor and Henri Fayol
1910–1930	• World War and its legacy	• Rise of larger organisations and the consequent need for increased management control
1930s	• Crash: trade barriers erected to protect some countries	• Formal management control mechanisms developed, e.g. budgeting and management accounting, particularly in the USA • Early human resource experiments in USA
1940s	• World War and its legacy	• Strong US industry and the birth of formal strategy • Beginnings of organisational theory
1950s	• Sustained economic growth coupled with first European trade and political block: European Economic Community	• First real strategy writings in formal series of papers • Organisational theory is applied to management tasks
1960s	• Continued growth until first oil price rise late in the decade	• Corporate strategy techniques are researched • Separate parallel development in organisational research
1970s	• Growth becomes more cyclical with another oil price shock	• Formal corporate strategy techniques adopted • First research writings objecting to same techniques
1980s	• Far East and global developments • Computer data handling develops fast	• Major strategic emphasis on competitive aspects of formal corporate strategy • Search continues for new strategy concepts emphasising the human rather than the competitive aspects of the process
1990s	• Telecommunications, global corporations, high growth in the Pacific Rim but currency problems in Japan	• Global concepts of strategy • Greater emphasis on the organisation's own resources rather than competition as the basis for strategy development

North America, Europe and Japan were more or less the only areas that had begun to industrialise by the end of the nineteenth century. Countries such as China, India, Korea, Malaysia, Singapore, the Philippines, Saudi Arabia, Iran and Iraq, Nigeria, South Africa were still largely without industry; they supplied commodities and raw materials to world markets but had not yet begun to industrialise.[1] Corporate strategy which is principally associated with increased industrialisation was therefore more likely to develop in Europe, North America and Japan than other areas around the world.

2.1.1 Corporate strategy in the early twentieth century

During the early twentieth century, particularly in the United States and Europe, managers rather than academics began to explore and define the management task. F W Taylor in the USA and Henri Fayol in France are examples of senior industry figures who started to research and write on such issues. Taylor and Fayol were industrialists rather than academics, holding senior positions in industry for some years. Among other industrialists, we can identify Adamiecki in Poland who was investigating 'principles of organisation'; around the same time, Hellmich in Germany did much to establish the place of the engineer in senior management – a tradition that continues to this day in German industry in contrast to the UK.[2] Although such managers regarded human beings as capable of rational thought, their prime concern was not with the strategic direction of the enterprise. They were rather concerned with the detailed analysis of specific organisational functions in order to perfect individual management tasks. The move towards a broader perspective for corporate strategy would only come later in the century.

At the same time and extending into the period after the First World War, other senior industrialists were faced with what today we would probably identify as major strategic issues: industrialisation had brought economies of scale, greater competition between countries and between companies, along with mass markets for such items as the motor car. In a pragmatic way, owner proprietors such as Henry Ford set about experimenting in their companies to produce their goods more cheaply and thus fulfil growing market demand. Strategies that we still recognise today were developed by Ford in the period 1908–15[3] and included those outlined in Exhibit 2.1.

Henry Ford did not believe in major model variations and market segmentation, however, unlike his great rival from the 1920s, General Motors, headed by Alfred P Sloan.[4] Nor did Ford believe in the importance of middle and senior management. He actually sacked many of his senior managers and ultimately left his company in real difficulties when he died.[5] Hence, his rival in the 1920s and beyond, General Motors, was ultimately more successful with other strategies that we also still recognise today (*see* Exhibit 2.1).

These developments took place against a business environment of growing international tension culminating in war and slump. But the principal market of Ford and General Motors in North America was large, growing rapidly and insulated from the effects of the First World War until 1917. Indeed, the massive investment during wartime is advantageous to an economy as long as the country is able to avoid the destruction that usually accompanies conflict.[6]

| Exhibit 2.1 | Early strategies still recognised today |

From the period 1908–1915: Henry Ford

- Innovative technology
- Replacement of men by machines
- Search for new quality standards
- Constant cost-cutting through factory redesign
- Passing on the cost reductions in the form of reduced prices for the model T car

From the period 1920–1935: Alfred Sloan and colleagues

- Car models tailored for specific market niches
- Rapid model changes
- Structured management teams and reporting structures
- Separation of day-to-day management from the task of devising longer-term strategy

Other companies began to follow these successful policies; they were introduced into Japan and Europe during the 1920s and 1930s. The business environment also began to change, however: after the First World War came the great economic depression of the 1930s. This brought the need for a new order in international currency and, just as importantly, the desire for greater controls to cut superfluous costs and return to profitability. The economic depression had been particularly acute in North America, so it was perhaps not surprising that new forms of management accounting were developed during this period in the USA and Canada.

2.1.2 Corporate strategy in the mid-twentieth century

The Second World War brought its specialist demands for military equipment coupled with more destruction across much of Europe and Japan; North and South America went largely unscathed. At this time, the Middle East and Far East still remained largely outside the scope of industrial development. This period was hardly the time for corporate strategists to influence events.

The late 1940s probably witnessed the period of the greatest power of North American industry and companies. It was also the real beginning of corporate strategy development and this then continued into the 1950s. It was accompanied by the reconstruction of industry across Europe and the beginnings of the Asian development period, particularly in Japan.

By the late 1950s, writers such as Ansoff were beginning to develop corporate strategy concepts that would continue into the 1970s. During the 1960s the early concepts of what would later become one of the main approaches to corporate strategy – *prescriptive corporate strategy* – began to take shape. Ansoff[7] argued that there were environmental factors which accelerated the development of corporate strategy. Two trends can be identified:

- *The accelerated rate of change*. Corporate strategy provided a way of taking advantage of new opportunities;

- *The greater spread of wealth*. Corporate strategy needed to find ways of identifying the opportunities provided by the spread of increasing wealth, especially in Europe.

It was during this same period that the early research was conducted which subsequently led to the development of the second main approach to corporate strategy – *emergent corporate strategy*, although this really only came to prominence in the 1970s and 1980s.

2.1.3 Corporate strategy in the late twentieth century

The 1970s saw the major oil price rises. They came as a result of the world's increased need for energy and Middle Eastern success in organising an oil price cartel. The business environment was subject to a sudden and largely unpredicted change that caused some corporate strategists to reconsider the value of prediction in corporate strategy.

The 1980s and 1990s have witnessed six further environmental developments, all of which are still impacting on corporate strategy:

- increased global competition for many businesses;

- the consolidation and development of trading blocks;

- the development of telecommunications and computers that have transformed the scope of the environment (along with the absence of major wars), making global communication reliable and cheap;

- the collapse of Eastern European controlled economies;

- the rise of the highly competitive and low-wage economies of Far Eastern countries, such as Singapore and Malaysia;

- increased levels of training and knowledge of workers.

These trends have had the following effects on corporate strategy:

1 *Free market competition*. This has become a stronger element in strategy. According to various United Nations and World Bank studies, free market competition has been one element in supporting and encouraging growth in many newly developing countries.[8] Corporate strategy has therefore become more international in scope.

2 *Asia–Pacific competition*. Corporate strategy has moved out of being the preserve of North American and European countries. Because of the lower labour costs in the new region, this has put pressure on Western companies to cut costs or move east.

3 *Global and local interests*. In addition to economic growth, the world market place has become more complex in cultural and social terms. Markets have become more international thus making it necessary to balance global interests and local demand variations.

4   *Need to empower and involve employees in strategic decisions*. The higher levels of training and deeper levels of skills of employees mean that they are no longer poorly trained and no longer have difficulty making a contribution to corporate strategy, especially in some Western countries.

These trends have led to increasing interest by corporate strategists in theories that reflect this greater diversity of global backgrounds. The 1980s and 1990s have therefore seen a move away from *wealth creation* associated purely with Western concepts of profit maximisation to more complex concepts that introduce *social and cultural elements* into corporate strategy, such as the work of researchers Marris and Granovetter (see later in this chapter).

All the environmental trends identified above and their implications for corporate strategy will be examined during the course of this book. The overall conclusion is perhaps that the *pace of change* would appear to be increasing and corporate strategy needs to cope with this important structural variable.

Key strategic principles

- Corporate strategy responds to the environment existing or developing at that time.

- The early twentieth century was characterised by the increased use of science and technology. This was reflected in greater structuring of management and strategy. Mass production of quality products became possible.

- In the mid-twentieth century, the accelerated rate of technological change and the greater spread of wealth led to new demands for formal strategy development.

- In the late twentieth century, there were four distinct pressures on corporate strategy: free market competition; the rise of the Asia–Pacific economies; global competition; and greater knowledge and training of managers and employees. All four elements in the environment have directed the development of corporate strategy.

2.2 PRESCRIPTIVE CORPORATE STRATEGY IN PRACTICE

2.2.1 The basic concept

A prescriptive corporate strategy is one where the *objective* has been defined in advance and the *main elements* have been developed before the strategy commences.

1   In Chapter 1 we showed that prescriptive strategy starts with the search for an agreed objective, such as the maximisation of the return on the capital involved in a business (Ansoff, Porter).[9] It should be noted that the objective is not

necessarily profit maximisation: for example, in a publicly-owned enterprise or social co-operative, the objective could have social service standards as its major aim.

2 The environment within which the organisation operates is then analysed and projections made for the future. For example, economic and political considerations are analysed for their strategy implications.

3 Based on this work, forecasts then form the background for the organisation's strategic plan. At this point, the objectives may be reviewed: if the forecasts are particularly positive or negative, then the objectives may be changed. For example, the US$1 billion objective for breakfast cereals' market share at CP might have been altered if there had been a sudden health scare associated with cereals.

4 After making a forecasted projection of the expected environment, various options are identified to enable the business to achieve the agreed objectives – there is usually more than one way of achieving an objective.

5 One option is then selected which has the ability to meet the objective.

6 The chosen option is implemented by the organisation's managers. For example, at CP, the breakfast cereal company surveyed the options for entry into each country and chose the one that fitted their criteria, including ease of entry and likelihood of success. The launch was then implemented in that country.

This prescriptive process is shown in Fig 2.1.

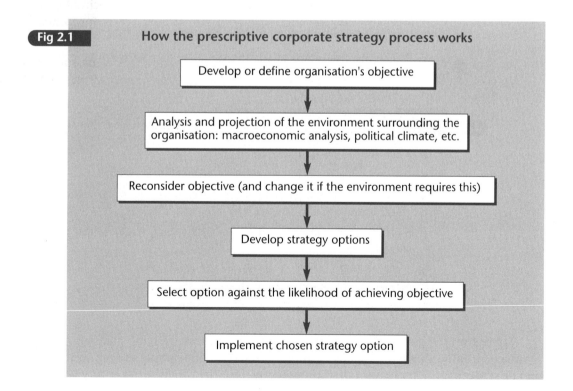

Fig 2.1   How the prescriptive corporate strategy process works

Develop or define organisation's objective

Analysis and projection of the environment surrounding the organisation: macroeconomic analysis, political climate, etc.

Reconsider objective (and change it if the environment requires this)

Develop strategy options

Select option against the likelihood of achieving objective

Implement chosen strategy option

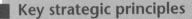

Key strategic principles

- Prescriptive strategy usually has a clear and well-defined objective that is agreed in advance.
- The objective may be adjusted if the environment or other circumstances change.
- To test for prescriptive strategy, it is essential to examine whether a clearly defined, main objective has been identified.

2.2.2 Typical strategic practice for prescriptive strategy

1 *The objective*. This is the starting point. A typical profit maximisation objective is that stated by Alfred Sloan,[10] the former President of General Motors (US), the largest car company in the world. Writing in 1961, he commented that the key strategic issue for a company is to manoeuvre its products into markets where they could earn the maximum return:

   The strategic aim of a business is to earn a return on capital and, if in a particular case the return in the long run is not satisfactory, the deficiency should be corrected or the activity abandoned.

2 *Options, selection and implementation*. These have been seen by many prescriptive strategists as capable of rational analysis and action. Case study 2.1 illustrates the experience of Spillers, where some of the practical issues were tackled and management decisions were assisted by prescriptive strategic planning.

In general terms, the practical advantages of such a prescriptive process have been found to be those summarised in Exhibit 2.2.

Exhibit 2.2   **The advantages of the prescriptive process**

- A complete *overview* of the organisation.
- The possibility of making a *comparison* with the defined objectives.
- A summary of the *demands on the resources* of the organisation, including people, physical assets, finance and cash flow.
- A picture of the *choices* that the organisation may need to make if resources are limited.
- The possibility for the organisation to *monitor* the agreed plan as it is implemented, so that it can evaluate the progress that is being made.

Strategical influences on corporate strategy   In studies of the practice of prescriptive strategy, close parallels have been drawn with what happens in *military strategy*. For example as seen in the early Chinese military historical writings of Sun Tzu; the nineteenth-century German strategist,

Clausewitz;[11] and Captain B H Liddell Hart[12] who wrote about the First World War. All these have been have quoted by corporate strategists.[13]

Prescriptive business strategy is seen as being similar to sending the troops (*employees*) into battle (*against competitors*) with a clear plan (*the prescriptive strategic plan*) that has been drawn up by the generals (*directors*) and then has been implemented (by launching innovatory products, etc.). The Kelloggs/CP breakfast cereals' strategic battle is a good example.

Prescriptive strategic analysis has borrowed from *economic theory*. Adam Smith, writing in the eighteenth century, took the view that human beings were basically capable of rational decisions that would be motivated most strongly by maximising their profits in any situation.[14] Moreover, individuals were capable of rational choice between options, especially where this involved taking a long-term view. Adam Smith has been quoted with approval by some modern strategists, economists and politicians. However, it should be noted that he lived in the eighteenth century and wrote about an era before modern organisations were conceived: for example, he had never seen a factory; only the craftsman's workshop.[15]

Subsequently, modern strategy theorists, such as Professor Michael Porter[16] of Harvard University Business School, have translated profit maximisation and competitive warfare concepts into strategy techniques and structure that have contributed to prescriptive strategic practice. Porter suggested that what really matters is *sustainable competitive advantage* versus competitors in the market place: only by this means can a company have a successful strategy.

Others have taken this further: for example, the Boston Consulting Group used market data to develop a simple, strategic matrix that presented strategic options for analysis (we will explore this in Chapter 3). One of the early writers on corporate strategy was Professor Igor Ansoff, at that time at Vanderbilt University, Tennessee, who wrote a number of books and papers over the period from 1960–90[17] that explored the practice of prescriptive strategy. Strategists such as Chakravarthy and Lorange[18] follow in the long line of those writing about strategic planning systems who employ many of these basic concepts. They are still widely used in many organisations around the world.

The prescriptive strategic process is claimed to be logical, rational and capable of real insight into the problems of an organisation. It focuses on the major issues that each company needs to address.

The strategy techniques employed in this approach are explored in the later chapters of this book. In our breakfast cereals case, the development of CP's worldwide strategy in breakfast cereals was based on such an approach.

Despite the advantages claimed for a prescriptive strategy system operating at the centre of organisations, there have been numerous critics of the whole approach. One of the most insightful is Professor Henry Mintzberg of McGill University, Canada. Mintzberg, along with other commentators, has researched decision making at corporate strategy level and suggested that a prescriptive strategy approach is based on a number of dangerous assumptions as to how organisations operate in practice (summarised in Exhibit 2.3).[19] There is significant research to show that these assumptions are not always correct. For example, the

| Exhibit 2.3 | Some major difficulties with the prescriptive strategic process |

Mintzberg has identified six major assumptions of the prescriptive process that may be wholly or partially false.

1 *The future can be predicted accurately enough to make rational discussion and choice realistic.* As soon as a competitor or a government does something unexpected, however, the whole process may be invalidated.

2 *It is possible and better to forgo the short-term benefit in order to obtain long-term good.* This may be incorrect: it may not be possible to determine the long-term good and, even if it were, those involved may not be willing to make the sacrifice, such as jobs or investment.

3 *The strategies proposed are, in practice, logical and capable of being managed in the way proposed.* Given the political realities of many companies, there may be many difficulties in practice.

4 *The Chief Executive has the knowledge and power to choose between options. He does not need to persuade anyone, nor compromise on his decisions.* This may be extraordinarily naive in many organisations where the culture and leadership seek discussion as a matter of normal practice.

5 *After careful analysis, strategy decisions can be clearly specified, summarised and presented; they do not require further development, nor do they need to be altered because circumstances outside the company have changed.* This point may have some validity but is not always valid.

6 *Implementation is a separate and distinctive phase that only comes after a strategy has been agreed: for example, a strategy to close a factory merely requires a management decision and then it just happens.* This is extraordinarily simplistic in many complex strategic decisions.

market place can change, or employees may not like an agreed solution and will find ways to delay it or not implement it at all. Given this evidence, *emergent strategy* has developed, as an alternative view of the strategy process.

Although highly critical of the formal prescriptive planning process, Mintzberg has modified his views in recent years and accepted that some strategic planning may be beneficial to the organisation.[20]

In conclusion, the period of the 1970s was the era when prescriptive corporate strategic planning was particularly strong. Further strategic competitive concepts, such as generic strategies, would be proposed in the 1980s (*see* Chapter 15), but the basic process of analysis, strategic choice, selection and implementation formed the best practice of many companies. The major UK food company, Spillers, was just one example of prescriptive strategy in action (*see* Case study 2.1). Another more recent example of prescriptive strategy is that of the major German mail order company, Otto Versand (*see* Case study 2.2).

Prescriptive strategic planning at Spillers plc

Under the guidance of a leading North American consulting company, a strategic corporate planning system was introduced into Spillers plc in 1978–79.[21] The company had a turnover of around £700 million (US$1200 million) and had been largely without any form of central direction up to that time.[22]

Spillers plc consisted of a number of operating companies:

- Flour milling and bread baking (Spillers Homepride Flour)
- Food coatings (Lucas Food Ingredients)
- Meat slaughtering and processing (Meade Lonsdale Group)
- Branded petfoods (Winalot)
- Restaurant chain (Mario and Franco Italian Restaurants)
- Branded canned meats and sauces (Tyne Brand)

The new strategic planning system consisted of an annual plan prepared to a common format by each of the above operating groups. Each plan had to address how it conformed with the Spillers' mission statement and objectives, e.g. on return on capital, market share, capital investment, etc. The plans were gathered together and presented by the operating groups to the Spillers Group Board.

This prescriptive strategy process certainly gave the centre of Spillers a degree of central knowledge and direction that it had never possessed before. It allowed the centre to debate with the senior managers and directors representing the various parts of

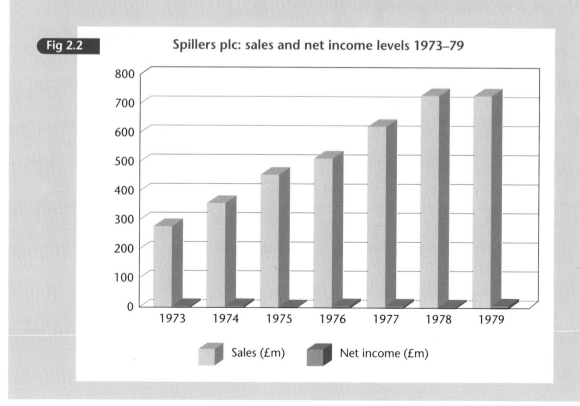

Fig 2.2 Spillers plc: sales and net income levels 1973–79

the group what they judged to be the major strategic issues facing the company. Moreover, for the first time, it gave the company an ability to allocate scarce resources among the competing requests of the operating companies within the group:

- £2 million investment in a new ingredient production line at Lucas Ingredients near Bristol, UK.

- £1.5 million investment in a major expansion of the Mario and Franco restaurant chain.

- Expansion of Spillers petfood branded products and production facility in Cambridgeshire, UK – estimated cost £3 million capital and a net loss for two years of £2 million in this product group.

- £20 million capital requirement spread over three years for a new abattoir at Reading UK. (The existing facility cannot meet the new higher EU standards in the long term, yet it provides over half the profits of the Spillers Meat Group.)

The company did not have the financial resources to meet all the requests. It had to make a selection; techniques such as portfolio matrices [see Chapter 6] were used to analyse and present the results. Even under the new system, however, few strategic options were ever presented by the operating companies to group headquarters: for example, the proposal was for a new abattoir or nothing. Nevertheless, rational choice was considered by the main Board. Moreover, beyond the centre, shareholders could now be told about the future plans and direction of the company. Employees were equally interested in the success of their own areas of the group.

Group strategic planning at Spillers had not previously existed. The success of Spillers' operating subsidiaries in obtaining funds up to that point had depended upon which operating company had asked first and who happened to make the most attractive financial case at the time when funds were available. Once, prescriptive strategic analysis and rational debate were introduced into this process during 1979, the main Board at last had a clear picture of the strategies of each major operating company and their requests for funds to implement these proposals. There had been a few complaints by the operating companies that the estimated system had been too rigid. Overall, however, the new Spillers' system was fairer and less open to individual favouritism.

In practice, for Spillers in 1979 the prescriptive solutions offered by its corporate strategic planning process were too little and too late; the strategic problems that would ultimately lead to its downfall were already evident.

CASE QUESTIONS

1 Using Mintzberg's critique of prescriptive processes, what are the main weaknesses of the Spillers' proposals?

2 Bearing these in mind, was it a worthwhile exercise for Spillers in your judgement?

Prescriptive strategy at Otto Versand

In 1992, Otto Versand was the largest mail order company in Europe. It had annual turnover of US$9678 million and was reasonably profitable. It had been expanding outside its German home territory for some years.

Otto Versand had developed a prescriptive corporate strategy approach for its expansion programme:

- Acquire a small mail order or joint venture in a new country.

- Find a new market niche in mail order in the country concerned.

- Use the company's international expertise in mail order to build the business in that country.

- Avoid tackling the leading companies already in that country head-on.

- Choose countries with well developed postal systems and high population density.

By 1992, Otto had become the second largest mail order company in Germany, France, Belgium and the Netherlands. It had also started operations in most other European countries, including the acquisition of Grattan in the UK. It was in the process of buying its first company in Japan.

Source: Lynch, R (1994) *European Business Strategies*, 2nd edn, Kogan Page, London, p202. © Copyright Aldersgate Consultancy Limited 1994. All rights reserved.

CASE QUESTION

Compare the country-by-country approach to market entry developed by Cereal Partners with the Otto Versand standardised country formula outlined above. How would you decide which prescriptive formula would be most appropriate?

Key strategic principles

- A prescriptive strategy is a strategy whose objective has been defined in advance and whose main elements have been developed before the strategy commences.

- The objective may be adjusted if circumstances change significantly.

- After defining the objective, the process then includes analysis of the environment, the development of strategic options and the choice between them. The chosen strategy is then implemented.

- The advantages of the prescriptive process include the overview it provides; the comparison with objectives; the summary of the demands made on resources; the picture of the choices to be made; and the ability to monitor what has been agreed.

- Mintzberg identified six assumptions made by the prescriptive process that may prove suspect in practice and invalidate the process.

◼ 2.3 ◼ EMERGENT CORPORATE STRATEGY IN PRACTICE

2.3.1 The basic concept

Emergent corporate strategy is a strategy whose *final objective* is unclear and whose *elements* are developed during the course of its life, as the strategy proceeds.

Deriving from the observation that human beings are not always the rational and logical creatures assumed by prescriptive strategy, various commentators have rejected the dispassionate, long-term prescriptive approach. They argue that strategy *emerges*, adapting to human needs and continuing to develop over time. Given this, they argue that there can be only limited meaningful prescriptive strategies and limited value from long-term planning.

Although this approach probably has its roots in the Hawthorn experiments of Elton Mayo in the 1930s,[23] it was not really until the research of Cyert and March in the 1960s[24] and Herbert Simon[25] around the same period that real progress was made. Research into how companies and managers develop corporate strategy in practice has shown that the assumption that strategies are always logical and rational does not take into account the reality of managerial decision making.

- Managers can only handle a selected number of options at any one time.
- They are biased in their interpretation of data.
- They are likely to seek a satisfactory solution rather than maximise the objectives of the organisation.
- Organisations consist of coalitions of people who form power blocks. Decisions and debate rely on negotiations and compromise between these groups, termed political bargaining. Researchers found that the notion of strategy being decided by a separate, central main board does not accord with reality.
- To take decisions, managers rely on a company's culture, politics and routines, rather than on a rational process of analysis and choice. (Who you know and how you present it is much more important that what you know.)

More recently, the research of Pettigrew,[26] Mintzberg,[27] Johnson[28] and others has further developed the *people* areas of strategy. Their empirical research has shown that the development of corporate strategy is more complex than the prescriptive strategists would imply: the people, politics and culture of organisations all need to be taken into account. Strategists such as Senge[29] have emphasised the *learning* approach to strategy: encouraging managers to undertake a process of trial and error to devise the optimal strategy.

As a result, according to these researchers, corporate strategy can best be considered as a process whereby the organisation's strategy is derived as a result of trial, repeated experimentation and small steps forward: in this sense, corporate strategy is *emergent* rather than *planned*. Figure 2.3 presents a simplified and diagrammatic view of the emergent process. The process then proceeds as market conditions change, the economy develops, teams of people in the company change, etc. Clearly such a process is hard to define in advance and therefore difficult to analyse and predict in a clear and structured way. For example, when entering new breakfast cereal markets, Cereal Partners adopted different strategies in accordance with the particular market circumstances.

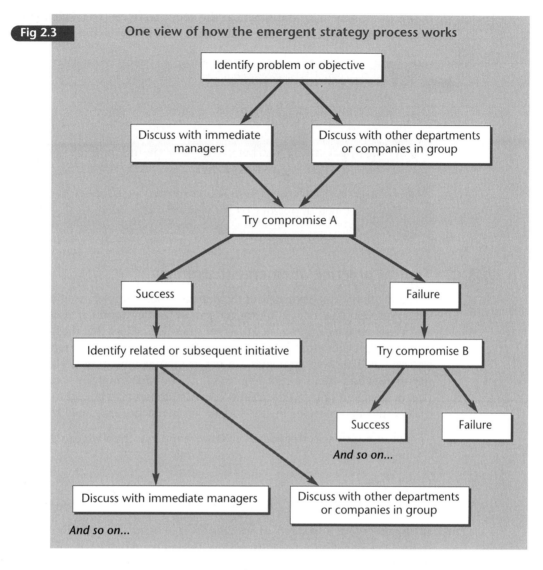

Fig 2.3 One view of how the emergent strategy process works

If the emergent view of the strategy process is correct, then the implications for corporate strategy are profound.

1 Strategies emerge from a confused background and often in a muddled and dis- organised way: the resulting strategies themselves may therefore be confused.

2 The process is unlikely to reflect reality: options identified will not be compre- hensive and the selection process will be flawed.

3 Considering 'implementation' after the rest of the strategy process does not reflect what usually happens.

4 Managers are unlikely to seek the optimal solution: it may not be capable of identification and, in addition, may not be in their personal interests.

5 Working within an organisation's routines and culture will allow the optimal culture to emerge rather than be forced by an artificial planning process.

In practice, many organisations treat the above comments as *limitations* on the pre-scriptive approach, rather than issues that cannot be overcome.

Key strategic principles

- Emergent strategy does not have a single, final objective; strategy develops over time.

- In fast-developing markets, the time period may be short; in slow-developing markets, it is likely to be longer.

- To test for emergent strategy, it is essential to examine how the strategy has developed in practice over a defined time period.

2.3.2 Typical practice of emergent strategy

According to the emergent view of the strategy process, implementation does not follow strategy development but is an integral part of the development. It can best be considered therefore as a compromise. Emergent strategists believe that the rational and logical analysis of the prescriptive process towards achieving the highest return on shareholders' capital is flawed. Strategies are better seen as emerging during the process of negotiation and discussion.[30] Objectives may not maximise the good of the organisation or even add value. Options and selection do not always lead to rational decision making and are not wide-ranging[31]. Managers in practice are more likely to say:

> 'Let us try this strategy and see what happens; then we can adjust it as we implement it.'

rather than:

> 'Here is our new strategy for the next five years. Let's go out and implement it.'

In the emergent approach, strategies emerge from an ongoing system of experimentation, negotiation and discussion. Research evidence has suggested that many strategies take time; they are not necessarily implemented immediately.[32] They may also involve learning and change in the organisation itself: there may be no instant results as envisaged by the prescriptive strategy route. Attitudes may need to alter and this is a slow, exploratory process.[33]

To see how strategy can emerge, refer to Case study 2.3 at the end of this section. The strategy of Spillers plc can be examined from a different, longer-term perspective over the period 1970–80. An *extended time perspective* is essential in order to see how strategic decisions take shape according to the emergent approach.

Those who favour emergent strategy argue that market place comparisons with competition rarely produce the real strategy insights and development. Sustainable competitive advantage has some value but what really matters is the organisation's own skills, resources and knowledge; these must form the basis of the development of the unique advantage that will allow the organisation to survive in the long term.

Exhibit 2.4

The advantages of the emergent process

- It accords with actual practice in many organisations.
- It takes account of the people issues – such as motivation – that make the prescriptive process unrealistic in some circumstances.
- It allows the strategy to develop as more is learnt about the strategic situation.
- The role of implementation is redefined so that it becomes an integral part of the strategy development process.
- It provides the opportunity for the culture and politics of an organisation to be included in the process.
- It delivers the flexibility to respond to changes, especially in fast-moving markets.

The practical advantages of the emergent strategy process are summarised in Exhibit 2.4.

Those who favour prescriptive strategic approaches have a number of basic concerns about emergent strategy (summarised in Exhibit 2.5).[34]

Exhibit 2.5

Concerns about the emergent strategic process

1 It is entirely unrealistic to expect Board members at corporate level to simply sit back and let operating companies potter along as they wish. The HQ consists of experienced managers who have a *unified vision* of where they wish the group to progress. It may take several steps to arrive at this vision, but the group should make visible progress rather than just muddling along.

2 Resources of the group need to be *allocated* between the demands of competing operating companies; this can only be undertaken at the centre. It therefore demands some central strategic overview.

3 It is entirely correct that there are political groups and individuals that need to be persuaded that a strategy is optimal, but to elevate this process to the level of corporate strategy is to *abdicate responsibility* for the final decisions that need to be taken.

4 In some industries where long time frames are involved for decision making, decisions have to be taken and adhered to or the organisation would become completely muddled: for example, building a new transport infrastructure or telecommunications network may take years to implement. Experimentation may be appropriate in the early years but, beyond this, strategy has to be *fixed for lengthy projects*.

5 Although the process of strategy selection and choice has to be tempered by what managers are prepared to accept, this does not make it wrong; rational decision making based on evidence has a greater likelihood of success than hunch and personal whim. Thus the debate should take place but be *conditioned by evidence and logic*.

6 Management control will be *simpler and clearer* where the basis of the actions to be undertaken has been planned in advance.

Emergent strategy at Spillers Baking

In the face of fierce competition in the UK bread baking industry, Spillers Bakeries tried a series of strategies in the 1960s and 1970s. Their aim was to turn around the ailing business. The strategic trial-and-error process was essentially emergent, rather than prescriptive. This case describes the moves that were made and the eventual outcome which was to leave the group exposed to acquisition by an opportunistic predator.[35]

Background to the 1970s

Under its major shareholder Garfield Weston, the baking subsidiary company of Associated British Foods (ABF) came to dominate the bread baking market in the UK in the 1950s and 1960s. This was achieved through strategies involving heavy investment in baking plant and the takeover of rival baking companies. At the time, bread was regarded as one of the staple elements of the British diet and was the subject of Government price controls. The main rivals of ABF were Ranks Hovis McDougall (RHM) and Spillers; they both struggled to compete against aggressive ABF competition. RHM began investing heavily in new bakeries to achieve similar economies of scale to ABF; Spillers did not have the funds for such investment and needed to seek other strategies.

Spillers' first emergent strategy: merge with rivals (1970–74)

By 1970, Spillers was a poor third in the bread baking market. The company decided to build market share by merging its bread baking interests with those of two smaller rivals, J Lyons and CWS. It formed a new company, Spillers French Baking Ltd. This company then lost £7 million over the period 1970–74.

This was not quite as disastrous as it might appear; Spillers French was purchasing flour for baking from its associated milling company at high prices. Nevertheless, Spillers French was unable to gain a strategic advantage by its attempt to grow larger by merger.

Spillers' second emergent strategy: Invest and consolidate (1974–76)

Investment in new plant and marketing was then undertaken by the Spillers French group; the com-

pany invested £5 million in new baking plant around the country. It also attempted a series of marketing initiatives associated with new product launches and bread advertising. These produced some moderately memorable advertising campaigns, but brand loyalty in the bread market was low in the face of strong and sustained price competition.

By contrast with the Spillers investment, ABF and RHM invested £68 million and £62 million respectively in new baking plant over the same period. For both companies, the strategy was to reduce substantially their manufacturing costs below those of Spillers French. Moreover, both ABF and RHM were opening up their own bakery shops to distribute their products: ABF had 1800 shops plus a supermarket chain (then called Fine Fare, now part of Safeway, UK) and RHM had over 1000 shops. Spillers French had around 200 shops.

Spillers French Baking losses continued – £5 million in 1975, £1 million in 1976 and £1 million in 1977. The losses were accompanied by increasing labour militancy in the Spillers French bakeries; workers feared redundancy. The company then tried its third strategy.

Spillers' third emergent strategy: Divest (1978–79)

In early 1978, there was a major strike by the bread trade unions at Spillers French Baking. The company lost £9.7 million in that year. New drastic strategies were required. Simply closing the bakeries was not an option: this would have cost £33 million in capital write-downs and £20 million in redundancy payments under the labour laws that existed at that time.

A strategy of divestment that included sale of some of the better bakeries to ABF and RHM coupled with continuing contracts from ABF and RHM to take flour from Spillers was therefore negotiated with its two rivals. After difficult discussions, Spillers French managed to sell 13 bakeries to ABF and RHM for £15.5 million and it simply closed the rest. After allowing for the bakery sale, the net cost to Spillers plc was £22 million with another £7 million to its partners, J Lyons and CWS. To protect its profitable milling interests, Spillers French also negotiated a continuing deal to supply flour to ABF and RHM for around another five to ten years. The company was then in a position to embark on its fourth strategy.

Spillers' fourth emergent strategy: attempt to block a hostile takeover bid (1979–80)

Having resolved its bread baking strategy by withdrawal, Spillers plc then made more substantial profits in 1979. However, its share price still reflected the under-investment it had made in other areas of the business while it had tried various strategies to sort out the baking problems between 1970 and 1979. The company was therefore exposed to predator activity. In August 1979, the international food conglomerate Dalgety plc launched a takeover bid for Spillers; by January 1980, the slimmed-down, breadless Spillers had been taken over by Dalgety as a result of its disastrous emergent strategies.

We will return to the fortunes of the new Dalgety plc, including Spillers, later in this chapter. The strategy continued to emerge.

CASE QUESTIONS

1 The Spillers' emergent approach to strategy development required at least a year to elapse between each phase. What might be the reasons for this? Are there any disadvantages in this timing from a strategic perspective?

2 Critically evaluate the Spillers Bakeries' strategies during the 1970s. Was the company wise to spend nearly ten years pouring funds into such an operation? What would you have done?

Key strategic principles

● Emergent corporate strategy is a strategy whose final *objective* is unclear and whose *elements* are developed during the course of its life, as the strategy proceeds.

● The process is one of experimentation to find the most productive route forward.

● The advantages of the process include its consistency with actual practice in organisations; it takes account of people issues such as motivation; it allows experimentation about the strategy to take place; it provides an opportunity to include the culture and politics of the organisation; it delivers flexibility to respond to market changes.

● Six problems have been identified with the emergent strategic process that make it difficult to operate in practice.

2.4 PRESCRIPTIVE THEORIES OF CORPORATE STRATEGY

Corporate strategy has now been explored and set in its historical and international context. It is now possible to turn to the theories that underlie these processes. This section examines prescriptive strategy theories, while emergent strategy theories are explored in Section 2.5. It should be noted, however, that there is some overlap between the two areas. This will be explored further later in this chapter.

Prescriptive strategy usually ends up with some form of corporate plan for the medium term. By definition, the process uses logical thought processes and well publicised strategy concepts to derive its results. As long as the same planning theories, logic and evidence are used, it might initially be thought that similar strategies would result everywhere in the world and for all sizes of business. However, this is not the case. This is because the objectives of the organisation will vary. While the maximisation of profit is a common objective in most organisations in the West, there are many types of organisation and cultures where profit is not of supreme importance.

Table 2.2

Corporate objectives in US and Japanese companies: ranking by importance

Objective	USA	Japan
Return on investment	8.1 (1st)	4.1 (2nd)
Share price increase	3.8 (2nd)	0.1
Market share	2.4 (3rd)	4.8 (1st)
Improved product portfolio	1.7	2.3
Rationalisation of production and distribution	1.5	2.4
Increase equity ratio	1.3	2.0
Ratio of new products	0.7	3.5 (3rd)
Improve company's image	0.2	0.7
Improve working conditions	0.1	0.3

Note: The sample was 227 US companies, 291 Japanese companies. Method: rank factors from 10 (most important) to 1 (least important).
Source: Abegglen, J C and Stalk, G: 1985, *Kaisha: The Japanese Corporation*, New York, Basic Books. Reproduced with permission.[36]

The size of the company will also influence objectives and so in turn strategies. For example, small companies will have substantially different strategies to large multinationals. The form of shareholding will also have an effect on objectives – private shareholders may well have different company dividend expectations compared to a government shareholding.

Table 2.2 shows the results of a survey of over 500 US and Japanese companies in the early 1980s. It asked the corporations to rank their objectives from highest to lowest priorities. The results indicate that the US and Japanese corporations in the mid-1980s had substantially differing views on objectives.

Whatever their strategic processes may be, it is evident from Table 2.2 that US and Japanese companies have different approaches to company development. The contents of their plans will therefore almost certainly differ. For example, a plan to increase market share preferred by a Japanese company may well involve expenditure on advertising and promotions that will impact adversely on return on investment which would prove unattractive to a US company. We will explore shortly the reasons for these differences, but essentially they are the result of structural, social and cultural differences between the countries.

Even for companies within one country, the content may also change. The strategic plan of a large corporation with a mass of shareholders may well have different content to a small, privately owned and entrepreneurial organisation with perhaps only one shareholder; earnings for shareholders may be important for the former, whereas survival or market development may be the main objective for the latter.

For similar reasons, government-owned companies, whether large or small, may also have different objectives: for example, social or service objectives that are, at least in part, determined by government policy. These considerations will inevitably affect the logic and content of the prescriptive strategies adopted by such companies.

Although there are clearly differences between countries, many commentators have argued that there are common principles that will apply to all countries; such theorists argue that as the world becomes more global in its nature the apparent differences that exist will become less important.[37] Other theorists argue that the differences outlined above are still paramount.[38] Nevertheless in broad terms, there are three main areas of prescriptive corporate strategy theory:

- profit-maximising, competition-based theories of strategy;
- resource-based theories of strategy;
- socio-cultural theories of strategy.

2.4.1 Profit-maximising, competition-based theories of strategy

For some companies, *profitability* is the clear goal, and the content of the corporate strategy therefore addresses this objective; over the long term, this is likely to override all other objectives. This profit is delivered by *competing in the market place*. Figure 2.4 shows where the emphasis lies within the context of prescriptive strategy.

Such concepts derive from the assertion that organisations are rational, logical and driven by the need for profitability. They can be related back to two areas:

- the eighteenth-century Scottish economist, Adam Smith, and his view that man was rational, logical and motivated by profit;
- the concepts of military warfare quoted earlier in this chapter that show how the competitive war can be won.

In terms of the development of strategy theory, much of this material only really came together in the 1960s. Igor Ansoff,[39] Alfred Chandler[40] and Alfred Sloan[41] were all early influencers in this area. More recently, writers such as Wheelen and Hunger[42] have laid out the model for rational, analytical and structured development of strategy. During the 1980s, the work of Porter[43] added significantly to this material; he was a dominant influence during this period. Much of his work was based on the study of large companies and the application of economic concepts to strategy, as has been pointed out by Rumelt, Schendel and Teece.[44] The contributions of these researchers will be examined in greater depth later in the book.

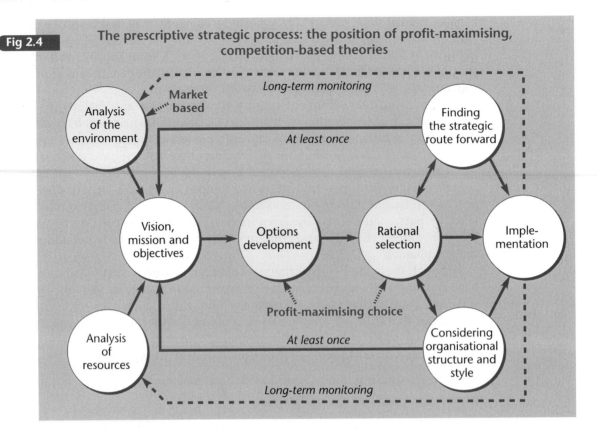

Fig 2.4 The prescriptive strategic process: the position of profit-maximising, competition-based theories

In fairness, it should be pointed out that researchers such as Ansoff never saw their work in quite such stark prescriptive terms. For example, an Ansoff 1968 research paper on corporate strategy[45] refers with approval to the emergent strategy work of Cyert and Marsh on human resources strategies, which we explore later in this chapter.

For all these writers, strategy involves formal, analytical processes. It will result in a specific set of documents that are discussed and agreed by the board of directors (or public sector equivalent) of an organisation – a tangible corporate plan for some years ahead. Typically, the plan will include sections predicting the general economic and political situation; analysing competitors, their strengths and weaknesses; considering the resources available to the organisation; and recommending a set of strategies to meet these requirements.

The strategy will primarily (but not exclusively) be driven by the objective of maximising the organisation's profitability in the long term (such profits may particularly accrue to the shareholders). The major argument of the theorists is that the purpose of strategy is to develop sustainable competitive advantage[46] over competitors.

Although these views were broadly endorsed by Kenichi Ohmae,[47] head of the Japanese part of the well-known consulting company, McKinsey, it has been pointed out by Wilks that they remain largely western and Anglo-American in their orientation.[48] They are primarily concerned with profit and leave only limited room for social, cultural, governmental and other considerations. This view of strategy is therefore unlikely to appeal to countries which demand a higher social content from company plans – for example, within Europe, France, Poland, the Netherlands and Scandinavian countries.

Outside Europe, India has insisted on a strong social content to plans for many years and has only recently come to accept that strong social policies needed tempering by market forces.[49] Japanese companies have also other criteria, as we have already seen. Malaysian and Singaporean companies with their strong relationships with the governments of their respective countries might well also sacrifice profitability to other objectives, such as building market presence or providing extra training for workers.[50] Content for companies in these countries will inevitably be broader.

These nation-state arguments are, however, a matter of degree and do not deny the need to make long-term profits in order to ensure the survival and growth of the enterprise. A more fundamental criticism of profit-maximising theories has been made by Hamel and Prahalad[51] and Kay.[52] They argue that, although competitors are important, the emphasis on competitive comparisons essential to such theories is misleading: it simply shows where organisations are weak. Such theories do not indicate how the company should develop its own resources and skills – the key strategic task in their view. This is explored further in the next section.

Hannan and Freeman[53] argued that markets are so powerful that seeking sustainable competitive advantage for the majority of companies is not realistic; only the largest companies with significant market share can achieve and sustain such advantage. For all the others, complex and detailed strategies are a distraction. Moreover, as soon as all companies have access to Porter's writings on sustainable competitive advantage, Hamel and Prahalad[54] and Kay[55] have argued that the advantage ceases.

From a different perspective, Mintzberg[56] and others have criticised the approach by arguing that this is simply not the way that strategy is or should be developed in practice. Thus human resource-based theories of strategy would suggest that seeking to maximise performance through a single, static strategic plan is a fallacy. There are no clear long-term mission statements and goals: just a series of short-term horizons to be met and then renewed. Techniques that purport to provide long-term insights may be too simplistic. Using such arguments, Mintzberg in particular has been highly articulate in his criticisms of the formal strategic planning process. However, he has subsequently modified his criticisms and accepted that some strategic planning may be beneficial to the organisation.[57]

2.4.2 Resource-based theories of strategy

Resource-based theories concentrate on the chief resources of the organisation as the principle source of successful corporate strategy. The source of competitive advantage lies in the organisation's resources (*see* Fig 2.5).

Writing in the 1960s, Drucker[58] points out that it is important to '... build on strength ... to look for opportunities rather than for problems'. Many basic economic texts have also stressed the importance of resources as the basis for profit development.

One particular aspect of resource-based strategy, emphasised by US and Japanese strategists beginning in the 1960s and 1970s, was operations (manufacturing) strategy and the emphasis on total quality management. Although Henry Ford had developed these areas early in the twentieth century, little emphasis was subsequently given to them. They were probably considered to be too ordinary and

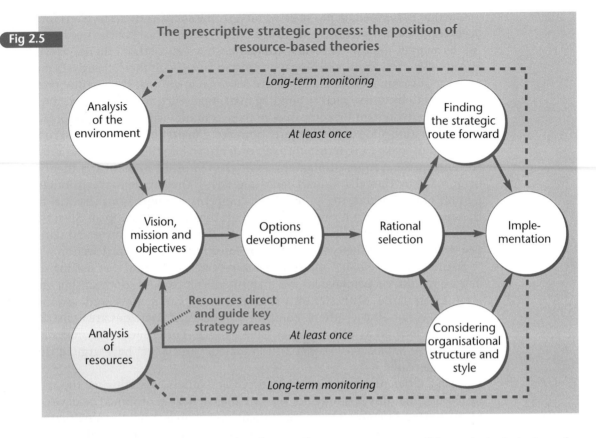

Fig 2.5

The prescriptive strategic process: the position of resource-based theories

Long-term monitoring

Analysis of the environment

Finding the strategic route forward

At least once

Vision, mission and objectives

Options development

Rational selection

Imple-mentation

Resources direct and guide key strategy areas

Analysis of resources

At least once

Considering organisational structure and style

Long-term monitoring

insufficiently concerned with overall corporate strategy. (Many strategic texts make no mention of them even in the late 1990s.) Deming, Ishikawa and Taguchi[59] worked on quality issues and Ohno[60] and many others worked on manufacturing strategy issues. Chapter 10 will attempt to redress the balance in this area; some of the major practical advances in corporate strategy during the last twenty years have occurred in this area.

Although such developments are not new, they have been given new emphasis in the 1990s. Hamel and Prahalad believe that distinctive *core competences* internal to the organisation are what will deliver winning strategies over competitors, rather than the external comparisons in themselves. Developing such competences may be a slow laborious process:

> *The traditional competitive strategy paradigm* [e.g. Porter 1980] *with its focus on product–market positioning, focusses only on the last few hundred yards of what may be a skill-building marathon.*[61]

Kay[62] has developed the argument further by suggesting that there are three possible areas of core competence: the organisation's resources in terms of architecture (e.g. links with customers and suppliers), reputation and innovative ability. These are explored in Chapter 7.

Resource-based theories of strategy do not deny the importance of competition but they lay greater emphasis on the internal resources of the organisation. They represent new strategy areas in the 1990s and have not yet had the depth of analysis afforded other areas in this review.

2.4.3 Socio-cultural theories of strategy

Socio-cultural theories seek clearly defined, prescriptive strategies, but they stress the importance of the social and cultural frameworks and beliefs of nations as the starting point for strategy development. Figure 2.6 shows where they fit into the overall model.

Such theories have arisen in recent times as a result of the increasing prominence of cultures beyond the Anglo–American mould; the rise of Europe during the 1970s and 1980s, the emergence of Asia–Pacific during the 1980s and 1990s have led to greater awareness of the need for a broader range of parameters and values to measure and drive objectives and other aspects of the organisation.

For example, in countries such as Korea and Japan, the whole structure of society is different from the countries that gave rise to the profit-maximising theories. Both these countries have major structural differences that will influence strategy content – for example; in the areas of wage costs, industry organisation, relationship with government, and cultural expectations of workers and shareholders. Ultimately, these cultural differences may make the content of strategic plans very different.

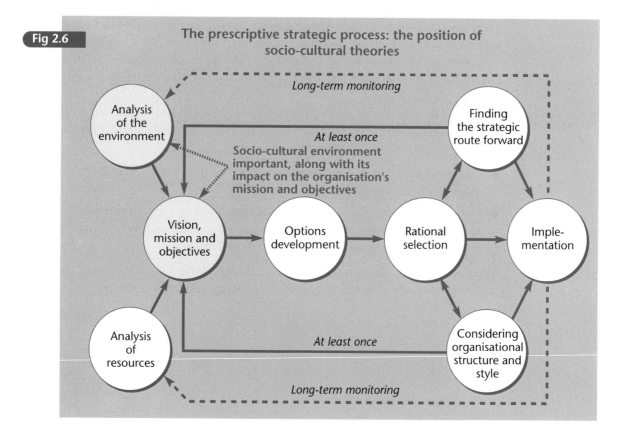

Fig 2.6 The prescriptive strategic process: the position of socio-cultural theories

Marris,[63] Granovetter[64] and Whittington[65] have all explored aspects of this important, global topic. The essence of their research and arguments is that all companies and their managers are embedded in social and cultural systems that influence their decision making and thus the strategies they develop. Economic activity cannot be separated from the society in which it operates. Networks exist that constrain, direct and influence the strategies for all members both at the *national* level and the more *local* level of ethnic, religious and other communities in local catchment areas. Prescriptive strategic plans may well be written but they will cover more than profit-maximising.

In south-east Asia, Whitley[66] showed that business varies with regard to strategic actions according to the intermingling of state, family and market structures. South Korea has always been a strong state, so this has resulted in the formation of powerful industrial conglomerates, the Chaebol. In Taiwan, state influence has been more muted and Chinese family enterprise culture is stronger, resulting in more small and medium-sized companies. The content of strategic plans in these countries will inevitably reflect these influences.

Prescriptive planning may not even be appropriate in some cultures. One of the underlying assumptions of such planning is that companies have the freedom and ability to alter their future. In countries where there is a strong belief in luck and fate, a corporate strategy to alter the direction may be totally inconsistent with such beliefs (*see* Boyacigiller and Adler[67]). For the purposes of this book, however, we can observe that in countries such as Saudi Arabia, Iran, Korea and Malaysia such beliefs have not stopped companies developing strategies in industries as diverse as petrochemicals, consumer electronics and cars. Thus, we may conclude that, even where strong social and cultural influences will certainly affect prescriptive strategy, they will not completely inhibit such developments, but content will change in a major way.

It could be argued that socio-cultural issues, although important, are only one of many influences on corporate strategy. Other issues that will clearly influence strategy are:

- *Company size.* Small companies are likely to develop substantially different strategies from those of large multinationals.
- *Shareholding.* Shareholders have in formulating strategy, company dividend expectations, which must be taken into account in formulating strategy, whereas public sector expectations will be different.

As compared with these, however, socio-cultural issues are so important that they can fundamentally alter the nature of the strategy under development.

> ## Key strategic principles
>
> - Profit-maximising, competition-based theories emphasise the importance of the market place to deliver profits. Strategy should seek sustainable competitive advantage.
>
> - Resource-based theories stress the resources of the organisation in strategic development. Core competences need to be identified.
>
> - Socio-cultural theories focus on the social and cultural dimensions of the organisation in developing its corporate strategy. They have arisen as a result of greater awareness of cultures beyond the Anglo–American mould. It is possible that in some cultures the profit objective may not even be appropriate.

2.5 EMERGENT THEORIES OF CORPORATE STRATEGY

When strategies emerge from a situation rather than being prescribed in advance, it is less likely that they will involve a long-term strategic plan. This does not mean that there is no planning but rather that such plans are more flexible, feeling their way forward as issues clarify and the environment surrounding the company changes. Planning is short term, more reactive to events, possibly even more entrepreneurial.

To understand the background to emergent strategy theory, it is necessary to look back to the 1970s. At the time, prescriptive strategies with detailed corporate plans were widely used. Suddenly, oil prices rose sharply as a result of a new, strong Middle East oil price consortium. Many industrial companies around the world were hit badly in an entirely unpredictable way; the prescriptive plans were thrown into confusion. Emergent strategies that relied less on precise predictions about the future were sought. In practice, it is likely that even companies which relied heavily on prescriptive strategies would move over, at least temporarily, to emergent strategies during such a period of uncertainty.

In the light of the uncertainties of the oil price shock of the 1970s, a number of researchers have argued that the whole basis of prescriptive strategy is false. Even during periods of relative certainty, they would argue that organisations are better served by considering strategy as an emergent process.

For our purposes, we can usefully distinguish three sets of emergent strategy theories:

- survival-based theories of strategy;
- uncertainty-based theories of strategy; and
- human resource-based theories of strategy.

2.5.1 Survival-based theories of strategy

Survival-based theories of strategy start from Darwin's theory of 'the survival of the fittest'. Such theorists take the view that strategy is primarily decided in the jungle that is the market place. Corporate strategy is about how to survive in an environment which is shifting and changing. There is little point in sophisticated *prescriptive* solutions: much better to dodge and weave as the market changes, letting the strategy *emerge* in the process. Figure 2.7 shows where the emphasis is placed by survival-based strategies.

As section 2.4 explained, profit-maximising, competition-based approaches are concerned with selecting the optimal strategy to maximise the organisation's profitability and then implementing that strategy. Critics have long known that this simple economic model is far from reality. For example in the late 1930s, Hall and Hitch[68] surveyed companies and showed that they did not set output at the theoretical maximum level, that is, where marginal cost equals marginal revenue. This was partly because decisions were not necessarily rational and partly because it was unclear what the revenue and cost relationships were anyway.

However, this does not mean that companies just muddle through. The competitive jungle of the market place will ruthlessly weed out the least efficient companies; survival-based strategies are needed to prosper in such circumstances. Essentially, according to the survival-based strategy theorists, it is the market place that matters more than a specific strategy; hence, the optimal strategy for survival is to be really efficient. Beyond this, companies can only rely on chance.

To overcome these difficulties, Henderson[69] suggested that what most companies needed to survive in these highly competitive circumstances was differentiation. Products or services that were able to offer some aspect not easily available to competitors would offer some protection. However, other strategists doubt that true differentiation is possible because it takes too long to achieve and the environment changes too quickly. In these circumstances, theorists suggest that survival-based strategies should rely on running really efficient operations that can respond to changes in the environment. As Williamson commented:

'*Economy is the best strategy.*'[70]

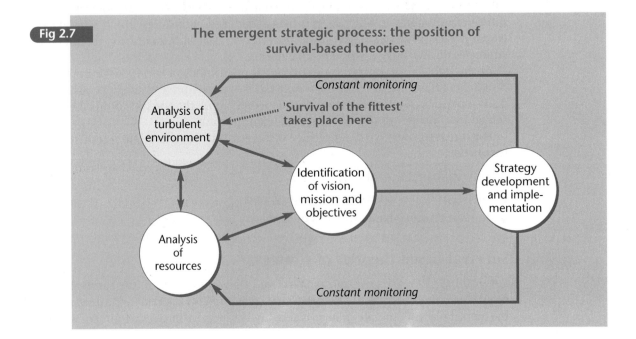

Fig 2.7 — The emergent strategic process: the position of survival-based theories

If the environment matters more than a specific strategy, then survival-based strategists argue that the optimal strategy will be to pursue a number of strategic initiatives at any one time and let the market place select the best.[71] Selection of strategy is therefore incorrect according to this theory. It is better to experiment with many different approaches and see which emerges as the best through natural selection. For example, Whittington[72] points to the example of Sony's Walkman strategy in the 1980s. The company launched 160 different versions in the North American market, never retaining more than about 20 versions at any one time. Ultimately, the market selected the best.

If survival-based theories are correct, then we need to study the organisation's environment carefully (we begin this process in Part 2). In addition to this, we would need to treat the strategy selection process of Chapters 15 and 16 with a great deal of circumspection.

Other strategy writers believe survival-based theories are too pessimistic; there are practical problems in a strategy that only takes small cautious steps and keeps all options open. Major acquisitions, innovative new products, plant investment to radically improve quality would all be the subject of much anxious debate and little action. The bold strategic step would be completely ruled out.[73]

2.5.2 Uncertainty-based theories of strategy

Uncertainty-based theories use mathematical probability concepts to show that corporate strategy development is complex, unstable and subject to major fluctuations, thus making it impossible to undertake any useful prediction in advance. If prediction is impossible, then setting clear objectives for corporate strategy is a useless exercise. Strategy should be allowed to emerge and change with the fluctuations in the environment. Figure 2.8 illustrates where the emphasis lies in such theories.

As a result of the major difficulties in predicting the future environment surrounding the organisation in the 1970s, the development of long-term strategic planning was regarded by some theorists as having little value. Strategic planning could still be used but it had to have much greater flexibility and did not have the absolute certainties of the 1970s. This approach to strategy led not only to survival-based strategies that seek to keep all options open to the last possible opportunity but also to uncertainty-based strategies.

Since the 1960s, chaos theory and mathematical modelling of changing states have been used to map out the consequences of scientific experiments; such procedures were not developed for the business community but for other scientifically oriented topics such as the mathematical modelling of weather forcecasting. Essentially, such techniques were able to demonstrate that, in certain types of uncertain environment, small perturbations in the early stages of a process can lead to major variances in the later stages – not unlike the multiplier effect in macroeconomics. A major implication of such environments – often called *chaotic systems* – is that it is simply not possible to predict sufficiently accurately many years ahead (*see* Gleick).[74]

One variant of this approach to strategy is provided by the empirical research study conducted by Miller and Friesen.[75] They found that significant corporate strategy occurs in revolutionary ways: there are sudden major shifts in the whole strategy and organisational structure of the company before they reach a new steady state. From a mathematical perspective, it is possible to model such systems

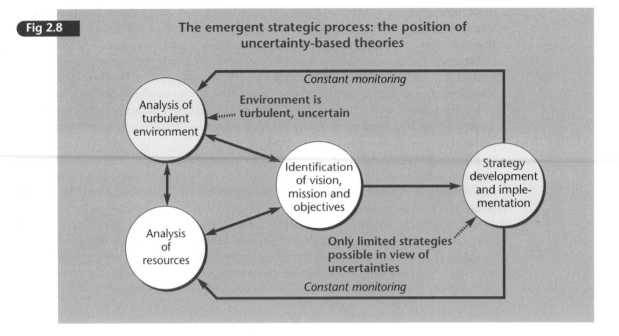

Fig 2.8

The emergent strategic process: the position of uncertainty-based theories

and show that they oscillate between steady and turbulent states. Strebel[76] has used a similar argument, pointing particularly to changes in technology that are likely to lead to 'breakpoints' in the development of the organisation.

Business has been identified as such a chaotic system. Stacey[77] has suggested that the environment of many businesses, particularly those in rapidly growing industries such as computers, is inherently unstable. It will never be possible to forecast accurately profits five or ten years into a new project: hence, for example, the apparent accuracy of discounted cash flows and cash projections is largely spurious. It follows that business strategy has to emerge rather than try to aim for the false certainties of the prescriptive approach.

Some companies would regard this approach as being partially true but probably too pessimistic. Although the weather is a chaotic system and cannot be predicted accurately, we do know that the Sahara Desert is hot and dry, Singapore is warmer and more humid than London, and so on. Similarly, it can be argued that there are some certainties about business, even though we are unable to predict accurately.

There are patterns of behaviour and trends that may be subject to change but can still be predicted with some accuracy. Business strategy may need to emerge and be adaptable, but it is not necessarily totally random and uncertain. However, strategy does need to identify and estimate risk. (We will return to the problem of risk and risk management in Chapter 16.)

2.5.3 Human resource-based theories of strategy

These theories of strategy emphasise the *people* element in strategy development and highlight the motivation, the politics and cultures of organisations and the desires of individuals. They have particularly emphasised the difficulties that can arise as new strategies are introduced and confront people with the need for change and uncertainty. Figure 2.9 shows where these theories fit into the emergent process. They involve people and occur wherever human resources are prominent and it is therefore difficult to identify a precise position.

We have already examined the important findings of researchers such as Cyert and March[78] and the work of Herbert Simon[79] – corporate strategy needs to have a human resource-based dimension. Organisations consist of individuals and groups of people, all of whom may influence or be influenced by strategy; they may make a contribution, acquiesce or even resist the corporate strategy process, but they are certainly affected by it.

The human resource aspects of strategy development will be explored in much greater detail in Chapter 8. However, according to some writers, these matters are not just about peripheral issues of implementation; they are fundamental to the strategy process itself. Nelson and Winter[80] argued that organisations have in reality limited strategic choice. The strategy available is:

> not broad, but narrow and idiosyncratic; it is built on a firm's routines, and most of the 'choosing' is also accomplished automatically by those routines.

Strategic logic is restricted by the processes and people already existing in the organisation.

Mintzberg[81] has also developed this theme and argued that strategy thus emerges from an organisation as it adapts continuously to its environment. Implementation is not therefore some separate phase tacked on to the end of the strategy process but intermingled with corporate strategy as it develops. Quinn[82] has described this gradualist, emergent approach that accepts that it is looking at only a limited number of feasible options as *logical incrementalism*. In the words of Mintzberg's famous phrase:

> Smart strategies appreciate that they cannot always be smart enough to think through everything in advance.

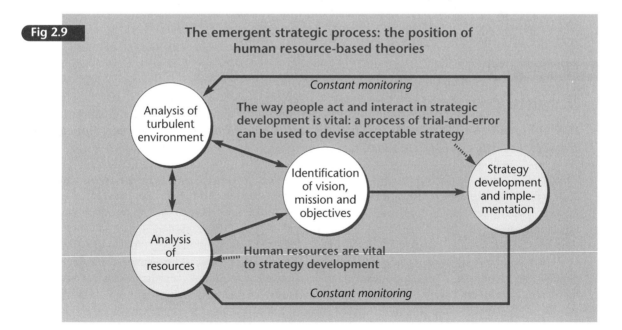

Fig 2.9

The emergent strategic process: the position of human resource-based theories

Constant monitoring

Analysis of turbulent environment

The way people act and interact in strategic development is vital: a process of trial-and-error can be used to devise acceptable strategy

Identification of vision, mission and objectives

Strategy development and implementation

Analysis of resources

Human resources are vital to strategy development

Constant monitoring

We will explore these areas in greater depth in Chapter 17.

More recently, there has been considerable emphasis on the *learning* aspect of strategy development. Mintzberg emphasised the importance of learning. After him, Senge[83] and others have developed the learning concept – encouraging managers involved in strategy to undertake a process of trial and error to adopt the optimal strategy (*see* Chapter 21).

The main criticisms of the emergent approach to strategy development listed in Section 2.3 apply especially to human resource-based strategy. Similar comments may have prompted Mintzberg to move more recently towards the modification of his argument outlined above.[84]

Key strategic principles

● Survival-based theories of strategy are based on the survival of the fittest in the market place. It is difficult to plan strategy actively and possible to survive by differentiation as events unfold.

● Uncertainty-based theories of strategy regard prediction as impossible because of the inherently unstable nature of business and its environment. Strategies must be allowed to react to the changing environment and emerge from the chaos of events. Some would regard this as being a pessimistic view of strategy.

● Human resource-based theories emphasise the importance of the people element in strategy development. They highlight the motivation, the politics and culture of organisations and the desires of individuals. They also suggest that strategy would benefit from an element of learning and experimentation that empowers individuals.

CASE STUDY 2.4

Dalgety corporate strategy continues

After its acquisition by Dalgety, Spillers became part of a new company: Dalgety plc. This case describes the fortunes of Spillers under its new owners.

Dalgety 1980–89: diversification strategy

During the 1980s, the new group started by consolidating its Spillers acquisition, particularly in agricultural cattle feeds – its *agribusiness*. It invested in new mills and divested others that were poorly located to build market share against the market leader – part of Unilever – and build towards the economies of scale that were available in such a business. This is a typical resource-based strategy and worked well for the new company.

It took Dalgety several years to recognise the high added-value businesses that it had acquired from Spillers in branded products, petfood and ingredients in particular. (It is difficult for a business to see potential when it has no previous knowledge of a market area.) However, it eventually invested further in these areas.

At the same time, Dalgety was acquiring other companies without any real sense of strategic logic; it made 15 acquisitions in the first six months of 1988 alone. Few of these seemed to add anything to existing parts of the group such as economies of scale or market share. This reflected the buoyancy and confidence of the UK and the international economy at that time. Then came the stock market crash of 1987 which was unpredicted by many. It left companies like Dalgety with a ragbag of businesses bought at inflated prices and difficult to sell.

Overall, Dalgety had done a reasonable job investing in agribusiness, but it had conducted a company acquisition and disposal policy that was, at best, unclear. This perhaps contributed to the sudden departure of the chief executive officer in July 1989.

Dalgety Spillers 1990–95: focus on three core businesses

Dalgety chose to concentrate on what it called its 'three legs', although some might see this as more than three:

- animal feeds and pig breeding;
- food ingredients;
- pet food.

Dalgety claimed that there were real benefits in terms of cost savings between them. These came from shared technology and from specialist expertise which also acted as an entry barrier for potential competitors. Sales and net income levels are shown in Fig 2.10.

In practice, pig breeding has proved highly profitable because of the special expertise in genetics required. Animal feeds were largely UK based and thriving. Food ingredients had come from the Spillers acquisition ten years earlier; the strategy was to expand this with some further acquisitions. Petfood was expanded in 1983 by the acquisition of Paragon Petfood from British Petroleum for £42 million[85] and another company in Spain.

This increased focus on the three core businesses was taken a stage further in 1995 when the company announced that it was purchasing all the

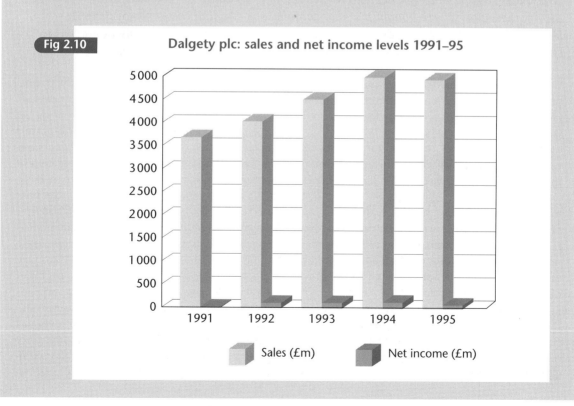

Fig 2.10   **Dalgety plc: sales and net income levels 1991–95**

Sales (£m)   Net income (£m)

CASE STUDY 2.4 continued

European petfood business of the Quaker Oats company for £442 million.[86] At the same time, to help provide funds for the deal and to focus further, the company announced that it wished to sell its Golden Wonder crisps, snacks, Homepride sauces, flour and baking mixes. Specifically in crisps and snacks, over-capacity, price pressure from retailers and competition from PepsiCo and United Biscuits, were making the market less profitable. At last, it was really beginning to focus its strategic resources.

CASE QUESTIONS

1 For much of this period, Dalgety concentrated on acquisitions. Is this approach prescriptive or emergent? Within this approach, can you identify any particular strategy route? What does this tell you about the Dalgety strategy?

2 During the 1990s, Dalgety decided to concentrate on 'three legs'. What is the main danger that comes from focussing its strategic resources?

CASE STUDY 2.5

Strategy at Saes Getters[87]

Saes Getters will never be a household name like Sony or Philips, but there is a chance that the new television set you bought last year contains one essential component – a 'getter' – manufactured by this small, Milan-based, high technology company. This case examines the corporate strategy of the company over recent years.

The getter is the chemical pump which maintains the vacuum in a television or computer's cathode ray tube. Saes Getters has a staggering 82 per cent share of the world market in colour TV getters.

Saes was founded in 1940, and started manufacturing getters in the 1950s. It currently has more than 600 employees, nine plants in Europe, the US and East Asia and turnover in 1994 is forecast to top L130 billion (US$80 million), with 99 per cent of sales outside Italy. In the first half of 1994, Saes reported net consolidated profits of L12 billion – a net margin of 18 per cent on sales, and an increase of 58 per cent over the first six months of the previous year.

Paolo Della Porta, the chief executive, invented the modern getter at the beginning of the 1950s. He now describes Saes as a multinational, but he is not ready to hang up his lab coat and retire. Growth, he says, is set to continue.

Della Porta knows from experience the importance of continuing innovation. Semi-conductors made the radio valves using his original getter obsolete, but Saes switched to producing getters for black-and-white and then colour tubes. This is why Saes invests the equivalent of 10 per cent of turnover in research and development, making itself a training ground for specialists in the next generation of getter-based products . It is also why Della Porta is not frightened by talk of tubeless flat-screen televisions. Certain flat screens still require a vacuum, analysts point out, and mass-produced liquid crystal displays of sufficient quality are still at least five years away.

In any case, the company is already diversifying. Traditional barium getters accounted for only half of Saes's 1993 sales. The other half came from industrial applications and the growing gas purification division. This area should account for about

25 per cent of sales in 1995. Potentially lucrative industrial applications could include a new getter for vacuum panels in refrigerators.

Saes has been quoted on the Italian stock market since 1986, but last year it broadened its shareholder base with an offer of ordinary shares, putting new pressure on management to sustain progress. Della Porta has no doubts about the company's ability to do so, but demands the same rigour from his investors as from his research staff. He is scathing, for example, about outgoing investors who did not have the patience to wait five years for returns on the company's investment in the US.

So far his long-term vision has paid off. His family is still the company's biggest shareholder with 30.5 per cent of Saes ordinary shares and the company's only rivals have fallen by the wayside. Della Porta says simply:

> Competitors are always disappearing ... Large factories decide to stop internal production and use our products because they are more advanced.

Source: Case adapted from an article by Andrew Hill, *Financial Times*, 27 February 1995, p11.

CASE QUESTIONS

1 *How would you categorise the company's strategy?*

2 *What are the implications for its future strategic development?*

KEY READING

What is business strategy?

In this extract from an article from **The Economist**[88] *we consider the nature of business strategy. Top managers of big firms devote the bulk of their efforts to formulating strategy, though there is remarkably little agreement about what it is ...*

No single subject has so dominated the attention of managers, consultants and management theorists as the subject of corporate strategy. For the top managers of big companies, this is perhaps understandable. Served by hordes of underlings, their huge desks uncluttered by the daily minutiae of business, they often consider setting strategy as their most valuable contribution. And it is also understandable that there is a great deal of debate about which strategies work best; business is, after all, complicated and uncertain. More puzzling is the fact that the consultants and theorists jostling to advise businesses cannot even agree on the most basic of all questions: what, precisely, is corporate strategy?

In the January–February 1993 issue of the *Harvard Business Review*, Gary Hamel and C K Prahalad, professors at the London Business School and the University of Michigan, turn much of their recent thinking upside down by asserting that the real function of a company's strategy is not to match its resources with its opportunities, as many businessmen assume, but rather to set goals which 'stretch' a company beyond what most of its managers believe is possible.

The authors cite a number of well-known cases of smaller companies defeating bigger companies with deeper pockets, stronger reputations and larger market shares. Toyota *v* General Motors, Cable News Network *v* CBS, British Airways *v* Pan Am and

Sony v RCA are all competitive battles in which most observers would have predicted defeat for the challenger. In all these examples, overwhelming ambition and gritty determination may well have been a vital ingredient in the smaller firm's success. But this is not what most people would call a 'strategy'.

The authors' reduction of strategy to little more than a rallying cry is the apotheosis of a trend away from formal planning at big firms which has been gathering pace for the past 30 years. In a vast outpouring of writing on the subject during this period, management theorists have come up with so many alternative views of what a corporate strategy should contain that they have undermined the entire concept. A growing number of businessmen now question whether thinking consciously about an overall strategy is of any benefit at all to big firms. Grabbing opportunities or coping with blows as they arise may make more sense.

Soon after the Second World War, when a new class of professional managers began to search for ideas about how to run big firms, the original views of strategy were borrowed from the military. Managers still talk about 'attacking' markets and 'defeating' rivals, but the analogy between generalship and running a firm was quickly abandoned when businessmen realised that slaughtering your opponents and outselling them had little in common.

By the 1960s, corporate strategy had come to mean a complex and meticulously wrought plan based on detailed forecasts of economies and specific markets. That view was endorsed by two celebrated books: Alfred Sloan's *My Years with General Motors*, a memoir by the man who made the car maker the world's biggest industrial enterprise; and Alfred Chandler's *Strategy and Structure*, a history of big, successful American firms in which the Harvard professor argued that their strategies had produced their multi-divisional form.

This approach to strategy fell into disrepute for several reasons. Many people blame it for the over-zealous diversification of the following decade and the creation of poorly performing conglomerates. In the 1970s, the success of Japanese firms which seemed to eschew detailed planning, cast further doubt on its usefulness. The two sudden oil-price rises of the 1970s also meant that firms found that the reams of statistics and targets, once assembled, sat gathering dust. Occupied with running their operations, few managers at any level of the firm ever bothered to refer again to its handsomely bound corporate strategy.

Then in 1980 came another book: *Competitive Strategy* by Michael Porter, an economist at Harvard Business School. He argued that a firm's profitability was determined by the characteristics of its industry and the firm's position within it, so these should also determine its strategy. Applying the analytical techniques common to industrial economics, Professor Porter said that a firm's primary task was to find niches it could defend from competitors, by becoming the low-cost producer, by differentiating its products in a way which would allow it to command a higher profit margin, or by erecting barriers to the entry of new rivals. Professor Porter's book was an instant hit.

Nevertheless, his ideas have had little impact on how most big firms go about formulating strategy. One reason is that Professor Porter's work is descriptive, not prescriptive. His vast checklists provide little guide to what firms should actually do, or avoid doing. Every firm would like to be in an industry with high barriers to entry, weak rivals and high profits. But few are so lucky.

About the same time as Professor Porter's book appeared, James Quinn, a professor at Dartmouth College's Amos Tuck business school, published the results of a study of how big firms actually went about formulating strategy. He found that they proceeded by trial and error, constantly revising their strategy in the light of new experience. He called this *logical incrementalism*. To a lot of people this sounded suspiciously like 'muddling through' (i.e. no strategy at all), though Professor Quinn vehemently denied this, arguing that there were great benefits to formalising the process.

The most influential strain of theorising about strategy in the 1980s has stressed expanding a firm's skills – a rapid product development, high-quality manufacturing, technological innovation and service – and then finding markets in which to exploit those skills. This is the argument made by Professors Hamel and Prahalad themselves in a 1990 *Harvard Business Review* article.

Despite the changing fashions, decades of theorising have not been entirely useless. How a company views strategy does depend largely on its circumstances. Small firms determined to challenge behemoths may find it helpful to call their aspirations a 'strategy'. Big companies defending a dominant market position may find Professor Porter's industry analysis illuminating. All firms should try to exploit and hone their skills. But there is no single way to approach the future. The next time your boss proudly boasts that he is off to a strategic planning meeting, give him your condolences.

© Copyright *The Economist*, London, 20 March 1993.

QUESTIONS

1 *Does the writer accurately summarise some of the main theories? What strategy areas, if any, need to be added?*

2 *Does the lack of quoted references invalidate the comments of the writer?*

3 *The writer appears to dismiss many of the major strategy developments of the last thirty years. Do you agree?*

SUMMARY

● Prescriptive and emergent strategies can be contrasted by adapting Mintzberg's analogy:[89]

Prescriptive strategy is Biblical in its approach: *it appears at a point in time and is governed by a set of rules, fully formulated and ready to implement.*

Emergent strategy is Darwinian in its approach: *an emerging and changing strategy that survives by adapting as the environment itself changes.*

Given the need for an organisation to have a corporate strategy, much of this chapter has really been about the *process* of achieving this strategy. As has been demonstrated, there is no common agreement on the way this can be done.

● One the one hand, there is the *prescriptive* process which involves a structured strategic planning system. There is a need to identify objectives, analyse the environment and the resources of the organisation, develop strategy options and select among them. The selected process is then implemented. There are then writers who caution against having a system that is too rigid and incapable of taking into account the people element in strategy.

● On the one hand, there is the *emergent* process that does not identify a final objective with specific strategies to achieve this. It relies on developing strategies whose final outcome may not be known. Managers will rely more on trial and error and experimentation to achieve the optimal process.

● In the early part of the century when industrialisation was proceeding fast, the prescriptive process was the main recommended route. As organisations came to recognise the people element and their importance to strategic development during the middle part of the century, emergent strategies were given greater prominence. In recent years, emphasis has switched between market-based routes and resource-based routes in the development of strategy. Social and cultural issues have also become more important as markets and production have become increasingly global in scale.

● Within the *prescriptive* route, three main groups of strategic theory have been identified:

1 *the profit-maximising, market-based route* – the market place is vital to profit delivery;

2 *the resource-based route* – the resources of the organisation are important in developing corporate strategy;

3 *the socio-cultural-based route* – focussing on the social and cultural dimensions of the organisation, especially for its international implications.

Each of these has different perspectives on the development of strategy.

● Within the *emergent* route, three main groups were also distinguished:

1 *the survival-based route* – emphasising the 'survival of the fittest' in the jungle of the market place;

2 *the uncertainty-based route* – regards prediction as impossible because of the inherently unstable nature of the environment;

3 *the human resource-based route* – places the emphasis on people in strategic development. Motivation, politics, culture and the desires of the individual are all important. Strategy may involve an element of experimentation and learning in order to take into account all these factors.

QUESTIONS

1 Is it possible for organisations to follow both prescriptive and emergent strategies or do they need to choose?

2 Examine the criticisms of prescriptive strategies in Section 2.2 and those of emergent strategies in Section 2.3. To what extent, if at all, do you agree with them? Why?

3 Consider the three emergent approaches to strategy outlined in Section 2.5. Which would you judge most closely described the route taken by Spillers in Case study 2.3. What conclusions do you draw from this about the viability of the Spillers' approach?

4 What predictions would you make for the environment over the next ten years? What influence will your predictions have on developments in corporate strategy over this period?

5 Take an organisation with which you are familiar. Analyse whether it has been following prescriptive or emergent strategies or both. Within these broad categories, how would you characterise its strategies according to the classifications laid out in Sections 2.4 and 2.5?

6 If you were asked to develop corporate strategy for the following companies, which corporate strategy theory might you pick as a starting point for your assessment? A large, international car company; an advertising agency with global links; a government institution; a small travel agent company with four branches, all in one region of a country.

7 'When well-managed major organisations make significant changes in strategy, the approaches they use frequently bear little resemblance to the rational–analytical systems so often touted in the planning literature.' Professor J B Quinn. Discuss

8 'In turbulent environments, the speed at which changes develop is such that firms which use the emerging strategy formation advocated by Mintzberg endanger their own survival. When they arrive on a market with a new product or service, such firms find the market pre-empted by more foresightful competitors who plan their strategic moves in advance.' Professor I Ansoff. Explain and critically evaluate this comment.

STRATEGIC PROJECT

Corporate strategy in the food industry

Several of the cases in the chapter have examined aspects of corporate strategy in the food industry. You will find other cases later in this book. Such companies face real strategic problems because of the increasing power of grocery retailers. They have attempted to hit back using branding, pricing and even supplying products under the brand name of the retailer, especially in the UK. Consider what further activities the food companies should undertake.

- Should they merge into larger enterprises?
- Should they move further into supplying the retailer?
- Should they cut down their product range so that they can invest heavily behind a narrower focus (that is, the Dalgety strategy)?

Examine the French company, Danone, which has used a strategic mix of product innovation and acquisitions with some success. Alternatively, explore the UK company United Biscuits, which has had significant problems (*see* Chapter 21).

FURTHER READING

Richard Whittington's *What is Strategy and does it matter?* (Routledge, London, 1993) is a lucid, well-structured and thought-provoking book. I have acknowledged some of its interesting research references as this chapter has progressed and it has certainly influenced some elements of the material. Read Chapter 2 of Whittington for an alternative view and structuring of strategy theories and practice.

Bob de Wit and Ron Meyer's *Strategy: Process, Content and Context* (West Publishing, St Paul, Minn, 1994) is a book of academic readings that would provide excellent source material for essays and projects. The selection of material is perceptive and helpful and has been used to provide the references in several places in this book. Read the first two chapters: in particular, you might find the dispute between Mintzberg and Ansoff (pages 69–83) worthy of critical study and possibly even entertaining.

Richard Pascale's *Managing on the Edge* (Viking Penguin, London, 1990) has a useful review of the development of corporate strategy in this century (*see* Chapter 4).

J L Moore's *Writers on Strategy and Strategic Management* (Penguin, London, 1992) has a useful survey of some leading writers and theories. Helpful for essay references and revision.

REFERENCES

1 Kennedy, P (1990) *The Rise and Fall of the Great Powers*. Fontana Press, Ch 5. The historical description of this chapter draws on this well researched and documented book.
2 Urwick, L (ed) (1956) *The Golden Book of Management*, Newman Neame, London. The book contains brief records of the lives and work of seventy of the early management pioneers, including their publications and a comment on their contribution. The historical material in this chapter draws on this score.
3 Williams, K, Haslam, C, Johal, S and Williams, J (1994) *Cars: analysis, history and cases*, Berghahn Books, New York, Ch 7.
4 Abernathy, W J and Wayne, K (1974) 'Limits of the Learning Curve', *Harvard Business Review*, Sept–Oct, pp109–19.
5 Drucker, P (1961) *The Practice of Management*, Mercury Books, London, Ch 10.
6 Kennedy, P (1990) Ibid, p697.
7 Ansoff, H I (1969) *Business Strategy*, Penguin, Harmondsworth.
8 World Bank (1994) *World Development Report 1994*, Oxford University Press, New York, Ch 3.
9 Ansoff, I (1969) Ibid; Porter, M E (1980) *Competitive Strategy*, The Free Press, Harvard, MA, Introduction.
10 Sloan, A P (1963) *My Years with General Motors*, Sedgewick & Jackson, London, p43.
11 Clausewitz, C von, *On War*, Routledge and Kegan Paul, London, quoted in Kotler, P and Singh, R (1981) 'Marketing Warfare', *Journal of Business Strategy*, pp30–41.
12 Liddell Hart, B H (1967) *Strategy*, Praeger, NY, also quoted in reference 4 above.
13 *See*, e.g., James, B G (1985) *Business Warfare*, Penguin, Harmondsworth. Also Ries, J and Trout, A (1986) *Marketing Warfare*, McGraw-Hill, Maidenhead.
14 Whittington, R (1993) *What is strategy – and does it matter?*, Routledge, London, p16.
15 Wiles, P J D (1961) *Price, Cost and Output*, Blackwell, Oxford, p78.
16 Porter, M E (1985) *Competitive Advantage*, The Free Press, Harvard, MA.
17 Ansoff, H I (1965) *Corporate Strategy: an analytical approach to Business Policy for Growth and Expansion*, McGraw-Hill, NY.
18 Chakravathy, B and Lorange, P (1991) *Managing the Strategy Process*, Prentice Hall, Upper Saddle River, NJ. The first chapter is usefully summarised in: De Wit, B and Meyer, R (1994) *Strategy: Process, Context and Content*, West Publishing, St Paul, Minn.

19 Mintzberg, H (1990) 'The Design School: reconsidering the basic premises of strategic management', *Strategic Management Journal*, 11, pp176–95.

20 Mintzberg, H (1994) 'The fall and rise of strategic planning', *Harvard Business Review*, Jan–Feb, pp107–14.

21 The evidence in this case comes from personal experience: the author was senior manager at Spillers plc corporate strategy headquarters and acted as liaison manager with the consultancy company.

22 Lester, T (1979) 'Slow Grind at Spillers', *Management Today*, Jan, pp59–114.

23 Mayo, E, *Human Problems in Industrial Civilisation*, along with other research on the *Bank Wiring Observation Room*, described in Homans, G (1951) *The Human Group*, Routledge and Kegan Paul, London, Ch III.

24 Cyert, R M and March, J (1963) *A Behavioral Theory of the Firm*, Prentice Hall, Upper Saddle River, NJ.

25 March, J G and Simon, H (1958) *Organisations*, Wiley, New York.

26 Pettigrew, A (1985) *The awakening giant: continuity and change at ICI*, Blackwell, Oxford.

27 Mintzberg, H (1990) Ibid.

28 Johnson, G (1986) *Managing strategic change – the role of strategic formulae*, published in: McGee, J and Thomas, H (ed) (1986) *Strategic Management Research*, Wiley, Chichester, Section 1.4.

29 Senge, P M (1990) 'The leader's new work: building learning organisations', *Sloan Management Review*, Fall, pp7–22.

30 Cyert, R M and March, J (1963) Ibid.

31 Whittington, R (1993) Ibid. Repeats Weick's true story of the Hungarian troops who were lost in the Alps during the First World War but found a map which they used to reach safety. They then discovered that they were using a map of the Pyrenees. Whittington makes the point that taking *some* action, *any* action, will constitute strategy in these circumstances, even if the particular choice of strategy is wrong. The issue is not whether the *right* strategic choice has been made and then implemented, but rather whether *any* choice has been made that will give choice to the people concerned.

32 Lindblom, C E (1959) 'The Science of Muddling Through', *Public Administrative Review*, 19, pp79–88, as quoted in Whittington, R (1993) Ibid.

33 Cyert, R M and March, J G (1956) 'Organisation Factors in the Theory of Monopoly', *Quarterly Journal of Economics*, 70(1), pp44–64, as quoted in Whittington, R (1993) Ibid.

34 These comments are taken from a variety of sources: many of the prescriptive strategists have been so confident of their approach that they have not bothered to criticise the emergent strategists.

35 Lester, T (1979) Ibid.

36 Whittington, R (1993) Ibid, p33.

37 *See*, e.g., Levitt, T (1983) 'The Globalisation of Markets', *Harvard Business Review*, May–June, pp92–102. Reprinted in De Wit, R and Meyer, B (1994) *Strategy: Process Content and Context*, West Publishing, St Paul, Minn.

38 *See*, e.g., Douglas, S and Wind, Y (1987) 'The Myth of Globalisation', *Columbia Journal of World Business*, Winter. Also reprinted in De Wit, R and Meyer, B (1994) Ibid.

39 Ansoff, I (1965) *Corporate Strategy*, Penguin, Harmondsworth.

40 Chandler A (1962) *Strategy and Structure*, MIT Press, Cambridge, Mass.

41 Sloan, A P (1963) *My Years with General Motors*, Sedgewick & Jackson, London.

42 Wheelen, T and Hunger, D (1992) *Strategic Management and Business Policy*, Addison-Wesley.

43 Porter, M E (1980) and (1985) Ibid.

44 Rumelt, R, Schendel, D and Teece, D (1991) 'Strategic Management and Economics', *Strategic Management Journal*, 12, pp5–29. This contains an extensive and valuable review of this area.

45 Ansoff, I (1968) 'Toward a strategy theory of the firm', in Ansoff, I (ed) (1969) *Business Strategy*, Penguin, Harmondsworth, p39.

46 Porter, M E (1980) Ibid.

47 Ohmae, K (1983) *The Mind of the Strategist*, Penguin, Harmondsworth.

48 Wilks, S (1990) *The Embodiment of industrial culture in bureaucracy and management*, quoted in Whittington, R (1994) Ibid, p160.

49 *See*, e.g., the leading article in the *Financial Times Survey on India*, 8 Nov 1994.

50 *See*, e.g., the leading article in the *Financial Times Survey on Singapore*, 24 Feb 1995.

51 Hamel, G and Prahalad, C K (1990) 'The Core Competence of the Corporation', *Harvard Business School Review*, May–June. Their 1994 book *Competing for the Future* picks up many of the same themes.

52 Kay, J (1993): *see* 'Key Reading' in Ch 1.

53 Hannan, M T and Freeman, J (1988) *Organisational Ecology*, Harvard University Press, MA.

54 Hamel, G and Prahalad, C K (1990) Ibid.

55 Kay, J (1993) *Foundations of Corporate Success*, Oxford University Press.

56 Mintzberg, H (1987) Ibid.

57 Mintzberg, H (1994) 'The fall and rise of strategic planning', *Harvard Business Review*, Jan–Feb, pp107–14.

58 Drucker, P (1967) Ibid, Ch 9.

59 Slack, N, Chambers, S, Harland, C, Harrison, A and Johnston, R (1995) *Operations Management*, Pitman Publishing, London, p812.

60 Williams, K, Haslam, C, Johal, S and Williams, J (1994) Ibid, Ch 7.

61 Hamel, G and Prahalad, C K (1990) Ibid.

62 Kay, J (1993) Ibid, Part III.

63 Marris, R (1964) *The Economic Theory of Managerial Capitalism*, Macmillan, London, quoted in Whittington, R (1993) *What is strategy – and does it matter?*, Routledge, London.

64 Granovetter, M (1985) 'Economic action and social culture', *American Journal of Sociology*, 91(3), pp481–510, quoted in Whittington, R (1993) Ibid.

65 Whittington, R (1993) Ibid, p28.

66 Whitley, R (1991) 'The social construction of business systems in East Asia', *Organisation Studies*, 12(1), pp1–28, quoted in Whittington, R (1993) Ibid.

67 Boyacigiller, N and Adler, N (1991) 'The parochial dinosaur: organisation science in a global context', *Journal of Management Studies*, 28(4), pp262–90.

68 Hall, R C and Hitch, C J (1939) 'Price Theory and Business Behaviour', *Oxford Economic Papers*, 2, pp12–45, quoted in Whittington, R (1993) Ibid.

69 Henderson, B (1989) 'The Origin of Strategy', *Harvard Business Review*, Nov–Dec, pp139–43.

70 Williamson, O (1991) 'Strategising, economising and economic organisation', *Strategic Management Journal*, 12, pp75–94.

71 Hannan, M T and Freeman, J (1988) Ibid.

72 Whittington, R (1993) Ibid, p22.

73 Pascale, R (1990) *Managing on the Edge*, Viking Penguin, London, p114.

74 Gleick, J (1988) *Chaos*, Penguin, London.

75 Miller, D and Friesen, P (1982) 'Structural change and performance: quantum versus piecemeal-incremental approaches', *Academy of Management Journal*, 25, pp867–92.

76 Strebel, P (1992) *Breakpoints*, Harvard Business School Press, Boston, MA. A summary of this argument appears in De Wit, B and Meyer, R (1994) Ibid, pp390–2.

77 Stacey, R (1993) *Strategic Management and Organisational Dynamics*, Pitman Publishing, London.

78 Cyert, R and March, J (1963) Ibid.

79 March, J and Simon, H (1958) Ibid.

80 Nelson, R and Winter, S (1982) *An evolutionary theory of economic change*, Harvard University Press, MA.

81 Mintzberg, H (1987) 'Crafting Strategy', *Harvard Business Review*, July–Aug, pp65–75.

82 Quinn, J B (1980) *Strategies for change: Logical Incrementalism*, Irwin, Burr Ridge, Minn.

83 Senge, P M (1990) Ibid.

84 Mintzberg, H (1994) Ibid.

85 de Jonquieres, G (1993) 'Dalgety buys petfood arm of BP for £42 million', *Financial Times*, 30 Nov, p22.

86 Oram, R (1995) 'Dalgety in £442 million pet food purchase', *Financial Times*, 4 Feb, p20 and Oram, R (1995) 'Dalgety picks an interesting time to sell Golden Wonder', *Financial Times*, 20 Feb 1995, p19.

87 Case adapted from an article by Hill, A (1995) *Financial Times*, 27 Feb, p11.

88 *The Economist*, 20 March 1993.

89 Mintzberg, H (1990) 'The Design School: Reconsidering the basic premises of strategic management', *Strategic Management Journal*, as adapted by De Wit, R and Meyer, B (1994) Ibid, p72.

PART 2

ANALYSIS OF THE ENVIRONMENT

Both the prescriptive and the emergent approaches to corporate strategy consider an organisation's ability to understand its environment – its customers, its suppliers, its competitors and the social and economic influences in its operations – to be an important element of the strategy process.

This part of the book begins by examining the basic analytical tools and frameworks used in a study of an organisation's environment and then goes on to tackle particular aspects of this task in more detail, namely the basic market conditions and influences, the organisation's competitors and its customers and marketing resources.

ANALYSIS OF
THE ENVIRONMENT

- **The *prescriptive* strategic process**

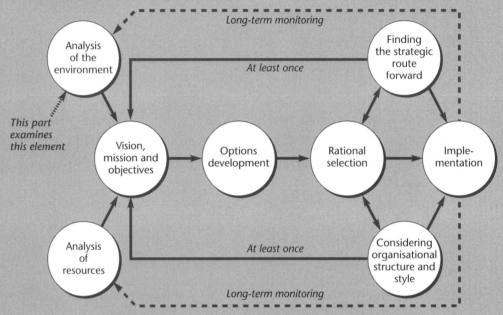

- **The *emergent* strategic process**

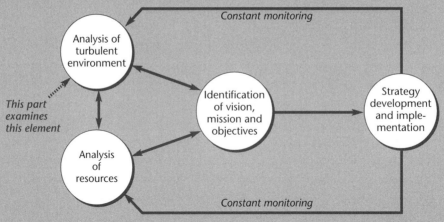

Chapter 3
ANALYSING THE ENVIRONMENT

- What is the environment and why is it important?
- What are the main background areas to be analysed?
- How are the more immediate influences on the organisation analysed?
- What is the importance of market share and market growth?
- How important is the customer?

Chapter 4
ANALYSING THE MARKET

- What is the strategic significance of market growth?
- What influence can governments have on corporate strategy?
- What is the impact of globalisation and internationalisation on corporate strategy?

Chapter 5
ANALYSING COMPETITORS

- How are competitors analysed?
- How do competitors compete with each other and what is the nature of competition?
- How important are distributors and suppliers?
- What is market attractiveness and does it really matter?

Chapter 6
ANALYSING CUSTOMERS

- How are customers analysed?
- What is the strategic role of price and value for money?
- What contribution do branding and the other aspects of the marketing mix make to strategy?
- How important are innovation and new product development?

3

Analysing the environment

When you have worked through this chapter, you will be able to:

- outline the main environmental influences on the organisation and relate the degree of change to prescriptive and emergent strategic approaches;

- undertake a PEST analysis of the general influences on the organisation;

- understand the importance of key factors for success in the environment;

- carry out a Five Forces analysis of the specific influences on the organisation;

- undertake a competitor profile and a product portfolio analysis of the organisation and its competitors;

- explore the relationship between the organisation and its customers.

INTRODUCTION

In recent years, the term 'the environment' has taken on a rather specialised meaning: it involves 'green' issues and the poisoning of our planet by human activity. These concerns are certainly part of our considerations in this book, but we use the term 'the environment' in a much broader sense to describe *everything and everyone outside the organisation*. This includes customers, competitors, suppliers, distributors, government and social institutions.

Before examining aspects of the environment in depth in Chapters 4 to 6, it is useful to begin by exploring the six basic factors in the environment that influence corporate strategy (*see* Fig 3.1). As elements of the environment change, the organisation needs to adjust its corporate strategy accordingly. Prescriptive strategies will want to *anticipate* how the environment will change in the future in order to meet future needs ahead of competing organisations. Emergent strategies will be content with an *understanding* of the environment.

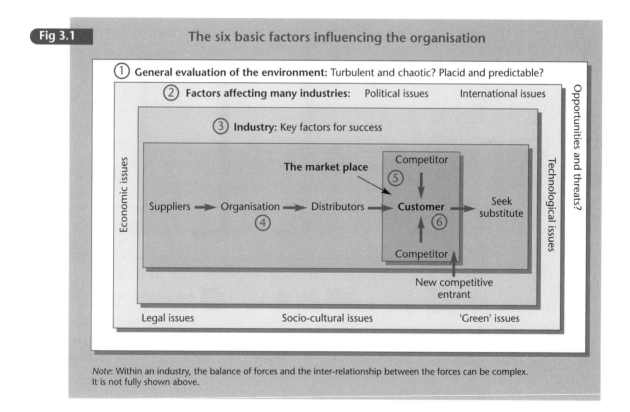

Fig 3.1 The six basic factors influencing the organisation

Note: Within an industry, the balance of forces and the inter-relationship between the forces can be complex. It is not fully shown above.

Usinor–Sacilor copes with a difficult environment

Over the last ten years, Europe's steel companies have had to operate in a very uncertain environment. This case examines how Europe's largest steel manufacturer, the French steel company Usinor–Sacilor, has coped with this task.

Usinor–Sacilor, and the steel industry in general, have been affected by the following factors in recent years:

● economic downturn;
● European Union and national government interference;
● major changes in technology; and
● increasing low-cost competition from outside Western Europe.

All these areas have led to major profit problems for many of the companies, with Usinor–Sacilor posting two years of losses in the mid-1990s (*see* Fig 3.2).

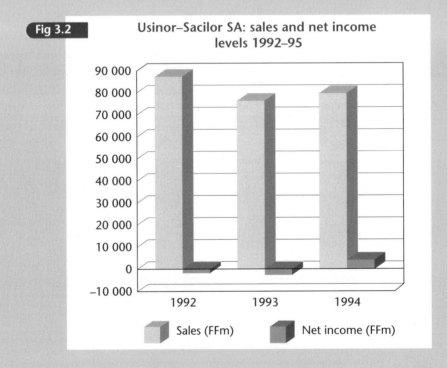

Fig 3.2 Usinor–Sacilor SA: sales and net income levels 1992–95

Back in 1985, the state-owned French steel company, Sacilor, was merged with its French rival, Usinor, to form Europe's largest steel company. But in the steel industry, however, size is no guarantee of profitability and the group was only just breaking even. To generate profits in the industry, the key components are:

● new and efficient plant;
● low labour costs;
● modern technology;

- a range of specialist, high-priced steels; and
- secure distribution outlets.

At the time, Usinor–Sacilor (U–S) had few of these assets.

The company was brought together by the French government, who wanted France to remain powerful in European steel. They recruited a new chief executive, M Francis Mer, from a subsidiary of the major French glass company, St Gobain. He subsequently appointed several former colleagues to U–S, with the comment that he wanted to recruit from outside the steel industry in order to change working practices inside the company.

During the period 1986–91, Europe was expanding, with economies buoyant and the industry profitable. U–S was relatively weak, however, with poor representation in the most profitable steel sectors, limited distribution outlets across Europe and inefficient plant. Corporate strategy was therefore aimed at a series of acquisitions, joint ventures and alliances to overcome these problems.

Over this period, the company was aided by support from the French banks and a benign view about such support from the European Commission in Brussels. By 1993, the company had debts of FF 23 billion and shareholders' funds of FF 21 billion. This was not a healthy situation, particularly as French interest rates were beginning to rise rapidly to support the French franc in the European Exchange Rate Mechanism.

During the period 1992–95, corporate strategy shifted and involved consolidation rather than expansion.[1] Three major strategies were undertaken in France especially:

- *Major reductions in the workforce.* The size of the workforce had come down from 96 000 in 1989 to 62 000 in 1994, with much of this reduction occurring in the later years. This trend was expected to continue.
- *Retraining of the workforce.* This brought new opportunities for promotion in order to change the company culture from one of *production orientation* to one of *profit orientation*.[2]
- *Some investment in new technology.* This was an attempt to simplify and integrate steel production;[3] arguably the company could have done more in this area.

By 1995, Usinor–Sacilor was the third largest steel producer in the world, behind Nippon Steel in Japan and Posco in South Korea. It had moved back into profit but accepted that this was partly as a result of the cyclical upswing during 1994 in the European steel industry. The profit improvement was useful as there had been a change of government in France, with the new regime of President Chirac favouring increased privatisation – the company was a prime target. M Francis Mer was still chief executive of the company and he was quoted as saying that he was looking forward to moving the company into the private sector. It was not known whether his enthusiasm was affected by the possibility of his receiving the same generous and largely unjustified managerial payouts that had accompanied privatisations in the UK.

CASE QUESTIONS

1 *What were the main changes in the environment of Usinor–Sacilor? What was their impact on company strategy?*

2 *Which single factor seems to have been more important than any other? What implications, if any, does this have for corporate strategy at the company?*

3.1 EXPLORING THE ENVIRONMENT

3.1.1 The connection with corporate strategy

Strategists are agreed that an understanding of the environment is an essential element of the development of corporate strategy. However, there are three difficulties in determining the connection between the organisation's corporate strategy and its environment.

1 *The prescriptive versus emergent debate.* The first problem arises from the fundamental disagreement about the corporate strategy processes that was explored in Part 1 of this book. Some prescriptive strategists take the view that, in spite of the various uncertainties, the environment can usefully be predicted for many markets. Some (but not all) emergent strategists believe that the environment is so turbulent and chaotic that prediction is likely to be inaccurate and serve no useful purpose. Each of these interpretations implies a quite different status for the same basic topic. This difficulty is explored further in Section 3.2.

2 *The uncertainty.* Whatever view is taken about prediction, all corporate strategists regard the environment as uncertain. New strategies have to be undertaken against a backdrop that cannot be guaranteed and this difficulty must be addressed as corporate strategies are developed. For example, Usinor–Sacilor acquired a steel-making company in the USA in the late 1980s for over US$500 million. This was undertaken on the basis that the American steel market was attractive and its future reasonably certain. However, there was inevitably a residual risk related to the environment that needed to be accepted by the French company. Such a risk could only be assessed by analysing the environment.

3 *The range of influences.* It is conceivable, at least in theory, that every element of an organisation's environment may influence corporate strategy. One solution to the problem posed by such a wide range of factors might be to produce a list of every element. This would be a strategic mistake, however, because organisations and individuals would find it difficult to develop and manage every item. In corporate strategy, the production of comprehensive lists that include every major eventuality and have no priorities has no value. A better solution is to identify the *key factors for success* in the industry and then to direct the environmental analysis towards these factors. For example, in the European steel industry, the Usinor–Sacilor case identified several items that were particularly important in delivering profitability to the companies. These items could then be used to select and direct an environmental analysis undertaken by Usinor–Sacilor.

3.1.2 The main elements of environmental analysis

To analyse an organisation's environment, while as the same time addressing the three difficulties outlined in Section 3.1.1, certain basic analytical procedures can be undertaken (*see* Table 3.1).

Table 3.1 Six basic stages in environmental analysis

Stage	Techniques	Outcome of stage
1 Consideration of the *nature* of the environment, both for *many* organisations and for the *specific sector* associated with the organisation. (*See* Section 3.2.)	General considerations: <ul><li>Change: fast or slow?</li><li>Repetitive or surprising future?</li><li>Forecastable or unpredictable?</li><li>Complex or simple influences on the organisation?</li></ul>	General strategic conclusions: <ul><li>Is the environment too turbulent to undertake useful predictions?</li><li>What are the opportunities and threats for the organisation?</li></ul>
2 Factors affecting *many* organisations. (*See* Section 3.3.)	PEST analysis and scenarios.	<ul><li>Identify key influences.</li><li>Predict, if possible.</li><li>Understand interconnections between events.</li></ul>
3 Factors specific to the industry: what delivers success? (*See* Section 3.4.)	Key factors for success analysis.	<ul><li>Identify factors relevant to strategy.</li><li>Focus strategic analysis and development.</li></ul>
4 Factors specific to the competitive balance of power in the industry. (*See* Section 3.5.)	Five Forces analysis.	Static and descriptive analysis of competitive forces.
5 Factors specific to immediate competitors. (*See* Section 3.6.)	Competitor analysis and product portfolio analysis.	<ul><li>Competitor profile.</li><li>Analysis of relative market strengths.</li></ul>
6 Customer analysis. (*See* Section 3.7.)	Market and segmentation studies.	Strategy targeted at existing and potential customers.

Note that the first two stages in Table 3.1 relate, partly at least, to *all* organisations; the final four stages are mainly concerned with a *specific industry*.

3.2 CONSIDERATION OF THE STRATEGIC ENVIRONMENT[4]

Before exploring specific aspects of environmental analysis, it is important to give some general consideration to the basic conditions surrounding the organisation. Special attention needs to be directed to the nature and strength of the forces driving strategic change – the *dynamics* of the environment. One reason for this consideration is that, if the forces are exceptionally turbulent, they may make it difficult to use some of the analyses discussed later in this chapter. Another reason is that the nature of the environment may influence the way that the organisation is structured to cope with such changes.

The environmental forces surrounding the organisation can be assessed according to two main measures:

- *Changeability* – the degree to which the environment is likely to change.
- *Predictability* – the degree with which such changes can be predicted.

These measures can each be subdivided further. Changeability comprises:

- *Complexity* – the degree to which the organisation's environment is affected by factors such as internationalisation and technological, social and political complications; and
- *Novelty* – the degree to which the environment presents the organisation with new situations.

Predictability can be further subdivided into:

- *Rate of change* of the environment (from slow to fast); and
- *Visibility of the future* in terms of the availability and usefulness of the information used to predict the future.

Using these factors as a basis, it is then possible to build a spectrum that categorises the environment and provides a rating for its *degree of turbulence* (*see* Table 3.2).

Table 3.2 Assessing the dynamics of the environment

Environmental turbulence	Repetitive	Expanding	Changing	Discontinuous	Surprising
Changeability — Complexity	National	National	Regional Technological	Regional Socio-political	Global Economic
Changeability — Familiarity of events	Familiar	Extrapolable		Discontinuous Familiar	Discontinuous Novel
Predictability — Rapidity of change	Slower than response		Comparable to response		Faster than response
Predictability — Visibility of future	Recurring	Forecastable	Predictable	Partially predictable	Unpredictable surprises
Turbulence level Low	1	2	3	4	5 High

Source: *Implanting Strategic Management* by Ansoff, I and McDonnell, E, © 1990. Reprinted by permission of Prentice-Hall, Inc., Upper Saddle River, NJ.

When turbulence is low, it may be possible to predict the future with confidence. For example, Usinor–Sacilor might be able to use data on its major customers along with national economic data to predict future demand for its steel products.

When turbulence is higher, such predictions may have little meaning. The changeability elements influencing the organisation may contain *many* and *complex* items and the *novelty* being introduced into the market place may be high. For example, new services, new suppliers, new ideas, new software and new payment systems were all being launched for the Internet at the same time. Turbulence was high. Predicting the specific outcome of such developments was virtually impossible.

Corporate strategy needs to involve an assessment of these factors and then a consideration of how these factors can be dealt with. This can be done in two main ways:

1 *By careful organisation.* If the environment is turbulent, the organisation needs to remain responsive and flexible so that it can adapt quickly, while at the same time developing new initiatives – this is essentially an *emergent* approach to the development of corporate strategy. Organisations can also be structured in such a way that decisions can be taken at local level and thus opportunities can be seized without referral to some slower central authority.

   If the environment is calmer, then the organisation has the opportunity to examine its options and engage in a more measured exercise – more probably a *prescriptive* approach to the development of corporate strategy.

2 *By information processing.* A *computer model* could be built to simulate the various influences. The model's usefulness will, however, depend on the changeability of the factors involved: if there are many novel features and many discontinuous changes, the value of such a model is likely to be limited.

In practice, during turbulent periods, the solutions would probably rely on developing the flexible organisation outlined in point 1.

If the level of turbulence is high, and as a result the environment is difficult to study, the analysis recommended in some of the sections that follow may need to be treated with some caution. However, for most fast-growing situations, including the Internet, there is merit in at least attempting to understand the main areas of the environment influencing the organisation. It may not be possible to undertake formal predictions but it will certainly be possible to identify the most important elements.

Key strategic principles

- It is important to begin an analysis of the environment with a general consideration of the degree of turbulence in that environment. If it is high, then this will make prediction difficult and impact on prescriptive approaches to strategy development.

- There are two measures of turbulence: changeability, i.e. the degree to which the environment is likely to change; and predictability, i.e. the degree to which such change can be predicted.

- Each of the two measures can then be further subdivided: changeability can be split into complexity and novelty; predictability can be divided into rate of change and visibility of the future. All these elements can then be used to explore turbulence.

- When turbulence is high, the organisation will need to structure itself so that it can respond rapidly to changing events.

3.3 ANALYSING THE GENERAL ENVIRONMENT

In any consideration of the factors surrounding the organisation, two techniques can be used to explore the general environment (as opposed to the specific industry or service): these are the PEST analysis and scenarios.

3.3.1 PEST analysis

It is already clear that there are no simple rules governing an analysis of the organisation. Each analysis needs to be guided by what is relevant for that particular organisation. However, it may be useful to begin the process with a *checklist* – often called a PEST analysis – of the **P**olitical, **E**conomic, **S**ocio-cultural and **T**echnological aspects of the environment. Exhibit 3.1 presents some of the main items that might be considered when undertaking a PEST analysis.

Exhibit 3.1   **Checklist for a PEST analysis**

Political future

- Political parties and alignments at local, national and European or regional trading-block level
- Legislation, e.g. on taxation and employment law
- Relations between government and the organisation (possibly influencing the preceding items in a major way and forming a part of future corporate strategy)
- Government ownership of industry and attitude to monopolies and competition

Socio-cultural future

- Shifts in values and culture
- Change in lifestyle
- Attitudes to work and leisure
- 'Green' environmental issues
- Education and health
- Demographic changes
- Distribution of income

Economic future

- Total GDP and GDP per head
- Inflation
- Consumer expenditure and disposable income
- Interest rates
- Currency fluctuations and exchange rates
- Investment, by the state, private enterprise and foreign companies
- Cyclicality
- Unemployment
- Energy costs, transport costs, communications costs, raw materials costs

Technological future

- Government and European Union investment policy
- Identified new research initiatives
- New patents and products
- Speed of change and adoption of new technology
- Level of expenditure on R&D by organisation's rivals
- Developments in nominally unrelated industries that might be applicable

---

Like all checklists, a PEST analysis is really only as good as the individual or group preparing it. Listing every conceivable item has little value and betrays a lack of serious consideration and logic in the corporate strategy process. Better to have three or four well thought-out items that are explored and justified with evidence than a lengthy 'laundry list' of items. This is why this book does not recommend simple + and – signs and accompanying short bullet points, although these would provide a useful summary.

To the prescriptive strategists, although the items in a PEST analysis rely on *past* events and experience, the analysis can be used as a *forecast of the future*. The past is history and corporate strategy is concerned with future action, but the best evidence about the future *may* derive from what happened in the past. Prescriptive strategists would suggest that it is worth attempting the task because major new investments make this hidden assumption anyway. For example, when Usinor–Sacilor invested US$500 million in its US acquisition, it was making an assumption that the US market would remain attractive; it might as well *formalise* this through a structured PEST analysis, even if the outcome is difficult to predict.

The emergent corporate strategists may well comment that the future is so uncertain that prediction is useless. If this view is held, a PEST analysis will fulfil a different role in *interpreting* past events and their inter-relationships. In practice, some emergent strategists may give words of caution but still be tempted to predict the future. For example, one prominent emergent strategist, Herbert Simon, wrote a rather rash article in 1960 predicting that, 'We will have the technical ability, by 1985, to run corporations by machine.'[5] The emergent strategists are correct in suggesting that prediction in some fast-moving markets may have little value. Overall, when used wisely, the PEST analysis has a role in corporate strategy.

3.3.2 Scenario–based analysis

In the context of a scenario-based analysis, a scenario is a model of a possible future environment for the organisation, whose strategic implications can then be investigated. For example, a scenario might be developed to explore the question: 'What would happen if green environmental concerns forced private cars off the road by the year 2020 and demand for steel in cars collapsed as a result? What impact would this have at Usinor–Sacilor?'

Scenarios are concerned with peering into the future – not predicting the future. Prediction takes the *current* situation and extrapolates it forward. Scenarios take *different* situations with *alternative* starting points. The aim is not to predict but to explore a set of possibilities; a combination of events is usually gathered together into a scenario and then this combination is explored for its strategic significance. Exhibit 3.2 provides some guidance on the development of scenarios.

Exhibit 3.2   Some guidance on building scenarios

- Start from an *unusual viewpoint*. Examples might include the stance of a major competitor, a radical change of government or the outbreak of war.

- Develop a *qualitative description* of a group of possible events or a *narrative* that shows how events will unfold. It is unlikely that this will involve a quantitative projection.

- Explore the *outcomes* of this description or narrative of events by building two or three scenarios of what might happen. More than three scenarios is usually difficult to handle. Two scenarios often lend themselves to a 'most optimistic outcome' and a 'worst-possible outcome'.

- Include the inevitable *uncertainty* in each scenario and explore the *consequences* of this uncertainty to the organisation concerned – for example, 'What would happen if the most optimistic outcome was achieved?' The PEST factors may provide some clues here.

- Test the usefulness of the scenario by the extent to which it leads to *new strategic thinking* rather than merely the continuance of existing strategy.

Key strategic principles

- The PEST analysis – the study of Political, Economic, Socio-cultural and Technological factors – provides a useful starting point to any analysis of the general environment surrounding an organisation. It is vital to select among the items from such a generalised list and explore the chosen areas in depth: long lists of items are of no use.

- Prescriptive and emergent strategists take different views on the merits of projecting forward the main elements of the PEST analysis. The prescriptive approach favours the development of projections because they are often implied in major strategic decisions in any event. Emergent strategists believe the turbulence of the environment makes projections of limited value.

- A scenario is a picture of a possible future environment for the organisation, whose strategic implications can then be investigated. It is less concerned with prediction and more involved with developing different perspectives on the future. The aim is to stimulate new strategic thought about the possible consequences of events, rather than make an accurate prediction of the future.

CASE STUDY 3.1

Steeled for global action

Recent world economic and political trends may encourage the development of worldwide steel companies.

After years of variable profits, there is evidence that the good times are rolling again for the world steel industry. For once, there is more to look forward to than a few years of profits and flat-out production before the next recession arrives. Steelmakers have their best opportunity ever to break out of the rut in which the industry has languished for the past 20 years. The end of state interference and the creation of a commercially driven, international or even global steel industry are within sight.

In the mid-1990s, the end of the recession in the industrialised countries was cause enough for celebration. After three years of decline, demand for steel products in the 25 member countries of the Organisation for Economic Co-operation and Development (OECD) rose 6.8 per cent to 326 million tonnes in 1994, with a further 2.5 per cent rise expected in 1995. Increased production in the main steel-consuming industries stimulated demand in almost all the OECD countries. The main exception was Japan, though even here demand was forecast to rise in 1995. 'We're in the best steel market we've had for 20 years,' said Robert Darnall, chairman and chief executive of Inland Steel Industries, the fifth-largest US steelmaker.

Mr Maarten van Veen, chairman of Hoogevens, the Dutch steelmaker believes that there are two ways forward for the industry. The first, which he calls 'déjà vu', would be a return to the old ways of the industry. These were characterised by steelmakers' refusing to look beyond national boundaries, sheltering behind trade barriers and state subsidies, viewing the global market as a threat, manufacturing standard products and 'struggling on'.

The second way forward, which he calls the 'new era', would be to create an international steel market with free competition and fair conditions. Steelmakers would adopt a global approach, view their market as an opportunity and make 'dedicated' products tailored to customers' needs.

Rather than struggle, steelmakers would proceed vigorously into the twenty-first century.

Mr van Veen naturally hopes (and expects) the industry will have 'the collective wisdom and foresight' to choose the second path – an optimism shared by others in the industry. This optimism is based on three factors: the trend towards privatisation, the changing nature of the steel market and the growing importance of developing countries. In contrast to industries such as chemicals, there are no true multinational steel companies. Steel may be sold across world markets, but it is still largely produced and supplied by national companies.

Government views of the steel industry

In the past, particularly in Europe, steel was viewed by national governments as 'strategic', partly because of its importance in making arms and partly because it provided high levels of employment in steelmaking regions. A steel industry was considered a symbol of national virility, and to preserve it many governments took some or all of their steelmakers into state ownership. However, times have changed. Steel is no longer so important to defence because of the increasing importance of other materials, such as plastics and composite materials. Modern steel plants require far fewer employees than in the past. As a result, political attitudes to steel are changing, and this is evident in the trend towards privatisation (*see* Table 3.3). In 1986, more than half the steel capacity in the European Union was publicly owned. With the privatisation of Usinor–Sacilor of France and the sale by the Italian state holding company of Ilva Laminati Piani, the flat steel producer, to Riva (one of Italy's biggest private steelmakers), the figure drops to between 20 and 25 per cent.

▶

CASE STUDY 3.1 continued

Table 3.3   State-owned companies' share of crude steel capacity (%)

	1968	1986	1992
Developing countries	62	68	45
Industrialised countries	14	24	15

Source: International Iron and Steel Institute

Steel privatisation plans continue in Portugal and in Turkey. Further afield, India has been rapidly reducing its stake in the Steel Authority of India (Sail) (which accounts for 60 per cent of Indian steel production). In Latin America, the Brazilian steel industry has been entirely in private hands since 1993, even though, as recently as 1988, the government owned 70 per cent of Brazil's production capacity.

Privatisation has generally invigorated national steel industries, exposing steelmakers to market pressures and freeing managements to take the decisions necessary to be competitive. In Brazil, for example, according to Mr Sylvio Nobrega Coutinho, President of Companhia Siderurgica Nacional (CSN) the removal of the state from the decision-making process gave the sector a free hand to cut costs and raise productivity. CSN has cut its workforce from 19 100 in 1990 to 15 000 with productivity rising over the same period from 160 tonnes of steel produced annually by each worker to 314 tonnes.

Privatisation of government-owned companies

In Europe, privatisation has been particularly welcomed by the private steelmakers, which have suffered what they have seen as unfair competition from subsidised state producers. According to Dr Ruprecht Vondran, President of the German Steel Federation, the private steel companies have tended to react more flexibly and efficiently to market conditions. The private companies have increased output faster in times of expansion and been better able to survive recessions through cost-cutting. Freed from the need to act as national champions, privatised European steelmakers ought also to be able to merge across borders. Ultimately, this should help reduce over-capacity and build bigger, more specialised – and hence more powerful – companies.

Some progress has been made, but M Francis Mer, Usinor's President, believes the European steel industry is still too fragmented, compared with producers of competing materials such as glass or aluminium, who are in a similarly weak position in relation to the manufacturing industries that use their products, such as producers of cars and home appliances. The expected downturn in the economic cycle in 1997 or 1998 would be the crucial test of whether governments were willing to let the industry fend for itself.

In Europe at least, the omens did not look good in the mid-1990s. In late 1994, the European Commission's two-year effort to restructure the industry ended in partial failure. As the market began to recover, steelmakers failed to offer the capacity cuts to Europe, considered by Brussels as the minimum necessary. Mr Karel Van Miert, the European competition commissioner, said that an opportunity to find a long-term solution to the industry's over-capacity problem had been missed in late 1994. However, with continuing privatisation, he thought it unlikely that there would be a return to widespread state subsidies for steelmakers.

Steel industry in the developing world

The growth of the steel market in the developing world was expected to force western steelmakers to step outside their national markets to exploit the new opportunities. According to preliminary estimates by the International Iron and Steel Institute, China and other developing countries accounted for 223.1 million of the total 723.3 million tonnes of crude steel produced worldwide in 1994. Their share of world output was 30 per cent in 1994 compared to 20 per cent in 1988 – a share expected to rise further because of high economic growth rates and relatively low per capita consumption of steel. China overtook the US in 1994 to become the world's second largest steel producer behind Japan. (*See* Table 3.4.)

Table 3.4 Top steel producing countries (m tonnes)

	1988	1989	1990	1991	1992	1993	1994 est	Annual change in 1994 (%)
Japan	105.7	107.9	110.3	109.6	98.1	99.6	98.3	−1.3
China	59.4	61.6	66.3	71.0	80.9	88.7	91.5	3.2
US	90.7	88.8	89.7	79.7	84.3	88.8	88.9	0.2
Russia	–	–	–	–	67.0	58.3	48.6	−16.7
Germany	41.0	41.1	38.4	42.2	39.7	37.6	40.8	8.5
South Korea	19.1	21.9	23.1	26.0	28.1	3.0	33.8	2.3
Italy	23.6	25.2	25.5	25.1	24.8	25.7	26.1	1.5
Brazil	24.7	25.1	20.6	22.6	23.9	25.2	25.7	1.9
Ukraine	56.4	54.8	52.6	45.0	41.8	32.4	23.9	−23.6
India	14.3	14.6	15.0	17.1	18.1	18.2	18.2	0.4
France	19.1	19.3	19.0	18.4	18.0	17.1	18.0	5.4
UK	19.0	18.7	17.8	16.5	16.2	16.6	17.4	4.4

Source: International Iron and Steel Institute

The traditional approach of OECD producers to such markets has been to export from home-based facilities. According to Mr Brian Moffat, British Steel's Chairman and Chief Executive, however, transport costs will make them uncompetitive in these new markets. Instead they need to make steel in the growth markets, via joint ventures and alliances with local companies in those markets. Mr Moffat believes the outlook in developing countries gives the western steelmakers an opportunity to 'break out of the past structural rigidities'. The more forward-looking steel companies are already building the partnerships to exploit these opportunities. In 1994, for example, British Steel, LTV Steel of the US and Japan's Sumitomo Metal Industries announced they were forming a company, Trico Steel, that could become a vehicle for expansion in developing markets. According to one steel analyst, it has the potential to be the world's first 'global steel company'.

Exploiting the developing markets will require the type of imaginative approach to new markets many steelmakers have hitherto lacked, and a culture committed to making profits rather than making steel for the sake of it. As the state relinquishes its grip on the sector, privatised steelmakers can break free from their national straitjackets, and by chasing the world's growth prospects, they can at least partly insulate themselves from the business cycles in their traditional home markets.

Source: Case adapted from the article by Andrew Baxter in *Financial Times*, 22 March 1995, p17.[6]

CASE QUESTIONS

1 *What particular aspects of the environment does the case highlight?*

2 *According to the case, the main alternative to **national** steel companies is the **global** steel company. What arguments and data, if any, does the case contain to justify this position? Given the case is only a summary of a more detailed analysis, what would you expect such an analysis to contain?*

3 *The case argues that one of the problems in the European steel industry is production over-capacity. How does the case suggest that the strategy of moving onto a global scale can help to overcome this problem? Do you find this strategy persuasive?*

3.4 KEY FACTORS FOR SUCCESS IN AN INDUSTRY

In a strategic analysis of the environment, there is an immense range of issues that can potentially be explored, creating a problem for most organisations, who have neither the time nor the resources to cope with such an open-ended task. The analysis can be narrowed down by identifying the *key factors for success* in the industry and then using these to *focus the analysis* on particularly important environmental matters.

The key factors for success (KFS) are those resources, skills and attributes of the organisations in the industry that are *essential* to deliver success in the market place. Success often means profitability, but may take on a broader meaning in some public service or non-profit making organisations.

KFS are common to all the major organisations in the industry and do not differentiate one company from another. For example, in the Usinor–Sacilor case, the factors mentioned – low labour costs, a range of specialised steel products, etc. – are common to many steel companies. Such factors will vary from one industry to another. For example, by contrast, in the perfume and cosmetics industry the factors will include branding, product distribution and product performance, but they are unlikely to include low labour costs.

When undertaking a strategic analysis of the environment, the identification of the KFS for an industry may provide a useful starting point. For example, the steel KFS item of 'low labour costs' would suggest an environmental analysis of the following areas:

- general wage levels in the country;
- government regulations and attitudes to worker redundancy, because high wage costs could be reduced by sacking employees;
- trade union strength to fight labour force redundancies.

In the steel industry, these elements of the environment would benefit from careful study, whereas, in the cosmetics and perfume industry, they may have some relevance but would be far less important than other areas.

It is therefore important to identify the KFS for a particular industry. Many elements relate not only to the environment but also to the *resources* of organisations in the industry. For example, 'labour costs' will relate to the numbers employed and the level of their wages in individual companies. To identify the KFS in an industry, it is therefore usual to examine *the type of resources* and *the way that they are employed* in the industry and then to use this information to analyse the environment outside the organisation. Hence, KFS require an exploration of the resources and skills of an industry before they can be applied to the environment. Part Three of this book will explore resources while the way in which KFS are developed is covered in greater detail in Chapter 7.

Key strategic principles

● Key factors for success (KFS) are the resources, skills and attributes of an organisation that are essential to deliver success in the market place. They are related to the industry and are unlikely to provide differentiation between organisations in the industry.

● KFS can be used to identify elements of the environment that are particularly worth exploring.

● KFS are developed from an examination of the type of resources used and the way in which resources are employed in an industry. They need therefore to be developed from an analysis of the organisation's resources.

3.5 ANALYSING THE INDUSTRY ENVIRONMENT

An industry analysis usually begins with a general examination of the forces influencing the organisation. The objective of such a study is to use this to develop the *competitive advantage* of an own organisation to enable it to defeat its rival companies.

This type of analysis is often undertaken using the structure proposed by Porter;[7] his basic model is illustrated in Fig 3.3. This is often called *Porter's Five Forces Model* because he identifies five basic forces that can act on the organisation:

Fig 3.3 — Porter's Five Forces Model

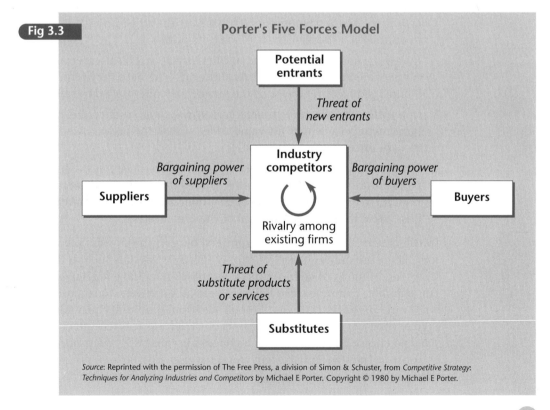

Source: Reprinted with the permission of The Free Press, a division of Simon & Schuster, from *Competitive Strategy: Techniques for Analyzing Industries and Competitors* by Michael E Porter. Copyright © 1980 by Michael E Porter.

- the bargaining power of suppliers;
- the bargaining power of buyers;
- the threat of potential new entrants;
- the threat of substitutes;
- the extent of competitive rivalry.

The objective of such an analysis is to investigate how the organisation needs to form its strategy in order to develop opportunities in its environment and protect itself against competition and other threats.

The basic assumption of the model is that all organisations will wish to benefit and protect their *own interests* first. Certainly, commercial companies will wish to protect themselves in an essentially competitive environment. This is not necessarily true, however, of some charitable and not-for-profit service organisations, where their own interests are intimately bound up with those of customers and possibly suppliers. Porter himself cautiously described[8] his analysis as being concerned with the 'forces driving industry competition'. However, the general principles can be applied to public service and not-for-profit organisations where they compete for resources, such as government funding or charitable donations.

3.5.1 The bargaining power of suppliers

Virtually every organisation has suppliers of raw materials or services which are used to produce the final goods or services. Porter suggested that suppliers are more powerful under the following conditions:

1 *If there are only a few suppliers.* This means that it is difficult to switch from one to another if a supplier starts to exert its power.

2 *If there are no substitutes for the supplies they offer.* This is especially the case if the supplies are important for technical reasons – perhaps they form a crucial ingredient in a production process or the service they offer is vital to smooth production.

3 *If suppliers' prices form a large part of the total costs of the organisation.* Any increase in price would hit value added unless the organisation was able to raise its own prices in compensation.

4 *If a supplier can potentially undertake the value-added process of the organisation.* Occasionally a supplier will have power if it is able to integrate forward and undertake the value-added process undertaken by the organisation; this could pose a real threat to the survival of the organisation.

In the case of European steel, suppliers' bargaining powers are in some respects **low**. There are many sources of supply for raw materials such as coal and iron ore. However, in terms of energy supply, suppliers may have **higher** bargaining power. For example, Usinor–Sacilor will rely heavily on energy to smelt the steel and this will come partially from the French national electricity provider, Electricité de France (EDF). If EDF were to raise its electricity prices, the steel company would have no choice but to accept such changes because EDF is a monopoly supplier. By contrast in the UK, British Steel could bargain with several potential suppliers for the supply of electricity because there is a more open market.

3.5.2 The bargaining power of buyers

In his model, Porter used the term *buyers* to describe what might also be called the *customers* of the organisation. Buyers have more bargaining power under the following conditions:

- *If buyers are concentrated and there are few of them.* When the organisation has little option but to negotiate with a buyer because there are few alternative buyers around, the organisation is clearly in a weak position: national government contracts in defence, health and education are obvious examples where the government can, in theory at least, drive a hard bargain with organisations.

- *If the product from the organisation is undifferentiated.* If an organisation's product is much the same as that from other organisations, the buyer can easily switch from one to another without problems. The buyer is even more likely to make such a shift if the quality of the buyer's product is unaffected by such a change.

- *If backward integration is possible.* As with suppliers above, the buyer's bargaining power is increased if the buyer is able to backward integrate and take over the role of the organisation.

- *If the selling price from the organisation is unimportant to the total costs of the buyer.*

In the case of European steel, small companies or private buyers are unlikely to have much bargaining power with companies of the size of Usinor–Sacilor or British Steel; a letter from an individual to Usinor–Sacilor, threatening to switch from its products to those of British Steel or Krupp unless its prices are lowered, is unlikely to have much impact – the threat is **low**. However, if a major steel distributor or steel user, such as an engineering company, were to make such a threat, then it would clearly have to be taken more seriously because of the potential impact on sales. In this latter case, the threat is **high**. Steel companies have reduced this threat by acquiring most of the leading European steel distributors. The European Commission does not seem to have realised the potential distortion of the Treaty of Rome and has been more concerned to regulate the shape of bananas!

3.5.3 The threat of potential new entrants

New entrants come into a market place when the profit margins are attractive and the barriers to entry are low. The allure of high profitability is clear and so the major strategic issue is that of barriers to entry into a market.

Porter argued that there were seven[9] major sources of barriers to entry:

- *Economies of scale.* Unit costs of production may be reduced as the absolute volume per period is increased. Such cost reductions occur in many industries and present barriers because they mean that any new entrant has to come in on a large scale in order to achieve the low cost levels of those already present: such a scale is risky. We have already examined the computer and steel industries where such cost reductions are vital.

- *Product differentiation.* Branding, customer knowledge, special levels of service and many other aspects may create barriers by forcing new entrants to spend extra funds or simply take longer to become established in the market. Real barriers to entry can be created in strategic terms by long established companies in a market (*see* Chapter 7). Retailers such as IKEA with strong branding and specialist product lines and expertise are examples of companies with differentiated products.

● *Capital requirements.* Entry into some markets may involve major investment in technology, plant, distribution, service outlets and other areas. The ability to raise such finance and the risks associated with such outlays of capital will deter some companies. For example, the high capital cost of investing in a new paper making machine will be covered in Chapter 4.

● *Switching costs.* When a buyer is satisfied with his existing product or service, it is naturally difficult to switch that buyer to a new entrant. The cost of making the switch would naturally fall to the new entrant and will represent a barrier to entry. Persuading buyers to switch their purchases of computer software from Microsoft Windows to Apple has an obvious cost and inconvenience to many companies that would need to be overcome. In addition to the costs of persuading customers to switch, organisations should expect that existing companies will retaliate with further actions designed to drive out new entrants. For example, Microsoft has not hesitated to upgrade its products and reduce its prices to retain customers that might otherwise switch.

● *Access to distribution channels.* It is not enough to produce a quality product; it must be distributed to the customer through channels that may be controlled by companies already in the market. For many years, the leading petrol companies have owned their own retail petrol sites to ensure that they have access to retail customers.

● *Cost disadvantages independent of scale.* Where an established company knows the market well, has the confidence of major buyers, has invested heavily in infrastructure to service the market and has specialist expertise, it becomes a daunting task for new entrants to gain a foothold in the market. Korean and Malaysian companies are now attempting to enter the European car market and face these barriers against well entrenched companies such as Ford, Volkswagen and Renault.

● *Government policy.* For many years, governments have enacted legislation to protect companies and industries: monopolies in telecommunications, health authorities, utilities such as gas and electricity are examples where entry has been difficult if not impossible. The European Commission has been working alongside European governments to remove some but not all such barriers over the last few years.

In the case of the European steel market, it is not easy for small companies to enter the market because there are major economies of scale. For these companies, entry barriers are **high**. However, technology is now beginning to develop that will allow smaller companies to make steel economically so entry barriers may be reduced. For the larger companies, such as Usinor–Sacilor, there have been real problems: governments, trade unions and closed ownership structures have made acquisition difficult. British Steel made several abortive attempts to enter the German steel market without success. Moreover, the cost of building distribution channels has been such that this has proved a difficult route as soon as the major steel stockholding distributors have been acquired.[10] Hence even for large steel companies, the entry barriers have been **high**.

3.5.4 The threat of substitutes

Occasionally, substitutes render a product in an industry redundant. For example, SmithKline Beecham lost sales from its product Tagamet in the treatment of ulcers due to the introduction of more effective products – first the introduction of Zantac from Glaxo in the 1980s and then, in the 1990s, Losec from the Swedish company, Astra. Tagamet is still on sale as an over-the-counter remedy but its major public health sales have largely ceased. More recently, Zantac sales have also suffered, although the difference in performance between that product and Losec is still the subject of dispute between the two companies.

More often, substitutes do not entirely replace existing products but introduce new technology or reduce the costs of producing the same product. Effectively, substitutes may limit the profits in an industry by keeping prices down.

Substitutes may also affect products in neighbouring markets that might not have originally been expected to provide competition. For example, the trend for increased snack eating has been accompanied by a move in taste towards more savoury and less sweet products: this has led crisps and nuts to be substituted for confectionery products in some markets.

From a strategy viewpoint, the key issues to be analysed are:

- the possible threat of obsolescence;
- the ability of customers to switch to the substitute;
- the costs of providing some extra aspect of the service that will prevent switching;
- the likely reduction in profit margin if prices come down or are held.

In the steel market, there is possibly substitution between steel and lighter metals such as aluminium, depending on the usage. The threat of substitution may therefore be **high** but this depends on the technology and end-use.

3.5.5 The extent of competitive rivalry

Some markets are more competitive than others. In highly competitive markets, companies engage in regular and extensive monitoring of key competitor companies. For example:

- examining price changes and matching any significant move immediately;
- examining any rival product change in great detail and regularly attempting new initiatives themselves;
- watching investment in new competing plant and having regular drives to reduce their own costs levels;
- attempting to poach key employees; and so on.

These areas are explored more formally in Chapter 6. In other markets, companies certainly compete but without the same degree of intensity.

All the factors outlined in Sections 3.5.1 to 3.5.5 may have an effect on the extent to which competitors compete but there are some conditions in the industry that may lead specifically to higher competitive rivalry.

- *When competitors are roughly of equal size and one competitor decides to gain share over the others*, then rivalry increases significantly and profits fall. In a market with a dominant company, there may be less rivalry because the larger company is often able to stop quickly any move by its smaller competitors. In the European steel industry, companies are roughly of equal size with no company dominating the market – one of the reasons why rivalry is so intense.

- *If a market is growing slowly and a company wishes to gain dominance*, then by definition it must take its sales from its competitors – increasing rivalry.

- *Where fixed costs or the costs of storing finished products in an industry are high*, then companies may attempt to gain market share in order to achieve break-even or higher levels of profitability. Paper making, steel manufacture and car production are all examples of industries where there is a real case for cutting prices to achieve basic sales volumes – thus increasing rivalry.

- *If extra production capacity in an industry comes in large increments*, then companies may be tempted to fill that capacity by reducing prices, at least temporarily. For example, the bulk chemicals industry usually has to build major new plants and cannot simply add small increments of capacity. In the steel industry, it is not possible to half-build a new steel plant: either it is built or not.

- *If it is difficult to differentiate products or services*, then competition is essentially price-based and it is difficult to ensure customer loyalty. Markets in basic pharmaceutical products such as aspirin have become increasingly subject to such pressures. In the steel market, flat-rolled steel from one manufacturer is much the same as that of another, so competition is price-based. However, where specialist steels are made with unique performance characteristics, the products are differentiated on performance and price rivalry is lower.

- *When it is difficult or expensive to exit from an industry* (perhaps due to legislation on redundancy costs or the cost of closing dirty plant), there is likely to be excess production capacity in the industry and increased rivalry. The European steel industry has suffered from problems in this area during the last few years.

- *If entrants have expressed a determination to achieve a strategic stake in that market*, the costs of such an entry would be relatively unimportant when related to the total costs of the company concerned and the long-term advantages of a presence in the market. Japanese car manufacturing in the European Union will have advantages for Toyota and Nissan beyond the short-term costs of building plant, as EU car markets are opened to full Japanese competition around the year 2000.

In the European steel market, some sectors of the market clearly have intense rivalry – for example, basic steel products competing on price and possibly service. Overall, an analysis would probably conclude that competitive rivalry was **high** in the market place, but would certainly seek to explain the differing reasons in the different segments and draw out the implications for strategy.

3.5.6 Strategy implications from the general industry and competitive analysis

In corporate strategy, it is not enough just to produce an analysis; it is important to consider the implications for the organisation's future strategy. Some issues that might arise from the above include:

1 *Is there a case for changing the strategic relationships with suppliers?* Could more be gained by moving into close partnership with selected suppliers rather than regarding them as rivals? The Japanese car industry has sought to obtain much closer co-operation with suppliers and mutual cost reduction as a result.[11] (*See* Chapter 10.)

2 *Is there a case for forming a new relationship with large buyers?* Manufacture of own label products for large customers in the retail industry may be undertaken at lower margins than branded business but has proved a highly successful strategy for some leading European companies.[12] Even Cereal Partners (from Chapter 2) is now engaged in this strategy in order to build volume through its plants.

3 *What are the key factors for success that drive an industry and influence its strategic development?* What are the lessons for the future that need to be built into the organisation's corporate strategy? We will return to these questions in Chapter 7.

4 *Are there any major technical developments that rivals are working on that could fundamentally alter the nature of the environment?* What is the time span and level of investment for such activity? What action should we take, if any?

3.5.7 Criticisms of the Five Forces Model

Porter's Five Forces Model is a useful early step in analysing the environment, but it has been the subject of some critical comment:

- It assumes that the organisation's own interests come first; for some charitable institutions and government bodies, this assumption may be incorrect.

- It assumes that buyers (called customers elsewhere in this book) have no greater importance than any other aspect of the micro-environment. Other commentators such as Aaker,[13] Baker[14] and Harvey-Jones[15] would fundamentally disagree on this point: they argue that the customer is more important than other aspects of strategy development and is not to be treated as an equal aspect of such an analysis.

- In general, its starting point is that the environment poses a threat to the organisation – leading to the consideration of suppliers and buyers as threats that need to be tackled. As pointed out above, some companies have found it useful to engage in closer *co-operation* with suppliers; such a strategy may be excluded if they are regarded purely as threats.

- Porter's strategic analysis largely ignores the human resource aspects of strategy: it makes little attempt to recognise, let alone resolve, aspects of the micro-environment that might connect people to their own and other organisations. For example, it considers neither the country cultures, nor the management skills aspects of corporate strategy (*see* Chapter 8).

- Porter's analysis proceeds on the basis that, once such an analysis has been undertaken, then the organisation can formulate a corporate strategy to handle the results: *predictive* rather than *emergent*. As we saw in Chapter 2, some commentators would challenge this basic assessment.

In spite of these critical comments, the approach taken in this book is that Porter's model provides a very useful starting point in the analysis of the environment. It has real merit because of the issues it raises in a logical and structured framework. It is therefore recommended as a useful first step in corporate strategy development.

Professor Porter presented his Five Forces Model as an early stage in strategic analysis and development. He followed it with two further analyses: an analysis of *industry evolution* – the extent to which the micro-environment is still growing or has reached maturity[16] – and the study of *strategic groups* within a market. (*See* Chapters 5 and 6 respectively.)

Key strategic principles

- The purpose of industry and competitive strategic analysis is to enable the organisation to develop competitive advantage.

- Porter's Five Forces Model provides a useful starting point for such an analysis.

- Suppliers are particularly strong when they can command a price premium for their products and when their delivery schedules or quality can affect the final product.

- Buyers (or customers) are strong when they have substantial negotiating power or other leverage points associated with price, quality and service.

- New entrants pose a substantial threat when they are easily able to enter a market and when they are able to compete strongly through lower costs or other means.

- Substitutes usually pose a threat as a result of a technological or low-cost breakthrough.

- Competitive rivalry is the essence of such an analysis. It is necessary to build defences against competitive threat.

- The model has been the subject of some critical comment but it remains a useful starting point for competitive strategic analysis.

3.6 ANALYSING THE COMPETITIVE ENVIRONMENT

In any analysis of competitors and their relationship to the organisation, it is useful to undertake two forms of analysis: competitor profiling and product portfolio analysis.

3.6.1 Competitor profiling

As a starting point, it is useful to undertake competitor profiling – that is, the basic analysis of a leading competitor covering its objectives, resources, market strength and current strategies.

In many markets, there will be more than one competitor and it will not be possible to analyse them all. It will be necessary to make a choice – usually the one or two that represent the most direct threat. In public service organisations where the competition may be for *resources* rather than for *customers*, the same principle can be adopted with the choice being made among the agencies competing for funds. In small businesses, the need to understand competitors is just as great although here it may be more difficult to identify which company will pose the most direct threat; a *typical* competitor may be selected in these circumstances. Once the choice has been made, the following aspects of the competitor's organisation need to be explored:

- *Objectives*. If the competitor is seeking sales growth or market share growth, this may involve an aggressive stance in the market place. If the company is seeking profit growth, the company may choose to achieve this by investing in new plant or some other means that might take time to implement. If this is the case, there will be less of an immediate impact on others in the market place, but new plant may mean lower costs and a longer term impact on prices. Company Annual Reports and press statements may be helpful here in defining what the competitor says it wants to do. These need to be treated with some caution, however, since the company may be bluffing or using some other competitive technique.

- *Resources*. The scale and size of the company's resources is an important indicator of its competitive threat – perhaps it has superior or inferior technology, perhaps over-manning at its plants, perhaps financial problems. Chapter 5 will provide a more detailed checklist and Chapter 7 examines resources in more detail.

- *Past record of performance*. Although this may be a poor guide to the future, it is direct evidence that is publicly available through financial statements and stockbrokers' reports.

- *Current products and services*. Many companies buy competing products or services for the sole purpose of tearing them apart. They analyse customers, quality, performance, after-sales service, promotional material and some will even interview former employees – unethical perhaps, but it does happen.

- *Present strategies*. Attitudes to subjects, such as innovation, leading customers, finance and investment, human resource management, market share, cost reduction, product range, pricing and branding, all deserve investigation. The marketing areas are explored further in Chapters 5 and 6 and resources are examined in Part 3.

Competitor profiling is time-consuming but vital to the development of corporate strategy. Some larger companies employ whole departments whose sole task is to monitor leading competitors. Small businesses also often have an acute awareness of their competitors, although this may be derived more informally at trade meetings, social occasions, exhibitions and so on. In corporate strategy, it is vital to gain a 'feel' for competitors.

3.6.2 The product portfolio analysis

The majority of companies offer more than one product or service and many serve more than one customer. There are good strategic reasons for this: to be reliant on one product or customer clearly carries immense risks if, for any reason, that product or service should fail or the customer should go elsewhere. Decisions on strategy usually involve a range of products in a range of markets. This is the subject of portfolio analysis and strategy. It was originally suggested by the Boston Consulting Group (BCG) in the 1970s, and as a result one version of the approach is sometimes called the *BCG Matrix* – the matrix described in this section.

When an organisation has a number of products in its portfolio, it is quite likely that they will be in different stages of development: some will be relatively new and some much older. Many organisations will not wish to risk having all their products in the same markets and at the same stages of development. It is useful to have some products with limited growth but producing profits steadily, as well as having others that have real potential but may still be in the early stages of their growth. Indeed the products that are earning steadily may be used to fund the development of those that will provide the growth and profits in the future.

According to this argument, the key strategy is to produce a *balanced portfolio of products* – some low risk but dull growth, some higher risk with future potential and rewards. The results can be measured in both *profit* and *cash* terms. (Cash is used as a measure here because, both in theory and in practice, it is possible for a company to be trading profitably and yet go bankrupt. This is because the company is earning insufficient *cash* as the profits are being reinvested in growth in the business. It is important to understand this distinction.)

3.6.3 The product portfolio matrix

The product portfolio matrix is one means of analysing the balance of an organisation's product portfolio. According to this matrix, two basic factors define a product's strategic stance in the market place:

- *Relative market share* – for each product, the ratio of the share of the organisation's product divided by the share of the market leader.

- *Market growth rate* – for each product, the market growth rate of the product category.

Relative market share is important because in the competitive battle of the market place, it is advantageous to be larger than rivals: this gives room for manoeuvre, the scale to undertake investment and the ability to command distribution. Some researchers, such as Buzzell and Gale[17], claim to have found empirical evidence to support these statements. For example, in a survey of major companies, the two researchers found that businesses with over 50 per cent share of their markets enjoy rates of return three times greater than businesses with small market shares. There are other empirical studies that also support this broad conclusion.[18] Jacobsen and Aaker[19] have questioned this relationship. They point out that such a close correlation will also reflect other differences in businesses. High market share companies do not just differ on market share but on other dimensions as well: for example, they may have better management and may have more luck. However,

Aaker himself in a more recent work[20] has conceded that portfolios do have their uses, along with their limitations.

Market growth rate is important because markets that are growing rapidly offer more opportunities for sales than lower growth markets. Rapid growth is less likely to involve stealing share from competition and more likely to come from new buyers entering the market. This gives many new opportunities for the right product. There are also difficulties, however, perhaps the chief being that growing markets are often not as profitable as those with low growth. Investment is usually needed to *promote* the rapid growth and this has to be funded out of profits.

Relative market share and market growth rate are combined in the portfolio matrix, as shown in Fig 3.4. It should be noted that the term 'matrix' is misleading. In reality, the diagram does not have four distinct boxes, but rather four areas which merge into one another. The four areas are given distinctive names to signify their strategic significance.

● *Stars.* The upper-left quadrant contains those products with high market shares operating in high growth markets. The growth rate will mean that they will need heavy investment and will therefore be cash users. However, because they have high market shares, it is assumed that they will have economies of scale and be able to generate large amounts of cash. Overall, it is therefore asserted that they will be cash neutral – an assumption not necessarily supported in practice and not yet fully tested.

● *Cash cows.* The lower-left quadrant shows those product areas that have high market share but exist in low growth markets. The business is mature and it is assumed that lower levels of investment will be required. On this basis, it is therefore likely that they will be able to generate both cash and profits. Such profits could then be transferred to support the stars. However, there is a real strategic danger here that cash cows become under-supported and begin to lose their market share.[21]

Fig 3.4	**The product portfolio matrix – individual products or product groups categorised by market growth and share**

	High relative market share	Low relative market share
High market growth rate	**Star** Cash neutral	**Problem child** Cash user
Low market growth rate	**Cash cow** Cash generator	**Dog** Cash neutral

- *Problem children.* The upper-right quadrant contains products with low market shares in high growth markets. Such products have not yet obtained dominant positions in rapidly growing markets or, possibly, their market shares have become less dominant, as competition has become more aggressive. The market growth means that it is likely that considerable investment will still be required and the low market share will mean that such products will have difficulty generating substantial cash. Hence, on this basis, these products are likely to be cash users.

- *Dogs.* The lower-right quadrant contains those products that have low relative market shares in low growth businesses. It is assumed that the products will need low investment but that they are unlikely to be major profit earners. Hence, these two elements should balance each other and they should be cash neutral overall. In practice, they *may* actually absorb cash because of the investment required to hold their position. They are often regarded as unattractive for the long term and recommended for disposal.

Overall, the general strategy is to take cash from the *cash cows* to fund *stars* and invest in future new products that do not yet even appear on the matrix. Cash may also be invested selectively in some *problem children* to turn them into *stars* with the others being milked or even sold to provide funds for elsewhere. Typically in many organisations, the *dogs* form the largest category and often represent the most difficult strategic decisions. Should they be sold? Could they be repositioned in a smaller market category that would allow them to dominate that category? Are they really cash neutral or possibly absorbing cash? If cash absorbers, what strategies might be adopted?

Clearly the strategic questions raised by the approach have a useful function in the analysis and development of strategy. In Chapters 13 and 14, we will examine these further in the context of strategic options. Some care needs to be taken in calculating the positions of products on the matrix and Chapter 13 has a worked example to show how it can be done.

3.6.4 Difficulties with the product portfolio approach

There are a number of problems associated with the product portfolio. The most obvious difficulty is that strategy is defined purely in terms of two simple factors and other issues are ignored. Further problems include:

- *The definition of market growth.* What is high market growth and what is low? Conventionally, this is often set above or below 5 per cent per annum, but there are no rules.

- *The definition of the market.* It is not always clear how the market should be defined. It is always possible to make a product dominate a market by defining the market narrowly enough. For example, do we consider the *entire* European steel market, where Usinor–Sacilor would have a small share, or do we take the *French segment* only, when the U–S share would be much higher? This could radically alter the conclusions.

- *The definition of relative market share.* What constitutes a high relative share and a low share? Conventionally, the ratio is set at 1.5 (organisation's product to share of market leader's product) but why should this be so?

- *Dubious recommendations*. Can we really afford to eliminate dogs when they may share common factory overheads with stars and cash cows? Are we in danger of under-investing in valuable cash cows and diverting the funds into inherently weak problem children?

- *Innovation*. Where do innovative new products fit onto the matrix? Do they have a small share of a tiny market and so deserve to be eliminated before they have even started?

- *Divesting unwanted product areas*. In many western countries there may be substantial redundancy costs that make divestment unattractive. Even if there are not, it also assumes that other companies might be interested in buying such a product range at a fair market price which may be equally dubious.

- *The perceived desirability of growth*. This assumption is not necessarily appropriate for all businesses. Some may make higher longer term profits by seeking lower levels of growth.

- *The assumption that competitors will allow the organisation freedom to make its changes*. Competitors can also undertake a product portfolio analysis for both their own and competing products. Competitor reactions may negate the proposed changes in the organisation's portfolio.

Although the development of the product portfolio is useful in raising and exploring strategic issues, it is not a panacea for the development of corporate strategy. To overcome some of the issues raised above, various other formats for the product portfolio have been developed. Aaker[22] has provided a useful recent review of these. In 1977, Day[23] concluded that product portfolios were useful as a starting point in strategic analysis; such a comment still holds today. Nevertheless, it may be useful to consider an alternative product portfolio approach (*see* Chapter 5).

Key strategic principles

- Competitor profiling is an essential first step in analysing immediate competitors. It will explore objectives, resources, past performance, current products and services and present strategies for at least one competitor.

- Portfolio analysis provides a means of analysing a company that has a range of products.

- The BCG portfolio analysis is undertaken using only two variables: relative market share and market growth. It is clearly a weakness that other variables are not included.

- The portfolio is then divided into four areas: stars, cash cows, problem children and dogs. These outline categories are then used as the basis for developing a balanced product portfolio. The technique is useful as a starting point only in the analytical process.

3.7 ANALYSING THE CUSTOMER AND MARKET SEGMENTATION

Since customers generate the revenues that keep the organisation in existence and deliver its profits, customers are crucial in corporate strategy. In this context it is perhaps surprising that much greater emphasis has been given in some aspects of strategic development to *competition* rather than to the customer.[24] The reason is that the focus of the purchase decision for the customer is a competitive selection between the different products or services on offer. While this is undoubtedly true, it is easy to lose sight of the direct strategic importance of the customer.

There are three useful dimensions to an analysis of the customer:

● identification of the customer and the market;

● market segmentation and its strategic implications;

● the role of customer service and quality.

3.7.1 Identification of the customer and the market

Back in the 1960s, Levitt[25] wrote a famous article that argued the main reason some organisations were in decline was because they had become too heavily product-oriented, and were not sufficiently customer-oriented. As a result they defined their customer base too narrowly.

Levitt gave the example of the American railway industry which identified its market during the 1950s as being that for *railway transport*. As a result, each company in the industry saw its environment as being largely a matter of competition among the railway companies. This was just around the time when the vast geographical distances in North America, coupled with the decreasing prices and increasing reliability of air transport, were attracting customers away from rail to air travel. The new airlines were growing rapidly *at the expense of rail*. The corporate strategies of the railways were directed primarily at each other and ignored the customer move to air travel; they were fundamentally flawed. Modern-day examples of the same need to identify the market environment correctly include:

● *Snack markets*. Defining sweets (e.g. chocolate bars) and savoury snacks (e.g. crisps and nuts) as operating in separate markets would miss the fact that customer tastes have switched from sweet to savoury products over the last ten years.

● *Construction materials*. Aluminium door and window frames have increasingly replaced wooden structures over the last 20 years. They are lighter, more resistant to some types of atmospheric pollution and can be moulded into shapes that cannot be replicated in wood.[26]

To help this process, a useful distinction can be made between:[27]

● *immediate customer base* – such as the railway journeys or crisp flavours above; and

● *wider customer franchise* – which will allow for the substitution effects discussed above between, for example, different forms of transport or between snacks and confectionery.

The importance in defining accurately this aspect of the environment lies in developing strategies that identify customers and competitors. Ultimately, if the market environment is incorrectly defined, then competitors may creep up and steal customers without the company realising it until it is too late. Furthermore, it is vital to analyse *future* customers as well as the *current* customer profile (*see* Chapter 6).

3.7.2 Market segmentation and its strategic implications

Most markets have now moved beyond *mass marketing* – where one product is sold to all types of customer – *to targeted marketing* – where the seller identifies market segments, selects one or more of these and then develops products or services targeted specially for the segment. Market segmentation is the identification of specific parts of a market and the development of different market offerings that will be attractive to those segments[28] – an important element of any market analysis.

Market segmentation is important for strategy for several reasons:

- *Some segments may be more profitable and attractive than others*. For example, large segments may have low profit margins but their size may make them attractive, even at these levels of profitability.
- *Some segments may have more competition than others*. For example, a specialist segment may have only a limited number of competitors.
- *Some segments may be growing faster and offer more development opportunities than others*.

Porter[29] uses market segmentation to draw a basic distinction between two major areas of strategy:

- *broad target segments* that involve large numbers of customers, e.g. basic flat-rolled steel bars that have wide customer demand; and
- *narrow target segments* that involve small niches in the market place, e.g. small specialist steel products that are sold for their particular performance characteristics at high prices to a small number of buyers.

In conclusion, careful analysis of segments and their characteristics is therefore important (*see* Chapters 6 and 13).

3.7.3 The role of customer service and quality

With corporate strategy in the late 1990s, it is often no longer sufficient to sell a product or deliver a service on one occasion. In order to compete in some markets, it has become essential to offer *superior service*. For example, some retail banks have begun to distinguish themselves on their ability to offer exceptional levels of service such as 24-hour banking by telephone. The starting point for such a development is to understand the customers' potential needs in such areas.

In addition, considerable emphasis has been laid on *quality*, as perceived by the customer. For example, Japanese cars have gained a reputation for quality and reliability as they have extended their distribution and sales across Europe over the last 20 years.

Both service and quality have provided real opportunities in corporate strategy. Their particular strengths lie in their attractiveness to customers and the difficulty that competitors face in attempting to match them.

Key strategic principles

- In identifying markets, it is important to identify the customer base sufficiently broadly. A useful distinction can be drawn between the immediate customer base and a wider franchise based on product substitution. It is also important to explore future customers as well as the current customer base.

- Market segmentation is fundamental to the development of corporate strategy: some parts of markets may be more attractive than others. Careful analysis of segments and their characteristics is therefore important.

- Customer service and quality have proved powerful corporate strategies for the 1990s. They have provided a means for companies to compete for customers in the market place.

3.8 CONCLUSIONS

Given the amount of analysis that can potentially be undertaken, the question is raised as to whether each aspect of analysis has equal priority. Although there are no absolute rules, it is usually the case that the customer comes first, the immediate competition second and the broader environment surrounding the organisation then follows behind this. In other words, the analytical process may well be arranged in the *reverse order* of this chapter.

In many respects, the real danger in analysing the environment is to limit the process to examining past events and ways of thinking. It is absolutely essential to break out of the current mould and examine alternative routes and ideas. This is particularly likely to be the case if an emergent approach is adopted, because it relies essentially on taking small steps from the current position. As Egan[30] has pointed out:

> *While expedient for conditions of relative environmental stability, [the emergent approach] is likely to be unacceptable in periods of discontinuous change. The rapid demise of Nixdorf Computer and Wang Computer should have sent rapid signals to IBM that more of the same was wholly inappropriate in the rapidly changing computer industry.*

CASE STUDY 3.2

Benefon keeps in touch[31]

Benefon is a small Finnish company producing mobile telephones, which is highly dependent on a fast-growing environment with a strong regulatory infrastructure and keen customer interest.

Quitting a top management job with Nokia and setting up as a direct competitor to the Finnish telecommunications giant requires nerve. The gamble appears to have paid off for Jorma Nieminen who left Nokia (along with 12 colleagues) in 1987 and now presides over Benefon, a fast growing mobile telephone specialist.

After an unsteady start, Benefon now operates in nearly 40 markets worldwide, and has enjoyed strong growth with $17.8 million profit on revenues of $58.2 million in 1994. The company has more than 230 employees and has exceeded its target of growing by at least 30 per cent a year; its operating margins are the envy of rivals.

Yet Benefon remains a pigmy in the cellular phone market, with a global share of around half a per cent. Its main competitors are the world's top three producers of mobile handsets – Motorola (US), Nokia (Finland) and Ericsson (Sweden) – whose size gives them a muscle Niemenen can only dream about. He admits:

> We are not well-known; we cannot afford to offer discounts; we have less R&D and marketing people than our rivals.

Benefon growth

In spite of this, Benefon, based in Salo, about an hour's drive west of Helsinki, has managed to thrive and not just because the mobile phone business is booming. By targeting niche areas at the top end of the market, it has been able to sell its products for premium prices and limit the impact of trade wars on performance. It offers good-looking, high-quality phones with more functions than rival models, and this enables Benefon to charge up to 30 per cent more than its competitors. 'A typical Benefon customer is not buying their first phone, but their second or third one, ' Niemenen notes, adding that customers come to appreciate the sophistication of Benefon phones after relying on more basic models. According to Niemenen a Benefon phone can be used for longer without

being recharged, performs better on the fringes of field strength and can withstand extreme weather.

In its main segment – the NMT 450 standard – Benefon is second only to Nokia with a market share of 20 per cent. Part of the reason for its success is its strong position in emerging East European markets, where analogue systems offer operators a cheaper starting point than digital ones. In some East European markets, Benefon claims to be the number one supplier.

The group's other main markets are in Scandinavia, central Europe, the Middle East and Asia. Displaying a small company's paranoia about giving too much information away to rivals, Niemenen will not disclose unit sales or individual market penetration rates, nor is he particularly informative about the group's future strategy.

The key will be the group's ability not just to develop a new generation of analogue products but to penetrate the digital sector too. Benefon has arguably been slow off the mark, given that digital is the faster growing market. The weakness is being addressed, however, and the first digital (GSM) products are now being developed. Competition will undoubtedly be fierce, but if the digital launch is a success, the group will really have joined the big league.

Source: Financial Times, 26 June 1995.

CASE QUESTIONS

1 *Given the limited resources and geographical spread of Benefon, how would you approach the task of analysing the environment for corporate strategy development? What process would you recommend and what data would you collect?*

2 *Undertake a PEST analysis and a Five Forces Analysis for this company's future development.*

3 *From the many possible environmental factors, choose the three which you consider to be the most significant in preparing a corporate plan. Why?*

The importance of environmental analysis[32]

In this extract from his book, Strategic Management: an introduction, *Ronald Rosen links environmental analysis with its implications for corporate strategy in the organisation.*

An organisation does not exist in a vacuum; it interacts with its environment. A business offers its goods and services in the market place – usually against competition – while the environment provides sources of labour, energy, raw materials, finance, information, etc., over which it has little control.

If the environment were relatively unchanging, an organisation might after a period of adaptation, settle down to a fairly stable relationship with its customers, suppliers, competitors, channels of distribution and investors. There would be little motivation to make major changes to the objectives or strategy if all parties more or less accepted the status quo. However, this stable state is rare; customers' needs change, a new competitor arises or a superior product is offered, sales decline, shareholders become dissatisfied with the return on their investment, a source of supply dries up or important retail outlets are denied to a manufacturer, a new market opens up. These, or innumerable other changes in the environment, might require a rethink about objectives, strategy, or both.

In other words, changes in strategy or objectives are frequently – although not always – made in response to, or in anticipation of, an environmental change: either reacting to a threat, or taking advantage of an opportunity. These changes may, in turn, provoke a response in the environment which must then be dealt with: for example, reducing prices in order to gain market share may spark off a price war, or launching a new product might trigger competitors to take their new product off the shelf, where it has been awaiting such an eventuality. Conversely, if an organisation responds too late to environmental changes, it runs the risk of failure. Hence, adapting an organisation to its environment is an essential aspect of strategic management.

If the environment were relatively unchanging, the process of strategic management would appear to be fairly simple, largely a matter of keeping an eye on the environment just to make sure that nothing much has changed – or is likely to do so – and concentrating mainly on good housekeeping: keeping costs under control, maintaining quality and productivity levels by monitoring actual levels of performance against established standards, taking any necessary corrective action to keep on course. In other words, the emphasis would be on the *maintenance* of existing strategy – keeping the trains clean and running on time – rather than *adapting* or changing it, although the strategy might still need to be tweaked because of slight changes in the environment or in order to make it more effective.

In a more turbulent environment, the process of strategic management becomes more complex and demanding. Information systems must be sufficiently sensitive to detect change as early as possible in order to analyse the existing, and probable future, situation and to adapt to it in good time. Matching the organisation to its environment may require a more suitable structure, different systems and, in particular, an appropriate organisational culture, all of which are aspects of strategic management.

Source: Rosen, R (1995) *Strategic Management: an introduction,* Pitman Publishing.

◖■ SUMMARY

In analysing the environment surrounding the organisation, six main factors were identified.

● *A general consideration of the nature of the environment and, in particular, the degree of turbulence.* When events are particularly uncertain and prone to sudden and significant change, corporate strategy needs to become more flexible and organise its procedures to cope with the situation.

● *A general analysis of the factors that will affect many industries.* This can be undertaken by two procedures: the PEST analysis and scenarios. The PEST analysis explores political, economic, socio-cultural and technological influences on the organisation. It is important when undertaking such an analysis to develop a short list of only the most important items, not a long list under every heading. In developing scenarios, it should be recognised that they provide a different view of conceivable future events, rather than predict the future.

● *The identification of key factors for success.* Moving towards an analysis the environment surrounding the organisation itself, it is useful to establish the key factors for success in the industry (not the organisation). This requires a consideration of the resources of the organisation (*see* Chapter 7).

● *A Five Forces Analysis.* This will involve an examination of buyers, suppliers, new entrants, substitutes and the competition in the industry. The aim is to analyse the balance of power between each force and the organisation in the industry.

● *A product portfolio analysis.* This plots market growth and relative market share for the organisation's main group of products. It identifies four major categories of products: stars, cash cows, dogs and problem children. It permits some consideration of their contribution to the organisation and a comparison with competition.

● *A study of customers.* The final area of analysis is concerned with actual and potential customers and their importance to the organisation. Segmentation of markets derives from customer analysis and plays an important role in corporate strategy development.

QUESTIONS

1 Using Table 3.2 and your judgement, determine the degree of turbulence in the global steel industry. Give reasons for your views.

2 Undertake a general environmental analysis of an industry of your choice, using both the PEST format and scenarios to draw out the major strategic issues.

3 Develop and compare the key factors for success in the following three industries: computer industry (Chapter 1), food industry (Chapter 2) and steel industry (Chapter 3).

4 For the European steel industry, analyse the competitive forces within the industry using the Five Forces Model.

5   Based on your answers to the previous questions, what strategic advice would you offer Usinor–Sacilor? Use Section 3.5.6 to assist you.

6   Construct a product portfolio matrix for a company in an industry of your choice. What strategic conclusions would you draw for the company concerned? Comment on the conceptual difficulties of the matrix in reaching your conclusions.

7   Prepare a full environmental analysis for an industry of your choice and make recommendations on its future corporate strategy.

8   Undertake a customer analysis for your own organisation. What segments can you identify? What role is played by customer service and quality? What strategic conclusions can you draw?

9   Do you agree with the statement that stable environments favour prescriptive approaches to strategy whereas turbulent environments demand emergent strategies? Consider carefully the impact technology may have on a stable environment and the problem of long-term investment, even in turbulent industries.

10 To what extent can competitive analytical techniques be applied to the public sector and charitable institutions?

STRATEGIC PROJECT

International steel strategy

This chapter has examined the steel industry. You might like to take this a step further. For example, look at the strategies of British Steel to build its low-cost efficient British operations and its difficulties in making acquisitions in other European countries.

FURTHER READING

M E Porter's *Competitive strategy: techniques for analysing industries and competitors* (The Free Press, Harvard, Mass, 1980) has careful and detailed studies for analysis of the immediate competitive environment.

L Fahey and V K Narayanan's *Microenvironmental analyses for strategic management* (West Publishing, St Paul, Minn, 1986) explores the way that the environment influences organisational strategy.

R Rosen's *Strategic management: An introduction* (Pitman Publishing, London, 1995) has some useful strategic planning worksheets that will help to structure a study of the environment. However, it is important to treat them as a useful framework rather than a rigid format.

REFERENCES

1 Articles in the *Financial Times* will provide more detail: 16 July 1991, 31 Jan 1992, p21; 22 Apr 1992, p25; 28 Oct 1994, pp21 and 26; 8 Feb 1995, p30.

2 *See* Dawkins, W (1994) 'How the nightmare faded', *Financial Times*, 24 Oct.

3 *See* Leadbeater, C (1991) 'Usinor strives for edge in technology', *Financial Times,* 15 July.

4 The early part of this section is based on Ansoff, I and McDonnell, E (1990) *Implementing strategic management*, 2nd edn, Prentice Hall, Englewood Cliffs, NJ.

5 Simon, H 'The Corporation: will it be managed by machine?' in Leavitt, H and Pondy, L (eds) (1964) *Readings in Managerial Psychology*, University of Chicago Press, pp592–617.

6 Case adapted from an article by Andrew Baxter, *Financial Times*, 22 March 1995, p17. ©*Financial Times*. Reproduced with permission.

7 Porter, M E (1980) *Competitive Advantage*, The Free Press, New York, *See* also Porter's article, 'How competitive forces shape strategy', (1979) *Harvard Business Review*, Mar–Apr, pp136–45 which is a useful summary of the main points from the early part of his book.

8 Ibid, p4.

9 Porter actually refers in his book to 'six' areas and then goes on to list seven!

10 *See* Lynch, R (1994) *European Business Strategies*, 2nd edn, Kogan Page, London, pp188–9.

11 Cusumano, M and Takeishi, A (1991) 'Supplier relations and management: a survey of Japanese, Japanese-transplant and US auto plants', *Strategic Management Journal*, 12, pp563–88.

12 Nielsen, A C (1988) *International Food and Drug Store Trends*, Nielsen.

13 Aaker, D (1992) *Strategic Marketing Management*, 3rd edn, Wiley, New York.

14 Baker, M (1993) *Marketing Strategy and Management*, 2nd edn, Macmillan.

15 Harvey-Jones, J (1991) *Getting it Together*, Heinemann, London, Ch 14.

16 Porter, Ibid, Chs 7 and 8.

17 Buzzell, R D and Gale, B T (1987) *The PIMS Principles*, The Free Press, New York.

18 Aaker, D (1992) Ibid, pp160–61.

19 Jacobsen, R and Aaker, D (1985) 'Is market share all that it's cracked up to be?' *Journal of Marketing*, Fall, pp11–22. A vigorous debate still continues in the academic press on the benefits of portfolio analysis. For example, a research paper from Armstong and Brodie in the *International Journal in Research in Marketing* (11(1), Jan 1994, p73 *et seq*) criticising such matrices produced a strong defence from Professor Robin Wensley in the same journal and a further reply from the two authors.

20 Aaker, D, (1992) Ibid, p176

21 *See* McKiernan, P (1992) *Strategies for Growth*, Routledge, London, Chapter 1 has an excellent discussion of some of the problems that can arise.

22 Aaker, D, Ibid, p167 *et seq*.

23 Day, G S (1977) 'Diagnosing the product portfolio', *Journal of Marketing*, April, pp29–38.

24 For example, Porter, M E (1980) *Competitive Strategy*, The Free Press, New York.

25 Levitt, T (1960) 'Marketing Myopia', *Harvard Business Review*, Jul–Aug, p45.

26 *See* for example, Baxter, A (1994) Clash of two metals, *Financial Times*, 20 Oct, p21.

27 Davidson, H (1987) *Offensive Marketing*, Penguin, Harmondsworth.

28 Adcock, D, Bradfield, R, Halborg, A and Ross, C (1995) *Marketing: Principles and Practice*, 2nd edn, Pitman Publishing, London, p386.

29 Porter, M E (1980) *Competitive Strategy*, The Free Press, New York, Ch 2.

30 Egan, C (1995) *Creating Organisational Advantage*, Butterworth–Heinemann, Oxford, p83.

31 Based on an article in the *Financial Times*, 26 June 1995, p13. © *Financial Times*, Reproduced with permission.

32 Extracted from Rosen, R (1995) *Strategic Management: an introduction*, Pitman Publishing, London.

4

Analysing the market

When you have worked through this chapter, you will be able to:

- understand the implications of market growth and maturity for corporate strategy;

- identify the specific strategic issues associated with cyclicality in a market;

- outline the role that governments can play in the development of corporate strategy;

- explore the inter-relationships between governments, nations and companies in the development of corporate strategy;

- undertake an analysis of the main elements involved in international markets.

INTRODUCTION

Before discussing competitors and customers in Chapters 5 and 6, it is useful to examine the market itself. From an analytical perspective, there are three main considerations:

1 *The rate of growth in the market place* – with different rates of growth posing completely different strategic problems.
2 *The role of government* – especially the extent to which government policies support or hinder the corporate strategies of organisations.
3 *The opportunities for global market development* – ranging from limited internationalisation to a major opportunity to build a global organisation.

These three areas may operate totally independently of each other. Alternatively, there may be substantial interconnections. For example, governments may wish to encourage global-scale companies as a matter of national policy or simply to bring foreign revenue into the country. Equally, companies may seek to expand overseas to offset low growth in their home countries. The possible interconnections are shown in Fig 4.1.

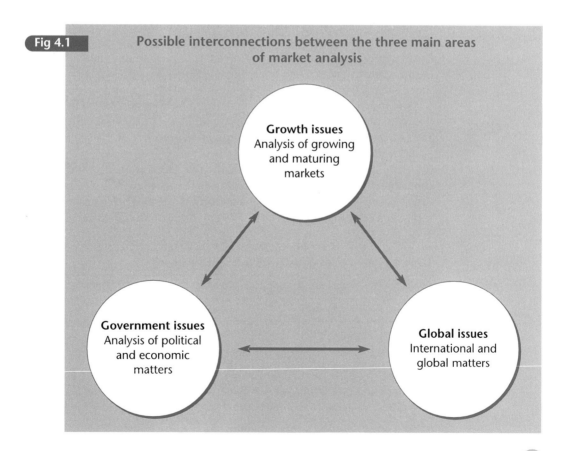

Fig 4.1 **Possible interconnections between the three main areas of market analysis**

Growth issues
Analysis of growing and maturing markets

Government issues
Analysis of political and economic matters

Global issues
International and global matters

Stora expands through acquisition and internal growth

With sales of over US$7 billion, Stora AB is one of Europe's largest pulp and paper companies. Its compound rate of sales growth has been around 25 per cent each year for the last ten years. This case examines the strategies it has used to achieve this phenomenal growth rate.

Back in the early 1980s, Stora set itself the task of becoming Europe's largest pulp and paper company. The reasons for this objective were:

● to achieve substantial economies of scale in pulp and paper manufacture; and
● to secure raw material supplies – that is, forests and cheap hydroelectric power – as cheaply as possible.

To achieve this objective, Stora then employed the following strategies:

● the acquisition of paper companies;
● internal sales growth of specialist products;
● the acquisition of distributors, especially to support the sale of office paper products;
● investment in new, more cost-efficient production facilities.

Stora acquired a series of paper companies during the 1980s and 1990s, some in Sweden and some with a wider European base. The companies taken under full Stora control were: Billerud (1986), Papyrus (1987), Swedish Match (1988) and Feldmuhle Nobel (1990) – all Swedish with the exception of Feldmuhle Nobel, which was German. Swedish Match had other interests as well as paper and pulp and these were soon sold to a third party.

More recently, Stora began by acquisition to build its distribution network for paper and office products across Europe. This contributed 12 per cent to the total 1995 sales and represented the most significant growth in turnover of the last three years. The profits from distribution operations were rather smaller, however. The strategy here was not just to increase size, but to ensure that Stora products, rather than those of competitors, were available to the final customer. When there is little product differentiation between one brand of paper and another, the *bargaining power of distributors* is high. Stora overcame this difficulty by buying distribution companies.

Table 4.1 Stora sales growth 1986–95 (SEK million)

1986	1988	1992	1994	1995
12 996	39 868	46 895	48 894	57 106*

* Growth in 1994/95 was almost entirely due to the acquisition of paper distributors.

During the early 1990s, the European market for many paper products such as newsprint and office supplies was flat (*see* Case study 4.3). In this market sales are dependent on economic growth. When economies are flat, organisations advertise less; smaller newspapers are printed and so less newsprint is sold by companies like Stora. Europe accounts for around 89 per cent of Stora's sales and so this downturn in economic activity had a strong impact on the growth of Stora's sales.

To generate new sources of sales, Stora pursued the remaining higher growth areas in pulp and paper, such as specialist printing papers, technical office papers, and packaging and board. New products were launched and existing ranges expanded.

Within Europe, Sweden, Germany and the UK account for 48 per cent of total sales; arguably Stora could expand further in such countries as France, Italy and Poland, but it would probably need to do so by acquisitions. Target companies may not be for sale or, more likely, a high acquisition price could not be justified in terms of the profit that would then be earned after the purchase.

The depressed European economy has prompted another element of Stora's strategy – investment in more modern facilities for its products to reduce its costs further and stay ahead of competition.

To consolidate its position in paper and pulp over the period, Stora also disposed of its subsidiaries in other product groups, such as chemicals and floorings.

Although overtaken in terms of size by the merger of Finnish pulp and paper companies to form UPM/ Kymmene, by 1995 Stora had become the second largest pulp and paper company in Europe. It had achieved its major objective. The impact on profits of such sales expansion was not unacceptable: it averaged 10 per cent return on capital employed over the period 1991–5 and 13 per cent over the period 1986–95, compared with its objective of 13 to 14 per cent.

CASE QUESTIONS

1   *How important was the objective for Stora's strategy development? Should the company be disappointed that it was still only second largest?*

2   *Is growth important in itself in corporate strategy? Give reasons for your views.*

4.1 THE RATE OF GROWTH IN THE MARKET PLACE

The well-known strategic writer, Professor Michael Porter from Harvard University Business School, has described the *industry life cycle* as 'the grandfather of concepts for predicting industry evolution'. The basic hypothesis is that an industry – or a market segment within an industry – goes through four basic phases of development, each of which has implications for corporate strategy. These phases can be loosely described as introduction, growth, maturity and decline and are shown in Fig 4.2.

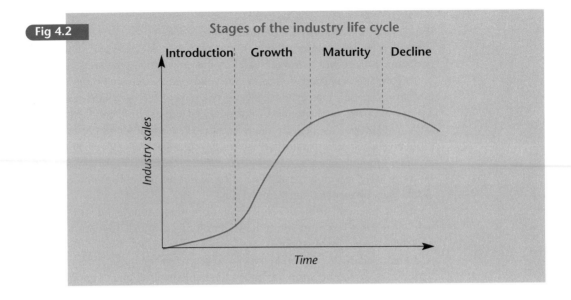

Fig 4.2 Stages of the industry life cycle

4.1.1 Industry life cycle

The nature of corporate strategy will change as industries move along the life cycle. In the *introductory* phase, organisations attempt to develop interest in the product. As the industry moves towards *growth*, competitors are attracted by its potential and enter the market: from a strategic perspective, competition increases. As all the available customers are satisfied by the product, growth slows down and the market becomes *mature*. Although growth has slowed, new competitors may still be attracted into the market: each company then has to compete harder for its market share which becomes more fragmented – that is, the market share is broken down into smaller parts. Sales enter a period of *decline*.

To explore the strategic implications, it is useful to start by identifying what stage an industry has reached in terms of its development. For each stage in the cycle there are a number of commonly-accepted strategies (*see* Table 4.2). In the case of customers, for example, the *introduction* phase will be used to present the product or service to new customers, whereas the *maturity* phase assumes that most customers are aware of the product and little new trial is required.

As in other areas of corporate strategy, there are differing views regarding the choice of appropriate strategies for each phase of the industry life cycle. Table 4.2 represents the *conventional* view of the appropriate strategy for a particular stage in the industry's evolution. In corporate strategy, however, there are often good arguments for doing *the unconventional*, so this list would be seen as a starting point for analysing the dynamics of an industry. The most innovative strategy might well come by doing something different and breaking the mould.

Table 4.2 The industry life cycle and its strategy implications – a conventional view

	Introduction phase	Growth phase	Maturity phase	Decline phase
Customer strategy	• Early customers may experiment with product and will accept some unreliability • Need to explain nature of innovation	• Growing group of customers • Quality and reliability important for growth	• Mass market • Little new trial of product or service • Brand switching	• Know the product well • Select on basis of price rather than innovation
R&D strategy	• High	• Seek extensions before competition	• Low	
Company strategy	• Seek to dominate market • R&D and production particularly important to ensure product quality	• React to competition with marketing expenditure and initiatives	• Expensive to increase market share if not already market leader • Seek cost reductions	• Cost control particularly important
Impact on profitability	• High price, but probably making a loss due to investment in new category	• Profits should emerge here but prices may well decline as competitors enter market	• Profits under pressure from need for continuing investment coupled with continued distributor and competitive pressure	• Price competition and low growth may lead to losses or need to cut costs drastically to maintain profitability
Competitor strategy	• Keen interest in new category • Attempt to replicate new product	• Market entry (if not before) • Attempt to innovate and invest in category	• Competition largely on advertising and quality • Lower product differentiation • Lower product change	• Competition based primarily on price • Some companies may seek to exit the industry

As an example of the conventional view of such an analysis, the industry life cycle suggests that in the *early stages* of an industry's development there may be more opportunities for new and radical R&D. When an industry is more *mature*, rather less investment is needed in R&D.[1] However, the unconventional view argues that it is the mature industry that requires new growth and therefore R&D or some other strategic initiative. In the Stora case, the company needed to invest in more modern facilities to reduce costs further, showing that, even in the mature phase of a market, heavy investment is often necessary to remain competitive in the market. It is for this reason that the life cycle concept can best be seen as a starting point for growth analysis.

It is important to note in the development of strategy the two consequences of the industry life cycle that can have a significant impact on industries:

● *Advantages of early entry*. There is substantial empirical evidence that the first company into a new market has the most substantial strategic advantage. For example, Aaker[2] quotes a study of 500 mature industrial businesses showing that pioneer firms average a market share of 29 per cent, early followers 21 per cent and the late entrants 15 per cent. Although there are clearly risks in early market entry, there may also be long-term advantages that deserve careful consideration in strategic development.

● *Industry market share fragmentation*. In the early years, markets that are growing fast attract new entrants. This is both natural and inevitable. The consequence as markets reach maturity is that each new company is fighting for market share and the market becomes more fragmented. Again, this has important implications for strategy because it suggests that mature markets need revised strategies – perhaps associated with a segment of the market (*see* Chapter 6).

For strategic purposes, it may be better to examine different *segments* of an industry, rather than the market *as a whole*, as different segments may be at different stages of the industry life cycle and may require different strategies (*see* the European ice cream industry example in Case study 4.1). An industrial example can be taken from the European pulp and paper industry where during the same period coated magazine papers were showing strong growth, kraft papers were beginning to mature and fluff pulps were definitely in the mature stage of the life cycle.[3]

CASE STUDY 4.1

Different strategies in the ice cream market

During the 1990s, the European ice cream market underwent significant change: some segments were relatively mature while some were experiencing strong growth. This case study shows how the positions of the main segments can be plotted in terms of the industry evolution (see Fig 4.3) and how strategies vary from one segment to another.

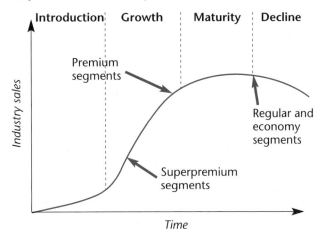

Fig 4.3 Industry evolution in European ice cream market in mid-1990s

The market can be divided into four distinct segments:

- *The super-premium segment*, typified by Häagen-Dazs, was still in the early stages of its growth at this time. New companies were still entering the segment, e.g. Ben and Jerry's from the USA, Ranieri from Unilever. New products were being tried using new methods of carton presentation and new high prices.

- *The premium segment* had developed significantly in 1989 with the introduction of premium-priced Mars ice cream. There were few new companies entering the market. The basic product ranges had become established among the leading players; the strategic battle was for distribution.

- *The regular and economy segments* were typified by Unilever's bulk packs, sold under the name Carte d'Or across much of Europe. These had existed for many years but were still growing at around 5 per cent per annum (still regarded as a growth market according to some definitions). The segment also had a large number of other suppliers, not all of whom were national, let alone European. There was keen competition on price and with own-label products from grocery retailers. There was relatively little product innovation.

4.1.2 Comment on the industry life cycle

The concept of the industry life cycle has both supporters and critics. Smallwood[4] and Baker[5] defend its usefulness and offer empirical support for the basic concept. Dhalla and Yuspeh[6] have led the criticisms, some of which certainly have a degree of validity (*see* Exhibit 4.1).

| Exhibit 4.1 | Criticisms of the industry life cycle |

1   It is *difficult to determine the duration* of some life cycles and to identify the precise stage an industry has reached. For example, the Mars Bar was launched in the 1930s and is certainly not in decline: but is it in the growth or mature phase?

2   Some industries miss stages or *cannot be clearly identified* in their stages, particularly as a result of technological change. For example, has the bicycle reached the mature phase or has it reached a new lease of life as the petrol-driven car pollutes city atmospheres?

3   Companies themselves can instigate change in their products and can as a result *alter the shape of the curve.* For example, new life has been brought into the camera industry by the introduction of miniaturisation and more recently by the use of electronic storage in place of film.

4   At each stage of evolution, the *nature of competition may be different*: some industries have few competitors and some have many regardless of where they are in the cycle. This may be a far more important factor in determining the strategy to be pursued. For example, in Chapter 5 we will examine the fragmented shoe industry and the concentrated grocery retailing industry: both are relatively mature with corporate strategy being determined not by evolution but by other factors.

There are certainly some difficulties with the industry life cycle approach, but the reason for such an analysis at the corporate strategy level is to identify the *dynamic factors that are shaping the industry's evolution.* The industry life cycle helps us to do this; it will then be possible to compare the organisation's own strategy with this analysis.

4.1.3   Cyclicality: its strategic implications

One industry condition that is only partially covered in the industry life cycle concept is the *cyclicality* of a market. In cyclical markets, the size of the market grows for a period, declines, grows again and declines again on a repeating basis. This may occur as a result of economic or political cyclical conditions over which the industry has no control – for example, the growth and decline in a national economy.

During the *upward* part of such a cycle, companies experience high profitability and during the *downward* part of the cycle, some companies face major profit problems, particularly those with high fixed costs and a lack of flexibility in their variable costs. Stocks of products tend to run down during the upward part of the cycle and build up during the downward part. These stockbuilding changes only make matters worse: as the downturn begins, a company may try to unload its stocks onto the market. Even though it may have to sell at lower prices, it may still make sense for a company to unload its stocks rather than hold onto the investment it has made in unwanted stock during the downturn. One result of cyclicality is that *prices rise during the upswing and fall during the downswing* with a severe and immediate impact on profits. Figure 4.4 shows the effects of this.

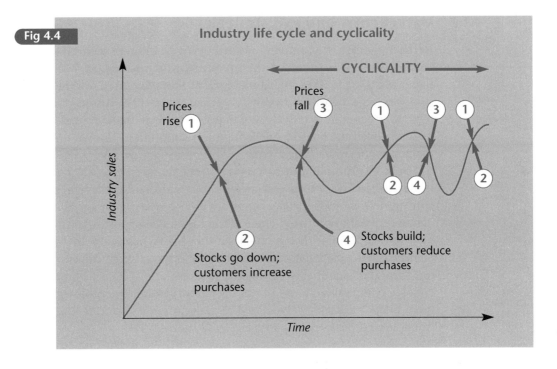

Fig 4.4 Industry life cycle and cyclicality

Cyclicality has an impact on *market demand*. There are three ways in which this may occur:

- *Replacement demand can be delayed.* In mature markets, demand slows down by definition. In the case of durable goods and capital items (such as televisions, domestic appliances, cars and chemical plant), customers will mainly buy as the product wears out – *replacement demand*. This will be delayed during periods of economic decline.

- *Purchases can be temporarily halted.* Even in markets where goods are regularly replaced, such as disposable paper and packaging, it may be possible to *halt purchasing* temporarily until the economic prospects have improved – for example, the same paper is reused rather than new paper being purchased.

- *A depressed national economy may reduce demand.* In a depressed economic climate there may be *reduced demand* that is never recovered for a product such as paper – for example, newspapers are shorter during an economic downturn.

As economic prospects change, so demand fluctuates – this is *market cyclicality*. Such factors are critical to strategic development: *timing* new developments to meet the upswing in the business cycle may well make the difference between the success and failure of a strategy.

Predicting such cycles and estimating their impact on the industry becomes a very important part of corporate strategy. The effects of cyclicality can be seen in the world prices for wood pulp in Case study 4.3. These reached a peak in August 1989 and another peak in March 1995, with company profits soaring and declining in consequence.

4.1.4 Market entry and exit strategies

In the Stora case the company needed to invest in more modern facilities to reduce costs further. This involved the investment of around US$ 400 million in a new paper plant – the KM8 Board machine at Stora Skoghall, Sweden. For Stora, this sum was large, being approximately equal to the 1994 profits of the company. For reasons of economies of scale, it was not possible to build a smaller factory or half a factory. Given the level of investment in relation to its annual profits, Stora had to make a major strategic decision.

The Stora example shows that even in the mature and cyclical phase of a market, it may be necessary to invest heavily to remain competitive in the market place. During such periods, it may therefore be necessary to make substantial financial demands on the company. The resulting financial exposure means that companies have to be certain of their strategies if they are to justify the investment. (It should be noted that a *prescriptive* strategy may be essential here: an *emergent* strategy may not solve the issue that the company faces.)

Some companies choose to *exit the industry* rather than to continue with investment plans – a strategy associated with mature markets. (*See* Case study 4.3 for an example in the European paper and pulp industry.)

4.1.5 Strategies for maturity: the importance of the company

Before we become too carried away by the influences of the industry on corporate strategy, it is important to remind ourselves of the argument developed by Baden-Fuller and Stopford:[7] what really matters in strategy is *company* activity, not the industry. They argue that many of the firms in such mature industries become incapable of generating the growth, so that it appears that the industry is mature. However, they believe that it is misleading to see *industries* as becoming mature: what really happens is that *each individual company* has become mature and lacking in innovation.

They point to the evidence developed by Rumelt[8] that only 8 per cent of a business unit's profitability can be explained by the *industry*; 46 per cent can be explained by the *choice of strategy* within the industry. The interpretation applied to this research by Baden-Fuller and Stopford is probably overstated: it relies on the sweeping statement that profitable industries are populated by 'imaginative and creative companies' and unprofitable industries consist of 'sleepy, uncreative businesses'.[9]

Nevertheless, there is no denying it is the *company* that will need to act if it wishes to escape low growth. Stora is a good example of what can be done. Companies can still find growth but they need to look beyond their existing markets.

Key strategic principles

- The industry life cycle – charting the development of a market from introduction, through growth and maturity to decline – is useful to identify the dynamic factors shaping the industry's evolution, although there are criticisms of its use.

- It also helps to specify the conventional view of the strategies that are appropriate to each stage of the cycle, even if these are then changed for logical reasons.

- Aspects of life cycle analysis that are worthy of special consideration include: the advantages of early entry, the fragmentation of market share as markets mature, the incidence of cyclicality and its effect on demand in mature markets.

- There are benefits in examining different *segments* of an industry, rather than the market as a whole.

- Especially in mature markets, it is the company that matters, not the industry. Although industries may appear to be mature, the company should be able to generate new growth opportunities by looking beyond its existing markets.

4.2 THE ROLE OF GOVERNMENT

At government policy level, politics and economics are inextricably linked. Corporate strategy is not concerned with forming such policies but does need to understand the implications of the decisions taken. Governments can stimulate national economies, encourage new research projects, impose new taxes and introduce many other initiatives that affect the organisation and its ability to develop corporate strategy.

4.2.1 History and momentum in politics

Over the last four centuries, politics has been a great driver for industrial growth.[10] Much of this growth has come through a combination of wars, the search for power and the exploitation of resources. Corporate strategy will need to take into account the opportunities and the moral dilemmas that may arise. For example, the problems in China in the early 1990s did not stop major western companies investing in that country in the years that followed; indeed, some may argue that such wealth creation is a contribution to overcoming the difficulties.

Any corporate strategy that does not take account of the history and momentum of politics is ignoring an essential element of the environment. Looking back from the vantage point of the late twentieth century, five political trends can be highlighted that are relevant to corporate strategy (*see* Exhibit 4.2).

| Exhibit 4.2 | Five political trends that have affected corporate strategy |

1 *The decline of the centrally directed command economies of Eastern Europe and the move towards democracy and freer markets.* Even the great nation of China is now moving towards a larger element of *laissez-faire*, market-driven efficiency. This has provided major strategic opportunities for many companies, including those in China itself.

2 *The absence of world wars and the more recent end of the Cold War.* This absence of global conflict has started to shift the balance away from defence industries and towards civilian activities – a development counterbalanced by the concentration of military forces and strongly held religious beliefs in the Middle East.

3 *The relative weakness of African and South/Central American economies.* This has resulted from their struggle with high inflation, weak currencies, low value-added industries and political instability. The recent changes in countries such as South Africa and Argentina hold out hope for stronger corporate strategic development opportunities in the future.

4 *The rise of international trade, global companies and new trading nations,* such as the 'Tiger' economies of South-East Asia.

5 *The emergence of supportive international finance and economic institutions,* such as the International Monetary Fund (IMF), the World Bank and European Bank for Reconstruction and Development (EBRD). Their research, guidance and influence has had a positive effect on international development.

4.2.2 The role of the state in industrial development

In both the European Union and in the United States of America, there are differing views on the extent to which the state should become involved in industrial development. In France, Italy and Greece, it has long been the tradition that state-owned companies and state intervention are important elements of the national economy. In the UK, Germany and the USA, the opposing view has been taken. The approach adopted is essentially a *political* choice made by those in power. The two approaches – often referred to as *laissez-faire* and *dirigiste* – are summarised in Table 4.3. Adam Smith, Karl Marx and many other political commentators have all contributed to the important political debate in this area. Table 4.3 is intended merely to summarise areas that are the most relevant to the development of corporate strategy.

Table 4.3 Government and industrial policy

Laissez faire: free-market approach	Dirigiste: centrally directed approach
• Low entry barriers	• High entry barriers
• Competition encouraged	• National companies supported
• Little or no state	against international competition
support for industry	• State ownership of some
• Self-interest leads	key industries
to wealth creation	• Profit motive benefits
• Belief in laws of	the few at the expense
supply and demand	of the many
• High unemployment levels	• Failure in market mechanism
• Profit motive will provide	will particularly affect the
basis for efficient	poor and can only be
production and high quality	corrected by state
	intervention
	• Need to correct monopolies
	controlled by private companies

In practice, the distinctions drawn in Table 4.3 are very crude. Some countries offer a *balance* between strong infrastructural support in some areas – for example, education, favoured industries (as in Singapore), investment in roads, power and water – and then couple this with a free-market approach in other areas – for example, privatisation of state monopolies, lower barriers to entry to encourage Multinational Enterprise (MNE) investment. (MNEs are the large global companies such as Ford, McDonald's and Unilever.) Each country will have its own approach so that any corporate environmental analysis will have to be conducted on a country-by-country basis.

In the late 1990s, it might be argued that state intervention is dead: the industrial chaos resulting from the collapse of communism in Eastern Europe certainly highlights the problems. During the period 1945–90, all the communist regimes in Eastern Europe operated with large state-run industries that had no competition and little, if any, incentive to operate efficiently. After these regimes disappeared, it became clear that the inefficient industries that remained were witness to the problems of a monopolistic, command economy. As one post-communist Bulgarian put it: 'Lenin said that the system which guaranteed higher productivity would prevail, and this turned out to be capitalism.'[11]

The evidence from Eastern Europe only applies to the totalitarian state, however: it does not follow that all state intervention is useless. State involvement in the 'Tiger' economies of South-East Asia (Singapore, Malaysia, Hong Kong, Thailand, Korea) and selective intervention in Japan, the EU and the USA suggest that some governmental policy can be beneficial.[12]

Corporate strategy should therefore anticipate that politics will continue to be a part of the equation. Companies may benefit from policies such as higher state subsidies, better education and international trade incentives; it may be hindered by measures such as new laws restricting competition, new taxes on profits, limited investment in country infrastructure (e.g. roads, telecommunications).

Hence, corporate strategy needs to be acutely aware of the benefits and problems associated with government policies. It will certainly wish to press for policies that it regards as beneficial during the formation and implementation of strategic decisions. Influencing major political decisions is part of corporate strategy. As long as this is done openly and with integrity, there can be no objection by those with other interests.

4.2.3 Broader government policy and state institutions

In addition to direct state intervention in industry, governments influence companies by a whole variety of other mechanisms:

- *Public expenditure.* In the EU through the European Commission in Brussels, public expenditure is quite low as a percentage of GDP when compared with the expenditure concentrated at national government level. In the USA, public expenditure is higher at federal (central) level in some areas, e.g. defence.

- *Competition policy.* This is strong at EU central level and likely to become stronger; similar strength in USA at federal level.

- *Taxation policy.* This is weak at EU central level with taxes largely left to individual nations; in the USA, there are clear federal taxes with further taxes raised at state level.

- *Regional policy.* There is clear EU support for weaker nations and parts of nations with infrastructure investment, etc.; in the USA, individual states are more likely to fulfil this role but federal support is still important in some industries.

All the above policies can have a major influence on where companies locate and whether they are profitable; in practice, organisations often make considerable efforts to obtain government grants and other forms of support as part of their corporate strategy.

At the international and global level, countries around the world have joined together in essentially politically inspired international institutions, trade agreements and trading blocks (*see* Section 4.3).

Macroeconomic analysis: the national economy

Governments have some direct control over the economy of a country. It is easier for organisations to launch a growth or survival strategy when the national or international economy is showing steady growth with low inflation. Conversely, if economic decline is likely, the company might be well advised to take a more prudent view of strategic expansion. It follows that the *macroeconomic conditions* – that is, economic activity at the general level of the national or international economy – surrounding an organisation are an important element in the development of corporate strategy.

It is for this reason that all the usual issues in macroeconomic analysis are relevant here: growth, interest rates, inflation, unemployment, balance of payments, etc. It should be noted that this analysis is concerned with the *prediction* of the future – an activity that some emergent strategic thinkers consider largely worthless when applied to corporate strategy (*see* Part One). Although macroeconomic prediction is not an exact science, it does have a well validated and broadly accurate track record: on this basis, it may usefully be applied in strategic analysis.

In practice, when exploring corporate strategy, many organisations, both large and small, use their own managers to make economic forecasts, buy in reputable forecasts or simply use published forecast material. The forecasts are usually made on key macroeconomic issues such as:

● Gross Domestic Product (GDP), total and per head of the population
● Growth in GDP
● Retail and consumer price indices
● Trade flows in imports, exports and the balance of payments
● Private sector share of GDP; agricultural share of GDP
● Foreign Direct Investment, total and as a percentage of total investment.

Many readers will be familiar with these areas. For companies operating in more than one country, these forecasts may usefully be estimated for all the major countries in which they operate with the addition of *currency fluctuation* as another important variable.

In addition to the collection of this relatively straightforward data, organisations may need to implement a more structured and extensive analysis. Mesch[13] used his industrial experience at Sun Exploration and Production Company to develop seven criteria for exploring whether the organisation really needed to take matters further (*see* Exhibit 4.3).

| Exhibit 4.3 | Seven criteria to establish whether an organisation needs to undertake a more extensive macroeconomic analysis |

1 Does the external business environment influence capital allocations and the decision-making process?

2 Have the previous long-range plans been scrapped because of unexpected changes in the environment?

3 Have there been any unpleasant surprises in the external business environment?

4 Is competition growing in the industry?

5 Is the business more marketing oriented and more concerned about the ultimate customer?

6 Do more and different kinds of external forces seem to be influencing decisions, and does there seem to be more interplay among them?

7 Is management unhappy with past forecasting and planning efforts?

If any of the above are answered affirmatively, then further analysis may need to be undertaken; an increase in the number of positive answers means that the need may be greater.

4.2.5 Analysis of economic conditions at the government/industry level

In addition to changes in the macroeconomic conditions, organisations will also be concerned with government changes in the economic environment, *specific to the industry* in which they are involved. For example:

● The rising price of petrol and international environmental concerns have impacted on car engine design in the car industry; in turn, this has meant that companies have altered their model ranges and changed their plant investment strategy. Some companies have coped better than others.

● Changes in government policy on the purchase of drugs (the industry's biggest customers) are reducing the profitability of the major pharmaceutical companies. In response, new company strategies have been varied: some have moved more into non-government sales and others are pursuing more complex strategies.

Such conditions are specific to a particular industry, and so there can be no generalised list of items, nor any common body of theory in the industry environment that will always influence strategy. The types of issue that are usually worth considering are those shown in Exhibit 4.4. The impact that such economic changes will have on corporate strategy will vary with the organisation: essentially, the demand and cost structures of the industry and the company will be the prime determinants. The *key factors for success* can be used to highlight major areas (*see* Chapter 3). There is further consideration of the cost structures of an industry in Chapter 7.

Exhibit 4.4 **Typical economic issues involving both government and industry**

- Government tax and legislative activity.

- Specific impact of macroeconomic growth on an industry. (For example, house construction particularly relies on a buoyant economy in a way that food does not – we need to eat but may be able to delay moving house.)

- Cyclicality of demand and investment in an industry.

- The level of derived demand. Some companies, particularly in the industrial area, depend on their *customers'* economic prospects for their demand – for example, bricks and door frames depend partly on demand derived from the construction industry.

- Raw material supplies and costs.

- Industry negotiations on wages and conditions of work.

Key strategic principles

- Politics has been an important driver of industrial growth. Corporate strategy needs to consider the opportunities and difficulties that derive from such policies.

- Government policies can have a general impact on corporate strategy: some countries have adopted a *laissez-faire*, free-market approach, while others have followed a *dirigiste*, more centrally directed approach to industrial development. Corporate strategy needs to be acutely aware of the benefits and problems of these areas.

- Other areas of government interest, such as public expenditure, competition policy and taxation issues, also need to be analysed. Influencing political decisions in these areas is an important part of corporate strategy.

- Macroeconomic conditions – that is, economic activity at the general level of the national economy – can have a significant impact on corporate strategy, which needs to be explored and assessed.

- Economic conditions at the industry level are also important. Such matters as government policy, raw material supplies and industry wage negotiations can have a significant impact on strategy.

CASE STUDY 4.2

Coping with politics after apartheid[14]

As a result of sanctions and the role of the South African government, Shell South Africa has never known competition in the oil industry. This case explains how politics and profitability have become mixed.

Shell South Africa, a wholly owned subsidiary of Royal Dutch/Shell, has maintained a constant presence in South Africa since 1912. It was the second biggest oil company in South Africa in 1996 with a turnover in 1995 of Rand 4.5 billion.

The legacy of oil sanctions imposed by the United Nations during the apartheid era shows an oil industry that includes seven domestic oil companies but has known no competition. Each company is bound by law to purchase crude stock in proportion to its market share from Sasol, a synthetic fuels producer which manufactures crude oil from coal. All other crude stocks are imported and retail pump prices are set by the Central Energy Fund (CEF), which manages the country's strategic oil reserves.

Koosum Kalyan, general manager of Shell SA, says it is a highly efficient environment. The Durban refinery (which Shell co-owns with British Petroleum) is 'one of the most capital-intensive and technologically advanced refineries in the world'. Profit margins, fixed by the CEF at a flat level for all companies on the basis of a nominal import price, are 'very low'.

The 1993 Oil Petroleum Act lifted the veil of secrecy shrouding the industry and laid the foundations of a more competitive market. Oil companies can now bid openly for crude oil imports on the international market. Miss Kalyan commented:

There are now monthly adjustments to the pump price, and more transparency. We welcome further deregulation and we believe there will be new entrants to the market in the years ahead.

Shell is increasing capacity at its Durban plant to meet the growing demand for liquid fuels – a market which is growing by 5 per cent a year. Meanwhile, the industry growth rate was 10 per cent in 1995, reflecting growing confidence in the deregulation process which is widely expected to result in the phasing-out of price controls by 2000. With a market share of 18.5 per cent, Shell's net income last year was Rand 230 million after tax – about 1 per cent of Royal Dutch/Shell's total earnings.

Source: Financial Times, 28 March 1996.

CASE QUESTIONS

1   *Should Shell South Africa seek actively to support the end of the controlled market on the basis that it is well placed to make higher profits, or should its policy simply be to accept what is decided by the government?*

2   *How will this influence its corporate strategy?*

4.3 THE OPPORTUNITIES FOR GLOBAL MARKET DEVELOPMENT

4.3.1 The role of international trade in corporate strategy

In 1994, world merchandise trade – the exporting and importing activities of countries and companies around the world – amounted to US$4000 billion, an increase of 9 per cent over the previous year.[15] At the same time, world output of goods – the total production of goods by companies and public organisations aggregated together across the world – increased by 3.5 per cent. In fact, as shown in Table 4.4, world merchandise *trade* outstripped world *output* for the ten years from 1984 to 1994.[16] Countries are trading more with each other and faster than they are increasing their output. This should present continuing opportunities for the development of corporate strategy.

Table 4.4 Comparison of world exports and world manufacturing value added

	1960–70	1970–80	1980–90
Annual growth in world trade (%)	9.2	20.3	6.0
Annual growth in manufacturing value added (%)	N/A	3.1	2.1

Source: UNIDO[17]

In many respects, world merchandise trade has come to be an important *driver* of output growth around the world. Corporate strategy has played a significant part in achieving this and, equally, has benefited from it. We are concerned here with the way international markets and industry structure interact with international company activity. Some industries cannot survive without overseas trade: for example, aerospace and defence companies such as Boeing and McDonnell Douglas need sales beyond their home country of the United States to make a profit. Other industries simply benefit from being able to sell their products or services internationally. The role of overseas trade has changed significantly for many companies and has come to be a direct part of corporate strategy.

The international significance for corporate strategy goes beyond trade, however:

● *Low-cost sources of raw materials, expertise and labour* might exist in other countries beyond the home country of the company: for example, Japanese companies make consumer electronics goods in South-East Asia because labour costs are lower than in Japan.

● *Increased globalisation* – that is, the worldwide sourcing of components and sale of goods, production and investment coupled with international finance and capital markets – has transformed the environment in which companies now operate. For example, computer companies might make hard disk drives in Singapore, microchip-sets in Taiwan and assemble the finished product in the USA with the whole deal financed from a bank in the City of London.

The international environment in which trade operates has changed dramatically over the last 20 years. For our purposes, it is useful to distinguish two types of environment within which companies operate:

- *The Developed Countries Environment, such as the USA and the EU.* Corporate strategies have been designed to gain market share in these countries, which are generally attractive as sources of trade for international companies. However, *trade barriers* have been erected to protect native industries in developed countries. Increased *foreign direct investment* (FDI) and *on-site production* by the international companies have been used to circumvent these. For example, Toyota and Nissan have set up car production factories in the UK to gain share of the EU market and overcome barriers to direct car imports from Japan.

- *Developing countries environment, such as South-East Asia or Latin America.* Corporate strategies take into account the potential of such markets, but recognise that the lower levels of wealth in such countries mean that, at present, they may not be particularly important as targets for trade. Their real attraction for now is that they may well have lower labour costs and access to raw materials. A major part of their output may be *re-exported* to the developed countries. For example, the largest source of hard disk drives in the world is Singapore – a country with a population of just 2 million.

In spite of treaties to encourage world trade such as the GATT (described in Section 4.3.3), governments have been fearful of the effects of unbridled international competition on their home trade. They have used at least five types of mechanism to restrict international trade:

- *Tariffs* – taxes on imported goods which do not stop imports but do make them less competitive.
- *Quotas* – a maximum number placed on the goods that can be imported in any one period.
- *Non-tariff or technical barriers* – with governments imposing local laws or other technical means to make it difficult for imports to enter the country.
- *Financial subsidies for home producers.*
- *Exchange controls* – with governments controlling the access that their citizens have to foreign currency so that it becomes difficult to pay for imports.

In the short term, the barriers may be small and outside the more fundamental scope of corporate strategy. However, at a deeper level, the effect on the international environment may need to be addressed by corporate strategy, if it is to survive. The case of Japanese car production in the EU is a direct strategic response to problems in this area. In particular, we should note that it is predicted that the completion of the Uruguay Round of the General Agreement on Trade and Tariffs will have a steady real impact on international trade over the next 20 years.[18]

In the example of Shell, described in Case study 4.2, the South African oil market, isolated from the rest of the world for political reasons up to the mid-

1990s, was beginning to change. Oil markets are global, so it is likely that over the next 20 years there will be increased international trade in this area between South Africa and other parts of the world. However, this does not mean that Shell will disappear in South Africa because local sales and distribution facilities will still be required: the company has a strong strategic position which it can easily defend as long as it is not undercut on price by cheap oil imports as the market opens up.

4.3.2 Theories of international trade and the development of nations

Over the last 200 years, economists have been developing theories to explain the growth and advantages of international trade. They have been particularly concerned to explore the benefits and problems in the context of empirical evidence that increased trade has generally been beneficial to those countries that have engaged in it.[19] The importance of such theories for corporate strategy lies in:

- their explanation of the *environment* in which corporate strategy is defined; and
- the *framework* they provide for analysing corporate strategy international opportunities and threats.

For the purposes of this text, three theories of international economic growth can usefully be identified and contrasted for their impact on corporate strategy (*see* Table 4.5). There is no agreement among economists as to which is the correct theory; they probably all have some merit. Overall, they point to the important role of government in several areas:

- *Developing basic infrastructures* – such as water supplies, telecommunications and roads. It is difficult for corporate strategy to make much headway in a country if governments are unwilling to invest in such areas.

- *Training and the quality of education.* The stock of human capital is an important element in the development of new investments because of the need to recruit and train nationals to work for the company.

- *Economic stability and selected export stimuli.* Most organisations are able to work better if inflation is low and the economy is stable. In the early stages of development, there is also some evidence that governments can usefully support certain industries in terms of export assistance to stimulate early growth.

- *Competitive and open home market.* Although there is a risk that home industries may be swamped by large international companies entering the home market, this is not what has tended to happen in practice. When the home market is open, it has stimulated new entrants to open factories, create jobs and thus wealth. India has for years had home markets that were partially closed to international trade. Singapore and Malaysia have opened up their markets and benefited accordingly.

Table 4.5 Three theories of international trade and country development

	Comparative advantage of nations	Competitive advantage of nations	Limited state intervention to develop the infrastructure and open competition
Source	David Riccardo, 19th century economist	Michael Porter (1990) *Competitive Advantage of Nations*, Free Press, Boston, Mass	World Bank (1994), *World Development Report 1994*, Oxford University Press, NY
Some key elements of the theory	• Countries should specialise in those areas of production in which they are particularly efficient • Countries then exchange these goods with countries who have advantages in other goods and services	Four major factors are important: • demanding home customers • quality and quantity of institutions to support production, e.g. universities and technical training • highly competitive home markets • strong supporting and supplier industries In addition, two other factors were also identified: • government policy • chance	Government policy in the early stages of development to produce: • economic stability • low inflation • stable finances and currency • agricultural development policies • export support for selected areas • quality civil service and training institutions In addition, two other areas also supported growth: • open market competition with low tariffs • government providing infrastructure in early years and then allowing free market to operate as the economy strengthens
Relevance for corporate strategy (organisations should be seeking evidence of these matters)	• Natural resources may provide the basis for economic growth, e.g. pulp and paper with their reliance on forests and cheap energy	• Emphasis on the importance of competition • Institutional excellence to provide resources and stimulus • Relationships with suppliers important	• Role of government to stimulate growth in the early years • Openness to international trade as a growth stimulant • Need for stability in the economy and currency • Government investment in infrastructure and education

Influence of institutions involved in international trade

In any analysis of international trade, it is useful to include some background information on the main institutions involved, their role and background.

The period of trade between 1918 and 1939 was characterised by countries attempting to protect their industries by erecting trade barriers against what were regarded as unfair practices. The result was a serious decline in international trade during the 1930s, making the major economic depression of this period even worse. After 1945, countries resolved that they would avoid these mistakes by establishing the *General Agreement on Tariffs and Trade* (GATT): there were originally 23 signatory countries but now over 140 have signed.

Since 1947, GATT has sponsored eight major rounds of tariff and other trade barrier reductions to encourage world trade – each round being named after the country in which it began. The latest completed round was the Uruguay Round which started in 1986 and was signed in 1993. The GATT agreement embodies two major principles:

- *Non-discrimination.* Each country will give all other countries the same rates on import duties. Giving more to one country means giving more to all signatories (called *Most Favoured Nation* status).

- *Consultation.* When disputes arise, GATT brings the parties together and encourages compromise, rather than the squabbles of the 1930s.

This agreement gave important protection to small countries when they opened their barriers to large and powerful partners. However, the small, developing countries of the world still felt that GATT assisted industrialised goods; it is a fact that their share of world trade was declining. The developing countries therefore encouraged the United Nations to form the *United Nations Conference on Trade and Development* (UNCTAD) – a body concerned to highlight the trade concerns of the developing nations.

In addition to trade, another major area of concern in 1945 was *exchange rates* for currency between countries. There is little point in fixing a price, regardless of tariffs, if the unit in which it is quoted then collapses. There had been real problems in this area of international trade in the 1930s. A system of largely fixed exchange rates was agreed internationally in 1944 – the *Bretton Woods agreement*. This lasted until 1973 but was then replaced by floating exchange rates around the world. The *International Monetary Fund* (IMF) was set up to oversee the fixed system but did not disappear when the fixed system collapsed. It has more of a background role now but still lends funds to countries in balance of payments difficulties and helps to support international trade stability through co-operation and discussion.

Around the same time as the IMF was being formed, the International Bank for Reconstruction and Development (usually called the *World Bank*) was set up to provide long-term capital for reconstruction projects, mainly in developing countries. It provides lending for infrastructure, tourism and other projects with the aim of long-term improvement in growth. It also undertakes background studies on development issues: for example, investigating the reasons why some types of government development are more productive than others. Such data has been used in this book and will provide much good source material for those engaged in strategic environmental analysis.

In addition to these global institutions, various *trade blocks* have also developed around the world – for example, the European Union (EU), the Association of South-East Asian Nations (ASEAN) and the North American Free Trade Area (NAFTA). The purpose of a trade block is to encourage trade between its members on the basis of the *theory of comparative advantage* between its members (*see* Table 4.5). In the case of the European Union, the trade block which was originally set up to encourage trade between its member states – the European Community – was subsequently extended to cover more direct political matters. As a result of the Treaty of Rome 1957, the Single Europe Act 1986 and the Maastricht Treaty 1992, the trade block became the *European Union* in 1993. There are 15 member states with other European countries waiting to join as soon as possible. It is governed[20] by three main institutions:

- *European Commission* – a relatively small group of civil servants (approximately 20 000), located principally in Brussels who initiate legislation and other changes and co-ordinate all major activities.
- *Council of Ministers* – gives the final agreement on all major decisions. It consists of the Prime Ministers (President in the case of France) or their representatives in particular functional areas (e.g. finance or agriculture ministers).
- *European Parliament* – with limited powers, but directly elected by voters in all the member states.

The main concern of the last few years is the future political and economic direction of the EU. Areas of under discussion include:

- the possibility of a single currency across the member states;
- increased powers for the central institutions of the EU; and
- stronger accountability in Brussels for decisions made.

These issues are still to be explored and agreed and will have a substantial impact on corporate strategy for European companies. For example, the trade of every European Union country is now inextricably linked in a largely beneficial way with the other member states of the EU. The political agreement will also influence the strategies of those companies outside the EU but *exporting* into Europe.

4.3.4 Political analysis

Over the last 25 years, world trade has increased for essentially political reasons. Countries have wanted to raise their levels of trade with each other because they believe such activity brings increased wealth. As a consequence, the growth in world trade has substantially exceeded that in manufacturing value added (*see* Section 4.3.1). For any company involved in world trade or threatened by world competitors, the world political environment is of great importance in the development of corporate strategy and corporate strategy needs to define the trends for its own industry.

World trade has expanded faster than manufacturing growth for the following reasons:

1 *New or enhanced trade areas have been agreed* over the last 20 years: for example, the Single European Act 1986 certainly encouraged and supported trade across the EU. The ASEAN pact has been extended because benefits have been identified. New trade agreements are expected to maintain this momentum for the immediate future. There are many recent examples:

- The Uruguay Round of the General Agreement on Trade and Tariffs (GATT), signed in December 1993, is expected to increase global welfare by between US$213 billion and US$274 billion (measured in 1992 dollars) by the year 2002.[21]

- The Mercosur Treaty will bring together Brazil, Argentina, Paraguay and Uruguay in South America to form a new regional trade pact.

- The North American Free Trade Area (NAFTA) Treaty was signed in late 1994 and will bring increased trade between the USA, Mexico and Canada.

2 *World and regional trade organisations have themselves been strengthened and reformed*: for example, the European Bank for Reconstruction and Development (EBRD) has been renewed following a difficult early period and has now begun to offer significant funds for development in Eastern Europe. The World Bank and the IMF have also been strengthened (*see* Section 4.3.3).

3 *Multinationals have become an important source of world sales and investment.* According to UN estimates,[22] foreign sales by transnational corporations reached US$5500 billion in 1992. The same companies have accumulated US$2000 billion worth of foreign direct investment.

Over the last ten years, the dominant thinking by governments has moved from managed and centrally planned international trade to allowing market forces to take over. The *competitive advantage of nations* (*see* Table 4.5) has taken over as a guiding approach. Any increase in such market opportunities will provide corporate strategy with openings not previously available. The *laissez-faire* market theory (described in Table 4.3) has been applied to international trade: it suggests that the efficiencies to be found in the theoretically perfect market can contribute real benefits to nations engaged in international trade and real opportunities for corporate strategy. As the United Nations Industrial Development Organisation has commented:[23]

> *'The market provides a decentralised and efficient system of coordinating and reconciling millions of decisions taken daily by countless economic agents in an economy. Guided by the "invisible hand" of self-interest and collective social welfare, the market imparts stimulus to growth and technical change through incentives and flexibility, and leads to a harmony between the pursuance of individual self-interest and collective social welfare, while ensuring a fairly close relationship between costs and prices ... The role of the state is confined to defence, law and order, provision of public goods and enforcing competition. The remaining vast area of economic affairs is left to the guidance of laissez-faire or free market forces.'*

Three major preconditions are then needed for the price mechanism to achieve optimal dynamic resource allocation and production:

- perfect information and resource mobility with numerous economic agents, none of which is big enough to influence prices and conditions in any market – whether product, labour, financial or capital;

- an absence of economies of scale;
- complete tradeability – that is, all products can be substituted for each other with no trade barriers.

In practice, these economic conditions are highly unlikely to occur. This does not mean that corporate strategy will not obtain benefits from economic dynamics, however; on the contrary, it is precisely the *absence* of these perfect market conditions that may provide corporate strategy with its competitive advantage – for example, economies of scale.

4.3.5 The shift towards market forces: implications for international corporate strategy

In many countries, there are a number of political decisions that distort the perfect market mechanism described in Section 4.3.4. From a theoretical economic perspective, these further limit the presumed benefits of the perfect market or at least render it less useful. These distortions can be grouped as:

- *Labour market distortions* – minimum wage legislation and trade union rights as in the EU Social Chapter (which the UK has refused to join in order to provide competitive advantage in terms of lower wage costs in the UK).
- *Labour training* – which companies cannot own since employees can easily move to other firms (Singapore has had a problem here).
- *Information and technology initiatives* – which have been developed by one entrepreneur but are then available to others without significant cost. This may cause the original inventors to under-invest in this area. (Patenting may offer little protection for the medium-sized company because of the expense of implementing this route.)
- *Economies of scale* – where a firm produces at a price equal to average costs but below marginal costs, that is, a socially suboptimal price.
- *Finance and capital markets* – which may be less efficient in developing countries, thus inhibiting growth.

From an international political and economic viewpoint, the main issue is the extent to which the state or group of states (such as the EU) should intervene and bring about structural change. This involves the third theory of international trade highlighted in Table 4.5 – the *Limited State Intervention theory*.

The relevance of this issue to corporate strategy lies in the relationship between the organisation and the state: any state intervention will affect the economic environment of the organisation. The firm therefore needs to understand and establish the situation clearly and negotiate with the state, if necessary: in practice, many companies, particularly multinationals, regard a relationship with the state as an important part of their corporate strategy.

If the state should intervene, then it follows that it may be necessary for corporate strategy to pinpoint where, when and in what way this intervention should take place. Political analysis which questions government policy on essential infrastructures is vital – for example, there is little point in setting up paper-making plant if there is no power supply. There are real advantages for companies needing advanced telecommunications facilities in investing in Singapore, given the country's well advanced plans for optical fibre networks throughout the country.

In spite of the enthusiasm of some commentators for market-led solutions, Japan and the Asian 'Tiger' countries have not hesitated to intervene politically in crucial areas of industry over the last 20 years. As a result, they have an economic growth record that has impressed other countries around the world. Dr Mahathir bin Muhammed has led Malaysia to major success during this period. The former Prime Minister of Singapore, Lee Kwan Yew, has been a visionary driving force behind this growth in his own country. He is on record as saying that some countries benefit from not having too much democracy: they need central decision making to make rapid progress. Singapore, along with Hong Kong and Taiwan, has also benefited from the ancient Chinese traditions of diligence and filial obedience, rather than the delays introduced by democratic discussion.

The considerable success of the Asian Tigers over the last 20 years holds some lessons for corporate strategy. However, it is important not to overstate the case for state involvement in industrial development. The European steel industry described in Chapter 3 shows just what can go wrong when the state continues to intervene and prevent necessary rationalisation from taking place. State intervention can be a mixed blessing.

With regard to the Asian 'Tiger' economies, the following points should also be noted:

1 Companies who have invested in ASEAN countries have been highly successful in terms of growth and profitability. Early corporate strategic analysis identifying these countries was successful.

2 Such companies have had to follow closely the policies laid down by their respective governments. For example, in the case of Singapore, the government identified four strategic areas of economic expansion for the country: banking and finance, international transport, construction and electronics. Companies involved in these industries or able to direct their strategy to support these industries have been particularly well placed to reap the rewards. Detailed analysis of the country concerned is required.

3 When trading with and investing in such countries, it is important for European and American companies to be sensitive to the relevant government policies and reflect these in their corporate strategies. There is plenty of scope for the company to import new ideas and technology, but it is essential to understand and support the nation state and its political aspirations and goals. The need for analysis is evident.

The interesting analytical question is when should the power of the state to intervene be reduced and the power of the market take over. There are no conclusive answers but it has been suggested[24] that intervention might be scaled back as a nation becomes more industrialised: In the early stages of industrialisation the state invests in infrastructure projects, transport, power, water, institution building, etc.; in the later stages of industrialisation the state has increasing difficulty in intervening in the more complex structures that are beginning to emerge. Its role becomes restricted to maintaining a competitive environment.

In practice, the two stages are likely to form part of a continuing national process of industrialisation and negotiation between state and company. When analysing countries for corporate strategy opportunities, companies may wish to identify where the states are in relation to the above continuum. This may then have implications for the type of dealings the firm might expect to have with the state and the expectations of future growth.

4.3.6 Global corporate strategic growth

Over the last ten years, there has been a fundamental shift in the international environment regarding corporate growth – providing major opportunities for international corporate strategy. Formerly, barriers were raised to protect domestic industries and governments sought to develop home industries that would substitute for imports. More recently, some countries have instituted market reforms and liberalised trade; investment has been oriented to producing strong export growth rather than import protection.[25] Even India, which has had a long tradition of protecting its home industries and suffering the consequences, has begun to change its policies.[26] Barriers have begun to come down and companies such as Coca-Cola and Unilever have been allowed to develop further: Hindustani Lever has had a long tradition of involvement in India. Chapter 3 pointed out that the Indian state had plans for reducing its holding in the largest steel company in India.

Corporate strategy needs to analyse such environments with care, but the analytical data has not always been available, especially in Eastern Europe which until a few years ago saw no need to discover what its customers might actually want.[27] Other examples include such countries as China which it has offered major growth opportunities but also analytical problems that are not easily resolved.

During the 1980s and early 1990s, the vigorous and privatised British Steel made several unsuccessful attempts to acquire major European companies: by 1994, it had changed its strategy and, after analysis, saw its future in the Far East.[28] In 1986 it started a joint venture with Jardine Matheson and it followed this with a network of sales offices. In a sense, this is a substitute for analysis: by setting up offices British Steel was able to test local market conditions without detailed advanced study.

Key strategic principles

- Over the last ten years, global trade has increased faster than manufacturing output. Trade growth has become an important driver of output and represents opportunities for corporate strategy development.

- Theories of international trade and the development of nations provide the framework within which to analyse international corporate strategy, especially its opportunities and threats. Theories differ but many highlight the importance of the role of government in developing basic country infrastructures such as roads. Training and quality educational institutions are also vital. Economic stability and selected trade stimulants need to be developed. To stimulate growth, governments also need to encourage increasingly competitive home markets with low barriers to international trade.

- Global political developments have served to enhance world trade over the last 25 years. Corporate strategy needs to analyse and determine the relevant trends for its own products or product groups.

- World trade institutions have also had a substantial impact on global activity.

- In developing international corporate strategy, one of the main issues is the relationship of the state with individual organisations. The success of the Asian 'Tiger' economies holds some lessons for corporate strategy. Conversely, the problems of state support in Europe highlights the problems that can arise.

CASE STUDY 4.3

Corporate strategy in the world paper and pulp industry

This case study explores the links between market growth, economic and political changes and corporate strategy in this major world industry.

North America and Scandinavia produce between them the bulk of the world's pulp and paper. Their ability to make a profit is highly dependent on the price of wood pulp (most paper, and thus wood pulp, goes into making newsprint for the world's newspapers and magazines). The price of wood pulp is characterised by strong cyclical patterns that peak roughly every four years.

Since wood pulp makes up by far the largest part of total costs, corporate strategy in the pulp and paper industry is therefore highly dependent on commodity prices for pulp over which corporations have no control. It is against this background that companies have to devise their corporate strategy.

Table 4.6 Leading companies in the world pulp and paper industry

Company	Country	Sales (1995) (Tonnes million)
International Paper	USA	9.6
UPM/Kymmene	Finland	7.2
Stone Container	USA	7.1
Jefferson Smurfitt	Ireland	7.0
Georgia-Pacific	USA	6.3
Stora	Sweden	5.9
SCA	Sweden	5.3
Enso/Vietsiluoto	Finland	5.2
Champion International	USA	4.5
Nippon Paper Industries	Japan	4.3

Source: Stora

Industry background

In 1994, Stora was Europe's second largest pulp and paper company. It announced that it was to start work on a new paper plant costing SEK 3.1 billion (US$400 million) capable of handling 290 000 tonnes of wood pulp per year. By comparing this capital expenditure with the company's 1994 pre-tax profit of SEK 3.2 billion, it will be evident that the investment was a significant strategic decision. One of its major competitors, Modo (Sweden), was also planning a new plant with a capacity of around 270 000 tonnes at that time.

The reason for these investments was that Scandinavian and North American pulp and paper plants were working near capacity to meet world demand: for example, Scandinavian plant was working at 94 per cent of production capacity in 1994. However, this was the industry at the peak of its cycle. In addition, not all parts of the industry were growing at the same rate (*see* Table 4.10).

Industry key factors for success

At that time there were four key factors for success which would deliver profitability in the industry.

High plant capacity breakeven

The difficulty in adding new capacity was that plant economies of scale in this industry were massive. As mentioned above, Stora needed to spend a sum roughly equivalent to its 1994 annual profits on a new plant.

Once a plant was built, the profits came from keeping it operating as near to capacity as possible. Breakeven was between 75 and 80 per cent of capacity; below these plant utilisation levels, the companies made a loss. It was not feasible for the companies to smooth their production schedules by supplying for stock in times of low demand. It was therefore necessary for pulp and paper companies to price their product to keep production running as steadily as possible. Because of its direct impact on profitability, pricing was therefore used among the pulp and paper companies to stimulate demand.

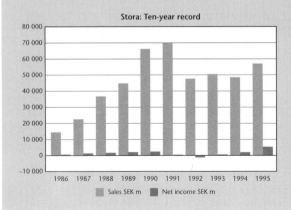

Exploitation of derived demand from newspapers and magazines

Inevitably, pricing policies made the pulp and paper industry highly dependent on the demand of its customers, especially the world's newsprint industry. Small swings in demand from the newspaper and magazine world caused major changes in profitability in pulp and paper companies.

In newspapers and magazines, one of the main factors that governed the demand for newsprint was the size of the publication. In turn, this depended on the state of the national and world economy: in times of boom, newspapers grew in size to advertise jobs, more products and new services; in times of depression, the reverse applied.

The pulp and paper industry was therefore dependent on *derived demand* – that is, demand derived from the demand of another industry – from the newspaper and magazine industry. A major strategic estimate was therefore required by the pulp and paper industry of both the national and world economies and the derived demand from the newspaper industry.

Excess plant capacity

When times were good in the paper industry in 1989, companies tended to invest in new and larger plant.[29] As demand then fell during the early 1990s, there was then excess plant capacity in the industry – for example, 21 plants closed in Canada in the years 1990 to 1993. Closing down plant is a major strategic decision.

The paper and pulp price cycle

With producers even more anxious to keep production running during times of economic difficulty, paper prices inevitably fell. Since pulp is the main ingredient of paper, the price of pulp also dropped – between 1989 and 1993, the price per tonne of one kind of standard pulp more than halved from US$840 to US$390 (*see* Table 4.7).

Short term, the price of paper and pulp was the biggest single factor in delivering profitability. Pricing in this industry was therefore a major strategic decision.

Table 4.7   World pulp prices and the environment (US$ per tonne)

Date	Price of bleached softwood kraft pulp	Environment
April 1988	570	World economy begins to rise rapidly
August 1989	840	Spending spree on new pulp capacity and company acquisitions
August 1990	700	Downturn begins: Gulf War, etc.
August 1991	580	Weak demand just as some new plant capacity planned in 1989 now comes on stream
August 1992	500	No upturn yet: continued plant closures in Canada
August 1993	390	Gloomy comments about real paper industry profit problems
December 1993	430	Was the cycle turning or was this just a blip?
August 1994	620	'Near panic' as demand from the rising US economy and from the still booming Asian economies starts to cause capacity problems
October 1994	700	Paper companies now dusting off plans for new plant
March 1995	925	Bid from Stora for PWA, Germany's major paper producer
October 1995	990	Stories begin to appear about a new technology threat: electronic media needing no newsprint
March 1996	600	Modo warns of further price falls: inventories high amongst producers

Corporate strategies to overcome pulp and paper price cyclicality

Pulp and paper companies around the world are well aware of the problems caused by cyclicality in the industry. They were constantly examining the following corporate strategy options to overcome the difficulties:

1 *Invest in new plant with greater efficiency and lower costs.* This would reduce breakeven. Importantly, it would replace existing capacity so the costs of closure and redundancy would need to be included in the estimates.

2 *Reduce transport costs by building plant closer to customers.* Local production – for example, in UK, France, Southern USA – was considered rather than selling throughout the world from Canada and Scandinavia. The higher costs from smaller plants in such countries would be offset by the lower cost of transport of the finished product.

Fletcher Challenge (New Zealand) has successfully located plant in Canada, Brazil, Chile, Australia and New Zealand itself with this strategy.

3 *Invest in higher added value production.* Fine papers, graphic papers, hygiene and tissue papers command higher prices than newsprint. They have higher added value through the need for specialist production skills, coatings and ingredients that are then reflected in higher prices. However, it should be noted that such a strategy is well known and may bring basic paper companies into competition with other buyers of paper products.

In 1989, SCA (Sweden) acquired the French company Peaudouce disposable nappies (called diapers in North America). The objective was to move into the higher added value use of paper fibres in nappies. Since that time, SCA has been involved in a highly expensive war in the European baby market with the US company, Procter & Gamble, who make Pampers, the European market leader in nappies.

Higher added value is easy to prescribe but is hardly the exclusive right of any one company. As soon as a new market becomes attractive, other companies think of the same strategy.

4 *Close plant capacity.* If closure does not work, then the next strategy might be to exit the industry, but even this strategy may have a cost in redundancy payments, etc.

5 *Export to Asia.* Throughout the period of economic problems in Europe and North America, many Asian economies continued to grow, with a resulting demand for newsprint.

6 *Invest in plant to recycle newsprint.* It is estimated that around 50 per cent of paper from newspapers was recovered in 1994. By the year 2000, it is likely that environmental legislation will require this to rise to 65 per cent of all newsprint. New, specialised plant is better at recycling than some existing machinery.

7 *Exit the industry.* If it was no longer possible to generate real profits from the industry without massive investment, then some companies chose to exit the industry (*see* Table 4.8).

In order to survive and prosper in the European packaging industry, it is the larger companies that have on balance been the most successful. Their corporate strategies have been derived from their larger relative size so they have been able to:

● invest in new, lower cost means of manufacture;

● develop new technologies;

● create new products;

● set up new means of marketing and distribution.

In practice, this has also meant that over the period 1980 to 1995 those companies that have not had the resources or willingness to grow have had to exit the industry (*see* Tables 4.8 and 4.9).

Economies of scale have been only one element of corporate strategy in the European packaging industry, however. It has also involved the following areas of strategy:

● *Market strength.* In terms of brand share and geographic coverage, market dominance may be crucial to controlling the market.

Table 4.8 Exit strategies in the European packaging industry 1980–95

BSN (F)	Left glass except for bottles in 1979
BAT (UK)	Broken up: sold as Wiggins Teape in 1990: now Arjo Wiggins Teape
Feldmuehle (G)	Sold to Stora
DRG Group (UK)	Broken up: sold to US holding company in 1989
Reed Elsevier (UK/Neth)	Sold Reedpack to concentrate on publishing in 1989
St Gobain (F)	Left paper and packaging in 1994 (but strengthened glass interests)

Table 4.9 Growth strategies in the European packaging industry 1980–95

	Company acquired	Year	Cost (US$ million)
Wiggins Teape (UK)	Arjomari (F)	1990	966
St Gobain (F)	Oberland Glass (G)	1991	n/a
Stora (Sweden)	Feldmuehle (G)	1990	2560
Svenska Cellulosa (Swe)	Reedpack (UK)	1989	1832
	Peaudouce (F)	1988	350
	Launkirchen (A)	1988	350
	Otor (F)	1994	540
	PWA (G): 60% share	1995	745
Modo (Swe)	Alicel (F)	1991	257
Pilkington (UK)	Italiano Vetro (I)	1994	135
Jefferson Smurfit (Ire)	Cellulose du Pin (F)	1994	1038

- *Distribution strength*. It is not enough to have good products; they need to be distributed to customers.

- *High R&D investment*. Innovation in the face of products that are basically similar or the need to reduce costs is important.

- *Move to higher added-value products*. Too many products have had little added value and have thus been strategically weak.

However, corporate strategy does not end with the identification of these major issues. To achieve the cost savings resulting from the acquisitions, it is necessary to make substantial changes in the companies acquired. Rationalisation is vital if the savings are to be made and new products are to be introduced. This may well mean for the employees: change, uncertainty, retraining and possible redundancy. For the company, it may mean that its culture will need to change.

CASE QUESTIONS

1 *Which of the possible strategies in the industry were followed by Stora?*

2 *In which strategic areas will it be important to gain government involvement? How would you approach this task?*

3 *Most pulp and paper companies are strong in regions of the world. Is there a case for developing a global strategy? What elements might it contain?*

Continuing low growth[30]

Dr Kenichi Ohmae was formerly the head of the Japanese division of the well-known management consultants, McKinsey. In this extract from his book, **The Mind of the Strategist,** *he comments on the strategic implications of low growth markets.*

It is not news that low economic growth is likely to continue. But not enough has been said in practical terms about the concrete changes in business activities that conditions of prolonged low growth require. We hear plenty of fine generalizations about new perspectives, but they do not often result in concrete, practical proposals.

Possibly the most alarming effect of low growth is the way it drastically limits the margin of error in managers' decisions and narrows the leeway within which mistakes in judgement can be accommodated. Over-optimism and other judgemental errors that frequently may escape serious penalty in times of prosperity may turn out to be catastrophically costly in a period of economic stagnation. This is why, directly after the 1973 oil crisis, some companies wisely conducted an urgent across-the-board examination of all the important managerial decisions they had taken over the previous ten years. The object: to screen out those which were no longer appropriate from those which were still valid in the new situation and then to make the corrections necessary to keep the company on course.

During a period of rapid economic growth, it is clearly important to be investing, even though it may not be clear how much investment is appropriate. Over-investment is not a very serious worry, since the excess is likely to be absorbed in a year or two by the growth of the market. If the investment should prove insufficient, additional sums can be injected right away. Thus there is considerable room for errors of judgement.

By contrast, continuing low growth amplifies the painful consequences of strategic mistakes. Suddenly the market no longer forgives errors of judgement. This is why companies in which an ingrained scepticism toward accepted assumptions, the habit of analysis, and the practice of strategic thinking have become a way of life are the companies that seem to prosper so remarkably in bad times as well as good.

In growing markets, a basic principle is that a company should try to increase its market share by investing in advance of market growth, accepting the increased risk for the sake of building its sales faster than the growth of the market. If all its competitors are participating to some extent in the growth of the market, a disproportionate gain in share by one company is a great deal less likely to provoke a backlash from the others.

When market growth slows down or stops, however – in other words when a market reaches maturity – market shares more often than not become fixed, and competition approaches a condition of stalemate. In a stalemated market, where the market-share pattern has become rigid, customers' expectations and ideas about particular products tend to become rigid as well so that it becomes hard to stimulate additional new demand. Any change, in fact, becomes difficult and costly.

When a company takes various strategic steps to acquire a share of a mature product market, it often finds that the required investment far exceeds the gain. Experience has repeatedly shown that such moves as price reductions, advertising and development of new products undertaken in this situation can almost always put profitability at risk.

Even maintaining a company's existing share may be expensive in a stalemated market. Usually a gradual widening takes place in the gap between companies with large shares and those with small shares. This is because the factors that enable companies to win a large share during the period of growth – a vigorous investment in production facilities, expansion of sales networks, and introduction of new or improved products – often continue to operate as important management assets even after the emphasis of the strategy may have shifted from taking an aggressive approach to maintaining the company's present position. This is particularly noticeable in markets in which competition is centred on a single main product such as beer, tyres, cars or motorcycles.

Source: Ohmae, K (1983) *The Mind of the Strategist*, © Copyright The McGraw-Hill Companies, Inc 1983. Reproduced with permission of McGraw-Hill, Inc.

SUMMARY

● In any market analysis, three key areas for investigation can be identified: growth characteristics, government influence and global trends.

● *Growth characteristics* can be explored using the industry life cycle concept. Markets are divided into a series of development stages: introduction, growth, maturity and decline. In addition, the maturity stage may be subject to the cyclical variations associated with general economic or other factors over which the company has little control.

● Different stages of the life cycle demand different corporate strategies. The early stages probably require greater investment in R&D and marketing to develop and explain the product. The later stages should be more profitable on a conventional view of the life cycle. However, there is an argument that takes a more unconventional stance: it suggests that it is during the mature phase that investment should increase in order to restore growth.

● *The role of government* can be seen through its involvement in both political and economic issues. Politics has been an important driver of industrial growth. Corporate strategy needs to consider the opportunities and difficulties that derive from such government influences. Government policies can be broadly classified as *laissez-faire*, free-market or *dirigiste*, more centrally directed. More specifically, policies on such matters as public expenditure, competition and taxation will all influence organisations and their corporate strategies. Organisations may wish to develop links and influence government policy on relevant aspects of corporate strategy.

● Government policies also influence national economic growth and may affect the market growth of particular sectors. Both these areas need careful study when developing strategy.

● Over the last ten years, *global trade* has increased faster than manufacturing output: countries are trading more with each other. It has come to represent a significant factor in corporate strategy.

● Theories of international trade provide a framework within which to develop corporate strategy. The role of government in providing economic stability and sound infrastructure development has been emphasised. To stimulate growth, governments also need to encourage an increasingly competitive home market with low barriers to international trade. Corporate strategy needs to identify the relevant trends in its own product groups.

● In developing international corporate strategy, one of the main issues is the relationship of the state with companies. State support and encouragement may be both beneficial and problematical for individual companies. In international markets, companies may also wish to develop relationships with governments as part of the development of corporate strategy.

QUESTIONS

1 Using the data on market growth in Table 4.10 and the industry life cycle as a guide, undertake an analysis of the European pulp and paper industry and identify the implications for corporate strategy.

Table 4.10 Demand trends for pulp and paper in Western Europe 1985–95 (Annual change (%))

	1985–90	1991	1992	1993	1994	1995
Fluff pulp	2	2	2	0	0	-1
Newsprint	6	0	3	4	6	2
SC (uncoated magazine paper)	4	-4	-3	-6	10	10
LWC (coated magazine paper)	10	4	10	3	10	5
Liquid packaging board	5	3	3	3	5	5
Folding boxboard	3	2	-1	-5	12	-1
Sack paper	-2	-3	-4	-4	2	0
Kraft paper	3	5	5	3	6	2
Coated fine papers	12	7	10	6	16	-4
Uncoated fine papers	5	4	5	3	12	-8

Source: Stora

2 What are the strategic implications of industry cyclicality? Does it make any difference if such implications are treated from a prescriptive or emergent perspective?

3 Professors J Stopford and C Baden-Fuller commented: '*It is the firm that matters, not the industry. Successful businesses ride the waves of industry misfortunes; less successful businesses are sunk by them.*' Explain this statement and comment on its implications for corporate strategy.

4 Outline for your own country the relationship between politics and corporate strategy. Do you think it is acceptable for companies to try to influence governments favourably on corporate strategy issues? Give examples to illustrate your points.

5 You are managing a Scandinavian pulp and paper company and seeking expansion in South-East Asia. What political and economic considerations would you wish to consider in drawing up your corporate strategy?

6 Taking a market with which you are familiar, explain how the *government* has influenced corporate strategy in that industry, both directly and in a general way. How has the European Union or another *trade block* influenced such strategy? Have these influences been beneficial or otherwise, in your opinion?

7 If you were reviewing the possibility of expanding your company into a new country, what areas of corporate strategy would you explore in relation to that country? Why?

8 'World trade has increased faster than manufacturing output.' Discuss the implications of this statement for corporate strategy. In particular, explain the relationships with the theories of international trade explored in this chapter.

9 Taking a foreign country with which you are familiar, what strategic lessons would you wish to draw about the entry of new companies? How would you structure your analysis in terms of the data you would seek and the areas you would investigate?

STRATEGIC PROJECT

International pulp and paper strategy

Explore further the pulp and paper industry examined in some depth in this chapter. For example, why did UPM/Kymmene combine together? How are North American companies now making major inroads into European markets? What strategy has been followed by SCA (Sweden) and how has it come up against a major US multinational determined to take market leadership?

FURTHER READING

Industry life cycle issues Michael Baker's *Marketing Strategy and Management* (2nd edn, Macmillan, London 1992) (Chapter 5) has a general review. Peter McKiernan's *Strategies for growth* (Routledge, London, 1992) has an extensive and thoughtful discussion on mature market strategies. Charles Baden-Fuller and John Stopford's *Rejuvenating the mature business* (Routledge, London, 1992) has the provocative views referred to in the chapter.

Government issues Few books discuss politics and corporate strategy. Paul Kennedy's *The rise and fall of the great powers* (Fontana, London, 1992) is recommended. The *World Bank Report 1994* (*see* below) also has some useful views. *See also* Yves Doz (1986) *Strategic Management in Multinational Companies,* Pergamon.

Global issues The *World Bank Report 1994* (Oxford University Press, New York) has an excellent and thoughtful commentary on development issues. The *Industry and Development Global Report 1993–94* by the United Nations Industrial Development Organisation, Vienna has some interesting comments on the shift in the involvement of governments. A book that will help on the theories: Alan Rugman and Richard Hodgetts' *International Business* (McGraw-Hill, New York, 1995). A book that will help on the trends and the strategic implications: John Ellis and David Williams' *International Business Strategy* (Pitman Publishing, London, 1995). Two books that will help on globalisation: John Dunning's *The globalisation of business* (Routledge, London, 1993) and Michael Porter's (ed) *Competition in global industries* (Harvard Business School Press, Mass, 1986).

REFERENCES

1 Porter, M E (1980) *Competitive Strategy*, The Free Press, Harvard, Mass, Ch 8.

2 Aaker, D (1992) *Strategic Marketing Management*, 3rd edn, Wiley, p236.

3 *See STORA Annual Report 1995* which has an excellent summary of the industry statistics.

4 Smallwood, J E (1973) 'The Product Life Cycle: A Key to Strategic Marketing Planning', *MSU Business Topics*, Winter, pp29–35.

5 Baker, M (1993) *Marketing Strategy and Management*, 2nd edn, Macmillan, p100 *et seq* presents a stout defence and interesting discussion of the main areas.

6 Dallah, N K and Yuspeh, S (1976) 'Forget the product life cycle concept!', *Harvard Business Review*, Jan–Feb, p101 *et seq.*

7 Baden-Fuller, C and Stopford, J (1992) *Rejuvenating the Mature Business*, Routledge, Ch 2.

8 Rumelt, R (1991) 'How much does industry matter?' *Strategic Management Journal*, Mar, pp167–86.

9 Arguably, their reasoning is unclear in that they categorise a whole industry while drawing the conclusion that it is the company that matters.

10 Kennedy, P (1990) *The Rise and Fall of the Great Powers*, Fontana Press, London, pxvii.

11 Pryce-Jones, D (1995) *The war that never was*, Wiedenfeld and Nicholson, London.

12 World Bank (1994) *World Development Report 1994*, Oxford University Press, New York. Chapter 2 certainly supported selective state support and policies.

13 Quoted by Ginter, P and Duncan, J (1990) 'Macroenvironmental Analysis', *Long Range Planning*, Pergamon, Oxford.

14 This case was adapted by Richard Lynch from an article by Mark Ashurst in the South African Supplement of the *Financial Times*, 28 Mar 1996. © Copyright *Financial Times* 1996. Reproduced with permission.

15 United Nations Industrial Development Organisation (UNIDO) (1993) *Industry and Development Global Report 1993/94*, Vienna, p81. Interesting and thoughtful material with additional references useful for essays and assignments.

16 Williams, F (1995) 'World Trade rise sharpest for 20 years', *Financial Times*, 4 Apr, p3.

17 UNIDO (1993) Ibid, pp88 and 89.

18 *See Financial Times*, 16 Dec 1993 for an excellent summary of the Uruguay Round deal that had been negotiated over many months.

19 Kennedy, P (1992) *The Rise and Fall of the Great Powers*, Fontana Press, London, Ch 7.

20 *See Lynch, R (1992) *European Marketing*, Kogan Page, for an extended description of all these areas.

21 Woolf, M (1993) 'Doing good despite themselves', *Financial Times*, 16 Dec, p19.

22 UNIDO (1993) Ibid, p81.

23 UNIDO (1993) Ibid, p82.

24 UNIDO (1993) Ibid, p83.

25 UNIDO (1993) Ibid, p81.

26 Wagstyl, S (1994) 'The mending of India's Backbone', *Financial Times*, 9 Dec, p17.

27 *See* for example, Lynch, R (1992) *European Marketing*, Kogan Page, London, Ch 5.

28 Baxter, A (1994) 'British Steel sees future in the east', *Financial Times*, 21 June, p22.

29 *Financial Times* (1993), 1 Dec, p49.

30 Extracted from Ohmae, K (1983) *The Mind of the Strategist*, Penguin, Harmondsworth, pp166–7. © Copyright McGraw-Hill.

5

Analysing competitors

When you have worked through this chapter, you will be able to:

- understand the importance of sustainable competitive advantage;

- explore the intensity of competition and assess its strategic implications;

- outline the range of aggressive activities undertaken by competitors and assess their strategic significance;

- undertake a strategic group analysis;

- analyse individual competitors and their influence on strategy;

- explore and assess the importance of distributors.

■ INTRODUCTION

A corporate strategy will only succeed in a competitive market place, if it is based on a thorough analysis of the organisation's competitors. Any such analysis can usefully begin with a general consideration of the advantages that competitors have in the market place. The intensity of competition and the aggressive strategies that may be employed should then be reviewed in detail.

In addition to these general considerations, it is important to examine three inter-related areas that may affect the *specific* immediate competitive environment of the organisation: strategic groups (that is, close competitors that can usefully be grouped together), individual competitors and distributors. Competitor analysis is summarised in Fig 5.1.

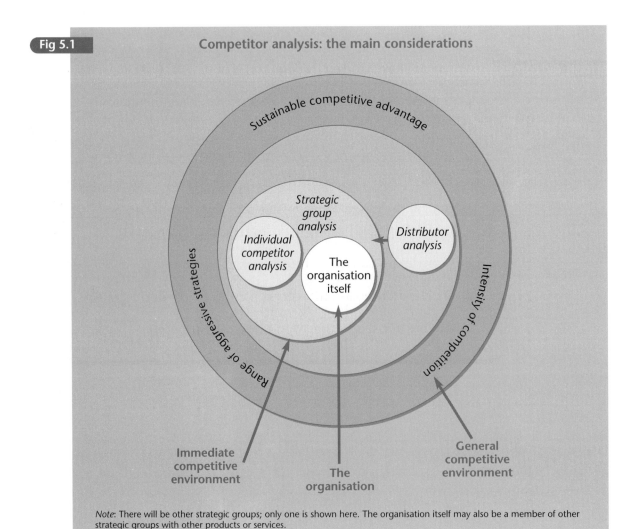

Fig 5.1 — Competitor analysis: the main considerations

Note: There will be other strategic groups; only one is shown here. The organisation itself may also be a member of other strategic groups with other products or services.

Unilever Ice Cream defends its European market share[1]

With around 40 per cent of the European ice cream market involving sales of US$2.3 billion, Unilever has much to defend. The company operates across Europe not under the name of Unilever but using a series of operating companies that employ strategies which combine both pan-European and national activities.

Unilever has been involved in the European ice cream market for many years, but during the 1980s and 1990s has faced an increasing threat as its main competitor, Nestlé, began to realise the profitability of ice cream and started acquiring ice cream companies across Europe. Major competition also came from another formidable challenger, Mars, who introduced new innovations into the ice cream market by using its well-known branded confectionery products and finding ways of freezing them in the late 1980s – for example, Mars Ice Cream. By the mid-1990s, Nestlé had followed with Kit Kat Ice Cream. Branded ice cream strategy involved heavy advertising, strong product innovation and major drives to secure distribution in retail freezer cabinets.

Unilever's strengths lie in its dominance of the market. It has traditional, well-known brand names. As a result of its long history and extensive resources in many European countries, Unilever can implement a strategy at both a pan-European level and a national level:

● In the 1980s and 1990s, Unilever successfully adopted a new strategy of developing *pan-European* product categories – in terms of overall name, pack design and basic formulation – ranging from premium speciality ice creams, like Magnum, to family packs, such as Carte d'Or.

● At the same time each of Unilever's operating companies has a *national* name (*see* Table 5.1) and each company adds to its range some national products that are targeted at customers in that market alone. This strategy builds on nationally known brand names that would be too costly to extend to other countries (such as Miko in France) and takes account of national taste and price variations that still exist in food products across Europe.

Over the years, the company has developed strong distribution links with retailers, especially the smaller outlets that can only take one freezer cabinet (which in many cases Unilever has supplied free of charge). The large brand share has also led to economies of scale that newer entrants cannot match, preventing them from achieving the same low-cost structure.

Table 5.1 Unilever's operations in the European ice cream market

Country	Main Unilever company	Unilever market share	Competing companies
Germany	Langnese–Iglo	40% (60% of impulse market)	Schoeller Mars Dr Oetker
France	Cogesal Ortiz-Miko (see text)	45%	Gervais/Nestlé Mars Pilpa
Italy	Algida/Findus	40%	Italgel/Nestlé Mars Sammontana
Netherlands/Belgium	Iglo-Ola	30%	Schoeller Mars Isboerke Artic
Ireland	HB Ice Cream	60%	Nestlé
UK	Birds Eye/Walls	40%	Nestlé/ Lyons Maid Mars Treats

Probably Unilever's greatest weakness is that the group has no involvement in the confectionery market, unlike Nestlé and Mars. Unilever has thus had difficulty in responding to the 1990s' trend to employ confectionery brands in ice cream. (Mars and Nestlé activities in this area will be explored in Case studies 5.4 and 5.5.) Unilever has thus had to make arrangements with national chocolate manufacturers – for example, its UK deal with Cadbury to reproduce Cadbury's Dairy Milk Chocolate in an ice cream as CDM. CDM is largely a national UK brand and cannot be easily presented on a pan-European scale.

CASE QUESTIONS

1   What is the source of Unilever's advantages over its competitors?

2   What are Unilever's main strengths? Where do its weaknesses lie? What, if anything, would you do about its weaknesses?

3   Should Unilever go further in launching truly pan-European products, like those associated with Mars Ice Cream and Nestlé Kit Kat Ice Cream? How important, if at all, are such products to the overall Unilever strategy?

5.1 SUSTAINABLE COMPETITIVE ADVANTAGE

5.1.1 The importance of sustainable competitive advantage

The main reason for analysing competitors is to enable the organisation to develop *competitive advantages* against them, especially advantages that can be *sustained* over time. Sustainable competitive advantage (SCA) involves every aspect of the way that the organisation competes in the market place – prices, product range, manufacturing quality, service levels and so on. However, some of these factors can easily be imitated: for example, prices can be changed virtually overnight or other companies can make ice cream just like Unilever.

The real benefits come from advantages that competitors cannot easily imitate, not those that give only temporary relief from the competitive battle. To be *sustainable*, competitive advantage needs to be more deeply embedded in the organisation – its resources, skills, culture and investment over time. Unilever's advantages in ice cream come from its brand investment, its well developed distribution service and its sheer size in the market place, which should deliver economies of scale.

More generally, the development of sustainable advantage can take many forms. Such activities may possibly involve seeking something *unique* and *different* from competition, and so it follows that there will be a wide range of possibilities. Table 5.2 presents some possible sources of advantage for certain industries.

Table 5.2 Some possible sustainable competitive advantages in different areas of business

High technology	Services	Small business	Manufacturing market leader
● Technical excellence	● Reputation for quality of service	● Quality	● Low costs
● Reputation for quality	● High quality and training of staff	● Prompt service	● Strong branding
● Customer service	● Customer service	● Personalised service	● Good distribution
● Financial resources	● Well-known name	● Keen prices	● Quality product
● Low-cost manufacturing	● Customer-oriented	● Local availability	● Good value for money

Sources: see[2]

For many strategists, the development of sustainable competitive advantage lies at the core of corporate strategy development. Professor Michael Porter wrote persuasively about its importance in the 1980s in two classic strategy texts – *Competitive Strategy* (1980)[3] and *Competitive Advantage* (1985)[4] – which have influenced both academic and industry developments. For example, Stephen South, Corporate Planning Director at Clark Equipment (USA) commented:

'The process of strategic management is coming to be defined, in fact, as the management of competitive advantage – that is, a process of identifying, developing and taking advantage of enclaves in which tangible and preservable business advantage can be achieved.'[5]

There are other aspects to the development of corporate strategy – for example those associated with the strategy process and the purpose of an organisation (*see* Chapters 8 and 12) – and so the statement may over-emphasise the importance of competitive advantage. Nevertheless, it is a vital aspect of corporate strategy development.

5.1.2 Public service and not-for-profit organisations

Most businesses face competitors, so the need for a sustainable advantage to help them compete is evident. It is more questionable, however, whether public service and not-for-profit organisations need sustainable competitive advantages. In one sense, they may not because their services are often provided free to the consumer and without competition – for example, police services, hospitals, charitable institutions and so on.

However, many public services and charities depend for financial support either on government funds or private donations. Such support is usually not unlimited, and so in this sense such organisations *compete for finance* from potential providers. Developing arguments and evidence to maintain and enhance the funds distributed will be important. Such organisations could usefully consider the decisions that have to be made by the fund providers and the *incremental advantages* that their service provides to the general public and which therefore justify extra funding.

5.1.3 Prescriptive and emergent approaches to sustainable advantage

By definition, if an advantage is to be sustainable, then it cannot be quickly copied by others. It is likely that it will have taken some time, possibly years, for the organisation to have developed the advantage. A prescriptive approach, requiring a sustained period of development, is therefore likely to be required in principle at least. For example, it takes some years to develop and establish a new branded product such as Mars Ice Cream.

Emergent approaches are not excluded, however. The development of sustainable competitive advantage may well require a degree of experimentation along with adjustments based on the developments by competitors. For example, the introduction of super-premium ice creams, such as Häagen-Dazs, will benefit from experimenting with new forms of distribution – such as the supply of freezer cabinets in pizza restaurants – in order to overcome the hold that the traditional ice cream suppliers have on more familiar outlets.

Hence, the development of SCA will probably require elements of both prescriptive and emergent strategic approaches.

5.1.4 Developing sources of sustainable competitive advantage

In seeking the advantages that competitors cannot easily copy, it is necessary to not only examine the competitors, but also the organisation itself and its resources.

Resources are explored in depth in Part 3 of this book, but it is appropriate here to identify some possible sources of advantage as a starting point for later study.

- *Differentiation.* This is the development of unique features or attributes in a product or service that position it to appeal especially to a part of the total market. Branding is an example of this source.

- *Low costs.* The development of low-cost production enables the firm to compete against other companies either on the basis of lower prices or possibly on the basis of the same prices as its competitors but with more services being added. For example, production in some South-East Asian countries may involve lower labour costs that cannot be matched in the West.[6]

- *Niche marketing.* A company may select a small market segment and concentrate all its efforts on achieving advantages in this segment. Such a niche will need to be distinguished by special buyer needs. Fashion items such as Yves St Laurent or Dunhill are examples of products that are especially targeted towards specialist niches.

- *High performance or technology.* Special levels of performance or service can be developed that simply cannot be matched by other companies – for example through patented products or recruitment of especially talented individuals. The well-known global consulting companies and merchant banks operate in this way.

- *Quality.* Some companies offer a level of quality that others are unable to match. For example, some Japanese cars have until recently provided levels of reliability that western companies have had difficulty in reaching.

- *Service.* Some companies have deliberately sought to provide superior levels of service that others have been unable or unwilling to match. For example, McDonald's set new levels of service in its fast food restaurants that were unmatched by others for many years.

- *Vertical integration.* The backward acquisition of raw material suppliers and/or the forward purchase of distributors may provide advantages that others cannot match. For example, in Chapter 4, the Stora paper company owned both forest raw materials and some of its distributors.

- *Synergy.* This is the combination of parts of a business such that the sum of them is worth more than the individual parts – that is, 2 + 2 = 5. This may occur because the parts share fixed overheads, transfer their technology or share the same salesforce, for example. Claims are often made for this approach when an acquisition is made, but this synergy is not necessarily achieved in reality. Nevertheless, it remains a valid area of exploration.

- *Culture, leadership and style of an organisation.* The way that an organisation leads, trains and supports its members may be a source of advantage that others cannot match. It will lead to innovative products, exceptional levels of service, fast responses to new market developments and so on. This area is more difficult to quantify than some of the other areas above, but this only adds to its unique appeal. It is unusual to find such an area listed in strategy texts, but it is a theme of this book.

Some organisations and strategists have become almost obsessed with the first three of these sources – Porter's *generic strategies*, as they are often described – and these are discussed under this heading in Chapter 13. This is completely misleading, however, as Professor Porter's books explore all the above areas and more in considerable detail.

It could also be argued that several of the sources in the list involve some form of differentiation. To group these all under differentiation, however, would be to ignore the *specific nature* of the form of advantage and to deny the important individual areas of strategy opened up by such concepts.

More generally, Professor John Kay, the British strategy writer still linked with the London Business School, has argued that competitive advantage is more generally based on the *stability* and *continuity* in relationships between different parts of an organisation.[7] He argues that major advantages are not developed overnight or by some special acquisition or other miraculous strategy. Substantial advantages take many years to develop and involve the whole culture and style of an organisation. To this extent, it may even be misleading to see advantages as being summarised by the short list of items above. However, this does provide a starting point for further analysis.

Ultimately, there is no single route to achieving sustainable competitive advantage. The question that arises is therefore whether it is possible to test whether it has been achieved. Three possible tests for such advantages are shown in Exhibit 5.1.

Exhibit 5.1　　　　　　Three tests for sustainable competitive advantage

The advantage should be:

- *Sufficiently significant to make a difference.* Modest advantages that hold no real benefits to the customer or the organisation are unlikely to be persuasive.

- *Sustainable against environmental change and competitor attack.* The market as a whole may move forward in terms of technology or tastes. Equally, competitors may be able to copy advantages developed by the organisation. In both cases, these advantages are not sustainable.

- *Recognisable and linked to customer benefits.* An advantage needs to be translated from a functional advantage inside the organisation – for example, low costs – into something that the customer will value – for example, low prices. Advantages that cannot be linked in this way may ultimately prove to have no persuasive and competitive edge.

Key strategic principles

- One of the main purposes of analysing competitors is to explore where and how sustainable competitive advantage (SCA) can be generated. The search for SCA will be wide and deep within the organisation.

- Public service and not-for-profit organisations may also wish to explore SCA as they may be in competition for finance from external bodies, such as the government, even if there is no competition for customers.

- SCA will probably require elements of both emergent and prescriptive strategy approaches to strategy development.

- There are numerous sources of SCA. These include: differentiation, low costs, niche marketing, high performance or technology, quality, service, vertical integration, synergy and the culture, leadership and style of the organisation. Importantly, SCA develops slowly over time, such a list is only the starting point of a more detailed study.

5.2 THE INTENSITY OF COMPETITION IN AN INDUSTRY

It is useful to start any analysis of competition with Porter's *Five Forces analysis* (*see* Chapter 3). This will provide a basic starting point in any development of the major factors driving the dynamics of the industry.

In addition to such an analysis, it is possible to examine two further areas:

- *the degree of concentration of companies in a market* – examined here; and

- *the range of aggressive strategies of competitors in the market.* (*See* Section 5.3).

In microeconomic theory, the degree of concentration of companies in a market can be seen as being somewhere between two extremes, each of which will have strategic consequences for companies:

- perfect competition

- pure monopoly

In *perfect competition*, there are numerous buyers and sellers with no single firm able to influence market prices: it is assumed that products are identical in every respect and that the firm accepts the price set by the market. The perfectly competitive firm sets its level of production output to maximise profits. From a strategic viewpoint, this leaves the firm at the mercy of market pressures and is therefore undesirable. It would be much better strategy for the firm to *differentiate* its product, dominate a sector of the market and thus influence that sector's market price – in other words, to gain sustainable competitive advantage.

At the other extreme to perfect competition, there exists the state of *pure monopoly*. In this case, there is no competition and the company has total control over its prices; it erects barriers to entry and maximises profits and value added. It does this at the expense of its customers, but from a corporate strategy viewpoint, it might be argued that the corporation has no responsibility to such customers and should seek to maximise profit and value added regardless of their views: strategies would therefore include raising prices to the maximum that the market will bear and setting output accordingly.

In practice for many companies, the environment is neither one of perfect competition nor one of pure monopoly. Corporate strategy needs to deal with a wide range of industrial structures in the middle. For some industries where there are economies of scale, it may actually be more efficient for the state and more profitable for individual companies to have a few large companies in an industry – that is, *an oligopoly*. Corporate strategy in such industries will therefore be directed towards obtaining and sustaining the oligopoly, if this is possible.

Some of the strategic implications of these different types of industry structure are explored in Case studies 5.1 to 5.3, using examples from European Union markets. Industry structure and market characteristics have a significant impact on corporate strategy. However, the actions that companies take go well beyond the pricing activity often highlighted in microeconomic theory – for example, cost reduction, product differentiation, linkages with other companies through alliances and joint ventures. In the chapters that follow, these areas will be explored further.

The *concentration ratio* is often used to measure the degree to which value added or turnover is concentrated in the hands of a few or a large number of firms in an industry. It is usually defined as the percentage of industry value added or turnover controlled by the largest four, five or eight firms – the C4, C5 or C8 ratio respectively. Typically, C5 averages around 55 per cent in UK manufacturing industries and C4 averages around 34 per cent in US industries. After the ratio has been calculated, two areas of strategic significance can be analysed:

- The *total number of firms in an industry* may influence their ability to exert buying power over suppliers. If there are few, then buying power may increase as in the case of grocery retailers (*see* Case study 5.3); if there are many, as in case of the shoe manufacturers (*see* Case study 5.1), then their buying power will be lower.

- The *mix of firms making up the industry* will also impact on profitability. If there are a few companies that are roughly equal in size, then there may be some tacit understanding between them to allow profits to grow. As the numbers increase and there is a likelihood of some giants and some smaller companies, then there is a lower possibility of a tacit understanding so profits will suffer.

Overall, it is likely that corporate strategy will vary with company size and the degree of market competition. Smaller companies, such as small shoe manufacturers, may have to adopt different strategies from larger organisations, such as the large shoe companies that can afford to set up retail chains to sell their products. Fiercely competitive markets, such as retailing, may require different strategies from the more collaborative environment of the national telephone monopolies (*see* Case study 5.2).

This has profound significance because it suggests that corporate strategy will vary with industry; there may be no single 'corporate strategy' that will suit all industries.

The fragmented European footwear market

Within the European Union, the footwear market was worth ECU 16 billion in 1992[8] and was growing annually at around 6 per cent in monetary terms. Sports footwear was particularly strong with brand names such as Adidas (Germany), Nike (US) and Reebok (UK) offering major technical and fashion initiatives in a very price-competitive sector. Outside the few large companies, the industry structure is highly fragmented with many small businesses having no control over market prices. In 1990, there were nearly 16 000 footwear companies across the EU, each employing only 21 workers on average. Across the EU, employment fell by 15 per cent in total in the period 1983–92.

Since companies have no control over price, corporate strategies have partly been to reduce costs, especially labour costs which can form a high proportion of total costs. (This explains why employment has declined in high-wage economies such as France and Germany and has stabilised in lower-wage countries such as Spain and Portugal.) However, the trend masks even stronger cost-cutting strategies. Imports of footwear from very low-wage countries such as Indonesia, China and the Philippines have increased significantly. Larger companies such as Adidas and Puma have now transferred much of their production to the Far East in order to remain competitive. From a value-added viewpoint, low prices have meant that value has been sustained partly by cutting wage costs.

The other major corporate strategy adopted by some of the larger manufacturers has been to open up their own retail stores: Bata Organisation (based in Switzerland), Bally (Switzerland) and Salamander (Germany) are all examples of footwear companies that have moved into retailing. This has occurred because the fragmented industry has meant that the footwear manufacturers have had little bargaining power with retailers, who have always had plenty of alternative sources of supply.

CASE QUESTIONS

1   *What strategies would you be seeking, as a small shoe company, to develop sustainable competitive advantage?*

2   *How does market fragmentation affect corporate strategy for such companies?*

CASE STUDY 5.2

Monopoly in Europe's national telecommunications companies[9][10]

Europe's top telecommunications companies have operated until recently as state-owned monopolies to all intents and purposes. With the moves toward a truly single European market, however, their corporate strategies will have to be adapted to reflect their changing environment.

During the period up to 1992, most of the top European telecommunication companies were state-owned, with the exception of the two British companies – British Telecom and Cable & Wireless – which were in private hands (*see* Table 5.3). All were monopolies, except British Telecom, but even British Telecom had over 95 per cent of the market. Prices were set accordingly and reflected the ability of nationalised industries to collude with government on price setting.

During the late 1980s the situation became more complicated, however, as the European Commission and some large customers began to agitate for a single European market. The Single European Act 1986 and the Treaty of Rome both enshrine open competition in EU law. The national telecommunications companies with the support of some of their respective governments – especially France, Belgium, Italy and Spain – fought a strong rearguard action to stop open competition across Europe and maintain barriers. Early agreement was reached to free *data communications* across Europe, but since these accounted for less than 5 per cent of all telephone traffic this was something of a hollow victory. *Voice traffic* will now be opened up to free competition in 1998. In consequence, it is likely that telephone call prices will be reduced in real terms over the next few years; value added will decrease as a result.

CASE QUESTIONS

1 What strategies would you be seeking, as a monopolistic telephone company, to develop sustainable competitive advantage?

2 How might this advantage change as competition opens up across Europe?

Table 5.3 Europe's top telephone companies

	Country	Turnover (1992) (US$ m)	Return on capital
Deutsche Telekom	Germany	36 956	10.5%
France Telecom	France	23 005	N/A
British Telecom	UK	20 645	14.6%
STET	Italy	17 500	N/A
Telefonica de Espagna	Spain	11 430	10.0%
Cable & Wireless	UK	9 647	15.1%
PTT Schweiz	Switzerland	6 500 (est)	N/A
Televerket	Sweden	6 251	10.7%
PTT Nederlands	Netherlands	6 050 (est)	N/A

Note: the above sales figures exclude revenue from postal services

Oligopoly in European grocery retailing

The importance of a small number of major chains in the European grocery retailing market brings both advantages and disadvantages.

Table 5.4 Europe's top grocery retailers

Company	Country	Turnover 1992 (US$ million)
Aldi	Germany	20 204
Leclerc	France	20 100
Intermarché	France	20 089
Carrefour	France	16 081
J Sainsbury	UK	15 207
Auchan	France	15 007
Ahold	Netherlands	12 910
Tesco	UK	12 528
Casino	France	12 218
Delhaize	Belgium	10 675

Over the last 20 years, large grocery retailing chains have been set up in many European countries, giving the customer the advantages of one-stop shopping for a very wide range of goods at competitive prices. For the retailers, there have been real economies of scale from the large size of individual stores and the negotiating power that their turnover has given them with their suppliers. The environment that has resulted has not been monopoly, but rather oligopoly – a concentration of retailing into the hands of a few major retailers in each European country.

The degree of competition between the retailers has then varied by country. In those countries where price discount retailers have been strong – for example, Aldi in Germany – there has been strong price competition; in those countries where price discounters have been weaker – for example, in the UK – there have been occasional price wars but competition has not been so fierce. Profit margins have been reported as being higher in the UK than some other European countries as a result. By the mid-1990s, the price discounters were beginning to open up in the UK with retailer margins in the UK suffering as a result. Value added was beginning to decline.

CASE QUESTIONS

1 *What strategies would you be seeking, as a large grocery retailing company, to develop sustainable competitive advantage?*

2 *How does the degree of concentration in this industry influence corporate strategy?*

Key strategic principles

● Intensity of competition in an industry can be studied by examining the two extremes of perfect competition and monopoly. Corporate strategies differ under these two conditions.

● In practice, most industries follow neither of the above models. The concentration ratio can be used to measure the competitive intensity of an industry. The ratio measures the percentage of value added or turnover controlled by the largest four, five or eight firms in an industry.

● Overall, corporate strategy will vary with the size of companies and the degree of competition in the industry.

5.3 AGGRESSIVE COMPETITIVE STRATEGIES[11]

There are a whole range of aggressive strategies that competitors can undertake. These need to be analysed for two reasons:

● to understand the strategies competitors may undertake;

● to assist in planning appropriate counter-measures.

In practitioner literature and even some more academic articles in this area, the language and style is often *militaristic* in tone.[12] For example:

● 'Find a weakness in the leader's strength and attack at that point.'

● 'Strong competitive moves should always be blocked.'

Professor Porter eschews some of the more colourful language but is in no doubt about the importance of this area. Professor Philip Kotler from North Western University, USA, has developed the material in his well-known marketing text, *Marketing Management*[13] and has collaborated with Singh to write an influential article on the topic.[14] The analytical process is summarised in Fig 5.2.

5.3.1 Market intelligence

In accordance with the well-known saying, 'Knowledge is the basis of power', many companies monitor the activities of their competitors constantly. Occasionally a few

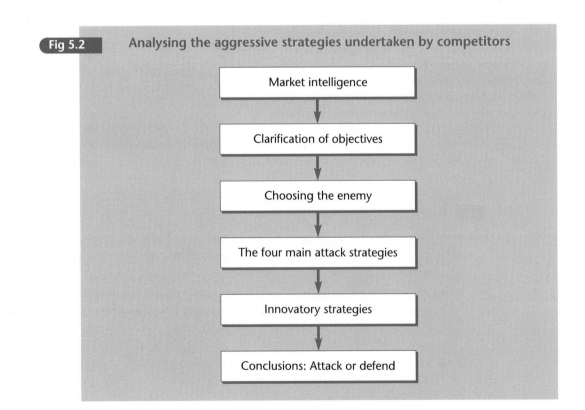

Fig 5.2   Analysing the aggressive strategies undertaken by competitors

Market intelligence

↓

Clarification of objectives

↓

Choosing the enemy

↓

The four main attack strategies

↓

Innovatory strategies

↓

Conclusions: Attack or defend

may undertake snooping or eavesdropping activities which may be illegal and are probably unethical. While not condoning such behaviour, it is entirely correct for companies to seek an understanding of their competitors' strategies. There are many entirely legitimate means for investigating this area. For example:

- company annual reports;
- newspaper articles;
- stockbroker analyses;
- exhibitions and trade fairs.

5.3.2 Clarification of the objectives of competitors

In military situations, the objective is often the total defeat of the enemy. This is rarely appropriate in corporate strategy for the following reasons:

- It may contravene monopoly legislation, certainly in the European Union, the USA and many other countries around the world.
- It often becomes increasingly costly to pursue the last remnant of share.
- A weakened opponent that is still in the market may be easier to handle than a new aggressive entrant.
- A defeated opponent may be acquired cheaply in a takeover by a new powerful entrant (*see* Spillers in Chapter 2).

Even military strategists have recognised that the objectives of war may be better served by some form of stalemate or understanding. As Captain B H Liddell-Hart[15] commented:

> The objective of war is a better state of peace, even if only from your own viewpoint.

To develop this, it is necessary to understand the competitor's objectives, especially in such areas as market share and sales. Subsequently, the organisation itself will also need to develop its own objectives.

The optimal corporate strategy may define its ideal objective as being a *new market equilibrium* – that is, one that allows all competitors a viable and stable market share accompanied by adequate profits. This may be a more profitable solution than the alternative of continuing aggression, especially if this involves a price war in which competitors outbid each other downwards in the pursuit of market share. Even under strict national competition legislation, it is often possible for companies to develop such an equilibrium.[16]

For example, in UK grocery retailing, the leading supermarkets have engaged in minor price wars but have been willing to settle for shares that allow them all to make high returns on their capital. By contrast, some other European retailing markets have been the subject of continuing aggressive price wars, especially where price discounters – such as Aldi and Netto – have become major players. The result has been that German and other retailers tend to operate with returns on capital that are below those of the UK. In this context, cut-throat competition may serve no one well: the profits of all companies are then reduced.[17]

From a strategic perspective, it is therefore important to clarify the true objectives of competitors in the industry.

5.3.3 Choosing the enemy

Not all competitors are the same: some may be immensely aggressive with large financial resources, relatively passive shareholders, long-term objectives to take market share and considerable determination. Some well-known Japanese companies provide examples here. These are not the companies to choose to fight, although it may be inevitable that the organisation will compete with them.

Equally, attacking a market leader directly is a high-risk strategy because of the strength of such a competitor, even if the payoff appears to be attractive. Military strategists state that a superiority in people and machinery of 3:1 is needed before launching an attack, if the approach is to be successful. By definition, this is highly unlikely where the market leader is involved.

For these reasons, it may be better to analyse and target competitors of more equal size. Their weaknesses might then form the basis of an aggressive move. They might even be available for takeover.

5.3.4 The four main attack strategies

In any analysis of competitors, it is important to recognise the four main strategies that they may use against each other and any new entrant. It should also be noted that these represent a *checklist of strategy options* for use in Part 5 when it comes to further development of corporate strategy (*see* Chapter 13).

Exhibit 5.2   **The four main attack strategies**

1 **Head-on against the market leader**

  ● Unless resources are sustained, the campaign is unlikely to be successful.

  ● Attack where the leader is weak.

  ● Pick a narrow front to open up the campaign.

2 **Flanking or market segmentation**

  ● Choose a flank that is relatively undefended.

  ● Aim to take a significant market share.

  ● Expect to invest in the flank for some years.

  ● Pricing and value for money are often distinguishing features of a successful flank.

3 **Occupy totally new territory, that is, where there is no existing product or service**

  ● Innovate if possible.

  ● Seek market niches.

4 **Guerrilla, that is, a rapid sortie to seize a short-term profitable opportunity**

  ● Relies on good information to identify opportunities.

  ● Fast response needed and rapid withdrawal after success.

  ● Important not to stand and fight leaders on their own ground but pick new areas.

The four main attack strategies are shown in Exhibit 5.2. These are based on three main principles:

- *the need to concentrate the attack on competition*, so that it is overwhelming at that particular point and therefore more likely to be successful;
- *the element of surprise* so that gains can be made while the competitor is still recovering (perhaps involving rewriting the rules of the game);
- *the need to consolidate the attack* by continuing to invest for some period (except in the last option which is based on rapid withdrawal and limited losses).

The principles are derived from those used in military strategy.

- They involve a reliance on brute force to achieve an objective, only when it is useful and achievable.
- They recommend concentrating such force so that it will achieve maximum effect.
- They suggest following up the use of force by longer term strategies that will secure the position permanently.

For these reasons, the head-on strategy is rarely successful.

It should be emphasised that other strategies are also possible and, for the underdog, may be crucial. They often involve some form of *innovation* in the competitive environment (*see* Section 5.3.5).

5.3.5 Innovatory strategies

There are many forms of innovation but it is useful to identify four for our purposes:

- rewriting the rules of the game
- technological innovation
- higher levels of service
- partnerships.

Rewriting the rules of the game
In competitive strategy, the existing players in the market will work according to a mutual understanding of how competitors are engaged – the rules of the game. For example, life and household insurance was sold by agents who personally advised their customers on the best product for their circumstances. All the major companies invested vast sums in recruiting and training their people to undertake this task. Ultimately, their heavy investment meant that it was in the interests of such insurance companies not to offer any alternatives. Then along came telephone insurance selling. It changed the rules of the game and sold the product without the same heavy overhead of a large salesforce, so that it was possible to offer much lower prices. The revolution is still taking place in the European insurance industry. Rewriting the rules of the game is important in corporate strategy.

Technological innovation
Especially in the case of new, smaller players, it may be essential to introduce some form of innovation in order to take market share. This does not mean that this is the only way to enter a market and survive, but in certain types of industry, it may represent a viable route.

Higher levels of service In some industries, technology may not be a dominant feature but service levels may still be important. For example, in the shoe industry, there have been technical advances but some companies have survived because they have offered high levels of personalised service and shoe design. Even in retailing, small shops have been able to survive by staying open for long hours in their local communities.

Partnerships Formal partnerships or some other form of joint activity have proved useful innovatory strategies in the 1990s. Joint ventures, alliances and other forms of co-operation have been used with success to beat larger rivals (*see* Chapter 13).

Key strategic principles

- In assessing the aggressive strategies of competitors, it is important to begin by monitoring competitive activity on a regular basis.

- Although total defeat may be appropriate as a military objective, it is rarely relevant in business. A new market equilibrium may be much more profitable, involving stable market shares, no price wars and viable levels of profitability.

- Some competitors may be naturally more aggressive than others and have more substantial resources. If it is possible to choose, then these may be the competitors to avoid.

- Choosing an enemy that can provide a successful outcome is important. Attacking the market leader is not usually wise.

- The four main attack strategies are: head-on, flanking, occupy totally new territory and guerrilla.

- Innovatory strategies may prove particularly significant, especially for the underdog. These include rewriting the rules of the game, technological innovation, higher levels of service and partnerships. (*See* further Chapter 11.)

5.3.6 Conclusions: attack or defend

In a static market, every company that identifies a market opportunity will present another company with a market problem. Attack strategies therefore invite defensive responses, but they are two sides of the same coin and need to be treated as such in corporate strategy.

The analysis of the range of aggressive strategies open to competitors is a useful starting point in the development of corporate strategy. However, Kay[18] has urged caution in the use of military analogies for two reasons:

1 *It may exaggerate the importance of size and scale.* The use of brute force is supported by the financial resources and market share that can be brought to bear. Kay points out that business success comes from *distinctive capabilities* rather than destroying the enemy. It is therefore important to recognise size and scale as useful but not conclusive devices in strategic terms.

2 *It invites excessive emphasis on leadership, vision and attack.* The generals plotting the strategy are the primary engines for successful military strategy. He also points out that many successful companies rely on *teams*, rather than charismatic leaders – a theme that will be explored throughout this book.

In many respects, it is the *prescriptive* view of strategy that is best served by concepts of aggressive attack with plans that are carefully drawn up in advance. The more adaptive approach of *emergent* strategy does not lend itself so readily to such recipes, although the militarists would no doubt recognise the need for adaptation as the battle proceeds.

5.4 STRATEGIC GROUPS WITHIN AN INDUSTRY

Having examined the forces acting throughout an industry, the next analytical stage is to explore in more detail the competitive forces acting within parts of an industry – *the analysis of strategic groups*. This is particularly useful because the Five Forces Model undertakes only a general analysis of competitors.

Porter[19] has suggested that most industries contain *strategic groups* of close competitors – groups of firms within an industry that follow the same strategies or ones that have very similar dimensions. For example, similar strategies might include the targeting of the same market segments, the use of identical or similar technology and the employment of the same specialist distributors.

Importantly, some groups are more attractive than others: their profitability may be higher, the competition less intense, the market trends may favour them. For example, in the European ice cream market in the mid-1990s, arguably the super-premium sector with its high profit margins and growth was more attractive than the economy sector. According to McGee and Segal-Horn,[20] the key to strategic groups is the *mobility barrier* – the barrier that stops other firms entering and inhibits existing members of the group from threatening each other. As a result, some groups may be able to protect their group interests better than others and some groups may have more aggressive strategies that make competition fierce for other members. The analytical process for strategic groups is shown in Exhibit 5.3.

Exhibit 5.3　　　　　**The analytical process for strategic groups**

1　Identify the competitive characteristics that specify strategic groups: for example, geographic coverage, product range, product quality, price ranges such as high/medium/low, common customers, etc.

2　Identify the leading pairs of independent variables associated with 1 above.

3　Plot the pairs as a matrix or as a two-variable map.

4　Assess which competitors should be grouped together using the two variables. Alternatively, identify competitors but leave them as individual companies.

5　Plot the groups or individual competitors as positions on the map.

6　Draw circles centred at the group or competitor with the radius or area representing turnover for the competitor or group.

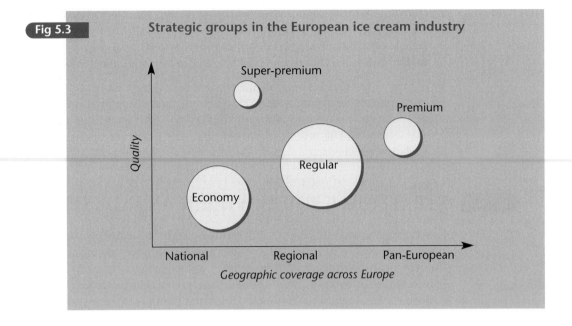

Fig 5.3 **Strategic groups in the European ice cream industry**

Figure 5.3 shows how strategic groups can be constructed for the European ice cream industry. They are based on the segment analysis of the European ice cream market described in Chapter 6 and the geographic coverage that each product had across Europe in 1995. Other dimensions could also have been plotted but these illustrate some useful strategic issues such as the small size of the super-premium segment.

Strategic groups have another important use in strategic analysis: they can be used to identify current gaps in an industry that represent a strategic market opportunity – a concept often called *strategic space*. This has been explored by McGee and Segal-Horn[21] and is consistent with the Hamel and Prahalad discussion of 'white space' which we will explore in Chapter 13.

By exploiting industry segments, the analysis of strategic groups is a useful extension of the Five Forces Model, in that it develops the competitive analysis further. It also helps to identify the gaps that might exist in markets and highlights the barriers that need to be analysed to defend the group. There are two problems, however:

- Such an analysis often requires a leap of imagination to arrive at the 'correct' two dimensions.

- This type of grouping is not always relevant to industries: for example, where *every* firm is separated or some are really *distinctive* in themselves.

Key strategic principles

● Most industries contain strategic groups of close competitors – groups of firms within an industry that follow the same strategies or ones that have very similar dimensions.

● Some groups are more attractive than others: their profitability may be higher, the competition less intense, the market trends may favour them.

● The key to strategic groups is the mobility barrier that stops other firms entering and inhibits members of the group from threatening each other.

● Strategic space is a system for identifying where there are gaps in the market that might be filled. However, it has the weakness that it is necessary to find the 'correct' two dimensions that will detect such a space.

5.5 INDIVIDUAL COMPETITOR ANALYSIS

During the 1980s, great emphasis was laid on the development of competitive strategy. Although, more recently, the focus has shifted to customer strategy and the organisation's resources, competitors are still important. Competition has probably increased in many areas over the last ten years. For example:

● Further markets have been privatised in many countries around the world – for example in Europe, the Far East and South America.

● Much of Eastern Europe has been opened up to market pressures.

● Global trade barriers have been reduced and global companies have become more powerful.

As a result of such changes, competitor analysis has become more complex. The danger is that any analysis is either reduced to long, but largely meaningless, lists of possible factors or, alternatively, to intelligent but over-complex interactions that are strong on analysis but weak on useful conclusions. The starting point for resolving this is to return to the purpose of competitor analysis – *to identify the sustainable competitive advantages*, especially those that Rumelt[22] described as most telling, enduring and most difficult to duplicate.

Competitive analysis will seek to explore the *differences* between the organisation and its competitors. In particular, it will search for those differences that provide real, long-term advantages in the market place and that impact in a significant way on profits. For example, one of the problems that Unilever faces in the European ice cream market is that all ice creams are similar to one another. The differences between Unilever and its competitors lie in branding, distribution contracts and the economies of manufacturing and distribution scale that are available to a company with a dominant market share. Its competitive advantage lies in its long-established brands, its factory and distribution networks and its distribution contracts. These are so substantial that competitors have found it difficult to enter the market; its rival, Nestlé, has done so by acquiring competing production companies and rival distribution agreements (*see* Case study 5.5).

In competitive analysis, one of the early questions that arises is the *choice of competitor* for analysis. In highly concentrated industries, such as the aerospace and defence markets, this is not an issue. In fragmented industries, such as machine tools or European ice cream, however, it can be a problem. For example, there are several thousand ice cream manufacturers across Europe alone: do we analyse them all? Some commentators[23] suggest grouping competitors together and using the *strategic groups* method described in Section 5.4. Another method is to select the industry leader (for example, Unilever) and a couple of other companies of roughly comparable size to the organisation against which the comparison is being made (for example, Nestlé and Mars) plus possibly one or two new entrants that raise interesting strategic issues (for example, Grand Met/Häagen-Dazs).

Competitor analysis then needs to examine five key areas:

1 *Market share, growth and profitability* are obvious areas for investigation. Share strength in the market place will impact on its ability to compete. Large companies are not always profitable. Ability to grow may also be a measure of whether the company is likely to prove a formidable competitor or just follow market trends. Performance in the market place is a useful guide to future action.

2 *Resources and organisation* are major topics (*see* Part 3). While such an analysis may be lengthy, many companies in industry do in fact devote considerable time and resources monitoring and analysing competitors in depth. Many of the multinationals employ whole departments that undertake this task for leading competitors. Even small companies are often highly aware of the activities of their immediate competitors, perhaps with regard to pricing activity and whom their rivals are hiring and firing. Any serious competitor analysis would do well to devote some resources to this area.

3 *Cost structures* for competitors are not easy to estimate since the information is confidential. Nevertheless, some form of comparison is necessary and such data may be calculated from published material on such items as:

- number of employees and managers;
- plant size and type;
- planned and announced new investments;
- share and bank financing structure;
- relative costs of raw materials and bought-in components;
- sales levels and sales/marketing expenditure;
- degree of vertical integration.

None of the above is likely to be wholly accurate, but it should be possible to use the financial press, business press, mutual suppliers and customers to obtain some indication. Part 3 explores these areas in more detail.

4 *Competitor objectives and ambitions* are important in deriving future competitor moves. These are often published in such documents as annual company reports and press articles. For larger companies, bank reports and stockbroker commentaries may also provide some information.

5 *Current and past strategies* are clearly relevant to the assessment of the competitor and its future. These will give an indication of its future intentions by focussing on its performance up to the present.

What is really important in all the above is not just a list of attributes but some indicator of the *style and tone* of future competitive activities. Is the company an aggressive competitor or just passive? Does it have real ambitions in the area or is it rather more interested in another area of its activities? Does it really have the resources and skill to carry out its announced objectives or are they without real substance? The Nestlé example in Case study 5.5 raises such questions. This Chapter's Key Reading by Professor Michael Porter also presents material that emphasises the same mental process: some competitors are easier to handle than others because some do not compete all that hard. Competitor analysis must explore and answer such issues.

The same considerations apply in small business competitor analysis and in analysis of rivals for funds in the public services. Market share will probably have little meaning in fragmented local industries or in public service monopolies. However, other aspects of the marketing analysis on price and service can be coupled with the resource analysis areas outlined above to produce a meaningful competitor profile.

5.6 DISTRIBUTOR ANALYSIS

An important area of strategy for many organisations is *distribution* or *channel strategy* – covering all the activities that happen beyond the factory gate, such as physical distribution, salesforce activity and customer service actions. To illustrate the strategic importance of distribution in certain markets, we have only to examine pharmaceutical industry strategy: in 1993–94, two US pharmaceutical companies spent over US$10 billion buying US drug distributors because of a fundamental reappraisal of their corporate strategies.[24] European car companies have also invested substantial sums in distribution of their products and regard it as a vital part of overall company strategy.

With regard to distributor analysis, Lynch[25] has suggested that it is useful to distinguish between two types of customer to whom products are distributed:

1 *Direct end-users* – who buy and consume the product that is purchased. They do not buy for stock and do not sell to third parties. They often buy in large quantities and usually obtain direct supplies from the manufacturer.

2 *Distributors* – who buy a product for stock and then sell it to other customers. They may be agents, stockholders or other trade combinations. What distinguishes this group is that a 'sale' is not really made until they sell out their stock and re-order.

From a corporate strategy perspective, we are concerned not with the detail of such issues, but with the basic issue of how we distribute our product or service to the customer and the costs that are involved. The most striking opportunity in corporate strategy may well be to distribute the product differently. The most difficult problem in some industries has been to obtain any significant distribution for a product at all. Case study 5.4 describes the problems that the well resourced and skilled company, Mars, has had in obtaining distribution for its highly popular ice cream products in the 1990s. Customer demand did not solve the distribution strategy problem.

Areas that the analysis will need to cover include:

1 *Direct end-user or distributor objectives*. Many purchasers will be concerned not just with price but also with product quality, levels of service and technical support. At a more fundamental level, it will be important to deliver the levels of profitability or other objectives demanded by the end-user or distributor.

2 *Service levels*. Important items under this heading include timetables for delivery but also levels of back-up service, order-taking policies and general after-sales service.

3 *Technical and quality specifications*. For many end-users and distributors, specifications are vital. While the detail of such issues is not the subject of general strategy, the principles are important and their internal impact on the organisation will be explored further in Chapter 10. It should be noted here that international customers may well have more complex requirements than those from the home country.

4 *Distributor pricing and discounts*. Competitor information is often just as important in this area as basic data for the organisation itself.

5 *Distributor support*. In many cases, the product or service has not really been 'sold' until the distributor has sold it out of the warehouse, supermarket shelf or service centre. Promotional support to help the distributor may be a vital part of the organisation's strategy. In capital goods, design support, commissioning of the new machinery and continued technical advice are often required. The computer software company Microsoft recognised the importance and substantial costs of this when it launched its product Windows '95 in August 1995.

All these areas need careful analysis as part of the strategic development process. There are no strategic 'models' to consider: solid, careful study of the many complex factors and costs involved needs to be set against the sales to be gained. The main general principle to be followed is that of assessing the costs and benefits of each of the distribution options that have been identified.

Key strategic principles

- In distribution analysis, it is useful to distinguish between the use of distributors and delivery to direct end-users.

- Objectives for the two groups need to be established because they will have an important effect on the distribution that results.

- Service levels, quality, pricing and discounts and support from the distributor are all issues that then need to be investigated. There are few general models that govern these areas beyond that of an assessment of the costs and benefits that are available from the various options.

Mars ice cream: distribution strategy problems

From the launch of its first product in 1989, Mars has built a European market share, reported as being between 5 per cent and 10 per cent of the total market, with a share of between 10 per cent and 20 per cent of the chocolate ice cream bar segment. Its market penetration has not been without setbacks, however, particularly in the area of distribution.

Mars' share of the European ice cream market has been achieved through the launch of a range of products that largely build on its well-known confectionery products which are pan-European in branding and widely distributed. The ice cream products are all branded exactly the same across Europe and are nearly all produced at one factory in Eastern France.

Ice Cream Mars was the first of the product range, followed by others from its confectionery range such as Snickers and Opal Fruits. Its chosen strategy deliberately used high-quality ingredients, such as real cream and real chocolate, the use of significant advertising support across Europe and the establishment of a new premium-price category in the market place. By 1990, Unilever's UK subsidiary was commenting:

> *Fierce competition brought on by new players like Mars has helped to change the face of impulse ice cream. Ice cream is now coming of age with confectionery values becoming linked more and more with ice cream bars.*

European ice cream distribution
In addition to its confectionery branding revolution, Mars has invested considerable effort in freezer distribution as part of its business strategy. Its excellent and long-standing relationships with the grocery trade meant that it had no major difficulty in this sector in obtaining distribution for its multi-pack items. However, problems have arisen in other sectors of the trade that account for a substantial share of the ice cream market.

Ice cream distribution to retail outlets involves high costs because of the need for frozen storage and vehicle transport. This is made worse by several factors:

- *The low unit cost of the items carried* (particularly impulse ice cream). At only US$1 per item, it is necessary to sell many items to balance out transport costs.
- *The small drop sizes of orders to non-supermarket outlets.* Small shops can only sell limited numbers.
- *The related difficulty of making up economic loads within a sufficiently compact geographic area.*

As a consequence, all ice cream manufacturers have devoted considerable time and expense to ice cream distribution. In the UK, Ireland, the Netherlands, Germany, Denmark, Spain and Greece, Unilever has followed a policy of offering free freezer cabinets to retailers for the *exclusive use* of its products. Large supermarkets and multiple retailers have generally not taken up this offer but many small outlets have done so. In countries where it has some distribution strength, Nestlé has followed the same policy where possible. It has even done this where it was clearly in a weaker marketing position than Unilever.

Mars ice cream distribution strategy
Mars has faced an uphill struggle to gain distribution. Essentially, the company has been denied access to Unilever, Nestlé and Schoeller freezer cabinets in many European markets. Mars formally lodged protests against these practices with the governments of the UK and Ireland and with the European Commission in the case of Germany. Mars argued that freezer exclusivity was anti-competitive and against Articles 85 and 86 of the Treaty of Rome. Its rivals have defended their practices. Essentially, they have said that 'it would be a very odd interpretation of the Act to regard as restrictive of competition a refusal on the part of those who

had invested in freezers to give a free ride to those who had not … The cabinet was a selling tool. It did not dictate winners and losers; success derived from service, brand, quality range and price.' All retailers had the option to install their own freezers.

Mars has been forced to operate schemes to either make loans or sell freezers, depending on the outlet. It has also attempted to negotiate distribution agreements with companies that were in second or third position in various national markets across Europe. In the UK, it had a deal with Lyons Maid before that company was taken over by Nestlé in 1993. In France, it negotiated an arrangement with Ortiz-Miko before it was bought by Unilever in 1994.

From the viewpoint of a retail customer, Mars' strategy is not always attractive because it does not sell dessert ice creams, bulk packs or children's novelty ice creams for which there is also demand. The retailer thus has to seek alternative suppliers of these items and Mars has to allow them into its cabinets in order that a complete range is stocked.

Overall, it is not surprising that the Mars company said that it had made no profit on its ice cream activities up to 1993. It was unclear whether its chosen strategies would overcome this difficulty by the late 1990s.

CASE QUESTIONS

1 *How would you summarise the strategies adopted by Mars to launch its ice cream products?*

2 *Do you think that Mars will ever make significant profits from its ice cream operations? Why? How?*

5.7 INTERNATIONAL COMPETITION

Given the evidence from the previous chapter that growth in world sales has consistently outstripped growth in manufacturing output over the last 20 years, it follows that international competition has increased. The key issue is whether international competitors pose similar or increased threats to those from the home country. There is good evidence that they present additional problems in at least three areas:

● *International ambitions* to deliver world sales volume will certainly pose an additional threat to domestic manufacturers. Global objectives of some companies have been well documented since the early 1980s.[26] Companies like Caterpillar (US) and Komatsu (Japan) in construction equipment, Ericsson (Sweden) in telecommunications equipment, Honda (Japan) in cars and motorcycles are examples of companies who have taken share from domestic manufacturers.

● *Lower costs* arise for a number of reasons. These include economies of scale from operating on a larger, international market and lower labour costs through sourcing some products in countries with this benefit.

● *Global strategies* have been deliberately pursued in some industries to integrate worldwide strategy. Essentially, strategy is centralised for the whole world, with an integrated network of production and market positions in all the leading countries on a broadly similar platform. Not all industries are global, but those that hold this position present additional competition to domestic competitors.[27]

Nestlé ice cream: attacking through acquisition and branding

Nestlé is one of Unilever's global rivals, but it has come late to the European ice cream market. Its main growth strategies have been the acquisition of ice cream companies and the introduction of some of its confectionery branded items into ice cream.

Before 1992, Nestlé's involvement in ice cream was largely confined to its French operations. It owned the company France Glace Findus and had around 15 per cent of the French market, selling its ice cream products under the brand names Gervais and Nestlé. Then in 1992, Nestlé bought the second largest Italian ice cream producer, Italgel. This company had around 30 per cent of the Italian market with brand names like Motta and the premium brand La Cremeria.

(It should be noted that brand ownership across Europe is complicated. Nestlé owns the brand name Motta in Italy and Unilever owns the same brand in France. Unilever owns the Findus brand in Italy, whereas Nestlé owns this brand in France, the UK and elsewhere.)

Nestlé expansion

In 1993, Nestlé purchased the Clarkes Foods company in the UK. This company owned the second largest ice cream manufacturer in the UK, trading under the brand name Lyons Maid. By chance, Nestlé was able to buy a company that had just invested in new production plant (and had gone bankrupt in the process). It had also purchased an important share of a leading European ice cream market; however, its share was still only around 15 per cent of the total. Importantly for the future, however, Nestlé said that it had bought the distribution infrastructure and management expertise to build this share over the subsequent years.

By pan-European standards, Nestlé was not a strong player in the ice cream market. However, it was much stronger than the market leader, Unilever, in confectionery brands. It therefore borrowed a strategy from Mars: it was beginning to reformulate its confectionery brands as ice cream. During the mid-1990s, it introduced such new ice creams as Kit Kat, Dairy Crunch and Lion Bar. It also launched a revolutionary new Rowntree's Fruit Pastil-Lolly to its European range. However, there were a number of countries where it was under-represented – for example, Germany, Belgium, the Netherlands and Scandinavia. No doubt the company was examining medium-sized companies operating in the ice cream market for acquisition candidates.

Ideally, the acquisition of a company such as Schoeller (Germany) would fit well into the Nestlé portfolio. Unilever would also have identified such a move by Nestlé, but might be unable to prevent it. If Unilever attempted to take over Schoeller itself, its combined market share might become too dominant for EU policy. Moreover, in 1994, it was not known whether Schoeller was for sale.

CASE QUESTIONS

1 *What are the advantages and disadvantages of the strategies adopted by Nestlé?*

2 *From Unilever's viewpoint, how would you summarise the main Nestlé strengths and weaknesses?*

3 *Is Nestlé following a clear international strategy, or is it just opportunistic?*

What makes a good competitor?[28]

In this extract from his book, **Competitive Advantage,** *Professor Michael Porter asks: 'What makes a good competitor?' His comments need to be understood in the context of his view that some competitor strategies can reduce the profits for all companies in an industry. His aim is to maximise the profits for those currently in the industry. Potential new entrants to the industry might choose exactly the opposite strategies to those outlined below.*

Competitors are not all equally attractive or unattractive. A good competitor is one that can perform some beneficial functions without representing too severe a long-term threat. A good competitor is one that challenges the firm not to be complacent but is a competitor with which the firm can achieve a stable and profitable industry equilibrium without protracted warfare. Bad competitors, by and large, have the opposite characteristics.

No competitor ever meets all the tests of a good competitor. Competitors usually have some characteristics of a good competitor and some characteristics of a bad competitor. Some managers, as a result, will assert that there is no such thing as a good competitor. This view ignores the essential point that some competitors are a lot better than others, and can have very different effects on a firm's competitive position. In practice, a firm must understand where each of its competitors falls on the spectrum from good to bad and behave accordingly.

Tests of a good competitor

A good competitor has a number of characteristics. Since its goals, strategy and capabilities are not static; however, the assessment of whether a competitor is good or bad can change.

Credible and viable. A good competitor has sufficient resources and capabilities to be a motivator to the firm to lower cost or improve differentiation, as well as credible with and acceptable to buyers.

Clear, self-perceived weaknesses. Though credible and viable, a good competitor has clear weaknesses relative to a firm which are recognised. Ideally, the good competitor believes that its weaknesses will be difficult to change. The competitor need not be weaker everywhere but has some clear weaknesses that will lead it to conclude that it is futile to attempt to gain relative position against a firm in the segments the firm is interested in.

Understands the rules. A good competitor understands and plays by the rules of competition in an industry, and can recognise and read market signals. It aids in market development and promotes the existing technology rather than attempting strategies that involve technological or competitive discontinuities in order to gain position.

Realistic assumptions. A good competitor has realistic assumptions about the industry and its own relative position. It does not overestimate industry growth potential and therefore overbuild capacity, or underinvest in capacity and in so doing provide an opening for newcomers. A good company also does not overrate its capabilities to the point of triggering a battle by attempting to gain share, or shy from retaliating against entrants because it underestimates its strengths.

Knowledge of costs. It knows what its costs are, and sets its prices accordingly. It does not unwittingly cross-subsidise product lines or underestimate overhead.

Moderate exit barriers. A good competitor has exit barriers that are significant enough to make its presence in the industry a viable deterrent to new entrants, but yet not so high as to completely lock it into the industry. High exit barriers create the risk that the competitor will disrupt the industry rather than exit if it encounters strategic difficulty.

Has moderate stakes in the industry. It does not attach high stakes to achieving dominance or unusually high growth in the industry. It views the industry as one where continued participation is desirable and where acceptable profits can be earned, but not one where improving relative position has great strategic or emotional importance.

Has a comparable return-on-investment target. It is less likely to undercut prices or make heavy investments to attack a firm's position.

Has a short time horizon. It does not have so long a time horizon that it will fight a protracted battle to attack a firm's position.

Source: Reprinted with the permission of The Free Press, a division of Simon & Schuster, from *Competitive Advantage: Creating and Sustaining Superior Performance* by Michael E Porter. Copyright © 1985 by Michael E Porter.

SUMMARY

- *Sustainable competitive advantage* has been placed at the centre of the development of corporate strategy. The real benefits of developing this area derive from those aspects of the organisation that cannot easily be imitated and can be sustained over time. Such advantages can take many forms: differentiation, low costs, niche marketing, high performance or technology, quality, service, vertical integration, synergy and the culture, leadership and style of the organisation.

- In exploring the intensity of competition in an industry, it is useful to begin by exploring the *degree of concentration* in a market – ranging between the two extremes of perfect competition and pure monopoly. The concentration ratio itself can also be calculated – that is, the percentage of an industry turnover or value added controlled by the largest four, five or eight firms.

- Military language and concepts are often used to describe the *aggressive strategies* of competitors. The four main attack strategies are: head-on, flanking, totally new territory and guerrilla. In addition, *innovatory strategies* may be employed, especially those that rewrite the rules of the game in a market. Within the context of competitive analysis, it is often helpful to explore groups of immediate competitors more extensively: the *analysis of strategic groups*. In addition, it is usually useful to identify one or more *immediate competitors* for detailed analysis. Such a study will examine the competitor's market share, resources, cost structures, objectives and current strategies.

● Another area of investigation is that concerning *distributors* – that is, those companies that purchase the product and then resell it to small end-consumers. In some markets, distributors are a vital part of the chain of sale and need to be analysed in detail. Service levels, quality, pricing and discounts and the support from the distributor are subjects for investigation.

● *International competition* has increased over the last 20 years. This has taken many forms but three areas can be usefully highlighted: ambition of some companies for global expansion, low costs through careful sourcing of production and global strategies to integrate worldwide strategy.

QUESTIONS

1 Consider the three case studies on shoes (5.1), telecommunications (5.2) and retailing (5.3) and identify where and how sustainable competitive advantages might be developed in each case.

2 Use the three tests for SCA in Exhibit 5.1 to analyse Mars Ice Cream and other products in the range. What are your conclusions for the Mars company?

3 Take an industry with which you are familiar and estimate its degree of concentration. For example, you might pick the university and college of higher education market in a particular country. What strategic conclusions would you wish to draw from your analysis?

4 Analyse the aggressive strategies undertaken by competitors against Unilever in the European ice cream market. How would you classify their attack strategies?

5 Can you think of any examples of innovatory aggressive strategies? If you are having trouble, then you might like to skim through some of the cases in this book to find those that fit this role. Give reasons for your selection.

6 'Military principles and strategies are not the whole answer to competitive strategy, but they do provide insight into what it takes for a company to succeed in attacking another company or in defending itself against an aggressor.' Philip Kotler and Ravi Singh

   To what extent do you agree with this statement?

7 Choose an industry familiar to you and identify the strategic groups existing in that industry. What distinguishes them from each other? What strategic conclusions can you draw?

8 Using the procedures outlined in this chapter, prepare a competitive analysis of the European telecommunications industry over the next five years from the viewpoint of British Telecom. *Or*, if you prefer, take the South-East Asian market or the North American market and prepare the same review from the viewpoint of Singapore Telecom or MCI respectively. *Or*, if you prefer, you can use your own national telecommunications operator and consider the issues as global competition increases.

9 Bruce Henderson, founder of the Boston Consulting Group, commented:

   'Induce your competitors not to invest in those products, markets and services where you expect to invest most ... that is the fundamental rule of strategy.'

   Briefly explain this statement and comment on its usefulness.

10 What general conclusions can you draw from the Mars Ice Cream case about the nature and importance of distributor strategy? What lessons does it imply for other companies, if any?

Branded ice cream markets

This chapter has explored the European ice cream market. Take this further by examining the progress Ben & Jerry's ice cream has made into Europe and the more recent results of Mars Ice Cream. Several companies in this survey are developing *global* ice cream businesses: find out which ones and assess the likelihood of their success.

FURTHER READING

Professor Porter's two books are the classic texts in this area – *Competitive Strategy* (1980) and *Competitive Advantage* (1985) – both published by The Free Press, New York. They are strongly recommended. In addition, the book by Professor David Aaker, *Strategic Market Management* (Wiley, 1992) has a well balanced and detailed approach to the development of sustainable competitive advantage that merits careful reading.

REFERENCES

1 The study of the European ice cream market in this chapter is based on data from published sources. These include: UK Monopolies and Mergers Commission (1994) *Report on the supply in the UK of ice cream for immediate consumption*. March, HMSO, London Cmd 2524; *Financial Times*: 19 May 1993, p24; 17 Mar 1994 and 13 Jun 1995, p18; *Dairy Industry International*: May 1994, p33; Aug 1994, p17 and Sep 1994, p19; *Food Manufacture*: June 1994, p24 and July 1994, p28; *Sunday Times*: 7 June 1992, pp1–8.
2 High technology and services columns developed from Aaker, D (1992) *Strategic Marketing Management*, 3rd edn, Wiley, New York, p186; others from author.
3 Porter, M E (1980) *Competitive Strategy*, The Free Press, New York.
4 Porter, M E (1985) *Competitive Advantage*, The Free Press, New York.
5 Quoted in Aaker, D (1992) Ibid, p182.
6 For those obsessed with the generic strategies outlined in Professor Porter's two books, it should be noted that no mention has been made of being the lowest cost producer. This book will argue that sustainable advantage may be achieved by having both low costs and other qualities that take the company beyond being merely the lowest cost producer.
7 Kay, J (1993) *Foundations of Corporate Success*, Oxford University Press, Oxford, p367.
8 Some data for this case study has been extracted from Office for Publications of the European Communities, *Panorama of EC Industry 1993*, pp14–24.
9 Leadbeater, C (1991) 'Cut-off point for telecoms giants', *Financial Times*, 15 Jan and Adonis, A (1994) 'Lines for the global village', *Financial Times*, 17 Sep, p8.
10 *See* Lynch, R (1994) *European Business Strategies*, 2nd edn, Kogan Page, London, pp203–5 for a longer description of telecommunications strategy.

11 This section is based on the work of Professors Porter and Kotler (*see* refs 13 and 14) and on a lecture given by Professor Ken Simmons at the London Business School in 1988.

12 For example, *see* Ries, A and Trout, J (1986) *Marketing Warfare,* McGraw-Hill, New York.

13 Kotler, P (1994) *Marketing Management: Analysis, Planning, Implementation and Control*, 8th edn, Prentice Hall, New York.

14 Kotler, P and Singh, R (1981) 'Marketing Warfare in the 1980s', *Journal of Business Strategy*, Winter, pp30–41.

15 Liddell-Hart, B H (1967) *Strategy*, Praegar, New York.

16 Kay, J (1994) Ibid, pp236–8 provides an interesting discussion of the circumstances under which such an understanding can emerge without contravening monopoly legislation.

17 Lynch, R (1994) Ibid, pp119–21 supplies some evidence here.

18 Kay, J (1994) Ibid, p364.

19 Porter, M E (1980) Ibid, p129.

20 McGee, J and Segal-Horn, S (1990) 'Strategic Space and Industry Dynamics', *Journal of Marketing Management*, No. 3, pp173–93.

21 McGee, J and Segal-Horn, S (1990) Ibid.

22 Rumelt, R (1980) 'The evaluation of business strategy', in Glueck, W F (ed) (1980) *Business Policy and Strategic Management*, McGraw-Hill, and reprinted in De Wit, R and Meyer, R (1994) *Strategy: Process, Content and Context*, West Publishing, pp186–92.

23 Aaker, D (1992) Ibid, p65.

24 Green, D (1995) 'Takeover Fever', *Financial Times*, 22 Aug, p12.

25 Lynch, R (1994) Ibid, Ch 22.

26 Hout, T, Porter, M E, Rudden, E (1982) 'How global companies win out', *Harvard Business Review*, Sep–Oct, p98.

27 Porter, M E (ed) (1986) *Competition in global industries*, Harvard Business School Press, Mass, Chs 3 and 4.

28 Extracted from Porter, M E (1985) Ibid.

6

Analysing customers

When you have worked through this chapter, you will be able to:

- explain the importance of a customer-driven organisation and the significance of unmet customer needs;

- analyse customers and the segments to which they belong;

- outline the basic principles involved in communicating with customers and their strategic implications;

- understand the main elements of pricing strategy;

- explain the customer/competitor matrix and its importance for strategy development;

- identify some of the main international issues in customer strategy.

INTRODUCTION

Customers are essential to any organisation engaged in corporate strategy. It is important for an organisation both to understand its customers and to develop policies that will encourage them to stay with the organisation.

This chapter considers the process of analysing customers. It begins by estimating market demand. Market segments are examined and any that currently remain unfilled are identified. In addition, the process of customer analysis examines how the company communicates with its customers and how it undertakes its pricing strategy. Finally, the analysis of customers explores the complex relationships that exist between customers, the organisation and its competitors so that the strategy implications can be better understood. The process of customer analysis is outlined in Fig 6.1.

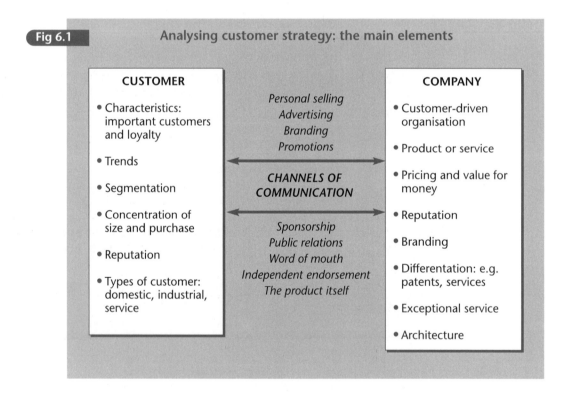

Fig 6.1   Analysing customer strategy: the main elements

CUSTOMER

- Characteristics: important customers and loyalty

- Trends

- Segmentation

- Concentration of size and purchase

- Reputation

- Types of customer: domestic, industrial, service

Personal selling
Advertising
Branding
Promotions

CHANNELS OF COMMUNICATION

Sponsorship
Public relations
Word of mouth
Independent endorsement
The product itself

COMPANY

- Customer-driven organisation

- Product or service

- Pricing and value for money

- Reputation

- Branding

- Differentation: e.g. patents, services

- Exceptional service

- Architecture

Estimating demand for the Airbus SuperJumbo[1]

During 1996 and 1997, Europe's player in the world civil aircraft market, Airbus Industrie, had to make an important strategic decision: was there sufficient customer demand for its proposed new SuperJumbo aircraft, the A3XX, to justify up to US$12 billion investment?

Background

Airbus Industrie was set up in 1975 as a special consortium called a Groupement d'Intérêt Économique (GIE). It had an advisory board and its own central management. However, it consisted essentially of the four European aircraft makers who shared out its work and profits according to their shareholdings. The four were:

● Aerospatiale (France) – 37.9 per cent share

● Dasa (Germany) – part of Daimler-Benz Aerospace, 37.9 per cent share

● British Aerospace – 20 per cent share

● Casa (Spain) – 4 per cent share

The company built up its share of the world civil aircraft market from nothing in 1975 to around 30 per cent in 1996. In total, it had sold 1334 aircraft to 130 airline customers worldwide. Its corporate strategy had enabled four medium-sized European manufacturers to compete in the market for large civil aircraft against the two major US companies, Boeing and McDonnell Douglas. Airbus sales in 1993 were US$8.5 billion and in 1994 US$9.6 billion.

Competitive rivalry

Up to the 1990s, Airbus had been highly successful in taking sales from its great US rival, Boeing. For example, Airbus actually won more orders in 1994 than Boeing. This was the first time ever that the US company had been beaten. However, Boeing hit back in 1995 with 346 orders compared with only 106 for Airbus. The whole process showed how variable order-taking could be in such an industry, where typically orders were taken over a year before the sales were finally made to the customer. Orders could be cancelled at any time by the customers.

Airbus had been particularly successful with its wide-bodied mid-range aircraft, the A330 and the A340. Boeing had responded with its new 777 in 1994/95 (*see* Case Study 6.3).

Estimating demand for the SuperJumbo

Airbus had a problem regarding its future product range: it did not have an aircraft to match the larger Boeing 747-400 model which had around 400 seats. It was known that Boeing planned to use the design of this aircraft to aid its development of a new aircraft over the following two years – the 500-seat Boeing 747-600X.

It was against this background that Airbus was now considering whether to develop an even larger model – the A3XX. This would have 550 to 800 seats arranged in two decks (or layers) in the aircraft. The price of the new aircraft was unknown but, as a guide, the price of the latest Boeing aircraft – the 777 – was US$120 million before special discounts to favoured customers. Hence on a similar basis, the price of the new

A3XX could be around US$150 million. The development costs of the new aircraft could be between US$5.5 and 12 billion. The strategic issue facing Airbus was whether to go ahead with the A3XX. There would clearly be *some* demand for the new A3XX, but would there be enough to make a profit?

CASE QUESTIONS

1 *How should Airbus go about estimating demand?*

2 *Should they even try to estimate demand, or just go ahead for strategic reasons?*

6.1 CUSTOMERS AND CORPORATE STRATEGY

Customers buy the organisation's products or services and in this way realise the value that the company has added to its products. Customers are thus vital to corporate strategy development. Indeed, the well-known marketing writer Theodore Levitt is on record as saying:

> *The purpose of an enterprise is to create and keep a customer.*[2]

From much of the literature on corporate strategy, it would appear that customers are only a part of the analysis: greater emphasis is sometimes given to competitive advantage, core competences, learning organisations and other matters. Yet it is the *customer* that has to choose the products or services of the organisation, if it is to survive and prosper.

However, as long as customers have a choice, the development of corporate strategy will also need to consider the customer options available from competitors. Customer strategy needs to be linked to competitor strategy. These two areas are therefore considered together later in this chapter, but our starting point is a careful exploration of the customer and the relationship with the organisation.

6.1.1 Estimating customer demand

In turbulent markets, estimating customer demand will be difficult (*see*, for example, the Hewlett-Packard comment on hand-held calculators in Chapter 1) and as a result strategy will follow an emergent approach and move forward step-by-step without over-exposing the organisation's resources. Where demand can be estimated with more certainty, then various methods of forecasting will be used:

● PEST analysis of major background influences;

● study of historic trends of existing sales;

● marketing research for evidence of new initiatives;

● examination of competitor reactions and new strategies;

● market tests to provide further evidence.

Corporate strategy will usually leave the more detailed analysis to specific business groups. However, it will wish to take a broad view of the likely levels of demand in each of its major product categories over the following few years as long as markets are not too turbulent. For example at Airbus, the future demand for aircraft has guided the number of employees who have remained in work at the various factories making parts and assembling finished aircraft.

6.1.2 Unmet customer needs

In the development of corporate strategy, one area that constantly delivers new initiatives is the search for needs among existing customers that are currently not being fulfilled by existing products. Unfortunately, it is not always possible to research these adequately. The reason is that customers have difficulty seeing beyond their current horizons towards the *vision* of the revolutionary new product. Fax machines, mobile telephones, the Internet and credit cards are recent examples of products that clearly fulfil needs, but were difficult to research in advance of the products actually being available.

It is easier to research reactions to existing products than to elicit responses to the largely unknown. For example, realistic research with passengers on the proposed new Airbus SuperJumbo may be difficult because the whole concept of a *double-decker aircraft* is unfamiliar. Yet it may be this latter category of the revolutionary product that will deliver the important new corporate strategy initiative. To quote Hamel and Prahalad:

> *Any company that can do no more than respond to the articulated needs of existing customers will quickly become a laggard.*[3]

Unmet customer needs are difficult to research and require close co-operation between technologists and strategists. They may benefit from mock-ups, structured marketing research and trial products to test reactions.

6.1.3 Customer-driven organisation

As a deliberate part of their corporate strategy, some organisations have set out to become driven by the customer.[4] There are three main strands to this approach to strategy:

- understanding the customer;
- responsiveness by the organisation to customer needs;
- provision of real value for money by the organisation.

The essence of such a strategy is that it goes way beyond the functions of the organisation that have traditionally had direct contact with the customer – that is, marketing and sales. The concept is that *everyone* becomes involved. Some of the main areas are summarised in Exhibit 6.1.

| Exhibit 6.1 | Some examples of customer-driven strategy |

Understanding the customer

- Direct customer contact at many levels
- Widely disseminated research on key customer findings, e.g. on segmentation
- Knowledge of why customers choose the organisation

Responsiveness of the organisation to customer needs

- Regularly receive and act upon customer satisfaction surveys
- Responsive to customer complaints and suggestions
- Track key customer data on company image

Provision of real value for money

- Monitor quality relevant to the positioning of products in the market place
- Conduct comparative surveys of competitive prices and service offerings
- Rewards inside the organisation based on performance with customers

Comment Although customer-driven strategy sounds fine in principle, it is sometimes reduced to exhortation and hyperbole. No real evidence is available that short-term slogans make a significant difference. However, a long-term commitment to customer excellence has characterised some of the world's most successful enterprises – for example, Toyota (Japan), McDonald's (US) and BMW (Germany).

6.1.4 Emergent and prescriptive approaches to customer strategy

Both emergent and prescriptive approaches are usually employed in the development and maintainance of customer strategy.

An *emergent strategy* approach may be needed in the context of unmet customer needs or more general marketing research in difficult areas. It may also be required to ensure that customer service and quality are *continually* improved.

A *prescriptive strategy* approach will be required in other contexts, especially where the customer is concerned. If the customer is to be assured of value for money, then it will be necessary to have a clear understanding of the product or service being sold at the price quoted: there can be no sense of trial and error. All this demands the greater clarity and precision of the prescriptive approach.

> **Key strategic principles**
>
> - Customers are vital to corporate strategy development. Demand needs to be estimated where possible. A broad view of likely levels of demand may be essential for future development plans.
>
> - Some companies have set up customer-driven organisations as a deliberate part of strategy. This is a long-term task rather than a matter of short-term exhortation.
>
> - Both emergent and prescriptive approaches are needed in customer analysis and strategy development.

6.2 ANALYSING CUSTOMERS

6.2.1 Identifying customers and competitors

The first task is to identify who the customers are now and who they might potentially be in the future. This might seem to be abundantly clear to many corporations but nothing is ever obvious in corporate strategy. It was Theodore Levitt, a marketing professor at Harvard Business School, who pointed out in the 1960s that some large North American companies had made major strategic mistakes by incorrect identification of customers. If customers are not correctly identified, then it is quite possible that companies who are competing for the same customers will also be left out of consideration.[5]

In identifying customers, a *broad view* of who they are should be taken initially in corporate strategy. Once this has been considered, a *narrower view* can then be adopted. Levitt[5] gave the example of the American railway industry who identified its market during the 1950s as being that for *railway transport*. As a result, each company in the industry saw its environment as being largely a matter of competition between the railway companies. This was explored further in Chapter 3, Section 3.7.1; refer back to this section for a discussion of this important topic.

The importance in defining accurately this aspect of the environment lies in developing strategies that target customers properly and in ensuring that competitors have been properly identified. Ultimately, if the market environment is incorrectly defined, then competitors may creep up and steal customers without the company realising it until it is too late.[6, 7]

6.2.2 Profiling customers and their purchase decisions

To continue the strategy development process, it is essential to understand customers and the reasons that they have for choosing particular products and services. Even those customers that have no choice in public service and charities may be better served by a deeper understanding of their needs. This means profiling them and their purchase decisions using marketing research.

Customer profiles describe the main characteristics of the customer and how they make their purchase decisions. Table 6.1 provides some examples of typical customer profiles using information that would normally be available in more depth from marketing research. The main categories of customer are:

- *Domestic customers.* These customers buy products or services for themselves or their families. This is called *primary demand,* since demand does not depend on any other group. The customers seek immediate satisfaction from their purchases – for example, eating ice cream. There are a large number of customers each of whom makes a small purchase so their individual bargaining power is low. Groups of customers can often be distinguished by some further feature of their lifestyle or consumption – for example, family consumption of bulk packs of ice cream creating a family segment. Domestic customers can often be persuaded to purchase products by the branding of goods and advertising. Primary demand will be influenced mainly by factors from the industry itself.

- *Large business customers.* These customers tend to buy for more rational and economic reasons – for example, performance measures and cost considerations such as aircraft from Airbus that meet particular travel specifications and criteria. Each business customer may be different – for example, British Airways and Lufthansa (Germany) will have different requirements. It may not be practicable to group customers together but often each has a large enough individual order to justify the individual attention that it will receive. Demand is often *derived demand* – that is, it is dependent on the demand from another industry. For example, the demand for aircraft will be derived from the demand for air travel. Derived demand requires analysis of factors outside the immediate industry.

- *Small business customers.* These customers have many of the same characteristics as their larger counterparts. However, the size of their potential orders may not justify the same level of individual attention.

- *Large service customers.* These customers often sell products to domestic customers for immediate consumption. Examples of such organisations are retail banks and major hotel chains. Importantly, the *product* includes the person providing the service, the ambience of the buildings and location of the service and the process by which the service is dispensed – for example, with a friendly smile.

- *Public service customers.* These customers may well exhibit considerable similarities with large service customers. However, commercial considerations may be less important.

- *Not-for-profit charity customers.* These customers will also involve service, but may be driven by a stronger sense of beliefs and the need to keep voluntary workers interested. These may guide its strategies towards a more co-operative approach.

In considering the strategy implications of typical customer profiles, it is important to note that some areas are specific to the industry and cannot be generalised across all strategic categories.

Table 6.1 Typical customer profiles

	Domestic consumer	Large industrial	Large private service	Not-for-profit charity	Public service	Small business	Strategic implications
Example	Unilever ice cream	Airbus aircraft	McDonald's restaurants	UNICEF	Health service hospital	Hairdresser or local builder	
Nature of demand	Primary	Derived or joint	Primary	Primary	Primary	Derived or joint	
Selling message	Immediate satisfaction: status can be important	Economic and non-economic needs	Immediate service: quality is part of service	Driven by belief in charity	As private service, but tempered by public service guidelines	As large industrial, but may place greater value on personal service	Major areas of difference may require industry-level strategies
Customer needs	Customers can be grouped into those with similar needs: segmentation	Each customer different	Customers grouped as in domestic	Customers may be grouped but individual service also important	Customers may be grouped but individual service also important	Customers may be grouped but many will be different	Strategies for segments and individual buyers
Purchase motivation	Individual or family	Buy for company	Will partly be driven by location, style	Receive for others and self	Receive for others and self	Local and national service	Major areas of difference may require industry-level strategies
Product	Branding, possibly low technical content	Perhaps technically sophisticated	People providing service are part of product	People providing service are part of product	People providing service are part of product. Also technical content	Possible technical content. Also possibly high and personal service	Technical sophistication in some areas. People as part of service in others

6.2.3 Market segmentation

In the development of customer strategy, customer analysis will often move rapidly to an examination of market segmentation.[8] Market segmentation may be defined as the identification of specific groups (or *segments*) of customers who respond differently from other groups to competitive strategies.

The advantages of identifying a market segment include:

- *Strength in (and possibly dominance of) a group*, even though the overall market is large. It may be more profitable to have a large share of a group than a small share of the main market.

- *Closer matching of customer needs and the organisation's resources* through targeting the segment. This will provide sustainable competitive advantage.

- *Concentration of effort on a smaller area*, so that the company's resources can be employed more effectively.

Hence from a strategic viewpoint, the key advantage of market segmentation is probably the ability to dominate a sector of a market and then target benefits that will sustain this position. For example, Boeing dominated the 400-seat aircraft market segment. Typical bases for segmentation in consumer and industrial markets are listed in Table 6.2. However, markets can be segmented by any criteria that prove helpful and do not necessarily need to conform to this list.

Table 6.2 Typical bases for market segmentation

Consumer products	Industrial products
• Geography	• Geography
• Demography (age, sex, education, etc.)	• End-use
• Socio-economic grouping and income	• Customer business
• Ethnic group	• Buying situation
• Benefits sought	• Market served
• Usage rate and brand loyalty	• Value added by customer
• Attitudes	• Source of competitive advantage
• Lifestyle	(price, service, etc.)
• Situation (where the consumption	• Emphasis on R&D and innovation
takes place)	• Professional membership

Having established the segments, strategic customer analysis then proceeds to identify the *usefulness* of each segment. It is not enough for a segment to be different. There are four important characteristics of any segment if it is to be useful in strategic customer analysis:

- *Distinguishable*. Customers must be distinguishable so that they can be isolated in some way.

- *Relevant to purchasing*. The distinguishing criteria must relate to differences in market demand. For example, they may pay higher prices for higher quality.

- *Sufficient size*. If the segment is too small, then it will not justify the resources needed to reach it.

- *Reachable*. It must be possible to direct the strategy to that segment.

It is also important to assess the future growth prospects of the segment. An example of market segmentation is explored in Case 6.1.

Two ways of segmenting the European ice cream market

The European ice cream market can be usefully segmented into impulse buys and take-home packs. This case study considers the implications of this segmentation for strategy and looks at an alternative segmentation for the 1990s.

European ice cream purchases can usefully be segmented into impulse and take-home: the former are bought for immediate consumption while the latter are usually taken home in bulk for consumption later. Impulse purchases typically take place in small shops such as beach kiosks and newsagents' stores, whereas take-home products are normally bought in grocers and supermarkets. It would be wrong to draw a rigid distinction between the two segments: bulk packs are purchased by retailers to sell as scoops for impulse demand; impulse items such as chocolate bars are sold in multi-packs and may then be consumed on impulse later at home.

In practice, detailed segment data is available for some national markets but no true pan-European study has been published. Best estimates from a variety of sources for some leading European markets are shown in Table 6.3.

Interpreting the data in Table 6.3 is complex since there are several factors at work. In France, eating ice cream is sometimes regarded as a luxury and eating occasions may therefore be taken more seriously, rather than on impulse. In Italy, ice cream is also an expensive item with many luxury ingredients, individual variants and local manufacturers but it is bought more casually from cafés and gelaterias. In the UK, ice cream has traditionally been manufactured using lower quality ingredients, for example vegetable oils in place of real cream. During the 1980s, there was substantial growth across Europe in the take-home trade of economy packs and, more recently, more expensive, higher quality bulk packs. In Germany, ice cream has traditionally been bought on impulse; but more recently, there has been substantial growth in the take-home market: in both market segments, expectations have remained high with regard to ingredients and taste.

During the 1990s, Europe has seen a marked growth in ice creams with expensive ingredients, high prices and exotic flavours: some customers (but not necessarily all) have become more adventurous in taste, more wealthy and more demanding in terms of quality. There has been a new attempt to redefine customers by *price* and *quality*. Table 6.4 shows the main areas.

Table 6.3 Customer segmentation in ice cream by purchase intention

	France	Italy	UK	Germany
Impulse	30%	40%	30%	50%
Take-home	70%	60%	70%	50%

Source: author's estimates based on various trade articles

Table 6.4 Customer segmentation by price and quality

Segment	Product and branding	Pricing	Market growth in the mid-1990s
Super-premium	High quality, exotic flavours, e.g. Häagen-Dazs Mint Chocolate Chip	Very high unit prices: very high value added	Over 15% per annum from a small market base
Premium	Good quality ingredients with individual, well-known branded names such as Mars and Magnum	Prices set above regular and economy categories but not as high as super-premium: high value added	10% per annum from a larger base than super-premium
Regular	Standard quality ingredients with branding relying on manufacturer's name rather than individual product, e.g. Walls, Schoeller	Standard prices: adequate value added but large volume market	Over 5% per annum from a large base
Economy	Manufactured by smaller manufacturers with standard quality ingredients, possibly for retailers' own brands	Lower price, highly price competitive: low value added but large market	Over 5% per annum from a large base, particularly in some countries such as the UK and Ireland

Source: author's estimates from trade articles

The segments in Table 6.4 need to be treated with some caution: no precise information on the four market segments has been published. The categories probably have too much overlap with customers buying from several segments depending on the meal occasion. In spite of the problem of accuracy, the above segments are certainly large enough to justify separate marketing and distribution activity. Many have been targeted accurately through appropriate media – for example, the use of up-market, young-profile colour magazines to reach potential Häagen-Dazs customers with a sexually suggestive campaign and the use of TV advertising to present the new Ice Cream Mars branded range to a wider TV audience. Thus some segments have real marketing potential in spite of difficulties in precise definition.

CASE QUESTIONS

1 What other methods of segmenting the ice cream market are available?

2 Using the tests for segmentation, what conclusions do you draw on the usefulness of the two methods above?

6.2.4 Identification of segmentation gaps

From a strategy viewpoint, the most useful analysis often emerges from a study of the *gaps* in the segments of an industry: among others, Porter[9] and Ohmae[10] recommend this route. The starting point for such work is to map out the current segmentation position and then place companies and their products into the segments: it should then become clear where segments exist that are not served or are poorly served by current products. This is shown in Exhibit 6.2 using the European ice cream case as an example.

Exhibit 6.2 New or under-utilised segment gaps illustrated in Unilever's presence in the European ice cream market, 1995

Market basis for possible segmentation

	Buyer type 1	Buyer type 2	Buyer type 3 etc.
Product variety 1			
Product variety 2			
Product variety 3 etc.			

Step 1 Existing segments with Unilever's European presence shown

	Grocery supermarkets	Small grocery stores	Restaurants and takeaways	Newsagents and leisure facilities
Super-premium	✓ market test only	✓	✓	✓ some
Premium	✓	✓		✓ most
Regular	✓			
Economy	✓	✓ some		

Step 2 Some possible new segments *in addition* to the above

	Garages	Temporary facilities at sporting and cultural events	Factory canteens and restaurants: contract catering
Super-premium		✓	
Premium	✓		
Regular			✓
Economy			✓

For the sake of clarity, only Unilever's presence is shown in Exhibit 6.2. Moreover, the example is *illustrative only* and may not represent the actual practice of the Unilever subsidiaries in each country. Further segmentation analyses based on criteria, such as the geographical country, might also produce some useful additional information.

It will be evident from Exhibit 6.2 that there are some gaps in existing coverage of the market. The segmentation criteria outlined in Section 6.2.3 could be used to assess whether it would be worth while filling the gaps. One obvious area where Unilever could take action was in the super-premium sector.

6.2.5 Strategy implications arising from customer profiling

In addition to identifying possible segment gaps in the market place, there are three other issues related to customer profiling that deserve attention:

1 *Sustainable competitive advantage.* The use of customer profiling may well suggest areas where sustainable competitive advantage could be developed by the organisation. For example, price or branding may be important for domestic customers.

2 *Customer switching costs.* This is the cost to the customers of changing their purchase from the organisation and moving to another supplier. If the cost is *high*, then switching may not occur and this will enhance the organisation's power over the buyer. For example, the switching cost from Boeing to Airbus may be substantial if engineers have been trained to service Boeing aircraft and spare parts have been purchased. If the switching cost is *low*, then change may occur at any time. For example, switching costs for an individual ice cream customer between Mars and Magnum ice cream are zero.

3 *Customer bargaining power.* Buying power is reduced in the following cases:
- if there is a large number of small customers so that there is no danger of one large customer suddenly removing its business;
- if maintainance, service or some other technical support contract ties the customer to the organisation;
- if customer purchase is being financed by the seller through leasing or some other deal.

Key strategic principles

- When identifying customers, a broad view of who they are should initially be taken. Having considered this, a narrower view can then be adopted.
- Marketing research can be used to profile customers and provide a deeper understanding of their needs.
- Market segmentation is the identification of specific groups of customers who respond differently from other groups to competitive strategies. They can be important in strategy development because they provide the opportunity to dominate part of the market.
- Identification of gaps in segment provision may provide the basis of new strategic opportunities.
- Customer profiling may also clarify the organisation's strengths when faced with customers who wish to switch to rival products.

6.3 COMMUNICATING WITH CUSTOMERS AND STAKEHOLDERS[11]

Organisations communicate with their customers in order to:

● inform them about their products; and

● persuade them to purchase or continue buying products or services.

In communicating with customers, the organisation also sends signals to the world at large – its employees, shareholders, the government and many other bodies. This group, including the customers, is often given the title *stakeholders* in the organisation.

Although the main emphasis of this chapter is with the customer, corporate analysis needs to consider not only the communications impact on customers but also on the wider group of stakeholders.

6.3.1 Cost effectiveness in persuasion

In most situations, personal persuasion is the most effective method of communication because the message can be tailored to the individual customer. However, for many domestic consumer products, it is not cost-effective to call on each customer, every time he or she fancies an ice cream, for example. Mass marketing is required – advertising, branding and promotion.

The key criterion in measuring communication strategy proposals is *cost effectiveness* – that is, the cost of obtaining an effective communication with the customer with the effect usually being measured as a product sale. The difficulty is that it is usually substantially easier to estimate the *cost* of such items as operating a sales force or mounting a campaign on television, than it is to measure the *effects* on sales of such activity. For example, even if the sales go up, it is not always clear that it was the result of the specific communications activity.[12]

Quantitative measures of the effects of such activity are in use, however. They work well in some areas such as direct mail – that is, promotions addressed and posted to individuals. However, they are incomplete in other areas such as advertising and sponsorship where there is often a time lag before the impact is fully realised. This means that there is an element of judgement involved in investment decisions in such areas but this does not usually inhibit strategic decisions to invest in brands, advertising and other communications areas.

Some commentators go further: although communications are important for corporate strategy, the impact of advertising is essentially difficult to assess. Professor John Kay[13] comments:

> This leads us to the conclusion that the effectiveness of modern advertising is fundamentally an irrational phenomenon.

He then goes on to defend the role of advertising in building and supporting the *reputation* of the company, but still leaves the impression that it is essentially wayward and unquantifiable. Certainly it is not easy to assess the effectiveness of advertising. However, the empirical research evidence of its measurement and effectiveness is greater than that implied by the above comment. Other areas of communication *can* be assessed accurately, e.g. direct mail and personal selling.

6.3.2 Communications options to reach customers

If an organisation wishes to communicate with customers, there are substantial differences of approach depending on the customer profile. These are shown in Table 6.5.

Essentially from a corporate strategy perspective, the communications issues are related to the methods of persuading customers to remain with the organisation. They may include:

- *Branding* – that is, the additional reassurance provided to the customer over the intrinsic value of the assets purchased by the customer. This can be a powerful method of retaining customer loyalty in mass-market products.
- *Personal selling* – that is a personal relationship and individually tailored message for a single customer to purchase the product. Each selling occasion is expensive and can only be justified if the order that is placed is sufficiently large.
- *Technical promotions* – that is, the use of the technical presentation of data on the product or service to persuade the potential customer of its merits. This may be conducted through research papers, magazines, technical advertising, exhibitions and trade conferences.
- *Consumer promotions* – that is, devices that promote the product without building any fundamental relationship. These may be effective where customer loyalty is low or a new product is being introduced.
- *Public relations and sponsorship* – that is, the more general activities undertaken by the organisation that will have an impact on a customer and other stakeholders. These will include lobbying of governments and other public bodies as mentioned in Chapter 4. They may also cover a broader range of corporate objectives such as support for the community and charities that take them beyond customer communications.

The choice of communications methods is likely to depend on the nature of the customer (*see* Table 6.5).

6.3.3 Communicating with stakeholders

Inevitably, any communications directed at customers will also be seen by other stakeholders. For example:

- employees
- shareholders
- consumer groups
- government
- suppliers
- trade unions

As a result, some organisations are now beginning to take a broader view of communications in corporate strategy. Customers may be the primary target but the broader public group will be influenced by the messages. For these reasons, internal communications to employees within the organisation and external messages are now being linked. *Public relations* has an important role in all these broader areas: many organisations now seek professional advice and planning in these sectors,

Table 6.5 Different types of communication for different customers

	Domestic consumer	Large industrial	Large private service	Not-for-profit charity	Public service	Small business	Strategic implications
Example	Unilever ice cream	Airbus aircraft	McDonald's restaurants	UNICEF	Health service hospital	Hairdresser or local builder	
Branding and advertising	Yes	Not usually beyond technical press	Yes	Possibly but doubts about cost-effectiveness	Possible but unlikely	No, except local advertising	Mass market, scatter-gun effect but can be cost effective
Personal selling	No, except to large distributors	Yes: important	Yes in the sense of personal service	Unlikely: against the culture	Personal attention but no real selling	Important part of promotion	Targeted and personal but often expensive
Consumer promotions	Yes	Yes, possibly	Yes	Mailing letters important	Not usually	Simple cost-effective methods constantly being tried	Mass market but effect can often be carefully assessed
Technical promotions and exhibitions	No	Yes	No	No	No	Yes	Carefully targeted but some areas difficult to assess
Sponsorship, PR and other third-party events	Yes	Yes	Yes	Yes for fund raising	Possibly	Yes on small scale	One of the most difficult to assess impact, but can be vital

even relatively small companies and those in the public sector. *Lobbying governments* and management in the event of a *corporate crisis* are examples of the important strategic activities included in this area.

Additionally, *sponsorship* is increasingly being used to provide a focus of communications activity. This is particularly true for those organisations that believe their role is more than just making a profit: cultural, charity and sporting events can be linked to communications in a wider and more socially acceptable way.

The general policy issues surrounding all these areas are part of overall corporate policy, rather than customer analysis and are explored further in Chapter 12.

6.3.4 Strategic implications of communications policy analysis

There are three strategic implications:

- *Integrated communications policy.* In view of the wider impact of customer communications, it is advisable for corporate strategy to develop a broader policy in this area. Such a policy must be consistent with customer communications.

- *Need to examine competitor activities.* Although these have not been discussed explicity above, no customer communications can stand in isolation from those of immediate competitors.

- *Consider innovative approaches.* In the light of the analysis results, it might be better to rewrite the rules. For example, it might be better to avoid the investment of consumer branding by supplying retailers with their own retailer brands. This would involve a totally different approach to communications in that part of the market.

In many cases, it is perfectly possible to assess with some accuracy the *effects* as well as the *costs* of communications. The areas where this is more difficult have been identified. Cost-effectiveness remains the major criterion for judging the strategic impact of communications.

CASE STUDY 6.2

Different communications approaches at Häagen-Dazs and Boeing

Large aircraft are sold to sophisticated airline customers. Premium ice cream is sold to domestic customers. They have totally different communications strategies.

International aircraft customers

Boeing aircraft are purchased by the world's leading airlines: British Airways, American Airlines, Lufthansa, Air France, Singapore Airlines and so on. Their general requirements are for technically safe and cost-efficient travel. In addition, there are substantial efforts to personalise the aircraft to the airline: design space, livery and engine capacity are examples. The final product is priced somewhere between US$80 and 120 million.

Ice cream customers

These customers buy what is largely a standardised product. They often buy brands that have their own personalities by association with the advertising and other forms of promotion. In the case of Häagen-Dazs, customers are purchasing a product that is positioned up-market with high-quality ingredients and an adult appeal. All these elements are used to justify the price of around US$4 per tub of product.

Communications

As a result, Boeing communications emphasise the technical performance, safety and global nature of the product. By contrast, Häagen-Dazs emphasises the adult overtones of its ice cream in a striking and original way that sets the product apart from what it claims are boring, normal products.

Corporate strategy and advertising

For Boeing, advertising is just a small part of its overall corporate strategy. For Häagen-Dazs, advertising moves beyond conveying basic product information. Figure 6.2 shows how it has been used to build the brand image. In strategic terms, it differentiates the product and helps to justify its premium price. It builds the product's *strategic reputation*.

CASE QUESTIONS

1 *What brand image do you derive from the advertisement? How important is such communication to the overall strategy of the brand?*

2 *Is brand building part of the basic corporate strategy of Häagen-Dazs? If so, how should its contribution be assessed?*

3 *How precisely should the company decide the level of advertising investment in this product and estimate the price premium to be charged?*

Fig 6.2   **Häagen-Dazs – building the brand image**

Copyright Jeanloup Sieff, Hamiltons Photographers Ltd. Agency: Bartle Bogle Hegarty Ltd.

> ■ **Key strategic principles**
>
> ● Organisations communicate with their customers in order to inform and persuade them about the merits of their product and services.
>
> ● Cost-effectiveness is the main criterion when assessing communications proposals. Costs are usually relatively easy to estimate but the effects of some promotional areas may be more difficult to assess.
>
> ● Different types of customers will need different forms of communication.
>
> ● Communications policy may need an integrated approach across the organisation. It will also need to examine activities of competitors and possibly consider innovative approaches to communications.

6.4 STRATEGIC PRICING AND VALUE FOR MONEY

Short-term pricing does not usually form the basis of sustainable competitive advantage because any price changes can be imitated very quickly by competitors. Nevertheless, pricing is strategically important for several reasons:

● *The impact of price changes on profitability.* This is explained below.

● *The positioning of products in the market place.* The price can be used to signal more general forms of competitive advantage – for example, there are no cheap Rolls Royce or Porsche cars.

● *The value-for-money impression created about the organisation.* Price needs to be coupled with quality, after-sales service and other aspects of the product.

The impact of price changes on the organisation's profitability is often immediate. For example, Table 6.6 shows the impact of a ±5 per cent change in price and

Table 6.6 The sensitivity of price and volume changes at Stora

	Effect on earnings due to ±5% change in	
	Price (SEK m)	*Volume* (SEK m)
Fluff pulp	60	30
Newsprint	330	160
SC (uncoated magazine paper)	120	50
LWC (coated magazine paper)	320	160
Liquid packaging board	90	40
Other board	220	100
Packaging paper	170	90
Fine papers	430	150
Other grades	10	50
Total	1840	830

Source: Stora Annual Report and Accounts 1995

volume on the earnings of different product areas at Stora Paper and Pulp Company (discussed in Chapter 4). Price changes have more than twice the impact on earnings compared with volume changes at the company. Although other companies may not show the same sensitivity, the evidence does show how important it can be for companies to set and control pricing in the context of profit objectives.

6.4.1 The pricing decision: the basic considerations

As a starting point for customer analysis, the pricing decision can be considered as a balance of two main factors:

- *Costs*. Setting the market price below the marginal cost of production will certainly lose the company money.
- *Competition*. Pitching the market price significantly above competition will result in minimal sales even if there is some product differentiation.

Figure 6.3 shows how these factors can be balanced out to provide some basic considerations in price setting. Beyond this basic structure, the factors that will then influence pricing include:

- *Price elasticity* – the sensitivity of volume to changes in price.
- *Stage in the product life cycle* – early stages may need some special pricing strategies.
- *Strategic role of price*.

It is this last element that will benefit particularly from further analysis. In some product categories and competitive situations, pricing forms a key part of overall company strategy. For example:

- *Price discounting* – where a company deliberately offers cut-price goods on a permanent basis such as Aldi (Germany and Holland) and Kwiksave (UK) in grocery retailing.

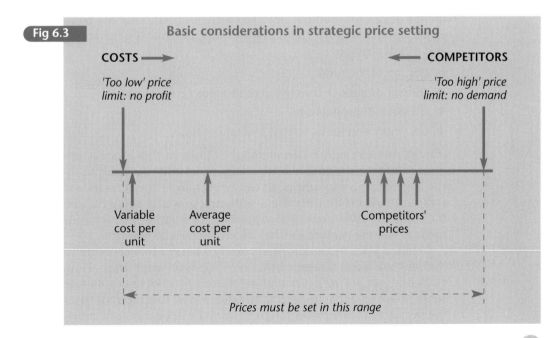

Fig 6.3   **Basic considerations in strategic price setting**

COSTS ➝   ⬅ COMPETITORS

'Too low' price limit: no profit   'Too high' price limit: no demand

Variable cost per unit   Average cost per unit   Competitors' prices

Prices must be set in this range

● *Premium pricing* – where a company sets out to price its goods at permanently high prices such as Yves St Laurent, Dunhill and Gucci.

These are basic strategic decisions of the organisation that need careful analysis at an early stage. They will then form part of the strategic options considerations of Part 3 of this book.

6.4.2 Value for money

For many customers, considerations other than the quoted price also apply – quality, availability of stock, product performance, after-sales service, brand value and many other issues. For example in purchasing aircraft, performance, special financing deals and the currency of purchase may well clinch the deal for a company. For these reasons, *value for money* which includes these broader elements may be a more appropriate method of analysing pricing.

All these items make simple pricing decisions more complex. Determination of costs and prices is not an exact science. Therefore, there are real issues to be resolved in advance of any price negotiations.

6.4.3 Negotiated pricing deals

Some customers purchase mainly on the basis of competitive price comparisons: for example in commodity products, such as some areas of paper and pulp, price is crucial and any significant difference from competition will impact quickly on sales levels. In these cases, products usually perform to acceptable industry standards and are readily available for delivery. The key considerations are:

● the *quoted* price; and
● the price *negotiated* by customers.

Price negotiation will depend primarily on the relative buying power of customers (Five Forces analysis will assist here) and may well include elements other than the quoted price – for example, delayed payment, finance for the purchase, other credit terms, special volume discounts, etc. All these may be the subject of negotiation and will depend on:

● the size of the order;
● the importance of the customer in terms of annual sales;
● the costs of production;
● the prices and terms offered by competitors.

Inevitably there may be an element of bluff in this process, especially over the prices and terms available from competitors and the freedom that is available to the negotiator to vary prices. As can be seen from the Stora data in Table 6.6, there is often a case for limiting the negotiating power in some circumstances: at Stora, the company gives priority to *supporting prices* rather than chasing every extra element of volume because this has a lower impact on profits.

Detailed price negotiations are rarely a matter for corporate strategy, except in the case of a major strategic initiative such as an acquisition. However, the general guidelines on *pricing policy* and *negotiation freedom* may well form a basic area of strategy. For example in negotiating major new contracts for the supply of aircraft, the degree to which prices might be varied will be carefully considered in advance of the commencement of negotiations. If it is a new and attractive long-term customer, then greater flexibility may be entirely appropriate. However, there are matters that need to be controlled carefully:

1 Price reductions must not go below the costs of producing the goods, otherwise a loss will be made.

2 A precedent should not be set for future prices so that the customer always expects low prices in the long term.

In addition to these issues, it needs to be recognised that pricing negotiations will not affect every price contract (*see* Table 6.7).

Table 6.7 Customer strategy: pricing and value-for-money considerations

	Domestic consumer	*Large industrial*	*Large private service*	*Not-for-profit charity*	*Public service*	*Small business*	*Strategic implications*
Example	Unilever ice cream	Airbus aircraft	McDonald's restaurants	UNICEF	Health service hospital	Hairdresser or local builder	
Turbulent environment?	Not normally: depends on product	Quite possible	Not normally	No	No	Quite possible	When turbulent, more flexibility and rapid reaction to events necessary
Discounts and special terms?	No	Yes, many	No	n.a.	Tough negotiating with finance providers	Yes, many	Discounts need more initiative with individual managers, less centralised pricing
Negotiation	No	Yes	No	n.a.	No	Yes	Bargaining power important in negotiation
Strategic role of price	Affects positioning and competition	Technical and complex negotiation	As domestic	Largely irrelevant	Fixed but financial providers may need evidence of value for money	Technical and personal negotiation	Can be complex and specific to industry

6.4.4 Target pricing

One major pricing technique that deserves careful analysis is target pricing because of its strategic significance. *Target pricing* sets the price for goods and services primarily on the basis of the competitive position of the company, almost regardless of the costs of producing the goods. Having established the target price, engineers, production workers, marketers, designers, suppliers and others are then given target costs that must be met for profit targets to be met.

This process contrasts sharply with the traditional practice of *cost-plus pricing:* all the costs are added up, a percentage profit margin is applied and the final price is then determined. The two routes to pricing are shown in Fig 6.4.

Target pricing has been used for some years by Japanese car companies to achieve their profit and marketing objectives.[14] It has been highly successful but relies on close co-operation between all elements and the use of innovative ideas at the design stage to reduce costs (*see* Chapter 10). The detail of the procedures is not a matter of corporate strategy. However, the principle of target pricing is fundamental as an option for customer strategy analysis.

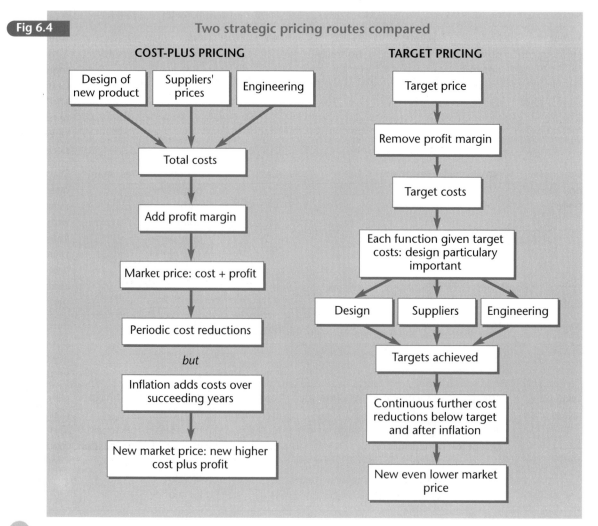

Fig 6.4   Two strategic pricing routes compared

Clearly, target pricing can put real pressure on competitors. It has actually been used by Airbus Industrie to compete against Boeing, though it is not entirely clear whether this was intentional or the only way that the company could operate. As the opening case explained, Airbus is structured as a conglomerate GIE. This means that Airbus has no production facilities of its own but uses those of its shareholders: Dasa, Aerospatiale, BAe and Casa. Airbus therefore has only very limited information on its costs and simply negotiates a price with its customers. It then calculates the *target price* it is prepared to pay its shareholders for their components and tells them. If the aircraft price falls, Airbus drives a harder bargain with its shareholder-suppliers, forcing them to cut costs if they wish to make a profit.[15]

Key strategic principles

- Pricing strategy can have strategic significance at three levels: rapid impact on profitability, positioning of the product and value for money.

- The price decision will be determined by a balance of factors under the general headings of costs and competitor analysis.

- Value for money, which includes quality, branding and other factors, represents the broader elements that will determine and condition pricing for many customers.

- Negotiated price deals need to be constrained by customer analysis and corporate strategy.

- Target pricing places the main emphasis on competitors' prices and has proved an important element in the success of some companies over the last few years.

6.5 CUSTOMER/COMPETITOR MATRIX

It will be evident that customer and competitor analyses are interlinked and can therefore usefully be brought together. One method of undertaking this task is the *customer/competitor matrix*. The purpose of such an analysis is to explore the types of strategy and the difficulties of entering or staying in such an industry. The matrix is shown in Fig 6.5 and combines two main elements:

1 *Customer needs – providing* sources *of competitive advantage.*
   - Some customers have essentially the same needs as others, for example when purchasing commodities such as sugar, cotton or electricity. The *sources* of competitive advantage will therefore be *limited* for such products – minor variations in the price and quality of cotton, for example.
   - Some customers have infinitely varied needs. For example, hairdressing and strategy consulting where no two jobs are ever exactly the same. The *sources* of competitive advantages here are *many* and *varied* – for example, type of service, quality of product, length of assignment, etc.

Fig 6.5	Customer/competitor matrix

Customer needs

	Small, so easily imitated	Large, so difficult to imitate
Very varied, so many sources of competitive advantage	Fragmented strategies	Specialised strategies
Largely the same, so few sources of competitive advantage	Stalemate strategies	Volume strategies

Small, so easily imitated · Large, so difficult to imitate

Competitor advantage

2 *Competitor advantages – based on economies of scale and differentiation.*

- Some companies will have small competitive advantages because either scale is low or there is little differentiation possible. For example, coal mining and an average country hotel represent areas where the products are easily imitated.

- Some companies will have large competive advantages because there are economies of scale and the product is well differentiated and difficult to imitate. For example, branded ice cream products at Unilever and Boeing aircraft.

From this matrix, four types of strategic situation emerge:

1 *Fragmented strategies.* Customer needs are highly varied and provide sources of competitive advantage but the advantages they deliver are easily imitated. Speciality retailing, hairdressing and other small businesses are examples. Some accountancy companies fall into this category. However, the large, multinational accountancy companies have managed to break out and supply a service that relies on scale to audit their multinational clients: they employ *specialised* strategies (*see* below).

2 *Specialised strategies.* These involve special or corporate skills, patents, proprietory products that are sold to many different customers who all have varied needs often on a large scale. Examples are some of the major drug companies, with varied end-markets and strongly patented products, and international consulting companies.

3 *Volume strategies.* These are often based on economies of scale and branding but involve customers who want basically standard products with little individual variation. Examples include branded products and some types of basic industrial chemicals. Hospitals are increasingly offering services in this area such as standard operations and medical checks.

4 *Stalemate strategies.* The products are easily imitated and most customer needs are essentially the same. It is therefore difficult to raise the value added because customers can easily switch to another supplier. Examples are some staple food products and many commodities.

Key strategic principles

● The customer/competitor matrix links together two important aspects: the extent to which customers have common needs and the possibilities of achieving competitive advantage in the market place based on differentiation and economies of scale.

● It identifies four main types of strategic situation: fragmented, specialised, volume and stalemate. The strategic significance of each can then be explored.

6.6 INTERNATIONAL CUSTOMER CONSIDERATIONS

Disney, Benetton, Sony, Heineken and Adidas are all examples of international brands that are instantly recognisable in many countries around the world. Products, tastes and markets are becoming increasingly international. In this sense, customer analysis also needs to become more international in its approach.

Probably the most famous article arguing for an international approach to strategy development was written by Theodore Levitt in 1983 – 'the Globalisation of Markets'.[16] He acknowledged that there were real differences in taste, culture and language around the world but argued that the pressures for globalisation would more than outweigh them. Everyone was developing global tastes:

> *Cosmopolitanism is no longer the monopoly of the intellectual and leisure classes; it is becoming the established property and defining characteristic of all sectors everywhere in the world.*

Levitt's main arguments are summarised in Exhibit 6.3. To support his enthusiasm, Levitt quoted the evidence of a washing machine manufacturer who had *not* followed a global approach,[17] as well as brief examples of companies that had successfully internationalised. The most significant point in developing international analysis is that it is *far more important to seek the similarities between nations* than to analyse the differences: this remains true in the late 1990s. Levitt also lays great emphasis on international economies of scale to deliver really low prices and thus overcome any differences in taste.

- Price competition is important and persuasive for customers.
- It is possible to change national tastes if prices are low enough.
- Globalisation will emerge from a standardisation of products and services.
- Tariffs and quotas will not protect national industries against the international attack.
- Major economies of scale are possible and will lead to increased international price competition.
- Global branding is meaningful and attractive to customers.

Comment   Written in enthusiastic tones, bordering on the lyrical, Levitt's article has certainly been influential. However, the quality of evidence in the article is poor, the assertions inaccurate and the argument open to question at several points. Douglas and Wind produced a critique that was both accurate and helpful several years later.[18] Nevertheless, the central argument that it is better to seek the similarities rather than the differences is still useful today.

 Key strategic principles

- International analysis needs to concentrate on the similarities rather than the differences between nations.
- There are numerous potential advantages from operating internationally. However, they depend on some assumptions about customers that need careful validation in reality.

CASE STUDY 6.3

Boeing's customer and competitor strategies for its new airliner – the Boeing 777[19]

When it set about building a new aircraft for the 1990s, the world's largest aerospace company, Boeing, developed new competitive strategies to link with its customers and fight its main competitor, the European company, Airbus Industrie.

On a grey and blustery day in Seattle in May 1995, a new Boeing 777 took off from the local airfield to the cheers of the company's employees. It was the company's first new model in 13 years and was likely to be the last passenger aircraft model launched by any manufacturer this century. On it, rested Boeing's hopes of remaining the world's leading aircraft maker and resisting the challenge of Airbus Industrie, its increasingly confident European competitor.

Boeing's executives say that building the aircraft which carries up to 400 passengers changed the way the company operated, breaking down barriers between its specialists, introducing new technology and making closer contact with its customers. The new aircraft, priced at US$120 million before discounts, was developed against a background of some of the worst market conditions the industry has seen. When Boeing decided to build the aircraft in 1990, it employed 161 000 people and recorded annual net earnings of US$ 1.9 billion. By the end of 1994, staff numbers were down to 117 000 and net earnings were US$856 million (*see* Fig 6.6). Another 12 000 job losses were expected in 1995.

In 1994, Boeing had a shock when Airbus recorded more orders than it did – the first time Boeing had been deprived of the top slot since the arrival of the jet age. However, by the end of 1995, the situation was much changed with Boeing's success in obtaining major new orders for its 777. Nevertheless, the shadow of Airbus has hung over the entire 777 project on which analysts estimate

Boeing has spent US$5 billion. For example, Mr Gordon McKinzie, the airline buyer at the US air carrier United Airlines, openly admits to playing off Boeing and Airbus against each other in a bid to gain a better deal and better aircraft. Towards the end of the 1980s, United realised that it would need a replacement for its McDonnell Douglas DC-10 fleet which would be 25 years old in 1996. In October 1990, the airline invited Boeing, Airbus and McDonnell Douglas to Chicago to present their arguments for re-equipping the United fleet: United was the world's largest airline so this was an attractive contract. United had to choose between Boeing's 777, the Airbus A330 and A340 and the McDonnell Douglas MD-11. The company was impressed by Airbus' 'fly-by-wire' technology which allows the wing and tail surfaces to be controlled electrically rather than mechanically. However, it decided that the 777 seemed the better aircraft. However, it told Boeing that the aircraft would have to be designed and made differently from the manufacturer's previous models.

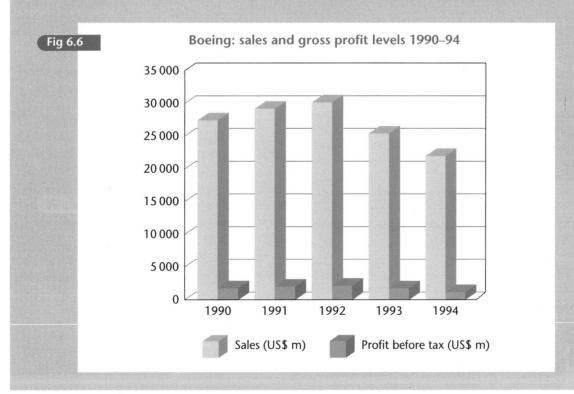

Fig 6.6

Boeing: sales and gross profit levels 1990–94

Sales (US$ m) Profit before tax (US$ m)

First, United said that the aircraft would have to work properly from the day it was delivered. United did not want a repeat of its experience with the Boeing 747-400 when it and other airlines had to sort out early faults. Mr McKinzie said:

What we had in mind was orchestrating a departure from our past practice of ordering an aeroplane, waiting five years, then giving Boeing a final payment hoping everything aboard was as we expected.

Second, United would help Boeing design the 777 from the beginning.

We moved into Boeing. We virtually infiltrated the Boeing process.

Boeing customers

Boeing decided to go further, inviting eight airlines to help it design the aircraft – United, American Airlines, Delta Air Lines, British Airways, Cathay Pacific, Qantas, Japan Airlines and All Nippon Airways. Three Japanese companies were to make 20 per cent of the airframe – Mitsubishi, Kawasaki and Fuji Heavy Industries. The airlines and Boeing decided it would have fly-by-wire technology. It was designed entirely by computer so that no mock-up had to be built.

The involvement of its airline customers saved Boeing from making several errors. United told Boeing that the level of the 777's fuelling panels meant the aircraft would need different fuelling trucks from those used for the 747. Boeing agreed to change the positioning of the 777 panels so that the same trucks could be used on both models. United said it did not want silver-plated wiring in the fuel tanks because past experience had shown that this corroded. Nickel-plated wiring was used instead.

777 sales

Before the 777 was completed, it had attracted 144 firm orders and 99 options. United was the largest customer with 34 orders and 34 options. Boeing claims that since work on the 777 started in 1990, the aircraft has taken a clear sales lead over the A330 and A340 and the MD-11. Airbus

concedes that the 777 has outsold its aircraft but the two companies disagree on how big a lead Boeing has. Airbus scoffs, however, at Boeing's claims that it has broken new ground in the design of the 777. Airbus says its A320 aircraft which entered service in 1988 was 90 per cent computer-designed. The A340 which went into service in 1993 was completely computer-designed.

Airbus also asks why Boeing should regard listening to customers as such a feat. Mr Gerald Greewald, Chairman of United, has an explanation: 'Historically, aeroplanes have been designed by engineers for engineers and the engineers have been left to determine what's good for everyone else.'

Mr Philip Condit, the man who headed the Boeing 777 project, explained that while other manufacturers were being forced to listen to their customers many in the airline industry thought of themselves as a special case: 'There's always a temptation to say that aeroplanes are different. We have a product that leaves the ground.'

Boeing's Chairman, Mr Frank Schrontz, says he is confident that the company can maintain a worldwide market share of 60 to 65 per cent, in spite of the progress Airbus has made. The challenge now will be to begin earning a return on the large investment in the 777. The orders accumulated in 1990 dried up in 1994 when the aircraft did not attract any new buyers. Of the eight airlines that helped design the 777, three – American, Delta and Qantas – have not ordered any. However, Boeing says airlines will buy more than 15 000 aircraft over the next 20 years. An independent financial analyst commented that Boeing's ability to produce a new aircraft with fewer people has made him optimistic about the future. 'Boeing's ability to remain competitive is not going to be challenged.'

Source: Financial Times, 6 June 1995.

CASE QUESTIONS

1 *What was the customer strategy of Boeing for the 777? What had it been previously? Why?*

2 Do you agree with the Airbus comment that the new customer strategy was nothing special? Or do you take the view that Boeing could hardly have become the leading aircraft manufacturer in the world if it had little idea of customer needs?

3 How significant do you consider the desire of Boeing and its customers to adopt the 'fly-by-wire' technology of its rival? To what extent was this just a catching-up process? How, if at all, might it give a competitive design edge to Boeing?

4 How convincing do you find the Boeing estimate of 15 000 sales over the next 20 years? What does this imply with regard to its investment of US$5 billion?

5 If you were working in corporate strategy at Airbus Industrie and had read the article in the Financial Times on which this case study is based, what would it indicate about the strategies that Airbus needed to adopt over the next five years?

KEY READING

The competitive triangle[20]

In this extract from their book, Dennis Adcock, Ray Bradfield, Al Halborg and Caroline Ross explore the key relationship between the company, its customers and its competitors.

The competitive triangle is inspired by the work of Kenichi Ohmae. It is an excellent way of remembering that customers have choices. From the apex of the triangle customers can assess the different offerings of all companies and their competitors.

Obviously, customers will choose to do business with that company which best matches requirements. Of course, the workings of customers' decision processes are not simple. Nevertheless, the match between the various offerings and particular customers, or groups of customers, should not happen by chance. The role of strategists is to try to influence factors in such a way that their organisations are chosen.

The object of this is to try to gain a sustainable advantage over competitors. Writing in the *Harvard Business Review* on this subject, Pankaj Ghemwat stated:

> For outstanding performance, a company has to beat competition. The trouble is that competition has heard the same message.

He summarises three areas of potential advantage from cross-industry findings:

1 *Product innovation.* Competitors secure detailed information on 70 per cent of all new products within a year of their development. Patenting usually fails to deter imitation. On average, imitation costs a third less than innovation and is a third quicker.

2 *Production.* New processes are even harder to protect than new products. Incremental improvements to old processes are vulnerable too. If consultants are to be believed, 60 per cent to 90 per cent of all 'learning' ultimately diffuses to competitors. Production often blurs competitive advantage: recent studies show that unionised workers pocket two-thirds of the potential profits in US manufacturing.

3 *Marketing.* Non-price instruments are usually ascribed more potency than price changes, partly because they are harder to match. Rivals often react to a particular move, however, by adjusting their entire marketing mix. Such reactions tend to be

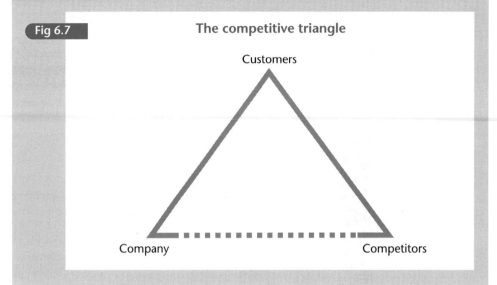

Fig 6.7

The competitive triangle

intense; limited data on advertising suggest that the moves and countermoves frequently cancel out.

Nevertheless, Peters still suggests that the goal should be uniqueness. He advises:

> *Uniqueness most often comes not from a breakthrough idea, but from some accumulation of thousands of tiny enhancements.*

In the early days of marketing, it was suggested that organisations looked for one Unique Selling Proposition (USP). In fact, as Peters points out, it is much more complex. Therefore, to achieve competitive advantage, a strategist needs to be involved with the total offering, both inside and outside the organisation.

The study of competitors' activities is vital. But it must be closely linked to a study of potential buyers, how those buyers behave and how they are likely to behave in the future. It is necessary for marketers to study both customers and competitors. A focus on one alone is not enough, as it leaves the triangle incomplete. If there is a failure to appreciate the ever-changing competition, then these words of warning are even more relevant:

> *There are three types of companies. Those who make things happen. Those who watch things happen. And those who wonder what happened.*

Source: Adcock, D, Bradfield, R, Halborg, A and Ross, C (1995) *Marketing Principles and Practice*, Pitman Publishing.

SUMMARY

- Customers are important because they buy the products or services of the organisation and therefore turn its products into profits. At its most basic level, corporate strategy will wish to determine the levels of demand for its goods. In addition, corporate strategy may wish to investigate the customer needs that are currently not being met by existing products: these may provide possible future opportunities. Some companies have oriented their strategy towards developing the customer-driven organisation.

- In analysing customers, both prescriptive and emergent approaches are useful. In addition, customers need to be carefully defined from both a broad and a narrow perspective: if this is not done, important areas of customer need and competitor attack may be missed.

- Market segmentation is the identification of specific groups of customers who respond differently from other groups to competitive strategies. The advantages of segmentation in corporate strategy relate to the development of sustainable competitive advantage and to the ability to target products to that segment.

- Communicating with customers is important both to inform them and to persuade them about the organisation's products and services. Cost-effectiveness is the main criterion when it comes to assessing the methods to employ. Costs are relatively easy to determine but the effects of some forms of promotion may be more difficult.

- Pricing is important because of its short-term impact on profits, because it allows a product to be positioned against others and because it is a measure of the value for money delivered by the organisation. To develop pricing strategy, it is necessary to examine both costs and competitive prices. The result also needs to be balanced by a number of other factors in the market place, such as price elasticity, the position in the product life cycle and the role of pricing in the product. Target pricing is one approach to pricing strategy: it places the emphasis on matching competitive prices.

- The customer/competitor matrix is one method of drawing together some of the strategy issues that arise out of these two areas. It combines the extent to which customers have common needs with the possibilities of achieving competitive advantage in the market place. Four main types of strategic situation result.

- Business is undoubtedly becoming more international. Customer analysis therefore needs to follow this trend. It has been argued that, although there are national differences in taste and culture, it is more important to seek out the similarities than to examine the differences. The greater economies of scale from operating internationally will be reflected in lower prices that will overcome any lingering problems over differences in taste.

QUESTIONS

1 Take the global market for large aircraft and explain the areas of customer analysis you would wish to consider in developing the corporate strategy for Airbus Industrie.

2 To what extent is it worth while estimating demand when a market is turbulent? What are the reasons for undertaking the task and what are the problems?

3 On the subject of customer needs, Professor G Hamel and Professor C K Prahalad comment:

> *Any company that can do no more than respond to the articulated needs of existing customers will quickly become a laggard.*

Explain briefly the argument that is being used here and then comment on its validity. Are unmet needs so very important for strategy development?

4 Take a market with which you are familiar and assess one of the leading organisations as a *customer-driven* organisation. Use Exhibit 6.1 to assist you. How might the chosen organisation improve its performance?

5 Compare and contrast the purchasing behaviour, communications strategy and pricing policies of the following three companies: a branded breakfast cereal manufacturer, a large retail bank and a national charitable institution of your choice.

6 What are the arguments in favour of cost-effectiveness in communicating with the customer? What are the difficulties? In view of your answer, what problems do you foresee in assessing the usefulness of the Häagen-Dazs and Boeing advertising campaigners described in Case study 6.2? Are they likely to be cost-effective?

7 Arguably Airbus Industrie over the last few years has followed a strategy of attempting to catch up with Boeing's initiatives. Is this the best approach to aircraft corporate strategy development? Or would Airbus have been better to seek out a new, unmet customer need?

8 What are the likely dangers of target pricing? Is it worth while? Are there any circumstances where it could not be used?

9 '*A powerful force drives the world toward a converging commonality and that force is technology...the globalisation of markets is at hand.*' Professor Theodore Levitt

Discuss.

10 Identify where the following would fit on the customer/competitor matrix: a large hospital; a major league football team such as Real Madrid, Juventus or Manchester United; the Ford Motor Company; and Airbus Industrie. What are the strategy implications?

STRATEGIC PROJECT

The world market for regional aircraft

This chapter has concentrated on the market for international *long-haul* aircraft. There is another market for *regional* aircraft which have between roughly 20 and 80 seats. Many of the same companies are or were involved such as Dasa, Aerospatiale, British Aerospace and Casa along with Fokker (Netherlands) and Alenia (Italy). After growth during the 1980s, the regional aircraft market has been a disaster for all concerned during the 1990s. Some companies have lost very large sums of money. Investigate the reasons and explore the corporate strategies necessary for the late 1990s.

FURTHER READING

There are two books that explore the subjects of this chapter in much greater detail: Philip Kotler's *Marketing Management* (Prentice Hall, NJ, 1994, 8th edn) and Michael J Baker's *Marketing Strategy and Management* (Macmillan, London, 1992, 2nd edn).

REFERENCES

1 *See Financial Times*: 13 Sep 1990; 29 Jan 1993, p17; 3 Mar 1993, p19; 11 May 1994, p33; 19 Apr 1995, p17; 23 Feb 1996, p15.
2 Levitt, T (1960) 'Marketing Myopia', *Harvard Business Review*, July–Aug, pp45– 56.
3 Hamel, G and Prahalad, C K (1994) *Competing for the Future*, Harvard Business School Press, Mass, p102.
4 Aaker, D (1992) *Strategic Marketing Management*, 3rd edn, Wiley, New York, p213.
5 Levitt, T (1960) Ibid, p45.
6 *See* for example, Baxter, A (1994) 'Clash of two metals', *Financial Times*, 20 Oct, p21.
7 Davidson, H (1987) *Offensive Marketing*, Penguin, Harmondsworth, p126.
8 Aaker, D (1992) Ibid, p48.
9 Porter, M E (1985) *Competitive Advantage*, Free Press, New York, p233.
10 Ohmae, K (1983) *The Mind of the Strategist*, Penguin, p103.
11 This whole subject is relatively poorly discussed in corporate strategy literature. Professor J Kay is the only recent strategist to deal in any depth with the issues raised in this chapter: *Foundations of Corporate Success* (Oxford University Press, Oxford, 1994) has two chapters but they treat the subject from an economics rather than a marketing perspective and are rather limited as a result.
12 Baker, M (1992) *Marketing Strategy and Management*, 2nd edn, Macmillan, Ch 17.
13 Kay, J (1994) Ibid, p252.
14 Cusumano, M A and Takeishi, A (1991) 'Supplier relations and management: a survey of Japanese, Japanese transplant and US Auto plants', *Strategic Management Journal*, 12, pp56–8.
15 Skapinker, M (1996) 'A struggle to fly to the top', *Financial Times*, 23 Feb, p15.
16 Levitt, T (1983) 'The globalisation of markets', *Harvard Business Review*, May–June, pp92–102.
17 Readers may care to note that some of this evidence is reduced in the shortened version of this article that appears in books such as that by De Wit, R and Meyer, B (1994) *Strategy: Content, Context and Process*, West Publishing. It is a pity that the flimsy nature of the empirical evidence has been emasculated.
18 Douglas, S and Wind, Y (1987) 'The Myth of Globalisation', *Columbia Journal of World Business*, Winter. This is also reprinted in De Wit, R and Meyer, Bob (1994) Ibid.
19 Adapted from an article in the *Financial Times*, 6 June 1995, p19. © *Financial Times*. Reproduced with permission.
20 Adcock, D, Bradfield, R, Halberg, A and Ross, C (1995) *Marketing Principles and Practice*, 2nd edn, Pitman Publishing. Also source for Fig 6.7. Reproduced with permission.

ANALYSIS OF RESOURCES

Both the emergent and prescriptive strategy processes regard the organisation's resources as the foundation stone of strategy development.

The resources are the means by which the organisation generates *value*. It is this value that is then distributed to the employees as salaries, to government as taxes, to the shareholders as dividends or retained in the organisation to be reinvested for the future. This part introduces the concept of generating value and its fundamental importance to corporate strategy. The three resources of the organisation – human, financial and operations – are then explored in turn.

PART 3

ANALYSIS OF RESOURCES

• The *prescriptive* strategic process

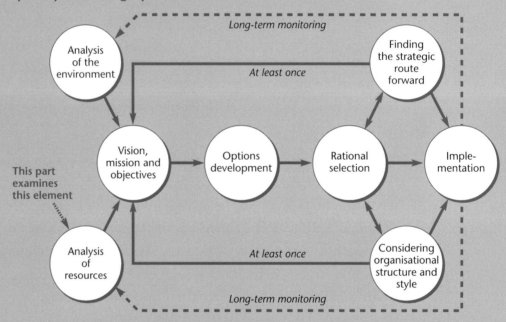

• The *emergent* strategic process

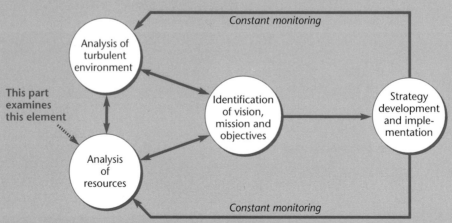

Chapter 7
ANALYSING RESOURCES

- What key industry factors deliver the objectives of the organisation?
- How do resources add value to the organisation?
- What is the role of the value chain in adding value?
- How does cost reduction contribute to added value?
- What are the core resources of the organisation and how do they contribute to value added?
- What are the organisation's strengths, weaknesses, opportunities and threats?

Chapter 8
ANALYSING HUMAN RESOURCES

- How do human resources add value? And how do they contribute to sustainable competitive advantage?
- What is the organisation's culture? How does it take decisions and develop its strategy?
- How does the organisation undertake change?
- How does the politics of the organisation affect change?

Chapter 9
ANALYSING FINANCIAL RESOURCES

- How do financial resources add value? And how do they contribute to sustainable competitive advantage?
- What are the main sources and the cost of finance?
- What are the financial consequences of strategic expansion?
- What is the relationship between financial and corporate objectives?

Chapter 10
ANALYSING OPERATIONS RESOURCES

- How do operations resources add value? And how do they contribute to sustainable competitive advantage?
- What impact do changes in technology have on corporate strategy?
- What areas of operations strategy make a major contribution to corporate strategy?
- What are the main elements of operations strategy?

7

Analysing resources

When you have worked through this chapter, you will be able to:

- identify the key factors for success in an industry;

- explore the main resources of an organisation;

- explain the concept of value added;

- analyse the value chain of an organisation and comment on its strategic significance;

- identify the main routes for cost reduction in an organisation;

- outline the core resources of an organisation, including its core competences;

- undertake a SWOT analysis for the organisation.

INTRODUCTION

Analysing the resources of an organisation involves not only drawing up a list of the main resources, but also developing an understanding of the way the organisation operates, what its strengths and weaknesses are and how it can serve its customers better and build advantage over its competitors.

This chapter begins by considering the factors that deliver success in an industry as a whole, covering both the resources and the environment – *the key factors for success*.

The *purpose and use* of resources are then explored. Essentially, the organisation takes goods from its suppliers and turns them into finished goods or services that are then sold or delivered into the environment. In particular, the organisation *adds value* to the inputs it receives from its suppliers. This chapter covers two ways in which an organisation does this: *cost reduction* and *core competences*. The chapter ends by examining the organisation's strengths, weaknesses, opportunities and threats – *the SWOT analysis* – another concept which combines both the organisation's resources *and* its environment. Figure 7.1 summarises the main elements.

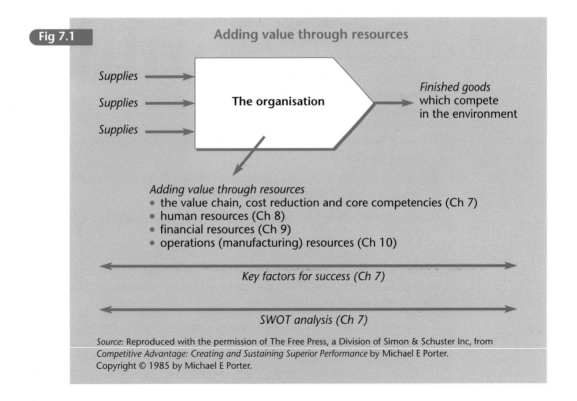

Fig 7.1   **Adding value through resources**

Supplies →
Supplies → **The organisation** → *Finished goods which compete in the environment*
Supplies →

Adding value through resources
- the value chain, cost reduction and core competencies (Ch 7)
- human resources (Ch 8)
- financial resources (Ch 9)
- operations (manufacturing) resources (Ch 10)

Key factors for success (Ch 7)

SWOT analysis (Ch 7)

Source: Reproduced with the permission of The Free Press, a Division of Simon & Schuster Inc, from *Competitive Advantage: Creating and Sustaining Superior Performance* by Michael E Porter. Copyright © 1985 by Michael E Porter.

Utilising resources at Glaxo Wellcome Pharmaceuticals[1]

After its acquisition of Wellcome (UK) in 1995, Glaxo (UK) became the biggest drug company in the world. This case study examines the strategic resources employed by the new Glaxo Wellcome company to maintain its competitive position.

Ever since the early 1980s, Glaxo had been highly dependent on its drug Zantac which is used for treating stomach ulcers. Although the drug was revolutionary and highly effective, the company was relying heavily on a drug that was due to run out of basic patent protection in 1997. Zantac accounted for 44 per cent of sales and 50 per cent of profits in 1994. The drug was coming under increased competitive threat as its patents ran out and its sales suffered from a new rival drug from a Swedish company. However, Glaxo had used its profits over the years to develop substantial company resources:

- *Research and development* produced unique new drugs that were difficult, if not impossible, for competitors to copy. This provided long-term competitive advantage that was sustainable. However, R&D was expensive and uncertain.

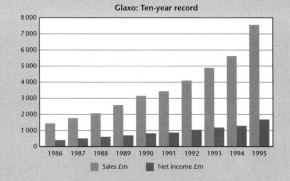

Glaxo: Ten-year record

- *Promotion and marketing* to doctors and health authority customers was developed by Glaxo's own teams and by alliances with other drug companies where these were particularly strong geographically.

- *Product manufacturing and quality* clearly needed to be highly advanced given the life-saving nature of the resulting products.

- *Cash reserves* of US$3.3 billion in mid-1994 formed the basis for a major strategic thrust.

Most pharmaceutical companies rely on a company strategy that places heavy emphasis on new drugs and hence research and development. This was particularly true during the 1980s. As the 1990s developed, three new pharmaceutical corporate strategies began to emerge:

1 *The need to control distribution channels.* Drug distribution has become increasingly concentrated. Some leading manufacturers with substantial financial resources (but not Glaxo) have acquired leading distribution companies. After such take-overs, their resource analyses change with greater costs being expended in the distribution and stock control area.

2 *Mergers with or acquisitions of competitors.* This was the route chosen by Glaxo with its take-over of Wellcome (UK) to form what was the largest drug company in the world in 1995. Glaxo paid US$13.5 billion for the acquisition. The aim was to achieve greater efficiencies through combining manufacturing, research and development and marketing costs.

3 *Move from biochemical to biogenetic new product development.* The major growth area is currently biogenetics, although the profits have yet to emerge. In addition to its purchase of Wellcome, Glaxo also paid US$533 million for the Affymax biotech group in 1995.

After acquisition, Glaxo began to reassess the combined resources of the two groups. Duplication of administration and marketing could clearly be eliminated cutting 2600 jobs in a key resource area. Another 3000 jobs were expected to be lost in manufacturing. Finally, around 1800 jobs were to be lost as the two R&D teams were combined together. This was assessed through a resource review in 1995.

Although the total annual saving from these measures was expected to be over US$1 billion, there was a real risk. The threat of the job cuts and major change unsettled everyone. There was a period from the time of the acquisition in March 1995 to the announcement of the results of the resource review in September 1995 when morale was low and no one was certain of a job. This was felt particularly keenly in the R&D area.

CASE QUESTIONS

1 *What are the major resources of a company like Glaxo Wellcome?*

2 *What were the strategic implications for those resources of the acquisition of Wellcome by Glaxo?*

3 *What were the risks involved? Did the results justify the risks?*

4 *The case suggests that other pharmaceutical companies are following alternative strategies. What are these? Do they involve a lower risk?*

7.1 PRESCRIPTIVE AND EMERGENT APPROACHES TO RESOURCE ISSUES

Both emergent and prescriptive approaches to strategy development regard resources as important. However, their perspectives are very different.

Prescriptive strategists take the view that it is important to use resources efficiently and build on resource strengths. Resources are to some extent regarded as inanimate objects without feeling. Hence it is possible for strategy to manipulate and mould resources in order to provide a more efficient organisation. For example, the Glaxo Wellcome merger benefited from the 7400 jobs that were to be cut and the resultant annual savings of over US$1 billion. Prescriptive strategists argue that the company will be stronger as a result.

Although there is not complete agreement among emergent strategists, they would certainly all question the certainties of the prescriptive view of resources. For some, doubts centre on the assumption made by prescriptive strategists that change is achievable. Emergent strategists probably lay more stress on the impact of human resources than their prescriptive counterparts. For example, the Glaxo Wellcome job cuts were accompanied by considerable uncertainty and worry which must have affected the ability of those carrying out the changes: some emergent strategists argue that people resources are not just objects but human beings who can help or hinder strategic change.

For other emergent strategists, the environment is changing so fast as a result of forces beyond the control of the organisation that resources need to be flexible and aimed at survival. In this sense, the Glaxo Wellcome merger could be regarded as being unwelcome if it produced a larger and less flexible organisation.

These differences of views are reflected in the two models used in this book. In the prescriptive model, resources deliver a definite result to the organisation and its future strategies. In the emergent model, the resources and subsequent strategies are much more fluid and inter-related.

This chapter concentrates on the prescriptive approach as it forms the basis of resource analysis for strategy development. This is because it is well developed with useful insights and, in addition, even those who doubt its usefulness still need to understand it first.

In Chapter 8 and subsequent chapters, the emergent approach is explored further.

Key strategic principles

- Prescriptive approaches regard resources as objects to be moulded for maximum strategic benefit.

- Emergent approaches do not have a consistent theme with regard to resources. However, they tend to value the human element more highly: this is inherently less predictable. They also emphasise the need for a close relationship between the environment and the resources.

- This chapter concentrates on the prescriptive view because it is well developed and has useful strategy insights.

7.2 KEY FACTORS FOR SUCCESS IN AN INDUSTRY

By now, it will be evident that corporate strategy encompasses the whole organisation. Whether the strategic process is prescriptive or emergent, it needs to consider every part of the organisation and, most importantly, do so with limited resources.

Potentially, this raises a major strategic problem: corporate strategy analysis could be overwhelmed by the size of the task. An analytical process is needed that will examine the many factors that can potentially impact on strategy.

The Japanese strategist, Kenichi Ohmae,[2] the former head of the management consultants, McKinsey, in Japan, has suggested a way of tackling this matter by identifying *the key factors for success* that are *likely* to deliver the company's objectives. He argued that, when resources of capital, labour and time were scarce, it was important that they should be *concentrated* on the key activities of the business – that is, those most important to the delivery of whatever the organisation regards as 'success'.

This concept of key factors for success is also consistent with Porter's view[3] that there are factors that determine the relative competitive positions of companies within an industry. Moreover, the foundation of the approach of Kay[4] is that it is important to concentrate resources on the specific areas of the business that are most likely to prove successful. All the above have said that identifying the key factors is not an easy task.

7.2.1 Starting with the company mission and objectives

How does an organisation determine whether a factor is a key factor or not? The answer given by some commentators is to consider potential factors against the *company mission and objectives*. For example, in the case of Glaxo Wellcome, a strategy issue impacting on drug marketing or R&D would be likely to be critical. The importance of exploring the mission and objectives at the same time as discussing key factors for success should be clear.

7.2.2 Identifying the key factors for success in the industry

Key factors concern not only the *resources* of organisations in the industry but also the *competitive environment* in which organisations operate. There are three principal areas that need to be analysed – Ohmae's *three Cs*[5]:

- *Customers*. What do customers really want? What are the segments in the market place? Can we direct our strategy towards a group?
- *Competition*. How can the organisation beat or at least survive against competition? What resources and customers do they have that make them particularly successful? How does the organisation compare on price, quality, etc. Does the organisation have a stronger distributive network than its competitors?
- *Corporation*. What special resources does the company itself possess and how do they compare with competitors? How does the company compare on costs with its rivals? Technologies? Skills? Organisational ability? Marketing?

Exhibit 7.1 sets out some key questions in more detail. No single area is more important than another. The *customer* and *competition* issues were examined in Chapters 5 and 6 and it is not proposed to repeat this analysis here. The *corporate* factors relate to the *resource* issues which are explored in detail in the remainder of this chapter.

| Exhibit 7.1 | Identifying key factors for success |

Note that key factors for success are directed at *all companies in an industry*, not just the target company for strategy development.

1 Customers
Who are our customers? Who are our potential customers? Are there any special segments that we dominate? Why do customers buy from us? And from our competitors?

- *Price.* Is the market segmented by high, medium and economy pricing? (Example: European ice cream.)
- *Service.* Do some customers value service while others simply want to buy the product? (For example, top class fashion retailers versus standard clothing shops.)
- *Product or service reliability.* Is product performance crucial to the customer or is reliability useful but not really important? (For example, heart pace makers and pharmaceuticals.)
- *Quality.* Some customers will pay higher prices for actual or perceived quality differences. Does this provide a route to success? (For example, organic vegetables.)
- *Technical specifications.* In some industrial and financial services, technical details will provide major attractions for some customers. Is this relevant to the organisation? (For example, specialist financial bond dealers.)
- *Branding.* How important is branding for the customer? (For example, Coca-Cola and Pepsi Cola.)

2 Competition
Who are our competitors? What are the main factors in the market that influence competition? How intense is competition? What is necessary to achieve market superiority? What resources do competitors possess that we lack and vice versa?

- *Cost comparisons.* Which companies have the lowest costs? Why? (For example, Toyota until the mid-1990s.)
- *Price comparisons.* Which companies have high prices? (For example, Daimler Benz does not make cheap cars.)
- *Quality issues.* Which companies have the highest quality? Why? How? (For example, Xerox (USA) in the light of fierce competition from Japanese companies such as Canon.)
- *Market dominance.* Which companies dominate the market? (For example, Nestlé with strongest coffee product range in the world and the largest market share.)
- *Service.* Are there companies in the industry that offer superior service levels? (For example, industrial markets, such as those served by Asea Brown Boveri, which need high levels of service to operate and maintain sophisticated equipment.)
- *Distributors.* Which companies have the best distributive network? Lowest costs? Fastest delivery? Competent distributors that really know the product or service? (For example, major glass companies such as St Gobain (France) and Pilkington (UK).)

3 Corporation

What resources do we have? How do they compare with competitors? What do they deliver to customers? Where are the majority of our costs concentrated? A small percentage reduction to a large part of our total costs will deliver more than an equally large percentage reduction in an area of lower total costs.

- *Low cost operations*. Are we low cost operators? How do we compare to competitors? (For example, Aldi (Germany) and KwikSave (UK).)

- *Economies of scale*. Do these exist in the industry? How important are they? (For example, large-scale petroleum chemical refinery operations such as those operated by Royal Dutch/Shell.)

- *Labour costs*. Does our industry rely heavily on low labour costs for competitive operations? (For example, Philips (Netherlands) which has moved its production to Singapore and Malaysia to lower labour costs.)

- *Production output levels*. Does our industry need full utilisation of plant capacity? (For example, European paper and packaging companies.)

- *Quality operations*. Do customers need consistent and reliable quality? How do we compare with others in the industry? (For example, McDonald's has applied the same standards around the world in its restaurants.)

- *Innovative ability*. Does our industry place a high reliance on our ability to produce a constant stream of new innovations? (For example, computer hardware and software companies such as Apple, Epson and Microsoft.)

- *Labour/management relations*. Is our industry heavily reliant on good relations? Are there real problems if disputes arise? (For example, European large-scale steel production, at companies such as Usinor–Sacilor.)

- *Technologies and copyright*. Does the industry rely on specialist technologies – especially those that are patented and provide a real competitive advantage? (For example, News International (Australia) which has exclusive global control over the decoder cards for satellite television and as a result a virtual monopoly of viewer payment satellite channels.)

- *Skills*. Does the organisation possess exceptional human skills and people? (For example, advertising agencies and leading accounting companies.)

7.2.3 The importance of key factors for success in directing strategic analysis

Key factors for success are rather easier to define in principle than examine in practice. However, if they prompt a thorough examination of what drives profitability or other measures of success in an industry and in the company itself, then they are worth while considering. In the context of strategy, key factors may be particularly concerned with adding value to the organisation. When key factors for success have been correctly identified, they can provide a checklist for the rest of the strategic analysis process. For example, if we know that service levels are crucial to adding value then any strategic analysis that fails to address this issue is bound to be weak. This does not mean that such an analysis should address only these factors but rather that they should feature prominently in the result.

Key strategic principles

- Identifying the key factors for success shapes the key areas of strategic analysis.

- They need to be consistent with the company's mission and objectives and selected on the basis of providing significant value added to the organisation.

- Such factors can conveniently be considered under three headings: customers, competition and corporation. By 'corporation' is meant the resources of the organisation.

- Key factors can be found in any area of the organisation and relate to skills, competitive advantage, history and background of the company, special technologies or customer contacts.

CASE STUDY 7.1

How three European companies attempt to utilise their resources

In this case study, three totally different companies are explored to see how each utilises its resources and achieves its corporate objectives. The first two companies operate in the pharmaceutical and national railway service industries respectively; the third is a holding company with a range of activities from construction to water supply.

The three companies under consideration are the UK pharmaceutical company, Glaxo, the Dutch national railway company, Nederlandse Spoorwegen, and the French services holding company, Générale des Eaux. Each has totally different resources, skills and methods of working, and each is involved in very different environments, including healthcare, transport services and the construction of roads. The purpose of this case is to identify the *key* strategic resources – that is, those that will make a difference to the company's corporate strategy.

Mission and objectives

As a starting point for any strategic analysis, it is important to consider *why* these three organisations are utilising the resources. What are they attempting to achieve? In principle, each is setting out to accomplish its *mission and objectives*. These need to be identified and explored.

Key resource analysis

Each of these companies brings totally different types of resources, skills and methods of operation to the achievement of its objectives. Figure 7.2 has used data taken from recent annual reports to construct the *cost profiles* for each of the three companies in this case study. The costs of each major item of company expenditure are expressed as a percentage of sales, coupled with profits before tax and interest as a percentage of sales. It is calculated by taking each cost item and dividing it by the sales figure and expressing this as a percentage. The profile demonstrates how each element of *resource* in the company contributes to profit and sales.

Resources for Glaxo
The information for Glaxo is included in the case study at the beginning of this chapter.

Resources for Nederlandse Spoorwagen

● *Increased utilisation of existing railway lines and rolling stock.* The investment in track and trains in most companies is largely complete. The key is to obtain greater usage of what is already present.

● *Marketing, sales and special prices.* These are to encourage customers to use the railways in preference to their competitors: road, air and bus traffic. This is particularly true in the Netherlands with its extensive and well-developed transport infrastructure.

● *High levels of service.* These involve the employees of the company and investment in new equipment

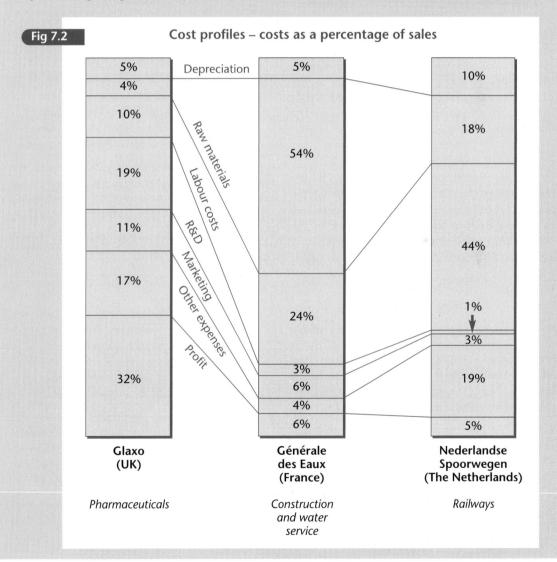

Fig 7.2

Cost profiles – costs as a percentage of sales

	Glaxo (UK)	Générale des Eaux (France)	Nederlandse Spoorwegen (The Netherlands)
Depreciation	5%	5%	10%
Raw materials	4%		18%
Labour costs	10%	54%	
R&D	19%		44%
Marketing	11%		
Other expenses	17%	24%	1%
			3%
Profit	32%	3%	19%
		6%	
		4%	
		6%	5%

Pharmaceuticals

Construction and water service

Railways

CASE STUDY 7.1 continued

on information and signalling to inform customers better of transport network problems.

Most national European railway companies are competing mainly within their national boundaries.[6] Resource analysis therefore needs to concentrate on national transport competitors in the first instance.

With the high fixed investment already made in track, signalling and rolling stock, corporate strategy has relied largely on encouraging *greater utilisation of the existing facilities* – that is, the marketing and sales activities mentioned above.

Another aspect of strategy that is important for most railway companies is *the relationship with government*. During the period from which the data shown in Fig 7.2 were taken, the Dutch railway company was receiving grants from the Netherlands Government that amounted to 9 per cent of its total revenue. These were used to subsidise train fares and freight passage so that railways would be used in preference to roads.

Resources for Générale des Eaux

In this case, the resources will be dictated by the precise nature of each of the activities in which the company is engaged. In theory, it will be necessary to analyse each of the 2250 companies in the group. In practice, three areas of the company accounted for around 70 per cent of sales in 1992:

Building, construction and public works	29.7%
Water distribution and waterworks construction	25.3%
Thermal and electrical energy supply	21.0%

For the purposes of *strategic* analysis, it is acceptable to ignore the remaining collection of areas. This is not a financial audit of the company, simply an overall judgement on the *main thrust* of the company's business. Clearly, this judgement would be invalid if the remaining areas of the business contained:

1 a business that was growing fast (for the reasons we explored in portfolio analysis);

2 a business that was taking up a large amount of the group's resources (which might not necessarily be one of those above); and

3 a business that was making large losses (again not necessarily one of those above).

None of these applies in this case. We can therefore comment on the resources involved in each of the three main areas of business:

1 *Building and public construction work resources*:
● Raw materials for roads and buildings
● Labour construction costs coupled with skills and efficiency
● Design costs

2 *Water distribution and waterworks construction resources*:
● Quality of finished product
● Quality of service, especially the absence of breakdowns
● High utilisation of heavy fixed investment
● Consideration for environment

3 *Thermal and electrical energy supply resources*:
● Continuity of supply
● Efficiency and cost-effectiveness of supply
● Raw material costs such as oil and coal
● High utilisation of heavy fixed investment.

It will be evident that analysing the resources in a diversified holding company is a major task. It has been simplified by concentrating on certain key areas of the business. However, this is a compromise.

CASE QUESTIONS

1 *An examination of the cost profiles of the three companies reveals that research and development (R&D) feature more prominently in Glaxo than in the other two companies. Why is this? What risks, if any, are associated with heavy R&D expenditure? What implications might this have for strategic decisions?*

2 *Marketing and related expenditures are much higher as a proportion of sales in Glaxo than Nederlandse Spoorwagen. What are the reasons for this? Can you make out a strategic case for higher levels of marketing expenditure at the Dutch railway company?*

3 *The case study suggests that holding companies have a more complex task in managing their resources. Do you agree?*

7.3 RESOURCE ANALYSIS AND ADDING VALUE

In an analysis of key factors for success, the only area that the organisation has direct control over is its own resources. Some researchers, such as Hamel and Prahalad,[7] argue that resources are particularly important in the development of corporate strategy: their starting point is the contribution that resources make to the organisation.

7.3.1 Adding value – the role of resources in the organisation

The fundamental role of resources in an organisation is to *add value.* Resources add value by working on the raw materials that enter the factory gate and turning them into a finished product. Added value can be defined as the difference between the market value of output and the cost of inputs. The concept is basically an economic one and is outlined, using Glaxo as an example, in Fig 7.3.

When calculating the value that the company's resources add, it is important to consider three areas of costs: *labour, raw materials* and *capital* costs. The first two of these areas are reasonably clear for a company to calculate: the company's management accounts will record this data. Capital costs are more complex. The value of land and buildings, plant and machinery, stocks and work in progress needs to be assessed. *The replacement value* of this capital (not just historic cost depreciation) and the *Cost of capital* allowing for an element of risk for the company (*see* Chapter 9), must also be calculated. The detailed calculation is not easy, even when inside information on the organisation concerned is available. Consequently, the value-added calculation is not usually undertaken in detail in strategic analysis.

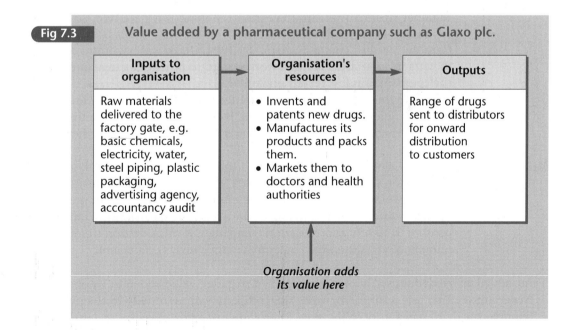

Fig 7.3   **Value added by a pharmaceutical company such as Glaxo plc.**

Inputs to organisation	Organisation's resources	Outputs
Raw materials delivered to the factory gate, e.g. basic chemicals, electricity, water, steel piping, plastic packaging, advertising agency, accountancy audit	• Invents and patents new drugs. • Manufactures its products and packs them. • Markets them to doctors and health authorities	Range of drugs sent to distributors for onward distribution to customers

Organisation adds its value here

Nevertheless, added value is an important strategic concept. As Kay[8] points out, a commercial organisation that adds no net value to the inputs it receives from its environment has no long-term reason for existence. Some organisations actually have a *negative* added value: they are not recovering the full costs of their inputs and may be in danger of survival. In Table 7.1 we return to the three companies of Case study 7.1 and calculate their value added with some interesting strategic consequences. (Data was not available to make direct comparisons for all years but the latest information has been used at the time of writing.)

Table 7.1   Value added in three large European companies in (US$ million)

	Glaxo		Générale des Eaux 1992	Nederlandse Spoorwagen 1993
	1994	1990*		
Sales/outputs	8 701	5 096	25 155	2 080
Wages & salaries	2 000	1 152	6 917	1 155
Capital costs	978	557	2 854	692
Raw materials	3 526	1 948	16 212	1 050
Value added	2 197	1 439	(828)	(817)

* Recalculated from Kay[9]
Source: Annual reports and accounts calculated by the author

Value added at Glaxo Clearly, Glaxo adds real value to its inputs. In fact, in a survey quoted by Kay,[10] Glaxo added more value to its inputs than any other large European company between the years 1981 and 1990. It did this by using the competitive advantage it had in its pharmaceutical markets: this was its main drug, Zantac, an anti-ulcer drug which was clearly superior in performance to its chief rival during the 1980s, Tagamet (from SmithKline Beecham). Zantac was patented, so it had a unique advantage. However, it was under threat in the early 1990s from a new drug, Losec, from the Swedish company, Astra. By 1994, Glaxo was beginning to lose advantage to Astra in some areas but had worked hard to produce a range of new drugs so that the company was less reliant on Zantac.

During the 1980s, Glaxo also benefited from the market conditions that allowed prices for unique drugs to remain high. By the mid-1990s, the health authorities across Europe were beginning to negotiate lower prices for all drugs that they purchased.

Value added at Générale des Eaux In 1992, Générale des Eaux appeared to be losing value rather than creating it. The explanation is difficult to discover in a holding company. In this case, it is probable that its construction companies were unable to recover fully the costs they were incurring due to the beginning of the economic recession in France and the competition from other construction companies. If this situation were to continue for a number of years then the company would clearly be in trouble.

Value added at Nederlandse Spoorwagen Nederlandse Spoorwagen also had negative value added in its operations in 1993. This is less surprising since the company was essentially in the public-service area and had a duty to the state to provide low-price travel for its customers.[11] Its costs were not being recovered fully from its passengers in that year: it was making a loss.

Strategic implications of value added

For non-profit, public and commercial companies, long-term value needs to be generated in order for them to survive. From the above definition of value added (that is, outputs minus inputs), it follows that value can be added in an organisation:

- *either* by raising the value of outputs (sales) delivered to the customer;
- *or* by lowering the costs of its inputs (wages and salaries, capital and materials costs) into the company.

Alternatively, both routes could be used simultaneously. Strategies therefore need to address these two areas.

Raising the value of outputs may mean raising the level of sales either by raising the volume of sales or by raising the unit price. Both these methods are easy to state and more difficult to achieve. Each will involve costs – for example, the cost of advertising to stimulate sales – which need to be set against the gains made. *Lowering the costs of inputs* may require investment – for example, new machinery to replace workers – at the same time as seeking the cost reduction.

These two strategic routes need to be examined in detail. *Outputs* have already been covered in Part 2; inputs are considered in the remainder of this chapter.

A strategic analysis of value added needs to take place at the market or industry level of the organisation, not at a corporate or holding company level. If this analysis were to be undertaken at the general level, the performance of individual parts of the business would be masked. Value added is therefore calculated at the level of individual product groups.

Key strategic principles

- The added value of an organisation is the difference between the market value of its output and the costs of its inputs.

- The market value of its output is typically its sales revenue. The costs of its inputs are the costs of its labour, its materials and its capital costs, including land, plant and machinery and stocks and work in progress.

- All organisations need to ensure that they do not consistently lose value in the long term or they will not survive. For commercial organisations, adding value is essential for their future. For non-profit organisations, adding value may only be a minor part of the reason for their existence, other purposes being centred on social, charitable or other goals.

- In principle, there are only two strategies to raise value added in a commercial organisation: increase the value of its outputs (sales) or lower the value of its inputs (the costs of labour, capital and materials). In practice, this implies detailed analysis of every aspect of sales and costs.

- In companies with more than one product range, added value is best analysed by considering each group separately. Some groups may subsidise others in terms of added value. Not all groups are likely to perform equally.

7.4 ADDING COMPETITIVE VALUE: THE VALUE CHAIN AND THE VALUE SYSTEM

In order to develop competitive advantage, it is necessary to examine all aspects of the organisation. It is not possible to undertake this task at a broad corporate level: a systematic approach is necessary involving two related routes – the *value chain* and the *value system.*

Every organisation consists of activities that link together to develop the value of the business: purchasing supplies, manufacturing, distribution and marketing of its goods and services. These activities taken together form the *value chain* of the organisation.

When organisations supply, distribute, buy from or compete with each other, they form a broader group of value generation: the *value system.*

The *contributions* of the value chain and value system to the development of competitive advantage, and the *links between the two areas,* which may also deliver competitive advantage, are explored in this section.

7.4.1 The value chain

The value chain links the value of the activities of an organisation with its main functional parts. It then attempts to make an assessment of the contribution that each part makes to the overall added value of the business. The concept was used in accounting analysis for some years before Professor Michael Porter[12] suggested that it could be applied to strategic analysis. Essentially, he linked two areas together:

● the added value that each part of the organisation contributes to the whole organisation; and

● the contribution to the competitive advantage of the whole organisation that each of these parts might then make.

In a company with more than one product area, he said that the analysis should be conducted at the level of product groups, not at corporate strategy level, as the Générale des Eaux example in Section 7.3. The company is then split into the *primary activities* of production, such as the production process itself, and the *support activities*, such as human resources management, that give the necessary background to the running of the company but cannot be identified with any individual part. The analysis then examines how each part might be considered to contribute towards the generation of value in the company and how this differs from competitors.

Porter's outline process is shown in Fig 7.4. He used the word 'margin' in the diagram to indicate what we defined as *added value* in Section 7.3: *'margin is the difference between the total value and the collective cost of performing the value activities'.*[13]

According to Porter, the *primary activities* of the company are:

● *Inbound logistics.* These are the areas concerned with receiving the goods from suppliers, storing them until required by operations, handling and transporting them within the company.

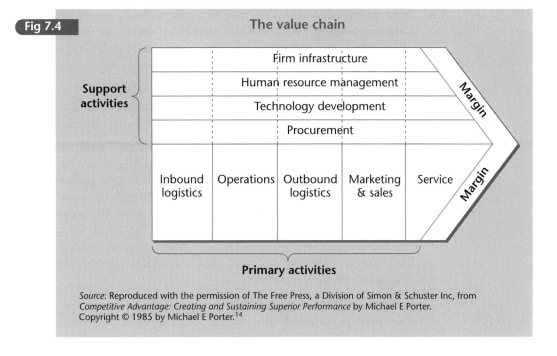

Fig 7.4 The value chain

Source: Reproduced with the permission of The Free Press, a Division of Simon & Schuster Inc, from *Competitive Advantage: Creating and Sustaining Superior Performance* by Michael E Porter. Copyright © 1985 by Michael E Porter.[14]

- *Operations*. This is the production area of the company. In some companies, this might be split into further departments – for example, paint spraying, engine assembly, etc. in a car company; reception, room service, restaurant, etc. in a hotel.

- *Outbound logistics*. These distribute the final product to the customer. They would clearly include transport and warehousing but might also include selecting and wrapping combinations of products in a multi-product company. For a hotel or other service company, this activity would be reconfigured to cover the means of bringing customers to the hotel or service.

- *Marketing and sales*. This function analyses customers' wants and needs and brings to the attention of customers what products or services the company has for sale. Advertising and promotions fall within this area.

- *Service*. Before or after a product or service has been sold, there is often a need for installation or after-sales service. There may also be a requirement for training, answering customer queries, etc.

Each of the above categories will add value to the organisation in its own way. They may undertake this task better or worse than competitors: for example, higher standards of service, lower production costs, faster and cheaper outbound delivery and so on. By this means, they provide the areas of *competitive advantage* of the organisation.

The *support activities* are:

- *Procurement*. In many companies, there will be a separate department (or group of managers) responsible for purchasing goods and materials that are then used in the operations of the company. Their function is to obtain the lowest prices and highest quality of goods for the activities of the company, but they are only responsible for purchasing, not for the subsequent production of the goods.

- *Technology development.* This may be an important area for new products in the company. Even in a more mature industry, it will cover the existing technology, training and knowledge that will allow a company to remain efficient.

- *Human resource management.* Recruitment, training, management development and the reward structures are vital elements in all companies.

- *Firm infrastructure.* This includes the background planning and control systems – for example, accounting, etc. – that allow companies to administer and direct their development. It includes corporate strategy.

These support activities add value, just as the primary activities do, but in a way that is more difficult to link with one particular part of the organisation. In Table 7.2 value added was quantified precisely at Glaxo, Générale des Eaux and Nederlandse Spoorwagen. However, this value related to the *overall* inputs and outputs of the companies.

To develop sustainable competitive advantage, it is necessary to undertake more detailed analyses of where value is added. This is normally undertaken *without* any quantification for three reasons:

1 Such assessments are difficult to quantify with accuracy. For example, how do you calculate accurately the precise added value of procurement? Salary costs? Lower prices gained? Higher quality obtained and quantified?

2 Even if known for the company itself, the same data would be needed for competitors, since a competitive assessment is then made.

3 Such detailed quantification is unnecessary in the broad general discussion of strategy.

Value chain analysis is therefore usually undertaken without detailed quantification of the value added. It concentrates on the main areas and makes broad comparisons with competitors on this basis.

Comment   The problem with the value chain in strategic development is that it is designed to explore the *existing* linkages and value-added areas of the business. By definition, it works within the existing structure. Real competitive strategy may require a revolution that moves *outside* the existing structure. Value chains may not be the means to achieve this.

7.4.2 The value system

In addition to the analysis of the company's own value chain, Porter argued that an additional analysis should also be undertaken. Organisations are part of a wider system of adding value involving the supply and distribution value chains and the value chains of customers. This is known as the *value system* and is illustrated in Fig 7.5.

Except in very rare circumstances, every organisation buys in some of its activities: advertising, electricity, product packaging design, management consultancy, electricity power are all examples of items that are often acquired even by the largest companies. In the same way, many organisations do not distribute their products or services directly to the final consumer: travel agents, wholesalers, retail shops might all be involved in this role.

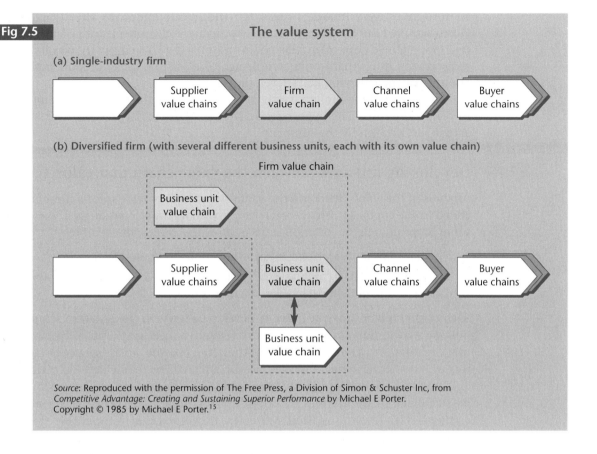

Fig 7.5

The value system

(a) Single-industry firm

Supplier value chains → Firm value chain → Channel value chains → Buyer value chains

(b) Diversified firm (with several different business units, each with its own value chain)

Firm value chain

Business unit value chain

Supplier value chains → Business unit value chain → Channel value chains → Buyer value chains

Business unit value chain

Source: Reproduced with the permission of The Free Press, a Division of Simon & Schuster Inc, from *Competitive Advantage: Creating and Sustaining Superior Performance* by Michael E Porter. Copyright © 1985 by Michael E Porter.[15]

Competitors may or may not use the same value system: some suppliers and distributors will be better than others in the sense that they offer lower prices, faster service, more reliable products, etc. *Real* competitive advantage may come from using the *best* suppliers or distributors. New competitive advantage may be gained by using a new distribution system or obtaining a new relationship with a supplier. An analysis of this value system may also therefore be required. This will involve a resource analysis that extends beyond the organisation itself.

Value chain and value system analysis can be complex and time consuming for the organisation. This is where the *key factors for success* (*see* Section 7.2) can be used. If these have been correctly identified, then they will provide the focus for the analysis of added value that follows. Key factors may well be those factors that add value to the product or service.

In Section 7.3 we concluded that value added can only be raised by either increasing the outputs (sales) or by lowering the inputs (costs) of a company. Along with the key factors for success, these two value-added options now provide a method of analysing the value-added resources in the company. Such an enquiry will need to examine both the costs and the benefits of any proposed changes.

In the case of Glaxo, the company might be advised to concentrate its value analysis initially at least on its identified key factors for success: R&D, marketing and product performance. In fact, the company's strategy during the 1990s has been to invest very heavily in research and development. As already explored, Glaxo acquired the UK pharmaceutical company Wellcome plc for US$13.5 billion in 1995.[16] One of the main reasons for purchasing this company was its strong range of new drugs that would complement the existing Glaxo product portfolio – another way of achieving R&D development.

Glaxo might also usefully investigate ways of raising the value of key *outputs* and lowering key *costs*. The opening case showed that this is precisely the strategic activity undertaken by the company.

7.4.3 Developing linkages between the value chain and value system

Analysis of the value chain and the value system will provide information on value added in the company. For an organisation with a group of products, there may be some common item or common service across the group, for example:

- *a common raw material* (such as sugar in various food products); or
- *a common distributor* (such as a car parts distributor for a group with subsidiary companies manufacturing various elements in a car).

Such common items may be *linked* to develop competitive advantage. Such possible linkages may be important to strategic development because they are often *unique* to that organisation. The linkages might therefore provide advantages over competitors who do not have such linkages, or who are unable to easily develop them.

It was Porter[17] who suggested that value chains and value systems may not be sufficient in themselves to provide the competitive advantage needed by companies in developing their strategies. He argued that competitors can often imitate the *individual* moves made by an organisation; what competitors have much more difficulty in doing is imitating the special and possibly unique *linkages* that exist between elements of the value chain and the value systems of the organisation.

In addition to analysing resources for value chains and value systems, therefore, competitive strategy suggests that there is a third element. It is necessary to search for special and possibly unique linkages that either exist or might be developed between elements of the value chain and between value systems associated with the company. Figure 7.6 illustrates this situation.

Examples of such linkages abound:

- Common raw materials used in a variety of end-products: for example, petrochemical feedstocks are used widely to produce various products.
- Common services, such as telecommunications or media-buying, where a combined contract could be negotiated at a lower price than individual series of local deals.
- Linkages between technology development and production to facilitate new production methods that might be used in various parts of a group – for example, direct telecommunications links between large retail store chains such as Marks & Spencer and their suppliers.

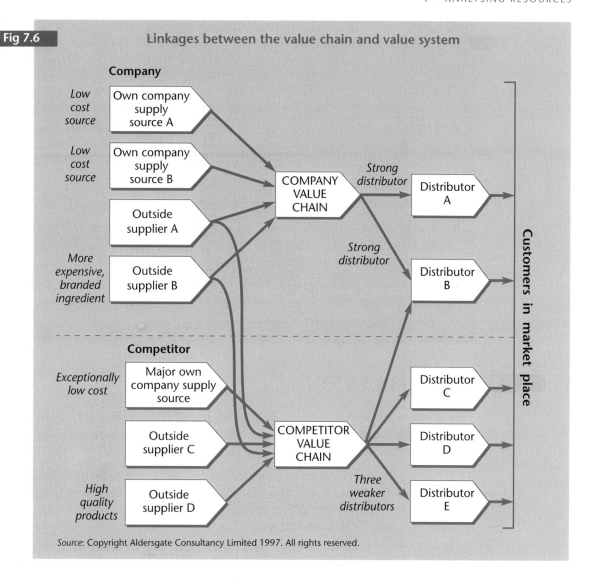

Fig 7.6 Linkages between the value chain and value system

- Travel computer reservation systems that link the airlines with travel ticket agents (proving to be so powerful that the European Commission has investigated their effects on airline competition).

- Joint ventures, alliances and partnerships that often rely on different members to the agreement bringing their special areas of expertise to the relationship (*see* Chapter 14).

All the above suggest that linkages that enhance value added may provide significant ways for companies to improve their resources.

> ### Key strategic principles
>
> - The value chain breaks down the activities of the organisation into its main parts. The contribution that each part makes can then be assessed for its contribution to sustainable competitive advantage.
>
> - The value chain is usually analysed without any detailed quantification of the added value that each element contributes. It is undertaken at a broad general level and is compared with competitors.
>
> - Most organisations are part of a wider system of adding value involving supplier and distributor channels: the value system.
>
> - Analysing value chains and the value system can be complex. One way of reducing such difficulties is to employ the key factors for success as a means of selecting the items.
>
> - Possible linkages of elements of the value chain and value systems need to be analysed because they may be unique to the organisation and thus provide it with competitive advantage.

7.5 COST REDUCTION

One of the main routes to increasing value added through resource analysis has been identified as the *reduction of costs* by the organisation. There are many methods of cost reduction but five deserve to be highlighted:

1 *Designing-in cost reduction.* In some industries, large cost reductions come, not from activity in the production plant, but *before* the product ever reaches the factory. By carefully designing the product, for example, so that it has fewer parts or is simpler to manufacture, real reductions in costs can be achieved.

2 *Supplier relationships.* If a supplier is willing and able to maintain quality and reduce costs, then the organisation will achieve a cost reduction.

3 *Economies of scale and scope.* For large plant, unit costs may reduce as the size of the plant increases. It may also be possible for different products to share some functional costs.

4 *The experience curve.* As a company becomes more experienced at production, it may be able to reduce its costs.

5 *Capacity utilisation.* Where plant has a high fixed cost, there may be cost reductions to be obtained by running production as close to capacity as possible.

The first two areas deserve detailed consideration and are explored under the subject of operations (production) in Chapter 10. These are headlined here because it is important to have a sense of proportion about the options available and these two areas can be major contributors to the process. The discussion here is therefore confined to the last three areas.

7.5.1   Economies of scale and scope

When it is possible to perform an operation better or differently at large volumes, then the increased efficiency – the economies of scale – may result in lower costs: for example, in a major petrochemical plant and in pulp and paper production.

Economies of scale need to be distinguished from *capacity utilisation* of plant. In the latter case, costs reduce as the plant reaches capacity but would not reduce further if an even larger plant were to be built. With economies of scale, the larger plant would lead to a further cost reduction.

Economies of scope occur when cost savings are available as a result of providing two distinct products from the same company compared with providing them from separate companies. An example might be those products that share the same retail outlets and can be delivered by the same transport.

Economies of scale are also available in areas outside production. They may occur in areas such as:

- *Research and development.* On some occasions, only a large-scale operation can justify special services or items of testing equipment.

- *Marketing.* Really large companies are able to aggregate separate advertising budgets into one massive fund and negotiate extra media discounts that are simply not available to smaller companies.

- *Distribution.* Grouping and selecting loads to maximise the use of carrying capacity on transport vehicles travelling between fixed destinations.

In the analysis of resources, economies of scale are an important area for analysis. It is worth while making an assessment for at least one leading competitor, if possible. Factors to investigate will include not only size of plant, but also age and efficiency of equipment.

Although writers such as Porter[18] are clear about the basic benefits of economies of scale and scope, there have been real doubts expressed about the true reductions in costs to be derived from them (*see* for example, Kay[19]). The doubts centre on the argument that larger plant will have lower costs. When Henry Ford built his massive new Baton Rouge car plant in the 1930s, he was driven by this view. In practice, he encountered a number of problems.[20] They included:

- *Machine-related issues* – the increased complexity and inflexibility of very large plant.

- *Human-related issues* – the increasingly depersonalised and mechanistic nature of work in such plant, which made it less attractive or interesting for workers to perform to their best ability.

Although there were other management problems associated with the relative failure of this plant, some of the major reasons lay in the above areas. In the 1990s, large-scale steel plant was considered as providing lower costs but new technologies have now allowed much smaller scale operations to make the same profits.

Moreover, the competitive advantage of large plant is lost if the market breaks into segments that are better served by higher cost plants that produce variations on the basic item which more directly meet customers' needs. Car markets and consumer electronics markets are examples where four-wheel drive vehicles and specialist hi-fi systems are not the cheapest in terms of production but meet real customer demand.

The conclusion has to be that economies of scale have their place but are only part of a broader drive for competitive advantage.

7.5.2 The experience curve

In the 1960s, a large number of unrelated industries were surveyed[21] in terms of their costs and the *cumulative production achieved*, as opposed to the production in a particular year. It was shown that an empirical relationship could be drawn between a cost reduction and cumulative output. Moreover, this relationship appeared to hold over a number of industries from insurance to steel production. It appeared to show dramatic reductions in costs: typically, costs fell by 15 per cent every time overall output doubled. In Fig 7.7, for example, Company B has produced more units than Company A, so it has more 'experience' and consequently lower unit costs. The relationship was explained by suggesting that in addition to economies of scale, there were other cost savings to be gained:

● technical progress;

● greater learning about the processes;

● greater skills from having undertaken the process over time.

The cost/experience concept can be seen both at the *company* level and the *industry* level.

● At the company level, the market leader will, by definition, have produced cumulatively more product than any other company. The leader will have the lowest costs and other companies should be at a disadvantage.

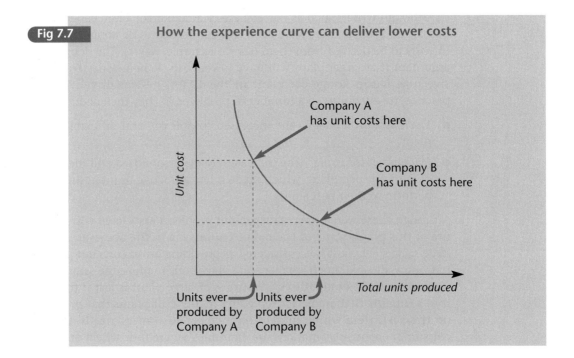

Fig 7.7   How the experience curve can deliver lower costs

- At the industry level, costs should reduce as the industry overall produces more. Every company should benefit from knowledge that is circulated within the industry.

These insights into the ways that production costs can be reduced have had a significant impact on cost strategies in some companies. According to the concept, costs should always trend downward, especially when a market is growing rapidly and volume-doubling is relatively easy to achieve. From the evidence, however, it follows that even when a market ceases to grow, the company should still be learning about its production processes and should therefore still seek cost reductions.

The former Chairman of the Unilever UK detergents company, Lever Brothers, has written with conviction on the benefits of cost experience.[22] But he points out that it is necessary to work to achieve the cost savings: they do not come automatically. His experience was that production managers at his company's Warrington plant were very proud of their plant. For its size and kind, it was understood to be one of the most efficient in Europe. They had great difficulty in accepting the cost experience curve concept: even though it was already highly efficient, further cost reductions were always possible but needed to be sought out.

When comparisons are drawn across different and unrelated industries, the similarities in the relationship are remarkable for industries as far apart as aircraft manufacture and chicken broiler production. However, this is misleading. The broad lessons for corporate strategy are more limited. As Kay[23] points out, the only similarity between chicken and aircraft is that they both have wings. There may be an *apparent relationship* at the numerical level, but the *causes* are entirely different and as a result the strategy implications are entirely different. Aircraft production is essentially global (*see* Case study 6.3). Chicken production relies largely on national markets and requires somewhat less sophisticated technology and totally different forms of investment to aircraft manufacture and assembly. It is essential to consider the concept of experience within an industry only.

Even within an industry, there are ways of overcoming experience curve effects, the most obvious being by new technology or by enticing an employee of a more experienced company to join the organisation. As Abernathy and Wayne[24] point out, there are real limits to the benefits:

- Market demand in market segments for a special product change or variation cannot easily be met: to achieve scale, production flexibility may have to be sacrificed.

- Technical innovation can overtake learning in a more fundamental way: a new invention may radically alter the cost profile of an existing operation.

- Demand needs to double for every significant proportionate cost reduction. In markets where growth is still present but slowing down, this is only possible if an ever-larger market share is obtained. As market share becomes larger, this becomes progressively more difficult and expensive to achieve. In a static market where a company already has around 50 per cent market share, this becomes logically impossible.

Within a defined market, the experience curve may suggest a significant route to cost reduction, but it is not always a key source of cost advantage.

7.5.3 Capacity utilisation

In the study of the European pulp and paper industry in Chapter 4, we saw an example of the cost benefits to be gained by full utilisation of plant capacity. We also saw how companies cut their prices as they scrambled to fill their plant, thus reducing their profit margins. High capacity utilisation is useful but relies on competitors allowing such activity to take place which may weaken its effect.

Key strategic principles

- There are at least five routes to cost reduction: design, supplier relationships, economies of scale and scope, the experience curve, capacity utilisation.

- Economies of scale and scope are generally seen to reduce costs and raise value added, but the lack of production flexibility and the depersonalised nature of the work may be significant drawbacks.

- The experience curve suggests that significant reductions in costs are achieved as companies and the whole industry produce more product. The cost reductions relate to the cumulative production ever achieved, not just in one year.

- Experience curve cost reductions arise from a whole series of sources. They need to be sought and do not just happen automatically.

- Comparisons of experience curves across industries have little meaning in terms of the strategy lessons to be drawn.

- Utilising existing plant capacity is an important consideration in cost reduction.

7.6 CORE RESOURCES, SKILLS AND COMPETENCES

Within resource analysis, the area of core resources, skills and competences may be difficult to quantify in terms of added value but is fundamental to strategy development. It relates particularly to research undertaken in the late 1980s and into the 1990s that seeks to explore a basic strategic question: *How is it possible for companies with a small share of a market to gain a significant share of an industry?* How did Canon photocopiers (Japan) make headway against the dominance of Xerox (US)? How did Airbus Industrie (Europe) take market share from Boeing (US)? Part of the answer lies with their *resources* and how they used them competitively. We examine this under separate headings but the reader should be aware that there is some overlap.

7.6.1 Core resources: architecture, reputation and innovative ability

In analysing the resources of organisations, Kay[25] identifies architecture, reputation and innovative ability as being important company resources in strategy development. They are complex and not necessarily capable of quantified analysis but they will undoubtedly contribute to the distinctive development of a company's strategy. He introduced and explored them by explaining that an organisation has a series of contracts and more informal relationships:

- with its employees inside the organisation;
- with its suppliers, distributors and customers outside in the environment; and
- possibly with a group of collaborating firms inside and outside the immediate industry.

This can apply to small as well as large businesses. The relationships have been built over time. Some are formal and some informal. They are similar to, but extended from, the linkages explored in the value system of Section 7.3.2. They provide the organisation with three major ways for their resources to be distinctive from competitors.

1 *Architecture.* This is the network of relationships and contracts both within and around the firm. Its importance lies in its ability to create knowledge and routines, to respond to market changes and to exchange information both inside and outside the organisation. Long-term relationships with other organisations can lead to real strategy benefits that competitors cannot replicate. Examples include:

- the contacts between major construction companies such as Générale des Eaux and government departments who let out substantial contracts;
- rail companies such as Nederlandse Spoorwagen and their negotiations with trade unions on new working practices to introduce new technologies and reduce costs;
- pharmaceutical companies such as Glaxo Wellcome and Merck engaged in corporate negotiation with governments on new drug price structures.

2 *Reputation.* This allows an organisation to communicate favourable information about itself to its customers. It is particularly concerned with long-term relationships and takes lengthy periods to build up. Once gained, it provides a real distinctiveness that rivals cannot match. Examples include:

- *Reputation for good quality work, delivered on time and to budget.* Construction companies can gain immensely over time as they consistently perform in this area.
- *Reputation for a quality service that is usually punctual and reliable.* Railway companies can win or lose in this area, particularly when they are competing for business against alternative forms of public transport such as buses.

3 *Innovative ability.* Some organisations find it easier to innovate than others because of their structures, procedures and rewards. They may even innovate and then fail to take advantage of this against competitors. This is a highly important area of strategy that deserves careful study. It is therefore explored more fully in Chapter 11.

Architecture, reputation and innovative ability will apply to a greater or lesser extent to most organisations. In themselves, they are important but uncontroversial.

Comment   All three areas usually require years of development. The first two are easier to define than they are to develop in terms of options: the *method* by which architecture and reputation are to be improved begs numerous questions about their nature that are difficult to explore. They may tend towards worthy, but largely meaningless, wish-statements about the desirability of improving them. Kay offers no clear exposition in this area.

The real point is how they are understood and used to gain competitive advantage. Resource analysis in these areas needs to take into account the changes that can take place over time and the need to explore not only the area itself but how it can be developed further.

7.6.2   Core skills and competences

In a related area of study, Hamel and Prahalad[26] have explored the area of core skills and competences. They define a core competence as a group of production skills and technologies that enable an organisation to provide a particular benefit to customers. Core competence underlies the leadership that companies have built or wish to acquire over their competitors.

Core skills are a basic fundamental resource of the organisation. The two authors describe the example of Sharp and Toshiba who identified flat-screen electronic technology as an opportunity area that they expected to see grow in the future. Both companies invested hundreds of millions of dollars in developing their technology and skills in the market for flat screens that would then be used in miniature televisions, portable computers, digital watches, electronic video recorders and other areas. Importantly, this investment was made *before* it was possible to build a product-specific business case that would justify this level of investment.

Core competence covers an integration of skills, knowledge and technology. These then build into core products which then form the basis of the business areas of the company. This combination can then lead to competitive advantage. Figure 7.8 illustrates the linkages. The analysis of such areas is derived from a study of its components in an individual organisation. A skills analysis needs to be conducted at a level that is detailed enough to reveal useful strategic insights but not so detailed that it is unmanageable. Hamel and Prahalad suggest that if only three or four skills are identified then this may be too broad but if 40 or 50 are identified then this may be too detailed. They suggest there are three areas that distinguish the major core competences:

- *Customer value.* Competence must make a real impact on how the customer perceives the organisation and its products or services.

- *Competitor differentiation.* Competence must be competitively unique. If the whole industry has the skill, then it is not core unless the organisation's skills in the area are really special.

- *Extendable.* Core skills need to be capable of providing the basis of products or services that go beyond those currently available. The skill needs to be removed from the particular product group in which it currently rests. The organisation needs to imagine how it might be exploited throughout its operations.

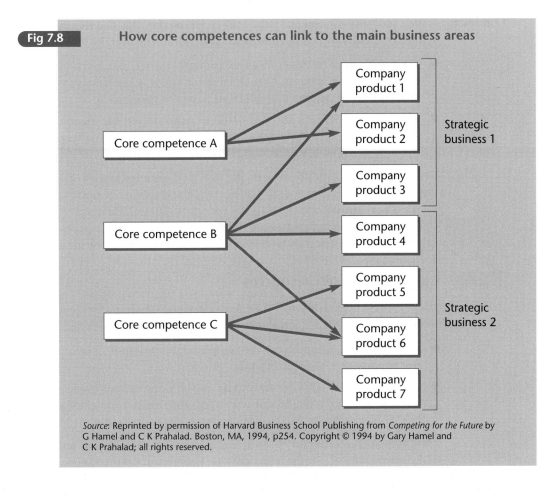

Fig 7.8 **How core competences can link to the main business areas**

Importantly, core competence is a vital *prerequisite* for the competitive battle that then takes place for market share: the development of key resources has to come before and not during market place activity. It should be noted that Hamel and Prahalad couple core competences with the organisation's *vision of the future*: this is explored in Chapter 11.

Examples of core skills will include:

- *Glaxo Wellcome* will have core skills that cover not just its ownership of the Zantac patents, but also the whole range of skills and contacts that the company has in the pharmaceutical market place with customers, distributors and health authorities.

- *Nederlandse Spoorwagen* will have core skills related to its operation of a rail network. More importantly, from a competitive viewpoint, it will have skills in customer handling, timetabling, service scheduling and so on versus buses and aircraft.

- *Générale des Eaux* has core skills in road building that relate to road design and construction. However, many companies will have such skills. Its real competences will relate to its ability to gain large contracts and manage such assignments once agreed. It will need to deliver on-time to an agreed standard and within the agreed budget.

Comment   David Sainsbury, Chairman of the leading UK retailer, has said that he believes the concept of core skills and competences has real merit. However, he also comments that:[27]

- Core skills may be easier to apply to larger rather than smaller companies, who may not have the depth of management talent. Certainly, the examples on core skills quoted in the text are all from large companies.

- The ideas have been most thoroughly developed for electronics and related markets. The concepts may need to be adapted for others – for example, medium-sized engineering companies.

Beyond these comments, one of the practical problems with core competences is that the developers never really offer any clear checklist of points for their development: they are all rather vague. Ten guidelines that explore resource-based competences and capabilities are offered in Exhibit 13.2 on page 473. Further critical comment on core competences is contained at the end of the next section.

7.6.3 Capability-based resources

Stalk, Evans and Shulman[28] draw a distinction between *core competences* and their own concept of broader, *capabilities-based resources* in the organisation.

- *Core competences* emphasise the underlying technological and production expertise at particular areas of the value chain.

- *Capability-based resources* cover the entire value chain, especially areas that go beyond the core elements of resources. For this reason, they are more likely to be directly visible to the customer than core competences.

The three authors suggest that capabilities-based competition will be broader and will complement the more basic core technological competences approach. It will include people, financial and market-based resources that are not fully covered by core competences.

According to the authors, resource-based capabilities will focus on four principles throughout the organisation:

- *Business processes*, rather than markets and products. This is the dynamic inter-linking of various functions of the business to provide superior customer service. It involves considering carefully the links across the organisation. For example, the business process that allows Glaxo to introduce a new drug may be enhanced if the various parts of the business are more integrated. These links need to be studied and codified as the business process.

- *Transformation of business processes* into superior capabilities so that they can react to rapidly changing market opportunities. For example, Glaxo might transfer its knowledge of the introduction of new drugs from one country to another or from one customer segment to another.

- *Investment in support infrastructure* to link together the resources, regardless of where they are based in existing strategic business units and functions. Thus in Glaxo, the company may wish to formalise the arrangements for the development and introduction of new drugs through formal links across the group by investing in the appropriate computer networks, co-ordinating management and meetings.

● *A chief executive officer* to provide the cross-functional viewpoint on resource capabilities. For many years until his retirement in the mid-1990s, Sir Paul Girolami fulfilled this role at Glaxo.

Comment on core competences and capabilities In both the Hamel and Prahalad book and the above article, the authors make major claims for their strategic concepts. For example, from Hamel and Prahalad:[29]

Because core competencies are the highest level, longest-lasting units for strategy making, they must be the central subjects of corporate strategy.

The Stalk, Evans and Shulman article[30] suggests that:

...the combination of core competences and [resource-based] capabilities may define the universal model for corporate strategy in the 1990s and beyond.

The reader is justified in being suspicious of such claims. They appear to suggest that if you adopt these few concepts, then you, too, will have a global world-beating company. This does not mean that the concepts make little contribution to the development of strategy: but they need to be treated with some caution.

Overall, there seems to be some overlap between core competences and capabilities. The view taken in this book has been to take a broader view of core competences. In this sense, we have combined capability-based resources together with core competences. There is some support for this view in the book by Hamel and Prahalad published in 1994[31] after the comments by the three authors above, which were based on the Hamel and Prahalad's original article published in 1990.[32] On this basis, the guidelines outlined in Exhibit 13.2 have been developed. We will return to the analysis of core competences and capability-based analysis in Chapter 13.

Key strategic principles

- Core skills and competences may be difficult for organisations to quantify as resources. However, they represent real areas where competitive advantage may be developed.

- Core resources relate to three areas of the organisation: *architecture* – the relationships that are developed internally and externally; *reputation* – the knowledge that customers acquire over time about the organisation; *innovative ability* – the skill to produce new ideas and initiatives.

- Core skills and competences add up to a group of skills and technologies that allow a company to gain long-term advantage over competitors. They need to be identified early in the strategy development process. They may take many years to develop, perhaps before all the business opportunities have been fully recognised.

- Core capabilities take the core skills framework into the broader area of people, financial resources and production resources. There may be some overlap with the core skills concept.

7.7 THE SWOT ANALYSIS

Part 2 examined the organisation's *external* environment and this chapter has explored the *internal* environment. One useful way of drawing these together is to produce a SWOT analysis for the organisation:

● Strengths and Weaknesses based on the *internal* analysis; and

● Opportunities and Threats based on the *external* analysis.

Clearly, each analysis will be unique to the organisation for which it is being devised. However, some general pointers based on the issues explored in Part 2 can be drawn up. Table 7.2 provides a checklist of some possible SWOT factors.

In devising a SWOT analysis, there are several factors that will enhance the quality of the material:

● Keep it brief: pages of analysis are usually not required.

● Relate strengths and weaknesses, wherever possible, to key factors for success.

● Strengths and weaknesses should also be stated in competitive terms, if possible. It is reassuring to be 'good' at something, but it is more relevant to be 'better than the competition'.

● Statements should be specific and avoid blandness: there is little point in stating ideas that everyone believes in.

● Analysis should distinguish between where the company *wishes to be* and where it *is now*. The gap should be realistic.

● It is important to be realistic about the strengths and weaknesses of one's own and competitive organisations.

Probably the biggest mistake that is commonly made in SWOT analyses is to assume the analysis is bound to be 'correct' if it contains every conceivable issue and is truly comprehensive. This is not the case: it merely demonstrates that little serious consideration and a lack of strategic judgement have been employed in its preparation.

Another common error is to provide a long list of points but little logic, argument and evidence. A short list with each point well argued is more likely to be convincing. Table 7.2 with its bullet points and lack of any explanation should therefore be regarded with some caution.

Table 7.2 Some possible factors in a SWOT analysis*

Internal

Strengths	Weaknesses
● Market dominance	● Share weakness
● Core strengths	● Few core strengths and low on key skills
● Economies of scale	● Old plant with higher costs than competition
● Low-cost position	● Weak finances and poor cash flow
● Leadership and management skills	● Management skills and leadership lacking
● Financial and cash resource	● Poor record on innovation and new ideas
● Manufacturing ability and age of equipment	● Weak organisation with poor architecture
● Innovation processes and results	● Low quality and reputation
● Architecture network	● Products not differentiated and dependent on few products
● Reputation	
● Differentiated products	
● Product or service quality	

External

Opportunities	Threats
● New markets and segments	● New market entrants
● New products	● Increased competition
● Diversification opportunities	● Increased pressure from customers and suppliers
● Market growth	● Substitutes
● Competitor weakness	● Low market growth
● Strategic space	● Economic cycle downturn
● Demographic and social change	● Technological threat
● Change in political, economic environment	● Change in political or economic environment
● New takeover or partnership opportunities	● Demographic change
● Economic upturn	● New international barriers to trade
● International growth	

*Note: danger of lists and bullet points as described in text!

FT

Nolan Helmets[33]

This case study describes a small company that has made some attempt to identify the key factors for success in its market and the consequences in terms of the resources needed. It is now awaiting the results of its new strategies.

That most of the world's motorcycle helmets are produced in Italy, one of the last European countries to make helmet-wearing compulsory, is an irony particularly appreciated at Nolan Helmets.

Helmetless moped-riders (exempt from the 1986 law) can be seen dodging traffic outside Nolan's headquarters near Bergamo in northern Italy. For Nolan, this is evidence not of commercial failure – the company and its compatriots Bieffe and AGV dominate the Italian market anyway – but of potential to be exploited. Alberto Lanfranchi, Nolan's chairman, comments:

> Standards worldwide are getting tougher, which is fine by us, because higher norms exclude the improvisers from the market.

Born in 1971, Nolan Helmets was one of the first to take advantage of polycarbonate technology, developed by General Electric of the US, to challenge the dominance of more expensive fibreglass and composite helmets. However, the sale of the founding family's shares in the late 1980s ushered in a period of unstable ownership, which only ended in 1992 when Lanfranchi rallied a consortium of investors to buy the company. They included Nolan managers, helmet distributors and a group of Bergamo professionals – backed by 3*i*, the British venture capital group, which owns bonds convertible into 27 per cent of Nolan's capital. They have financed a heavy capital investment programme – L10 billion (US$6 million) over three years – aimed at revitalising the brand and cutting costs.

The group decided to halve its factory floor to a mere 12 000 square metres producing a growing number of helmets – about 700 000 a year. At the same time, Nolan set out to renew the range of products and the machinery, relaunch the marketing effort and reorganise the internal structure of the group. Investors' faith is based on the strength of the brand name. Italian producers, including Nolan, tend to concentrate on mid-price helmets – the 'touring' market – leaving mainly Japanese companies to fight it out in top-range composite helmets. In the middle range, as Manchester Business School MBA students pointed out in a 1992 study of the market:

> ... helmets are sold on individual technical features, helmet detail and on brand image and design.

Investment in marketing should also give Nolan the edge at the point of sale where most decisions about mid-range helmets are taken, according to the Manchester study.

Early results indicate that the investment effort has already put Nolan back on the growth path. In the year to August 1994, net profit rose to L 934 million, against L 740 million the previous year, against sales of L 43 billion. For 1994–95, profits are forecast to rise by more than 60 per cent to L 1.5 billion on turnover of L 51 billion.

Nolan already sells 80 per cent of its helmets outside Italy, 32 per cent of them in Germany. If the investment in new technology proves its worth, Nolan may be able to seek out new partners which can apply Nolan's expertise in other sports, or to other markets, such as Eastern Europe.

Source: Financial Times, 24 July 1995.

CASE QUESTIONS

1 *What would you estimate to be the key factors for success for the industry in which Nolan is located?*

2 *Undertake a value-chain analysis for this company and point out the most likely areas where value is being added. What value linkages does the case suggest this company might have? How important might they be?*

3 *How would you characterise the company's resources? How have they changed over the last four years? With what result?*

4 *What are the core strengths of the company? How has the company exploited these over the last few years? What does the case suggest about exploiting them further in the future? Do you judge these arguments to have any merit?*

KEY READING

Defining strategy in an uncertain world[34]

The chapter has taken a prescriptive approach to resource analysis. In part at least, it has relied on a quantified view of added value and its financial effects on the organisation. In this extract from his book, **Strategic Management and Organisational Dynamics,** *Professor Ralph Stacey explains how an emergent strategic perspective might take the view that the whole procedure is largely worthless.*

When we try to use measures of performance, benchmarks, and associated analytical techniques to select acceptable strategies for the future, we face the problem of forecasting. Using financial measures in a future-oriented way requires forecasts of what will happen to an organisation's cash flows and profit levels over long periods into the future. While everyone recognises the great difficulty of doing this, most continue to believe that it is possible to forecast accurately enough to justify using the criterion of financial acceptability. Under what conditions will this belief be justified?

It is possible to predict the performance outcome of a sequence of actions if, and only *if*, there are clear-cut connections between causes and effects. Only when this is true can we say that, in principle at least, if we pursue action A in circumstance B it will lead to performance C. We may still have great difficulty in forecasting because we may not be sure whether circumstance B will actually occur or not and we may not accurately know the quantitative relationship between A and C. But we will be able to make some kind of forecast with some probability of success. However, if a sequence of actions is being generated in a system in which the relationships between cause and effect are lost in the minute detail of what happens, then it becomes impossible in principle even to predict, let alone forecast, specific outcomes.

To summarise then, the prescription to select a strategy well in advance of acting that satisfies the criterion of acceptable financial performance makes the following unquestioned assumptions:

● Organisations are systems that are driven by laws producing predictable long-term futures. Although it is difficult to identify what those laws are, and it is also difficult to use them to make accurate forecasts, it is nevertheless possible to do so in principle. Progress therefore lies in gathering data and researching the laws and the techniques of forecasting.

● Those laws establish clear-cut links between cause and effect, between an action and an outcome.

● Organisations are successful when they are close to a state of stable equilibrium, i.e. when their behaviour regularly repeats its past.

● The dynamics of successful organisations are therefore those of stability, regularity and predictability where any tensions or contradictions have been resolved.

The most widely accepted view of the cause of organisational success today is based on a particular set of assumptions about the nature of organisational dynamics. These assumptions indicate that success is achieved when an organisation gets close to a position of stable equilibrium. Here the organisation produces regular patterns of behaviour over time; it displays internal harmony and external adaption to its environment. According to this view organisations can reach success by selecting strategies that are acceptable, feasible and suitable. Successful organisations stick to one of a number of configurations. Because of the assumptions of the dynamic, it is assumed to be possible to predict the long-term outcomes of strategies to some extent, even if that extent is only a qualitative vision. Successful strategies can therefore be selected in advance and systems put in place to deliver success. Leaders choose future strategies and are in control of the organisation and plan its future direction.

Recent studies, however, are increasingly raising question marks over this widely-accepted view. The differences centre around what we are assuming about the dynamic.

Looking at the pattern of development of successful companies over a period, we find that they make incremental adjustments much of the time, but occasionally they experience crises that provoke revolutions or sudden jumps to new configurations. The idea here is that creativity is closely related to destruction; that instability is required to shatter existing paradigms, thus making way for the new.

Some of the latest work on strategic management is pointing away from equating success with a movement to stable equilibrium. It seems to be pointing to success as having to do with being away from equilibrium and [instead being] in a state of contradiction and instability. It seems to be doing so in the context of feedback systems that show self-reinforcing and amplifying behaviour, generating virtuous and vicious circles. It seems to be behaviour characterised by qualitative patterns that are irregular. And development over time for this far-from-equilibrium, amplifying feedback system occurs through paradigm-shattering crises and revolution that produces newly negotiated paradigms and configurations.

Source: Stacey, R D (1993) *Strategic Management and Organisational Behaviour*, 1st edn, Pitman Publishing.

SUMMARY

● For both prescriptive and emergent strategists, the resources of the organisation are an important element in strategy. Prescriptive approaches emphasise the need to build on strengths, whereas the emergent view favours flexibility and harnessing the more unpredictable human element. This chapter has concentrated on the prescriptive view.

● In seeking to understand the key factors for success in an industry, the three 'Cs' can be used as a basis for analysis: *customers*, *competitors* and *company*. The purpose of such an approach is to identify those strategic factors that are common to most companies in an industry and are essential to delivering the objectives of such companies. The key factors for success can be used to focus on other areas of strategy development.

● Resources add value to the organisation. They take the inputs from suppliers and transform them into finished goods or services. The *value added* is the difference between the market value of outputs of an organisation and the costs of its inputs. It is possible to calculate this accurately for an overall company but very difficult for individual parts of the company. When used in developing competitive advantage for the individual parts of the company, the concept is therefore often left unquantified.

● In order to develop sustainable competitive advantage, it is necessary to consider the various parts of the organisation and the value that each part adds, where this takes place and how the contribution is made. The *value chain* undertakes this task. It identifies where value is added in different parts of the organisation.

● It may also be necessary to consider the *value system*, that is, the way that the organisation is linked with other parts of a wider system of adding value involving suppliers, customers and distributors. Unique linkages between elements of the value system may also provide competitive advantage.

● Cost reduction is a major way to increase value added. There are five main areas of cost reduction: designing-in such reductions, supplier relationships, economies of scale and scope, the experience curve and capacity utilisation.

● Resource analysis will also seek to determine the core skills and competences of the organisation. These add up to a group of skills and technologies that allow the organisation to gain long-term advantage over competitors. They may take many years to develop fully but represent a major resource area for corporate strategy development.

QUESTIONS

1 Using your judgement, determine the key factors for success in the following industries: pharmaceuticals, fast food restaurants, charities helping homeless people, travel tour companies offering package tours.

2 Outline the value chain for an organisation you know. Explain the implications of your study for competitive advantage.

3 Take the value added and other data for Glaxo and outline the value chain for the company. Develop the value system within which the company operates. What strategy conclusions can you draw?

4 How do economies of scale contribute to corporate strategy? What are their limitations?

5 'To make the [experience] curve evolve successfully, the manufacturer needs a standard product. Under conditions of rapid product change, s/he cannot slash unit output costs [because the product keeps changing].' Professors W Abernathy and K Wayne. What are the implications for corporate strategy of this conclusion?

6 Take an organisation with which you are familiar and identify its core resources, using the key guidelines to assist the process. Compare the organisation with its competitors and comment on the strategy implications.

7 Identify the core competences of pharmaceutical companies in general and Glaxo Wellcome in particular. What do your observations mean for corporate strategy development at Glaxo Wellcome?

8 Can a core competence be bought in as a short-term strategic solution or does it have to be developed over the long term? Use an example to support your answer.

9 Undertake a SWOT analysis for Glaxo Wellcome. What strategic conclusions can you draw?

10 How would you rate human resources in relation to other aspects of resources in the development of corporate strategy? Do you think the value chain adequately captures your answer?

11 The writer in the Key Reading argues that successful new strategy comes from crisis, provoking revolutions and new configurations. Can this view be reconciled with those outlining a more analytical approach, as described in this chapter? Do you agree or disagree with the writer? Give reasons.

STRATEGIC PROJECT

The global pharmaceutical industry

This chapter has examined the pharmaceutical industry. You might like to explore this global industry further – for example, the strategies that have been adopted by the large US and European companies to build scale and acquire distribution companies. Why did companies such as Merck and SmithKline Beecham spend large sums on such activities?

FURTHER READING

For key factors for success: Ohmae, K (1983) *The Mind of the Strategist*, Penguin, London.

For value chain and value system: Porter, M E (1985) *Competitive Advantage*, The Free Press, NY.

For core competences: Hamel, G and Prahalad, C K (1994) *Competing for the Future*, Harvard Business School Press, Mass.

REFERENCES

1 Glaxo Wellcome references: *Financial Times*: 7 Dec 1993, p22; 16 July 1994, p10; 24 Jan 1995, p17; 27 Jan 1995; 9 Mar 1995, p33; 24 Mar 1995, p27; 24 Apr 1995, p11; 8 Sep 1995, p15; 9 Nov 1995, p25.

2 Ohmae, K (1983) *The Mind of the Strategist*, Penguin, New York, Ch 3.

3 Porter, M E (1985) *Competitive Advantage*, The Free Press, New York, Ch 7.

4 Kay, J (1993) *Foundations of Corporate Success*, Oxford University Press, Chs 5 to 8.

5 Ohmae, K (1983) Ibid, p96.

6 Lynch, R (1994) *European Business Strategies*, 2nd edn, Kogan Page, London, p43.

7 Hamel, G and Prahalad, C K (1994) *Competing for the Future*, Harvard Business School Press, Boston, Mass.

8 Kay, J (1993) Ibid, p24.

9 Kay, J (1993) Ibid, p24.

10 Kay, J (1993) Ibid, p28.

11 Kay, J (1993) Ibid, discusses this further in Ch 12.

12 Porter, M E (1985) *Competitive Advantage*, The Free Press, New York, Ch 2.

13 Porter, M E (1985) Ibid, p38.

14 *Source*: Porter, M E (1985) Ibid.

15 *Source*: Porter, M E (1985) Ibid.

16 Cookson, C and Luesby, J (1995) 'Glaxo Wellcome giant changes the drug mixture', *Financial Times*, 9 Mar, p33.

17 Porter, M E (1985), Ibid, Chs 9, 10 and 11.

18 Porter, M E (1985) Ibid, Ch 3.

19 Kay, J (1993) Ibid, pp170 to 175. It is difficult to convey fully the interesting data that Kay brings to this discussion in summary format in the text.

20 Abernathy, W and Wayne, K (1974) 'Limits of the Learning Curve', *Harvard Business Review*, Sep–Oct, p108.

21 Kay, J (1993) Ibid, pp140–2.

22 Hardy, L (1987) *Successful Business Strategy*, Kogan Page, London, pp90–92.

23 Kay, J (1993) Ibid, p116 where he reproduces the two charts.

24 Abernathy, W and Wayne, K (1974) Ibid, p128.

25 Kay, J (1993) Ibid, Chs 5, 6 and 7.

26 Hamel, G and Prahalad, H K (1994), Ibid, Chs 9 and 10.

27 Sainsbury, D (1994) 'Be a better builder', *Financial Times*, 2 Sep, p11.

28 Stalk, G, Evans, P and Shulman, L (1992) 'Competing on Capabilities', *Harvard Business Review*, Mar/Apr.

29 Hamel, G and Prahalad, C K (1995) Ibid, p220.

30 Stalk *et al* (1992) Ibid.

31 *See*, for example, Hamel, G and Prahalad, C K (1994) Ibid, p223 which lists some core competences that are directly customer-related.

32 Hamel, G and Prahalad, C K (1990) 'The Core Competence of the Corporation', *Harvard Business Review*, May/June.

33 Adapted from an article by Andrew Hill in the *Financial Times* of 24 July 1995. © *Financial Times*. Reproduced with permission.

34 Stacey, R (1993) *Strategic Management and Organisational Dynamics*, 1st edn, Pitman Publishing, London, pp85–7 and 113–15. © R D Stacey. Reproduced with permission.

8

Analysing human resources

When you have worked through this chapter, you will be able to:

- conduct a human resource audit of an organisation and explore the strategic implications;

- outline the strategic issues involved in organisational culture and analyse the culture of the organisation;

- understand the impact of strategic change on strategy development;

- comment on the impact of downsizing and business process re-engineering in the context of human resources;

- analyse the political network of an organisation and assess its strategic implications;

- appraise the impact of international culture on strategy development.

■ INTRODUCTION

For many organisations, people are a vital resource. Their strategic significance extends beyond the resource context, however, because strategy development often involves change and some people may resist change to such an extent that it becomes impossible to implement the planned strategy. Human resource analysis is therefore essential during the development of corporate strategy and cannot simply be left as a task to be undertaken after the strategy has been agreed.

The starting point for the analysis is an *audit* of the human resources of the organisation – the people, their skills, backgrounds and relationships with each other. An assessment of the *culture* of the organisation is also required – the style and learned ways that govern and shape the organisation's people relationships. *Strategic change* is analysed and its forces explained (although covered in greater detail in Chapter 21). Finally, *power and politics* may guide and direct the organisation in its strategy development and therefore need careful assessment. The relationship between these subjects is circular – that is, no single area is dominant and all are inter-related – and is shown in Fig 8.1.

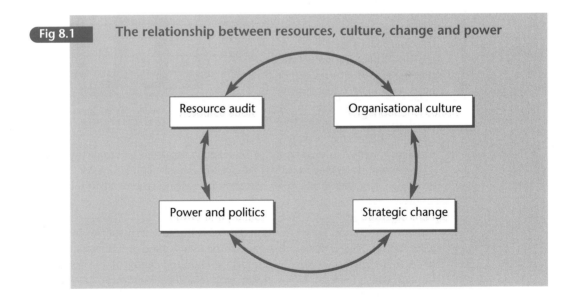

Fig 8.1   **The relationship between resources, culture, change and power**

Barons swept out of fiefdoms at Royal Dutch/Shell

In 1995, Royal Dutch/Shell faced two major strategic problems: it was beginning to run out of growth and its profitability was insufficient for long-term survival. This case study describes the far-reaching shake-up devised to tackle the difficulties.

Background

When the Royal Dutch/Shell's results were announced in 1995, there was no obvious reason for the company to embark on such a major exercise. It had just announced record earnings of £4 billion for the previous year, an increase of 24 per cent. Its return on capital employed – the main measure of financial efficiency – was given as 10.4 per cent, which was back into double figures for the first time since 1990. This was the result of a shakeout of the operating companies which had led to the loss of more than 10 000 jobs out of about 100 000 in 1994 and the sale of Shell's mining interests. Shell's international management systems were famous for their smoothness: the company's culture was good at breeding the right corporate types and fostering a co-operative atmosphere.

However, Mr John Jennings, the chairman of the UK side of the UK–Dutch company, said that the rate of return was not high enough to sustain the company in the long term. By 1994, further cost-cutting had become necessary. Further-

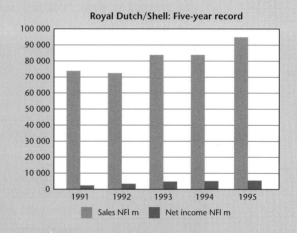

Royal Dutch/Shell: Five-year record

more, the Shell culture was good at breeding committees – hundreds of them – which, once created, never went away. 'There is a committee culture,' says Mr Ernst van Mourik-Broekman, who was in charge of human resources and co-ordinating the review.

Proposed changes

The proposed changes were shaped in consultation with staff over six months and were radical. They did more than attack the overstaffing and bureaucracy that threatened to weigh down Shell. They also eliminated many of the regional fiefdoms through which Shell ran its worldwide empire and which allowed local barons to wield a great deal of power. For historical reasons, Royal Dutch/Shell was organised mainly on geographical lines. Each country or region had its own companies and managers. These reported back through layers of command to the corporate centre which was split between London and the Hague. At the top was the four-strong committee of managing directors – the CMD – each responsible for one of Shell's four regions and a number of businesses.

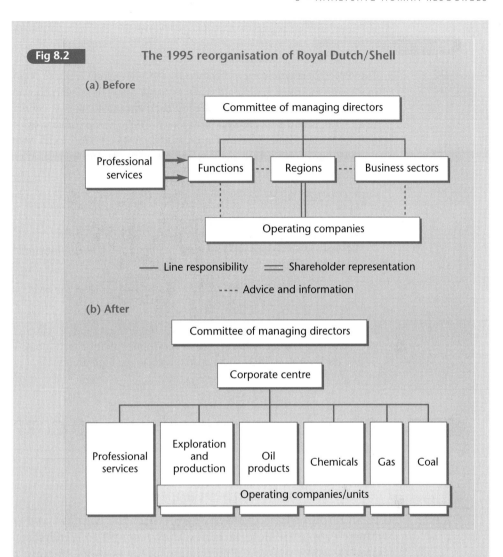

Fig 8.2 The 1995 reorganisation of Royal Dutch/Shell

(a) Before

Committee of managing directors

Professional services → Functions --- Regions --- Business sectors

Operating companies

—— Line responsibility ══ Shareholder representation

---- Advice and information

(b) After

Committee of managing directors

Corporate centre

Professional services | Exploration and production | Oil products | Chemicals | Gas | Coal

Operating companies/units

From 1995 onwards, the group was reshaped around five business organisations covering Shell's main activities: exploration and production, oil products (refining and marketing), chemicals, gas and coal. Each operating company would report to whichever of those organisations was relevant to its activities. The *shape* of the operating companies would not be altered by the proposals, only their *relationship* with the rest of the group. The organisational changes are shown in Fig 8.2.

Some results of the changes

For Shell's internal politics, these changes could be dramatic. At a stroke, they cut the larger regional baronies and reduced layers of regional co-ordination which accounted for many of the 1170 jobs expected to go at the centre. However, the changes also created a new senior officer corps in the members of the Business Committees.

MINICASE continued

These members would be nominated by the Managing Directors during 1995 and represented a moment that would make or break many highflying Shell careers.

By early 1996, 900 jobs had already been cut but there was considerable resistance to change. It had proved more time-consuming than originally envisaged. Consultation with staff councils in the Netherlands had been 'laborious'. Moreover, the main benefits had shifted from savings in staff wages to the increased performance that would result from a new slimmed-down organisation.

Source: Financial Times, 30 March 1995 and 15 February 1996.

CASE QUESTIONS

1 *What were the reasons given for the reorganisation? Were they sufficient to justify the upheaval involved?*

2 *What problems, if any, did Shell foresee in implementing the proposed changes? How did it propose to solve them?*

3 *How would you describe the previous culture and values of people in Shell? In what way might they change with the new organisation? What effect, if any, would you expect the announced changes to have on morale in the organisation?*

8.1 HUMAN RESOURCE ANALYSIS AND CORPORATE STRATEGY

8.1.1 Prescriptive and emergent approaches

Human resource-based analysis emphasises the *emergent* approach to corporate strategy. People are not machines: they respond to leadership, enthusiasm and shared decision making. Emergent strategy is more in tune with these issues because it encourages consensus and experimentation. Prescriptive stategy with its emphasis on the rational solution is less flexible and amenable to this stance.

Some prescriptive strategists have taken the view that human resources should be considered *only after the basic strategy has been derived*. Their view is based on two areas of evidence and thinking:

● Alfred Chandler's highly influential research text, *Strategy and Structure*.[2] This book analysed strategy development at four leading US companies during the early twentieth century. Among its many conclusions, it said that it was necessary to formulate the strategy of the company *before* considering how the company should be organised to implement the strategy.

● The focus on *important* strategy issues might be diluted by the consideration of other matters, such as human resource issues. For example, Porter's two books on *Competitive Strategy*[3] and *Competitive Advantage* certainly include human resource issues but lay the emphasis on competitive strategy development.

In fact, the Chandler text does not preclude the discussion of leadership and human resources in the formulation of strategy. On the contrary, it accurately describes their role in strategy development in some situations.[4] Moreover, Porter's concept of competitive strategy is consistent with the comparative analysis of human resources in an organisation versus competitors. Nevertheless, the fact remains that some prescriptive strategists only consider human resource issues *after* the formulation of strategy.[5]

However, human resources need to be considered *during* the strategic resource analysis phase for three related reasons:

1 People-related strategies may form an integral part of the new strategy – for example, a change in the organisation's way of conducting its business. The purpose of such a change might be to achieve greater responsiveness and efficiency from people within the company, as at Royal Dutch/Shell.

2 The increased technological skills and knowledge-based complexities of many commercial processes have meant that an analysis of the existing human resources is essential for an accurate assessment of the options that are available.

3 Research and writings on organisational change and culture[6] have emphasised the importance of values and cultures in the *development* of organisational structure. These cannot simply be added on afterwards.

8.1.2 Sustainable competitive advantage

For most organisations, people are a vital resource. There are some industries where people are not just important but are the *key factor* for successful performance, for example:

- *Leisure and tourism,* where a company has a direct, intangible interface that relies on individual employees to give interest and enjoyment to customers;
- *Management consultancy and the advertising industry,* where client relationships are vital to successful outcomes;
- *Hospitals and the medical profession*, where people and personal relationships are essential to the delivery of quality services.

Even in organisations where there are other key factors for success, such as oil resources at Royal Dutch/Shell, human resources clearly play a major part in the process. The smooth-running Shell man or woman is an essential feature of the company.

In this context, the ability of people in some organisations to be more *adaptable to changes* in the environment is a real skill. It may even be a source of competitive advantage in fast moving markets[7]. Arie De Geus, the former head of planning at Royal Dutch/Shell has said:

> The ability to learn faster than your competitors may be the only sustainable competitive advantage.[8]

Such skills are essentially people-related and the strategic approach is emergent.

8.1.3 Strategic change

The recognition that the threat posed to people by strategic change can be a significant barrier to the development of corporate strategy has come in the last 30 years. They fear that they may lose their jobs or their status: the Royal Dutch/Shell reorganisation in 1995 shows the results in terms of slow implementation and lower levels of cost savings than originally envisaged.

To quote Whittington, writing about corporations in crisis:[9]

> *'History is littered with managers apparently unable to adapt to new and threatening circumstances, and suffering the penalty of dismissal.'*

Even when companies are not in crisis, some writers take the view that the ability of people in the organisation to cope with change is a vital element in the development of strategy. This issue is explored later in this chapter and further in Chapter 21.

Key strategic principles

- Human resource-based analysis emphasises the emergent approach to strategic development. It is essential to consider human resources during the development of corporate strategy because of the need to explore people-related strategies at an early stage.

- People are a vital competitive resource in most organisations. The adaptability of people in the organisation may be a source of real competitive advantage in fast-moving markets.

- The analysis of strategic change needs to be explored and built into the development of corporate strategy.

8.2 HUMAN RESOURCE AUDIT

8.2.1 Audit

In undertaking the human resource audit of the organisation, it is important to give careful thought to a basic list of important areas in the business. Exhibit 8.1 shows a suggested list.[10] The main principles are:

- to obtain some basic information on the people and policies involved in the organisation;

- to explore in detail the role and contribution of the human resource management function in the development of corporate strategy.

Exhibit 8.1 Human resource audit

People in the organisation

- Employee numbers and turnover
- Organisation structure
- Structures for controlling the organisation
- Use of special teams, for example for innovation or cost-reduction
- Level of skills and capabilities required
- Morale and rewards
- Employee and industrial relations
- Selection, training and development
- Staffing levels
- Capital investment/employee
- Role of quality and personal service in delivering the products or services of the organisation
- Role of professional advice in delivering the product or service

Role and contribution of human resource strategy

- Relationship with corporate strategy
- Key characteristics of human resource strategy
- Consistency of human resource strategy across an organisation with several divisions
- The responsiveness of human resource strategy to changes in business strategy and the environment
- The role of human resource strategy in *leading* change in the organisation
- The monitoring and review of human resource strategy
- The time frame for the operation of human resource strategy

8.2.2 Strategic implications

The difficulty is to move beyond a list to something of strategic significance. Three factors need to be added to the above:

1 analysis of the list using the *key factors for success*;
2 comparative data for a *leading competitor* or, in the case of a smaller company, several competitors of comparable size; and
3 consideration, if appropriate, of the *international dimensions* of human resources in the organisation.

Using these additional factors, it should be possible to develop a human resource analysis that is rather more focussed on the *key strategic issues* related to the company. Equally, it should be possible to define and explore the role of human resources in the development of *competitive advantage*. The development of such advantages is likely to derive both from:

● *Issues common to all organisations in the industry* – for example, levels of service expected in all organisations, such as the frequency of oil deliveries by Shell to an industrial customer.

● *Factors that are unique to the organisation itself* – for example, aspects of the service that only the organisation itself can provide such as rapid local backup by Shell.

> ## Key strategic principles
>
> ● The human resource audit will have two main elements: people in the organisation and the role and contribution of human resources to the development of corporate strategy.
>
> ● The development of sustainable competitive advantage will derive both from issues common to all organisations in the industry and to factors that are unique to the organisation itself.
>
> ● A basic analysis of human resources can be constructed for the company. However, from a strategy viewpoint, it would be more valuable if this were filtered using key factors for success, competitive comparisons and, if appropriate, international considerations.

8.3 ANALYSIS OF ORGANISATIONAL CULTURE

8.3.1 The elements of organisational culture

Every organisation has a culture – its set of beliefs, values and learned ways of managing – and this is reflected in its structures, systems and approach to the development of corporate strategy. Its culture derives from its past, its present, its current people, technology and physical resources and from the aims, objectives and values of those who work in the organisation.

Because each organisation has a different combination of the above, each will have a culture that is unique. Analysis is important because culture influences every aspect of the organisation and has an impact on the performance of organisations.[11] Specifically, it is the filter and shaper through which the leaders, managers and workers develop and implement their strategies. For these reasons, it will be one of the factors that influences the development of corporate strategy.

The main elements of organisational culture are set out in Fig 8.3.

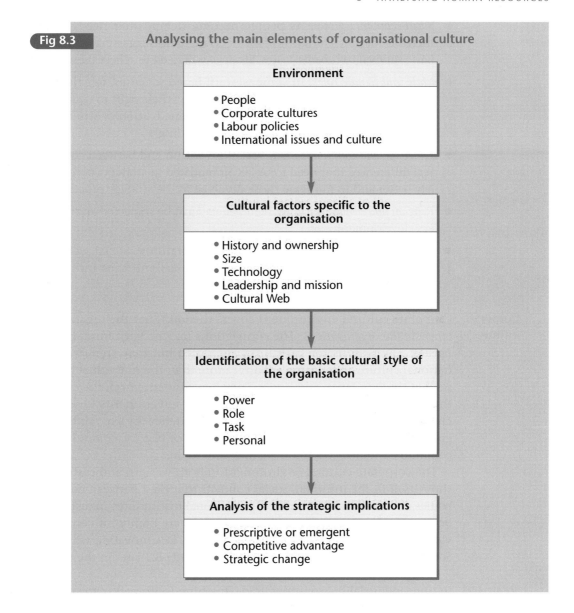

Fig 8.3   **Analysing the main elements of organisational culture**

8.3.2   Environmental influences on organisational culture

Outside the organisation itself, there will be a whole series of influences on the organisational culture of the organisation.

People   We are concerned here with the impact on the organisation of people in the environment: such people will include customers and suppliers, along with government and professional advisors. The main areas are:

- *Age profile.* As the population grows older, so tastes change, recruitment changes and those in employment must pay more from their remuneration for those already in retirement. The company burden will also increase.

● *Socio-economic group.* As people become richer, their needs and aspirations increase: Maslow's *hierarchy of needs*[12] is useful in suggesting how these alter from basic survival to broader tastes. Strategy will need to reflect these differences.

● *Male and female roles.* In some western-based societies, females have not only extended their working lives but are asserting their right to equal status with the male. In other societies, this has not happened. Strategy will need to be sensitive to such variations and be devised accordingly.

● *Language and communication.* Variations within and between countries represent real differences that need to be accommodated in strategy: both to control strategy better and to motivate those involved in the strategy process better.

● *Religion and beliefs.* Strongly held beliefs must be respected and reflected in strategy development.

● *Government policy.* Policy on education, training, social welfare provisions, health and pensions provisions will have a significant influence on people development inside the organisation.

Corporate cultures[13]   Corporate cultural environment covers the *links* that the organisation has with *other similar organisations*. The connections may be both formal and informal in nature. The reasons for such links are varied but may stem from an aspect of national cultures: group goals matter more than the individual in some societies such as those in Japan and Korea. They may also arise from the common interests that organisations share such as petitioning governments for grants, laws and favourable economic status. There is also a tendency for like-minded companies to group together in many countries for reasons of history, common shareholdings, common customers, common enemies and so on.

The corporate cultural environment in both western and eastern societies will show itself in the informal, social contacts that exist between companies in such bodies as chambers of commerce, professional institutions, industry representative bodies. In some countries, such organisations are highly influential and can provide an important outlet for informal contacts in connection with strategy issues. Some examples are explored further in Case study 8.1 later in the chapter.

Labour and employment policies   In some industrialised countries, trade unionism forms part of the environment that needs to be considered. However, the influence of organised labour has been declining over the last few years with union membership declining around the world.[14]

International issues   International cultures may have a significant impact on corporate culture (*see* Section 8.5).

To explore these matters further, Case study 8.3 tracks the corporate strategy and cultural changes introduced as a result of market and competitive pressures on Rank Xerox in the 1990s.

8.3.3 Cultural factors specific to the organisation

To understand the culture of an organisation, it is useful to consider the factors that have influenced its development.

History and ownership A young company may have been founded by one individual or a small group who will continue to influence its development for some years. Centralised ownership will clearly concentrate power and therefore will concentrate influence and style. Family firms and owner-dominated firms will have clearly recognisable cultures.

Size As firms expand, they may lose the tight ownership and control and therefore allow others to influence their style and culture. Even if ownership remains tight, larger companies are more difficult to control from the centre. More typically, as organisations grow, they need to introduce more control mechanisms and engage in more formal control procedures. All this will lead to a new and more formal culture with less flexibility and more rigid reporting structures.

Technology This will influence the culture of the company but its effects are not always predictable.[15] Those technologies that require economies of scale or involve high-cost and expensive machinery usually require a formal and well structured culture for success: examples might include large-scale chemical or beer brewing production. Conversely, in fast changing technologies, such as those in telecommunications, a more flexible culture may be required.

Leadership and mission Individuals and their values will reflect and change the culture of the organisation over time, especially the chief executive and immediate colleagues. These issues are vital to the organisation (*see* Chapter 12).

Cultural Web The Cultural Web is a useful method of bringing together the basic elements that are helpful in analysing the culture of an organisation (*see* Fig 8.4).
The main elements are:

- *Stories*. What do people talk about in the organisation? What matters in the organisation? What constitutes success or failure?
- *Routines*. What are the normal ways of doing things? What are the procedures (not always written down)?
- *Rituals*. Beyond the normal routine, what does the organisation highlight? For example, long service? Sales achievement? Innovation? Quality standards? How does it highlight and possibly reward such rituals?
- *Symbols*. What are the symbols of office? Office size? Company car size? Separate restaurants for different levels of managers and workers? Or the absence of these? How do employees travel: first, business or tourist class?
- *Control systems*. Bureaucratic? Well documented? Oriented towards performance? Formal or informal? Haphazard? (*See* Part 6.)
- *Organisational structure*. Who reports to whom in the organisation on a formal basis and who has an informal relationship?
- *Power structures*. Who makes the decisions? Who influences the decisions? How? When? (*See* Section 8.3.4.)

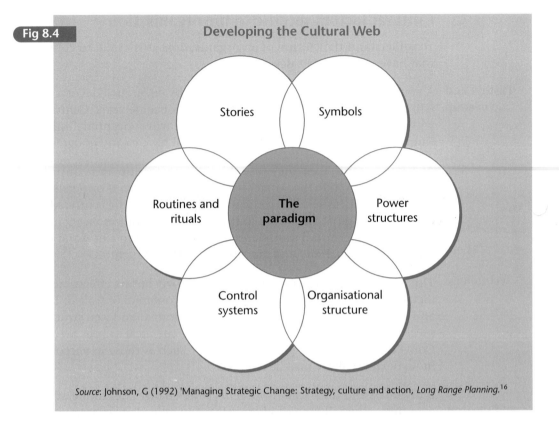

Fig 8.4

Developing the Cultural Web

Stories

Symbols

Routines and rituals

The paradigm

Power structures

Control systems

Organisational structure

Source: Johnson, G (1992) 'Managing Strategic Change: Strategy, culture and action, *Long Range Planning*.[16]

The paradigm not only links the elements but may also tend to *preserve* them as 'the way we do things here'. It summarises the culture of the organisation. Chapter 12 contains a worked example of the Cultural Web.

8.3.4 Identification of the basic cultural style of the organisation

Although each organisation has its own unique culture, Handy[17] has used the work of Harrison to suggest that there are four main types.

The power culture The organisation revolves around and is dominated by one individual or a small group. Typically, it can result from an entrepreneur setting up a new company. It may be buccaneering and risk taking. All decisions refer back to the centre and so do beliefs and work styles. Experts are either overvalued or treated with suspicion and disdain.

As the organisation grows in size, it becomes increasingly difficult for the centre to keep control. Either the organisation changes or it spawns a new subgroup with its own leader who, in turn, reports back to the original centre. The corporate plan, if it exists at all, reflects the individual at the top, her/his whims, interests and passions. *Examples*: small building companies, some former newspaper proprietors. *Strategic change*: fast or slow depending on the management style of the leader.

The role culture This organisation relies on committees, structures, logic and analysis. There is a small group of senior managers who make the final decisions, but they rely on procedures, systems and clearly defined rules of communication. It might even be regarded as bureaucratic but has a thoroughness and solidity that make it a reliable and fair employer. Expert opinions are treated with caution as they represent outsiders to the organisation.

As long as the outside environment is stable, the organisation can handle difficult situations. However, senior managers often do not see the changes that are coming and, even if they do, they do not know how to manage them. Change in such a culture comes through a new set of managers being appointed. Strategic planning in a formal way would characterise such a culture. *Examples*: civil service, retail banks. *Strategic change*: likely to be slow and methodical.

The task culture The organisation is geared to tackle identified projects or tasks. Work is undertaken in teams that are flexible and tackle identified issues. The teams may be multidisciplinary and adaptable to each situation. Power rests with the team, which may contain some experts to facilitate group decisions. Expert opinions are valued.

The culture is flexible and sensitive to change, but it works best on small-team issues. It is less capable of large-scale work such as that required in a major factory. Control relies largely on the efficiency of the team with top management having to allow the group considerable day-to-day autonomy. Strategic planning is both flexible and task-oriented but will focus largely on the task in hand. *Examples*: advertising agencies, consultancies. *Strategic change*: will depend on the circumstances but may be fast where this is needed.

The personal culture The individual works and exists purely for her- or himself. The organisation is tolerated as the way to structure and order the environment for certain useful purposes, but the prime area of interest is the individual. Such organisations exist infrequently in business, but may exist in non-profit institutions. Such individuals are not easy to manage and feel little loyalty to the organisation.

Changes are coped with easily or with difficulty depending on the inclination of the individual. Strategic planning is largely meaningless except in a very personal sense. *Examples*: co-operatives, communes and also individual professionals such as architects or engineers working as lone people in larger organisations such as health authorities. *Strategic change:* can be instant, where the individual decides that it is in his or her interests to make such a move.

8.3.5 Analysis of the strategic implications

To explore the four cultures in the context of corporate strategy, three criteria related to corporate strategy can be used:

- fit with prescriptive or emergent strategy routes;
- delivery of competitive advantage;
- ability to cope with strategic change.

The four cultural types are analysed against these criteria in Table 8.1.

Table 8.1 Conclusions on the four types of culture

	Prescriptive or emergent strategy	Delivery of competitive advantage	Ability to cope with strategic change
Power culture	Presciptive	Enhanced but individuals may miss competitive moves	Depends on individual or group at centre
Role culture	Prescriptive	Solid, slow and substantive	Slow, will resist change
Task culture	Emergent	Good where flexibility is important	Accepted and welcomed
Personal culture	Possibly emergent	Depends on individual	Depends on individual

In examining the four main types of organisational culture, there are three important qualifications:

1 *Organisations change over time.* The entrepreneur, represented by the *power culture*, may mature into a larger and more traditional business. The bureaucracy, personified by the *role culture*, may move towards the more flexible structure of the *task culture*. Hence, an analysis may need to be reassessed after some years.

2 *Several types of culture usually exist in the same organisation.* There may be small task-teams concentrating on developing new business or solving a specific problem and, in the same organisation, a more bureaucratic set-up handling large volume production in a more formal structure and style. Corporate strategy may even need to consider whether different parts of the organisation should develop *different* cultures – for example, a team culture for a radical new venture, a personal culture for the specialist expertise required for a new computer network.

3 *Different cultures may predominate depending on the headquarters and ownership of the company.* Hofstede's research[18] indicates that national culture will also have an influence and will interact with the above basic type (*see* Section 8.5).

For these reasons, strategy cultural analysis needs to be approached with caution. Nevertheless, there are many organisations both large and small where the mood, style and tone are clear enough as soon as you walk through the door. There is one prevailing culture that permeates the way that business is done in that organisation. The implications for competitive advantage and strategic change follow from this.

8.3.6 Conclusions on organisational culture

Exhibit 8.2 lists ten guidelines for analysing cultural issues within an organisation. Both Brown[19] and Handy[20] have provided longer questionnaires than are shown in Exhibit 8.2. From a strategy viewpoint, they are useful but the danger with such an analysis is that it becomes another descriptive list of possible factors. The analytical process needs to be evaluated against possible areas of strategic interest. For example, it is *interesting* to know that the organisation's culture is risk-averse, but it is much more *relevant* to set this against a new corporate strategy that requires a higher degree of risk-taking than was previously the case. Hence, Exhibit 8.2 also provides some possible criteria to test for relevance. This is sometimes referred to as *testing for strategic fit* with the current strategy.

Exhibit 8.2   **Ten guidelines for analysing organisation culture and its strategy implications**

1 How old is the organisation? Does it exist in a stable or fast changing environment?

2 Who owns it? Shareholding structure? Small company owner–proprietor? Government shareholding? Large public company? What are the core beliefs of the leadership?

3 How is it organised? Central board? Divisions? Clear decision-making structure from the top? Are structures formal or informal? Is competition encouraged between people in the company or does the organisation regard collaboration as being more important?

4 How are results judged? Sympathetically? Rigorously? What elements are monitored? Is the emphasis on looking back to past events or forwards to future strategy?

5 How are decisions made? Individually? Collectively and by consensus? How is power distributed throughout the organisation? Who can stop change? And who can encourage it?

6 What qualities make a good boss? And a good subordinate?

7 How are people rewarded? Remuneration? Fear? Loyalty? Satisfaction in a job well done?

8 How are groups and individuals controlled? Personal or impersonal controls? Enthusiasm and interest? Or abstract rules and regulations?

9 How does the organisation cope with change? Easily or with difficulty?

10 Do people typically work in teams or as individuals? What does the company prefer?

Overall: Is the *whole* organisation being analysed or just a *part*?

Tests for strategic relevance might include:

● *Risk.* Does the organisation wish to change its level of risk?

● *Rewards.* What reward and job satisfaction?

● *Change.* High or low degree of change needed?

● *Cost reduction.* Is the organisation seeking major cost reductions?

● *Competitive advantage.* Are significant new advantages likely or will they be needed?

Key strategic principles

- Organisational culture is the set of beliefs, values and learned ways of managing that govern organisational behaviour. Each organisation has a culture that is unique.

- Culture influences performance and corporate strategy. It is the filter and shaper through which strategy is developed and implemented.

- Factors within the organisation influencing culture include: history and ownership, size, technology, leadership and mission, along with the cultural web of the organisation.

- The cultural web provides a method of summarising some of the cultural influences within an organisation: stories, routines and rituals, symbols, power structures, organisation structure, control systems.

- Factors external to the organisation influencing culture include: people, national cultures, corporate cultural environment, labour and employment policies.

- There are four main types of culture: power, role, task and personal. Their importance for corporate strategy lies particularly in their ability to encourage or cope with the *strategic change* that is likely to be needed with specific strategic initiatives and to deliver *competitive advantage*. Some types are better able to cope and manage strategic change than others.

- Guidelines can be developed for analysing organisational culture. For the purposes of strategy development, such an analysis needs to be assessed against the strategy in areas such as attitudes to risk, change, reward, cost reduction and competitive advantage.

CASE STUDY 8.1

Culture, crisis and power at British Petroleum[21]

In early 1990, Bob Horton, the new Chairman of British Petroleum, announced major changes in the management organisation, processes and culture of Europe's second largest oil company. Over the next two years, the implementation process brought him into open conflict with fellow board members. Horton was ousted in a board room coup in June 1992.

After gaining something of a reputation as an 'axeman' at BP Chemicals and BP Oil in North America, Horton was appointed Deputy Chairman at British Petroleum (BP) in 1989. Horton had inherited a company in 1990 with some major business problems. Principally, BP had incurred major debts when it purchased back a block of its shares from the Kuwait Investment Office in 1987. By 1992, it had a 100 per cent gearing ratio and US$16 billion of debts (*see* Chapter 9). The world economic markets were also depressed so oil consumption was weak.

The company certainly knew Horton's management style well. He called BP's first group management conference in March of that year and identified major problems with BP's structures, systems and management: they were over-bureaucratic, sluggish and committee-driven. His intention was to revise the structure and achieve a new 'tight–loose' structure in the phrase of the strategy book, *In Search of Excellence*. The new form would be leaner, have more delegated powers and be able to respond faster to the market place.

Rather than asking his main board colleagues to mastermind the changes he had outlined, Horton recruited from within BP a team of seven 35- to 40-year-old mid-ranking executives to take a fundamental look at the whole corporation. From March to December 1989 the team interviewed all the senior management and employed outside advisors to help develop recommendations for streamlining BP. The team also sent questionnaires to one in six BP employees seeking their views on the company. Two thirds (4000) responded. Their opinions made dismal reading and confirmed all the team's worst fears.

During Autumn 1989, the team met weekly with Horton to put together proposals for the new slimmed down BP. In November, the team had a major meeting with Horton, who by this time had been confirmed as Chairman- and Chief Executive-

designate of BP from March 1990. The team highlighted particularly the gap between where BP was at that time and where it wanted to be. They said that BP should seek clear vision, open communication, empowered people, deep trust and team accountability. What they had identified was no shared vision, poor communications, excessive emphasis on asset trading, little trust, with BP as a company being held in low esteem.

At the same time, Horton's project team leader, David Pascall, was feeding some of this message to other main board members on an informal basis. The aim of this process had been to fire them up for the major review meeting with Horton scheduled for December 1989. This meeting duly took place outside London and in great secrecy with all the Managing Directors (MDs) attending. In general, the meeting accepted the changes that were needed in culture and style. Some proposals went through quite quickly, such as the need to give the MDs more authority over capital spending limits. Others led to more lengthy debate – for example, whether the head office central planning and control functions should be cut as drastically as proposed. This was only finally settled after the meeting.

There was only one open revolt at the meeting over an appeal by Horton for BP to work its managers less hard. Various senior MDs had supported the view, but Horton's Deputy Chairman designate, David Simon, then disagreed: 'I wouldn't overdo the chances of the system changing.' Two other MDs supported this view, so Horton backed off. More importantly, one MD on leaving the meeting was heard to comment that the MDs themselves were having a meeting the following day without Horton; his opinion was that the proposals might be overturned at that session. In fact they were not, but the comment epitomised the resentment shown by many senior managers.

Over the next two years, Horton, who was now Chairman, moved to put in train his changes in the programme which had been named *Project 1990*. Over US$30 million was spent on workshops, communications and training programmes. There was to be a transformed view of human resource management in the company. There was a major drive to change the culture to one of 'ownership' of problems by individuals rather than committees.

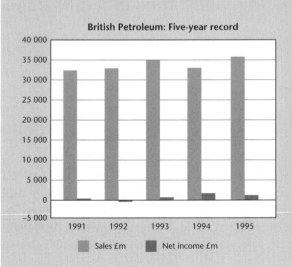

British Petroleum: Five-year record

■ Sales £m   ■ Net income £m

Horton had come to BP headquarters with a reputation as a straight-talking manager. His attitude was that there would be many managers, especially those over 40, who might well obstruct his attempt to introduce a new culture at BP. He was quite open that he was not prepared to let such people get in the way of strategic and cultural reforms which he regarded as essential. He even went on record to the press to say that the biggest mistake he had made when reorganising BP Chemicals some years previously was 'to allow some guys to stay in place whom I should have got rid of on day three'. He understood that not all managers would find this acceptable but felt that it was sometimes necessary to take difficult decisions. That was the function of senior management.

Slowly, the resentment began to build during 1990 and 1991. 'Culture change teams' were introduced to bring about the new era. The baronies were attacked, revised job descriptions were introduced and job cuts were achieved. It was inevitable that some managers would be feeling discomfort. Satirical stories began to circulate in the company about Horton himself: one likened him to Napoleon. He was described as autocratic and quick-tempered by a senior colleague. Horton himself became increasingly restive about the pace of change, but judged that what he was doing was for the benefit of BP.

Finally, his board turned on him in June 1992. His Deputy, David Simon, took over as Managing Director. Simon was reported to represent the more traditional BP culture. An outside Chairman was also brought in, Lord Ashburton, a City merchant banker. The culture change programme continued and some 6000 people left the company during 1992 and 1993. However, BP had decided that Bob Horton was part of the problem rather than the source of the solution.

After Horton's departure, the company immediately cut its dividend as it struggled to reduce debts. The company also drastically cut its debt with a programme of asset disposals and job cuts.

CASE QUESTIONS

1 *What was the significance of involving 35- to 40-year-old managers for Horton? And his fellow board members?*

2 *How important do you consider the comment by Horton about the over-40-year-old managers?*

3 *What is your assessment of the cultural changes that took place in the period 1990–92 against the cultural change models outlined in the chapter?*

4 *Horton took the view that his decisions may have been autocratic but were for the good of the company. Moreover, the board knew his personality when it appointed him. On this basis, he was entitled to expect more support than he received. Do you agree with this view of the politics of BP?*

8.4 ANALYSIS OF STRATEGIC CHANGE IN ORGANISATIONS

Although some organisations may continue successfully with their current strategies, many will need to change. Any change brings uncertainty and some organisations and individuals are better able to cope with this than others. Some may even resist proposed new strategies and put at risk the new proposals. Strategic change can usefully be explored as the three inter-related topics shown in Fig 8.5.

Fig 8.5 The analysis of strategic change in organisations

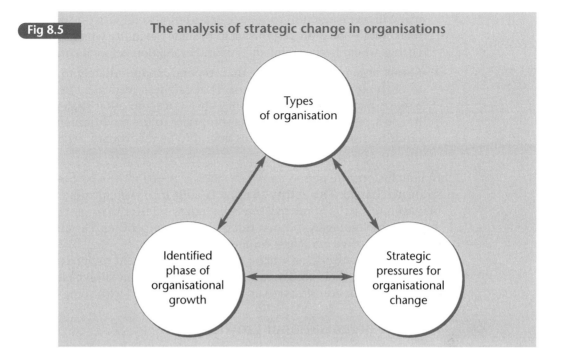

8.4.1 Types of organisation and their ability to cope with strategic change

Given the uncertainties that usually come with strategic change, organisations need to be analysed in advance for their ability to cope with this process. If they are likely to have difficulty, then there may be an argument for adjusting the proposed strategy to reflect this situation. There is no overall agreement on an analytical procedure for examining the link between organisation and strategic change. Commentators have proposed various ways of analysing the process.

Miles and Snow[22] proposed four main strategic types of organisation which can be analysed for their ability to cope with change:

1   *Defender organisations* produce products or services with the objective of obtaining market leadership. They may achieve their objectives by concentrating on a market niche through specialisation and cost reductions. The market may be mature and stable. The organisation is able to cope with sudden strategic change but would be more comfortable with steady strategic change.

2   *Prospector organisations* are involved in growing markets where they actively seek new opportunities through innovation. They are typically flexible and decentralised in their approach to the market and able to respond quickly to change. Their objectives are to seek new opportunities. Strategic change is no problem for such companies.

3   *Analyser organisations* seek to expand but also to protect what they already have. They may wait for others to innovate and delay while others prove new market opportunities before they enter. Large and small organisations can take this route

using mass production to reduce costs but also relying on some areas such as marketing to be more responsive to provide flexibility where required. Strategic change would need careful analysis and evaluation before it could be adopted.

4 *Reactor organisations* are those that respond inappropriately to competitors and to the more general environment. They rarely, if ever, take the initiative and, in a sense, may have no strategy: they always react to other strategies. Even if they have a strategy, it is entirely inappropriate to the environment and hence the resulting reactor organisation is bound to be inadequate. Strategic change will therefore be a problem.

In conclusion, the *prospector organisation* is probably the best able to cope with strategic change. The ability to cope is built into the culture, organisation and management style. Some markets are changing faster than previously, especially with new technologies and new international competition. The ability to cope and even enjoy change is a major competitive advantage.

For strategy purposes, it will be essential to analyse the various parts of an organisation against their ability to cope with change. The above classification may over-simplify the real situation and needs to be treated with some caution.

8.4.2 Phase of organisational growth

Whatever organisational classification is used in the analytical process, some changes may be more rapid and more dramatic than others. It is probably the case that the more intense the debate, the more difficult the change process and the more problems there are with the strategy. It is appropriate therefore to examine the *type of change* that might be expected. Greiner[23] identified two major determinants to clarify this process:

- *The age of the organisation.* Young organisations are typically full of ideas, creative, perhaps a little chaotic but actively seeking change. As they grow older and achieve success, there is more to defend and more to co-ordinate.
- *The size of the organisation.* Small organisations may be closer to the market place and have simpler administration. As the organisation becomes larger and acquires more people, it sets up systems and procedures to cope.

Greiner's five phases of growth are shown in Fig 8.6. They are not meant to be taken literally – organisations can overcome their problems – but they are helpful in identifying the main issues to be met and the types of strategic change that may be needed.

Particular types of organisation will experience particular pressures for change.

- *Small business.* As a small business expands, the owner–proprietor begins to lose control because s/he can no longer keep in contact with everyone personally. Moreover, the administration becomes more complex. Hence, it may become increasingly difficult to take rapid decisions and respond to changes in the environment. One strategic solution is to remain small and refuse to grow. Another solution is to sell out to a new group.
- *Large organisations that were formerly in government ownership.* Having previously relied on government funds, there is now a need to undertake marketing and other related business areas. However, the organisation is large and has little experience of business pressures and culture. It is used to the bureaucracy that is

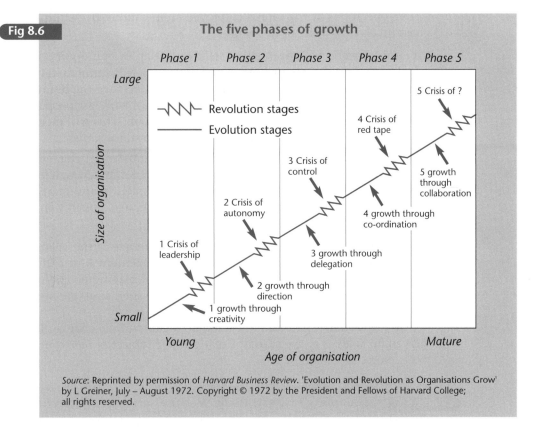

Fig 8.6 The five phases of growth

demanded of government systems. Strategic change needs to be seen as a shift in *culture* just as much as new business-oriented *strategies*.

● *Not-for-profit institutions*. Relying on public donations and voluntary help, there is an increasing problem as the organisation grows older and expands in size. It needs to set up systems to manage its finances and services while at the same time keeping the personal touch and enthusiasm of its individual helpers. Change will present real problems.

● *Medium-sized business*. With expansion, it may no longer be possible to control every aspect of strategy from the centre. There will be a need for greater autonomy and delegation. Some managers are better able to delegate than others. The change strategy may involve not only new strategies but *new managers* recruited into the organisation.

8.4.3 Strategic pressures driving organisational change

As corporate strategy is analysed and developed, there are two main strategic pressures that may drive organisational change:

● *internal* – desire for increased profitability, growth or some other objective, such as quality or innovation.

● *external* – competitive pressures or other environmental change.

For example, the objective might be stated as an *increase in the return on capital employed*. Since the return on capital employed is calculated by dividing the profits from operations by the capital employed in operations, by definition, this objective can involve only one of two routes:

1 *Raising profits* will mean either selling more at lower proportional costs or reducing the total costs or both. Such activities will immediately impact on the organisation as the instructions are given to achieve the results: perhaps it will mean producing and selling the same amount with less people; perhaps longer working hours for the same money; and so on. This will mean organisational change, possibly loss of jobs, certainly upheaval for some.

2 *Reducing capital employed* may also involve substantial change. There may be a need to cut back stocks, introduce new computer-driven systems, negotiate with suppliers to deliver raw materials more frequently and many other areas. All these will bring pressure for organisational change, possibly entailing retraining and even the loss of jobs.

Two specific strategies driving organisational change in the 1990s include *delayering*, which involves removing layers of management and administration, and *business process re-engineering*, which involves replacing people in administrative tasks by technology. Exhibit 8.3 explains how such strategic pressures will drive change in the organisation.

Strategic change will lead inevitably to organisational change. The starting point is careful *analysis* of the current situation. The subject of *managing* strategic change is explored in Chapter 21.

Exhibit 8.3   Examples of two strategic pressures driving organisational change

Delayering
Traditionally big companies believed that one manager could only control a certain number of people – the *span of control* – often between 7 and 10. Several *layers* of management were therefore needed to allow one senior person to control several hundred lower down in the organisation. With the new computer and telecommunications control systems, there is now a view that managers can control 30 people. This reduces the need to have so many managerial layers and thus opens the way for companies to cut costs – for example, the process undertaken by Shell to reduce its headquarters workforce by 1170 employees.

To work properly, delayering needs to be undertaken with careful planning: this means examining the paperwork and bureaucracy that often accumulate in large companies and cutting these down at the same time. It also needs to be done radically once rather than in piecemeal fashion, because of the impact on morale every time cuts are made.

Business process re-engineering[25]
This is the process of using modern computer technology to simplify radically the organisation's handling of administrative tasks. This may accompany delayering but is a different process. It is more likely to occur in the lower levels of the company, rather than at managerial level. It is likely to involve combining departments such as customer handling , complaints, stock ordering, stock delivery and control. Typically, there will be a dismantling of demarcation between departments and a radical reduction in the number of employees. The human resource aspects of such a strategy are obvious. (*See* Case study 8.2.)

- Given the uncertainty that usually comes with strategic change, organisations need to be analysed for their ability to cope with this process.

- There are no agreed procedures for such an analysis but they usually involve categorising an organisation into specific strategic types: four have been identified. The ability of each type to cope with change is then assessed.

- As strategies are developed in organisations, they may grow in size and certainly in age. In consequence, the nature of the strategic problems changes. Five stages of growth have been identified: creativity, direction, delegation, co-ordination and collaboration.

- Change also needs to be assessed against the pressures that are on the organisation. These will be both internal and external. Strategies such as delayering and business process re-engineering are specific modern examples of such influences.

8.5 ANALYSIS OF POLITICS, POWER AND STRATEGIC CHANGE

When writing about his life in politics, the British politician Lord Butler called his book *The Art of the Possible*. Although certain changes in national life might be *desirable*, he argued that they were not always *possible*, given the electorate and the environment of that time. In politics, he believed that people needed to be persuaded and this was an art, not an exact science. Business and not-for-profit organisations also involve people. The early twentieth-century view of management pioneers such as F W Taylor and Henry Ford was that there was one best way to achieve results and organisations were machines that could be directed to these ends. Views are now more sophisticated, especially where strategic change is concerned.

In organisations, there will be individuals and groups who are likely to have an interest in any strategic change. There may be pressure groups, rivalries, power barons and brokers, influencers, arguments, winners and losers. Some dispute may be disinterested and rational and some may be governed by strongly held views and interests. All these areas form the *politics* of the organisation. Strategic change cannot be separated from such issues.

Strategy too is about 'the art of the possible'. An analysis of the organisation's political situation is important in the early stages of strategic development. It may be highly desirable to alter radically a company's structure, but the cost in terms of management time may be too high in some circumstances, even with an imposed solution. Case study 8.1 explored the difficulties that faced the new Chairman of BP over the period 1990–92 as he attempted to achieve radical change and impose his preferred solutions on the organisation.

8.5.1 What are the main components of politics in organisations?

Taking an emergent strategy perspective, Handy points out[26] that it is wishful thinking to attempt to 'manage change' in the sense that it is possible not only to know where the organisation is heading but also to instruct everyone to take the same route. It is much more realistic and rewarding to 'cultivate change', suggesting that a positive attitude to change coupled with learning and persuasion is more likely to be productive.

There is nothing wrong with healthy competition between groups and individuals in an organisation. It can stretch performance and help groups to become more cohesive. It also helps to sort out the best. The difficulty arises when it gives rise to conflict and the political manoeuvring. There are two principle reasons for organisational conflict:

- *Differing goals and ideologies.* For example, different groups or individuals within an organisation may have different goals, make different value judgements, be given different and conflicting objectives, etc. There may also be a lack of clarity in the goals and objectives. It should be possible in the context of strategic change to ensure that conflict and confusion over goals is minimised.

- *Threats to territory.* For example, some groups or individuals may feel threatened by others doing the same jobs, become jealous of other roles, be given instructions that cut across other responsibilities, etc. It is in this area that the greatest strategic difficulty is likely to arise. If savings are to be made or improved performance to be obtained, then it may be necessary to accept the conflict here.

Addressing the strategic change issue, Mintzberg[27] suggests that there are benefits from competition in organisations. They can be a force for achieving change. In this sense, politics is an inevitable consequence of strategic change and needs to be accepted and channelled for the best results.

8.5.2 How can strategic change be analysed in a political context?

It is important to clarify right at the start the organisation's objectives and the implications for individual parts of the organisation. If it is true that conflict arises as a result of confusion over objectives, then it follows that these need to be fully explored before other matters are raised.

In addition, five areas would benefit from analysis at this early stage:

1 *The extent to which the organisation has developed a culture of adaptation or experiment.* Such an approach will help when it comes to implementing agreed strategies later.

2 *The identification of major power groups or individuals,* whose influence and support is essential for any major strategic change.

3 *The desirability or necessity of consultation rather than confrontation,* as the strategic analytical process continues.

4 *The role and traditions of leadership in the organisation* and the extent to which this may enhance the success and overcome problems associated with strategic change.

5 *The nature and scope of the external pressures on the organisation.*

These are the subjects that need to be analysed in the context of strategic change. They are interconnected as a *network* of relationships (*see* Fig 8.7). Once the main outline of strategies have been agreed, it will be necessary to return to the politics of strategic change again. We will do so in Chapter 21.

Key strategic principles

- Strategic change needs to take into account what is possible in terms of change, rather than what is desirable.

- Competition is healthy in organisations, except when it degenerates into unhealthy conflict and political manoeuvring.

- During the analysis phase of strategic development, there are political issues that can usefully be explored. In analysing the political network, it is necessary to survey power groups, leadership, the change style of the organisation, the adoption of a learning-adaptive culture and the nature of the external pressures.

Fig 8.7　　　**The political network of an organisation**

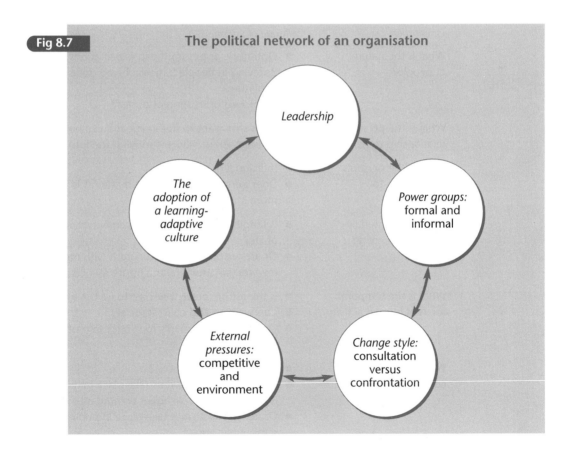

8.6 INTERNATIONAL CULTURAL PERSPECTIVES

In one sense, *national culture* is just one of the organisational culture issues explored in Section 8.3. However, from a strategy viewpoint, it is important enough to be highlighted on its own. The reason is that some corporate strategies may be desirable in theory but extremely difficult to implement in practice, once national culture is considered. It would therefore be better to identify any national culture problems in the analysis phase and develop a different and more acceptable strategy.

There is no single agreed definition of national culture, but for our purposes we will use that of Hofstede:[28]

> *The collective programming of the mind which distinguishes the members of one human group from another ... Culture, in this sense, includes systems of values; and values are among the building blocks of culture.*

National culture governs so much of the way that society operates, and so it needs to be taken into account in deriving corporate strategy. Asking members of a company to undertake tasks that they do not understand or find unacceptable to their culture and beliefs will lead to a failed strategy. Kluckhohn and Strodtbeck[29] defined six basic cultural orientations and these are listed in Table 8.2.

Table 8.2 Six basic national cultural orientations

Orientation	Range of variations
What is the nature of people?	● Optimistic or pessimistic in expectations about people? ● Believing in people basically being good or evil or a mixture? ● Suspicious or trusting of others?
What is the person's relationship to nature?	● Does s/he want to dominate and exploit nature or remain fatalistic about nature and what the future holds?
What is the person's relationship to other people?	● Individual or collective? ● Does personal achievement matter or is the group's goal more important?
What is the modality of human activity?	● Is tangible reward and achievement important as a way of life? ● Or are we born to a certain path with merit being rewarded in after-life or a future re-incarnation?
What is the temporal focus of human activity?	● Is the future, present or past to be the focus of activity? ● Can we plan and control society? ● Or should we primarily look back to past events to guide the future?
What is the conception of space?	● Private, mixed or public? ● Do meetings and events take place behind closed doors? Is it easy to visit colleagues without an invitation? ● Or do most activities take place in public or semi-public areas?

National culture governs both the style and content of the way business is done internationally. To a large extent, the basics are learnt in the early years of life before individuals ever encounter the business world. As people then move into different companies, they then encounter aspects of culture which their previous cultural expectations allow them to cope with easily or with varying degrees of difficulty.

Probably the most comprehensive study undertaken of the importance of different national cultural groups was that undertaken by Hofstede.[30] Over a number of years, he surveyed 116 000 employees at IBM in 50 countries and three regions (note the specialist nature of the sample). He grouped the data he obtained against four, and later five, dimensions which were largely independent of each other.

- *Power distance* – the extent to which those who were poorest in a society were willing to accept their position. Countries such as Panama, Malaysia and Venezuela emerged as being those where such acceptance was common. Israel, Denmark, Ireland and Sweden were countries where such inequalities were less acceptable.

- *Individualism/collectivism* – the extent to which societies are collections of individuals or are bound together in a cohesive whole. The USA, UK, Australia and the Netherlands were among the more individual with South American countries such as Guatamala, Panama and Columbia being typical of those who were more collectivist.

- *Masculinity versus femininity* – the extent to which a country is placed on a spectrum from masculine to feminine. In *male* cultures, there is a sharp distinction between the role the two sexes play in society and at work: males are expected to emphasise the importance of work, power and wealth. In *female* cultures, there is more equality between the two with achievements being measured in terms of the environment and human contacts. Japan, Austria and Italy were typical masculine cultures and Sweden, the Netherlands and Finland typical feminine cultures.

- *Uncertainty avoidance* – the extent to which members of a culture feel threatened by the unknown. Where uncertainty avoidance is *weak*, people are willing to embrace uncertainty and ambiguous situations: precision and punctuality for meetings were useful but not essential. In *strong* uncertainty avoidance countries, people need certainty, planning and order. Strong country cultures include Japan, Portugal, Greece and Belgium. Weak countries covered Singapore, Denmark, Jamaica and Hong Kong.

- *Confucian versus dynamism.* Hofstede later added this category to those above. He discovered that different cultures have different time horizons – long-termism versus short-termism – which were also linked with the Confucian concept of 'virtue' versus the more Western concept of 'truth'. Thus *long-termism* emphasises the importance of taking a long view and adapting traditions to a modern context, while stressing perseverance. *Short-termism* seeks not only the short-term view but also the importance of status, social obligations and quick results. China, Hong Kong and South Korea typify the former, whereas the USA, Nigeria, Canada and the UK were typical of the latter.

For a critique of the Hofstede research, *see* Meade.[31]

Such cultural variation will also be reflected in the corporate group cultures of various countries. These are explored in Case study 8.2.

CASE STUDY 8.2

Industry groups in Japan, Korea, Hong Kong and Italy

Companies often coalesce into informal industry groupings within a country. These can have a substantial influence on the strategy of group members, ranging from support in time of trouble to mutual benefits and co-operation on new strategic initiatives. Occasionally, such co-operation may be in danger of breaching anti-monopoly legislation.

As an example of such groupings, we can look at the Far East and Europe. In Japan, such groupings are called *Keiretsu* and in Korea *Chaebol*. (It should be noted that they are not quite the same in the two societies but they fulfil similar roles. The Keiretsu is more informal while the Chaebol are effectively conglomerates.) From a strategy viewpoint, the links between the companies in the Keiretsu or Chaebol can be mutually supportive of new business initiatives. They can be used to help in difficult times and can be used to secure business deals that might otherwise prove difficult. The regular meetings of senior managers from such groupings can also be a source of useful business information. For competitors, such groupings need to be understood and their mutual support anticipated in any negotiations.

Mitsubishi and Mitsui are examples of Keiretsu in Japan: they had 25 and 22 companies respectively in 1993 in their organisational orbit. The top six Keiretsu controlled 38 per cent of Japan's market capitalisation, 16 per cent of sales and 17 per cent of listed company profits in 1993.[32] In the same way, the three leading Korean Chaebol controlled over US$15 billion sales in 1993. Samsung, Hyundai and Lucky-Goldstar were the three biggest with sales of US$5.6, 4.6 and 3.5 billion respectively.[33]

Such links are not confined to these two countries: networking has long been an important characteristic of Chinese families. The *Riady* Family connections through their Lippo Group of companies in China, Hong Kong, USA and Indonesia is an example of a group that has now grown to a capitalised value of around US$2.5 billion.[34]

This should not be seen as a purely Eastern phenomenon. The *Agnelli* family in Italy have extensive interests that go well beyond Fiat cars into chemicals, aerospace and banking.[35] The *Seagram* family in the USA in 1995 completed their purchase of MCA for US$2 billion. In both cases, there is a web of companies that have interconnections that extend across the corporate environment. They add to the complexity of the analysis of corporate strategy.

CASE QUESTIONS

1 *Compared to the other cultural areas outlined in this chapter, how important do you believe corporate cultures are for the companies above?*

2 *What are the main features of such a culture in terms of their influence and control over individual companies?*

3 *Can you identify a corporate culture close to your own organisation? For example, how about the student union? Or a trade association to which the company belongs? What are its chief distinguishing features? How does it influence the strategy of its members, if at all?*

From a national strategy perspective, the implications may be significant.

● For organisations engaged primarily in one national market, it will have some relevance if people from a number of cultural backgrounds are employed. For example, in South Africa, there are white and black communities with quite different cultural backgrounds working together.

● For organisations with a range of national companies in different countries, possibly across Europe, Africa or South-East Asia, the implications are equally important. There will be a need to devise a strategy that takes account not only of central HQ issues but also local cultures and styles, values and expectations. For example, a mission statement or a timetable for strategic change may need to reflect national cultural values and sense of urgency.

- For global companies, the cultural issue is more likely to be how to bring together the many cultures that exist. This may involve special integration programmes to break down cultural barriers.

Beyond these national-specific cultural issues, Olie[36] has pointed out that some management theories may be *culture specific* – in other words, they may not 'work' outside the national country in which they were invented. As an example, we might take Peters and Waterman's loose–tight principle:[37]

> 'Organisations that live by the loose–tight principle are on the one hand rigidly controlled, yet at the same time, allow (indeed, insist on) autonomy, entrepreneurship and innovation from the rank and file.'

This may operate well in the United States but not in other cultures such as Korea where there is a stronger need for certainty and collectivism.

Although no research has been undertaken, it may also be that some of the organisation types described in Section 8.3 are more prevalent in some national cultures than others. For example, *power cultures* and *personal cultures* may be largely lacking from those countries where individualism and entrepreneurship do not form a significant part of the way the culture of a country operates. If this is true, it would have important implications for the development of international and global companies.

More generally, it should be said that national culture is by no means the only driver of business style. Many companies large and small will develop their own ways of doing their work that go well beyond national culture. However, the root of some of these areas of behaviour may lie in the learned culture of a country or group: imposing such a culture on others will inevitably lead to tensions and misunderstandings that need to be overcome for strategy to be successful.

Key strategic principles

- National culture is defined as the collective programming of the mind which distinguishes the members of one human group from another.

- National culture governs both the style and content of the way business is done internationally. It may therefore influence corporate strategy.

- Hofstede developed five dimensions that help to define and describe national cultures: power distance, individualism/collectivism, masculinity versus femininity, uncertainty avoidance, confucian versus dynamism.

- The evidence from these national characteristics would suggest that they can have a profound effect on the human aspects of corporate strategy. They need to be taken into account during the development of strategy, not later.

- It may even be the case that *national* culture will influence some aspects of *organisational* culture.

How Rank Xerox shifted its strategy and changed its organisation[38]

During the 1990s, Rank Xerox has reduced the size of its workforce, reorganised its operating companies and introduced a new organisation and culture to the company. This case study examines the shift in its strategy and structure.

Background

For 30 years, the US company Xerox has been engaged in a major global battle with its Japanese rivals, especially Canon and Ricoh. From dominance of the photocopying market in the 1960s, Xerox market share has slowly been reduced. Its sales have risen but not as fast as the market has grown. It has been the Japanese companies who have made all the running in terms of new products, higher quality, ease of use and maintenance-free equipment.

Outside the Americas, Xerox has managed its operations in Europe, Africa and parts of Asia including Japan through *Rank Xerox*, a UK-based company in which it had a controlling share interest and total management control. In 1993, Rank Xerox had sales of around US$5.5 billion and profits of US$226 million. This case study examines the shift in strategy and organisation at Rank Xerox during the 1990s.

Markets, competitors and customers

When Japanese companies decided to enter international photocopying markets in the 1960s, they had to find a way to overcome the dominance of Rank Xerox. They chose to open up a new market segment: copiers for medium and small businesses that needed little maintenance and no regular service support. Rank Xerox had a policy of always leasing its machines and then providing service engineers to maintain them: this was attractive to large companies with heavy printing demands but smaller companies rapidly found the Japanese offerings more acceptable.

By the 1990s, Rank Xerox had lost market share of the overall market, but still continued to maintain its market leadership in the high-end segment. Its competitive strengths still lay in its ability to pro-vide a high level of service to customers. This was an area that the Japanese companies had never really attempted to match because of the high set-up costs and difficulty in obtaining minimum levels of business to make profits.

Rank Xerox had made several attempts to break into the lower end of the market. However, its strengths and cost structures were still largely geared to large company customers. In 1993, it undertook a survey of its customers' photocopying requirements: it found that they were spending 8 per cent of their turnover creating and managing documents, including creating and developing printed material, photocopying it, and filing and recording the results. This compared with 3 per cent of turnover spent on information technology. Moreover, up to 60 per cent of their customers' time was regularly spent on various activities associated with documentation.

Shift of mission statement and strategy

Given the time spent by its customers and its own strengths in servicing large customers, Rank Xerox decided during the early 1990s to shift the emphasis of its mission statement and basic business strategy. It changed from servicing photocopying to becoming *The Document Company*. This implied higher degrees of service for all the document requirements of its customers, not just the photocopying part. The strategy shifted from simple photocopying towards offering a wider range of services and products to cater for the *document management needs* of its customers. Naturally, it continued to offer photocopying to those customers who preferred this.

Rank Xerox commented that it would take time for customers to see the benefits of its broader range. It noted that its rivals soon picked up the same theme: 'document management' and the 'document solution' were soon appearing. However, it was convinced that its strategy was sound: it was built on its core skills and based on service. When done well, a service competitive advantage is immensely difficult for competitors to match because service is localised. However, quality of service is vital.

For some years, the company had been operating a company culture based on quality. This was defined as providing customers with innovative ways of working. Importantly, 'customers' were defined as other departments from the quality provider *inside* Rank Xerox, as well as customers *outside* the company. The company had introduced new employee training to improve quality. It also developed a system to validate the quality processes of each of its departments. This was based on issuing a 'business excellence certificate'. It was later picked up by Xerox, USA, and extended worldwide. [We examine quality as part of strategy in Chapter 11.]

New strategy initiatives

Between 1992 and 1994, Rank Xerox reorganised the company and introduced new strategies that would strengthen its profitability. There were four main areas:

Customer business units

Up to the mid-1990s, the operation of customer services was based on national boundaries. However, the company found that, whatever the economic environment, it was the smaller countries that always performed better – Austria, Portugal, Switzerland, Belgium. Rank Xerox investigated and discovered that the ideal company size for customers contained around 400 employees, corresponding to the size in the smaller countries. Hence all the larger countries were split in 1992/93 into smaller units, including the major markets of France and Germany. Country and regional managers became Customer Business Unit (CBU) managers.

Devolved power

The CBU changes were accompanied by a devolution of power and decision making to individual CBUs, including profit and loss responsibility. Managers can now make a whole range of decisions as to how the unit operates. The effect in some cases has been highly beneficial on profitability. For example in Italy, the country was divided into three CBUs. After years of consistent losses, revenues increased 25 per cent and profitability was in sight.

Re-engineering processes

Rank Xerox has set out to re-engineer some of its major processes with the aim of a 20 per cent reduction in costs. Re-engineering is the detailed examination of every process to see how costs are built up and hence where costs can be saved. It is usually beneficial to approach the processes with a radical and open mind. For example, Rank Xerox does not define its processes by functional areas such as marketing, sales, services, but by the way the customer orders are picked up and processed through the company. The four areas for re-engineering were:

- *market to collection* – the organisation of the sales force and business development
- *invoice to collection* – customer payments including debt collection
- *integrated supply chain* – all areas from purchases through to deliveries
- *service quality* – including product maintenance.

By concentrating on these areas, the company was able to make major cost savings: percentage inventory to revenue reduced from 15 per cent to 12 per cent with 10 per cent the aim, for example.

Benchmarking

Rank Xerox set up an international team to explore how it was that a business unit in one country managed to sell the same product range more successfully than others? The team took the top performing units as a *benchmark* for the others. It then set out to strip down the performance of the marketing function in this unit in a very detailed way. The group drew up a list of ten key benchmarking practices which it circulated to all CBUs.

CASE STUDY 8.3 continued

CASE QUESTIONS

1 *How would you summarise the strategies adopted by Rank Xerox in the face of strong Japanese competition? Do you think they will be successful?*

2 *The company argued that there were real benefits from moving to CBUs: what were they? Is it possible that the company has lost out on central control and economies of scale as a result of these moves? Do you think CBUs will still be around in five years' time?*

3 *Rank Xerox laid great emphasis in its strategy initiatives on re-engineering and benchmarking: what organisational, morale and human resource problems might arise as a result?*

4 *How would you characterise the company culture of Rank Xerox from the material in the case and using the categorisation in Section 8.3?*

KEY READING

Organisational culture, strategy and performance[39]

In this extract from his book, **Organisational Culture,** *Dr Andrew Brown comments on the process of strategy development.*

While it is tempting to think of strategy as a dependent variable determined and constrained by the culture in which it develops, such a view is not sustainable. Strategy does not merely reflect or externalise culture, but influences and modifies it. An organisation's strategy makes visible its culture, expressing it in much the same way that speech creates meanings in language. This is an important point.

It is vital to remember that organisational strategy is not just a reflection of organisational culture. The formulation of strategy is generally influenced by a wide variety of non-cultural environmental factors such as the activities of competitors, customers and suppliers. Certainly the resulting trends, activities and events will be interpreted through the perception filter of culture, but this fact does not make a new technological breakthrough or a reduction in the number of supplier companies any less real. This means that it is impossible to accurately predict an organisation's strategy from knowledge of its culture alone. It also means that when we observe an organisation it is possible for its strategy to appear not to match its culture because of the influence of external exigencies.

If it is true that as a general rule strategy gives voice to culture, then in analysing the relationship between any particular culture and strategy we should expect to find a number of coughs, splutters and hiccups that distort the pattern.

Source: Brown, A (1995) *Organisational Culture*, Pitman Publishing.

◖ SUMMARY

- The analysis of human resources is important for strategy development for two reasons. People are a vital resource. In addition, strategy development often involves change and some people may resist it. There are four areas to explore in the analysis of this area: resource audit, organisational culture, strategic change and its implications in terms of the power and politics of the organisation.

- Human resource-based analysis emphasises the emergent approach to corporate strategy. Sustainable competitive advantage will often depend on human resources. In fast moving markets, the adaptability of people inside the organisation becomes a special and important skill. Coping with strategic change is a vital element in the development of corporate strategy.

- The human resource audit will have two main elements: *people* in the organisation and the *contribution* of human resources to the development of corporate strategy. A basic analysis will reflect these two areas but also needs to consider key factors for success, competitive comparisons and possibly international issues.

- Culture is the set of beliefs, values and learned ways of managing the organisation. Each organisation has a culture that is unique. In analysing culture, there are four main areas: environment, cultural factors specific to the organisation, the basic cultural type of the organisation and the strategic implications.

- Factors within the organisation influencing culture include: history and ownership, size, technology and leadership. These can be coupled with the cultural web of the organisation to provide a method of summarising the main cultural influences. The cultural web includes stories, routines and rituals, symbols, power structures, organisation structure and control systems.

- The four main types of culture are power, role, task and personal. Their importance for corporate strategy lies in the ability of each type to cope with strategic change and to deliver competitive advantage.

- Analysis of strategic change needs to consider three areas: the type of organisation, the phase of organisation growth and the strategic pressures for organisational change. Four types of organisation have been identified with each having a different response to strategic change. The age and size of an organisation will provide information on its phase of growth. The strategic pressures for organisational change need careful assessment. They may include such concepts as delayering – the reduction of the number of reporting layers in an organisation – and business process re-engineering – the use of new technology to reduce the administrative task and reduce costs.

- Strategic change needs to take into account what is possible in terms of change in the organisation, rather than what is theoretically desirable. Political issues in the organisation therefore need to be carefully explored – the political network.

- International cultures may have a profound impact on corporate strategy. They may even make some strategy proposals very difficult to implement.

QUESTIONS

1 Use Exhibit 8.1 to audit the human resources of an organisation with which you are familiar. What conclusions can you draw with respect to corporate strategy?

2 You have been retained by a well-known fast-food restaurant chain to advise them on corporate strategy. You are aware that human resources are important in this work. What considerations would you wish to explore initially? How would you approach this task?

3 Analyse the culture of British Petroleum over the period of Case study 8.1. Compare it with the Royal Dutch/Shell culture.

4 *'There is no robust, generalisable evidence that business process re-engineering has made any significant impact on business performance.'* Professor Colin Egan.[40]
If you were a senior manager at Rank Xerox, what would you make of this?

5 What are the general environmental influences on the culture of higher education at present? What are the strategic implications for institutions involved in this area?

6 Develop the cultural web for Rank Xerox from Case study 8.3 and identify the basic cultural style of the company. Give reasons for your views.

7 Use the criteria from Table 8.1 to characterise the culture of the following four organisations: a multinational car company; a small, new computer software company; a recently privatised national telecommunications company (such as British Telecom or Deutsche Telekom); a local police station.

8 Analyse the strategic change implications of an organisation of your choice. Use the typology of Section 8.4 to explore the *type* of organisation, the *phase* of organisational growth, and the *pressure* for strategic change.

9 *'An organisation's strategy makes visible its culture, expressing it in much the same way that speech creates meaning in language.'* Dr Andrew Brown.

How important is culture to strategy development when compared with other aspects of the analytical process?

10 Is *delayering* feasible in every national culture? Use Hofstede's analysis of culture to explain your answer.

STRATEGIC PROJECT

International oil companies

This chapter has explored companies in the oil industry mainly from a human resource angle. You might like to take a broader look at strategy in the oil industry. For example, you might like to compare the strategies of Elf (France) with Repsol (Spain). At the time of writing one has been more successful than the other.

FURTHER READING

For a well developed exposition of culture: Brown, A (1995) *Organisational Culture*, Pitman Publishing, London.

For some excellent and provocative reading on the relationship between human resources and strategy: Egan, C (1995) *Creating Organisational Advantage*, Butterworth Heinemann, Oxford.

For some excellent articles on international aspects that are well linked together: Harzing, Anne-Wil and Van Ruysseveldt, J (eds) (1995) *International Human Resource Management*, Sage, London with the Open University of the Netherlands.

Daniels, J and Radebaugh, L (1995) *International Business – Environments and Operations*, Addison-Wesley, Ch 3. Useful for the general environment surrounding business and organisations.

REFERENCES

1 Case adapted from articles by David Lascelles, *Financial Times*, 30 Mar 1995, p19 and Robert Corzine, *Financial Times*, 15 Feb 1996, p28. © *Financial Times*. Reproduced with permission.

2 Chandler, A (1962) *Strategy and Structure: Chapters in the History of the Industrial Enterprise*, MIT Press, Cambridge, Mass, p14.

3 Porter M E (1980) *Competitive Strategy* and (1985) *Competitive Advantage*, The Free Press, Boston, Mass.

4 Chandler, A (1962) Ibid. See for example the roles of Durant, Du Pont and Sloan in Chapter 3 on General Motors.

5 There are several well-known strategic management texts that take this approach.

6 Handy, C (1989) *The Age of Unreason*, Business Books.
  Handy, C (1991) *The Gods of Management*, Business Books.
  Tyson, S (1995) *Human Resource Strategy*, Pitman Publishing, London, Chs 4, 5 and 6.
  Brown, A (1995) *Organisational Culture*, Pitman Publishing, London, p198.

7 Pettigrew, A and Whipp, R (1991) *Managing change for competitive success*, Blackwell, Oxford.

8 De Geus, A (1988) 'Planning as Learning', *Harvard Business Review*, Mar–Apr, p71.

9 Whittington, R (1993) *What is strategy and does it matter?* Routledge, London, p122.

10 This exhibit has been derived from Tyson, S (1995) *Human Resource Strategy*, Pitman Publishing, London, pp171–4 and Rosen, R (1995) *Strategic Management: an introduction*, Pitman Publishing, London, p166.

11 Brown, A (1995) *Organisational Culture*, Pitman Publishing, London p198.

12 Maslow, A H (1943) 'A Theory of Human Motivation', *Psychological Review*, 50, pp370–96.

13 This subject area does not seem to have been the subject of any major research study. It is included because of the practical experience of many companies.

14 International Labour Office (1993) *World Labour Report*, Geneva.

15 Handy, C (1993) *Understanding Organisations*, 4th edn, Penguin, London, pp193–4.

16 Johnson, G (1992) 'Managaing Strategic Change: strategy, culture and action', *Long Range Planning*, 25, pp28–36.

17 Handy, C (1993) Ibid, p183. Handy uses the work of Harrison, R (1972) 'How to describe your organisation', *Harvard Business Review*, Sep–Oct. Handy uses Greek gods to typify the four cultural types: they make an interesting read, but mean rather less to those of us who studied *The Aeneid*.

18 Hofstede, G (1980) *Culture's Consequences: International differences in work-related values*, Sage, Beverly Hills.

19 Brown, A (1995) Ibid, pp62–5.

20 Handy, C (1993) Ibid, pp210–16.

21 References for BP Case: *Financial Times*: 23 Mar 1990; 25 Mar 1990, p20; 10 May 1991; 26 June 1992, pp1, 18 and 19; 28 June 1993, p17; 15 Mar 1995, p29.

22 Miles, R E and Snow, C C (1978) *Organisational Strategy, Structure and Process*, McGraw-Hill, New York. *See* also Miles, R, Snow, C, Meyer, A and Coleman (1978) 'A Strategy Typology of Organisations', *Academy of Management Review*, July and reprinted in De Wit, R and Meyer, R (1994) *Strategy: Content, Context and Process*, West Publishing. There is clearly some overlap here with the classification developed by Handy on types of culture. It is hardly surprising that the two areas are consistent: it would be alarming if they were not.

23 Greiner, L (1972) 'Evolution and Revolution as Organisations Grow', *Harvard Business Review*, July–Aug.

24 *Source*: Greiner, L (1972) Ibid, p265.

25 Readers may care to note that there is a useful critique of this strategy in Egan, C (1995) *Creating Organisational Advantage*, Butterworth Heinemann, Oxford, pp109–11.

26 Handy, C (1993) Ibid, p292.

27 Mintzberg, H (1991) 'The Effective Organisation: Forces and Forms', *Sloan Management Review*, Winter.

28 Hofstede, G (1980) Ibid.

29 Kluckhohn, C and Strodtbeck, F (1961) *Variations in Value Orientations*, Peterson, New York, quoted in Meade, R (1994) *International Management Cross Cultural Dimensions*, Blackwell, Oxford, p50.

30 Hofstede, G (1991) *Cultures and Organisations, Software of the Mind*, McGraw-Hill, Maidenhead, and *Images of Europe: Valedictory Address* given at the University of Limberg, 1993.

31 Meade, R (1994), Ibid, pp73–6.

32 *Financial Times* (1994) 30 Nov, p15.

33 *Financial Times* (1994) 16 Sep, p26.

34 *Financial Times* (1993) 14 Apr, p30.

35 Friedman, A (1988) *Agnelli and the Italian Network of Power*, Mandarin.

36 Olie, R (1995) 'The culture factor in personnel and organisation policies', Chapter 6 in Harzing, A and Van Ruysseveldt (1995) *International Human Resource Management*, Sage, London in association with Open University, Netherlands.

37 Peters, T and Waterman, R (1982) *In Search of Excellence*, Harper and Row, New York, p318.

38 References for Rank Xerox Case: *Financial Times:* 24 Sep 1991; 25 Aug 1992, p5; 13 Jan 1995, p19; 13 Feb 1995, p19; 28 Apr 1995, 2-page advertisement; Lynch, R (1994) *European Business Strategies*, 2nd edn, p87; *Xerox USA Annual Report 1992*.

39 Extracted from Brown, A (1995) Ibid, p182. © Andrew Brown.

40 Egan, C (1995) Ibid, p109.

9

Analysing financial resources

When you have worked through this chapter, you will be able to:

- identify the sources of funds available to an organisation;

- carry out an analysis of an organisation's current financial resources;

- assess an organisation's potential for further funding and the costs and risks involved;

- identify and quantify the financial benefits of strategies and their cash flow implications;

- understand the impact on the organisation of greater international activity;

- appreciate the importance of balancing the organisation's financial objectives with its other corporate objectives.

INTRODUCTION

Many corporate strategies involve the organisation's financial resources: investment in the organisation's activities now will be rewarded by profits or other benefits later. This chapter explores the *relationship* between the financial resources that are available for corporate strategy – their sources, costs and the risks involved – and the returns that may be achieved (*see* Fig 9.1).

Financial analysis deals primarily with the precision of numbers, and therefore tends to be prescriptive rather than emergent in its approach. However, leading financiers are well aware that in practice there is a judgmental element to the subject. This chapter considers both approaches and then goes on to explore the importance of maintaining the fine balance between the financial objectives of the organisation and those objectives involving more general issues, such as the public good, better pay and job satisfaction. The implications for those organisations engaged in international trade are also considered.

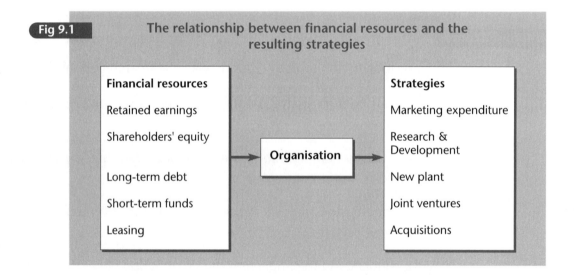

Fig 9.1 The relationship between financial resources and the resulting strategies

Financial resources

Retained earnings

Shareholders' equity

Long-term debt

Short-term funds

Leasing

Organisation

Strategies

Marketing expenditure

Research & Development

New plant

Joint ventures

Acquisitions

Global expansion: brewing at Heineken NV

As Heineken and other leading European brewers expand internationally, the financial implications of this process need careful and consistent analysis.

Heineken claims to be the world's second largest company brewing beer and lager. Table 9.1 shows its sales against those of leading European competitors.

Table 9.1 Annual sales of Europe's leading brewers, 1994

Company	Country	World beer sales (million Hectolitres)	Comment
Heineken	Netherlands	60	Focussed on worldwide growth but real strengths in some parts of Europe.
Carlsberg	Denmark	28	Limited representation in some countries.
Guinness	UK	25	Company strengths also in spirits, e.g. whisky, brandy.
Danone/ Kronenbourg	France	24	Company strengths in dairy products and other food areas, where company is world leader.
Interbrew	Belgium	18	See Case study 9.2.
Bass	UK	14	Also a world leader in hotels through ownership of Holiday Inn brand.
Oetker	Germany	10	Mainly in Germany, where the market is fragmented and highly competitive.
Maerz	Germany	9	Also mainly in Germany.
Whitbread	UK	8	Mainly in UK.

Sources: trade estimates and company annual reports.
Note: The above list excludes the world's largest brewer, Anheuser–Busch, the US company, whose leading brand is Budweiser. It also omits other major world brewers: Kirin (Japan), San Miguel (Philippines), Fosters (Australia) and Tsing Tao (China).

Heineken sales have experienced strong growth during the 1990s – rising almost 10 per cent in Europe between 1993 and 1994, at a time when the European market for beer and lager was actually decreasing slightly. Major growing markets, such as China, Indonesia and Japan, contributed to an 18 per cent rise in sales to Asia over the same period – an extremely high growth rate for a beverage product.[1]

The company achieved this level of sales by implementing the following strategies, all of which involved the use of substantial financial resources:

1 *Carrying out company acquisitions in Europe.* Heineken bought breweries, particularly in Eastern Europe, including Hungary, Bulgaria, Poland. The company also bought control of Interbrew Italia.

2 *Setting up* new plants *in countries such as Indonesia, China, Vietnam and Malaysia.* A typical plant might cost US$5 million. Local partners will develop some plant but still need a major capital injection from Heineken. It should be noted that there are some cost savings from economies of scale in brewing plant,[2] but larger plants need more capital.

3 *Advertising, promoting and distributing the new premium speciality beers.* This product group segments the market and is sold at higher prices. Heineken has been supporting its Heineken and Amstel brands with sponsorship of the Rugby World Cup in South Africa, US Open Tennis and the World Badminton Championships in Vietnam. A typical major sponsorship deal might cost US$1 million per event. There are cost economies of scale in branding and sponsorship, but these are related to the funds invested.

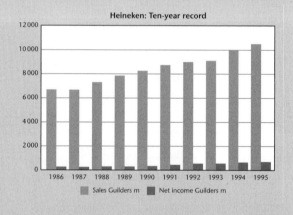

4 *Carrying out* research and development *into new plant processes and product and packaging innovations.* Examples include the new ice beers and the successful introduction in the UK of a version of Murphy's Irish Stout in a can. Again, economies of scale can clearly be obtained. Research and development costs are not normally published by brewers but could easily total US$5 million per year.

5 *Developing joint ventures and licensing* in countries such as the UK, Greece, Brazil and China to share the costs of distribution with other partners. It is not possible to estimate typical costs since these will depend on the size of the joint venture or other deal, but significant funds are usually involved.

None of the above could be carried out without extra capital to finance them. Moreover, it should be noted that, even if none of the above activities had taken place, there might still have been a need for increased financial resources, due to the 10 per cent increase in Heineken's sales in 1994 compared with 1993 (9974 million guilders versus 9049 million guilders). When sales increase, there is often a need to extend the company's credit terms to new customers: extra finance is required for this purpose alone. Sales can be increased without an attendant rise in credit, but this cannot be assumed.

According to Heineken, the strategic consequence for the leading companies in the brewing industry worldwide of the high market growth, economies of scale and significant investment has been an increased concentration of market share.[3] However, it may also be significant that, before global expansion, the major global brewers already had high market shares in their home countries (*see* Table 9.2). High home market share may provide a useful *cash cow* strategy (*see* Chapter 6) from which to launch an expansion programme.

Table 9.2 Market share in home country of some of Europe's leading brewers

Company	Home country	Market share in home country
Heineken	Netherlands	50%
Carlsberg	Denmark	70% including Tuborg
Guinness	Ireland (for beer and stout)	60% but note that home market small
Kronenbourg	France	35% but 81% of all the company's beer sales are in France and another 17% in the rest of Europe
Interbrew	Belgium	60%
Bass	UK	23% in highly competitive market
Oetker	Germany	6% in the fragmented German beer market

Source: trade estimates

CASE QUESTIONS

1 *Using the following information:*

- *one company acquired every three years at typically US$50 million.*
- *one new Far Eastern plant per annum*
- *ten events sponsored per annum for the new speciality beers*
- *research and development costs as stated in the case*
- *joint ventures and licences cost US$10 million per annum*

   estimate the order-of-magnitude finance required by Heineken for new strategies in a typical year.

2 *Compare this with the Heineken balance sheet and profit and loss statement located at the end of this chapter. You will need to convert the financial data to US$, using 1.82 N Fl = 1US$.*

3 *Does Heineken have any problems financing such strategies?*

9.1 ANALYSING THE SOURCES OF FINANCE

Company ownership varies greatly around the world. In some countries, such as the UK and USA, there is a strong tradition of private share ownership with public share quotation. In other countries such as Germany, Italy and Spain, rather more companies may be at least part-owned by banks, private trusts, families and government institutions. As a starting point, we ignore these differences and simply identify the main *sources of finance* for strategic development or retrenchment. As an example, Fig 9.2 shows the sources of finance used by Heineken in 1994.

9.1.1 Sources of finance

Retained profits Instead of distributing profits as share dividends to the shareholders, these are retained and invested in new ventures. Although full evidence is not available,[4] this probably represents the most common method of funding the organisation's strategy when it is conducting its normal operations.

Fig 9.2

Sources of finance at Heineken (1994)

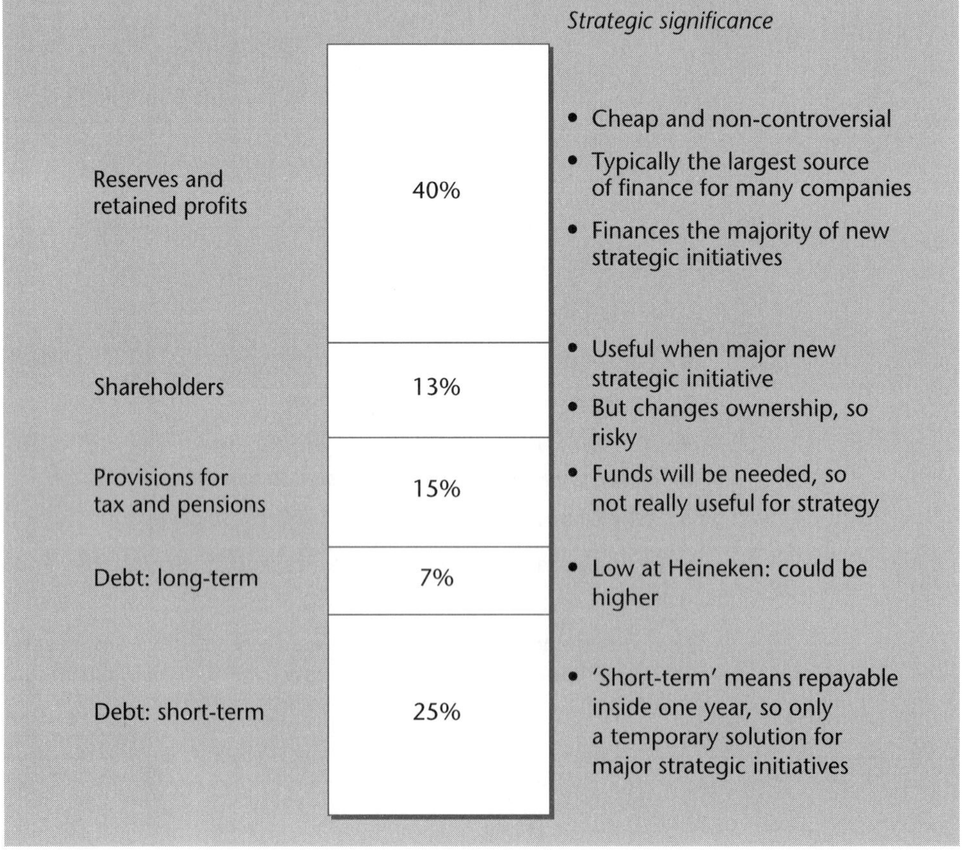

Strategic significance

Source	%	
Reserves and retained profits	40%	• Cheap and non-controversial • Typically the largest source of finance for many companies • Finances the majority of new strategic initiatives
Shareholders	13%	• Useful when major new strategic initiative • But changes ownership, so risky
Provisions for tax and pensions	15%	• Funds will be needed, so not really useful for strategy
Debt: long-term	7%	• Low at Heineken: could be higher
Debt: short-term	25%	• 'Short-term' means repayable inside one year, so only a temporary solution for major strategic initiatives

Advantages: The company does not have to ask any outside group or individual. There are no issue costs involved in raising the funds and the company does not need to reveal its plans to outsiders such as banks in order to gain agreement. It is essentially non-controversial.

Disadvantages: Profits that are retained and not distributed to shareholders represent dividends forgone to the owners. Owners may demand a regular dividend from the company. The company needs to be generating adequate profits, so this route is not suitable for those in financial difficulties.

Share issues Share issues are often called the *equity capital* method of raising funds because they involve the 'equity' or shareholding of a company. It is often possible to seek further funds from existing shareholders through a *rights issue* – that is, the right to purchase new shares is issued to current shareholders in proportion to their existing voting rights in the company – although the success of such an issue clearly depends on how enthusiastic existing shareholders are about the company's prospects. An alternative method might be to issue a block of shares to a new specialist purchaser such as a bank or other company. However, such issues would usually need the permission of the existing shareholders since the latter's share in the company would be diluted by such an issue.

Even with a rights issue, it would be unusual if *all* the existing shareholders took up their right-to-buy allocation. For example, they might not have the money at that time or they might not want to invest more of their funds in the one company. Such an issue is therefore usually *underwritten* by institutional investors – that is, the sale of the shares is guaranteed at a price agreed in advance with the company. The aim is to ensure that the issue of new shares does not depress the existing share price. Like any insurance policy, underwriting has a significant cost.

With new investors coming in, the share ownership profile is likely to change. New shareholders may be hostile and it will not always be possible to identify them in advance. They may even try to take control of the company: in the UK and USA, new shareholders have to declare their interest if it is over 4.9 per cent of the shareholding. Other countries may have less stringent rules.

Advantages. This method is useful when a large tranche of new capital is needed – for example for an acquisition. Unlike a bank loan (*see* below), there is no automatic commitment to pay interest, nor repay the capital: dividends are paid only if the new funds earn profits. It rewards those shareholders who have stayed with the company.

Disadvantages. It can clearly change the shareholding structure and allow predators to enter. Any share issue will have significant administrative costs, such as the cost of underwriting the issue.

Loans Loans from banks and financial institutions are a major source of funds in those countries where large and widespread shareholding is not a part of normal operations. It is also much more common in countries where banks have traditionally played a major role in the shareholding life of companies – for example, Germany and Japan. It is often called the *loan* or *debt capital* method of raising funds, for obvious reasons.

Loans can be made in various ways to the organisation, with the rates of interest and the duration periods of the loan being either fixed or varied. Larger loans may carry exceptionally onerous terms depending on how desperate the organisation is to obtain the funds. Such loans are usually secured on the assets of the organisation so, if there is a default, the lender can seize the asset. Because of this security, loan capital is often cheaper than equity capital. However, it carries the penalty that interest *must be paid* even if the company is earning little profit, whereas equity capital could forgo the dividend during that period. There are also limits on the amount of debt financing (*see* Section 9.2).

Risk assessment plays a large part in the lender's view of the loan and the company. Past company performance, the prospects for the new strategy, the quality of the secured assets and the long-term personal relationship between the parties will all have an influence on the source of funds.

Advantages: Loans can be cheap, quick and retain the existing shareholding structure. This method of finance is also confidential and discreet. It may be essential where widespread public shareholding is not available.

Disadvantages. This method can be painful, intrusive and involve increased risk for the company. The date of repayment and the need to pay interest in most circumstances can be a major burden if the strategy begins to show signs of weakness.

Leasing Leasing from specialist companies can be important in those countries where there are tax advantages and the company does not need to own the assets. It has limited and specialised use usually where a physical asset needs to be purchased as part of a new corporate strategy – for example, a new computer system. Essentially, it involves an independent company buying the asset and then renting ('leasing') it out to the organisation wishing to use it in return for a regular payment. Clearly, the leasing company retains ownership of the asset and can reclaim it if payment is defaulted.

In addition to possible tax advantages in some countries, the other obvious advantage to the organisation taking out the lease is that it does not have to find the capital. Often, it only has to carry out simple maintenance and can give the product back after an agreed number of years and trade up to a new model.

Advantages. Leasing is clear, quick and perhaps tax-efficient.

Disadvantages. This method has limited scope. No ownership at the end of the period.

A reduction in short-term debt An organisation can reduce its short-term debt by introducing one of the following measures:

● *Paying creditors more slowly*. Taking longer to pay means that such funds are kept in the company for a longer period and are therefore available for investment;

● *Reducing stocks*. An organisation's *stock turn* – its ratio of turnover divided by stock – is a measure of its ability to operate with lower stocks. A lower level of funds invested in stocks will increase the organisation's ability to raise funds for use elsewhere.

● *Insisting on more prompt payment by debtors*.

Such creditors and debtors are usually referred to as *current liabilities* and *current assets* in the balance sheet of the company. The reason is that any such debt is usually loaned for a short period of less than one year. In practice, this has occasionally provided a significant source of new long-term finance for most companies. Although by definition it is short term, a permanent reduction in stocks (a form of assets) or a permanent change in payment arrangements with debtors and creditors, even by a few days, can have a major impact on the amount of funds an organisation needs to keep tied up in these areas. Many companies have taken advantage of such funding over the last few years – for example, through the introduction of new computer stock control. Usually, such savings can only be made once.

> *Advantages*. This method has many of the advantages of retained profits in the sense that it involves the more efficient use of the organisation's existing funds.

> *Disadvantages*. This method may be difficult for the organisation to achieve if it is already operating reasonably efficiently. There may need to be significant expenditure to achieve the saving – for example, a new computer system to control stocks will mean investment in the new system along with the subsequent stock reduction.

Sale of assets Sale of some existing company assets to finance expansion elsewhere has proved to be a major strategy for some companies in the 1990s. For example, Gogel and Larreche[5] suggested that companies should consider selling part of their product portfolio and reinvest the funds in the remainder. We will explore the full implications of this proposal in Chapter 12. Companies such as Dalgety Spillers (*see* Chapter 2) planned to divest their snack food interests in 1995–96 in order to concentrate on petfood. On the strength of this plan, it then raised the funds to purchase the European petfood interests of Quaker (US).

The route clearly has merit when resources are limited and spread too thinly. Following from the logic of *core strengths* (*see* Chapter 7), it will be evident that this approach may have real benefits for some companies.

> *Advantages*. This method of finance is simple, clear, concentrates on core strengths, and clearly involves no dilution in shareholding interests.

> *Disadvantages*. This method is drastic, no going back, and forces choice when not essential. The sale of assets may have to be undertaken at less than their full value depending on the timing of the sale.

The financing of brewers' growth

With extensive business activity taking place in the brewing industry, this case study examines the sources from which the brewing companies have financed their expansion.

Heineken's expansion of recent years was funded from the following sources:

- *Shareholders.* Heineken is a family-controlled company and so issuing new shares would dilute the family's control over the firm and be unacceptable. Heineken made three *bonus share issues* in 1986, 1989 and 1992. These simply split existing shares into smaller amounts and make no attempt to raise fresh capital. By definition, they are issued in proportion to existing shareholdings and have no impact on the family interests.

- *Retained profits.* Heineken has used this method more than any other to expand. Because it is family-controlled, it does not have the same pressures to pay a dividend each year. It is therefore able to ignore any outside pressures, so long as the family members themselves continue to agree.

- *Increased long-term debt.* Heineken has not used this method of financing in any significant way. Danone/Kronenbourg, on the other hand, has used loans from banks or other lending institutions extensively to expand its worldwide interests.

- *Short-term funds.* If brewery companies can negotiate it, there is nothing to stop them paying their creditors more slowly and insisting that those who owe them money pay faster. For example, Heineken increased its stock turn by nearly 40 per cent over the period 1990–94.

Table 9.3 shows how Heineken raised its funds up to 1994. For comparison, two other leading European brewers are also shown. (It is important to point out that the companies do not have the same year-end, and figures have been translated into a common currency (US$) at rates that may not be those used by the individual companies themselves. All this makes comparison only

approximate.) An additional item in the table – *Provisions for tax, pensions, etc.* – relates to the need for companies to set aside funds that are owed to the government as tax and to their former employees as pensions. Because of the special purpose of such funds, they should not be used for financing the business and are therefore excluded from the above list of the sources of funds.

Table 9.3 Sources of capital in some of Europe's leading brewers

Source of funds	Heineken	Danone /Kronenbourg*	Carlsberg
Reserves and retained earnings	40%	22%	33%
Shareholders	13%	24%	10%
Provisions for tax, pensions	15%	7%	16%
Debt: long-term	7%	23%	15%
Debt: short-term	25%	24%	26%
Total	100%	100%	100%
Total capital	US$ 5 125 m	US$ 14 863 m	US$ 2 954 m

Source: Company annual reports
*Note that capital is used for non-beer trading, which is the majority of total turnover at Danone/Kronenbourg.

In terms of sources of finance, the financial resources of the three brewers shown in Table 9.3 need to be considered in the context of the *objectives* and *values* of the companies concerned.

Heineken is a family-controlled company with little desire to raise funds from outside shareholders or the debt from banks. If this has meant that it has grown more slowly, then the company has been willing to accept this as the price of family control.

Carlsberg is controlled by a Danish trust. Typically, such organisations do not have great ambitions for the future. However, Carlsberg has become more expansionist in recent years and has raised some debt on a long-term basis.

Danone/Kronenbourg has its shares quoted on European stock exchanges and has wide share ownership. It has followed a vigorous and imaginative strategy of expansion over the last ten years with a mix of acquisitions, divestment and internally generated growth activities. Its product range includes not only Kronenbourg beer, but also Danone dairy products (in which it is world leader), biscuits, glass containers, mineral waters and grocery products. All these areas have benefited from its ability to raise substantial finance, especially from the banks through long-term debt financing.

CASE QUESTIONS

1 *If you were Heineken, would you raise more finance through long-term debt and expand faster?*

2 *If you were Carlsberg, what arguments would you wish to consider about how you raised new finance? From whom would you seek advice?*

3 *If you were Danone/Kronenbourg and had observed the increased segmentation in the beer market and global trends, what strategy would you follow with to extend the company's beer sales beyond France? Where would you go? Why? What factors would you consider in the financing of any such expansion?*

Key strategic principles

- There are six main sources of finance for strategic activities. Each has its merits and problems.

- Retained profits: the most common method of funding new strategy.

- Equity finance, i.e. the issuance of new shares to either existing or new shareholders, is one clear route but it has numerous disadvantages associated with the costs of issue and the possible loss of control in the company.

- Long-term debt finance is simpler and cheaper, but there are limits to the amount and major difficulties if the company defaults on paying the interest charges.

- Leasing (renting) of plant and machinery has some specialist uses and attractions: it can have tax benefits and lower costs. However, the equipment remains the property of the lessor at the end of the period.

- Savings from reductions in short-term debt can be a substantial source of funds to a company, but these can usually be made only once.

- The sale of some existing assets to fund development elsewhere is useful but drastic.

9.1.2 Constraints on sources of finance

After reviewing the main sources of finance for an organisation, we now need to consider two important constraints on the ability of the organisation to act:

● difficulties with debt financing; and

● difficulties with the dividend payout policy on equity shareholdings.

Difficulties with debt financing

As we saw in Section 9.1.1, debt financing means that the organisation agrees to pay interest on the debt it acquires. The rate of interest is usually fixed and has two constraints:

● If there is a drop in profits, payment of interest *takes priority* over payment of dividends to shareholders.

● The interest *must be paid*, regardless of how profits might fluctuate. (Clearly, if the company goes into loss then the interest cannot be paid and the company is technically bankrupt.)

It is, therefore, the *shareholders* who bear the risk of profit fluctuation, not the *debt lenders*, such as the banks. As a result, because the shareholders are bearing this greater risk, they look for a higher return on their funds than the debt lenders. Debt financing is therefore usually cheaper than equity financing and as a result some companies prefer a proportion of debt capital.

In spite of its lower cost in relation to equity financing, however, companies restrict their level of debt financing because when debt capital is present, it causes any fluctuation in profits at the organisation to be reflected *disproportionately* in retained profits and dividends. Debt interest takes priority in payments from the organisation's profits. It is a simple mathematical task to show that the remainder, available as retained profits and dividends to shareholders, is bound to fluctuate more widely than if there had been no debt finance. Since retained earnings may well fund strategy, any fluctuation as a result of higher gearing – that is the proportion of debt finance to total shareholders' funds (*see* Exhibit 9.1) – will impact disproportionately on corporate strategy.

Exhibit 9.1   **The gearing ratio**

Most companies begin life with financing by shareholders – *equity financing*. They then generate some profits and retain part of those profits in the company, paying the rest out as dividends, tax, etc. The *total shareholders' funds* that then exist in the company are the original equity finance plus the retained profits.

At some stage in its life, the company may then acquire significant amounts of long-term debt – *debt financing*. The ratio of debt finance to total shareholders' funds is called the *gearing ratio* of the company – often called *gearing* for short – and is usually expressed in percentage terms. For example, if a company with US$10 million of shareholder's funds raises US$5 million of debt finance, it has a gearing ratio of:

$$\text{Gearing ratio} = \frac{\text{Debt finance}}{\text{Total shareholders' funds}} = \frac{\text{US\$5 million}}{\text{US\$10 million}} \times 100 = 50\%$$

Thus any company *with* debt is more exposed to fluctuations in dividends than one *without* debt – the higher the gearing, the more the exposure. Although debt finance is cheaper, there is therefore a limit to the amount of debt that a company can usually accept. Typically, companies with strong growth strategies and widespread public share ownership (such as Danone in Case study 9.1) will have a gearing ratio of 50 per cent. When the gearing of a company reaches 100 per cent then banks and other lenders become nervous because the company is so reliant on a steady, non-fluctuating stream of profits. It is for this reason that some companies are reluctant to *gear up* their company – that is, raise the proportion of debt to equity. Heineken is an example of a company with low gearing at 13 per cent.

However, lower gearing means that fewer funds are available for growth strategies. Although Heineken does not seem to have suffered excessively from lower gearing, it has been unable to grow at the same rate over the last ten years as Danone. Earnings per share almost tripled at Danone over the ten years between 1984 and 1993 (FF 18.4 to FF 50.96 per share), whereas they doubled at Heineken over a roughly comparable period from 1985 to 1994 (54.8 to 108.5 guilders per share). These considerations reflect the risks over gearing that the company is willing to take and the value the company puts on growth as part of its objectives.

Difficulties with the dividend payout policy on equity shareholdings In addition to constraints arising from gearing, it is also necessary to consider the *dividend payout policy* of the company on its ordinary shares. The higher the dividend, the lower the profit retained in the company and the more difficult it becomes to fund new strategies. In theory,[6] there is a balance to be struck between maximising the dividend payout and retaining profit for the company. In practice, companies usually prefer to keep the dividend payout *steadily and gently rising*. It is a reward for loyalty and is often reflected back in shareholder confidence and a stable share price. The data for Heineken in Table 9.4 shows that dividends have not tracked profit, but have gone up in three stages.

The implication of a stable dividend policy on retained earnings is clear: if dividends are steady, then any fluctuation in profits must be taken up by *retained earnings*. The reasons are just the same as those for debt capital interest above. Since it is retained earnings that fund corporate strategy, it is the *strategy area* that suffers disproportionately if there are major variations in profitability.

Table 9.4 Heineken NV profits and dividends per share (guilders)

	1994	1993	1992	1991	1990	1989	1988	1987	1986	1985
Net profit per share	15.03	12.92	11.53	10.21	9.11	8.11	7.24	7.14	7.11	6.61
Dividend per share	3.50	3.50	3.50	2.80	2.80	2.80	2.24	2.24	2.24	1.68

Source: Annual Report and Accounts

Overall, the choice between the funding methods for strategy will depend on a balance of the factors outlined above along with one other consideration – the cost of each route to the company – which we examine in Section 9.2.

> ### Key strategic principles
>
> - There are three main constraints on debt financing:
>   1. the need to fund the interest payments regardless of profit fluctuations;
>   2. the company with debt is more exposed to profit fluctuation than the one without;
>   3. the reluctance of banks to offer finance that would gear companies above 100%.
>
> - The main constraint on equity financing is the need in many companies to establish a steady increase in dividend payouts, regardless of profit variations.
>
> - As a result of the debt and equity payout constraints, fluctuations in profits impact disproportionately on the funding needed for strategic change.

9.2 COST OF FUNDS AND THE OPTIMAL CAPITAL STRUCTURE

In order to assess alternative sources of capital, we need to start by examining their costs to the company. There are two principal sources of funds to the company: equity and debt. We will examine each of these separately and look at the problems, mainly in estimating the costs of equity capital. We then consider the factors surrounding the optimal combination of the two different sources and why calculating the cost of funds is important.

9.2.1 Costing equity capital using the Capital Asset Pricing Model

It may seem slightly surprising to consider *equity capital*, that includes the company's retained profits and its original share capital, as having a *cost*. The cost comes in the organisation's refusal to distribute profits to its shareholders who could, in theory, have invested this money in shares in other companies. They might even have purchased a government bond in their home country. (Such bonds usually pay interest that is *guaranteed* and *virtually risk-free*, unless the state itself goes bankrupt. Naturally, the rate of interest on government bonds is lower than would be expected from commercial organisations that carry greater risks of failure.)

In both theory[7] and practice, it is often the case that the organisation invests part of its own funds *outside* the organisation, rather than in its own corporate strategies. Indeed, for reasons of high market risk and low profitability in an industry, companies occasionally find that their proposed new strategies are so unattractive that they actually invest some of their funds outside the company.[8] Investing in corporate strategies *inside* the organisation therefore has a *financial cost* associated with it. As a *minimum*, this cost would be the interest that might have been obtained from the alternative investment of the same funds *outside* the organisation. However, this still does not estimate the *actual* cost of the capital inside the company, only this *minimum* threshold.

The *Capital Asset Pricing Model*[9] is an attempt to estimate the actual cost of equity capital inside the company. It starts by estimating what a company could earn if it invested its money in a *risk-free bond*, such as a government security. We will call this rate of interest R_i. The interest rate of the government bond will include an element relating to the rate of inflation of the country concerned. In other words, R_i will be higher in countries with historically higher rates of inflation (such as the UK) than it is in countries like Japan.

In addition to the risk-free rate of interest, the Capital Asset Pricing Model then adds a factor for the *equity market overall*. This is estimated by taking the average rate of interest that might have been obtained by investing in all the securities traded in that national market. This rate of interest is usually called R_m.

Finally, the Capital Asset Pricing Model adds an element for the *company itself*. This is a coefficient that measures the volatility of the company's return *relative* to the market overall. It is called the *beta coefficient* and is represented by the Greek letter ß.[10] It is calculated by monitoring the rate of return on the *company's* shares in relation to that of the *market overall* and then plotting the slope of the line using statistical regression techniques. A beta coefficient of 1.0 would mean that the company's rate of return was historically fluctuating exactly in line with the market. A high beta coefficient of 1.5 would mean that the company's shares were fluctuating 1.5 times the market average. A low beta coefficient of 0.2 would mean that the company's shares only fluctuated 0.2 times the market average.

In practice, the beta coefficient is difficult to estimate due to the problems related to factors such as the link between returns for the company and the market overall, the forecast changes in such rates of return and their timing. If it is being used on international projects, it will also need to take into account the differing tax regimes in different countries. Moreover, the beta coefficient may need to take into account the *nature of the strategy* being funded by new equity within the company. Some projects will carry inherently more risk than others: for example, replacing existing equipment with a life of 20 years has higher certainty and is probably less risky than research and development.[11]

The full Capital Asset Pricing Model then estimates the cost of equity, E(R), for a company. It can be determined by the formula:

Cost of equity for the company $= E(R) = R_i + ß(R_m - R_i)$

In other words, the cost of equity for a company is equal to the *risk-free cost of equity* (R_i) plus a factor calculated as the average cost of equity in the *market* ($R_m - R_i$) multiplied by a beta factor (ß) for the *company* concerned.

For example, let us assume the risk-free rate of interest, R_i, was 7 per cent and the return on all market securities, R_m, was 11 per cent. In addition, the company had a marginally volatile share price with a ß of 1.4. Then the cost of equity for the company would be calculated as follows:

Cost of equity $= 7\% + 1.4 (11\% - 7\%) = 12.6\%$

9.2.2 Problems in the use of the Capital Asset Pricing Model

In practice, it is not difficult to determine the risk-free rate of interest in most countries: governments issue bonds to fund their future programmes and they publish the interest rates. Although there is some variation in such rates on a monthly and annual basis, the rates quoted provide the basis for R_i.

The return on all market securities, R_m, can also be estimated from publicly available data in countries with wide share ownership such as the UK and USA. However, R_m is more difficult to estimate in those countries with limitations on or limited share ownership such as Italy or Singapore. In this case, some estimate of average rates of return on widely available investment opportunities is probably required. The lack of a widely available market portfolio of alternative share opportunities is a problem in using this method to estimate the cost of equity.

In the case of those companies that have no public quotation of their share price at all, greater reliance may need to be placed on alternative investment opportunities for the funds. An allowance also needs to be made for the degree of risk. R_i will still be available, but R_m may need to be estimated from some form of average alternative return on commercial investments.

The beta value, ß, can be estimated from historical data on the share price of the company, provided that:

● the shares of the company are quoted on the stock market; and

● there is a widely available portfolio of shares against which to monitor price variation.

If either or both of these conditions are absent, it is no longer possible to apply well validated statistical techniques to calculate the beta factor. In these circumstances, some estimate may still be made but it will inevitably be largely judgmental. Such a calculation could perhaps be based on variations in the company's profit record and the impact this might have had on the price of its shares, if they had been traded. An alternative is to use the method described in Section 9.2.3.

9.2.3 Cost of equity capital using risk-free rates of interest

Where there is no widespread share ownership, a much simpler alternative has been used to estimate the cost of equity capital. It begins by estimating the value of the risk-free bond rate, R_i. This should be readily available in most countries. It then adds several percentage points to this rate to take into account the risks of dealing with shares where the returns are not guaranteed. We will call the additional interest rate, R_R. The cost of equity, E(R), is then defined by the equation:

Cost of equity $= E(R) = R_i + R_R$

The difficulty with this method comes in estimating the additional rate of interest, R_R. It is usually derived from an examination of rates of return available on commercial bonds, other shares if available and other types of commercial contract. (A practical example of this method is contained in the Key Reading at the end of the chapter.) There are no clear rules and the method relies on judgement, but it does have the merits of simplicity and flexibility.

An additional possible weakness of the models described in Sections 9.2.1 and 9.2.3 is that all the factors used in the calculation are based primarily on *historical* data, while the model is being used to assess *future* strategies. Naturally, an attempt will be made to estimate future rates of interest in R_i and R_m and also a future ß coefficient. However, estimates of the future are rarely perfect and the emergent strategist would decry the whole approach.

With all these problems, some will question whether it is important to calculate the cost of capital. We return to this issue once we have considered long-term debt capital.

9.2.4 Cost of long-term debt capital

The cost of debt capital is rather more straightforward. For existing funds, it is simply *the weighted average of the interest costs* of the individual loans already made to the company, after deducting the tax. Consider the example of Company XYZ with two main loans from banks:

Loan A	Taken out several years ago when interest rates were favourable. Funds raised at 12% and amounting to 55% of the company's total loan capital.
Loan B	Raised recently when interest rates had gone up. Funds raised at 15% and amounting to 45% of the company's total loan capital.
Tax rate	30%

The cost of debt capital for Company XYZ can be calculated as follows:

$$\text{Cost of long-term debt} = \{\,(12\% \times 0.55) + (15\% \times 0.45)\,\} \times \{1 - 0.3\}$$
$$= 9.345\%$$

It will be noted that the *rate of tax* has been deducted in the cost of debt calculation, but not in the cost of equity capital calculation in the previous sections. This is because, in some countries, interest on debt capital is paid out of profits *before* the company is assessed for tax. The tax rate therefore needs to be deducted from the cost of debt capital.

In the same countries, shareholder dividends are paid *after* tax and so tax does not have to be deducted in calculating the cost of equity capital. In practice, the international treatment of tax is extremely complex (*see* Section 9.4).

9.2.5 The Weighted Average Cost of Capital

The *Weighted Average Cost of Capital* (WACC) is simply the combination of the two costs for equity and debt above – the cost of equity capital and the cost of long-term debt capital – weighted in proportion to their part in the overall capital of the company. In practice, it is the average cost of raising additional funds for the company since the two elements are largely valued on the basis of their current and future interest rates. Hence, WACC is defined by the following formula:

$$\text{WACC} = \frac{(\text{cost of long-term debt}) \times (\text{long-term debt})}{(\text{total company capital})} + \frac{(\text{cost of equity}) \times (\text{equity})}{(\text{total company capital})}$$

In the example of Company XYZ, the amount of debt in the company was US$50 million and the amount of equity was US$100 million. If the individual costs of long-term debt and equity were those calculated above, then the WACC could be calculated as follows:

$$\text{WACC} = (9.345\%) \times \frac{(50)}{(100 + 50)} + (12.6\%) \times \frac{(100)}{(100 + 50)} = 11.515\ \%$$

Clearly, such a calculation is relatively simple. The problems arise in estimating the costs of the individual parts, particularly the cost of equity.

9.2.6 The optimal capital structure

The overall aim of an analysis of the cost of capital will be to arrive at the optimal balance between equity and debt capital. In undertaking this task, it will be evident that each organisation has a unique set of circumstances that need to be taken into account. Financial strategy will wish to take the mathematical formulae shown above and adjust them for other factors that are more difficult to quantify. Factors that need to be considered include:

- the risk involved in the organisation's future strategies;
- company attitudes to risk (for example, entrepreneurs might relish the risk whereas multinationals might be more dubious);
- the risk in the industry (some markets have greater uncertainty than others);
- competitors' costs of capital and capital structures (others may have good ideas, access to their own unique sources of funds, different attitudes to risk, etc.);
- possible trends in interest rates and factors that might substantially alter these, such as national economic performance.

Some of these considerations cannot easily be quantified but will have an important influence on the final choice of funding route. Having taken these considerations into account, it is now possible to address the questions:

- Can the organisations raise *more funds*?
- If so, *from what source* and *at what cost*?
- How does the cost of new funds *compare* with the cost of existing funds?
- What are the *risks involved* in tapping the new sources of funds?

The many sources of finance were discussed in Section 9.1, retained profits, equity and debt capital being the most common.

The cost of *new debt-financed funds* will be the subject of negotiation between the organisation and the banks or other lenders: after such discussion, the cost should be clear. These are most unlikely to involve any advertising of the new funds issue. The professional fees should be limited to those of the organisations merchant bank and to the legal fees involved in drawing up the appropriate deeds. However, fees might typically amount to several million US dollars and so it is evident that the costs of *new* debt finance will go beyond the simple calculation outlined above.

The costs of *new equity* are more complex and will relate to *timing* and *regulatory* issues in most stock markets that go beyond the matters calculated above. Moreover, there will certainly be advertising costs, professional fees from merchant banks, share issue underwriting expenses and other items that will take the costs of *new* equity way beyond the simple calculations undertaken above.

The risks involved in tapping new sources of funds were discussed in Section 9.1.

9.2.7 The importance of calculating the cost of funds

With all the complexities and uncertainties already mentioned, we may ask whether it is really necessary to calculate the cost of funds. Knowing the cost of funds is important for two reasons:

- All the stakeholders need to be re-assured that their efforts are worth while. There is no point in undertaking years of effort and investment if the financial resources could earn more in a lower risk fund outside the organisation. The only rational way of approaching this is to start, however crudely, by estimating the cost of the funds being used inside the enterprise.

- More specifically, the cost of funds is the starting point for the analysis of new strategies. If the return on the new proposals does not even match the cost of the funds that are required to undertake this task, then such projects should not be pursued. We consider this further in Section 9.3.

Key strategic principles

- The cost of equity capital can be calculated using the Capital Asset Pricing Method but it only really works where there is wide public shareholding.

- An alternative method starts with the cost of risk-free government bonds and then adds a factor for the risk of owning shares.

- The cost of long-term debt is calculated from the weighted average of the individual loans made to the company.

- For the company overall, the combined cost of debt and equity is called the Weighted Average Cost of Capital (WACC). It combines equity and debt in proportion to their use in the company.

- The optimal capital structure for a company will also involve the assessment of risks, in addition to the costs estimated above.

- Calculating the cost of capital matters because it reassures the stakeholders that their efforts are worth while and because it provides a benchmark for assessing the profitability of future strategies.

Interbrew: the Stella Artois strategy[12]

International expansion strategies at Belgium's Interbrew will have important financial implications.

Born of a difficult merger in 1988 between Stella Artois and Jupiler breweries, Interbrew of Belgium has been developing into one of the few European brewers with a coherent global strategy. In Spring 1995, it purchased the Dutch brewery operations of the UK company, Allied Domecq, and it entered its fourth Eastern European country. These two activities exemplified its two-pronged strategy for growth:

- to offer segmented brands in the static western European market for beer;

- to forge ahead with the new launches and joint ventures in the emerging markets of Eastern Europe and Asia.

Other brewers, such as Heineken and Guinness, chose to market a few big volume brands, but Interbrew decided to draw on Belgium's rich brewing heritage and offer a portfolio of some 20 distinctive beers. They ranged from premium lagers, led by Stella Artois, to speciality products such as wheat and cherry beers. With people drinking less but spending more on each drink, the strategy was value, not volume.

'The days of going for volume are over,' says Mr Hans Meerloo, Interbrew's Chief Executive. However, trying to persuade other countries to try Belgian speciality beers 'takes a very, very long time and to some extent cannibalises other beers.'

In 1995, Interbrew was pushing Stella and the speciality beers in both emerging countries and western European markets. It was the largest brewer in Belgium, the second in the Netherlands, third in France and eighth in Italy. In the UK, Stella Artois – brewed under licence and distributed by the UK brewer Whitbread – was the leading premium lager brand with about 30 per cent of the market. No European brewer had as much as 10 per cent of the EU market with five brewers, including Interbrew, competing for third place with roughly 4.5 per cent each. If the market consoli-

dated, however, the top 10's share could rise from 50 per cent to 70 per cent by 2000.

Growth abroad, particularly through consolidation, was the only option for Interbrew, given its 60 per cent share of its home market. Interbrew's early days were difficult, exacerbated by the Flemish and Wallonian origins of the precursor companies. The families relinquished management and brought in a succession of chief executives from outside the industry. Mr Meerloo, a Dutchman, was the third since 1988 and took over in 1993. He had joined Interbrew in 1990 after a career spanning the J Walter Thompson advertising agency, a US car parts maker and senior jobs with Philips (Netherlands) in its consumer durable goods sector. Total quality management and a mission statement are but two techniques he brought with him.

> 'We've had some turbulent times to get here. It was a difficult job to put together different breweries and cultures and develop them into a company culture. It has become a very international company.'

Breweries too were revamped at a cost of US$800 million during the years 1992 to 1995. The main brewery at Leuven, for example, produces 4 million hectolitres of beer a year with only eight workers per shift in the brewhouse. Some of the cost was funded by the sale of Interbrew's Belgian Coca-Cola franchise. Net profits were flat for the years 1986 to 1991 at about Bfr 2 billion (US$60 million). They dipped to around [Bfr 1.5 billion in the year ended September 1992 at the depth of the European recession, recovering to Bfr 2 billion in the year to 1993, with further progress in the year to September 1994. Profits were still only marginally up on previous years, however.

Investment banks occasionally tried to persuade debt-free Interbrew to float some or all of its shares on the Belgian stock exchange. However, according to Mr Meerloo, there is neither a financial need nor a family desire to make the company public. Management stays in close touch with board members from the three owners – the de Spoelberch, Van Damme and de Mevius families. All big decisions require unanimous board approval, reducing the risk of dissenting family factions. Dividends are rising and, as far as Mr Meerloo is aware, there is little share trading. Interbrew does have some potential weaknesses, however:

● Its beers are sold in some 45 countries, mostly under licence, but conflicts are creeping into some of these relationships. In the UK, for example, Whitbread produces both Stella and a competitor, Heineken Export, while other brewers handle Interbrew's other beers.

● Interbrew has its own production in fewer than ten countries. Most of these are either small shares of big markets – for example Italy – or big shares of relatively small markets – for example Belgium. Thus it does not have the size for real economies of scale.

● Penetrating a new market is easier with the big global brands such as Heineken, Carlsberg or Guinness. Stella carries less punch and building specialist brands is a long-term proposition.

● In the crowded race for new markets, it is jockeying for position against larger companies with broader international experience – again Heineken and Guinness.

● Cautious family ownership has meant that Interbrew has restrained any excessive spending, for example, on the acquisition of other companies. This saved it from over-paying for Cruzcampo in Spain, a prize that went to Guinness. It has so far kept out of the Czech market where consumption is, along with Germany, the highest in Europe at some 140 litres per person per year.

But given Interbrew's strengths, Mr Meerloo is confident the group can grow. Expansion will carry one small additional cost, however: outside the Leuven headquarters a flag flies for each of the countries where the group brews. There are only ten flagpoles: it may be time to widen the circle.

Source: Financial Times 20 January 1995.

CASE QUESTIONS

1 *What are the benefits for Interbrew of its strategy of building specialist beers? What are the problems?*

2 *What are the reasons for the restrained financial resources of the last few years? How do these relate to the culture of the company?*

3 *Should Interbrew abandon its strategy of a series of small specialist beers and back at least one larger brand, say Stella Artois? What are the financial implications of whatever strategy you recommend? What are the human resource implications?*

9.3 FINANCIAL APPRAISAL OF STRATEGY

When an organisation implements a policy of strategic expansion, this essentially means that funds are invested today for benefits that will accrue in the future. In this section, we explore the *general concepts* of financial resource appraisal in relation to that initial investment (some of the more detailed aspects of this process are covered in Chapter 16). Because of its implications for the survival of the organisation, we separate out the analysis of cash flow from more general financial analysis.

9.3.1 General concepts of strategic financial appraisal

Prescriptive strategists have a very clear view of financial appraisal for strategic decisions. They take the investment to be made and predict the financial returns in the future. They use forecasts of demand, resources, inflation and likely tax regimes in the country or countries in which the investment is being made. The whole process is often built using a computer spreadsheet and has a precision and consistency that is a model of rational decision making. To this is then added some more judgmental evaluation of:

● the *risks* involved;

● the *financial exposure,* if the project were to fail;

● the *opportunity cost* of the strategy, that is, the benefits that would arise if the funds were used for an alternative investment.

It was probably Joel Dean[13] in 1954 who introduced the concept of *discounting* future funds into financial analysis. He argued that the practice in government bonds of treating earnings several years away as worth less than money today should be extended to company analysis. He also pointed out that the *time pattern* of future flows must also be appraised – that is, the fact that future funds do not always accrue evenly over time but may be bunched. Hence, it was important to predict accurately the expected future cash flows and reduce them by a discounting factor based on the *cost of capital* of the company. In the 1960s, Merrett and Sykes[14] were among several writers who wrote persuasively in the UK and across Europe on this approach. For the last 30 years, *discounted cash flow* (DCF) techniques have been widely employed to reduce the future value of strategies to their present value (*see* Fig 9.3).

More recently, among others, Grant[15] has argued that for international investment decision making it is essential to follow discounted cash flow procedures. Competitive pressure for excellence on a global basis is so intense that every strategy needs to be ruthlessly appraised for its contribution to long-term profit maximisation. Although there are some difficulties over the projection of future cash flows in uncertain fast-moving environments, it is essential to ensure that the post-tax rate of return for the strategy exceeds the company's cost of capital. These techniques are widely used in many institutions.

There are four difficulties with this approach.

Accurate prediction There can be little doubt that if markets are fast moving, then there are real difficulties in predicting future cash flows accurately. Even markets with steady growth will have real uncertainties as technology changes, government policies alter, social values and awareness evolve, wars occur and so on. This is the most difficult problem to overcome with discounted cash flow techniques.

By 1982, Hayes and Garvin[16] were pointing out that firms often coped with such uncertainties by setting tougher criteria. The net result of the need for accurate prediction coupled with the increased uncertainty was that many US companies were seeking extraordinarily high rates of return on strategic investments. Many investments were then mistakenly rejected because they did not meet these demanding criteria.

Arbitrariness of investment assumptions Hayes and Garvin also pointed out[17] that investment decisions rely on three rather arbitrary assumptions:

● *The profitability of the project.* Arbitrary estimates are sometimes used regarding the funds that will be needed to undertake the strategy.

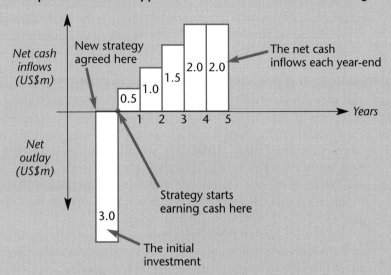

Using DCF to assess a typical new strategy

Example: US$3 million approved investment in new beer-brewing facility

Cost of capital: Project needs to earn a minimum 10%
so use 10% discount factor and discount tables

DCF calculation

End of year	Discount factor	×	Cash inflow		Present value (US$m)
1	0.9091	×	0.5	=	0.455
2	0.8264	×	1.0	=	0.826
3	0.7153	×	1.5	=	1.073
4	0.6831	×	2.0	=	1.366
5	0.6208	×	2.0	=	1.242
	Present value of cash inflows				4.962
	Less: net outlay initially				3.000
	Net present value				US$ 1.962 million

Source: Adapted from Glautier, M W E and Underdown, B: 1994[18]

- *The deterioration of the assets employed.* Estimates that may be relevant for accounting and tax purposes may be arbitrary as far as the real life of the assets is concerned.

- *The external investment opportunities.* It may be somewhat arbitrary to assume that government bonds, alternative stocks and other investment possibilities are available.

Moreover, unless care is taken, *new* investments are treated on the same basis as the replacement of *existing* businesses.[19] This is highly dubious because new business is likely to be less well-known and therefore have a higher degree of risk than existing business. This could perhaps be reflected in the calculation by using two different interest rates for new and existing business in the DCF calculations. However, the *choice* of the two interest rates will have a largely judgmental and arbitrary element.

Differing country approaches to investment appraisal

Williams *et al*[20] studied investment appraisal in Japanese companies around 1990. They discovered that the electronics company NEC never used discounted cash flow techniques at all. Toyota calculated DCF but explicitly did not use it in strategic appraisal. Kenwood also used a rather different approach in assessing strategic opportunity. Payback and wider criteria connected with market share and global intent were employed, rather than strict financial appraisal techniques. In addition, more attention was paid to customer demands on price and quality and the need to meet such demands, whatever cost reduction was required. The authors commented that the whole approach was probably a reflection of the lower status of the financial function in Japanese companies.

Carr *et al*[21] reported that some German managers also took a rather different view on the use of appraisal techniques. They tended to favour simpler payback techniques rather than the more elaborate DCF approach. Specifically, German family firms were more ready to support strategically important projects, even if they produced returns *below* the cost of capital. Again there is some evidence that the financial function has a lower status in German companies than Anglo–American concerns.

Incorrect application of techniques

Even in those western countries that strongly favour the DCF approach, there has been evidence that DCF techniques are incorrectly used or even ignored. Marsh *et al*[22] showed in their survey of three British companies that strategic decisions often ignored the formal guidelines laid down in their financial manuals. Whittington[23] describes other research that supports the contention that there are widespread problems in the use of DCF techniques in some UK companies. For example, one British manufacturer adopted a segmentation strategy and proceeded to make the financial investment *before* the financial calculations had even been undertaken. According to these researchers, the idealised techniques described above do not accord with the reality of use.

The implications of these difficulties for strategy are explored in Section 9.3.3.

9.3.2 Basic cash flow analysis

Profit projections of the future strategy are the basis for DCF calculations. However, *profit* differs from *cash* in at least four ways:[24]

- timing differences between when cash is paid or received and when transactions appear on the profit and loss (P&L) statement;
- the effect of depreciation;
- accounting transactions which are recorded on the balance sheet but do not go through the P&L account;
- changes in working capital requirements.

Although there may be some debate over the use of financial appraisal techniques such as DCF, there can be no doubt that a basic cash flow analysis – that is an analysis that does *not* involve discounting the future cash flows – of every strategic decision is essential. As Ellis and Williams[25] point out, without cash a business cannot survive. It is usually possible to adjust sales, costs and profits so that they fit whatever financial appraisal technique is being used and produce an acceptable return on capital, but 'creating *cash* is virtually impossible'. It is therefore vital to undertake some form of cash flow analysis for new strategies, however difficult the projections.

In strategic investment appraisal, the difficulties with cash flow usually arise in two areas:

1   in the initial period, where the project is likely to be a cash user rather than a cash generator; and

2   with projects that have a long payback, where there may be a major cash requirement some years into the venture before it starts to earn major revenues.

Cash flow analysis is particularly important in periods of uncertainty such as national economic decline or rapid currency fluctuation. The additional pressures from such events can worsen an already tight cash situation and cause real problems. Hence, in addition to conducting a normal cash flow analysis, it is usual to undertake a *sensitivity* or *worst-case analysis* for such events – that is a cash flow analysis of the worst possible combination of events for that particular strategy.

9.3.3   Impact on corporate strategy

Whatever the problems, prescriptive strategists take the view that there is merit in conducting a thorough financial appraisal of the financial results against the costs of capital. It may be that some companies are incompetent in their approach but this does not invalidate the technique. Certainly, there are also real problems in projecting future profits and cash in some projects, as the Channel Tunnel financial appraisal has proved. However, there is no real alternative.

Emergent strategists take the view that there are real uncertainties in the whole process: it is so difficult to predict the future that there is little point in trying. Moreover, there is evidence to support the view that corporate strategy decision making is not the rational process assumed by analytical formulae.

From the narrow viewpoint of strategic analysis, it is evident that there is little compromise between these views. This book takes the approach that there is merit in both arguments but that ultimately it is better to undertake some analysis, however flawed. What really matters is that the corporate strategy appraisal is undertaken with *imagination* and *vision, in addition to* the narrower financial criteria that have been explored in this chapter. We will explore this further in Chapter 11.

Moreover, judgement does play an important role in determining both the sales, costs and profits on the one hand, and the risks and attractions, on the other, of a major new strategic initiative. This means that accurate projections are unlikely and some decisions will be wrong. For many companies, there is a need to accept the uncertainties that real life analysis will bring, while taking the positive decisions demanded of the highly original strategies that bring real competitive advantage.

Key strategic principles

- Strategic expansion is often analysed using discounting techniques to reduce future projected profits back to their value in today's monetary terms.

- Several difficulties have been identified with this approach. Probably the most substantial is the difficulty of producing accurate projections of future profitability.

- DCF is not to be confused with basic cash flow analysis, which is not discounted but projects net cash flows during the life of the project. Cash flow analysis is essential for project assessment in order to identify and avoid bankruptcy.

- Overall, while there are certain difficulties involved in the techniques, it is probably better to undertake these analyses rather than ignore them.

CASE STUDY 9.3

SCA's financial objectives[26]

This case study explores the relationship between group and financial objectives at the Swedish paper and packaging company, Svenska Cellulosa (SCA)

Extract from SCA 1992 Report and Accounts	Comment
'The SCA Group's financial targets combine growth with financial balance. As a result of the divestment of the Energy business group, the capital structure changed substantially, reducing financial risk.'	A good example of the need to balance different business and financial requirements.
'Visible shareholders' equity almost doubled, at the same time as net debt decreased significantly. The objective is to sustain this reinforced capital structure. Therefore, a certain downward adjustment of the return requirement on shareholders' equity is justified, from the current 15 per cent to 13 per cent.'	The company decreased its gearing substantially and reduced its reliance on heavy debt finance. Such a major change would reduce the risk to shareholders and allow a reduction in shareholder return targets.
'Profitability is the overriding guideline. Accordingly, expressed as return on shareholders' equity after tax, the requirement is 13 per cent, calculated as an average over an economic cycle.'	The company has chosen to define profitability in terms of its shareholders only. Other stakeholders are ignored. It has calculated this over the whole economic cycle because of the cyclicality of the paper industry (see *Case study 4.3*). It means that in some years profitability needs to be above this level and in other years below it.

Extract from SCA 1992 Report and Accounts	Comment
'This is based on yield on a risk-free, long-term investment in the European money market and a 3 per cent risk premium for share investments.'	The calculation of 13 per cent is clearly explained with a reference to R_i. Instead of trying to calculate R_m, the company simply added 3 per cent to R_i for the risk involved in shares on a stock exchange. The company does not explain why it chose 3 per cent.
'Considering the current tax situation, interest and equity/assets ratio, this requires a consolidated return on capital employed of slightly less than 15 per cent.'	From the 13 per cent shareholder-return, the company has then calculated the amount that it needs to earn on its assets to deliver this figure – that is, just below 15 per cent.
'The [15 per cent] requirement varies between the business groups.'	Some markets are inherently more profitable than others, and so the company varies the 15 per cent by different business groups within the overall portfolio of its products. Some will be above 15 per cent and some below in order to average at 15 per cent overall.
'Individual operations within each business group are managed on the basis of the return required on its operating assets, as differentiated, taking into account local inflation rates and the age structure of the assets.'	Within each business group, further distinctions are then made for each operating asset. Where country inflation is high, this will inflate the profit figure so the target is also set higher – a good example of country management. The comment on age structure is unclear. For old assets, they may peform worse and be less profitable. However, they may have been largely depreciated in which case they would easily achieve the return on capital targets.

SCA: Ten-year record

Source: SCA Annual Report and Accounts 1992.

9.4 RELATIONSHIP BETWEEN FINANCIAL AND CORPORATE OBJECTIVES

Without adequate financial performance, the survival of all commercial organisations would be put at risk. The same is also at least partially true of the many not-for-profit organisations that need to survive, if only to provide the services they offer. Much of this chapter has considered the analysis of financial resources against the background of maximising profits, retaining part of those profits, delivering attractive earnings per share, paying steadily increasing dividends and similar objectives. It has been argued that a basic criterion against which to judge strategy is the opportunity cost of capital.

All these matters have been judged in terms of the shareholder returns. For example, in Case study 9.3 SCA states that its main guideline is the profit delivered to shareholders, as represented by shareholder's equity after tax. Equally, the Capital Asset Pricing Model is essentially a quantification based on the primacy of shareholder interests. There are two reasons for suggesting that this view is oversimplistic and incomplete:

- long-term *versus* short-term objectives; and
- the importance of key stakeholders.

9.4.1 Balancing long-term and short-term objectives

It is perfectly possible to maximise shareholder profits after tax by stopping research and development, cancelling all advertising and promotional expenditure, and by implementing such policies as a run-down of stocks and zero maintenance of the factory and so on. *In the short term*, profits and shareholder equity would rise substantially. *In the long term*, the organisation would die, which is clearly undesirable. The strategic issue is how to strike a *balance* between the short term and long term.

There is a subsidiary problem with the short-term approach to objectives. As soon as there are unfavourable variations in the external environment, the short-term view would suggest that longer term investment should be cut back and the short term protected. For example, economic downturn might mean a major strategic capital project being delayed, even though its benefits were significant. Corporate strategy needs to consider how to manage the organisation so that this balance is not thrown off course at the first sign of difficulty.

9.4.2 Importance of key stakeholders

Some key stakeholders in a business – such as management and workers – seek rewards from the firm other than the maximisation of profit – job satisfaction and rewards, for example. A variety of research sources suggests that reasonable rather than maximum profits may be a more accurate reflection of their views. This is reflected in the Ford Motor Company mission and objectives statement (*see* Exhibit 12.5 on p441) which refers to its mission as 'allowing us to prosper as a business and to provide a reasonable return for our stockholders, the owners of the business'. The implication for financial evaluation is that there is a need to explore what 'reasonable' profit means and then to assess the organisation's financial resources in that context.

This does not mean that organisations should not raise new funds and explore the means of achieving this as cheaply as possible. It is perfectly rational to explore the cost of the capital that has been raised or is being sought. It is always desirable for the benefits of a strategy to be greater than the cost of capital, however calculated. It is important, however, for the benefits to be seen in a broader context than simply the maximisation of profit.

9.4.3 Distinction between strategic and financial objectives

It is important for a distinction to be drawn between an organisation's financial and strategic objective. The starting point is to recognise the need to invest in the long-term future of the business and to establish the legitimate interests of other stakeholders in the business. Both of these aspects then need to be reflected in the organisation's objectives which make up the organisations broad strategies for the future. Essentially, this will lead to *strategic* rather than *financial* objectives. The distinction is shown in Table 9.5.

There can be little doubt that strategic objectives are essential for the long-term development of strategy.

Table 9.5 Financial and strategic objectives[27]

Financial objectives	Strategic objectives
● Faster revenue growth	● Bigger market share
● Faster earning growth	● Higher, more secure industry rank
● Higher dividends	● Higher product quality
● Wider profit margins	● Lower costs relative to key competitors
● Higher returns on invested capital	● Broader or more attractive product line
● Stronger bond and credit ratings	● Stronger reputation with customers
● Bigger cash flows	● Superior customer service
● A rising stock price	● Recognition as a leader in technology and/or product innovation
● Recognition as a 'blue chip' company	● Increased ability to compete in international markets
● A more diversified revenue base	● Expanded growth opportunities
● Stable earnings during recessionary periods	● Higher salaries and other employee benefits

Source: Thompson A and Strickland A, *Strategic Management*, 9th edition.

© Richard D Irwin, a Times Mirror Higher Education Group, Inc. Company, Burr Ridge, IL, USA, p31. Adapted with permission of the publisher.

Key strategic principles

● To define objectives purely in terms of the organisation's short-term financial profitability would be over-simplistic and incomplete.

● There are two principle reasons. First, it is often possible to sacrifice long-term profits to boost the short term at the expense of the survival of the organisation. Second, such an approach ignores the interests of other stakeholders in the organisation such as employees.

● Hence, a distinction needs to be drawn between strategic and financial objectives.

9.5 INTERNATIONAL ASPECTS OF FINANCIAL RESOURCES

In examining international financial resources, there are many similarities with the techniques outlined in Sections 9.1 to 9.4. This section will therefore concentrate on the differences. There are five main areas to be considered:

- capital structure of overseas holdings;
- international fund remittances;
- risk management, including currency;
- taxation considerations;
- cost of capital variations across countries.

9.5.1 Capital structure of overseas holdings

In principle, the same mixture of equity, debt and other forms of finance is available in overseas companies as in the home country. Retained earnings are often the main method of financing overseas subsidiaries but debt capital can also sometimes be high.[28] Special considerations that might be applied to overseas companies include:

- Where the company is located in a country with widely fluctuating exchange rates, there is a case for using as much *local* debt finance as possible. This allows the company to avoid the uncertainties of using its own funds.
- Special grants and investment loans from sources such as the European Union and World Bank may make a substantial difference to strategy profitability.

9.5.2 International fund remittances

Paying funds to and obtaining dividends from foreign subsidiaries will almost certainly need careful thought. For example, some years ago a South American government had a policy that allowed only limited repatriation of company profits back to Europe from activities in that country. There was no point in evaluating the cost of capital without taking this into account.

One way round the problem was to seek payment from foreign subsidiaries for other services beyond dividends on shares – for example, royalties on the use of brand names, patents, management services, goods supplied from the home country and so on. Naturally, these other payments were all agreed with the government authorities of the country concerned, but they did make the financial resource evaluation task more complex and hence the strategic analysis more difficult.

9.5.3 Risk management

When companies are forced to rely on payments from countries with weak currencies, they always face the risk that their earnings will decline from the projections made at the time when the strategy was devised. There are a number of mechanisms for reducing such risks but none is without its problems. Essentially, they all amount to some form of insurance and have a cost that needs to be built into the analysis of financial resources. Judging by some major corporate disasters of the last few years, probably the most important area of risk is that of *currency management*.

9.5.4 Taxation considerations

Among the many matters to be evaluated, there are the issues of:

- the choice of the country in which to take any profits earned;
- the possibility of moving funds to countries that have no corporation tax;
- the complexities of different national tax systems on profits.

Even within the European Union, there has been no real harmonisation of the important tax rates, nor is there likely to be in the near future.[29] Tax matters make the evaluation of financial resources for overseas companies sufficiently complex to require specialist advice and consultation.

9.5.5 Cost of capital variations across countries

For reasons associated with levels of inflation, currency and national resources, different countries have differing costs of capital. A study by McCauley and Zimmer[30] examined the cost of capital in four leading industrial countries. Some of the results are shown in Table 9.6. Such factors will need to be given careful consideration when it comes to deciding the country in which to raise funds. The obvious conclusion is that international financial analysis needs to be conducted on a country-by-country basis.

Table 9.6 The cost of capital in four leading industrial countries (1989)

Country	Research and development project with 10 years payoff	Equipment and machinery with physical life of 20 years	Expensed item with physical life of 3 years
US	20.3%	11.2%	40.4%
Japan	8.7%	7.2%	34.9%
Germany	14.8%	7.0%	34.8%
UK	23.7%	9.2%	37.4%

Key strategic principles

- When international operations are involved, financial resource analysis becomes more complex.
- The capital structure of equity and debt is broadly similar, but sending funds to and obtaining dividends from overseas companies is more difficult because of barriers to trade, country differences on tax and economies' growth and currency uncertainties.
- Probably the greatest single area of risk in many overseas operations is currency fluctuation.

> ### Key strategic principles continued
>
> - Taxation and cost of capital are both subjects that require in-depth and possibly specialist financial analysis.
>
> - For a variety of reasons, the cost of capital will vary between countries. This means that the financial analysis of strategic projects will need to be conducted on an individual country basis.

CASE STUDY 9.4

Financing growth at MorphoSys[31]

As conversation stoppers in Germany's financial community, the topics of venture capital and biotechnology would be hard to beat. Risk financing is scarce and genetic engineering often viewed sceptically. However, the southern state of Bavaria likes biotechnology companies and is keen to finance them. One beneficiary is Munich-based MorphoSys, which is not yet in profit, but has caught the attention of pharmaceutical companies due to its pioneering biomedical research.

'Venture capital is difficult here, there's no question about it,' says Simon Moroney, the Chief Executive. 'But you can get a lot of soft money on a scale that's unprecedented anywhere.' As a result the company is embarking on a third financing round in which each D-Mark of venture capital will be matched by two from state and federal funds.

MorphoSys is researching drugs for cancer and other diseases by seeking to optimise the properties of proteins and peptides (amino acid compounds), especially as antibodies. Some companies in the US and UK do this by working with transgenic animals such as pigs and sheep and others build up synthetic molecule libraries. The unique MorphoSys method, stemming from the work of Andreas Plückthun, a German biochemistry professor, is to select the best biochemical variants from a vast number and repeat them over and over again. In the case of cancer treatment, an antibody variant

would be chosen which binds best to the malignant cell and this would be repeated constantly.

'It's molecular evolution', says Alex Korda, joint Managing Director of Korda and Company – a UK venture capital company that invested in MorphoSys in 1993. Korda, the German federal government and Technostart – a Stuttgart-based technology finance operation – together put in DM 2.1 million (US$1.5 million) at that time. A further DM 3.7 million was provided in 1994 with Atlas Venture Capital (Dutch-based with a German operation), Standard Life of the UK and Jafco (part of Nomura Securities) of Japan also participating. The company hoped a UK institution would participate in the 1995 financing round of DM 8.0 million.

'Sales don't exist at this stage,' says Moroney. 'It's purely venture capital.' All the money now goes into research and development. He hopes for 'cash neutrality' in about 1997, but adds, 'the potential rewards are enormous.' The company is pinning its hopes on the big drugs companies' desire to put out more research to specialised companies. MorphoSys is in advanced talks with a British group on development of a prophylactic for septic shock (associated with invasive surgery) and with a German company on a diagnostics kit.

Moroney says the company's techniques are widely applicable: 'any disease is associated with some aberrant molecule'. In about two years,

MorphoSys hopes to give its investors (who own 75 per cent of the company) an exit through a share flotation – possibly on Easdaq, the planned European version of the US's Nasdaq – or a trade sale. It may then link up with another company, possibly in the US, to give it greater strength in the field of antibody engineering.

Source: *Financial Times*, 12 June 1995.

CASE QUESTIONS

1   What elements of the strategy of MorphoSys justi-fied the share investments made by companies and the Bavarian and federal government in the company?

2   How would you estimate the cost of capital for MorphoSys? Do you think that such a calculation would provide a useful guide for shareholders?

3   Would you have invested in the company's DM 8 million financing programme in 1995? Give reasons for your views.

KEY READING

The accounting function and strategy[32]

In this extract from their book, Accounting Theory and Practice, *Professors M Glautier and B Underdown comment on the relationship between the accounting function, finance and the development of corporate strategy.*

Given that long-range planning is concerned with the totality of the enterprise's strategy in every sphere of action, it is evident that the information that is needed goes much beyond that which normally is defined as accounting information.

In the final analysis, cash flows into and out of a business enterprise are the most fundamental events upon which accounting measures are based. Management and investors, in particular, are very concerned with the cash flows generated by corporate assets. These cash flows are not only central to the problem of corporate survival, but they are essential to the attainment of corporate objectives. The size, timing and risks inherent in estimating future cash flows are critical aspects of this process.

The recognition of the importance of future cash flows has led many writers to define *the* objective of business corporations in terms of maximising corporate wealth, defined as the present value of the future stream of net cash flows to be earned by corporate assets. This objective is also expressed as the maximisation of shareholders' wealth, since they are deemed by law to be the owners of the enterprise.

There is general agreement that the return on capital employed (ROCE) is the most important performance measurement for long-range planning and for setting long-range profit targets. It is a common practice to compute the ROCE for each year covered by the long-range plan in order to show whether planned increases in annual profits will keep pace with annual increases in assets. This analysis also indicates the effectiveness with which management will be required to use corporate assets.

The accountant's task is not to attempt the impossible by deciding what should be the maximum possible long-range profit on the basis of assumed long-range resources for planning purposes: his/her job is to quantify the size of the profit which is required as the profit objective. The required profit as a planning goal is never a theoretical ideal, such as the 'maximum long-term profit' or 'the maximum long-term return to shareholders', but represents rather the outcome of discussion as to what is a possible and desirable target for the time-span considered. As a guide to selecting the profit target, one of the most influential factors is the minimum rate of return expected by investors and creditors. A satisfactory profit ensures that debt and dividend payments may be made, thereby reducing the risks attached to investing in the firm.

Source: Glautier, M W E and Underdown, B (1994) Accounting Theory and Practice, 5th edn, Pitman Publishing, Chapter 28.

◼ SUMMARY

● Organisations need to finance their existing and proposed new strategies. There are six main sources of funds for such activities, each with its own merits and problems. *Retained profits* are the first source of finance for most organisations: probably the largest and cheapest source of funds. *Equity finance* – that is, the issuance of new shares to either existing or new shareholders – is another way of raising funds. *Long-term debt finance* is simpler and cheaper than equity but there are limits to the amount that can be raised. There are also major constraints on debt finance. These relate to the need to pay interest on the debt regardless of the profit fluctuations in the business.

● Other sources of finance include *leasing* (renting) plant and machinery, *savings* from reductions in short-term debt and the *sale of existing assets*. They all have their advantages and problems.

● All capital raised by the organisation has a cost associated with it. Calculating the cost matters because it reassures the stakeholders that their efforts are worthwhile and because it provides a benchmark for assessing the profitability of future strategies.

● The cost of equity capital can be calculated using the Capital Asset Pricing Method, but it really only works where there is wide public shareholding. The cost of debt is calculated from the weighted average of the individual loans to the company. For the company overall, the combined cost of debt and equity is called the Weighted Average Cost of Capital (WACC).

● When assessing new strategic proposals, it is normal to undertake a financial appraisal. Discounting techniques are often used as part of this in Western companies. They reduce future net cash flows back to their value in today's terms. Several difficulties have been identified with this approach. Probably the most substantial is the problem of producing accurate projections of future profitability.

● Basic cash flow analysis is also undertaken. It should not be confused with the discounting techniques above. Analysing cash flow is essential to ensure that the company avoids bankruptcy.

● To define objectives purely in terms of the organisation's short-term financial profitability would be over-simplistic and incomplete. A distinction needs to be drawn between strategic and financial objectives.

● When international operations are involved, financial resource analysis becomes more complex. Probably the greatest source of risk for many companies is currency fluctuation. Taxation and the cost of capital are both subjects that require in-depth and possibly specialist financial analysis.

QUESTIONS

1 You have been commissioned to comment upon a proposal to invest US$100 million in a new mobile telephone service. The company already operates such a facility but it has seen opportunities for expansion into new geographical areas. Competition is strong and the market is growing around 12 per cent per annum. The company currently has gearing around 90 per cent and a WACC of 12 per cent. The new funds would double the total already invested in the company. What would you advise?

2 Use Section 9.1 to analyse the financial resources of an organisation with which you are familiar. Comment particularly on the strategic implications.

3 Explain the constraints on sources of finance likely to be experienced by Heineken, Carlsberg and Danone. To what extent can these constraints be overcome?

4 'Marketers and finance people seldom see eye to eye. The marketers say, 'This product will open up a whole new market segment.' Finance people respond, 'It's a bad investment. The discounted rate of return is only 8%.' Why are they so often in opposition?' Professors Patrick Barwise, Paul Marsh and Robin Wensley.

How would *you* approach this issue?

5 Investigate the cost of capital for an organisation of your choice. How would you calculate it? With what result? What are the implications for the development of corporate strategy?

6 Compare the shareholding structures of the brewery companies named in the chapter and comment on the financial and strategic implications.

7 There appears to be a conflict in companies between financial and strategic objectives. Do you agree? How can any such conflict be resolved?

8 'Capital investment represents an act of faith, a belief that the future will be as promising as the present, together with a commitment to making the future happen.' Professor Robert Hayes.

Discuss the implications for financial and strategic appraisal of new corporate strategies.

STRATEGIC PROJECT

International brewing strategy

This chapter has examined the brewing industry. Develop this study further. For example, Interbrew acquired John Labatt, the Canadian brewer, in 1995 for US$2 billion. The company is building an international strategy, but some competitors have been unimpressed.

FURTHER READING

For a general survey of financial issues: Glautier, M W E and Underdown, B (1997) *Accounting Theory and Practice*, 6th edn, Pitman Publishing, London.

For a most useful summary of basic financial issues and their relationship to strategy: Ellis, J and Williams, D (1993) *Corporate Strategy and Financial Analysis*, Pitman Publishing, London.

For a critical look at DCF techniques: Hayes, R (1982) 'Managing as if tomorrow mattered', *Harvard Business Review*, May–June.

For the link between finance and strategy: Barwise, P, Marsh, P and Wensley, R (1989) 'Must finance and strategy clash?' *Harvard Business Review*, Sep–Oct.

For a discussion of cost of capital and financial issues: Franks, J R and Broyles, J E (1979) *Modern Managerial Finance*, John Wiley, Chichester. Very useful text.

APPENDIX I

Heineken NV

Extract from the consolidated accounts for the year ended 31 December 1994 (million guilders)

Balance sheet

	1994	*1993*
Assets		
Fixed assets		
Tangible fixed assets	4695	4362
Financial fixed assets	646	541
	5341	4904
Current assets		
Stocks	687	690
Accounts receivable	1150	972
Securities	134	195
Cash at bank and in hand	1606	1371
	3578	3228
Total assets	8919	8132
Liabilities		
Group funds		
Shareholders' funds	4354	3973
Minority interests	354	239
	4708	4212
Investment facilities equalization account	119	130
Provisions	1362	1281
Debts		
Long-term debts	503	462
Current liabilities	2226	2046
	2729	2508
Total liabilities	8919	8132

Profit and Loss Statement

	1994	*1993*
Net turnover	9974	9049
Raw materials	5450	4908
Excise duties	1359	1198
Personnel costs	1684	1643
Depreciation	586	501
Total operating expenditure	9079	8251
Trading profit	895	798

Earnings of non-consolidated participants	39	19
Interest	16	2
Profit on ordinary activities before taxation	950	814
Taxation	318	320
Group profit on ordinary activities after taxation	631	494
Minority interests	28	24
Net profit on ordinary activities	603	519
Net extraordinary income	59	–
Net profit	662	519
Dividends	140	140
Retained profit	522	379

Shareholder data (guilders per share)

	1994	1993
Net profit	15.03	12.92
Dividend	3.50	3.50
Shareholders' equity	108.47	98.98

APPENDIX II

Checklist of the main financial ratios

Note: it is important to obtain comparative data for competitors and to analyse the trends over several years.

Liquidity – measures the ability to survive and avoid default

$$\text{Current ratio} = \frac{\text{Current assets}}{\text{Current liabilities}}$$

$$\text{Acid test} = \frac{\text{Current assets} - \text{Stocks}}{\text{Current liabilities}}$$

Gearing – examines the financial strength and the different forms of finance

$$\text{Gearing} = \frac{\text{Long-term borrowing}}{\text{Capital and reserves}}$$

$$\text{Interest cover} = \frac{\text{Earnings before interest and tax (EBIT)}}{\text{Interest}}$$

Profitability

$$\text{Profit margin} = \frac{\text{EBIT}}{\text{Sales}}$$

$$\text{Return on capital employed} = \frac{\text{EBIT}}{\text{Capital employed}}$$

Investor ratios – measures the earnings available to those who own the company

Usually uses profit after tax and interest, i.e. *net profit*.

$$\text{Net profit margin} = \frac{\text{Net profit}}{\text{Sales}}$$

$$\text{Earnings per share} = \frac{\text{Net profit margin}}{\text{Number of shares}}$$

$$\text{P/E ratio} = \frac{\text{Price per share}}{\text{Number of shares}}$$

$$\text{Earnings yield} \quad = \quad \frac{\text{Earnings per share}}{\text{Price per share}}$$

$$\text{Dividend per share} \quad = \quad \frac{\text{Dividends}}{\text{Number of shares}}$$

Trading activity

$$\text{Stock cover} \quad = \quad \frac{\text{Cost of sales}}{\text{Stock}}$$

$$\text{Debtor days} \quad = \quad \frac{\text{Debtors} \times 365}{\text{Sales}}$$

$$\text{Creditor days} \quad = \quad \frac{\text{Other creditors} \times 365}{\text{Sales}}$$

$$\text{Fixed asset turnover} = \quad \frac{\text{Sales}}{\text{Fixed assets}}$$

REFERENCES

1 *Heineken Annual Report* (1994), p14.
2 Groupe MAC (1988) *Cost of Non-Europe Volume 1*, OOPEC, Luxembourg, p431.
3 *Heineken Annual Report* (1994) Ibid.
4 There is evidence for the UK which showed that in 1990 it accounted for around 50 per cent of the total source of funds: *Annual Abstract of Statistics*, HMSO, 1993. Such data does not appear to have been researched for a broader range of countries. However, sampling of company accounts would appear to confirm this at least for Europe and the USA.
5 Gogel, R and Larreche, J-C (1989) 'The Battlefield for 1992: product strength and geographic coverage', *European Management Journal*, 7(2), p132.
6 Gitman, L J (1982) *Principles of Managerial Finance*, 3rd edn, Harper and Row.
7 Franks, J R and Broyles, J E (1979) *Modern Managerial Finance*, Wiley, Ch 2.
8 For example, the UK company General Electric has held large cash balances for many years rather than invest these in company projects.
9 Franks, J R and Broyles, J E B (1979) Ibid, p106 *et seq.*
10 Wensley, R (1981) 'Strategic Marketing: Betas, Boxes or Basics', *Journal of Marketing*, 45, Summer, p175. This contains a useful discussion and references in the context of the use of ß for strategy projects and a comparison with product portfolio evaluation.
11 McCauley, R and Zimmer, S (1989) 'Explaining international differences in the cost of capital', *Federal Reserve Bank of New York, Quarterley Review*, Summer.
12 Adapted from an article by Roderick Oram in the *Financial Times* of 20 Jan 1995, p17.
13 Dean, J (1954) 'Measuring the productivity of capital', *Harvard Business Review*, Jan–Feb, p21.
14 Merrett, A J and Sykes, A (1966) *Capital Budgeting and Company Finance*, Longman, Harlow.
15 Grant, R M (1991) *Contemporary Strategy Analysis*, Blackwell, Oxford.

16 Hayes, R and Garvin, J (1982) 'Managing as if tomorrow mattered', *Harvard Business Review*, May–June, p71.

17 Hayes, W and Garvin, J (1982) Ibid, p75.

18 Extracted from Glautier, M W E and Underdown, B (1994) *Accounting Theory and Practice*, 5th edn, Pitman Publishing, London, p494.

19 Hayes, W and Garvin, J (1982) Ibid, p76.

20 Williams, K, Haslam, C, Williams, J with Makato Abe, Toshio Aida and Isutomo Mitsui (1991) *Management Accounting: the Western problematic against the Japanese application*, Annual Conference on the Labour Process, UMIST and mimeograph from the University of East London.

21 Carr, C, Tomkins, C and Bayliss, B (1991) 'Strategic Controllership – a case study approach', *Management Accounting Research*, 2, pp89–107.

22 Marsh, P, Barwise, P, Thomas, K and Wensley, R (1989) *Managing strategic investment decisions in large diversified companies*, London Business School Centre for Business Strategy, London.

23 Whittington, R (1993) *What is strategy and does it matter?*, Routledge, London, pp64–5. The comments in this reference include a much more extensive discussion of the problems than is possible in this text.

24 Ellis, J and Williams, D (1993) *Corporate Strategy and Financial Analysis*, Pitman Publishing, London, p172.

25 Ellis, J and Williams, D (1993) Ibid, p168.

26 Extracts from 1992 Report and Accounts.

27 Adapted from Thompson, A and Strickland, A (1993) *Strategic Management*, 7th edn, Irwin, Homewood, ILL, p28.

28 Brooke, M Z (1992) *International Management*, 2nd edn, Stanley Thornes, Cheltenham, Ch 8.

29 *See* Citron, R (1991) *Getting into Europe*, Kogan Page, London, for a more detailed discussion of this area.

30 McCauley, R and Zimmer, S (1989) Ibid.

31 Adapted from an article by Andrew Fisher, in the *Financial Times*, 12 June 1995, p13. © *Financial Times*.

32 Extracted from Glautier, M W E and Underdown, B (1994) *Accounting Theory and Practice*, 5th edn, Pitman Publishing, London, Ch 28.

10

Analysing operations resources

When you have worked through this chapter, you will be able to:

- assess the contribution of operations strategy to the corporate strategy process;

- identify the competitive advantage and value-added contributions that the operations function makes to the organisation;

- analyse the operations environment for relevant trends, especially major changes in technology;

- identify how and where operations strategies contribute to value added;

- analyse operations in organisations for the specific areas that are most likely to impact on corporate strategy;

- understand the importance of the main elements of operations strategy;

- explore the differences that exist between operations in manufacturing and in service industries.

◼ INTRODUCTION

Operations management covers all manufacturing processes in an organisation and includes raw material sourcing, purchasing, production and manufacturing, distribution and logistics – in other words, the contribution of the production function to the organisation's ability to add value to its goods or services. Importantly, human resource aspects of the function are just as significant as machinery. In many corporate strategy texts, operations management barely rates a mention, and yet it has delivered real benefits to organisations in both the commercial and public sectors over the last 20 years.

There are four main topics in this chapter: the environmental forces that have been a powerful influence on operations development; the contribution of operations to value; the role of technology in operations and corporate strategy; and the application of operations concepts to the service industry (*see* Fig 10.1).

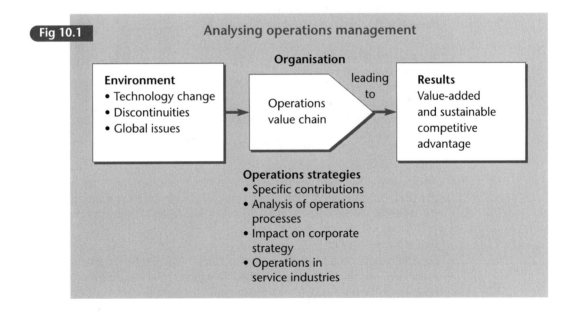

Fig 10.1 — Analysing operations management

Kvaerner's strategy to improve productivity at Govan Shipyard[1]

The Norwegian company, Kvaerner, acquired the Govan shipyard on the River Clyde in Scotland from the British Government for £1 in 1988. Ever since, Kvaerner has been seeking to increase profitability through new operations strategies.

Background
The world shipbuilding market has excess production capacity. It is dominated by major Japanese and Korean yards that have based their lower costs on the strategies of new technology and flexible workforces over the last 20 years. The high-cost European yards have been forced to close or accept heavy government subsidies.

Against this background, Kvaerner made the strategic decision in the 1980s to move into shipbuilding. It bought the Govan yard cheaply because it was taking over a record of 30 years of loss-making activities. Subsequently, the company has purchased shipyards in Finland and the former East Germany on a similar knock-down price basis. However, it has still been faced with the problem of turning them around.

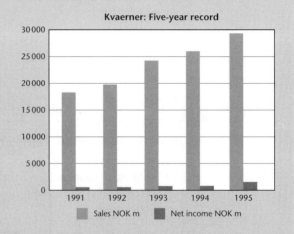

Kvaerner: Five-year record

The problem at Govan
There is a long and proud tradition of building ships at the Govan yard in Glasgow. For this reason, Kvaerner approached its new acquisition with caution. It quickly discovered that attitudes towards costs and customers were still rooted in the days of its former government owners: the state would always subsidise any losses. This showed in its working practices. For example in 1990, Govan took 50 per cent more man-hours to build exactly the same ship as the Kvaerner shipyard in Norway. Major change was needed.

New strategies
New Norwegian and UK management was installed. *The Govan Productivity 2000 Plan* was drawn up. Six areas were identified for action. They ranged from design and planning through production and production services to sub-contracting, skills and organisation. Importantly, more responsibility was devolved to the shop floor – *empowerment*. Information on the work in progress was increased and greater co-ordination put in place. Real co-operation between the management and the trade unions was beginning to produce results.

10.1 OPERATIONS AND CORPORATE STRATEGY

10.1.1 Why operations matters to corporate strategy

Operations management is an important element of corporate strategy for three reasons:

1 *The rewards from the successful implementation of such strategies can be very high –* for example, *see* Case study 10.1 on Toyota and the resulting delivery of US$1.5 billion annually to that company.

2 *Major investment in physical and human resources is necessary to achieve the identified results –* for example, *see* the large investments needed in production plant in European paper companies described in Chapter 4.

3 *Fundamental changes in both people and machines need to be addressed by every company –* for example, *see* the Ford Motor Company's new global strategy described in Chapter 12. The Kvaerner case also shows the importance of major changes in these areas if improvement is to be obtained.

As Hill comments,[2] operations strategy has two major contributions to make to corporate strategy:

1 It aims to provide manufacturing and related processes that will give the organisation competitive advantage over competition.

2 It supplies co-ordinated support for products so that they will win sales orders in a competitive market place.

As a result, operations resource analysis is important to strategic development because it can lead to *competitive advantage* in areas such as:

● *variable production* to make products that are more precisely tailored to individual customer requirements;

● *lower costs* than competitors for the same product performance;

● *product quality* that it is superior to competition;

● *enhanced services and delivery* associated with the product that is superior to rivals.

10.1.2 Prescriptive and emergent approaches

Traditionally, the operations function has seen itself as using machines to undertake tasks as efficiently as possible. Professionally, it has an engineering and science background and has viewed its tasks as essentially oriented towards the same goal. Its management roots go back to Taylor, Gantt, the Gilbreths and Knoeppel – all pioneers in the field of 'scientific management'.[3] In keeping with these traditions, operations management has often been *prescriptive* in its solutions to strategy issues.

The one-sidedness of this approach has been recognised for many years. In 1945 a number of psychologists formed a group to redress the balance – the Tavistock Institute in London and the Socio-Technical Round Table in the USA, for example.[4] The *emergent* strategy approaches of team-working and empowerment, as described in the Kvaerner case study, were pioneered during that period. At the same time, similar Japanese developments were being initiated by people such as Ohno (*see* Case study 10.1) and others. In a similar way German and French social reconstruction was also being initiated that took the same broader view of the nature of work and its social role.

Corporate strategy needs to take both this broader emergent perspective, and the important prescriptive approaches. All the topics in this chapter therefore need to be explored from both emergent and prescriptive perspectives.

Key strategic principles

- Operations needs to be considered as part of corporate strategy because of the rewards it brings, the major investments that may be required and the fundamental changes that may be needed.

- Traditionally, operations has taken a prescriptive approach to strategy issues. It is becoming increasingly recognised that emergent perspectives are also required.

10.2 ANALYSIS OF THE OPERATIONS ENVIRONMENT

Over the last 30 years, there have been many fundamental changes in the environment surrounding operations at the strategic level. Although factors are specific to the organisation itself, three general trends deserve investigation:

- technological environment;
- discontinuities in technology;
- global activity and cost reductions.

10.2.1 Technological environment

Due to the impact of technology, the world has changed more dramatically over the last 150 years than it did in the previous 2000 years.[5] Arguably, the pace is increasing: this will have an even greater effect on the corporate environment. Hill[6] identifies five factors that have allowed Far Eastern countries, particularly Japan, to move ahead of the West, although it should be noted that Germany and France are perhaps less guilty than the others.

1 The increased pace of technological change.

2 The failure to appreciate the impact of increased world manufacturing capacity. In some markets, there is now substantial excess capacity, which impacts particularly during a downward trade cycle. Shipbuilding is an example. Competition is inevitably keener.

3 Lack of willingness to invest in research and development in some countries.

4 Top management lack of experience in manufacturing.

5 The production manager's obsession with short-term output, rather than the longer term strategic viewpoint.

In analysing technological change, the pervasiveness of electronics and the rapid pace of electronic development have led to shorter life cycles in some industries, particularly industrial.[7] In addition, better communications have meant that any technological advance is now shared much more quickly around the world, so that it is difficult to sustain technological advantage without patents. At the same time, research and development are becoming more expensive. Analysis of technology will need to examine both the life cycle of the organisation's major products and, at a more fundamental level, the technological resources available to the company.

When the Swiss pharmaceutical company, Roche, lost its exclusive patents to the tranquiliser Valium in the 1960s, it faced the real problem of how to generate the same profitability from new drug sources. It invested heavily in research for many years and achieved some success. The real breakthrough in technology, however, was its acquisition of 60 per cent of the shares in the US biotechnology company Genentech in 1990 for US$2 billion. This was a company with sales of US$500 million and hardly any profit, but its acquisition opened up a window of new technology opportunity for Roche.

However, not all organisations are at the white heat of technological development: many parts of the poorer nations and many markets in richer nations rely on more mundane activities for the production of their goods. For example, technology is unlikely to be the main strategy in some of the more traditional parts of the food industry. While some markets may see rapid technological change, others are better seen as being more mature. Technology strategies need to be seen in the context of industry life cycles (*see* Chapter 7).

10.2.2 Discontinuities in technology

Many students will be aware of the powerful, portable personal computers that have coloured liquid crystal displays and are used to undertake complex calculations. These are likely to be battery driven and cost upwards of US$1000. Compare them with the 'calculating aids' that have been available over the last 40 years:

1950s	Slide rules and logarithm tables
1960s	Mechanical calculating machines, each with a turning lever that was cranked around to undertake the calculations
1970s	Large, simple electronic calculators with an electronically-lit display
1980s	The first liquid crystal displays, but the calculations were still simple.

What is striking is not just the change of technology but the drastic implications for those businesses still producing the older versions of the above equipment – for example, the slide rule manufacturers. These companies changed or went out of business many years ago because of a discrete change in the technology – a *discontinuity*.

For shareholders, managers and employees, the impact of a discontinuity on an organisation is significant. It may be caused by anything from a change in fashion to a radically new technology. Essentially, it is a change in the organisation's environment that makes a radical difference to its strategy. One of the more likely reasons for this in the 1990s is a change in technology and its consequent impact on manufacturing.

Due to its radical nature, it is often not possible to predict such a change. It is therefore important, not to predict, but rather to develop a strategy that needs to be followed once a discontinuity has occurred. According to Strebel,[8] there are two distinct phases after such an event has taken place:

- *Development phase.* Competitors attempt to develop the value of the product, its functionality, uses and benefits. An industry standard of performance is developed. Strebel points to the example of the IBM personal computer which set a standard in that market. The phase is often characterised by product innovation, new technologies, new suppliers and new entrants.

- *Consolidation or cost reduction phase.* Having established an industry standard, competition then moves on to produce this at increasingly lower costs. For example in personal computers, Far Eastern manufacturers successfully reduced the cost of personal computer components once the standard was set. The phase will typically include price wars and similar products. The bargaining power may shift from manufacturers to distributors.

At a later stage, Strebel suggests that there may well be another phase that links back towards development again, as technology makes another breakthrough. The cycle may then repeat itself with periods of *divergence* (the development phase) followed by periods of *convergence* (the consolidation or cost reduction phase). It is important for organisations to understand what phase of the industry development they are engaged in and develop appropriate operations and other strategies. Naturally, there will be many that will attempt to analyse or, at least, be sensitive to discontinuities as they begin to occur.

10.2.3 Global activity and cost reductions

During the 1970s and 1980s, the Italian sportswear company Fila slowly transferred its production from Italy to a range of sub-contract manufacturers in the Far East, such as China and Indonesia. Its workforce in Italy declined from 2500 employees in the 1950s, through 1800 in the 1960s to around 250 in the mid-1990s. In 1994, a further 670 employees, spread worldwide, were working on design, distribution, marketing and liaising with their manufacturing operations.

The reason for this shift was that it was the only way for Fila to survive. By 1994, it was around eight times more expensive to produce the goods in Italy than in China. The company faced low-priced competition using low-cost labour and could only respond by moving its own operation onto a global basis.

To take another example from the textile trade, Great Future Textiles Ltd of Taipei was described by the World Bank[9] as an important supplier to Modern Fashions Gmbh in Düsseldorf, Germany. Fashions are designed in Taipei, but are made up in a factory near Bangkok, Thailand. The factory imports cloth from Rajasthan, India, cotton from Texas, USA and yarn from Java, Indonesia. The finished product is air-freighted directly from Bangkok to Düsseldorf. This system is operated to take advantage of the *comparative advantages* of the various nations involved and the low barriers to trade that exist in the world textile industry.

In practice, the world is beginning to return to the policies of free trade of the early twentieth century.[10]

There are two main implications for operations strategy:

1 *World trade barriers have been reduced.* These will come down further as the 1993 GATT Uruguay Round of tariff cuts is implemented over the next few years.

2 *World manufacturing has become more complex.* Some companies now source products in one country and market in another.

More generally, markets around the world have been subject to slower growth and to the attack of new industrial competitor nations, such as Singapore and Malaysia. This had led to pressure on costs, fragmentation in market share, rapid copying of competitors' products and increasing globalisation of market demand. Customers have also become more demanding, especially in terms of quality and value for money. The implication is that production machinery has needed to be more flexible and workers have either been forced to adapt or face the possibility that their company will not survive. Western manufacturers have had to reduce costs and increase quality to remain competitive.

In the consumer electronics market, the two factors identified above have both been at work. Japanese companies such as Sony and Matsushita dominate the world industry. Key components are made in Japan but much of the basic assembly now takes place in the Asian 'Tiger' economies – Singapore, Malaysia, Thailand, Korea and Hong Kong.[11] Components and parts are imported into such countries, assembled using low-cost labour and exported again. This is done inside the countries using free-trade zones which do not attract import and export tariffs and controls. As the Japanese yen increased in value against world currencies in the 1980s, such manufacturing strategies became even more important. If the companies had kept their production in Japan, their products would probably have been priced out of world markets.

The implications for the operations of companies all around the world need to be carefully explored. Importantly, it does *not* automatically follow that all production should be shifted to low labour-cost countries. Higher labour cost countries may have other advantages in terms of higher productivity through better training and knowledge that can offset their labour cost disadvantages. However, such skills are most likely to be best used in the more sophisticated manufacturing operations. In turn, these are likely to be those with higher value added that can support higher labour costs.

Moreover, global activities are only possible for some goods and for services. Other important conditions might include:

● high value-added consumer products that can support the transport costs;

● long shelf-life items that will not perish during transport;

● industrial goods with a high labour cost content.

(*See* Section 10.3.8 for a European context.)

Other considerations apply to *service products*, such as consultancy, restaurants and hotels. If these services require various forms of direct and ongoing contact with the customer, then they are often wholly unsuited to production on the other side of the globe, although they may still be part of a *global services network*.

When considering global manufacturing, operations strategy will need to consider where the balance of cost, services, feasibility and skill is likely to rest over the coming years.

Key strategic principles

● Particularly in the area of operations, new technology can shape future strategy. The pace of change is growing. There are other environmental difficulties facing some companies, especially a lack of awareness of the implications of new manufacturing capacity and the impact of new production techniques.

● Discontinuities, i.e. major changes in technology and markets, can have a substantial impact on strategy. By definition, they are difficult to predict so organisations should sensitise themselves to the environment in these circumstances. Typically, after a discontinuity, industries go through two phases: divergence, which is a development phase, then convergence, which is a cost reduction or consolidation phase.

● The lowering of trade barriers around the world and the movement of some company production to low labour-cost countries has had a significant impact on operations strategy in some industries. However, not all industries are affected by such trends.

Toyota: taking out costs and adding value

Over the last 30 years, Toyota Motor Corporation has become one of the top three global car companies, alongside General Motors (US) and Ford (US). Its rise centres on twin strategies related to operations and marketing. This case study concentrates mainly on its operations successes but also touches briefly on marketing, since the two areas are interlinked. The Toyota operations strategies have been copied around the world.

Background

In the year to end-June 1994, Toyota sold over 4 million vehicles around the world. The company had only started car production in the 1930s. Even in the early 1950s, it was still only averaging 18 000 vehicles per annum.[12] The increase in production and sales between 1950 and 1990 was, by any standards, remarkable.

Many of the production successes between 1950 and 1980 have been accredited to the Toyota Production System and its chief engineer during that time, Taichi Ohno. He started experimenting to improve production in the late 1940s, but it took many years to develop the systems described below, such as *kaizen* and *kanban*, and to have them widely adopted across the company. Even in the 1990s, experimentation and change were still taking place to improve production. Indeed, such change was by definition an *integral* part of the process of achieving production improvements: it was called 'continual improvement'[13] or *kaizen* in Japanese.

During the same period of time, Toyota operated a separate marketing company that essentially sold Toyota production. It was headed by Shotaro Kimaya, who had trained in US marketing methods after the Second World War. He is credited with many marketing innovations in the company during the 1960s and 1970s. They slowly propelled Toyota to market leadership in Japan with over 40 per cent of the market. Among other initiatives, he set up dealer networks, cheap car finance for customers and a strong, dedicated salesforce. He also developed Toyota exports so that by the 1970s around 40 per cent of all production was being sold outside Japan, especially in the USA.[14]

Operations initiatives at Toyota between 1950 and 1980

During this period, Toyota introduced a whole series of operations initiatives that assisted car and truck production – essentially a repetitive, mass-manufacturing process. The new procedures were designed to achieve three main objectives:

1 to reduce costs;
2 to increase quality;
3 to control the production process more tightly, thus reducing the inputs needed and making the company more responsive to market demand.

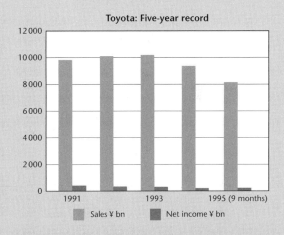

Toyota: Five-year record

The first two objectives had an immediate impact on added value in the plant; the last had an indirect influence on added value. To achieve these objectives, Toyota had a number of key operations strategies:

● *Design*. More costs can be taken out at the design phase of operations than at any other stage. For example, Toyota have consistently used research and development to undertake

| Fig 10.2 | Axle-stand production line at a car accessory factory |

(a) Before Kaizen

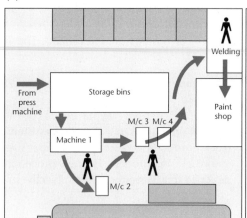

(b) After Kaizen

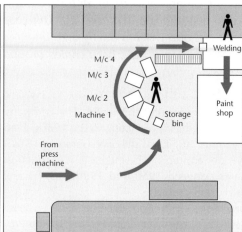

Source: Financial Times, 4 January 1994.

such tasks as combining components together so that they can be produced by one process rather than two.

- *Kaizen*. This means 'continuous improvement' across every aspect of production. Toyota's engineers invented this approach to operations strategy.[15] It is reflected in Toyota's attention to detail that is legendary.[16] The result of *one stage* in Kaizen is shown in Fig 10.2.

- *Kanban system*. This was originally a system of coloured cards on the factory floor that were associated with the amount of stock available for production. These were used to signal when stock needed to be replenished and provided a simple but extremely effective visual system both to tell operatives when to reorder and to keep stocks controlled and low up to that time.

- *Layout*. Instead of long, linear layouts for production lines, cellular layout arrangements of plant machinery were designed. They allowed workers to operate a number of machines and allowed them to work in teams to provide support and backup more effectively. The teams

had to be flexible in their willingness to operate any machinery in the layout and needed to be highly trained to complete the varied range of tasks. Some other Japanese companies, such as Nissan, have had difficulty in achieving the same results,[17] probably because of the sophistication needed to operate this system.

- *Supplier relationships*. Close co-operation was obtained and maintained with a small group of leading suppliers to Toyota. It was used to work jointly on cost reduction schemes and seek higher quality from bought-in components. This was particularly important in the value-added process at Toyota because the company had a higher proportion of bought-in items from suppliers than its main international rivals. This arrangement applied to other companies in Japan but was extended when Toyota opened its plants overseas – for example in 1993 at Burnasten in the UK.[18]

- *Just-in-time systems*. Toyota pioneered the arrival of stock from suppliers using methods which involve close contacts with suppliers. When stocks in the factory run low, they are replaced by stocks from suppliers very rapidly using computer linkages and daily or even more frequent deliveries – *just-in-time for production*. The clear advantage to companies such as Toyota is that their capital investment in stock is permanently kept lower than otherwise. The company is not unique in the use of such systems.

Each of these developments was equally important at Toyota. All contributed to the general improvement in the production efficiency of the company.

By the early 1980s, the Toyota Manufacturing System was being described and recommended for introduction into Western companies.[19] Japanese rivals such as Nissan and Honda also attempted to introduce the same or similar schemes. During the 1990s, the Toyota plant at Takaoda was compared as a model of production against the worst North American plant.[20] Toyota was used as a pointer to the changes required in the USA. However, there are cultural and industry-structure problems that make complete adoption of the Toyota System difficult: for example, team-working and flexibility may be closer to the Japanese model of society than Western cultures.[21] Toyota itself saw the techniques it had developed as being a set of evolving production strategies with no single ideal solution: *kaizen* meant what it said.

Production at Toyota in the 1990s

During the early 1990s, Toyota experienced real problems in the macroeconomic environment. They were:

● downturn in worldwide demand for cars, including for the first time ever a drop in demand in its key Japanese home market;

● significant rise in the value of the Japanese yen, making exports from Japan more expensive.

These developments prompted a major reappraisal of its production methods at the company and a redoubling of efforts to achieve new, lower costs. As a result, all Japanese car manufacturers including Toyota were forced to shift in a major way the focus of their operations strategy from quality and rapid model changes to cost reductions.[22] Toyota responded to the pressures by setting up a major cost reduction programme. By 1994, the company was claiming that it had found savings at an annual rate of US$1.5 billion.[23]

Some would question how Toyota could have been so efficient during the 1980s if it was still able to generate such massive savings in the 1990s. They might point to the Toyota Annual Accounts which showed that the ratio of sales to inventories actually dropped from 26.1 in 1993 to 23.5 in 1994. Essentially, this showed that it was turning over its inventories more slowly in 1994 than the previous year. In fact, it was the *finished stock* component of inventories (for example, completed cars) that rose rapidly, as the company kept its factories operating even though sales had dropped worldwide. Hence, even the Toyota Production System was subject to the pressures of worldwide demand and the implications for production at its factories.

Toyota said that such difficulties made it work even harder. *Kaizen* became even more significant. For example, Toyota's Annual Report for 1994 states:

> *People in Toyota plants and offices in Japan came forward with 929 257 ideas for improvements in the past year. And workplace teams implemented 99 per cent of those ideas.*

However, *kaizen* also implies criticism and Toyota had no intention of hiding its past errors in the 1990s. In the same document, it admitted that there had been a mood of complacency in the company during the 1980s:

> *Business was good. We might not have been as efficient as we could have been. But we were able to turn a profit and keep our people employed without subjecting ourselves to the rigors of lean production. Then came the slump. That lit a fire in us.*

Personal and team motivation were then renewed and remain an important part of the Toyota system.

According to the *Annual Report 1995*, the result has been that, 'Everyone has become an expert at identifying waste and discovering ways to eliminate it.' There is more training, further expansion of *kaizen* into new areas of the company such as the distribution and logistics system[24] and the salesforce:[25] the same levels of stock in warehouses and car showrooms are no longer required to provide the same service.

At the same time, the company has continued

to win awards for the quality of its products from national quality bodies in countries such as the USA and Germany.[26]

CASE QUESTIONS

1 Using the definition of corporate strategy in Chapter 1, identify which of the operations strategies undertaken by Toyota (kaizen, kanban, design, etc.) have a corporate strategy perspective and which are mainly the concern of operations management alone.

2 Examining the Toyota Manufacturing System overall, to what extent do you judge this to be critical to the company's strategic success? If you believe it to be critical, then how does this fit with strategy theories that lay stress on the market aspects of corporate strategy, such as Porter's Five Forces Model? If you believe operations to be relatively unimportant, then how do you explain the remarkable success of Toyota globally since the 1950s?

3 Some commentators argue that it is relatively easy for market leaders such as Toyota to undertake the investment in machinery and training programmes to achieve strategic success but more difficult for smaller organisations. Do small companies have anything to learn from Toyota? If so, what?

4 The case describes how Toyota became complacent in the 1980s. Do you believe that this was the company's main strategic problem in the 1990s or does it lie elsewhere?

10.3 THE ROLE OF OPERATIONS IN ADDING VALUE AND ACHIEVING SUSTAINABLE COMPETITIVE ADVANTAGE

10.3.1 Value added, competitive advantage and operations strategy

Operations strategy has two major structural constraints:

1 Operations resources take time to plan and build: for example, many factories take years.

2 Once installed, they are difficult and expensive to change: for example, bulldozing the completed factory is not an easy option.

Moreover, resource analysis in the operations area is *complex* because it often involves the bulk of the organisation's assets and employees.

Ideally, operations strategy really needs to be split into a series of separate, but interlinked, analyses. Each of these would cover the different parts of the operations process and would be different for each organisation. Porter's *value chain* from Chapter 7 can be used as a starting point for such studies (*see* Fig. 10.3). Importantly, much of this is *not* corporate strategy, in the sense that the detailed day-to-day operations are outside the definition of corporate strategy. Nevertheless, corporate strategy will set the *focus*, *agenda* and *priorities* in these areas – for example, on issues such as which customers take priority, how quality is improved, the relationships between subsidiaries of the same company. The strategies are then translated into decisions that are then followed in detail by the managers concerned.

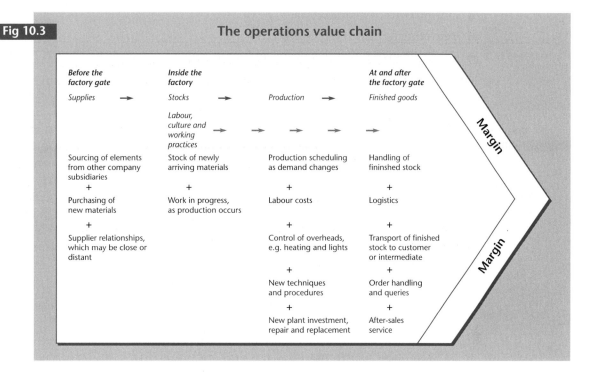

Fig 10.3   The operations value chain

Before the factory gate	Inside the factory		At and after the factory gate
Supplies →	Stocks →	Production →	Finished goods
	Labour, culture and working practices →		
Sourcing of elements from other company subsidiaries	Stock of newly arriving materials	Production scheduling as demand changes	Handling of fininshed stock
+	+	+	+
Purchasing of new materials	Work in progress, as production occurs	Labour costs	Logistics
+		+	+
Supplier relationships, which may be close or distant		Control of overheads, e.g. heating and lights	Transport of finished stock to customer or intermediate
		+	+
		New techniques and procedures	Order handling and queries
		+	+
		New plant investment, repair and replacement	After-sales service

When dealing with strategy in such tangible areas as building a new factory or producing an existing product, corporate strategy might be primarily *prescriptive* rather
than *emergent* in its approach: after all, the factory or product is a physical entity. In
practice, the corporate strategy of operations resources has elements of *both*.

● After taking the strategic decision to build a new factory, the actual building
process will typically be lengthy. The decision to embark on this process can
only be based on assumptions and predictions about the future. Moreover, in
existing factories, sales estimates are often required in advance of the sales order
actually being taken, so that production can be scheduled smoothly and at the
lowest costs. This is essentially *prescriptive* in its strategic approach.

● However, after the new factory has been built and certainly in existing sites,
many aspects of the production process rely heavily on worker attitudes, culture
and motivation. Typically, change is undertaken in small steps. Some companies even refer to this process as 'continuous improvement' with no specified
final end-point. This is essentially *emergent* in its strategic direction.

10.3.2   Operations' contributions to value and competitive advantage

These can be grouped into six areas:

● market adaptability;

● winning against competition;

● adding value through enhanced performance or service;

- cutting costs of manufacture;
- delivering human resource objectives;
- the link between manufacturing and marketing.

The additional task of improving quality and dependability will be explored in Chapter 11.

Market adaptability Where a repetitive product is being made by mass-production such as a car or food product, there is usually a need to match production of an individual type, brand, model, colour, etc. with consumer demand. Otherwise significant costs may be incurred in holding finished stock. *Production needs adapt to market demand.* This is an important part of the production/marketing interface and is well described in the literature (*see*, for example, Hill[27] and Wild[28]). However, the detailed planning that is necessary does not take place at the level of corporate planning. It is a day-to-day or week-to-week task depending on the length of time it takes to produce variations in the products and the nature of the customers.

There are two corporate strategy aspects of market adaptability:

1 *The extent to which an organisation will wish to respond to individual customer needs.* In essence, this will depend on two balancing factors:

   - the size of the customer's individual order – whether it is sufficiently large enough to justify the time and costs of producing a product that is specialised to that customer; and
   - the capacity and adaptability of the production machinery to reduce the costs involved.

2 *The contribution that market adaptability might make to beating competition.* Some customers may find the option of customised production highly attractive.

Winning against competition The development of manufacturing strategy to win orders against competition is an important aspect of operations resource analysis. Hill[29] explains that this process may be market-led but manufacturing has a major role in two areas: contributing to the debate and delivering the successful products that beat competitors.

Adding value through enhanced performance or service We explored this in Chapter 7. Many of the operations areas are directly concerned with adding value to the supplies that are brought into the company. Although the detail of such matters does not come within corporate strategy, the basic arrangements made by the organisation are at the centre of the strategy process.

Value can be added to a product not just by physical production but also by the performance or the quality of the service that is related to the product. Technology can also contribute to product added value by providing new opportunities and variations from competition.

Cutting costs of manufacture As the Toyota case showed, many of the strategies in the operations area have the basic objective of cutting costs. For the sake of clarity, it is important to distinguish here between the *objective* of cutting costs – for example, in order to raise profits at Toyota – and the *strategy* by which this is achieved – for example, by redeploying labour in the Toyota plant.

Delivering human resources objectives

This objective is naturally a part of the human resource analysis of the company. In addition, it appears here for two reasons:

- the large number of people often employed in the operations function;
- the crucial need, in many instances, to obtain the co-operation of such people in order to deliver the other objectives.

The link between manufacturing and marketing

From the above factors, it will be evident that successful operations strategy demands that there is a strong link between these two functional areas. Hill[30] lists five steps to achieving this:

Step 1   Define corporate objectives.
Step 2   Determine marketing strategies to meet these objectives.
Step 3   Assess how different products win orders against competitors.
Step 4   Establish the most appropriate mode to manufacture these sets of products – *process choice*.
Step 5   Provide the manufacturing infrastructure required to support production.

Importantly, it is essential to see the steps as *sequential,* but also *interactive,* with feedback loops connecting the first three in particular.

Key strategic principles

- Operations faces two structural constraints: the length of time to build new resources and the difficulty of altering them once they are installed. For these reasons, it is useful to apply the value chain concept to the process and analyse every element individually.

- It is essential to clarify the purposes to be served by operations and technologies strategies, because they are complex and may need to be prioritised.

- Market adaptability, winning against competition, added value through enhanced performance or service, cutting the costs of manufacture, improved quality and human resource objectives are the main elements that need to be considered.

- The five steps that enable marketing and manufacturing strategy to link together are a vital part of the development of operations analysis. They will determine the manufacturing processes and infrastructure required for the corporate strategy.

Cutting costs and increasing customer satisfaction at SKF[31]

Roller Bearings are used virtually every time a wheel turns. The Swedish company SKF is the largest manufacturer in the world. During the early 1990s, they introduced what they called 'the new industrial revolution' to transform their production processes around the world. The company describes below how they developed their new strategy.

A production company working on low profit margins needs to be paid as quickly as possible by its customers. Moreover, it cannot afford to purchase large volumes of materials in advance. It is necessary to reduce lead times – that is the time between order and delivery. It also requires using only the minimum materials to complete the order required.

In the past, companies like SKF achieved highly creditable results in the development of production processes. With constantly improving machine technology, the time required for a machine to produce a bearing has been reduced by 95 per cent during the past four decades. However, even financial analysts with no insight into production processes could see that in the late 1980s lead times were too long. They simply had to compare the inventories in the balance sheet with the annual sales of SKF. Among the reasons were:

● The production process required an excessive amount of work in progress.

● A portion of the benefits deriving from the efficient manufacturing process was lost due to products constantly forming bottlenecks at various intermediate storage phases in the plants.

SKF customers who knew that a product only required a few hours of effective manufacturing time wondered why they had to wait up to four months for the processing of a special order.

Comparison with competition

Although comparisons with other leading bearing manufacturers in 1990 showed that SKF was a little better than its main German competitor, FAG, they also showed that Japanese competitors turned over their inventory quicker than either company.

In Japan, awareness of the importance of lead times is so great that the country's leading banks

use it as a ratio in their lending activities. Any company whose lead times are more than 100 times greater than the manufacturing time on the machines is refused credit. Instead they are recommended to release funds from their inventories. For a company to be ranked favourably, its lead times must not exceed ten times its manufacturing time.

By comparison, European companies can have lead times that are a thousand times greater than manufacturing time. However, this has been changing rapidly with many European companies

SKF: Seven-year record

changing their approach. In future, an ever-growing portion of the flow of products will be manufactured against a direct order. By 1992, SKF itself had reorganised to achieve such changes with most of the company now using new organisational forms.

Changes in production procedures at SKF

In the early stages of the reorganisation, it was inevitable that the production channels for particular products would cross each other, since certain machines and people were shared by several channels. In time, this pattern was expected to change so that each channel ran independently and much more directly. The individual worker was no longer responsible for a particular process but instead shared responsibility for entire production channel flow. The result was measured for entire channels rather than one manufacturing process. This also changed the basis for cost accounting. SKF accountants claimed:

> This was a change for the better... Now we have a language that can be understood by everybody, not just production technicians.

Initially, the focus was on reducing the size of the various intermediate inventories. Levels were halved in just a few years, releasing SEK 600 million and saving the interest expenses that would otherwise have resulted from such capital. However, according to SKF, that was not the most important part of the achievement.

The whole process was like reducing the water level in a power station reservoir. One obstacle after another was revealed as the water receded. In a plant with substantial intermediate inventories, it was difficult to identify where the production bottle-necks were actually located. There was a considerable risk that time and resources were sometimes allocated to flow difficulties that did not even exist. The real benefit was that it was now possible to identify the real problems.

The differences between the old and new systems are shown in Table 10.1. The company commented that not everyone was able to handle the mental adjustment and most people had problems, at least at the beginning. In essence, these problems arose because the nature of the job changed: it moved from consisting of small, individual demarcated duties to less well defined team joint responsibility work on the complete flow. Moreover, the formal barriers between salaried staff and shop floor workers were removed and a complete level of management in the company disappeared.

Table 10.1 Comparing the old and the new at SKF

Old system	New channel system
Pressure from organisation	Stimula from customer orders
Planned system	System reacts
Uniform flow desirable	Only exactly the amount needed is produced
Few machine resettings	Many resettings
Buffer inventories	Natural flows
Planning in stages	Information integrated into the system
Bottlenecks hidden by buffer inventories	Bottlenecks clearly visible and priorities made
High quality costs more	High quality costs less
Substantial investments	Minor investments
Shop floor personnel and staff	Team-mates
Permanent positions at a work station	Flexible positions in a work area
Follow the rule book	Act on own initiative
Others monitor quality	The team measures its own performance
Always do as much production as possible	Do only what is necessary at exactly the right time
Work-point based cost accounting	Accounting by channel
Functional organisation in plant	Flow organisation: each channel contains built-in functions
Achieve best possible results	Eliminate faults
Major improvement campaigns to make changes	Many small regular improvements

The pressure to which some individuals were exposed was significantly greater than what they had previously experienced and against which they were helpless as individuals. However, team members did have the opportunity to influence factors causing the stress and the system was eventually supported by most at SKF.

Progress using the new system

In 1989, it took 18 weeks for a roller bearing order to proceed from raw material to delivery of the finished product, of which lead time relating to steel operations accounted for eight weeks. At the end of 1992, the average time had been reduced to 12 weeks with a goal of 9 weeks by the end of 1993. At the same time, manufacturing inventories had been halved between 1989 and 1992, as had the number of reject products. Over several years, it was hoped to reduce this by a further 50 per cent, but this process had no finite end goal.

Because flow had improved, there were fewer bottlenecks, less reprocessing and fewer unnecessary stages. There were fewer opportunities to make mistakes and the intensity of the production process meant that those on the production learnt

more. Consequently, quality was also improved and motivation increased with reduced employee absenteeism and turnover. SKF commented that the new self-instructional units had replaced the large bureaucratic production systems based on the principles of Taylorism.

Source: Adapted from the SKF 1992 Annual Report and Accounts. Used with permission.

CASE QUESTIONS

1 *What were the principle objectives of SKF in introducing the changes they proposed? How do they compare with the list of possible objectives in Section 10.3?*

2 *The case describes a number of detailed procedures adopted by the company to improve productivity at its main factories: to what extent do you regard such processes as being part of corporate strategy? And, in contrast, detailed manufacturing strategy?*

3 *SKF described the impact on workers of the changes they had implemented. Would the impact have been less if they had discussed the procedures further before they were introduced? What would have been the problems of such discussion?*

10.4 OPERATIONS AND TECHNOLOGY STRATEGY

In examining this area from a corporate strategy perspective, the difficulty is the large number of possible strategies that are available. There are dangers for the analytical process from:

● becoming immersed in the detail that is important to those undertaking the strategy but largely irrelevant to the corporate strategist;

● failing to identify those strategies that will have a *real* impact on the future direction of the business, as against those that are useful but not crucial.

Corporate strategy really needs to confine itself to an awareness of the areas to be probed and a sense of priority regarding the areas that will deliver the organisation's objectives. A strong analysis will start by considering this matter rather than plunging into long lists of specific strategies. As guidance, the criteria shown in Table 10.2 are suggested. With these words of caution, we can now turn to consider the areas that may need to be analysed in more detail. We tackle this under several headings that broadly follow the way that value is added during the manufacturing process and link with basic texts in this area:[32]

- Make or buy?
- Supplier relationships
- Manufacturing strategy
- Product design prior to manufacture
- Factory layout and processes
- Logistics and transport
- Human resource implications
- International manufacturing
- Conclusions

Table 10.2 Criteria for the relevance of manufacturing strategy to corporate strategy

Strategic area	Issues to be explored
Organisation objectives	Possible impact? Some strategies may be more important than others.
Added value	To what extent does the strategy add significant value?
'What if?' questions	Explore what would happen if certain conditions were changed and assess the impact on objectives – e.g. what would happen if we were able to reduce supply prices by 10%? Would this have a substantial impact or not make much difference?
Key factors for success	In Chapter 7, we explored this area. They may well guide the selection of the most appropriate manufacturing strategies.
Human resource implications	Operations strategy often involves change in working practices, responsibilities and reporting relationships. Some strategies may be difficult to operate unless these human factors are explored against the organisation's human resource objectives.

10.4.1 Make or buy?

Instead of buying products from suppliers, some manufacturers will choose to make the products themselves. The strategic decision on the best route to take is complex but can be summarised as:

Make, when:

- the company has specialised needs;
- it needs to have a really secure source of supply; or
- the cost of supply is a high part of the total costs.

Buy, when:

- the company wants to maintain flexibility in its sources of supply;
- the company has only limited skills and resources in the supplier's area.

The decision is clearly related to *vertical integration* of the organisation back into its suppliers. However, in the case of such integration, the company would actively market the products that formerly came from its supplier, as against merely supplying its own factories.

Analysis will clearly need to examine not just the costs of each alternative make-or-buy decision but also the skills, resources needed and broader strategic direction of the company. It will also look at what competitors do and explore the reasons for any differences.

10.4.2 Supplier relationships

Two different and opposing trends[33] can be observed in the strategies adopted by manufacturing companies:

- *Closer relationships with suppliers.* As used by Toyota, this will involve sharing technical and development information in order to lower the cost of the finished product. It implies closer co-operation over many years, often with a small number of key suppliers. Inevitably, some of the value added is passed from the manufacturer to the supplier. However, it can help to drive down costs overall and raise quality.

- *More distant relationships with suppliers.* This will involve aggressive negotiating to obtain the lowest possible price for an agreed specification. For example, Saab Cars (part-owned by General Motors) actually telephoned its suppliers of car mirrors twice a day for two weeks requesting lower quotes before deciding.[34] In this case, supplier relationships are at arms length and obtain the lowest prices. However, there may be only limited involvement in the development process and the contributions to quality improvement are strictly defined rather than a joint ideas process. This supplier system is used by General Motors and Volkswagen, Germany (who recruited the GM Purchasing Director in 1994).

As described in Section 10.2.3, there is also increasing *globalisation* in the sourcing of supplies. This makes the purchasing task more complex and demanding.

10.4.3 Manufacturing strategy

To analyse this area, it is useful to examine the six basic areas of manufacturing strategy. In addition to the make-or-buy decision above, there are five other key areas:[35]

- *Factory location and size.* Most organisations start with an existing configuration from one site to several. For example, Ford Motors has a number of plants in several different European countries; each has different products and capacities and many are linked together in the production chain.

- *Processes.* Each factory will have certain types of equipment and procedures for making products, dealing with variations in demand and so on. For example, Toyota makes different models at different plants; each plant has different production equipment relevant to the models at that location. Each factory has links with sales to vary demand accordingly.

● *Production capacity*. From a strategic perspective, the capacity of the plant to meet customer demand is an important consideration. Clearly, in the long term this will change as markets grow and decline. In addition, there are short-term plant capacity scheduling issues which are largely outside the interest of corporate strategy. For example, Chapter 3 explored the strategic implications of excess production capacity in the European steel industry.

● *Manufacturing infrastructure*. Planning and control of stocks, quality, work-in-progress inventories and the flow of goods are vital to factories. The overall principles by which this is done are part of corporate strategy but the detail is not. For example, Case study 10.2 on SKF showed how the company introduced the principles and then allowed the factory floor to follow them up.

● *Links with other functions*. Manufacturing has started to move towards production that meets *precise* customer demand through *flexible manufacturing*. This is only possible from close links with sales. The *range of the products* that are manufactured will also depend on such links. In both cases, there are often economies of scale from manufacturing a limited range in large quantities, but this may not match market demand. With new modern flexible equipment and telecommunications links, a new strategy may be to introduce shorter production runs and rapid changeover to other products. For older plant and some manufacturing processes, a *compromise* is needed and this is a strategic decision. For example, the prime objective of a factory which regularly produces six months' supply of some confectionery lines, such as Hazlenut Brittle, is to reduce the cost of its production, rather than the cost of its finished goods stock and the fresh quality of its finished product.

Overall, Skinner[36] comments that:

1 It is not necessary to be the lowest cost producer – quality and service being more important for some customers – but this implies an understanding of competition and how they compete on costs, quality and service.

2 Factories need to *compromise* regarding a number of variables. For example, the flexible, low-volume product with frequent model changes needs to be balanced by the lower costs of large-volume production runs and the stock-holding that may result. Another example is the need for investment to increase plant capacity against the need to house it in a new building because existing ones are full.

3 Simple repetitive tasks in mass-manufacturing are more likely to lead factories down the cost experience curve described in Chapter 7.

10.4.4 Product design prior to manufacturing

In some cases, up to 70 per cent of the cost of manufacturing a product is determined at the design stage – that is, before the product ever reaches the factory.[37] The reason is that it is at the design stage that major savings can be made on components, plant and procedures. It is more difficult to make them once products have reached the factory floor because of the inflexibility of installed machinery and the high cost of changing over time.

Design procedures might include analysing the product for the *number of parts* it contains: the smaller the number, the quicker it will be to assemble. Procedures might also cover *methods of assembling the product*. For example, by careful design, it may be possible to put the product together without using a machine to grip or hold the product (commonly called a *jig*). The advantage of such a procedure is that any variation in the product might involve resetting the jig, which takes unproductive time and adds no value to the product. Clearly, the detail of such procedures is not part of corporate strategy but the *principle* of careful and adequate expenditure on design is vital.

In addition, efficiency in the design procedures themselves has become an important element in the process. It can take years to design some products with all the consequent costs involved. If time can be saved, this reduces the cost of the process. For example, Renault Cars (France) announced a new design and development facility in 1995 costing US$1.22 billion.[38] The aim was to reduce design time from 58 months to 38 months for a new car launch in the year 2000. The facility's current cost per car was between US$1 and 5 billion depending on the model: this would be reduced by US$200 million per model simply by producing each design more quickly.

Again, analysis of this topic needs a study of *competition*. For example, Renault may have invested a large absolute amount in design but comparison with the amounts invested by other car companies would show:

- whether it would improve the French company's competitive position; or
- simply mean that Renault was catching up with others, especially some Japanese car companies.

10.4.5 Factory layout and procedures

Within an existing factory installation, it is possible to make substantial cost savings and other improvements by changes in the factory layout. For example, Case study 10.2 showed how changes in factory procedures at SKF had a dramatic effect on three areas:

- *Efficiency* – the output increased.
- *Stock control* – stocks employed reduced substantially.
- *Quality* – significant improvements were obtained.

In the case of SKF, these three improvements arose primarily from how the factory machinery was laid out and operated. Seven central principles of such procedures can be identified and analysed:[39]

1 *Eliminate waste.* All excess stock is removed from the factory floor. All excess movements of workers beyond those required to complete the manufacturing task are eliminated.

2 *One-piece production.* All the consecutive processes necessary to make one piece are undertaken by one worker at one work location, where possible. This can be contrasted with the Taylorist approach, where one worker repeatedly made only a small part of the piece and then passed it along for another part to be added by another worker, each having inventory and set-up time to keep production flowing.

3 *Elimination of low value-added processes.* Walking between machines, waiting, carrying parts and setting up equipment such as jigs are all reduced, where possible.

4 *Team-working.* Teams support each other in multi-skilled roles, looking after a number of machines and moving flexibly to solve problems as they occur.

5 *Factory floor responsibility.* Team workers can stop the production line to clear faults. They can make improvements and changes without seeking prior permission. Responsibility is broader and more comprehensive at the workplace. Continuous discussion of the best procedures is encouraged.

6 *Automation is used only where it really assists the process.* Instead of the moving assembly line of traditional plants, there may be flexible computer-controlled individual transportation of products.

7 *Attention to detail.* Every aspect is explored and investigated.

Clearly, the detail of most of the above is not part of corporate strategy, but the basic introduction of the whole process certainly is a part, not only in terms of the machinery but also the change in mental attitude of the workforce.

10.4.6 Logistics and transport

Once the product is ready to leave the factory, there are further decisions on two areas:

- *Logistics* – where to hold the finished product, in what quantity and with what delivery schedule to customers; and

- *Transport* – what product to send, in what economic delivery quantity, by what transport method and from what location.

Essentially, these decisions involve a balance between the customers, who might like small amounts of the product frequently, and the costs involved in such lengthy and detailed procedures. According to Christopher,[40] there are five basic elements to balance in the analytical process:

1 *Facility decisions.* This involves deciding where warehouses and factories are to be located. Clearly, this is a long-term issue.

2 *Inventory decisions.* Stockholding has a cost but may be necessary to provide adequate customer service.

3 *Communications decisions.* Information is essential to deliver the correct goods to the customer. Thus, ordering, processing and invoicing goods all form part of the essential information. A system for handling normal customer queries and complaints is also needed.

4 *Utilisation decisions.* Pallets, containers and other means of transporting the goods need to be resolved.

5 *Transport decisions.* The method of transport, ownership, leasing or hiring of vehicles all need resolution; the choice of road, rail, ship and air may all be key decisions.

As Lynch comments,[41] the balance of these issues will vary with the type of industry, as well as with the customer. It will also depend on competitors and the level of service that they are offering. Industry distribution costs for the above have been published and provide a basis for comparison for national and international expansion.

10.4.7 Human resource implications

When the Norwegian engineering company Kvaerner acquired the Govan shipyard in Scotland in 1988, it needed to boost productivity dramatically (*see* Case study at beginning of chapter).[42] Part of the change came through the investment of US$52 million in the yard by the new owners. However, just as important, the company introduced new procedures for working that involved many of the concepts described above. They involved:

- devolved responsibility;
- frequent progress reports to management on progress;
- improved internal communications;
- changed staff attitudes;
- shared responsibility and commitment;
- joint management and workers committee to monitor progress.

In each of the cases, there was a significant human resource element that needed to be analysed during the formative phase of the corporate strategy process. The impact on workers, their attitudes and the degree of co-operation required are all important elements to be estimated in assessing the feasibility of strategy. Specifically, worker participation is a key element in many aspects of manufacturing strategy.

10.4.8 International manufacturing

Manufacturing strategies have been developed that cover *regions* of the world, such as the North American Free Trade Area, Association of South-East Asian Nations and the European Union. As an example of pan-regional activity, the *European single market* was designed to help deliver economies of scale, reduce excess production capacity, integrate operations across the EU and deliver significant cost savings to companies.

In 1994, Collins and Schmenner[43] surveyed 93 European manufacturing companies to examine how, if at all, they had benefited from this change in their environment. Many of the strategies described in this chapter had been employed across Europe over this period. At least 70 per cent of the companies had achieved increased standardisation of company products and operations over the previous five to ten years. In the area of product quality, the standardisation percentage was even higher. Obstacles to pan-European manufacturing strategies among the sample are shown in Table 10.3. They show the importance of human relations factors in achieving the results: power, status and esteem have been threatened as factory responsibility has been shifted from national companies to a pan-European operation.

Table 10.3 Obstacles to pan-European manufacturing strategies

Obstacle	Percentage of respondents citing each criterion	
	Process industries	Non-process industries
Reorganisation would involve demotion of senior executives and a loss of status or esteem	45	40
Moving personnel from country to country	33	39
Cultural differences among managers that affect attitudes, performance, etc.	38	34
Governmental regulations	26	29
Problems in harmonising products from different countries	29	17
Union/management relations	19	23
Environmental concerns	24	6
Incompatible computer-based informations systems	12	23
Incompatible cost or performance measurement systems	10	14
Unchanging, uncompromising tastes or fashions in consumers	7	3
Other obstacles cited	12	9

Source: Reprinted from *European Management Journal*, Vol 13(3), R Collins and R Schmenner, 'Taking manufacturing advantage of Europe's single market', p257, copyright 1995, with kind permission of Elsevier Science Ltd, The Boulevard, Langford Lane, Kidlington, OX5 1GB, UK.[44]

10.4.9 Conclusions

There are some broader lessons to be learned from the research. The increased standardisation has allowed some companies to tackle such problems as:

- over-capacity in production;
- stock reduction;
- critical production mass from fewer locations;
- more efficient transport and logistics operations;
- better planning, processes and procedures.

To summarise operations strategy, there are ten guidelines for analysing the operations and technology manufacturing strategies of organisations. These are shown in Exhibit 10.1.

| Exhibit 10.1 | Ten guidelines for analysing operations and technology manufacturing strategy |

1 Does the company buy or make all its supplies? How do competitors handle this decision?

2 What relationship does the company have with its suppliers? Distant or close? Why?

3 Where is value added in the production process? What stage of the production process is really important? How does this compare with competition?

4 What is the role of technology? High? Low? What investment normally takes place in R &D? How does this compare with competition?

5 How does at least one competitor organise its production? What factories? Stock levels? Age of factories, plant and machinery? Investment programmes? Comparative costs?

6 How is production organised in our own factories? What factories and departments? What machines and workflow? How old are the machines and what is their capacity? What costs of production? How does the organisation, its machinery and costs compare with competition?

7 How are stocks organised and controlled? Before, during and after production? How does competition organise this area?

8 What is the style of operation? Centre dominated? Workplace and co-operative?

9 How are links organised with other departments? Are they good or poor?

10 Is there organised labour? And what is its role and style? Co-operative or conflict?

Key strategic principles

- Before starting on a detailed analysis of manufacturing strategy, it is useful to establish what areas are particularly important. Six tests can be employed to assist this process but it is essentially judgmental.

- Whether a company makes or buys in its products will depend on the balance between the costs and benefits of the two routes. It is useful to explore what competitors do in this area.

- Supplier relationships can be close or distant. This will depend on the company's basic management style and culture. There are no conclusive reasons for choosing one approach.

- Manufacturing strategy is complex and depends on a number of inter-related factors: factory location, size, production capacity and infrastructure. In addition, links with other functions such as sales are important in determining both efficiencies and customer service. Comparison with competition is an important element in the analysis.

Key strategic principles continued

- With many products, greater cost savings are achieved during the design stage of the process than during the subsequent procedures. Expenditure in this area usually has a clear positive payback. Competitor expenditure and effort in this area needs also to be analysed.

- Factory layout and procedures need to be governed by attention to detail and co-operation with the workforce. Coupled with specific techniques, the corporate strategy interest lies mainly in initiating the task rather than in the detail that then follows.

- Logistics and transport need careful planning both to reduce costs and to provide adequate service to customers. The level of service that competitors offer will be a factor in deciding the optimal configuration.

- The human resource implications of all the above need to be considered during the analysis phase of corporate strategy, not later.

CASE STUDY 10.3

ISS cleans up against its European competitors[45]

The Danish office cleaning company, ISS, has a major task ensuring that its operational procedures and services are the same across Europe

With much of its work done in the hours of darkness, the cleaning business occupies a twilight zone of the service industry. Yet providing sparkling environments for offices, hospitals and industrial premises can offer Europe-wide growth opportunities comparable to those in much higher-profile sectors.

ISS, the Danish cleaning group which is the world's leader in this field, has built up a European network of high-quality cleaners. Mr Waldemar Schmidt, the 53-year-old Managing Director of ISS's European operations, responsible for turnover of US$500 million a year, says: 'If other people can have pan-European businesses, we asked ourselves, why shouldn't this apply to cleaning?'

Cleaning is traditionally a fragmented, regional business, given scant attention by customers. By offering high standards and encouraging companies to take a cost-conscious look at their cleaning bills, ISS claims it can lower overheads and promote efficiency. The company prides itself on higher wages and better training than competitors. Mr Theo Dilissen, Managing Director of Belgian operations comments:

> Cleaning is generally thought of as a job nobody wants to do. We offer incentives and training courses so people can upgrade. Our workforce is our product. We're helping customers to become competitive.

ISS customers range from multinationals, such as IBM, Philips and Monsanto, to the European Commission, and Vienna and Geneva airports. Cleaning budgets can be surprisingly large. The annual cleaning costs of ASEA Brown Boveri, the international engineering group, exceed US$75 million. 'If you have an in-house cleaning team, it's not part of the core business,' says Mr Schmidt. He believes the key to better productivity is to bring in quality-conscious outsiders, sometimes combining cleaning with other duties.

Under a 1994 contract with Slovenian railways, ISS arranged to have 300 cleaners on the country's trains and stations (down from 600 previously). In an annual US$3 million contract with the British Airports Authority, 130 ISS cleaners work in three shifts at Heathrow's Terminal One. They are encouraged not merely to sweep floors but also to give directions to travellers. ISS is also developing additional services for its hospital customers, such as catering, portering, technical maintenance and equipment supply.

With 120 000 employees in 20 countries, ISS was present in 1994 in every main European country apart from France and Italy. Its share of the cleaning market was between 20 and 40 per cent in Scandinavia where it was market leader. Its share in the UK was 6 per cent, where it is the number three cleaning company, and its share in Germany was 2 per cent, where it was the number eight.

Mr Schmidt says expansion is customer-driven. Many companies still undertake their own cleaning

and do not contract this out to outside companies such as ISS. Mr Schmidt estimates annual growth rates of the 'contracted out' cleaning market at 5 per cent in Austria, Switzerland, Germany and France, 7 per cent in the UK and 10 per cent in Belgium and Greece. If ISS is right, more and more companies will be coming round to the view that cleanliness and competitiveness belong together.

Source: Financial Times 1 March 1994.

CASE QUESTIONS

1 *In what way does the case indicate that ISS undertakes to ensure that its services are of the same high standard across Europe?*

2 *What are the similarities between a manufacturing and a service business in terms of operations strategy? And what are the differences?*

3 *Can service companies learn lessons from manufacturing experience in operating pan-European businesses?*

10.5 SERVICE OPERATIONS STRATEGY

A survey of research published in the area of operations strategy,[46] seemed to show that most of the research has concentrated on *manufacturing* strategy – that is strategy that is concerned with making products in factories – and yet, in 1989, *services* such as telecommunications, travel and banking accounted for almost 50 per cent of the Gross Domestic Product of Japan and the European Union and 54 per cent in the USA.[47] Moreover, the services sector continued to grow faster than manufacturing.

From an operations strategy perspective, the difficulty is that services have a number of major differences from products, for example:

● *Retail banking counter services* depend heavily on the performance of the employees behind the counter at the time of the service. The employees are part of the product.

● *Rail commuter services* cannot be stored as finished goods in a warehouse.

Service operations involve people and immediate responses that need special consideration when it comes to operations strategy development.

10.5.1 Services and products compared

Although there are differences in *nature* between products and services, it is important to keep this in perspective, since there are likely to be service elements in the supply of most products. The service content might range from a pre-sales personalised training course to an after-sales maintenance contract. From the extensive research on services marketing, five main differences between services and products have been identified and these are outlined in Table 10.4.[48]

Table 10.4 The five main differences between services and products

Distinguishing features at the point of service	Description	Example	Impact on operations strategic analysis
Intangibility	Cannot be seen or tasted like a product	● Bank counter service ● Airline booking	More difficult to define but important for setting standards. Hence, difficult to analyse
Inseparability	● Cannot be separated from the person of the seller ● Consuming and selling may be undertaken at virtually the same time	● Telephone selling of car insurance ● McDonald's 'Big Mac'	● High reliance on the people delivering the service ● Need for careful selection and training
Heterogeneity	● Difficult to standardise service output ● Reliant on human element	● Hospital in-patient care ● Reception welcome at Holiday Inns Hotel	Decision on whether it is necessary, desirable or even possible to standardise service
Perishability	Services cannot be stored	● Empty hotel room ● Telephone call not made	● Concept of stock may be irrelevant ● Strategy needs to address issue of immediate utilisation of service
Ownership	Customer may not own what is being consumed	Cinema, night club, football stadium	No physical need for logistics and transport

In addition to the five distinguishing features at the point of service, there will also be various *tangible* elements that are clearly product-oriented. For example, telephone lines, hotel beds, hospital reception areas and advertising agency studios are physical areas that are part of the service. These areas are part of the operation. They can be quantified and be the subject of a normal manufacturing-type analysis – for example, a stock analysis.

10.5.2 The value chain in operations services

It is now possible to examine how the value chain will change for services operations (*see* Fig 10.4). Many of the early operations aspects do not change radically. For example, there is still a need to obtain raw materials and also likely to be a requirement for after-sales service, albeit of a different kind. In truth, many service businesses rely heavily on *repeat business*, in just the same way as many products. This directs the operations task closer to that of products than might otherwise be the case.

10.5.3 Implications for the analysis of service operations strategy

With the growing importance of service industries, the detail of their operations strategy needs careful analysis. It will be evident that many of the early aspects of the analysis are not significantly different from manufacturing: at least the same elements apply in principle. Where services differ is in *the direct customer interface*. It is here that operations need to be redefined.

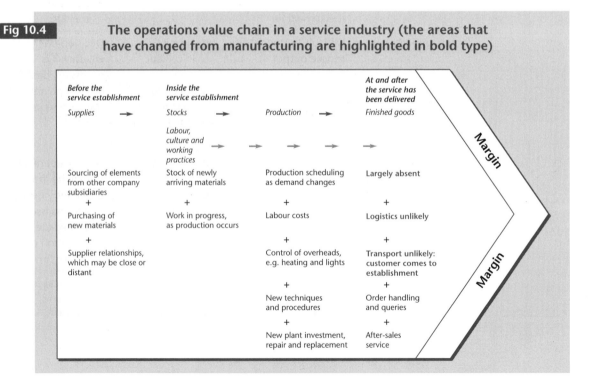

Fig 10.4   **The operations value chain in a service industry (the areas that have changed from manufacturing are highlighted in bold type)**

From a competitive strategy perspective, we should also note that service has become an increasingly strong element in manufacturing strategy. This is not a new idea. As Levitt[49] observed in 1972:

> *There is no such thing as service industries. There are only industries whose service components are greater or less than those of other industries. Everybody is in service.*

This has important implications for corporate strategy for three reasons:

1   Operations needs to consider carefully the service requirements of its customers. If the service is to run smoothly, there needs to be a direct link connecting production to the customer. Such an arrangement has to be part of the organisation's strategy.

2   One way of enhancing sustainable competitive advantage might be to strengthen the service element associated with a product – for example, more comprehensive after-sales and follow-up.

3   In those markets that have become increasingly global, one defence strategy is to offer higher levels of service. The reason is that, almost by definition, services are difficult to offer from a distance. They are best delivered locally. The cost and local knowledge required to set up and maintain such services will benefit the national operator against the global organisation.

Overall, the whole approach to service is likely to need an increased reliance on human resources and investment in training and education if it is to be successful.

Key strategic principles

- The people element and the need for immediate responses mean that services need special consideration from operations.

- There are five main points of difference between products and services that have implications for operations analysis: intangibility, inseparability, heterogeneity, perishability, ownership.

- Nevertheless, there are many points of similarity along the value chain for both products and services, so many of the same basic principles apply to both areas.

- Even in manufacturing strategy, services have become an increasingly strong element in the overall mix. They may provide a means to support and enhance competitive advantage.

Manufacturing strategy[50]

In this extract from his book, Manufacturing Strategy, *Professor Terry Hill comments on the interface between manufacturing strategy and corporate strategy.*

Companies invest in processes and infrastructure in order to make products and sell them at a profit. Consequently, the degree to which manufacturing is aligned to the product needs in the market place will make a significant contribution to the overall success of a business. The size and fundamental nature of the manufacturing contribution is such, however, that the wrong fit will lead to the business being well wide of the mark. Many executives are still unaware that what appear to be routine manufacturing decisions frequently come to limit the corporation's strategic options, binding it with facilities, equipment, personnel and basic controls and policies to a non-competitive posture which may take years to turn around.

The reason for this is that companies having invested inappropriately in process and infrastructure, cannot afford to reinvest to put things right. The financial implications, systems development, training requirements and the time it would take to make the changes would leave it, at best, seriously disadvantaged.

In the past, manufacturing's role in terms of its corporate contribution has been perceived by the company as a whole as being the provider of requests. The corporate strategy debate has stopped short of discussing the implications of decisions in terms of manufacturing. And this has been based on two incorrect assumptions, that:

1   within a given technology, manufacturing is able to do everything;

2   manufacturing's contribution concerns the achievement of efficiency, rather than the effective support of the business needs.

The result for many companies is that not only have the profit margins they once enjoyed been eroded, but also the base on which to build a sound and prosperous business in the future is no longer available. Without the frequent manufacturing strategy checks necessary to evaluate the fit between the business and manufacturing's ability to provide the necessary order-winning criteria of its various products, then the absence of these essential insights leaves a business vulnerable and exposed.

In times of increased world competition, being left behind can be sudden and fatal. In many cases, averting the end is the only option left. Turning the business around, however, will only be achieved by switching from an operational to a strategic mode, and one which will require a corporate review of the marketing and manufacturing perspectives involved in the alternatives to be considered and the financial implications of the proposals involved.

Source: Extracted from Hill, T (1993) *Manufacturing Strategy*, 2nd edn, Macmillan, London, pp 25, 56–7. Reproduced with permission.

◼ SUMMARY

- Operations includes raw materials sourcing, purchasing, production and manufacturing, distribution and logistics. Its coverage of the organisation's resources is therefore wide and comprehensive. Its importance in the strategic process is in delivering competitive advantage and in providing co-ordinated support for products – that is, every aspect of order handling, delivery and service to the customer – so that sales orders can be won by the organisation.

- There are two major constraints on operations:

1 they take time to plan and build; and

2 once installed, they are expensive to change.

These constraints mean that great care needs to be taken in arriving at the optimal strategy. The analytical process that accompanies such considerations will need to examine *where* and *how value is added* in the operations process from raw materials arriving at the factory gate through to finished goods being shipped to the final customer.

- It is evident from any analysis of the operations environment that the pace of technological change has clearly increased. Major changes in technology, often called *discontinuities*, also deserve careful analysis, as does global activity, particularly where it is aimed at cost reduction through the use of low-cost labour.

- Value added is an important part of the analytical process. It is likely to occur in the following areas:

1 adapting products to meet customer needs;

2 delivering better products than competitors;

3 adding value through enhanced performance or quality;

4 cutting the costs of manufacture.

The methods of achieving operations strategy involve both human resource considerations and the link between manufacturing and marketing.

- In any detailed analysis of operations strategies, part of the problem is the size and complexity of the resources under consideration. Tests can be applied to identify the major factors affecting the achievement of corporate objectives, adding value and the critical success factors identified for an industry. In addition to these basic procedures, operations strategy needs to examine eight strategy areas:

1 make or buy decisions

2 supplier relationships

3 manufacturing strategy

4 product design prior to manufacture

5 factory layout and procedures

6 logistics and transport

7 human resources implications

8 international manufacturing

When analysing organisations involved primarily in services, such as banking or travel, some special considerations apply. Services are different in five areas: intangibility, inseparability, heterogeneity, perishability and ownership. However, they still cover areas that have much in common with manufacturing – for example, raw materials, supplier relationships, stocks and work in progress.

● In practice, service has become an increasingly strong element in manufacturing strategy. Service usually needs to be delivered locally, and as a result this has provided some protection against increased globalisation of manufacturing. More generally, service is heavily reliant on human resources and investment in training and education.

QUESTIONS

1 Operations strategy has made major contributions to corporate profitability over the last 20 years, yet has not always featured in some descriptions of corporate strategy. What are the reasons given in the chapter for this? Do you think that they are likely to continue to apply over the next few years?

2 Hill contends that manufacturing strategy needs to be led by changes in customer demand. If this is the case, how is it possible to develop products that are revolutionary in their technology and essentially unknown to the customer?

3 The chapter argues that the low-cost labour strategies of some developing countries can be offset by more sophisticated operations strategies in Western countries. If you were managing a Western company, what type of manufacturing would you seek to keep in the West and what would you move to a developing country?

4 In Section 10.4, the comment is made that some detailed operations decisions are more likely to be outside the scope of corporate strategy. For each *element* of Section 10.4, explain the extent to which corporate strategy is involved and the extent to which it is not.

5 Analyse the world car industry for the contribution that operations strategy has made to the corporate strategies of companies in these industries. Comment also on the future potential of operations strategy in these industries. Use the references at the end of this chapter to assist the process.

6 Operations strategy has become more international over the last 20 years. Do you think this trend will be reflected in services? What are the problems in the services area?

7 Apply the ten guidelines for analysing operations to an organisation of your choice. What are the implications of your analysis for corporate strategy?

8 *'Design is a strategic activity whether by intention or default.'* Daniel Whitney. Discuss.

International engineering companies

This chapter has taken several examples of international engineering companies and shown how they have used operations to improve their overall strategic capability: SKF and Kvaerner are examples. You might like to take this further. For example, what real differences have occurred at SKF since the introduction of the new procedures? What happened to profitability? Has it really picked up as a result?

Hill, T (1993) *Manufacturing strategy*, 2nd edn, Macmillan. Clear, basic text that is well referenced and directed at exploring corporate strategy issues.

Harrison, M (1993) *Operations Management Strategy*, Pitman Publishing. Thoughtful with useful academic references.

Voss, C A (1992) *Manufacturing Strategy – process and content*, Chapman and Hall. Series of individual academic papers that address strategic and other issues: high-quality debate.

Slack, N, Chambers, S, Harland, C, Harrison, A and Johnston, R (1995) *Operations Management*, Pitman Publishing. Comprehensive text, clearly written and presented. This book explores manufacturing issues in further detail.

Whitney, D (1988) 'Manufacturing by design', *Harvard Business Review*, July–Aug. This explores some of the areas outlined in the chapter, especially concentrating on the strategic implications of design and technology.

REFERENCES

1 *Sources* include: *Financial Times*, 7 Aug 1995, p9 and Ohmae, K (1983) *The Mind of the Strategist*, Penguin, London, Ch 3.
2 Hill, T (1993) *Manufacturing Strategy*, 2nd edn, Macmillan, Basingstoke, p18.
3 Urwick, L (1956) *The Golden Book of Management*, Newman Neame, London.
4 Mumford, E (1996) 'Restructuring: values, visions, viability', *Financial Times*, 9 Apr, p12. A really interesting article on the history of this subject.
5 Kennedy, P (1989) *The rise and fall of the great powers*, Fontana, London, p259.
6 Hill, T (1993) Ibid, Ch 1.
7 Lorenz, C (1991) 'Competition intensifies in the fast track', *Financial Times*, 28 June.
8 Strebel, P (1992) *Breakpoints*, Harvard Business School Press, Harvard, Chs 1 and 2.
9 World Bank Report (1991), *Trade and Industry Logistics in Developing Countries*, H J Peter.
10 Kennedy, P (1989) Ibid, p535.
11 Wong Poh Kam (1991) *ASEAN and the EC*, ASEAN Economic Research Unit, Singapore, p170 *et seq.*
12 Williams, K, Haslam, C, Johal, S and Williams, J (1994) *Cars: Analysis, History and Cases*, Berghahn, Providence, p108.
13 Toyota (1994) *Annual Report and Accounts*, p11 (English language version).
14 Williams, K *et al* (1994) Ibid, p118.

15 Gourlay, J (1994) 'Back to basics on the factory floor', *Financial Times*, 4 Jan, p7.

16 Griffiths, J (1993) 'Driving out the old regime', *Financial Times*, 20 Aug, p8.

17 Williams, K *et al* (1994) Ibid, p115.

18 Griffiths, J (1995) '£200m Toyota expansion may create 3,000 jobs', *Financial Times*, 17 Mar, p9.

19 Hartley, J (1981) *The Management of Vehicle Production*, Butterworth, London.

20 Womack, J, Jones, D and Roos, D (1990) *The Machine that Changed the World*, Rawson Associates, New York.

21 Williams, K *et al* (1994) Ibid, p115.

22 Butler, S (1992), 'Driven back to basics', *Financial Times*, 16 July, p16.

23 Toyota (1994) *Annual Report and Accounts*, p1 (English language version).

24 Ibid, p9.

25 Toyota (1995) *Annual Report and Accounts,* p12 (English language version).

26 Ibid, p7.

27 Hill, T (1991) *Production and Operations Management*, 2nd edn, Prentice Hall.

28 Wild, R (1984) *Production and Operations Management*, 3rd edn, Holt, Reinhart and Winston.

29 Hill, T (1993) Ibid, Ch 2.

30 Hill, T (1993) Ibid, p36. (*See* also pages 55 and 56 for further clarification of these matters).

31 Adapted from the SKF *Annual Report and Accounts* 1992.

32 Hill, T (1991) Ibid.

33 *See*, for example, Cusumano, M and Takeishi, A (1991) 'Supplier relations and Management; A survey of Japanese, Japanese-Transplant and US Auto Plants', *Strategic Management Journal*, 12, pp563–88.

34 Marsh, P (1995) 'Car mirror rivalry turns cut-throat', *Financial Times*, 14 June, p10.

35 Hill, T (1991) Ibid.

36 Skinner, W (1974) 'The focussed factory', *Harvard Business Review*, May–June.

37 Whitney, D (1988) 'Manufacturing by design', *Harvard Business Review*, July–Aug, p83.

38 Ridding, J (1995) 'Renault unveils plant to speed launches', *Financial Times*, 17 Feb, p24.

39 Adapted from Hill, T (1993) Ibid and Gourlay, R (1994) 'Back to basics on the factory floor', *Financial Times*, 4 Jan, p7.

40 Christopher, M (1992) *Logistics and Supply Chain Management*, Pitman, London. (*See* also Christopher, M (1993) 'Logistics and Competitive Strategy', *European Management Journal*, June, pp258–61.)

41 Lynch, R (1992) *European Marketing*, Kogan Page, London, p214.

42 Carnegy, H (1995) 'Time to chart a different course', *Financial Times*, 7 Aug, p9.

43 Collins, R and Schmenner, R (1995) 'Taking manufacturing advantage of Europe's single market', *European Management Journal*, 13(3), p257.

44 Collins, R and Schmenner, R (1995) Ibid.

45 Adapted from an article by David Marsh in the *Financial Times*, 1 Mar 1994, p4. © *Financial Times* 1994.

46 Adam, E A and Swamidass, P M (1989) 'Assessing operations management from the strategic perspective', reprinted as Ch 19 in Voss, C (1992) *Manufacturing strategy – process and content*, Chapman and Hall.

47 *See* 'Can Europe compete?', *Financial Times*, 1 March 1994, p14.

48 *See*, for example, Cowell, D (1984) *The Marketing of Services*, Butterworth Heinemann, Ch 2.

49 Levitt, T (1972) 'Production line approach to service', *Harvard Business Review*, Sep–Oct, pp41–52.

50 Extracted from Hill, T (1993) *Manufacturing Strategy*, 2nd edn, Macmillan, London, pp25, 56–7.

PART **4**

THE PURPOSE OF THE ORGANISATION

It is impossible to develop corporate strategy without first establishing the general direction of the organisation. Building on the analyses of the organisation's environment and resources this part of the book now explores the purpose of the organisation. It considers three further background areas – technology, innovation and quality. It also explores the need for the organisation to think imaginatively about its vision for the future.

The mission and objectives of the organisation are then developed in the context of the organisation's stakeholders. In a prescriptive approach, they are likely to be defined in general terms for some years to come. In an emergent approach and in turbulent markets, they will be more fluid and contingent upon unfolding events.

THE PURPOSE OF THE ORGANISATION

● The *prescriptive* strategic process

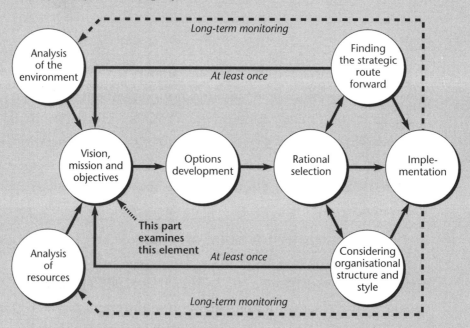

● The *emergent* strategic process

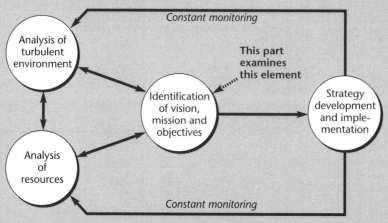

Chapter 11
BACKGROUND ISSUES

- *What vision does the organisation have for its future?*
- *What are the strategic implications of new technologies?*
- *Can innovation contribute to the organisation's purpose? If so how?*
- *What is the organisation's policy on quality?*
- *In what areas does the organisation have competitive advantage?*

Chapter 12
MISSION AND OBJECTIVES

- *What is the purpose of the organisation?*
- *Who are the stakeholders in the organisation and what do they want from it?*
- *What is the leadership style of the organisation?*
- *What are the ethical values of the organisation?*
- *What is the organisation's mission?*
- *What are the objectives of the organisation?*

11

Background issues

When you have worked through this chapter, you will be able to:

- explore the organisation's vision for the future and its strategic implications;

- examine the implications of developments in technology for the organisation's strategy;

- identify the main innovation processes relevant to strategy development;

- understand and develop the organisation's policy on quality issues;

- identify the area where the organisation is likely to have competitive advantage and consider the implications for the purpose of the organisation.

◖▬ INTRODUCTION

In developing the purpose of the organisation, there is a need to take the process beyond the current horizons and to explore future opportunities and challenges. Some may conclude that the future is too turbulent to predict and therefore the result is worthless. However, in many strategic situations, this will not be the case, even in turbulent markets. The vision of the future will set the boundaries and stretch the organisation as it develops its mission and objectives.

There are three areas which are important in developing the purpose of an organisation and yet, due to the wide scope of corporate strategy, do not fall neatly into a particular functional category. These are: the impact of technology, innovation and quality. These are considered in this chapter before we return to the issue of competitive advantage and examine its relationship with the purpose of the organisation. These areas are shown in Fig 11.1.

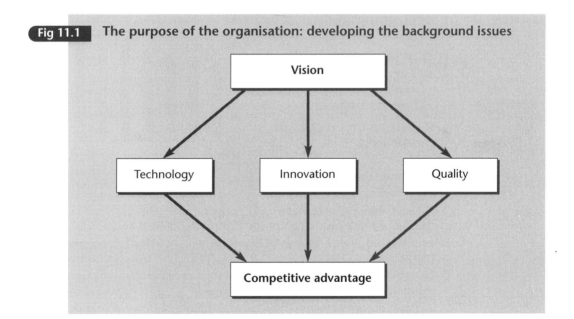

Fig 11.1 **The purpose of the organisation: developing the background issues**

Imperfect vision at Daimler–Benz[1]

In 1985, the new Chairman of Daimler–Benz, Edzard Reuter, developed a new vision for the future of the company. Over the next ten years, it turned out to be flawed. This case study explores the reasons.

Background

Daimler–Benz had been making quality cars for many years when Edzard Reuter became Chairman in 1985. With the support of its powerful shareholder, Deutsche Bank, the company then proceeded to announce a major shift in strategy: it was to become an 'integrated technology group'. It would use its highly profitable cars and trucks to fund a strategic move into other businesses, whose main connection with the car business would be shared technology.

Over the next four years, the company spent US$4.7 billion building an industrial conglomerate that made the group into the third largest company in Europe in terms of total sales. It acquired companies in the following areas:

- *Aerospace and defence*: Messerschmitt–Bolkow–Blohm, Fokker, Dornier, as well as investing in Airbus.

- *Electrical engineering, electronics, rail engineering and domestic appliances*: AEG.

- *Financial services and software*: Debis.

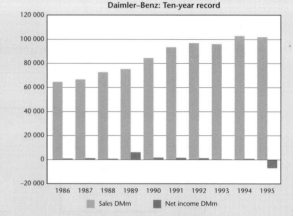

Daimler–Benz: Ten-year record

Sales DMm   Net income DMm

1986 1987 1988 1989 1990 1991 1992 1993 1994 1995

Reasons for the acquisitions

The reasons for the shift in strategic thinking were essentially linked to a new vision of the company. Daimler–Benz decided that it would emulate the highly successful Japanese and American conglomerates, such as Mitsubishi and General Electric. It was also keen to develop German industry as a global power in high technology companies and to transform the European aerospace industry, where it could see real opportunities.

The process was seen to be a long-term move to develop Daimler–Benz into new areas that would be *mutually supportive* through technology. For example, as car pollution and traffic flow became greater problems in European cities, the vision was that cities would seek new ways to balance public and private transport. Daimler–Benz would draw up the new strategy for a city through its Dornier subsidiary, build the trains at AEG, the buses at Daimler–Benz and the new traffic control systems at TEMIC – a joint venture between AEG and Daimler Aerospace (Dasa). This process would require careful and complex co-ordination of the various large subsidiaries of the group by the centre. At the same time, each of these subsidiaries had its own product ranges to develop and sell – cars, aircraft, electronics, etc.

If all these aspects seem rather vague and unconvincing, they appeared that way to some employees at the time. They resented the interference from the centre in individual businesses. For example, the Chairman of Dasa, Mr Jürgen Schrempp, is on public record[2] as describing the Daimler–Benz headquarters in Stuttgart as 'Bullshit Castle'.

Results of the new approach

There were several unforeseen environmental factors that caused problems for the company.

- German currency became even stronger, making Daimer–Benz exports more expensive.
- Just as Daimler–Benz was investing in aerospace and defence, the political situation changed. There were substantial defence cutbacks as the Cold War between the USSR and the West was coming to an end.
- There was a major downturn in the mid-range aircraft market (*see* Chapter 6) with the acquisition of Dornier being particularly expensive and ill-judged.

In addition, the most expensive acquisition of the expansion period, AEG, proved to have some major difficulties. These related both to the culture of the companies acquired, which were not easy to assimilate into the new group, and to the product ranges which were too broad and needed more focus. At one stage, AEG was producing everything from nuclear power stations to refrigerators and typewriters. There was no attempt to focus on core areas of strength. The result was that between 1990 and 1995 AEG made a cumulative loss of around DM 3.7 billion (US$2 billion).

During the late 1980s and early 1990s, the profits from Daimler–Benz cars and trucks continued to subsidise much of the above. In 1995, the situation had become so bad that more drastic action was required. Edzard Reuter retired from the company. Daimler–Benz effectively transferred some assets of AEG to other subsidiaries and closed the rump of the company. It also withdrew its financial support from Fokker, the Dutch aircraft maker, which was forced to close, but continued its development of Airbus.

The company had begun to define its new vision as being essentially involved in *transport-based manufacture*. A new Chairman was appointed – Mr Jürgen Schrempp from Dasa.

CASE QUESTIONS

1 *With the future so uncertain, was there any point in Daimler–Benz developing a vision as the basis of its strategy?*

2 *Can a future vision be essentially very broad, as it was at Daimler–Benz? Or should vision be more focussed by constraints such as the existing core skills of the group?*

11.1 DEVELOPING A STRATEGIC VISION FOR THE FUTURE

When developing the strategic options of an organisation, it is important to develop a vision of the future within which it will operate – that is, an awareness of why, where and how the organisation and its competitors will be competing in the future. There are five reasons for this:

1 Most organisations will compete for business and resources. They will have ambitions that go well beyond the immediate future and it is important for options to reflect this vision. Even not-for-profit organisations or those in the public sector usually need to compete for charitable or government funds and often wish to increase the range of services that they offer: such organisations will also benefit from a picture of where they expect to be in the future.

2 The organisation's mission and objectives may be stimulated in a positive way by the strategic options that are available from a new vision.

3 There may be major strategic opportunities from exploring new development areas that go beyond the existing market boundaries and organisation resources.[3]

4 Simple market and resource projections for the next few years will miss the opportunities opened up by a whole new range of possibilities, such as new information technologies, biogenetics, environmental issues, new materials and lifestyle changes. Virtually every organisation will feel the impact of these significant developments. Extrapolating the current picture is unlikely to be sufficient.[4]

5 Vision provides challenge for both senior and junior managers without the rigidities of an agreed mission and objectives.

Vision is therefore a backdrop for the development of the purpose and strategy of the organisation. It is not the same as mission and objectives: vision is the *future* picture; mission and objectives describe the role and tasks that the organisation chooses to adopt, based on the *current* situation. However, it may be that the vision will lead to the mission and objectives: for example, the Daimler–Benz vision of an integrated technology group led directly to its acquisitions of AEG and the aircraft companies.

However, vision will not always lead to mission. For example, a small grocery store competing against a new hypermarket might see its *vision* as being increased competition from a newly opened hypermarket. It might then change its *mission and objectives* to that of moving from that geographical area, rather than being driven out by the larger store in two years' time.

Hamel and Prahalad have suggested five criteria for judging the relevance and appropriateness of a vision statement. These are shown in Table 11.1. They are important because it would be all too easy to develop some wild and worthy vision that bore no relationship to the organisation, its resources and the likely market and competitive developments – for example, Daimler–Benz during the period between 1985 and 1995.

Table 11.1 Five criteria for judging the organisation's investigation of its vision[5]

Criterion	Indicative area to be investigated
Foresight	What imagination and real vision is shown? Over what time frame?
Breadth	How broad is the vision of the changes likely to take place in the industry? And of the forces that will lead to the changes?
Uniqueness	Is there an element of uniqueness about the future? Will it cause our competitors to be surprised?
Consensus	Is there some consensus within the organisation about the future? If not, there may be a problem if too many different visions are pursued at once.
Actionability	Have the implications for current activity been considered? Is there basic agreement on the immediate steps required? Have the necessary core competences and future market opportunities been identified?

Source: Reprinted by permission of Harvard Business School Publishing from *Competing for the Future* by G Hamel and C K Prahalad. Boston, MA, 1994, p122. Copyright © 1994 by Gary Hamel and C K Prahalad; all rights reserved.

The important action points that arise out of the vision investigation are connected with two issues:

● *Core competences.* Do we have the technology and skills to meet this vision?

● *Market opportunities.* What will this mean for market development? How can we take the opportunies as they arise?

It is also necessary to consider *how* the vision of the organisation is to be developed. It is likely that this will be guided by the Chief Executive Officer. To quote Warren Bennis and Burt Nanus in their well-known text on leadership:[6]

> '*To choose a direction, a leader must first have developed a mental image of a possible and desirable future state of the organisation ... The critical point is that a vision articulates a view of a realistic, credible, attractive future for the organisation, a condition that is better in some important ways than what now exists.*'

However, other strategists would argue that this should not be just a task for the leader but should involve many in the organisation. There is a strong case for using multi-functional teams that are brought together to investigate an area of the business. The precise format will depend on the prevailing culture of the organisation (*see* Chapter 8).

Key strategic principles

● When developing strategy, it is necessary to develop a vision of the future within which the organisation will operate. The main reason is to ensure that every opportunity is examined.

● Vision is not the same as the organisation's mission, though the two may be related.

● There are five criteria that may assist in developing the organisation's vision: foresight, breadth, uniqueness, consensus and actionability.

Motorola provides a competitive advantage[7]

For some years now, Motorola (US) has not only sponsored one of the world's leading teams of racing cyclists, but has backed it with the information technology to help it win races.

Traditionally, cycle racing teams have communicated with the team manager and the support group by shouting at them, even while moving at speeds up to 60 miles per hour (100 km per hour) on fast downhill sections. When a team member had a puncture or the whole team needed to change its race strategy in the middle of a race, the manager drove the team car up to the moving pack of cyclists for a hurried and dangerous conversation.

Motorola is the world's largest manufacturer of mobile telephones. It has sponsored a cycle racing team for some years. The company used its information technology to improve cycle race communications. It redesigned its two-way radio device to provide instant and continuous communication.

After installation, the team members received their orders through their helmets and one member was able to speak back through a microphone on her/his handlebars with a transmitter under the seat.

The competitive advantages have been significant. For example, in the Paris–Nice Race in 1993, the Motorola race leader broke away from the main pack but he was considering dropping back again to preserve his energy. A team member still in the main group was able to tell him that the pack itself was also fatigued, so he should hang on. He did so and won. On other occasions, precious minutes have been saved in repairing damaged cycles as a result of being able to direct the back-up team to where they were needed.

Motorola: Ten-year record

	Sales US$ m	Net income US$ m

(Bar chart showing Sales US$ m and Net income US$ m for the years 1985–1994, with Sales rising from about 5000 in 1985 to about 22000 in 1994.)

CASE QUESTIONS

1 *Can you name* business *situations where such a system might provide competitive advantage?*

2 *What is the main long-term competitive strategy problem with such a technical advance?*

3 *What other elements of competitive strategy should the Motorola team pursue to ensure success?*

11.2 USING TECHNOLOGY TO DEVELOP COMPETITIVE ADVANTAGE

11.2.1 Technology and competitive advantage[8]

Given the pace of change over the last 20 years, technology has come to play an important role in the development of sustainable competitive advantage. Even in mature industries, not-for-profit organisations and small businesses, it is technology that has on occasions added the extra element to differentiate the organisation. For these reasons, technology strategy deserves careful investigation.

New technology developments are just as likely to alter the vision and purpose of the organisation as any other area: They can extend and enhance the existing position of the company. However, it should be noted that this will take time and resources: there may be no short-term impact on strategy. There are two main phases to this task:

Phase 1   Survey of existing technologies
Phase 2   Development of technology strategy

This phase has four elements:

**Phase 1
Survey of
existing
technologies**

1   *An organisation-wide survey of existing technologies.* This should examine areas in detail rather than making broad generalisations, as this ensures that no opportunities are missed. The result will be an *audit* of which technologies are used and where in the organisation they are used. The audit data is then classified into three areas:

- *base technologies* that are common to many companies;
- *core technologies* that are exclusive to the organisation itself, possibly delivering real competitive advantage;
- *peripheral technologies* that are useful but not central to the organisation.

2   *An examination of related areas inside the organisation.* For example, patents and intellectual property may form the basis of important areas of competitive advantage. Some companies have special skills that have never been patented but come from years of experience and training: these may also present real advantages over competitors.

3   *A technology scan external to the organisation.* This will identify opportunities that are available for later consideration.

4   *A technology/product portfolio.* A matrix can be constructed relating products and technologies (*see* Fig 11.2).

Fig 11.2   **Technology/product portfolio matrix**

	Mature technologies	New technologies
New products	Possible growth opportunities in new areas	Embryonic, new stars
Mature products	Cash cows	New possible opportunities and, importantly, competitive threats

Phase 2 Development of technology strategy

To develop technology strategy, it is important to take one technology at a time or risk muddle and confusion. It may also be important to develop both the *technology* and the *operations* (manufacturing) processes at the same time because the two areas are inter-related and because lead times need to be shortened.

The technology development initiative then needs to be analysed in two ways:

- the technological developments of the organisation compared with those of competitors; and
- the costs of further development compared with the time that this will take. (There is always a trade-off here.)

In addition to these two tasks, it is important to consider the possibilities of *acquiring* new technology – possibly through company acquisition, joint ventures or the purchase of a licence to use technology, probably from a company outside the home market.

Two final issues then need to be considered:

- *The speed of imitation*. It is important to estimate how quickly any technology development could be imitated by competitors.
- *Issues of globalisation*. It may be possible to exploit the new area on a worldwide scale and thus alter the attractiveness of the business proposition.

The above procedure may be too elaborate for some small companies and for not-for-profit organisations. However, small companies often gain their initial advantage from a technology edge. Larger companies may fail to consider the benefits of a clear drive on technology development, especially when they are operating in mature industries. The area has considerable potential strategic importance.

Technology developments are probably *prescriptive* in their overall approach in the sense that there needs to be a definite objective. However, they may be *emergent* in their detailed processes and by the nature of the experimental process.

Key strategic principles

- An internal and external scan of technologies is vital to corporate strategy development. It may alter the purpose of the organisation over time.
- Technologies should be classified into base, core and peripheral. Base areas are common to many companies. Peripheral areas are not mainstream to the organisation. The core areas are most likely to deliver competitive advantage, along with patenting and special skills.
- Taking each technology separately, it can then be assessed against competition and for the costs of further development against the time taken.
- The speed of imitation and possible global exploitation also deserve examination.

11.2.2   Information technology and its implications for corporate strategy

Whether it needs to make a profit or not, every organisation needs information to survive. It needs data to monitor its progress and inform its members of the present status. Information and the way it is gathered can also make a contribution to competitive advantage. The provision of effective information systems is therefore an important part of the corporate strategic task.

Global
information
environment

With the active encouragement of the many companies involved, it is evident that the computer industry, telecommunications operators and media companies are now converging in terms of the services they offer:

- Computers come supplied with CDs, sound and fax cards and a link to the global Internet.
- Telecommunications are able to transmit film and home shopping to the domestic TV screen.
- Media companies are linking commercially with consumer electronics companies.

We are in the middle of what has been called the third industrial revolution – *the information age*. Moreover, the information is global, not just local or national. For example, a major UK company now has a permanent *three-way* telecommunications link between its engineering design teams in the USA, UK and India. The communications use the specialist engineering knowledge of the American team, the skilled but low labour costs of their Indian colleagues and the overall co-ordination and marketing skills of the UK headquarters. Such activity was simply not possible some years ago.

Other information examples include:

- The development of global treasury links, as multinationals and banks transfer overnight funds around the world to obtain the most favourable currency deals and interest rates.
- Major cost savings across Europe as warehouses no longer have to be sited in each country. As trade barriers have come down, operating one centre to service several countries has led to major reductions in inventory with no loss of service to the customer.
- Higher service levels using mobile telephone systems to contact salesforce and delivery vehicles, internationally as well as nationally.
- New production techniques, such as just-in-time, that require much closer co-operation between supplier and customer, relying heavily on communications technology.

New information technology has thus opened up the possibility of *greater strategic control* in companies. It has allowed corporations to be better informed and to monitor events more closely. At the same time, it has allowed subsidiaries to have greater strategic freedom, within defined parameters. One commentator has even argued that the greater spread of information will actually make it more difficult for the centre to control events because the subsidiaries may know so much and can communicate with each other, bypassing the centre.

Whatever view is taken of information and its influence on control, the information age will certainly mean that *knowledge* will be central to corporate strategy. Moreover, such information will go well beyond basic market share, financial data and management accounting information, involving people and unquantifiable assets. To paraphrase Professor Gary Hamel,[9] Madonna may have been 'the material girl' but what sets her apart are her *immaterial assets* – her knowledge-based copyrights, recording deals, television and film contracts and so on. These items are less easy to measure but represent the real wealth and knowledge at the centre of the global information environment. They are Madonna's sustainable competitive advantage.

Information resource analysis and competitive advantage

In Chapter 7, we explored Professor John Kay's view that the *architecture* of an organisation – that is, its network of formal and informal relationships – links the business together and helps to drive it forward.[10] He argued that this was one of the four distinctive areas that helped shape corporate strategy. Information resources and capabilities are a key part of an organisation's architecture.[11] Specifically, the *way* that information is gathered and the *substance* of that information will have a profound effect on architecture. Analysis of information needs therefore needs to address these two topics.

The involvement of less easily measurable assets, such as people, time and the immaterial assets mentioned above, means that the full cost of the information resource is difficult to determine. However, it usually amounts to a substantial investment and represents a significant part of the organisation's architecture. In this sense, information is a substantial asset for the organisation seeking to develop competitive advantage.

According to this view of strategy, competitive advantage can be developed from an organisation's information resources by what is essentially a prescriptive process. Specifically, information technology (IT) may influence competition in three ways:[12]

1 *Change of industry structure*. Porter's Five Forces Model explores the forces that influence industry strategy. Fast and accurate information can alter the *balance* of the forces, particularly where an industry needs a high information content. For example:

- Airline ticketing relies heavily on computer networks.
- Large supermarket chains employ linkages between their barcode readers at cash tills and their warehouses for restocking goods sold out.
- Bank networks employ computerised cash transfer systems between branches and rivals.

As computer usership becomes more widespread and sophisticated, it may be that such advantages will settle into a new balance of power based on higher levels of IT usage.

2 *Creation of competitive advantage*. Faster information and the lower costs of acquiring data will provide advantage to those companies that update their information systems more quickly and use it more effectively. There are two main ways that IT can be used:

- to lower labour costs by automating manual tasks; and

- to differentiate companies so that they are able to charge higher prices or offer a unique service.

For example:

- The introduction of direct insurance and banking services by telephone has both lowered costs and improved levels of service. It has given substantial competitive advantage to those companies that introduced such services across Europe earlier than their rivals. This has proved to be one of the major successes of competitive advantage using information systems in the 1990s. Direct Line, a subsidiary of the Royal Bank of Scotland, swept into UK market leadership in private car and house insurance by this route. Other UK insurers are now using the technology to attack Allianz (Germany), Europe's largest insurance company, in its home territory.

- The use of computer networks and computer design in architectural and media practices has provided real competitive advantage and service to customers for some companies.

3 *Ability to reach new customers.* With the creation of the Internet and the development of new forms of telecommunications between individual homes and the supplier, there are real opportunities to conduct shopping and other services from an increased number of locations. Examples include home shopping which is beginning to develop, especially for those who are housebound, and home banking on a 24-hour basis in some countries.

In analysing the potential for strategic information technology (IT) systems, there are two approaches consistent with the above:[13]

1 *The impact approach.* IT is concentrated on specific information projects that will build measurable competitive advantage. It is probable that it will be *prescriptive* in its strategic approach because it involves planning and installing a new system.

2 *The align approach.* IT is spread throughout the organisation, according to demand, in support of broader strategy developments. It is likely that this will be *emergent* in its strategic approach because it will entail developing and adapting the system only where required.

Hence, the analysis needs to explore whether there is a specific requirement to develop competitive advantage through IT or a more general need in the organisation or both these routes. Such approaches will therefore examine *customer* needs but will also explore what *competitors* are offering in terms of service.

Key strategic principles

- New information technology has opened up the possibility of greater strategic control in organisations.

- The information that is collected will go well beyond basic market share, financial data and management accounting information, involving people and unquantifiable assets.

- Analysis of information needs to explore the way that it is gathered and the substance of the information.

- Information technology (IT) may influence the competitive situation in three ways: a change in the balance of power in industries, the creation of competitive advantage in some companies and the ability to reach new customers.

- Analysis of IT will need to examine whether it is concentrated on specific information projects designed to build competitive advantage – *the impact approach* – or spread throughout the organisation to support a wider range of strategy developments – *the align approach*.

- Technology developments are probably prescriptive in their overall approach but emergent in the detailed processes.

CASE STUDY 11.2

FT

Innovation at Corning[14]

The US company, Corning, has produced three innovations that have revolutionised mankind over the last hundred years. This case study describes the company's approach to the process.

The small town of Corning, in the northern hills of the Appalachian mountains in the USA, might seem to the casual observer a parody of Victorian capitalism. From their mansions high above the town, the ruling Houghton family – the company Chairman and his brother, the congressman – look out on the workers below.

The old glassworks, founded by their great-grandfather, has been knocked down and replaced by a gleaming office block. In a town of 12 000 inhabitants, 6000 are still employed by Corning. Intensely traditional companies are not uncommon in the US; Corning is also intensely innovative. The company's laboratories in the town made the first

light bulb for Thomas Edison and were the first to mass-produce glass tubes for TV sets. They also invented optical fibre, thus laying the pathway for the information revolution. As Mr Jamie Houghton, Corning's Chairman, says:

> Very few companies can say they have produced inventions that changed the lives of mankind. We've produced three.

The heart of Corning technology

At the heart of Corning is the technology of inorganic materials. From the starting point of the old glassworks, the company has followed some curious paths. Like most glass companies, it is heavily involved in the motor industry. However, instead of making windscreens, Corning is the world's biggest producer of ceramic honeycombs for catalytic converters for car exhausts. Similarly, it has developed from its starting point in laboratory glass to become a leading provider of blood tests, as well as working on drug development and biotechnology manufacture for the pharmaceutical industry. In electronics, it is the main producer of glass substrates for the flat screens used in personal computers.

Corning makes nose cones for spacecraft, giant mirrors for astronomical telescopes and projection lenses for high definition TV sets. 'Virtually everything we do', says Mr Roger Ackermann, Corning's Chief Executive, 'goes back to an invention in our laboratories.'

Problems at Corning

Not all these inventions have turned out to be benign. In the 1930s, a Corning scientist invented silicone. Unsure what to do with it, Corning formed a joint venture with Dow, the US chemicals company. Dow Corning went on to become one of the biggest makers of silicone breast implants, and is currently facing enormous damages claims. The venture, Corning insists, is ring-fenced, so that no liability can be attached to its parent. Nevertheless, the affair has depressed its share price and is a blot on its reputation with investors. However, it has not dampened the company's enthusiasm for joint ventures. Corning has an extraordinary array of these, with partners ranging from Siemens of Germany to Mitsubishi of Japan and Samsung of Korea. There is an unwritten company rule that these ventures should not make up more than half the company's business. Nevertheless, as Mr Ackermann makes plain, they are a fundamental part of Corning's philosophy:

> The joint venture is a financial hedge. More important, it shortens the time you take to get to market.

Besides Dow Corning, the company has one other headache: its consumer division – the world's largest producer of tableware and cookware, such as heat resistant Pyrex (another Corning invention). After several years of losses, the division made a meagre US$56 million operating profit in 1993 on US$780 million sales. Mr Ackermann says:

> The business is in critical care. It's climbed out of the cellar, but if it doesn't meet the goals that the board has set for it, we'll have to do something about it.

Business pressures

One of the difficulties the company faces is the downward pressure on prices from big retailers. The problem is not confined to the consumer division. As Mr Ackermann observes, Corning may be big in niches but some of its customers have purchasing power of US$30 billion to US$40 billion apiece.

> The auto industry says real costs have to come down by 2 to 3 per cent a year, or you won't be a supplier. Optical fibre has to keep coming down by 5 per cent. In healthcare, we're under pressure from managed care organisations. I operate on the assumption that over time, our costs must go down 3 to 5 per cent a year in real terms.

Part of the answer lies, once again, in technology. In optical fibre, the company reckons to have worked through eight generations of manufacturing technology since the early 1980s. Mr Houghton says:

> It wasn't so long ago that we were selling fibre at US$1 a metre. Now it's five cents, and our margins have been very good throughout.

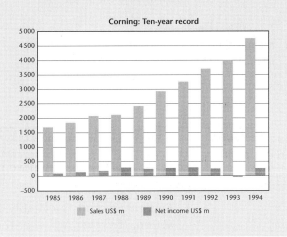

Corning: Ten-year record

The long-term commitment, in Mr Houghton's view, owes much to Corning being a family company. It has been run by Houghtons since its foundation, his immediate predecessors being his elder brother, Amory – now the local congressman – and his father. However, family share ownership in the company is now estimated to be only about 20 per cent. Mr Houghton, now 59, must face the fact that the only other family members in the company are his son, James, 31, and nephew, Carter, 24. 'So far they're both doing well,' he says. 'But the days are clearly over when you could assume the top position by having the right name.'

If the family nature of the firm is open to question, one might also query its location. The town of Corning may be in the state of New York, but it is so far from the metropolis that employees shuttle up and down by company plane. Would it not make sense to move? Mr Houghton replies:

We've been here since 1886. Yes, it's inconvenient in some ways. But the fact is we have a very tightly wired connection here between technology, manufacturing and management.

There is also, he makes plain, an element of paternalism.

If somebody's been around here a long time and they're over a certain age, we're not happy about throwing them out on the street.

Invention

Meanwhile, the process of invention continues. According to Mr Houghton:

Our major task is to keep scanning the horizon to see what could be the next big one. If you ask me whether there will be another one like fibre optics in my tenure, probably not. These things take a long time to develop.

The question still arises of what the next big one might be. Mr Houghton has a surprising answer:

I think you'd have to try solar energy. If there's going to be a major breakthrough in storing it and making it visible, I hope Corning will be responsible. But I'm not betting the lab on it.

Source: *Financial Times*, 17 March 1994

CASE QUESTIONS

1 *The case implies that innovation arises primarily as a result of a strong research and development (R&D) team. Is this all that is required for innovation? How would you judge the amount of funds to be made available for R&D in the first place and how would you assess the results? Based on your answer, what is your assessment of innovation at Corning?*

2 *Do customers have a role in the innovation process beyond passively examining the ideas produced by R&D boffins? If so, what is that role and how does it relate to corporate strategy?*

3 *Comment is made in the case study that the company is seeking to find another major innovation to match the three it claims to have pioneered already. Is this really the process of innovation or are there more modest ways that require smaller, incremental steps but still achieve competitive advantage?*

11.3 INNOVATION AND CORPORATE STRATEGY

The analytical process described in the earlier parts of this book brings with it three potential dangers:

1 *Backward looking.* Inevitably, historical data form the starting point for future action. However, whether the strategy intends to build on past success or to

fight its way out of problems, it cannot rely just on the past. There needs to be a determined attempt to move forward.

2 *Sterility*. Too much analysis may stifle creativity. New ideas, new approaches to old problems may be weakened by over-emphasis on analysis and data collection.[15]

3 *False sense of security*. Because they have already happened, events in the past can be viewed with some certainty. However, it would be wrong to see the future in the same way. Whatever is predicted stands a high probability of being at least partially incorrect.[16]

Innovation is an important antidote to these real problems. In corporate strategy, we need to move beyond the obvious and comfortable into the new and interesting.

11.3.1 The strategic role of innovation

By definition, innovation moves products, markets and production processes beyond their current boundaries and capabilities. Innovation is the generation and exploitation of new ideas. It also provides organisations with the ammunition to move ahead of the competition. Hence, innovation can deliver three priceless assets to corporate strategy:

● substantial future growth;

● competitive advantage;

● ability to leapfrog major competition, even dominant competitors.

However, none of the three above areas will automatically deliver future profitability to innovating companies (*see* Fig 11.3). Consider the cases of Canon (Japan) and EMI (UK). Both companies developed major new innovations during the 1970s.

● *Canon* set out to compete with and beat Xerox (US) in world photocopying markets. It developed a series of new processes that did not infringe the Xerox

Fig 11.3

This was profitable . . .   . . . so was this

. . . this made a loss.

1922 Austin Chummy
Courtesy of Austin Rover

Sony Walkman
Courtesy of Sony Consumer
Products Group

Concorde

patents yet produced products that turned Canon into one of the world's lead-ing photocopying and printing companies. By the mid-1990s, it had a larger market share than Xerox.[17]

● *EMI* was so badly wounded by its foray into medical electronics that its scanner business had to be sold off at a knock-down price. This happened despite the fact that its product was truly innovative and was the first in the market place by a significant period.[18]

Innovation is not without risk. Yet, if it is successful, the payoff is significant. There are two principle sources of innovation to be examined, neither of which is sufficient in itself:

● Customer needs analysis – *market-pull*.

● Technology development analysis – *technology-push*.

Customer needs analysis: market-pull

Baker[19] suggests that innovation occurs when companies identify new market opportunities or a segment of an existing market that has been neglected. Essen-tially, it is important to develop such opportunities in terms of the *customer need served* in broad general terms – for example, transport, convenience – rather than by examining current products and how they meet demand. For example, Canon photocopiers were innovatory in meeting the general demand for photocopying rather than the needs of the existing customer base which was biased towards large companies. The company developed new machines requiring little maintenance or repair which were sold to a much broader range of customers – the medium-sized and small businesses. This process is known as *market-pull*.

As Whittington points out,[20] the importance of market-pull in successful inno-vation has been well validated by research. It relies on identifying a market need that needs to be satisfied by a technological advance – essentially a *prescriptive* approach to corporate strategy. It is used in research and development of some new pharmaceuticals, consumer electronics and other areas of technology that are market driven.

Technology development analysis: technology-push

Market-pull procedures do not fully describe the way that many real innovations happen, however.[21] Innovation may be born out of developments at small compa-nies, often in a two-way process with their customers who may be larger companies. Alternatively, innovations may start as narrow solutions to particular problems. For example, Thomas Watson, President of IBM said that a new calcula-tor built by his company in 1947 (the Selective Sequence Electronic Calculator) would be able to solve many of the world's major scientific problems but had no commercial applications. It proved to be one of the first IBM computers.

Successful technology often takes time to diffuse through to other industries. It follows that, in addition to monitoring customer needs, an innovatory company should also survey other industries for their technology developments and assess their relevance to its own – essentially an emergent approach to corporate strategy. This process is sometimes known as *technology-push*.

11.3.2 The routes to delivering innovation

Innovation often occurs through a diffusion process.[22] It may well be adopted slowly at first, then the pace quickens until finally there are just a few late-adopters left to take up the process. Diffusion thus follows the S-shaped curve shown in Fig 11.4.

Sometimes the early pioneering companies fail to make profits because there are still few purchasers and large sums have been invested in developing the process. It is at this stage that business failures like the EMI Scanner occur. The real profits are made during the rising part of the curve when there is major demand, pricing is still high to reflect the genuine innovation or costs have been dramatically reduced as a result of a technological breakthrough.

In some respects, corporate strategy may therefore be better served by those who are 'fast seconds' into the market place: the curve is still rising and the original innovator has still not come to dominate the market. For example, the anti-ulcer drug Zantac (Glaxo Wellcome, UK) was second into the market after Tagamet (SmithKline Beecham, UK/USA) yet came to dominate the market eventually and make a substantial contribution to Glaxo profitability. This is supported by the research of Mansfield[23] who tracked innovations over a 30-year period. He estimated that on average those who were second into a market could make a new product for two-thirds of the cost and time of the original innovating company. The strategic problem is how to identify correctly and react quickly to the truly new innovation – not an easy task.

For the original innovators, the payoff can be substantial with the right product. Professor James Quinn[24] of Dartmouth College, USA, investigated the innovation process of a variety of companies and concluded that large companies need to behave like small entrepreneurial ventures to be truly successful. He suggested that innovatory companies should ideally follow the process he called 'controlled chaos' (*see* Exhibit 11.1).

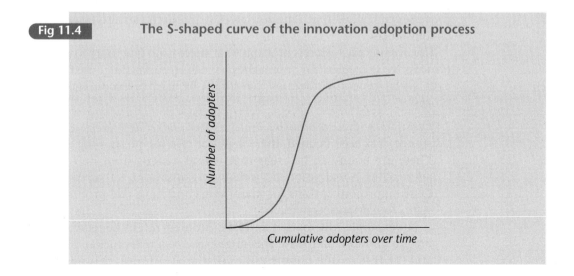

Fig 11.4   **The S-shaped curve of the innovation adoption process**

Number of adopters

Cumulative adopters over time

| Exhibit 11.1 | The controlled chaos approach to generating innovation |

- *Atmosphere and vision* – with chief executives providing support, leadership and projecting clear, long-term ambitions for their company.

- *Small, flat organisation* – not bureaucratic, but flexible.

- *Small teams of innovators* – multi-disciplinary groups of idea makers.

- *Competitive selection process* – with innovatory ideas selected from a range in the company, and encouragement and support, not penalties, for the losing team.

- *Interactive learning* – random, even chaotic, consideration of ideas from many sources and from a range of industries.

Quinn believed strongly in the *emergent process* for innovation strategy. Writing around the same time, Fred Gluck[25] of the consulting company, McKinsey, took largely the opposite view. He argued that the really innovatory achievements needed a *'big-bang'* approach. They need masses of information, a decision-making process that can discern patterns in this undigested data and the functional skills to implement the decisions once they were made. He urged the larger corporations, to whom he was addressing his remarks, to become more sensitive to major environmental changes and to create a better climate to explore *big-bang* ideas.

This conflict of view of the best way forward for innovation would appear to be equally true for Japanese researchers. One study[26] describing Japanese practice was based on a survey of products in eight major companies including Honda, NEC, Epson and Canon. It found that the process was informal, multifunctional and involved excess information over that initially identified to solve the problem. The conclusion was that the most successful innovation processes often involved redundant information that interacted through chance, even chaotic, processes to produce the innovatory result. By contrast, another study[27] of Japanese innovation processes concluded that a more analytical approach can also be employed in some circumstances.

The overall conclusion is probably that there is no one route to innovation: both prescriptive and emergent approaches have been successfully used. There are, however, seven general guidelines that might be used to encourage the innovation process.[28]

1 *Question the present business strategies and market definitions.* Once the present strategy has been defined, there is a clear case for questioning every aspect of it. There are bound to be areas that would benefit from new definitions and approaches. A real problem for many organisations is that they live with their existing preconceptions for many years and have real problems raising their sights to new perspectives.

For example, the market and its customers might be redefined either more broadly or more narrowly. This might lead to a redefinition of the competitors and the threats and opportunities that arise. In turn, this might suggest new insights into areas where the organisation has a competitive advantage – some real leverage over others in the market. Walt Disney Corporation redefined its market in the 1970s as one of providing pleasure using themed characters such as Mickey Mouse and Donald Duck: it used these ideas to develop another way of delivering such entertainment with the first of its Disney theme parks in Anaheim, California.

2 *Consider carefully the purpose served by the current products or services.* Exploring carefully the purpose served by the current offerings may lead to ideas about the future. It may be possible to reach the same end by new and more rewarding means. While some piano manufacturers were unable to compete for the attention of youngsters against the attractions of computer games such as Nintendo and Sega, Yamaha had other ideas. It redefined its piano as a keyboard and added new designs, sizes and technology to provide the same fun as a game.

3 *Explore external timing and market opportunities.* There are often strategic windows of opportunity that may provide real benefits if they can be tackled. Resources then need to be concentrated on such areas to ensure progress is quick, but the rewards are significant. Timing is vital, however. For example, Asea Brown Boveri (Switzerland/Sweden) and Deutsche Babcock have seized opportunities to develop products in the area of environmental control engineering over the last few years, building on the new concerns of some governments, especially those in northern Europe and the USA.

4 *Seek out competitors' weaknesses.* Most organisations have areas in which they are weak. These might provide opportunities for others to expand. However, such an approach does invite competitive retaliation and so needs to be considered carefully. For example, Microsoft has dominated world markets for computer software for years with its *Windows* system. The company did not notice that Netscape Communications had quietly developed software for the Internet 'browser' market and by 1995 had come to dominate this segment. Microsoft was then involved in some expensive joint deals to recover the situation in this area.

5 *Deliver new and better value for money.* Companies sometimes become locked into assumptions about the possibilities of further reductions in costs and improvements in quality. However, design and technology development is moving at such a pace in some markets that new opportunities have arisen. For example, all the Japanese car manufacturers were able to make real share gains in the 1970s and 1980s not only by competitive prices but also by offering superior quality and performance standards.

6 *Search wide and far.* Examining areas such as lifestyles, technology, regulatory regimes and demographics can generate significant opportunities. For example, Motorola (US) and Nokia (Finland) have both benefited from the rise of the mobile telephone, having developed expertise in this market over the last ten years. In the same way, Sharp (Japan) was the leading company in the launch of pocket computer organisers because it recognised trends to busier and more complex lives that needed to be managed.

7 *Seek to challenge conventional wisdom.* Acceptance of the current market and resource status is unlikely to lead to major new developments. There is a need to challenge every aspect of what is believed to be the generally held view in markets. This might include a challenge to areas such as *key factors for success*, perhaps by finding a totally new method of delivering a product or service. Some managers are better at the challenge process than others and need to be encouraged and supported as they engage in this task. For example, as late as the 1980s it was considered impossible for personal car insurance to be sold over the telephone: it was far too complicated and customers would not accept it. This has proved to be totally false. By the mid-1990s, telephone selling had become the dominant mode of selling in several of Europe's largest markets. As a result, the new companies such as Direct Line (now a subsidiary of the Royal Bank of Scotland) have taken over market leadership in the UK.

It will be evident that there is no one piece of conventional strategic theory that will prompt innovative developments, but the strategic payoff from such processes can be substantial.

11.3.3 International perspectives on innovation

International country comparisons on innovation pose significant problems. This is because innovation is dependent on the *product group*: for example, innovation is likely to be higher in biotechnology and lower in food products because of the state of technological development in these two categories. Different countries have different strengths in different product groups (*see* Chapter 6 for an exploration of this area). Hence, it is difficult to make generalisations about countries without assessing the product groups with which they are involved.

Nevertheless, the reasons why the pace of innovation seemed to be higher in some countries than in others were explored in the 1980s.[29] Three inter-related groups of factors were identified:

● Factors that influence *inputs* to the innovation process, such as the quality of the country's scientific community, especially its educational institutions.

● Factors that influence *demand*, such as receptive and interested customers.

● An *industrial structure* that favours intense competition to stimulate growth and provides some method for companies to spread the cost and results of scientific research, such as through a government agency.

These conclusions are similar to those of Porter when exploring the competitive advantage of nations (*see* Chapter 6).

The role of government may also be important. In France, the UK and the USA, it was 'top down' directed at specific industries, such as defence, and with specific measurable objectives. In other countries such as Sweden, Switzerland and Germany, government acted in a more 'diffusion-oriented' way. It responded to market signals and provided education and training and set industry standards that raised quality and diffused technology.

In terms of competitive advantage, over the centuries nations have come to rely less on the possession of raw material wealth, which can be bought through international trade. They also place less emphasis on being close to markets, since transport costs have come down dramatically. Countries now rely heavily on scientific skills, not only to invent products but also to manufacture those that have been developed. In turn, such developments require a highly skilled workforce and investment by the state in education. In seeking sources of innovation, organisations will wish to consider the role that the state has played and is continuing to play in investing in its future workpeople. Countries such as Singapore and Malaysia have recognised the importance of investment in education to provide the structural basis for the innovatory process.

Key strategic principles

- Innovation contributes growth, competitive advantage and the possibility of leapfrogging major competition.

- However, innovation can be risky and can result in major company losses.

- There are two major drivers for innovation: customer needs analysis (often called *market-pull*) and technology development analysis (often called *technology-push*).

- Innovation development often follows an S-shaped curve with the real profit being made during the growth phase, after the initial development.

- The innovation process can be *emergent* with ideas freely generated from many sources. It can also be *prescriptive* with a more analytical and directed approach to the task.

- The seven guidelines offered on innovation to start this process do not claim to be comprehensive. They have as their central theme the need to challenge conventional understanding and wisdom.

- International perspectives in innovation suggest that a strong national education structure is useful.

CASE STUDY 11.3

How Perrier Water lost its sparkle and its independence[30]

In early 1990, minute traces of the cancer-inducing chemical benzene were found in bottles of Perrier mineral water on sale in the USA. There had been a failure in quality control that was to cost the company dear. This case study examines the quality problems and their consequences for the whole company.

Mineral waters are bottled from natural country or mountain springs and sold for their purity, naturalness and healthy qualities. There is little real competitive advantage between the different brands so they rely heavily on marketing campaigns to explain and exploit their benefits.

During the 1970s and 1980s, Perrier Water was developed by the family-controlled company into one of the world's leading mineral water brands. Perrier undertook this task using a series of branding campaigns that were witty and confident. Each leading country was allowed to develop its own style but the central core remained: the familiar light green bottle with its claim that Perrier was 'naturally sparkling'.

By the early 1990s, the market was growing in the West by a remarkable 30 to 40 per cent per annum, mainly on the basis of healthy life style claims. The world market was worth around US$8 billion in 1990. Perrier was market leader in France, the UK and the US: sales in the US alone were worth around US$2.5 billion. Perrier also had other mineral water brands such as Volvic and Vichy, but the lead brand was Perrier. The company did not publish full, separate data on its mineral water operations, but combined them together with its other commercial activities in dairy products and other areas. Its main competitor was Danone (France) with brands such as Evian and Badoit.

Key factors for success

Since mineral water is simply drawn out of the ground and competitive products are largely the same, the key factors for success for Perrier and other companies were:

- running the bottling plants close to production capacity;
- brand marketing to sell the purity and quality;
- strict controls on production to guarantee the purity.

Perrier's quality problem

In early February 1990, Perrier North America was told by US regulatory authorities that traces of benzene, a chemical that can produce cancer, had been found in its product. For a company where purity was critical, its reaction was curiously slow. Initially, Perrier announced that it was halting production completely, but the problem was confined to North America. It backed this up two days later by stating that the product's North American bottling line, which was located in France, had become contaminated by benzene that had been used to clean the plant. As it turned out subsequently, this was at best disingenuous – the company had actually still not traced the problem.

After another two days, Perrier finally found the real cause: quality control had failed. Company employees had not changed the charcoal filters that were used to extract minute traces of harmful gases present in the water emerging from the Perrier Spring. It was discovered that all production over the previous six months was involved. Perrier then acted immediately and scrapped all its product worldwide at a cost of US$200 million. Rather more reluctantly, the company had to admit that the natural product contained impurities that had to be removed during the production process. Its slow response to the problem meant that it was accused of failing to react with openness as the situation developed.

Perrier's action and its consequences

Over the following six months, Perrier relaunched the product but still faced battles with US regulators, EC officials and UK supermarket chains over the claims made on the Perrier bottle: it was forced to withdraw the product claim 'naturally sparkling'. By 1991, it had recovered its market share in France, but its North American and UK shares were still only running at half their former levels.

The company's share price had not suffered significantly because there were a whole range of other products in the Perrier Group. However, the company had been greatly weakened in terms of its drive and energy. In late 1991, the Italian Agnelli family (who controlled Fiat) made a bid to gain control. In early 1992, the Swiss-based food multinational Nestlé made a counter-offer. There followed a series of complicated bids and deals that had to be approved eventually by the European Commission. Nestlé finally won control of Perrier in mid-1992 at a cost of US$1.6 billion. After investigation by the European Commission,

Nestlé had to sell Volvic to Danone in 1993. The cost of inadequate quality control had indeed been substantial and involved the complete break-up of the Perrier group.

CASE QUESTIONS

1 *Given that the purity of the product was so important, what two explanations did Perrier offer for its contamination? What does this imply about the company's procedures at that time with regard to quality?*

2 *Once the situation was clear, Perrier decided to scrap all its product stock worldwide at a cost of US$200 million. Was this the total cost of failure? If not, what other costs might have been involved?*

3 *With hindsight, how would you assess the cost of preventing such a quality breakdown in the company? Could such a cost be set against a new quality improvement programme? What items might be included in the programme?*

11.4 QUALITY AND CORPORATE STRATEGY

Quality is important for most organisations but needs to be defined in the context of customer expectations about the product, its price and other issues. For example, quality does not mean the same thing to Rolls Royce or Mercedes as it does to a market trader. Although both should attempt to deliver quality to their customers as part of their overall strategy, not all quality issues are strategic.

Total Quality Management (TQM) is the modern approach to the management of the whole organisation that emphasises the role of quality in meeting the needs and expectations of its customers.[31] It is essential to operate this as part of the corporate strategy of the organisation. Not every organisation operates TQM although virtually all have some form of *quality control* – that is, the regular inspection of goods and services to ensure that they meet minimum standards. Quality control is involved with day-to-day detail and is *not* strategic in its approach.

TQM *is* strategic for three reasons:

- the TQM emphasis on the *whole* organisation;
- the TQM requirement for active support from *senior* management;
- the significant contribution that TQM can make to competitive advantage.

Quality procedures in general and TQM in particular can be considered as having an influence on corporate objectives, such as profitability, by a series of interconnected routes. These are shown in Fig 11.5 and are backed up by empirical research. The PIMS database of 3000 companies showed a strong correlation between quality and profitability.[32] (*See* Chapter 16.)

11.4.1 Origins and international nature of TQM

TQM has a strategic role because of the success of some companies in developing quality and reliability as competitive weapons in the international market place. Although it was first conceived in the USA in the mid-1950s, it was Japanese interest and persistence that really developed this area during the period between 1955

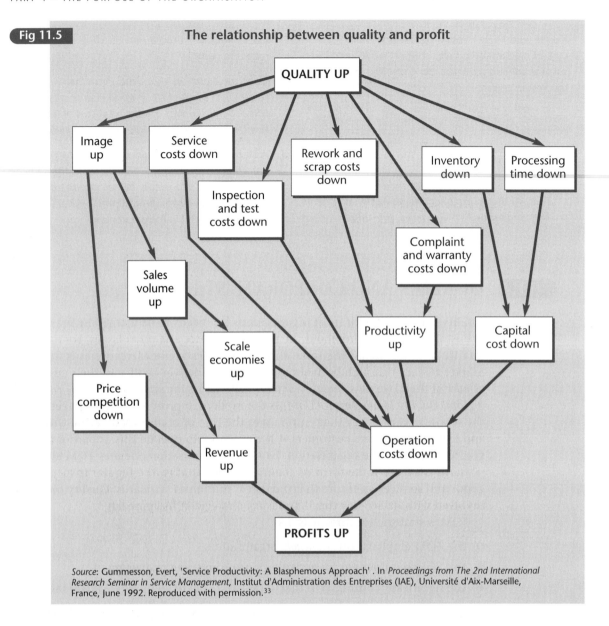

Fig 11.5 **The relationship between quality and profit**

Source: Gummesson, Evert, 'Service Productivity: A Blasphemous Approach' . In *Proceedings from The 2nd International Research Seminar in Service Management*, Institut d'Administration des Entreprises (IAE), Université d'Aix-Marseille, France, June 1992. Reproduced with permission.[33]

and 1985. Pioneers worked mainly in Japan and included Deming, Juran, Ishikawa, Taguchi and Crosby.[34]

After the proven success of Japanese companies in slowly and painfully developing new procedures over 30 years,[35] TQM was then picked up by Western companies. This does not mean that Western companies had no quality procedures prior to this time: they simply used more limited and different methods. With the benefit of hindsight, some would argue that such Western procedures were less successful but this has not been conclusively proved. Many Western companies do not operate TQM procedures at the present time but do place significant and successful emphasis on quality control.

11.4.2   The difference between quality procedures and TQM

Typically in Western companies in the period between 1960 and 1980, quality procedures were seen to be a function of a separate quality department that set standards for the manufacturing operation. The department then tested regularly the products that were made on the factory floor and rejected those that fell below the defined performance standards. Rejected products had to be scrapped or reworked. There were statistical control procedures for sampling and testing products. However, in order to keep down the expense, only a sample of products were tested. Hence, some defective products were likely to be passed on to customers, who then either returned them for compensation or took their business elsewhere.

TQM lays the emphasis rather differently. It places much more responsibility on the workers to monitor their own output of products, rather than a separate quality department. It seeks to 'get things right first time' rather than have defects that need to be picked up by a statistical testing method. Hence, TQM rejects the concept of *optimum* quality and attempts to eliminate *all the errors and failures* that might happen. It involves everyone in the organisation including those who might judge that their normal responsibility is not for quality – for example, telephone operators are important in TQM because they interface with customer service. TQM seeks to identify the true and total costs related to quality – for example, the cost of reworking the material that has been rejected.

To illustrate the difference between a TQM and non-TQM company, Slack *et al*[36] retell the story of a plant in Ontario, Canada, of IBM, the computer company. It ordered a batch of components from a Japanese manufacturer and specified that the batch should have an acceptable quality limit of three defective parts for every 1000. When the parts arrived in Ontario they were accompanied by a letter which expressed the supplier's bewilderment at being asked to supply defective parts as well as good ones. The letter also explained that they had found it difficult to make parts which were defective, but had indeed managed it. These three defective parts per thousand had been included and were wrapped separately for the convenience of the customer.

The details of all quality and TQM procedures are evidently beyond the scope of corporate strategy but there are two aspects that are our legitimate concern:

● *Differences in management approach.* A TQM business is likely to be more co-operative in its style.

● *Results in terms of customer relationships with the organisation.* A TQM business is likely to have a deeper, more quality-based relationship with its customers.

Both of these might possibly form the basis of competitive advantage; however, TQM is not without its costs and difficulties.

11.4.3   Analysing the benefits and costs of TQM

Japanese companies such as Honda, Nissan, Toyota and Matsushita have been working for over 35 years on TQM. Among the earlier Western companies to adopt the approach, Motorola (US) and Texas Instruments (US) began operating TQM procedures in the early 1980s.[37] One of the real problems found by all the companies, including the Japanese, is that the benefits take time to emerge but the costs are only too obvious from an early stage. For example:

- the development and running costs of an organisation-wide strategy on quality;
- the cost of a steering group to monitor quality progress;
- the selection and training of teams as the basis of quality improvement;
- the recognition of success through reward schemes, though these do not have to be expensive;
- the restructuring of the organisation so that each part is considered to have a customer relationship with another part – that is, the *internal market*;
- extra quality procedures;
- training schemes to improve worker control;
- the cost of empowering worker teams;
- the administrative costs involved in setting up and running internationally recognised quality procedures, such as ISO 9000.

These and other costs, as well as the basic shift in attitudes to quality, mean that the fundamental decisions required need to be taken at the level of corporate strategy. Some benefits usually emerge quickly as early procedures tighten and then the rest come slowly over a period of years: to this extent, TQM is probably best seen as an *emergent* rather than *prescriptive* process, in spite of the clear decision needed to undertake the task at the outset.

Key strategic principles

- Quality is vital for most organisations. Total quality management (TQM) is the modern strategic approach to quality delivery. It is not the same as quality control.

- Total Quality Management (TQM) is an approach to the management of the whole organisation that emphasises the role of quality in meeting the needs and expectations of its customers. Not every organisation operates TQM procedures, though virtually all have some form of quality control.

- TQM lays the emphasis on workers being responsible for quality, rather that using a separate quality department. It aims to 'get things right first time' rather than have defects corrected later.

- There are real differences in the approach to managing TQM-based organisations and the relationships with customers. These may form the basis of competitive advantage.

- Although there are benefits from TQM, there are many costs. It often takes years for the full benefits to emerge but the costs are often obvious from an early stage.

11.5 COMPETITIVE ADVANTAGE AND THE PURPOSE OF THE ORGANISATION

So far in this book emphasis has been placed on *sustainable competitive advantage* in the development of corporate strategy. Having identified and developed their competitive advantage, many organisations then make this part of the purpose of the organisation. For example:

- *Corning*: 'We are dedicated to the total success of Corning Glass Works as a worldwide competitor.'

- *Daimler–Benz*: 'We aim to offer the world's most advanced products, systems and services.'

Purpose and sustainable competitive advantage need to be linked together. To have a purpose that is *exactly the same* as all other organisations may pose problems for long-term strategy, because it implies that the organisation can see no long-term advantages for itself whatsoever. An element of difference therefore needs to be built into the purpose. To explore this further, it is useful to consider several specific types of organisation:

1 *Diversified holding companies*. A diversified conglomerate company such as Hanson plc (UK) or General Electric (US) either needs to establish its purpose in very general terms for the whole group or allow each part to develop its own mission. The central *group* route may be considered an imposition and discourage diverse businesses from developing their own individual areas.[38] For diversified companies, it may therefore be better to allow each area to develop its own mission.

2 *Small companies*. For small companies, it may be more difficult to be better than every other company, but it may be possible to be better in a local area or better at one aspect of the total business. Small company strategy is often more successful when it allows the company to stand out from all those around it.

3 *Government-owned institutions*. Government-owned institutions providing a service may not have the financial resources to be better at everything. However, they may be best able to provide service in a *local area* because of their geographic location. For example, a university or a hospital may be unique in this respect. In addition, it may also be possible to provide excellence in some functions or subjects as an additional aspect of the search for advantage.

4 *Charitable organisations*. Many of these organisations are specialists in their approach with clear areas of distinction. However, there are some larger general charities with a variety of roles. Arguably, there is a case for some degree of focus here, but the case is less clear.

Key strategic principles

- Purpose needs to be linked to sustainable competitive advantage.

- This needs to be undertaken at the *business* level rather than the *corporate* level in organisations.

KEY READING

Technology and corporate strategy[39]

Technology can revolutionise corporate strategy. In this extract from their book, **The Corporate Environment,** *Huw Morris and Brian Willey explore the factors that cause technological change and its impact on society and business.*

An important question for policy makers in government and business is: what causes technological change? The answer to this question has important implications for the research and development strategies pursued by different countries and companies. New inventions and discoveries offer people the opportunity of better standards of health and education. They also provide the physical basis for an expansion of the wealth of nations and their citizens.

Conventionally, the opinions of scientific and economic historians about the causes of technological change could be divided into roughly two groups. One group of writers believed that the role of scientists and engineers engaged in pure research was central. The breakthroughs made by these specialists, they argued, produced the technological push for the development of new products, processes and organisational forms. By contract, another group tended to highlight the role of customers and financial backers who, they suggested, provided the demand for new ways of doing things. This approach emphasised the power of the market place and the importance of the final consumer, who, they maintained, provided the demand pull which inspired new approaches.

In recent years, this polarisation of the debate between advocates of the technological-push theory and believers in market pull has been superseded by more complex explanations which combine elements of each approach. Freeman (1987)[40] provides a good example of this approach with his distinction between four forms of innovation:

- Incremental innovations
- Radical innovations
- Changes of technology system
- Technology revolutions.

Incremental innovations
Incremental innovations happen continuously in any industry or service activity. They arise as a consequence of engineers, managers and workers making suggestions to improve the goods or services being produced.

Radical innovations

Radical innovations occur irregularly and often as a result of deliberate research and development activity by companies, universities or government laboratories. The causes of these developments are difficult to ascertain. Radical innovations often provide the stimulus for the development of new markets and industries.

Changes of technology system

In this case a number of related innovations appear simultaneously and they can provoke fundamental changes in the corporate structure and composition of specific industries. Comprising a combination of incremental and radical innovation, these developments can give rise to the emergence of new industrial sectors as well as rapid and turbulent restructuring or decline within established industries.

A recent example of this type of technological change is provided by the development of multimedia forms of entertainment which combine digital communication with established television and computer technologies.

Technology revolutions

In these circumstances changes to technology are so substantial and far-reaching that they have the capacity to change the way in which people think and behave within an entire economy. These revolutions happen relatively infrequently and take many years to affect everyone; however, when they occur, they necessitate changes in the knowledge, skills and systems of working for entire populations.

A number of writers have suggested that technological revolutions occur in cycles or waves. These waves, it is argued, provide the impetus for economic growth as people find ways of exploiting these technologies.

Source: Morris, H and Willey, B (1996) *The Corporate Environment*, Pitman Publishing.

SUMMARY

● When developing corporate strategy, it is necessary to develop a *vision* of the future within which the organisation will operate. The main reason is to ensure that every opportunity is examined. There are five criteria that may assist in developing the vision: foresight, breadth, uniqueness, consensus and actionability.

● An internal and external scan of *technologies* is vital to the development of corporate strategy. It may alter the purpose of the organisation over time. Technologies need to be classified into base, core and peripheral. It is the core area that is most likely to deliver sustainable competitive advantage. Each technology then needs to be assessed against its competitors and for the time and costs of development.

● New *information technology* (IT) has opened up the possibility of greater strategic control in organisations. The control that can be exercised needs to go beyond basic financial data into people aspects of the organisation. At the same time, IT has presented new opportunities to develop sustainable competitive advantage. This can be done through concentration of specific areas – the impact approach – or through a wider spread of IT – the align approach. Technology developments are probably prescriptive in their approach overall, but emergent in the detailed processes.

● *Innovation* contributes growth, competitive advantage and the possibility of leapfrogging competition. However, it can also be risky and result in major losses to the organisation. There are two major drivers for innovation: customer needs analysis (market-pull) and technology development analysis (technology-push). The innovation process can be both prescriptive and emergent.

● *Quality* is vital for most organisations but needs to be defined in the context of the expectations of its customers. Total Quality Management (TQM) is the modern approach to quality delivery. It involves the whole organisation and emphasises the role of quality in meeting the needs and expectations of its customers. Not every organisation operates TQM but every organisation needs to place quality high in priority with regard to corporate strategy. This means providing the appropriate emphasis as strategy is developed. Although there are benefits from TQM, there are many costs. It often takes years for the full benefits to emerge, but the costs are often obvious from an early stage.

● Overall, purpose needs to be linked to *sustainable competitive advantage*. Such a process needs to be undertaken at the *business* level, rather than the *corporate* level, in most organisations.

QUESTIONS

1 Take an organisation with which you are familiar and classify its technologies into basic, core and peripheral. What conclusions can you draw on sustainable competitive advantage for the organisation's strategy?

2 Daimler–Benz claimed around 1990 that it was developing itself as an 'integrated technology group.' Is this the same as core technologies that can be exploited? Do you believe the claims the company was making at that time?

3 With the introduction of the new information superhighway, it has been argued that this: '*will give consumers increased access to a vast selection of goods but will cause a restructuring and redistribution of profits amongst stakeholders along the [value] chain.*' Robert Benjamin and Rolf Wigand.

   Discuss the strategic implications of this comment from the viewpoint of (a) a major retailer and (b) a small to medium-sized supplier of local building services.

4 Do you think that the increased use of IT will affect all organisations equally? Will some remain relatively unaffected apart from the introduction of a few computers and a link to the Internet? What are the strategic implications of your answer?

5 Identify some recent innovations and classify them into market-pull and technology-push. Explain how each innovation has been delivered into the market, using the S-shaped curve to show the process.

6 Quinn argues that large companies need to behave like small entrepreneurial ventures to be truly innovative. Gluck suggests that major innovations only come from a 'big-bang' push that needs major resources. Can these two views of the innovative process be reconciled? (*See* references 24 and 25.)

7 Take an organisation with which you are familiar and assess the importance of quality to the organisation. How is quality defined? How is it monitored? In your view, is the process successful?

8 If quality should form part of the strategy of the organisation, is it appropriate to emphasise this in preference to other elements of the strategy? What are the benefits and the dangers of this approach?

9 Can the concept of purpose and competitive advantage be applied to the whole of Daimler–Benz, even in its new slimmer form? And Corning at the corporate level? Compare your answers with the statements in the text from these companies and comment on any differences.

STRATEGIC PROJECT

Daimler–Benz

Even though the company has been in difficulty during the 1990s, it is a massive enterprise with substantial resources and many well respected managers. The story of its continuing strategic development is still unfolding. You might like to explore this further.

FURTHER READING

On vision: Tregoe, B B *et al* (1989) *Vision in action*, Simon & Schuster, London. At the practical end of a difficult subject.

On technology and corporate strategy: Contractor, F J and Narayanan, V K (1990) 'Technology Development in the Multinational Firm', *R&D Management*, Basil Blackwell, republished in Root, F R and Visudtibhan (eds) (1992) *International Strategic Management*, Taylor and Francis, London, pp163–83. Well developed, thoughtful and comprehensive.

On IT and corporate strategy: Porter, M E and Millar, V E (1985) 'How information gives you a competitive advantage', *Harvard Business Review,* July–Aug. *See* also Benjamin, R and Wigand, R (1995) 'Electronic markets and virtual value chains on the information superhighway', *Sloan Management Review*, Winter, p62.

On innovation: June Henry and David Walker (1994) *Managing Innovation*, Sage/Open University.

On TQM, read the chapters in Slack, N, Chambers, S, Harland, C, Harrison, A and Johnston, R (1995) *Operations Management*, Pitman Publishing, London. A good starting point.

REFERENCES

1 References for Daimler–Benz case study: *The Economist:* 27 Apr 1991, p87; 26 June 1993, p77; *Financial Times:* 7 Apr 1993, p26; 23 Sept 1993, p24; 1 Dec 1993, p49; 16 Dec 1993, p21; 20 Dec 1993, p13; 21 Dec 1993, p3; 11 July 1995, p24; 8 Aug 1995, p13; 20 Dec 1995, p25; 18 Jan 1996, p27; 14 Feb 1996, p23; 7 Mar 1996, p28; 12 Apr 1996, p23.
2 *Financial Times*, 11 July 1995, p24.

3 Hamel, G and Prahalad, C K (1994) *Competing for the future*, Harvard Business School Press, Boston, Mass, p31.

4 Hamel, G and Prahalad, C K (1994) Ibid, p29.

5 Adapted from Hamel, G and Prahalad, C K (1994) Ibid, p122.

6 Bennis, W and Nanus, B (1985) *Leaders: the strategies for taking charge*, Harper & Row, New York.

7 Some technical data taken from an article in the *Financial Times*, International Telecommunications Supplement, 17 Oct 1994, pXV.

8 This section has benefited from Contractor, F J and Narayanan, V K (1990) 'Technology Development in the Multinational Firm', *R&D Management*, Basil Blackwell, republished in Root, F R and Visudtibhan (eds) (1992) *International Strategic Management*, Taylor and Francis, London, pp163–83. Well developed, thoughtful and comprehensive.

9 Hamel, G (1995) 'Foreword', *FT Handbook of Management*, Financial Times, London. *See* also his article in *Financial Times*, 5 June 1995, p9 for an abridged version of the article.

10 Kay, J (1994) *Foundations of Corporate Success*, Oxford University Press, Ch 5.

11 Farbey, B, Targett, D and Land, F (1994) 'The great IT benefit hunt', *European Management Journal*, 12, Sept, p270.

12 Porter, M E and Millar, V E (1985) 'How information gives you a competitive advantage', *Harvard Business Review*, July–Aug. *See also* Benjamin, R and Wigand, R (1995) 'Electronic markets and virtual value chains on the information superhighway', *Sloan Management Review*, Winter, p62.

13 Lederer, A L and Sethi, V (1992) 'Meeting the challenges of information systems planning', *Long Range Planning*, Apr, pp69–77.

14 Case study adapted from an article by Tony Jackson in the *Financial Times* 17 Mar 1995, p19.

15 Hamel, G and Prahalad, C K (1995) Ibid, p274.

16 Stacey, R (1993) *Strategic Management and Organisation Dynamics*, Pitman Publishing, London, p115.

17 Harvard Business School (1983) *Canon (B)*, Case 9–384–151 plus note on world photocopying industry.

18 Harvard Business School (1984) *EMI and the CT Scanner (A) and (B)*, Case 383–194 and the *Economist Survey on Innovation*, 11 Jan 1992, p21.

19 Baker, M (1992) *Marketing Strategy and Management*, 2nd edn, Macmillan, London, p28.

20 Whittington, R (1993) *What is strategy and does it matter?*, Routledge, London, p82.

21 *The Economist* (1992) Ibid, p21.

22 Baker, M (1992) Ibid, p110 and *The Economist* (1992) Ibid, p22.

23 *The Economist* (1992), Ibid, p22.

24 Quinn, J B (1985) 'Managing Innovation: controlled chaos', *Harvard Business Review*, May–June, p73.

25 Gluck, F (1985) 'Eight big makers of innovation', *McKinsey Quarterly*, Winter, p49.

26 Nonaka, I (1990) 'Redundant, overlapping organisations: a Japanese approach to managing the innovation process', *California Management Review*, Spring, p27.

27 Kawaii, T (1992) 'Generating innovation through strategic action programmes', *Long Range Planning*, 25, June, p42.

28 Developed principally from two sources: Hamel, G and Prahalad C K (1994) Ibid, Ch 4 and Day, G S (1987) Ibid, Ch 6.

29 Ergas, S, quoted in *The Economist* (1992) Survey on Innovation, 11 Jan, p23.

30 References for Perrier case study: *Financial Times*: 13 Feb 1990, 15 Feb 1990, 16 Feb 1990, 17 Feb 1990, 27 Apr 1990, 21 Aug 1990, 5 Apr 1991, 10 July 1991, 29 Nov 1991, 18 Dec 1991, 21 Jan 1992, 24 Jan 1992, 1 Apr 1992, 5 June 1992, 18 July 1992, 23 July 1992, 10 Feb 1993; *The Economist*: 3 Aug 1991, p69 and 21 Mar 1992, p102.

31 Slack, N, Chambers, S, Harland, C, Harrison, A and Johnston, R (1995) *Operations Management*, Pitman Publishing, London, p684.

32 Buzzell, R D and Gale, B T (1987) *The PIMS Principles*, The Free Press, New York, Ch 6.

33 *Source*: Slack, N *et al* (1995) Ibid, p683, based on Gummeson, E (1993) 'Service productivity, service quality and profitability', *Proceedings of the 8th International Conference of the Operations Management Association*, Warwick, UK.

34 Slack, N *et al* (1995) Ibid, pp812–14.

35 *See* 'The cracks in quality', *the Economist*, 18 Apr 1992, p85.

36 Slack, *et al* (1995) Ibid, p824.

37 *The Economist* (1992) Ibid, p86.

38 Campbell, A and Yeung, S (1991) 'Creating a sense of mission', *Long Range Planning*, Aug.

39 Morris, H and Willey, B (1996) *The Corporate Environment: A Guide for Human Resource Managers*, Pitman Publishing, London, pp136–8.

40 Freeman, C (1987) 'The Case for Technological Determinism' in Finnegan, R, Salaman, G and Thompson, K (eds) (1987) *Information Technology: Social Issues. A Reader*, Hodder and Stoughton, Sevenoaks/the Open University.

12

Mission and objectives

When you have worked through this chapter, you will be able to:

- identify the main stakeholders and conduct a stakeholder power analysis;

- understand the role that organisation culture and leadership play in establishing the organisation's mission and objectives;

- identify the main issues involved in business ethics and their influence on the development of the organisation's mission;

- develop a mission statement for the organisation;

- develop the objectives consistent with this statement;

- distinguish between corporate, functional and business unit objectives.

INTRODUCTION

Having explored the background issues related to the purpose of the organisation, it is now time to define the purpose more precisely. This chapter tracks the development of the organisation's mission and objectives, stressing the need to take into account during this process several important sets of interests – the stakeholders (shareholders, employees, etc.) in the organisation, its culture and its leadership – as well as the more general matters of values and business ethics. The process is shown in Fig 12.1.

Fig 12.1   **Developing the organisation's mission and objectives**

The Ford Motor Company objective – to develop a global organisation[1]

Ford, the world's second largest vehicle maker, threw down the gauntlet to its industry rivals in April 1994. This case study explores how the company sought to expand its operations onto a global scale.

For the first time in its history, Ford was seeking to become a global corporation, breaking down national and regional barriers that had blocked its drive to create common vehicles for the world market. 'This is a worldwide business that requires the broadest thinking and execution,' explained Mr Alex Trotman, Ford Chairman and Chief Executive Officer.

In a bold move aimed at freeing it from the shackles of history, Ford planned to move to a single set of processes and systems throughout its product development, manufacturing, supply and sales activities. If it succeeded, Ford would set new benchmarks that would be hard for most of its competitors to match.

In the 1990s all the world's car makers faced the same challenge of trying to increase the efficiency of their enormous investment programmes, while at the same time producing a greater diversity of products. They needed to increase the speed at which they brought products to the market while jumping into emerging markets, be it for multi-purpose vehicles, sport-utility vehicles or micro cars. They had to be able

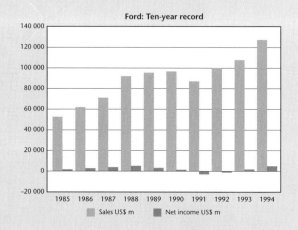

to squeeze their massive materials purchasing bills by moving to global sourcing for parts and systems. What they could no longer afford in a world of over-capacity and shrinking margins was the luxury of duplication. It was too wasteful, for instance, for Ford to develop an Escort-sized car for Europe, and in parallel to develop a similar but yet entirely different vehicle for North America. With its deeply entrenched traditions of independent regional fiefdoms, that was exactly what Ford had been doing. However, in 1994, Ford decided to call a halt.

Mr Trotman commented:

> *By integrating all our automotive processes and eliminating duplication of effort, we will use our creative and technical resources.*

He claimed that Ford's new way of doing business would provide customers with a broader array of vehicles in most markets and would ensure that the group was fully competitive in quality and value against the best in the world. At the same time, the simplification of engineering, purchasing and other processes would 'substantially reduce the cost of operating the automotive business'. Ford estimated the potential cost-saving from the reorganisation to be at least US$2 billion to US$3 billion a year by the end of the decade.

The group had been feeling its way for more than a decade towards ways of increasing the global punch of its organisation. Its top management had long been tantalised by the holy grail of the so-called world car, and by the savings that could be achieved by developing a product once for both manufacture and sale in different continents. It tried in the late 1970s with a common programme for Ford Escorts in Europe and in North America, but the cars launched at the beginning of the 1980s ended up with little more than the name and the blue Ford oval badge on the bonnet in common. Now there would be a new mission and objectives.

Source: Financial Times, 22 April 1994.

CASE QUESTIONS

1 *Who should be involved in devising the mission and objectives of the company?*

2 *Should they stress the global issue or is globalisation a strategy to achieve the objective and therefore inappropriate for this statement?*

3 *What should happen to such a statement when it has been prepared? Does it need to be circulated beyond senior managers? If so, to whom?*

12.1 DEVELOPING THE MISSION AND OBJECTIVES

The *mission* of an organisation outlines the broad directions that the organisation should and will follow and briefly summarises the reasoning and values that lie behind then.

The *objectives* are then a more specific commitment consistent with the mission over a specified time period. These may be quantified, but this may be inappropriate in some circumstances.

As explored in Chapter 1, the strategies that will achieve the objectives then follow from this. The mission and objectives define the whole strategic process and are therefore important in the development of corporate strategy.

12.1.1 Prescriptive approach to mission development

Under prescriptive theories of strategy, the organisation will set out its mission and objectives for the next few years. It then develops strategies consistent with the mission and aimed at achieving the objectives – for example, Ford's global ambitions.

The analysis of the environment and resources is used to develop the mission and objectives of the organisation. After this, a prescriptive *mission statement* is then developed setting out the organisation's purpose over a period of time. Several examples are given later in the chapter.

12.1.2   Emergent approaches to mission development

In contrast to the prescriptive approach, some emergent strategists argue that it is a contradiction in terms to couple the concept of purposeful planning with the idea of a strategy emerging in the organisation. By definition, they would argue that purposes do not emerge.

For some emergent strategists – the *uncertainty-based* strategy theorists of Chapter 2 – the whole idea of purpose for an organisation is largely incomprehensible. For example, they would argue that Ford's global ambitions outlined at the beginning of the chapter are a waste of time; too many chance events may blow the company off its chosen route. They would reject those parts of this chapter concerning mission and objectives. They would probably accept the stakeholder and cultural sections of the chapter but would see them as supporting their view that the uncertainties they introduce only make it more difficult to set out clearly an organisation's purpose.

For other emergent strategists – the *survival-based* theorists and the *human-resource based* theorists of Chapter 2 – the situation is less clear. Certainly, they would have doubts about a mission that was developed without consideration of the external forces and without careful discussion between the interested parties in the organisation.

However, they would not reject the concept of purpose completely: they would accept it with reservations. Ford's global ambitions would probably meet their criteria for acceptance since they were developed out of Ford's views on the way that external forces were moving and were discussed among senior managers before being introduced.

Some emergent strategists would want the complexity of the interests of the *stakeholders* in the business to become part of the purpose – that is, the interests not only of the shareholders but also the senior managers and the employees who all have a share in the success of the organisation. They would be impressed by Ford's attempts to communicate the new global purpose to all employees and, as we will see, to take account of employee-stakeholders in the Ford mission statement.

As will be explored more fully in Section 12.2, stakeholders may well have conflicting interests – for example, shareholders' desire for profits versus the employees' desire for continued employment even when it may not be profitable. The organisation's purpose, according to the human-resource theorist, may need to be tempered by *compromise* between the various interested parties.

12.1.3   Developing the mission

This chapter concentrates first on *prescriptive* approaches before returning to the *emergent* route at the end of the chapter. This is because most organisations find it helpful to have some clear statement of their purpose, whether they take a prescriptive or emergent approach to its achievement.

Even small businesses, government institutions and not-for-profit organisations have come increasingly to regard the development of a mission statement as a useful starting point for strategy development. The advantages are:

- It can be circulated and discussed among those involved in the organisation.
- It provides a sense of direction and focus.
- It draws the organisation together.

Key strategic principles

- The *mission* of an organisation outlines the broad directions that an organisation should and will follow and briefly summarises the reasoning and values that lie behind them.

- The *objectives* are then a more specific commitment consistent with the mission over a specified time period. They may be quantified, but this may be inappropriate in some circumstances.

- Prescriptive approaches emphasise the need to set out a mission and objectives for the next few years for the organisation.

- Some emergent approaches doubt the usefulness of a mission and objectives because the future is so uncertain. Other emergent approaches accept the need for a mission and objectives but place great emphasis on the need to include the managers and employees in its development.

12.2 STAKEHOLDER ANALYSIS

12.2.1 Identifying the stakeholders

An organisation's mission and objectives need to be developed bearing in mind two sets of interests:

- the interests of those who have to carry them out – for example, the managers and employees; and
- the interests of those who will be interested in the outcome – for example, the shareholders, government, customers, suppliers and other interested parties.

Together these groups form the *stakeholders* – the individuals and groups who have an interest in the organisation and as such may wish to influence its mission and objectives.

Given this situation, it is perhaps not surprising that the organisation's mission is not formulated overnight. It can take months of debate and consultation within the organisation. When the implications of the organisation's mission are clearly set out for the directors, managers and employees, they may not necessarily accept the mission without question: there may be objections as it is realised, for example, that individuals will have to work harder, undertake new tasks or face the prospect of leaving the company. The individuals and groups affected may want to debate the matter further.

This concept of stakeholding extends *beyond* those working in the organisation. Shareholders in a public company, banks who have loaned the organisation money, governments concerned about employment, investment and trade may also have legitimate stakeholdings in the company. Customers and suppliers will also have an interest in the organisation. These interests may be informal, such as government involvement in a private company, or formal, such as through a shareholding in the company. All stakeholders can be expected to be interested in and possibly wish to influence the future direction of the organisation.

12.2.2 Conflict of interest among stakeholders

The organisation needs to take stakeholders into account when formulating its mission and objectives. If it does not, they may object and cause real problems for the organisation: for example, major shareholders may sell their shares and key employees may leave.

A difficulty arises when the interests of individual stakeholders or groups of stakeholders are in conflict. For example, workers may want more pay at the expense of profits and dividends for the shareholders. Other areas where interests may conflict are summarised in Table 12.1. Consequently, the organisation will need to resolve which stakeholders have priority: *stakeholder power* needs to be analysed.

Table 12.1 Stakeholders and their expectations

Stakeholder	Expectations	
	Primary	*Secondary*
Owners	Financial return	Added value
Employees	Pay	Work satisfaction, training
Customers	Supply of goods and services	Quality
Creditors	Creditworthiness	Payment on time
Suppliers	Payment	Long-term relationships
Community	Safety and security	Contribution to community
Government	Compliance	Improved competitiveness

Source: Adapted with permission from Cannon, T (1994) *Corporate Responsibility*, Pitman Publishing.[2]

Importantly in many organisations, it is no longer the case that the shareholders who own the organisation automatically have absolute power. Ever since the 1930s, there has been evidence of an increasing gap between shareholders and senior managers in large companies. Berle and Means[3] surveyed top management in the USA and produced evidence that there was an increasing gap between senior managers and shareholders. In about half of the 2000 American companies studied, 'ownership' had become separated from 'control'. Stakeholder *managers* did not necessarily have the same interests as stakeholder *shareholders*.

Managers may be more interested in size than profits: as companies grow, they are more protected from take-over and can afford to offer larger and more prestigious rewards to their leading managers.[4] By contrast, owners are more likely to be concerned with maximising profits and seeking only moderate growth. Unless managers in large organisations are threatened by take-over or incentivised financially, they may take a broader view of the purpose of the organisation than shareholder.[5][6][7] For example, shareholder dividends may be less important to senior managers than power and prestige. Shareholding is fragmented in large companies, and as a result such managers have considerable power.

12.2.3 Analysing stakeholder power

Stakeholders can have both a positive and a negative influence on an organisation's mission and objectives: many organisations will welcome the contributions and discussions with many who have power.

Some of the major groups of stakeholders are shown in Fig 12.2. The analysis of their relative power is likely to vary from country to country. In addition, there is likely to be variation by industry: the volume car industry may well have a different profile from a more fragmented industry, such as the textile garment industry with its smaller companies and family shareholdings. It is difficult to generalise but the checklist in Exhibit 12.1 may provide a useful guide to assist in analysing the relative power of stakeholders in a particular organisation.

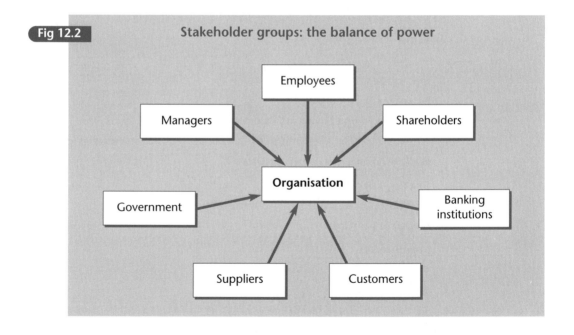

Fig 12.2   **Stakeholder groups: the balance of power**

However welcome contributions may be to the development process, the fact remains that there are likely to be conflicts of interest. Those stakeholders with the most power need to be considered most carefully. A *stakeholder power analysis* can be broken down into five discrete steps:

1 Identify the major stakeholders.

2 Establish their interests and claims on the organisation, especially as new strategy initiatives are developed.

3 Determine the degree of power that each group holds through its ability to force or influence change as new strategies are developed.

4 Develop mission, objectives and strategy development, possibly prioritising to minimise power clashes.

5 Consider how to divert trouble before it starts, possibly by negotiating with key groups.

Exhibit 12.1　　　　　　　　**Checklist for the analysis of stakeholder power**

Managers

- Large or small company? Relative remuneration versus employees?
- Style of company on hire and fire?
- Company profitability versus industry?

Employees

- Trade union legislation?
- Presence of workers representation on supervisory board?
- Widespread presence and acceptance across company?
- Presence of workers' co-operative?
- National traditions on unionisation and influence?

Government

- *Laissez-faire* or *dirigiste*?
- Shareholding and ownership policy beyond national institutions?
- Support for favoured industries? Encourage registration of shares in companies?
- Favour world trade or protectionist?

Banking institutions

- Shareholding or just loan involvement?
- Presence on supervisory board?

Shareholders

- Have full voting shares?
- Elect management to supervisory board?
- Have blocking or cross-shareholdings that make external pressure difficult?
- Family influence (still) strong?
- Can they sue the company for poor performance? (They can in the USA.)

Customers and suppliers

See the Five Forces analysis in Chapter 3.

Key strategic principles

- Stakeholders are the individuals and groups who have an interest in the organisation. Consequently, they may wish to influence its mission and objectives.

- The key issue with regard to stakeholders is that the organisation needs to take them into account in formulating its mission and objectives.

- The difficulty is that stakeholder interests may conflict. Consequently, the organisation will need to resolve which stakeholders have priority. Stakeholder power needs to be analysed.

- Stakeholder Power Analysis covers five stages: identification of stakeholders, establishment of their interests and claims, estimation of their degree of power, prioritised mission development, negotiation with key groups.

12.3 COMPANY CULTURE AND MISSION

Power and stakeholders are not the only influences on the future direction of the company: a more subtle, but equally important, area is *company culture*. This was explored in Chapter 8. Achievement of company mission and objectives will be influenced by the company's culture – 'the way we do things around here'.

The behaviour that reflects an organisation's culture is for much of the time instinctive.[8] For example, when individuals join a new organisation, there is a period of socialisation when they fine-tune their approach to the new culture. After this period, only in specific circumstances do they become conscious of the culture in which they are operating. One of those situations is the development of the company's mission and objectives. The way things are done will almost certainly be reflected in the development of such vital issues.

Company culture will show itself in such issues as *attitudes to risk* – for example, the company may go for a really challenging and risky mission or a more cautious one? It will also be reflected in the organisation's *ability to undertake change* – for example, significant changes were planned as Ford went global in 1994. The company's ability to carry change through will depend on the company culture: the cultural web is a useful starting point.[9] Exhibit 12.2 shows how it might be developed for the Ford globalisation example. However this is only part of a broader consideration of culture that needs to be undertaken in the context of mission and objectives (*see* Chapter 8).

| Exhibit 12.2 | Ford company culture as it started to 'go global' in 1994[10] |

Stories. Too early for clear development but Alex Trotman, the Chairman and CEO was UK-born (unusual in a US company), only in the job six months before the global changes began, worked his way up from the bottom of the organisation.

Routines. New matrix structure was introduced to manage the global business: there will be both functional and vehicle programme teams; long hours of work typical with the extensive foreign travel becoming part of the new routine. Expectations of long work hours and total commitment to Ford continued as part of the culture.

Rituals. Rewards innovation, cost saving, being on-time with projects.

Symbols. Trotman abolished executive privileges such as separate dining rooms; he wanted to signal a 'sea change' in attitudes; worldwide meetings from April to December 1994 to announce and discuss global change.

Organisation. New matrix structure; aimed at destroying national fiefdoms; global centralisation of research and development, production and purchasing.

Control. Detailed documentation; new computer systems so that they can operate in real-time globally.

Rewards. Still to come in the new organisation but past performance was reflected in the promotions announced.

Power. 'Far reaching' management shakeup with a new structure, introducing uncertainty and many new faces into the senior positions. Power change was signalled in a major way.

Key strategic principles

- The culture of the organisation will also influence and be reflected in the mission and objectives.
- Typically, attitudes to risk and the ability to undertake change will form and guide the development of such areas.

12.4 LEADERSHIP AND MISSION

12.4.1 Understanding the influence of leadership

General Electric's Jack Welch, Francois Michelin of Michelin Rubber, Lord Hanson, Akio Morita of Sony, Gianni Agnelli of Fiat are all examples of leaders who have guided and directed their companies. *Leadership* is defined as:

> '*influence, that is the art or process of influencing people so that they will strive willingly and enthusiastically toward the achievement of the group's mission.*'[11]

The organisation's mission does not always result from a process of discussion, but may be actively directed by an individual with strategic vision.

Visionary leadership inspires the impossible: fiction becomes truth.[12]

Leadership is a vital ingredient in inspiring organisations to new horizons. The potential that leaders have for influencing the overall direction of the company is arguably considerable. There is substantial anecdotal evidence to support this observation. In drawing up the mission statement and developing corporate strategy, it would therefore be wise to consider carefully the personality, role and power of the leading person in the organisation.

Given the evident power that leaders may have in developing the company's mission and strategy, it is important to note some areas of caution based on research:

- Leaders should to some extent *reflect* their followers[13] and may need to be good team players in some company cultures if they are to effect change or they will not be followed.
- Vision can be eccentric, obsessed and not always logical.[14]
- It is certainly possible to exaggerate the importance of individuals when they are leading large and diverse groups.

Certainly, these latter features are important in the modern, complex world of corporate strategy. Companies such as Philip Morris (US), Royal Dutch Shell (UK/Netherlands) and Toyota (Japan) may all be more comfortable with a corporate leader who is inclined to be evolutionary rather than revolutionary. To this extent, we may be suspicious of the hero worship of management saviours who have come to the rescue of failing businesses with vision and purpose.

The same variations can be found in small business, not-for-profit and government organisations. In every case, leadership can have a profound effect on mission.

12.4.2 Analysing leadership

Although the subject of leadership has been studied extensively, there is no general agreement on the method of analysis.[15] The *best-fit* analytical approach is perhaps the most useful for the purposes of corporate strategy because it allows each situation to be treated differently. It identifies three key elements:

- the chief executive officer,
- the senior/middle managers who carry out the tasks, and
- the nature of the strategies that will be undertaken.

Each of these is then plotted on a common scale, ranging from rigid (or heavily structured) to relaxed (or supportive and flexible). The best fit is then sought for these three elements. An example is shown in Fig 12.3. The result is inevitably vague but may prove useful in identifying the balance of style and its influence on people and strategies.

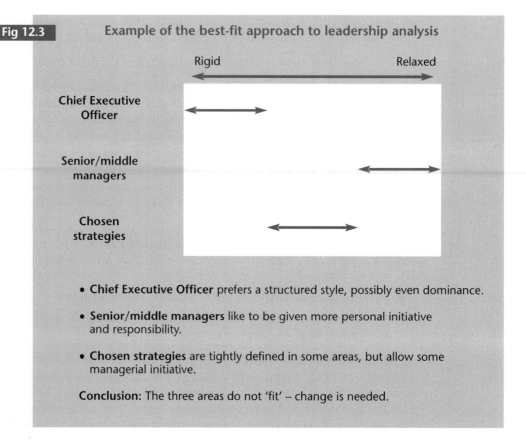

Fig 12.3 Example of the best-fit approach to leadership analysis

- **Chief Executive Officer** prefers a structured style, possibly even dominance.

- **Senior/middle managers** like to be given more personal initiative and responsibility.

- **Chosen strategies** are tightly defined in some areas, but allow some managerial initiative.

Conclusion: The three areas do not 'fit' – change is needed.

12.4.3 Leadership style

Leadership style can vary from the *shared vision* approach of Senge to the *dominance* of individuals, such as the first Henry Ford or Margaret Thatcher in the UK in the late 1980s.

Shared vision approach Senge had a useful perspective on the relationship between the organisation and its leadership.[16] It is the *leaders* of the organisation that can show the way. However, he argued that, in well-managed development, the *whole organisation* is involved in developing the mission and objectives. The way an organisation evolves is a function of its leadership as much as its strategy. However, the leader does not dominate and decide for the organisation, rather he or she helps the organisation to develop a *shared vision* of its future and the changes required to achieve it. It is the leader who focusses on the underlying trends, forces for change and their impact on the organisation. To explain his view, Senge quotes an age-old vision of leadership by Lao Tsu that expresses this relationship between the leader and the organisation:

> *The wicked leader is he who people despise.*
> *The good leader is he who people revere.*
> *The great leader is he who the people say, 'We did it ourselves.'*

Dominance approach The words of Lao Tsu read well, but may not be appropriate in some strategic situations. If a company is in crisis, then it may need strong and firm central leadership to enable the company to survive. When a company is in the early stages of development with a new vision about its future, it may also benefit from a strong, entrepreneurial leader with a quite different style and approach to the mission.

12.4.4 Conclusion

The leadership system that best describes the management style of the leader of the organisation needs to be taken into account in devising the mission and objectives. Where the leader is dominant then he or she will be involved early. Where the leader is more consultative then early involvement will be on a more participative basis. In addition, the style of the leader will be conditioned by the style and culture of the organisation and the development of mission and objectives will also need to take this into account in devising its procedures.

Key strategic principles

- Leaders can have a profound influence on mission and objectives. They may be particularly important in moving the organisation forward to new challenges.

- There is no agreement on how to analyse leadership. The best-fit analytical approach can be used. It is useful in strategy because it allows each situation to be treated differently.

- Leadership style can vary from shared vision to dominance. The style needs to be modified to suit the strategic situation.

12.5 BUSINESS ETHICS IN CORPORATE STRATEGY

Business ethics encompasses the standards and conduct that an organisation sets itself in its dealings within the organisation and with its external environment. Given the ability of modern businesses to contribute to the world at large or inflict damage beyond the business itself, most companies would now accept that some form of ethical standard should govern and guide their activities. There is no one appropriate time to introduce such standards but they should be reflected in the development of the organisation's mission statement and so deserve to be highlighted here. An example can be seen in the Ford mission statement in Exhibit 12.5.

It is not the function of this book to explore the vast topic of ethics in a general sense. There are three areas that might be explored in the context of corporate strategy:

1 *The extent of ethical considerations.* Beyond the legal minimum, to what extent does the organisation wish to consider the ethical issues that could arise in its conduct of its business? Does it wish to be involved in every area or lay down some basic principles and then leave parts or individuals to conduct themselves appropriately?

2 *The cost of ethical considerations.* Some actions will have a cost to the organisation. Many of the real conflicts arise here because if such measures were without cost then they would be easily undertaken. There are no abstract rules but each organisation will need to consider this area.

3 *The recipient of the responsibility*. Is it considered that the organisation has a responsibility to the state? To the local community? To individuals? To special interest groups? These matters will need careful consideration in the light of the particular circumstances of the organisation.

Furthermore, ethical considerations may influence corporate strategy at a number of levels:

● *The national and international level* – the role of the organisation in society and the country. Political, economic and social issues such as those explored in Chapter 3 will impact here: *laissez-faire* versus *dirigiste*, the role and power of trade blocks and closer economic union. The organisation is entitled to have a view on these matters and to seek to influence society, if it so desires.

● *The corporate level* – ethical and corporate issues over which the organisation has some direct control. Such matters as the preservation of the environment, contributions to political parties, representations to the country's legislative parliament are all examples of direct corporate activities that need to be resolved.

● *The individual manager and employee level* – standards of behaviour set by the organisation for individual managers and workers. Some of these matters may not be strategic in nature in the sense that they are unlikely to affect the future direction of the organisation overall but rather the future of individuals. However, there may well be some general policies – for example on religious, ethnic and equality issues – that both involve the individual and fundamental matters relating to the direction of the organisation. These general matters of policy deserve to be treated at the highest possible level and therefore come within the ambit of corporate strategy.

The values of the organisation will need to be reflected in its mission statement; even the absence of values in the mission statement will serve as an indication of the organisation's position and its perceived role in society.

It should be noted that not all commercial organisations believe that they have a role beyond their own business: they take the view that society is perfectly capable of looking after itself and the prime responsibility of the enterprise is to care for its shareholders. In such a case, the company's mission statement is unlikely to include any comment on business ethics. It should be emphasised that this does *not* mean such a company would behave unethically; simply that there is no need to reflect this in its mission.

There are other companies who take the view that it is in the long-term benefit of both the company and the shareholders for the company to play a role in society beyond the minimum described by law. Sponsorship, welfare provisions, strong ethical beliefs and standards may all follow from such a view and be reflected in comments *associated with* the mission statement, but not directly in the mission statement which will still have a largely commercial purpose.

Beyond this again, there are organisations that exist primarily or wholly for their social function in society – for example, those engaged in providing social services. Clearly, for this group, it will be vital to specify the relationship with society. This group may well wish to include some statement of their beliefs and values in their mission statement.

As an example of how business can both work within the community and at the same time focus on its more obvious commercial concerns, Case study 12.1 on the UK charity, Business in the Community, provides a useful model. Essentially, it allows those businesses who believe that they should have a role in the community to *channel their efforts* while at the same time focussing on what they do commercially. Similar organisations exist in other countries, ranging from chambers of commerce to some specific industry initiatives.

CASE STUDY 12.1

Mission and objectives at Business in the Community[17]

The UK charity, Business in the Community, spans the divide between the commercial demands of business and the ethical responsibilities of businesses to the community in which they operate. Its mission and objectives reflect this dual role.

Established in 1982, Business in the Community (BITC), is a not-for-profit organisation with a membership of 450 companies, including 80 of the *The Times* Top 100. Operating through a network of regional offices covering England, Northern Ireland and Wales, it has a staff of 140, a third of whom are secondees from business or the public sector. BITC has a sister organisation, Scottish Business in the Community, which operates independently.

BITC works with member companies to help raise business awareness of community issues, promote action through campaigns, encourage partnerships across the public, private and voluntary sectors and match business resources to community needs. Membership is by annual subscription, based on company size and structure and level of service desired.

BITC is headed by its President, HRH The Prince of Wales, and is governed by a board of business, public and voluntary sector leaders. Campaigns are led by leadership teams of senior business men and women. It had an income of £4.86 million, of which 85 per cent came from business through membership fees or contributions to campaigns.

It defined its mission as:

> To support the social and economic regeneration of communities by raising the quality and extent of business involvement and by making that involvement a natural part of successful business practice.

In 1994 the organisation conducted a strategic review of all its activities in conjunction with a wide range of BITC member companies and community partners. As a result of this review, it defined its objectives, and these have been updated for 1996 as follows.

During the next three years, Business in the Community is committed to:

- Measurably improving the quality, impact and sustainability of private sector investment in the community;
- Increasing the number of key companies at national, regional, branch and subsidiary levels, which are engaged in corporate community involvement;
- Acting as an effective broker between business and voluntary organisations serving community needs;
- Raising employer awareness and capacity to contribute effectively to the economic and social well-being of Britain by conducting selected campaigns;
- Serving as the leading authority on corporate community involvement and developing as a centre of expertise on corporate social responsibility.

BITC will achieve these objectives by:

- Using skills and resources of business to address community needs through an effective network of Regional offices;
- Raising the awareness and commitment of business leaders through an expanded programme of Seeing is Believing visits and targeted communications strategy;
- Assisting companies to develop effective community investment strategies through improved account management, increased information exchange, skill building and advisory services;
- Increasing the extent and quality of business involvement through a limited number of high quality campaigns;
- Significantly expanding the capability of companies to support their employees, at all levels, to participate in community affairs through volunteering, management assignments and contributed expertise;

CASE STUDY 12.1 continued

- Promoting and expanding our relations with partner organisations including Training and Enterprise Councils, City Challenge, local government and key voluntary organisations at national and local level;
- Influencing public policies affecting business investment in the community and the future development of public/private partnerships.

The principles which will guide our activities are:

- Focus activities on those companies most likely to lead and influence the behaviour of others;
- Customise our support to meet the varying levels of resource and capability of member companies and of partner organisations;
- Undertake only those campaigns which are consistent with our mission, generate private sector financing and have a significant impact on employer behaviour and the community;

- Work increasingly with and through local partnerships to achieve our objectives;
- Establish clear, measurable outcomes for all our work and make public our results;
- Act as a catalytic, high performance organisation with the skills, practice and values to make BITC a centre of excellence in its field.

CASE QUESTIONS

1 *In what ways do this statement and its contents differ from those of a commercial organisation?*

2 *Are there any areas that you think would benefit from greater clarity or other developments? Can you improve on it?*

Key strategic principles

- Business ethics means the standards and conduct that an organisation sets itself in its dealings within the organisation and with its external environment. These need to be reflected in the mission statement.

- There are three prime considerations in developing business ethics: the extent of ethical considerations, their cost and the recipient of the responsibility.

- There are numerous differences between organisations over what should be covered under ethics, reflecting fundamentally different approaches to doing business.

12.6 DEVELOPING THE MISSION STATEMENT

As discussed in Section 12.1 the mission statement outlines the broad directions that the organisation will follow and briefly summarises the reasoning and values that lie behind it. The purpose of the mission statement is to *communicate* to all the stakeholders inside and outside the organisation what the company stands for and where it is headed. It therefore needs to be expressed in a language and with a commitment that everyone of those involved can understand and relate to his or her own circumstances.[18]

12.6.1 What is a mission statement?

There is some dispute among strategists over the definition of a mission statement.[19][20] There has been a high degree of interest by companies and other practitioners but relatively limited definition and research of a more academic nature.

There are considerable differences of view on the form, purpose and content of such statements. Some researchers have questioned the lengthy nature and content of such statements: some[21][22] have even suggested that companies should concentrate on short and concise statements of their 'strategic intent'. At the same time, many leading companies in Europe and North America have developed and quoted their mission statements in their Annual Reports and Accounts. Even if there is no agreed definition, companies still find the process of developing their mission useful.

12.6.2 How to formulate mission statements

No two organisations are exactly the same in terms of ownership, resources or environmental circumstances, and as a result the mission statement is peculiar to each organisation. Essentially, there are six elements:

- Consideration must be given to the *nature* of the organisation's business. Typical questions include What business are we in? What business should we be in?
- The responses need to be considered from the *customer* perspective, rather than the perspective of the organisation itself: 'We are in the business of developing books that will inform and educate our readers about strategy' *rather than* 'We are in the business of developing textbooks on strategic issues.'
- The mission needs to reflect the basic *values and beliefs* of the organisation:[23] 'We believe it is important to respect the environment and offer employment that is free from any prejudices associated with culture, race or religion.'
- Where possible, the mission needs to refer to *sustainable competitive advantage*[24]: 'It is our aim to be a leader in this field.' This may not be possible in a diversified holding company. It may also be more appropriate to adjust this to reflect *distinctiveness* in an organisation which has no direct competitors – for example, a charity. It may be that the business is unable to be truly distinctive. For example, the Ford mission statement refers to the company being a 'worldwide leader' which implies some distinctiveness while at the same time recognising that it will be difficult for the company to be unique in such a mass market.
- The mission needs to summarise the *main reasons* for its choice of approach: 'We are a team. We must treat each other with trust and respect' is a good example from the Ford mission statement.

All the above will rely on *business judgement*, which is imprecise and difficult to define by its very nature. Business judgements are usually made by senior managers in the company.

A mission statement needs to summarise the organisation's purposes and be communicated easily. As a result it needs to be worded carefully. It needs to be written in language that is commonly understood.

As mentioned above, mission statements need to include some statement of the logic and values of the organisation in order to capture better the spirit of the statement and to facilitate its communication within and outside the organisation. Managers sometimes find it easier to explore and articulate the strategy areas specific to their business, rather than the human values that underly them. However, if there is to be true commitment to the mission, then those underlying values need to be explored and made part of the mission. Such a process may take some years to complete but is an important part of the overall development.

Finally, some criteria for judging the effectiveness of a mission statement are shown in Exhibit 12.3.

Exhibit 12.3	Some criteria for judging mission statements[25]

A mission statement should:

- be specific enough to have an impact upon the behaviour of individuals throughout the business;
- reflect the distinctive advantages of the organisation and be based upon an objective recognition of its strengths and weaknesses;
- be realistic and attainable;
- be flexible enough to take account of shifts in the environment.

12.6.3 Clarity in mission statements

Lack of clarity in a mission statement means that there is potential confusion when it comes to developing the objectives and strategy associated with the mission. Exhibit 12.4 gives examples of mission statements taken from the Annual Reports of the companies concerned. In fairness, these statements may have greater clarity within the company than they appear to have in the published summaries below, but, nevertheless, they do illustrate the potential for confusion.

Exhibit 12.4	Examples of potentially confusing mission statements

British Airways (UK) Annual Report 1992
'Our mission: to be the best and most successful company in the airline industry.'
'Our goals ... include being

- financially strong
- global leader: to secure a leading share of air travel business worldwide
- service and value: to provide overall superior service.'

Comment: What do 'best' and 'successful' actually mean? Largest? Most profitable? Greatest customer satisfaction? What does a 'leading share' mean? What does 'superior service' mean?

Daimler–Benz (Germany) Annual Report 1993
'The corporate principles of Daimler–Benz include ... Our work at Daimler–Benz serves people and their environment. We aim to offer the world's most advanced products, systems and services. Our core businesses include vehicles for passengers and freight transportation ... aerospace ... energy systems. In these areas, Daimler–Benz aims to be a world leader.'

Comment: Plenty of companies aim to serve people and their environment. Where is the distinctiveness? Do people really want the world's most advanced systems? What does being a world leader mean?

Chargeurs (France) Annual Report 1992
'Chargeurs is a diversified industry group which operates in textiles and entertainment. It is also active in automobile transportation, leisure cruises and protective surfacing. One of France's leading international companies, Chargeurs has 10 500 employees worldwide ... Chargeurs is committed to being a leader in the markets in which it operates.'

Comment: It may desire to be a 'leader', but how can this be realistic when it is up against such giants worldwide as Time Warner and other Japanese/US companies in entertainment?

The need for precision and care in the development of mission statements is an important part of their analysis and development. The examples in Exhibit 12.4 are just short extracts from longer material. As an example of a complete mission statement, Exhibit 12.5 returns to the Ford Motor Company of the opening case in this chapter and presents the material circulated within the company.

Exhibit 12.5

Ford Motor Company
Company mission, values and guiding principles

MISSION

Ford Motor Company is a worldwide leader in automotive and financial products and services. Our mission is to improve continually our products and services to meet our customers' needs, allowing us to prosper as a business and to provide a reasonable return for our stockholders, the owners of our business.

VALUES

How we accomplish our mission is as important as the mission itself. Fundamental to success for the Company are these basic values:

▶ **People** – Our people are the source of our strength. They provide our corporate intelligence and determine our reputation and vitality. Involvement and teamwork are our core human values.

▶ **Products** – Our products are the end result of our efforts, and they should be the best in serving customers worldwide. As our products are viewed, so are we viewed.

▶ **Profits** – Profits are the ultimate measure of how efficiently we provide customers with the best products for their needs. Profits are required to survive and grow.

GUIDING PRINCIPLES

▶ **Quality Comes First** – To achieve customer satisfaction, the quality of our products and services must be our number one priority.

▶ **Customers are the Focus of Everything We Do** – Our work must be done with our customers in mind, providing better products and services than our competition.

▶ **Continuous Improvement is Essential to Our Success** – We must strive for excellence in everything we do: in our products, in their safety and value – and in our services, our human relations, our competitiveness, and our profitability.

▶ **Employee Involvement is Our Way of Life** – We are a team. We must treat each other with trust and respect.

▶ **Dealers and Suppliers are our Partners** – The Company must maintain mutually beneficial relationships with dealers, suppliers and our other business associates.

▶ **Integrity is Never Compromised** – The conduct of our Company worldwide must be pursued in a manner that is socially responsible and commands respect for its integrity and for its positive contributions to society. Our doors are open to men and women alike without discrimination and without regard to ethnic origin or personal beliefs.

Source: Copyright © Ford Motor Company 1996. Reprinted with permission.

> **Key strategic principles**
>
> ● The mission statement outlines the broad directions that the organisation will follow and briefly summarises the reasoning and values that lie behind it.
>
> ● The purpose of the mission statement is to communicate to all the stake-holders inside and outside the organisation what the company stands for and where it is headed.
>
> ● There are six elements in formulating a mission statement: nature of the organisation, customer perspective, values and beliefs, competitive advantage or distinctiveness, main reasons for the approach.
>
> ● Mission statements rely on business judgement but criteria can be developed to assess the results.

12.7 DEVELOPING THE OBJECTIVES

Objectives take the generalities of the mission statement and turn them into more *specific* commitments: usually, this will cover *what* is to be done and *when* the objective is to be completed. Objectives may include a *quantified* objective – for example, a specific increase in market share or an improvement in some measure of product quality. But the objective will not necessarily be quantified.

The purposes of objectives therefore are:

1 to focus the management task on a specific outcome;
2 to provide a means of assessing whether the outcome has been achieved after the event.

12.7.1 Different kinds of objectives

In the 1960s and 1970s, several writers were keen to make the objectives quantified and thus measurable.[26] It is now generally recognised that some objectives cannot easily be quantified – for example, those associated with business ethics and employee job satisfaction – yet they may represent extremely important parts of the activities of companies.

Nevertheless, a company that has a mission but no quantified objectives at all would be in danger of engaging in meaningless jargon. As we saw in Chapter 9, it is usual for companies to set objectives in two areas, the first of which is likely to be quantified and the second only partially:

● *Financial objectives* – for example, earnings per share, return on shareholders' funds, cash flow.

● *Strategic objectives* – for example, market share increase (quantified), higher product quality (quantified), greater customer satisfaction (partially quantified), employee job satisfaction (supported by research survey, but not necessarily quantified).

None of the above areas is necessarily more important than any other. Individual organisations will devise their own lists depending on their stakeholders, culture, leadership, mission and future direction.

12.7.2 Conflict between objectives

There are some objectives that ensure the *survival* of the organisation – for example, adequate cash flow, basic financial performance. These need to be considered early in the process. However, for many organisations, survival is not their main concern for the future: for example, the two organisations in this chapter, Ford and BITC, are not about to disappear tomorrow. A major issue for these organisations concerns *development and growth*: for example, the Ford statement refers to 'survive and grow'.

Development and growth take time and require investment funds. Money invested in growth is not available for distribution now to shareholders. Potentially, growth objectives are therefore in conflict with the short-term requirement to provide returns to shareholders, the owners of the company. Taking money out of the business today will not provide the investment for the future. Objectives therefore need to reach a *compromise* between the short and long term. It is for this reason that the Ford statement refers to providing a '*reasonable* return for our stock-holders, the owners of our business'. This comment will then be translated into a numerical objective in terms of a dividend payout at Ford that reflects the need to invest as well as satisfy the shareholders.

Where a *competitive environment* exists, as in the global car industry, it is particularly important to recognise that any funds distributed now make it much more difficult to maintain performance against competitors in the future. For any organisation that needs to distribute the value that it adds, there will always be a potential conflict between the short and long term.

12.7.3 Implications of shareholder structure

The conflict between the long and short term becomes even more acute in some national markets where *shareholder power* is particularly strong. The North American and UK stockmarkets have a reputation for *short-termism*[27] – that is companies face the need to maintain their dividend record or face the threat of being acquired. Other European, Japanese and South-East Asian companies have had less pressure in this respect because their shares are often held by governments and banking institutions who have been able to take a longer term view. For example, German car companies such as Volkswagen and Mercedes Benz have had large share interests held by leading German banks. By contrast, Ford and General Motors have had their shares largely held on the open stock exchanges of Europe and North America. The US companies have faced more acute shareholder pressures than the German companies. These priorities are bound to be reflected in how the objectives for the company are devised initially and monitored later.

12.7.4 Challenging but achievable objectives

When developing objectives, one of the real issues that arise is just how *challenging* the objectives should be. Do we merely set objectives that are easy to achieve so that we can then show real success beyond this? Or do we set objectives that are more challenging but still achievable? If we set the latter, to what extent are these open to negotiation with those who will be responsible for delivering them? Do we need a contract? And a reward?

These are difficult questions to resolve and answers will depend on the culture and style of the organisation and its senior managers, along with the nature of the organisation's mission and its competition, if any. Some will set demanding objectives and assess performance accordingly; others will discuss and agree (rather than set) a balance between demanding and easy objectives. In spite of Peter Drucker's optimism that this might be done more scientifically by the late-1990s,[28] this aspect of objective setting still requires great business judgement.

Key strategic principles

- Objectives take the generalities of the mission statement and turn them into more specific commitments: usually, this will cover what is to be done and when the objective is to be completed.

- Different kinds of objectives are possible. Some will be quantified and some not.

- There may be conflict between objectives, particularly between the long- and short-term interests of the organisation.

- Shareholding structures will impact on objectives. UK and USA companies are under greater pressure for short-term performance.

- Objectives need to be challenging but achievable.

12.8 CORPORATE, FUNCTIONAL AND BUSINESS OBJECTIVES

The development of corporate strategy is not just a task for the Chief Executive Officer (CEO) and the main board. It usually involves many others in the organisation, whether it is in the commercial, state or voluntary sector. The discussion that takes place often requires a number of meetings between the CEO and managers in the area concerned. Strategies take time to emerge. Even after this, they are subject to review and change depending on such matters as changes in the environment. Strategies that remain fixed for a number of years usually do so because of the lead times on the activities involved: for example, it may take several years to invest in a new car model, so that the strategy is fixed over this time frame.

Small
organisations

In a small organisation, such discussions take place without excessive formality. Typically, the CEO might chair a meeting on the topic and then talk further with the participants several weeks later after background analysis has been undertaken. Executives from different functional areas of the business might be asked for their opinions as the strategy is explored. After agreement, functional executives (marketing, finance, human resources, production, etc.) might take both the overall strategy and specific aspects of it back to their own areas. For example, the cash flow implications of a new car launch, as stocks of the new model are built up prior to the launch date, will clearly be a matter that will concern finance; the need to recruit additional staff to work on production will clearly matter both to human resources and production. It is thus quite possible that the *corporate* objectives will need to be *translated* into *functional* objectives. Clearly, functional objectives are subordinate to the overall corporate objective.

Larger
organisations

In larger organisations and those with scarce resources, the situation may be more complicated. Very often such organisations are split up by the type of business: for example, in the Ford example at the beginning of the chapter, there were five groups, each responsible for a different car model range. Such groups are often called *divisions* or *Strategic Business Units* (*SBUs*): each may be so large that it has its own CEO and functional managers. In these circumstances, the corporate objectives need to be examined by each of the divisions or SBUs. In addition, the corporation may not have unlimited funds and will need to allocate those that it has. Where an SBU has received less than the funds it requested, it may be inappropriate for the headquarters to set an objective as demanding as it might otherwise have been.

For these reasons, corporate objectives will not necessarily translate into the same objective for each SBU. For example:

● There may be limited financial resources which are *rationed* between the SBUs; it would not be realistic to expect all the SBUs to perform against the group objectives.

● Some divisions may be in rapidly growing markets that will need substantial funds but will deliver well above any standardised group-wide objective; other divisions may be in decline and struggle to perform against any averaged corporate objective regardless of the resources they are given.

In larger organisations, a distinction needs to be drawn between what the overall corporation will achieve and what it will expect each of its divisions to achieve. The *corporate objectives* will need to be *translated* into *divisional* or *SBU objectives*. The divisional objectives will also be subordinate to the corporate objectives.

Key strategic principles

● In developing objectives, the overall corporate objective needs to be translated into objectives for different functions or business units.

● In larger organisations and those with scarce resources, the objectives may need to be adjusted to take into account the circumstances and trading situation of different parts of the organisation.

12.9 EMERGENT STRATEGY PERSPECTIVES

In this chapter, we have been exploring mission and objectives from the viewpoint of the *prescriptive* corporate strategist. This has been done because it is occasionally easier to explore aspects of a topic without all the qualifications that might apply in practice. The work of Professor J B Quinn on 'logical Incrementalism' has been ignored up to this point.[29]

Quinn began his seminal 1978 paper with a quote from an interview he undertook with a manager who commented:

> *'When I was younger, I always conceived of a room where all these [strategic] concepts were worked out for the whole company. Later I didn't find any such room …The strategy [of the company] may not even exist in the mind of one man. I certainly don't know where it is written down. It is simply transmitted in the series of decisions made.'*

Quinn went on to comment that when well managed major organisations make significant changes in strategy, the approaches they use frequently bear little resemblance to the rational–analytical systems so often touted in the planning literature. He was reacting (with justification, in my view) to the formalised planning systems that were being recommended in the 1970s: strategy was almost seen to be a mathematical formula rather than the craft it actually is. An important issue is whether his comments should still be applied to some of the processes described in this chapter, especially in the later sections.

Stakeholder analysis and company culture analysis would probably not cause a problem. Business ethics might also be acceptable. However, Quinn would have a difficulty with the idea of a mission statement. It was for this reason that Campbell and Yeung[30] commented on the need to see a mission statement not just as a statement of purpose, but also as an expression of the *values of the organisation*. Nevertheless, the practice of producing mission statements might cause Quinn and other emergent strategists some concern. However, as we have seen, they are extensively used by companies in the late 1990s. Translating these into objectives involves such an element of business judgement that Quinn might consider that his original research was still valid.

Key strategic principles

- There is a danger in being too rational in the development of mission and objectives.

- Mission statements need to reflect the *values* of the organisation as well as a statement of its purpose.

12.10 SHAREHOLDER AND STAKEHOLDER POWER AROUND THE WORLD

Much of the shareholder research appears to have been conducted in an Anglo–American context. In the UK and North America, stock markets have been described as demanding short-term results from quoted companies. Shares are widely held and many larger companies have *public share quotations*. This does not imply that shareholders always put direct pressure on senior company managers but company shares can always be sold as a means of applying pressure. Privatisation has largely taken place so that most companies are only influenced indirectly by governments. Some unions are still powerful in the US in certain industries, but unions lost their substantial power base in the UK through the Thatcher labour law reforms of the 1980s.

Owner–stakeholder interests across other parts of Europe are not necessarily the same. Specifically, *large commercial banks* have much larger shareholdings in major companies in Germany,[31] France,[32] Italy[33] and Spain.[34] For example, in Germany, the large German banks have traditionally held large share blocks in leading German companies: Deutsche Bank in 1994 owned 28 per cent of Daimler–Benz, 10 per cent of Allianz and 25 per cent of Karstadt – Germany's largest car, insurance and department store chain respectively. Such banks will certainly be interested in the long-term profitability of their investments but do not have the short-term profit horizons of the Anglo–American model. The banks can afford to wait for years because each shareholding is only a small part of their total portfolio and because they are able to spread the risk. Banking power has usually been benign and supportive.

Across Europe, it is not just a question of bank shareholding. For example, it was estimated in 1991 that only seven of the top 200 companies listed in Milan had over half their shares in public hands.[35] There has been some resistance to the widespread ownership of shares in Germany.[36] In France, the state has been the traditional owner of companies some of which were privatised in the 1980s with more to come in the mid-1990s.

We must also not forget the strong tradition in some European countries of *worker-co-operatives* and other mutual and non-profit organisations, where the workers and others own the shares of the enterprise. These are shown in Exhibit 12.6. In these organisations, power will be distributed differently. There will be more worker involvement, open discussion and employee representation on senior company councils.

| Exhibit 12.6 | Worker co-operatives and similar forms of power[37] |

These are particularly strong in the following areas:

- Co-operative banks.
- Production co-operatives such as farmers' agricultural organisations, including, for example, the largest milk producer in the EU, the Dutch company Campina MelkUnie.[38]
- Consumer co-operatives, such as retail and wholesale shops, including CWS in the UK and Migros in Switzerland.[39]
- Social pharmacies where legislation permits.
- Social tourism organisations – for example, in France, where they represent 12 per cent of the overall tourist activity of the country.[40]
- Housing and social accommodation co-operatives.

In addition to all the above, there are also a range of *mutual* companies whose shares are essentially owned by their members. The UK has a particularly strong tradition in this area. These include, for example, some of the larger insurance companies in Europe. In all these cases, it would be quite correct to envisage co-operative organisations having a rather broader perspective on the purposes of the organisation.

Moving beyond Europe, Japanese share ownership is widespread but the structure of industry is different with strong groupings and interlocking shares of companies.[41] Hostile take-overs are almost unheard of: the Japanese word for take-over is the same as that for hijack and indicates the same degree of enthusiasm. The threat of hostile shareholder activity is muted. Union membership is low and has been in decline,[42] so stakeholder power from this source is also not high. Government involvement in industry development has traditionally been high in certain industries.[43] Power relationships are therefore more complex. The same considerations apply in other Asian countries such as Korea, Malaysia and Singapore.

Although the same depth of research has not been conducted on employee influence on the mission of organisation, the history of twentieth-century labour relations would suggest that there have periodically been conflicts in some Western countries (but not all) between managers and workers. Stakeholder interests may not be the same.

Around the world, it is not at all clear how the balance of stakeholder interests will develop. What is certainly evident is the need to conduct a thorough analysis of stakeholders early in the process of developing corporate strategy.

Key strategic principles

- In developing mission statements, recognition needs to be given to the different power of shareholders in different countries around the world. There are greater pressures on companies in the UK and USA for short-term results.

- Mutual and non-profit co-operatives will approach power issues in the development of mission statements in a different way to other more commercial institutions.

Pink Elephant Company[44]

This case study describes the mission and strategy of a 15-year-old computer service company and its parent company in the Netherlands

It takes a leap of faith to entrust the valuable, weighty and serious contents of a company's computer centre to a computer services business with the name 'Pink Elephant'. However, that has not stopped hundreds of Dutch businesses commissioning Pink Elephant to sort out their computer centres, proving that a computer business does not have to find a new variation on the old stand-bys 'compu-', 'data' and 'technology' to come up with a winning name.

In the early days, Michael Westermann, one of the student-founders of Pink Elephant at the Technical University of Delft in 1980, asked his clients whether the name should be changed. The answer was no. 'One of them said to me, "It's the only computer company name that I don't have trouble remembering",' he recalls. Pink Elephant is now one of 11 computer services companies loosely allied within a holding company called Roccade, based in Zoetermeer outside The Hague. The name may not be as memorable as Pink Elephant, but it will probably become better known, when it is opened to outside investors, possibly from overseas, in a government privatisation.

The story of how Pink Elephant – an entrepreneurial start-up – became part of government-owned Roccade encapsulates the 45-year history of computing in the Netherlands. Roccade's nucleus is the former national computer agency, called 'Rijkscomputercentrum' or RCC. Set up in the early 1950s in the dawn of data processing, RCC was turned into a private company at arm's length from the government in 1990. RCC began buying other computer service companies, including Pink Elephant. The name Roccade is a reflection of the fact that about half of the group's Fl 480 million (£192 million) annual turnover is generated by RCC. In 1991, the first year after RCC's new private-

sector status, the company generated Fl 273 million in turnover. This jumped to Fl 416 million a year, thanks to acquisitions, and has been growing at double-digit rates ever since.

The long-term goal, says Westermann, is to double the company's sales, ensuring its ability to invest in research and development. Each of the 11 operating companies, all involved in computer services, has relative autonomy and retains its own 'label'. The group as a whole ranks among the largest computer service providers in the Netherlands, along with such competitors as Getronics and Cap Volmic.

The company is hoping that the 1996 share sale preserves its character but also proves to be a springboard for further growth. The privatisation options range from a bourse flotation to a sale to another company. An unspoken assumption is that the group's individual companies will retain their identities, preserving the name Pink Elephant as a tribute to irreverent thinking in the Dutch computer services industry.

Source: Financial Times, 20 March 1995

CASE QUESTIONS

1 *Do you think the company is wise to set an objective of boosting sales two- to threefold in the long term? What are the problems with this approach?*

2 *RCC has kept the identities and names of the companies it has acquired in order to preserve the entrepreneurial spirit of each company. Do you think that in these circumstances RCC itself can have any useful 'mission'? If so, what should this be?*

3 *Do you think that the privatisation of RCC should be reflected in its mission and objectives? If so, in what way?*

Balancing the objectives[45]

In this extract from his book, **The Practice of Management,** *Peter Drucker considers the importance of balancing objectives.*

In addition to balancing the immediate and the long-range future, management also has to balance the objectives. What is more important: an expansion in markets and sales volume, or a higher rate of return? How much time, effort and energy should be expended on improving manufacturing productivity? Would the same amount of effort or money bring greater returns if invested in new-product design?

There are few things that distinguish competent from incompetent management quite as sharply as the performance in balancing objectives. Yet, there is no formula for doing the job. Each business requires its own balance – and it may require a different balance at different times. The only thing that can be said is that balancing objectives is not a mechanical job, and is not achieved by 'budgeting'. The budget is the document in which balance decisions find final expression; but the decisions themselves require judgement; and the judgement will be sound only if it is based on sound analysis of the business. The ability of a management to stay within its budget is often considered a test of management skill. But the effort to arrive at the budget that best harmonises the divergent needs of the business is a much more important test of management's ability. The late Nicholas Dreystadt, head of Cadillac and one of the wisest managers I have ever met, said to me once: 'Any fool can learn to stay within his budget. But I have seen only a handful of managers in my life who can draw up a budget that is worth staying within.'

Objectives in the key areas are the 'instrument panel' necessary to pilot the business enterprise. Without them management flies by the 'seat of its pants' – without landmarks to steer by, without maps and without having flown the route before. However, an instrument panel is no better than the pilot's ability to read and interpret it. In the case of management, this means ability to anticipate the future. Objectives that are based on completely wrong anticipations may actually be worse than no objectives at all.

Source: Drucker, P (1961) *The Practice of Management* Butterworth-Heinemann, Oxford. Reproduced with permission.

SUMMARY

● The *mission* of an organisation outlines the general direction that it should follow in the future and outlines the rationale and values that lie behind it. The *objectives* are a more detailed commitment consistent with the organisation's mission and specify a particular time period. They may be quantified in some cases; this may be inappropriate in others. Prescriptive approaches emphasise the need to set out a mission and objectives for the next few years for the organisation.

● Some emergent approaches doubt the usefulness of a mission and objectives because the future is so uncertain. Other emergent approaches accept the need for a mission and objectives but place great emphasis on the need to include the managers and employees in its development.

● Stakeholders are the individuals and groups who have an interest in the organisation and as a result may wish to have a say in its mission and objectives. The organisation needs to take stakeholders into account in formulating its mission and objectives.

● Problems arise because stakeholder interests often conflict. Consequently, it is necessary for the organisation to determine which stakeholders have priority. Stakeholder power needs to be analysed and this can be done in five stages: identification of stakeholders, establishment of their interests and claims, estimation of their degree of power, prioritised mission development, negotiation with key groups.

● The culture of the organisation will also influence and be reflected in the mission and objectives. Typically, attitudes to risk and the ability to undertake change will form and guide the development of such areas.

● Leaders can have a profound influence on mission and objectives. They may be particularly important in moving the organisation forward to new challenges. There is no agreement on how to analyse leadership. The best-fit analytical approach can be used. It is useful in strategy because it allows each situation to be treated differently. Leadership style can vary from shared vision to dominance. The style needs to be modified to suit the strategic situation.

● Business ethics are the standards and conduct that an organisation sets itself in its dealings within the organisation and outside with its environment. These need to be reflected in the mission statement. There are three prime considerations in developing business ethics: the extent of ethical considerations, their cost and the recipient of the responsibility. There are numerous differences between organisations over what should be covered under ethics, reflecting fundamentally different approaches to doing business.

● The purpose of the mission statement is to *communicate* to all the stakeholders inside and outside the organisation what the company stands for and where it is headed.

● There are six elements in formulating a mission statement: nature of the organisation, customer perspective, values and beliefs, competitive advantage or distinctiveness, main reasons for the approach. Mission statements rely on business judgement but criteria can be developed to assess the results.

● Objectives translate the general directions of the mission statement into more specific commitments – usually covering what is to be done and when the objective is to be completed. Different kinds of objectives are possible – some quantified and some not. There may be conflict between objectives, particularly between the long- and short-term interests of the organisation. Shareholding structures will impact on objectives. UK and USA companies are under greater pressure for short-term performance. Objectives need to be challenging but achievable.

● There is a danger in being too rational in the development of mission and objectives. Mission statements need to reflect the *values* of the organisation as well as a statement of its purpose.

QUESTIONS

1   In the Ford case study at the beginning of the chapter, why do you think the company makes no mention in its mission of its desire to establish a global company? Does this desire need to be in there? What reasons might it have for excluding it?

2   Critically evaluate the form and content of the Ford mission and values in this chapter against its global objective.

3   The chapter suggests that the development of mission statements should be conducted from a customer viewpoint. Do you agree with this? What are the difficulties of this approach?

4   Choose two organisations with which you are familiar: one from the commercial sector (perhaps from work or from your place of study) and one voluntary body (perhaps from a hobby, sport or society to which you belong). Analyse their leadership and culture and show how these relate to their objectives.

5   Do small companies really need mission statements and objectives? What might be the problems of setting these in small companies? Does the Pink Elephant need a mission and objectives?

6   Do companies always need to behave ethically, regardless of the costs?

7   What are the benefits and problems of short-termism? How might this affect the development of the mission and objectives of an organisation?

8   Take an organisation with which you are familiar and suggest some areas where it has both quantified and unquantified objectives. Is it important that some are unquantified?

STRATEGIC PROJECT

Mission statements

Search out the mission statements and objectives of some large companies from their Annual Reports and Accounts. Critically evaluate the content of such statements.

FURTHER READING

On mission statements: Campbell, A and Yeung, S (1991) 'Creating a sense of mission', *Long Range Planning*, Aug.

On business ethics: Cannon, T (1994) *Corporate Responsibility*, Pitman Publishing, London.

On leadership: Handy, C (1994) *Understanding Organisations*, Penguin, London, Ch 4.

REFERENCES

1 Adapted from an article by Kevin Done in the *Financial Times*, 22 Apr 1994.

2 Adapted from Cannon, T (1994) *Corporate Responsibility*, Pitman Publishing, London.

3 Berle, A A and Means, G C (1967) *The Modern Corporation and Private Property*, Harvest, New York (originally published in 1932).

4 Marris, R (1964) *The Economic Theory of Managerial Capitalism*, Macmillan, Basingstoke.

5 Holl, P (1977) 'Control type and the market for corporate control in large US corporations', *Journal of Industrial Economics*, 25, pp259–73.

6 Lawriwsky, M L (1984) *Corporate Structure and performance*, Croom Helm, London.

7 Whittington, R (1993) *What is strategy and does it matter?*, Routledge, London.

8 Vielba, C (1995) 'Teaching managers about culture', *Journal of European Industrial Training*, Spring.

9 Johnson, G (1992) 'Managing strategic change: strategy, culture and action', *Long Range Planning*, 25(1), pp28–36.

10 Based on Griffiths, J (1994) 'Dark horse sets the pace', *Financial Times*, 22 Apr and other articles in the same paper on 17 Feb 1992, p14; 29 Mar 1994, p30; 11 Apr 1994, p20; 23 Apr 1994, p11; 4 Oct 1994, pVII; 2 Dec 1994, p17; 6 Jan 1995, p17; 23 Jan 1995, p10.

11 Weihrich, H and Koontz, H (1993) *Management: Global Perspective*, 10th edn, McGraw-Hill, p490.

12 Westley, F and Mintzberg, H (1989) 'Visionary leadership and strategic management', *Strategic Management Journal*, 10, pp17–32.

13 Homans, G (1965) *The Human Group*, Routledge and Kegan Paul. Chapter 7 on the 'Norton Street Gang' is illuminating and reflects research by Whyte in 1943.

14 Whittington, R (1993) Ibid, pp47–9.

15 Handy, C (1994) *Understanding Organisations*, 4th edn, Penguin, London, Ch 4.

16 Senge, P (1990) 'The Leader's New Work: building learning organisations', *Sloan Management Review*, Fall. Reprinted in De Wit, R and Meyer, R (1994) *Strategy: Process, Content and Context*, West Publishing, St Paul, Minn, pp132–41.

17 Business in the Community (1995) *Annual Report and Accounts*.

18 Christopher, M, Majaro, S and McDonald, M (1989) *Strategy: a guide for senior executives*, Wildwood House, Aldershot, Ch 1.

19 Campbell, A and Yeung, S (1991) 'Mission statements: selling corporate values to employees', *Long Range Planning*, 24(3).

20 Hooley, G, Cox, A and Adams, A (1991) 'Our five-year mission to boldly go where no man has been before', *Proceedings of the Marketing Education Group Annual Conference*, Cardiff, pp559–77.

21 Prahalad, C K and Doz, Y (1987) *The multinational mission*, Free Press, New York.

22 Hamel, G and Prahalad, C (1989) 'Strategic Intent', *Harvard Business Review*, May–June, pp79–91.

23 Campbell, A and Yeung, S (1991) Ibid.

24 Christopher, M *et al* (1989) Ibid.

25 Adapted from Christopher, M *et al* (1989) Ibid, p8.

26 Ansoff, I (1968) *Corporate Strategy*, Penguin, p44.

27 There are many papers on this controversial topic: *see*, for example, Williams, K, Williams, J and Haslam, C 'The hollowing out of British manufacturing and its implications for policy', *Economy and Society*, 19(4).

28 Drucker, P (1993) *The Practice of Management*, Butterworth-Heinemann, Oxford, p54. Reproduced with permission.

29 Quinn, J B (1978) 'Strategic Change: Logical Incrementalism', *Sloan Management Review*, Fall.

30 Campbell, A and Yeung, S (1991) Ibid.

31 For example, in Germany Deutsche Bank has major shareholdings in some of Germany's leading companies: Simonian, H, *Financial Times*, 27 Oct 1989. *The Economist*, 30 Nov 1991, p81; Waller, 'German group's reluctant to list', *Financial Times*, 21 Feb 1994, p21 takes this into Germany's family-owned *Mittelstand* – the middle rank private companies; Waller, 'Resisting the bait of equity ownership', *Financial Times*, 14 July 1994, p27 takes this further.

32 For example, banks such as Indo-Suez and Credit Lyonnais have been much criticised for their extensive relatively non-productive shareholdings in French companies during 1995.

33 For example, see the labyrinthine bank shareholdings controlled by Italy's largest merchant bank, Mediobanca, and described in Friedman, A·(1988) *Agnelli and the Network of Power*, Mandarin.

34 For example, *see* Bruce, P (1991) 'Climate Control in corporate Spain', *Financial Times*, 16 July.

35 *See The Economist*, 30 Nov 1991, p81.

36 *See* reference 12 above, *Financial Times*, 14 July 1994.

37 Panorama of EC Industry 1991–92, *Co-operative, Mutual and non-profit Organisations in the EC*, Luxembourg: OPOCE, pp121–41. Note that because they were not members of the EU at the time, Sweden and Finland with some very large co-operative organisations are not included in this survey.

38 *See* Lynch, R (1994) *European Business Strategies*, 2nd edn, Kogan Page, p62.

39 Lynch, R (1994) Ibid, pp119 and 120.

40 Panorama of EC Industry 1991–92, Ibid, p129.

41 Tasker, P (1987) *Inside Japan*, Penguin, London, p307.

42 Jetro, *Nippon 1990: Business Facts and Figures*, p131.

43 Tasker, P (1987) Ibid, p68.

44 Adapted from an article by Ronald van de Krol in the *Financial Times*, 20 Mar 1995, p11.

45 Extracted from Drucker, P (1961) Ibid. Reproduced by permission of Mercury Books Ltd.

PART **5**

DEVELOPING THE STRATEGY

Having explored and defined the purpose of the organisation, it is now possible to develop the strategy. With no single process agreed by all strategists, in this part of the book we first introduce the *prescriptive* approach to the development process – the generation of a number of strategic *options*, followed by a *rational selection* between them, using agreed strategic criteria – and then in later chapters we apply the *emergent* approach to adjust the basic recommendations.

The routes suggested by the prescriptive approach may need to be re-examined. Some strategists may choose to introduce the emergent approach at an earlier stage.

Finally, the organisation structure and the style of the company are explored as these elements may have an important influence on the strategy, possibly even entailing a further reworking of it. It should be noted, however, that some strategy writers regard the structure as something to be resolved *after* the strategy has been agreed and as a result would not include a consideration of the organisation structure at this stage in the development process. For the reasons explained in Chapter 17, this book takes the view that it is better to consider strategy, structure and style together.

Note: There are no separate key readings in this part of the book because the treatment of corporate strategy includes the main elements of such topics.

DEVELOPING THE STRATEGY

● The *prescriptive* strategic process

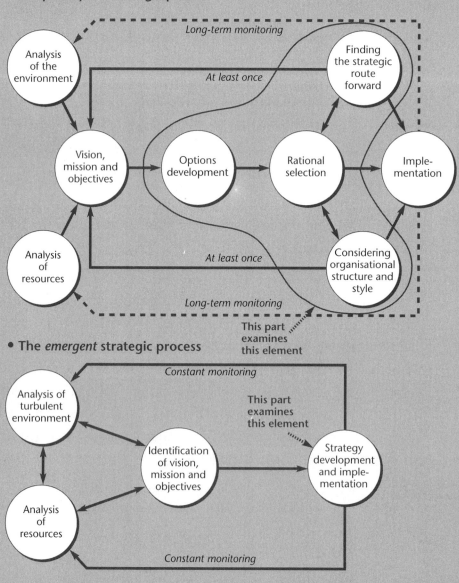

● The *emergent* strategic process

Chapter 13
RESOURCE-BASED STRATEGIC OPTIONS

- *What are the main resource opportunities available to the organisation?*
- *What strategy options arise from these resources?*

Chapter 14
MARKET-BASED STRATEGIC OPTIONS

- *What are the main market opportunities available to the organisation?*
- *What strategy options arise from these options?*

Chapter 15
STRATEGY EVALUATION AND SELECTION 1

- *Which options are consistent with the purpose of the organisation?*
- *Which options are particularly suitable for the environment and deliver competitive advantage?*
- *Which options make valid assumptions about the future?*

Chapter 16
STRATEGY EVALUATION AND SELECTION 2

- *Which options are feasible?*
- *Which options contain acceptable business risk?*
- *Which options are attractive to stakeholders?*

Chapter 17
FINDING THE STRATEGIC ROUTE FORWARD

- *How do emergent strategic considerations alter the decisions?*
- *What are the consequences for the chosen strategies?*

Chapter 18
STRATEGY, STRUCTURE AND STYLE

- *What organisation structures and styles are necessary for the chosen strategies?*
- *Do the chosen strategies need to be altered as a result?*

13

Resource-based strategic options

After working through this chapter, you will be able to:

- develop the options based on the resources of the organisation;

- assess their importance to the strategic development process;

- consider the value chain in the development of resource options;

- explain how small businesses can organise their resources;

- outline the implications of resource strategy for not-for-profit organisations;

- explore the contribution made by the headquarters of multi-product organisations – the concept of parenting.

INTRODUCTION

From the analysis of the organisation and its environment in Parts 2 and 3, it is now possible to develop options for strategy development. The development process may be supported by a consideration of the vision, innovation and technology outlined in Part 4 and will certainly be focussed on achieving the mission and objectives of the organisation.

This chapter concentrates on the strategic options that might arise from the *resources* of the organisation. Chapter 14 will explore the options that arise from the market place. In practice, these two areas are likely to be interlinked, but for reasons of clarity, they are considered separately here.

In theory, there are a very large number of options available to an organisation: probably more than it can cope with. This chapter begins by considering how these options can be reduced down to a more manageable size. In developing resource-based options, the *value chain* is a useful starting point. *Core competences* and *core resources* are then explored. Finally, some special resource considerations for particular business circumstances are discussed, namely those of small businesses, not-for-profit organisations and large organisations with several diversified product groups. These are summarised in Fig 13.1.

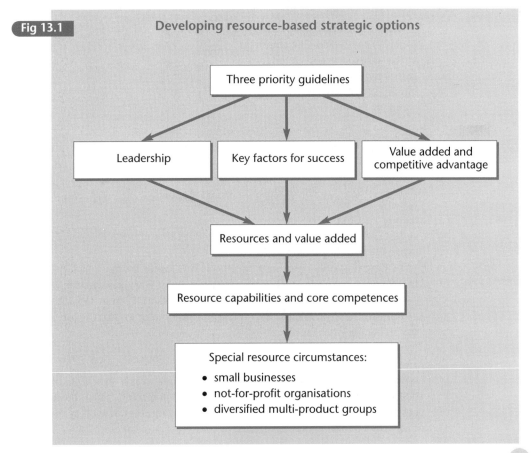

Fig 13.1 Developing resource-based strategic options

Hachette Media rescued, but what was the strategic logic?[1]

In 1992, the world's fifth largest media group, Hachette (France) was rescued by a merger with the aerospace company, Matra (France). This case examines the reasons for the deal which had little strategic logic beyond saving the company from bankruptcy.

Background

In 1981, Jean-Luc Lagardère acquired a controlling stake in the French media company, Hachette. During the course of the decade, he built up the company into the fifth largest media group in the world. For example, the company bought the encyclopaedia publisher, Grolier, and the US magazine group, Diamandis, to accompany its famous women's fashion magazine, *Elle*. The company was also the world's largest distributor of newspapers, being particularly strong in France.

During the same period, M Lagardère was also Chairman of the aerospace and defence company, Matra. His family interests had controlled the company for some years.

Hachette expansion

As a result of the 1980s' acquisitions, Hachette was heavily geared financially. However, it was still able to raise the funds to buy La Cinq – the second largest private TV channel in France – when it came up for auction in 1990. This was to prove Hachette's undoing.

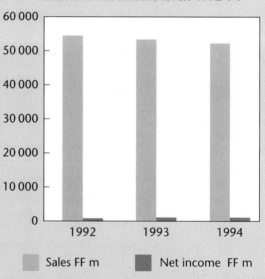

Lagardère Group (formerly Matra-Hachette): **sales and net income levels 1992–94**

Sales FF m   Net income FF m

La Cinq had only been sold because it was losing money. Hachette was confident that it could make the TV channel profitable, but it was unsuccessful. During 1990 and 1991, Hachette lost a total of around US$660 million. Even in 1992, there was no end in sight to these problems. As a result of these major losses, the whole media group was in danger of collapse.

The 1992 merger of Hachette with Matra

It was then that M Lagardère prompted a merger with Matra. To explain the merger, he cited the example of the US company, General Electric, which has been highly successful at operating a range of engineering companies as well as owning NBC, the national American TV channel. The new company would be called Matra–Hachette and would be 'an eagle with two heads'. It would be a communications and technology company with combined sales of around US$12 billion. Financial analysts remained totally unconvinced by this sophistry. 'Lagardère's solution to Hachette's problems has stupefied the French financial community.'

The merger went through, however, probably because it was supported by the French banks. They stood to lose more if Hachette was put into liquidation than if it was taken over by the friendly Matra and allowed slowly to recover. However, the prospects at Matra were not attractive. The company was heavily involved with the defence industry, which was also going through a difficult period, and so was not in a position to give any guarantees.

Nevertheless, the merged group was able to survive. In 1996, Matra–Hachette was fully absorbed by M Lagardère's family company, the Lagardère Group.

CASE QUESTIONS

1 *Why would bankruptcy at Hachette have been particularly unattractive to M Lagardère? And to the banks?*

2 *What are the advantages of merging with another company that has similar strategic interests?*

3 *If you were M Lagardère, what other options might you have considered?*

13.1 PRIORITISING STRATEGIC OPTIONS

The whole business of developing options can be a complex and tortuous process.[2] The director of a major British food processing company described the options process in his company as:

> **griping** (grumbling about the problem) ⟶
> **groping** (fumbling for options) ⟶
> **grasping** (for solutions)

In theory, the number of strategic options open to a company is vast. Many organisations experience major difficulties in *coping* with all the options that can be generated. For example at Hachette, these might have included selling different assets of the group, each of which would need to have been considered separately.

It is important to avoid the 'laundry list' approach to corporate strategy options as some options have little competitive advantage and add little value to the company. With such a broad range of options, some shape needs to be given to the development procedure. There is no single way to achieve this, but three priority guidelines are suggested: leadership, key factors for success and value added and competitive advantage.

13.1.1 Leadership

In the logical world of strategic options and selection, corporate leadership does not often feature in the considerations: indeed, it may be argued that options generation should be rational and unbiased.[3] In the real world of commerce, government and not-for-profit organisations, however, chairmen and chief executives guide the organisation forward – for example, M Jean-Luc Lagardère in the case of Hachette. In a similar way, other companies are guided by their chief executives – for example, Bill Gates at Microsoft (US), Akio Morito at Sony (Japan) and Gianni Agnelli at Fiat (Italy). As Drucker pointed out over 30 years ago,[4] it is *leadership* that lifts a person's vision to higher sights and challenges managers to consider new areas. Judgement, experience and knowledge are rolled into this guideline for shaping the options chosen by the company.

13.1.2 Key factors for success

Key factors for success were explored in Chapter 7 and can be used here in the development and selection of options. In essence, those options that address the key factors are more likely to be relevant than those that do not. This means that there should be some connection between the key factors for success and the strategies adopted. However, the link will not be absolute; there will be other reasons for developing strategies.

13.1.3 Value added and competitive advantage

The purpose of strategy development is to *add value* to the organisation – that is, the value of the outputs needs to exceed the cost of the inputs – and to gain *competitive advantage*. These areas need to be explored carefully at the outset of the option development process. Ultimately, they may well be reflected in the mission and objectives of the organisation and need to be considered early in the process.

> ### Key strategic principles
>
> - A major difficulty in the strategy development process is coping with the number of options that can quickly arise. There are three ways in which the process can be focussed.
>
> - *Leadership*. Leading managers in the organisation can provide the guidance and vision to direct the search process.
>
> - *Key factors for success*. Identifying these areas will inevitably focus the options search on relevant areas.
>
> - *Value added and competitive advantage* coupled with the organisation's mission and objectives will provide strategic purpose to the process. These need to be considered early in options development.

13.2 RESOURCE OPTIONS BASED ON VALUE ADDED AND COMPETITIVE ADVANTAGE[5]

When developing resource options, it is useful to return to the *value chain* of Chapter 7 because of its importance in the development of competitive advantage.

13.2.1 Source of value added

Value can be added early in the value chain, *upstream*, and later in the value chain, *downstream*. Examining where and how value can be added by the resources of the organisation will generate strategic options.

- *Upstream sources of value added* – those activities that add value early in the value chain. Such activities might include procurement of raw materials and the production processes. To add value here, it is useful to buy in bulk and make few changes in the production process, thus keeping costs low and throughput constant. This is assisted if the organisation produces *standardised* items. Upstream value is added by low-cost efficient production processes and process innovations, such as those described in Chapter 10. Value is also added by efficient purchase of raw materials and other forms of procurement.

- *Downstream sources of value added* – those activities that add value later in the value chain. These may rely on *differentiated* products for which higher prices can be charged. Such product variations may mean stopping the production line and making changes which incurs extra costs. The resources may also involve elements of advertising or specialised services to promote the differentiated items. Downstream value is also added by research and development, patenting, advertising and market positioning.

The value chain can itself be associated with upstream and downstream activities (*see* Fig 13.2).

Of course many organisations are involved in adding value both upstream and downstream. For example, Matra–Hachette would clearly have resources in the downstream part because its magazines and books are targeted at specific groups of customers. However, it would also use largely undifferentiated newspaper and printing inks to produce its products which would be located upstream.

Nevertheless, some organisations are *primarily* located either upstream or downstream. Some examples for different industries engaged in one main business are shown in Table 13.1.

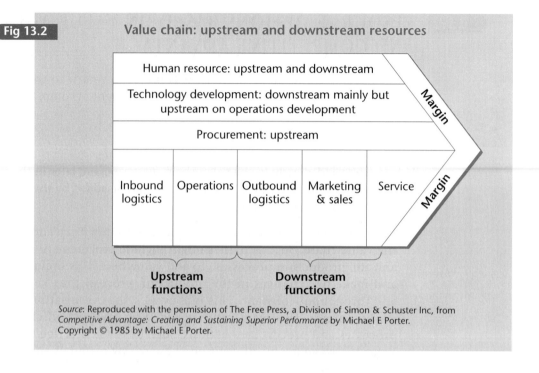

Fig 13.2 Value chain: upstream and downstream resources

Source: Reproduced with the permission of The Free Press, a Division of Simon & Schuster Inc, from *Competitive Advantage: Creating and Sustaining Superior Performance* by Michael E Porter. Copyright © 1985 by Michael E Porter.

Table 13.1 The location of the main source of value added in different single-product industries

Main resources	Examples of industries	Location: Primarily upstream or downstream?
Raw material extraction	Coal, oil, iron ore	Upstream
Primary manufacture to produce standardised output	Paper and pulp, iron and steel, basic chemicals	Upstream
Fabrication of primary manufacture	Paper cartons, steel piping, simple plastics	Upstream
Further added value through more complex manufacture, patents and special processes	Branded packaging, cars, specialist plastic products	Downstream
Marketing and advertising	Branded products	Downstream

13.2.2 Resource implications of upstream and downstream value added

Using the concept of upstream and downstream value added it is possible to develop resource options. For example, if *standard* products are required, then economies of scale may be possible. Other resource options that might produce standardised products more cheaply will also deserve investigation – the upstream activities of Exhibit 13.1.

With *differentiated* products that are carefully targeted at niche markets, very specific promotion will be necessary with resources based on downstream activity. The resource options more likely to be associated with downstream activities are also shown in Exhibit 13.1.

Exhibit 13.1   **Possible resource options associated with upstream and downstream activities**

Upstream resource strategies might include:

- Increased standardisation of products
- Investment to lower the costs of production
- Operations innovation to lower the costs of production or improve the quality
- Capital investments that add value
- Developing a customer base from a wide range of industries that require a common product without variation.

Downstream resource strategies might include:

- Varied products targeted at particular market segments
- R&D and product innovation to add more value
- Advertising investment and branding
- New increased services to add value.

Key strategic principles

- Resource options can be developed by considering the value chain of the organisation. This is particularly important because the chain will help to identify competitive advantage.

- Value can be added early in the value chain, *upstream*, or later in the value chain, *downstream*. Examining where and how value can be added will generate strategic resource options.

- Upstream activities add value by processing raw materials into standardised products. Resource options concentrate on lower costs.

- Downstream activities use intermediate products to manufacture differentiated items targeted at specific customer needs. Resource options focus on R&D and marketing areas.

News Corporation builds a global television network – 1⁶

Starting from a base in Australian and UK newspaper publishing, News Corporation (Australia) is developing a worldwide television network. This case study is in two parts. This first part examines the company's futuristic vision, the key factors for success in television networking and the core competences of the company. Remarkably, it has built a global network from scratch over the last few years. (The second part of the case study follows in Chapter 14.)

Background

Until recently, the newspaper industry has been highly competitive in many countries of the world, but the television industry has not. Technical limitations on the numbers of TV channels that could be broadcast and the profound influence of television on its audience meant television companies were often controlled by the state or a small number of commercial interests.

With satellites, cable TV and digital broadcasting in the 1990s, this situation is now changing dramatically. Many more channels are becoming available and television is becoming more global: CNN news broadcasts, MTV pop music, BBC World TV, Deutsche Welle radio and TV are all examples of this trend. At the same time, some television remains firmly regional – for example, Hindu drama on Doordarshan, the government-controlled Indian TV channel, Chinese films on Star TV based in Hong Kong and Portuguese-language soap opera from Globo TV in Brazil.

New profit streams

Traditionally, profits were made on commercial TV channels by charging for advertising space. In many European countries such as the Netherlands, Sweden and Germany, this was severely restricted or not allowed at all until the late 1980s. In South-East Asia and parts of Africa, there were also major restrictions on TV advertising.

In the 1990s, television companies still make profits from advertising but, increasingly, two new streams of revenue have become an important addition to the advertising that is carried:

- *Cable* – rental of the line to the cable company.

- *Satellite* – rental of a special box that decodes the TV signal using a smart card available only from the TV company.

For these reasons, new companies are entering the market through a range of competitive strategies:

- *Delivery of attractive programmes* – such as live sport or recent films.

- *Restrictive access* – that is, the viewer has no choice but to buy into the network.

- *Outright acquisition of old films.*

- *Heavy investment in new cable channels* – for example, cable companies are investing around US$10 billion in the US and a similar amount in the UK.

- *Company acquisitions and joint ventures* – for example, Disney acquired the ABC TV network and other assets for US$19 billion.

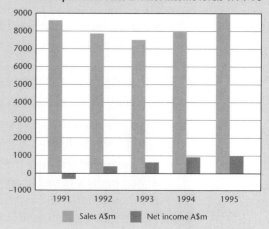

News Corporation: sales and net income levels 1991–95

Sales A$m   Net income A$m

- Cross-promotion deals across the different media – for example, from book to film or video to satellite.

Television business strategies

There is some disagreement between the leading companies over the most effective business strategies for the 1990s. Viacom (US) believes the best approach is through *software* – that is, the purchase of exclusive rights to films, TV programmes and books. Other companies such as News Corporation and Disney have spent at least part of their efforts on *hardware* – the devices that deliver the television signal to the final customer through ownership of TV stations in some countries, satellite or cable channels. Both these routes can produce high barriers to entry in terms of the substantial investment required.

The necessary investment often amounts to billions of dollars, and so companies may not have the resources to pursue *both* strategies and need to make a choice. It should be noted that this was not the view held by News Corporation (*see* below).

Key factors for success in television

There is some disagreement on business strategy across the television industry, and as a result the key factors cannot be identified with certainty. However, it is likely that on a global basis these would include:

- highly creative and innovative people to create programme content;
- strong financial base in order to fund the high market growth;
- real strengths in selected markets in terms of market share at least in some market segments, possibly built using sports contracts, media contracts, a strong film library and even total control over subscribers to their channels;
- means of overcoming barriers to entry – either access to programmes or channels of distribution.

News Corporation believed that it was also important to have *vertical integration* of the television company from film production (*software*) to television service delivery to individual homes (*hardware*).

As mentioned above, other companies took a different view on the importance of this issue.

News Corporation: newspapers

Over the last 20 years, News Corporation has really been shaped by its Chairman and Chief Executive, Rupert Murdoch. From a chain of newspapers in Australia, he acquired control of a similar range in the UK during the 1960s and '70s. These included the brash and breezy *Sun* and the prestigeous *Times*. His companies were prepared to take risks and innovate in order to advance strategically.

News Corporation: television

In the 1980s, News Corporation was one of the earliest companies to see the potential for satellite broadcasting. By a series of bold moves in the UK, it launched a TV service 18 months ahead of the official government-sponsored rival. The early days were difficult with the venture being a major drain on cash: at one stage, the whole group was within hours of bankruptcy. Eventually, his own and the rival channel were merged to form British Sky Broadcasting (BSB), in which News Corporation held a 50 per cent share. When BSB was floated on the stock exchange in 1994, it had a valuation of US$8.7 billion.

In the late 1980s, Murdoch had also identified the USA as having major television potential. His company acquired the film company, 20th Century Fox, in 1985. He then made a typical bold move and announced that he was going to build a fourth national US TV channel to rival the existing three networks – ABC, CBS and NBC. He used the Fox Studios as a base for four years of expansion by buying or setting up cable, satellite and terrestrial broadcast stations across the USA. When it was pointed out to him that only US citizens could own TV stations in the USA, he renounced his Australian nationality and became an American citizen.

During the 1990s, News Corporation has begun building TV networks in the Far East. The company has acquired Star TV in Hong Kong as a basis for expansion into China. It has also acquired TV channels on several Far Eastern satellites in order to broadcast over much of Asia. The financial position of the company in 1995 is shown in Table 13.2.

Table 13.2 Financial performance of New Corporation 1995 (US$ million)

	Revenue	Profit before depreciation, interest and tax
US	6283	932
UK and Europe	1563	300
Australia and Pacific Rim	1147	177

Total assets: US$21.5 billion
Total debt: US$5.8 billion

News Corporation future vision

The key to understanding the News Corporation television strategy is its vision of the future:

Our evolution from primarily a newspaper publisher to an electronic media powerhouse.

This sums up the company's intentions. It also envisaged only four or five leading global television companies by the end of the decade and News Corporation would be one of them.

The primary focus during the 1990s has been on TV, but by the mid-1990s new links were being built with the Internet – the electronic media highway that connects computers worldwide. All their resources have been focussed on achieving this vision of *the electronic media powerhouse*.

News Corporation's core competences and resources

Over the ten years to 1995, the company had enhanced its core competences and resources in the development and management of global television operations. Specifically, these included:

- Entertainment and news gathering skills coupled with television production knowledge.

- Adequate library of entertainment programmes, though it was weaker in the Far East, Latin America and Africa. It also had nothing like the library of the really large US companies, such as Disney, Viacom (Paramount Films) and Time Warner (Warner Brothers Films).

- Satellite encryption technology.

- Range of satellite and cable channels for global coverage.

- Ability to negotiate useful deals with other broadcasters and owners of attractive media opportunities such as sport.

- Skill in identifying revolutionary and imaginative new media opportunities.

News Corporation was the first company to identify satellite encryption technology as being an important aspect of business strategy. The TV signal from its satellite channels is scrambled on broadcast and then decoded using a special machine and smart card in the individual home. Smart cards are purchased from News Corporation on a monthly or annual subscription. The company owns the exclusive world rights to the technology. By 1995 in developed world markets such as the UK and Germany, News Corporation was receiving about five times more revenue from subscription to the smart cards than it was from advertising on its channels. Cable companies have a similar ability to control the signal that is delivered to individual homes. They do not need encryption but simply disconnect homes that do not pay.

CASE QUESTIONS

1 *How and where does News Corporation add value to its services? Where does it obtain its competitive advantage? What strategies has it adopted on barriers to entry?*

2 *How has the company's vision of its future been translated into reality over the last ten years?*

3 *If you were a competitor of News Corporation, what strategies would you investigate to counter any possible threat posed by encryption?*

4 *If you were developing the corporate strategy of a smaller company amid these industry giants, what strategy options would you investigate?*

13.3 RESOURCE-BASED OPTIONS AND CONSTRAINTS

From Drucker[7] to Hamel and Prahalad,[8] the development of strategy options based on resource considerations is reasonably well established. There was a period in the 1970s and '80s when the focus shifted to market-based opportunities (*see* Chapter 14), but the resource-based approach has now regained its deserved role as a means of generating options. It is particularly relevant when market opportunities are limited, either because the market is only growing slowly or because the organisation itself has very limited resources which are better devoted to internal activities. For example, public sector organisations with limitations placed on their resources by government may find that resource-based options provide more scope than market-based opportunities.

Resource-based options are those that arise from the analysis of the organisation's resources considered in Part 2 (*see* Fig 13.3). Options can derive from any resource within the organisation – people, finance, operations, etc. In addition, there are three resource areas that are cross-functional in approach and may provide important strategy options:

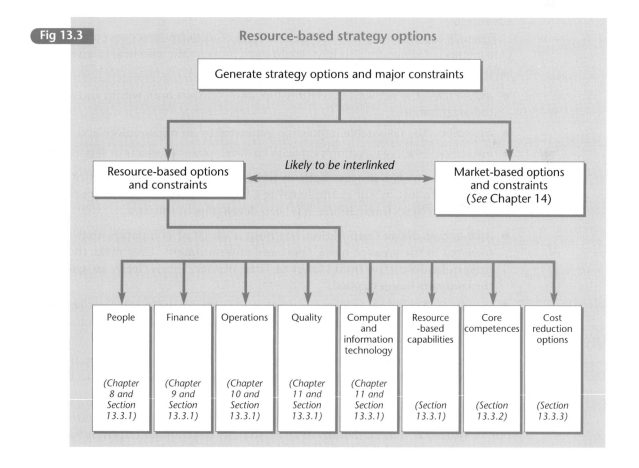

Fig 13.3 **Resource-based strategy options**

469

- *Resource-based capabilities* – the resource assets of the organisation. For example at News Corporation, these would include the library of film and television entertainment programmes, the TV and film studios.

- *Core competences* – the skills, technologies and knowledge of the organisation built over many years. For example at News Corporation, these would include the entertainment and news gathering skills of the organisation. These are less tangible and easily measured than resource-based assets.

- *Cost reduction options* – the opportunities that exist in many organisations to reduce the costs incurred by the resources of the organisation.

13.3.1 Resource-based capabilities

Resource strategies need to consider the broad range of resource-based capabilities present in the organisation: for example, people or financial resources. Other capabilities might also include areas such as patents, technology licensed from other companies and information technology.[9]

There are no detailed structures regarding how to conduct such an examination because every organisation is different. It may be necessary to survey each of the functional areas of the organisation for their capabilities. The aim of such an exercise is to explore those areas for their contribution to value added and competitive advantage.

Resource capabilities need to offer some form of *distinctiveness* over competitors. One method of generating options would be to measure the resources of an organisation against the following criteria:

- *architecture* – the network of relationships and contracts both within and around the organisation;

- *reputation* – the favourable impression generated by an organisation; and

- *innovation* – the organisation's capacity to develop new products or services.

This would focus the process both in terms of current resources and of those needed for the future. For example using Chapter 7 (Kay[10]), we can specify the ways in which News International has been developing in this area:

- *Architecture.* News Corporation has built a range of companies that are all focussed in the areas of news, sport and entertainment. They make the company quite distinctive from Disney or Time Warner. This is clearly an asset that the company has developed.

- *Reputation.* News Corporation has developed a clear image in this area, based on its newspapers in particular. Its aggressive, open and iconoclastic style has set it apart from its rivals. This is clearly an asset of the organisation.

- *Innovation.* Several examples of the innovative ability of News Corporation are recorded in Case study 13.1. This may well cover *core competences* as well as *resource assets* at the company.

Hence, there may be some overlap between core *capabilities* and core *competences* in one or two areas. Ten guidelines to assist strategy development options for both areas are shown in Exhibit 13.2.

13.3.2 Core competences

Core competences are defined as a group of skills and technologies that enable an organisation to provide a particular benefit to customers. These were explored in Chapter 7 and can be used to guide the development of strategy options.

Core competences are important in the development of strategy because they are usually unique to the organisation and therefore important in delivering *sustainable competitive advantage*. Options that do not address core competences are less likely to contribute to strategy than those that do. This suggests that a careful exploration of core competences in the context of strategy development is desirable.

During the 1980s,[11] the approach to the development of strategy options emphasised markets and products. Renewed emphasis was given to resource-based strategic options by the concept of core competences developed in the late 1980s by Gary Hamel and C K Prahalad, professors of strategy at the London Business School and University of Michigan respectively. (It should be noted that they were not the first strategists to emphasise the importance of resources.)

In the examination of core competences, it is important to recognise that the organisation may not at present have all the competences it really needs to fulfil its strategic vision. For example in the case of News Corporation, it might be argued that it needs to develop further skills and competences if it is to develop successfully its television activities to India: in late 1995, it had a limited programme library of films, few native Indian producers and minor involvement in the country. However, through the Star TV satellite system, it was able to broadcast directly to that vast and important Indian market. Organisations need to consider the acquisition of new core competences.

To illustrate the opportunities that core competences can provide in the market place, Hamel and Prahalad developed the matrix shown in Fig 13.4. The four categories need a word of explanation:

1 *Fill in the blanks*. This area clearly relates to existing market areas and core skills.

2 *Premier plus 10*. This area refers to the organisation's vision in 10 years' time and the new core competences that will be needed at that time. These new competences will be used to cope with enhanced demand in its existing markets.

3 *White spaces*. This area relates to new market areas that could be supplied by the existing core competences of the company. This is similar to the *strategic groups analysis* of Section 6.2.

4 *Mega-opportunities*. These are self-evident but need to be developed out of the existing resources of the company.

Comment Despite its intrinsic appeal, the concept of core competences has two problems:

● There are no precise tests to select and establish the core competences of the organisation. There is a strong element of judgement required to identify them and group them correctly.

● Even if core competences are identified correctly, it is unclear how they should be developed further for new products. This again leaves a considerable amount to business judgement.

Fig 13.4	Strategic opportunities suggested by core competences[12]

		Existing	New
CORE COMPETENCE	**New**	*Premier plus 10* What new core competences will we need to build to protect and extend our franchise in current markets?	*Mega-opportunities* What new core competences would we need to build to participate in the most exciting markets of the future?
	Existing	*Fill in the blanks* What is the opportunity to improve our position in existing markets by better leveraging our existing core competences?	*White spaces* What new products or services could we create by creatively redeploying or recombining our current core competences?
		Existing	**New**
		MARKET	

Source: Reprinted by permission of Harvard Business School Publishing from *Competing for the Future* by A Hamel and C K Prahalad. Boston, MA, 1994, p227. Copyright © by the President and Fellows of Harvard College; all rights reserved.

To aid the development of core competences, ten guidelines are shown in Exhibit 13.2. There is a distinction between core competences and resource capabilities, but they are combined here as there is often an overlap between the two concepts in organisations.

13.3.3 Cost reduction options

Strategic options are not only concerned with expansion into new resource capabilities and core competences. The organisation may also need to consider cutting back its current operations in order to reduce costs. Given the increasingly global nature of competition in some markets, it is quite possible that low-wage settlement countries such as Korea, Malaysia and the Philippines will provide real competition. This will mean that companies are unable to survive in western countries unless they can cut costs drastically. Cost reduction strategy options therefore need to be considered.

We explored the basic issue of cost reduction in Chapter 7. However, Ohmae has suggested a model which structures this process in a logical and cross-functional way (*see* Fig 13.5). Overall, the model does not pretend to be comprehensive but rather to show the options that are possible, their logical flow and the interconnections between the various elements. For example, News Corporation over the last five years has emphasised the need to cut costs in order to remain competitive. It has introduced various programmes to achieve this.

| Exhibit 13.2 | Ten guidelines for developing core competences and resource capabilities |

1 What *technology* do we have? Is it exclusive? Is it at least as good as that of competitors? Is it better?

2 What *links* are there between the products that we manufacture or services that we operate? What common ground is there?

3 How do we generate *value added*? Is there anything different from our competitors? Looking at the main areas, what skills are involved in adding value?

4 What *people skills* do we have? How important is their contribution to our competences? How vital are they to our resources? Are there any key workers? How difficult would they be to replace? Do we have any special values? What is our geographical spread?

5 What *financial resources* do we have? Are they sufficient to fulfil our vision? What is our profit record (or financial record in not-for-profit organisations)? Is the record sufficiently good to raise new funds? Do we have new funding arrangements, tax issues or currency matters?

6 How do our *customers* benefit from our competences and resources? What real benefits do they obtain? Are we known for our quality? Our technical performance against competition? Our good value for money (*not* low cost)?

7 What *other skills* do we have in relation to our customers? What are the core skills? Are they unique to our organisation or do many other companies have them? How might they change?

8 What *new resources*, *skills* and *competences* do we need to acquire over the next few years? How do they relate to our vision?

9 How is the *environment* changing? What impact will this have on current and future core skills and resources?

10 What are our *competitors* undertaking in the area of resources, skills and competences?

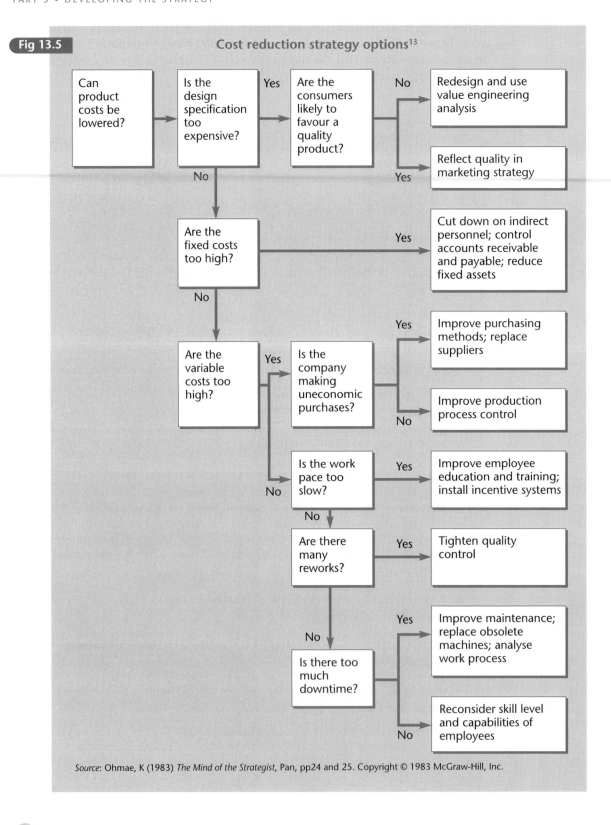

Fig 13.5   Cost reduction strategy options[13]

Source: Ohmae, K (1983) *The Mind of the Strategist*, Pan, pp24 and 25. Copyright © 1983 McGraw-Hill, Inc.

- Resource options can be developed from three main areas of the organisation.

- *Resource-based capabilities* explore the options that can be generated by the functional areas of the organisation such as its plant and finance.

- *Core competences* explore options deriving from such areas as the basic skills, knowledge and technology of the organisation.

- When related to market opportunities, core competences may lead to options for the organisation in four main areas, ranging from small opportunities using current skills to major new areas that will deliver real scope for the future.

- New core competences may be needed to meet important new options.

- In addition to resource-based options, there is also the possibility of *cost-cutting* as a strategy. It is possible to develop a model which examines this in a structured and cross-functional way.

13.4 RESOURCE OPTIONS IN SOME SPECIAL TYPES OF ORGANISATION

Some specific types of organisation present special opportunities and problems in terms of managing resources. It is useful to identify three situations:

- Small businesses
- Not-for-profit organisations
- Diversified multi-product groups

13.4.1 Small business resources

By definition, small businesses are unlikely to have at their disposal the range of resources available to the larger companies. There will be fewer people, more limited finance and so on. The strategic issue is how to manage this special resource situation. There are three main methods:

- *Employ outside advisers such as consultants.* This can be expensive but is probably appropriate for some specialist skills. Outside resources are hired temporarily.

- *Concentrate resources on particular tasks that are more likely to yield added value and competitive advantage.* The problem here is that other areas of the organisation are inevitably neglected. Correct choice of the selected area is therefore vital. For these reasons, resources are often concentrated on a segment or niche of the market that is likely to bring long-term benefit. The limited resources are focussed.

- *Offer superior service*. This can be an area where smaller companies can win against larger competitors. By being unencumbered by the slow decision making of large companies, smaller organisations can react faster and more flexibly to customers. This may even justify slightly higher prices than the larger competitors. Resource strategies here may involve extra training and possibly even the hiring of extra service staff in some cases.

13.4.2 Resources in not-for-profit organisations

This sector includes organisations such as small charitable organisations as well as large government-funded institutions. They need to be considered separately.

Charitable organisations These organisations have two unique areas of resource:

- *Beliefs*. These drive the organisation forward in terms of the charitable purpose. This means that everyone is likely to be highly motivated. It is a real resource in terms of the extra work that people are prepared to undertake on occasions.

- *Voluntary workers*. These people can put exceptional effort into the enterprise and undertake major tasks. However, because of the voluntary nature, such a resource needs to be handled with care. People can become demotivated. Some need to be given a greater degree of freedom than would be appropriate in a commercial organisation.

Government-funded institutions These organisations often have highly professional resources but may be excessively bureaucratic. The culture of such organisations needs to be taken into account in devising resource options. Resources may be large and unwieldy and slow to respond to outside events.

13.4.3 Diversified multi-product groups

Some companies have major subsidiaries engaged in a number of quite different markets – for example, Matra–Hachette. Sometimes the subsidiaries have little or no trading connection with each other – for example, book publishing at Hachette and missile launchers at Matra. Each of these subsidiaries will have its own resources. In addition, the whole enterprise will have a corporate headquarters. It is this special resource – the *parent* of the subsidiaries – that is explored here.

In some texts,[14] the words 'corporate strategy' refer *exclusively* to strategies pursued by such a corporate headquarters. In this book, the term corporate strategy has been used more freely, as explained in Chapter 1.

Parenting is another term covering the same general areas. It means the special strategies pursued at the headquarters of the diversified group. The parenting resource of corporate headquarters can offer:

- *Corporate functions and services* – such as international treasury management and central human resource management.

- *Corporate development initiatives* – such as centralised R&D and new acquisitions.

- *Additional finance for growth areas* – on the principle of the product portfolio outlined in Chapter 3.

- *Formal linkages between businesses* – such as the transfer of technology or core competences between subsidiaries.

For example at News Corporation, the film library of 20th Century Fox was available to both its TV stations in the US and the UK, even though they were operating totally independent schedules and were completely independent companies. In addition, the centre was the major provider of funds for the main growth areas such as the Far Eastern satellite ventures and the new exclusive sports channels and contracts.

Clearly such parenting resources are formidable if carefully developed. Each group will have its own combination of resources depending on its mix of businesses and the relevant strategic issues. However, a corporate headquarters has a cost. The purpose of parenting is to add value to the subsidiaries that are served, otherwise the parental cost cannot be justified.[15] Subsidiaries need to perform better with the parent than they would independently.

To perform better with the parent requires that the parenting resource itself, the corporate headquarters, comes under careful scrutiny. It is not enough for the parent to provide a few add-on services, as might be the case at Matra–Hachette. This means understanding the core skills of the parent itself – the *parenting characteristics* of the headquarters.[16]

The parent needs two attributes:

1 an understanding and familiarity of the *key factors for success* relevant to all of the diverse industries in which each of its subsidiaries is engaged.

2 an ability to *contribute something extra* beyond the subsidiaries that it manages. These might be from any of the four areas listed earlier in this section – for example, R&D, finance.

Some parents do not understand the key factors for success of their subsidiaries. In the case of Matra–Hachette, the Chairman certainly did understand both industries well because he had worked in them for many years. Some parents are unable to contribute much extra to the subsidiaries. It is perhaps here that Matra–Hachette HQ had rather less to offer. By contrast, News Corporation HQ was able to offer a range of resources that would be relevant to its subsidiaries at various times because it was more focussed on a narrower range of operations.

Key strategic principles

- Some specific types of organisation present special opportunities and problems in the management of resources.

- Small businesses are unlikely to contain the range of resources of larger enterprises. However, this problem can be overcome by employing outside advisers and concentrating resources. A more flexible service may provide a real competitive advantage.

Key strategic principles continued

- Charitable organisations benefit from exceptional resources: the beliefs that drive the society and the use of voluntary workers. However, they may need to give such people extra freedom to keep them motivated.

- Government institutions have highly professional resources but may be bureaucratic in their approach. Resources may be unwieldy and slow to respond to events.

- Diversified multi-product groups can gain from the special resource of their corporate headquarters – the parent of the subsidiaries.

- Parenting may provide special functions, new initiatives, additional finance for growing areas, and formal linkages between the subsidiaries. The key issue is whether the parental resource adds extra value beyond those of the individual businesses.

- Parenting is more likely to add extra value when two conditions are fulfilled. First, the parent needs to understand the key factors for success of all the industries in which its subsidiaries are involved. Second, the parent itself needs to contribute or arrange some service or resource that is beyond that of its subsidiaries.

CASE STUDY 13.2

Developing resource options at Eastman Kodak[17]

During his five years running Motorola, the US electronics group, George Fisher achieved a formidable reputation as a manager and strategist. So when he resigned late in 1993 to take on the chairmanship of photo giant Eastman Kodak, Wall Street's delight was mixed with puzzlement.

Why would a man who had won such plaudits and profits at a company in the forefront of America's digital revolution trade them for a business that, despite its proud history and powerful brand name, could best be described as demoralised and floundering?

Several years on, Fisher, a trim and thoughtful man with a straightforward manner, offered an answer that had started to win over doubters. The traditional photographic business, he said, was set for significant growth around the world for as long as he could foresee.

'When I came here, the mental set was that this was a slow growth industry and that the way to keep going was you keep cutting. The new mind set that I think I've succeeded in establishing within the company is that there are tremendous growth opportunities; we have to go develop them ...'

Fisher's approach was indeed a departure. When he took over, Kodak was struggling after waves of cuts to maintain profits at the level of a decade before. Its traditional lines of silver halide film and photographic paper were stagnating, and seemed doomed to erosion by new technology which Kodak did not fully understand.

To the dismay of some in the investment community, Fisher – an engineering graduate who spent 10 years at Bell Telephone laboratories before

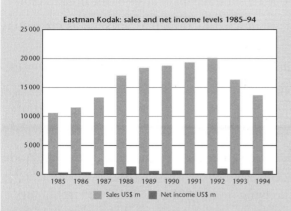

Eastman Kodak: sales and net income levels 1985–94

Sales US$ m   Net income US$ m

ment already growing strongly. However, digital was still a marginal business and would not make profits for another couple of years at least.

Fisher's immediate preoccupations were cutting costs.

'I think our costs are too high still. We have a lot of room to improve quality and our costs of production. Our overhead costs are also too high. In every one of our businesses I have areas where we're dissatisfied.'

Source: Financial Times, 18 December 1995.

moving to Motorola – concluded early on that the answer was not more cuts.

Instead, he rapidly set about disposing of the pharmaceutical and consumer health businesses Kodak had bought during an ill-conceived diversification spree, and went on to a trade and marketing offensive in Kodak's traditional product lines. He also brought a new singlemindedness to the company's efforts to exploit new digital technologies. Digital imaging, he insisted, was not a threat to the traditional business of film and paper but an opportunity to expand it. By early 1996, results were already being achieved with sales of digital equip-

CASE QUESTIONS

1 *How would you advise Mr Fisher to analyse his resources? What should he examine first? How should he approach the task?*

2 *What are the core resources, competences and skills of Kodak?*

3 *Do you agree that there is still plenty of scope for development in the traditional film and photographic business?*

4 *Is Mr Fisher following the correct strategy?*

SUMMARY

● It can be difficult for organisations to cope with the number of potential strategy options that can quickly arise. There are three ways in which the process might be focussed.

1 *Leadership* can provide the guidance and vision to direct the search process.

2 *Key factors for success* can be identified to focus the options search into relevant areas.

3 *Value added, competitive advantage, and the organisation's mission and objectives* will provide strategic purpose to the process – these need to be considered early in options development.

● Resource options can be developed by using the organisation's value chain, which will help to identify competitive advantage. Value can be added early in the value chain (*upstream*) or later (*downstream*), and the choice of where and how to add value will generate strategic resource options.

● Upstream activities add value by processing raw materials into *standardised* products – options will concentrate on achieving lower costs. Downstream activities involve *differentiated* products targeted at specific customer needs with resource options focussing on R&D and marketing.

- Resource options can be developed from three main areas of the organisation:

1 *resource-based capabilities* – the resource (functional) assets such as machinery and finance;

2 *core competences* – the basic skills and knowledge accumulated over many years;

3 *cost reduction options* – the opportunities that often exist for reducing the costs of resources.

- It is important to understand the distinction between:

1 *resource-based capabilities* – the options that can be generated by the functional assets of the organisation;

2 *core competences* – the options deriving from skills, knowledge and technology.

- When related to market opportunities, *core competences* may lead to options for the organisation in four main areas, ranging from small opportunities using current skills to major new areas of future development – new core competences may be needed to meet such important major options.

- There is also the possibility of cost-cutting as a resource-based strategy. It is possible to develop a model which examines this in a structured and cross-functional way. Some specific types of organisation present special resource-based opportunities and problems.

1 *Small businesses* may have a limited range of resources, but can overcome this by employing outside advisers and concentrating resources. A more flexible service may provide a real competitive advantage.

2 *Charitable organisations* benefit from exceptional resources: the beliefs that drive them and the use of voluntary workers. However, they may need to give such workers extra freedom to keep them motivated.

3 *Government institutions* have highly professional resources but may be bureaucratic in their approach, unwieldy and slow to respond to events.

4 *Diversified multi-product groups* can gain from the special resource of their corporate headquarters, the parent of the subsidiaries. *Parenting* can provide special functions, new initiatives, additional finance for growing areas, and formal linkages between the subsidiaries. The key issue is whether the parental resource adds extra value to the individual businesses. To do this, first, the parent needs to understand the key factors for success of all the industries in which its subsidiaries are involved. Second, the parent itself needs to contribute or arrange some service or resource that is beyond that of its subsidiaries.

QUESTIONS

1 Choose an organisation with which you are familiar and identify the upstream and downstream parts of the value chain for that organisation. Which is the most important for that organisation or do they contribute equally?

2 Where is value added at Eastman Kodak? How does this impact on its resource options? Give reasons for your views.

3 Identify the probable core competences of the following: a charity like UNICEF; a major consumer electronics company; a holiday travel tour operator; a multinational fast-moving consumer goods company.

4 *'During the 1990s, top executives will be judged on their ability to identify, cultivate and exploit the core competences that make growth possible.'* Professors Gary Hamel and C K Prahalad. Discuss.

5 If core competences are important, can they be acquired in the space of a few months or do they take years to develop? What are the implications of your response for the development of competitive advantage?

6 Distinguish between core competences and core assets. Give examples of both from Eastman Kodak.

7 To what extent could parenting strategy be used to justify the merger of Matra with Hachette?

8 *'Good corporate parents constantly search for ways in which they can improve the performance of their businesses.'* Michael Goold. Is it wise for corporate parents to interfere in the strategies of their multi-diversified businesses?

9 Take a small student society or charitable institution with which you are familiar. What strategic options based on its resources does it have for development?

10 It has been argued in this chapter that small businesses can develop competitive advantage over larger companies by offering higher degrees of service. What are the possible problems with this approach?

STRATEGIC PROJECT

Media companies

This chapter has examined two media companies. Chapter 14 explores News Corporation further. There have been major strategic opportunities during the 1990s for such organisations – for example, the battle to supply new satellite channels to Germany. You might like to explore these areas further.

FURTHER READING

On core capabilities *see* readings in earlier chapters.

On core competences: read Hamel, G and Prahalad, C K (1994) *Competing for the Future*, Harvard Business School Press, Boston, Mass. *See* also by the same authors, 'The Core Competence of the Corporation', *Harvard Business Review*, May–June 1990.

On parenting strategy: Campbell, A, Goold, M and Alexander, M (1995) 'Corporate Strategy: the quest for parenting advantage', *Harvard Business Review*, Mar–Apr. *See* also their book, *Corporate-level strategy: Creating value in the multibusiness company*, Wiley, New York, 1994. Michael Goold has also written a useful article: Goold, M (1996) 'Parenting strategies for the mature business', *Long Range Planning*, June, p359.

Professor Michael Porter also wrote an influential article on corporate strategy, meaning parenting: Porter, M E (1987) 'From competitive advantage to corporate strategy', *Harvard Business Review*, May–June. A brief commentary on this article was written by Goold, M and Campbell, A, 'From corporate strategy to parenting advantage', *Long Range Planning*, Feb, p115. These two articles were republished in De Wit, B and Meyer, R (1994) *Strategy: Process, content and context*, West Publishing.

REFERENCES

1 References for Matra–Hachette case: *Sunday Times*, 2 Feb 1992, Business Section; *Financial Times*, 6 May 1992, p24; 19 Feb 1993, p14; 23 Feb 1996, p17; 18 May 1996, p7.
2 Day, G S (1987) *Strategic Market Planning*, West Publishing, St Paul, Minn, p60.
3 Most of the most popular texts take this viewpoint.
4 Drucker, P (1961) *The Practice of Management*, Mercury, London, p138.
5 This section has benefited from the paper by Galbraith, J R (1983) 'Strategy and Organisational Planning', *Human Resource Management*, Spring–Summer. Republished in Mintzberg, H and Quinn, J (1991) *The Strategy Process*, Prentice Hall, New York, pp315–24. Galbraith's concept has been applied to the value chain, although he did not use this terminology.
6 References for Case study 13.1: *Financial Times*: 16 Feb 1994, p32; 20 Feb 1995, p16; 28 Mar 1995, p21; 21 Apr 1995, p27; 1 Aug 1995, p17; 3 Aug 1995, p19; 31 Aug 1995, p11. *Sunday Times*: 6 Aug 1995, p23. News Corporation Annual Report and Accounts for 1995. The direct quote comes from this document.
7 Drucker, P (1964) *Managing for Results*, Pan, London, p163.
8 Hamel, G and Prahalad, C K (1994) *Competing for the Future*, Harvard Business School Press, Boston, Mass, Ch 1.
9 Stalk, G, Evans, P and Shulman, L (1992) 'Competing on Capabilities', *Harvard Business Review*, Apr–May. Hamel and Prahalad make no reference to this paper and its criticism of core competences in their book published in 1994.
10 Kay, J (1993) *Foundations of Corporate Success*, Oxford University Press, p64.
11 Hamel, G and Prahalad, C K (1994) Ibid, p221 and Ch 10 that follows.
12 *Source*: Hamel, G and Prahalad, C K (1994) Ibid, p227.
13 *Source*: Ohmae, K (1983) *The Mind of the Strategist*, Pan, London, pp24–5. © McGraw-Hill 1983.
14 *See*, for example, Porter, M E (1987) 'From competitive advantage to corporate strategy', *Harvard Business Review*, May–June.
15 Goold, M (1996) 'Parenting strategies for the mature business', *Long Range Planning*, June, p359.
16 Campbell, A, Goold, M and Alexander, M (1995) 'Corporate Strategy: the quest for parenting advantage', *Harvard Business Review*, Mar–Apr.
17 Adapted from an article by Andrew Gowers and Tony Jackson in the *Financial Times*, 18 Dec 1995, p9.

14

Market-based strategic options

After working through this chapter, you will be able to:

● explore generic strategy options and evaluate their potential;

● understand the Market Options Matrix and its contribution to developing market-based options;

● investigate the options prompted by the Expansion Method Matrix and their implications for market-based options;

● critically evaluate the contributions of all three routes to the strategic development process.

■ INTRODUCTION

Market-based options are those that arise from market opportunities and constraints. They complement those resource-based options explored in Chapter 13. Although market-based options face outwards toward the environment, they also include elements of resources and other factors internal to the organisation.

Market-based options build on the analysis of customers and competitors explored in Part 2, especially the portfolio matrix, the value chain and sustainable competitive advantage. There are *three* main groups of market-based options: generic strategies, the Market Options Matrix and the Expansion Method Matrix. These are explored in this chapter using the structure outlined in Fig 14.1.

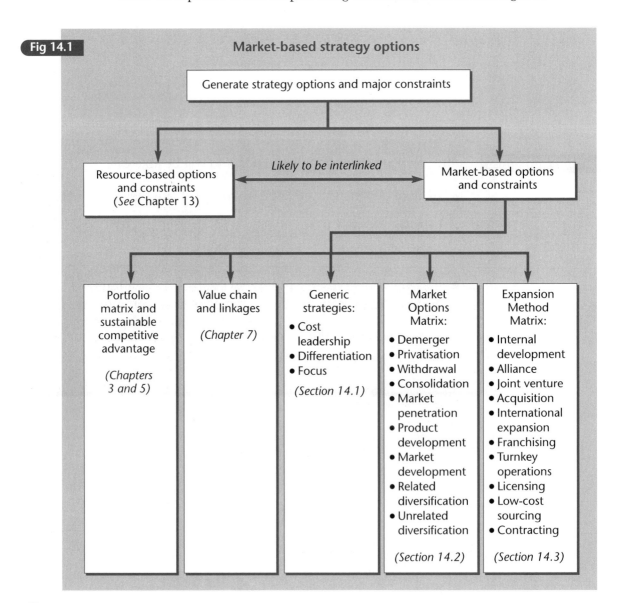

Fig 14.1   **Market-based strategy options**

Market opportunities at Muzak Europe[1]

This case study explores the small Dutch company, Muzak Europe, and its search for new market opportunities for a well-known American service.

As in many industries, the world of 'muzak' has big and small players. At the very top, there is Muzak of the USA – a 61-year-old company whose name has become a generic term for background, or functional, music (sometimes referred to unkindly as 'elevator music'). There is also Alcas, a Dutch specialist in background music. Although only a fraction of the size of Muzak, Alcas became in 1995 the US company's partner in a new venture across Europe. The purpose of the new company was to bring satellite-based functional music to Europe's department stores, hotels and petrol stations.

Their 50/50 partnership was called Muzak Europe and was designed not just to beam music across Europe but also to provide in-store advertising, business television and data communication. If successful, it would catapult Alcas into faster growth than it had obtained up to that time.

The genesis of the Muzak joint venture was an article in a Dutch magazine about Muzak's 60th birthday. Eric van der Horst, Managing Director of Alcas, said the article made clear that Muzak was at the forefront of satellite broadcasting. This led to letters and telephone calls to Muzak of Seattle and a visit to the US company's headquarters several weeks later. Van der Horst's opening line was, 'Hello, we're the small fry from Europe.'

The difference in size was indeed dramatic. Muzak, a privately held company, had a turnover estimated in 1995 at US$150 million, mainly in the USA, through 230 000 links of which 80 000 were by satellite. Alcas with a turnover of US$6 million (Fl 10 million) had a reach of 2 million people in Benelux, Germany and Spain. With the new venture, it hoped to develop a turnover of US$15 million by the year 2000.

For Muzak of the US, the venture with an established player in the Benelux area promised to provide access to Europe's fragmented market. For Alcas, the partnership offered a chance to find swift growth through satellite technology, an important diversification from its base in the distribution of music using cassettes and compact discs. The ultimate target customers would remain the same, but it would be possible to offer much wider geographic coverage with speed and cost-effectiveness.

'We can reach them from the north of Norway to the north of Africa, including Israel,' said Rob van den Berg, Managing Director of Muzak Europe. The plan was to find distributors in Germany, Britain and Scandinavia in 1996, and then to spread across Europe by finding additional distribution companies in Italy and Spain in 1997. In a sense, the marketing target customers were also the new distributors that it was seeking, as well as the final customers in the form of department stores, etc.

In the new venture, the music was programmed by Alcas at its base in the Dutch town of Naarden, and broadcast from the joint venture's office in neighbouring Hilversum. The music reflected European rather than American roots. 'To appeal to people in Europe, you have to have Irish bands too,' said Van den Berg. 'You have to be able to include the occasional French language hit.'

Source: Financial Times, 27 November 1995.

14.1 GENERIC STRATEGIES

During the 1980s, generic strategies were regarded as being at the forefront of strategic thinking. They still have a useful contribution to make to the consideration of strategic options. They were published in two books by Professor Michael Porter, *Competitive Strategy*[2] in 1980 and *Competitive Advantage*[3] in 1985 (the second book contained a small modification of the concept). The original version is explored here. After exploring the basic elements, two cases are considered and some comments on their theoretical validity and practical usefulness are offered. Professor Porter confined his books to business situations and did not explore not-for-profit organisations.

14.1.1 The three generic competitive strategies

Professor Porter argued that there were three basic – that is, *generic* – strategies open to any business:

● Cost leadership

● Differentiation

● Focus.

According to Porter, every business needs to choose one of these in order to compete in the market place and gain sustainable competitive advantage. Each of these three strategic options represents an area that every business and many not-for-profit organisations can usefully explore. The three options can be explained by considering two aspects of the competitive environment:

● *The source of competitive advantage.* There are fundamentally only two sources of competitive advantage: *differentiation* of products from competitors and *low costs*. We explore these two areas below.

● *The competitive scope of the target customers.* It was possible to target the organisation's products as a *broad* target covering most of the market place or as a *narrow* target focusing on a niche within the market.

Porter then brought these two elements together in the well-known diagram shown as Fig 14.2.

In his second book, Porter modified the concept to split the niche sector into:

● Niche differentiation

● Niche low-cost leadership.

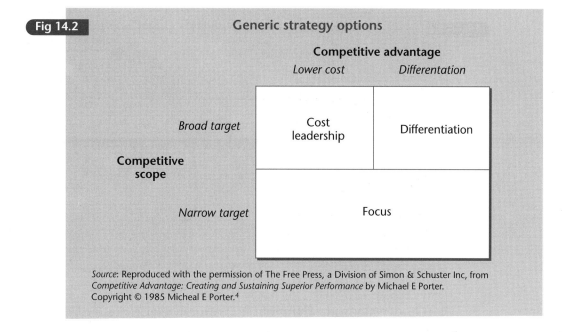

Fig 14.2 **Generic strategy options**

Competitive advantage

Lower cost *Differentation*

Broad target Cost leadership Differentiation

Competitive scope

Narrow target Focus

Source: Reproduced with the permission of The Free Press, a Division of Simon & Schuster Inc, from *Competitive Advantage: Creating and Sustaining Superior Performance* by Michael E Porter. Copyright © 1985 Micheal E Porter.[4]

14.1.2 Low-cost leadership

The low-cost leader in an industry has built and maintains plant, equipment, labour costs and working practices that deliver the lowest costs in that industry.

Readers will recall from Chapter 7 that there are a number of ways of reducing costs: these can be summarised in the cost experience curve (*see* Fig 7.7). Any firm able to achieve the lowest costs has a clear sustainable competitive advantage. However, low-cost producer status involves more than just going down the experience curve. A low-cost producer must find and exploit *all* the sources of cost advantage. Low-cost producers typically sell a standard, or no-frills, product and place considerable strategic emphasis on reaping scale or absolute cost advantages from all sources. In practice, low-cost leaders achieve their position by shaving costs off every element of the value chain; the strategy comes from attention to detail.

The profit advantage gained from low-cost leadership derives from the assertion that low-cost leaders should be able to sell their products in the market place at around the average price of the market (*see* line AA in Fig 14.3). If such products are not perceived as comparable or their performance is not acceptable to buyers, a cost leader will be forced to discount prices below competition in order to gain sales. Compared to the low-cost leader, competitors will have higher costs (*see* line YY). After successful completion of this strategy option, the costs of the lowest-cost producer will be lower by definition than other competitors (*see* line XX in Fig 14.3). This will deliver *above-average profits* to the low-cost leader.

To follow this strategy option, an organisation will lay the emphasis on cost reduction at every point in its processes. It should be noted that cost leadership does not necessarily imply a low price: the company could charge an average price and reinvest the extra profits generated. Referring back to Chapter 6, an example of

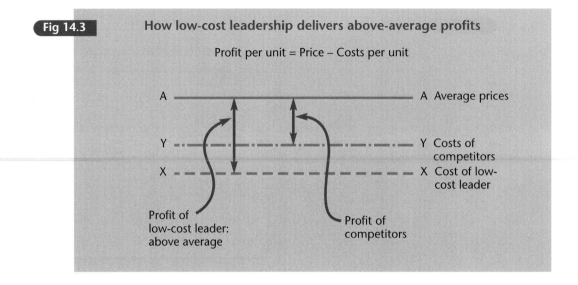

Fig 14.3   How low-cost leadership delivers above-average profits

Profit per unit = Price – Costs per unit

A ———————————————— A Average prices

Y — · — · — · — · — · — · — Y Costs of competitors

X — — — — — — — — — — X Cost of low-cost leader

Profit of low-cost leader: above average

Profit of competitors

cost leadership in the European ice cream market would be Unilever's product range across Europe. The company enjoys the advantage of the substantial cost benefits of being market leader in a high fixed cost industry.

14.1.3   Differentiation

Differentiation occurs when the products of an organisation meet the needs of some customers in the market place better than others. When the organisation is able to differentiate its products, it is able to charge a price that is higher than the average price in the market place.

Underlying differentiation is the concept of *market segmentation* which was explored in Chapter 6 – that is, the identification of specific groups who respond differently from other groups to competitive strategies. Essentially, particular groups of customers will pay more for a differentiated product that is targeted towards them. Examples of differentiation include better levels of service, more luxurious materials and better performance. Benefon in Chapter 3 is a classic example of a differentiated product. Another example can be taken from the European ice cream industry. The Mars Ice Cream range is clearly differentiated by its branding and as a result it can be sold at a price premium.

In order to differentiate a product, it is necessary for the producer to incur *extra* costs. The differentiated product costs will therefore be higher than those of competitors (*see* line ZZ in Fig 14.4). The producer of the differentiated product then derives an advantage from its pricing: with its uniquely differentiated product it is able to charge a premium price – that is, one that is higher than its competitors (*see* line BB in Fig 14.4).

There are two problems associated with differentiation strategies:

● It is difficult to estimate whether the extra costs incurred in differentiation can be recovered from the customer.

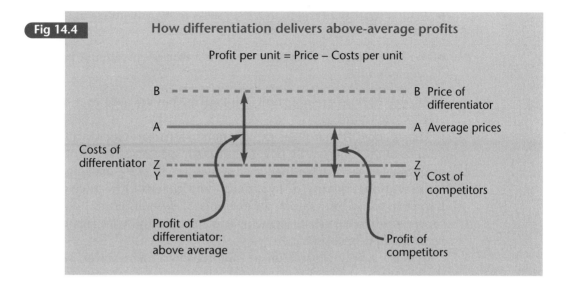

Fig 14.4   **How differentiation delivers above-average profits**

Profit per unit = Price – Costs per unit

- The successful differentiation may encourage competitors to copy the differentiated product and enter the market segment. There are often costs associated with being first into a market, so there may be additional cost advantages from moving in second – for example, other companies have followed the lead of Mars Ice Cream.

Neither of the above problems is insurmountable but they do reduce the attractiveness of this option.

14.1.4   Focus strategy (sometimes called niche strategy)

Sometimes neither a low-cost leadership strategy nor a differentiation strategy is possible for an organisation across the broad range of the market. For example, the costs of achieving low-cost leadership may require substantial funds, which are not available. Equally, the costs of differentiation, while serving the mass-market of customers, may be too high: if the differentiation involves quality, it may not be credible to offer high quality and cheap products under the same brand name so a new brand name has to be developed and supported. For these and related reasons, it may be better to adopt a *focus* strategy.

A focus strategy occurs when the organisation focuses on a specific niche in the market place and develops its competitive advantage by offering products especially developed for that niche.

Hence the focussed strategy selects a segment or group of segments in the industry and tailors its strategy to serve them to the *exclusion* of others. By optimising its strategy for the targets, the focuser seeks to achieve a competitive advantage in its target segments, even though it does not possess a competitive advantage overall.

It may undertake this process either by using a cost leadership approach or by differentiation:

- With a strategy of *cost focus* a firm seeks a cost advantage in its target segment only.

- With a strategy of *differentiation focus* a firm seeks differentiation in its target segment only.

These two options are not shown in Fig 14.2 but are used in the case studies (*see* Figs 14.5 and 14.6).

The essence of focus is the exploitation of a narrow target's differences from the balance of the industry. By targeting a small, specialised group of buyers it should be possible to earn higher than average profits, either by charging a price premium for exceptional quality or by a cheap and cheerful low-price product. For the European ice cream market, an example of differentiation focus would be the super-premium ice cream segment, while the economy ice cream segment would be an example of cost focus.

In music supply, Muzak Europe was probably a niche player: it had only a small percentage of the European market. However, the definition of its niche was unclear since it was neither premium priced, nor clearly low cost.

There are some problems with the focus strategy.

- By definition, the niche is small and may have limited long-term growth.

- Cost focus may be difficult if economies of scale are important in an industry such as the car industry.

- The niche is clearly specialist in nature and may disappear over time.

Each of these problems can be overcome. Many medium and small companies have found that this is the most useful strategic area to explore.

14.1.5 The danger of being stuck in the middle

Professor Porter concluded his analysis of the main generic strategies by suggesting that there are real dangers for the firm that engages in each generic strategy but fails to achieve any of them. *It is stuck in the middle.* A firm in this position:

> ... *will compete at a disadvantage because the cost leader, differentiators, or focuser will be better positioned to compete in any segment ... Such a firm will be much less profitable than rivals achieving one of the generic strategies.*

Several commentators, such as Kay,[5] Stopford and Baden-Fuller,[6] and Miller[7] now reject this aspect of the analysis. They point to several empirical examples of successful firms that have adopted more than one generic strategy: for example, Toyota cars and Benetton clothing manufacturing and shops, both of which are differentiated yet have low costs.

CASE STUDY 14.1

Two examples of generic strategy options analysis: the European ice cream industry and the global TV industry in the mid-1990s

It is useful to explore some of the benefits and problems of options that have been developed from generic strategies. We can use the data from Chapters 6 and 13 and Case study 14.2 (see later in this chapter), to analyse the possible strategy options in these two industries in the mid-1990s.

The generic strategies of the leading companies in the two industries are set out in Figs 14.5 and 14.6.

Although the European ice cream market is still growing, it is relatively easy to position the main companies in the market. The position of a company such as Nestlé is highlighted because it is neither the low-cost leader, nor does it have a strong range of branded lines that will allow a price premium to be charged. Nevertheless, the direction in which the company appears to be moving can be identified from the matrix.

In the global TV market, there are clearly competitors who compete primarily on a broad-target differentiated basis: they produce films or TV series that are targeted towards mass markets but are unique and highly branded, such as *Star Trek*. Other world channels include MTV pop music and the CNN news channel. However, it is arguable that the latter two examples are niche products on a world scale. From a *global* perspective, there are then the *national* TV channels which clearly address the television needs of one country only: BBC, TF1, RAI and so on. There are also some small local town channels that operate on very small budgets that might be considered the low-cost option.

Ostensibly, there appears to be an option for low-cost leadership in global TV. No company or channel has yet achieved this position.

Fig 14.5   **Generic strategies in the European ice cream industry**

Competitive advantage

		Lower cost	*Differentiation*
Competitive scope	*Broad target*	**Cost leadership** Unilever	**Differentiation** • Mars ice cream • Nestlé?
	Narrow target	**Cost focus** Economy ice cream made by small, local ice cream companies with low overheads	**Differentiation focus** Super-premium, e.g. Häagen-Dazs

CASE STUDY 14.1 continued

Fig 14.6 **Generic strategies in the global TV industry**

		Competitive advantage: *Lower cost*	Competitive advantage: *Differentiation*
Competitive scope	*Broad target, i.e. the global market only*	**Cost leadership** Opportunity here???	**Differentiation** • News Corporation • Time Warner • Disney • Viacom, e.g. MTV
	Narrow target, e.g. national, regional and local TV stations or specialist global markets	**Cost focus** • Local town TV channels • Channels with old movies and game shows	**Differentiation focus** • National TV state broadcasters, e.g. BBC, ZDR, TF1, Singapore TV, South African Broadcasting Company, etc. • Specialist news channels e.g. CNN • Specialist business channels, e.g. CNBC

CASE QUESTIONS FOR BOTH ICE CREAM AND GLOBAL TV

1 *If you were Nestlé in the European ice cream market, what strategy options would you pursue?*

2 *If you were News Corporation and someone recommended a low-cost option, what would your reaction be?*

3 *Can Porter's generic strategies be used with equal confidence in both the European ice cream market and the global TV market?*

14.1.6 Comment on Porter's generic strategies

Hendry[8] and others have set out the problems of the logic and the empirical evidence associated with generic strategies that limit its absolute value. We can summarise these as follows:

Low-cost leadership

- If the option is to seek low-cost leadership, then how can more than one company be *the* low-cost leader? It may be a contradiction in terms to have an *option* of low-cost leadership.
- Competitors also have the option to reduce their costs in the long term, so how can one company hope to maintain its competitive advantage without risk?

- Low-cost leadership should be associated with moving down the experience curve (*see* Chapter 7). However, it was pointed out in Chapter 7 that there are limitations to the usefulness of this concept. They will also apply here.

- Low-cost leadership assumes that technology is relatively predictable, if changing. Radical change can so alter the cost positions of actual and potential competitors that the concept may only have limited relevance in fast changing, high technology markets.

- Cost reductions only lead to competitive advantage when customers are able to make comparisons. This means that the low-cost leader must also lead *price* reductions or competitors will be able to catch up, even if this takes some years and is achieved at lower profit margins. Permanent price reductions by the cost leader may have a damaging impact on the market positioning of its product or service that will limit its usefulness.

Differentiation
- Differentiated products are assumed to be higher priced: this is probably too simplistic. The form of differentiation may not lend itself to higher prices.

- The company may have the objective of increasing its market share, in which case it may use differentiation for this purpose and match the lower prices of competitors.

- Porter discusses differentiation as if the *form* this will take in any market will be immediately obvious. The real problem for strategy options is not to identify the *need* for differentiation but to work out *what form* this should take to be attractive to the customer. Generic strategy options throw no light on this issue whatsoever. They simply assume that once differentiation has been decided then the problem has been solved.

Focus
- The distinction between broad and narrow targets is sometimes unclear. Are they distinguished by size of market? Or by customer type? If the distinction between them is unclear, then what benefit is served by the distinction?

- For many companies, it is certainly useful to recognise that it would be more productive to pursue a niche strategy, away from the broad markets of the market leaders. That is the easy part of the logic. The difficult part is to identify *which* niche is likely to prove worthwhile. Generic strategies provide no useful guidance on this at all.

- As markets fragment and product life cycles become shorter, the concept of broad targets may become increasingly redundant.

Stuck in the middle
As was pointed out above, there is now useful empirical evidence that some companies do pursue both differentiation and low-cost strategies at the same time. They use their low costs to provide greater differentiation and then reinvest the profits to lower their costs even further. Companies such as Benetton (Italy), Toyota (Japan) and BMW (Germany) have been cited as examples.

Conclusions Given these arguments, it might be concluded that the concept of generic strategies has no merit. This would miss the basic point that it is a useful tool for generating *basic options* in strategic analysis. It encourages exploration of two major aspects of corporate strategy: the role of *cost reduction* and the use of *differentiated products* in relation to customers and competitors. However, it is only a starting point in the development of such options. When the market is growing fast, it may provide no useful routes at all.

More generally, the whole approach takes a highly prescriptive view of strategic action. We will leave our consideration of this issue until Chapter 17.

Key strategic principles

- Generic strategies are a means of generating basic strategy options in an organisation. They are based on seeking competitive advantage in the market place.

- There are three main generic options: cost leadership, differentiation and focus.

- Cost leadership aims to make the organisation among the lowest cost producers in the market. It does not necessarily mean having low prices. Higher than average profits come from charging average prices.

- Differentiation is aimed at developing and targeting a product against a major market segment. The product is especially developed, and so it should be possible to charge a small premium to the average price. Differentiation has a cost but this should be more than compensated for in the higher price charged.

- Focus involves targeting a small segment of the market. It may operate by using either a low-cost focus or differentiated focus approach.

- According to the theory, it is important to select between the options and not to be 'stuck in the middle'. Some influential strategists have produced evidence that has cast doubt on this point.

- There have been numerous criticisms of the approach based on logic and empirical evidence of actual industry practice. Undoubtedly these comments have validity, but generic strategies still represent a useful starting point in developing strategy options.

CASE STUDY 14.2

News Corporation builds a global television network – 2

From a standing start in the mid-1980s, News Corporation has built one of the world's largest television networks. This case study explores the strategies it has used to achieve this position. Many of these are market-based and derive from the rapid growth in world electronic media.

In some respects, News Corporation's main strategy has been opportunistic. It has seized the market and technical opportunities that have emerged over the last few years: for example, its acquisition of Star TV was clearly dependent on the Chinese owners being willing to sell; its encryption technology relied on this technical development at that time. It has also attempted to negotiate an interest in the major Italian TV companies controlled by the former Italian Prime Minister, Silvio Berlusconi, but without success at the time of writing.

Underlying these emerging business opportunities, News Corporation has itself identified its four basic strategies:

● *Vertical integration from film-making through to delivery of the electronic signal to the final customer.* Thus it acquired the film company, 20th Century Fox, as well as having an interest in the satellite broadcaster, BSB.

● *Content creation not only through creative skills but also negotiating exclusive new sports deals that buy up the media rights to world sporting events.* For example in 1995, the company proposed to the Rugby Unions of Australia, New Zealand and South Africa a totally new regional championship with new funds from the company and exclusive TV coverage of the matches.

● *Globalisation to give world coverage of electronic media.* This is particularly important for news and sports events. It is less important for entertainment which is more culture-specific. For example, News Corporation announced in late 1995 that it would use its UK-based TV news channel to develop a world news network to rival CNN. There are competitive risks from such a strategy (*see* below).

● *Convergence of newspapers, books and TV so that they all support each other and promote each other's*

interests. For example, the cross-promotion of News Corporation's TV channels in the company's newspapers that had a much wider audience was an important contributor to their early success. (*See* also the comment under 'Risks' below.)

In practice, News Corporation has also chosen to add several more strategies that are particularly important in delivering competitive advantage. They have not been acknowledged in public by the company (unlike those above) but have been identified by writers and researchers in the industry. It should be noted that News Corporation is following widely accepted business practice: publishing some strategies might allow rival companies to counter them more easily. Other strategies include:

● *Exclusive sports deals that have revolutionised TV sport worldwide.* These have also helped the company: for example, its deal to snatch the US TV rights to American Football from its rival, NBC, in 1994 added a substantial new audience to Fox TV in the USA.

● *Encryption technology to capture viewers.*

● *Strong finances.* The company paid little tax in the period 1986–95. Part of the reason was the substantial losses made on BSB between 1989 and 1990, but the company had also been adept at managing its finances beyond that time.

● *Low programming costs.* Nearly all the News Corporation channels use relatively cheap programmes, such as quiz shows and old US soaps, with the exception of the large sports deals. They simply do not produce the same range of new drama, documentaries and comedies of their national rivals. In spite of this, however, the company was still losing money on some of its services. For example, the UK-based Sky News 24-hour TV service made a loss in 1995 of around US$30 million: it needed to find more advertising or more broadcasters willing to take its service in order to cover the heavy fixed costs involved in such an operation.

● *Alliances and joint ventures.* To extend its global network, the company has entered into a number of deals with companies in individual countries or regions of the world. Some of these are shown in Fig 14.7.

Finally, it should be noted that Mr Murdoch himself did not believe in economies of scale in the industry: 'There may be diminishing returns to being bigger.' However, this had not stopped his rivals growing.

Competition

In the rapidly changing global media market, it was difficult to keep track of competitors and their particular strengths.

In every area of its operations, News Corporation faces aggressive rivals. This is partly because it is competing against North American companies where this is part of the culture. It has also arisen because of the world opportunities that leading companies have identified over the coming years: they judge that now is the time to establish their position.

The intensity of the rivalry was highlighted in 1995 when News Corporation announced its intention to launch a new 24-hour *global* news channel, probably based at Sky News. This would compete directly with Mr Ted Turner's Cable News Network (CNN) channel. Mr Murdoch had previously tried to buy CNN but the deal became impossible when CNN became part of Time Warner. On hearing that Rupert Murdoch was planning a rival channel, Ted Turner commented:

We look forward to a fight with anybody who wants to get in the ring with us. We're going to squash Rupert like a bug. He's tried to figure out a way to compete with CNN for years. He tried to buy us and we wouldn't sell to him.

Risks for News Corporation

After nearly collapsing in 1990, the company has strongly recovered its finances. Not only has it had an injection of funds from the public flotation of its UK/European TV channel but the American telephone company, MCI, took a share stake during 1995, contributing US$1 billion. The purpose was to take the strategy of *convergence* even further by adding a link with telecommunications services. What precisely this meant for both companies and how it was to operate was unclear: such a new venture may therefore carry some risk.

There are four other risks faced by the company:

1 *Creativity.* It is impossible to guarantee box office success with films and TV series and the exposure can be high. For example, Kevin Costner's film *Waterworld* needed US$135 million in 1995 from its owner, the Hollywood studio MCA. For comparison only, this sum was one third of the profits before depreciation and tax of News Corporation in the same year.

2 *Government regulation.* The Chinese and Singaporean governments were both concerned at unrestricted access of TV signals to their population. The Indian and Indonesian governments were also reported to be concerned about the impact of News Corporation TV programmes in their countries.

3 *Political and ethical backlash against exclusivity.* Governments and individuals were slowly coming to realise that sporting events that had previously been free or low-cost now had to be paid for. Some regarded this as the application of market forces but others were beginning to take the view that their citizens had inherent rights to view such occasions. At the time of writing, there was a major investigation by the UK Monopolies and Mergers Commission in progress into this area.

4 *Competition.* Clearly the intensity of the rivalry may impact on industry profitability.

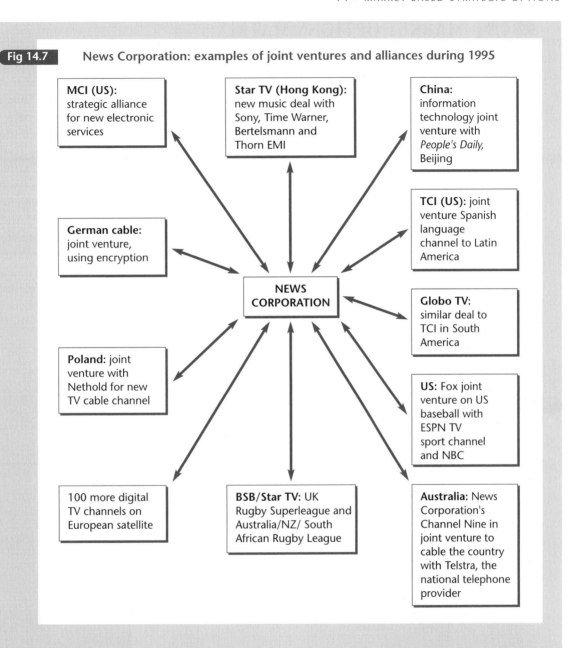

Fig 14.7 News Corporation: examples of joint ventures and alliances during 1995

MCI (US): strategic alliance for new electronic services

Star TV (Hong Kong): new music deal with Sony, Time Warner, Bertelsmann and Thorn EMI

China: information technology joint venture with *People's Daily*, Beijing

German cable: joint venture, using encryption

TCI (US): joint venture Spanish language channel to Latin America

NEWS CORPORATION

Globo TV: similar deal to TCI in South America

Poland: joint venture with Nethold for new TV cable channel

US: Fox joint venture on US baseball with ESPN TV sport channel and NBC

100 more digital TV channels on European satellite

BSB/Star TV: UK Rugby Superleague and Australia/NZ/ South African Rugby League

Australia: News Corporation's Channel Nine in joint venture to cable the country with Telstra, the national telephone provider

CASE QUESTIONS

1 Among the media companies, there is disagreement on the best route forward for corporate strategy: the **software** route versus the **hardware** route. Where does News Corporation stand in this debate? Do you judge that News Corporation has chosen the most successful long-term strategies?

2 In such a fast changing market, is it possible to select a **range** of strategies and follow these through as the market changes? Or would a company such as News Corporation be better advised to have a **general** vision and then grab **individual** business opportunities as they arise?

3 What arguments and evidence would you investigate to judge whether Mr Murdoch was right about economies of scale?

14.2 MARKET OPTIONS MATRIX

The Market Options Matrix identifies the product and market choices open to the organisation. The distinction is drawn between *markets*, which are defined as customers, and *products*, which are defined as the items sold to customers. Thus for example, one customer could buy several different products depending on need.

The Market Options Matrix examines the options available to the organisation from a broader, strategic perspective than the simple market/product matrix (called in some texts the *Ansoff Matrix*). Thus the Market Options Matrix not only considers the possibility of launching new products and moving into new markets, but explores the possibility of *withdrawing* from markets and moving into *unrelated* markets. Nevertheless, the format is based on product/market options[10] and is shown in Fig 14.8. It should be noted that although the developments are shown as *options* in separate boxes in Fig 14.8, there may be in reality a *gradual* movement from one area to another. They are not absolutes.

Each of the strategic options is now considered in turn. To avoid confusion, it should be noted that market *penetration* differs from market *development* because penetration concentrates on existing *or* potential customers, whereas development seeks totally new segments of customers or totally new customer groups.

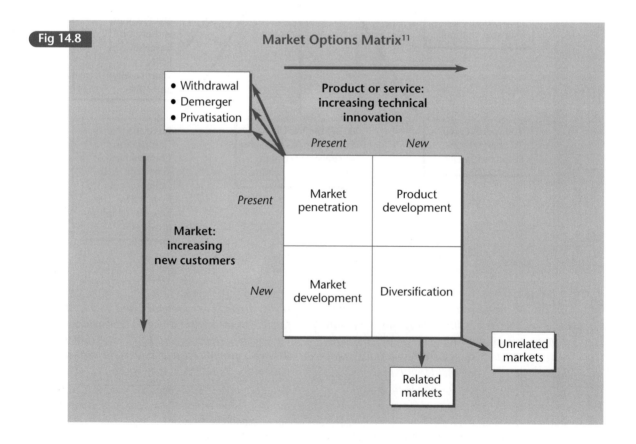

Fig 14.8 — Market Options Matrix[11]

- Withdrawal
- Demerger
- Privatisation

Product or service: increasing technical innovation

Market: increasing new customers

	Present	New
Present	Market penetration	Product development
New	Market development	Diversification

Related markets

Unrelated markets

14.2.1 Withdrawal

It may seem perverse to begin the consideration of market options by the possible strategy of withdrawing from them. However, strategy must always consider the unpredictable if it is to develop competitive advantage. There are a number of circumstances where this option may have merit, for example:

● *Product life cycle in decline phase with little possibility of retrenchment*. We looked at examples in Chapter 3. In the context of global TV, the time will come in the next 20 years when digital TV channels will take over from analogue broadcasts and all the old products will simply be scrapped. Many companies have now stopped producing LP records.

● *Over-extension of product range which can only be resolved by withdrawing some products*. In television, some of the many channels now being offered may have such small audiences that they do not justify even the minimal expense of keeping them operating. Other industries such as the food industry regularly weed out underperforming products from their total range in order to concentrate on the leading lines.

● *Holding company sales of subsidiaries*. Such companies often see their subsidiary companies, perhaps in diverse industries, as being little more than assets to be bought and sold if the price is attractive. US television companies regularly sell local TV stations and withdraw from that market for reasons associated with finance, ability to link with other stations, change of corporate objectives, etc. Even though it was a core element of the businesses, Virgin Records (UK) sold its retail store chain to Thorn EMI (UK) for the right price.

● *Raise funds for investment elsewhere*. Organisations may be able to *sell* the asset they are planning to withdraw from the market. Even without a sale, the working capital and management time devoted to the asset might be redeployed to other more productive uses. Government-owned companies faced with restrictions on outside funds might regard withdrawal and sale as a useful strategy here.

14.2.2 Demerger

In a sense, this is a form of withdrawal from the market, but it has a rather specialist meaning with some attractive implications. For some companies whose shares are openly traded on the stock exchange, the value of the *underlying assets* may be rather higher than the value implied by the *share price*. For example, the UK-based chemical company ICI was split into two companies in 1993 by issuing two sets of shares to its existing shareholders. The shares of the two companies were then separately traded on the London Stock Exchange at a greater value than when they had been combined together. The reason was that one company's product range was in basic chemicals and the other in pharmaceuticals, the latter being highly attractive to stockholders. ICI was *demerged*.

This strategy has been used increasingly to realise the underlying asset values in publicly quoted companies. It also has the benefit that companies with totally unrelated market activities allow each part to focus on its own business without competing for scarce resources. It has the disadvantage that it may destroy the benefits of size, cross-trading and uniqueness of a larger company.

14.2.3 Privatisation

In many countries around the world, there has been a trend to privatise government-owned companies – that is, to sell its shares into private ownership. This has become a major option for some institutions. For example, many national telecommunications companies have now been privatised, with the exception of the USA where they have always been in the private sector. The results in terms of management style, public accountability, ownership and strategy changes have been substantial. The changes in the product range, levels of service and public perceptions have also been significant.

14.2.4 Market penetration in the existing market

Without moving outside the organisation's current range of products or services, it may be possible to attract customers from directly competing products by penetrating the market. Market penetration strategy should begin[12] with *existing* customers. A direct attack on competitors' customers invites direct retaliation that can nullify the initial gains and erode the company's profit margins. Retaining an existing customer is usually cheaper, especially in consumer goods markets. Car companies such as Toyota and BMW make great efforts to retain customers when they change cars.

If a direct attack is to be mounted on a competitor in order to penetrate the market, it is likely to be more effective[13] if a *combination* of activities is mounted: for example, an improvement in product quality and levels of service along with promotional activity. Clearly this is likely to be more expensive in the short term but should have long-run benefits in terms of increased market share. News Corporation satellite operations regularly combine new TV channels with advertising and special deals on decoders as part of their strategy to penetrate the market.

Market penetration may be easier if the market is *growing*. The reason is that existing customer loyalties may be less secure and new customers entering the market may still be searching for the most acceptable product. The most attractive strategy in these circumstances will vary with the company's market share position:

- Existing companies with *low relative market share* in a growing market have little to lose from attacking aggressively the market or a segment of it. For example, the smaller Burger King (Grand Metropolitan, UK) has mounted a concerted attack on McDonald's over the last few years with some success.

- Existing companies with a *high relative market share* in a growing market have potentially an attractive position which might be lost. Predatory price cutting is a strategy sometimes employed to keep out the smaller new entrants. It will work well and move the company down the experience curve, as long as it has the production capacity. This strategy has been employed to launch new-generation computer chips by Intel and hold off the smaller new entrants such as Cyrix and AMD (all US companies).

14.2.5 Market development using existing products

For this strategic route, the organisation now moves beyond its immediate customer focus into attracting new customers for its existing product range. It may seek new *segments* of the market, new *geographical areas* or new *uses* for its products or services that will bring in new customers.

Expansion to bring in totally new customers to the company for its existing products could easily involve some slight repackaging and then promotion to a new market segment. It will often involve selling the same product in new international markets: there are many examples of such a strategy throughout this book. Using core competences and a little ingenuity, it may be possible to find new uses for existing products. For example, the pharmaceutical company Glaxo (UK) has sought to develop the markets for its anti-ulcer drug Zantac as markets have matured in western Europe and North America. Thus it has marketed the product to an increasing range of countries and it has also developed a lower-strength version to be sold without prescription as a stomach remedy in place of antacid remedies.

We explore the methods by which organisations can undertake such expansion in Section 14.3.

14.2.6 Product development for the existing market

We refer here to significant new product developments, not a minor variation on an existing product. There are a number of reasons that might justify such a strategy:[14]

- to utilise excess production capacity
- to counter competitive entry
- to exploit new technology
- to maintain stance as a product innovator
- to protect overall market share.

Understanding the reason for such a strategy is the key to selecting the route that product development will then follow. Probably the area with the most potential is that associated with innovation: it may represent a threat to an existing product line or an opportunity to take market share from competition. There are two key elements to highlight from the extensive literature on new product development:

1 the importance of a genuine improvement in performance, if new products are to be successful;[15] and

2 the significant contribution to sales and profits from new product introductions across a wide range of industries.[16]

Sometimes product development strategies do not always fall neatly into an existing market. They often move the company into markets and towards customers that are not currently being served. This is part of the natural growth of many organisations.

14.2.7 Diversification: related markets

When an organisation diversifies, it moves out of its current products and markets into new areas. Clearly, this will involve a step into the unknown and will carry a higher degree of business risk. However, this risk may be minimised if it moves into related markets. (*Related* here means a market that has some existing connection with its existing value chain.) It is usual to distinguish three types of relationship based on the value chain of Chapter 7:

● *Forward integration*. A manufacturer becomes involved in the activities of the organisation's *outputs* such as distribution, transport, logistics – for example, the purchase of glass distributors by Europe's two leading glass manufacturers, St Gobain (France) and Pilkington (UK).[17]

● *Backward integration*. The organisation extends its activities to those of its *inputs* such as its suppliers of raw materials, plant and machinery – for example, the purchase by the oil company Elf (France) of oil drilling interests in the North Sea.[18]

● *Horizontal integration*. The organisation moves into areas immediately related to its existing activities either because they compete or they are complementary. For example, the acquisition by BMW (Germany) of the UK car company, Rover, in 1994.

News Corporation has engaged in forward integration by purchasing cable and satellite channels to deliver television programmes directly to customers. It has integrated backwards into film production companies. It has undertaken horizontal integration by extending the range of its activities from newspapers into books, television and electronic media.

Synergy is the main reason given for such activities.[19] It means essentially that the whole is worth more than the sum of the parts: the value to be generated from owning and controlling more of the value chain is greater because the various elements support each other. This concept is relatively easy to understand but rather more difficult to analyse precisely and as a result it is difficult to assess its specific contribution to corporate strategy. It is related to the concept of the *linkages* in the value chain that were explored in Chapter 7 and is probably best assessed using these concepts.

14.2.8 Diversification: unrelated markets

When an organisation moves into unrelated markets, it runs the risk of operating in areas where its detailed knowledge of the key factors for success is limited. Essentially, it acts as if it were a *holding company*. Some companies have operated such a strategy with success, probably the best known being Hanson plc (UK but with strong interests in the USA) and General Electric (US). The logic of such an expansion is unlikely to be market-related, by definition, since the target market has no connection with the organisation's current areas of interest. This does not mean that the strategy is without merit for two reasons:

● There could be other connections in finance with the existing business that would justify such expansion.

● There may be no connection but the diversification could still be operated successfully if the holding company managed such a venture using tight but clear financial controls. Hanson has used this method with some success. (*See* Chapter 22 for more details on Hanson.)

Clearly, such strategies are directly related to the discussion on *strategic parenting* in Chapter 13.

14.2.9 Comment

The Market Options Matrix is a useful way of structuring the options available. However, it does not in itself provide many useful indicators of which option to choose in what circumstances. Thus its value lies in *structuring* the problem rather than *solving* it. The main strategic insights come from the possibilities that it raises to challenge the current thinking by opening up the debate.

Such routes may involve the expenditure of some funds on new product development, research, advertising and related matters. Hence, the options are more likely to be favoured by those organisations with significant financial resources. Many of the options are more likely to be considered by profitable companies, rather than those attempting to recover from substantial losses. However, by disposing of some assets, market-based options may actually *raise funds* and provide greater freedom of action for those remaining in the organisation. Typically, these might include the sale of parts of companies.

The Market Options Matrix may be more appropriate in the commercial, non-government owned sector because state companies are usually set up to fill a specific role with little room for development beyond this definition.

Key strategic principles

- By examining the market place and the products available, it is possible to structure options that organisations may be able to adopt: the overall structure is called the Market Options Matrix.

- Options include moving to new customers and new products. As these are developed further, they may involve the organisation in diversifying away from its original markets.

- Synergy is the main reason behind diversification – the whole being more than the sum of the parts. This concept is associated with linkages in the value chain.

- The Market Options Matrix is a method of generating options but provides no guidance on choosing between them. The main strategic insights come from the possibilities that it raises to challenge the current thinking by opening up the debate.

14.3 EXPANSION METHOD MATRIX

The Expansion Method Matrix explores in a structured way the methods by which market options might be achieved. By examining the organisation's *internal* and *external expansion opportunities* and its *geographical spread* of activity, it is possible to structure the various methods that are available.

In addition to exploring the ways of developing strategy options, it is also important to consider the methods by which these can be achieved: for example, launching a new product could be done using an existing company or an acquisition, merger or a joint venture with another firm. As companies have moved outside their home countries, the range of methods used to achieve such a development have also increased. We have already seen how News Corporation has used a variety of contractual arrangements in different countries in the world to develop its global presence. The full list of options available to organisations is set out in Fig 14.9.

Although it is appropriate to generate *options* using the Expansion Method Matrix, there may still be problems. There is empirical evidence that some options do not deliver the promised benefits: this is explored in Chapter 16 in the context of selecting between the options.

14.3.1 Acquisitions

Probably the most important reason for this method of market expansion is that associated with the particular assets of the company: brands, market share, core competences and special technologies may all represent reasons for purchase. News Corporation acquired its encryption technology by buying a company in 1990. The obvious disadvantage is that, if a company really has an asset, there may be a substantial premium to pay over the asset value of the company. For example, Nestlé paid double the value at which the shares of Rowntree had been previously quoted on the Stock Exchange, when it bought the chocolate company in 1989.

Fig 14.9

Expansion Method Matrix

Company

	Inside	Outside
Home country	• Internal development	• Merger • Acquisition • Joint venture • Alliance • Franchise
International	• Exporting • Overseas office • Overseas manufacture • Multinational operation • Global operation	• Merger • Acquisition • Joint venture • Alliance • Franchise • Turnkey • Licensing

Geographical location

Note: All the above methods must add value to the organisation if they are to justify their costs.

Acquisitions may also be made for competitive reasons. In a static market, it may be expensive and slow to enter by building from the beginning: for example, in the slow growing coffee market, Philip Morris/ Kraft General Foods has made a series of company purchases to add to its Maxwell House brand: Café Hag and Jacob's Coffee. In fast growing markets, acquisitions may be the means to achieve presence more rapidly: for example, the purchase of the Biogen Company by Roche (Switzerland) moved the Swiss company from its traditional drugs into the totally new area of biomedical sciences at a stroke.

14.3.2 Mergers

Mergers are similar to acquisitions in the sense of two companies combining together. However, mergers usually arise because neither company has the scale to acquire the other on its own. This has the potential benefit of being more friendly but requires special handling if the benefits are to be realised. In other respects, it is similar to an acquisition in terms of the main strategic issues.

14.3.3 Joint ventures and alliances

A *joint venture* is the formation of a company whose shares are owned jointly by two parent companies. It usually shares some of the assets and skills of both parents. Cereal Partners Inc. is a 50/50 joint venture between Nestlé and General Mills (US) whose purpose is to attack Kelloggs Breakfast Cereals around the world except in North America.

An *alliance* is a form of weaker contractual agreement or even minority shareholding between two parent companies: it usually falls short of the formation of a separate subsidiary. Several of the European telecommunications companies have built alliances as the basis for international expansion.

14.3.4 Franchise

A franchise is a form of licensing agreement in which the contractor provides the licensee with a pre-formed package of activity. It may include a brand name, technical service expertise and some advertising assistance. The payment is usually as a percentage of turnover. McDonald's Restaurants are among the best-known franchises.

The main advantages and disadvantages of the various methods of market expansion are summarised in Exhibit 14.1.

Exhibit 14.1　　　Methods of expansion: advantages and disadvantages[20]

Advantages	Disadvantages
Acquisition	
● Can be relatively fast	● Premium paid: expensive
● May reduce competition from a rival, although such a move usually has to be sanctioned by government competition authorities	● High risk if wrong company targeted
	● Best targets may have already been acquired
● Cost savings from economies of scale or savings in shared overheads	● Not always easy to dispose of unwanted parts of company
● Maintenance of company exclusivity in technical expertise	● Human relations problems that can arise *after* the acquisition: probably the cause of more failures than any other.
● Extend to new geographical area	
● Buy market size and share	
● Financial reasons associated with purchase of undervalued assets that may then be resold	● Problems of clash of national cultures particularly where target 'foreign'
Joint venture	
● Builds scale quickly	● Control lost to some extent
● Obtain special expertise quickly	● Works best where both parties contribute something different to the mix
● Cheaper than acquisition	
● Can be used where outright acquisition not feasible	● Can be difficult to manage because of need to share and because parent companies may interfere
● Can be used where similar product available	● Share profits with partner
Alliance	
● Can build close contacts with partner	● Slow and plodding approach
● Use joint expertise and commitment	● Needs constant work to keep relationship sound
● Allows potential partners to learn about each other	● Partners may only have a limited joint commitment to make alliance a success
● Locks out other competitors	
	● Unlikely to build economies of scale
Franchise	
● Lower investment than outright purchase	● Depends on quality of franchise
● Some of basic testing of business proposition undertaken by franchise holder: lower risk	● Part of profits paid over to franchise holder
	● Risk that business built and franchise withdrawn
● Exclusive territory usually granted	

14.3.5 International options

In spite of the publicity on some occasions across Europe, acquisitions are relatively infrequent outside the UK and North America.[21] They are also used sparingly in many countries of South-East Asia and Japan. There are two main reasons: shares are more openly traded in Anglo-Saxon countries than in parts of Europe and Asia, where bank and government holdings are more important. In addition, there is a stronger tradition in some countries of inter-locking shareholdings that makes outright acquisition difficult, if not impossible.

Beyond this basic issue, the greater degree of global trading has made options that might have applied in a few western countries now available around the world. There are two that have some importance for overseas operations:

- *Turnkey*. A contractor has total responsibility for building and possibly commissioning large-scale plant. Payment can take many forms.

- *Licensing*. Technology or other assets are provided under license from the home country. Payment is usually by royalty or some other percentage of turnover arrangement.

More generally, overseas expansion for many companies may take the form of the following sequence:[22]

- *Exporting* is a possible first expansion step.

- *An overseas office* may then be set up to provide permanent presence.

- *Overseas manufacture* can take place but this clearly increases the risk and exposure to international risks such as currency.

- *Multinational operations* may be set up to provide major international activity.

- *Global operations* may be introduced. The distinction from multinational operations lies in the degree of international commitment and, importantly, in the ability to source production and raw materials from the most favourable location anywhere in the world.

There are various risks and opportunities associated with all the above operations. Probably the most important of these is currency variation – that is, the difficulty of trading in currencies that are volatile and may cause significant and unexpected losses.

14.3.6 Comment

The Expansion Method Matrix suffers from the same disadvantage as the previous matrix: namely, it is useful at structuring the options but offers only limited guidance on choosing between them.

■ Key strategic principles

- The Expansion Method Matrix explores in a structured way the methods by which market options might be achieved. By examining the organisation's internal and external expansion opportunities and its geographical spread of activity, it is possible to structure the various methods that are available.

- Within the home country, the four main methods of expansion are: acquisition, joint venture, alliance and franchise. Each has its advantages and problems.

- Beyond the home country, there are additional means of international expansion, including exporting, setting up overseas offices and undertaking full manufacturing. The most important risk associated with international expansion is probably currency fluctuation.

CASE STUDY 14.3

Strategic choice at British Aerospace[23]

Having pulled back from the brink of collapse in 1995, British Aerospace had to face the challenge of emerging US aerospace giants. This case study describes the main options now available for the company.

In mid-1995, all Europe defence and aerospace executives were deeply concerned by reports that Boeing and McDonnell Douglas of the US were considering a merger. It would create a major global aerospace corporation with US$35 billion sales. For perhaps the first time, there was a real threat to the very survival of European companies. The main solution was the consolidation in Europe that had already taken place among some US companies. The problem in Europe was that no one had been able to agree the way forward.

Although it had been the sick person of European industry four years earlier, British Aerospace (BAe) was better placed in 1995 than its continental counterparts to meet the challenge. It had been through much of the internal reconstruction that French and German companies were only just beginning to contemplate and had restored its financial position. The reforms at BAe had bought the company time to undertake the harder task of negotiating its way through UK national priorities

and its own corporate ambitions. BAe's overall objective was to secure its place in one of the three or four groups which were likely to dominate the global industry in the next century.

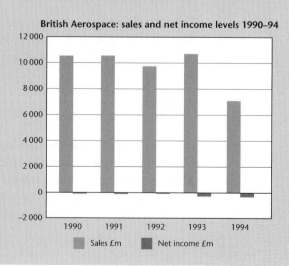

British Aerospace: sales and net income levels 1990–94

Dick Evans, BAe's Chief Executive says:

Aerospace is a very long-term business, and we have to plan now for the way that the industry will be in 20 or 30 years' time. We will act both internally and externally to protect the long-term prospects for BAe.

Translated, this meant that BAe needed to forge partnerships with other companies. Given the pace of consolidation in the USA, it needed to act sooner rather than later.

Core competences

BAe saw its central skill as being the management of very large and complex high technology programmes. In the years 1993–95, it had tried to expand its presence in the UK defence market beyond its traditional aircraft and missiles business to make use of its prime contracting skills. It had attempted to become the main supplier to a new Franco–German Tiger helicopter and it had also tried to buy a UK submarine maker. However, both attempts were beaten by rival UK companies, Westland and GEC respectively. Domestic UK expansion through bolt-on acquisitions now appeared unlikely. By late 1995, it was seeking to use its core competence to develop larger, strategic alliances. They would have to be agreed deals because of their size.

In addition to these moves, BAe also had high-quality technical skills in aerospace research and development. For example, it had developed the highly successful Harrier vertical take-off aeroplane. It also had extensive knowledge and trained workers in many aspects of the complex construction of aircraft and other defence systems. For example, it was a main contractor to the European Airbus consortium.

BAe options

The company had three main options:

- It could use its long-standing links to the US and become part of a rationalised Anglo-Saxon market.

- It could turn inward to the UK, which would in practice mean striking a heavily predicted merger with the main aerospace interests of its chief rival, GEC.

- It could seek alliances in continental Europe.

The rest of this case describes these three options in more detail and explores the opportunities and problems.

Option 1: US link

Ties with the US had superficial attractions for BAe. It had had a close relationship with McDonnell Douglas (US) over 20 years: BAe and the US-based company made BAe Harrier and Hawk aircraft for the US Marines and Navy. A formal merger would have given both companies better access to each other's markets, and their product ranges were complementary. McDonnell Douglas made current generation fighters which would have a role well into the next century, but at present it had little stake in the next generation of aircraft. BAe made Tornado strike aircraft and was also playing a big part in the Eurofighter project, which had yet to enter production but had good long-term export prospects.

The two companies also worked at adjacent sites in Saudi Arabia on huge defence contracts and in the civil field they had aircraft businesses which could be rationalised. BAe already worked with the US on specific projects, such as the Joint Advanced Strike Technology programme, whose aim was to produce a replacement for the vertical take-off Harrier. However, any deal with an American company has serious drawbacks. US law means that British board members could not see details of secret US projects. Any overall control of a US project had to rest solely with Americans. Besides, the sheer scale of the US market would inevitably force BAe to become the junior partner in any alliance.

In practice, any deal with the US would almost certainly have meant that over time BAe became a sub-contractor to a larger American company, losing the skills of running whole programmes and developing the intellectual property which was one of its main sources of wealth creation. A full-scale merger therefore seemed a very remote possibility.

Option 2: Link with GEC, UK

Tying up with GEC was an idea that had been around for a long time. At one stage, it was thought that GEC might bid to acquire BAe. However, as BAe increased its profitability, it also raised

CASE STUDY 14.3 continued

its share price. This made it highly unlikely that GEC would mount a bid. Certainly, during 1992 and 1993, there were extensive discussions between the two companies when BAe had been in difficulties. It was BAe itself that had terminated them, however. By 1995, BAe's negotiating position had improved so that any discussions were bound to be on a more equal footing.

A pooled BAe–GEC aerospace company would have a greater size and would therefore be better able to compete in world markets or negotiate a subsequent, more strategic deal with US or European companies. It would also rationalise the supply chain for the British defence industry and help avoid some of the problems that had dogged the Eurofighter project, by combining the technical teams of the two companies. However, while the defence industry was increasingly a competition between US and European teams, the creation of a single large UK defence company might worry the British Ministry of Defence because its national buying choice would be restricted. Furthermore, since there was little overlap between GEC's electronics, avionics and shipbuilding businesses, and BAe's aircraft and missiles operations, there would be limited scope for rationalisation.

Most importantly, the two companies had widely differing cultures and management styles. The risk of clashes would be high. BAe was created in 1977 from the merger of several defence businesses and had taken a long time to gel into a single company. Forming a genuine bond with GEC would be even more difficult. Besides, BAe had an eye to the Continent. Dick Evans commented:

> Part of the success that we have made for ourselves in the last few years is the creation of strategic options for the company, many of which lie in Europe.

Option 3: Links with Continental Europe

Continental Europe was certainly the most fertile area for links, but it had also proved the most difficult arena in which to conclude deals. Cross-border mergers between aircraft makers – for example, between BAe and Daimler–Benz Aerospace (Dasa)

of Germany – could save large sums by eliminating duplicated research effort and plant capacity. Similarly mergers between electronics companies – such as GEC and the French company Thomson–CSF – could create component and sub-systems with the scale to challenge US firms. Yet the barriers were as great as the prizes. Up to 1996, national ambitions and security concerns had prevented integration. To reap the full benefits of consolidation, companies would need to work within co-ordinated, and preferably integrated defence markets – something which showed little sign of happening. In France, most of the industry was state-owned and heavily loss-making. In Germany, it was at least concentrated in private hands in Dasa, but even the Dasa civil operations were losing money.

Even before the announcement of a joint research venture in late 1995, links had been mooted between BAe and the French aircraft maker, Dassault. However, the deal was small in scale and, in reality, just showed how far apart the two companies remained. More generally, the two companies were working on very different programmes for the current generation of aircraft. Thus the benefits of any alliance would only flow in the long term. Moreover, in practice, the complex Dassault shareholding structure made a deal difficult to organise.

More credible perhaps was a deal between BAe and Dasa, which would have big advantages. It would bring together the two largest partners in the US$50 billion Eurofighter project and strengthen the programme's central management, while merging two of the partners in Airbus. A unified company would retain within Europe the prime contracting skills and intellectual property that BAe would lose if it went to the US. It was possible to conceive of a single BAe–Dasa company, perhaps with BAe running the military aircraft business and Dasa running the civil operations, structured along the lines of Unilever or Royal Dutch Shell. BAe expertise might help Dasa solve its civil aircraft difficulties which were similar to those the British company faced in 1990. As private sector companies, a deal would be comparatively easy to structure.

Such an entity could be the focus for further consolidation. The logical first French partner for BAe–Dasa would be Aerospatiale. The three companies were the largest shareholders in Airbus, the European airliner consortium. Bringing together the British and German companies would be a powerful incentive to France to rationalise its industry to prevent it being relegated to the margins. Other French groups such as Dassault might eventually join such a grouping.

Yet BAe was well aware of how difficult it was to agree such deals. It had spent almost three years trying to agree a relatively simple joint venture in missiles with Matra (France) without managing to cement a deal.

Conclusions

In examining its options, BAe had to weigh up the strategic, if complex, benefits of a European rationalisation, against a simpler more limited UK consolidation or the large market size of the North American option. In late 1995, Dick Evans commented:

> BAe has long maintained that Europe must come together. Recent developments in the US provide a challenge for Europe. BAe is determined to be at the centre of the changes in the European industry.

Action was unlikely to be delayed, given the possibility of the Boeing–McDonnell merger and the previous deal in 1994 between two other leading US companies, Lockheed and Martin Marietta. Having waited too long, the European industry might be about to move. BAe was considering whether to lead the charge.

Source: Financial Times, 19 December 1995.

CASE QUESTIONS

1 *Examine the three options in the case in the context of the guidelines for core competences and decide what extra information would be needed for the company to pursue this resource area further.*

2 *Use the criteria for generating innovation to produce some additional options for BAe.*

3 *Taking the three options identified in the case, where would you place them in Porter's generic strategies? Does such an analysis add significantly to the strategy considerations in this case? If so, in what way? If not, why not?*

4 *Use the Expansion Method Matrix to analyse the advantages and disadvantages of the three options in the case. What conclusions can you draw on the opportunities and problems already identified above? (**Clue**: for example, there is at least one possible problem in the BAe–Dasa link that is not even mentioned in the case.)*

SUMMARY

● Generic strategies are a means of generating basic strategy options in an organisation, and are based on seeking competitive advantage in the market place. There are three main generic options:

1 *Cost leadership* aims to make the organisation's among production costs the lowest in the market. It does not necessarily mean having low prices, as higher than average profits can come from charging average prices.

2 *Differentiation* aims to develop and target a product especially for a major market segment, enabling it to be priced at a small premium. The cost of differentiation should be more than compensated for in the higher price charged.

3 *Focus* involves targeting a small segment of the market by using a low-cost focus or differentiated focus approach. Some theorists consider it is important to

select between the options and not to be 'stuck in the middle', but a number of influential strategists have produced evidence that has cast doubt on this point. Criticisms of the approach, based on logic and empirical evidence of actual industrial practice, undoubtedly have validity, but generic strategies still represent a useful starting point in developing strategy options.

● *The Market Options Matrix.* By examining the market place and the products available, it is possible to structure options that organisations may be able to adopt. Such options may include moving to new customers and new products. Developing these options may involve the organisation in diversifying from its original markets. The main reason behind such diversification is synergy – the whole being more than the sum of the parts. This concept is associated with linkages in the value chain. The Market Options Matrix is a method of generating options, but provides no guidance on choosing between them. The main strategic insights come from the possibilities that are raised to challenge the current thinking by opening up the debate.

● *The Expansion Method Matrix* explores in a structured way the methods by which market options might be achieved. By examining the organisation's internal and external expansion opportunities and its geographical spread of activity, it is possible to structure the various methods that are available. Within the organisation's home country, the four main methods of expansion are: acquisition, joint venture, alliance and franchise. Each has its advantages and problems. Outside the home country, there are additional means of international expansion, including exporting, setting up overseas offices and undertaking all manufacturing abroad. The greatest risk associated with international expansion is probably currency fluctuation.

QUESTIONS

1 Plot the position of Muzak Europe on the generic strategies matrix in Fig 14.2. What conclusions can you draw about future strategies for the company from this?

2 *'Generic strategies are a fallacy. The best firms are striving all the time to reconcile opposites.'* Professors Charles Baden-Fuller and John Stopford.
Discuss.

3 Do small firms have anything useful to learn from a consideration of the options available from generic strategies?

4 Take an organisation with which you are familiar, such as a small voluntary group, and consider the possibilities of expansion. Apply the Market Options Matrix and Expansion Method Matrix to your choice. What conclusions can you draw on future expansion strategy?

5 Use the Market Options Matrix to take a broader look at the options available to British Aerospace in Case study 14.2. Has the company identified all the main options?

6 To what extent is the Expansion Method Matrix useful in examining the options now available to Muzak Europe as it pursues further growth? Are there any strategic recommendations that you would make to the company?

7 *'A recurring theme to criticisms of strategic planning practice is the pedestrian quality of the strategic options that are considered.'* Professor George Day.
By what methods might this legitimate concern be overcome?

8 If successful strategy is only built slowly over many years, how useful is it to consider such concepts as the Expansion Method Matrix which often rely on a rapid strategic development such as an acquisition?

9 There has been no discussion in this chapter on human resource issues. Does this matter at this stage? Can it be left for consideration later?

STRATEGIC PROJECT

Mobile telecommunications around the world

Benefon has already managed to develop its operations worldwide. There are many other companies examining the same rapid developments with considerable interest. You might like to explore the companies, strategies and challenges of this new and exciting market opportunity.

FURTHER READING

On generic strategies: Porter, M E (1980) *Competitive Strategy*, The Free Press, Boston, Mass. and Porter, M E (1985) *Competitive Advantage*, The Free Press, Boston, Mass. It should be noted that they also provide a much broader view of strategy than this single topic.

On the Market Options Matrix and Expansion Method Matrix: these are covered in many marketing texts in a more limited form. Professor George Day's book is probably the best at providing a breadth of viewpoint beyond the marketing function: Day, G S (1984) *Strategic Marketing Planning*, West Publishing, St Paul, Minn.

REFERENCES

1 Case adapted from an article by Ronald van der Krol in the *Financial Times*, 27 Nov 1995, p13.
2 Porter, M E (1980) *Competitive Strategy*, The Free Press, Boston, Mass.
3 Porter, M E (1985) *Competitive Advantage*, The Free Press, Boston, Mass.
4 *Source*: Porter, M E (1985) Ibid.
5 Kay, J (1993) *Foundations of Corporate Success*, Oxford University Press, Ch 1.
6 Stopford, J and Baden-Fuller, C (1992) *Rejuvenating the Mature Business: The Competitive Challenge*, Routledge, London.
7 Miller, D (1992) 'The Generic Strategy Trap', *Journal of Business Strategy*, 13(1), pp37–42.
8 Hendry, J (1990) 'The Problem with Porter's Generic Strategies', *European Management Journal*, Dec, pp443–50.
9 References for Case study 14.2: *Financial Times*: 4 Sep 1993, p6; 5 Mar 1994, p11; 3 Aug 1994, p22; 10 Aug 1994, p14; 6 Jan 1995, p15; 24 Jan 1995, p23; 13 Feb 1995, p3; 14 Feb 1995, p25; 3 Apr 1995, p13; 7 Apr 1995, p1; 11 Apr 1995, p17; 27 May 1995, p8; 14 June

1995, p1; 18 June 1995, p9; 27 July 1995, p25; 2 Aug 1995, p15; 19 Aug 1995, p17; 30 Aug 1995, p15; 8 Nov 1995, p33; 30 Nov 1995, p8. *Guardian*: 5 Dec 1995, p12.

10 Kotler, P (1994) *Marketing Management*, 8th edn, Prentice Hall, Upper Saddle Road, NJ, p77. The matrix also uses concepts outlined by Day, G S (1987) *Strategic Market Planning*, West Publishing, St Paul, Minn, Ch 5.

11 *Source*: author based on Kotler and Day.

12 Day, G S, Ibid, p104.

13 Buzzell, R and Wiersema, F (1981) 'Successful Share-Building Strategies', *Harvard Business Review*, Jan–Feb, pp135–44.

14 Kuczmarski, T and Silver, S (1982) 'Strategy: the key to successful product development', *Management Review*, July, pp26–40.

15 Davidson, J (1987) *Offensive Marketing*, 2nd edn, Penguin, Harmondsworth, p336.

16 Baker, M J (1992) *Marketing Strategy and Management*, 2nd edn, Macmillan, London, p328.

17 Lynch, R (1994) *European Business Strategies*, 2nd edn, Kogan Page, London, p208.

18 Lynch, R (1993) *Cases in European Marketing*, Kogan Page, London, p31.

19 Synergy is explored in Ansoff, I, *Business Strategy*, Penguin, Harmondsworth, Ch 1, p22.

20 Adapted from Lynch, R (1994) *European Business Strategies*, 2nd edn, Kogan Page, London.

21 Kay, J (1993) Ibid, p146.

22 More information on international expansion is available in Lynch, R (1992) *European Marketing*, Kogan Page, London, Ch 8.

23 Adapted from Gray, B (1995) 'Time to seek a grand alliance', *Financial Times,* 19 Dec, p7.

15

Strategy evaluation and selection – 1

After working through this chapter, you will be able to:

- identify the criteria against which an organisation wishes to judge its strategies;

- explore any criteria that are particularly important;

- evaluate the organisation's strategies against the chosen criteria;

- make an initial selection from the options.

■ INTRODUCTION

Once the options available have been identified (*see* Chapters 13 and 14), according to classical *prescriptive* corporate strategy[1] the next task is to select from the identified options. This chapter gives an overview of the entire selection process with Chapter 16 exploring some aspects of the selection process in further detail.

This chapter examines the *main criteria* used in the selection process and suggests ways of prioritising them to make the selection process more manageable. The *initial evaluation* of the options against the criteria that have been chosen for the organisation is then considered.

Chapter 16 then looks at some particular areas in more depth. Specifically, *empirical evidence* on what strategies are likely to work best and the *logic* of particular strategic situations are both investigated. *Business risk* and the specific interests of different *stakeholders* are also considered further.

Figure 15.1 shows the full evaluation and selection process covered by the two chapters.

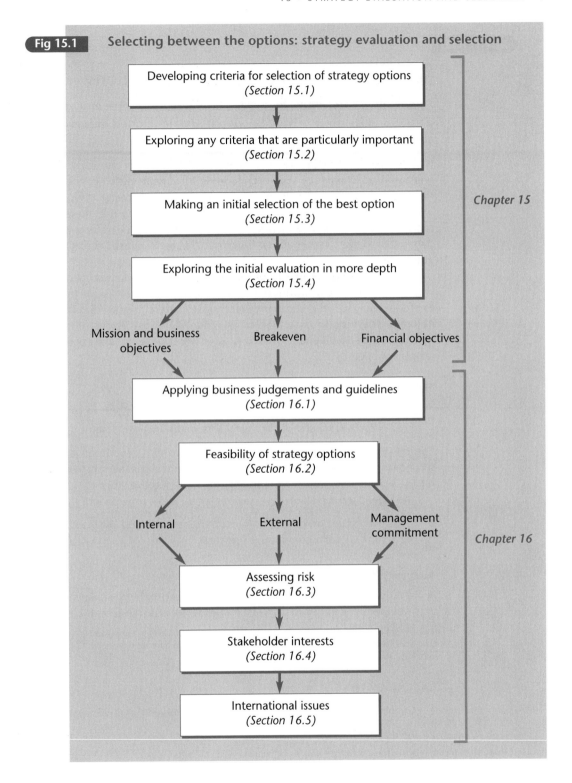

Fig 15.1   Selecting between the options: strategy evaluation and selection

Eurofreeze evaluates its strategy options – 1

As a result of competitive pressures, Eurofreeze faces some important strategic decisions. It is now reviewing its options and has started the process by considering its mission and objectives.

With annual sales of US$1.105 billion, the European freezer company, Eurofreeze, was one of the larger producers of frozen foods in the European Union. It had freezer factories in the Netherlands, UK, Belgium, France, Italy and Germany. It supplied every type of grocery store from small foodstores to large hypermarkets in all these countries. Customers included national supermarket chains such as Aldi (Germany, Benelux, France, UK), Albert Heijn (Netherlands), Carrefour (France), Sainsbury (UK), GB Inno (Belgium).

Factories were dedicated to producing particular product ranges – for example, vegetables, fish, meat products and desserts. The products were then transported to strategically located company warehouses where they were gathered together before distribution to customers across the EU. Foodstore customers were served by cross-border deliveries from the closest warehouse, regardless of the European country of origin.

Mission and objectives

The company had developed the following *mission statement*:

> *To be a leading producer of frozen products in the European Union.*

This mission was based on its current core strengths, its competitive position as the second largest producer in the EU and the way it envisaged freezing technology would retain its position in preserving food over the following five years.

It had identified the following *objectives* for the same time period:

- to raise its return on capital from the current level of 12 per cent by 0.5 per cent per annum, despite competitive pressures, to a level of 15 per cent over a six-year period;

- to raise its earnings per share at a similar rate;

- to hold its overall market share in existing geographical markets but to shift this from low-value added items to higher value items within this objective.

CASE QUESTIONS

1 *Are these objectives suitable for selecting from a range of strategic options?*

2 *Are they consistent with each other?*

15.1 EVALUATION CRITERIA FOR STRATEGY OPTIONS

Corporate strategy has taken the approach that a rational and fact-based analysis of the options will deliver the strategy that is most likely to be successful: logic and evidence are paramount in choosing from the options. In this and the following chapter, the main techniques and basis of this approach are explored. We leave the difficulties that this raises in connection with *emergent* corporate strategy until Chapter 17: first, we need to understand the *prescriptive* process and examine its merits. Certainly, the process described in these two chapters is used, in some form or other, by many organisations around the world.

Strategy options need to be evaluated for their contribution to the organisation. To undertake this task, the evaluative process needs to take place against criteria that are relevant to the organisation: for example, evaluating the strategy for its profitability will be important in most commercial organisations.

The main objectives of corporate strategy for an organisation are to *add value* and to *develop sustainable competitive advantage*. The strategic options offer a number of ways in which these might be achieved. The first task is to develop a means of assessing the options – that is some ground rules that can be used to test each of the options and discover which is best at delivering the objectives. In other words, we need *evaluation criteria*.

There are six main criteria[2] that can be used to evaluate strategy options: *consistency, suitability, validity, feasibility, business risk* and *attractiveness*. Their relationships with strategy are summarised in Fig 15.2.

15.1.1 Criterion 1: Consistency

The main purposes of the organisation are defined through its *mission and objectives* (Chapter 12 explored this in detail). Whatever the purpose of the organisation – for example, adding value, developing sustainable advantage or, in the case of a non-profit making organisation, the provision of a service – a prime test of any option has to be its *consistency* with this purpose.

In a business context, this is likely to be the mission and its ability to deliver the agreed objectives of the organisation. If an option does not meet these criteria, there is a strong case for:

- *either* changing the mission and objectives, if they are too difficult or inappropriate;
- *or* rejecting the option.

If the mission and objectives have been carefully considered, then the rejection option is the most likely course. For example, the US telecommunications company MCI has a minimum required rate of return on investment of 15 per cent. This means that strategy options that do not deliver at this level of profitability *in the long term* are rejected by the company. There may well be a period in the early years of a new option when the project will lose money, but it must justify itself at the identified level of profitability over a longer period.

Fig 15.2 Selection criteria and proposed strategies

Strategies need to be consistent with the mission and objectives

Strategies need to be suitable for the organisation and its environment

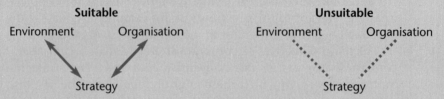

Strategy assumptions must be valid and tested where possible

Strategies must be feasible if they are to be successful

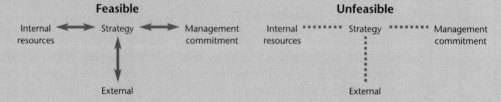

Strategies must involve an acceptable level of business risk

Strategies need to be attractive to the organisation's stakeholders

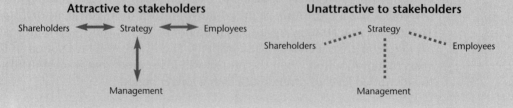

15.1.2 Criterion 2: Suitability

Some options may be more *suitable* for the organisation than others: how well does each option match the organisation's environment and how well does it deliver competitive advantage?

The *environment* can be explored according to the mixture of opportunities to be taken and threats to be avoided. *Competitive advantage* can be built on the organisation's strengths, especially its core competences, and may try to rectify weaknesses that exist. The *SWOT Analysis* at the end of Part 2 summarises the main elements identified here. Strategy options can also be examined for their consistency with the elements of the SWOT Analysis. For example, Eurofreeze has strengths in marketing to the main supermarket groups across Europe. A new option that ignored these strengths and pursued a policy of new freezer outlets, such as canteens and restaurants, would need careful study and possibly (but not necessarily) rejection.

15.1.3 Criterion 3: Validity

Most options will involve some form of *assumptions* about the future, which need to be tested to ensure that they are *valid* and reasonable.

In addition, many options will use *business information* that could be well supported by background material or, alternatively, of dubious value. In the case of Eurofreeze, some of the information it holds about its competitors is soundly based, for example, the market share data, while some is likely to be rather more open to question, for example, information on its competitors' future plans and intentions.

It will be necessary to test the validity of the assumptions and information in each option. In practice, there is some overlap between suitability and validity. We will explore both criteria in Section 16.1.

15.1.4 Criterion 4: Feasibility

Although options may be consistent with the mission and objectives, there may be other difficulties that limit the likelihood of success. An option may, in practice, lack feasibility in three areas:

- culture, skills and resources *internal* to the organisation;
- competitive reaction and other matters *external* to the organisation;
- *Lack of commitment* from managers and employees.

Constraints internal to the organisation
As we explored in Chapters 8, 9 and 10, an organisation might not have the *culture, skills* or *resources* to carry them out. For example, there might be a culture in the organisation that is able to cope with gradual change but incapable of the radical and sudden changes required by a proposed strategy option. The difficulties experienced by the highly centralised company Metal Box (UK) when it merged with the decentralised company Carnaud (France) were largely in this area and caused the group major problems.[3]

Equally, an organisation may lack the necessary technical skills for a strategic option. It may not be possible for a variety of reasons to acquire them by recruiting staff.

In addition, some organisations have insufficient finance necessary for an option to succeed. For example, the French computer company, Groupe Bull, had real problems financing its strategic development during the mid-1990s as it struggled to survive after a series of over-ambitious strategy initiatives earlier in the decade.[4]

Constraints external to the organisation

Competitive reactions can make a strategy option less likely. In Chapter 5, we observed that competitors who are affected by a strategy option may react and make a strategy option difficult to achieve. For example, the US software company, Microsoft, has around 90 per cent of the world market for personal computer software with its *Windows* operating system. It has been accused by competitors of deliberately pre-announcing some of its products to stall sales of new, competing software products.[5] The likelihood of competitive response is an area that must be assessed.

In addition to competitors, there are other difficulties external to the organisation that reduce the likelihood of success: these are covered in the *PEST Analysis* explored in Chapter 3.

Lack of commitment from managers and employees

If important members of the organisation are not committed to the strategy, it is unlikely to be successfully implemented. For example, the major US toy retailer, Toys 'R' Us, had major problems implementing its business strategy in Sweden during 1995 because the local managers and employees considered it to be inconsistent with the Swedish approach to labour relations.[6]

These three areas are explored in Section 16.2.

15.1.5 Criterion 5: Business risk

Most worthwhile strategies are likely to carry some degree of risk which needs to be carefully assessed. Ultimately, the risks involved may be unacceptable to the organisation.

There are countless examples in corporate strategy of organisations taking risks and then struggling to sort out the difficulties. For example, Germany's largest industrial company, Daimler–Benz, took considerable risks with its expansion strategy in the late 1980s (*see* Chapter 12). The *mission* was to create 'an integrated technology concern'. By the mid-1990s, the company was stretched financially and engaged in a major cost-cutting strategy to cut back many of the ventures which had become loss-making.[7] The company was engaged in a major exercise to reduce its risks.

Strategic risk is explored in Section 16.3.

15.1.6 Criterion 6: Attractiveness to stakeholders

As we explored in Chapter 4, every organisation has its stakeholders – for example, the shareholders, employees and management. All the stakeholders will be interested in the strategic options that the organisation has under consideration because they may be affected by them. However, individual stakeholder interests and perspectives may not always be the same. For example, an option might increase the *shareholders'* wealth, but also mean a reduction in *employees* in the organisation. Hence, stakeholders may not find all the strategic options equally attractive. This subject is explored in Section 16.4.

15.1.7 The international variations in criteria

It must not be assumed that organisations in different countries will all take the same approach to strategy assessment: stakeholders differ, government involvement differs, the levels of financial and economic risk differ and so on. For example, contrast Siemens in Germany with GEC in the UK. Both have strong business interests in high technology markets but German and UK shareholders differ in their attitudes to share dividends: the UK is more short term than Germany. As a result, the UK company has been more risk-averse than the German company and has maintained large cash holdings whereas the German company has been more adventurous and spent its funds.[8] Hence, those organisations that are developing international strategy options will need to explore the implications for the countries involved. Some more general issues of international strategy development are explored in Section 16.5.

Key strategic principles

- There are six main criteria for evaluating strategy options: consistency (especially with the organisation's mission and objectives), suitability, validity, feasibility, business risk and attractiveness to stakeholders.

- Consistency with the purpose of the organisation is a prime test for evaluating and selecting strategies.

- Suitability of the strategy for the environment within which the organisation operates is clearly important.

- Validity of the projections and data used in developing the option must be tested.

- Feasibility will depend on three factors: constraints internal to the organisation, such as technical skills and finance; constraints external to the organisation, such as the response of competitors; and the commitment from the management and employees.

- Business risk also needs to be assessed because it may be unacceptable to the organisation.

- Attractiveness to stakeholders such as shareholders and employees is an important consideration. Some options may be more attractive to some stakeholders than others.

- There may be international variations in evaluation criteria depending on national differences in the interests of stakeholders, governments and other national characteristics.

Eurofreeze evaluates its strategy options – 2

To understand fully the company's new strategy options, it was necessary for Eurofreeze to explore the background to the frozen food market and the competitive trends that were operating.

Frozen food products and added value

The first products to be frozen commercially were vegetables and fish in the 1940s. For many years, the higher food quality resulting from the freezing process allowed such products to be sold at premium prices compared with those of the competition – cans, glass jars and other forms of preserved food.

As freezing process technology became more widely available from the 1960s onwards, it became easier for small companies to freeze and pack such items as fresh vegetables. Such products required no significant processing, and so there was little added value in them, beyond that delivered by the immediate packing process. By the 1990s, obscure brands without advertising support from companies such as farmers' co-operatives were widely available. In addition, the major supermarkets were developing their own branded versions of many basic products: keen prices were negotiated from suppliers such as Eurofreeze. By the mid-1990s, the profit margins on basic vegetables and other commodities were very low: added value was minimal.

Over the same period, household incomes rose across Europe and tastes became more international: for example, people across Europe had come to know and enjoy a wider range of fresh recipe dishes and international products, everything from Quattro Stagione Pizza to Double Layer Chocolate Gateaux. Home freezers had also become more widespread. From the manufacturing viewpoint, technology was developed further to make and pack a much wider range of goods.

As a result, new products that required more processing beyond merely freezing a raw product were launched. They had higher added value because they involved more processing and packaging and more opportunity for branding. Over the period,

many new items had been added to supermarket frozen food cabinets: complete meals, chinese recipe dishes, slimmers' meals and so on. These were sold as branded items, usually under a brand name that had been well-established over the years – for example, *Birds Eye, Dr Oetker, Heinz Weight Watchers* and *Findus*. The brand name was used across all products from the company so that it supported the strong, well advertised products along with the weaker ones – a group branding policy.

Key factors for success

The following were considered to be key factors for success in the industry:

- experienced and talented buyers to negotiate price and quality on low value-added items;
- fast and efficient freezing processes coupled with good freezer storage;
- excellent relationships with the main supermarket chains;
- strong and consistent group branding;
- a vigorous and innovative new product development programme.

Eurofreeze core competences

As a result of its history and present market position, the company had core competences in the following areas:

- purchasing of raw materials such as vegetables, including the buying function;
- freezer technology;
- recipe development for new frozen dishes;
- frozen food distribution;
- supermarket negotiating and service;
- developing branded food products (with a well-known brand name across Europe).

The competition

During the 1980s and 1990s, companies such as Eurofreeze sought new strategies to avoid the low-priced competition: the own-branded supermarket sales of vegetables and other low added value items had become a real problem. Profit pressures were such that Eurofreeze was even considering phasing out its ranges of branded vegetables.

In addition, many large grocery store chains wanted only one market-leading frozen brand to put alongside their own brands. In this context, Eurofreeze faced a specific problem: in some European product categories, it was not the market leader. Eurofreeze was second in its markets to its major rival, Refrigor.

Refrigor had invested heavily in frozen food brands, manufacturing and grocery distribution over the last few years at a rate in excess of Eurofreeze. However, the company had been rather less profitable. It had much the same grocery customers as Eurofreeze. Both competitors offered a full range of frozen branded food products and, at the same time, supplied own label versions to the leading grocery chains.

In total, Eurofreeze faced four competitive threats:

- The market leader, Refrigor – the low-cost leader.

- In many supermarkets such as Sainsbury (UK) and Albert Heijn (part of Ahold, Netherlands), an increasing volume of freezer space previously occupied by manufacturer's branded products was given to supermarket chains' *own branded* products.

- In other supermarkets with a strong cut-price positioning, such as Aldi and Kwiksave, the same freezer space was used for *local* or *regional branded* products that had no national advertising or promotional support but were low-priced.

- In some specific product lines, such as french fries or gateaux, specialised companies such as McCain (US) and Sara Lee (US) respectively, sold branded products that had a significant share of that particular market segment.

Overall, the market was becoming volume driven and highly competitive in many sectors. It was becoming increasingly difficult to afford the investment in advertising and promotions to support branded lines.

© Copyright Aldersgate Consultancy Limited 1997. The case is based on real companies which have been disguised to protect confidentiality. Market share and financial data have also been changed.

CASE QUESTIONS

1 *Now that you know more about the market trends and increased competition of the industry, what is your assessment of the mission and objectives of Eurofreeze?*

2 *Should the objectives be expanded? What about branded and non-branded items, for example? Clearer on the competitive threat? Further reference to financial objectives such as dividend payout policy? Specific reference to other matters such as ecological issues and employee job satisfaction? If your answer is **yes** to any of these questions, then what considerations should Eurofreeze have taken into account in making its decision? If your answer is **no**, then what are the implications for strategy selection?*

3 *What are the possible implications of the customer and competitive trends on the development of strategy options for Eurofreeze? You may wish to undertake some of the analyses contained in Chapters 13 and 14 in preparing your answer.*

15.2 PRIORITISING CRITERIA

In examining the many criteria that can be employed, it is sometimes useful to consider whether some criteria are more important than others. It is possible that no useful prioritisation can be undertaken in this respect.

If some selection of criteria is useful, then this can initially be undertaken by considering the *purpose* of the organisation. In addition, it is important to consider the *viewpoint* of those developing the criteria: for example, the headquarters of an organisation may be less enthusiastic about an opportunity than its subsidiary, because it sees other possible opportunities. The criteria important to HQ may not be the same as those important to the subsidiary.

Importantly, in not-for-profit organisations, the criteria may go beyond consideration of the generation of the value-added necessary for survival and may consider other matters – for example, the levels of service to the community or to the individuals it has chosen to serve. In addition, the culture and style of some of these organisations do not always lend themselves to *precise* evaluation: this is explored more fully below. Some of the main considerations are shown in Fig 15.3.

15.2.1 Criteria in commercial organisations

For most organisations, the criteria will be prioritised by the mission and objectives. They will also involve a need to balance the interests of different stakeholders (*see* Chapter 16).

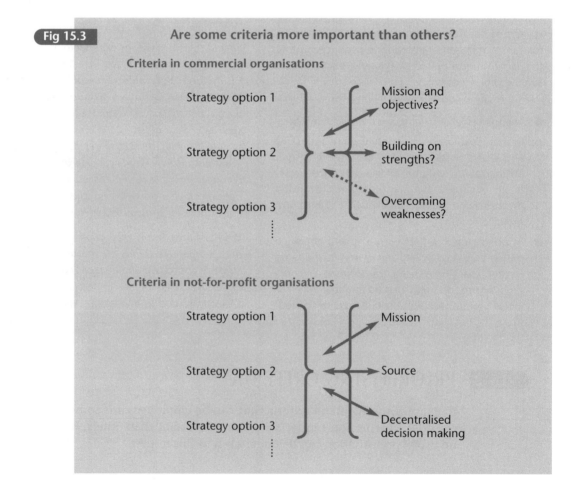

Fig 15.3   Are some criteria more important than others?

Within the mission and objectives, the following questions indicate the areas that may need exploration:

1 Is each strategy option consistent with the mission of the organisation? How well does each option deliver the objectives? For example at Eurofreeze, how does each option meet the stated desire for a return on capital of 15 per cent and rising? How does each option contribute to the shift to higher value-added products?

2 Does each option build on the strengths of the organisation? Does each option exploit the opportunities that have been identified (*see* Chapter 7 on SWOT Analysis)? And the core competences (*see* also Chapter 7)? Thus at Eurofreeze, it should be possible to test each option for usefulness in contributing to freezer technology or to supermarket opportunities. If an option is not consistent with these issues, then there *may* be a case for rejecting it. However, it should be noted that rejection is not automatic.

3 Does each option avoid, or even overcome, the weaknesses of the organisation? Does each option do the same for the threats that have been identified? At Eurofreeze, an option that involved development of its basic vegetable business would move the company further into this weak area and would invite rejection.

Question 3 has *lower* priority than Questions 1 and 2.[9] It is much more important to deliver the organisation's mission and objectives and to build on its strengths than to worry about its weaknesses. However, there will be occasions when the weaknesses cannot be ignored and strategy options need to consider these.

It would be a great mistake to consider only those criteria that can be put into numbers. For example, many organisations will have guidelines related to *customer quality* and *satisfaction*. Others will include *service to the broader community*. These may not be easy to quantify, but are no less important in spite of this. All of these need to be reflected in the criteria for selection of strategy options. Such matters simply underline the importance of defining carefully the purpose of the organisation (*see* Part 4).

15.2.2 Criteria in not-for-profit organisations

Great care needs to be taken in not-for-profit organisations that any quantified criteria do not come to dominate the strategy selection when such selection measures are inappropriate. All not-for-profit organisations will need to create added value. However, beyond this, the criteria may need to reflect strongly the important aspects of the service or the value to the community appropriate to the mission.

Criteria in not-for-profit organisations also need to take into account the different decision-making processes and beliefs that motivate many such organisations. The reliance on voluntary support, the strong sense of mission and belief in the work of the organisation and the style of the organisation may not lend themselves to the simple choice from a series of options.

Not-for-profit organisations may involve a high degree of loyalty to a mission, which is often clear, but the organisation may be decentralised with local decision making. If this is the case, then a centralised evaluation of options is difficult. A comparison of the criteria with those of commercial organisations is shown in Table 15.1. Strategy option evaluation in not-for-profit organisations may be more diffuse and open-ended.

Table 15.1 Comparison of possible criteria in commercial and not-for-profit organisations

Commercial organisation	Not-for-profit organisation
● Quantified	● Qualitative
● Unchanging	● Variable
● Consistent	● Conflicting
● Unified	● Complex
● Operational	● Ambiguous
● Clear	● Non-operational
● Measurable	● Non-measurable

15.2.3 Considering differing perspectives

Different parts of the organisation will have varying perspectives on the evaluation criteria. For example, the centre represented by corporate headquarters is likely to have a different view from a strategic business unit (SBU) or geographical division located far from the centre. In addition, some options may be exceptionally large in scope and may need to be treated on an individual project basis, outside the SBUs – for example, a major acquisition. To ensure that the optimal decision is made, there is a need to recognise these different perspectives and attempt to reconcile them through discussion. These are summarised in Table 15.2.

Table 15.2 Differences in perspective on mission and objectives

Level in organisation	Perspectives on mission and objectives	
	Strengths	Weaknesses
Corporate headquarters	● Clearly perceives overall group picture ● Strong on core competences and synergies across group ● Able to allocate resources across the whole group ● Financial perspectives in terms of gearing and cash management ● Group and global direction strong	● Makes limited distinction between the different business activities across the group ● More difficult to identify market opportunities, niche segments, etc. ● Differences in culture and national or regional variations ignored
Strategic Business Units	● More focussed strategy ● Clearer on customers and competitors ● Able to identify specific market opportunities ● Can apply human resource management policies specific to that SBU or industry	● Synergy and core competences weaker ● Corporate overview and links more difficult ● Cash and currency management ● Shareholder interests
Individual project, e.g. acquisition	● Easiest to evaluate at outset and judge success later ● Focus on special opportunity ● Clear, specific appraisal	● Links across corporate structure weaker ● Synergy, core competences need to be defined and strengthened

Key strategic principles

- It is important to clarify the basis on which an initial selection of the best option is to be done. Evaluation against the mission and objectives is useful but needs to be carefully considered if it is to provide real benefit. Non-quantified objectives may be just as important for some organisations.

- In a not-for-profit organisation, the criteria need to reflect the broader aspects of its service or contribution to the community. They also need to take into account the different decision-making processes and beliefs that motivate many such organisations. This may make strategy option evaluation more diffuse and open-ended.

- Additional criteria for evaluation include the ability to build on the strengths and core competences of the organisation and avoid its weaknesses. Generally, in evaluation, strengths are more important than weaknesses, but occasionally a weakness cannot be ignored.

- It is important to recognise during selection that different parts of an organisation such as the HQ, the Strategic Business Units (SBUs) and those involved in individual projects will have different perspectives on the evaluation process.

15.3 MAKING AN INITIAL SELECTION OF THE BEST OPTION

15.3.1 Some immediate questions

Before exploring the problems associated with strategic options, it is usual to make an initial selection of one or more options. There are some immediate questions that deserve careful exploration:

- *What does 'best option' mean?*
  Unless there is an answer to this question, the whole exercise will be meaningless. It can only be answered in the specific context of the organisation and its purpose. For this section, we will assume that it is the option or options that most closely match the mission and objectives.

- *For whom are we making the selection?*
  The selection is being made for the stakeholders, but *which* stakeholders in particular? Are there any priorities? In this section, we will assume that the owners of the organisation take precedence, that is, its shareholders[10] (*see* Chapter 16).

- *Who is undertaking the selection process?*
  The company itself? An investment analyst on behalf of outside interests? A student studying the organisation?

Each of these will have her/his own perspectives and depth of knowledge. For example, those inside the company will have access to information that is not published for competitive reasons to those outside. For the purposes of this chapter, we will assume the company perspective, where possible.

● *On what basis is the selection process being undertaken?*
Each organisation will develop its own criteria. There are no absolute rules. For the purposes of this chapter, we will follow some generally accepted criteria on profitability, cost of capital and so on. However, one of the first tasks for anyone examining a specific organisation (especially when working closely with it through consultancy or employment) is to establish that organisation's criteria. As discussed above, it may be useful to prioritise the criteria.

15.3.2 The initial evaluation sequence

To some extent, the initial evaluating sequence will depend on the type of business. In commercial circumstances, the selection might start with the *profitability* of the venture. In a not-for-profit situation, other factors such as *the ability to deliver the service* might be more important. This is why the careful exploration of the mission and objectives is so important.

In any event, it would be usual to *screen out* those options that are unlikely to deliver the basic objectives and concentrate on the remainder.

For each of the remaining major options, the following calculations are then undertaken:

● *Profitability* – often known as the return on capital employed (ROCE). This is the ratio of profits to be earned divided by the capital invested in the new strategy. Profits are usually calculated *before* any tax that might be charged, because tax matters go beyond the assessment of individual strategy options. Profitability and other similar measures are explored more fully in Section 15.4.

● *Breakeven* – the point at which the total costs of undertaking the new strategy are equal to the total revenue. It is often restated as the number of units of a product that need to be sold before a product has covered all its fixed costs. This is explored more fully in Section 15.4.7.

● *Net cash flow* – the sum of pre-tax profits from the new strategy option *plus* depreciation *less* the capital to be invested in the new strategy.

Having undertaken these basic calculations for each option, an initial assessment then explores the *strategic implications* of each option:

● whether each option meets the agreed strategic objectives such as profitability;

● whether the number of units required to break even is easily attainable or somewhat unrealistic;

● whether the cash flow is more negative than is reasonable for the resources of the group; and

● whether the sales levels required are unrealistic in relation to the existing market share or some other common-sense evaluation. For example, if the sales levels required market share to double from 2 per cent to 4 per cent, this might be perfectly reasonable. However, if the sales levels required the market share to double from 30 per cent to 60 per cent, this might be regarded as highly unlikely in normal circumstances.

The steps that might be involved in the initial evaluation are summarised in Exhibit 15.1.

Exhibit 15.1   **Ten steps towards an initial strategy evaluation**

1 Screen out any *early no-hopers* that are highly unlikely to meet the objectives.

2 Estimate the *sales* of each of the remaining options based on market share, pricing, promotional support and competitive reactions.

3 Estimate the *costs* of each of the remaining options.

4 Estimate the *capital and other funds* necessary to undertake each option.

5 Calculate the *return on capital employed* for each option.

6 Calculate the *breakeven* of each option.

7 Calculate the *net cash flow* effects of each option.

8 Evaluate whether the *projected sales levels* imply exceptional levels of market share or *unusually low costs*. Are these reasonable? Real strategic weaknesses can emerge here.

9 Assess the likely *competitive response* and its possible impact on each strategy option.

10 Assess the *risks* associated with each option (*see* Chapter 16).

Key strategic principles

- In making an initial evaluation of the best option, it is important to establish and define what is meant by 'best'. It is also useful to examine what is required by the stakeholders for whom the evaluation is being undertaken, the perspective of the evaluation and the criteria that will be employed for the selection process.

- Ten steps can be undertaken to make an initial evaluation.

- In the initial evaluation in commercial organisations, it is usual to calculate for each option the profitability, breakeven and net cash flow.

- From a strategic perspective, it is particularly useful to examine whether the projected sales levels of each option imply exceptional levels of market share or low costs in order to achieve their targets. If these occur, then it may imply that the option has real weaknesses.

15.4 EXPLORING THE INITIAL EVALUATION IN MORE DEPTH

15.4.1 Evaluation against the mission

When evaluating the strategy options for an organisation, the obvious starting point is the agreed mission. If an option does not contribute to this, then there is a strong case for rejection. It is usually worth exploring this area carefully and understanding fully its implications for strategy selection. For example, the mission of Eurofreeze is rather vague: what does 'to be a leading producer of frozen products' really mean?

- What is the definition of a leading producer? Leader of what market exactly? (Any company can be a leader if the market is defined narrowly enough.)
- Does this include both high and low added-value products? (The company is considering whether it wishes to pull out of low added-value vegetables.)
- Leadership defined by market share? Or profit? (A reduction in profit is often required to build market share in the short term.)
- Low-cost leadership?
- How many other producers are involved in the group of which it aspires to be a leader?
- What is the purpose of the company?

For the sake of comparison, the Eurofreeze vagueness might be compared with the greater clarity of the mission of the Ford Motor Company in Chapter 12. It will be difficult to select from the options when there is confusion in this area.

15.4.2 Evaluation against the objectives

When evaluating options against the objectives of an organisation, it is useful to distinguish between:

- *general business objectives*, such as profitability, market share, quality standards and performance, job satisfaction of employees; and
- *specific financial objectives* such as earnings per share, cash flow, breakeven, shareholder satisfaction and dividend record.

This distinction was explored in Chapter 9. It should be emphasised that most organisations usually have a combination of criteria: those listed for Eurofreeze in the opening case are typical, if rather brief. They might be extended by some further definition of quality and some more specific comments on shareholders' dividend policy and employee job satisfaction.

Each option must be individually assessed for its contribution to the objectives of the company. This will mean estimating for each option such areas as sales, the cost of sales, capital expenditure, depreciation, tax implications, cash flow and all the other areas that are normally undertaken in a major project assessment. For not-for-profit organisations, the same principles will apply but some of the benefits may be unquantifiable and therefore more difficult to assess. Even in commercial organisations some benefits are more difficult to express numerically – for example, quality improvements, job satisfaction and the like where the measures used may not do justice to the underlying evaluation.

More generally, there has been considerable emphasis on the need to provide a steady increase in earnings per share as a measure of a company's success for shareholders among UK and US companies, as explored in Chapter 9. This has not been the case among companies in Germany, Japan and some other parts of the world where shares have been held by banks, conglomerates and even governments, who have been willing to take a longer term view of events.

15.4.3 Evaluation of value added

Value added is an important determinant for the selection of strategy options. It is usually undertaken using the value chain concept outlined in Chapter 7. The *value chain linkages* between various parts of the business can also be examined. For reasons of complexity, the detailed chain is rarely quantified. However, it needs to be explored for its implications in developing sustainable competitive advantage.

An example of value-added linkages occurs at Eurofreeze. The benefits of high added value recipe dishes and their inter-relationship with the low added value vegetables need careful exploration. It might be argued that the best solution would be to drop the low-value items. However, if they are carried on the same transport as the high value-added items and the transport then operates half-empty, dropping some items would not be the optimal solution.

There are difficulties in quantifying the value chain and its linkages, and as a result there are some problems with its application in selecting the best option. It might not even appear in the selection process of those commercial companies that lay great emphasis on the numerical quantification for choice. However, this would simply demonstrate the poor criteria employed by such companies.

15.4.4 Evaluation of profitability[11]

Most evaluations of strategic options in commercial organisations make some attempt to analyse the profit against the capital employed. It is important to note that extra capital will be needed in most organisations[12] as soon as sales rise: there is a need to fund debtors and pay for the extra stocks required for the new business activity. There are three main measures of profitability (*see* Exhibit 15.2).

1 Return on capital employed (ROCE)
2 Payback period
3 Discounted cash flow (DCF)

| **Exhibit 15.2** | Definitions of profitability |

$$\text{Return on capital employed} = \frac{\text{Profit before tax and interest} \times 100}{\text{Capital employed}}$$

Payback = Time in years to recover the intitial capital investment

Discounted cash flow = Future cash flows after tax discounted back to the initial year

Return on capital employed

Return on capital employed (ROCE) is commonly used to assess strategies. The expected operating profit is assessed after the strategy has been in operation for an agreed number of years, usually defined before tax and interest. It is divided by the capital employed in the option, which is commonly averaged across a year to take into account the tendency of capital to vary during the course of a year.

One of the major difficulties is defining the *incremental* capital used purely for that strategy: it is easy where a new piece of plant has been installed, but more difficult where the strategy involves using existing plant or involves a service where the capital involved cannot be easily distinguished from more general trading.

For ongoing business investments, companies often have *hurdle rates* for ROCE: if they do not earn at these rates then the abandonment of that strategy is given serious consideration. Such rates are usually set in relation to the company's *cost of capital*: if capital is cheap, then a lower rate can be set (*see* Chapter 9).

Payback

Payback period is used where there is a significant and specific capital investment required in the option. In the early years of the option, capital is invested in it. As the company earns profits from the venture, it recovers the capital that has been invested. Payback is the time it takes to recover the initial capital investment and is usually measured in years. The cash flows in payback are not discounted but are simply added and subtracted equally, whatever year they occur.

Typically, payback on a capital project in the car industry will be around 5 to 7 years. This is because of the large amounts of capital involved (often into US$ billions) and the competitive nature of the industry making profit margins low. In consumer goods, the period may be shorter, not because markets are any less competitive but the profit margins on some items are higher, for example in fashion clothing and cosmetics. By contrast, the payback period may be 20 to 60 years for some highly capital-intensive items such as telecommunications infrastructure and roads.

Discounted cash flow

Discounted cash flow (DCF) is now used extensively in some western countries for the assessment of strategic options. Essentially, DCF, unlike payback, takes account of the fact that cash in five years' time is worth less than cash today. It begins by assessing the net cash flow for each year of the life of the option. The cash is usually assessed after subtracting the taxation to be paid to the government. Each annual cash amount is then discounted back to the present using the organisation's *cost of capital* (*see* Chapter 9). It is probably negative in the early years as capital is expended and then positive as the option increases its sales. There are discounting tables or computer spreadsheet programmes that make this process relatively easy. The Net Present Value (NPV) is the sum in today's values of all the future discounted cash flows. Case study 16.2 shows the procedure for some Eurofreeze options.

Comment Following on from the discussion in Chapter 9, there are some clear difficulties with these methods of appraisal of strategic options:

- The cost of capital is a vital element in two of the calculations. The difficulties associated with its calculation were explored in Chapter 9. It is especially difficult to estimate when investment takes place over a lengthy period.

- There are real problems in estimating the future sales accurately up to ten years away, which is a typical period in many DCF calculations, even in consumer goods companies. However, direct costs can usually be estimated satisfactorily. The projections are therefore doubtful. Payback may be better here.

- With shorter product life cycles and greater product obsolescence in some product categories such as computers, the DCF process may rely on an over-extended time span. Payback may again be better here and is the justification used by some Japanese companies for using this approach.

- The difficulty of isolating incremental from ongoing capital applies not only to ROCE calculations but for all such appraisals.

- With the emphasis on cash generated by the project itself, the appraisal tends to concentrate on the quantified financial benefits and may ignore some of the broader strategic benefits that are more difficult to quantify – for example, synergies and value chain linkages.

- ROCE is by definition an accounting calculation that looks back at a project's past rather than forward to its future potential. It may not therefore be suitable for strategic use.

There are other broader criticisms of this prescriptive approach that will be covered in Chapter 17. There are also some special considerations which apply when value-ing acquisitions (*see* also Chapter 17).

15.4.5 Evaluation using the Shareholder Value Approach (SVA)[13]

Although many western companies continue to use DCF techniques in their evaluation of strategies,[14] they became conscious in the 1980s of the difficulties of ignoring the broader strategic benefits. There were two further developments:

1 Professor Michael Porter's work emphasising the value chain and its relevance in strategy development (*see* Chapter 7).

2 Other writers[15] began to doubt the wisdom of seeking a steady increase in earnings per share as a measure of shareholders' wealth. Such wealth can be measured in terms of a company's share price. It was shown empirically that share price was more closely correlated with long-term cash generation in a business than it was with earnings per share.

Taking the goal of a public company as maximising shareholder value, the concept of the Shareholder Value Approach (SVA) was developed out of DCF techniques and these difficulties. Its purpose is to develop corporate strategy 'maximising the long-term cash flow of each SBU'.[16] Thus SVA evaluation differs in the following areas from the profitability approaches above:

● SVA takes the concept of cash flow but applies it to *complete business units* rather than individual strategy options.

● It argues that strategy options need to be considered in the *broader context* of their contribution to the SBU, rather than be judged in isolation.

● It lays particular emphasis on the *key factors for success* (KFSs) of the business, defining these as the factors that are particularly important in generating cash or value added. It calls these KFSs *value* or *cost drivers*, but they are much the same as the KFSs explored in Chapter 7.

● It supports the *inter-relationship* of KFSs in the development of cash generation. In this sense, it differs from the more simple DCF view that an option can be analysed by itself.

Comment   Although SVA represents an advance on some simpler DCF techniques, it still relies on a prescriptive view of strategy projections: a projection of future cash over an extended period of time is required. Moreover, it makes the crucial assumption that maximising shareholder value is the prime objective of strategy development. This may be true in UK and US companies but does not necessarily apply in some other leading industrialised countries. Further broader criticisms of this prescriptive approach are considered in Chapter 17.

15.4.6   Evaluation using a cost/benefit analysis[17]

Ever since cost/benefit analysis was used to assess the justification for building London Underground's Victoria Line in the 1960s, this has been an appraisal method favoured where the benefits go beyond simple financial benefits. For example, they might include lower levels of pollution or greater use of recycled materials. It is regularly used in public service investment decisions. It attempts to quantify a much broader range of benefits than sales, profits and costs.

When the benefits of some forms of public service go beyond simple financial appraisal, cost/benefit analysis may be used. It may be especially valuable where the project delivers value to users who are not directly investing their own funds. For example, in the case of the new Victoria Line analysis on London Underground, it attempted to assess:

● the faster and more convenient travel to be enjoyed by passengers on the London Underground;

● the ability of road transport to move more freely because roads would be less congested.

As well as the benefits, there may also be social costs that need to be assessed: in the case of underground transport, these might include building subsidence or inconvenience while the line is being built.

The key point in cost/benefit analysis is that all such broader benefits and costs are still assessed in monetary terms. Much of such research is concerned with the quantification of such benefits and also the costs that may be associated with them. The direct investment costs are usually rather easier to determine and form another element in the equation.

The difficult part of such a cost/benefit analysis is usually where to place the limit on the possible benefits and costs. For example, it might be argued that easier travel would mean that there would be less atmospheric pollution, more healthy people and therefore a need to quantify the health benefits. There might also be benefits in terms of a more stress-free lifestyle that need to be quantified. In spite of the difficulty of determining the scope of the analysis and the more general problem of quantifying the intangible, cost/benefit analysis does serve a useful function in the appraisal of public projects and strategy initiatives.

15.4.7 Breakeven analysis[18]

Breakeven analysis is directed at the *breakeven point* – that is, the point where fixed and variable costs equal total revenue. It is based on a number of assumptions that make its use in practice rather crude:

- Costs can easily be split into fixed and variable elements.
- Fixed costs are constant.
- Variable costs and revenue are linear in their relationship with volume over the range used in the analysis.
- Variable costs vary proportionately with sales, within given limits.
- It is possible to predict the volume of sales at various prices.

Although these remain only rough approximations, they may be used to provide a basic analysis of some strategic options. To calculate the breakeven point, it is first necessary to calculate the *contribution margin*.

Contribution margin = Revenue per unit – Variable costs per unit

Having calculated the contribution margin, it is then possible to calculate the breakeven point in terms of the numbers of sales units required.

$$\text{Breakeven} = \frac{\text{Fixed costs}}{\text{Contribution margin}}$$

In strategic terms, the breakeven point will provide an estimate of the sales needed before profits start to be earned. Expressing this in unit terms and relating it to the total number of units sold in the market place will provide the *market share* required to break even. Clearly, if such a share were to turn out to be really high, then it would call into question the proposed strategy option.

We can illustrate this calculation using an example from the Eurofreeze case. Eurofreeze is considering a new range of deep-pan pizzas. From market research, the company knows that the total market volume is around 250 000 per annum. The company is investigating two new price points for its product: US$10 and US$6 per pizza. It has estimated that it will sell substantially increased volumes at the lower price, so it expects some economies of scale at the lower prices. Hence, its estimates of the variable costs are US$4 and US$3 at the higher and lower prices respectively. Its calculations are shown in Table 15.3.

Table 15.3 The calculation of breakeven at Eurofreeze

	High-price strategy	Low-price strategy
Unit price (US$)	10	6
Unit costs (US$)	4	3
Contribution margin per unit (US$)	10 – 4 = 6	6 – 3 = 3
Fixed costs (US$)	150 000	150 000
Breakeven in units needed	150 000 ÷ 6 = 25 000	150 000 ÷ 3 = 50 000
Market share to breakeven	25 000 ÷ 250 000 = 10%	50 000 ÷ 250 000 = 20%

Many strategists would argue that expecting to achieve a 20 per cent share of the market merely in order to break even is probably optimistic. The low-price strategy therefore needs some further justification if it is to be successful.

Key strategic principles

- Evaluation usually employs common and agreed criteria across the organisation, such as contribution to value added and profitability. The strengths and weaknesses of these criteria need to be understood.

- The Shareholder Value Approach takes a broader perspective on evaluation than that provided by the specific project. It seeks to determine the benefit of such developments in the context of the whole SBU in which the project rests. However, it still relies on the assumption that shareholders are always the prime beneficiaries.

- Cost/benefit analysis has been successfully employed in public sector evaluation where it is important to assess broader and less quantifiable benefits. The main difficulty is where to place the limit on such benefits and costs.

CASE STUDY 15.2

European expansion in the central heating market[19]

Several years ago, the UK company, Blue Circle, decided to develop a standardised product in the pan-European market for central heating boilers. This is a sector in which it has proved particularly difficult to unify the marketing and design processes that are needed across the single Europe. The key issue is whether the strategy the company has developed is likely to prove successful.

The project started when Blue Circle began to create a high-efficiency boiler called a condensing system. These boilers – which account for only about 5 per cent of the annual US$4.5 billion European domestic gas-boiler business – recycle energy normally lost to the atmosphere, in order to cut fuel bills and reduce carbon dioxide emissions. The boilers have seen high sales growth in Germany and the Netherlands, and are thought to have good potential in other countries as environmental issues become more important. However, they are significantly more expensive than conventional wall-hung boilers because of their greater technical complexity.

In 1993, after spending more than US$900 million acquiring heating companies across Europe, Blue Circle realised that it did not have a condensing system to compete with those offered by rival groups, including Hepworth of the UK , France's Geminox and Bosch, Vaillant and Buderus of Germany. Buderus owns Nefit of the Netherlands, one of the most successful European makers of condensing boilers. All these companies had strong strategic positions in their home markets. Blue Circle was itself leader in its home market in the UK.

The product design process

In contrast to traditional practice in the European boiler industry, Blue Circle decided to design a boiler for which 90 per cent of the components were common to all the main countries. It created a design team composed of 40 boiler engineers from four Blue Circle heating companies around Europe. The team was based in the UK with a third of the group being French, German or Dutch, and used English as its working language. Other key people remained in their home countries and met the rest of the team once a month for design conferences in Blue Circle offices in the UK or the Netherlands.

Across Europe, there are major variations in housing, climate and plumbing techniques. As a consequence, of the thousands of boiler types on sale across Europe, hardly any have been designed with an eye to selling them anywhere other than in a particular nation. Boiler companies interested in a pan-European approach – in the mid-1990s this applied to most of the big companies – usually took an existing boiler intended for sale in, for example, Germany and adapted it for use in another nation. After analysing the industry, using techniques borrowed from white goods sectors such as washing machines, Blue Circle reasoned that this approach could be improved on, and that a relatively high level of standardisation could be applied in the case

of its new condensing system, leading to substantial savings in development and manufacturing costs.

Markets and marketing for Blue Circle

European boiler company acquisitions had cost Blue Circle US$900 million in the late 1980s and early 1990s. They gave the company a heating division with sales in 1994 of boilers worth about US$450 million throughout Europe, roughly about 10 per cent of the Continent's gas-fired central heating boiler market. Included in this definition was the market for condensed boiler systems mentioned above.

Half the UK company's boiler sales were in the UK, where it traded under the brand names of *Potterton* and *Myson* and was the market leader in gas-fired boilers. Its heating division was called Compagnie Internationale du Chauffage (known as Celsius) in France, Bröttje in Germany and Burnham in the Netherlands. Blue Circle had not attempted to integrate these companies because of the fragmentation of the boiler market across Europe. However, it reasoned that integration of production and design would make sense for the new condensing boiler.

Customers for boiler systems were similar across Europe. First, there were the small builders who were installing systems in new houses and the specialist plumber craftsmen, who worked individually or in small companies to undertake the same task on behalf of builders or house owners. Small customers bought their products through wholesalers and not direct from the manufacturer. During the1990s, there had been periods of growth and decline broadly in line with the economic cycles of individual countries.

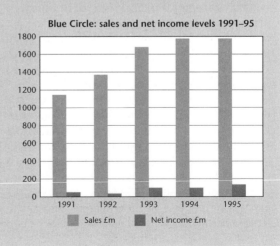

Blue Circle: sales and net income levels 1991–95

Second, there were the larger building companies, some of whom were privately owned and some part of either local, regional or national government activities. All such building companies placed large orders and expected volume discounts on their purchases. All customers were technically well informed and were seeking performance as well as price from the products they purchased. Once installed, it was important that the product performed well without maintenance for lengthy periods of time. Larger customers often bought their products direct from the manufacturers. In this market segment, demand had also varied with the economic cycle of the country concerned. The cyclicality of demand was probably typical of a maturing market.

Company project development process

Organisation of the project was handed to two Blue Circle strategists, David Williams and Nick Whitwell (who subsequently became Managing Director and Marketing Director of the company's heating business in the UK). Between 1990 and 1992, they researched the European market by travelling around the area visiting about 40 established heating companies, many of them rivals to the business they were attempting to create. 'The best way of finding out about an industry is to walk around it,' says Williams. Most companies were happy to talk to him on the grounds that they might later get a chance to become involved with Blue Circle's plans through ventures such as marketing or licensing deals.

Williams was particularly impressed with the skills of Nefit, with which Blue Circle had talked tentatively in the 1980s about a joint venture in condensing systems. Two other companies also stood out: Vaillant for its 'product quality' and Saunier Duval, a French company owned by Hepworth (UK), because of its 'solid long-term approach to investment'.

Using ideas from the Williams/Whitwell research plus ideas from the 40-strong design team, Blue Circle devised a specification for its condensing system based around a list of 80 to 90 technical factors. These covered everything from the shape and size of the heat exchanger to burner efficiency and the concentration of specific vapours in the exhaust gases. 'For all these factors, we had to strike a balance between what it would be nice to

have for a particular market and what we had to have,' commented Michelle Fabre, a member of the design team and Manufacturing Director of Celsius. 'The debate was about trade-offs between technical complexity and cost,' says Whitwell.

Single Europe considerations

Another challenge was to ensure that of the 150 key components in the boiler, 90 per cent were common to boilers sold in any of the main European countries. The remainder would differ according to the needs of specific nations. It was also essential that some components could easily be varied depending on whether the boiler was the heating-only type most common in the UK or a combination boiler that heats water without a separate tank, which is popular elsewhere in Europe.

Components were designed to fit into a product that could be manufactured at one UK site – the main Potterton Myson boiler factory in Warwick, UK – and shipped abroad. The design process had to address key questions such as the type of gas used in each country. French boilers, for example, must be able to run on several variations of natural gas, piped in from the North Sea, Algeria or the former Soviet Union.

Other variations – in spite of a new European Commission procedure which set minimum design requirements for boilers for each individual nation – made setting common standards difficult. For example, flue (chimney) systems in different countries varied widely, largely because in the UK boilers were usually sited in kitchens, in the Netherlands they were often sited in the attic and in Germany in the cellar. Electronic controls in different countries normally followed different principles, while French fixtures for fitting boilers to walls were completely different to those in other countries. The design which the team came up with focussed on a central boiler unit containing main components such as heat exchanger and burners, with other parts which could be fitted or removed to take into account the technical design variations required for specific markets.

Lessons from the European-wide design approach

Hans Christian Pargman, Sales Director at Bröttge and a member of the design group, says thinking about technical or marketing problems from the vantage point of other countries also proved useful in a broader sense. For example, engineers from one country were able to learn about specific design features from those of others; so the German engineers rethought their approach to, among other things, flue design, and came up with a better system based on practice in other nations.

Through studying the UK approach to design, Pargman himself thought for the first time about using price competition as a sales tool. He commented:

In Germany consumers have traditionally paid high prices for sophisticated products. So designers have not generally thought of attempting to sell more products by cutting down on specifications, still selling a good product but at a somewhat lower cost.

Total costs of the exercise have been around US$30 million. Some of this resulted from a US$10.5 million revamp of the Warwick factory to make the cast aluminium heat exchangers needed for the new boilers. Borrowing ideas from Nefit, a set of new casting techniques was introduced at the plant to make a small and light heat exchanger so the boiler would fit into a small space. Blue Circle also invested US$10.5 million in a computerised warehouse in Warwick to handle distribution of the products around Europe.

Results so far

In August 1995, it was too early to say whether the project would succeed. The company is taking on stiff competition, particularly in Germany and the Netherlands, where Blue Circle's own boiler companies had only a fairly small marketing presence.

The condensing boiler went on sale in the UK and the Netherlands in Summer 1995, under the names *Envoy* and *Runner* respectively. In the UK, it sold at a wholesale price of US$855 – US$180 more than a non-condensing Blue Circle boiler. Launches in other countries were planned for the remainder of 1995. The new product would be called the *Ecoterm* in Germany.

Blue Circle was expecting great things of the product. But whatever happens, says Whitwell, the company has learned important lessons from the project, particularly about teamwork and how to use modular design and manufacturing techniques, which it hopes can be applied in future.

Source: Financial Times, 21 August 1995.

CASE QUESTIONS

1 *Identify the market growth and competitive position characteristics of the European market and use these to assess the strategies that were developed.*

2 *How did the company overcome the cultural problems involved in developing across countries? What lessons, if any, can be drawn from this for strategy development?*

3 *The strategy process appeared to make only a limited attempt to develop a series of options and then select from them: it concentrated on a pan-European route. What are the problems and opportunities of taking such a single-minded approach? Would you have investigated other options? If so, what options and why?*

4 *Do you judge that its strategy will be successful? Are there any areas that you would like to see developed further?*

◼ SUMMARY

● This chapter has provided an initial overview of the evaluation process. Such a process relies on developing criteria as a starting point for selection. These need to be developed bearing in mind the nature of the organisation: for example, commercial organisations will clearly require different criteria from non-profit-making organisations.

● There are six main criteria usually employed for evaluating strategy options in commercial organisations: consistency, especially with the organisation's mission and objectives, suitability, validity, feasibility, business risk and attractiveness to stakeholders.

1 consistency with the purpose of the organisation;

2 suitability for the organisation's environment;

3 validity of the projections and data used in developing the option;

4 feasibility, bearing in mind internal and external constraints on the organisation, such as technical skills, finance and competition; and the commitment of management and employees;

5 business risk, which must be at a level acceptable to the organisation;

6 attractiveness of the option to stakeholders, including shareholders and employees.

● Internationally, evaluation of these criteria may be affected by national characteristics and by differences in the interests of stakeholders and governments.

● It is important to clarify the basis on which an initial selection of the best option is to be done. Evaluation against the mission and objectives is useful to find the best strategic option, but non-quantified objectives may prove just as important for some organisations.

● In non-profit organisations, the criteria also need to reflect the broader aspects of the service or contribution to the community and to take into account the different decision-making processes and beliefs that motivate many such organisations. This may make strategy option evaluation more diffuse and open-ended.

● Additional criteria for evaluation include the ability to build on the strengths and core competences of the organisation and avoid its weaknesses. Generally, in evaluation, strengths are more important than weaknesses, but occasionally a weakness cannot be ignored. Different parts of an organisation, such as the HQ, the Strategic Business Units (SBUs) and those involved in individual projects, will have different perspectives on the evaluation process. It is important to recognise this in selection.

● Evaluation usually employs common and agreed criteria across the organisation, such as contribution to value added and profitability. The strengths and weaknesses of these criteria need to be understood.

● The Shareholder Value Approach takes a broader perspective on evaluation than that provided by the specific project. It seeks to determine the benefit of such developments in the context of the whole SBU in which the project rests. However, it still relies on the assumption that shareholders are always the prime beneficiaries.

● Cost/benefit analysis has been successfully employed in public sector evaluation where it is important to assess broader and less quantifiable benefits. The main difficulty is where to place the limit on such benefits and costs.

QUESTIONS

1 Using Section 15.1, consider what criteria would be particularly important if you were evaluating strategy options in the following organisations: a small chain of petrol stations; a large multinational developing a global strategy; a government telecommunications company that was about to be privatised; a student career planning service?

2 If you were developing strategy for a small company with 50 employees and a turnover of around US$5 million, would you use all the selection criteria outlined in Section 15.1 or would you select only some for this purpose? Give reasons for your answer and, if only choosing some, then explain which you would pick.

3   A strategic business unit of a major multinational has proposed a new acquisition of one of its immediate competitors. Who should evaluate this proposal? Against what criteria?

4   Japanese companies have tended to favour payback criteria while US/UK companies have been more inclined to use DCF criteria in evaluating strategic options. What are the merits of the two approaches? Can you suggest any reasons why one might be preferred to another?

5   'Discounting techniques rest on rather arbitrary assumptions about profitability, asset deterioration and external investment opportunities.' Professor Robert Hay. Explain the implications of this comment for strategy evaluation and comment on its application in strategy selection.

6   What are the dangers, if any, of using quantified and precise evaluation criteria in strategy selection?

7   'Strategy evaluation is an attempt to look beyond the obvious facts regarding the short-term health of a business and appraise instead those more fundamental factors and trends that govern success in the chosen field of endeavour.' Professor Richard Rumelt. Discuss.

8   Do the merits of Shareholder Value Analysis justify its use in preference to Discounted Cash Flow? Or would you recommend using neither? In which case, what criteria would you use for strategy evaluation?

9   If you were advising the Blue Circle company (Case study 15.2) on its new pan-European strategy, what evaluation procedures and criteria would you adopt? Give reasons for your views.

STRATEGIC PROJECT

Strategies for world regions

In its approach to new strategic opportunities, Blue Circle chose a pan-European approach. You might like to explore the possibilities of strategies that cover a region of the world: pan-American, South-East Asian and pan-African being other examples.

FURTHER READING

On criteria for selection: see Day, G S (1987) *Strategic Market Planning*, West Publishing. Tiles, S (1963) 'How to evaluate business strategy', *Harvard Business Review*, July–Aug, pp111–22. Rumelt, R (1980) 'The evaluation of business strategy', originally published in Glueck, W F, *Business Policy and Strategic Management*, McGraw-Hill, New York.

On financial evaluation: Glautier, M W E and Underdown, B (1994) *Accounting Theory and Practice*, 5th edn, Pitman Publishing, London is a useful summary of the main areas. *See* also Grundy, A N (1992) *Corporate Strategy and Financial Decisions*, Kogan Page, London. Ellis, J and Williams, D (1993) *Corporate Strategy and Financial Analysis*, Pitman Publishing, London.

For an alternative and rational view on the use and abuse of investment criteria: Hay, R (1982) 'Managing as if tomorrow mattered', *Harvard Business Review*, May–June, pp72–9.

REFERENCES

1 *See*, for example, Gilmore, F and Brandenburg, R (1962) 'Anatomy of Corporate Planning', *Harvard Business Review*, Nov–Dec, pp61–9.

2 Different commentators have employed other criteria: the criteria used here have been developed from Day, G S (1987) *Strategic Market Planning*, West Publishing. Tiles, S (1963) 'How to evaluate business strategy', *Harvard Business Review*, July–Aug, pp111–22. Rumelt, R (1980) 'The evaluation of business strategy', originally published in Glueck, W F, *Business Policy and Strategic Management*, McGraw-Hill, New York.

3 *See* Lynch, R (1993) *Cases in European Marketing*, Kogan Page, London, Ch 16.

4 *See Financial Times*: 15 Apr 1995, p9; 13 Oct 1994, p2; 1 Mar 1994, p29; and Lynch, R (1994) *European Business Strategies*, 2nd edn, Kogan Page, London, p84. Groupe Bull is a company with some real strategic problems that would make an interesting strategy project.

5 Kehoe, L (1995) 'Restrictive practice claims put Microsoft back in firing line', *Financial Times*, 6 Feb, p6.

6 Carnegy H (1995) 'Bitter Swedish dispute to end', *Financial Times*, 3 August, p2.

7 Munchau, W and Norman, P (1995) 'Planes, trains and automobiles', *Financial Times*, 7 Nov, p19. This company is explored further in Chapter 11.

8 Gray, B (1994) 'Still sitting tight in the electric chair', *Financial Times*, 25 July, p12 and Lynch, R (1994) Ibid, p27 and p252. Compare also the Annual Report and Accounts of the two companies for 1994.

9 This is consistent with the emphasis on core competences in Chapter 12.

10 Much of the literature on strategy evaluation makes this assumption. One of the difficulties with the current state of development in corporate strategy is that there needs to be further exploration of this area.

11 Further detailed exploration of the techniques outlined in this chapter is contained in the recommended reading at the end of the chapter: Grundy (Kogan Page), Ellis and Williams (Pitman Publishing), Glautier and Underdown (Pitman Publishing).

12 The main exceptions are the large grocery multiple retailers who sell for cash to the general public and buy on credit from the manufacturers. Retailers have relied on their suppliers to fund increased sales for many years, but they do need careful stock control procedures to handle the situation.

13 This was essentially proposed by Rappaport, A (1983) *Creating Shareholder Value*, Free Press, Harvard. *See* also Rappaport, A (1992), 'CEO and Strategists: forging a common framework', *Harvard Business Review*, May–June, p84. A clear and careful discussion of this area is also contained in Ellis, J and Williams, D (1993) *Corporate Strategy and Financial Analysis*, Pitman Publishing, London, Ch 10.

14 It is not true of some Japanese companies according to the work of Williams, K, Haslam, C and Williams, J (1991) *Management Accounting: the Western problematic against the Japanese application*, 9th Annual Conference of Labour Progress, University of Manchester Institute of Science and Technology. The authors examined car and electronics companies only and made no claim to have extended their research to the *whole* of Japanese industry. Professor Toyohiro Kono also comments that 'DCF is not used very often' in his interesting survey of Japanese practice, which is more broadly based: Kono, T (1992) *Long Range Planning of Japanese Corporations*, de Gruyter, Berlin, pp277 and 281.

15 Rappaport, A (1983) Ibid, and Woolridge (1988) 'Competitive decline and corporate restructuring: Is a myopic stock market to blame?', *Continental Bank Journal of Applied Corporate Finance*, Spring, pp26–36, quoted in Ellis, J and Williams, D, Ibid.

16 Quoted from the UK chemist retailer, Boots plc's definition of strategy: Buckley, N (1994) 'Divide and thrive at Boots', *Financial Times*, 4 July, p12.

17 *See*, for example, Rowe, A, Mason, A and Dickel, K (1985) *Strategic Management and Business Policy*, 2nd edn, Addison-Wesley, New York.

18 This section is based on the example in Chapter 31 of Glautier M W E and Underdown, B (1994) *Accounting Theory and Practice*, 5th edn, Pitman Publishing, London, p540.

19 Adapted from Marsh, P (1995) 'Down in the boiler room', *Financial Times*, 21 Aug, p8.

16

Strategy evaluation and selection – 2

After working through this chapter, you will be able to:

- apply business judgement to the inevitable uncertainties that arise from the selection of strategies;

- appraise the feasibility issues that will limit the selection of strategies;

- assess the risks of each major strategy and the implications for the organisation;

- identify the main stakeholders and consider how their interests are best served by the strategy options available;

- consider the implications for strategy selection of operating in an international environment;

- undertake a strategy evaluation and selection.

■ INTRODUCTION

This chapter examines in greater depth some aspect of the selection and evaluation process introduced in Chapter 15.

Although the 'best' option may have been selected, there are a number of factors that can alter the decision. *Business judgement* can be used to explore the competitive situation and suggest a route forward. *Empirical evidence* of successful strategies is also available.

Furthermore, scarce resources and the pressure of events outside the organisation mean that it is important to appraise the *feasibility* of the options that the organisation can undertake. In most strategic decisions, there will be residual uncertainties and *risks* that cannot be overcome and need to be carefully assessed before the final decision is made. The interests of *stakeholders* must also be taken into account. Finally, the implications of operating in an *international* environment are considered.

None of the above considerations has any particular priority and each plays a role in the strategy selection process (*see* Fig 16.1).

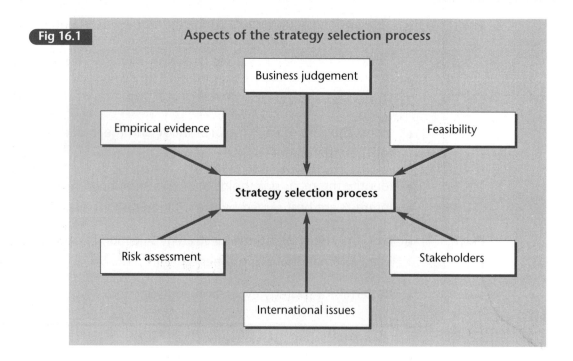

Fig 16.1 Aspects of the strategy selection process

Business judgement

Empirical evidence

Feasibility

Strategy selection process

Risk assessment

Stakeholders

International issues

Swatch to the rescue[1]

Back in 1984, some major Swiss banks turned down investment proposals for a new Swiss disposable watch, the Swatch. It went on to become one of the strategy successes of the decade.

Background

During the 1970s and early '80s, Japanese watch-making companies, such as Seiko and Citizen, developed wrist watches with new standards of accuracy and display. They used new quartz technology and liquid crystal display which they coupled with new production methods. The result was that by the early 1980s they had come to dominate the world watch industry.

It was the previous leaders in the world watch industry who had suffered from this onslaught. The Swiss watch industry had been the largest but suffered a devastating drop in employment between 1974 and 1983 from 90 000 to 30 000 people. Swiss production was also slashed, falling from 91 million pieces to 43 million pieces in the same period. The effects were felt not only in the cheaper watch segment directly hit by Japanese innovation. The more expensive Swiss watches were also affected: their greater accuracy and reliability could now be replicated in the new cheaper Japanese models. Brands such as Omega, Tissot and Longines were among those that suffered.

Industry rescue

Two companies controlled about one third of Swiss watch production: Asuag and SSIH. It was decided that these would form the basis of a rescue attempt in 1984 through a new company called SMH. A well-known Swiss entrepreneur, Nicholas Hayek, was brought in to spearhead the revival. He ran an established Swiss engineering consultancy and had a flair for aiding weak companies.

Mr Hayek proposed to tackle the Japanese threat to the Swiss industry head-on. He commented:

> No other area in the world is as richly gifted as western Europe. If we use our people well, we can always make high-quality, low-cost consumer products and make them better than people in Singapore, Hong Kong, South Korea and Japan.

Nevertheless, some of the Swiss banks were extremely dubious and refused to support this strategy. Hayek put up some of his own finances to move the strategy forward.

The new Swiss strategy: 1984–90

There were two main elements to the strategy: manufacturing and marketing. In addition, the new Swiss strategy was also helped by the rising Japanese yen which made Japanese watches more expensive.

In manufacturing, the company invented a totally new process that cut the number of components necessary to make a watch. This reduced the costs dramatically, even in high-wage Switzerland. Hayek also insisted that other Swiss watches used standardised parts so that economies of scale could be achieved across a wide range of watches, even the expensive ones that still kept their well-known brand names. Over the years, this aspect of the strategy has proved a major success.

In marketing, the company launched the Swatch – a plastic, well-designed fashionable watch at a reasonably competitive price (around S FR 50). The new watch was branded around the world with new watch-face designs every few months in bright colours and limited quantities. By the mid-1990s, some of the earlier models had become highly prized collectors' items. However, the watch was less successful in North America and Asia, where plastic was seen to be cheap.

By 1995, the Swiss watch industry had recovered its position as the world's leading producer of *finished* watches and clocks. However, the leadership of the highly automated manufacture of watch *movements* stayed firmly with Japan.

CASE QUESTIONS

1   *Do you have any sympathy for the judgement of the Swiss bank investors in 1984?*

2   *What elements of business judgement would have persuaded you to support Mr Hayek's strategy selection?*

16.1 APPLYING BUSINESS JUDGEMENTS AND GUIDELINES

In assessing strategy options, no one can be certain about sales, profits, costs and capital requirements over a time horizon that spans years. Some emergent strategists argue that this difficulty makes the whole options selection process largely irrelevant (*see* Chapter 17). Even the most ardent prescriptive strategist would accept that there are residual uncertainties and as a result we need to test the *suitability* of the strategy for the organisation and the *validity* of the data – criteria 2 and 3 from Chapter 15.

Prescriptive strategists take the view that *sound logical thought in the form of a study of generic industry environments and empirical evidence* will reduce these difficulties, though not eliminate them.

16.1.1   Generic industry environments[2]

Some strategies have been shown through logical thought to provide a higher chance of success than others. Such insights may aid the selection of strategy options. Exploration and understanding of the main concepts is called the study of *generic strategy environments*.[3] Essentially, it is proposed that strategies can be selected on the basis of their ability to cope with particular market and competitive circumstances. Five specific types have been identified for examination in this chapter: four are explored below. The fifth concerned with *international industries* is examined at the end of this chapter. This section begins with a more general viewpoint that also relies on the same logic – the ADL matrix.

16.1.2 Overall generic viewpoint: the ADL or Lifecycle Portfolio Matrix

The well-known management consultants, Arthur D Little (ADL), developed an overall approach during the 1970s which involves matching an organisation's own strength or weakness in a market with the lifecycle phase of that market – the Lifecycle Portfolio Matrix. Specifically, it focusses on:

● *Stage of industry maturity* – from a young and fast growing market through to a mature and declining market.

● *Competitive position* – from a company that is dominant and able to control the industry through to one that is weak and barely able to survive.

It is important not to over-simplify the strategies that can be adopted depending on a company's competitive position in the above matrix. As a starting point, the matrix shown in Table 16.1 (*see* p550) was developed in order to illustrate some of the choices that might be made. The boxes indicate suggested strategies depending on lifecycle and share position held by the company: they can be used both to *stimulate* options and to *evaluate* proposed options to ensure that they are consistent with the company's strategic position. For example, if a company is in a *strong* position in a *mature* market, then the strategic logic of the matrix would suggest that it:

● seeks cost leadership *or*

● renews its focus strategy *or*

● differentiates itself from competition

● while at the same time growing with the industry.

Hence, if other strategy options for this market and competitive combination were presented and they did not conform with one of the above proposals, there would be a case for rejecting them. However, it will be evident from the Swatch case that such analyses can be flawed where major technological change and marketing initiatives are introduced.

16.1.3 Selecting strategies in fragmented industries

There are some markets that are unlikely to produce dominant companies. The market is often local or regional – for example, laundry services or taxi companies. Dominant companies are unlikely, either because:

● value added is not high for technical reasons, thus making it difficult to fund differentiation; or

● the service is essentially personal and difficult to operate on a large scale.

Table 16.1 Evaluation using The Lifecycle Portfolio Matrix[4]

Competitive position \ Maturity	Embryonic	Growing	Mature	Ageing
Clear leader	**Hold position** Attempt to improve market penetration *Invest slightly faster than market dictates*	**Hold position** Defend market share *Invest to sustain growth rate (and pre-empt potential competitors)*	**Hold position** Grow with industry *Reinvest as necessary*	**Hold position** *Reinvest as necessary*
Strong	**Attempt to improve market penetration** *Invest as fast as market dictates*	**Attempt to improve market penetration** *Invest to increase growth rate (and improve position)*	**Hold position** Grow with industry *Reinvest as necessary*	**Hold position** *Reinvest as necessary or reinvest minimum*
Favourable	**Attempt to improve position selectively** Penetrate market generally or selectively *Invest selectively*	**Attempt to improve position** Penetrate market selectively *Selectively invest to improve position*	**Maintain position** Find niche and attempt to protect it *Make minimum and/or selective reinvestment*	**Harvest, withdraw in phases, or abandon** *Reinvest minimum necessary or disinvest*
Defensible	**Attempt to improve position selectively** *Invest (very) selectively*	**Find niche and protect it** *Invest selectively*	**Find niche or withdraw in phases** *Reinvest minimum necessary or disinvest*	**Withdraw in phases or abandon** *Disinvest or divest*
Weak	**Improve position or withdraw** *Invest or divest*	**Turn around or abandon** *Invest or disinvest*	**Turn around or withdraw in phases** *Invest selectively or disinvest*	**Abandon position** *Divest*

Source: Reproduced with permission from Arthur D Little. Copyright © Arthur D Little, Inc 1996.

Barriers to entry are often low and economies of scale may be absent. Companies typically have little bargaining power with customers and suppliers. In some cases, transport costs make it difficult to operate across a dispersed geographic area: for example, a bottling plant for milk or beer needs to be operated reasonably close to the local market. This does not mean that consolidation is impossible: as an industry matures, this may become more viable, especially where a standardised product can be developed. Strategies that might have a higher chance of success include:

- *Attempting to devise a 'business formula' that can be applied in multiple locations and restructure the industry away from fragmentation.* Franchising of services and restaurants are examples where companies have begun to transform highly fragmented industries: McDonald's (US) is now the biggest restaurateur in France, for example.

- *Specialising in some customers or products.* This may overcome some scale problems and provide greater bargaining power against suppliers and customers. Customer specialisation might take the form of specialised services which require unique knowledge of an industry – for example, law companies specialising in certain types of commercial law. Product specialisation can take many forms but would typically concentrate on one area of a more general service – for example, rapid replacement of exhaust systems and car tyres by national chains specialising in such services.

- *Concentrating on low-cost production* may provide protection. Low overheads, low wage costs, tight control of all costs, 'no-frills' operations can still operate in such circumstances.

Figure 16.2 shows one way in which the strategy in such industries might be developed.

16.1.4 Selecting strategies in emerging industries

When a market is new and fast growing, it is not clear how it will develop. Technology may be still in its early stages with little agreement on industry standards. Companies will still be low on the learning curve (*see* Chapter 7). Dominant market shares may have less meaning because the market is changing fast. New

Fig 16.2 **Possible strategic choice in fragmented industries**

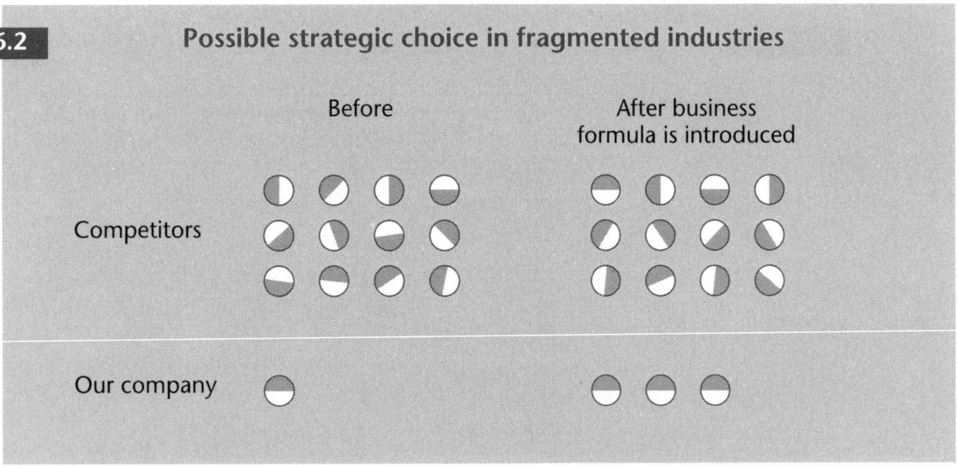

customers will still be entering the market and will need to be introduced to the products. Competitors should all be experiencing significant sales growth, with the problem being the provision of adequate finance for this and for further research at the same time. For example, the SMH company and the Swatch were the belated Swiss strategic responses to this situation in the world watch and clock industry.

Strategies that might be particularly successful include:

- bold initiatives to capture market share and build on cost experience effects;
- significant investment to develop the basic technology and adapt it to customer tastes;
- search for a viable customer base beyond the initial trialists – for example, a market segment.

Examples of such markets in the 1990s include mobile telephones and some parts of the computer industry. International expansion may provide an important additional strategic opportunity and is explored in Section 16.6.

Figure 16.3 summarises a possible strategic choice in this situation.

16.1.5 Selecting strategies in markets that are beginning to mature[5]

In maturing markets there are fewer opportunities for natural sales expansion. Thus, companies seeking growth are forced to take share from their competitors. This is likely to intensify market competition with companies particularly aware of how they compare against each other. In these circumstances, some companies may decide that it is more realistic to take profitability and cash as objectives, rather than attempt a major growth initiative. However, this will clearly depend on competitors and their objectives: if a competitor decides that growth is needed, then all the companies in the market have to respond or face a loss of sales. The entry of Japanese, Korean and Malaysian cars into the mature western European car markets of the 1990s is an example of the problems that existing European manufacturers face. The choice of strategy will vary according to the competitive position of the company.

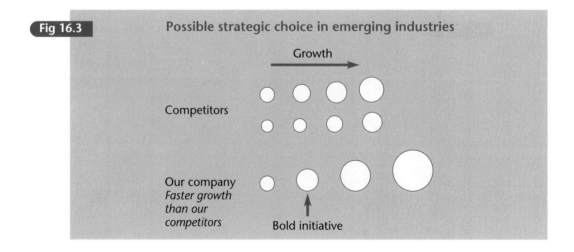

Fig 16.3   **Possible strategic choice in emerging industries**

For a company that *is not the market leader*, the strategies that are more likely to deliver consistent profits are those that:

● seek to develop market niches;

● aim to differentiate their products or services from the leader;

● may also involve investment in innovation and renewal.

Strategies that attempt to attain cost leadership invite strong retaliation from the existing leader and are likely to fail.

If the company *is the market leader* in a mature market, different strategies will be appropriate. Prescriptive strategies suggest that the company should attempt to:

● maintain its market leadership by continuing to hold cost leadership;

● deter others from entering by aggressively producing and marketing its products;

● increase sales to existing customers by extending the product range offered, selling complementary services and doing more for the existing customer.

For both the leader and follower, there may also be opportunities from international expansion (*see* Section 16.6). Figure 16.4 summarises a possible strategic choice for a company that is not a market leader in a mature market.

16.1.6 Selecting strategies in declining markets

Some markets inevitably are in the decline phase, but there may still be good profits to be earned by the survivors. Such markets will have only limited opportunity for sales growth, possibly only when other companies exit from the industry. The starting point for strategy for all companies is to determine *the rate of decline*: if decline is fast (for example, the markets for hoola hoops, straw hats, LP records) then all companies will have to consider leaving those markets. More often than not, decline is slow and the issue becomes who will survive in these circumstances.

In addition, a distinction needs to be drawn in an ageing industry between a leader and a follower: a *follower company* will have to consider carefully whether survival is desirable or even possible, while the *leading company* may be able to survive, for a period at least, because of its larger scale.

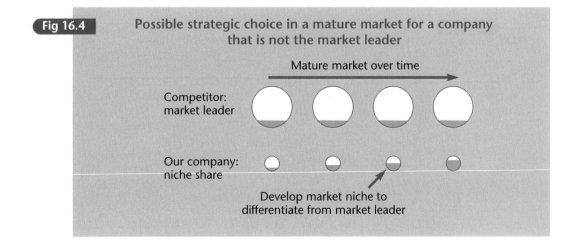

Fig 16.4 **Possible strategic choice in a mature market for a company that is not the market leader**

Mature market over time

Competitor: market leader

Our company: niche share

Develop market niche to differentiate from market leader

For both leaders and followers, industry strategies might attempt to:

- specialise in niches where the product or service has some specific continuing need;
- consider the core competences and recombine them in entirely new ways for moves into growing markets;
- acquire companies that are exiting the industry cheaply in order to buy their remaining sales and scale economies;
- seek innovation, so that any market-extension growth areas are exploited;
- drive hard to reduce costs: manufacturing processes, distribution channels and every aspect of the value chain might be usefully examined;
- seek international expansion (*see* Section 16.6).

Figure 16.5 shows a possible strategic choice in a declining market for a company that is not market leader.

16.1.7   Comment on industry solutions

The problem with industry solutions is that they are available to *everyone* in the industry and are therefore unlikely to deliver sustainable competitive advantage to a specific company. Although Professor Michael Porter has produced some logical and useful books, many have read and studied them. They are thus unable to deliver the unique solution necessary for long-term strategic growth. To quote Professors Baden-Fuller and Stopford:[6]

> It is the firm that matters, not the industry.

However, the industry solution to strategic choice still has merit for two reasons:

- It is a useful starting point in developing the strategic proposal.
- Its logic is useful in removing options that do not deserve further consideration.

The firm does matter in strategic choice but the industry cannot be dismissed completely.

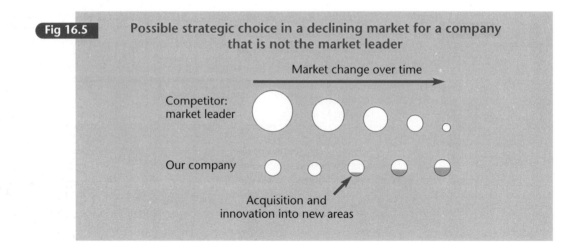

Fig 16.5 **Possible strategic choice in a declining market for a company that is not the market leader**

Market change over time

Competitor: market leader

Our company

Acquisition and innovation into new areas

> ### ◖ Key strategic principles
>
> - Business judgement needs to be applied to selection because no one can be certain about the outcomes of strategy proposals.
>
> - Generic industry environments have been analysed to provide some guidance on strategy evaluation. They are based on two broad categories: the stage of industry maturity and the competitive position of the organisation involved. After identifying where the organisation is positioned according to these two parameters, simple choices then suggest themselves.
>
> - Beyond this general work, further guidance on appropriate strategies has been developed for specific types of industry situation: fragmented industries, emerging industries, mature markets and declining markets have all been identified.

16.2 ◖ EMPIRICAL EVIDENCE OF SUCCESSFUL STRATEGIES[7]

In addition to the logic of strategy development covered in Section 16.1, there is also empirical evidence of strategies that have succeeded or failed which provides guidance that can be used to select the optimal strategy.

16.2.1 ◖ General evidence of successful strategies

The greatest contributor to corporate strategy may well be the strategic business unit level of an organisation rather than the higher, corporate level or the level of the industry overall. The evidence for this comes from a study of US Corporations in the 1970s.[8] It examined the contribution to profits from various sources including the industry, its cyclicality, the corporation owning the business unit and the SBU itself. The results appear in Table 16.2 and for this North American sample, they appear to show that who owns the business unit matters little. Even industry and cyclical effects (*see* Chapters 3 and 6) matter less than the activities undertaken by the business unit. Value is added at the individual strategic business unit (SBU) level rather than through corporate activity. Whether this finding is true for other countries and industry samples cannot easily be established, but it does suggest that the starting point for strategy selection should rest with the SBU, not with its links with the corporation or its particular position in the industry.

Table 16.2 Contributions to the variance of profitability across business units[9]

Source within corporation	Contribution to the total profitability of the corporation
Corporate ownership	0.8%
Industry effects	8.3%
Cyclical effects	7.8%
Business unit specific effects	46.4%
Unexplained factors	36.7%
Total across corporation	100%

Source: Rumelt, R (1991).

16.2.2 Evidence of quality and its role in strategy development

The evidence in this area comes from the Strategic Planning Institute (SPI) located in the USA. For the last 20 years, the SPI has been gathering data on around 3000 companies (some 600 of which are located in Europe). The information collected covers three major areas:

- the results of strategies undertaken (profits, market share, etc.);
- the inputs by the company to this activity (plant investment, finance, productivity, etc.);
- the industry conditions within which the company operates (market growth, customer power, innovation, etc.).

The data is often described as the *PIMS Databank* (PIMS means Profit Impact of Market Strategy) and is unique in terms of the size of its empirical database on corporate strategy coupled with its inputs and outputs. It collects data and calculates statistical correlations between various elements: whether such relationships have any real meaning has been the subject of fierce academic debate.[10] This book takes the view that it has made a useful contribution to empirical strategy research. The overall results have been published and a few of the key findings are explored below. In addition to its general work, the results are also fed back to contributing companies on a detailed and more confidential basis for them to assess their performance and draw relevant conclusions.

In the long run and according to the PIMS Database, the most important single factor affecting a business unit's performance is the quality of its products and services relative to those of its competitors. The evidence for this is shown in Table 16.3.

Strategy options that seek to raise quality are more likely to be successful than those that do not. This supports much of the activity described in Chapters 10 and 11 in this area on the subject of TQM, etc. This does not mean that there are no opportunities for a low quality/low value for money route: on the contrary, among the most profitable retailers across Europe are those such as Aldi and Kwiksave that have followed such an approach: *value for money* is just as important as the *absolute* pursuit of quality. However, it does mean that strategic options that emphasise quality have a greater chance of long-run success than those that do not.

Table 16.3 PIMS data showing that both quality and market share drive profitability[11]

Relative quality	Relative market share		
	Low to 25%	Medium	High above 60%
Inferior	7	14	21
Roughly equal	13	20	27
Superior	20	29	38

Numbers inside matrix are the return on investment expressed as a percentage.

Source: PIMS Associates Ltd, 1996.

16.2.3 Evidence of the importance of market share and marketing activity

In Chapters 3 and 6, we explored the strategic importance of a company having significant power in the market place. This is usually measured using market share. PIMS monitors market share and has shown a strong correlation with return on investment, as shown in Table 16.4. High market share is associated with high profitability.

The reasons for this probably relate to the experience curve: as companies increase their market share, they move down the curve for all the reasons explored in Chapter 7 – for example, economies of scale, greater purchasing power, more efficient use of transport and other activities. Strategy options that seek to raise market share may be worth pursuing.

However, it should be noted that the evidence is circular in the sense that, if high-share firms have higher profits, then they have more funds to invest in cost-saving devices, higher quality and more marketing activity. This will, in turn, raise their market share and profitability even further. Moreover, it may be of little strategic help to the majority of companies who do not have a high share. It may be prohibitively expensive to invest in marketing and plant economies. However, Japanese car and electronics companies were in much the same position in the 1960s, but have developed to become a major force in the world car industry. Innovation and the mistakes of the market leaders provide clues on the strategies needed.

A related question is the issue of the *level of marketing support activity* – that is, investment in advertising, branding and salesforce teams. Marketing expenditure compared to sales revenue is a rough measure of this level of activity. The results measured against relative market share are also shown in Table 16.4. They suggest that there is a correlation between high levels of marketing activity and market share. For those companies that already have a high share, there is merit in maintaining their levels of expenditure. For those companies with low market share, the correlation implies that it may not be the best strategy to spend funds on marketing activity to increase market share. Strategy options that attempt to buy market share with additional marketing activity may result in low return on investment.

Table 16.4 The PIMS relationship between marketing activity and market share[12]

Relative market share	Market/Sales ratio			
	Low	5%	10%	High
Low 25%	18	15	9	
60%	20	20	21	
High	33	32	33	

Numbers inside matrix are the return on investment expressed as a percentage.

16.2.4 **Evidence of capital investment**

In the context of the operations strategies reviewed in Chapter 10, it could be argued that it will usually be worthwhile to invest in extra mechanisation to improve productivity and thus return on investment. The PIMS Database suggests that this does not necessarily follow. Companies that have high levels of capital investment as a percentage of their sales tend to also have lower profitability. The higher productivity gained from such capital investment may not completely offset the damage. This is shown in Table 16.5.

There are several reasons for this: capital-intensive plant usually needs to be run at high production capacity to make profits, as the European paper industry case demonstrated in Chapter 4. Such production requirements need steady or increasing sales to deliver the profits and, as we have seen, this can be a dubious assumption. There may even be a temptation to keep production running at capacity by offering special deals to customers, stealing sales from competitors and so on – all reducing profitability. By contrast, direct labour is more flexible and can be switched around when demand fluctuates. Moreover, if the company decides to exit the industry, the investment in fixed capital may make it more difficult, as we saw in the European steel industry in Chapter 3. Such companies may be tempted to reduce prices in order to survive which will in turn reduce the profitability of all companies in the industry, even those who have invested in the latest capital-intensive equipment.

Strategy options that rely on heavy capital expenditure to generate profits need to be examined carefully. In some industries, there may be no choice, but there is no guarantee that such expenditure will always deliver the results.

Table 16.5 Evidence showing that heavy investment as a percentage of sales drags down profitability and high productivity only offsets part of this effect[13]

Productivity*	Investment/Sales ratio		
	Low to 40%	Medium	High above 60%
Low to US$60	23	14	4
Medium	35	22	11
High above US$90	41	28	15

*Productivity is defined as value added per employee in US$ thousands, 1995.
Numbers inside matrix are the return on investment expressed as a percentage.

Source: PIMS Associates Ltd, 1996.

16.2.5 **Evidence of mergers and acquisitions[14]**

Mergers and acquisitions often form part of the strategy options that are expected to transform company performance. However, it should be stated that these activities are mainly confined to the UK and USA. They are less common in the rest of Europe and the Far East. Although there are clear reasons for seeking mergers and acquisitions, the empirical evidence on their performance suggests that they add little value to the companies undertaking the activity.

Given the amount of energy and publicity expended, this conclusion may be regarded as somewhat disappointing. Professor John Kay has gathered together the main evidence which is summarised in Table 16.6. Essentially, it shows that when pre- and post-merger profitability is compared, even the most optimistic interpretation of the results concluded:[15]

> 'No consistent pattern of either improved or deteriorated profitability can therefore be claimed across the seven countries. Mergers would appear to result in a slight improvement here, a worsening there.'

Table 16.6 The performance of mergers[16]

Method of evaluation	Major studies	Conclusions
1 Subjective opinions of company personnel	Hunt *et al* (1987)	Around half were successful
2 Whether acquired business is retained in the long term	Ravenscraft and Scherer (1987)	More divested than retained
3 Comparison of overall profitability before and after the merger	Meeks (1977), Mueller *et al* (1980), Ravenscraft and Cosh *et al* (1990), Scherer (1987)	Nil to negative effect
4 Effect on stock market valuation	Franks and Harris (1986), Franks, Harris and Mayer (1988)	Positive initial impact

Source: Kay, J (1993).

None of the evidence suggests that it is impossible for mergers or acquisitions to succeed in adding value. What the evidence does suggest is that many do not and the main reason would appear to be over-optimistic and vague objectives rather than some more inherent flaw. Generally, mergers and acquisitions are more likely to be successful where the partners are of similar size but, beyond this, there are no absolute guidelines. Hence, the merger option has no proven record of success in terms of delivering value.

16.2.6 Evidence of diversification strategies[17]

In the Market Options Matrix in Chapter 14, diversification options were explored as a means of providing new expansion routes for a company. A number of attempts have been made over the last 20 years to research the links between diversification and financial performance with generally unclear results. The overall conclusion from the empirical work that has been undertaken is that it is very difficult in practice to achieve successful diversification. Even *related* diversification which might be thought to have a greater chance of success, cannot be relied upon to deliver the expected results.

The evidence suggests that profitability does increase with diversity up to the point where the new organisation becomes too complex to manage. Then, the relationship reverses. Moreover, many researchers have found that there are no universal rules that can be applied to ensure the success of diversification: the success is highly likely to depend on the specific circumstances of the company and the business situation it was facing at the time. Overall, it is possible that organisations may choose diversification strategies when the opportunities in their current markets appear to be limited.

According to the evidence, strategy options that rely on diversification may not deliver the expected results.

Key strategic principles

- Empirical evidence based on the PIMS Database also exists on the connection between strategic actions and the financial results in terms of profitability and other criteria.

- According to PIMS, high quality and strong market share can make a positive contribution to profitability. High capital intensity is less likely to have a positive impact. Some researchers doubt the cause and effect relationships here.

- Acquisitions and mergers have also been studied for their impact on profitability. The evidence is, at best, mixed and, at worst, suggests that many are unsuccessful. Diversification may be successful, depending on the circumstances.

CASE STUDY 16.1

Strategy transformation at Nokia[18]

The Finnish company, Nokia, has undertaken a major transformation in its strategy over the last few years. This required careful consideration of the constraints within which the company had to work.

Background

In 1991 and 1992, Nokia accumulated losses on its major businesses of FIM 482 million (US$120 million). The company had to find new strategies to remedy this situation. After careful consideration, it chose to develop two existing divisions: mobile telephones and telecommunications equipment (switches and exchanges). There were four reasons for this strategic choice:

1 The mobile telephone market had great worldwide growth potential and was growing fast.

2 Nokia already had profitable businesses in this area.

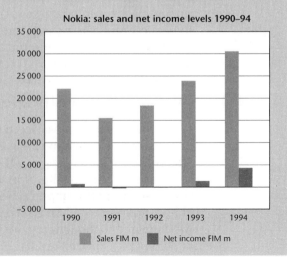

Nokia: sales and net income levels 1990–94

■ Sales FIM m   ■ Net income FIM m

3 Deregulation and privatisation of telecommunications markets around the world were providing specific opportunities in telecommunications equipment.

4 The pace of technological change was providing major market opportunities.

Constraints on strategy

The heavy losses of the group overall were a severe financial constraint. Moreover, it was still involved in a whole range of other industries – paper businesses, aluminium smelting, power generating and tyre making – many of which were making losses. Furthermore, it was not able to afford the same level of expenditure on research and development as its two major rivals, Motorola (US) and Ericsson (Sweden).

Although it had the in-house skills and experience of working with national deregulated telecommunications operators through competing in Nordic markets in the 1970s and '80s, the company needed many more employees if it was to develop with the market opportunities.

Resolution of the problem

Although the constraints were significant, Nokia solved them by:

- *Selling off most of its interests outside telecommunications.* These not only provided some funds but also reduced the drain on resources that had been required just to keep them in operation.

- *Concentrating its R&D on a few identified market opportunities rather than spreading them across many areas.* However, this ran the risk of picking the wrong areas for development.

- *Investing heavily in major training programmes both in Finland and beyond for its factories and sales operations.* Numbers employed in mobile telecommunications tripled to 9000 in the three years to 1995. Numbers employed in telecommunications equipment almost doubled to 11 000 in 1994 and 1995.

- *Careful communication of its culture and style using special training programmes.* Not all its foreign employees were able to cope immediately with Nokia's informal Finnish-style management approach.

CASE QUESTIONS

1 Why did Nokia select only two areas for development? What is the strategic risk involved in selecting two areas out of six?

2 Nokia appeared to decide on its strategy first and then consider the constraints. Is this wise? What would have happened if the strategy had not been feasible?

16.3 FEASIBILITY ISSUES

Feasibility issues may limit the selection of strategies because if a strategic option is proved to be infeasible, it becomes difficult, if not impossible, to carry out.

16.3.1 Internal feasibility issues

There may be constraints within the organisation that need to be considered before a final decision is taken to select a particular strategic option. These include such matters as the provision of finance, the availability of appropriately qualified people, and the existence of technical and manufacturing knowledge relevant to the new option.

The following types of question should be explored in this context:

1 Do we have the *people skills*? How difficult would it be to recruit them? Do we need to train them, if they are being brought in from outside?

2 Do we have the necessary *technical skills*? Can we meet the quality standards? How long will it take us to install the necessary machinery and how does this relate to the strategy timetable?

3 Do we have the *financial resources* or will we be stretched? Do we have the cash resources? What will be the breakeven of this venture?

4 Do we have the *marketing and sales resources* to meet the objectives? Salesforce numbers and organisation? Advertising and promotions experience and professional advisers?

In this context, you may like to examine the Eurofreeze case (Case study 16.2) and in particular, Option 5. This is the most revolutionary option. The feasibility of that option has to be investigated carefully. The ten-point checklist in Exhibit 16.1 may provide some useful areas, though even this could easily be extended.

Exhibit 16.1	Ten-point checklist on internal feasibility

1 *Capital investment required.* Do we have the funds?

2 *Projection of cumulative profits.* Is it sufficiently profitable?

3 *Working capital requirements.* Do we have enough working capital?

4 *Tax liabilities and dividend payments.* What are the implications, especially on timing?

5 *Numbers of employees and, in the case of redundancy, any costs associated with this.* What are the national laws on sacking people and what are the costs?

6 *New technical skills, new plant and costs of closure of old plant.* Do we have the skills? Do we need to recruit or hire temporarily some specialists?

7 *New products and how they are to be developed.* Are we confident that we have the portfolio of new products fully tested on which so much depends? Are they real breakthrough products or merely a catch-up on our competition?

8 *Amount and timing of marketing investment and expertise required.* Do we have the funds? When will they be required? Do we have the specialist expertise such as advertising and promotions agency teams to deliver our strategies?

9 *The possibility of acquisition, merger or joint venture with other companies and the implications.* Have we fully explored other options that would bring their own benefits and problems?

10 *The communication of the strategy.* How are these areas to be communicated to all those involved? Will we gain the commitment of the managers and employees affected?

It will be evident that some areas of feasibility may be difficult to achieve, if not impossible. Internal feasibility needs to be investigated *before* the option is chosen.

16.3.2 External feasibility issues

There may also be constraints outside the organisation that make strategy options difficult if not impossible. For example, in Case study 16.1 Nokia had to consider carefully the implications of the reduction in *government control* over telecommunications markets. This was not only an opportunity but also a problem because governments were still sensitive over their national interests in this area.

In addition, it is important to consider *competitive responses* which are external to the organisation. An aggressive competitor response might affect the feasibility of an option. These areas were explored in Chapters 4 and 5. In the Nokia case there were no significant competitor responses that needed to be considered: the market was growing too fast for these to have any impact.

The issues to be explored in this area are those covered by Porter's *Five Forces* and *PEST analysis* models of Part 2. Questions that might probe this area are summarised in Exhibit 16.2.

Exhibit 16.2 **Four-point checklist on external feasibility**

1 How will our *customers* respond to the strategies we are proposing?

2 How will our *competitors* react? Do we have the necessary resources to respond?

3 Do we have the necessary support from our *suppliers*?

4 Do we need *government* or *regulatory* approval? How likely is this?

For example, in Option 5 of the Eurofreeze case at the end of this chapter, the main external constraints were:

- *Customer response from the main supermarkets to new initiatives.* These were likely to be favourable, if only because they had little to lose.

- *Competitor reaction to its drive to become low-cost leader.* This was probably the most significant constraint on Option 5.

16.3.3 Management commitment

This constraint may arise because some organisations make a clear distinction between strategy development by senior managers and day-to-day management by more junior managers.[19] In such organisations, junior managers and employees are unlikely to have been involved in the strategy development process: in essence, they have the results *communicated* to them and they may not feel committed to its implications. In Chapter 17 and much of the rest of this book, an alternative approach will be explored – *the learning organisation* – where employees and junior managers are encouraged to contribute to the strategy process at an earlier stage and feel greater commitment.

For now, it should be noted that some strategic decisions may need to be made by a senior management centralised group – for example, the Nokia decision to divest some companies. In spite of Nokia's commitment to an open Finnish culture, the key decisions on the new strategy were taken by a group of senior managers. The more junior managers and employees were not really consulted: since the proposals included divesting part of Nokia, this is not really surprising. Most turkeys do not vote for Christmas, nor ducks for the Chinese New Year feast.

When the workers have not been consulted in advance and may be set challenging objectives, it is particularly important to gain their commitment. There are two prime conditions:[20]

1   *The strategy must be communicable.* It must be capable of explanation without appearing too complicated. It must not be misunderstood or misinterpreted in order to ensure that it is properly carried out.

2   *The strategy must challenge and motivate important members of staff.* It must include elements that are in their interests and these must be clearly communicated to them.

In the Eurofreeze Option 5, it would appear that at this stage the company had given no significant thought to this important matter. This is a serious weakness in this option.

Key strategic principles

●   In examining whether an option is feasible internally, the four main areas to explore are human resources, technical skills, financial resources and marketing and sales resources.

●   Feasibility external to the organisation is also an important test. Customer and competitor reactions to a proposed new strategy will be major constraints in the selection process.

●   Where strategy has not been discussed in advance with employees, their degree of commitment may also be a constraint. The new strategy needs to be communicated clearly and in a way that challenges and motivates staff.

16.4 BUSINESS RISK

The Japanese strategist, Kenichi Ohmae, comments that when companies are working out their strategies, they may start by thinking of all the things that cannot be done – that is, the constraints. If the company then merely asks itself what possibilities remain, it may be unable to break out of the existing situation.[21] Yet business risk is involved in most worthwhile strategy development. The important aspects are:

●   to make an explicit *assessment* of the risks;

●   to explore the *contingencies* that will lessen the difficulties, if things go wrong;

●   to decide whether the risks are *acceptable* to the organisation.

There is no single method of assessing risk in the organisation, but there are a number of techniques that may assist the process:

1 Financial risk analysis

2 Sensitivity analysis

3 Scenario projections

4 Simulation modelling.

16.4.1 Financial risk analysis[22]

For most strategy proposals in both the private and public sectors, it is important to undertake some form of analysis of the financial risks involved in strategy options. There are a number of types of analysis that can be undertaken:

- *Cash flow analysis*. This is essential. An organisation can report decent levels of profitability at the same time as going bankrupt through a lack of cash. Each option needs to be assessed for its impact on cash flow in the organisation.

- *Breakeven analysis*. This is often a useful approach: it calculates the volume sales required to recover the initial investment in the business. It is important to explore whether this volume is reasonable or not (*see* Chapter 15). Breakeven analysis of the main options at Eurofreeze would be useful.

- *Company borrowing requirements*. The impact of some strategies may severely impact on the funds needed from financial institutions and shareholders. This area was explored in Chapter 9 and represents a real area of risk for strategy analysis.

- *Financial ratio analysis*. Liquidity, asset management, stock holding and similar checks on companies can be usefully undertaken. It might be argued that these analyses are not needed since the company should already have this information. But what about key suppliers? And key customers? The knock-on effects of bankruptcy in one of these, when the company itself is stretched financially, deserve consideration (*see* Chapter 9).

For international activities, there is one other area that is also important – *currency analysis*. A major shift in currencies can wipe out the profitability of an overseas strategy option overnight (or, more optimistically, increase it). A number of major companies have discovered the impact of this over the last few years. Specialist help may be required.

16.4.2 Sensitivity analysis

This is a most useful form of analysis and would be regarded as part of the basic strategy process in many organisations. Essentially, it explores the 'What if...?' questions for their impact on the strategy under investigation. The basic assumptions behind each option – for example, economic growth, pricing, currency fluctuation, raw material prices, etc. – are varied and the impact measured on ROCE, cash and other company objectives. The key factors for success may be used to identify the major factors that need to be considered.

The sensitivity of each of these factors, as they are affected by arbitrary variations, is then assessed in order to determine which are crucial. For example at the Stora company in Chapter 4, it was shown that *price* variations of an arbitrary plus or minus 5 per cent had over double the impact on profit compared to *volume* variations of the same amount (*see* Table 4.4). Those variations that turn out to be particularly sensitive can then be re-examined carefully before the strategy is accepted. They can also be monitored after the strategy has been put into operation.

For example, the key assumptions on which the Eurofreeze Option 5 is built might be tested by examining what would happen if they varied:

- What impact would result if Refrigor carried on with its current rate of investment? This is quite a specific question and the answer could be used to assess the strategy.

- What impact would there be if there were only limited cost savings available in the industry? Perhaps only another 10 per cent cost savings instead of the 20 per cent assumed in the plan? Again a specific calculation could be undertaken to test the sensitivity of this change.

- What impact would there be if market leadership was not achieved? Perhaps the simplest calculation would be to assume that the two companies ended up with equal shares and to work out the result on that basis. The sensitivity to share variation could then be assessed.

Clearly, the results of all sensitivity analyses can provide those selecting the strategies with a useful estimate of the risks involved.

16.4.3 Scenario projections

Scenario analysis was explored in Chapter 3 and is useful here. Building scenarios are less concerned with the *most likely* picture of the future, but rather with *contrasting* pictures of the future.

> 'Ideally a scenario should be a description of a possible future in which social, political, economic and technological developments evolve in an internally consistent order.'[23]

Readers are referred back to Chapter 3 for a further discussion.

16.4.4 Simulation modelling

Simulation modelling involves the use of statistical and other econometric techniques on the variables involved in strategy to predict the outcomes of future strategy options. With the complexity that is evident in much of corporate strategy, it is unlikely that simulation modelling will be able to produce major evaluative results at the present time. There are three major difficulties:

- the difficulty in generating high-quality data not only for the target option but also for the major competitor;

- the problem of including non-quantified but vital elements of strategy associated with human resources;

- the need to over-simplify the inter-relationships between the elements in order to model them, thus making the model of limited value.

However, these represent issues to be resolved over time. There are already some useful models in economic and financial modelling that provide evidence of what may be possible. The PIMS Database has also been used in recent years to investigate these areas using multiple regression analysis on up to 20 different factors. For these reasons, there is a case for using simulation modelling in some circumstances alongside other methods in the assessment of business risk.

Key strategic principles

- Business risk assessment is important for strategy selection. It usually includes an analysis of financial risks, especially cash and the impact on the organisation's borrowing requirements.

- Sensitivity analysis examines the impact of variations in the immediate assumptions underlying the evaluation. It is usually undertaken in the form of an optimistic assessment and a pessimistic assessment.

- Scenarios can also be built up to take a broader view of the way the future may change. They can be used to explore future possibilities in qualitative as well as quantitative terms.

- Simulation modelling using computers has not yet been able to replicate the complex decisions needed in corporate strategy. Nevertheless, it has been used successfully in some situations. There is a case for employing it alongside other methods of risk assessment.

16.5 STAKEHOLDER INTERESTS

As was explored in Chapter 12, different stakeholders may have different interests and perspectives – for example, shareholders in increased dividends, employees in job preservation. Hence each group may not find all strategic options equally attractive.

One way of resolving this issue is to *prioritise* the stakeholder interests – for example, by putting the shareholders' interests first and raising dividends, cutting costs and possibly even sacking some workers. Some writers and companies would have no hesitation in pursuing this route, but it may be over-simplistic for corporate strategy.

Three examples will demonstrate the point:

1 Where major banks have significant shareholdings in a company, their interests may be better served by options that preserve their holdings and current risks rather than strategic options that extend these: for example, the Spanish banks, Banesto and Banco Central, were reported to have followed these policies during the privatisation of the Spanish oil industry in 1990–91.[24]

2 When the co-operation of employees is essential for the implementation of a strategic option, it may be that it is necessary for the option to be attractive to them. For example, the acquisition of Lotus Software by the major US computer company, IBM, in 1995 was accompanied by an IBM strategy to retain the Lotus employees who were a crucial asset of the company.[25]

3   When the organisation is government-owned or funded, then there will also be keen interest in the strategies that are being pursued and their implications for government policy – for example, the legitimate interests of the French government in its relationships with its major French suppliers of defence equipment, Aerospatiale and Dassault.

These areas need to be carefully considered in the context of evaluation criteria with such questions as:

1   Will the strategy option have high and unacceptable levels of *financial risk*? How will the shareholders react?

2   Does the option involve an increase or reduction in *employment levels*?

3   Will there be a need for *management* to be recruited or made redundant?

4   Are there any broader community issues such as *environmental 'green' issues*? Will these make the strategy unattractive to local or national citizens?

5   What is the likely *government* response to the new proposals?

As with the other items raised above, these examples have implications for the attractiveness of the strategy options to interested stakeholders.

Key strategic principles

- Stakeholders also need to be assessed for their reactions to major strategy initiatives. It may be necessary to prioritise the interests of stakeholders: shareholders may or may not come first.

- Stakeholder reactions need to be assessed under at least five headings: financial risks for shareholders, employment levels for employees, management opportunities or redundancies, broader community issues such as pollution, the government response to strategy initiatives.

16.6 INTERNATIONAL CORPORATE STRATEGY SELECTION[26]

Strategy selection across international boundaries is more complex because additional factors such as currency, national cultures, tariff barriers and other matters need to be considered. These aspects have been explored in previous chapters.

Probably the single most important aspect from a selection perspective is to clarify the *objectives* for international expansion. This will provide the direction for the development and selection of the relevant international activities. In practice, there are many variations. Exhibit 16.3 contains some examples of possible links between international objectives and strategic choice.

In international strategy it is difficult to find a basic pattern and logic for such developments in order to facilitate their selection. There are three significant areas:[27]

- the possible need for a global strategy;

- the possible need to be responsive to national interests;

- the history and culture of the organisation.

Exhibit 16.3		Two examples of the connection between international objectives and strategy selection
1	Objective	International expansion because the home market is mature
	Key factors for success	Include economies of scale
	Implication	Retain home-base production to obtain increased economies of scale
	Strategy choice	Select low-cost strategy based on production economies of scale from home-base factory and then export production
	Example	BMW car production is still based largely in Germany, but sales are international
2	Objective	International expansion because trade barriers are high
	Key factors for success	Need to obtain distribution inside the barrier, as well as economies of scale in production
	Implication	Need to set up manufacturing operation inside trade barrier
	Strategy choice	Select country that represents a useful entry point behind the trade barriers, but also allows good communications with the home country
	Example	Nissan and Toyota cars have set up operations in the UK and Spain behind the trade barriers represented by the European Union

Global strategy Global strategy may result from two main sources:

- *Components or complete products may be more economically manufactured on a global basis.* This was explored in Chapter 10. It is often the case in the consumer electronics industry where there are considerable cost savings by manufacturing labour-intensive items in countries with low labour costs, such as some Asian countries. Companies such as Sony (Japan) and Philips (Netherlands) now operate in this way.

- *Customer demand may be essentially the same around the world.* Companies such as Coca-Cola (US) and Nike (US) make products that are essentially branded in the same way in all countries. This was explored in Chapter 6.

Responsiveness to national interests This clearly pulls in the opposite direction to the pressure for global activity. There are three main reasons contributing to this:

- *Customer tastes may vary between countries.* This was examined in Chapter 6.

- *National governments may be concerned that the interests of their countries are better served by some variation special to that country.* This was explored in Chapter 4.

- *Different technical standards, different legislation and other social issues may make it essential to produce products especially for a specific country.* For example, it is still necessary for cars to be produced especially for the UK and Ireland because of the rule that traffic drives on the left.

The history and culture of the organisation This may make it difficult or easy to undertake agreed international policies depending on the organisation's background. This was explored in Chapter 8. For example:

- A company that has acquired another outside its home country may have to live with the need to continue to satisfy its newly purchased local management and provide some local autonomy to its new subsidiary.

- By contrast, the company that has set up an overseas operation from the beginning may have taken longer over the process, but will have been able to recruit, train and develop its people in exactly the way that it wishes without any previous history.

In practice, many supposedly global initiatives also need to incorporate significant national responsiveness. Even companies like Coca-Cola, Walt Disney and McDonald's provide some local variations in tastes, languages or national menu items respectively. The difficult strategic choice is often to find the *balance* between global expansion and local responsiveness. The global/national issues are summarised in Table 16.7.

Some companies may face pressures for *both* a global strategy *and* for national responsiveness. Some companies may face *neither* of these pressures but still see opportunities to sell their products or services internationally.

Table 16.7 The balance between global expansion and national responsiveness

Pressure for global strategy	*These are not mutually exclusive* ◄—— ——►	*Pressure for international strategy but also responsiveness to national variations*
• Global or multinational customers		• Differing customers or customer segments by nation or region
• Global or multinational competitors		• Differing competitors or distributors by nation or region
• High levels of investment or technology that need large sales for recovery, e.g. in production, branding or R&D		• Need to adapt product extensively to meet national needs
• Need to cut costs by seeking low labour sources		• Pressure from governments for national activity, e.g. tariff or quota restrictions on global activity
• Global sourcing of raw materials or energy		• National purchasing of key supplies essential

As a result of such considerations, some specific international strategies have been identified. They are given various titles with the following being representative:

- *Multicountry strategy*. This targets individual countries or groups of countries according to their customer potential and competitor presence. International co-ordination is secondary to a country-by-country expansion programme. For example, Danône (France) has marketed biscuits across Europe according to the local expansion opportunities rather than using a pan-European brand.

- *International low-cost strategy*. This sources production where production costs are lowest and then sells globally. For example, Philips (Netherlands) manufactures radios in Hong Kong and sells them in Europe.

- *International niche strategy*. The same product is sold in the same market niche in all countries of the world. For example, Dunhill (UK) and Yves St Laurent (France) products are presented in the same upmarket fashion in all countries.

- *International combination strategy*. Regions of the world will have their own production and there will be some regional or national variation in the products made and marketed, but the global underpinning of strategy is clear. For example, most car companies such as Toyota (Japan) and General Motors (US) follow such a strategy.

There are other strategy variations that may also be chosen.

In some of the literature, there is little consideration of the real strategic difficulties faced by organisations as a result of *history and cultural* influences. These can have a significant effect on strategic choice. For example even at international companies like Walt Disney pictures and Renault cars, the senior management is largely North American and French respectively. More recently, several authors[28] have produced useful analyses on this subject. The general conclusion seems to be that much of the key strategic decision making still remains centred on the home country, even if national responsiveness is needed. There is a need to consider these matters when international strategic selection is being undertaken.

Key strategic principles

- International strategy selection is more complex. The starting point is clarity on the objectives and reasons for international expansion.

- In international strategy it is difficult to find a basic pattern and logic for such developments in order to facilitate their selection. There are three significant areas: the possible need for a global strategy, the responsiveness to national interests, the history and culture of the organisation.

- The need for a global strategy is often contrasted with the need for national responsiveness. However, there are some circumstances where both may be required. Even for many so-called global products, there is often a need to provide some degree of local variation.

- The history of an organisation and its cultural values will have a significant impact on the strategic choice and also the way that the organisation is managed. It is important to consider these matters when international strategic selection is being undertaken.

Eurofreeze evaluates its strategy options – 3

With its mission and objectives defined, this case study now examines the strategy options that were available to Eurofreeze and the important strategic decisions that would follow.

Future strategy options for Eurofreeze

The company was now considering a number of strategy options. It had undertaken the basic analysis using a cost of capital of 9 per cent. To consider the options, it gathered basic market data for its own products and those of its main competitor,

Table 16.8 Market data on the European frozen products market 1995

	Eurofreeze		Refrigor		Market growth of product category	
	Sales US$ m	Market share of product category (%)	Sales US$ m	Market share of product category (%)	1995/94	2004/2003
Branded vegetables and fruit	400	10	800	20	+2%	–
Private label vegetables and fruit	200	5	300	7.5	+2%	
Branded meat & fish	300	30	200	20	+4%	+6%
Private label meat & fish	150	15	100	10	+4%	+6%
Branded savoury dishes including pizza	30	6	80	16	+8%	+5%
Private label savoury dishes including pizza	none	–	40	8	+8%	+5%
Branded cakes and gateaux	25	12	25	12	+9%	+6%
Private label cakes and gateaux	none	–	20	9.6	+9%	+6%

The European frozen foods market: portfolio matrices for Eurofreeze and Refrigor

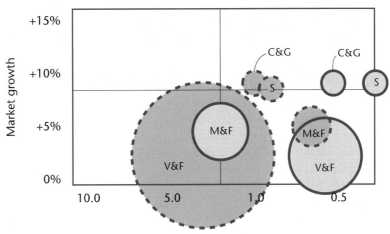

Relative market share (log scale)

Diameter of circle proportionate to size of sales for each company in that product category.

Eurofreeze

Refrigor

V&F = Vegetables and Fruit
S = Savoury
C&G = Cakes and Gateaux
M&F = Meat and Fish

Table 16.9 Summary of the Eurofreeze strategy options

Option	Implication for sales
1 Stop selling branded and own label vegetables and fruit	Sales decline US$400m in Year 1, US$200m in Year 2
2 Stop selling branded vegetables and fruit but continue own label	Sales decline US$400m in Year 1
3 Extend specialist branded food ranges, e.g. pizza and gateaux	Sales gain US$50m each year
4 Major cutback of range in first two years, then rebuild specialist areas from Year 4 onwards	Sales decline US$205m in Year 1, US$300m in Years 2 and 3.
	Sales gain US$50m in Year 4, US$100m in each year from Year 5 onwards
5 Become lowest cost producer through major investment	Build sales by at least US$100m per annum

CASE STUDY 16.2 continued

Refrigor. The information covered all its main European markets and is shown in Table 16.8. Within the product groups, there was little useful additional information: product sales data was available on individual items, but it varied so much by country and by store chain that there was little to be gained from analysing it.

Refrigor was market leader in vegetables and fruit. Eurofreeze was market leader in branded meat and fish dishes with Refrigor second. Neither company was market leader in savoury dishes (including pizza) or gateaux. (McCain was leader in savoury dishes with a 30 per cent share and Sara Lee in gateaux with a 25 per cent share.)

The company undertook a Portfolio Analysis in 1995. This is shown as Fig 16.6. The calculation of the relative market shares for this analysis is shown in the Appendix at the end of the chapter.

Eurofreeze then proceeded to consider each of the options that were available to it. The results are outlined below. (There could be some further combination of options but it was felt that the following reflected the main routes available to the company.)

The strategic options available to Eurofreeze are summarised in Table 16.9; their financial implications are then explored in the following text.

Option 1
Stop supplying all basic frozen products including its branded and own brand (that is, with the retailer's private brand name) vegetables. Dropping this range would mean that the overhead contribution made by carrying these products would no longer be available to the group. The financial implications are shown in Table 16.10.

Option 2
Cancel its current branded range of basic frozen food products such as vegetables, but continuing to manufacture own brand versions. This would keep some overhead contribution but would have very low added value. At the same time, the company would keep and slowly extend its range of higher added value branded items. (*See* financial implications in Table 16.11.)

Table 16.10 Financial projection for Option 1 (US$ millions)

	Current	Projected on option										Option 1
	1995	1996	1997	1998	1999	2000	2001	2002	2003	2004	2005	NPV*
Sales	600	200	–	–	–	–	–	–	–	–	–	–
Incremental profit impact	24	(5)	(8)	(8)	(8)	(8)	(8)	(8)	(8)	(8)	(8)	(48.6)**
Capital impact: working capital	–	10***	20***	–	–	–	–	–	–	–	–	26.0****
Capital impact: fixed capital	–	–	–	–	–	–	–	–	–	–	–	

Note: Current position shows the situation for the option only. All other sales and profits operate as previously.
* NPV = Net Present Value at 9% cost of capital 1995 = (5) x 0.917 + (8) x 0.842 + (8) x 0.772 + etc.
** Net effect of lower sales and some lower overheads, but freezer transport and warehousing would still be needed for other products.
*** Working capital no longer required to support sales.
**** US$26m working capital released from lower sales when discounted back to base year 1995.

Table 16.11 Financial projection for Option 2 (US$ millions)

	Current	Projected on option										Option 2
	1995	1996	1997	1998	1999	2000	2001	2002	2003	2004	2005	NPV
Sales	600	200	200	200	200	200	200	200	200	200	200	–
Incremental profit impact*	24	(5)	(6)	(6)	(6)	(6)	(6)	(6)	(6)	(6)	(6)	(37.6)
Capital impact: working capital	–	8**	12**	–	–	–	–	–	–	–	–	17.4
Capital impact: fixed capital	–	–	–	–	–	–	–	–	–	–	–	–

Note: Current position shows the situation for the option only. All other sales and profits operate as previously.

* Highly efficient to deliver own label to few supermarkets with no branded advertising. However, this is offset by the need to continue to deliver branded savoury, meat and fish dishes to all outlets.

** Reduction in working capital proportionately larger on smaller outlets: US$17.4m released.

Option 3

Drive hard to redevelop and substantially extend some specialist branded ranges, for example, its range of frozen cakes and gateaux and its market-leader range of meat and fish products. This would take time and resources but would produce higher added value. It would keep its broader range of branded products, including its low value-added items, as long as they made a contribution to overheads. (*See* financial implications in Table 16.12.)

Option 4

Become a specialist producer. This would be done by dropping almost all of its low added value basic range, closing a number of freezer factories, contracting out its freezer distribution, investing heavily in specialist menu ranges, advertising these ranges only. Clearly this is a more radical solution, but would emulate the success of several US companies across Europe such as McCain and Sara Lee. (*See* Table 16.13 for financial implications.)

Table 16.12 Financial projection for Option 3 (US$ millions)

	Current	Projected on option										Option 3
	1995	1996	1997	1998	1999	2000	2001	2002	2003	2004	2005	NPV
Sales	1105	1150	1200	1250	1300	1350	1400	1450	1500	1550	1600	–
Incremental profit impact*	80	(5)	(5)	4	6	8	10	12	14	14	14	35.7
Capital impact: working capital	–	(2.5)**	(2.5)	(2.5)	(2.5)	(2.5)	(2.5)	(2.5)	(2.5)	(2.5)	(2.5)	(16.0)
Capital impact: fixed capital***	–	–	(5)	–	(10)	–	–	–	–	–	–	(11.3)

Note: In this option, the current column considers total sales and profits because they will all be affected by the option.

* Net effect of increase in sales less the branded expenditure needed to achieve this.

** Steadily increasing sales so extra working capital required.

*** Some new capital investment required in plant and equipment to handle extra sales.

CASE STUDY 16.2 continued

Table 16.13 Financial projection for Option 4 (US$ millions)

	Current	Projected on option										Option 4
	1995	1996	1997	1998	1999	2000	2001	2002	2003	2004	2005	NPV
Sales	1105	900	600	600	650	700	800	850	900	1000	1200	–
Incremental profit impact*	80	(50)	(100)	(40)	(20)	10	30	100	225	250	300	258.7
Capital impact: working capital	–	10	30	–	(2.5)	(2.5)	(5)	(2.5)	(2.5)	(5)	(10)	19.0
Capital impact: fixed capital**	–	(50)	(100)	(50)	–	(50)	–	–	–	–	–	(201.1)

Note: In this option, the current column considers total sales and profits because they will all be affected by the option.
* Quite difficult to calculate the profit impact with certainty: need to explore detailed projections for each major product area but not presented above for reasons of space.
** Need to provide for factory closure costs and, in year 2000, for factory reinvestment.

Option 5
Becoming the lowest cost producer. This would be done by building on existing sales to all major customers: major investment in new factories, new warehouses and new transport networks would be needed. This would be coupled with major (and largely unknown) manufacturing innovation, all with the aim of reducing costs, so that they would move below those of its competitor, Refrigor. Although this option was available in theory, it was based on three assumptions that carried some risk:

- Refrigor would slow down its current rate of investment and allow itself to be overtaken.
- Major cost savings of the order of 20 per cent below existing costs were still available in the industry.

Table 16.14 Financial projection for Option 5 (US$ millions)

	Current	Projected on option										Option 5
	1995	1996	1997	1998	1999	2000	2001	2002	2003	2004	2005	NPV
Sales	1105	1400	1500	1600	1800	2000	2200	2400	2600	2800	3000	–
Incremental profit impact*	80	5	5	10	12	20	30	40	50	60	70	160.0
Capital impact: working capital	–	(15)	(5)	(5)	(10)	(10)	(10)	(10)	(10)	(10)	(10)	(60.7)
Capital impact: fixed capital**	–	(100)	(300)	(150)	(50)	(50)	–	(200)	–	(200)	–	(729.4)

Note: In this option, the current column considers total sales and profits because they will all be affected by the option.
* Profit attempts to take into account the increased move to build higher value-added products less the extra advertising and promotional costs to support these, especially in the early years.
** Substantial investment in new factories and other facilities will be required.

- Market leadership could be gained through a low-cost route.

For this option, it was recognised that it would also be necessary to provide substantial extra advertising and promotional support to sustain and build the brands. Overall, this was the option with the highest investment. (*See* Table 16.14.)

CASE QUESTIONS

1   *What are the relative merits and problems of each option?*

2   *In what way does the use of the portfolio matrix help the strategic debate? And in what way might it mislead the strategic decisions?*

3   *Consider what other strategic analytical tools, if any, might provide useful insights into the strategic choice debate: you might wish to consider a PEST Analysis, a Five Forces Analysis, generic strategies, a Market Options Matrix, value chain, innovations checklist (in Chapter 11).*

4   *Which option would you recommend to Eurofreeze? Give reasons for your choice and explain the strengths and weaknesses of your choice.*

■ SUMMARY

- The chapter explores some aspects of strategy choice in greater depth.

- The outcomes of strategy proposals are uncertain and so *business judgement* needs to be applied in the selection of strategy.

- Some guidance is provided on strategy evaluation by an analysis of generic industry environments, giving two broad categories: the stage of industry maturity and the competitive position of the organisation. After identifying the organisation's position according to these two parameters, simple choices then suggest themselves.

- Further guidance on appropriate strategies for specific types of industry have identified: fragmented industries, emerging industries, mature markets and declining markets.

- *Empirical evidence* based on the PIMS Database relates strategic actions to their results in terms of profitability and other criteria. High quality and strong market share can make a positive contribution to profitability. High capital intensity is less likely to do so. Some researchers doubt the cause and effect relationships here. Acquisitions and mergers have also been studied for their impact on profitability, suggesting that many are unsuccessful. In some circumstances, diversification may be a successful strategy.

- The chapter then explored the *feasibility of options*. It considered the subject from three perspectives: internal, external and the need for management commitment. In examining whether an option is feasible internally, the four main areas to explore are: human resources, technical skills, financial resources and marketing and sales resources. Feasibility external to the organisation is also an important issue: customer and competitor reactions to a proposed new strategy will be major constraints in the selection process. Where management has not discussed a strategy in advance with employees, their degree of commitment may also become a constraint. The new strategy needs to be communicated clearly and in a way that challenges and motivates staff.

● Business risk assessment is also important in strategy selection. This usually includes an analysis of financial risks. Risk can be assessed by using:

1 Sensitivity analysis, which examines the impact of variations in the assumptions underlying the evaluation, usually in the form of optimistic and pessimistic assessments;

2 Scenarios, which can be built up to take a broad view of future change in qualitative and quantitative terms;

3 Simulation modelling, which uses computers, has been successful in some situations, but cannot yet replicate complex corporate strategy decision-making requirements.

● *Stakeholders* also need to be assessed for their reactions to major strategy initiatives, and to ascertain whether or not their interests should be prioritised, e.g. shareholders may or may not come first. Stakeholder reactions need to be assessed under at least five headings: financial risks for shareholders, employment levels for employees, management opportunities or redundancies, broader community issues such as pollution, and the government response to the strategy initiatives.

● *International strategy selection* is more complex, and the objectives and reasons for international expansion must first be clarified. The difficulty in international strategy is to find some basic pattern and logic for such developments in order to facilitate their selection. There are three significant areas: global strategy, responsiveness to national interests and the history and culture of the organisation.

● Even for many so-called global products, there is often a need to provide some degree of local variation. The history of an organisation and its culture values will have a significant impact on its management and on the strategic choice.

QUESTIONS

1 A well-known German company is primarily engaged in supplying motor components such as car radios and gear changes to car companies in the European Union, such as Ford and Toyota. It is considering acquiring a medium-size US company as the basis for its first expansion outside Europe. What would you advise in this relatively mature and fiercely competitive industry?

2 When considering new, fast growing markets such as that for mobile telephones, the ADL Matrix would suggest that weak and dominant companies face quite different strategic opportunities and problems. Is this really true when the market is changing so rapidly?

3 When markets are mature or declining at home, one possible strategy is to expand internationally. What problems are associated with this approach? What alternatives are available? How would you advise a medium-size manufacturer of tables and chairs currently engaged in the home market only?

4 Should the firm or the industry be the prime focus for strategy? Give reasons for your views.

5 Consider the implications of Table 16.1 for strategy in the multinational enterprise. Does the corporate centre matter?

6 What useful strategic guidance, if any, is provided for small businesses by the data from the PIMS Databank?

7 *'Merger and acquisition is the most common means of entry into new markets.'* Professor John Kay.

   What is the evidence of success from such ventures? What are the strategic implications of your answer for organisations considering this option?

8 Use the feasibility criteria to examine the changes at Nokia during the 1990s. What conclusions can you draw on the company's strategic activity?

9 Take an organisation with which you are familiar and consider the risks involved in doubling its size in terms of the number of people involved in the organisation. What would make the risk acceptable?

10 *'Most firms rarely engage in explicit formal strategy evaluation … rather, it is a continuing process that is difficult to separate from normal planning, reporting and control.'* Professor Richard Rumelt.

   Discuss the implications for the evaluation criteria explored in this chapter.

STRATEGIC PROJECT

Strategy evaluation and selection in small companies

The world watch and clock industry contains many small companies as well as some large industry giants. The strategic problems faced by small companies in fragmented markets deserve careful consideration: there are far more smaller companies in the world than there are large multinational enterprises. You might like to consider the strategy option and evaluation process in small companies. How can such companies survive and grow? What strategies are particularly useful and what should be avoided?

FURTHER READING

On generic strategy environments: Porter, M E (1990) *Competitive Strategy*, The Free Press, Harvard, Chs 9 to 13.

On the PIMS Databank: Buzzell, R and Gale, B T (1987) *The PIMS Principles*, The Free Press, New York.

On feasibility and other criteria: Professor Richard Rumelt's article 'The Evaluation of Business Strategy'. This was originally published in 1980 but has been republished in two more recent texts: De Wit, Bob and Meyer, R (1994) *Strategy: process, content and context*, West Publishing and Mintzberg, H and Quinn, J B (1991) *The Strategy Process*, Prentice Hall, New York.

On international issues: *see* the articles mentioned in Reference 27.

APPENDIX

Calculation of relative market shares for portfolio analysis in Case study 16.2

For Eurofreeze *Vegetables and fruit*: $(10\% + 5\%) \div (20\% + 7.5\%) = 0.54$
(Note that these could be redefined as separate branded and private product categories. Given the low added value from both routes, this has not been undertaken here. There are no clear rules.)

Meat and fish: $(30\% + 15\%) \div (20\% + 10\%) = 1.5$

Savoury dishes: $6\% \div 30\% = 0.2$
(Note that McCain is market leader in this category and it is this share that has been used.)

Cakes and gateaux: $12\% \div 25\% = 0.48$
(Note that Sara Lee is market leader in this category and it is this share that has been used.)

For Refrigor *Vegetables and fruit*: $(20\% + 7.5\%) \div (10\% + 15\%) = 1.83$

Meat and fish: $(20\% + 10\%) \div (30\% + 15\%) = 0.67$

Savoury dishes: $(18\% + 6\%) \div 30\% = 0.8$

Cakes and gateaux: $(12\% + 9.6\%) \div 25\% = 0.86$

REFERENCES

1 References for Swatch case: *Economist*: 18 Apr 1992, p90. *Financial Times*: 15 June 1990; 10 June 1991; 20 July 1992, p32; 26 Feb 1994, p13; 9 Nov 1994, p33; 9 Dec 1994, p25; Survey 18 Apr 1996.
2 This section is based on Porter, M E (1980) *Competitive Strategy*, The Free Press, Boston, Mass, Chs 9 to 13. The comments on leaders and followers also draw on Kotler, P (1994) *Marketing Management*, 8th edn, Prentice Hall International, New Jersey, Ch 15.
3 Porter, M E (1980) Ibid, p191.
4 © Arthur D Little, Inc (1997).
5 This short section and the one that follows on ageing markets hardly does justice to some insightful research and literature in this area. McKiernan and Baden-Fuller, C and Stopford, J (1992) *Rejuvenating the Mature Business*, Routledge, London, attempt to make amends. Also McKiernan, P (1992) *Strategies of Growth*, Routledge, London.
6 Baden-Fuller, C and Stopford, J (1992) Ibid, Ch 2. Republished in De Wit, B and Meyer, R (1994) *Strategy: process, content and context*, West Publishing, Minn, p405.
7 This section relies heavily on Buzzell, R and Gale, B T (1987) *The PIMS Principles*, The Free Press, Boston, Mass, plus other researchers that are individually acknowledged below.
8 Rumelt, R (1991) 'How much does industry matter?', *Strategic Management Journal*, Mar, pp64–75, John Wiley, New York.
9 *Source*: Rumelt, R (1991) Ibid.
10 Described in Buzzell, R and Gale, B T (1987) Ibid.
11 *Source*: PIMS Associates Ltd, London. © PIMS Associates Ltd 1996.

12 *Source*: PIMS (1991) 'Marketing: in pursuit of the perfect mix', *Marketing Magazine*, London, 31 Oct. © PIMS Associates Ltd 1991.

13 *Source*: PIMS Associates Ltd, London. © PIMS Associates Ltd 1996.

14 This section relies essentially on the work and data in Kay, J (1993) *The Foundations of Corporate Success*, Oxford University Press, Ch 10.

15 Mueller, D (1980) *The determinants and effects of merger: an international comparison*, Oelschlager, Gunn and Hain, quoted in Kay, J (1993) *Foundations of Corporate Success*, Oxford University Press.

16 Compiled by Kay, J (1993) Ibid.

17 This section relies heavily on the useful summary of research findings prepared and reviewed by Johnson, G and Scholes, K (1993) *Exploring Corporate Strategy*, 3rd edn, Prentice Hall, Hemel Hempstead, pp268–70.

18 *Sources*: Carnegy, H (1995) 'Scared of growing fat and lazy', *Financial Times*, 10 July, p11. For earlier data and comment on Nokia, *see* Lynch, R (1994) *European Business Strategies*, 2nd edn, Kogan Page, London, p151.

19 *See* Chapter 2 for details.

20 Rumelt, R (1980) 'The evaluation of business strategy', pp359–67 in *Business Policy and Strategic Management*, 3rd edn, McGraw-Hill, New York.

21 Ohmae, K (1982) *The mind of the strategist*, Penguin, Harmondsworth, p86.

22 For a more detailed treatment of this topic, *see* Glautier, M W E and Underdown, B (1994) *Accounting Theory and Practice*, 5th edn, Pitman Publishing, London, Chs 28 and 29.

23 Leemhuis, J P (1990) 'Using scenarios to develop strategies at Shell', Ch 13 in Taylor, B and Harrison, J (eds) (1990) *The Managers' Casebook of Business Strategy*, Butterworth–Heinemann, Oxford. *See* also Smith, R J (1994) *Strategic management and planning in the public sector*, Longman, Harlow, Essex.

24 Lynch, R (1993) *Cases in European Marketing*, Kogan Page, London, Ch 2.

25 Kehoe, L *et al* (1995) 'IBM's bid to hit the high notes', *Financial Times*, 6 June, p21 and 'The risks of adopting the Lotus position', *Financial Times*, 13 June, p21.

26 This section is based on Porter, M E (1980) Ibid, Ch 13; Thompson, A and Strickland, A (1993) *Strategic Management*, 7th edn, Irwin, Ill, pp136–7; Lynch, R (1994) *European Business Strategies*, 2nd edn, Kogan Page, London.

27 This section is based on the extensive research into international and global markets during the last 20 years. No single research paper has provided the basis for the typology used. Among the important papers consulted were: Hout, T, Porter, M E, Rudden, E (1982) 'How global companies win out', *Harvard Business Review*, Sep–Oct, p98; Hamel, G and Prahalad, C K (1985) 'Do you really have a global strategy?', *Harvard Business Review*, July–Aug, p139; Bartlett, C and Ghoshal, S (1989) *Managing across borders: The Transnational Corporation*, Harvard Business School Press, Boston, Mass; Prahalad, C K and Doz, Y (1986) 'The Dynamics of Global Competition', extracted from *The Multinational Mission*, The Free Press, NY. Reprinted in De Wit, B and Meyer, R (1994) Ibid; Doz ,Y (1986) *Strategic Management in Multinational Companies*, Pergamon Press, Oxford. Some of these articles are dated and do not reflect the latest field evidence. Their guidance has been updated in the comments in this text.

28 *See* Bartlett, C and Ghoshal, S (1989) *Managing across borders: The Transnational Corporation*, Harvard Business School Press, Boston, Mass. *See also* Turner, I and Henry, I (1994) 'Managing International Organisations: Lessons from the field', *European Management Journal*, Dec, p417.

Finding the strategic route forward

When you have worked through this chapter, you will be able to:

- understand and critically evaluate the arguments suggesting that the prescriptive model has limited validity;

- establish whether a single prescriptive strategy is appropriate for an organisation or whether an uncertainty-based, survival-based, learning-based or negotiated-based process is more appropriate;

- understand how bargaining and contracts in the decision-making process affect strategic outcomes;

- decide the extent to which a learning-based strategy is needed as part of an organisation's strategy process;

- assess the implications for the strategy process where an organisation operates internationally.

INTRODUCTION

The prescriptive model is probably the most widely-used representation of the corporate strategy process and appears in different forms in organisations in the private, public and not-for-profit sectors. Yet, in recent years, it has been the subject of increasing criticism by some corporate strategists. In this chapter we identify their main concerns, which are centred on the strategy process, and suggest alternative models to overcome these difficulties – the survival-based, uncertainty-based, learning-based and negotiation-based processes.

It is argued that it is the learning approach which needs to be added to prescriptive strategy in order to find the strategic route forward for any organisation. Finally, we examine the implications for those organisations with international involvement.

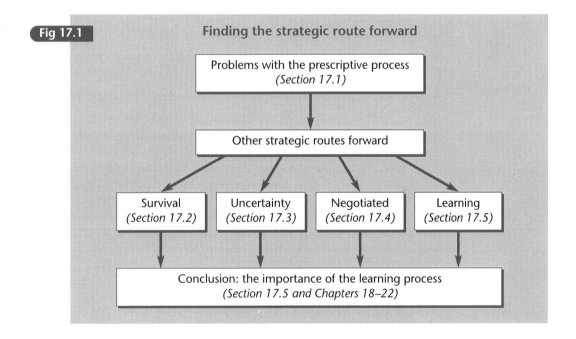

Fig 17.1   **Finding the strategic route forward**

Problems with the prescriptive process
(Section 17.1)

Other strategic routes forward

| Survival (Section 17.2) | Uncertainty (Section 17.3) | Negotiated (Section 17.4) | Learning (Section 17.5) |

Conclusion: the importance of the learning process
(Section 17.5 and Chapters 18–22)

How Honda came to dominate two major motorcycle markets

This case study describes how Honda Motorcycles achieved its dominant market share of the USA and UK markets. Although the strategic approach was originally seen as prescriptive, it was shown that, in reality, the strategies were much more emergent in their development.

During the period 1960–80, Honda Motorcycles (Japan) came to dominate motorcycle markets in the USA and UK. Professor Richard Pascale has researched and described two perspectives on the process that Honda used to develop its strategies over this period.[1] They resulted in Honda moving from zero market share to domination of the US and UK markets, leaving the home-based industries with only small, niche-based market shares.

Professor Pascale first examined a study undertaken by Boston Consulting Group for the UK motorcycle industry in 1975 on the strategic reasons for the success of Honda. Two key factors for the success of Honda were identified:

● An advantage in terms of Honda's economies of scale in technology, distribution and manufacturing.

● The loss to other companies of market share and profitability as a result of the Honda attack.

The diagnosis appeared to be an example of the classical model and its prescriptive solutions in action.

Professor Pascale then interviewed the Honda executives who had actually launched the motorcycles in the USA and subsequently in the UK. He discovered that Honda's strategy had at first been a failure and that it was as a result of sheer desperation that they had stumbled on the strategy that proved so successful. The executives at Honda had a full range of motorcycles that could be imported into the USA. They ranged from small scooters to very large machines. All were more reliable and had higher performance than equivalent US competitors.

Honda US initially tried to compete head-on against the US main competition by using their large machines. However, Japanese motorbikes lacked credibility in the US market against the well-known US brands, even though the Honda bikes were better. The launch programme was unsuccessful. By chance, Honda then tried to sell some small scooters into the US market purely for local transport. They were immediately

Honda: Four-year record

successful and provided the platform for Honda to launch its attack on the main motor-bike market several years later.

If corporate strategists had listened to the consulting company, they might have concluded that a major strategic initiative had been undertaken by Honda, based on careful strategic analysis and evaluation of options. But the reality was more haphazard and opportunistic, especially in the early days of the programme.

In conclusion, Pascale commented that Japanese managers at Honda and elsewhere did not use the term *strategy* to outline a *prescriptive* strategic plan. They were more inclined to see the process as providing an *emerging* process of trial-and-error, with the strategy evolving from experimentation as the process unfolded. According to his findings, Japanese companies were unlikely to develop a single strategy that was set to guide the company unerringly forward into the future.

In the Honda case, the strategy was developed from the managers in the market experimenting to find the most effective strategy. As each success was obtained, the Honda managers reported this back to Japan, with their ideas and suggestions for the next phase. There was frequent dialogue between Japan and the individual markets, with consensus being far more important to the emergence of the final strategy. Professor Pascale concluded that strategy needed to be redefined as:

> All the things necessary for the successful functioning of an organisation as an adaptive mechanism.

It should be noted, however, that during the 1980s Professor Toyohiro Kono repeatedly surveyed strategic planning in Japanese companies.[2] His conclusions suggested that, in large Japanese companies at least, there is rather more strategic planning than was observed by Professor Pascale. Other examples also exist that suggest that Japanese companies have now adopted some aspects of the prescriptive process, although there is still a strong element of experimentation and consensus in deriving the final plans.

CASE QUESTION

Does prescriptive strategy need to be modified or would it be better, as Pascale suggests, to redefine the strategic process completely?

17.1 PROBLEMS WITH THE PRESCRIPTIVE STRATEGIC MODEL

In the preceding chapters we have been using elements of the prescriptives model of corporate strategy to explain the process of strategy development, as this is the most common representation of the strategy process. However, there have been a number of criticisms of this approach in recent years.

17.1.1 The prescriptive process of corporate strategy

In describing their version of the prescriptive model, Wheelen and Hunger[3] state that the process of corporate strategy involves five major elements:

● *Environmental scanning.* The external opportunities and threats of the SWOT analysis.

- *Internal scanning.* The strengths and weaknesses of the SWOT analysis.
- *Strategy formulation.* Mission, objectives, strategies and policies.
- *Strategy implementation.* Including programmes, budgets and other procedures.
- *Evaluation and control.* Ensuring that the strategic process remains on its predicted path.

Some commentators on this classical model, such as Jauch and Glueck,[4] put the mission and objectives before environmental scanning. This book has taken the view that the process is circular and there is no single 'correct' sequence. Table 17.1 sets out a *typical* sequence for the classical model.[5]

The process in Table 17.1 is largely linear but with feedback mechanisms at various points to ensure that the objectives, analysis and strategies are all consistent with each other. It is shown in the table by the *arrow directions*, whose significance will become clearer when we examine alternative processes later in this chapter.

Table 17.1 The prescriptive model of the corporate strategy process

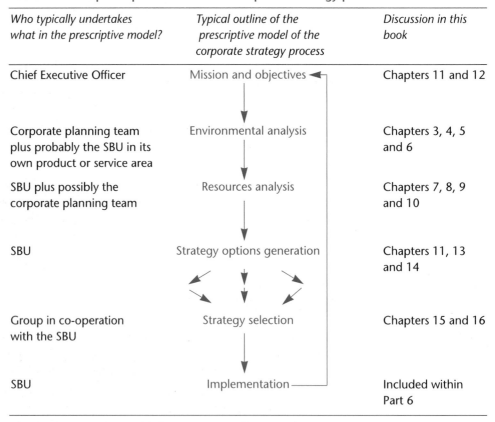

Who typically undertakes what in the prescriptive model?	Typical outline of the prescriptive model of the corporate strategy process	Discussion in this book
Chief Executive Officer	Mission and objectives	Chapters 11 and 12
Corporate planning team plus probably the SBU in its own product or service area	Environmental analysis	Chapters 3, 4, 5 and 6
SBU plus possibly the corporate planning team	Resources analysis	Chapters 7, 8, 9 and 10
SBU	Strategy options generation	Chapters 11, 13 and 14
Group in co-operation with the SBU	Strategy selection	Chapters 15 and 16
SBU	Implementation	Included within Part 6

Just as important as the precise sequence of events in the process is *who* undertakes them. This becomes particularly acute when the organisation consists of a group of industries that are possibly unrelated. In these circumstances, it is likely that there will be a corporate centre that might undertake some tasks and Strategic Business

Units (SBUs) that will undertake others. But who does what tasks? The SWOT analysis is usually undertaken at the corporate level and it is also the corporation that defines the overall mission and objectives. The reason is that only the corporation can have the overview needed to undertake these tasks. The results are then passed down for the strategy *option* process to be developed by the SBUs. The strategy *selection* might then be undertaken at corporate headquarters, in consultation with the SBU and in the context of the available funds that the group has at its disposal. The SBUs then implement the agreed strategies.

The process is therefore usually driven by corporate headquarters, on the basis that it is the only part of the organisation to have a complete picture of all aspects. Alfred Chandler,[6] one of the earliest writers and researchers on this approach, commented:

> *'Strategic plans can be formulated from below, but normally the implementation of such proposals requires the resources which only the general office* [i.e. the corporate HQ] *can provide. Within the broad policy lines laid down by that office and with the resources it allocates, the executives at the lower levels carry out tactical* [i.e. day-to-day, non-strategic] *decisions.'*

Although many companies around the world have adopted the classical process, there are a number of well-documented problems with this.

17.1.2 Some problems with the prescriptive process

There are a number of assumptions or simplifications in the prescriptive process that may not be valid in reality. We summarise four here, but other difficulties have been identified.

1 *Environment.* It is assumed that this is predictable, so that a clear direction can be used to develop the opportunities and threats to the organisation. There have, however, been numerous instances of major variations in the environment that make such a direction difficult to sustain (*see* Sections 17.2 and 17.3).

2 *Planning procedure.* It is assumed that the major strategic decisions are initiated by a clear planning procedure that, once set in motion, can arrive at a clear and simple decision point: the strategy selection. In many organisations, however, planning procedures are complicated by the need to persuade managers to undertake specific strategies. Managers may be reluctant for a variety of reasons, from a loss of power to a personality clash (*see* Section 17.4).

3 *Top-down procedures.* It is assumed that top-down procedures from corporate HQ to the SBUs represent the most efficient method of developing new and innovative strategies. It is assumed that they can cope with the environment and gain commitment from the managers who will implement them. However, many research studies have shown that managers find such a process demotivating; by contrast, the Honda case studies showed that frequent consultation and dialogue may be far more effective. This difficulty will be explored further (*see* Section 17.5).

4 *Culture.* It is assumed that the culture of the organisation will allow the classical model to operate. Culture here has two meanings: the style, beliefs and practices of

the organisation itself and, more broadly, the culture of the country in which the organisation operates. Both of these are assumed to be consistent with the top-down classical model. In practice, however, some cultures are clearly more suited to a dominant top-down approach than others. (The ABB case study in Chapter 18 provides an example of how the company's culture was actually changed.)

All the above assumptions have therefore been shown to have significant flaws.

Commenting on Japanese companies, Pascale concluded that the strict classical strategy development process was not the most effective method for developing superior strategy:

- a greater flow of ideas was needed;
- the 'top-down' process from HQ to SBUs needed to be a two-way dialogue;
- strategy needed to be above all adaptive to the environment.

Although we may be concerned that Pascale appears to generalise about all Japanese companies from the study of the one company, Honda, he has produced some useful evidence. Moreover, there is evidence from North America to support these conclusions. Marx[7] quotes the Chairman of the giant US corporation, General Electric, Mr Jack Welch, on the problems encountered in strategic planning in the 1960s using the classical process:

'Our planning system was dynamite when we first put it in. The thinking was fresh, the form mattered little – the format got no points. It was idea-oriented. We then hired a head of planning and he hired two vice-presidents and then he hired a planner, and the books got thicker and the printing got more sophisticated, and the covers got harder and the drawings got better. The meetings kept getting larger. Nobody can say anything with 16 or 18 people there.'

Welch became increasingly concerned over the whole planning process in GE and moved to change it. More recently, he has moved to comment on what he regards as a fundamental shift now taking place in the way information is made available in both large and small companies through electronics and computer networks.[8] General Electric has fundamentally changed the way it operates: 'boundaryless' management has taken over. Between individuals and across the many divisions of GE, from electric turbines to the NBC television networks, intellectual openness has been encouraged, involving the taking of ideas and sharing them with others. The former rigid bureaucracy had difficulty in selecting which strategy options to choose because the HQ had only limited information: boundaryless management has helped to open things up. However, HQ is still left with the task of making a choice. Jack Welch commented:

'Here at head office we don't go deep into much of anything, but we do have the smell of everything. Our job is capital allocation – intellectual and financial. Smell, feel, touch, listen and allocate. Make bets with people and dollars. And make mistakes – but we're big enough to make mistakes. Once you have the critical mass and the momentum, you can take a swing at everything.'

GE has annual sales of around US$70 billion.

Mr Welch has been concerned about three areas:

- the *bureaucracy* that may breed under classical strategy processes;
- the *judgement* required to make choices, which may not be as rational as a simple choice;
- the need to encourage a *culture of ideas*, rather than a top-down approach as in the classical strategy process.

Again, this is anecdotal evidence but it makes the point that there can be real problems with the classical strategy process. However, in the case of GE, it was easier for Mr Welch to make his comments because the company had been operating the prescriptive process for a number of years and was ripe for the changes that he introduced. For a company that was newer to the prescriptive process, the same arguments would not necessarily apply: they would not have the same level of skills and familiarity that had led to the problems encountered at GE.

17.1.3 Solutions to problems within the prescriptive process

To explore the solutions available within the prescriptive process, it is useful to have a careful survey of the difficulties encountered. One such survey in the early 1980s observed that the prescriptive model had become excessively rational, bureaucratic and formalised.[9] Certainly strategic planning procedures were needed in both large and small organisations, but there was a real danger that they would come to dominate, shape and ultimately to interfere with optimal strategic development processes. Four major forces were identified that might contribute to this deteriorating state:

1 Professionalising the strategic planning job by turning it into a science, rather than the art that it partly is.
2 Unqualified acceptance of techniques, so that their conclusions were misapplied or incorrectly drawn.
3 Pressures for administrative efficiency that tended to over-formalise and distort ideas and concepts which needed to be nurtured and grown.
4 Excessive emphasis on numerical data and quantification of material – the opposite of Jack Welch's 'smell, feel, touch' approach.

There are a number of ways to overcome these problems. They involve a more open strategic planning culture with less emphasis on quantification of data. Stress can also be laid on two aspects of the actual process:

- *Exploring the assumptions on which the strategy is based with the proposers of that strategy.* When such assumptions are incorrect, the whole strategy is open to doubt.
- *During the strategy review sessions, requesting a simple verbal summary of the main proposals.* If this could not be done, then the proposals themselves may be suspect.

The whole process and system by which a strategy is developed should also be re-examined periodically by the organisation: this is a *planning process audit*. The aim would be to remove the impediments that creep in over time.

17.1.4 Conclusion

Overall, prescriptive strategists are aware of the problems that the process causes. They may attempt to overcome them by revising the process and renewing it. They may try to undertake this by more radical measures involving a change to the culture of the company. However, there are still residual problems and some strategists favour more radical solutions than the prescriptive process.

Key strategic principles

- The prescriptive model of the strategic process is largely linear. It has feedback mechanisms at various points to ensure that objectives, options and strategy choice are consistent with each other.

- Problems with the prescriptive approach are in four main areas: environmental unpredictability; planning procedures; top-down approaches driven by the centre; and the culture that will allow the model to operate in the organisation.

- Specific criticisms include the need for more dialogue, a greater flow of ideas and more adaptation to the environment.

- It may be possible to solve these problems within the prescriptive process but some strategists take a more critical view.

CASE STUDY 17.1

Developing strategy in European telecommunications service companies

Over the next ten years, the European companies supplying telephone services will undergo profound change. Some will be winners and some losers. What strategy processes should they adopt to come out on top?

From 1998, Europe's market for voice telecommunications opens up for full competition (prior to this, only the market for data transmission has been open). Since data transmission accounted for only 10 per cent of the sales of these companies, the real impact will be felt only with the newly liberalised European voice telephone market of 1998. For many years the mainly state-run monopoly companies have provided the bulk of services. In 1998 the environment for all the main companies will therefore change radically through increased competition. The present leading European companies are shown in Table 17.2. From 1998, some of these companies will experience competition for the first time: for example, France Telecom and Deutsche Telecom. There are real problems on pricing and other strategic areas as competition opens up.[10] Even where there has been a more open market, there is likely to be room for further competition, e.g. British Telecom was privatised in 1981 but still held around 87 per cent of the UK market in 1995.

Table 17.2 Leading European telephone companies ranked by turnover

Company	Country	Turnover US$m (1992)	Ownership status
Deutsche Telekom	Germany	36 956	Partially privatised
France Telecom	France	23 005	Public
British Telecom	UK	20 645	Private
Telecom Italia*	Italy	17 500	Private
Telefonica de Espagna	Spain	11 430	Likely to be privatised in 1990s
Cable and Wireless	UK but turnover mainly outside Europe	9 647	Private
PTT Schweiz	Switzerland	6 500	Public
Televerket	Sweden	6 251	Likely to be privatised in 1990s
KPN	The Netherlands	6 050	Partially privatised

*Although SIP is publicly quoted, it is 60 per cent owned by STET, the forerunner of Telecom Italia, and is therefore not listed separately.
Source: Lynch, R: 1994[11]

Apart from the competitive situation, the more general environment in the 1990s was reasonably favourable. The European market was worth around US$120 billion and growing by at least 8 per cent per annum. It was also reasonably profitable, after allowing for the large capital sums being invested by all the main operators to upgrade their facilities and provide extra capacity. Demand was buoyant and was projected to remain so. In the longer term, there was the threat of increased competition, not only from each other but also from the cable TV companies, which were also installing telephone capacity capable of taking telephone calls at speeds higher than the specialist telecommunications companies.

The monopolies also faced an important pricing issue: they needed to *rebalance* their pricing structure. Monopolies such as Deutsche Telekom and France Telecom used profits on their international calls to subsidise local prices. During the years to 1998, the subsidy has had to be reduced to prevent companies such as British Telecommunications plc, which had already undertaken this exercise,

being able to pick off customers who made large numbers of international calls by giving prices that undercut the domestic operator.

Key factors for success in the existing telephone companies
These included:

- The need to persuade customers to use the telephone more often: the companies had heavy fixed investment in existing facilities that would benefit from increased usage, especially outside peak telephone periods.

- Capital funds for investment in modernising their systems.

- Every effort to counteract threats from the low-cost TV cable operators, satellite and, in some cases, mobile telephone companies.

- Preservation of their domestic (i.e. national) markets, which accounted for 80 to 95 per cent of their total revenues, in spite of the Single European Act 1986.

- The need to reduce their fixed-cost base through greater labour efficiencies and possibly through redundancies.
- Successful targeting of high-usage telephone customers, especially business users.

Strategies employed by the leading national operators

As most of the companies' revenues were derived from calls within a country which they dominated, their strategies were naturally divided into those inside and those outside the home country.

1 *Strategies for home markets.* Companies devised strategies to protect and defend the national markets where they were still the dominant supplier. They attempted to:

- increase the quality of service;
- negotiate longer contracts with leading customers, even if this meant lower prices;
- launch products to fill all conceivable market niches and leave no gaps for future competitors;
- reduce costs, especially labour costs, through restructuring prior to market liberalisation.

2 *Strategies for the rest of Europe and for global markets.* Outside the companies' home countries, competition was already more fierce by the mid-1990s. There was also high capital investment required to provide services beyond the home country, and their services were restricted to data only in the EU until 1998. It was therefore difficult to start services in a new country without incurring investment levels that could not be justified by the available business at that time. As a result, they negotiated to:

- build alliances and other forms of partnership (some examples are given below);
- open offices across Europe;
- target multinational companies who were seeking truly international services that were cheap and reliable and not dependent on one country.

- form a partnership with a leading *non-telephone* company in a target country as a base for expansion in that country. Some British Telecom (BT) examples are given below.

Examples of the type of links that developed outside the home country include:

- France Telecom, Deutsche Telecom and the US company, Sprint;
- BT with Telenor, Norway, and TeleDenmark, Denmark, against the national operator in Sweden;
- BT wth Banco Santander to provide data services in Spain;
- BT with a subsidiary of the major German company, Viag, to form Viag Interkom and serve business customers;
- BT with the leading Italian bank, Banca Nazionale del Lavoro, to target leading business customers;
- A four-way partnership between KPN, Telefonica, PTT Schweiz and Telia to form Unisource and provide international services.

It should be noted that such links were not exclusive to European operators. Companies such as Singapore Telecom, NTT Japan, and their Chinese, Korean and Australian counterparts were also linking up to form alliances. The largest US company, AT&T, was a leading player in such moves; it was also linked to Unisource.

Conclusion

Each of the leading European telecommunications companies was seeking the strategies that would allow it to be one of the leading world players. Commentators were predicting that by the year 2010 there would be only five leading global companies and each of the European players wanted to be one of the survivors. The strategic process to achieve this objective was therefore important.

17.2   THE SURVIVAL-BASED STRATEGIC ROUTE FORWARD

As the European telephone market is liberalised from 1998 onwards, it is likely that competition will increase. Companies are already beginning to enter each other's markets on a limited basis and make the necessary investments. Markets are showing reasonable growth rates and these are likely to continue. However, the sales increases from such growth are unlikely to satisfy the objectives of the major companies. Moreover, some of the leading US companies – such as AT&T, Bell South, Nynex and Pacific Telesis – have indicated their interest in investing more heavily in European markets. One important conclusion that some strategists have therefore drawn about the European telephone industry is that by the year 2010 only five major European companies will remain. The rest will have been swallowed up in a shakeout of the industry. The contrast with the relative stability of the state monopoly companies of the 1980s and early 1990s is striking. Survival-based strategy processes provide one explanation of the likely outcome after liberalisation.

17.2.1   The nature of survival-based strategies

Essentially, the survival-based process begins with the concept of *natural selection* first introduced in the nineteenth century by Charles Darwin to explain the development and survival of living creatures. He argued that survival was a constant battle against the environment. The species most likely to survive were those best suited and adapted to their surroundings. On this basis in a business context, adaptation to the environment is the main strategy that needs to be developed. Those that fail to change quickly enough will be the ones that select themselves for extinction.[12] The fittest companies survive because they are selected on the basis of the demand for their goods or services and the profits that they make.[13]

In the survival-based process there are two mechanisms in operation:

1 Adaptation to the environment.
2 Selection among those present for survival.

Using these two processes, together with principles and concepts from sociology, researchers have analysed the way that some industrial companies have developed.[14] They noted that, of the top 500 companies listed in *Fortune* magazine in 1955, only 268 were still listed in 1975: 46 per cent had disappeared, merged or otherwise declined over the twenty-year period. They suggested that *adaptation to the environment* was the preferred mechanism for change in many companies because it was less painful than selection. This was influenced by a built-in inertia to change in many industrial situations (*see* Exhibit 17.1).

Exhibit 17.1　　　**Examples of inertia against change in company environments**

Internal inertia

● Existing investment in plant and machinery.
● Previous experience and history of the company.

For example, in European telephone companies the existing bureaucracy which had been built up during many years in government ownership was very difficult to shift.

External inertia

● Barriers to entry and exit from an industry.
● Difficulty and cost of acquiring information on how the environment itself might be changing.

For example, European telephone companies' existing investment in exchanges and telephone equipment, coupled with external government restrictions that would prevent new companies entering until 1998, had created an inertia to change within the industry.

Most strategy literature takes an *adaptive* perspective as its starting point in developing strategy options. Importantly, some survival-based strategists argue that this may not be sufficient. It may be necessary to add a *selection* perspective. There may come a time, precisely because of the inertia in the industry, that some organisations do not or cannot adapt quickly enough to the changes in the environment, and will not survive against the powerful forces ranged against them. Nevertheless, there may be an element of chance in selecting precisely who will disappear. For example, some European telephone companies may adapt to the changed environment of the late 1990s, while others will change too slowly, and the pressures on them will be so great that they will not survive in their present form and will have to amalgamate with more efficient or luckier enterprises.

From a strategy *selection* perspective, the industry environment is the main determining factor of strategy development and survival. There is only a limited amount that individual companies can do in the time available before changes arrives. The only companies for whom this may not apply are those who already have substantial market power and can influence the way their markets develop. However, even these may be overtaken by events – for example, in the case of European telecommunications, the advent of new communications technologies such as cable, satellite or worldwide web.

17.2.2 Consequences for the corporate strategy process

On this basis, corporate strategy has a limited ability, if any, to influence the environment. Moreover, an organisation may not be able to adapt quickly enough to change. In addition, the techniques recommended by the prescriptive process will be so well publicised that they will provide no competitive advantage to individual companies. As a result, and for those companies without real market power, Williamson[15] has recommended that the best strategy is to develop the most cost-effective operation possible, which he calls *economizing*. He distinguishes this from new strategic moves beyond basic cost-effectiveness, which he calls *strategizing*.

> '*I aver that, as between economizing and strategizing, economizing is much the more fundamental ... A strategizing effort will only prevail if a program is burdened by significant cost excesses in production, distribution or organisation. All the clever ploys and positioning, aye, all the king's horses and all the king's men, will rarely save a project that is seriously flawed in first-order economizing respects.*'[16]

What, therefore, can be done? Table 17.3 summarises the main strategies that can be undertaken if this view of the strategy process is correct. It is clearly important to be cautious. It will also be necessary to seek clues from the environment on possible change and what is needed to survive. Finally, it will be useful to generate plenty of options so that whatever happens in the environment can be accommodated by the organisation.

Overall, if this view of the strategy process is correct, then the organisation is severely restricted in its strategies. Arguably, the way that the European telephone companies have been building alliances and cross-shareholdings suggests that they cannot see the way ahead clearly and have chosen these mutually-supportive strategies as the best protection.

17.2.3 Comment

This is a pessimistic view of the role of corporate strategy and the ability of organisations to shape their destiny. It rejects the insights offered by the prescriptive process but offers little alternative. It is useful in rapidly-changing and turbulent environments, but offers only limited solutions in other circumstances.

Table 17.3 The survival-based strategy process compared with the prescriptive process

Typical outline of the prescriptive model of the corporate strategy process	Survival-based corporate strategy process
Mission and objectives	Short-term, conservative objectives
Environmental analysis	Analysis important for clues to survival but difficult to predict and inertia may be strong
Resources analysis	Internal factor analysis also important but note structural inertia
Strategy options generation	Vital to generate many options
Strategy selection	Do not choose: keep options open and let the *market* choose
Implementation	Survive and hold some capacity in reserve for unknown events

Key strategic principles

- Survival-based strategies emphasise the importance of adapting strategies to meet changes in the environment. The ultimate objective is survival itself.

- The approach adopted is to develop options for use as the environment changes. Options that seek low costs are particularly useful.

- Beyond taking the precaution of developing strategic options, there is little that the individual organisation can do. There is an element of chance in whether it will survive or not.

17.3   THE UNCERTAINTY-BASED STRATEGIC ROUTE FORWARD

According to uncertainty-based strategists, Europe's telephone companies are wasting their time developing corporate strategies to cope with the events of 1998. They would argue that the environment is too uncertain and the outcomes largely unknown. Even striving for survival-based efficiency is useless. To understand the reasoning behind this, we need to examine the origins and thinking behind this approach.

17.3.1   Rationale

The key to understanding this route forward is its assumption about the purposes of most organisations: success will come from the ability of an organisation to survive by *innovating* and *transforming* itself.[17] Uncertainty-based strategists argue that it is not enough for most organisations simply to co-exist with others. In today's rapidly changing world, renewal and transformation towards new directions are key tasks for corporate strategy.

Given this definition of success, the strategic process by which this is achieved will inevitably involve uncertainty. However, uncertainty can be modelled mathematically and its consequences set out in the science of *chaos theory*[18] – a system of modelling originally applied to scientific processes such as weather forecasting – which demonstrates that, in certain types of uncertain environment, *small* changes in the early stages of a process can lead to *major* variances in the later stages. This is not unlike the multiplier effect in macroeconomics.

In the classic strategy process, there is a mechanism of cause and effect that controls the dynamics of change. *Feedback* arises from an initial strategic decision, but goes *beyond* such a decision by multiplying its effects. *Uncertainty* is the unknown result of a strategic decision which may be affected by chance events along with those that are more predictable.

An example will help to clarify the concept. When the price of an item such as a telephone call is raised relative to competing products, the sales of the item are predicted to fall. According to uncertainty-based theory, this simple process may not represent the *full* outcome of events. The *feedback mechanism* suggests that the rise in telephone prices may affect not only sales but also feed back into a lower level of loading at the telephone exchange. This may in turn influence the ability of the company to recover overheads from the exchange. Thus, the exchange loading, overheads and overall profitability may all be influenced by the one pricing decision. As soon as these items are affected adversely, there may be some attempt to recover profitability by a *further* price increase, i.e. the initial problem has fed back on itself. This will have a deleterious effect on the organisation, and so is usually referred to as *negative feedback*.

Conversely in the above example, a reduction in price might have the opposite effect. It might cause profitability to rise more than the initial move in pricing as a result of other consequences in the organisation. This is called *positive feedback*.

Uncertainty theory then adds another possibility. It can be proved mathematically that, where positive and negative feedback mechanisms operate, the system can *flip* between the positive and negative states. Importantly, it is not possible to predict in advance which of these three outcomes – that is, positive, negative or flip – will occur. The long-term consequences are therefore unknown and cannot be foreseen.

17.3.2 Consequences for the corporate strategy process

Uncertainty-based strategists argue that, there is little to be gained by predicting the future, because virtually all strategy is composed of feedback mechanisms and involves uncertainty; therefore the outcome cannot be predicted. If the future is unknown, the effects of long-term strategic actions will also be unknown and the classical prescriptive process has little meaning.

This does not mean that uncertainty-based strategists believe that nothing can be done. They take the view, however, that actions should be much shorter term in nature. Organisations must be able to learn and adapt to changed circumstances. Thus workers and managers in organisations are capable of assessing the results of their actions – in the example above, the effects of raising or lowering the price of telephone calls. They are also capable of learning to adapt to the consequences. More generally for strategy purposes, they are capable of experimenting and innovating in the organisation and assessing the results of their work.

The implications of such theories are profound for corporate strategy. The majority of organisations need to innovate in order to survive and they exist in the increasingly turbulent world of the 1990s, and yet uncertainty-based strategists would suggest that it is not possible to predict how innovation will succeed in the long term. According to these strategists, however, new ideas and new directions are necessary to survival and growth and should be pursued using the learning mechanisms mentioned above in order to refine and adapt strategies to a rapidly-changing environment.

As an example of uncertainty-based strategy in action, you might like to return to the Perrier case study in Chapter 11. The consequences of the traces of benzene leaking into bottles of mineral water were ultimately the loss of independence for the company and its take-over by Nestlé and Danône/BSN. Such an outcome was clearly impossible to predict when the benzene problem was first discovered. According to the uncertainty-based theorists, corporate strategy based on, for example, a prescriptive approach would have been largely irrelevant in these circumstances.

For the uncertainty-based strategist, long-term strategy is a contradiction in terms. The only possible objectives are short term, possibly with a strong innovative content.[19] There is no point in undertaking environmental analysis because it is essentially unpredictable, but it is useful to understand the organisation's resources in order to assess their contribution to the innovative process. As for strategy options and selection, this has no relevance to the strategy process that actually occurs. What is important is the way the company is organised to learn and respond to its changing environment: loose, informal networks of managers, rather than rigid functional divisions.

Overall, there is no clear flow process, unlike in prescriptive strategy; only constant monitoring of the environment in order to take advantage of opportunities that occur. Table 17.4 makes a comparison between the prescriptive and uncertainty-based processes.

Table 17.4 Comparison of the uncertainty-based strategic route with the prescriptive process

Typical outline of the prescriptive model of the corporate strategy process	Uncertainty-based strategy process	Flow process
Mission and objectives	Short-term only: possibly some strategic intent with innovation as a stated aim	?
Environmental analysis	Unpredictable: waste of time	
Resources analysis	Important to be aware of internal factors but the analysis will not have the predictive thrust of the prescriptive approach	No clear flow process ?
Strategy options generation	Options generation is irrelevant since the outcomes are unknown and unpredictable	Chaotic only with constant monitoring of the environment
Strategy selection	Strategy selection is also irrelevant but spontaneous small groups and learning mechanisms might be involved in short-term selection	?
Implementation	Informal, destabilising networks are useful. It may also be worth holding some resources in reserve because of the unknown	Flexible response from informal groups depending on the opportunities that emerge

17.3.3 Comment

The approach may be useful when market conditions are turbulent, but the approach has few insights into some of the areas of strategic decision making such as the human resource aspects. However, the approach is still in its early stages of development.

Key strategic principles

- Renewal and transformation are vital aspects of strategy. Inevitably, they will involve uncertainty. Such uncertainty can be modelled mathematically. However, the long-term consequences are unknown and cannot be foreseen or usefully predicted.

- Uncertainty-based approaches therefore involve taking small steps forward. Management needs to learn from such actions and adapt accordingly.

- Because of the uncertainty about the future, strategy options and selection between them using the prescriptive approach are therefore irrelevant.

European mobile telephones and Hutchison Mobilfunk

Mobile telephones are a recent innovation. In some European countries, they have been subject to more intense competition and benefited from greater market growth than fixed-line telephone systems. This case study concentrates on a small German company as it refines its corporate strategy in this rapidly-changing environment.

In 1994, the European market for mobile telephone services was worth around US$6 billion compared with the market for fixed services at US$120 billion. However, it was growing much faster: at 25 per cent annually for mobile telephones versus 8 per cent for fixed line. The reasons were:

- The sheer convenience and usefulness of being able to make and receive telephone calls anywhere.

- The upmarket appeal, enhanced in some countries by the high prices of handsets. All countries charged a hefty premium over fixed-line prices to make and receive mobile telephone calls, even the countries where there was heavy competition.

- Marketing policies in some countries that encouraged trial and early use of the mobile system, for example the UK, Norway, Sweden and Italy.

- Open competition in some markets, which had the effect of stimulating marketing activity and growth.

One of the countries that had lagged behind was Germany. During the 1980s, handset prices had been high and calls particularly expensive. There had been no competition, the sole operator, DeTeMobil, being a subsidiary of the state monopoly. In the late 1980s the first competitor was introduced and in 1996 Deutsche Telekom itself was to be privatised. Around 11 companies were now offering competitive services among which was Hutchison Mobilfunk, owned by Hutchison Whampoa (Hong Kong).

The parent company

Hutchison Whampoa was a conglomerate holding company with diverse interests including property, shipping, energy, retailing and telecommunica-

tions. The company had a turnover in 1994 of around US$4 billion and profits available to shareholders of over US$1 billion. Its total turnover in telecommunications was not published.[20]

The company had been built up and was still largely owned by Mr Li Ka-Shing and his family. Since 1992 it had been investing heavily in southern China, after that country's decisive move away from central planning and towards a market economy.[21] However, it had also been investing in mobile telecommunications in the UK, France and Germany. It had set up the Orange network in the UK as part of a global strategy to develop such services. It had also started a small company in France and acquired Hutchison Mobilfunk in 1994. Traditionally, the group did not interfere in the detailed strategy of its European subsidiaries. It set broad guidelines and then left the European companies to set the pace and strategy to meet them.

Hutchison Mobilfunk, the German subsidiary

By comparison with the group, the German subsidiary was quite small. It had a turnover around US$160 million and 100 000 customers. It had been built up by Mr Rene Obermann over a number of years and sold to Hutchison in 1994.

Obermann had started the company to generate enough income on which to live which he was a 23-year-old student.[22] He started marketing mobile telephone services in Germany with an aggression that was in contrast with the more staid approach of rivals such as DeTeMobil. He offered a 'small and friendly service'. However, this was proving more difficult to maintain with the larger customer base which he had now developed and the increasingly competitive market place. Nevertheless, the small original size and special culture of the 200-strong workforce were still evident: people addressed each other on first-name terms, which was against the culture of many German companies.

In the past, Obermann had handled client problems personally, but this was no longer possible with the larger customer base. Recently, he had installed a customer retention unit to persuade customers to stay rather than switch to one of his ten competitors. He had also introduced a fraud prevention unit because it was too easy for customers to generate high telephone bills without the means to pay.

Differentiation from other mobile telephone operators in Germany was difficult. There was little differentiation in hard terms based on equipment. However, the company was attempting to differentiate itself by superior levels of service and by investing in a major service department in Münster so that its technicians were able on average to repair and return faulty mobiles within two days.

Life for the new subsidiary was beginning to change. Previously, Obermann had been able to talk openly about sales and profits, but Hutchison had stopped this because it was not group policy to reveal confidential details. Obermann had liked to see himself as one of the *Mittelständler* – the middle ranks of family companies who dominate much of German industry. He was now having to become used to referring to his company as being part of the *Konzern*, i.e. part of the Hutchison Whampoa group. However, there was one great advantage from the group. It was asking him and his other European colleagues to draw up a strategy for major expansion by the company over the next few years.

CASE QUESTIONS

1 *Apply the prescriptive strategy process to this company and indicate what conclusions you would draw about strategy.*

2 *Apply the survival-based and uncertainty-based strategy processes to the company and indicate what conclusions you would draw about strategy. Does it matter that it is more difficult to draw specific recommendations?*

3 *Identify the main elements of the company's likely resources and market position and use these to advise the company on whether any of the above three processes provides a useful model for strategy development. You can assume that the company faces the strategic task mentioned at the end of the case and that it has a viable, but not strong, share of the German market.*

17.4 THE NEGOTIATION-BASED STRATEGIC ROUTE FORWARD

Even if Hutchison Mobilfunk (*see* Case study 17.2) was able to develop an outline strategy for the next few years, there are other problems with the process because of the need to *negotiate* the strategy proposals with individuals and groups both outside and inside the organisation.

● *Within the organisation*, groups of workers and managers in particular functions may see their interests threatened or enhanced by new strategy proposals and react accordingly.

● *Outside the organisation*, groups of customers or suppliers may demand special services or prices based on their bargaining power (explored in Porter's Five Forces Model in Chapter 3).

The need to negotiate both inside and outside the company is evident. The theoretical background to the negotiation-based approach was developed by

Williamson in his concept of *transactional cost economics*.[23] This section extracts the main themes from his work.

Negotiation has two components that are sometimes muddled:

1 *Human resources*, dealing with individuals and groups inside the organisation.

2 *Game theory transactions*, involving structured methods of bargaining with customers and others.

These two elements are explored separately in terms of the following rationale.

17.4.1 Rationale: human resource aspects

Back in the 1960s, research showed the importance of coalitions and groups within organisations.[24] They might have some interests that were the same as those stated by the organisation, but other interests would not necessarily coincide. Typically, groups and individuals negotiated with each other inside the organisation and arrived at a compromise on important issues, including aspects of corporate strategy. For example, in Hutchison Mobilfunk, we can speculate that compromises will be achieved on the nature, power and status of the new customer services unit. The key point is that it may be difficult for senior management simply to define the customer service strategy in advance, because of the need for some form of negotiation: 'If we support you on this then will you support us in our negotiations?' Moss Kanter[25] provides graphic detail of how departments negotiate with each other in US companies. From a prescriptive strategy perspective, the negotiation process means that simple objectives such as profit maximisation are subject to the reality of the politics of the organisation.

Between 1968 and 1980, the British chemical company, ICI, needed to adapt its strategies to cope with an environment which had changed radically. However, the company was large and bureaucratic with a range of experienced and intelligent senior managers and groups who had vested interests in the current strategies. For example, some faced the loss of their jobs if the new strategy proposals were implemented. Pettigrew researched the long human resource process that was required to obtain the changes:[26]

> *'This kind of process management also necessitated patience and perseverance; waiting for people to retire to exploit any policy vacuum so created; introducing known sympathisers as replacements for known sceptics or opponents; using succession occasions to combine portfolios and responsibilities and integrate thought and action in an otherwise previously factious and deadlocked area of change; backing off and waiting, or moving the pressure point for change into another area when continuing downright opposition might have endangered the success of the whole exercise.'*

The point here is that, according to such strategists, this is not something added on to strategy after it has been formulated but is part of the strategy itself. As stated in Chapter 8: *strategy is the art of the possible.* Thus rational decisions on markets, finance or products are deeply influenced by the social and political texture of the firm. Corporate strategy is not a simple, unemotional process but is, in fact, interpreted by managers and groups of workers according to their own frames of reference, their particular motivations and information.[27] It is the *limits* to managerial action which are just as important to strategic decisions as the ability to choose any strategy option. In case this might be regarded as only a British phenomenon, it is worth pointing to the difficulties companies in Germany, such as Daimler–Benz and Volkswagen, have had during the mid-1990s in restructuring their workforces against low-cost EU and global competition.

The concept of a network of interest groups inside the organisation can also be extended to the outside environment. Salespeople over time may strike up relationships with customers, purchasing managers with suppliers and so on. Long-term relationships with outsiders may be a crucial element of the company's strategy, as will quickly be confirmed by those in the aerospace, defence, telecommunications equipment and other industries negotiating with government. Negotiation is a vital strategic aspect of such relationships and the process becomes effectively one of the key determinants of success. Thus, for example, governments may well be involved in the purchase or specification of such items as mobile telephones. More generally, government direct control may be achieved by access to preferential credit, joint ownership, a threat to call in new suppliers, the allocation of R&D contracts and assistance in export sales.[28] Developing corporate strategy without negotiating with a government may be an expensive luxury. The bargaining power that each side has in such negotiations will depend on the maturity of the market and the technology involved.

In many respects, therefore, the organisation can be seen as a *network of treaties,* both external and internal.[29] Moreover, if such agreements are important for the development of strategy, then it follows that it is important to understand the dynamics of these networks in order to develop optimal strategy.[30] The sheer complexity of this task means that it may be better to use *key factors for success* to focus attention on the important areas of the process (*see* Chapter 3).

17.4.2 Rationale: game theory transactions

In the negotiation process, the successful acquisition of a large contract may be crucial to the profitability or even the survival of the organisation. This has increasingly become the case in the former public sector as more industries are privatised. During the 1940s mathematical models were first developed to handle in a structured way the commercial decisions that are involved in negotiating: they are known under the general title of *game theory.*

Game theory attempts to predict customer reactions in the negotiating situation. The circumstances may be regarded as being similar to the game of chess, where anticipation of the opponent's moves is an important aspect of the challenge. Much of game theory has been modelled mathematically, with rules specifying how the scarce resources of the company can be employed and what benefits (often called *pay-offs*) will be obtained by particular moves or a combination of moves.[31]

- In a *zero-sum game*, there is ultimately no pay-off because the gains of one member are negated by the losses of another.

- In a *co-operative game*, the benefits may add up to a positive pay-off for all.

- In a *negative-sum game*, the actions of each party undermine both themselves and their opponents.

Although game theory has provided a useful basis for structuring negotiations and the consequences of each move, it has proved difficult to model strategic options and decisions which are often highly complex and inter-related.

The *Prisoner's Dilemma* is one example of game theory and is described in Exhibit 17.2. Essentially, it involves a negotiated outcome that is less than optimal for both parties but is also the likely result. Many organisations in highly competitive situations face similar decisions. For example, we can speculate that the strategic option is available to Hutchison Mobilfunk to reduce its prices and seek greater market share. This would be undertaken in the context of examining prices of all mobile telephone calls at present being charged at tariffs higher than those of other companies throughout Germany. However, if the company does drop its prices, it may generate a price war in which all mobile telephone companies would lose. Alternatively, by supporting the current strategy of premium pricing across the industry, the company is allowing its rivals to maintain their share of the market and denying any growth ambitions it may have.

It should be noted that the above pricing example is not idle speculation: Hutchison's UK company faced precisely this dilemma in 1994/95 with its bigger rivals, Cellnet and Vodaphone. It chose to undercut its rivals on price by 20 per cent during 1995 and became the fastest-growing company in the UK mobile telephone market in 1995/96, provoking a response from its competitors.

Exhibit 17.2 **The Prisoner's Dilemma**

The dilemma facing the two prisoners is mirrored in the strategic choice that organisations often face in trying to anticipate the reactions of competitors.

The dilemma concerns two prisoners each faced with a 10- or 20-year sentence for armed robbery and considering how they will respond to the police in an interview. The prisoners are kept isolated from each other and then interrogated by the authorities who know that they will only obtain a conviction in the courts if at least one of the prisoners confesses. Each prisoner is told that if he/she alone confesses then he/she alone will be freed and the other prisoner will receive a heavier 20-year sentence. If both confess, then they will both receive 10-year sentences. However, neither prisoner is allowed to communicate with the other before making the decision. Thus neither can negotiate the best strategy, which is that *neither* should confess and then they will both go free.

Thus each prisoner faces the dilemma:

- *Either to confess* and receive a 10-year sentence, or go free if the other has not confessed;

- *Or to offer no confession* and go free if the other has also offered no confession, or receive the heavier 20-year sentence if betrayed by their fellow prisoner.

Since they can neither communicate with each other nor trust each other, the likely outcome is that both will confess and receive 10 years. Clearly this is not the optimal strategy since they could both have been freed.

17.4.3 Consequences of both aspects for corporate strategy

Essentially, nothing is fixed and everything is open to negotiation. Therefore, objectives may need to be revised and selection may be compromised by the need to persuade groups to adopt a particular route. In a sense, the implementation process itself is now part of the selection process and part of the strategy.

Table 17.5 illustrates the major implications of such a negotiation-based route forward. It should be noted that the timetable for any strategic change may need to be lengthened to accommodate this process. It is not possible to show this adequately in the table.

Table 17.5 Comparison of the negotiation-based process with the prescriptive process

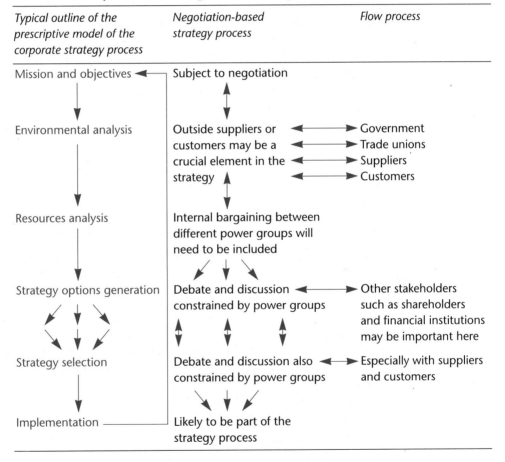

Typical outline of the prescriptive model of the corporate strategy process	Negotiation-based strategy process	Flow process
Mission and objectives	Subject to negotiation	
Environmental analysis	Outside suppliers or customers may be a crucial element in the strategy	Government / Trade unions / Suppliers / Customers
Resources analysis	Internal bargaining between different power groups will need to be included	
Strategy options generation	Debate and discussion constrained by power groups	Other stakeholders such as shareholders and financial institutions may be important here
Strategy selection	Debate and discussion also constrained by power groups	Especially with suppliers and customers
Implementation	Likely to be part of the strategy process	

17.4.4 Comment

There can be little doubt that politics and negotiations are a part of many organisations, both large and small. However, there is still a need to drive the strategy process forward. This is where *leadership* is probably vital. Negotiation-based strategies are unlikely to represent a complete route in themselves, but need to take place alongside prescriptive and learning-based strategy processes.

> ### Key strategic principles
>
> - Negotiation-based strategies emphasise the need to persuade colleagues and outside stakeholders. Coalitions and groups play an important part in strategy development.
>
> - Such a strategic approach also needs to be seen in the context of negotiations with powerful customers and suppliers where bargaining and trade-offs will take place.
>
> - Game theory attempts to predict the outcomes of customer reactions or, in some cases, to show how the outcome of negotiations may well produce a sub-optimal solution unless both sides of the negotiations realise the consequences of their actions.

17.5 THE LEARNING-BASED STRATEGIC ROUTE FORWARD

When there is considerable uncertainty, as in the European mobile telecommunications market, it may not be possible or prudent to develop a strategy that is firmly fixed for some years ahead. It may be better to have some basic business objectives, possibly even a vision of the future (*see* Chapter 11), but also be prepared to experiment and react to market events. These might include the launch or disappearance of rival companies. The process of adopting a flexible, emergent strategy that monitors events, reacts to them and develops opportunities is at the heart of learning-based strategies.

17.5.1 Rationale

In a persuasive article in 1987, Mintzberg argued that the rational analysis of such areas as markets and company resources was unlikely to produce effective strategy. A much more likely process was that of *crafting strategy* where 'formulation and implementation merge into a fluid process of learning through which creative strategies evolve'.[32]

Mintzberg was not denying the need for planning and formulation of strategy. However, he argued strongly for the flexibility that comes from learning to shape and reshape a strategy as it begins to be implemented. This was particularly important because strategy occasionally had to address a major shift in the market place or in internal practice – a *quantum leap*. At such a time, those strategists who had really *learnt* how the organisation operated would be better able to recognise the need for change and respond quickly to the signals of the major shift.

As an example to clarify the process, we can examine Royal Dutch/Shell, one of the world's leading oil companies. The company provided an example of the quantum leap and the learning process during the 1980s.[33] In 1984, oil was priced around US$28 per barrel. Against this background, the company's central planning department developed a speculative scenario based on the price dropping to US$16 per barrel. Purely as an exercise, they urged senior management to speculate on the consequences of such a radical price drop. Some senior managers felt it was unlikely but were willing to enter into the spirit of the exercise. The consequences were explored well enough so that, when the price actually dropped to US$10 per barrel in 1987, the company was well prepared.

One of Royal Dutch/Shell's leading planners later concluded:

> *'Institutional learning is the process whereby management teams change their shared mental models of their company, their markets and their competitors. For this reason, we think of planning as learning and of corporate planning as institutional learning.'*

The key words here are *change their shared mental models* and the process of *learning*. Most companies have a group of assumptions about the company and its environment and these need to be made explicit and shared. These may then need to be changed, depending on the circumstances – for example, a quantum leap as mentioned above.

There are a number of well-recognised mechanisms for developing and sharing mental models as part of the learning process.[34] Probably the best known of these are the five learning disciplines of Peter Senge.[35] They are crafted to help organisations and individuals learn. However, *learning* here does not mean memory work or even merely coping with a changing environment. Learning has a more positive and pro-active meaning: *active creativity* to develop new strategies and opportunities. The five learning disciplines developed to achieve this are summarised in Exhibit 17.3.

Exhibit 17.3   **The five learning disciplines**

- *Personal mastery* – not only developing personal goals but also creating the organisational environment that encourages groups to develop goals and purposes.

- *Mental models* – reflecting and speculating upon the pictures that managers and workers have of the world and seeing how these influence actions and decisions.

- *Shared vision* – building commitment in the group to achieve its aims by exploring and agreeing what these aims are.

- *Team learning* – using the group's normal skills to develop intelligence and ability beyond individuals' normal abilities.

- *Systems thinking* – a method of thinking about, describing and understanding the major forces that influence the group.

Source: Based on the writings of Peter Senge

To survive in today's turbulent business climate, it has been argued that strategy must include mechanisms that transfer learning from the individual to the group.[36] There are then three advantages from the learning process for the group and for the whole organisation:

1   It will provide fresh ideas and insights into the organisation's performance through a commitment to knowledge.

2   Adaptation through renewal will be promoted so organisations do not stultify and wither.

3   It will promote an openness to the outside world so that it can respond to events – for example, the quantum change of an oil price shock or the rapid developments in the European mobile telephone market.

It is often the well-educated, highly committed senior professional in an organisation who has the most difficulty with this process.[37] Such an individual may misunderstand the meaning of the word 'learning' and interpret it too narrowly as being purely about problem-solving. It may also not be understood that the *process* of learning is about more than just instructions from the teacher or the senior management. The implications for corporate strategy are that learning is a two-way process and is more open-ended than prescriptive strategy would suggest.

17.5.2   Consequences for the corporate strategy process

In the learning process, the concept of 'top-down' management handing semi-finished objectives to the more junior managers and employees clearly carries no meaning. Generative learning needs to have a greater element of co-operation and discussion. Nevertheless, the analytical element of the process can proceed, though perhaps more openly and with more people involved. This will inevitably slow it down but it may be a small price to pay for the greater commitment achieved. Strategy options and selection are still conceivable but the process may be more complex and multi-layered than the prescriptive route. However, it is clearly possible that the implementation phase may actually be faster because people will be better informed and more committed to strategies that they themselves have helped to form.[38]

Table 17.6 outlines the main elements of the learning-based process. The key point is that the learning process itself is part of the strategy, not something added after the strategy has been developed. This means that the fully-developed strategy only emerges over time.

17.5.3   Comment

The learning-based route has real value in the development of corporate strategy. However, it has to be said that it is sometimes vague and non-operational in its proposals, beyond the need to consult everyone. Moreover, there is still a need in some circumstances for senior managers to take decisions *without* consultation (*see* Case studies 16.1 at Nokia and 18.2 at Asea Brown Boveri). More generally, *how* and *when* organisations should adopt the learning-based approach has been the basis for fully-justified criticism of this route forward.[39] In spite of these weaknesses, the route does not preclude the use of the prescriptive process. It will be explored further in later chapters of this book.

Table 17.6 Comparison of the learning-based process with the prescriptive process

Typical outline of the prescriptive model of the corporate strategy process	Learning-based strategy process	Flow process
Mission and objectives ◄───	Need to be discussed and agreed ◄───	
↓	↑↓	
Environmental analysis	Need wide range of inputs from all areas of the organisation	
↓	↕ ↕ ↕	
Resources analysis	Also needs wide range of inputs	*Possibly*
↓	↘ ↕ ↗	
Strategy options generation	Open debate and discussion	
↙ ↓ ↘	↗ ↕ ↖	
↘ ↓ ↙	↘ ↕ ↗	
Strategy selection	Open debate and discussion	
↓	↓	
Implementation ───────────	Greater commitment from greater discussion	

Key strategic principles

- Learning-based strategy emphasises the importance of flexibility in developing unique strategies.

- Learning is not concerned with memory work, but with active creativity in developing new strategic opportunities.

- It has real value as a concept but is vague and lacks operational guidance in practice.

17.6 INTERNATIONAL CONSIDERATIONS

Differences around the world in cultures, social values and economic traditions, mean it is possible that some strategy processes may be difficult, if not impossible, to introduce and manage in certain countries. For example, the learning process of

Section 17.5 requires a relaxed and open relationship between superior and subordinate that is available in some northern European countries but much more rare in Malaysia and India.[40] Some writers have promoted the idea of the *borderless world* and the *global corporation*. Undoubtedly, in terms of common customer tastes and sourcing of production, there are real commonalities, but in terms of the strategy process, which is more detailed and requires more commitment, real differences still exist.[41]

International considerations may impact on the strategy process during every stage. However, they do not influence the process in a single, consistent fashion. Thus there is no 'international strategy process'.

17.6.1 Stakeholders

As we have seen, stakeholders and their relative power vary throughout the world: shareholders, employees, managers, financial institutions, governments and other interested groups. Importantly, their ability to influence the strategy process will also vary:

- In some areas of the Far East and Africa, government influence will be important in guiding strategy development.
- In the UK and North America, shareholders are often given the first consideration in developing strategy.

These differences have arisen for historic, cultural and economic reasons. In each country, different sets of values, expectations and beliefs will influence the strategic process: companies may not hold the simple economic, rational views that have been used to guide strategic processes in some Western countries. The influences may be more complex and embedded in culture and social values.[42] Explicit awareness of stakeholders expectations is an important part of the strategic process.

17.6.2 Mission and objectives

Strategic goals and processes are likely to reflect the social systems of the country in which the strategy is developed. Thus, the missions and objectives of companies need to be seen in the context of their countries of origin. However, it should be recognised that even within countries there will be major variations in ambitions, ideas and values. The importance of socio-cultural elements should, therefore, not be over-emphasised. As Whittington commented: 'Societies are too complex and people too individualistic to expect bland uniformity.'[43]

17.6.3 Environment

In one sense, the international environment is the same for all companies: they will all be subject to the same trends in economic growth as they compete in world markets, the same major shifts in political power and the same social changes and technological developments. However, because the *base country* of the stakeholders may differ, their responses to and expectations of environmental changes may give rise to major variations in strategy. For example, the mid-1990s saw a significant rise of the Japanese yen against the US dollar: the impact of this environmental change on the world car industry is entirely different depending on the base country of the stakeholders. Japanese car companies have suffered and US car companies benefited.[44]

17.6.4 Options and choice

The whole concept of the rational choice between options may be Western, even Anglo–American, in its cultural and social background. For example, some cultures place more emphasis on preordained fate as an important element of life, including business matters. If events are decided by fate, then this may significantly influence the options and choice process.[45]

Options and choice also require some basic agreement on the *method* and *criteria* by which they will be discussed and judged. These are also culture-specific, as one researcher has described:[46]

- *Anglo-Saxon* style is comfortable, with open debate about different perspectives, and sees compromise as the best outcome from disagreement.

- *Teutons and Gauls* both like to debate but prefer to undertake this with those from the same intellectual and social backgrounds. This makes for less antagonism but for a more limited exposure to different expectations. Teutons then seek rigour in the debate before the elegance of the theories, whereas the Gauls take the reverse viewpoint, preferring the aesthetic nature of the argument itself rather than the conclusion.

- *Japanese* do not debate, partly because they have no tradition and partly because of a desire not to upset the social relationships that have already been established.

It is perhaps not surprising that there are problems when it comes to operating strategic decision-making processes across international boundaries.

Key strategic principles

- International considerations may impact on the strategy process during every stage. The ability of stakeholders to influence the process will vary from country to country for historic, political and cultural reasons.

- The mission and objectives are likely to be rooted in the social and cultural systems of the country in which the strategy is developed. The environment may also be important to another aspect of strategy development: the *home country* of an organisation will influence the way that its international strategy is developed and managed.

- Options and choice in the selection process will be governed by the culture and social systems of the people involved in the process.

FT

Strategic choice at MCI[47]

Amid the chaotic changes overtaking the world of telecommunications, certain themes recur: the need for global partners, the challenge of multimedia and, in the USA, the looming confrontation between local and long-distance operators. This case describes the answers that the US telecommunications company, MCI, has developed to these difficult strategic issues.

MCI's advantage lay in having been first to seize business opportunites. While other companies like AT&T and France Telecom were wrestling to put world alliances together, MCI's joint venture with British Telecom was started in 1994. Similarly, while others were tinkering with multimedia, MCI invested US$1 billion in a joint venture with News Corporation, to be followed by another similar amount.

In two other business areas MCI refused to invest significantly. In *wireless telephone frequencies*, its US rivals spent US$7 billion in 1995 to buy these from the US government, while MCI ignored the opportunity. Equally, in *US telephone networks*, MCI invested less in *local networks* in 1996 than it had in 1995. This contrasted sharply with its rivals, who were spending billions.

US market competition

MCI's strengths were in long-distance rather than local telephone calls. It was second in the US long-distance telephone market. The company's competitors in this segment were AT&T, the largest telephone company in the US, and Sprint, somewhat smaller than MCI. However, in the *local* telephone market MCI had little strength. Here the company competed against a series of regional telephone companies which were known collectively as the *Baby Bells*. The latter had real strengths in local regions of the USA, for example Nynex in New York and Pacific Telesis in California. Several of the Baby Bells were also investing heavily in European opportunities, such as cabling in the UK and exchanges in Hungary, because of the limited opportunities for expansion in the USA until the deregulation expected in 1996. When deregulation came in this highly competitive market, many of MCI's competitors were expecting to invade each other's territories. They would

undertake this by investing heavily in new telephone networks. MCI, however, took the view that such a strategy was mistaken.

Market competiton outside the USA

In examining such markets for MCI services, two types of customer could be distinguished:

- the truly *global companies*, such as the major multinationals, with their requirements for worldwide service;

- the many more *national companies* with a demand for services that was mainly confined within national boundaries.

The global company market was highly competitive and still growing fast, with no dominant suppliers of telephone services. The supply of services to national organisations was still dominated by the monopoly national suppliers, though some of these were now being privatised, such as Deutsche Telekom in Germany and Telecom Italia in Italy.

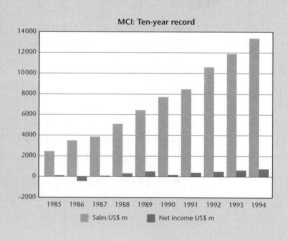

MCI: Ten-year record
Sales US$ m — Net income US$ m

Company origins

MCI's contrarian streak lay deep in its origins. As a tiny outfit 25 years ago, it hit on the idea of installing microwave towers along the route from Chicago to Seattle to allow truckers to call head office on mobile telephones. The plan was opposed by AT&T, then the official monopolist. MCI has been fighting AT&T and other monopolies ever since. Hence its claim not to be a phone company. Around the world, MCI argues, phone companies are monopolists or ex-monopolists and, as such, they are arrogant to their customers and vain about their technology. For MCI, customers are everything and technology is merely something bought off the shelf to provide a service.

MCI now claims to be the world's biggest telephone operator never to have enjoyed guaranteed rates or customers. While its competitors grew up on taxpayers' money or monopoly revenues, MCI's early ventures were financed by Mr Michael Miliken, the junk bond king. The resulting culture is still pervasive in MCI. Mr Jack Grubman, the telecoms analyst at the US securities firm Salomon Bros, says:

> It's tough to be an upstart when you have US$15 billion revenues. But, historically, companies like AT&T or the Baby Bells [the US local phone companies] all had unlimited access to capital. MCI was living hand-to-mouth up to the late 1980s. It hasn't forgotten where it came from.

Thus the company claims to have the best marketing database in the USA. Mr Tim Price, head of MCI's telecomms business, comments:

> No brag, just fact. For years we've rated our customers by 2000 variables – what they have for breakfast, what time they go to bed, what kind of music equipment they have. That's because when you go up against a monolith with 100 per cent market share, you have to pick your targets carefully.

MCI corporate strategies

MCI's decision not to bid for US wireless frequencies in 1995 was based partly on the expectation of a glut in the wireless market, which would allow it to buy cheap capacity from its rivals. However, there was also a more basic reason. Monopolists like the Baby Bells, according to MCI President Jerry Taylor, have to protect their interests: they have existing underground telephone cables in their local areas which they need to keep used. The threat from new wireless technology is that it would make such existing networks redundant. Mr Taylor says:

> We don't have a whole wired city that we have to defend. We don't need to own wireless, because we don't have to worry about an alien technology coming in to take our business away.

Above all, MCI argued, its penurious origins meant it was better at striking alliances. A company like AT&T needs to be in charge, according to Mr Taylor. In 1991 AT&T paid US$7.5 billion for computer maker, NCR. Then in 1994 it paid US$11.5 billion to absorb McCaw, the biggest US mobile phone company. In both cases, AT&T started as a partner. Mr Taylor comments:

> Partnerships are very difficult for the big guy. But we never had deep pockets and we always had to compete with the big guy, so we grew up with partnerships. Today there's no company on earth that's strong enough to do everything. The winners will be those who make partnerships work.

Though imprecise in detail, the partnership with News Corporation was plainly of central importance. The two companies have a certain maverick quality in common. As seen by MCI executives, the partnership was expected to cover both cross-marketing and joint ventures. An MCI telephone service might be marketed using characters from *The Simpsons*, News Corporation's cartoon show; or Fox studios could produce videos tailored to MCI subscribers. By early 1996, the partners had already started an embryonic joint venture on the Internet, and there was talk of MCI using News Corporation's TV satellites to beam down data to its business customers. If this sounded vague, there was a financial safety net. MCI's initial US$1 billion investment would pay interest at 6.25 per cent. Five years into the venture, MCI would end up owning about 14 per cent of News Corporation's equity shareholding. According to Doug Maine, MCI's chief financial officer, analysts' projections showed News Corporation making enough profit by then for MCI to earn its minimum required rate of return on investment of 15 per cent.

Concert, the joint venture with BT, was already selling products to 2000 multinational companies around the world. A typical instance was intra-company dialling, whereby employees could call colleagues around the world on a seven-digit number without using country codes. Such products had a finite application: one MCI executive said companies with sales of US$50 million probably could not afford them. At this early stage, the business was loss-making and, as Mr Taylor conceded, it might never enjoy particularly high margins, since big multinationals can secure cheap rates.

> But think of it like toilet paper. As a big company, you'll always get a better price. But the person selling to you has lower costs as well.

Future strategies

With both News Corporation and BT ventures, MCI had the advantage of being ahead of the game. There remained one game it could not control – the legislation to deregulate US national telecommunications which would determine the shape of the battle between the local and national telephone companies. Publicly, MCI was not worried by this. The thinking was that, if the legislation was even-handed, then the company would probably lose some market share in long-distance telephone calls to local operators but gain some local share in return. But not all industry analysts agreed. Mr Dan Reingold of stockbrokers Merrill Lynch says:

> You have to distinguish between the company's perspective and the investor's. The long-distance companies say that they are good enough to get through this and survive

and, of course, they are. But whether their survival will result in the cash flow and earnings which Wall Street expects is another question.

In contrast, Mr Jack Grubman of Salomon Brothers raised a further possibility. For at least some of the Baby Bells, partnership with a long-distance company could be an attractive solution to the perils of deregulation. AT&T was too big, while Sprint, the third biggest long-distance company, was already tied up to a group of cable TV companies in the US. What would be more natural than to turn to MCI, the established expert at alliances? Some such thinking might account for the relaxed air at MCI as deregulation was under way in a highly competitive market. Or perhaps it was simply relying on the belief that 'phone companies' were dumb, arrogant and easy to beat.

Source: Financial Times, 2 November 1995.

CASE QUESTIONS

1 How useful do you judge the prescriptive strategy process to be in analysing the strategy options available to MCI? The joint venture costing US$1 billion with News Corporation seemed to be rather vague at the time it was announced. Is this compatible with prescriptive strategy?

2 In the context of the uncertainties surrounding telecommunications, would you consider employing either the uncertainty-based or survival-based strategy routes? What are the benefits and problems of applying these two routes?

3 What changes, if any, would MCI need to consider if it were to employ the learning-based strategy process? Does the company's policy of partnerships constitute a learning-based strategy?

4 In the context of its highly competitive style, to what extent does the company already employ the negotiating-based process?

■ SUMMARY

- This chapter has reviewed the main methods of developing the strategy process. It commenced with an examination and critique of the prescriptive model. It then examined other models, especially those from the emergent strategy process.

- *The prescriptive model* of the strategic process was found to be largely linear. It has feedback mechanisms at various points to ensure that objectives, options and strategy choice are consistent with each other. Problems with the prescriptive approach lie in four main areas: environment unpredictability; planning procedures; top-down approaches driven by the centre; and the culture of the organisation that will allow the model to operate. Specific criticisms include the need for more dialogue, a greater flow of ideas and more adaptation to the environment. It may be possible to solve these problems within the prescriptive process but some strategists take a more critical view.

- *Survival-based strategies* emphasise the importance of adapting strategies to meet changes in the environment. The ultimate objective is survival itself. The approach adopted is to develop options for use as the environment changes. Options that seek low costs are particularly useful. Beyond taking the precaution of developing options, there is little that the individual company can do. There is an element of chance in whether the company will survive.

- *The uncertainty-based approach* concentrates on the difficult and turbulent environment that now surrounds the development of corporate strategy. Renewal and transformation are vital aspects of such strategy. Inevitably, they will involve uncertainty. Such uncertainty can be modelled mathematically. However, the long-term consequences are unknown and cannot be foreseen or usefully predicted. Uncertainty approaches therefore involve taking small steps forward. Management needs to learn from such actions and adapt accordingly. Because of the uncertainty about the future, it is argued that the perscriptive approach of looking at strategy options and selecting between them is irrelevant.

- *Negotiation-based strategies* emphasise the need to persuade colleagues and outside stakeholders to take a particular course of action. Coalitions and groups play an important part in strategy development. Such a strategic approach also needs to be seen in the context of negotiations with powerful customers and suppliers where bargaining and trade-offs will take place. Game theory attempts to predict the outcomes of customer reactions or, in some cases, to show how the outcome of negotiations may well produce a sub-optimal solution unless both sides of the negotiations realise the consequences of their actions.

- *Learning-based strategy* emphasises the importance of flexibility in developing unique strategies. Learning is not concerned with memory work, but with active creativity in developing new strategic opportunities. It has real value as a concept but in practice is vague and lacks operational guidance.

- *International considerations* may impact on the strategy process at every stage. The ability of stakeholders to influence the process will vary from country to country for historic, political and cultural reasons. The mission and objectives are likely to be rooted in the social and cultural systems of the country in which the strategy is developed. The environment may be important in another aspect of strategy development: the home country of an organisation will influence the way that the international strategy is developed and managed. Options and choice in the selection process will be governed by the culture and social systems of the people involved in the process.

QUESTIONS

1 Professor Charles Handy has described recent technological breakthroughs in global development as *discontinuous*. He has then commented: '*Discontinuous change required discontinuous upside-down thinking to deal with it, even if thinkers and thought appear absurd at first sight.*' Can discontinuities be handled by the prescriptive process or is an emergent process required? If so, which one?

2 To what extent, if at all, do the difficulties with the classic prescriptive process invalidate this route forward?

3 Thinking about an organisation with which you are familiar, to what extent does it plan ahead? How does it undertake this task? Is it reasonably effective or is the whole process largely a waste of time? To what extent does any planning process rely on 'people' issues and negotiation? What model from this chapter does the process most closely follow, if any?

4 Is it possible for the prescriptive strategy process to be creative?

5 Some have argued that the survival-based strategic route is over-pessimistic in its approach. Do you agree?

6 For organisations, such as the telecommunications companies, involved in lengthy investment decisions that take many years to implement, the uncertainty-based route forward with its very short time-horizons appears to have little to offer. Can this strategic route provide any useful guidance to such companies?

7 Why is negotiation important in corporate strategy? Why is it not better to have a strong leader who will simply impose his or her will on the organisation?

8 The learning-based strategic route emphasises creativity in strategy development. Why is this important and how might it be achieved?

9 '*Management theories are judged, among managers at least, by the demonstrable results that they deliver,*' comments Professor Colin Egan. Apply this comment to the strategic routes described in this chapter and outline your conclusions.

10 If you were advising Honda Motorcycles about its strategies in the 1990s, what strategic approach or combination of approaches would you adopt? Give reasons for your views.

STRATEGIC PROJECT

This chapter has examined some of the developments taking place in telecommunications strategy around the world. There is expected to be a revolution in this area over the next ten years, with some winners and losers. You might like to consider the strategies for survival and growth in this exciting area.

FURTHER READING

For a comparative review of strategic approaches, the book by Dr Richard Whittington remains one of the best: Whittington, R (1993) *What is strategy and does it matter?*, Routledge, London.

For a discussion of survival-based approaches, *see* Rumelt, R, Schendel, D and Teece, D (1991) 'Strategic management and economics', *Strategic Management Journal*, 12, pp5–29. This is a very useful general review and would provide a good link for those who have already studied economics.

For a description of the uncertainty-based approach, *see* Stacey, R (1996) *Strategic Management and Organisational Dynamics*, 2nd edn, Pitman Publishing, London.

For a useful discussion of learning approaches, *see* Senge, P (1990) *The Fifth Discipline: the art and practice of the learning organisation*, Doubleday, New York. For a critical examination of learning, Professor Colin Egan's book is strongly recommended: Egan, C (1995) *Creating Organisational Advantage*, Butterworth-Heinemann, Oxford.

REFERENCES

1 Pascale, R (1984) 'Perspectives on Strategy: the real story behind Honda's success', *California Management Review* XXVI, 3, pp47–72. This article was extracted in Mintzberg, H and Quinn, J B (1991) *The Strategy Process* 2nd edn, Prentice Hall, NJ, pp114–23. This is well worth reading to illustrate the problems of the classical model.
2 Kono, T (1992) *Long Range Planning of Japanese Corporations*, de Gruyter, Berlin.
3 Wheelen, T and Hunger, D (1992) *Strategic Management and Business Policy*, 4th edn, Addison-Wesley, Reading, Mass.
4 Jauch, L R and Glueck, W F (1988) *Business Policy and Strategic Management*, 5th edn, McGraw-Hill, NY.
5 In addition to references 3 and 4 above, similar versions of the prescriptive model presented here are to be found in the well-known text by Thompson, A and Strickland, A (1993) *Strategic Management*, 7th edn, Irwin, Homewood, Ill. A leading and well-respected European text is that by Johnson, G and Scholes, K (1993) *Corporate Strategy*, 3rd edn, Prentice Hall, Hemel Hempstead: this text is also essentially built around the options-and-choice model of prescriptive strategy, with implementation of the agreed strategic choice.
6 Chandler, A (1962) *Strategy and Structure*, MIT Press, Cambridge, Mass. This historical survey of three large US companies in the early twentieth century sought to discover what had made US industry so powerful. Chandler also examined General Motors, with reference to Sloan, A P (1963) *My years with General Motors*, Sedgewick & Jackson, London.

7 Marx, T (1991) 'Removing obstacles to effective strategic planning', *Long Range Planning*, 24 Aug. This research paper is reprinted in De Wit, R and Meyer, R (1994) *Strategy: Process, content and context*, West Publishing.

8 Jackson, T (1995) 'Big enough to make mistakes', *Financial Times*, 21 Dec, p13. Some very interesting insights on risk-taking in large companies are also in this article.

9 Lenz, R T and Lyles, M (1985) 'Paralysis by analysis: Is your planning system becoming too rational?', *Long Range Planning*, 18 Aug. This is also reprinted in De Wit, R and Meyer, R Ibid.

10 Cane, A (1996) 'Telecom competition hots up', *Financial Times*, 20 Jan, p2.

11 Lynch, R (1994) *European Business Strategies*, 2nd edn, Kogan Page, London.

12 Alchian, A A (1950) 'Uncertainty, evolution and economic theory', *Journal of Political Economy*, 58, pp211–21, first proposed this.

13 Hofer, C W and Schendel, D (1986) *Strategy Formulation: Analytical Concepts*, 11th edn, West Publishing, St Paul, Minn. This book used the same approach in the 1970s and 1980s.

14 Hannan, M and Freeman, J (1977) 'The population ecology of organisations', *American Journal of Sociology*, Mar, 82, pp929–64.

15 Williamson, O E (1991) 'Strategizing, economizing and economic organisation', *Strategic Management Journal*, 12, pp75–94.

16 This represents one particular view of the relationship between economics and strategy. For a more general discussion, *see* Rumelt, R, Schendel, D and Teece, D (1991) 'Strategic management and economics', *Strategic Management Journal*, 12, pp5–29.

17 Stacey, R (1993) *Strategic Management and Organisational Dynamics*, Pitman Publishing, London, p211.

18 Gleick, J (1988) *Chaos: the making of a new science*, Heinemann, London.

19 Lloyd, T (1995) 'Drawing a line under corporate strategy', *Financial Times*, 8 Sept, p10. This provides a short, readable account of some of the consequences of this strategic approach.

20 Hutchison Whampoa Annual Report and Accounts 1994.

21 Holberton, S (1995) 'Risk and reward in China', *Financial Times*, 23 Mar, p19.

22 Lindemann, M (1995) 'Hutchison Mobilfunk', *Financial Times*, 20 Nov, p10.

23 Williamson, O E (1985) *The Economic Institutions of Capitalism: firms, markets and relational contracting*, The Free Press, Boston, Mass.

24 Cyert, R and March, J (1963) *A Behaviour Theory of the Firm*, Prentice Hall, Englewood Cliffs, NJ.

25 Moss Kanter, R (1983) *The Change Masters*, Unwin Hyman (the book is full of examples).

26 Pettigrew, A (1985) *The Awakening Giant: continuity and change at ICI*, Blackwell, Oxford, p458. Note also his earlier book (1973) *The Politics of Organisational Decision Making*, Tavistock, London.

27 Pettigrew, A and Whipp, R (1991) *Managing Change for Competitive Success*, Blackwell, Oxford, p30.

28 Doz, Y (1986) *Strategic Management in Multinational Companies*, Pergamon, Oxford, pp95–6.

29 Reve, T (1990) 'The firm as a nexus of internal and external contracts' in Aoki, M, Gustafsson, M and Williamson, O E (eds) *The Firm as a nexus of Treaties*, Sage, London.

30 Johanson, J and Mattson, L-G (1992) 'Network positions and strategic action' in Axelsson, B and Easton, G (eds) *Industrial Networks: a new view of reality*, Routledge, London.

31 Dixit, A and Nalebuff, B (1991) *Thinking Strategically: the competitive edge in business, politics and everyday life*, W W Norton, New York.

32 Mintzberg, H (1987) 'Crafting strategy', *Harvard Business Review*, July–Aug.

33 De Geus, A (1988) 'Planning as learning', *Harvard Business Review*, Mar–Apr, p70.

34 *See The Economist* (1995) 'The Knowledge', 11 Nov, p107.

35 Senge, P (1990) 'The leader's new work: Building learning organisations', *Sloan Management Review*, Fall, and Senge, P (1990) *The Fifth Discipline: the art and practice of the learning organisation*, Doubleday, New York.

36 Quinn, S, Mills, D and Friesen, B (1992) 'The Learning Organisation', *European Management Journal*, 10, June, p146.

37 Argyris, C (1991) 'Teaching smart people how to learn', *Harvard Business Review*, May–June, p99.

38 Burgoyne, J, Pedler, M and Boydell, T (1994) *Towards the Learning Company*, McGraw-Hill, Maidenhead.

39 Jones, A and Hendry, C (1994) 'The learning organisation: adult learning and organisational transformation', *British Journal of Management*, pp153–62. *See also* a thoughtful critique of the learning approach in Egan, C (1995) *Creating Organisational Advantage*, Butterworth–Heinemann, Ch 5.

40 *See* the Hofstede research and the *power/distance* data in the last section of Chapter 8 of this book.

41 Hu, Y S (1992) 'Global or stateless firms with international operations', *California Management Review*, Winter, pp115–26.

42 Granovetter, M (1985) 'Economic action and social culture: the problem of embeddedness', *American Journal of Sociology*, 91(3), pp481–510.

43 Whittington, R (1993) *What is strategy – and does it matter?*, Routledge, London, p37.

44 *Financial Times* (1995) 'Hollowing out in Japan', 28 Mar, p21; Nakanoto, M (1995) 'Knocked off the road again', *Financial Times*, 20 Apr, p25.

45 Kluckhohn, C and Strodtbeck, F (1961) *Variations in Value Orientations*, Peterson, New York.

46 Furnham, A (1995) 'The case for cultural diversity', *Financial Times*, 8 Dec, p11. The author was Professor of Psychology at University College, London, at the time the article was written.

47 Case adapted from Jackson, T (1995) 'Plugged into partnerships', *Financial Times*, 2 Nov, p17.

Strategy, structure and style

After you have worked through this chapter, you will be able to:

- understand the historical background to the development of organisational structures to match chosen strategies;

- evaluate critically the arguments that strategy and structure have a more complex relationship that that suggested by the early strategists;

- assess the benefits and problems associated with the newer, learning-based organisational structures;

- explore how strategy and structure are inter-related;

- understand the concept of strategic fit;

- evaluate the importance of changing an organisation's management style at the same time as changing its strategy.

INTRODUCTION

A major debate has been taking place over the last 30 years regarding the relationship between the strategy and the structure of the organisation. In the past, it was considered that the strategy was decided first and the structure then followed. Some researchers have questioned this approach and taken the view that strategy and structure are inter-related. In this chapter we examine this important debate.

Since the 1980s, there has been another important strategic debate concerning the organisation's ability to change its style and culture. Such a change could have a profound impact on the organisation's development and choice of strategic options – for example, a more risk-taking style may well produce strategic options different from those of a more conservative style.

In this chapter we examine these important debates, and Fig 18.1 shows the overall structure of the chapter.

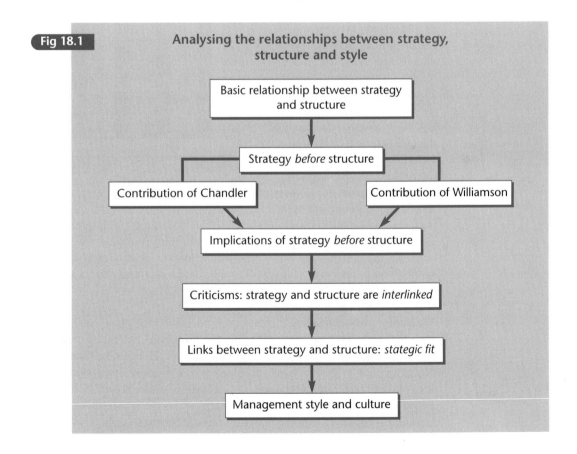

Fig 18.1   **Analysing the relationships between strategy, structure and style**

How Sony moved out across Asia[1]

Over a period of 20 years, Sony has developed its trading and manufacturing across the continent of Asia. This case examines the reasoning which lay behind their development strategy and the implications of the organisational links that have been formed.

Market progress

In 1997, Sony, the Japanese consumer electronics group, planned to make more than one million mobile telephones a year at an industrial plant near Beijing airport in China. The US$29 million joint venture was Sony's first on the mainland of China. It was typical of a great wave of Japanese investment flooding over many of its industrial neighbours, in particular focussing on China.

The potential political and financial risks of investing in China were significant but Sony, like others, could no longer afford to be over-cautious about entering a market of more than one billion people. Moreover, the Chinese market for consumer electronics was growing at 20 per cent per year. As Mr Kenji Tamiya, Sony's senior managing director explained, East Asia, including China, was a 'gold-mine for existing products'.

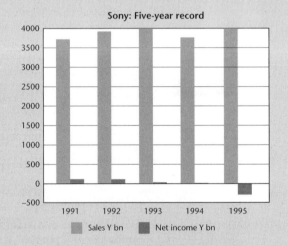

Sony: Five-year record

Sales Y bn   Net income Y bn

Sony's experience in East Asia is a good illustration of the Japanese investment trends in the region. The first cautious steps into local assembly used mainly imported components for export to third countries. There followed ever-larger investment now using higher proportions of locally-made components and selling into the local market as well as to other Asian countries, the US and, increasingly, back to Japan.

The history of the company

Sony first entered the market in East Asia in April 1967 almost by chance, when the acquisition of another Japanese company happened to include a radio and telephone production unit in Taiwan. Its second step into the region – a television tuner factory in South Korea – also came as the result of a company acquisition in 1973. Then followed a nine-year gap, during which Sony made no further investments in the region, focussing instead on the home market. That was understandable, in a period when the domestic market in Japan was experiencing unprecedented growth.

In 1984 Sony opened a radio, Walkman and telephone plant in Malaysia – the company's first greenfield site in Asia. This was followed the same year by a video-cassette recorder factory in Taiwan. It was not until after the 1985 Plaza Accord, when the world's leading economies agreed to co-operate to devalue an over-valued US dollar, that the turning point came. That year the yen touched ¥263 to the dollar, but has since moved to around ¥100 to the dollar, in the process rendering large areas of Japanese domestic manufacturing uncompetitive.

Sony's move into Asia

Like many other Japanese companies, Sony took the option to move its production off-shore in search of cheaper costs and easier exchange rates. 'We just had to do it, to keep our products competitively priced,' explained Mr Toshiyuki Takinaga, the general manager for consumer and audiovisual products. By the end of the 1980s, eight more Sony plants were in operation in Singapore, Malaysia and Thailand. These have subsequently been joined by another five – in Indonesia, Singapore, China, Vietnam and India. By 1995, some 25 000 of Sony's employees were in Asia, out of 135 000 employees worldwide, although most of the company's technical and production development was still conducted in Japan.

The Plaza Accord and the need to compensate for the high yen dictated the timing of Sony's Asian expansion. However, this was only part of the underlying rationale. Mr Tamiya explained: 'We were not only seeking inexpensive labour. We had a clear vision at that time that making investments would raise the purchasing power in Asian countries so that they would become more important markets for Asian products.'As workers gained higher wages, they would spend a portion on electronic goods.

Fig 18.2 — Sony manufacturing operations

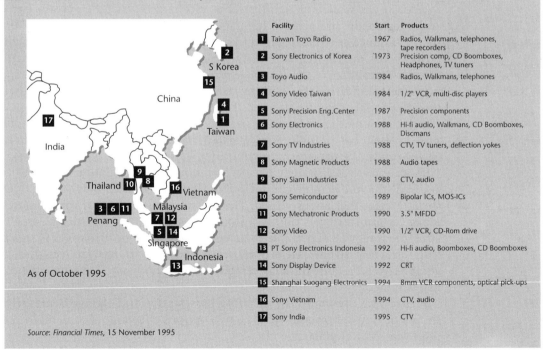

	Facility	Start	Products
1	Taiwan Toyo Radio	1967	Radios, Walkmans, telephones, tape recorders
2	Sony Electronics of Korea	1973	Precision comp, CD Boomboxes, Headphones, TV tuners
3	Toyo Audio	1984	Radios, Walkmans, telephones
4	Sony Video Taiwan	1984	1/2" VCR, multi-disc players
5	Sony Precision Eng.Center	1987	Precision components
6	Sony Electronics	1988	Hi-fi audio, Walkmans, CD Boomboxes, Discmans
7	Sony TV Industries	1988	CTV, TV tuners, deflection yokes
8	Sony Magnetic Products	1988	Audio tapes
9	Sony Siam Industries	1988	CTV, audio
10	Sony Semiconductor	1989	Bipolar ICs, MOS-ICs
11	Sony Mechatronic Products	1990	3.5" MFDD
12	Sony Video	1990	1/2" VCR, CD-Rom drive
13	PT Sony Electronics Indonesia	1992	Hi-fi audio, Boomboxes, CD Boomboxes
14	Sony Display Device	1992	CRT
15	Shanghai Suogang Electronics	1994	8mm VCR components, optical pick-ups
16	Sony Vietnam	1994	CTV, audio
17	Sony India	1995	CTV

As of October 1995

Source: Financial Times, 15 November 1995

MINICASE continued

Sony planning

Sony's planners were also guided by the company philosophy of keeping its sales split – supported by local production – in proportions roughly equal to the breakdown of the world consumer electronics market. Thus one-fifth of Sony's sales were in Asia, compared with a one-quarter share of the market in Europe and a one-quarter share in North America. Mr Tamiya aimed to keep the balance about the same for the foreseeable future. However, Asian economic dynamism was such that he believed that, while maintaining the balance, the area could double its world share of Sony's existing products to between 40 and 50 per cent in the next ten years.

Source: *Financial Times*, 15 November 1995.

CASE QUESTIONS

1 *What were the main reasons for Sony's expansion into East Asia?*

2 *How should Sony set up structures to manage such a range of manufacturing and market opportunities?*

18.1 THE BASIC RELATIONSHIP BETWEEN STRATEGY AND STRUCTURE

From a *prescriptive* strategy perspective, the purpose of an organisational structure is to allocate the work and administrative mechanisms that are necessary to control and integrate the strategies of an organisation.[2] Thus work is allocated to functions, such as finance and marketing, and recombined in divisions or departments, with power being distributed accordingly. Such a definition is consistent with other, broader definitions of structure taken from an organisational theory perspective.[3] Importantly, in this definition the strategy is developed first and only then is the organisational structure defined. For the prescriptive strategist, organisational structure is a matter of how the strategy is *implemented*: it does not influence the strategy itself. For example, Sony would define its strategy for moving into Asia and only consider the necessary structure after it had made the opening moves.

From an *emergent* strategy perspective, however, the relationship between strategy and structure is more complex. The organisation itself may restrict or enhance the strategies that are proposed. The existing organisational structure may even make certain strategies highly unlikely. For example, an informal, free-flowing structure might be better able to generate new strategic initiatives than a bureaucratic structure. In the case of Sony, for instance, the move into Asia through joint ventures could require different structures from those required where the company had wholly-owned subsidiaries.

Figure 18.3 illustrates the differing prescriptive and emergent perspectives. It should be noted, however, that the two options over-simplify the many combinations that exist in practice.

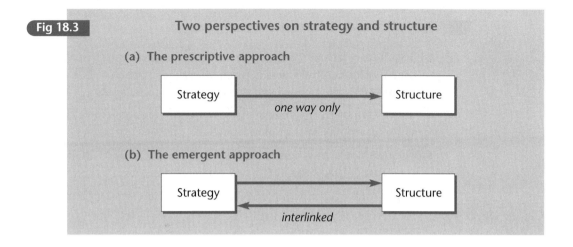

Fig 18.3   **Two perspectives on strategy and structure**

(a) The prescriptive approach

Strategy   *one way only*   →   Structure

(b) The emergent approach

Strategy   *interlinked*   Structure

Organisational structure therefore deserves careful consideration. In Chapter 8 we began the exploration of the organisation's culture and power structures. We now examine different types of organisational structure and how they relate to strategy.

From at least the 1960s[4] the *prescriptive* approach was employed. It was recommended that the formulation of strategy was studied *before* the development of the organisational structure to implement that strategy. There was empirical evidence to support this approach from the strategist Alfred Chandler and others.[5] In the 1970s, the economist Oliver Williamson explored the role of the centre as companies become larger and strategies more diverse.[6] Both Chandler and Williamson took the view that the organisation's strategy came first and structure second. These are not the only two approaches to organisational structure, however.

Since the 1960s, some strategists and organisational theorists have looked further at the evidence of how strategy is best developed. They have concluded that there are two problems with the concept of putting strategy before structure:[7]

● There is an artificial distinction between the *content* of strategy and the *process* by which that strategy is implemented.

● It is incorrect to describe the relationship between strategy and structure as being one-way only. They have argued that it is possible that a different organisational *structure* may actually lead to a different corporate *strategy*.

On these arguments, strategy and structure are more closely inter-related. Therefore structure needs to be considered while strategy is still being developed. For this reason, the relationship between these two elements is explored in Part 5 of this text, i.e. while strategy is still under development and before it is 'implemented' as explored in Part 6.

> **Key strategic principles**
>
> - For the prescriptive strategist, strategy is developed first and then the organisational structure is defined afterwards. Structure is a matter of how strategy is implemented and does not influence the strategy itself.
>
> - For the emergent strategist, the relationship is more complex. The organisation itself may restrict or enhance the proposed strategies.
>
> - Two well-known writers, Alfred Chandler and Oliver Williamson, took the view that strategy came first and structure second.
>
> - Other strategists and theorists have argued that strategy and structure are more closely inter-related and structure needs to be considered while strategy is being developed.

18.2 STRATEGY BEFORE STRUCTURE: CHANDLER'S CONTRIBUTION

To understand the logic behind this prescriptive approach to the development of organisational structures, it is helpful to look at the historical background. Prior to the early 1960s, the American strategist, Alfred Chandler Jr, studied how some leading US corporations had developed their strategies in the first half of the twentieth century.[8] He then drew some major conclusions from this empirical evidence, the foremost one being that the organisation first needed to develop its strategy and, after this, to devise the organisation structure that delivered that strategy.

Chandler noted how, during the late nineteenth and early twentieth century, American companies moved from craft industry production to mass production: their strategies changed fundamentally. Craftsmen had previously made individual items using their skills, knowledge and judgement. Steam power and electricity had already made manufacturing easier but, in many cases, it was still undertaken on a piece-by-piece basis. There were limited economies of scale. Then came the age of standardised products coupled with simplified engineering techniques. Machinery was developed that gave much lower costs and allowed customer prices to drop. Instead of such products only being available to the few who were rich, mass markets developed. This led to further economies of scale that reduced prices even further. Strategy changed fundamentally for such companies.

The classic example of such change took place under the guiding genius of Henry Ford with his development of the Model T car. Between 1909 and 1916, the price of the car dropped from US$850 to US$360 and the number of cars shipped rose from 14 000 per annum to 506 000 per annum.[9] New strategies and organisational structures were needed in every aspect of the company during this period.

Chandler studied a number of North American companies during the first half of the twentieth century, including Ford's rival, General Motors. He did not study Ford itself. He concluded that as companies grew in size and complexity they needed what he called a *general office* to handle the main planning and co-ordinating work of the various functions of a business, including the marketing, operations, finance and human resources (discussed in Part 2 of this book). The general office was concerned with the long-term health of the enterprise: it *devised the company's strategy*. Once the strategy was formulated, the general office then *implemented* it by designing a suitable organisational structure and allocating resources such as finance, equipment and people to the various parts of the organisation.

Chandler drew a clear distinction between *devising* a strategy and *implementing* it. He defined strategy as:

> *'The determination of the basic long-term goals and objectives of an enterprise, and the adoption of courses of action and the allocation of resources necessary for carrying out these goals.'*[10]

The task of developing the strategy took place at the centre of the organisation. The job of implementing it then fell to the various functional areas.

Chandler's research suggested that, once a strategy had been developed, it was necessary to consider the structure needed to carry it out. A new strategy might require extra resources, or new personnel or equipment which would alter the work of the enterprise, making a new organisational structure necessary: 'The design of the organisation through which the enterprise is administered,' to quote Chandler.

The principle that strategy came before organisational structure was formed, therefore, by considering the industrial developments of the early twentieth century.[11] Whether such considerations are still relevant as we move into the new millennium will be considered in Section 18.5 of this chapter.

Key strategic principles

- Chandler contended that it was first necessary to develop the strategy. After this task was completed, the organisation was then devised to deliver that strategy.

- His conclusion was based on his study of the way that North American businesses were formed and organised in the early part of the twentieth century. He only studied businesses that had developed from small enterprises into larger, more diversified structures.

18.3 STRATEGY BEFORE STRUCTURE: WILLIAMSON'S CONTRIBUTION[12]

Chandler's empirical studies showed that divisional structures became necessary to manage large corporations. At the same time, such organisational structures often became more diverse: for example, Case study 18.1 describes how in 1924 General Motors acquired property interests and set up facilities to make upholstery and spark plugs for cars. However, Chandler never explored the full implications of diversity. When corporations become really diverse, it is difficult to achieve the linkages across the parts of the corporation that deliver competitive advantage. The corporate centre adds little beyond acting as a holding company operation.

It is possible that diversified divisions would be even more efficient without any central direction at all, thus saving substantial costs. It may be better for such corporations to take the next logical strategic step and demerge.

Writing in the 1970s, the economist Oliver Williamson explored the role of the centre as organisations became more diverse in their business activities. However, unlike Chandler, his work was based on theoretical economic concepts and he undertook no new empirical research in reaching his conclusions. He agreed with Chandler that, as companies become more diverse, divisional structures were more efficient. He then proceeded to explore the contribution made by the centre to divisionalised companies. In particular, he raised the question of whether such divisions would be better served by being sold off and subject only to the pressure and scrutiny of outside capital markets – that is, national or regional stock exchanges where the shares of companies are bought and sold.

In essence, Williamson concluded that capital markets were not as efficient as the well-managed centre of a diversified company, for two related reasons:

1 Investors in capital markets skim across many companies and markets. The amount of information that they have tends to be widespread but lacking in the depth necessary for detailed strategy evaluation.

2 Capital markets could alert competitors to the organisation's plans, and so it may not be in the best interests of the organisation to reveal full and detailed information. The consequence is that investors in capital markets have to rely inevitably on this imperfect company data in making their decisions.

For Williamson, there was an important implication for the way the centre of a divisional structure was managed: it had to maintain an appropriate distance from the divisions. More generally, he suggested that optimum divisionalisation involved six elements:[13]

● identifying separable economic activities within the organisation (which we have called strategic business units (SBUs));

● according quasi-autonomous status (usually of a profit-centred nature) to each;

● monitoring the efficient performance of each division;

● allocating cash flows to high yield uses;

● performing strategic planning;

● awarding incentives to the best performing divisions.

Many of the above areas are explored further in Chapters 19 and 20. For our purposes, it is important to note that Williamson clearly took the view that the strategy needed to be resolved first and then the organisational structure followed from this. He concluded that an efficient form of organisational structure was to have a central headquarters allocating central resources to its divisions from a distance – in other words, acting as a holding company.

Key strategic principles

● Williamson explored the role of the centre in diversified businesses. He concluded that the centre should stand back from divisions when it came to allocating resources between them and, subsequently, to monitoring and controlling them.

● He supported Chandler's view that strategy came first and organisational structure came afterwards.

18.4 IMPLICATIONS OF DESIGNING STRUCTURES TO FIT STRATEGY[14]

At this stage it is useful to consider some basic implications of structure following from strategy, although the detailed design of organisational structures will be explored in Chapter 20. Once the organisation's strategy had been decided, Chandler recommended that there were four main questions to be explored in developing its structure:

● What are the work needs to be undertaken to implement the strategy?

● Who should undertake this work?

● Is any of the work inter-related?

● Are there limits to the size of the organisation?

In the early to mid-twentieth century, managers answered these questions by specifying the *formalised relationships* between employees, managers and directors in an organisation. They were supported by such early writers as F W Taylor and Henri Fayol and by later strategists, including Alfred Sloan, and Frank and Lilian Gilbreth. Many modern strategy texts also follow this approach, employing the following principles:[15]

● formal structures;

● clear responsibilities;

● identified lines of reporting;

● a *central directorate* whose strategy decisions are handed down to employees.

As we saw in Chapter 17, such concepts have been increasingly questioned in more recent years by strategists such as Senge and Mintzberg. However, in terms of clarity of purpose, formalised relationships do have real merit and may be particularly appropriate to certain companies and cultures. Moreover, even if some modification is required, they do present a clear approach to the development of organisational structure.

Beyond these general design issues, Chandler identified four key parameters for strategy growth that would influence organisational structure:

- expansion of volume;
- geographical dispersion;
- vertical integration (adding value by absorbing the tasks of the supplier or customer);
- product diversification.

He argued that, as any of the four changes occurred, new organisational structures were needed to handle them. Two principle consequences of this approach required to be explored.

1 *Increased bureaucracy* During the early twentieth century, some leading organisations grew substantially in size and required more complex organisational structures – for example, the growth of General Motors (US) as described in Case study 18.1. These larger units were often associated with increased bureaucracy but they were not necessarily less efficient. Research evidence suggests that larger companies performed better when they had more, rather than less, bureaucracy. However, larger companies were also often associated with lower job satisfaction, higher absenteeism and higher staff turnover.[16]

2 *Increased decentralisation* As an organisation becomes more diverse in its products or markets, there is a greater likelihood that it will need to reorganise its structures. Specifically, more complex forms of organisational structure may be necessary because the centre becomes increasingly isolated from the place where decisions are needed and can best be made. Separate divisions within the organisation may need to be set up and some power delegated to them. When an organisation changes from being a one-product company to including these more complex elements, it may need to move from *centralisation* to *decentralisation*.

In designing organisational structures, one important issue is the extent to which decision making is taken from the centre of the organisation and passed to subsidiaries or divisions.[17] There are no simple solutions to the *balance* that may need to be struck. According to many strategists, this should only be explored once the basic strategy has been agreed.

The main arguments are summarised in Exhibit 18.1. These are general issues affecting the direction of the organisation, of which strategy is one element. However, a series of issues also arises, using some of the same principles, directed at the way *strategic planning* is conducted in an organisation: should this be centralised or decentralised? The empirical work of Campbell and Goold[18] falls mainly in this latter area and is not to be confused with more general considerations on the subject. (We examine strategic planning in Chapter 19.)

| Exhibit 18.1 | The balancing considerations between centralisation and decentralisation |

Advantages of centralisation	Elements favouring decentralisation
● It is possible to produce a consistent strategy across the organisation	● Enables a strong response to local circumstances
● The greater likelihood of economies of scale	● When decisions are very complex or localised, centralised decision making may not be sensible
● It facilitates co-ordination of sub-units	● It is difficult to provide high-quality customer services from the centre
● Simpler control systems than with a decentralised structure	● Provides opportunities to develop general management talent
● Faster decision making, with less compromise	● Motivates staff in locations outside the centre
● Limited geographic distance between HQ and subsidiary	● A more diversified product range
● High degree of inter-relationship between sub-units	● A stable environment
● High technology content	● It is appropriate when unit is unimportant to the centre
● Resource allocation by the centre is much simpler	

Key strategic principles

● According to the early strategists, formal structures, clear responsibilities, identified lines of reporting and, for strategy development, a central directorate are all important elements of organisational design. They are undertaken after the basic strategy has been agreed.

● As organisations become larger and more complex, it may be necessary to form divisions and decentralise some power by delegating it to them.

● The centralisation versus decentralisation issue may be particularly important in designing the organisation's structure. According to many strategists, this should only be undertaken once the basic strategy has been decided. There are no simple rules to define where the balance needs to be struck between centralisation and decentralisation.

How General Motors organised its future

General Motors Corporation (US) is the world's largest manufacturer of cars and trucks. This case study examines the strategies and the organisational structures used by the company to gain and maintain its dominance of its chosen businesses. It contrasts the strategies and structures of 1924 with those of 1994.

General Motors gained market leadership from Ford in the 1920s and has maintained this position for the remainder of the century, in spite of what some strategists would regard as major strategic errors. The company has also grown in other directions but remains primarily a vehicle manufacturer.

General Motors in 1924[19]

After the near-collapse of GM around 1920, Réné Du Pont appointed a young manager with ideas to restructure the company: Alfred Sloan. The company was then reorganised by Sloan along the lines of what today we would recognise as the principles of *market segmentation*, e.g. Cadillac in the low-volume, high-price segment; Chevrolet in the high-volume, low-price segment. Each operation was set up as a separate division with its own marketing, finance and operations management structure. Specifically, the new organisation ensured that the divisions did not compete against each other in the market place. The organisation structure is shown in Fig 18.4.

To ensure that there was adequate co-ordination across the divisions on engineering, manufacturing and especially distribution, inter-divisional committees were also established. It was found that such co-operation worked more smoothly when the groups did not compete. Nevertheless, where products were sold between divisions (e.g. accessories), the goods were valued at the prices existing in the *market place*. This ensured that it was always possible to evaluate the performance of divisions, especially those parts and accessories groups supplying several divisions across GM.

In devising the new structure, special emphasis was laid on statistical and financial controls. These were considered essential for the monitoring of divisional performance by the central Executive Committee. The lack of such controls had been one of the reasons why the company had major problems around 1920. Advisory staff were also introduced to help co-ordinate and plan the provision of expert advice which was offered across the group.

It was the *Executive Committee* who made all the major entrepreneurial and strategic decisions for the group. This consisted of the Chairman, Chief Executive and heads of the leading Divisions. It was given time, space and commitment to examine the broad strategic direction of the company. Strategic control was vested in the centre with day-to-day operations firmly decentralised to the individual operating companies. This was a totally new policy for its time. The management principles developed for this type of organisation have been adopted subsequently by many companies around the world as they have grown in size and complexity.

Between 1924 and 1928, GM's new structure served the company well:

- Its market share rose from 18.8 per cent to 43.3 per cent. Sales in 1928 were US$276 million.

- Production more than doubled from 1.5 million cars per annum to around 4 million per annum.

GM was helped by major problems at its chief rival, Ford Motor Company. Ford completely closed down for 18 months during the period in order to reorganise and rebuild. However, even when Ford returned, GM maintained its market leadership, which it still held in North America in the 1990s.

General Motors in 1994[20]

By 1994, the company had grown from its base in cars and trucks into other areas. Total sales were US$155 billion, of which US$127 billion was in cars and trucks. The outline organisational structure at this time is shown in Fig 18.5.

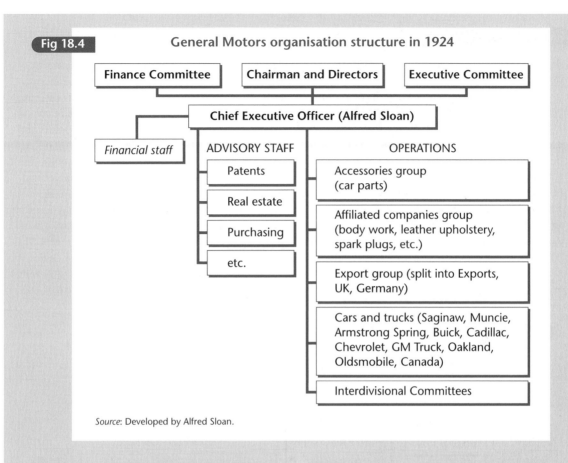

Fig 18.4 General Motors organisation structure in 1924

Source: Developed by Alfred Sloan.

During the 1980s, the company had expanded into two important new areas as a result of decisions taken by the then Chief Executive and his immediate colleagues. EDS and Hughes (*see* Fig 18.5) were acquired in 1984 and 1985 for US$2.55 billion and US$ 2.7 billion respectively, when GM decided that it needed to diversify out of cars. The purchases were funded with car profits earned between 1979 and 1985 when the North American car market had been protected from Japanese competition. Rather than using this period to lower its car production costs, GM moved outside the industry. At the same time, Japanese car manufacturers were reported to have lower production costs (by US$2000 per car) coupled with higher quality than most American cars.

Although the company was the world's largest producer of cars and trucks, it was heavily reliant on the massive North American market for nearly 80 per cent of its sales and was working on the low sales margin of just 0.7 per cent in its North American operations. Both its two leading rivals, Ford and Toyota, had lower production costs. Its international operations had clearly developed substantially since the early 1920s, but it still displayed the strategic insularity that has led some American companies to

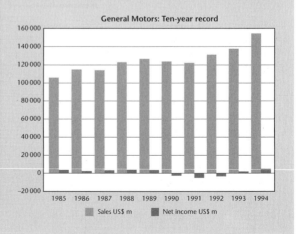

downgrade the importance of international expansion and involvement.

From an organisational viewpoint, its North American operations were still substantially the same in 1994, compared with 1924, even if they were rather larger. The main differences lay in the increased activities overseas and the two totally new business activities acquired during the 1980s. GM was also building a global purchasing operation for all its car and truck interests. More fundamentally, it had grown so large that it had no choice but to operate company divisions at a distance from each other. It was now a vast, major enterprise that was attempting to introduce new quality standards, lean manufacturing techniques and greater manufacturing flexibility (see

Chapter 10 for descriptions of these areas) across its North American and international operations. However, its whole strategy was geared towards catching up with the Japanese car producers who had become like-for-like more efficient, possessed lower costs and produced some more reliable products than GM. Even the advantage to GM of the rising Japanese Yen had diminished as the Japanese car companies continued to open up car manufacturing in the USA.

Global competition, over-capacity in a cyclical car market (see Chapter 3) and widely diversified operations had radically altered some aspects of GM's strategy in 1994 compared to seventy years earlier. It had become a major world company, but many of its problems were the result of its own strategic mistakes.

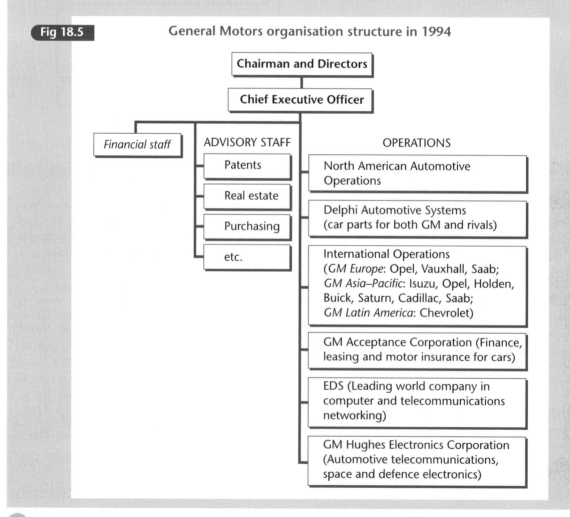

Fig 18.5 General Motors organisation structure in 1994

- **Chairman and Directors**
- **Chief Executive Officer**

Financial staff

ADVISORY STAFF
- Patents
- Real estate
- Purchasing
- etc.

OPERATIONS
- North American Automotive Operations
- Delphi Automotive Systems (car parts for both GM and rivals)
- International Operations (*GM Europe*: Opel, Vauxhall, Saab; *GM Asia–Pacific*: Isuzu, Opel, Holden, Buick, Saturn, Cadillac, Saab; *GM Latin America*: Chevrolet)
- GM Acceptance Corporation (Finance, leasing and motor insurance for cars)
- EDS (Leading world company in computer and telecommunications networking)
- GM Hughes Electronics Corporation (Automotive telecommunications, space and defence electronics)

CASE QUESTIONS

1 *Since the 1920s, the organisation structure of GM does not appear to have changed fundamentally: separate divisions still report to the centre. So what has changed about the company and its environment? What implications, if any, might this have for a change in the relationship between the centre and the divisions?*

2 *When a company grows as large as GM, what problems would you envisage in operating a divisional structure?*

3 *Are the learning strategy concepts of Senge relevant to GM's strategy and structure? (See Chapter 17 and Section 18.5.2 for guidance.)*

4 *Can strategy 'emerge' in such a large company? If so, why, where and how?*

18.5 CRITICISMS: STRATEGY AND STRUCTURE ARE INTERLINKED

According to some modern strategists, strategy and structure are interlinked. It may not be optimal for an organisation to develop its structure *after* it has developed its strategy. The relationship is more complex in two respects:

- Strategy and the structure associated with it may need to develop *at the same time* in an experimental way: as the strategy develops, so does the structure. The organisation *learns to adapt* to its changing environment.

- If the strategy process is emergent, then the learning and experimentation involved may need a *more open and less formal* organisation structure.

In recent years, it has been suggested[21] that the impact of process and organisation on strategy has been constantly underplayed. The contribution of employees in energising the organisation and promoting innovation may often be underestimated. Moreover, the quality of management and the organisational structure itself will all have an impact on strategy and may even be a source of competitive advantage. In this sense, it cannot be said that people and process issues arise after the strategy has been agreed.

It has also been pointed out that there are some companies which have broadly similar resources but differ markedly in their performance. The reasons for this disparity may be associated with the way that companies are organised and conduct their activities, rather than with differences in strategy. The five main weaknesses of the strategy before structure approach are explored in Exhibit 18.2.

Exhibit 18.2 — Summary of the five main criticisms of the strategy-first, structure-afterwards process

1 Structures may be *too rigid, hierarchical and bureaucratic* to cope with the newer social values and rapidly-changing environments of the 1990s.

2 *The type of structure* is just as important as the business area in developing the organisation's strategy. It is the structure that will restrict, guide and form the strategy options that the organisation can generate. A learning organisation may be required and power given to more junior managers. In this sense, strategy and organisational structure are inter-related and need to be developed at the same time.

Exhibit 18.2 continued

3 *Value-chain configurations* that favour cost cutting or, alternatively, new market opportunities may also alter the organisation required.

4 *The complexity of strategic change* needs to be managed, implying that more complex organisational considerations will be involved. Simple configurations such as a move from a functional to a divisional structure were only a starting point in the process.

5 *The role of top and middle management* in the formation of strategy may also need to be reassessed: Chandler's view that strategy is decided by the top leadership alone has been challenged. Particularly for new innovative strategies, middle management and the organisation's culture and structure may be important. The work of the leader in empowering middle management may require a new approach – the collegiate style of leadership.

18.5.1 Changes in the business environment and social values

To explain the movement from functional to divisional structures, we examined how corporations in the early twentieth century set up the first multi-divisional organisations. Since that time, the environment has changed substantially.[22] The workplace itself, the relationships between workers and managers and the skills of employees have all altered substantially. Old organisational structures embedded in past understandings may therefore be suspect. Exhibit 18.3 summarises how the environment has changed.

Exhibit 18.3 **A comparison of the early and late twentieth-century business environments**

Early twentieth century	Late twentieth century
● Uneducated workers, typically just moved from agricultural work into the cities	● Better educated, computer-literate, skilled
● Knowledge of simple engineering and technology	● Complex, computer-driven, large scale
● The new science of management recognised simple cause-and-effect relationships	● Multi-faceted and complex nature of management now partially understood
● Growing, newly-industrialising markets and suppliers	● Mix of some mature, cyclical markets and some high growth new technology markets and suppliers
● Sharp distinctions between management and workers	● Greater overlap between management and workers in some industrialised countries

18.5.2   The learning organisation, empowerment and organisational structure

According to Senge and others, the strategy processes of the late twentieth century need to be adaptive and involve *learning* throughout the organisation, not just top management (*see* Chapter 17). Learning must be matched by the appropriate organisational structure. It needs to be more responsive to the changing environment, adaptable and open to initiatives from middle and junior management. More junior managers need to be given more power – *empowerment.*

Importantly, Senge draws an important distinction between two types of learning, only one of which arises from the environmental changes outlined in Exhibit 18.3. These are:

- *Adaptive learning.* Understanding changes *outside in the environment* and adapting to these.

- *Generative learning.* Creating and exploring new strategy areas for positive expansion *within the organisation itself.*

Both types of learning will come from experimentation, discussion and feedback within the organisation. Rigid, formal, hierarchical organisations are unlikely to provide this. New, more fluid structures are needed, according to Senge. It is interesting to note that in the high growth economies of Japan in the 1970s and 1980s and in South-East Asia in the 1990s, one of the major distinguishing features has been participation in the planning process, coupled with flexibility and adaptability, rather than rigid, formal plans.[23][24]

Using similar evidence, the management guru, Tom Peters,[25] suggests that leaders and organisations need to be more adaptive if they are to have a greater probability of developing sustainable competitive advantage. If the organisational structure has been successfully developed as a flexible, adaptive organisation then it will be able to deliver what he has called the three main outcomes of strategy:

- total customer satisfaction;

- innovation;

- total commitment by all its members to provide service and quality.

Given these three prime outcomes, Peters argues that they will only arise if the organisation is flexible. Such a structure is more important than any specific strategy. Hence, structure comes *before* strategy. It is the process itself that will deliver the successful strategy rather than some pre-defined strategy handed down from top management.

A specific example of the link between organisation structure and strategy concerns the generation of the strategy options outlined in Chapters 13 and 14. Kanter[26] has argued that the way the company is organised is crucial to this task. Such a structure must come *before* the strategy options are explored in order to ensure that the most innovative options are developed: top management is unlikely to be able to generate these by itself.

Case study 18.2 on ASEA Brown Boveri describes a modern attempt to introduce into a large company the strategies of learning and empowerment. The implementation aspects of learning are explored in Chapter 21.

18.5.3 Value-chain implications for organisational structure

In Chapter 11, we examined Galbraith's view[27] that the value chain could be divided into two broad categories:

- *Upstream components* involving incoming logistics, purchasing and production.
- *Downstream components* covering marketing, service and R&D.

According to this basic division, typical strategies to add value might be:

- *Upstream*: cost reduction strategies, mass production strategies for unsegmented markets.
- *Downstream*: marketing, branding, innovation, often in segmented markets.

Although this two-way separation over-simplifies the complexities of strategy development, it does contain a useful and workable distinction. From a strategy viewpoint, the organisation required for upstream activities, according to the Galbraith definition, is very different from that required further downstream:

- *Upstream organisation structure.* A tightly controlled, centralised structure to achieve such strategies as economies of scale. Profits may be made by operating few plants that are centrally controlled and organised.
- *Downstream organisation structure.* Looser control and a more decentralised structure capable of responding to differentiated market initiatives. Profits are made by small, locally-flexible plants with management responsibility only loosely co-ordinated at the centre.

The above separation into two areas is an over-simplification of reality. For example, some recent advances in manufacturing processes have been designed to deliver greater product variety while maintaining low production costs. Equally, some differentiated marketing has been seeking underlying economies of scale from range-branding in order to make marketing more cost effective. However, for many companies involved in mass production of goods and services, it is quite likely that the upstream parts will tend to be more centralised and the downstream to be more decentralised. To this extent, the strategy and the organisation structure associated with it are at least partially inter-related: some strategies *demand* some structures. One does not come after the other, as outlined by Chandler.

18.5.4 Managing the complexity of strategic change

Much of the prescriptive approach is built around the notion that it is possible to choose precisely what strategies need to be introduced. The issue then becomes one of building the organisation and plans to achieve the chosen strategy. From empirical research, Professor J B Quinn[28] has suggested that this grossly over-simplifies the process in many cases:

- Simple strategic solutions may be unavailable, especially where the proposed changes are complex or controversial.
- The organisation structure may be unable to cope with the 'obvious' solution for reasons of its culture, the people involved or the political pressures.
- Organisational awareness and commitment may need to be built up over time, making it impossible to introduce an immediate radical change.

| Exhibit 18.4 | Quinn's Logical Incremental Strategy Process and its organisational implications[29] |

Strategic stage	Organisational implications
1 Sensing the need for change	Use informal networks in organisation
2 Clarify strategy areas and narrow options	Consult more widely, possibly using more formal structures
3 Use change symbols to signal possible change	Communicate with many who cannot be directly consulted: use formal structure
4 Create waiting period to allow options discussion and newer options to become familiar	Encourage discussion of concerns among interested groups: use formal and informal organisational structures
5 Clarify general direction of new strategy but experiment and seek partial solutions rather than a firm commitment to one direction	General discussion without alienation, if possible, among senior managers. Use formal senior management structure
6 Broaden the basis of support for the new direction	Set up committees, project groups and study teams outside the formal existing structures. Careful selection of team members and agenda is essential
7 Consolidate progress	Initiate special projects to explore and consolidate the general direction: use more junior managers and relevant team members from the existing organisation
8 Build consensus *before* focussing on new objectives and associated strategies	Use informal networks through the organisation. Identify and manage those people who are key influencers on the future strategic direction
Over time, possibly years	
9 Balance consensus with the need to avoid the rigidity that might arise from over-commitment to the now successful strategy	Introduce new members to provide further stimulus, new ideas and new questions
10 New organisation	*Reorganise the organisation's formal structure to consolidate the changes: at last!*

- Managers may need to participate in the change process, to learn about the proposed changes and to contribute specialist expertise in order to develop the strategic change required.

Quinn suggests that strategic change may need to proceed *incrementally*, i.e. in small stages. He called the process *Logical Incrementalism*. The clear implication is that it may not be possible to define the final organisation structure which may also need to evolve as the strategy moves forward incrementally. He suggests a multi-stage process for senior executives involved in strategy development: this is shown in Exhibit 18.4. Importantly, he recognises the importance of informal organisation structures in achieving agreement to strategy shifts (*see* Chapter 8). If the argument is correct, it will be evident that any idea of a single, final organisation structure is dubious.

Comment   The description of the process certainly accords with the evidence of other researchers. Formal organisation structures are important for day-to-day responsibilities and work, but are only part of the strategy process when it comes to implementing complex and controversial strategic change. The validity of the above description relies on the extent to which radical change is required. Quinn's assumption that change needs to be radical enables him to conclude that the final organisational structure may have to emerge at the end of this period.

18.5.5   Coping with changing strategies and organisations: the new collegiate leadership style

To cope with the uncertainties of strategy development, those who lead the organisation have a key role in guiding, controlling, initiating and employing considered value judgements to move the strategy process forward.[30] The work of leadership is crucial in the development of strategy and the optimal organisational framework. The *authoritarian* leader will continue to decide strategy and then define the organisation to achieve this. However, for leaders who have a different, more collegiate style,[31] strategy and organisation have more complex inter-relationships.

In the words of Peter Senge,[32]

> 'The old days when a Henry Ford, Alfred Sloan or Tom Watson [the founder of IBM], learned for the organisation are gone. In an increasingly dynamic, interdependent and unpredictable world, it is simply no longer possible for anyone to "figure it all out at the top". The old model "the top thinks and the local acts" must now give way to integrative thinking and acting at all levels. While the challenge is great, so is the potential payoff.'

If these comments are accurate, then it is possible that the structures of the early twentieth century are no longer appropriate. There may need to be a process of discussion *before* strategies and structures are finalised.

According to Senge,[33] there are three key dimensions to the role of the more collegiate leader in strategic change:

1   *Creative tension.* The tension that exists as a new leader moves to close the gap between her/his vision of the future and the current position of the organisation.

2 *New leadership role.* The former role of the authoritarian decision-maker may be too simplistic for the new millennium. The new role will involve:

● building the core values and purpose of the organisation;

● allowing strategy to emerge (*see* Mintzberg, Handy and others, Chapter 17);

● putting in place processes that allow an organisation to develop and renew itself;

● motivating, inspiring and coaching others in the organisation;

● adopting the role of custodian or steward of the organisation's people and its purpose.

3 *New skills.* None of the above will be achieved unless new skills are developed and employed both by the leader and others in the organisation. The four main skill areas are:

● building a shared vision so that members of the organisation are committed to its future purpose;

● challenging deeply-held assumptions without causing individuals to become overly defensive, so that new ideas can surface;

● identifying the key inter-relationships and the factors critical to the success of the organisation (*see* Chapter 3);

● distinguishing between the complex but unimportant details from the dynamic and important events that really shape strategy in the organisation.

The new role and skills imply more flexible relationships between the leader and the organisation. Such changes will include not only the organisational relationships but also the strategies associated with them: it is not possible to be a 'listening' leader while at the same time holding fixed, preconceived views on the strategic consequences. Hence, it follows that strategy, structure and leadership have more complex inter-relationships. Naturally, the authoritarian leader can define the organisation structure that will implement his or her chosen strategies but, for other leadership styles, the position is more complicated.

Comment Although the above values and comments may appear more in tune with some of the management thinking of the 1990s, caution is required in two areas:

1 It is not easy or necessarily appropriate to move quickly from a more authoritarian structure to a more collegiate organisation. Informing middle managers that they now have greater freedom may simply make older-style managers perplexed: they may have little experience, knowledge or skills in the new areas. It is too easy to underestimate the changes required in the *attitudes* and *skills base* to operate such an approach. Such changes involve both the leader and all the members of the organisation learning new roles and relationships over time.

2 According to Hofstede (*see* Chapter 8), some national cultures need greater certainty and dominance from their leaders. Learning and adaptive cultural solutions may not be appropriate in these circumstances. The problems may outweigh the benefits.

Key strategic principles

- According to some modern strategists, Chandler's concept of strategy first and then structure to deliver it may over-simplify the situation. There have been five major criticisms.

- Changes in the business environment and social values of the late twentieth century suggest that others beyond top management may need to contribute to strategy. This is called empowerment of the middle and junior ranks of managers. This can best take place before the final organisation structure is finalised.

- New processes for developing strategy are adaptive and involve learning mechanisms. They also need open, fluid structures that may not be best served by simple functional structures.

- The two broad parts of the value chain, upstream and downstream, suggest two broad organisation routes, one more rigid and centralised than the other. The implication is that strategy and organisation structure are more inter-related than previously suggested.

- When strategic change is radical, it may not be possible to define clearly the final organisation structure. It may be necessary to let the structure emerge as strategy changes and develops.

- Leadership style and content are key determinants of strategy, especially where they involve a more collegiate and less authoritarian approach. In these circumstances, new skills and roles will certainly alter the balance between organisation and the related strategy.

18.6 THE LINKS BETWEEN STRATEGY AND STRUCTURE AND THE CONCEPT OF STRATEGIC FIT

To provide an overview of the ongoing debate between prescriptive and emergent strategists regarding the relationship between strategy and structure, it is useful to examine the approach of the strategist, Professor Henry Mintzberg, to the links between strategy and structure. He is certainly of the opinion that the two are inter-linked, but he provides a thoughtful and useful starting point for exploring the *nature* of the relationship.

Additionally, the concept of the *strategic fit* between strategy and structure (as described by the American strategists, Galbraith and Kazanjian) does not claim to be conclusive, but it does provide another way of examining the relationship between the two areas.

18.6.1 The Mintzberg theory of the links between strategy and structure

Mintzberg[34] has provided a methodology for this task. There are two essential elements:

- the six parts of every organisation;
- the six basic co-ordinating methods that link them together.

We shall examine these two elements separately and then draw them together to explore the links with strategy.

The six parts of every organisation Mintzberg refers to these parts of every organisation that have to be connected together, because between them they add value to the organisation (*see* Fig 18.6). The six parts are:

1 *Operating core*. Where production takes place or services are provided, e.g. factory floor, restaurant, hospital ward.
2 *Strategic apex*. Where the overall management of the organisation is undertaken, e.g. chief executive and board of directors.
3 *Middle line*. This contains the managers that exist between the apex and the core.
4 *Technostructure*. Consisting of those staff who design the processes that monitor and control the operating processes, e.g. engineers, accountants, computer specialists.
5 *Support staff*. Who directly provide internal services to the operating core, e.g. secretarial, transport, canteen, laundry.
6 *Ideology*. The beliefs or culture that drive the organisation. This category is clearly less tangible than the others.

The above areas need to be co-ordinated in order for value to be added by the organisation.

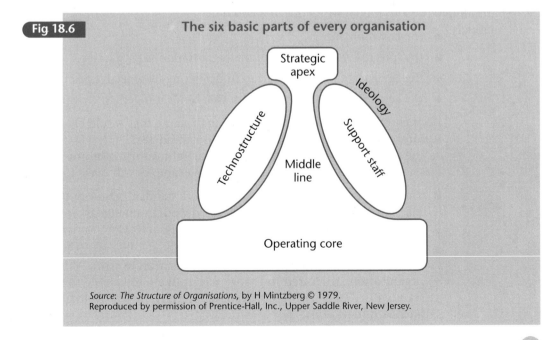

Fig 18.6 **The six basic parts of every organisation**

Source: *The Structure of Organisations*, by H Mintzberg © 1979.
Reproduced by permission of Prentice-Hall, Inc., Upper Saddle River, New Jersey.

Six co-ordinating methods

There are six co-ordinating methods that can be employed to link the six parts of the organisation together.

- *Mutual adjustment* may be carried out, using informal communications. This type of direct discussion is typical in small organisations, where people actually work closely together. It is also used in some complex circumstances to explore difficult issues, e.g. understanding of the research and development implications of strategic issues.

- *Direct supervision* may be implemented from the strategic apex to the middle line and operating core.

- *Standardisation of work processes* may be used to define the way that work is done. For example, factory engineers may be involved in detailed specifications to map out an engineering process and effectively standardise it. Vehicle assembly and quality procedures in car factories are examples of such standardised processes.

- *Standardisation of outputs* may be employed so that what comes out of a factory or service is predictable. For example, detailed specifications are used at McDonald's to ensure that the Big Mac burger is the same product wherever it is produced in the world: ingredients, cooking times, cooking temperatures, etc., are all carefully defined. Note that such procedures may involve the use of the standardised *processes* mentioned above as well as standardised *outputs*.

- *Standardisation of skills* involves the standardisation of the workers' skills (including knowledge in this definition), rather than the process or the output. Professional services in medicine or consultancy are examples in this area. They are assisted by the fact that some skills are common and shared.

- *Standardisation of norms* may also be introduced to ensure that workers share the same common beliefs. This may be important in voluntary organisations or those that are driven by strong social or religious convictions.

Combination of parts and methods

Using the above six parts and methods, Mintzberg then developed six major types of organisational structures that combine:

- the environment;
- the internal characteristics of the organisation (age, size, etc.);
- the key part of the organisation in delivering its objectives; and
- the key co-ordinating mechanism that binds it together.

He then gave each of these combinations a name that would characterise its main features. The configurations are shown in Exhibit 18.5.

The importance of the matrix lies in the light it throws on the types of *organisation* needed to deliver types of *strategy*. Two examples will make the point:

- The *machine organisation* is typified by work standardisation. Such an organisation may not wish to seek higher value-added work in small market segments because this would not be consistent with its current resources and work methods.

- The *innovative organisation* is typified by mutual adjustments between members of the organisation rather than standardisation of work, skills or output. An organisation structured in this way is unlikely to be able to start turning out standardised items, unless it changes radically, invests in totally new resources and learns new skills.

| Exhibit 18.5 | Mintzberg's configuration of organisations and the way they operate[35] | | | | |

Mintzberg's strategic configurations	Background: see Part 2 of this book		Structures and linkages		Example
	Environmental analysis	Resource analysis	Key part of organisation	Key co-ordinating mechanism	
Entrepreneurial organisation	Simple/ dynamic	Small, young Duplication of jobs	Strategic apex: the boss or owner	Direct supervision	Small computer service company
Machine organisation	High growth or cyclical	Older, large Defined tasks, techno-structure	Techno-structure	Standardisation of work	Computer assembly or car plant
Professional organisation	Stable, complex, closed to outsiders	Professional control by managers	Operating core	Standardisation of skills	Management consultancy or hospital
Divisionalised structure	Diverse	Old and large Strong links possible Standard criteria for resource allocation	Middle line	Standardisation of outputs	Fast-moving consumer goods group
Innovative organisation*	Complex and dynamic	Often young, complex work, experts involved	Support staff	Mutual adjustment	Advertising agency
Missionary organisation	Simple, static	Ideologically driven co-operative Small groups within total	Ideology	Standardisation of norms	Charity or social work

* Note that innovative organisation is called an *adhocracy* in some texts and versions of the above.

Source: Mintzberg, H, 'The Structuring of Organisations' in *The Strategy Process: Concepts and Contexts* 3/E by Mintzberg, H and Quinn, J B, © 1991, pp330–50. Adapted by permission of Prentice-Hall Inc, Upper Saddle River, New Jersey.

On this basis, when an organisation's structure is defined in broader terms than merely its reporting structure, then such a structure will guide the strategy options open to the organisation. To this extent, *strategy is linked to structure*.

It should be noted that most organisations will rarely match Mintzberg's six configurations precisely. However, they do provide guidelines that link the earlier characteristics with their strategy and structure implications. Moreover, they could be used to show the implications of what might happen as the organisation changes, for example becoming larger with a more complex product range.

Comment Mintzberg's configurations clearly over-simplify the possible organisational combinations. There are a number of more fundamental criticisms of the approach:

- It might be argued that Mintzberg's version of the *divisionalised structure* is so vague as to be limited in value: there may be a number of other different configurations contained inside the divisionalised configuration. In a sense, it is not discriminatory and could include a number of the other categories, each in its own division.

- It might also be said that some companies do not just standardise one variable above, such as work or processes, but standardise several and that the distinctions that Mintzberg draws between them may not reflect reality. In these cases, there is no single key co-ordination mechanism.

- There may be connections between the innovative and entrepreneurial organisation types: the way some entrepreneurial companies grow may involve a strategy of innovation.

- Chapter 10 showed how manufacturing innovation has made some real contributions to strategy over the last few years. However, in Mintzberg's categorisation, manufacturing is probably a *machine* rather than an *innovative* organisation.

- This book takes the view that *all* companies need to include innovation as part of all their strategies. To confine it to one configuration is dubious at best.

Overall, Mintzberg's configurations provide some useful guidelines on organisation structure and its relationship with strategy, but they need to be treated with caution.

18.6.2 The concept of strategic fit between strategy and structure

Having examined the relationships that exist between strategy and structure, there is a need to ensure that these two elements are consistent with each other. For an organisation to be economically effective, there needs to be a matching process between the organisation's strategy and its structure: this is the concept of *strategic fit*.[36]

In essence, organisations need to adopt an internally consistent set of practices in order to undertake the proposed strategy effectively. It should be said that such practices will involve more than the organisation's structure. They will also cover such areas as:

- The strategic planning process (*see* Chapter 19).

- Recruitment and training (*see* Chapter 20).

- Reward systems for employees and managers (*see* Chapter 19).

- The work to be undertaken (*see* Chapter 20).

- The information systems and processes (*see* Chapter 19).

This means that issues of strategic fit may not be fully resolved by considering only strategy and structure. It may be necessary to re-visit strategy, even when the implementation process is formally under consideration (*see* Chapter 19).

There is strong empirical evidence, however, whether it is from Chandler or Senge, that there does need to be a degree of strategic fit between the strategy and the organisation structure.

Although the environment is changing all the time, organisations may only change slowly and not keep pace with the outside. It follows that it is unlikely that there will be a perfect fit between the organisation's strategy and its structure. There is some evidence that a minimal degree of fit is needed for an organisation to survive.[37] It has also been suggested that, if the fit is close early on in the strategic development process, then higher economic performance may result. However, as the environment changes, the strategic fit will also change. We return to the consequences for organisation structure in Chapter 20.

Key strategic principles

- In designing organisational structure, it is important to consider the complex links that exist between the structure and strategy. Mintzberg has provided a process for this.

- There are six parts to every organisation and six methods by which they can be co-ordinated together. These can then be combined to produce six main types of organisational strategy and structure. They can be linked with typical key elements of the environment and mechanisms that link them together.

- By this process, the organisation's strategy and its likely structure can be inter-related. In this sense, strategy is linked to structure.

- Most organisations do not match the six different configurations precisely, but they do provide guidelines that link strategy to structure.

- At a broader level, the choice between strategies and organisational structures will be determined by the strategic fit between the two areas, i.e. the congruence between an organisation and its structure.

18.7 THE CHOICE OF MANAGEMENT STYLE AND CULTURE

18.7.1 Background

Although this chapter has explored the main discussions that have taken place over the last few years on the relationship between strategy and structure, there has been another equally vigorous debate about management style and culture, spanning both practitioner books and academic journals. Early writers included Professor Peter Drucker, who started writing in the 1950s but still produces books of interest in the 1990s.[38] In the 1980s, Peters and Waterman wrote their influential book *In Search of Excellence*, though Tom Peters has subsequently repudiated some of the guidance.[39] The writings of Charles Handy also represent a significant contribution.[40] Most are a good read but they also present research on how to operate companies, especially from the viewpoint of culture and style.

18.7.2 Culture, style and the relationship with strategy

Although every organisation is the result of its history, products and people, it periodically has the chance to renew itself. In other words, it is able to change its management culture and style. Inevitably, this will have an impact on strategy both in obvious ways, such as the attitude to risk-taking, and more subtle ways, such as the ability of the company to innovate.

To some extent, an organisation will evolve in response to its continually changing environment. Furthermore, the leadership and top management at any point in time will clearly influence the organisation's culture and style. Nevertheless, organisations can also make the deliberate choice to change their culture and style as part of a major shift in strategy. The issues are therefore:

● Should the organisation change its culture and style?

● If so, in what way should the company change these?

It should be noted that this is not just an issue of implementation *after* the strategy has been chosen, but a fundamental choice available as part of the process.

Most of the writers and researchers quoted earlier in this section would argue that a shift in culture and style is essential if a fundamental change in strategy is proposed. They would support this view for three reasons:

1 Fundamental strategic change needs to impact on people in the organisation as well as decision making. People issues are essentially summarised in culture and style.

2 Leadership is usually important for major changes in strategy. This is likely to encompass some shift in style and, occasionally, a change of leader.

3 Such a shift in culture and style is a *powerful symbol* of the related change in strategy.

18.7.3 The content of the new culture and style

As a starting point in exploring this area, the reader is referred back to the discussion of culture in Chapter 8. In addition, the final decision will clearly be related to the proposed strategic changes. There will also need to be a degree of *strategic fit* between the strategy and the style, just as there was between strategy and structure earlier in the chapter.

More generally, Hart has suggested a range of styles from which the choice can be made: they vary from the autocratic to the collegiate and are shown in Exhibit 18.6. The content of each style can be matched to how the organisation sees itself developing over the period of the strategy.

Importantly, it should be noted that culture and style do not change overnight: it is often possible to introduce a new strategy more quickly than bring about a related change in style. Culture and style take time to develop so the strategic fit may need some adjustment. Hence, the process of introducing a new style needs careful thought.

Exhibit 18.6 — Strategy and style options[41]

Descriptors	Command	Symbolic	Rational	Transactive	Generative
Style	Imperial Strategy driven by leader or small top team	Cultural Strategy driven by mission and a vision of the future	Analytical Strategy driven by formal structure and planning systems	Procedural Strategy driven by internal process and mutual adjustment	Organic Strategy driven by the initiatives of those empowered in the organisation
Role of top management	Commander Provide direction	Coach Motivate and inspire	Boss Evaluate and control	Facilitator Empower and enable	Sponsor Endorse and sponsor
Role of organisational members	Soldier Obey orders	Player Respond to challenge	Subordinate Follow the system	Participant Learn and improve	Entrepreneur Experiment and take risks

Source: Adapted from Hart, S (1992) 'An integrative framework for strategy-making processes', *Academy of Management Review*, Vol 17, pp 327–51. Also reprinted in Hart, S and Banbury, C (1994) 'How strategy-making processes can make a difference', *Strategic Management Journal*, Vol 15, pp 251–69.

> ### Key strategic principles
>
> ● Every organisation has the choice of changing its culture and style when it changes its strategy.
>
> ● In many cases, a change of style is essential when a fundamental change of strategy is proposed.
>
> ● The content of the culture and style depend on the strategies proposed. There needs to be a degree of strategic fit between the two areas. Importantly, culture and style take time to change and may move more slowly than the proposed strategy.

CASE STUDY 18.2

ABB empowers its managers[42]

When the world's largest electrical engineering company, ASEA Brown Boveri, was formed in 1987, one of its earliest strategic decisions was to reorganise and move power from the centre to its operating companies: empowerment. This case study explores the reasoning and consequences of this major shift in strategy and examines the strategy decisions that still remained with the centre.

Background

With 1994 revenue of over US$29.7 billion and 208 000 employees around the world, ABB is the world's largest electrical engineering company. Its products include electrical power generation and transmission equipment, railway rolling stock and industrial building systems. It operates in global markets and competes against such major companies as General Electric (USA), Westinghouse (USA), Siemens (Germany) and GEC Alsthom (UK/France) as well as with the major Japanese groups, Mitsui and Mitsubishi.

Company history

ABB was formed in 1987 from the engineering interests of the Swedish company, ASEA, and the Swiss company, Brown Boveri. Over the period 1988 to 1990, the company was completely reorganised. The central HQ in Switzerland was reduced to a total of 150 people with a matrix management structure introduced worldwide. The company was split into 1300 smaller companies

and around 5000 profit centres, functioning as closely as possible as independent operations. Several layers of middle management were stripped out and directors from the central HQ moved into regional co-ordinating companies.

At the same time, the company engaged in a major programme of acquisitions that grew the order intake of ABB from US$16 billion to US$25 billion over two years. Major companies

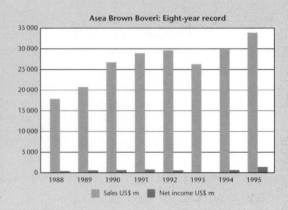

were purchased in the USA, Spain, Italy, the UK, France, Spain and Germany. All the negotiations for these major decisions were handled centrally by ABB.

Consolidation and restructuring

The period of consolidation that followed from 1991 to 1993 was accompanied by only selective acquisitions in several Eastern European countries along with some new Asian ventures. This period was also characterised by economic recession in the West which affected ABB's businesses. After the heady growth of the previous period, there was a period of further restructuring and reorganisation. This led to the loss of 47 000 jobs in North America and Western Europe. At the same time, 35 000 new jobs were added in Eastern Europe and Asia. ABB said that it was continuing to counteract severe pressure on selling prices by moving its labour-intensive activity to lower-wage Asian and Eastern European countries.

Restructuring to reduce costs continued from 1994 onwards and there was yet more reorganisation. It was also decided to introduce more co-ordination at the centre by reducing the number of product groups and by the creation of several senior corporate HQ posts designed to improve synergy across the group. The reasons for this shift in approach are described in the next section.

In addition to these moves, the drive to build Asian/Pacific business also continued.

Company strategy to empower management

Under the direction of its chief executive, Percy Barnevik, ABB has pursued its bold initiative of breaking up the company into 1300 smaller units, each with profit responsibility. At the same time, a new group co-ordinating structure was also introduced. The moves were essentially aimed at empowering managers to move closer to their customers and at giving them the incentives to act as smaller and more entrepreneurial units. Even research and development was decentralised with the new operating companies controlling 90 per cent of the group's US$2.3 billion budget.

Barnevik considered that the greatest strategic challenge in running a group of this size was motivating middle and lower managers and shifting entrenched corporate values. As he explained, previously managers had been happy to coast along with 2 per cent gross margins when a 5 per cent margin was possible with more commitment.

At the same time, each unit manager had to report to two more senior managers: a regional geographic manager and a worldwide business manager. The group then organised itself vertically into eight business areas (later reduced to four) and four geographic regions (later reduced to three) – a form of matrix management as described in Chapter 20.

Central controls over operating units

Each company unit was given considerable financial independence to control its own balance sheet, borrow money and retain earnings. All dealings between units were undertaken at market prices. Even working capital and inventory decisions by the units were reflected in their balance sheets so that they were held accountable for the decisions that they made. However, empowerment did not mean that the units had complete freedom: the group set up a sophisticated central computer system called Abacus to monitor unit performance. It supplied monthly updates of sales and orders and quarterly financial results to HQ. There was also a system of financial controls for managers to monitor their unit performance.

Two financial areas were excluded from unit control:

- independent speculation for foreign currency borrowings;
- independent raising of finance.

These two areas were handled centrally from ABB's World Treasury Centre based in Switzerland.

Results of the empowerment strategy

By 1991, the company was able to show that empowerment had become the norm for many managers. However, it was still necessary to reinforce the message: 'Now the problem is that they get too happy when they see profit doubled; they think 4 per cent margin is fantastic, and you have to tell them that American competitors can make 10 per cent.' Central management therefore continued to devote much of its time to 'indoctrinating' managers:

CASE STUDY 18.2 continued

- Two-day meetings of 200 to 400 senior managers were held regularly.
- Selective senior managers were invited to meet senior board members at seminars.
- Consultants were employed to operate empowerment training programmes.

Inevitably there were problems. Goran Lindahl, one of ABB's top-level executive team, was given the key role of identifying areas where ABB managers had become complacent or allowed their units to drift. He was given the power 'to shake things up to create an environment of learning'. For example, a power-transmission company reported to him that it was having difficulty sorting out the overlap in its factories and research facilities that had developed over time across several European countries. Lindahl became involved when he observed that several of the unit's senior managers were delaying decisions that would have favoured another facility over their own. Lindahl told them that he would not make the decisions for them but gave them clear guidelines on what decisions were unacceptable and by what date he wanted some answers.

When Lindahl realised that some managers were not committed to the collaboration that he had suggested, he replaced them. He contrasted his 'fingers in the management' style with a more abstract one where a director controls managers around the world only through sophisticated computer systems. He did not explain how his style was truly consistent with empowerment.

Changes in the empowerment strategy

By 1994, the company was able to comment that, 'Our strategy of delegating responsibility is a winning one ... we want to achieve management by motivation and goals instead of restrictions and directives.' ABB believed it was beginning to overcome its biggest strategic challenge, communications – 'mobilising thousands of managers'. Nevertheless, four real problems had begun to emerge:

1 *New environment.* More customers were requiring new contracts on major capital projects where the contractor did everything. The cus-

tomer simply took delivery of the finished, working plant after it had been finished and run in. The customer turned the key and started work – a *turnkey project*. ABB with its myriad small units was simply not geared up to supplying this type of operation.

2 *Major strains on senior staff.* Some senior managers were beginning to feel the strain of the complexity of their responsibilities.

3 *Lack of management experience in Eastern Europe and Asia.* Eastern European managers had previously been involved in command economies where there was no need to make profits. Some Asian managers had little previous business experience.

4 *Global managers.* Some international customers and some global projects demanded a new type of manager that could see beyond the home unit.

The solutions devised by ABB were to reduce the numbers of divisions, combining together areas where turnkey projects might be needed. Four senior corporate officers were also appointed with direct responsibilities for co-ordination and special cross-company projects. More responsibility was also pushed down to the next layer of management. New education and training schemes were introduced using outside institutions to help managers. Job rotation across countries was also begun to give managers experience beyond their home units.

Centralised strategic decision making

Although ABB had become famous over this period for its empowerment strategies, certain elements of its corporate strategy were still controlled centrally:

- the drive into the growing markets of Asia and Eastern Europe;
- the major shift of employment from the high labour cost areas of OECD countries to the low labour-cost areas of Eastern Europe and Asia;
- the Treasury function to raise finance for the group, handle currency issues and finance major contracts for major national and international customers;

● negotiations to acquire, rationalise and re-organise its many acquisitions, alliances, joint ventures and other major thrusts of business strategy. Units only had responsibility for their existing product areas.

CASE QUESTIONS

1 How important to the strategy of empowerment is the sophisticated financial control system, Abacus?

And how vital is the central monitoring (e.g. Lindahl)? What does this mean for empowerment?

2 If the world is becoming increasingly global, do you think that ABB's unit empowerment can continue? Or will it need to be more aggregated? If so, what does this mean for the empowerment strategy?

3 If empowerment is so valuable strategically, why are there companies that might not have followed the lead of ABB?

◼ SUMMARY

● For the *prescriptive* strategist, the strategy is developed first and then the organisation structure is defined afterwards. Thus, organisational structure is a matter of how the strategy is implemented and does not influence the strategy itself.

● However, from an *emergent* strategy perspective, the relationship between strategy and structure is more complex. The organisation itself may restrict or enhance the proposed strategies and may even make the implementation of certain strategies highly unlikely.

● Two well-known writers on strategy explored these areas in the 1960s and 1970s.

1 The strategist, Alfred Chandler, contended that it was first necessary to develop the strategy. After this task was completed, the organisational structure was then devised to deliver that strategy. His conclusion was based on his study of the way that US businesses were formed and organised in the early part of the twentieth century. However, he only studied businesses that had developed from small enterprises into larger, more diversified structures.

2 The economist, Oliver Williamson, explored the role of the centre in diversified businesses. He concluded that the centre should stand back from the corporate divisions when it came to allocating resources between them and, subsequently, to monitoring and controlling them. He supported Chandler's view that strategy came first and organisation structure afterwards.

● According to the early strategists, formal structures, clear responsibilities, identified lines of reporting and a central directorate for strategy development are all important elements of organisational design. They are undertaken after the basic strategy has been agreed. As organisations become larger and more complex, it may be necessary to form divisions and decentralise some power to them.

● The *centralisation* versus *decentralisation* issue may be particularly important in designing the organisation's structure. According to many strategists, this should only be undertaken once the basic strategy has been decided. There are no simple rules to define where the *balance* needs to be struck between centralisation and decentralisation.

● According to some modern strategists, Chandler's concept – strategy first and then structure to deliver it – may over-simplify the situation. There have been five major criticisms. Changes in the business environment and social values of the late twentieth century suggest that people other than top management may need to contribute to strategy. This is called *empowerment* of the middle and junior ranks of managers. This can best take place before the organisational structure is finalised.

● New processes for developing strategy are adaptive and involve learning mechanisms. They also need open, fluid structures that may not be best served by a simple functional organisation.

● The two broad parts of the value chain, *upstream* and *downstream*, suggest two broad organisation routes, one more rigid and centralised than the other. The implication is that strategy and organisation structure are more inter-related than was previously suggested.

● When strategic change is radical, it may not be possible to define clearly the final organisation structure. It may be necessary to let the structure emerge as strategy changes and develops. Leadership style and content are also key determinants of strategy, especially where they involve a more collegiate and less authoritarian approach. In these circumstances, new skills and roles will certainly alter the balance between the organisation and the related strategy.

● In exploring strategy and structure, it is useful to examine the links between the two elements, starting with the basic *design* of organisational structures. This will be governed by four main criteria: simplicity, the least-cost solution, motivation of those involved and the existing organisation culture.

● In designing organisation structure, it is also important to consider the *complex links* that exist between the structure and strategy. Mintzberg has provided a process to understand this. There are six parts to every organisation and six methods by which they can be co-ordinated.

● The parts and methods can be combined to produce six main types of organisational strategy and structure. They can be linked with typical key elements of the environment and other mechanisms. By this process, the organisation's strategy and its likely structure can be inter-related. In this sense, strategy is linked to structure. Most organisations do not match the six different configurations precisely, but these do provide guidelines that link strategy to structure.

● The choice between strategies and organisational structures will more broadly be determined by the *strategic fit* between the two areas, i.e. the congruence between an organisation and its structure.

● Every organisation has the choice of changing its *culture* and *style* when it changes its strategy. In many cases, a change of style is essential when a fundamental change of strategy is proposed. The content of the culture and style depend on the proposed strategies. There needs to be a degree of strategic fit between the two areas. Importantly, culture and style take time to change and may move *more slowly* than the proposed strategy.

1   Is Alfred Chandler's view of the relationship between strategy and structure correct? Give reasons for your views.

2   Should the Sony Corporation be centralised or decentralised in its manufacturing operations?

3   How should strategy and structure be developed in the following organisations?

   (a)   A large multinational involved in several different but interconnected product fields.

   (b)   A major local government department with a heavy administrative workload.

   (c)   A small manufacturing business with 25 employees.

   (d)   A small self-governing trust that administers a charitable foundation.

4   Examine each of the criticisms of the strategy first, structure afterwards argument. To what extent is each valid?

5   Does the comparison in the GM Case study between the business environments of the early and late twentieth century exaggerate the differences between the two periods? What are the implications of your view for the organisational structures and strategy?

6   '*Strategy deals with the unknowable, not the uncertain ... Hence logic dictates that one proceed flexibly and experimentally from broad concepts toward specific commitments, making the latter concrete as late as possible.*' Professor J B Quinn. Discuss the implications for the design of organisational structure.

7   What problems might there be with the new collegiate leadership style? Consider your answer both in terms of its introduction and its appropriateness for organisations.

8   Are the critical comments on Mintzberg's six strategic configurations outlined in Section 18.6 accurate and valid? What are the implications of your response?

9   Take an organisation with which you are familiar and characterise its management style according to the strategy and style options set out in Exhibit 18.6. What are the implications for the way that strategy is likely to be developed?

The global car industry has developed dramatically over the last few years, but there is over-capacity in world markets. There may well be a reduction in the number of companies involved. Investigate which companies are likely to survive such a shake-out.

FURTHER READING

J R Galbraith and R K Kazanjian (1986) *Strategy Implementation*, 2nd edn, West Publishing, St Paul, Min. An excellent book for its clarity of thought, research evidence and precision of argument. It has contributed significantly to the development of this chapter. It is a pity that it appears to be out of print. Highly recommended.

Professor Dan Schendel (1994) 'Introduction to competitive organisational behaviour: toward an organisationally-based theory of competitive advantage,' *Strategic Management Journal*, 15, pp1–4. This whole issue has an interesting review of the way in which strategy and organisational theory have developed since the 1960s.

Alfred Chandler (1987) *Strategy and Structure: chapters in the history of the American industrial enterprise*, MIT Press, Cambridge, Mass. Still a classic text.

Professor D Pugh (1984) *Organisation theory*, Penguin, London. This book brings together various papers, including those of other influential theorists of the early twentieth century such as F W Taylor and H Fayol.

Professor R M Kanter (1983) *The Change Masters*, Unwin, London. This is a well-researched, thoughtful and provocative book on innovation.

REFERENCES

1 This case is adapted from an article by William Dawkins (1995) Japan in Asia Supplement, *Financial Times*, 15 Nov, pVI.
2 Galbraith, J R and Kazanjian, R K (1986) *Strategy Implementation*, 2nd edn, West Publishing, St Paul, Min, p6.
3 Mullins, L (1996) *Management and Organisational Behaviour*, 4th edn, Pitman Publishing, London, Ch 10.
4 Schendel, D (1994) 'Introduction to competitive organisational behaviour: toward an organisationally-based theory of competitive advantage', *Strategic Management Journal*, 15, pp1–4. This whole issue has an interesting review of the way in which strategy and organisational theory have developed since the 1960s.
5 Chandler, A (1987) *Strategy and Structure: chapters in the history of the American industrial enterprise*, MIT Press, Cambridge, Mass.
6 Williamson, O (1975) *Markets and Hierarchies*, Free Press, Boston, Mass.
7 Schendel, D (1994) Ibid.
8 Chandler, A (1987) Ibid, pp8–14.
9 Williams, K, Haslam C, Williams, J and Johal, S (1994) *Cars*, Berghahn Books, p98.
10 Chandler, A (1987) Ibid, pp13–14.
11 Pugh, D (1984) *Organisation Theory*, Penguin, London. This book brings together various papers including those of other influential theorists of the early twentieth century such as Taylor and Fayol.
12 Williamson, O (1975) Ibid.
13 Williamson, O (1975) Ibid, pp148–9.
14 Mullins, L (1996) Ibid. Chapter 10 has a good general description of the principles of organisational design. However, the Mullins text treats such matters in a more general context than the specific requirements of strategy.
15 For example, *see* Thompson, A and Strickland, A (1993) *Strategic Management*, 7th edn, Irwin, Homewood, Ill, and Johnson, G and Scholes, K (1993) *Exploring Corporate Strategy*, 3rd edn, Prentice Hall, London.
16 Mullins, L (1996) Ibid, Ch 10.
17 Mullins, L (1996) Ibid, pp344–5.
18 Campbell, A and Goold, M (1987) *Strategies and Styles*, Basil Blackwell, Oxford.

19 Chandler, A (1987) Ibid. This section is based on parts of Chapter 3.

20 *Sources*: General Motors Corporation, *Annual Report and Accounts 1994*; Done, K (1994) 'Upbeat sounds in Motown', *Financial Times*, 19 Jan, p19; *The Economist* (1992) 'Survey of the car industry', *Supplement*, 17 Oct; *General Motors Case B*: Mintzberg, H and Quinn, J B (1991) *The Strategy Process*, Prentice Hall, New York, pp978–93.

21 Prahalad, C K and Hamel, G (1994) 'Strategy: the search for new paradigms', *Strategic Management Journal*, Summer Special Issue, p11.

22 This section has been adapted from the ideas of Kanter, R M (1983) *The Change Masters*, Unwin, London, pp42–3 and pp398–9. This is a well-researched, thoughtful and provocative book.

23 Pucik, V and Hatvany, N (1983) 'Management Practices in Japan and their impact on business strategy', *Advances in Strategic Management*, 1, JAI Press Inc, pp103–31. Reprinted in Mintzberg, H and Quinn, J B (1991) Ibid.

24 World Bank (1994) *World Development Report 1994*, Oxford University Press, NU, pp76–9.

25 Peters, T (1984) 'Strategy follows the structure: developing distinctive skills', *California Management Review*, Spring. Reprinted in Mintzberg, H and Quinn, J B (1991) Ibid.

26 Kanter, R M (1983) Ibid. *See* references at the end of Chapter 17.

27 Galbraith, J R (1983) Ibid. Galbraith's ideas have been re-expressed in 'value chain' terminology for the purposes of this book. He used the term 'industry chain'.

28 Quinn, J B (1980) 'Managing Strategic Change', *Sloan Management Review*, Summer. Reprinted in Mintzberg, H and Quinn, J B (1991) Ibid, and De Wit, B and Meyer, R (1994) Ibid.

29 *Source*: Lynch, R, based on reference 28.

30 These comments arise directly from the writings of both Quinn and Senge quoted above. They are also consistent with the conclusions of Chandler earlier in the century.

31 See Hart, S and Banbury, C (1994) 'How strategy making processes can make a difference', *Strategic Management Journal*, 15, p254 and Ch 17.

32 Senge, P (1990) 'The leader's new work: Building Learning Organisations', *Sloan Management Review*, Fall. Reprinted in De Wit, B and Meyer, R (1994) *Strategy*: *Process, Content and Context*, West Publishing, Min, pp132–41.

33 Senge, P (1990) Ibid.

34 *See also* Mintzberg, H (1991) 'The Structuring of Organisations', pp330–50 in Mintzberg, H and Quinn, J B (1991) Ibid.

35 *Source*: Adapted from Mintzberg, H (1991) 'The Structuring of Organisations', pp330–50 in Mintzberg, H and Quinn, J B (1991) *The Strategy Process*, Prentice Hall, New York.

36 Galbraith, J R and Kazanjian, R K (1986) Ibid, Ch 7.

37 Galbraith, J R and Kazanjian, R K (1986) Ibid, p113.

38 Examples: Drucker, P (1961) *The Practice of Management*, Heinemann/Mercury, and (1967) *Managing for Results*, Pan Books, London.

39 Peters, T (1992) *Liberation Management*, Macmillan, London.

40 Handy, C (1989) *The Age of Unreason*, Business Books, and (1991) *The Gods of Management*, Business Books.

41 *Source*: Adapted from Hart, S (1992) 'An integrative framework for strategy-making processes', *Academy of Management Review*, 17, pp327–51. Also reprinted in Hart, S and Banbury, C (1994) How strategy making processes can make a difference, *Strategic Management Journal*, 15, pp251–69. Reproduced with permission.

42 ABB Case study references:
Ghoshal, S and Bartlett, C (1995) 'Changing the role of top management: beyond structure to process', *Harvard Business Review*, Jan–Feb. *Financial Times*: 15 Nov 1989; 21 Mar 1990, p27; 5 Apr, 1991, p11; 15 Nov 1991; 20 Aug 1993, p15; 25 Aug 1993, p19; 15 Mar 1994, p32; 12 Aug 1994, p17; 18 Aug 1994, p18. *ABB Annual Report and Accounts*: 1993 and 1994. Video interview with Percy Barnevik on Tom Peter's 1993 video film: *Crazy times call for crazy organisations*. *See also* reference 39 above and the interview with Mr Barnevik.

THE IMPLEMENTATION PROCESS

This part of the book addresses implementation – the process by which the organisation's chosen strategies are put into operation. It may involve planning new activities, developing an organisational structure to undertake them and considering how to persuade stakeholders that their best interests will be served by undertaking the strategy.

However, empirical research has shown that the implementation process itself may influence the organisation's strategy. In other words, the distinction between the implementation process and the strategy choice may be overstated. Nevertheless, many organisations consider planning and control separately from the generation of strategy, while also recognising the interaction between the two. These issues are fully explored in the following chapters.

PART 6

THE IMPLEMENTATION PROCESS

• The *prescriptive* strategic process

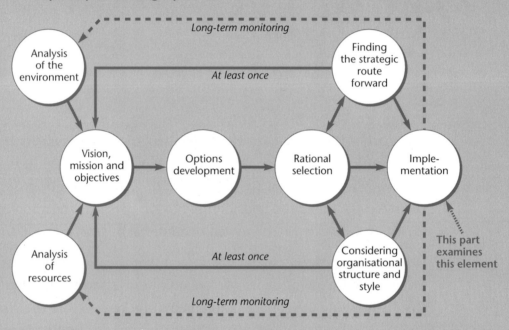

• The *emergent* strategic process

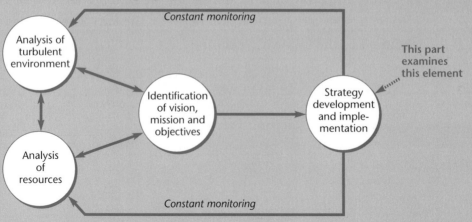

Chapter 19
RESOURCE ALLOCATION, STRATEGIC PLANNING AND CONTROL

- *What is the process of implementation?*
- *How are tasks and objectives set?*
- *How are resources allocated?*
- *How is strategic planning conducted and what is its influence on strategy?*
- *How is strategy controlled?*
- *What is the role of information processing and systems?*

Chapter 20
ORGANISATIONAL STRUCTURE AND PEOPLE ISSUES

- *What are the main principles involved in designing an organisation's structure to implement its strategy?*
- *What special considerations apply when seeking innovatory strategies?*
- *How are managers selected and motivated to implement strategies?*

Chapter 21
MANAGING STRATEGIC CHANGE

- *Why do people resist strategic change?*
- *What are the main principles involved in strategic change?*
- *How can we devise a programme to manage such change?*

Chapter 22
BUILDING A COHESIVE CORPORATE STRATEGY

- *How can the various elements of strategy be brought together?*
- *How are relationships changing between stakeholders?*
- *How is strategic management changing?*

19

Resource allocation, strategic planning and control

When you have worked through this chapter, you will be able to:

- outline the nature and limitations of the implementation process;

- identify the inter-relationships between strategy and implementation;

- understand the way that the objectives, tasks and timing are implemented;

- describe how resources are allocated between parts of the organisation;

- explore how strategic planning can be conducted and critically evaluate its merits;

- outline the main elements of control and monitoring, and investigate their importance for corporate strategy implementation.

INTRODUCTION

By whatever method strategies are selected, there will come a time when every organisation will need to put its strategies into practice, i.e. to implement them. This chapter explores the basic steps involved in this process and the possible links between strategy development and implementation.

As the prime aim in implementing strategy is to deliver the mission and objectives of the organisation, this chapter discusses these and considers especially the implications for the tasks to be undertaken by individuals and the allocation of the necessary resources. Detailed strategic plans are often developed, especially where there are elements of experimentation or uncertainty in the chosen strategies. As the strategies are implemented, they clearly need to be monitored and controlled. The way in which these activities are linked together is shown in Fig 19.1.

Importantly, the process of implementation relies on *human resources* to carry out these tasks. Changes in strategy may necessitate reorganisation. Individuals and groups may need to experiment and to learn about new areas. They need to be organised, given incentives and may possibly even require to be recruited. These areas are explored in Chapter 20.

Strategy implementation usually involves change: for chapter, change in responsibilities, work practices and the balance of power. *Strategic change* can either be a major opportunity or a significant threat to the people in the organisation and therefore to the implementation of strategy itself. To some extent, change can be managed positively to achieve the desired implementation. These matters are investigated in Chapter 21.

Chapter 22 then briefly explores some areas of modern strategic activity that form part of the implementation process and contribute also to current strategic debate.

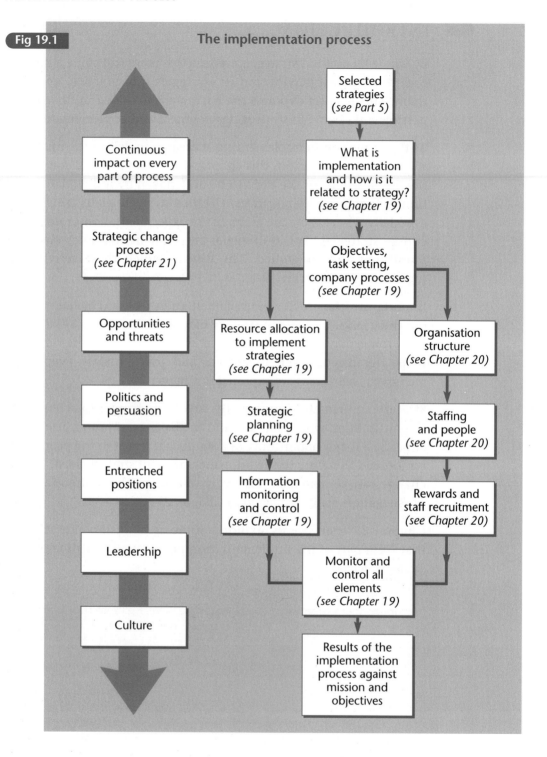

Fig 19.1   The implementation process

Implementing an unpopular strategy at Air France[1]

Air France, one of Europe's leading airlines, has been in trouble for much of the 1990s. It has been unable to reduce its costs sufficiently fast in the face of increased competitive pressures, employee resistance and inefficient working practices. The strategies were clear enough, but their implementation was proving difficult.

There was no doubt about the basic problem: Air France had made a net loss every year from 1990 to 1995. Over this period, its cumulative net loss came to over FF 14 billion (US$3 billion). However, the annual loss was beginning to decrease in 1995. The airline was government-owned and had received around FF 22 billion in direct subsidies to stop it collapsing and aid its reform strategies. Although the European Commission had approved this support in spite of severe opposition from other airlines, it had also made it clear that this would have to be the last. Air France was operating on borrowed time.

In terms of turnover, Air France was one of Europe's top three airlines in the 1990s. Its largest European competitors were Lufthansa (Germany) and British Airways (UK). Both the German and the UK airlines had been pursuing modernisation programmes during the 1980s and early 1990s that left Air France behind. By 1995, Air France was reported to have administrative costs and average salary costs that were respectively 40 per cent and 27 per cent higher than those of Lufthansa. BA (British Airways) was even more efficient than Lufthansa. Both these companies and other European and American airlines were able to put real pressure on Air France in terms of better value for money and higher service.

Air France: Four-year record

In the face of these difficulties, Air France had attempted a major overhaul of its position in the period 1990–93. The plans put before the French government and trade unions in 1993 included 4000 job cuts out of a workforce of 45 000, new employment conditions, reductions in routes flown by the airline and in the numbers of aircraft used. The plans were also accompanied by the proposed sale of non-core assets. Fierce confrontation followed with the airline's 14 trade unions. The Chairman of Air France, M Bernard Attali, was forced to quit but the difficulties did not go away.

Over the following two years, the new Chairman, M Christian Blanc, introduced some major measures. The airline was split into 11 profit centres, long-distance flights were upgraded and computer software was purchased from American Airlines that would allow the airline to adjust its booking and pricing arrangements so that it could raise revenues per seat. However, other strategies continued to face major union objections. M Blanc wanted to reduce the workforce by 5000 and change the bureaucracy and working practices. He also planned a new organisation structure that would merge Air France with its related domestic airline, Air Inter, and create a new European airline carrier with a shared cost structure. However, the unions feared the job cuts and the loss of privileges. At the same time, rival airlines, including the major global carriers, were continuing to offer fierce competition.

CASE QUESTIONS

Is this a problem of the correct strategy, but poor implementation? Or does the strategy itself need to be changed in the face of union opposition?

19.1 THE IMPLEMENTATION PROCESS

19.1.1 Basic elements of the implementation process

Whether the organisation faces the strategic problems of a company like Air France or the opportunities of new technologies such as the Internet, it will have to draw up plans to pursue its strategies. Essentially, these need to address the following questions:

- What activities need to be undertaken in order to achieve the agreed objectives?
- What is the timescale for the implementation of these plans?
- How will progress be monitored and controlled?

To turn general strategies into specific implementation plans involves four basic elements:[2]

- *Identification of general strategic objectives* – specifying the general *results* expected from the strategy initiatives.
- *Formulation of specific plans* – taking the general objectives and turning them into specific tasks and deadlines (these are often cross-functional).
- *Resource allocation and budgeting* – indicating how the plans are to be paid for (this quantifies the plans and permits integration across functions).
- *Monitoring and control procedures* – ensuring that the objectives are being met and that only the agreed resources are spent and that budgets are adhered to. Importantly, monitoring also takes place against the projections on which the strategies are based – for example, national economic change and competitive activity.

The relationship between these activities is shown in Fig 19.2.

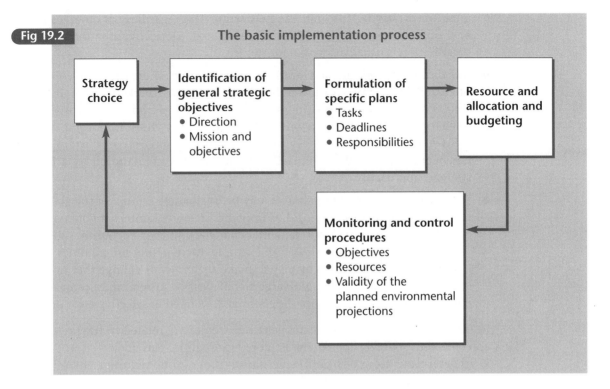

Fig 19.2   **The basic implementation process**

19.1.2   Types of basic implementation programme

Implementation programmes will vary according to the nature of the strategic problems which the organisation faces. These problems will range from the extreme and urgent need for change, such as at Air France, to the more ongoing strategic development processes of Canon or Nestlé (described in the case studies later in this chapter). The two essential causes of variation in implementation programmes are:[3]

● the degree of uncertainty in predicting changes in the environment;

● the size of the strategic change required.

In response to these issues, several types of basic implementation programme can be carried out. At one extreme, there is the *comprehensive implementation programme* for fundamental changes in strategic direction. At the other extreme, there is the *incremental implementation programme*, where implementation is characterised by small changes and short time spans within the general direction implied by the strategy. Both these approaches have their difficulties, so a compromise may be chosen in practice: the *selective implementation programme*.

● *Comprehensive implementation programmes* are employed when the organisation has made a clear-cut, major change in strategic direction, such as the Air France decision at the beginning of this chapter. Other reasons might include a new competitive or new technological opportunity. Implementation then becomes a matter of driving through the new strategies, regardless of changes in the environment and the reactions of those affected. Close co-ordination across the organisation is usually essential for success.

● *Incremental implementation programmes* may be used where there are conditions of great uncertainty – for example, rapidly changing markets or the unknown results of R&D. As a result, timetables, tasks and even objectives are all likely to change depending on the outcome of current activities. Important strategic areas may be left deliberately unclear until the outcome of current events has been established.[4] Essentially, the uncertainty is handled by a flexible strategic approach.

● *Selective implementation programmes* may be used where neither of the above represents the optimal way forward. Comprehensive programmes involving radical change may require such fundamental changes that they encounter substantial resistance, such as in the Air France example. Incremental programmes may be inappropriate when it is necessary to make a significant change that needs the impetus generated by a single, large step. Selective programmes represent the compromise required: a major programme developed in selective areas only.

Readers will recognise that the above two extremes are related to the prescriptive and emergent strategic approaches explored throughout this book.

To determine the type of implementation programme required, the following three criteria can be employed:

● Are clear and substantial advantages to be delivered in a specific area, e.g. investment in a new drug that will provide competitive advantage?

● Are there large increments that cannot be subdivided, e.g. a new factory with long lead times for construction?

● Is it important to protect some future step that may be required but cannot be fully justified on the basis of current evidence, e.g. an investment in a new distribution facility that will be needed if development programmes proceed according to plan?

For many organisations, it is useful to draw a basic distinction between:[5]

1 *ongoing, existing activities* with higher certainty and more predictable strategic change barring a major cataclysm;

2 *new activities* with higher uncertainty and possibly major strategic change.

Implementation programmes can then be drawn up for each of these groups, with plans being supplied for the new activities (*see* Table 19.1).

Table 19.1 How the nature of the activity affects the implementation

Activity	Typical implications for implementation	Typical implications for monitoring and control
Ongoing, existing activity	• General plans only • Predictable outcomes within limits	• Monitor major variations only • Monitoring undertaken against the experience of previous years and against the objectives for the plan (not necessarily the same)
New activity	• Careful, detailed plans • Perhaps incremental or selective • Staged release of funds for the strategy	• Monitor the programme in depth • Use detailed progress reports • Go beyond outline numbers into detailed discussions to understand the reasons

19.1.3 Implementation in small and medium-sized businesses

The basic elements of the implementation process – the identification of general strategic objectives, the formulation of specific plans, resource allocation and budgeting, and monitoring and control procedures are equally applicable to smaller organisations. All organisations need to specify the tasks to be undertaken and monitor progress. Moreover, choosing the correct type of implementation programme – comprehensive, incremental or selective – according to the nature of the problem and the particular environment of the organisation is also important to the small and medium-sized businesses. Indeed, any small or medium-sized business that attempts to obtain finance for a new venture will be asked to supply the essential information outlined above. Banks and other lending institutions no longer rely on vague promises and good intentions.

Key strategic principles

- Implementation covers the activities required for an organisation to put its strategies into practice. There are several basic elements to this process: general objectives, specific plans and the necessary finances, coupled with a monitoring and control system to ensure compliance.

- Within the implementation process, it is useful to draw a distinction between different types of implementation. There are three major approaches: comprehensive, incremental and selective.

- Implementation in small and medium-sized businesses may be less elaborate but needs to follow the same general principles.

19.2 ## RELATIONSHIP BETWEEN IMPLEMENTATION AND THE STRATEGY DEVELOPMENT PROCESS

Although many strategy researchers and writers have fully supported implementation as a separate stage after strategy choice,[6] over the last twenty years others have expressed significant and well-founded doubts. Their concerns have been based on empirical research of the way that strategy actually develops.

In the light of this research, it is important to view the basic implementation process as a series of small steps over time with complex learning and feedback mechanisms between implementation and strategy. This does not mean that Section 19.1 on basic implementation was incorrect; it does mean that implementation needs to be seen as a process over time that may well alter strategy. Consequently, it may even alter the organisation's vision and objectives.

The three main areas of research which contributed to this alternative view of the implementation process were:

- the empirical research of Pettigrew and Whipp;
- the concepts of intended rationality and minimum intervention of Hrebiniak and Joyce;
- the work of other emergent theorists, such as Quinn and Senge.

19.2.1 ### The empirical research of Pettigrew and Whipp

In a series of research studies between 1985 and 1990, the UK-based researchers Pettigrew and Whipp analysed how strategic change occurred in four sectors of British industry.[7] Their evidence did not extend beyond the UK but their conclusions are likely to be applicable to other geographic areas. They suggested that strategic change can most usefully be seen as a *continuous* process, rather than one with distinct stages such as the formulation of strategy and then its implementation. In this sense, they argued that strategy was not a linear movement with discrete stages but an experimental, iterative process where the outcomes of each stage were uncertain. A first small step might be actioned and then the strategy itself adjusted, depending on the outcome of the actions.

Comment The empirical evidence to support this view is significant. The description of the continuous process is similar to, but not necessarily the same as, the incremental implementation programme described in Section 19.1.2. According to this interpretation, the Air France strategy implementation at the beginning of this chapter might have been better served by a series of separate smaller actions, conducted on an experimental basis, rather than one major restructuring announcement. Chapter 21 will explore further the research of Pettigrew and Whipp.

19.2.2 ### Intended rationality and minimum intervention: Hrebiniak and Joyce

In exploring how managers develop their implementation plans, the strategists, Hrebiniak and Joyce,[8] have suggested that the implementation process is governed by two principles: intended rationality and minimum intervention.

● *Intended rationality* derives from the work of researchers Cyert and March (*see* Chapters 2 and 8). They showed that managers in practice have difficulty in considering every conceivable option. They therefore reduce their logical choices down to a more limited 'bounded' choice. Arguing in a similar way, Hrebiniak and Joyce suggest that implementation is also likely to be limited: managers will act in a rational way but will reduce the overall task to a series of small steps in order to make it more manageable. Thus the strategic goals and implementation are likely to be split into a series of smaller tasks that can be more easily handled but may not be optimal.

In addition, the authors suggest that *individuals* will make rational decisions but will include their *personal* goals in this process – not necessarily the same as those of the organisation itself. Implementation needs to ensure that there is consistency between personal and organisational goals.

● *Minimum intervention* has been summarised by the authors as follows:

'*In implementing strategy, managers should change only what is necessary and sufficient to produce an enduring solution to the strategic problem being addressed.*'

Practising managers might recognise this principle as the rather more basic sentence: 'If it ain't broke, don't fix it.' The implication here is that implementation may be constrained by the need to consider the impact on the strategy itself.

Comment Both these areas represent useful, if somewhat simple, guidance on strategy implementation. They suggest that implementation, strategy and goals are inter-related, which needs to be taken into account in the development of implementation plans.

19.2.3 Further emergent approaches to implementation

In Chapter 17, the work of Quinn, Senge and others on the strategy process was examined. They suggest quite clearly that implementation needs to be considered not just as a single event with fixed and rigid plans but rather as a series of implementation activities whose outcome will shape and guide the strategy. The full strategy will not be 'known' in advance but will 'emerge' out of the implementation.

This work has been complemented by that of Pettigrew and Whipp[9] who concluded that there were three interlinking aspects to strategic change:

● *Analytical aspects.* Implementation must involve many aspects of the organisation. These are the areas that have been emphasised in various strategic models and frameworks and are explored in Parts 2 and 3 of the book.

● *Educational aspects.* 'The new knowledge and insights into a given strategy that arise from its implementation have to be captured, retained and diffused within the organisation.' (Pettigrew and Whipp.) Thus implementation cannot be regarded as immutable and unchanging. The organisation will learn about its strategies as it implements them.

- *Political aspects.* 'The very prospect of change confronts established positions. Both formulation and implementation inevitably raise questions of power within the organisation. Left unattended, such forces can provide obstacles to change ... Indeed, in the case of Jaguar [Cars] in the 1970s, ultimately such forces can wreak havoc.' (Pettigrew and Whipp.) It might also be noted that these circumstances were not so different from those confronting Air France in the 1990s, described earlier in this chapter.

Comment   Educational and political aspects (examined further in Chapter 21) are important elements of the implementation process and again suggest that implementation and strategy formulation are interlinked. The three emergent perspectives that ask for implementation are summarised in Exhibit 19.1.

Exhibit 19.1   **Three emergent perspectives on the implementation process**

- Implementation must involve many parts of the organisation.

- Implementation needs to be seen as an ongoing activity rather than one major event with a finite outcome.

- Implementation needs to be flexible and responsive to outside and internal pressures.

Key strategic principles

- According to Pettigrew and Whipp, implementation is best seen as a continuous process, rather than one that simply occurs after the formulation of the strategy.

- Hrebiniak and Joyce placed boundaries on implementation in terms of the ability of managers to consider every choice rationally and to evaluate the impact of implementation on strategy itself.

- Emergent approaches to strategy imply that implementation needs to be considered not just as a single event but rather as a series of activities, the outcome of which may to some extent shape the strategy.

CASE STUDY 19.1

Strategic planning at Canon with a co-operative corporate style

Since 1957, the Japanese company Canon has operated strategic planning. However, it has not been a rigid, inflexible process imposed by top management. Instead, it has been a free-flowing, open approach driven by the strategic vision of its senior and other managers. This vision covered the values of the company, the market position it expected to hold over many years and the resources needed to develop and sustain it. The strategies and their implementation have proved highly successful. This case study examines the planning process in more detail.

Canon's sales have grown from Y4.2 billion in 1950 to Y1933 billion in 1994. The company has developed a strong market share in its leading products: for example, 70 per cent of the world laser beam printer engine market, 40 per cent of the world bubble jet printer market and second only to Hewlett-Packard. Overall, it has a strong global base in its major product areas: photocopiers, computer peripherals, computer and fax equipment, cameras, video recorders and optical products.

As an example of its strategic vision, Canon identified the world photocopying market back in the 1960s as an area for growth. Xerox Corporation (US) had been the world leader since the 1950s with its exclusive, patented technology. However, this did not stop Canon declaring its intention in 1967 of taking 30 per cent of the world market by the 1980s and its vision 'to catch Xerox through technological differentiation'. Through the 1960s and 1970s, it went about this by developing technology that was totally different from the Xerox patents and pursuing the small photocopier market niche, which remained poorly served by Xerox. Today, Canon is world market leader and has developed its core competences out of photocopiers into laser printers, digital scanners, colour bubble jet printing, digitised optical images and other areas. It will be noted that printing is only one of Canon's areas of competence in the 1990s (*see* Table 19.2).

Strategic planning at Canon, however, is not just a matter of vision and the identification of core competences. Exhibit 19.2 outlines the strategic planning process at Canon. It is driven initially by the centre and its strong belief in customer satisfaction. Typical of large Japanese companies, the

centre has also defined two elements of its overall philosophy which some Western companies would find vague and lacking in commercial directness:

- *Kyosei* – living and working for the common good.

- *Tsushin* – 'heart-to-heart and mind-to-mind communication' between the company and its customers in order to develop a bond of trust with the customer.

Such elements appear regularly in strategic planning in Japanese companies and are employed in order to shape the approach to strategy development in its early stages. They appear in the basic analysis along with the assumptions and projections about the future (as explored in Parts 2 and 3 of this book). In developing its long-range plan, Canon has to be directed and constrained by the distinctive features of its business. It is these characteristics that will determine the nature of the strategic planning process at the company:

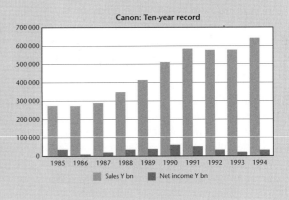

Canon: Ten-year record

Table 19.2 Canon's core competences and product development

	1950s	1960s	1970s	1980s	1990s
Core competences	● Optical ● Precision mechanical	● Electronics ● Fine optical	● Printing ● Materials technology ● Communications	● As 1970s but more advanced	● Biotechnology ● Energy saving
Additional new products	● Still camera ● Movie camera ● Lenses	● Reflex camera ● Calculators	● Copier ● Laser printer ● Word processing ● Fax	● Office automation ● Video recorders ● Computers	● Audio visual ● Information systems ● Medical equipment

- *Highly automated manufacturing plant* that takes years to design, install and bring to full efficiency. Planning therefore needs to be developed over a number of years, not just the short term. It also needs to take into account the possibility that new designs will need further work and detailed co-operation from all those working to install them.

- *High technology products* that take years to develop and perfect, including the possibility of some failures. Planning will again need to be experimental but will also need to be open and not involve criticism of failure to implement a new, experimental product.

- *Synergy and core competences* that provide linkages across a number of product areas. These take time and resources and rely on strong co-operation across different divisions. Planning will act as co-ordinator and will also direct the divisions towards the areas that have been identified: it is likely to be centralised.

Although the centre sets the long-term strategy, the product divisions begin the *medium-range planning* within the constraints set by the centre. Considerable emphasis is placed on scenarios and contingency planning so that Canon is not caught out by an unexpected event, such as a sudden rise in the value of the Yen. These plans are then consolidated by the centre.

For the short-term plan, financial objectives take greater precedence. They are usually prepared as budgets which are derived from the medium-term plan. Each division prepares its budget and these are then consolidated by the centre. From this amalgamation, the corporate HQ then prepares short-term plans on personnel, capital investments and cash flow. The data is also used to build the balance sheet and profit and loss account.

Although this might appear bureaucratic and unwieldy, Canon actually operates the process in an open, friendly and challenging fashion. Employees are encouraged to debate the issues, to take risks and to present new ideas. Strategy planning is regarded as an opportunity and a challenge, rather than a chore driven by hide-bound company rules.

CASE QUESTIONS

1 *What are the main problems of large companies such as Canon in managing the strategic planning process?*

2 *How has Canon succeeded in remaining innovative? Could it do even better? If so, how?*

Exhibit 19.2	The process of strategic planning at Canon	
Activity	*Content*	*Examples in 1994*
Basic assumptions, analysis and projections (*Prepared by the centre, but after open discussion*)	• Canon's strengths and weaknesses • Opportunities and threats • Business philosophy and beliefs	• Customer satisfaction • Kyosei • Tsushin
Long-range strategy: six years (*Decided by centre but with input and discussion from divisions*)	• Vision • Long-term objectives • Key strategic projects	• Beat Xerox • World-class • Develop Asian markets • TV broadcasting equipment • Colour personal copiers • Powersaving laser printers
Medium-range strategy: three years (*Started by divisions and then consolidated at HQ*)	• Canon itself: resources, cultures, etc. • Environment: general outlook; competition; scenarious if major shift in assumptions • Basic assumptions and projections • Resource allocation • Goals and policies • Contingency • Timetables	• Specific quantified goals developed • Resources include capital projects, human resources and the key strategic projects
Short-term plan: one year (*Developed by the divisions*)	• Budgeting: financial goals are stressed • Build on the medium-range plan	

19.3 OBJECTIVES, TASK SETTING AND COMMUNICATION PROCESSES

It is important to set out and agree clear guidelines with those individuals who will implement the strategies: typically, this process of task setting and communications will cover what is to be done, by what time and with what resources. This is a significant implementation issue and involves five basic questions, which are summarised in Exhibit 19.3.

Exhibit 19.3   **Task setting and communications: the basic questions**

- Who developed the strategies that are now being implemented?

- Who will implement the strategies?

- What objectives and tasks will they need to accomplish?

- How can objectives and tasks be handled in fast-changing environments?

- How will the implementation process be communicated and co-ordinated?

In reality, the answers to these questions will depend primarily on the way that the strategies have been developed. In this sense, the strategy development phase and the strategy implementation phase are interconnected.

19.3.1 Who developed the strategies that are now being implemented?

In the past, some strategy writers have taken the view that the strategies in large corporations will be largely developed at the centre:

> 'Most of the people in the corporate who are crucial to successful strategy implementation probably had little, if anything, to do with the development of the corporate strategy.'[10]

If this is the case, then the implementation process is very different from one where there has been a lengthy debate and agreement on the strategies. In this latter case, managers will know that they are likely to be responsible for implementing something that was discussed with them some weeks or months earlier. Importantly, ignorance will be higher and commitment to the new strategy will be lower among those managers who have had no involvement in developing the strategy.

For example, if strategies have been produced using the procedures described in the Canon Case study 19.1, then most managers will be clear on who will be doing what because they will have been closely involved in developing them. By contrast, in the case of Air France, where the centre was inevitably responsible, the implementation questions will need careful elaboration.

It is important therefore to address the question of who developed the strategy, rather than simply the question of who will implement it. For example, was it just a central team or was there full consultation? The response to this question will shape the implementation process.

19.3.2 Who will implement the strategies?

This question is important because it will define who is responsible for implementing a specific strategy. It is difficult to review progress at a later stage if no one is accountable for the way that it is being carried out. In many small companies, it is possible that a number of managers will be involved in the strategy development process because of the small size. The question needs more elaboration as organisations grow in size.

One important issue here is who makes the decision: is it the centre *telling* the managers or is the matter open for *discussion* and *negotiation*? Generally, this book takes the view that discussion is preferable because it is more motivating and rewarding all round. However, it may occasionally be necessary to instruct those involved.

19.3.3 What objectives and tasks will they need to undertake?

In Chapter 12, we examined the concept of the hierarchy of objectives – corporate, divisional and functional – cascading down from the top of the organisation. The main objectives and activities for implementation can also be considered as following a similar process. The overall corporate objectives need to be translated into objectives for each of the main areas of the business and then these objectives need to be reinterpreted into the tasks and action programmes that then need to be undertaken to achieve the objectives.

Figure 19.3 gives an example in a functional company of how the overall objective is reinterpreted in this way. The corporate objectives are translated into functional objectives that are each designed to make a contribution to the whole. This is not necessarily a simple task and may require several iterations before a satisfactory result is achieved. The marketing, operations and other tasks are then defined from the functional objectives. These are then broken down into plans: timetables, resources to achieve the objectives and other matters. Deadlines are usually set to indicate the date for completion of a particular task, as are *milestones* – interim indicators of progress so that those monitoring events can review implementation while there is still time to take remedial action.

In practice, the definition of objectives, tasks and plans may be simpler in smaller companies and more complicated in larger companies. For example at Canon, three sets of objectives and plans are prepared on six-year, three-year and one-year time horizons. They do not all have the same degree of detail but they are all fully co-ordinated across the company.

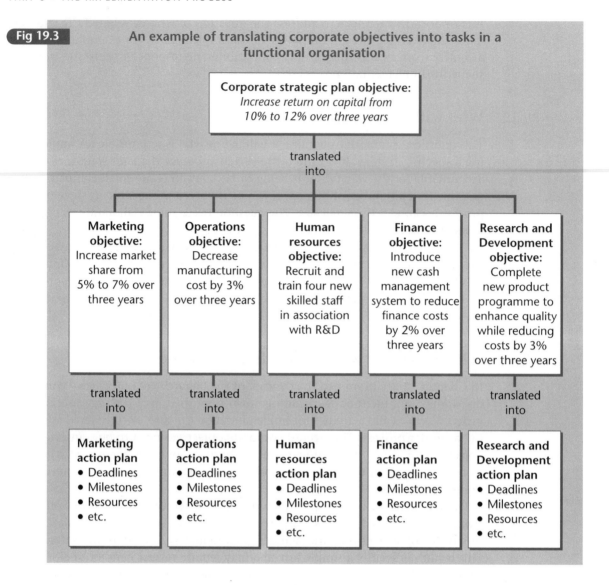

Fig 19.3 An example of translating corporate objectives into tasks in a functional organisation

Corporate strategic plan objective:
Increase return on capital from 10% to 12% over three years

translated into

Marketing objective:	Operations objective:	Human resources objective:	Finance objective:	Research and Development objective:
Increase market share from 5% to 7% over three years	Decrease manufacturing cost by 3% over three years	Recruit and train four new skilled staff in association with R&D	Introduce new cash management system to reduce finance costs by 2% over three years	Complete new product programme to enhance quality while reducing costs by 3% over three years

translated into

Marketing action plan
- Deadlines
- Milestones
- Resources
- etc.

Operations action plan
- Deadlines
- Milestones
- Resources
- etc.

Human resources action plan
- Deadlines
- Milestones
- Resources
- etc.

Finance action plan
- Deadlines
- Milestones
- Resources
- etc.

Research and Development action plan
- Deadlines
- Milestones
- Resources
- etc.

19.3.4 How can objectives and tasks be handled in fast-changing environments?

When environments are changing fast, it may be exceptionally difficult to specify satisfactory objectives and tasks: by the time they have been agreed and communicated, the environment may have changed. As changes occur, the objectives may rapidly become impossible or straightforward depending on the nature of the changes. In this situation, it makes little sense to adhere to objectives developed for earlier situations. Three guidelines can be applied:

1 flexibility in objectives and tasks within an agreed general vision;
2 empowerment of those closest to the environment changes, so that they can respond quickly;
3 careful and close monitoring by the centre of those reacting to events.

The purpose of such surveillance is to ensure that actions taken do not expose the centre itself to unnecessary strategic or financial risk. This is vital if the organisation wishes to avoid the fate of companies such as Barings Bank in 1995, which crashed with debts of over US$1.5 billion partly as a result of inadequate controls in such a rapidly-changing environment.

19.3.5 How will the implementation process be communicated and co-ordinated?

In small organisations, it may be unnecessary, over-complex or inappropriate to engage in the elaborate communication of agreed strategies. People who have explored the strategic tasks together during the formulation of the strategy and meet each other on a regular basis may not need lengthy communications during implementation. However, in larger enterprises, it is likely to be essential for four reasons:

- to ensure that everyone has understood;
- to allow any confusion or ambiguity to be resolved;
- to communicate clearly the judgements, assumptions, contingencies and possibly the choices made during the strategy decision phase;[11]
- to ensure that the organisation is properly co-ordinated.

This last point deserves particularly careful thought and action because co-ordination involves two major strategic areas: value-chain linkages and synergy.

In Chapter 7, the value chain was introduced and its ability to deliver *unique linkages* across the organisation was discussed. The purpose of such linkages is to develop competitive advantage because these are unlikely to be capable of exact replication by other companies whose history, competences and resources will be marginally different. Such linkages will be meaningless at the implementation stage if careful co-ordination is lacking.

In Chapter 16, the concept of *synergy* was examined – the situation where a corporate portfolio of businesses is worth more than their individual values as stand-alone enterprises. Co-ordination is essential if the synergistic values are to be realised. Campbell and Sommers Luchs have suggested four guidelines for synergy implementation, based on empirical research:[12] these are summarised in Exhibit 19.4. Similar consideration will also apply to value-chain linkages.

More generally, many organisations including small companies will create inter-functional or inter-divisional task forces to achieve the required co-ordination. Such mechanisms vary in their cost and their ability to cope with uncertainty and diversity.[13] For maximum effectiveness, they need to be designed in conjunction with management information systems (*see* Section 19.6) and reward systems (*see* Chapter 20).

> **Exhibit 19.4** **Four guidelines for implementing synergies and value-chain linkages**
>
> 1 Broad generalisations about the possible benefits of synergies or linkages are unlikely to be as useful as *detailed analysis* of precisely where they are likely to be obtained. This implies that detailed and precise studies need to be undertaken at the implementation stage and possibly earlier.
>
> 2 It is better to establish the *details* of what resources are to be shared or linked and how this is to be conducted at lower levels through local managers in charge of the local facilities. They will know better than others.
>
> 3 An *emergent approach* to synergy development and value-chain linkages is more likely to produce results because it avoids overloading those involved and gives time for experimentation.
>
> 4 The organisation's headquarters must *clarify in advance* what synergies or linkages are being sought. It must also be *sensitive* to the skills and concerns of those managers tasked with developing the synergistic or linkage benefits. For example, they may lose control of some elements of their work in order to provide benefits elsewhere which they may find unsettling.

> **Key strategic principles**
>
> ● When setting objectives and tasks, the first question to be established is that of who developed the strategy that is now to be implemented. The answer to this question will influence the implementation process.
>
> ● Individual objectives and tasks follow from the agreed overall objectives. It may be necessary to experiment to find the optimal combination of events.
>
> ● In fast-changing environments, it may not be possible or desirable to have rigid objectives because they may be made redundant by outside events.
>
> ● Communication and co-ordination are vital to satisfactory implementation. These are especially important where the organisation is seeking benefits from synergies or value-chain linkages.

19.4 RESOURCE ALLOCATION

Most strategies need resources to be allocated to them if they are to be implemented successfully. This section explores the basic processes and examines some special circumstances that may affect the allocation of resources.[14]

19.4.1 The resource allocation process

In large, diversified companies, the centre plays a major role in allocating the resources among the various strategies proposed by its operating companies or divisions.[15] In smaller companies, the same mechanism will also operate, although on a more informal basis: product groups, areas of the business or functional areas may still bid for funds to support their strategic proposals.

There are three criteria which can be used when allocating resources.

1 *The contribution of the proposed resources towards the fulfilment of the organisation's mission and objectives.* At the centre of the organisation, the resource allocation task is to steer resources away from areas that are poor at delivering the organisation's objectives and towards those that are good. Readers will recognise this description as being similar to that employed when considering the movement of funds in the BCG *product portfolio matrix* in Chapter 3: in that case, cash was diverted from *cash cows* towards *stars* and so on. The principle is similar here but relies on centrally-available funds rather than the diversion of funds.

2 *Its support of key strategies.* In many cases, the problem with resource allocation is that the requests for funds usually exceed the funds that are normally available. Thus there needs to be some further selection mechanism beyond the delivery of the organisation's mission and objectives. This second criterion relates to two aspects of resource analysis covered in Chapter 7:

- *the support of core competences*, where possible, in order to develop and enhance competitive advantage;
- *the enhancement of the value chain*, where possible, in order to assist particularly those activities that also support competitive advantage.

Although both of these should underpin the organisation's objectives in the long term, they can usefully be treated as additional criteria when resources are allocated.

3 *The level of risk associated with a specific proposal.* Clearly, if the risk is higher, there is a lower likelihood that the strategy will be successful. Some organisations will be more comfortable at accepting higher levels of risk than others so the criterion in this case needs to be considered in relation to the risk-acceptance level of the organisation.

19.4.2 Special circumstances surrounding the allocation of resources

Special circumstances may cause an organisation to amend the criteria for the allocation of resources. Still based on the common principle of *bargaining* for the centre's funds, some organisations will consider the following:

- *When major strategic changes are unlikely.* In this situation, resources may be allocated on the basis of a *formula*, e.g. marketing funds might be allocated as a percentage of sales based on past history and experience. The major difficulty with such an approach is its arbitrary nature. It may, however, be a useful short cut.
- *When major strategic changes are predicted.* In this situation, additional resources may be required either to drive the strategic process or to respond to an expected competitive initiative. In both cases, *special negotiation* with the centre is required rather than the adherence to dogmatic criteria.
- *When resources are shared between divisions.* In this situation, the centre may seek to enhance its role beyond that of resource allocation. It may need to establish the degree of collaboration and, where the areas disagree, *impose* a solution. The logical and motivational problems associated with such an approach are evident.

19.4.3 Caution regarding the resource allocation process

Hamel and Prahalad have reservations about the whole resource allocation process.[16] They view it as offering the wrong mental approach to the strategy task, arguing that it is more concerned with dividing up the existing resources rather than with using the resources more effectively and strategically.

> *'If top management devotes more effort to assessing the strategic feasibility of projects in its resource allocation role than it does to the task of multiplying resource effectiveness, its value-added will be modest indeed.'*

They make an important cautionary point.

Key strategic principles

- The resource allocation process is used to provide the necessary funds for proposed strategies. In circumstances of limited resources, the centre is usually responsible for allocating funds using various decision criteria.

- Criteria for allocation include the delivery of the organisation's mission and objectives, its support of key strategies such as core competences and its risk-taking profile. Some special circumstances such as unusual changes in the environment may support other resource allocation criteria.

- There is a risk that the resource allocation process will ignore the need to use resources more effectively and strategically.

CASE STUDY 19.2

Informal strategic controls at Nestlé[17]

Because of the diversity of its product portfolio, Nestlé has chosen to devolve strategy to its main operating areas and control them informally from the centre. This case study describes the processes and strategic planning procedures that have been developed.

With sales of over US$54 billion, Nestlé (Switzerland) is Europe's largest food and consumer goods company. Its main product areas include coffee (Nescafé), milk and baby foods, confectionery and frozen foods. It operates globally through a series of geographical *zones* and a set of product *strategic business units* (SBUs). For example, zone 1 is Europe and there is an SBU for the confectionery and ice cream product area operating on a worldwide basis.

Because of the wide variation in the SBUs in its portfolio, Nestlé has chosen to give *strategic*

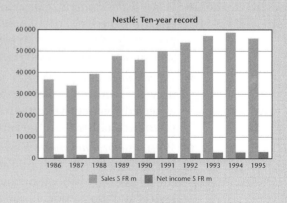

Nestlé: Ten-year record

Sales S FR m ■ Net income S FR m

control of its operations to the individual SBUs. Each SBU has a full range of functional expertise in its business area: marketing, production, research and so on. However, *operational* decisions rest with the zones and below them the national companies. The role of the centre is to co-ordinate and to allocate resources. The Nestlé structure for strategic planning, budgets and reporting is shown in Fig 19.4. The centre begins the process by issuing instructions to the SBUs for the next planning cycle. The SBUs then work on their three-year long-term plans (called LTPs). Every SBU prepares an LTP each year but some are merely updates from previous years. In order to promote strategic discussion with the centre, the LTPs are then circulated. They will include such areas as brand positioning, market

Fig 19.4

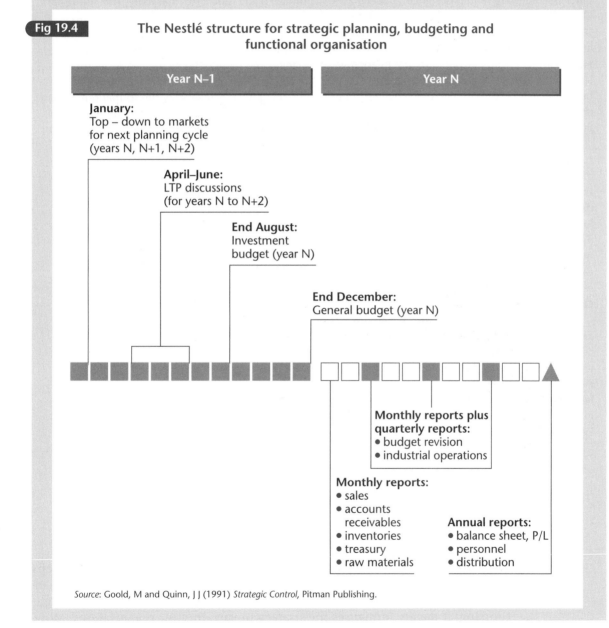

The Nestlé structure for strategic planning, budgeting and functional organisation

Source: Goold, M and Quinn, J J (1991) *Strategic Control*, Pitman Publishing.

share and competitive activity, pricing, capital proposals and new product development.

Because the company operates in relatively mature markets, it is able to operate a system of checks and balances with more lengthy debate between the centre and the SBUs than might be appropriate where markets are changing fast and quick decisions are required. Hence, following the LTP preparation early in the year, discussions are then held on content in the period from April to June between the SBUs, zones and the centre. The Nestlé Executive Committee has to give its approval. Later in the year, there is an investment and revenue budget review. The strategies and activities can be changed at this point if the market situation or competitive positions have altered significantly.

However, the controls and balances are more subtle than being simply the official committees described above. A Nestlé manager commented on the control procedures: 'You could achieve your monthly budget targets by disturbing the strategy; for example, by repositioning brands or change media expenditure. But if you did so, it would quickly be noticed by the product group director at the centre. This would not be through a formal report, but through informal contacts with the country in question.'

In a similar way, although the SBUs and zones are separated in decision-making terms from the centre, most are located in the same geographical location – at Nestlé's HQ in Vevey, Switzerland. Here is a senior manager talking about the chocolate strategy group, which was at one time located in York, England. 'I got increasingly sucked into Vevey because of the need to talk to the various zone managers, and to all the corporate functions and services ... I don't believe in electronic communication: face-to-face discussions are vital, especially in a group the size of Nestle.' This principle of direct informal contact is encouraged, even if it means that some managers have extensive travel commitments. The aims are to produce an integrated team and to maintain the informal communications that provide the real checks and balances to the Nestlé style of strategic planning.

Nestlé believes that such informal approaches to planning and monitoring by the centre are useful in guiding and developing corporate strategy. They are probably just as effective as the formal reporting against strategic objectives. Financial rewards for achieving strategic targets are not an important aspect of the strategic process. Peer pressures, promotion and personal competitiveness are greater incentives in ensuring that strategies are delivered. A longer-term view is taken of management performance and competence by the centre rather than specific achievement against targets. This is reflected in the tendency for managers to serve the company for many years in long and stable relationships.

CASE QUESTIONS

1 *What characterises the Nestlé style of strategic planning? To what extent is this a function of its large size? Its product range? Its geographical spread?*

2 *What, if any, are the dangers of informal strategic controls such as those operating at Nestlé?*

19.5 STRATEGIC PLANNING

19.5.1 What is strategic planning?

The purpose of strategic planning is to use a *formal planning system* for the development and implementation of the strategies related to the mission and objectives of the organisation. Importantly, strategic planning is no substitute for strategic thinking; it merely formalises the strategy process in some organisations. More specifically, the plan will *integrate* the activities of the organisation and specify the *timetable* for the completion of each stage.

Professor George Day is right when he suggests[18] that strategic planning should not be an isolated event that culminates in a clear-cut decision. Instead, it should be an ongoing activity that responds simultaneously to the pressure of events and the dictates of the calendar. To ensure organisational commitment, involvement in the planning process must come from many levels of the organisation – each with a distinct role in formulating the strategy and ensuring the integration of corporate resource allocations, strategies, objectives and action plans.

Strategic planning will plot the prescriptive strategic route forward but it also needs to contain strong elements of the emergent approach. Its subject matter is therefore not just implementation but the *whole strategy process* from mission and objectives through to control systems. It is discussed here at the implementation stage because the issues are essentially about how the whole process is actioned and monitored in a specific organisation.

19.5.2 The basic approaches to strategic planning

In the past, there have been three basic approaches to strategic planning in larger companies:

- *Top down*. Planning is initiated and conducted primarily by the centre of the organisation.
- *Bottom up*. Planning is primarily the responsibility of the individual parts such as divisions. Simple guidance is given by the centre as to what is required. The centre then sits in judgement on the plans provided.
- *Integrated*. There is continuing discussion involving both the centre (top) and the individual parts (bottom) of the organisation.

In the 1990s, many organisations choose the *integrated* approach. The route employed by Canon and Nestlé in the case studies described in this chapter. However, where the diversity of the company is large, there is a clear argument for the *bottom up* approach – for example, Hanson in Case study 19.3. Hanson in its own way also provides strong central guidance of a simple financial nature so it might be considered *top down* from this perspective.

In undertaking the strategic planning process, many companies believe that it is important to first establish the background assumptions and the basis on which business is conducted, including the key factors for success (*see* Chapter 3). Following this, the company will then explore its *long-term vision* and broad strategic direction: these might be only achieved over a number of years and would be expected to include the input of new technologies and ideas. A *medium-term plan* can then be developed for the next two or three years, where the environment is sufficiently stable. *Short-term annual plans* and budgets consistent with the medium term are then developed. It is important to see this process as not just happening in sequence but involving much iteration and revisiting before each stage is finalised. Figure 19.5 illustrates the basic process.

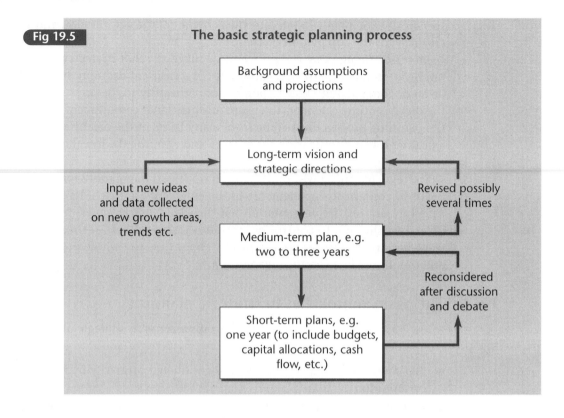

Fig 19.5   **The basic strategic planning process**

Sometimes such a cycle is repeated by the company every year – Case study 19.2 describes such a process at Nestlé. However, because of the potential complexity and length of such investigations, it would be most unusual if *every* aspect of the business was reviewed every year from a long-term perspective. Product groups, special topics, core competences, different group objectives are often chosen as starting points for exploring strategic issues and fed into the long-term review. As Arie de Geus, the former head of planning at Royal Dutch/Shell wrote:[19]

> *'The real purpose of effective planning is not to make plans but to change the … mental models that … decision makers carry in their heads.'*

19.5.3   The changing status of strategic planning

During the 1960s and 1970s, strategic planning promised to deliver superior financial returns. When these did not materialise and unpredictable events, such as the oil price crises of the 1970s, made a nonsense of planning (but not at Shell, as we saw in Chapter 17), strategic planning fell into some disarray.[20] Essentially, according to its critics, strategic planning had become too bureaucratic and rigid in its application.[21][22] These and similar comments were still being made in the 1990s.[23] Exhibit 19.5 summarises the major critical onslaught on strategic planning. It should be noted that some of the writers do not use the narrow definition of strategic planning, confined to formalising the broader process, as used in this chapter. Their criticisms rely on a broader view of the role of strategic planning and may therefore be inappropriate for the narrow definition used here.

| Exhibit 19.5 | Major reasons given for the failure of some forms of strategic planning[24] |

Poor direction from top management	Need for greater flexibility	Political difficulties	Corporate culture
● Planning replaced the flexibility and uncertainty needed in some environments ● Deep strategic thought replaced by planning formulae ● Short-term focus and financial emphasis ● Poor discussion of key issues ● Inadequate resources allocated for plans ● Whole process of resource allocation	● Annual budget took priority ● Accepted existing industry boundaries ● Over-emphasis on procedures and form-filling ● Tests for 'fit' between resources and plans rather than stretches for new resources ● Better to introduce improved systems to cope with flexibility rather than stick with rigid plan	● Planning was controlled by specialist staff and not by line managers who have the responsibility ● Power of some managers threatened by new procedures ● Ability of entrenched interests to delay decisions	● Need to develop organisation that can cope with uncertainty ● Short-termism ● Over-emphasis on financial results ● Lack of risk-taking and entrepreneurial flair ● Little toleration of the occasional failure

Note: Some comments might be regarded as applying to any form of strategy development rather than strategic planning as such. Note also the comment in the text on the research evidence used to support some of the comments.

Given all these considerations, it might be argued that strategic planning is no longer appropriate as a means of formalising the strategy process in the 1990s. However, many companies still need to look beyond the short term and to co-ordinate their main activities, especially where significant commitments have to be made over lengthy time spans. The three case studies in this chapter have all been chosen from successful companies who still use some form of strategic planning. Consequently, attitudes to strategic planning are beginning to change again. Even Mintzberg, who has been highly critical of strategic planning in the past, has now conceded that it does fulfil a useful function within certain limits.[25]

Specifically, Mintzberg has identified the main role of the strategic plan as being *to make plans operational*, after the basic strategic thinking has been undertaken;

that is, planning takes place in the implementation phase, as outlined in this chapter. Importantly, he recommends that planning is undertaken by the line managers responsible for implementing strategies, rather than by a separate planning department. He argues that it is only the line managers who have the detailed knowledge in advance and the commitment afterwards to carry out the strategy decisions. The role that he sees for strategic planning is therefore one of staff adviser, rather than one of major line responsibility.

Mintzberg also suggested three other ways that strategic planning, as he defined it, can assist the corporation:

1 to assist the communication process throughout the organisation by setting out the review and planning thinking;

2 to find new strategic insights by posing new or unusual questions outside normal operations;

3 to assist the presentation of alternative and possible radical ways of viewing strategic issues.

Comment
Some of Mintzberg's descriptions of strategic planning depend on which companies formed part of his sample and how representative they were of the total universe: this is not always clear. It is easy to paint a poor picture by choosing selected examples. Such a criticism also applies to some of the other comments made in Exhibit 19.5. For example, Hamel and Prahalad take strategic planning to task, but beyond the words 'in our experience' they actually quote *no specific research* evidence whatsoever, let alone presenting a representative sample.[26] These vague generalisations are unconvincing.

More generally, Mintzberg is right in his emphasis on the need for innovative thinking, which may not be best served by a strongly bureaucratic strategic planning process. Overall, this book takes the view that Mintzberg is correct in his identification of the role for strategic planning: it summarises the decisions taken elsewhere and is useful for making strategy operational. Strategic planning is no substitute for careful and innovative thinking on the main strategic issues.

It is sometimes argued that strategic planning with its emphasis on the 'one best way' to achieve the organisation's objectives is inherently weak: there can be no single route to strategic success because the environment, technology and customers/stakeholders are constantly changing. Strategic planning is not used in that sense in this book. It is used here because it forms a significant part of the strategic activities of many companies and has a role in making the strategic process operational.

19.5.4 Planning strategies and styles

Although a large number of companies undertake some form of strategic planning, it is important to understand that there are many variations in the way that it is conducted. The reasons for this include:

● *Environment.* Stable environments lend themselves to longer time horizons. Stability also favours a more centralised approach to planning, because there is less need to respond to rapid variations in the market, e.g. Nestlé.

● *Product range.* As products become more diverse across a company, it becomes more difficult to develop coherent core competences, synergies and linkages across the value chain. In these circumstances, the planning style may move from one seeking co-operation across divisions to one based on simple financial linkages, e.g. Hanson.

- *Leadership and management style.* Particularly in smaller companies, this will inevitably guide the approach to the development of strategy and its co-ordination across the company. It may also apply in some larger companies, e.g. Richard Branson at Virgin, Edvard Deutz at Mercedes-Benz and Akiro Morita at Sony.

There has been no wide-ranging international study on the range of management styles. However, Goold and Campbell conducted such a study during the 1980s on 16 diversified UK companies.[27] They distinguished several different styles for conducting strategic planning. The purpose of identifying the different approaches was to define the manner in which the *centre* added value to the company's separate businesses. The researchers suggested that there were two main ways in which value could be added:

- The centre could help to shape the plans of each business – the *planning influence*.

- The centre could control the process as the plans were being implemented – the *control influence*.

From the empirical research, three main styles of strategic planning were then identified as being most common:

- *Strategic planning.* The centre is involved in formulating the *plans* of the various businesses. Then the emphasis is on long-term objectives during the *control* process. Canon is an example that conforms approximately to this, although there is more collaborative effort at Canon than is perhaps implied by the definition.

- *Financial control.* The centre exercises strong short-term financial control but otherwise the businesses are highly decentralised and able to operate as they wish. The individual businesses are able to develop longer-term plans if they judge that it is useful. It should be noted that there is little attempt to co-ordinate across companies in such an arrangement. Synergies, value-chain linkages and core competences are largely absent. Hanson is an example.

- *Strategic control.* This lies between strategic planning and financial control. In *planning* terms, the company is not as centralised as a strategic planning company, nor as decentralised as a financial control company. Greater initiative is given to the individual businesses. In *control* terms, long-term strategic objectives are used but short-term profits are also required. Nestlé is a possible example here except that the centre is closely involved at various stages of the strategy development process.

A further style was also identified but not analysed in depth in the research: *the centralised style.* In this style, all the major strategy decisions are held at the centre with day-to-day implementation being delegated to the various businesses.

Within these broad types of planning, there were then further variations. The purpose of the research was not to choose between the styles but rather to explore how the resulting strategic process could be more successful. The researchers drew four conclusions:

- Style should be matched to the circumstances of the business: technology, product range, speed of environmental change, leadership and so on.

- Some styles demand greater understanding of the businesses than others: for example, the debate between the centre and its subsidiaries in the strategic control style is much more keen than the distant monitoring of financial performance in a financial control style.

- Successful styles benefit from openness and mutual respect between those involved across the company. Suspicion and lack of trust between the centre and the parts of the business will cause real problems.

- Shared commitment to work together to implement the agreed strategies is vital. This may come from inspired leadership or it may derive from the clarity of the objectives.

Comment   This research presents a useful and unique insight into strategic planning, but its attempt to categorise planning into a few distinct types is based on a sample of only 16 companies. There are other possible styles, e.g. entrepreneurial, that were not part of the sample. Moreover, styles change as companies, their environments and leaders change.

Exhibit 19.6 speculates on some possible styles in the public and not-for-profit sectors, where strategic planning is also possible.

| Exhibit 19.6 | Possible styles of strategic planning in the public and not-for-profit sectors |

1   Bureaucratic (e.g. civil service)

- clear goals
- great reliance on rules
- decisions follow standard operating procedures

2   Organised anarchy (e.g. some charitable trusts)

- unclear goals, difficult to quantify
- very decentralised organisation
- *ad hoc* decisions
- haphazard collection and use of information
- decisions not linked to goals, but rather to the intersection of persons, solutions and problems

3   Political power (e.g. university)

- goals consistent with social role but pluralistic in organisation
- shifting coalitions of interests
- disorderly decision making but becoming less so
- information used strategically or withheld strategically
- decisions bargained among interested parties

19.5.5 Strategic planning in small companies

By comparison with large diverse companies, there is a much narrower product range in smaller companies. By definition, the scope of the issues may also be narrower. Hence, there may be less need to go through a formal planning process and resource allocation procedure. Planning systems may also be simpler and shorter. Changes in the environment will be less of an issue in the planning sense: small companies should be able to react more quickly and responsively.

Nevertheless, the same basic planning process will apply: background assessment, vision for the future plus long-term aims, and then medium-term and short-term plans. The time horizon may differ and the planning style is likely to be more informal. As soon as external finance is needed to support or expand the business, however, basic plans will be required. Such plans will need the same strategic logic, evidence and justification that apply to larger organisations.

Key strategic principles

- Strategic planning operationalises the strategy process in some organisations. It is no substitute for basic and innovative strategic thinking.

- The basic process may well cover background assumptions, long-term vision, medium-term plans and short-term plans. Importantly, new ideas are input into the process and revisions are a significant element of its development.

- Strategic planning has been heavily criticised by some researchers as being too bureaucratic and rigid in its approach, but attitudes are beginning to mellow as long as the process is narrowly defined.

- There are a number of different styles for conducting the strategic planning process, for example, strategic planning, strategic control and financial control. The selection of a style depends on the circumstances of the company.

- Formal strategic planning in small companies may also prove beneficial, especially where external finance is being sought.

19.6 INFORMATION, MONITORING AND CONTROL[28]

19.6.1 Why are monitoring and controls important?

Monitoring and control procedures are an important aspect of implementation because information can be used:

- to assess resource allocation choices;
- to monitor progress on implementation;
- to evaluate the performance of individual managers as they go about the achievement of their implementation tasks;

- to monitor the environment for significant changes from the planning assumptions and projections;

- to provide a feedback mechanism and the fine-tuning essential for emergent strategy implementation, especially in fast-changing markets.

More generally, monitoring becomes increasingly important as the *concept* of strategy moves from being an isolated event towards being an ongoing activity.

> *Strategy creation is seen as emerging from the way a company at various levels acquires, interprets and processes information about its environment.*[29]

For all these reasons, companies like Nestlé and Canon spend significant resources on monitoring their activities. Because of the vast range of potential information, they may concentrate on the *key factors for success* as a first step (*see* Chapter 3). Some major companies have complete departments whose sole task is to monitor competitors. It is also a characteristic of some small businesses that they are acutely aware of their immediate competitors and customers, the market prices and other forms of strategic activity.

19.6.2 What are the main elements of a strategic control system?

Strategic control systems monitor the main elements of the strategy and its objectives. The crucial point from this is to obtain information in time to be able to take action. Information for its own sake has limited value: the real test is whether it is useful and timely in revising the implementation process, where required. These may include some financial measures but will also involve:

- customer satisfaction;
- quality measures;
- market share.

It may also be necessary to apply such indicators externally to monitor competition in order to assess the *relative* performance of the organisation against others in the market place.

It is important to distinguish between *financial monitoring* (cash flow, earnings per share, etc.) and *strategic controls* which may include these financial elements but will also have a broader perspective.

Effective systems need careful thought and some experimentation. Such systems will first assess the strategic control style of the company (*see* Section 19.5.4). Clearly, the financial control style will rely primarily on financial data. Other styles will require further strategic data, either in a formal or informal fashion. They will then need a period of experimentation to see whether they are producing the desired information. This means not only trying out the system but also obtaining feedback on its benefits and problems. It follows that the process of installing a strategic control system will involve *experimentation* and *learning*. Beyond these requirements, the main items that need to be included will then relate back to the strategic plans and associated targets that are being implemented.

19.6.3 How can strategic controls be improved?[30]

To some extent, this question cannot be fully answered unless the precise strategy style has been established. Nevertheless, there are some useful guidelines designed to obtain the best from such systems:

● *Concentrate on the key performance indicators and factors for success*. There is a real danger that too many elements will be monitored with resulting information overload.

● *Distinguish between corporate, business and operating levels of information and only monitor where relevant*. For example, not everyone at the centre needs to know that a minor product has just achieved its sales target. Equally, a division may have limited interest in market share data from another division even if this is important at the centre.

● *Avoid over-reliance on quantitative data*. Numbers are usually easier to measure but may be misleading and simplistic. Qualitative data and information that is difficult to quantify in such areas as service may be far more relevant to strategy monitoring.

● *As controls become established, consider relaxing them*. Eventually, they may interfere with the most important task of clear and insightful strategic exploration. For example, it was for this reason that Jack Welch at GE reduced them, but he did not do so until the principles had been learnt. Every organisation may need to go through this stage of learning before controls are relaxed.

● *Create realistic expectations of what the control system can do as it is being introduced or upgraded*. Some managers may regard strategic controls as a waste of time. Their reasoning is that it is difficult to see early results because of the long time scales involved. Such an objection cannot be avoided but can be anticipated. It is better to acknowledge that the benefits in terms of improved strategy, resources and results will not be immediately obvious.

19.6.4 Strategy control, budgets and cost accounting

Bungay and Goold[31] state that it is 'vital' to link strategy monitoring into the budget process. They argue that, if the two processes are controlled by two different departments, there is a danger that short-term budget considerations will take precedence over longer-term important strategic decisions. This is a realistic but short-term Anglo-American view of the way that business operates. It is particularly associated with the financial control style described in Section 19.5. It holds the real danger that *strategy controls* and *budgeting variances* will be confused. Budgeting is concerned with the achievement of targets planned monthly or quarterly on the basis of revenue and costs. Strategy rarely concerns itself with such short-term matters.

Moreover, much of traditional cost accounting in UK and US companies is concerned with monitoring and controlling variances from such budgets and plans. For some companies, this may have its place in assessing short-term performance, but the whole mentality of treating the 'plan' as sacrosanct and highly accurate is wrong at the strategic level. Although strategy monitoring is undertaken, the world of strategy is dynamic and is more concerned with exploration, debate and assessment. It is far removed from rigid budget short-term formulae and variances.

> ### Key strategic principles
>
> - Monitoring and control systems are important for their contribution to assessing how strategies are being implemented and how the environment itself is changing.
>
> - The important point about information and control is the necessity of obtaining information in sufficient time to take action, where required.
>
> - There are a number of ways in which strategic controls can be improved. All of them rely on the establishment of simple, cost-effective and useful information about the organisation and its environment.
>
> - It has been argued that strategy control and budgeting should be linked. This is not recommended because strategy monitoring is more concerned with exploration while budgeting is more focussed on achieving specific short-term targets.

19.7 IMPLEMENTATION OF INTERNATIONAL STRATEGY

International aspects of implementation are more complicated because of factors such as culture and geographical diversity. However, they essentially follow the principles already outlined in this chapter and the special comments elsewhere in this book.

CASE STUDY 19.3

Financial planning at Hanson plc

When the Anglo-American group, Hanson, acquired a company during the 1980s and early 1990s, it used a well-tested formula for imposing its own style of strategic planning on its new purchase. This case describes the main elements of its financial control strategy and shows how they were applied to its acquisition of the Imperial Group in 1987.

Background
During the 1970s and 1980s, the Hanson Group grew from a relatively small UK-based company to one of the largest conglomerates operating in the UK and USA. Growth was mainly through acquisition. Hanson had a reputation for identifying companies whose share price valuation was below the true worth of its underlying assets: they were *undervalued* on the UK or US stock exchanges. Hanson then made a generous bid by the standard of the existing share price, which shareholders

accepted. Each company was then reorganised with some parts sold off and others retained. Table 19.3 shows some assets and disposals made by Hanson over this period.

The Hanson holding company strategic style
Before making an acquisition, the Hanson Group subjected each target to a careful examination of its real worth. After purchase, each company was then reorganised with some parts being kept and others sold. For example, Hanson bought the

Table 19.3 Examples of assets and disposals at Hanson

Target	Acquisition cost (£ million)	Year	Disposal sale (£ million)	Year	Retained after disposal
Berec (Ever Ready Batteries)	95	1981	40	1983	Ever Ready, UK
			1	1989	
Imperial Group (hotels, food, tobacco)	2600	1986	1670	1986	Imperial Tobacco, UK
			23	1988	
			555	1988	
			88	1989	
			2	1990	
SCM (typewriters, office products)	930	1986	935	1986	SCM Chemicals, USA
			35	1987	
			118	1988	
			310	1989	
			42	1990	

Imperial Group in 1987 for around £2.5 billion. Over the following few years, it sold off much of the group and raised around £2.4 billion. However, it kept the tobacco interests under the company name Imperial Tobacco. Brand names included John Player cigarettes and Wills Tobacco with their major shares of the UK market.

Those parts that were retained were then subject to the Hanson style of management: *the stick and carrot*. This involved setting a few paramount financial targets and then giving the remaining management the autonomy and personal financial incentive to deliver against these. The company said that pairing discipline with freedom 'releases tremendous ingenuity' in management and the workforce. This freedom was extensive: for example, the Managing Director at the central HQ of Imperial Tobacco said that he and the small group of colleagues were responsible for Imperial, not Hanson.

There was no Hanson strategy debate with the Imperial Tobacco company. Headquarters set its subsidiary a few critical incentive targets on, for example, profits and capital employed and then left the tobacco company to work out how to achieve them. It also had a system of central approval for all capital budget items that was very

strict: any item over £1000 or US$2000 had to be approved by Hanson central HQ: this made the companies reluctant to submit bids. Approval was not usually given for research and development or other speculative investments. It was mainly reserved for cost-cutting new plant, factory closures that would reduce costs and similar ventures.

How this worked at Imperial Tobacco

After acquisition, Hanson installed its own senior managers and the Hanson financial controls at Imperial Tobacco. Reorganisation also started immediately with *delayering* taking place: nine layers of management were cut down to four, with resulting job losses. The remaining organisation was also subdivided into twelve largely autonomous units that reported directly to the new Hanson-appointed Imperial Tobacco Managing Director, each with profit responsibility.

Beyond this, in the first two years after acquisition, few physical changes were made to manufacturing and marketing arrangements. However, the new profit units were set very low transfer prices at which the plants sold their products to the distribution arm. These were fixed at prices which meant that the factories 'lost' £6 million in the first year after takeover. However, managers achieved a 70 per cent increase in productivity over the next three years, thanks to the new profit regime and the better management of manufacturing. For example, material costs fell over the first five years once buying of supplies was decentralised to the individual plants.

After the first two years, bigger gains came with the closure of two plants and the rebuilding of the other three. The capital for this was largely raised within the Imperial Group: capital employed fell from £200 million when annual sales were £750 million in 1987 to £30 million when annual sales were £707 million in 1994. Factory site rationalisation and drastic stock reductions were the key implementation factors: numbers employed dropped from 11 026 to 2910 over the same years.

Financial control at Hanson

Although the Imperial Tobacco company was guided by financial controls from the centre, this was not the complete story. There were some talented company managers at Hanson HQ who knew how to encourage new subsidiaries to work better, especially at middle-management level. Their strategies of *empowerment* by setting up new smaller profit centres and *delayering* to cut down central administration go beyond simple financial control. There was also *capital investment* to reduce costs. There was no substantive investment in innovation. However, for certain types of basic industry with limited growth prospects, such a combination of strategic principles was able to show its merits.

Source: © Copyright Aldersgate Consultancy Limited 1997. Developed by the author from published sources only.

CASE QUESTIONS

1 *How did Hanson achieve its results? What did the Hanson Group Headquarters contribute to this process?*

2 *To what extent could the Hanson style be considered as a form of empowerment of middle managers?*

3 *What are the dangers, if any, of the Hanson strategic style?*

Corporate planning: formality without bureaucracy[32]

In this extract from their book, Strategic Control, *Michael Goold and John Quinn suggest ways of overcoming a major problem in strategic planning.*

A formal and explicit strategic control process helps to clarify the criteria of good strategic performance. But formal processes can easily become rigid and bureaucratic. How can the strategic control process be formal and explicit but not bureaucratic?

Large departments and lengthy reports should be avoided. Line managers themselves should be in the best position to identify the sources of advantage in their businesses, and should not have to hire planners simply to fill in their corporate reports. Reports should focus on the few key targets that have been identified, and should not become glossy and extensive documents.

Most of the information should be readily available. If it is not, it should be specially gathered only if it is likely to help in running the business. Information on progress against key strategic objectives should, of course, be an important part of the data base of any business, whether or not it is called for as part of a corporate control process.

Face-to-face meetings and discussions help to prevent formal control reports from becoming simply a bureaucratic routine. Written reports that are greeted only with a resounding silence do not add value for the business, and should be avoided.

The existence of formal strategic control reviews should not preclude wider, less formal background reviews of progress that are not limited to the explicitly defined strategic objectives. These reviews, which should occur as part of the ongoing line management contacts between the businesses and the centre, are needed to allow the centre to gain an understanding of the sources of competitive advantage in the business and to determine what issues are most important for the business to address. They should also assist the centre in determining whether the agreed milestones are suitably stretching and in deciding on how to react to deviations from planned achievements.

A structured and systematic control process should not stop important decisions from being taken as and when issues arise. A formal strategic control process provides a safety net to prevent issues being missed, but it is not intended as a substitute for an effective and speedy line management decision process, and it should not interfere with the functioning of such a process.

Source: Goold, M and Quinn, J J (1991) *Strategic Control*, pp197–8. Reprinted with permission.

SUMMARY

● Implementation covers the activities required to put strategies into practice. The basic elements of this process are: general objectives, specific plans; the necessary finances; and a monitoring and control system to ensure compliance.

● There are three major approaches to implementation: comprehensive, incremental and selective. Implementation in small and medium-sized businesses may be less elaborate but should follow the same general principles.

● According to Pettigrew and Whipp, implementation is best seen as a *continuous* process, rather than as one following the formulation of the strategy. Hrebiniak and Joyce placed *boundaries* on implementation, depending on the ability of managers to consider every choice rationally and to evaluate the impact of implementation on the strategy itself. Emergent approaches to strategy imply that implementation needs to be considered not just as a single event but as a series of activities whose outcome may to some extent shape the strategy.

● When setting objectives and tasks, first establish who *developed* the strategy that is to be implemented. This will influence the implementation process.

● Individual objectives and tasks will follow from the agreed overall objectives. It may be necessary to experiment to find the optimal combination of events. In fast-changing environments, rigid objectives may be made redundant by outside events.

● Communication and co-ordination are vital to satisfactory implementation, and are especially important when the organisation is seeking benefits from synergies or value-chain linkages.

● The resource allocation process provides the necessary funds for proposed strategies. Where resources are limited, allocation of funds is usually from the centre of the organisation, using various decision criteria. Criteria for allocation include the delivery of the organisation's mission and objectives, the support of key strategies and the organisation's risk-taking profile, together with special circumstances, such as unusual changes in the environment. There is a risk that the resource allocation process will ignore the need to use resources more effectively and strategically.

● Strategic planning makes the strategy process operational in some organisations, but it is no substitute for basic and innovative strategic thinking. The basic process of strategic planning may well cover background assumptions, long-term vision, medium-term plans and short-term plans. Importantly, the input of new ideas and revisions to the process are significant elements of its development. Strategic planning has been heavily criticised by some researchers as being too bureaucratic and rigid in its approach, but attitudes are beginning to mellow as long as the process is narrowly defined.

● There are a number of different styles of conducting the strategic planning process, including strategic planning, strategic control and financial control. The selection of a style depends on the circumstances of the company and formal strategic planning in small companies may help when external finance is being sought.

● Monitoring and control systems are important in assessing strategy implementation and how the environment is changing. The necessity of obtaining information in sufficient time to take the required action is crucial. There are a number of ways in which strategic controls can be improved. All rely on having simple, cost-effective and useful information about the organisation and its environment. It has been argued that strategy control and budgeting should be linked. This is not recommended because strategy monitoring is concerned with exploration while budgeting is focussed on achieving specific short-term targets.

● International aspects of strategy implementation follow the same principles but are complicated by culture, geographical diversity and other factors.

QUESTIONS

1 Compare the Canon, Nestlé and Hanson styles of strategic planning and discuss why they are different. Is one better than the others and, if so, which?

2 Does a small company need a formal strategic plan?

3 Apply the basic implementation process outlined in Fig 19.2 to the current procedures of an organisation with which you are familiar. Where does it differ and where is it the same? What conclusions can you draw about the process?

4 'Nothing chastens the planner more than the knowledge that s/he will have to carry out the plan.' General Gavin, quoted by Professor George Day. Discuss this comment in the context of the implementation process.

5 What are the implications of intended rationality and minimum intervention in developing the strategic process?

6   How can objectives and tasks be communicated from senior management while at the same time motivating those who have to implement them?

7   'If top management devotes more effort to assessing the strategic feasibility of projects in its allocational role *than it does to the task of* multiplying resource effectiveness, *its value added will be modest indeed.*' Professors Gary Hamel and C K Prahalad. Discuss.

8   Is strategic planning dead or does it have a role to play in most organisations?

9   Explain briefly why strategic controls are necessary and indicate how they might be improved. Consider an organisation with which you are familiar and assess its strategic controls with reference to your explanation.

STRATEGIC PROJECT

This chapter has explored some of the criticisms of strategic planning. You might like to follow up this subject by consulting texts from the 1970s and 1980s that placed heavy reliance on this process and making a comparison with modern practice.

FURTHER READING

Hrebiniak, L and Joyce, W (1984) *Implementing Strategy*, Macmillan, New York. An abridged paper based on this book appeared in the following: De Wit, B and Meyer, R (1994) *Strategy: Process, Content and Context*, West Publishing, Minn, pp192–202.

The classic study of different types of strategic planning is that by Goold, M and Campbell, A (1987) *Strategies and Styles*, Blackwell, Oxford – well worth reading.

Arie De Geus wrote a useful article on strategic planning: (1988) 'Planning as learning', *Harvard Business Review*, March–April.

Professor H Mintzberg has changed his views on strategic planning: (1994) 'The fall and rise of strategic planning', *Harvard Business Review*, Jan–Feb, pp107–14. *See also* his book, Mintzberg, H (1994) *The Rise and Fall of Strategic Planning*, Prentice Hall, New York. Note that Professor Colin Egan provides a logical and well argued critique of Mintzberg's work in Egan, C (1995) *Creating Organisation Advantage*, Butterworth-Heinemann, Oxford, Ch 7.

REFERENCES

1   Sources for this case are: *Financial Times*, 15 Jan 1990, p19; 9 July 1992, p28; 26 Oct 1993, p19; 17 Feb 1994, p24; 11 Mar 1994, p20; 5 Oct 1994, p1; 15 Mar 1995, p33; 18 Sep 1995, p16.
2   Day, G S (1984) *Strategic Market Planning*, West Publishing, Minn, Ch 8.
3   Yavitz, B and Newman, W (1982) *Strategy in Action: The execution, politics and payoff of business planning*, Free Press, New York. It should be noted that Hrebiniak and Joyce also describe similar distinctions in their 1984 book (*see* below).

4 Day, G S (1984) Ibid, Ch 8.

5 Author's experience based on strategy development in fast-moving consumer goods, telecommunications and consultancy.

6 For example: Wheelen and Hunger, Jauch and Glueck, Thompson and Strickland, Johnson and Scholes, Hofer and Schendel.

7 Pettigrew, A and Whipp, R (1991) *Managing Change for Competitive Success*, Blackwell, Oxford, pp26 and 27.

8 Hrebiniak, L and Joyce, W (1984) *Implementing Strategy*, Macmillan, New York. An abridged paper based on this book appeared in: De Wit, B and Meyer, R (1994) *Strategy: Process, Content and Context*, West Publishing, Minn, pp192–202.

9 Pettigrew, A and Whipp, R (1991) Ibid, p176.

10 Hunger, J and Wheelen, T (1993) *Strategic Management*, 4th edn, Addison-Wesley, Reading, Mass, p238.

11 Day, G S (1984) Ibid, p186.

12 Campbell, A and Sommers Luchs, K (1992) *Strategic Synergy*, Butterworth-Heinemann, Oxford, p202.

13 Galbraith, J and Kazanjian, R (1986) *Strategy Implementation*, 2nd edn, West Publishing, Minn, p88.

14 Galbraith, J and Kazanjian, R (1986) Ibid, pp81–5.

15 Goold, M and Campbell, A (1987) *Strategies and Styles*, Blackwell, Oxford, p21.

16 Hamel, G and Prahalad, C K (1994) *Competing for the future*, Harvard Business School Press, MA, p159.

17 References for Nestlé case: *Financial Times,* 6 May 1992, p16; 15 May 1992, p13; 20 Apr 1994, p19. Goold, M and Quinn, J (1990) *Strategic Control*, Hutchinson Business Books, London, pp118–19.

18 Day, G S (1984) *Strategic Market Planning*, West Publishing, Minn, p189.

19 De Geus, A (1988) 'Planning as learning', *Harvard Business Review*, March–April.

20 Marx, T (1991) 'Removing the obstacles to effective planning', *Long Range Planning*, Aug, Pergamon Press, Oxford.

21 Loasby, B (1967) 'Long range formal planning in perspective', *Journal of Management Studies*, Oct.

22 Lenz, R and Lyles, M (1985) 'Is your planning becoming too rational?', *Long Range Planning*, Aug, Pergamon Press, Oxford.

23 Hamel, G and Prahalad, C K, *Competing for the Future*, Free Press, New York, p283.

24 Exhibit 19.6 is developed from references 18, 19 and 20.

25 Mintzberg, H (1994) 'The fall and rise of strategic planning', *Harvard Business Review*, Jan–Feb, pp107–14. *See also* his book (1994) *The Rise and Fall of Strategic Planning*, Prentice Hall, New York. Note that Egan provides a logical and well-argued critique of Mintzberg's work in Egan, C (1995) *Creating Organisation Advantage*, Butterworth-Heinemann, Oxford, Ch 7.

26 Hamel, G and Prahalad, C K, Ibid, p283.

27 Goold, M and Campbell, A (1987) *Strategies and Styles*, Blackwell, Oxford.

28 This section has benefited from Galbraith, J and Kazanjian, R (1986) *Strategy Implementation*, 2nd edn, West Publishing, Minn, pp85–7.

29 Pettigrew, A and Whipp, R (1991) Ibid, p135.

30 This section has benefited from the paper by Bungay, S and Goold, M (1991) 'Creating a strategic control system', *Long Range Planning*, June, Pergamon Press, Oxford.

31 Bungay, S and Goold, M (1991) Ibid.

32 Extracted from Goold, M and Quinn, J J (1991) *Strategic Control*, Hutchinson Business Books, London, pp197–8. © Copyright M Goold and J J Quinn and Pitman Publishing. Reproduced with permission.

20

Organisational structure and people issues

When you have worked through this chapter, you will be able to:

- understand the main principles involved in designing the structure of an organisation to meet its chosen strategy;

- outline the six main types of organisation structure and assess their advantages and disadvantages in relation to particular strategy;

- develop the special organisation structures that are more likely to lead to innovative strategies;

- make recommendations on the most appropriate organisation structure;

- explore how senior managers can be selected and motivated to implement the chosen strategies;

- outline the additional considerations that apply when developing structures for international organisations.

◼ INTRODUCTION

Whether strategy comes before or after structure, every organisation needs to build and maintain the optimal organisation structure to generate and develop its strategies. This chapter explores this process and has as its starting point the demands made on the organisation by its mission and objectives. Six general types of organisation structure are identified and then, given the importance of innovation in corporate strategy, particular emphasis is placed on the structures that are most likely to achieve this. We explore the role of effective reward structures and selection procedures in providing capable and well-motivated senior managers to implement strategy successfully. Finally, in the light of these considerations, an appropriate organisation structure can then be developed, as summarised in Fig 20.1.

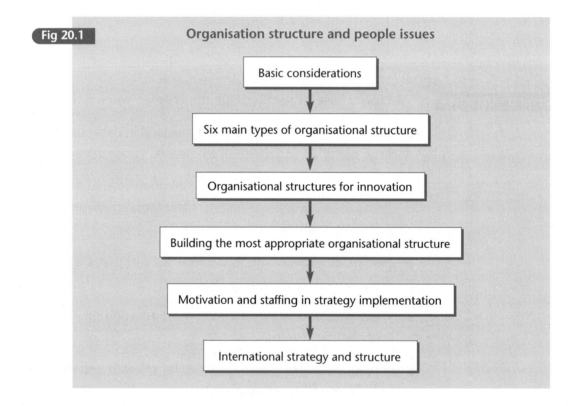

Fig 20.1   **Organisation structure and people issues**

Basic considerations

Six main types of organisational structure

Organisational structures for innovation

Building the most appropriate organisational structure

Motivation and staffing in strategy implementation

International strategy and structure

Organising for survival at Rolls-Royce Motors[1]

For a company with a world-famous name and a strong market niche strategy, Rolls-Royce considered its corporate strategy in 1990 to be soundly based: it had just made £24.4 million profit on turnover of £278 million. However, over the next two years, the company's sales collapsed and its cumulative losses were £150 million. New strategies for survival were required: they involved a major reorganisation of the company.

During 1991 and 1992, the world's major economies declined significantly. The Gulf War brought a major loss of confidence in car markets and the key US market was hit by a luxury tax. Rolls-Royce sales volumes dropped from their 1990 peak of 3300 cars per year to around 1400 cars per year in 1992. Although the company was part of a larger holding company (Vickers plc), its very survival was called into question. This became the focus of its new corporate strategy.

The Mulliner Park Ward factory was closed in May 1991 and the Corniche model transferred to the company's other factory at Crewe with the Phantom model being discontinued. Attention then focussed on achieving a complete reorganisation at Crewe along with a totally new culture. The shock of the factory closure and the associated loss of 2400 jobs out of 4900 in 1990 were powerful signals of the need for change.

The Crewe plant layout was changed to create 16 zones or factories within the factory, each with a manager responsible for cost, service, quality and continuous improvement. Craft demarcation lines were abolished and replaced by multi-functional teams. Trade union representation was substantially reduced but it was maintained at the level of the joint works council. The changes and pressures created significant pressures on the workforce and management.

Each factory zone was then organised to break down the old reporting relationships, empower individuals and encourage teamworking. For example, in developing new models, the company had previously used a system where the new car was first designed, then passed to engineering, before going to production and then commercial. As a result, design and other flaws were picked up too late and caused major delays. In the new set-up, all these actions were undertaken simultaneously with functional cross-co-operation being the norm. Other changes were also made: management was delayered. A further 4000 car components were bought in rather than being manufactured at Crewe.

By 1994, the results showed Rolls-Royce had stabilised the situation. Breakeven had fallen from 2800 cars per year to 1300. Output per person had doubled from 1.5 to 3.3 over the period 1991–94. The time to produce a new model had been halved.

CASE QUESTION

Can any useful lessons on organisation be drawn from Rolls-Royce cars for other companies whose survival is not in question? If so, what are they?

20.1 BUILDING THE ORGANISATION'S STRUCTURE

20.1.1 Consistency with mission and objectives

The organisation's structure is essentially developed to deliver its mission and objectives. Building the organisation structure must therefore begin at this point. Before considering the possible structures in detail, it is useful to explore some basic questions in the context of the analysis and development undertaken in Chapter 12.

1 *What kind of organisation are we?* Commercial? Non-profit making? Service-oriented? Government administration? (These questions are not an exhaustive list.)

2 *Who are the major stakeholders?* Shareholders? Managers? Employees?

3 *What is our purpose?*

4 *What does our purpose tell us in broad terms about how we might be structured?*

There is no simple or 'right' answer to question 4; this deserves careful thought. Every organisation is unique in size, products or services, people, leadership and culture. Exhibit 20.1 shows some of the possible implications. It can be useful to think in this general unformed way before plunging into the detail of organisation design.

20.1.2 The main elements of organisational design

Before embarking on the design process, it is worth reviewing the analysis of the organisation undertaken in Chapter 8. We will be using the work and insights described in that earlier analysis. It is important to remember that many organisations have existing structures and that the primary task of organisation design is usually not to invent a totally new organisation but to adapt the existing one. These matters are reflected in the nine primary determinants of organisational design:

1 *Age.* Older organisations tend to be more formal: for example, *see* Greiner in Chapter 8. The organisation structure needs to reflect the age of an organisation and the degree to which managers and employees have grown to rely on formal relationships in terms of reporting and job definition.

2 *Size.* The number of people involved will significantly change the organisational structure: *see also* Greiner in Chapter 8. Essentially, as organisations grow, there is usually an increasing need for formal methods of communication and greater co-ordination, suggesting that more formal structures are required.

3 *Environment.* Rapid changes in any of the *Five Forces* acting on the organisation will need a structure that is capable of responding quickly (*see* Chapter 3). If the work undertaken by the organisation is complex with strong inter-relationships between various parts of the organisation, then this will make its ability to respond more difficult to organise and co-ordinate.[2] The structure to handle such demands will need careful consideration depending on the precise nature of the environmental changes. If rapid responses are required, however, this argues for devolving responsibility towards those closest to the market place.

Exhibit 20.1	Examples of the connection between purpose and organisational design

Purpose	Implications for organisational design
'Ideas factory' such as an advertising or promotions agency	Loose, fluid structure with limited formalised relationships. As it grows in size, however, more formal structures are usually inevitable.
Multinational company in branded goods	Major linkage and resource issues that need carefully co-ordinated structures, e.g. on common suppliers or common supermarket customers for separate product ranges
Government civil service	Strict controls on procedures and authorisations. Strong formal structures to handle major policy directions and legal issues
Non-profit-making charity with a strong sense of mission	Reliance on voluntary members and their voluntary contributions may require a flexible organisation with responsibility devolved to individuals
Major service company such as a retail bank or electricity generating company	Formal structures but supported by some flexibility so that variations in demand can be met quickly
Small business attempting to survive and grow	Informal willingness to undertake several business functions such as selling or production, depending on the short-term circumstances
Health service with strong professional service ethics, standards and quality	Formalised structure that reflects the seniority and professional status of those involved while delivering the crucial complex service provisions
Holding company with subsidiaries involved in diverse markets	Small centralised headquarters acting largely as a banker with the main strategic management being undertaken in individual companies

4   *Centralisation/decentralisation decisions.* To some extent, most organisations have a choice over how much they wish to control from the centre. This was explored in Chapter 18. In summary, there are four main areas that need to be explored:

● the nature of the business, e.g. economies of scale will probably need to be centralised;

● the style of the chief executive: a dominant leader will probably centralise;

● the need for local responsiveness;

● the need for local service.

5 *Overall work to be undertaken.* Value-chain linkages (*see* Chapter 7) across the organisation will clearly need to be co-ordinated and controlled. They may be especially important where an organisation has grown and become more diverse. Divisional or matrix structures may be needed with the precise details depending on the specific requirements and strategies of the organisation.

6 *Technical content of the work.* In standardised mass-production, the work to be undertaken controls the workers and their actions. The more that the work controls the workers, the more necessary it will be to have standardised and bureaucratic procedures and structures. Mintzberg says that this will lead to greater specialisation in the work undertaken.[3] However, Japanese production methods have recently shown that flexibility may be highly desirable in mass-production (*see* Chapter 10) so that it does not necessarily follow that greater specialisation is inevitable. The organisation's structure will need to reflect the precise technical task of the organisation and its products or services.

7 *Different tasks in different parts of the organisation.* It is clear that the tasks of production are not the same as those of the sales and marketing areas. Mintzberg's description of the main *tasks* was explored in Chapter 18. What is less clear is that the *objectives* of different parts of the organisation may also differ: for example, production might prefer standard products with long production runs, whereas sales might favour products tailored especially for specific customers using short production runs. Strong *integration* between the various objectives of different parts of the organisation may require specific structures built into the organisation to overcome such difficulties.[4] In these circumstances, a specific group responsible for integration and co-ordination will need to be built into the organisation.

8 *Culture.* The degree to which the organisation accepts change, the ambitions of the organisation and its desire for experimentation are all elements to be considered. They all derive from the culture of the organisation and its leadership. Johnson's *Cultural Web* is one method of assessing the impact of culture on organisational design (*see* Chapter 8).[5]

9 *Leadership.* The style, background and beliefs of the leader may have an important effect on organisational design. This will be particularly true in *innovative* and *missionary* organisations which were explored in Chapter 18.

In bringing all the above elements together, there is a danger of over-complicating the considerations and arguments. *Simplicity in design* should guide the proposals because the structure needs to be understood and operated after it has been agreed. We return to this area later in this chapter.

It is usual in undertaking such an analysis to consider the *responsibilities* and *powers* of the main individuals and groups involved, even if they are deliberately left vague in some structures. Responsibility and power need to be *controlled* and *monitored* and this needs to be built into the organisational structure. However, the control systems of the organisation can usually be considered after the proposed structure has been resolved (*see* Chapter 19).

Individuals also need to be *motivated* to achieve the organisation's mission and objectives. This important consideration is discussed in Section 20.4.

- In building the organisation's structure, it is essential to start by considering its purpose. This will often provide some basic guidance on the structure required.

- There are nine main elements of organisational design: age, size, centralisation/decentralisation, overall work, technical content, tasks in different parts of the organisation, culture and leadership. All these elements will be inter-related with the organisation's strategy.

20.2 TYPES OF ORGANISATIONAL STRUCTURE

From all the above considerations, it is possible to identify some basic types of organisational structure that can serve to implement the chosen strategy:

- small organisation structure;
- functional organisation structure;
- multi-divisional structure (sometimes shortened to *M-form* structure);
- holding company structure (sometimes shortened to *H-form* structure);
- matrix organisation structure;
- innovative organisation structure.

20.2.1 Small organisation structure

In small organisations, there will often only be limited resources. Individuals will need to be flexible and undertake a variety of tasks. The informality of the structure will allow fast responses to market opportunities and customer service requirements. However, problems may be caused by the duplication of roles, confusion of responsibilities and muddled decision making, and it may not be realistic to draw up a clear organisational structure. Depending on the management style of the owner/leader, there may be many people or only the leader contributing to the organisation's strategy. Examples of such a company are a small family business or a specialist local computer service supplier.

20.2.2 Functional organisation[6]

As the organisation grows from being a small company, the functional organisational structure is often the first structure that is adopted (*see* Fig 20.2). It allows experts in a functional area to be grouped together and economies of scale to operate. For example, a single product range production or service company, such as a regional bus company, is likely to have a functional structure. Exhibit 20.2 lists some of the advantages and disadvantages of this type of organisation structure.

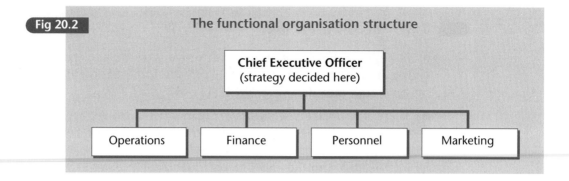

Fig 20.2 The functional organisation structure

Exhibit 20.2 Advantages and disadvantages of the functional organisation structure

Advantages	Disadvantages
● Simple and clear responsibilities	● Co-ordination difficult
● Central strategic control	● Emphasis on parochial functional areas in strategy development rather than company-wide view
● Functional status recognised	● Encourages inter-functional rivalry
	● Strategic change may be slow

20.2.3 Multi-divisional structure

This form of organisational structure was developed in the early 1920s by the future head of General Motors, Alfred Sloan, and was recorded by Alfred Chandler[7] (*see* Chapter 18).

As organisations grow, they may need to subdivide their activities in order to deal with the great diversity that can arise in products, geographical or other aspects of the business (*see* Fig 20.3). For example, there would be little to be gained by General Motors in Case study 18.1 by combining EDS, its separate computing networking subsidiary, with its Delphi Automotive Systems company, supplying car parts for the group. They have different customers, factories and methods of operation; the strategies of the two divisions are totally different. Chandler argued that strategy was decided at the centre, but in modern companies it is often partially determined by the divisions. However, the centre does influence strategy and allocate resources.

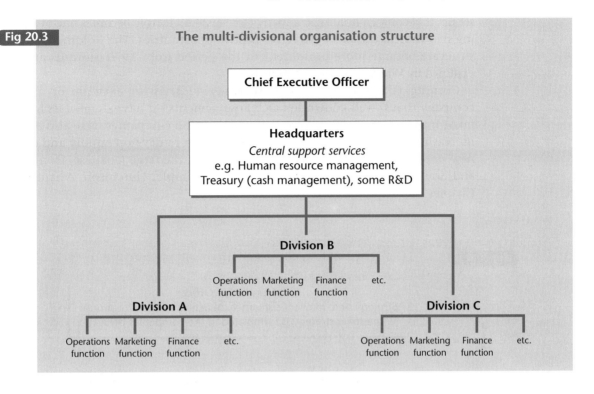

Fig 20.3 The multi-divisional organisation structure

Exhibit 20.3 Advantages and disadvantages of the multi-divisional organisation structure

Advantages	Disadvantages
● Focusses on business area	● Expensive duplication of functions
● Eases functional co-ordination problems	● Divisions may compete against each other
● Allows measurement of divisional performance	● Decreased interchange between functional specialists
● Can train future senior managers	● Problems over relationships with central services

20.2.4 Holding company structure

Further growth in organisations may lead to more complex arrangements between different parts of the organisation and outside companies. For example, joint ventures with totally new companies outside the group, alliances, partnerships and other forms of co-operation may be agreed. As a result the original company may take on the role of a central shareholder for the various arrangements that may be set up: it becomes a holding company (*see* Fig 20.4). Its role becomes one of allocating its funds to the most attractive profit opportunities. The holding company structure became more prominent in the period from 1970 onwards and was explored by Williamson (*see* Chapter 18).

Corning (US) (described in Case study 11.3) is an example of a larger company that is well known for such arrangements:[8] it has extended its involvement into new markets and products. Some small companies have also become increasingly involved in such strategies in order to develop rapidly and exploit new opportunities. This is also seen in some of the large Japanese, Hong Kong and South-East Asian conglomerates – for example, Hutchison Whampoa in Chapter 16.

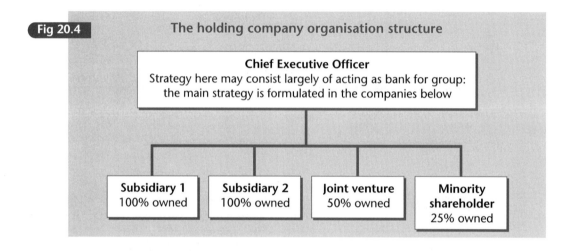

Fig 20.4 The holding company organisation structure

Advantages	Disadvantages
● Allows for the complexity of modern ownership	● Little control at centre
● Taps expertise and gains new co-operations	● Little group contribution beyond 'shareholding/banking' role
● New market entry enhanced	● Problems if two partners cannot co-operate or one partner loses interest
● Spreads risk for conglomerate	● May have very limited synergy or economies of scale

Exhibit 20.4 Advantages and disadvantages of the holding company organisation structure

20.2.5 Matrix organisation structure

In some cases, it may be disadvantageous for a large company to set up separate divisions. This is most likely to arise where close co-operation is still required between the groups that would form the separate divisions. For example, an oil company such as Royal Dutch Shell may need to take strategic decisions not only for its oil, gas and chemical products but also for countries such as the UK, Germany, USA and Singapore. It may be necessary to set up an organisation which has responsibilities along both product and geographical dimensions. Such dual-responsibility decision-making organisation structures are known as *matrix organisations*. The two dimensions do not necessarily have to be geography and product: any two relevant areas could be chosen (*see* Fig 20.5).

Fig 20.5

The matrix organisation structure

Chief Executive Officer

	Product group 1	Product group 2	Product group 3
Geographical area 1			
Geographical area 2		*Strategy perhaps decided in each of the matrix groups and perhaps at the centre*	
Geographical area 3			

Exhibit 20.5 Advantages and disadvantages of the matrix organisation structure

Advantages	Disadvantages
● Close co-ordination where decisions may conflict	● Complex, slow decision-making: needs agreement by all participants
● Adapts to specific strategic situations	● Unclear definition of responsibilities
● Bureaucracy replaced by direct discussion	● Can produce high tension between those involved if teamwork of some parts is poor
● Increased managerial involvement	

20.2.6 Innovative organisation structures

In some cases, large organisations need to lay special emphasis on their creativity and inventiveness – for example, advertising agencies, some service companies and innovative design companies. In these circumstances, there is a case for having strong teams that combine together experts from different functional areas and have an open style of operation. The free-flowing nature of the group and its ideas may be important in the development of some aspects of strategy. In essence, strategy will be developed anywhere and everywhere. No simple organisation diagram can usefully be drawn.

The choice of organisational structure is considered in Section 20.4.

Key strategic principles

- There are six main types of organisational structure, each having advantages and disadvantages.

- The small organisation has limited resources but an informal structure, allowing flexibility in response, but giving unclear lines of responsibility.

- The functional organisation has been used mainly in small to medium-sized organisations with one main product range.

- As organisations develop further ranges of products, it is often necessary to divisionalise them. Each division then has its own functional structure, with marketing, finance, production, etc.

- As organisations become even more diverse in their product ranges, the headquarters may just become a holding company.

- An alternative form of structure for companies with several ranges of products is the matrix organisation, where joint responsibility is held by two different structures, e.g. between product divisions and another organisational structure such as geographical or functional divisions. This type of organisation has some advantages but is difficult to manage successfully.

- Innovative organisations may have cross-functional teams.

- The place where strategy is developed depends on the organisational structure.

Organisation structure at Telepizza[9]

Telepizza is a young Spanish company that combines entrepreneurial flair with real growth. This case study explores how the company has grown and raises the question of what organisational structures are likely to be required over the next few years.

Telepizza realised before its competitors that Spain was changing rapidly. Gone were the days of siestas and elaborate family meals. Fast food was what Spaniards wanted and needed. The company was founded in 1988 as a single pizza parlour offering home deliveries in its immediate north Madrid neighbourhood. By late 1995, it had nearly 200 centres spread out across 120 Spanish towns and cities. By the end of 1995, Telepizza expected to post consolidated profits of more than Pta 800 million (US$6 million), more than double the Pta 375 million reported in the previous year. It was forecasting sales of Pta 19 billion for 1995, up from 1994's Pta 12.3 billion.

'The market was zero when we started,' says Mr Jose Maria Serrano, Telepizza's communications chief, 'but there was a terrific opportunity.' Mr Leopoldo Fernandez Pujals, the company's founder, spotted the gap in the market. He owns 40 per cent of Telepizza's shareholder capital and was its Chairman until a boardroom coup in mid-1995. Mr Fernandez Pujals was formerly an executive with the healthcare multinational, Johnson & Johnson. He knows a lot about marketing and consumer fads and nothing at all about fast food, but he knew what the Spanish public was prepared to buy. When he came across pizza home deliveries during a stay in the US, he had found the product he was looking for.

Market success

By 1995, Telepizza had a 54 per cent share of the pizza home deliveries market in Spain. Its success is as much the triumph of a concept as it is of a product. The company's management understood that Spain had undergone a profound sociological change that had brought young mothers out of the kitchen and into the workplace. Furthermore, office workers, like everywhere else, had begun to eat at their desks.

Home deliveries, as opposed to office deliveries, make up the bulk of Telepizza's business. They are ordered both by children battling with their homework while their parents are still at their jobs or by exhausted parents staggering home late because office hours in Spain can stretch into the night. Telepizza also understands that although Spaniards have belatedly come round to the concept of fast food, the domestic culture remains imbued with the tradition of good home-made cooking. This means that the company has to take special care over the quality of its product – fresh ingredients are delivered daily – and over the amount of choice it offers its customers. Having pioneered pizza home deliveries, Telepizza has stayed ahead of its competitors by introducing the do-it-yourself pizza: clients can summon up literally thousands of permutations of the product's 15 basic ingredients. Its most recent success was the Tex-Mex pizza called 'the Jalisco', dreamt up by its consumer research department.

Corporate culture

The corporate culture and growth strategy are no less important. Telepizza believes in decentralisation and cutting out bureaucracy. This ethos has set the tone of its staff relations and franchising. Telepizza has succeeded in creating a corporate culture and with it an expansion strategy that has multiplied its rewards. Employees who deliver pizzas by motorcycle within half an hour of receiving the order are, in the company's parlance, autonomous business people responsible for their own slice of the pizza market. These employees are allotted a specific area. It is up to them to develop a relationship with their clients. Spurred on by sales incentives and bonus packages, Telepizza's representatives will spend nearly as much time promoting the company in their allotted area as they do delivering its products to customers. Although numbers vary per outlet, there are approximately ten people, including five sales representatives, employed in each pizza parlour.

About half the 195 Telepizza centres in Spain are franchises. The company believes that this mix is the right one and that as it expands further franchises will, for the time being, be the property of the existing 50 or so franchise owners. 'For a franchise system to work, you have to love the company and what it produces,' says Mr Serrano. 'These are exactly the sort of people that we have got now and we want them to grow with us.'

Investment policy

Telepizza has pursued a strong investment policy, ploughing Pta 1.3 billion into new centres and equipment in 1994. It invested a further Pta 1.5 billion in 1995. One reason for the boardroom revolt that forced Mr Fernandez Pujal's resignation in October 1995 was that other shareholders were clamouring for dividends and objected to the drive for expansion that he was masterminding.

Firmly established in Spain, Telepizza has also tested foreign waters, again through a mixture of directly-owned outlets and franchises and has set up around 50 centres abroad. It is operating in Poland, Portugal, Greece and Belgium as well as in

Mexico, Chile and Colombia. The focus is on Spain, however, and its home market is far from saturated.

Source: Financial Times, 16 November 1995.

CASE QUESTIONS

1 *What organisational structure would you propose to match the strategy at Telepizza? In answering this question, you should consider that the company has recently undergone profound change with the shareholders pressing for greater returns on their investment.*

2 *To what extent does the structure need to remain loose in order to encourage the dynamic entrepreneurial spirit that has characterised its growth? What are the problems with this approach?*

3 *Is it inevitable that the company will begin to lose its entrepreneurial flair as it grows larger? How is it proposing to hold on to this approach?*

4 *What is your view of the company's international growth strategy – sensible expansion or a waste of scarce management resources, given the continued expansion possibilities in Spain and the resource difficulties of supervising foreign operations?*

20.3 ORGANISATIONAL STRUCTURES FOR INNOVATION

Innovative structures and processes were introduced in Section 20.2, but innovation is too important to the whole corporate strategic process for it to be described as only suitable for some specialist organisation types. *Every* organisation needs an element of innovation: hence, *every* organisation needs structures capable of producing this, even if these structures are only temporary, e.g. when a project team is disbanded once the work is completed.

20.3.1 Innovation needs to be commercially attractive

Before exploring how an organisation can best structure itself to be innovative, it is useful to examine what is required. In a competitive market place, it is not enough to be innovative: the new product or service has to be commercially attractive to potential customers, i.e. it must offer value for money compared with existing products and services. Gilbert and Strebel[10] call this the *complete competitive formula*.

It may be desirable to include a broader range of benefits in addition to the innovation itself. Often, the real breakthrough comes not with the technical development but with the extended package of promotion, distribution, support and customer service. All of these elements are geared towards making the innovation user-friendly and more commercially attractive. This requires an *integrated* organisation structure across all functions of the business. For example, one of the reasons that the World Web has taken off on the Internet over the last few years has been the introduction of innovative user-friendly software such as *Netscape*. However, the real breakthrough for the company came when it arranged for free distribution through computer magazines of certain types of its software for evaluation by personal use. The result has been that, at the time of writing, *Netscape* has become the dominant software on this new, growing medium. From the organisational viewpoint, such developments need integration and co-ordination across all the functions if innovative solutions are to be obtained.

20.3.2 The nature of the innovative process

In Chapter 11, we examined Quinn's use of the concept of 'controlled chaos' to describe the innovative process. Innovation is flexible, open-ended and possibly without a clearly defined or fixed objective. The process needs to be free-wheeling and experimental. Within this, it is useful to distinguish between:[11]

- *simple innovation*, which might be possible in any organisation and relies on one person or a small group, and
- *complex innovation*, which may require experts drawn from a variety of business functions to form project teams. This is likely to involve larger resources and greater organisational complexity.

Mintzberg's comments on the innovative process (*see* Chapter 18) had complex innovation particularly in mind when outlining three guidelines for organising project teams, which are summarised in Exhibit 20.6.

Exhibit 20.6	Guidelines for organising innovative project teams

1 *Flexible structures* that allow experts not just to exercise their skills but to break through conventional boundaries into *new* areas.
2 *Co-ordination* within the team needs to be undertaken by experts with a technical background in the area, rather than a superior with authority from outside.
3 *Power* in the team needs to be distributed among the experts, where appropriate. Much of the activity will consist of liaison and discussion among the experts as they progress their innovative ideas.

Ultimately, the strategy that emerges from the innovative process may remain vague and ill-defined. This has the advantages of being flexible, responsive and experimental. However, the disadvantages associated with a lack of definition may not satisfy the culture of organisations wanting quick and precise results.

20.3.3 Organisational structures and procedures for innovative companies

Kanter[12] surveyed a number of US companies in the 1970s and 1980s in an attempt to identify the organisation structures and processes that were most conducive to innovation. Among her conclusions were:

- *The importance of matrix structures.* These were more likely in innovative companies. They tended to break down barriers and lead to the more open reporting lines that were important to the innovative process. Decision making may have been slow and complex in matrix structures, but it provided the network for individuals to move outside their own positions and make the interconnections useful to innovation.

- *The need for a parallel organisation.* A separate group to run in tandem with the existing formal hierarchy was often highly valuable. It was specifically tasked with finding innovative solutions to problems especially where a matrix structure was not in operation. It was able to act independently without the day-to-day pressures and politics of the existing structure. It was then left to the existing organisation to define routine jobs, titles and reporting relationships. Instead of contacts and power flowing up and down the existing structure, the parallel organisation allowed new relationships and ideas to develop.

- *The work of a parallel organisation.* This had to be problem-solving, possibly focussed on a single business problem and structured around the team. The work was integrative, flexible and with little hierarchical division. The function of such a group was often to re-examine existing routines and systems, concentrating especially on areas that were partially unknown and needed challenging. It often provided a means of empowering people lower down in the organisation.[13]

- *Participative/collaborative management style.* This was often employed to encourage innovation. It involved persuading rather than ordering, seeking advice and comments and sharing the favourable results of successful initiatives.[14]

From her research, Kanter recommended five pointers to action that could be taken to encourage innovation in weaker organisations[15] (*see* Exhibit 20.7). The most successful global companies, such as Toyota and McDonald's, have been particularly successful at pursuing such policies.

Exhibit 20.7 **Five pointers to encourage innovation**

1 Publicise and take pride in existing achievements.

2 Provide support for innovative initiatives, perhaps through access to senior managers, perhaps through project teams.

3 Improve communication across the enterprise by creating cross-functional activities and by bringing people together.

4 Reduce layers in the hierarchy of the organisation and give more authority to those further down the chain.

5 Publicise more widely and frequently company plans on future activity, giving those lower down a chance to contribute their ideas and become involved in the process.

Comment   All of Kanter's ideas were researched and proposed in the context of the North American corporation. Some may not work at all or may need to be substantially modified in other national cultures. Moreover, the problems that were observed in terms of innovation may not be the same in other countries. What they do illustrate is that, for strategic innovation at least, the flexible, *open structure* of the organisation may need to come before the *innovatory strategies* that subsequently emerge.

Key strategic principles

- All companies need to be able to innovate as part of the strategic process.
- Such innovation needs to be commercially attractive if it is to be viable. An organisation structure that integrates and co-ordinates all the functional areas of a business is desirable.
- Innovation is open-ended and flexible, so the process needs to be experimental with flexible structures, close co-ordination and power distributed throughout the innovating group.
- In terms of structure, a matrix organisation may be more effective because it is more integrative. In some circumstances, a separate, parallel organisation tasked with developing innovative solutions can be usefully employed.

20.4 BUILDING THE MOST APPROPRIATE ORGANISATION STRUCTURE

The somewhat over-simplified discussion of strategy and structure in Sections 20.1 and 20.2 is now developed further.

20.4.1 Basic considerations

In developing organisation structures, there is a danger of losing sight of some basic criteria:

- *Simplicity*, where possible, so that the structure can be understood and operated by those involved.
- *Least cost solution*, avoiding, if appropriate, more complex organisations such as the matrix structure which may be more costly to administer and monitor.
- *Motivation of those involved* needs to be considered in the context of any proposed changes.
- *Existing organisation culture* is vital to the choice between structures – the 'way we do things around here' cannot be changed overnight, but only with difficulty and determination.

For most organisations to have no structure is not an option; the choice lies between what the organisation has now and what it might have as its strategy changes (*see* Chapter 8 on Greiner's depiction of organisational change and its relationship to structure and Johnson's *Cultural Web* – a useful analytical tool with which to examine the organisation's culture).

In addition to these issues, there is a connection between the range of an organisation's business and the most appropriate organisational structure[16] (*see* Exhibit 20.8).

Exhibit 20.8	Nature of business activity and organisational structure
Nature of business	*Likely organisational structure*
Single business	Functional
Range of products extending from a single business	Functional but monitor each range of products using separate profit and loss accounts
Separate businesses within group with limited links	Divisional
Separate businesses within group with strong links	Matrix (or divisional with co-ordination if matrix is difficult to manage)
Ideas factory	Innovative structure
Unrelated businesses	Holding company
Related businesses owned jointly or by minority shareholdings	Holding company

20.4.2 Environment

In Chapter 18, Mintzberg's configuration of six different types of organisation and their associated environments was set out. Although six were named, it is useful to concentrate on four main characteristics of the environment that influence structure (*see* Exhibit 20.9).

Exhibit 20.9	Environmental types and their impact on organisation structure	
Type of environment	*Range*	*Consequences for organisational structure*
Rate of change	Static ◄──► Dynamic	As rate increases, the organisation needs to be kept more flexible
Degree of complexity	Simple ◄──► Complex	Greater complexity needs more formal co-ordination
Market complexity	Involved in ◄──► Involved in single market diversified markets	As markets become more diversified, divisionalisation becomes advisable
Competitive situation	Passive ◄──► Hostile	Greater hostility probably needs the protection of greater centralisation

1 *Rate of change.* When the organisation operates in a more dynamic environment, it needs to be able to respond quickly to the rapid changes that occur. In static environments, change is slow and predictable and does not require great sensitivity on the part of the organisation. In dynamic environments, the organisation structure and its people need to be flexible, well co-ordinated and able to respond quickly to outside influences. The dynamic environment implies a more flexible, organic structure.

2 *Degree of complexity.* Some environments can be easily monitored from a few key data movements. Others are highly complex with many influences that interact in complex ways. One method of simplifying the complexity is to decentralise decisions in that particular area. The complex environment will usually benefit from a decentralised structure.

3 *Market complexity.* Some organisations sell a single product or variations on one product. Others sell ranges of products that have only limited connections with each other and are essentially diverse. As markets become more complex, there is usually a need to divisionalise the organisation as long as synergy or economies of scale are unaffected.

4 *Competitive situation.* With friendly rivals, there is no great need to seek the protection of the centre. In deeply hostile environments, however, extra resources and even legal protection may be needed: these are usually more readily provided by central HQ. As markets become more hostile, the organisation usually needs to be more centralised.

20.4.3 Resources and technical systems

For many years, it has been known that major resources such as mass production will influence organisational design.[17] The recommendation that was usually made was that the organisation needed a higher degree of *centralisation* in the organisation's structure. Traditionally, the main way to operate such resources has been to standardise working practices, to specialise job functions and to employ a greater degree of bureaucracy in the operating core.[18] However, with modern mass manufacturing, this is not necessarily correct from a technical and organisational perspective (*see* Chapter 10). The implication is clear: modern mass manufacture has begun to *decentralise* its work and empower workers. Decision making at individual units on the factory floor of modern, complex assembly-line operations has been an important strategy advance in the 1990s. However, it is not entirely clear whether this can happen in all situations.

Technical systems using computers, specialised controls and complex testing procedures have always relied on expert knowledge. There is little point in having such knowledge without the decision-making power to use it. Complex technical systems are usually *decentralised*.

20.4.4 The strategy to be implemented

Every organisation is to some extent unique – the result of its past, its resources and its situation. In addition, the key factors for success (*see* Chapter 7) and the major strategies chosen by whatever process will depend on the situation at that time. It is difficult to specify clear and unambiguous rules to translate strategy into organi-sational structures and people processes. Thompson and Strickland[19] recommend five useful steps that will assist this process but they caution against certainty:

1 Identify the tasks and people that are crucial to the strategy implementation.

2 Consider how such tasks and people relate to the existing activities and routines of the organisation.

3 Use key factors for success to identify the chief areas around which the organisa-tion needs to be built.

4 Assess the levels of authority needed to action the identified strategies.

5 Agree the levels of co-ordination between the units in the organisation neces-sary to achieve the strategy.

The above are all rather generalised but this is inevitable in view of the unique nature of each organisation.

20.4.5 Consequences for employment and morale

People implement strategies, not plant machinery nor financial resources. New organisational structures can provide new and interesting opportunities for man-agers and employees. Alternatively, structures may deliver a threat to their scope for work and possibly even their employment. Developing new organisational structures without considering the consequences for those who will be affected is clearly unsatisfactory. This is a major task for any strategy and is considered sepa-rately in Chapter 21.

Key strategic principles

- The basic design of organisation structures will be governed by four main criteria: simplicity, the least-cost solution, motivation of those involved and existing organisational culture.

- In any organisation, it is important to keep in sight the need for simple, cost-effective structures.

- Environmental factors such as market change and complexity will impact on the proposed structure. In general, increased change and complexity suggest more flexible, less centralised structures.

- Traditionally, it has been argued that increased standardisation and mass production have needed a more centralised organisational structure. With modern technical systems, decentralisation has been recommended with decision making being handed back to groups of workers in some cases.

- Each organisation is unique and so it is difficult to develop unambiguous rules to implement strategy in terms of organisation structure and people issues.

- The impact of strategic change on employees and managers is a major consideration that deserves separate and detailed work.

20.5 MOTIVATION AND STAFFING IN STRATEGY IMPLEMENTATION

Capable and well-motivated people are essential to strategy implementation, especially at senior management level. This section explores the *formal organisation* needed to achieve this:

● reward systems that can increase motivation;

● staffing and selection procedures that are necessary for a successful strategy.

The *informal* aspects of this subject, associated with strategy implementation, such as leadership and culture, are left to Chapter 21.

20.5.1 Reward systems

The measurement of achievement and the reward for good performance against the organisation's objectives can be powerful motivators for the delivery of corporate strategy. The linkage between reward and motivation has been extensively researched over the last few years and the connection well established.[20] Rewards need to be seen more broadly than simple payment: they may involve other forms of direct remuneration but also promotion and career development opportunities.

In designing reward systems to achieve strategic objectives, several factors need to be considered:

● *Strategic objectives.* These tend to have a longer-term element, whereas managers may well need to have short-term rewards. Hence, there may be a conflict between rewarding strategic objectives and a personal desire for short-term recompense. Moreover, not all strategic objectives are easily measurable, thus making accurate assessment difficult. To some extent, these problems have been resolved by rewarding individuals with shares in the enterprise but this incentive may not be available to all organisations and is still subject to manipulation.

● *Rewards focussing on individual performance.* These may not be appropriate when group objectives have been identified as crucial to strategy. Careful consideration of the impact of reward systems may therefore be required.

● *Rewards encouraging innovation and risk-taking.* These may need to move beyond quantitative measures of performance, such as an increase in return on capital or earnings per share, to qualitative assessments based on the number and quality of the initiatives undertaken. Inevitably, there may well be a greater element of judgement involved, which may in turn lead to accusations by others of unfairness unless handled carefully.

20.5.2 Formal organisation structures and staffing procedures

New strategies may well call for new business approaches, new skills and new knowledge. Existing members of staff will not necessarily have these. It may be necessary therefore to introduce formal structures and procedures to train existing staff or recruit new people in order to implement the strategy successfully.[21]

For motivational reasons, it is often appropriate to begin with existing staff members and assess their suitability for new positions. However, they may not possess the required knowledge and skill levels required, in which case outside recruitment becomes essential.

In corporate strategy, staffing issues primarily concern the most senior managers in the organisation. In cases of major strategic crisis, the Chief Executive Officer may need to be replaced: there are countless cases during the 1990s of this one act being crucial to strategic change. However, it should be said that this may only be the *beginning* of a new strategy, rather than its implementation. When Lou Gerstner was recruited to head IBM after its spectacular profit problems in 1994 (*see* Chapter 1), he was only hired on the basis that he had complete freedom to identify the main strategic problems, solutions and strategies. In this case, the first stage of the new IBM strategy was to hire an outsider to rescue the company. However, it should be pointed out that the previous Chief Executive was also aware of the difficulties and the need for change. It will be evident that, in general, recruiting senior talent to implement identified strategies can be a crucial element in an organisation's continued success or failure.

For the many companies that do not experience major crises, the provision of a sound *performance appraisal system* will be a major contribution to successful strategy implementation. This may be accompanied by *staff training* and broader *staff development programmes* to build up the people elements in corporate strategy. These are part of the area of human resource management strategy for the company. Coupled with recruitment and reward, they underline the crucial importance of this functional area at the highest levels of corporate strategy development.

Key strategic principles

- Measurement of achievement and the subsequent reward for good performance can be powerful methods for directing corporate strategy.

- However, reward systems may be difficult to develop that fully coincide with the organisation's strategic objectives for a variety of reasons.

- Staffing issues, such as recruitment, appraisal and training, are essential to the implementation of strategy. Formal procedures need to be built into the consideration of new or revised human resource management procedures.

20.6 STRATEGY AND STRUCTURE IN INTERNATIONAL ORGANISATIONS

As organisations become more international, their structures become more complex. Country and regional divisions join the product and functional interests in the organisation structure. This becomes particularly important when it is necessary to locate major resources, such as sales offices or manufacturing facilities, outside the home market.

As soon as companies move beyond the exporting of their existing products, international expansion strategy may become more complex. In Chapter 16 we saw that the development of the appropriate organisation strategy involved the exploration of the reasons behind:

● the possible need for a *global strategy*;
● the possible need to be *responsive to national interests*.

It should be noted that the two pressures are not mutually exclusive. Moreover, some organisations may face neither pressure but simply want to expand internationally. The reasons behind these pressures were explored in Chapter 16. We are concerned here with the organisational implications.

Global and national responsiveness can therefore be considered as the main factors in the design of international organisations.[22] Depending on the extent to which each of the two factors is present, we have four possible combinations of requirements for international and global companies. These are shown in Fig 20.6.

20.6.1 Global product company

In this type of company, products are essentially managed on a global basis, and therefore manufacturing, marketing and other functional aspects make few concessions to national demands. However, global co-ordination often goes much further, with production and supplies being *integrated* across national boundaries so that parts made in one plant may then be delivered to another for use in a further production process. For example, high value-added electronic items might be made in a plant in Japan and then shipped to Malaysia, where they are assembled using lower cost labour, before being exported as finished consumer electronic items to the USA or Europe.

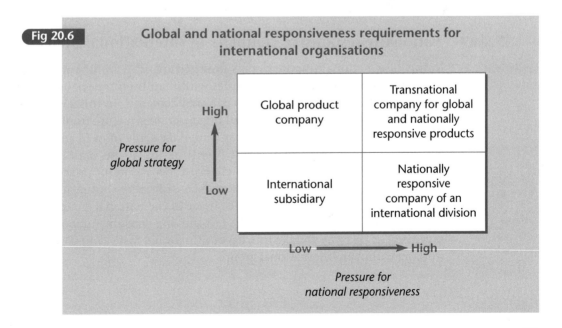

Fig 20.6 Global and national responsiveness requirements for international organisations

Clearly, extensive global co-ordination of production and sourcing is required. Cost savings resulting from major economies of scale might be expected. The extensive management control structures required make it difficult to respond quickly to changes in consumer demand even at the global level. However, in some markets this may not be a major disadvantage. We will explore global organisations further in Chapter 21.

20.6.2 Transnational company for global and nationally responsive products

In order to overcome some of the rigidities that may be present in global companies, some companies have attempted to gain the benefits of global operations while at the same time maintaining some responsiveness to national or regional markets – the *transnational company*. The global aspect is similar to that described in Section 20.6.1 so the real issue is how to achieve the local responsiveness within this. There are several possible mechanisms depending on the degree of local responsiveness required. They include:

- national manufacturing of some parts of the international company and national assembly;
- global production networks that allow national companies to pick-and-mix the items available on a global scale for national assembly;
- larger national companies within a global network given a degree of independence to act as they choose.

In terms of the organisation of such companies, there is a need for a high degree of co-ordination and information. Management decisions and responsibilities will involve matrix structures with both global and national managers needing to be consulted.

20.6.3 Nationally responsive company of international division

In this case, national responsiveness now becomes the dominant force in driving international strategy. Thus companies within an international division operate according to the need to respond to national demands. In this case, the company will need to have a complete national organisation structure from Chief Executive downwards. The parent company may undertake some form of annual review and will also monitor performance but it will be up to the national company to respond to market and production circumstances as appropriate. This does not mean that there will be no international co-ordination but rather that any that takes place will be on the basis of the choice of the national company rather than any direction from the parent. Some fast-moving consumer goods companies are organised in this way to take into account national tastes and competitors, while working within an international group.

20.6.4 International subsidiary

For some international companies, there is no need to provide nationally-responsive products and there are also no significant benefits to be gained from operating on a global scale. In this case, the home company may simply set up international subsidiary companies to sell or to manufacture and sell products similar to those produced in the home country. The organisation structure may be similar to that in the home country or it may only be a part of that structure depending on the extent of the international involvement. Co-ordination is simple and involves no day-to-day technological or marketing transfers.

Key strategic principles

- Four different types of international organisation were identified: global, transnational, nationally responsive and international subsidiary. Each will require a different form of organisation and relationship with the central part of the organisation.

- They derive from the twin strategic pressures for globalisation in some but not all markets and responsiveness to national or local needs. These trends are not mutually exclusive, so yielding the four configurations outlined above.

CASE STUDY 20.2

How Ford Motors went global[23]

In late 1993, the world's second largest vehicle company, Ford Motors, took the decision to develop a radical new global strategy and organisation structure. This case study traces the reasons for the decision and describes the new structures that emerged.

Background

In 1994, Ford had total sales of US$128 billion and a global workforce of 320 000. Its sales were more evenly spread geographically than its larger rival, General Motors. However, its profitability was below that of competitors such as Chrysler (US) and its quality ratings were lower than its Japanese rivals. The company decided that radical new strategies were required but it had to start from the constraints imposed by the existing multi-national organisation.

Although Ford had been involved in Europe and Asia–Pacific since the 1920s, it was operating these areas as independent profit centres with largely separate car development and manufacture. For example, the company had developed a Ford Escort model for Europe and North America in the 1970s and early 1980s, but it ended up with two versions that had little in common beyond the name and the blue Ford logo.

Even the subsequent Mondeo car development programme – aimed at replacing the Ford Sierra in Europe and the Ford Tempo/Ford Mercury Topaz in North America – was expensive by international standards (US$6 billion), took too long to develop and really only had one common feature, the Zetec powertrain (engine plus transmission). By contrast, Ford had observed that the Corolla from the Japanese Toyota company was essentially the same car around the world. In spite of being assembled on four continents, the Corolla had been designed and engineered only once.

Ford was therefore a multinational company but it was not global. Nevertheless, it had made its first moves in becoming more integrated: the Mondeo powertrain was the same on both sides of the Atlantic and it was a beginning.

New management and new global thinking

After Alex Trotman took over as Ford Chairman in 1993, he began considering how Ford could be managed more efficiently. He was helped by two colleagues, Ed HagenLocker and Wayne Booker. They had all been Ford employees for many years and were aware of the history, culture and power groups in the company that would need to be considered in any major strategic shift.

The three colleagues quickly decided that Ford needed to be more global and chose the Zetec powertrain as the most global starting point. A special team was set up consisting of a select number of European and North American managers to estimate whether Zetec could be globalised: in particular, whether this could happen without globalising the *remainder* of Ford. In the period from July to December 1993, the team studied the issues and concluded that:

- Different practices and systems existed in each Ford region around the world.
- These were so different that globalising the Zetec powertrain alone would only have limited benefits.

The team therefore recommended globalising all Ford's operations. This conclusion was also supported by a separate study team of senior Ford executives that had been meeting in parallel and had been examining Ford's global competitiveness.

As a result, the *Global Study Team* was set up for five intensive weeks in November/December 1993. Its conclusions were reported in December 1993 to Alex Trotman, to the Ford main Board and to senior executives from Europe and North America:

- By going global, Ford could save costs of around US$3 billion per annum by the year 2000.

- As a starting point, the two largest regions, North America and Europe, should be combined from January 1995. The other regions would follow later, possibly by January 1996.

- A detailed study by an expanded project team was needed to decide exactly how the new structure should operate: it would concentrate on key processes and practices and report back by March/April 1994.

- A public announcement and a notification to all Ford employees would be made in April 1994. This would be followed by briefing meetings around the world.

- A Transition Management Team would then operate from April to December 1994 to bring about the change: between 300 and 1000 employees would be involved.

- The new globalisation strategy was given the name *Ford 2000*.

New organisation structure and responsibilities

During 1994, the new organisation structure was agreed in detail. It would involve new global *product development* responsibilities and a new *matrix management* organisation structure.

The emphasis was placed on five vehicle programme centres (VPCs) to develop new models globally. Four of the five VPCs would be based in the USA but the one located in Europe, that for small cars, probably had the most potential for long-term growth at Ford and would account for 50 per cent of production by the year 2000. In addition to the VPCs, there would be functional management across all the main operations on a global basis. Figure 20.7 shows the agreed structure in outline.

As an example of how the global VPCs would operate, the European-based VPC started the development in 1995 of a new small Escort-type car which was planned to go into production from 1998/99. Annual worldwide volume would be around 1 to 1.5 million cars and it would be produced in plants in the UK, Germany, the USA, Mexico, either Brazil or Argentina and somewhere undecided in Asia–Pacific. Even with the new global

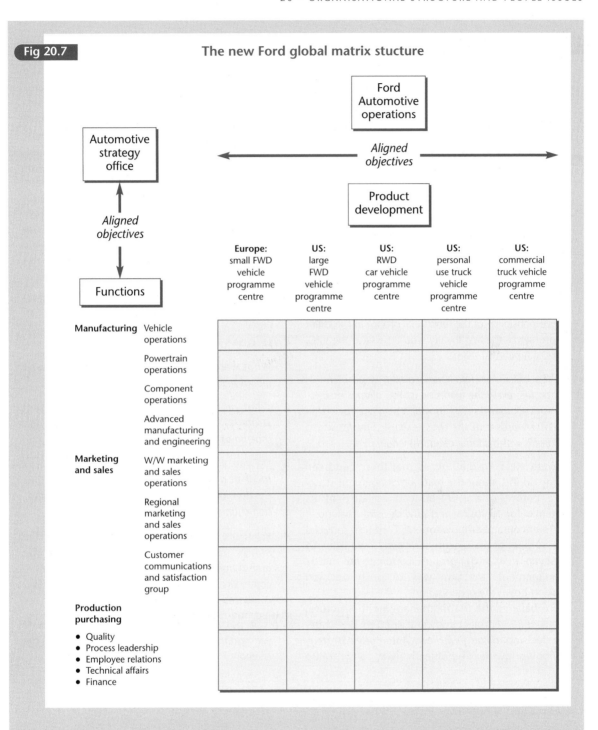

Fig 20.7

The new Ford global matrix stucture

design, Ford said that the car would be able to take account of regional customer preferences: the surface design and feel could be altered even though the under-the-skin components were all the same. Essentially, it would be substantially cheaper and quicker to design on a global scale.

To ensure that power was not over-centralised, Ford decided to push as much accountability and responsibility as possible down to the VPCs. In addition, the aim was to use the *Ford 2000* programme as a 'wrecking ball' against all the 'barriers, geographic or bureaucratic, that have complicated our lives for generations'. Thus the VPC structure was also accompanied by a new matrix management structure with VPCs being complemented by functional responsibilities inside the structure.

In the new organisation, most employees would report to two or more managers: a VPC manager and a functional head, such as manufacturing, marketing and sales or purchasing. The prime responsibility for an employee's performance evaluation would rest with the VPC, but career development would remain the responsibility of the functional group. In the event of problems, the first loyalty would be with the VPC, not the functional team.

> It's like a Formula One team. If a problem occurs, everyone works on it. You always race and you always race to win. It's no use saying afterwards that the chassis worked perfectly, but it was a shame about the engine.

Nevertheless, Ford admitted that there had been many doubts about the matrix management structure before it was introduced because of its potential for confusion and slow decision making.

To encourage empowerment, Ford also reduced the number of management layers: down from 14 to seven in its larger groups. Coupled with matrix management, the aim was to push decision making down the organisation.

To balance the matrix management structure, the *Ford 2000* project also centralised its key strategic decision making with one *Automotive Strategy Office* worldwide. The objective was to centralise the key strategic decision making by taking the widest possible view of global developments and opportunities. It was also to encourage the development of global cars, serving many markets that would increase the profit from every dollar spent on investment.

By mid-1995, the new global organisation was well under way. Europe and North America had been combined into the new VPCs along with the matrix structure. The Asia–Pacific and South American operations were planned to follow in 1996. However, the new strategy and structure had yet to produce the improved financial results and products that would outweigh the initial costs of the reorganisation.

CASE QUESTIONS

1 *What were the arguments in favour of the new global strategy?*

2 *What process was used to develop the global strategy? Did this help or hinder the decision making as Ford subsequently went global?*

3 *Do you consider that the global decision was made at a point in time or was there a sense that the decision to go global emerged as the organisation changed?*

4 *What are the advantages and problems of the matrix structure that has been set up to manage global operations? How does Ford plan to overcome the difficulties that can arise? Are you convinced by Ford's arguments?*

5 *Is it possible to have employee empowerment yet retain global strategy at the centre of the company?*

The importance of good structure[24]

In this extract from his book, **Management and Organisational Behaviour,**
Laurie Mullins provides an organisational behaviour perspective on design.
He emphasises the human and informal aspects of such a process.

The structure of an organisation affects not only productivity and economic efficiency but also the morale and job satisfaction of the workforce. Structure should be designed therefore so as to encourage the willing participation of members of the organisation and effective organisational performance.

The functions of the formal structure, and the activities and defined relationships within it, exist independently of the members of the organisation who carry out the work. However, personalities are an important part of the working of the organisation. In practice, the actual operation of the organisation and success in meeting its objectives will depend upon the behaviour of people who work within the structure and who give shape and personality to the framework.

The overall effectiveness of the organisation will be affected both by sound structural design and by the individuals filling the various positions within the structure. Management will need to acknowledge the existence of the informal organisation which arises from the interactions of people working in the organisation. The organisation is a social system and people who work within it will establish their own norms of behaviour, and social groupings and relationships, irrespective of those defined in the formal structure.

The human relations writers are critical of the emphasis on the formal organisation. They favour a structure in which there is increased participation from people at all levels of the organisation, greater freedom for the individual, and more meaningful work organisation and relationships. One of the strongest critics of the formal organisation is Agyris.[25] He claims that the formal, bureaucratic organisation restricts individual growth and self-fulfilment and, in the psychologically healthy person, causes a feeling of failure, frustration and conflict. Agyris argues that the organisation should provide a more 'authentic' relationship for its members.

The view of the human relations writers represents more of an attitude towards organisation than specific proposals, but it reminds us of the importance of the human element in the design of structure. Managers need to consider how structural design and methods of work organisation influence the behaviour and performance of members of the organisation.

The operation of the organisation and actual working arrangements will be influenced by the style of management, the personalities of members and the informal organisation. These factors may lead to differences between the formal structure of the organisation and what happens in practice. Building an organisation involves more than concern for structure, methods of work and technical efficiency. The hallmark of many successful business organisations is the attention given to the human element: to the development of a culture which helps to create a feeling of belonging, commitment and satisfaction.

Source: Mullins, L (1996). Reprinted with permission.

SUMMARY

- In building the organisation's structure, it is essential to start by reconsidering its purpose. This will often provide some basic guidance on the structure required. In addition, there are nine main elements of organisational design: age, size, centralisation/decentralisation, overall work, technical content, tasks in different parts of the organisation, culture and leadership. All these elements will be inter-related with the organisation's strategy.

- There are six main types of organisational structure, each having advantages and disadvantages. The *small organisation* structure is self-explanatory. The *functional organisation* structure has been mainly used in small to medium-sized organisations with one main product range. As organisations develop further ranges of products, it is often necessary to *divisionalise*. Each division then has its own functional structure – marketing, finance, production, etc. As organisations become even more diverse in their product ranges, the headquarters may just become a *holding company*. An alternative form of structure for companies with several ranges of products is the *matrix organisation*, where joint responsibility is held between the products structure and another organisational format such as the functional structure. This type of organisation has some advantages but is difficult to manage successfully.

- All organisations must be able to innovate as part of the strategic process, but such innovation needs to be commercially attractive if it is to be viable. An organisation structure that integrates and co-ordinates all the functional areas of a business is desirable. Because innovation is open-ended and flexible, the process needs to be experimental with flexible structures, close co-ordination and power distributed throughout the innovating group.

- In terms of innovative structures, a matrix organisation may be more effective because it is more integrative. In some circumstances, a separate, parallel organisation tasked with developing innovative solutions can be employed.

- In building the most appropriate organisation structure, it is important to keep in sight the need for simple, cost-effective structures. Environmental factors, such as market change and complexity, will also impact on the proposed structure. In general, increased change and complexity suggest more flexible, less centralised structures.

- Traditionally, it has been argued that increased standardisation and mass production need a more centralised organisational structure. With modern technical systems, decentralisation is recommended, with decision making being handed back to groups of workers. Because each organisation is unique, issues of structure and staffing make it difficult to develop unambiguous rules to implement strategy. The impact of strategic change on employees and managers is a major consideration that deserves separate and detailed discussion.

- Measurement of achievement and the subsequent reward for good performance can be powerful methods for directing corporate strategy. However, it may be difficult to develop rewards systems that coincide fully with the organisation's strategic objectives. Staffing issues, such as recruitment, appraisal and training, are essential to the implementation of strategy. Formal procedures need to be built into the consideration of new or revised human resource management procedures.

● Four different types of international organisation can be identified: global, transnational, nationally-responsive and international subsidiary. Each will require a different form of organisation and relationship with the central part of the organisation. They derive from the twin strategic pressures for globalisation in some markets and responsiveness to national or local needs. These trends are not mutually exclusive, and so give rise to the four different types of international organisation.

QUESTIONS

1   Explain the structure of an organisation with which you are familiar, using the elements outlined in Section 20.1 as your guide.

2   What structure would you expect the following organisations to have?

   (a)   A small management consultancy company based in one country only.

   (b)   A voluntary group providing volunteers to visit the elderly and house-bound.

   (c)   A medium-sized company with 1500 employees, two factories and a separate headquarters.

   (d)   A leisure park business owned and operated by a family company.

   (e)   A medium-sized computer software company with 80 employees which writes games for Sega-style machines?

3   *'If structure does follow strategy, why should there be a delay in developing the new organisation needed to meet the administrative demands of the new strategy?'* Alfred Chandler. How would you answer this question?

4   If you were asked to make Rolls-Royce cars more innovative, what would you do? In answering this question, you should take into account the existing culture of the company.

5   *'Every organisation needs an element of innovation'* (*see* Section 20.3). Is this correct?

6   *'All any company has to do to explore its own potential to become a more innovatory organisation is to see what happens when employees and managers are brought together and given a significant problem to tackle.'* Professor R M Kanter. Discuss.

7   Why is it difficult to develop reward systems to deliver the organisation's objectives? How might such difficulties be overcome in a small entrepreneurial business venture?

8   The managing director of a large company making bicycles has become worried by the lack of growth in sales, believing the company has lost its earlier innovative spark, and has turned to you for advice. What would you recommend?

9   *'The hallmark of many successful business organisations is the attention given to the human element.'* Laurie Mullins. Is the human element more important than competitive strategy?

STRATEGIC PROJECT

Restaurants and catering establishments have traditionally been fragmented industries, then came McDonald's, Burger King, Pizza Hut and Telepizza in Spain (*see* Case study 20.1). Branding and building up regional, national and international chains of restaurants has been one of the major strategy successes of the 1980s and 1990s. Investigate how this has been undertaken and evaluate the potential for further strategic development.

FURTHER READING

Professor Henry Mintzberg has a useful discussion on organisation structure and strategy in 'The structuring of organisations', p341 in Mintzberg, H and Quinn, J B (1991) *The Strategy Process*, 2nd edn, Prentice Hall, New York.

Laurie Mullins (1996) *Management and Organisational Behaviour*, 4th edn, Pitman Publishing, London, can be consulted for an extended discussion on organisational issues.

Professor Gerry Johnson's paper (1989) 'Rethinking incrementalism', *Strategic Management Journal*, Jan–Feb, is worth reading. It is reprinted in De Wit, B and Meyer, R (1994) *Strategy: process, content and context*, West Publishing, St Paul, Minn.

Professor Rosabeth Moss Kanter (1985) *The Changemasters*, Unwin, London, has a useful empirical study of innovative practice.

REFERENCES

1 Sources for Rolls-Royce Motors: Vickers plc *Annual Report and Accounts 1990–94* and Gemini Consulting 1995 report on their significant contribution to the turnaround at the company.
2 Laurence, P R and Lorsch, J W (1967) *Organisation and the Environment*, Richard D Irwin, Burr Ridge, Ill, contains a full discussion of this important area.
3 Mintzberg, H (1991) 'The Structuring of Organisations', p341 in Mintzberg, H and Quinn, J B (1991) *The Strategy Process*, 2nd edn, Prentice Hall, New York.
4 Lawrence, P R and Lorsch, J W (1967) Ibid.
5 Johnson, G (1989) 'Rethinking incrementalism', *Strategic Management Journal*, Jan–Feb. Reprinted in De Wit, B and Meyer, R (1994) *Strategy: Process, content and context*, West Publishing, St Paul, Minn.
6 Mintzberg, H (1979) *The Structuring of Organisations*, Prentice Hall, New York.
7 Chandler, A (1962) *Strategy and Structure*, MIT Press, Cambridge, Mass. *See also* Channon, D (1973) *The Strategy and Structure of British Enterprise*, for evidence in the UK.
8 For a discussion of Corning *see* Lynch, R (1994) *European Business Strategies*, Kogan Page, London, p263.
9 Adapted from an article by Tom Burns (1995) *Financial Times*, 16 Nov, pIII, Survey Section.
10 Gilbert, X and Strebel, P (1989) 'From innovation to outpacing', *Business Quarterly*, Summer, 54, pp19–22. Reprinted in De Wit, B and Meyer, R (1994) Ibid.
11 Mintzberg, H (1991) 'The Innovative Organisation', Ch 13 in Mintzberg, H and Quinn, J B (1991) Ibid, pp731–46.

12 Kanter, R M (1985) *The Changemasters*, Unwin, London, p146.

13 Kanter, R M (1985) Ibid, p205.

14 Kanter, R M (1985) Ibid, p237.

15 Kanter, R M (1985) Ibid, pp361–2.

16 Developed from Galbraith, J R (1987) 'Strategy and Organisation Planning', *Human Resource Management*, Spring–Summer. Republished in Mintzberg, H and Quinn, J B (1991) *The Strategy Process*, Prentice Hall, New York, pp315–24.

17 Woodward, J (1965) *Industrial Organisation: Theory and Practice*, Oxford University Press.

18 Mintzberg, H (1991) Ibid, p341.

19 Thompson, A and Strickland, A (1993) *Strategic Management*, 7th edn, Irwin, Ill, p220.

20 Galbraith, J and Kazanjian, R (1986) *Strategy Implementation*, 2nd edn, West Publishing, St Paul, Minn. Chapter 6 contains a thoughtful review of the evidence.

21 Hunger, J and Wheelen, T (1993) *Strategic Management*, 4th edn, Addison-Wesley, Reading, Mass,Ch 9.

22 This section is based on research in international and global markets since the late 1970s. No single research paper has provided the basis for the typology used. Some of these articles are dated and do not reflect the latest field evidence. Their guidance has been updated in the comments in this text. The full list of papers and books consulted is given at the end of Chapter 18.

23 References for this case study: *Financial Times* articles 29 Mar 1994, p30; 11 Apr 1994, p20; 22 Apr 1994, p17; 23 Apr 1994, p11; 6 Jan 1995, p17; 3 Apr 1995, p11; *Ford Annual Report and Accounts 1994*.

24 Extracted from Mullins, L (1996) *Management and Organisational Behaviour*, 4th edn, Pitman Publishing, London, pp337–8.

25 Agyris, C (1964) *Integrating the individual and the organization*, Wiley, Chichester.

Managing strategic change

When you have worked through this chapter, you will be able to:

- understand the nature of strategic change and its implications for strategy development;

- analyse the causes of change;

- outline the main approaches to managing strategic change;

- link a strategic change programme with the type of change required;

- draw up a programme of strategic change appropriate to the strategic task.

INTRODUCTION

Corporate strategy invariably involves change for people working in organisations. Sometimes they resist such proposals and make strategy difficult to implement; sometimes they are enthusiastic and make a significant contribution to the proposed developments. Understanding and exploring the impact of change on people is therefore important for strategy implementation.

As a starting point, it is useful to analyse the causes of strategic change. It is also important to understand the dynamics of the change process in the context of the strategies proposed. These can be used to suggest how such a change process can be managed in principle. Finally, a strategic change programme can be developed either on a one-off or permanent basis. The main areas to be explored are summarised in Fig 21.1.

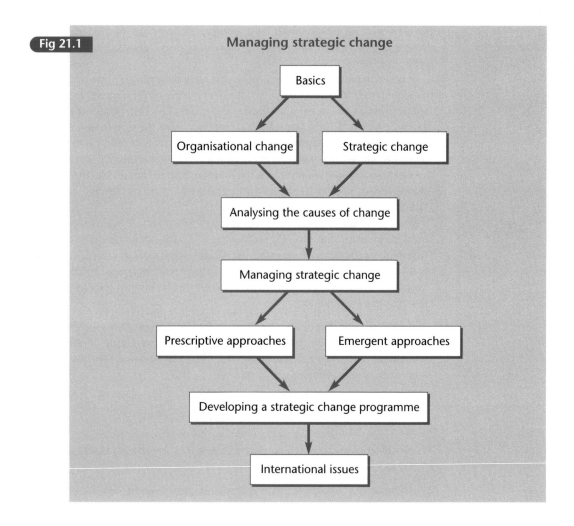

Fig 21.1 Managing strategic change

Basics

Organisational change

Strategic change

Analysing the causes of change

Managing strategic change

Prescriptive approaches

Emergent approaches

Developing a strategic change programme

International issues

Strategic change at Hoesch[1]

In mid-1992, the second largest German steel company, Krupp, undertook a hostile take-over of its rival, Hoesch Stahl, and its associated engineering companies. This case study examines what took place after the acquisition.

After the 1992 take-over, the Chief Executive of Krupp, Gerhard Cromme, set about the task of incorporating the new acquisition into Krupp. He encountered fierce resistance from some Hoesch workers who even spent months outside his home in protest at plans to shut down their steel plant. The implementation programme was fraught with problems.

By 1996, Herr Cromme was able to look back on the implementation programme and reflect on the events of that time. It was an operation that had been minutely planned. He occasionally admits that he was quite lucky that it all went as planned. What most definitely surprised him was what he describes as the 'energies' released by the take-over. He commented: 'Both companies had rigid, encrusted structures which came apart when people realised what new opportunities presented themselves following the merger.'

In order to harness those 'energies', he drew up a programme to review all tiers of management and peer into every nook and cranny of the sprawling conglomerate to work out what could be done better in future. The restructuring programme was drawn up by the Boston Consulting Group, but from the outset Herr Cromme wanted Krupp employees themselves to see the project through. 'I didn't want any clever consultants to come and make smart comments and then disappear again,' he said. Now the 4K programme – which stands for Kunden, Kosten, Kreativität and Kommunikation (clients, costs, creativity and communication) – is being applied at each of Krupp Hoesch's several dozen subsidiaries.

The 4K programme seems to be having some effect. The first time Herr Cromme stood up in front of about 100 employees at a subsidiary hoping to have a lively discussion about the shortcomings of the 4K project, hardly anyone spoke. On the most recent trip, employees straight off the shopfloor were prepared to take on their Chief Executive – even though most of them were meeting him for only the second time. As Herr Cromme commented:

> It became clear that at first the people in middle management were blocking the 4K programme because they were afraid it would reflect poorly on them. That has meanwhile changed. There is a certain layer of concrete that you have to get through to reach the workers themselves.

Source: Financial Times, 14 March 1996.

CASE QUESTIONS

1 *In acquiring Hoesch, what purpose was served by introducing the 4K programme? Why did such benefits outweigh the costs?*

2 *As a matter of implementation policy after a take-over, would you always attempt to introduce a new programme of that kind?*

21.1 THE BASIC CONCEPT OF STRATEGIC CHANGE

In this section, the concept of strategic change is explored and its importance for strategy implementation is explained. A distinction needs to be made between *organisational change*, which happens in every organisation and is inevitable, and *strategic change*, which can be managed.

21.1.1 Organisational change

Change takes place continuously within organisations. The pace of change can be represented by two extremes:

- *Slow organisational change*. This is introduced gradually, and is likely to meet with less resistance, progress more smoothly and have a higher commitment from the people involved.
- *Fast organisational change*. This is introduced suddenly, usually as part of a major strategic initiative, and is likely to encounter significant resistance even if it is handled carefully. However, some prescriptive change may be unavoidable, e.g. factory closure as part of a cost-cutting project.

Organisations usually prefer to choose slow change, where possible, because the costs are likely to be lower. In fact, much change follows this route, otherwise organisations would be in perpetual turmoil. Where there is a faster *pace* of change, it may be associated with strategic change, which is *pro-active* in its approach.

21.1.2 What is strategic change?

Strategic change is the *pro-active management of change* in organisations to achieve clearly identified strategic objectives. It may be undertaken using either prescriptive or emergent strategic approaches.

Because strategy is fundamentally concerned with moving organisations forward, there will inevitably be change for some people inside the organisation. However, strategic change is not just a casual drift through time but a *pro-active search* for new ways of working which everyone will be required to adopt. Thus strategic change involves the implementation of new strategies that involve substantive changes *beyond the normal routines* of the organisation. Such activities involve:

> the induction of new patterns of action, belief and attitudes among substantial segments of the population.[2]

Thus at one of the Hoesch steel plants workers changed their attitudes to the Chief Executive from Krupp and spoke up with their opinions on his second visit.

Many researchers and writers have explored the important topic of *organisational* change.[3] This text concentrates on those who have examined such concepts from a *strategic* perspective. Within this subject area, some researchers have seen the management of change as clear and largely predictable: the *prescriptive* approach (the actions of Krupp/Hoesch would probably fall into this category). Other researchers have formed the view that change takes on a momentum of its own and the consequences are less predictable: the *emergent* approach. (Emergent strategists might argue that in the Krupp/Hoesch case, although the initial consequences were well known, the longer-term results might be more difficult to predict and would take time to emerge.) In the emergent sense, change is not managed, but 'cultivated' (*see* Handy).[4]

It should be noted that emergent theorists may use the word *change* in a different way to prescriptive theorists:

- In prescriptive theories, change means the *implementation actions that result* from the decision to pursue a chosen strategy. In extreme cases, it is probable that the changes will be imposed on those who then have to implement them (such as the redundancies at Krupp/Hoesch).

- In emergent theories, change can sometimes mean the *whole process of developing the strategy*, as well as the actions that result after it has been developed. This may involve experimentation, learning and consultation for those involved in the change. (Because of the take-over, this could not happen at Krupp/Hoesch.)

We will return to this distinction in Sections 21.3 and 21.4.

21.1.3 Pressure points for strategic change

Strategic change is primarily concerned with *people* and the *tasks* that they perform in the organisation. They undertake their work through *formal organisation structures*, explored in Chapter 20. Groups of like-minded people also form *informal organisation structures* to pursue particular common interests: sometimes social groups such as the company sports club, sometimes commercial groupings such as a group seeking a minor change in working practices. All such groups inevitably discuss, formally or informally, any new developments that affect their lives such as the announcement or the rumours of strategic change. Importantly, such informal groups can abide by, interpret or change any element of the strategy implementation process: this can be advantageous but it can also be a focus for problems if the group does not like the proposed strategies.

Whether the groups are formal or informal, they provide a channel of opportunities for senior management to influence strategic change and to be influenced by the comments of those affected by such changes. In the Krupp case, Herr Cromme was engaged in precisely this task when he met the Hoesch workers for formal and informal discussion on the proposed changes after the take-over.

Identification of such groups and individuals constitutes an analysis of the *pressure points for influence* in the organisation (*see* Fig 21.2). The pressure points provide important links between the basic strategic change process and the people involved.

In more general terms, strategic change borrows from a number of academic disciplines and does not have a clearly defined set of boundaries.[5] The basic issues were outlined in Chapter 8 and the main themes will be explored during the course of this chapter.

21.1.4 Why is strategic change important?

In many cases, strategic change is accompanied by a degree of risk and uncertainty. Although risk assessment can be undertaken in an impersonal way at the corporate level,[6] uncertainty cannot be assessed in the same way at the *personal* level in an organisation.

Fig 21.2

People and pressure points for influencing strategic change[6]

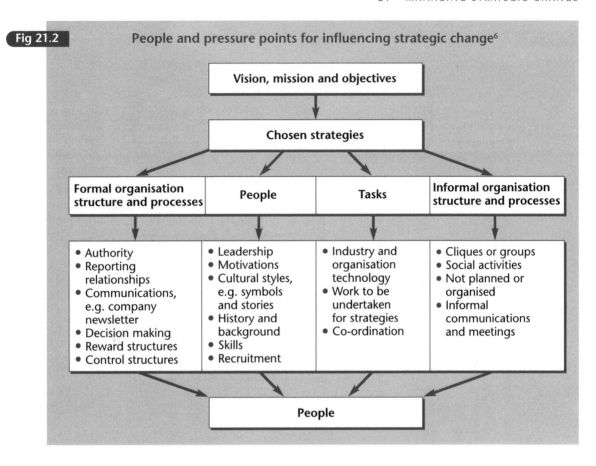

In some organisational cultures, individuals do not like the consequences of strategic change and seek to resist the proposals that are the cause of their problems. Strategic change may spark objections, thus making it difficult to implement. For example, the worker resistance at Hoesch was a typical and understandable response to the possibility that jobs might be lost.

In other organisational cultures, where learning and open debate have been part of the management process, change may be welcomed. However, even here, change will take time and will involve careful thought. Moreover, it will also be recalled from Chapter 18 that, even in a classic learning organisation such as ABB, there may still be some managers who do not like change.

To overcome problems associated with resistance to change, strategic change is therefore often taken at a slower pace – 'strategy is the art of the possible' to quote from Chapter 8. More consultation, more explanation and more monitoring of reactions are therefore involved in these circumstances. Figure 21.3 illustrates how the apparently simple process of strategic action is complicated by the reality of the many factors involved in successful strategic implementation.

All such discussion takes time and resources. For example, the cost at Krupp/Hoesch can be measured by the length of time – four years – it took to implement the takeover. Hence, strategic change is important because even successful change has an *implementation cost* for the organisation to set against the *direct benefits* identified from

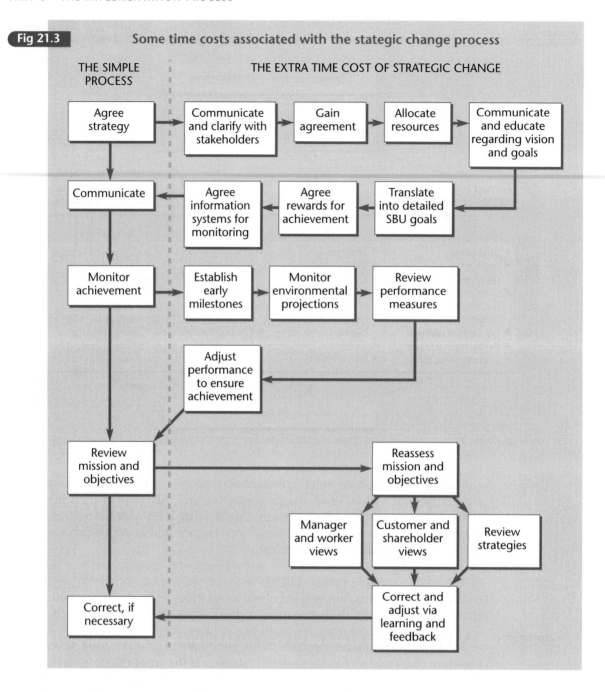

Fig 21.3   Some time costs associated with the stategic change process

the new strategies. Although there are costs involved in strategic change, it may be possible to reduce them. A partial test of a successful strategic change programme is the extent to which such implementation costs can be minimised.

However, it is important not to exaggerate the negative effects of strategic change on people. Strategic change can also be positive: people may feel enthused by the new strategies. Their contribution may be more than a passive acceptance of the proposed strategies, resulting in even lower costs. Hence, another test of a successful strategic change programme might be the extent to which such costs are *reduced* beyond those identified in the strategy itself. All this will depend on the context of the change – the culture of the organisation, the way in which strategic change is introduced and the nature of the changes proposed. In brief, strategic change is context-sensitive.

Key strategic principles

- A distinction needs to be made between the pace of change, which may be fast or slow, and strategic change, which is the pro-active management of change in an organisation.

- Strategic change is the implementation of new strategies that involve substantive changes to the normal routines of the organisation.

- In managing strategic change, it is useful to draw a distinction between prescriptive and emergent approaches.

- Prescriptive approaches involve the planned action necessary to achieve the changes. The changes may be imposed on those who will implement them.

- Emergent approaches involve the whole process of developing the strategy, as well as the implementation phase. This approach will also involve consultation and discussion with those who will subsequently be implementing the change.

- Strategic change is concerned with people and their tasks. It is undertaken through the formal and informal structures of the organisation. Understanding the pressure points for influencing change is important if such change is to be effective.

- Strategic change is important because it may involve major disruption and people may resist its consequences. Even where change is readily accepted, it will take time and careful thought. Strategic change carries important hidden costs.

21.2 ANALYSING THE CAUSES OF STRATEGIC CHANGE

In order to manage strategic change effectively, it is important to understand its causes. Strategic change can arise for all the reasons explored in Parts 2 and 3 of this book. Analysis of the specific causes is useful because it may provide clues to the best means of handling the change issues that arise. The two main classifications of the causes of change are:

- Tichy's four main causes of strategic change;
- Kanter, Stein and Jick's three dynamics for strategic change.

21.2.1 The four main causes of strategic change

Tichy[8] identified four main triggers for change:

- *Environment*. Shifts in the economy, competitive pressures and legislative changes can all lead to demands for major strategic change.

- *Business relationships*. New alliances, acquisitions, partnerships and other significant developments may require substantial changes in the organisation structure in order to take advantage of new synergies, value-chain linkages or core competences.

- *Technology*. Shifts here can have a substantial impact on the content of the work and even the survival of companies.

- *People*. New entrants to organisations may have different educational or cultural backgrounds or expectations that require change. This is especially important when the *leadership* of the organisation changes.

The implications of the above need to be considered in the context of the organisation's dynamic and complex structure. Tichy suggests that change is not only inevitable in such circumstances but can be managed to produce effective strategic results. This is explored later in the chapter.

21.2.2 Three dynamics for strategic change

Kanter, Stein and Jick[9] identified three causes of strategic change, one of which is the same as in the Tichy classification:

- *Environment*. Changes in the environment compared with the situation in the organisation can lead to demands for strategic change.

- *Lifecycle differences*. Changes in one division or part of an organisation as it moves into a phase of its life cycle that is different from another division may necessitate change. For example in a telecommunications manufacturer such as Nokia, mobile telecommunications would still be growing while network telecommunications might be in a more mature market phase. Typically, change issues relate to the size, shape and influence of such parts and involve co-ordination and resource allocation issues between them.

- *Political power changes inside the organisation*. Individuals, groups and other stakeholders may struggle for power to make decisions or enjoy the benefits associated with the organisation. For example, a shift in strategy from being production-oriented to customer-oriented would be accompanied by a shift in the power balance between those two functions.

The description of such changes suggests that they not only relate to strategic change but also to other complex factors, such as the interplay between people and groups. The researchers suggested that the causes were constantly shifting, sometimes slowly and at other times faster. Essentially, such causal effects prompted the need at various points for substantive strategic change.

21.2.3 Analysis of causality

In practice, there is a need to define more *precisely* the causes that apply to a particular organisation. The above interpretations may supply some general pointers but precision will prove more useful when it comes to managing strategic change. Equally, the causes described above raise important issues regarding how strategic change then takes place. This is examined in Sections 21.3 and 21.4 from the prescriptive and emergent change perspectives.

Key strategic principles

- To manage strategic change, it is important to understand what is driving the process. There are numerous classifications of the causes, two of which are explored in this text.

- Tichy identifies four main causes of strategic change: environment, business relationships, technology and new entrants to the organisation, especially a new leader.

- Kanter, Stein and Jick identify three dynamics for strategic change: environment, lifecycle differences across divisions of an organisation and political power changes.

- Precision regarding the causes of change is important in order to manage the change process effectively.

CASE STUDY 21.1

Owens-Corning reveals its strategies for change[10]

The US company Owens-Corning describes the strategy change procedures it used after the acquisition of the UK company, Pilkington Insulation. The company was purchased from the Pilkington Glass group for US$113 million in June 1994. If its 20 per cent increase in sales after take-over is taken as a guide, the change processes were successful.

The Owens-Corning executive in charge of the take-over was Mr Warren Knowles, President of the European building products division of the company. The lessons learnt were such that Mr Knowles now gives talks to senior Owens-Corning management on the experience gained in making the acquisition. According to Mr Knowles, a take-over is more about the aftermath than the deal itself. 'You have to think about integration before closing the deal,' he comments, quoting research that found that between 80 per cent and 90 per cent of acquisitions by US companies outside the US fail.

The deal, he stresses, is only the tip of an iceberg – making it work is the important bit. Furthermore, of all the elements making it work, communicating core messages and strategies to the workforce was perhaps the most crucial. Indeed, one of the goals Mr Knowles set for the acquisition was that employees should know both what was going on and what was in it for them.

He faced very worried employees in 1994: worried about the invasion of Americans, worried about the security of their jobs, and worried about their future. Mr Knowles explains: 'People had an emotional reaction and there was a tendency to deny the evil day. Productivity drains away in this situation and people lose sight of the customer. You have to get people refocussed on the customer.' He also faced a workforce used to being a non-core division with a consequent lack of interest on the part of senior management. Investment of about US$15 million helped persuade people that Owens-Corning was serious, followed up with constant repetition of the message of individual responsibility: 'I had to say: I cannot guarantee your jobs. Only you can do that.'

The introduction of gain-sharing and pay for performance hammered home the same message. According to Mr Knowles, 'People have to understand the drivers of the business and we learnt pretty quickly that if it affects their pay, people understand it.' Making clear the link between the factory line down-time and profitability brought the customer closer to the shop floor. 'Customer satisfaction is measured by market share. You have to focus on repeat business,' he says.

The other problem Mr Knowles had to tackle was integrating the European division. Having lived in Belgium for some time, he was not surprised by the lack of common European perspective, but he wanted to create a common set of values. 'There has to be a common set of expectations about how to behave so that, for example, everyone is trying to reduce cycle times. You have to speak a common language.'

One of the lessons of the acquisition that he feels companies ignore at their peril is that of 'soft' due diligence – relating to employees' needs and expectations, and their emotional response to the take-over. It is important, he believes, for senior managers to be accessible – but not only during official office hours. Being seen in the social club, going to sporting events or dances are just as important; being around when people are at their most relaxed can make a significant difference to the feel-good factor.

Source: Financial Times, 23 February 1996.

CASE QUESTIONS

1 *What were the main problems at the acquired company?*

2 *How would you categorise the strategic change analysis here?*

3 *Do you think the approach would have been the same if a substantial number of employees were to be made redundant as part of the take-over?*

21.3 PRESCRIPTIVE APPROACHES TO MANAGING STRATEGIC CHANGE

In developing and implementing strategy, managers will need to consider how to *manage* the change process. For example, in the Owens-Corning case, the acquiring company clearly set out to manage its take-over of its new UK subsidiary. Specifically, it undertook the following actions:

● It reassured its new employees by signalling new investment.

● It insisted that its new workers followed the Owens-Corning definition of best practice.

● It instituted new reward procedures to encourage new performance levels.

Two *prescriptive* routes for the management of change are examined in this section and then two *emergent* routes are examined in Section 21.4. The overall argument from the two sections is that the choice of prescriptive or emergent change is context-sensitive.

21.3.1 The three-stage prescriptive approach

During the late 1980s and early 1990s, research into change management by Kanter and her colleagues identified three major *forms* taken by the change process.[11] They linked these three forms with three *categories of people* involved in the change process, to produce a *three-stage process for managing change*. Their three forms were:

- *The changing identity of the organisation.* As its environment changes, the organisation itself will respond. For example, it may need to react to a shift in the political stance of a national government. The dynamic is likely to be slow rather than fast, unless a political or other major revolution occurs.

- *Co-ordination and transition issues as an organisation moves through its life cycle.* Relationships inside an organisation change as it grows in size and becomes older. Chapter 8 examined Greiner's depiction of the four stages of organisation development with each being associated with a 'crisis'. Whether such a precise event occurs or not, the dynamic shifts associated with such change are predictable with regard to their pressures on groups and individuals. For example, the decision to create a separate division for a product range that is growing increasingly wide will give rise to change issues that are well known, but need management.

- *Controlling the political aspects of organisations.* This results directly from the political pressures outlined in Section 21.2.2. Sometimes an orderly shift in power can be made but, occasionally, a more radical move is required. For example, the sudden departure of a chief executive 'after a clash over strategy and structure'.[12]

The three major categories of people involved in the change process were also identified:

- *Change strategists.* Those responsible for leading strategic change in the organisation. They may not be responsible for the detailed implementation.

- *Change implementers.* Those who have direct responsibility for change management (the programmes and processes that are explored later in this chapter).

- *Change recipients.* Those who receive the change programme with varying degrees of anxiety depending on the nature of the change and how it is presented. They often perceive themselves to be powerless in the face of decisions made higher up the organisation. In extreme cases, they may object strongly as was seen at Hoesch after the Krupp take-over.

Essentially, the researchers observed that, in their sample, managing change was a top-down, prescriptive process. Emergent strategists would point to the obvious weakness in such an approach: the lack of knowledge and co-operation in advance is quite likely to cause anxiety and resistance. Prescriptive strategists would counter this by pointing to the difficulty of exploring a hostile acquisition with the change recipients before the acquisition takes place. Prescriptive strategists might cite a famous case from 1993, in which contact *was* made with future employees prior to acquisition, resulting in the workers eventually rejecting the offer. Volvo Car workers joined its Swedish management and a majority of shareholders in repudiating the proposed joint venture with the French car company, Renault.[13]

Comment   Kanter *et al* offer one way of structuring and managing aspects of the change process. However, their categories of people only give limited indicators of how to manage the process. Their model may also be more suited to major changes rather than the more common ongoing strategic process.

21.3.2   Unfreezing and freezing attitudes

In the 1950s, Lewin developed a three-step model to explain the change process:[14]

● *Unfreezing current attitudes*. For change to take place, the old behaviour must be seen to be unsatisfactory and therefore stopped. Importantly, this need for change must be felt by the person or group themselves: it is a *felt-need* and cannot be imposed. This process might be undertaken by leaking relevant information or openly confronting those involved.

● *Moving to a new level*. A period of search for new solutions then takes place. This is characterised by the examination of alternatives, the exploration of new values, the changing of organisational structure and so on. Information continues to be made available to confirm the new position.

● *Refreezing attitudes at the new level*. Finally, once a satisfactory situation has been found, refreezing takes place at the new level. This may well involve positive reinforcement and support for the decisions taken. For example, good news about the new position might be circulated along with information about changes in status, changes in culture, reorganisation and reconfirmation of investment decisions.

Comment   This apparently simple model has been widely used to analyse and manage change. It tends to treat people as the objects of manipulation and does not involve them in the change process at all. However, it can be useful on occasions (*see*, for example, Fig 21.4 where the Owens-Corning case has been interpreted using the Lewin model).

21.3.3   Comment on prescriptive models of change

There are other similar models that take a prescriptive approach to organisational change.[15] We have explored the criticisms of the prescriptive approach elsewhere in this book and can summarise the issues here with regard to change models.

● The assumption is made in prescriptive models that it is possible to move clearly from one state to another. This may not be possible if the environment itself is turbulent and the new destination state therefore unclear.

● Where major learning of new methods or substantial long-term investment is needed for the new situation, it may not even be clear when the new refrozen state has been reached – the situation may be soft-frozen.

Fig 21.4 **Owens-Corning take-over using the Lewin model**

Typical activities in the organisation	Lewin model	Owens-Corning case study example
• Realisation among group of need for change • Signals from top management that 'all is not well' (perhaps even exaggerated news circulated) • Data on nature of the problem made known throughout the organisation	**Unfreezing current attitudes** ↓	• Information about the current situation given to all employees after take-over • News that productivity and performance have fallen to unacceptable levels
• Specific call for change coupled with discussion of what is required • Views gathered on possible solutions • Information built on preferred solution • Experiment	**Moving to a new level** (State of flux: reactions tested to proposed solutions; organised debate and discussion) ↓	• Emotional reactions • Productivity losses • Use of 'soft' management contacts to probe feelings • Senior managers present at social activities • Factory downtime linked to profits
• Make announcement • Reassure those affected • News circulated to show that new solution is working	**Refeezing attitudes at the new level**	• Introduction of gain sharing and performance pay • US$15 million investment • Common set of values across Europe

● The assumption is also made that agreement on the new refrozen state is possible. This may be unrealistic if the politics within the organisation remain in flux. Given that prescriptive models involve only limited consultation, this assumption can be shown to have real weaknesses in some cultural styles characterised by competition and power-building.

● Such models rely on the *imposition* of change on the employees concerned. This may be essential in some circumstances, e.g. factory closure, but where the co-operation of those involved is needed or the culture works on a co-operative style, the prescriptive models may be totally inappropriate.

> ### Key strategic principles
>
> - There are a number of prescriptive routes for the management of change: two were examined in this section.
>
> - Kanter *et al* recommend a three-stage approach involving three forms of change and three categories of people involved in the change. Essentially, the route is a top-down guide to managing planned change and its consequences throughout the organisation.
>
> - Lewin developed a three-stage model for the prescriptive change process: unfreezing current attitudes, moving to a new level and refreezing attitudes at the new level. This model has been widely used to analyse and manage change.
>
> - Prescriptive models of change work best where it is possible to move clearly from one state to another: in times of rapid change, such clarity may be difficult to find and such models may be inappropriate.

CASE STUDY 21.2

United Biscuits pulls out of the USA[16]

In 1995, United Biscuits announced a sudden strategic decision to pull out of its largest overseas operation. This case study explores the reasons and questions the implications for managing the strategic change.

With 1994 sales of US$5.2 billion, the UK-based company United Biscuits (UB) was the third largest biscuit manufacturer in the world. It was also joint equal market leader across Europe in crisps and nut snacks. European brands included McVities biscuits (UK), KP snacks (UK), Verkade biscuits (Holland and France), Fazer biscuits (Finland), Oxford biscuits (Nordic region). Asia–Pacific operations were centred on its 1993 Australian acquisition of the Smith's Snackfood company.

American brands were centred around the Keebler biscuits and snacks company which UB had purchased in 1979. The operation had moved into losses in 1993 and 1994 but the company was confident of turning events around. It added to its US interests in 1993 by acquiring America's foremost private label cookie company, Bake-Line. It announced an investment programme in 1994 amounting to US$160 million in the Keebler com-

pany. However, it later announced that it was withdrawing from some geographical areas of

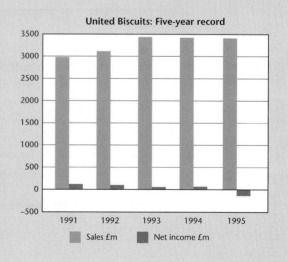

United Biscuits: Five-year record

the USA in order to consolidate its strengths in its main areas.

New global strategy: February 1995
In February 1995, UB was so confident of its trading future that it announced a new strategy and reorganisation aimed at producing:

- worldwide co-ordination of its biscuits and snacks activities in order to develop synergies, share experience, best practice and innovation;

- three new geographic areas – Europe, Asia–Pacific, USA – each with its own Director;

- increased worldwide co-ordination of R&D in order to 'champion' new product innovation around the world.

The statement was accompanied by a new detailed chart that identified senior members of the company and their new worldwide responsibilities. It also showed how the company's efforts would be increasingly co-ordinated to produce enhanced synergies in product development and innovation.

Withdrawal from the USA: July 1995
In July 1995, UB announced that it was pulling out of the USA completely and selling its Keebler and salty snack businesses for the best possible price. The Managing Director said: 'It's never easy to make statements like this, but this is decisive action that's right for the company.'

Keebler was finally sold in November 1995 for just under US$600 million, barely covering the asset valuation in its accounts. Since UB had invested another US$150 million in the previous two years in the USA, its exit had some additional financial consequences.

The reasons for the rapid turnaround in the US business were said to be:

- *inability to build volume beyond a modest 15 per cent market share* compared to the US market leader, Nabisco, with 55 per cent share;

- *major cost increases in raw materials in the US market* that could not be recovered because of competition from the market leader;

- *lower sales margins than the market leader* – 7 per cent versus 14 per cent, due to its provision of the same service level on much lower levels of sales.

UB had not been helped by the previous history of Keebler. From its acquisition up to 1993, it had been operated semi-independently from its other UB operations. The US Managing Director then quit, but this had made it difficult for UB up to that time to gain any synergies and to influence events.

Further pressures on UB in 1995
The overall reasons for the sudden shift in UB strategy were also influenced by three major strategic problems elsewhere in the world:

- *downturn in its most profitable market, the UK* – supermarkets were squeezing its leading brands;

- *fierce European competition in snackfoods from a powerful and increasingly aggressive rival* – PepsiCo, trading as Walkers in the UK and Frito in the rest of Europe. Pepsi was the biggest snack food maker in the world and had decided to build its European brands aggressively;

- *net debt at US$700 million was 64 per cent of shareholders' funds in December 1994.*

Some observers regarded it as no coincidence that a new Chairman, Mr Colin Short, was appointed to UB in Spring 1995 from outside the food industry. He had a reputation for facing unpleasant facts and taking hard decisions. By the end of 1995, the sale of its US interests had made UB more vulnerable to a hostile take-over bid than at any time in its history: it had a poor profit record and was unable to show the benefits of its US disposal.

CASE QUESTIONS

1 *What would be the effect on employees of the major strategic switch between February and July 1995? What actions would you have taken in July/August 1995 in these circumstances, if any?*

2 *Given the successful sale of its US interests in November 1995, what strategic change programme would you be seeking for the late 1990s?*

21.4   EMERGENT APPROACHES TO MANAGING CHANGE

From Section 21.3, it will be clear that there are occasions when prescriptive approaches to strategic change are essential, usually where some major shift in strategy is undertaken, such as in the United Biscuits case. However, the human cost may be high in terms of resistance to the changes and the consequences that follow from this. Emergent approaches therefore deserve to be investigated.

Within emergent theories, there is no one single approach. Some emphasise the need for responsiveness in an increasingly turbulent world. Others concentrate on the longer-term need to change an organisation's skills, style and operating culture fundamentally and over long time periods. It is these latter theories that are explored in this chapter since they are more closely related to issues of strategic change. The two emergent areas chosen for examination have already been explored:

- Learning theory, as developed by Senge and others.[17]
- The Five Factors theory of strategic change, as developed by Pettigrew and Whipp.

21.4.1   Learning theory

According to Senge,[18] the learning organisation does not *suddenly* adopt strategic change but is *perpetually* seeking it. The process of learning is continuous: as one area is 'learnt', so new avenues of experimentation and communication open up. In addition, the learning approach emphasises the following areas:

- team learning;
- the sharing of views and visions for the future;
- the exploration of ingrained company habits, generalisations and corporate interpretations that may no longer be relevant;
- people skills as the most important asset of the organisation; and, most importantly,
- systems thinking – the integrative area that supports the four above and provides a basis for viewing the environment.

It will be evident that the learning approach can work well where the company has the time and resources to invest in these areas. The objective is for the people in the organisation to shape its future over time. (The Owens-Corning acquisition included elements of this in the comment, 'I cannot guarantee your jobs. Only you can do that.')

Arguably, learning would not be so applicable where there was a sudden change in strategic direction – for example, the UB move out of the USA. The gradual assimilation of change and the ability of employees to guide their own destiny is limited, if rapid change is imposed for outside commercial reasons. The learning approach appeared to offer little in the short term for UB's 1995 predicament, for example.

Comment   The principle of the learning organisation appears to have a significant difficulty: precisely how and when should companies be developed into 'learning' organisations.[19] The outline concept is clear enough but the practicalities of how this is achieved are vague and lacking in operational detail. Egan has commented on the definitional and conceptual ambiguity in the learning concept 'which has stifled the practical adoption of what could otherwise be an extremely powerful idea'.[20] Garvin has attempted to answer these difficulties by exploring the management and measurement of such new processes.[21] He suggests some first useful steps that might be adopted to begin the process, e.g. *learning forums* or discussion groups in the organisation to tackle specific change issues.

21.4.2 The Five Factors theory of strategic change

Pettigrew and Whipp[22] (*see* Chapter 18) undertook an in-depth empirical study of strategic change at four companies: Jaguar cars, Longman publishing, Hill Samuel merchant bank and Prudential life assurance. They also undertook a more general examination of the industries in which the four companies were operating. Their conclusions were that there were five inter-related factors in the successful management of strategic change (*see* Fig 21.5):

1 *Environmental assessment.* This should not be regarded as a separate study by a separate function. All parts of the organisation should be constantly assessing the competition. Strategy creation emerges constantly from this process.

2 *Leading change.* The type of leadership can only be assessed by reference to the particular circumstances of the organisation. There are no universal 'good leaders'. The best leaders are always constrained by the actual situation of the firm. They are often most effective when they move the organisation forward at a comfortable, if challenging, pace: bold actions may be counter-productive.

3 *Linking strategic and operational change.* This may be partly prescriptive in the sense of a specific strategy for the organisation – 'This is my decision'. It may also be partly emergent in that the strategy may allow for evolution over time – 'But naturally our new strategy will evolve as we implement it.'

4 *Strategic human resource management – human resources as assets and liabilities.* These resources constitutes the knowledge, skills and attitudes of the organisation in total. Crucially, some people are better than others at managing people. It is a skill acquired over time and needing a learning approach (*see* Section 21.3.1). Long-term learning is essential for the organisation to develop its full potential.

5 *Coherence in the management of change.* This is the most complex of the five factors. It attempts to combine the four above into a consistent whole and reinforce it by a set of four complementary support mechanisms:

- *consistency* – the goals of the organisation must not conflict with each other;
- *consonance* – the whole process must respond well to its environment;
- *competitive advantage* – the coherence must deliver in this area;
- *feasibility* – the strategy must not present unsolvable problems.

Note that the five factors relate to the whole strategy development process, not just to the implementation process.

Overall, the organisation needs to be able to develop a *balanced approach* to change that is both focussed and efficient internally, while adapting successfully to external changes. To assist this process, the researchers included two additional components for each factor:

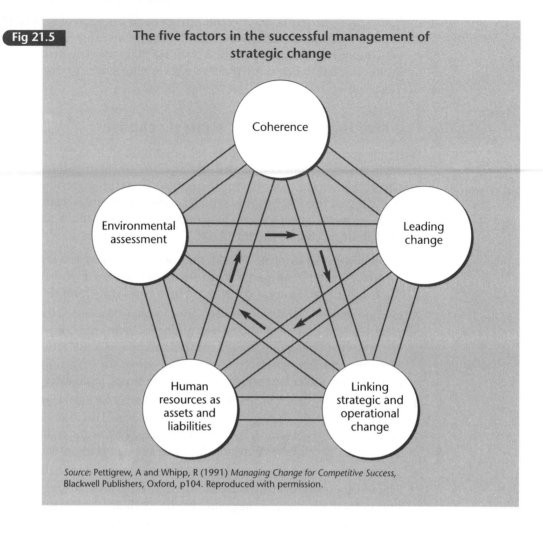

Fig 21.5

The five factors in the successful management of strategic change

Source: Pettigrew, A and Whipp, R (1991) *Managing Change for Competitive Success,* Blackwell Publishers, Oxford, p104. Reproduced with permission.

1 *The primary conditioning features*.
2 *The secondary actions and mechanisms* which can only come into effect once the primary conditioning features are present.

These additional components are shown in Fig 21.6.

To illustrate how the five factors might be used, the Owens-Corning take-over of Pilkington Insulation (*see* Case study 21.1) has been analysed using this approach. The results are shown in Table 21.1. The model provides a useful way of taking the facts from a strategic change situation and structuring them to highlight the important items. Where data has not been gathered on one of the five elements of change, it highlights this area. The model may also suggest additional areas that need to be explored in the organisation in order to understand the dynamic of change, especially in the area of coherence.

Fig 21.6

Characteristics of the five central factors

	Environmental assessment	Leading change	Linking strategic and operational change	Human resources as assets and liabilities	Coherence
PRIMARY CONDITIONING FEATURES	1 Availability of key people 2 Internal character of organisation 3 Environmental pressures and associated dramas 4 Environmental assessments as a multi-function activity	1 Building a receptive context for change; legitimation 2 Creating capability for change 3 Constructing the content and direction of the change	1 Justifying the need for change 2 Building capacity for appropriate action 3 Supplying necessary visions, values and business direction	1 Raising HRM consciousness 2 Use of highly situational additive features to create positive force for HRM change 3 Demonstrating the need for business and people change	1 Consistency 2 Consonance 3 Advantage 4 Feasibility
SECONDARY MECHANISMS	5 Role of planning, marketing 6 Construction of purposive networks with main stake-holders 7 Use of specialist task-forces	4 Operationalising the change agenda 5 Creating the critical mass for change within senior management 6 Communicating need for change and detailed requirements of the change agenda 7 Achieving and reinforcing success 8 Balance continuity and change 9 Sustaining coherence	4 Breaking emergent strategy into actionable pieces 5 Appointment of change managers, relevant structures and exacting targets 6 Re-thinking communications 7 Using the reward system 8 Setting up local negotiation climate for targets 9 Modifying original visions in light of local context 10 Monitoring and adjustment	4 *Ad hoc*, cumulative, supportive activities at various levels 5 Linking HRM action to business need with HRM as a means not an end 6 Mobilising external influences 7 Devolution to line 8 Construction of HRM actions and institutions which reinforce one another	5 Leadership 6 Senior management team integrity 7 Uniting intent and implementation 8 Developing apposite knowledge bases 9 Inter-organisational coherence 10 Managing a series of inter-related changes over time

Source: Pettigrew, A and Whipp, R (1991) *Managing Change for Competitive Success*, Blackwell Publishers, Oxford, p106. Reproduced with permission.

Table 21.1 Analysing the five factors for change at Owens-Corning

Factor	*Owens-Corning analysis*
Coherence	• Defined by the single act of acquisition • The clarity of the new owner's desire to make all areas successful • Common set of European values
Environmental assessment	• 'Drivers of the business' were identified • Emphasis on market share and customer satisfaction through repeat business
Strategic human resource management	• Clear understanding of the uncertainties of employees • Communication emphasis, especially core messages • 'Soft' due diligence
Linking strategic and operational change	• Pay linked to performance • Attendance of senior managers at informal functions • Motivation and customer focus
Leading change	• Individual responsibility: the role of Mr Knowles • Accessibility of senior managers • Clear vision and common set of values • Focus on key factors for success: customer, reduced cycle times, motivation

Note: The factors are in the order relevant to the Owens-Corning take-over.

Comment   Although the comprehensiveness of the model is its greatest strength,[23] it is also its most significant weakness. Some of the factors represent truths that most would agree with, but contain areas that are so generalised that they may provide only limited guidance on the difficult issues involved in strategic change. Thus, some of the Five Factors needed to be treated with caution.

- *Environmental assessment* is a well-known factor requiring constant monitoring. However, the more detailed comments against this heading in the model provide more limited guidance than those in Part 2 of this book.

- *Linking of strategic and operational change* is an important area of study, but many would regard this as being the same as the 'implementation' process discussed by other writers and explored in this book.

- *Leading change* and its complexity has been recognised as a change factor for many years.[24]

However, the emphasis on *human resource assets and liabilities* is a welcome emphasis not present in some other analyses, such as Porter's generic strategies or portfolio matrices. Moreover, the identification, definition and logic of *coherence* as a major factor is also useful.

21.4.3   Comment on emergent models of change

The UB case illustrates the difficulties of using emergent models of strategic change. For whatever reasons, between February and July 1995 the company found itself being forced to undertake a completely different approach to its strategy:

- worldwide and US activities were dropped in favour of a more modest European and Asia–Pacific programme;

- its major US subsidiary, Keebler, was sold off.

It could certainly be argued that the company had signalled the difficulties it was facing in North American markets during 1993/94, both to the Stock Exchange and to employees. However, the *emergent* models of strategic change, with their long-term approach to learning, provide only limited clues to interpreting the difficulties and suggesting how they might be tackled over this period. By contrast, the three-phase Lewin *prescriptive* model does provide a means of interpreting the events and their meaning for change (*see* Figure 21.7).

Emergent models of strategic change have a number of weaknesses that may make them difficult to employ:[25]

- The 'long-term learning' approach of Pettigrew and Whipp[26] necessary to achieve emergent strategies may have little practical value where an organisation faces a short-term unforeseen crisis. There is no guarantee that the 'learning' that has already taken place will be relevant to the crisis. Arguably, the crisis may partly have arisen because the learning was incorrect.

- In some emergent models, increased turbulence of the environment is assumed as a justification for the emergent strategies. Such generalisations about the environment need empirical evidence. There are a number of environments that are generally predictable.

Fig 21.7   **Unfreezing and freezing attitudes at UB in 1995**

Typical activities in the organisation	Lewin model	UB case study example
• Realisation among group of need for change • Signals from top management that 'all is not well' (perhaps even exaggerated news circulated) • Data on nature of the problem made known throughout the organisation	**Unfreezing current attitudes**	• Aggressive rival attacks market share across USA and Europe: 1994/95 • US subsidiary continues to make substantive losses after three years of investment: 1993/95
• Specific call for change coupled with discussion of what is required • Views gathered on possible solutions • Information built on preferred solution • Experiment	**Moving to a new level** (State of flux: reactions tested to proposed solutions; debate and discussion organised)	• Announce job losses in Europe and USA in 1994 • Executives undertake studies of UK and US markets: 1994/95 • Conclude that US position cannot be maintained • Announce withdrawal from part of US in 1994 • No real experimentation at this time: arguably took place in 1994
• Make announcement • Reassure those affected • News circulated to show that new solution is working	**Refeezing attitudes at the new level**	• Announce sale of all US interests: 1995 • 'It's never easy...' statement from Managing Director • Reorganise the remainder of the company • Reassure the remaining employees

● A reliance on a learning culture may be counter-productive for some managers and employees. Some managers may refuse to learn because they will realise that such a process will reduce their power.[27] Empowerment of some employees will certainly mean that others will have less power and may react accordingly.

Overall, the way forward proposed by some emergent strategists often amounts to the need to start earlier so that the organisation is able to adapt when the change comes. This may not be sufficient at the time when a sudden change hits the organisation.

21.4.4 The choice between emergent and prescriptive strategic change

The choice between the prescriptive and emergent routes is context-sensitive. Potentially, organisations may wish to choose emergent strategic change management because it is less disruptive and therefore has a lower cost. However, there may be occasions when the strategic circumstances force prescriptive change. The choice depends on the situation facing the organisation at the time.

Key strategic principles

- There are a number of emergent approaches to strategic change. The two explored in this section concentrate on the longer-term, learning culture routes to change.

- According to Senge, the learning organisation does not suddenly adopt strategic change but is perpetually seeking it. Hence, the organisation is using its learning, experimentation and communication to renew itself constantly. Strategic change is a constant process.

- According to Pettigrew and Whipp, their empirical study of strategic change identified five factors in the successful management of the process. They were environmental assessment, leadership of change, the link between strategic and operational change, human resource aspects and coherence in the management of the process.

- Emergent models of strategic change take a long-term approach and may have limited usefulness when the organisation faces short-term strategic crisis.

- The choice between prescriptive and emergent strategic change processes will depend on the situation at the time: ideally, emergent change should be chosen because it is less disruptive and cheaper. In reality, a prescriptive approach may be necessary.

21.5 DEVELOPING A STRATEGIC CHANGE PROGRAMME

The starting point for any programme of strategic change is *clarity* regarding the changes required. These will relate back to the organisation's objectives explored in Chapter 12 but may also include a more experimental element. They may also need to be modified by some aspects of the implementation programme – 'the art of the possible' from Chapter 8. A strategic change programme might also include the introduction of a 'learning culture' as part of its way forward.

Furthermore, most programmes of strategic change concentrate on certain key tasks: for example, they may identify individuals or groups with particular power to make or break a proposed change. In this context, the organisation has the ability to make changes among many variables and would be well advised to consider all of these before making its selection. Since one of the main problems may be the resistance to changes that are proposed and another will be the need to persuade people to support the proposals, it is also important to give these matters serious consideration at the commencement of the programme. The change programme needs to address four questions:

● What areas of change are available?

● What areas will we select and why?

● Will people resist change? If so, how can this be overcome?

● How will people use the politics of an organisation?

21.5.1 What areas of change are available?

In Section 21.1, four general areas of activity associated with people, referred to as pressure points for influence, were identified – formal organisation structure, people, tasks and informal organisation structure. These can be coupled with three main areas of strategic change activity[28] to produce the *change options matrix* shown in Fig 21.8. In practice, every organisation undertaking change will need to develop activities in most of these options. However, for most organisations, there will be a need to concentrate effort and monitor results. Hence, it will be useful to *focus and direct activities more tightly*: selection among the options will be a priority.

Fig 21.8 — Change options matrix

Three main areas of strategic change	Areas of people activity			
	Formal organisation structure	People	Tasks	Informal organisation structure
Technical and work changes from the strategy to be undertaken	• Organisation of work and reporting • Strategy and structure	• Selection, training • Matching of management style with skills • Routines	• Consider environment, technology, learning, competitor activity • Learn and carry out new tasks	• Understand and monitor • Feed with 'good news'
Cultural changes Style of company, history, age, etc.	• Managerial style • Minzberg's subcultures *(Chapter 15)* • Handy's cultures *(Chapter 8)*	• Individual and corporate values matched • Management of groups and teams • Leadership choice	• Symbols, stories • Unfreezing • Make role models of key people • Clarify values • New recipes	• Awards, symbols • Develop networks • Encourage useful groups • Develop social activities
Political changes Interactions and power inside the organisation	• Formal distribution of power • Balance of power between departments	• Use available skills and networks • Match with new strategies • Incentives and rewards	• Lobbying • Develop structures • Influence formal and informal groups	• Attempt to manage • Make contacts • Network and circulate

21.5.2   What areas will we select from the change options matrix and why?

The response to these questions will depend on the organisation, its culture and leadership. For example, organisations that have a history of top-down management might select items from the change options matrix that match this style of operating – that is, organisation of work and formal distribution of power.

However, organisations that have selected an open-learning, co-operative style of operating might select as their starting point team building and training and education.

The clear implication is that it is essential to review the organisation's culture analysis: Johnson's *Cultural Web* from Chapter 8 should provide a useful guide here.

There are no universal answers. As we have seen, some researchers have recently tended to favour the more co-operative, learning organisation approach. However, it should be recognised that this may be a fashion of the late 1990s: only time will tell.

Whatever route is chosen, a more detailed answer to the question then needs to be followed through. As an illustration of the issues that can then arise, the *assumption* is made here that the co-operative, learning approach has been chosen. Within this route, Beer *et al*[29] provide a detailed six-point plan on how to proceed, beginning by stressing that the areas to be selected for change should be chosen not by top management but by *those involved in the implementation process*. The six overlapping areas are:

1   *Mobilise commitment to change through joint diagnosis of business problems arising from the change objective.* One or more *task forces* might be employed here. They should represent all stakeholders in the organisation and be directed at specific aspects of the change objective.

2   *Develop a shared vision of how to organise and manage for competitiveness.* Senior management may lead the process but the identification of the new roles and responsibilities is undertaken by those involved in implementation. Typically, this will be through the task forces.

3   *Foster consensus for the new vision, competence to enact it and cohesion to move it along.* This book has already explored vision, competences and cohesion. The key new word is *consensus* which the researchers suggest needs to come from strong leadership at the top. New competences may be required, resistance may build and some individuals may turn out to be more reluctant than others. Difficulties may be overcome by teamwork coupled with training to provide support. However, it is likely that leadership will also be needed.

4   *Spread revitalisation to all departments pushing it from the top.* Change is spread to the departments that supplied the members of the task force. However, such change cannot be forced onto departments. They must be allowed some freedom, but they can be guided and revitalised by top management.

5   *Institute revitalisation through formal policies, systems and structures.* Up to this stage, the process has contained a degree of freedom of choice, experimentation and action. Now the time has come to 'refreeze' the procedures both to ensure commitment and understanding and to provide the basis for future monitoring and controls.

6 *Monitor and adjust strategies in response to problems in the revitalisation process.* Having 'learnt' an area, the organisation should be able to repeat the process as the environment continues to change and more is understood about the changes already introduced.

With the emphasis on joint task forces and learning through doing, it might well be asked what role senior management can perform. The researchers suggested they had three prime tasks:

- *To create the prime conditions for change* – forcing recognition of the need, setting the standards and monitoring performance. Owens-Corning senior management is a good example here.

- *To identify those teams and organisation units that had achieved successful change and then praise them as role models for the rest.* Educational visits to them and training by them can then be helpful in spreading best practice.

- *To identify individuals and promote them on the basis of their success in leading change.*

Finally, it should be emphasised again that this approach is suitable for one type of organisation but may not be appropriate for other types.

21.5.3   Will people resist change and how can this be overcome?

In practical terms, the issue of resistance to change is probably the chief obstacle to the successful implementation of strategic change. The reasons are many and the ways of overcoming them will depend on the circumstances. Exhibit 21.1 presents a list of some of the more common areas of resistance and suggests ways of overcoming them.

Exhibit 21.1   **Resistance to change**

Why people resist change	Overcoming resistance
• Anxiety, e.g. weaknesses revealed or loss of power or position	• Involving those who resist in the change process itself
• Pessimism	• Building support networks
• Irritation	• Communications and discussion
• Lack of interest	• Use of managerial authority and status
• Opposition strategy proposals	• Offering assistance
• Different personal ambitions	• Extra incentives
	• Encouraging and supporting those involved
	• Use of symbols to signal the new era

More positively, resistance will be less if the change is not imposed from outside but developed by those involved in the change procedures. Change will be more welcome if it is seen to reduce, rather than increase, the task of those involved and to be consistent with the values that they hold. Change is also more likely to be accepted if it offers an interesting challenge and a change from existing routine. Importantly, change is more likely to be appreciated if the outcome is genuinely valued by senior management, who have wholeheartedly supported the process as it has developed.

21.5.4 How will people use the politics of an organisation?

In the context of strategic change, politics starts by *persuading* people to adopt a new strategy. It may not be a question of meeting open resistance but rather one of different priorities, different power blocks or differences of opinion on the way forward. The first step is usually to establish the organisation's 'ground rules', that is, any criteria that it has for the acceptance of projects, such as minimum levels of profitability and so on.

The more difficult aspects of politics usually begin when these criteria have been met but there is still resistance. Politics then becomes *discussion, negotiation* and even *cunning* and *intrigue*. The Florentine diplomat and writer, Nicolo Machiavelli (1469–1527), remains well known to this day for his insights into the ways that people use the politics of the organisations to which they belong.[30] His writing appears cynical, devious and self-serving but he certainly understood management politics at its worst:

> *It is unnecessary for a good prince to have all the qualities I have enumerated but it is very necessary to appear to have them.*

On the subject of change:

> *There is nothing more difficult to take in hand, more perilous to conduct, or more uncertain in its success, than to take the lead in the introduction of a new order of things.*

Machiavelli saw little benefit in persuasion, except as a means of avoiding the alternative which was to use direct force and possibly end up making enemies. His attitude was that reason mattered less than power, and human nature was best considered as acting for the worst possible motives. He would have chuckled cynically at such strategic change concepts as communication, discussion and empowerment.

In some organisations, Machiavelli still remains relevant today. Certainly, it is highly unlikely that major strategic change can be implemented if it meets strong political barriers. Strategists therefore have to be skilled not only at devising their proposals but also at building support for them through the organisation's political structure. Hence, it is important to understand how the *decision-making system* works in the organisation: this will include not only any final presentation but also the preceding discussions, consultations and lobbying. It may be useful to call for advice from those who have had previous experience within its processes.

Inevitably, the politics of an organisation will take time to understand. It will include the activities of other people and their interaction with strategy across a whole range of activities. People will have many motives: some good and some less attractive. They may employ many different types of activity that could loosely be described as political. Table 21.2 lists some that have been shown by empirical research to be important.

Table 21.2 Politics in organisations[31]

Objective	Activities undertaken to achieve the objective	Reaction by superiors or rivals to the activities
Resist change or resist authority	● Sabotage ● Rebellion	● Fight back ● Institute new rules and regulations
Build power	● Flaunt or feign expertise ● Attach oneself to superior ● Build alliances with colleagues ● Collect subordinates: empire build ● Control resources	● Call bluff ● Find heir ● Reorganise department ● Reclaim control of resources
Defeat rival	● Battles between units ● Battles between staff and line ● Expose mistakes (we all make them)	● Good leadership should provide balance
Achieve fundamental change in strategy, authority and leadership	● Form power group of key executives ● Combine with other areas above ● Inform on opponent ● Leak damaging material to public media	● Intelligence essential ● Recognise and cultivate those who are particularly influential ● Seek out rival power groups ● Respond with own leaks

By definition, change involves moving from a previous strategy and therefore the starting point for the persuasion process might appear to be an attack on the existing strategy. However, politically this may be a mistake. It may force those who introduced the previous strategy to defend their decisions and therefore raise barriers to the new proposals. The people who are antagonised by the new strategies may be the very individuals whose support is vital for them.

Beyond these considerations, the person(s) responsible for seeking agreement to a new strategy will need to undertake several important tasks:

● Identify potential and influential supporters and persuade them to support the new strategy.

● Seek out potential opposition and attempt to change opinions or, at least, to neutralise them.

● Build the maximum consensus for the new proposals, preferably *prior* to any formal decision meeting.

Finally, it is important to keep political matters in perspective. They are important but this book has hopefully shown that strategy does not deal in certainties. It is an art as well as a science. This means that there is room for differing views and the use of judgement and debate in arriving at decisions. Strategy is the art of the possible.

Key strategic principles

- The change options matrix sets out the main areas where change is possible: it is important within this to focus and select options.

- Selection from the matrix needs to be undertaken. This can best be undertaken by an understanding of the culture of the organisation: the Cultural Web can be useful here. A more detailed process to achieve change can then be planned out with six overlapping areas providing a starting point.

- Resistance to change is probably one of the chief obstacles to successful strategy implementation. It is likely to be lower if strategies are not imposed from the outside.

- The politics of strategic change needs to begin by attempting to persuade those involved to adopt the new strategy recommendations. Beyond this, a Machiavellian approach may be necessary to ensure the desired changes are achieved. More generally, strategic change activities may include identifying supporters, attempting to change opposition views and building the maximum consensus for the new proposals. Preferably, this should be undertaken prior to any decision meeting.

21.6 CULTURE, STYLE AND CHANGE

An organisation's external environment is constantly changing, and so strategic change is inevitable. The issue for an organisation is therefore how to harness the energies of all its people to ensure success. In most organisations, there will be a measure of agreement on the way forward, but there will also be those who disagree. This is a sign of a healthy organisation: informed debate should not be stifled. There will come a time, however, when strategic decisions have to be made. It will then be necessary to move the organisation forward in a positive way. This is where the culture and style of the organisation are important – to ensure that it moves beyond the disagreements and relishes the positive strategic challenge.

Culture and style have been the stock-in-trade of a whole succession of management 'gurus' who often have their views of the 'one best way' to develop strategy. This book has deliberately avoided picking out one single approach because study should be eclectic and open to ideas from many areas. Moreover, strategy is too complex for simple solutions. However, there is one aspect of strategy associated with culture and style that does deserve careful thought: if change is inevitable, then the organisation should not simply wait for it to happen. In this sense, strategy is about seizing the initiative rather than reacting to change. In terms of culture and style, the implication is clear: the organisation should learn to welcome change. It should regard strategic change as a *positive challenge* and manage itself accordingly.

Culture and style are also linked with leadership. It is the leader or leading group that should set the tone and tasks for the organisation. From an empirical study of leadership, Bennis and Nanus[32] have derived four areas of competence for leadership that are relevant to change:

- *Vision.* This can instill confidence and a positive approach to the changes proposed.
- *Communication.* Visions need to be shared. Enthusiasms need to be communicated and groups inspired to meet the challenge of change.
- *Trust.* Consistency and integrity need to be part of the leader's approach if people are to follow willingly.
- *Self-knowledge.* Leaders also need to know their strengths and weaknesses and be able to acknowledge these. No one is good at everything, nor needs to be.

Although not covered by the researchers, it is important to add two more competences for leadership in strategy:

- *Responsiveness to the situation.* Leadership in strategy will occasionally require positive 'championing' of the new way forward. This may demand a degree of aggression to achieve the objective. At other times, leadership may need to be more participative and 'listening' in its style.
- *Creativity.* Strategy development needs innovation. The leader will not have all the answers but will know how to ask the right questions.

Key strategic principles

- Once change has been agreed, it is necessary to move beyond any past disputes and pick up the new challenge in a positive fashion. This will happen more easily if the culture and style of the organisation have been well prepared in advance to *welcome* change and not regard it as a threat.
- Leadership has an important role to play in managing strategic change: vision, communication, trust and self-knowledge are all desirable competences in good change leaders. They also need to be responsive to the situation of the time and to be creative so that innovative solutions can be found.

21.7 INTERNATIONAL ISSUES IN MANAGING STRATEGIC CHANGE

21.7.1 The need for multicultural teams

Given the importance of people-issues in strategic change and the need on occasions to work in groups, international co-operation requires careful thought: cultural differences between countries can make strategic change difficult to implement. There are special difficulties where team-working is required because different cultures have different ways of working, different expectations of success and different time scales. Some of these issues are illustrated in Exhibit 21.2.

> **Exhibit 21.2** **Examples of how cultural attitudes can affect working relationships**[33]
>
> Conclusions of a survey of 40 managers from 13 countries working at BP Oil in 1991.
>
> - Many Scandinavians expect to be called by their family names only. Germans do not anticipate being called by their first names even when they know each other well. Many UK managers are on first-name terms with their colleagues.
>
> - While shaking hands was a formal politeness on first meeting in the US and UK, French subsidiary managers did this every morning to the surprise of others.
>
> - French executives judged that their positions in the managerial hierarchy gave them the authority to make decisions, whereas Dutch, Scandinavian and UK managers anticipated that they might be challenged.
>
> - Germans were most comfortable in formal hierarchies, the Dutch the most relaxed. UK managers left more to individual initiative and expected more of individuals.
>
> - UK and US managers were proud to work late at the office, as this emphasised their commitment and ambition. Most others regarded working beyond the normal finishing time as a sign of inefficiency that needed training to overcome.
>
> A separate survey of 15 000 managers in 30 countries concluded:
>
> - Performance-related pay often fails in such countries as France, Germany, Italy and large parts of Asia where people tend not to accept that individual members of the group should excel in a way that reveals the shortcomings of other members.
>
> - Feedback sessions can motivate US managers but German managers may find them to be enforced admissions of failure.

Given the difficulties, it is worth asking whether the benefits outweigh the problems. The principal benefits are:

- it may be *essential* to create genuine involvement in a global strategy;
- it may also be *highly desirable* to obtain different national cultural contributions to the development of international strategy and its implementation;
- cultural diversity in general may promote creativity and should stimulate some rethinking about global and international activities.

21.7.2 Problems in multicultural team-working

Although the problems are recognised at the cultural level, the issue is how they impact on the working groups that operate within organisations. The usual barriers that appear as groups meet together for the first time can often be broken down quickly, if all the members come from one cultural background. For multicultural teams, however, there are differences in attitudes, values, behaviour, experience, background, expectations and language. Probably the biggest problem is a *lack of trust*: the need to overcome long-held prejudices and stereotypes. Students on international study programmes may experience this difficulty when they are asked to work on group assignments in mixed cultural teams.

The obvious way to overcome a lack of trust is for the team to explore this topic itself. This will take time. It is important to decide how much time to devote to this task before getting down to the *business* objective that the team is actually meant to tackle. Even this decision itself will have cultural implications: a typical US approach would be to attempt to 'fix' the team, while team members from some southern European countries, the Middle East and parts of Latin America would feel rushed and the attempt might backfire.

National cultures are important when addressing this lack of trust. For example:

- *Deadlines* in strategy implementation are usually important. For Germans, trust means honesty and punctuality with a deadline being renegotiated before it is missed. For Italians, trust is a more elastic concept with no literal deadline.

- *Misunderstandings* between members of a group will inevitably occur – perhaps a misunderstanding over a deadline or respect for a superior. This can be an acute problem where trust is already low. Even exploring the problem can carry risk because of differences in approach.

21.7.3 Overcoming difficulties

Probably the most important single factor is to have *time* to solve the problems. However, there also needs to be an acceptance on the part of those working in such teams that, as individuals, they are unlikely to be as confident nor as competent as they would be when working in the home environment.

Certainly it makes sense to start the teamwork slowly and end faster. Equally, it is better to address the cultural differences at an early stage rather than store up problems for later: 'How do we feel about deadlines? And commitment to the team objectives?' Humour can be used to defuse situations and explore cultural differences: when it is used successfully, the shared laughter itself shows a degree of trust. However, humour can lead to considerable misunderstanding: what might be considered mild humour in one culture, would be seen as biting sarcasm in another.

As Goffee and Jones state,[34] the main task is to understand other cultures and to operate within them. In addition, managers need to be able to explain or translate them to others. Like the anthropologist, managers also need to learn something of the background and history of the societies in which they manage. They need to explore how perceptions of the past shape the culture and actions of the present members of a national culture.

Key strategic principles

- Cultural differences between countries can make strategic change difficult to implement. There are special difficulties where team-working is required because different cultures have different ways of working, different expectations of success and different time scales.

- The most obvious problem for team-working can be a lack of trust. The best solution is for team members themselves to have the time to explore and resolve their problems. There is also a need to recognise that team members are unlikely to be as confident, or possibly as competent, as they are in their home environments.

Culture and change at merchant bankers, S G Warburg[35]

Sweeping changes have taken place in the culture and practices at SBC Warburg since its take-over in 1995.

Following the Swiss Bank Corporation July 1995 take-over of the UK's flagship investment bank, S G Warburg, there was a period of turmoil. Some 300 employees of the merged investment bank defected to other banks, prompting gossip of Warburg's disintegration. SBC Warburg was also hit by internal conflict as unresolved tensions were brought to the surface.

Mr Marcel Ospel, the Swiss chief executive who became chief executive of the whole of SBC in 1996, tried to draw a line under these troubles by announcing a new investment banking board composed mainly of younger faces. It would no longer be chaired by Sir David Scholey, and other veterans of S G Warburg were also leaving it. It was a symbolic act, intended to show that a new generation, untainted by mistakes of the past, was in charge.

Defections and upheavals

Defections and upheavals at an investment bank taken over by another are common. Investment banks are full of brokers and corporate financiers whose egos are fragile, and who can often find jobs elsewhere. This trauma was also accelerated at SBC Warburg, where Mr Ospel decided to cut 1000 of the 11 500 staff within a month of merging. But the level of tension took him and other by surprise.

One member of the 15-strong executive board which manages SBC Warburg said that S G Warburg was 'a sick firm that had to be healed'. He said SBC 'perhaps trusted some of the senior managers that were in place a little too much' at first in seeking advice on how to handle things. It transpired that many younger staff wanted a clear-out at the top.

After S G Warburg failed to pull off a merger with Morgan Stanley in December 1994, it seemed unable to survive alone and the younger employees became resentful at what they saw as the mismanagement during the 1990s.

'It was rocky for a time,' admitted Mr Ospel, a calm, analytical figure who had tried to introduce management disciplines that S G Warburg lacked. He seemed a little shaken at the reaction. Among the senior figures who departed where Mr Mark Seligman, head of S G Warburg's advisory business. Mr Ospel said there was only a handful whose departure he regretted; others could see their role would be diminished.

He said the worst was over. 'There are a few areas where we are facing problems, but by and large we should be pleased at where we are.' Yet SBC Warburg continues to face a problem in customer defections. Many of those quitting its corporate advisory business had long-standing relationships with large companies, which in turn could follow them to new banks.

It had already lost some. Burton, the clothes retailer, had replaced it with Schroders as an adviser, and other companies dispensed with its services as a corporate broker. SBC Warburg itself estimated that it lost seven and gained seven customers since the acquisition. But one executive admitted there were likely to be further departures among its customers following the staff defections.

Few regrets

At least one member of the old guard did not regret the departures of old-established names at Warburg. That was Mr Henry Grunfeld, the 92-year-old co-founder of S G Warburg. Mr Grunfeld was still coming to the office, and said his advice as a 'father confessor' had been in demand since the take-over. He was briskly dismissive of some star names who had departed.

'Some of those who left will not be missed,' said Mr Grunfeld firmly. He insisted some had exaggerated ideas of their own importance.

Sir David Scholey remained as chairman for four months, stepping down to be replaced by Mr Hans de Gier, a member of the SBC executive board. Sir David was given a role as chairman of SBC's council of international advisers. 'We had to show internally that room was being made for younger people,' said a senior figure from S G Warburg.

Yet the upheaval was a signal of more than *amour propre* among veterans and the release of tensions. It also stemmed from Mr Ospel's attempt to manage the firm in a fresh way, and organise everything differently, from how executives were paid to the way it handled customers.

Much of the impetus came from former partners of O'Connor, a Chicago derivatives firm taken over by SBC in 1991. Andy Siciliano, the head of foreign exchange, and David Solo, the head of fixed income, were former O'Connor partners who were now playing a central role in transforming Warburg.

New systems and styles

O'Connor built its reputation and profits from using the latest mathematical techniques to price and trade futures and options. Dominated by young mathematics and engineering graduates, it was run as a partnership. Bonuses were shared out evenly rather than allocated disproportionately to stars, or to particularly profitable departments. Mr Ospel now wanted to introduce a similar system at SBC Warburg.

O'Connor also stressed having precise figures on the profitability of its lines of business and its customers. This highlighted which were its best customers, and which ones should be targeted to sell more products. S G Warburg had only a hazy idea of such things, relying on maintaining relationships with companies in the hope that eventually it would gain a profitable transaction.

This meant opportunities were missed. Mr Rory Tapner, head of equity capital markets, said S G Warburg was surprised to find after the take-over that 66 of its 140 merchant banking customers had given business to SBC as well. Mr Tapner said Warburg 'did not have what it takes' to execute some types of financing. It was not innovative enough in having ideas, rather than relying on long-standing relationships.

'Some of the customers could see which banks were coming up with ideas and which weren't, and they were saying to us: "You need to do more", ' said Mr Tapner. SBC Warburg had belatedly followed US investment banks in grouping its advisers in specialist teams, in contrast to its former system of relying on generalist stars.

Mr Siciliano argued that SBC Warburg could no longer rely on pure advisory work, waiting for companies to make rights issues or pay for advice. 'The future looks pretty bleak for those that are pure advisers,' he said. Instead, SBC Warburg must sell foreign exchange services or underwrite bonds for companies that had used it only as a strategic adviser in the past.

New approaches

What happens if they do not want wider services? Mr Ospel said SBC Warburg would have to explain that it needed to sell more products to make a profit. 'It is a matter of making it transparent, so that both sides are properly rewarded by the relationship,' he said. He insisted that SBC Warburg would not arbitrarily freeze out a customer who was not providing an adequate return before giving its new approach long enough to work.

However, some customers had already seen a more analytical approach to business. For a decade, S G Warburg had acted as merchant bank adviser to some companies, and corporate broker to others. The twin roles came from the merger in the 1980s of S G Warburg and Rowe & Pitman, the broker. Its corporate brokers were cautious about selling other products, not wanting to offend the customers' merchant banks.

Mr Ospel said a traditional approach to corporate broking may have 'stood in the way of expanding our relationships into other areas' in some cases. Yet SBC Warburg had already been dropped by a few of the 260 companies to which it was broker. If others were disturbed by a more active approach and also left, it would have to compensate by making more money from the remaining advisory customers.

Global business

From Mr Ospel's perspective, such niggles to some extent missed the point. He was not attempting simply to preserve the strong UK business of S G Warburg. Instead, he was creating a global investment bank. He was trying to use its broking strength in Asia to create far stronger advisory and equity underwriting. He was also planning to bolster its US arm either by recruiting, or by buying a US investment bank.

Seen in such a context, the upheaval that followed the take-over is less significant. It seems like a local upset among some talented employees who no longer felt appreciated. Yet if they took other customers with them, SBC's attempt to capture S G Warburg would look somewhat shaky. Mr Ospel must hope the turmoil is over now that so many of the old regime have gone.

Source: Financial Times, 8 November 1995.

CASE QUESTIONS

1 *Undertake an analysis of the changes that have taken place in the culture and power balance across the company since the take-over. What conclusions can you draw for employees and management?*

2 *With hindsight, would you have managed the essential changes at the merchant bank differently from the senior managers who undertook them at the time?*

3 *Is the company likely to come through the change period with success or will there be permanent problems?*

Mobilising middle managers[36]

In this extract from their book, Rejuvenating the Mature Business, *Charles Baden-Fuller and John Stopford explain how middle managers are the key to the successful implementation of corporate strategy.*

Middle managers are the people who will make or break the organisation. Not only are they the key to 'the doing of management' but also they are vital to new thinking. The ideas that informed the choice of strategy in the first place can come from many sources in the firm, not just the top. Thus it is that those in the middle have to take the ideas from all quarters and make them work in daily operations. The common distinctions made among top-down, bottom-up and lateral processes of communication blur when considering what happens in practice: all have to be operative in entrepreneurial organisations. Unless middle managers are clear about their central role in company-wide affairs, they will inhibit progress.

Sometimes the difficulty of starting the process of mobilising the middle is that the chief executive may personally be unwilling or unable to provide the leadership needed to legitimise the effort. One of the less successful rejuvenators confessed to our survey that he had so far worked only with his top team of six people and had not 'got much further down'. He, like many others, once believed that the strategy was so commercially sensitive that it could not be shared. Like others he saw his mistake: 'We were initially afraid our competitors would get hold of the plan. But we then discovered they had it already and our employees were the only ones in the dark before our presentations.'

All too often middle managers wait until the corporate plan has been unveiled before they act. Top management must mobilise middle managers to look upwards, sideways and downwards as an essential part of their role in a complex network of relationships. Only then will they espouse the values of becoming more pro-active, more questioning and will not wait either for external events or instructions from above to trigger change. But to get to that state, considerable resistance must be overcome.

One common source of resistance is that initial enthusiasm may give way to fear. In pyramidal organisations whole layers of middle managers can exist merely to pass on – and often distort – information. They make no decisions of any competitive consequence. In the pre-information age they had a purpose in the control structure, but today they can become an endangered species. An example from one of our research sample shows the way forward. Reflecting on a controversial proposal to cut jobs at a time of business expansion, one chief executive recalled:

> *I set a man on the task of finding out what could be done. His evidence was so overwhelming that now everyone agrees that the cuts were necessary and obvious. Even the workforce agrees, though not the unions. Putting people on such projects releases ideas and adds further information and options. We aim to build consensus by discussion, where parochial feelings are eroded. Even where the functions of several directors were threatened, I heard no cries of 'it can't be done'.*

In other words, he had been careful to co-opt middle management in the process of seeking a solution. But he had done more. He had earlier built a climate in which it was possible for the evidence to be credible and become a force for action. He had set the target but he had not imposed a solution. As he added, 'The solution we finally adopted went far beyond what I had originally in mind.'

Perhaps even more importantly, he had reduced the personal risks to acceptable proportions for all involved. In another company we heard, 'You don't get fired for making mistakes; not learning from them is a sin.' Even when individuals fall by the wayside, the climate of progress can be retained. One chief executive commented, 'My dilemma is that too many of the team have fixed "achievement ceilings". We have to find homes for these people somewhere in the firm, for I do not believe in hire-and-fire.'

Such approaches place a high premium on frank and honest communications. The necessary climate for progress cannot be created when managers obfuscate. All too often, 'managers who are skilled communicators may also be good at covering up real problems'. Defensive routines and perhaps reluctance to risk personal friendships that grew up during earlier, less stressful periods can undermine the drive for progress and continuous change.

Learning organisations have to confront the persistent problem that many middle managers feel their status rests heavily on their power to tell others what to do. This is especially so in large organisations with long traditions of powerful specialist functions, such as engineering. Comfortable in a world of specific plans and actions, managers can find it acutely uncomfortable to ask themselves or their juniors to think through what the goals ought to be. This problem has been tackled head-on in Exxon Chemicals. Though progress has been rated as 'painfully slow', one corporate vice-president stated:

> *We're steadily improving performance. What we have done … is to drop plan reviews at the company level and replace them with strategy discussions. After all, if the top of the organisation isn't thinking in strategic terms, who is? … When objectives and strategies are clear and understood, planning is no problem and the reviews of plans at lower levels assume a different and more positive character.*

Source: Baden-Fuller, C and Stopford, J (1992). Reprinted with permission from International Thomson Publishing Services Limited. Copyright © Charles Baden-Fuller and John Stopford 1992.

SUMMARY

- In the management of strategic change, a distinction needs to be made between the *pace of change*, which can be fast or slow, and *strategic change*, which is the proactive management of change in an organisation. Strategic change is the implementation of new strategies that involve substantive changes beyond the normal routines of the organisation.

- In managing strategic change, it is useful to draw a distinction between prescriptive and emergent approaches. Prescriptive approaches involve the planned action necessary to achieve the changes. The changes may be imposed on those who will implement them. Emergent approaches involve the whole process of developing the strategy, as well as the implementation phase. This approach will also involve consultation and discussion with those who will subsequently be implementing the change.

- Strategic change is concerned with people and their tasks. It is undertaken through the formal and informal structures of the organisation. Understanding the *pressure points* for influencing change is important if such change is to be effective. Strategic change is important because it may involve major disruption and people may resist its consequences. Even where change is readily accepted, the changes will take time and careful thought. Strategic change carries important hidden costs.

- To manage strategic change, it is important to understand what is driving the process. There are numerous classifications of the causes, two of which are explored in this text, those of Tichy and Kanter *et al.*

1 Tichy identifies four main causes of strategic change: environment, business relationships, technology and new entrants to the organisation, especially a new leader.

2 Kanter, Stein and Jick identify three dynamics for strategic change: environment, lifecycle differences across divisions of an organisation and political power changes. Precision regarding the causes of change is important in order to manage the change process effectively.

- There are a number of *prescriptive routes* for the management of change, two of which are examined.

1 Kanter *et al* recommend a three-stage approach involving three *forms* of change and three *categories of people* involved in the change. Essentially, the route is a top-down guide to managing planned change and its consequences throughout the organisation.

2 Lewin developed a three-stage model for the prescriptive change process: unfreezing current attitudes, moving to a new level and refreezing attitudes at the new level. This model has been widely used to analyse and manage change.

- *Prescriptive* models of change work best where it is possible to move clearly from one state to another: in times of rapid change, such clarity may be difficult to find and such models may be inappropriate.

- There are a number of *emergent* approaches to strategic change. The two explored in this chapter concentrate on the longer-term, learning culture routes to change. According to Senge, the learning organisation does not suddenly adopt strategic change but is perpetually seeking it. Therefore, the organisation is using its learning, experimentation and communication to renew itself constantly. Strategic change is a constant process.

● According to Pettigrew and Whipp, their empirical study of strategic change identified five factors in the successful management of the process. These were environmental assessment, leadership of change, the link between strategic and operational change, human resource aspects and coherence in the management of the process. Emergent models of strategic change take a long-term approach and may have limited usefulness when the organisation faces short-term strategic crisis.

● The choice between prescriptive and emergent strategic change processes will depend on the situation at the time: ideally, emergent change should be chosen because it is less disruptive and cheaper. In reality, circumstances may make a prescriptive approach necessary.

● In developing a change programme, the *change options matrix* sets out the main areas where change is possible: it is important to focus and select options from the matrix. This can best be undertaken by an understanding of the culture of the organisation: the *Cultural Web* can be useful here.

● A more detailed process to achieve change can then be planned out, with six overlapping areas as a starting point. Resistance to change is probably one of the chief obstacles to successful strategy implementation. It is likely to be lower if strategies are not imposed from the outside.

● The politics of strategic change first require the persuasion of those involved to adopt the new strategy recommendations. Additionally, a Machiavellian approach may be necessary to ensure the desired changes are achieved. More generally, strategic change activities may include identifying supporters, attempting to change opposition views and building the maximum consensus for the new proposals. Preferably, this should be undertaken prior to any decision meeting.

● Once change has been agreed, it is necessary to move on from any past disputes and pick up the new challenge in a positive fashion. This will happen more easily if the culture and style of the organisation have been well prepared in advance to *welcome* change and not regard it as a threat. Leadership has an important role to play in leading strategic change: vision, communication, trust and self-knowledge are all desirable competences. They also need to be responsive to the current situation and to be creative in finding innovative solutions.

● Cultural differences between countries can make strategic change difficult to implement. There are special difficulties where *team-working* is required because different cultures have different ways of working, different expectations of success and different time scales. The most obvious problem in team-working is a lack of trust. The best solution is for the team to explore this itself and for team members to have the time to resolve their problems. It is also necessary to accept that team members are unlikely to be as confident, or possibly as competent, as they are in their home environments.

QUESTIONS

1 How would you characterise the strategic changes at the four companies in this chapter – fast or slow? How would you describe their strategic management process – as prescriptive or emergent?

2 *'The twin tasks for senior executives are to challenge misconceptions among managers and to foster a working environment which facilitates rather than constrains change.'* Professor Colin Egan. Discuss.

3 Identify the pressure points for influencing strategic change in an organisation with which you are familiar.

4 If strategic change is important, why do some people find it difficult to accept and what are the consequences of this for the change process? How can these difficulties be overcome?

5 *'The sad fact is that, almost universally, organisations change as little as they must, rather than as much as they should.'* Professor Rosabeth Moss Kanter. Why is this and what can be done about it?

6 Given the problems associated with prescriptive change, why is it important and what can be done to ease the process?

7 Does the comment in this chapter that the way forward proposed by some emergent strategists often amounts to the need to start earlier mean that emergent approaches have little useful role?

8 Examining United Biscuits in July 1995 (*see* Case study 21.2), what areas of change were available using the change options matrix? What areas would you select to enact the proposed changes and why?

9 Analyse the politics of an organisation with which you are familiar. If you were seeking significant strategic change in the organisation, how would you approach this?

10 Leadership may be important for strategic change, but is it essential?

STRATEGIC PROJECT

Follow up one or more of the cases of strategic change outlined in this chapter. What has happened since and with what results? Has there been any fundamental change in the management and its style?

FURTHER READING

Bernard Burnes (1996) *Managing Change*, 2nd edn, Pitman Publishing, London, has a most useful broad survey of the areas covered in this chapter.

Professor Charles Handy (1993) *Understanding Organisations*, Penguin, Harmondsworth, is still one of the best available reviews of organisational change.

Kanter, R M, Stein, B and Jick, T (1992) *The Challenge of Organisational Change: how companies experience it and leaders guide it*, Free Press, New York, has some thoughtful guidance on strategic change.

A most useful article is that by Garvin, D (1993) 'Building a Learning Organisation', *Harvard Business Review*, July–Aug, pp78–91.

Professors A Pettigrew and R Whipp (1991) *Managing Change for Competitive Success*, Blackwell, Oxford, has some important strategic evidence and insights.

REFERENCES

1 Adapted from an article by Michael Lindemann (1996) *Financial Times*, 14 Mar, p31. Reprinted with permission.
2 Schein, E H (1990) *Organisational Psychology*, 2nd edn, Prentice Hall, New York.
3 Burnes, B (1996) *Managing Change*, 2nd edn, Pitman Publishing, London. Part 1 of this book presents a useful broad survey of this area.
4 Handy, C (1993) *Understanding Organisations*, Penguin, Harmondsworth, p292 (*see* Chapter 8 for further discussion of Handy and note that his view is emergent rather than prescriptive).
5 Burnes, B (1996) Ibid, p173.
6 Ansoff, I (1987) *Corporate Strategy*, 2nd edn, Penguin, Harmondsworth.
7 Figure based on Tichy, N (1983) *Managing Strategic Change*, John Wiley, New York.
8 Tichy, N (1983) *Managing Strategic Change*, John Wiley, New York, pp18–19.
9 Kanter, R M, Stein, B, Jick, T (1992) *The Challenge of Organizational Change: how companies experience it and leaders guide it*, Free Press, New York.
10 Adapted from an article by Clare Gascoigne (1996) *Financial Times*, 23 Feb, p23.
11 Kanter, R M, Stein, B and Jick, T (1992) Ibid.
12 *Financial Times* (1996) 24 Apr, p1.
13 *Financial Times* (1993) 1 Nov, p19 and 6 Dec, p17.
14 Lewin, K (1952) *Field Theory in Social Science*, Tavistock, London.
15 Burnes, B (1996) Ibid, pp179–86 has a useful summary.
16 References for UB case: *UB press release* dated 3 Feb 1995. *Financial Times*: 22 Nov 1995, p30; 7 Nov 1995, p21; 15 Sep 1995, p18; 19 July 1995, p17; 18 July 1995, p1 and p20; 23 June 1995, p20; 25 Feb 1995, p8; 18 Mar 1994, p21; 16 Feb 1993, p23; 28 Jan 1993, p23.
17 For other writers and a wider review of the research, *see* Burnes, B (1996) Ibid, pp161–3.
18 Senge, P (1990) *The Fifth Discipline: the art and practice of the Learning Organization*, Doubleday, New York.
19 Jones, A and Hendry, C (1994) 'The Learning Organisation', *British Journal of Management*, 5, pp153–62. Egan, C (1995) *Creating Organizational Advantage*, Butterworth-Heinemann, Oxford, pp131–8 also has a useful critical discussion.
20 Egan, C (1995) Ibid, p135.
21 Garvin, D (1993) 'Building a Learning Organization', *Harvard Business Review*, July–Aug, pp78–91.
22 Pettigrew, A and Whipp, R (1991) *Managing Change for Competitive Success*, Blackwell, Oxford.
23 Egan, C (1995) Ibid, p178.
24 *See*, for example, Handy, C (1993) Ibid, Ch 4.
25 Burns, B (1996) Ibid, pp194–5.
26 Pettigrew, A and Whipp, R (1991) Ibid, p237.
27 Whittington, R (1993) *What is strategy and does it matter?*, Routledge, London, p30.
28 Tichy, N (1983) Ibid, pp126, 135 and 131.
29 Beer, M, Eisenhart, R, Spector, B (1990) 'Why change management programs don't produce change', *Harvard Business Review*, Nov–Dec, pp158–66.

30 Machiavelli, N (1961) *The Prince*, Penguin. There is a short article that summarises his work: Crainer, S (1994) *Financial Times*.

31 There are four sources for this table: Machiavelli, N (1961) Ibid; Mintzberg, H (1991) 'Politics and the Political Organisation', Ch 8 in Mintzberg, H and Quinn, J B (1991) *The Strategy Process*, 2nd edn, Prentice Hall; Handy, C (1993) Ibid, Ch 10; and the author's own experience.

32 Bennis, W and Nanus, B (1985) *Strategies for Taking Charge*, Harper Collins, New York.

33 *Sources*: Neale, R and Mindel, R (1992) 'Rigging up multicultural teamworking', *Personnel Management*, Jan, p36; Houle, V (1995) 'Cultural Exchanges', *Financial Times*, 5 Apr, p19. *See also* Trompenaars, F (1995) *Riding the Waves of Culture*, Nicholas Brearley, London.

34 Goffee, R and Jones, G (1995) 'Developing Managers for Europe: a re-examination of cross-cultural differences', *European Management Journal*, Sep, pp245–50.

35 Adapted from an article by John Gapper (1995) *Financial Times*, 8 Nov, p23.

36 Baden-Fuller, C and Stopford, J (1992) *Rejuvenating the Mature Business*, Routledge, London, pp186–8.

CHAPTER **22**

Building a cohesive
corporate strategy

Learning outcomes

When you have worked through this chapter, you will be able to:

- understand how the organisation's various elements can combine together to form the organisation's corporate strategy;

- consider whether there is one standard of excellence for all corporate strategy situations;

- examine the contention that contradictions and tensions assist the corporate strategy process;

- identify the tasks that need to be undertaken to implement the strategy process;

- outline the concept of the strategic staircase;

- evaluate some of the main issues involved in the longer-term task of developing corporate strategy.

INTRODUCTION

Although corporate strategy has been explored as a series of separate elements – such as the analysis of resources and the consideration of options development – it needs also to be considered as a whole. The purpose of this chapter is to bring these elements together under the general considerations associated with the implementation of corporate strategy.

In addition, it is important to recognise that corporate strategy will continue to develop for two reasons. First, the environment itself is changing and presenting new challenges. Second, issues in corporate strategy offer new challenges to researchers about the nature of the topic and its interrelationships. Both these areas need to be addressed in order to explore strategy as it is put into action in organisations around the world. The structure of the chapter is summarised in Fig 22.1.

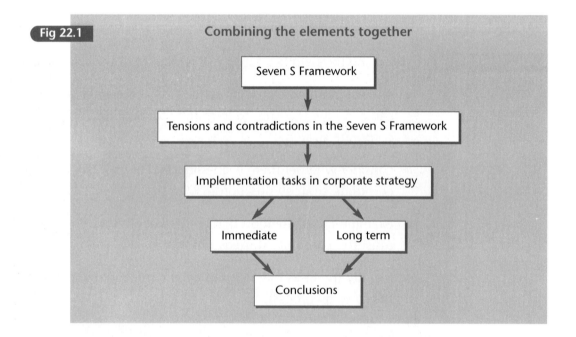

Fig 22.1 Combining the elements together

- Seven S Framework
- Tensions and contradictions in the Seven S Framework
- Implementation tasks in corporate strategy
  - Immediate
  - Long term
- Conclusions

The strategy implications of creating Novartis[1]

In March 1996, two major Swiss companies, Ciba and Sandoz, agreed to merge their worldwide operations under the new company name Novartis. This case study examines some of the strategy implementation issues that have arisen.

With 1995 sales of US$26 billion, Ciba was a medium-sized competitor in the global markets for pharmaceuticals and agricultural chemicals. In the same year, Sandoz had sales of US$18 billion and was more heavily involved in pharmaceutical markets with a range of products that complemented those of Ciba. Together after the merger, the two companies formed the world's second largest drugs company with a market share of 4.4 per cent: only Glaxo Wellcome was larger at 4.7 per cent. Both companies also had non-drug businesses that would need to be divested or merged into the new organisation.

The newly merged company was named Novartis and was to be located, as its two parents had been, in the Swiss city of Basel. However, some 13 000 job losses were expected from a combined workforce of 130 000 over the following two years. These would occur mainly in Basel but also in New Jersey, where both companies had their US headquarters. The restructuring was expected to cost around US$2.5 billion but would save US$2.2 billion annually by 1999.

In their merger, the two companies were following recent trends in the pharmaceutical industry which had seen some global consolidations in the preceding five years – for example, Smith Kline (USA) and Beecham (UK), Glaxo (UK) and Wellcome (UK), Pharmacia (Sweden) and Upjohn (USA). The strategy was to build size in order to spread heavy R&D costs and marketing expenditure across a wider range of products. It was also to counter the increasing negotiating power of distributors and government health bodies. However, some leading industrialists disagreed with this approach and regarded dominance in specific drugs and critical mass as being more important.

Ciba and Sandoz arranged the deal through an exchange of shares and so avoided the need to raise heavy debt to finance the merger. They now faced the problem of making the deal work in human terms. They may both have been Swiss companies with headquarters in the same city but their backgrounds were very different. Sandoz was the faster growing of the two, with a greater production concentration in drugs. Ciba had slower sales growth and had a stronger portfolio in lower-growth chemical products. In the past, the two companies had not been direct competitors but they had been rivals in terms of culture and local civic pride.

In both companies, their leading people faced uncertainty over job losses. Recent merger activity had shown that the best employees were willing to move outside the company rather than face the uncertainty of waiting to see whether they would survive inside. The workers' initial reactions were reported to be resigned to the losses because the industrial logic was clear. Swiss trade unions were asking Novartis to avoid redundancies and begin dialogue on the issue. One official said he hoped that the Ciba rather than the Sandoz personnel policy would be used, because the former was more enlightened.

CASE QUESTIONS

1 *Is personnel the main area to be tackled at this stage?*

2 *How important, if at all, is it to build a new combined corporate culture? What steps might be involved?*

22.1 COMBINING THE ELEMENTS OF CORPORATE STRATEGY: THE 'SEVEN S FRAMEWORK'

22.1.1 Background

Back in the 1970s, the well-known American consultancy company, Boston Consulting Group, was highly successful with its launch of the product portfolio matrix of problem children, cash cows, dogs and stars. One of its chief rivals, McKinsey & Co, charged four of its consultants with the task of finding a rival model to analyse organisations. The result was the *Seven S Framework*. The four consultants were Richard Pascale and Tony Athos (who published the diagram in their book *The Art of Japanese Management)*, and Tom Peters and Bob Waterman (who published the same diagram in their book *In Search of Excellence).*[2]

The purpose of the model was to show the *inter-relationships* between different aspects of corporate strategy. It was developed out of a realisation that the effective corporate strategy was more than merely a group of analytical tools, organisation structures and strategies: this is the disadvantage of the dissecting approach that has been adopted throughout this book. The elements need to be brought together. For example, the way that Novartis is now being combined into one company will involve a large number of elements, all of which are important in themselves but together will forge a totally new company.

22.1.2 The 'Seven S Framework'

The framework has no obvious starting point: *all the elements are equally important.* Moreover, all the elements are interconnected, so that altering one element may well impact on others. Fundamentally, the framework makes the point that effective strategy is more than individual subjects such as strategy development or organisational change – it is the relationship between strategy, structure and systems, coupled with skills, style, staff and superordinate goals.[3]

- *Strategy*. This is the route that the company has chosen to achieve competitive success (*see* Chapters 15 and 16).
- *Structure*. The organisational structure of the company (*see* Chapter 20).
- *Systems*. The procedures that make the organisation work – everything from capital budgeting to customer handling (*see* Chapter 19).
- *Style*. The way the company conducts its business, epitomised especially by those at the top (*see* Chapter 18).
- *Staff*. The pool of people who need to be developed, challenged and encouraged (*see* Chapters 8 and 20).
- *Skills*. Not just the collection of skills that the organisation has but the particular combinations that help it to excel. Core competences was a concept invented after the framework but may at least partially capture the special nature of skills (*see* Chapters 7 and 13).
- *Superordinate goals*. This means goals 'of a higher order' and expresses the values, concepts and vision that senior management brings to the organisation (*see* Chapters 11 and 12).

The Framework is shown in Fig 22.2.

Fig 22.2

The Seven S Framework

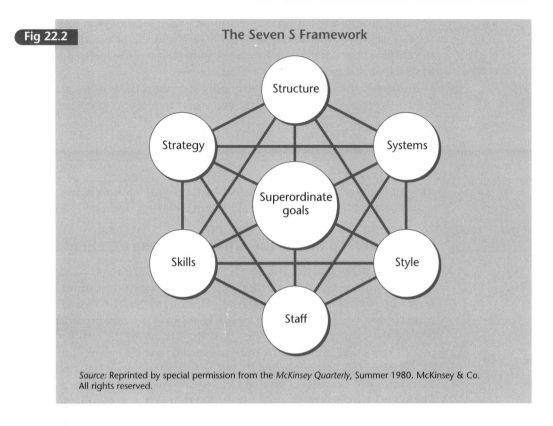

As a minimum, the framework provides a checklist of important variables for evaluation of proposed strategy developments. More fundamentally, it provides a structure for the network of inter-relationships that exist between the various elements, especially when an organisation is ensuring that they are all *coherent* during the strategy process. For example, its application to the Novartis merger would show the many varied links that need to be developed in the new combined organisation.

A particularly useful distinction is drawn by the developers between the *hard* elements in the framework – strategy, structure and systems – and the *soft* elements – style, skills, staff and superordinate goals. The hard elements are more tangible and definite, and so they are often the ones that gain the greater attention even in some books. However, the soft elements are equally important, even if they are less easy to measure, assess and plan. The comments of some Novartis workers on not wishing to wait and see if they had jobs in the new, merged company is a good example of soft issues at work: certainly Novartis fully accepted that the way the company treated its workers was just as important as its merger strategy.

Comment   The framework provides a way of examining the organisation and what contributes to its success. It is good at capturing the importance of the *links between the various elements* and, for this reason, it appears at this point in the text. However, Peters and Waterman used it only as the *starting point* for their search for more detailed interconnections. The framework shows that relationships exist and it provides some limited clues as to what constitutes more effective strategy and implementation.

Beyond this, however, it is not precise: for example, *strategy* is just that and nothing more. Essentially, the framework says little about the *how* and the *why* of inter-relationships. The model is therefore weak in explaining the logic and the methodology in developing the links between the elements.

Moreover, the model does not highlight or emphasise other areas that have subsequently been identified as being important for corporate strategy, such as:

● innovation;

● customer-driven service;

● quality.

At least three of the four originators of the framework were not entirely satisfied with its usefulness and decided to develop it further, addressing its weaknesses.

22.1.3 Is it possible to define the attributes of the excellent organisation?

Two of the developers of the Seven S Framework, Tom Peters and Bob Waterman, used the framework as a starting point for their exploration of the lessons to be learnt from America's best companies. During the late 1970s and early 1980s, they interviewed many senior executives in 43 major US companies on the reasons behind their success. They also tracked the history of the companies for the previous 25 years. The conclusions were presented in their best-selling book *In Search of Excellence* which was published in 1982.[4] Essentially, they attempted to identify the best American practice of strategy in action. Their conclusions are summarised in Exhibit 22.1, although it should be noted that it is not possible to do justice to the enthusiasm and vigour with which the authors made their comments. Exhibit 22.1 also includes three further observations from Peters and Waterman that were not highlighted as separate attributes in their list: they are included here because they are consistent with other conclusions reached throughout this text.

Without doubt, Peters and Waterman took the view that it *was* possible to define the attributes of the excellent organisation. They identified eight attributes that characterised the excellent, innovative companies. 'Most of the attributes are not startling. Some, if not most, are motherhoods.'[5] Not all the eight were present or conspicuous to the same degree in all of the excellent companies, but in every case a preponderance was present. The authors noted that when they presented the material to students who had no business experience, the response was occasionally boredom[6] because students felt that some of the conclusions were self-evident. In such cases, the authors pointed out that their empirical evidence showed that many American companies *did not follow* such 'self-evident' best practice.

Comment   Unfortunately, as Tom Peters himself pointed out in 1992,[8] many of the excellent company described in this book, *In Search of Excellence*, went through major strategic difficulties during the 1980s. For example, the original sample included extensive and enthusiastic endorsement of IBM's strategies: Chapter 1 showed what happened to that company in the 1980s and 1990s. The overall result has been to cast doubt on the evidence and conclusions of the original research. This has not stopped Mr Peters pursuing some of the major conclusions in his later research and writings. He remains one of the major *gurus* of the 1990s (*see* the Key Reading later in this chapter). Essentially, he has focussed even more on empowerment, innovation and the use of local initiatives rather than central direction in strategy.

| Exhibit 22.1 | Qualities of excellent companies: Peters and Waterman |

- *Operate on loose-tight principles.* The best companies were both tightly controlled from the centre and yet, at the same time, encouraged entrepreneurship.

- *Incline towards taking action.* There may be analysis, but there is always a bias towards practical and fast solutions where possible.

- *Close to the customer.* The best companies offered customers quality, reliability and service.

- *Innovative autonomy.* Responsibility is moved to individuals who are encouraged to be as innovative as possible.

- *Simplicity of organisational form.* Organisation structures work better when clear, simple and with well-defined lines of authority and responsibility. Matrix management structures were not to be encouraged because they were too complex. When organisations were organised simply, they were more able to combine quickly into effective teams, task forces and project groups.

- *The importance of the people resource, not just as an abstract concept but as individuals to be respected.* The better companies not only made tough demands on individuals but also treated them as individuals to be trained, developed and given new and interesting challenges.

- *Clarity regarding the organisation's values and mission.* In the best companies, many employees were clear both about the company's values and about *why* such values had been chosen. Better companies made a significant attempt to communicate, debate and seek to inspire all within the organisation.

- *Stick to the knitting.* Organisations may diversify into other related areas but the companies that do best are the ones that concentrate on their core skills. Companies should not move into unrelated areas.

In addition, three other elements of excellent companies can be identified from the Peters and Waterman research that are consistent with other areas of this book:

- *Excellent companies have flexible organisation structures.* This flexibility enables them to respond quickly to changes in the environment.

- *Excellent companies have quite distinctive cultures.* The company culture integrates the organisation's desire to meet its defined mission and objectives with two other important areas: serving customers and providing satisfying work for its employees.

- *Successful strategy emerges through purposeful, but essentially unpredictable, evolution.* Excellent companies are learning organisations that adapt their strategy as the environment changes through experimentation, challenge and permitting failure.

Source: Adapted from Peters, T and Waterman, R (1982).[7] (Copyright 1982 by Thomas J Peters and Robert H Waterman Jr. Reprinted by permission of HarperCollins Publishers.)

One of Peters's original co-developers of the 'Seven S Framework', Richard Pascale,[9] pointed out that, within five years of publication, two-thirds of the 'excellent' companies had slipped from their pinnacle, with some in serious trouble, e.g. Atari Computers and Wang Office Systems. He also criticised the *methodology* of the research:

> *'Simply identifying attributes of success is like identifying attributes of people in excellent health during the age of the bubonic plague ... The true path to insight required a study of both the sick and the healthy.'*

Two issues arise from the above:

- *How reliable are the conclusions of Peters and Waterman?* Pascale is correct: the methodology is flawed. However, the conclusions are not inconsistent with other areas covered in this book. For example, it was Lawrence and Lorsch who first produced empirical evidence of the *loose–tight* principle.[10] The conclusions are largely reliable because, as Peters and Waterman said, the recommendations are 'not startling'. In truth, they support some important areas of strategy development and perhaps over-simplify others. Moreover, their research is being assessed with hindsight. In fairness, it is easier to be wise after the events have taken place.

- *Is it possible to identify universal recipes for excellence?* This is one of the essential questions that we have been exploring throughout this book. Much of strategy development is context-sensitive, resource-sensitive and environment-sensitive. At best, this makes it difficult to derive universal solutions such as *recipes for excellence*; at worst, it is most unlikely.

Importantly, the *excellence* research was widely praised in the 1980s. Part of the reason for its inclusion here is to encourage the reader to review *critically* new evidence and theories in strategy development. A number of corporate strategy texts claim to offer the universal recipe. We examine another in Section 22.1.4.

22.1.4 Are there contradictions and tensions inherent in corporate strategy?

One of Peters' colleagues in the development of the 'Seven S Framework', Richard Pascale, worked independently of the others to produce his own insights in 1990 into the development of corporate strategy, *Managing on the Edge*. He reviewed the main areas of strategy research and development in a similar way to that of Chapter 2 of this book. He concluded that:

> *'A common thread runs through almost all ... organisational theories: each is predicated on seeking or maintaining order. Weber, Taylor and Chandler clearly belong to this school. The same is true of the writings of ... Herbert Simon and the Hawthorne Experiments as reported by ... Mayo. The contingency theorists, such as Lawrence and Lorsch, while acknowledging fluctuations in the environment, propose multiple strategies to retain coherence in the face of environmental uncertainty.'*

Readers will also recall the theory of Pettigrew and Whipp in Chapter 21 that laid great emphasis on *coherence*.

Pascale did not agree that organisations should seek stability. He used the 'Seven S Framework' to explore what he described as the *inherent contradictions* that exist in many aspects of business strategy development. For example, he highlighted the difficulties inherent in operating *planned strategies* at the same time as using *opportunistic strategies* that may arise as events unfold. For example, a new plant is being built to expand capacity when it is discovered that an existing competitor has suddenly gone bankrupt and its plant can be purchased cheaply. He explored each of the 'Seven S' elements in this way and concluded that there were inherent major tensions in each element (*see* Exhibit 22.2). From this argument, he concluded that every organisation had inherent tensions and contradictions that needed to be recognised in the development of corporate strategy, especially where change was the main objective. Strategy must *contend* with these contradictions and not try to reduce them. Thus coherence or the maintenance of order was not always appropriate.

Exhibit 22.2	Tensions and contradictions in the 'Seven S' elements: Pascale	
Strategy	*Planned*	*Opportunistic*
Structure	**Elitist** organisations tend to coalesce into groups which are often based on functions: focus is needed to drive strategy forward	**Pluralist** organisation structures are essential if teamwork and cross-functional activities are to be undertaken
Systems	**Mandatory** systems are used to ensure that meeting formats and reports are always prepared to an agreed standard	**Discretionary** systems are necessary if the organisation is not to be swamped with form-filling that will drive out entrepreneurial initiative
Style	**Managerial** style is essential for the administration necessary to keep the organisation operating smoothly	**Transformational** style is needed for the quantum leaps in performance that are essential for major new initiatives
Staff	**Collegiality** is important in large companies to obtain team spirit and support colleagues, but peer pressures to conform can be strong	**Individualism** is important where new ideas, heretical solutions to existing problems are required. It may be necessary to challenge the existing order
Shared values*	**Hard minds** are needed to deliver the bottom-line profit	**Soft hearts** are needed when issues such as responsibility for the environment, customers and employee rights are under discussion
Skills	**Maximise** skills essentially concentrate work activity on doing better what the organisation already does well	**Metamise** skills are involved when it is important to develop new skills that move competences to a completely new level

Source: Adapted from Pascale, R (1990).[11]

* Note that Pascale used the Peters and Waterman revision.

Pascale then highlighted what he described as 'compelling and surprising' research from Miller and Friesen.[12] They had established from empirical research of 26 companies over a prolonged period that *significant* change occurs in *revolutionary* ways. It does not just evolve and there is no question of 'seeking or maintaining order'. There is a wall of inertia that naturally blocks important new strategic initiatives. Pascale concluded from this that the way to encourage major strategic change was to seek a major disturbance of the existing state in an organisation, i.e. to seek to destabilise it by *managing on the edge*. It takes 'a concerted frontal assault to break through the wall'.[13] He then proceeded to produce his own evidence to support this contention with a study of six major US companies: Ford, General Motors, General Electric, Citicorp, Hewlett-Packard and Honda, US.

Overall, Pascale concluded that strategy must *transcend* these difficulties and create opportunities with a *new vision* that will transform the organisation (*see* Chapter 11). Importantly, the outcome is not entirely predictable. There will always be uncertainties that have to be taken as they come. The management itself will have to change as it enacts its new strategies. It will have to learn, experiment and adapt along the way.

To manage strategic transformation, Pascale suggested that there were four factors that influenced stagnation and renewal in organisations: *fit, split, contend* and *transcend*. All four are summarised in Exhibit 22.3.

Exhibit 22.3　　　**Factors that drive strategic stagnation and renewal (Pascale)**

Fit – *the consistencies, coherence and congruence of the organisation.* Specifically, this is the fit between objectives, strategies and identified elements of change. For example, a strategy of increased customer service will not 'fit' if funds are withdrawn from the customer service department and reward systems are defined simply by short-term profits. This is similar to the concept of *coherence* explored in Chapter 21.

Split – *the variety of techniques that can be employed to develop and sustain the autonomy and diversity of large organisations.* An example would be setting up profit-accountable subsidiaries or profit centres. This concept includes both divisionalisation and the multifunctional task forces to encourage innovation, as described in Chapter 20.

Contend – *the constructive conflict that every organisation needs.* For example, conflict generated between different functional areas needs to be channelled productively, not suppressed. Resolution of such conflicts is an ongoing management task.

Transcend – *given the inevitable complexities of the above three areas, organisations need an approach to management that will cope with the difficulties.* This cannot be achieved by compromise but needs a totally different mindset (or paradigm) that copes with conflict and uses it to move the organisation forward.

Source: Adapted from Pascale, R (1990).[14]

Comment   Having criticised Peters and Waterman for the inadequacy of their research, Pascale then proceeded to base his main conclusions on a sample of six companies that are not representative of the whole of US industry. It is possible that a wider sample would have produced some different evidence on the strategy development process.

To support his concept of underlying conflicts in an organisation, Pascale identifies *tensions* and *contradictions* based on the 'Seven S Framework' (*see* Exhibit 22.2). Some of these clearly make sense such as the contrast between 'planned' and 'opportunistic' strategy. However, others are less easy to accept as being at the root of strategy development. For example, 'elitist versus pluralist' organisations are only part of the characterisation of organisation structures: there are other aspects of organisations such as their political systems that may be far more important in the development of strategy. In a similar way, 'maximise versus metamise' is one aspect of skill development that is useful to explore but it over-emphasises a single factor in the skills continuum. In these circumstances, it is possible that the contending paradoxes that drive Pascale's view of strategy may be overstated.

Pascale argued that a totally new mindset or paradigm is needed to cope with the inevitable complexities and tensions of strategy development. He described this as *transcending* the existing difficulties and opportunities. However, it might be argued that this recipe for transformation is vague and unconvincing in terms of its usefulness. He describes no tests, gives no clear guidance and develops a concept that is difficult to define clearly, let alone manage.

Key strategic principles

- The 'Seven S Framework' can be used to bring the elements of strategy together. Each element is equally important and all need to be considered in the development of corporate strategy: strategy, structure, systems, style, staff, skills, superordinate goals. However, the model does little to explain the logic and the methodology of developing the links between the elements.

- Peters and Waterman used the 'Seven S Framework' as the basis for an empirical study on the attributes of the excellent American companies in the 1980s. They emerged with eight qualities, some of which were very basic and some more demanding. Included among the latter was an emphasis on innovation and on the devolution of power to individuals and groups.

- Pascale also used the 'Seven S Framework' when he investigated apparent tensions and conflicts between the various elements. His research established what he described as four factors that would drive stagnation or renewal in the strategic process: fit, split, contend and transcend.

- *Fit* relates to the coherence of strategy. *Split* describes the need to devolve responsibility in large organisations. More controversially, Pascale concluded that there would always be some tensions and contradictions in strategic development: he called this the *contend* factor. His research also suggested that the strategic challenge was to attempt to manage such difficulties: he called this the *transcend* factor. Some parts of the theory appear to suffer from a lack of operational usefulness.

22.2 IMPLEMENTATION TASKS IN CORPORATE STRATEGY

22.2.1 Immediate tasks

As Chapter 1 pointed out, the separation in prescriptive strategy of analysis, options and choice and implementation is useful but does not really capture much of the strategy work that occupies organisations on an ongoing basis. Even where major upheaval occurs, such as the creation of Novartis, the success of the venture will depend on how it is implemented over a relatively short space of time.

In general terms, *milestones and controls* need to be set up to oversee the implementation policy.

- *Milestones* are used to measure precisely what progress the strategy has made towards a final implementation goal at some intermediate point. These are important because it is only by assessing activity while it is still in progress that useful corrective actions can be taken.

- *Controls* are employed to ensure that financial, human resource and other guidelines are not breached during the implementation process. For example, they might include cash flow, cost expenditures against budget, training programme achievement, plant installation procedures and many other tasks. They differ from milestones in that they are more detailed, ongoing and function specific.

Some further guidelines on short-term implementation are shown in Exhibit 22.4.

Exhibit 22.4 **Some key guidelines on strategy implementation and control**

Problems of successful implementation tend to focus on how well or badly the organisation's reporting proves to be.

Problems arise:

- where implementation cuts across traditional organisational units;
- when information monitoring is poor;
- when an organisation resists change;
- when rewards for performance are geared to past performance rather than future action.

For successful implementation:

- allocate clear responsibility and accountability;
- pursue a limited number of strategies;
- identify the required actions and gain agreement from those who will implement them;
- produce 'milestones' so that it is clear earlier rather than later if implementation is off-course;
- above all, secure the active support of the chief executive.

Implementation using the strategic staircase

If an organisation has clearly identified its objectives over the following few years, then one useful method of considering the implementation process is using the *strategic staircase*.[15] This is the sequential development of the organisation's resources, competences and assets in order to reach a defined strategic objective. Asset development will include not only plant and equipment but also intangible areas, such as brand and service development.

Given that the final objective has been identified, the strategic staircase sequence can be developed by either going up or down the staircase:

● *Going up the staircase* by projecting *forward* from the current situation towards the objective and assessing the number and type of steps needed to reach the objective.

● *Going down the staircase* by projecting *backward* from the future objective to what needs to be undertaken at the start of the process.

Whichever route is chosen, they will both need to coincide in the long run. It is convenient to begin by projecting backward with the objective as the starting point (*see* Fig 22.3).

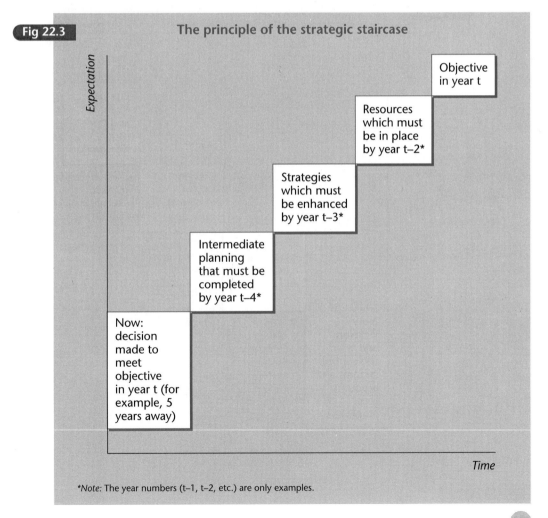

Fig 22.3 **The principle of the strategic staircase**

Expectation

Objective
in year t

Resources
which must
be in place
by year t–2*

Strategies
which must
be enhanced
by year t–3*

Intermediate
planning
that must be
completed
by year t–4*

Now:
decision
made to
meet
objective
in year t (for
example, 5
years away)

Time

Note: The year numbers (t–1, t–2, etc.) are only examples.

As an example of the strategic staircase, the objective of the Novartis merger can be taken as the starting point – *full integration of the two companies in the year 1999*. To achieve this, certain cuts in the number of employees will need to be undertaken during 1997 and 1998. In turn, this implies that certain strategies will need to be enacted in 1996/97 so that they can then be actioned in the following two years. In addition, other implementation activities will also be required. For example:

● quality and price issues as product ranges are merged;

● cost and control issues as the different accounting systems of the two companies are merged;

● organisation issues as those employees remaining accept new or enhanced responsibilities covering products from both Sandoz and Ciba.

If we put these together, the strategic staircase at Novartis might then look something like Fig 22.4.

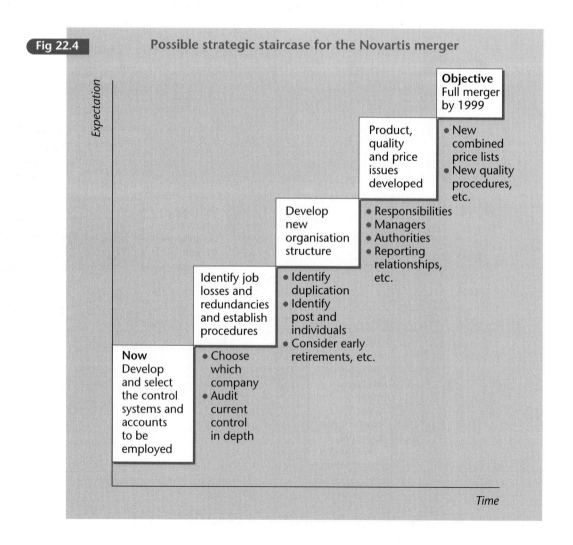

Fig 22.4 **Possible strategic staircase for the Novartis merger**

Thus implementation using the strategic staircase involves four elements:

1 *The final objective.* This must be clearly identified for the process to operate.

2 *Time sequence.* This is the period of time over which the staircase will operate.

3 *The chosen strategies.* These need to be selected.

4 *Trade-offs.* There may need to be some balancing between various elements as the implementation process is planned in detail.

Comment Clearly, the strategic staircase is dependent on knowing the final objective. This was relatively easy for the predictable Novartis merger but may be much more difficult where a new, speculative venture is being undertaken in a fast-moving, turbulent market.

As a first step, the strategic staircase ignores the *softer* issues of consultation, negotiation, power blocks, culture. These could be built into the steps but are not so easy to predict and therefore difficult to include.

The usefulness of the concept relies on its limitations being recognised. However, it does force consideration of deliberate, sequential development and the specific identification of the strategic consequences involved at each stage.

Key strategic principles

- When implementing corporate strategy, it is useful to identify the immediate tasks that need to be undertaken: these will include setting *milestones* to measure the progress along the way and setting up *controls* to ensure that overall guidelines on finance and other resources are not breached as the implementation proceeds.

- *The strategic staircase* is a useful concept for plotting out the implementation process. It is based on the assumption that it is possible and relevant to identify the final objective of a strategy. The steps backwards from this objective to the current time are then specified, including resources, strategies and intermediate plans.

- As a first stage, the strategic staircase ignores such softer strategic issues as negotiation with workers, power blocks and culture. These are more difficult to build in as separate steps because they are less predictable, but they may in practice be crucial to the implementation process.

CASE STUDY 22.1

Long-term purpose at TomTec Imaging Systems[16]

This case study examines a small German company that moved to the USA in order to raise sufficient new finance and be closer to some customers. It raises important strategic questions on the values of the founders in terms of the quality of life compared with the possibility of a major personal upheaval in order to enable the company to grow.

When small businessmen cross the Atlantic, they usually go to set up a local office not transplant a whole company. But TomTec Imaging Systems did just that, shifting its headquarters to the US from Germany to tap new sources of finance and find new markets.

In 1995, TomTec was still small with a turnover of US$21 million. However, it was the world leader in its highly specialised sector of the medical ultrasound technology market. It makes electronic equipment to capture digital images of the heart over a time interval. Its market share is at least 60 per cent across its product range. Its customers include General Electric, Hewlett-Packard and Toshiba as well as hospitals and heart centres. It expected to grow by 35 per cent during 1995 and achieve breakeven by the end of the year.

None of this would have been possible if it had stayed in its homebase near Munich, Germany. TomTec was able to raise the initial finance in Europe but not the bigger sums needed for its next stage of growth. Thus the company had to emigrate, according to its President and founder, Peter Klein, 41. It moved to Boulder, Colorado, USA, in 1993, when it employed only 25 people and had

sales of only US$1.5 million. The company has since raised US$20 million and taken over a US company, Prism Imaging. The larger company now has 145 employees and makes 25 per cent of sales in Asia, 28 per cent in Europe, 5 per cent in South America, with the rest in the USA.

The company had searched in vain for additional finance back in 1993 but had been unable to find it. Peter Klein explained: 'It seems that in Europe you can get money for technological development but when you need money to develop the market, you don't get the money. I think Europe is more technologically development-minded and the US more business development-minded.'

Source: Financial Times, 6 March 1995.

CASE QUESTIONS

1 *Would you be willing to take such a fundamental decision? What about your colleagues and their families?*

2 *What is the purpose of such a business? To make increased wealth? To enjoy a comfortable lifestyle, even if the full potential cannot be obtained?*

22.3 LONGER-TERM STRATEGY ISSUES

22.3.1 Re-examining the future environment

When examining strategy in action, organisations may take the view that it is useful to identify the main trends that are likely to affect them over the next few years. The TomTec Imaging company clearly took such a view in order to justify the risk of moving from Germany to the USA. Among the many issues that organisations might wish to investigate are those outlined in Exhibit 22.5.

| Exhibit 22.5 | Projecting the future strategic environment: some possible issues |

- Globalisation and global competition.

- Increasing ease, speed and low price of communications.

- Privatisation of government holdings and increase in market competition: deregulation.

- Environmental 'green' concerns.

- Mergers and acquisitions, and increasing alliances.

- Technological discontinuities.

- Excess production capacity in some industries, e.g. cars.

- Changing customer expectations: affluence, instant satisfaction, technological games and electronic shopping.

- Downsizing to smaller company units.

- Working from home instead of the office.

Independent research institutes, government and global forecasting bodies are often employed to provide extra input to such activities. In addition, individual hucksterism books have also been written extensively on trends that may provide opportunities – some of them sound and some of them merely hucksterism.

However, one of the most respected management writers, Peter Drucker, cautions against such predictions:

> 'It is not very difficult to predict the future. It is only pointless. Many futurologists have high batting averages – the way they measure themselves and are commonly measured. They do a good job foretelling some things. But what are always far more important are fundamental changes that happened though no one predicted them or could possibly have predicted them.'[17]

He goes on to mention such unpredictable developments as the major growth in the Republic of China and the economic growth in South-East Asia. He might also have mentioned the difficulties of predicting the implications of the information revolution and the collapse of the Eastern European bloc in such a short space of time.

In general, there are real problems with predicting the future, yet there is no denying its importance. It has even been argued that strategy should attempt to shape the future.[18] Some emergent strategists believe the process of prediction to be largely a waste of time (see Chapter 2). Possibly a useful route forward for those who believe in prediction is to adopt the scenario-building approach of companies such as Royal Dutch/Shell (see Chapter 16). However, it will be recalled that part of the reasoning for scenario building was not *prediction* but rather *preparation* for the unpredictable happening.

Re-examining the organisation

As well as examining their environment, organisations will need to reconsider their vision, purpose and mission. Organisations rarely stand still: some grow fast like TomTec. Some grow more slowly such as major multinationals, unless they make a major strategic shift like Novartis. Some decline for a whole variety of reasons. Some are changing beyond all recognition: the case of Hanson at the end of this chapter is an example.

The changes that take place raise fundamental questions about the purpose of the organisation. These were explored in Chapters 11 and 12 but deserve to be raised again here because they are part of the longer-term implementation programme, which becomes the *starting point* for the next round of corporate strategy. The three areas that deserve re-examination are:

- *The purpose of the organisation.* Does it actually matter if we decline? How important is it that we achieve our stated growth targets? The answers to these questions will relate to the values of the organisation and those of its management, employees and shareholders.

- *The culture and style of the organisation.* How do we undertake our work? What style do we wish to adopt? Again, these are fundamental questions that go beyond immediate implementation issues to the underlying philosophy of the business.

- *The values and ethical standards.* What values do we hold? Why? How do we wish to conduct ourselves? How do we measure up to these ideals? As organisations move towards the new millennium, some have questioned previously held views on sustaining the environment, equal treatment for minorities, political affiliations and so on. These are legitimate matters of corporate strategy and deserve to be revisited.

This book has argued in favour of customer-driven quality, innovation and the learning organisation. Such considerations will not necessarily be appropriate for all organisations, but all will need to determine their long-term perspectives, whatever they are.

Charles Handy has argued for a more fundamental re-examination of the organisation.[19] He has pointed out that, in the UK at least, over half the working population is now no longer working inside a large firm that will look after it: they are unemployed, temporarily employed or self-employed. Not everyone will feel comfortable in such an uncertain job environment, although it may apply especially to the UK and USA. Historically high unemployment levels when compared to the last thirty years are now also beginning to emerge in other developed countries such as Germany and France: these will also produce uncertainty.

In a separate development, increased company size will probably need to be accompanied by a need to decentralise. This book has explored the difficulties that arise particularly in a global and international context. Decentralisation can only work if there is increased *trust* among those who are seldom seen. Organisations may therefore need to meet up regularly in large meetings so that all those involved can truly understand what progress is being made, or find some other means of regular and easy communication and feedback.

Handy has also questioned the primacy of the shareholder when the stock market valuation is substantially in excess of the fixed tangible assets:

> 'This is the market's assessment of the intellectual property contained in the heads of the people in the business: their collective core competence, their experience, the brands, the research, the knowledge and expertise. In what sense is it moral, and in what sense is it practical for the people who provide the money to own the people who work in the business?'[20]

The Hanson example in Case study 22.2 also suggests that the relationship between the shareholder and the organisation has fundamentally changed, though not in the way suggested by Handy. Stakeholder relationships are likely to change over the next ten years in ways that will affect every organisation, both large and small.

Fundamental questions, such as those above, are legitimate issues in the exploration of corporate strategy and its impact on individuals and organisations. The role and purpose of both need to be kept constantly under review.

22.3.3 Conclusions on corporate strategy issues

Coupled with changes in the environment and in the organisation, new issues are constantly emerging in corporate strategy itself. The research papers, journals, books and magazines quoted throughout this book will provide guidance on the subjects that are currently under study[21] – the subjects that make corporate strategy dynamic, stimulating, controversial and relevant to our future.

Finally, it should not be forgotton that, in spite of all the corporate strategy attempts to guide and cope with the future, there are always the *unpredictable* elements that are beyond strategic theory, In the words of the German chemical company, Henkel, 'To succeed in business, you need skill, patience, money ... and a bit of luck.'[22]

22.4 CONCLUSION: PRESCRIPTIVE AND EMERGENT STRATEGIES

During the course of this book, both *prescriptive* and *emergent* strategies have been used to explore various strategic issues. In Parts 2 and 3 both were used at different times to develop corporate strategy. In Part 4 the purpose of the organisation had both in common. In Part 5 the process of developing strategy first considered the prescriptive route, but then considered the emergent approach in Chapters 17 and 18. Part 6 has used both approaches, where appropriate.

Some strategists might recommend that corporate strategy concentrates either on competitive advantage or, alternatively, on crafting learning approaches. Both these approaches would miss important aspects of corporate strategy development – there is one corporate strategy process which has two facets. The conclusion of this book is that the development of corporate strategy is better aided by using *both* the prescriptive and emergent approaches, rather than concentrating on either one of them.

Key strategic principles

● Many organisations attempt to re-examine the future environment. However, the most important elements may be difficult to predict. A useful route forward may be to adopt the scenario-building approach. Part of the reasoning for scenario building is not *prediction* but rather *preparation* in the event of the unpredictable happening.

● Organisations rarely stand still: it may also therefore be appropriate to re-examine the vision, purpose and mission of the organisation and also its culture and style. The values and ethical standards also deserve to be re-appraised, along with an examination of stakeholder relationships.

● There will always be an element of chance in corporate strategy. Luck will make a contribution to the development of workable proposals.

● Both prespective and emergent approaches are needed in the develoment of corporate strategy.

CASE STUDY 22.2

A fundamental shift in strategy at Hanson plc[23]

In early 1996, the major Anglo-US company, Hanson plc, announced that it was to demerge its activities into four areas. This case study examines the background and implications of this major change in strategic direction from one of the major growth companies of the last twenty years.

A popular interpretation of the shift in strategy is that Hanson is being forced to pay homage to changing corporate fashion. Conglomeration is out; focus is in; the management looked tired; Hanson was too big. Ergo, the conglomerate should be split into four principal businesses of energy, chemicals, tobacco and building materials, each with managements that will recapture the impetus in a new incarnation.

This makes sense up to a point, although Hanson itself prefers to portray the move as a natural evolution in the process of concentrating on fewer and larger businesses. Yet the prospects for the demerger which has been greeted with a marked lack of enthusiasm by the stock market, need to be seen in a wider perspective.

Development of the Hanson Group
Because of its entrepreneurial origins, Hanson has always been talked of as a highly personalised busi-

ness, in which competitive advantage derived from the deal-making talents of the late Lord White and the operational management capability of Lord Hanson. Yet all successful companies owe some-

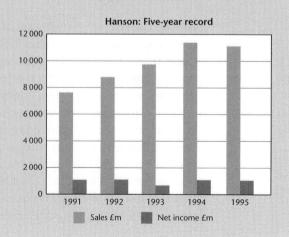

Hanson: Five-year record

thing, consciously or otherwise, to the environment of the time. One important feature of the 1960s, when the two men set about building what was then called Wiles Group, was that share ownership was more widely dispersed among smaller investors. With ownership divorced from control, management had a licence to perform in its own interest rather than that of the shareholders. By espousing the cause of shareholder value, Hanson and White helped provide an answer to this problem. Their aggressive acquisitions, which led to the imposition of tighter financial controls, delivered a much needed service to shareholders. It could also enhance industrial efficiency.

A second striking feature of the period in which Hanson has operated is that it experienced the greatest peacetime inflation in centuries. Against this background, a focus on low investment with short payback periods, a strong desire to minimise risk and a strategy of releasing value from under-utilised assets was a near-perfect survival kit. Friends of Hanson and White who borrowed heavily and took big risks in the 1970s – Jim Slater is an obvious case in point – were wiped out. In contrast, Hanson remained a boring company in low-risk, low-tech industries such as brick-making which generated plenty of cash. It survived.

In the 1980s, when the Thatcher administration provided a benign political climate for a style of management that involved growing redundancies, the Hanson formula produced exceptional returns for shareholders. The best example was the Imperial Group, where £2.4 billion of the original £2.5 billion purchase price was recouped from asset disposals, leaving Hanson with the tobacco business intact. A comparable trick was worked in the US, on SCM, the old Smith Corona typewriter business.

Doubts about Hanson in the 1990s

Even when Hanson did not succeed, as when it accumulated a stake in Imperial Chemical Industries (UK) without proceeding to a bid, it sometimes left a beneficial mark. ICI's subsequent decision to hive off its pharmaceutical businesses as a separate company, Zeneca, allowed the managers of the new company to escape from under the shadow of the older, cyclical chemicals busi-

ness. The battle over the chemical company revealed that Hanson's management style was less disciplined than many had thought.

After its failed interest in ICI, Hanson appeared to lose much of its edge. Acquisitions of Consolidated Goldfields, the mining company, and Beazer, the UK building group, appeared poorly timed. The earnings performance over the years 1992 to 1996, especially its dividend performance, disappointed observers. The share price has lagged dismally over the same period. With a market capitalisation of £10.5 billion before the demerger announcement, it has become increasingly difficult to find suitable acquisitions capable of making a big impact on earnings.

Fundamental changes in investor expectations

There is a more fundamental point about Hanson in the 1990s: it no longer delivers what investors want, because the investors have changed. In the UK and increasingly in the US, institutions such as insurance companies and pension funds dominate the market. Those institutions prefer to make their own decisions about which industries to back, rather than leaving judgements about diversification to industrialists. A conglomerate that continues to sustain exceptional performance, such as General Electric of the US, can still command a premium for management. But there are few such companies, and Hanson certainly is not one of them.

After the demerger announcement, the Hanson share price fell. This might have been taken to imply that the market expected the demerger to destroy some management value in the Hanson group. However, it was more likely that the fall reflected uncertainty over the ultimate outcome: there were fears that the overall tax charge in the demerged group would be higher and the dividends lower.

Criticism of the Hanson demerger strategy

A fundamental reason for questioning whether the demerger will transform the prospect for Hanson's businesses is that its traditional low-investment, short-payback approach looks less helpful in a low-inflation environment. Management gurus such as Gary Hamel argue that after constant re-engineering, delayering and downsizing, too many companies are suffering from corporate anorexia (the slimming disease). In Hamel's view, this is an era for a different kind of rule-breaker – time for more creative groups such as Virgin (UK), IKEA (Sweden) and Body Shop (UK).

From a wider economic perspective, Hanson's cost disciplines are less necessary because increased global competition, which has come increasingly from dynamic Asian economies with a big labour cost advantage, has imposed tougher constraints on the labour market. Moreover, for Hamel and others, the business culture of the Anglo-Saxon countries is still heavily biased towards cost reduction rather than revenue generation as a means of producing profits.

The Hanson response to criticism

Hanson's riposte is that it is changing its strategy. According to director Mr Christopher Collins, the company has moved into an era of higher investment. It believes that there are circumstances where capital investment can be a better way of developing a business than making acquisitions. Over the period 1994 to 1996, payback periods were lengthened although Mr Collins declined to say by how much.

Culture change needed?

But how easy will it be for Hanson companies to change their culture in this way? Another strain of current management thinking argues that the competitive advantage of more investment-intensive businesses comes from relationships of trust between employees, suppliers and customers, permitting a more flexible response to changing conditions. This is a lesson the US has learned from the Japanese. The approach underpins the dramatic turnaround in productivity at many US corporations. Yet such relationships are based on implicit contracts between companies and stakeholders. They stem from a view of the corporation as a social institution rather than the creation of private contract.

This is the very antithesis of the Hanson philosophy of shareholder value. Indeed, Hanson's critics have claimed that its post-acquisition profits are derived partly from breaking implicit contracts, for example, with the workforce over employment tenure and pensions. And if the distinctive capability of Hanson derives historically from a capacity for dealmaking and cost control, the cultural adjustment that will be required for its offspring to shift to a more investment-oriented bias will be huge, regardless of the view of the management theorists.

Hanson's strategic options

If Lord White had lived longer, Lord Hanson might have been tempted to ignore the markets and try to pull off another giant deal. However, it is hard to see what other route Hanson could now explore. Perhaps the most elegant way of combining shareholder value with a culture change would be for the demerged companies to fall victims to takeovers themselves. At 74, with plenty of money in the bank, Lord Hanson might feel a twinge of regret, but he could not, in principle, object.

Source: Financial Times, 3 February 1996.

CASE QUESTIONS

1 *What strategy did Hanson adopt so successfully until the early 1990s? Why did it suit the environment of that period?*

2 *In what way has the environment changed subsequently? To what extent did Hanson use such changes to justify the demerger?*

3 *What were the main doubts expressed about the demerger? How did they relate to a shift in strategic thinking over the last five years? What evidence does the case put forward to show that Hanson has recognised this strategic shift?*

4 *Do you think that the Hanson demerger will be successful? Give reasons for your views.*

Tom Peters: performance artist

The first book by Tom Peters, co-written with Robert Waterman, became the original management blockbuster. *In Search of Excellence* sold 1 million copies on its first printing in 1982 and turned both of its authors into millionaires. Since then Mr Peters has become a fixture on the international lecture circuit, outlasting and outearning such shooting stars as Ronald Reagan and Oliver North. Every year thousands of middle managers gape in awe as Mr Peters, arms flailing, brow sweating, voice hoarse, urges them to nuke hierarchy and thrive on chaos.

Mr Peters's prominence is not an unmixed blessing for his profession. Many people only have to watch him on television or read one of his many newspaper columns (which cover everything from 'power walking' to zen Buddhism) to have their prejudices about management theory redoubled. How can a 51-year-old parade around like that? How can he litter his books with phrases like 'Yikes', 'Wow' and 'Ho Hum'? As if to taunt his critics, his latest book, *The Tom Peters Seminar: Crazy Times call for Crazy Organisations*, has a cover picture of him dressed in his underpants.

There is a lot more to Mr Peters than that. True, he has contradicted himself spectacularly over the past decade; but then the business world has changed spectacularly, too. True, he has a penchant for dashing off fairly flimsy newspaper columns; but he also wrote an admirably obscure doctoral thesis, and churns out heavyweight articles for the *California Management Review* and the like. True, he is willing to rant to get his point over; but he has persuaded more managers to reflect on what they are doing than almost anyone else alive.

In addition, even Mr Peters's detractors have to grant him two talents. The first is an intimate knowledge of corporate life around the world, in Europe and Asia as well as the United States. Having started his career as a consultant with McKinsey, he continues to inveigle his way into hundreds of companies. Mr Peters cannot book into a hotel or park his car without finding an interesting management angle.

The second talent is an unfailing nose for business trends. Mr Peters senses where the corporate world is heading, usually correctly, and then shouts it from the rooftops. He was one of the first people to predict the fashion for 'downsizing', sensing that global competition would force firms to reduce labour costs, and that information technology would allow them to get rid of layers of middle managers. His 800-page tome, *Liberation Management* (1992), may ramble – Mr Peters has not extended his passion for downsizing to his own prose – but it is also a well-illustrated guide to the latest management fads, such as 'the fashionisation of everything' (Sony invents a new variant on the Walkman once every three weeks) and 'necessary disorganisation' (Asea Brown Boveri has subdivided itself into 5000 largely independent profit centres).

Mr Peters has the knack of saying the right thing at the right time. *In Search of Excellence*, which appeared in the week that American unemployment rose to 10 per cent, its highest level since the Depression, appealed to an America worried about declining competitiveness but sick of being told about the Japanese miracle. Sounding the 'morning in America' theme before Ronald Reagan, the book insisted that America had its own models of excellence. Five years later, *Thriving on Chaos* appeared on Black

Monday, as Wall Street fell 20 per cent: it articulated a widespread feeling that, in a world running out of control, businesses needed to reinvent themselves or die.

Add to his nose for the zeitgeist a genius for marketing – the Tom Peters Group churns out seminars, video cassettes and newsletters – and you begin to understand why Mr Peters is a multi-millionaire, with a house in Palo Alto, California, and a 1300-acre farm in Vermont, complete with cattle and llamas. But is he anything more than a shrewd trend-watcher with a talent for self-publicity?

Guru, guru on the wall

Two common criticisms are levelled at Mr Peters. One, which is hard to refute, is that he has often got it wrong: famously, two-thirds of the companies singled out as excellent in 1982 have now fallen from grace. Another is that he contradicts himself as frequently as the average politician. Having started his career genuflecting before big companies, he now preaches that small is beautiful. Having launched the 'excellence movement' with his first book, he opened his third book, *Thriving on Chaos*, with the flat assertion that 'Excellence isn't. There are no excellent companies.'

And yet, given such flagrant self-contradictions, there is a surprising amount of consistency in his work. Everything Mr Peters writes can be read as an extended critique of the ultra-rationalist school of management thinking, invented by Frederick Winslow Taylor (the father of stopwatch management) in the 1900s and embodied in the assembly line. Mr Peters learned to hate the rationalist model in the Pentagon, where he was posted for two years when he was a young naval officer, and at McKinsey, where he worked for eight years. He felt that it put too much emphasis on financial controls, too little on motivating workers or satisfying customers; that it worshipped size for its own sake; and that it rested on a simplistic reading of human nature.

It is as an antidote to all this that Mr Peters's intellectual contribution lies. For the past decade he has enjoyed the rare privilege of preaching from the heart and getting paid handsomely for it. The only thing he needed to do to sell more books was to get more radical. Lately, however, the corporate mood has started to change. Managers are wondering whether it has all gone too far: slimming, it seems, is turning into anorexia, delayering into disorganisation, anti-rationalism into insanity. Mr Peters may soon have to face a wrenching choice, between staying crazy and staying fashionable.

Source: © The Economist, London, 24 September 1994.

QUESTION

Choose one of Tom Peters's books, such as Liberation Management *or* In Search of Excellence, *and critically appraise it. You should take into account that his books are targeted at practising managers rather than students.*

◼ SUMMARY

● The 'Seven S Framework' can be used to bring the elements of strategy together. Each element is equally important and all need to be considered in the development of corporate strategy: strategy, structure, systems, style, staff, skills and superordinate goals. However, the model does little to explain the logic and the methodology of developing the links between the elements.

● Peters and Waterman used the 'Seven S Framework' as the basis for an empirical study on the attributes of the excellent American companies in the 1980s. They emerged with eight qualities, some of which were very basic and some more demanding – the latter including an emphasis on innovation and on the devolution of power to individuals and groups.

● Pascale also used the 'Seven S Framework' when he investigated apparent tensions and conflicts between the various elements. His research established what he described as four factors that would drive stagnation or renewal in the strategic process: fit, split, contend and transcend. *Fit* relates to the coherence of strategy. *Split* describes the need to devolve responsibility in large organisations. More controversially, Pascale concluded that there would always be some tensions and contradictions in strategic development: he called this the *contend* factor. His research also suggested that the strategic challenge was to attempt to manage such difficulties: he called this the *transcend* factor.

● In implementing corporate strategy, it is useful to identify the immediate tasks that need to be undertaken: they will include setting *milestones* to measure the progress along the way and setting up *controls* to ensure that overall guidelines on finance and other resources are not breached as the implementation proceeds.

● The *strategic staircase* is a useful concept for plotting out the implementation process. It is based on the assumption that it is possible and relevant to identify the final *objective* of a strategy. The steps backwards from this objective to the current time are then specified, including resources, strategies and intermediate plans. As a first stage, the strategic staircase ignores such *softer strategic issues* as negotiation with workers, power blocks and culture. These are more difficult to build in as separate steps because they are less predictable, but they may, in practice, be crucial to the implementation process.

● Many organisations attempt to re-examine the future environment, but the most important elements may be difficult to predict. A useful route forward may be to adopt the scenario-building approach. However, part of the reasoning for scenario building is not *prediction* but rather *preparation* in the event of the unpredictable happening.

● Organisations rarely stand still: it may also, therefore, be appropriate to re-examine the vision, purpose and mission of the organisation and also its culture and style. The values and ethical standards also deserve to be reappraised, along with an examination of stakeholder relationships. There will always be an element of chance in corporate strategy. Luck will make a contribution to the development of workable proposals. Finally, it is the conclusion of this book that both prescriptive and emergent approaches should be used in the development of corporate strategy.

QUESTIONS

1 Use the Seven S Framework to analyse the proposed changes at Novartis.

2 Is it possible to have excellent companies against which to compare performance?

3 What is your assessment of Pascale's theory of strategic change? Will there always be tension and is this endemic to change?

4 Examining a strategic decision with which you are familiar, use the strategic staircase to plot out the changes and comment on the usefulness of this concept.

5 This book has highlighted 'customer-driven quality, innovation and the learning mechanism' as being particularly important in the development of corporate strategy. Are there other areas that you would wish to select and, if so, what are they and why would you select them?

STRATEGIC PROJECT

Follow up the performance of the Hanson group since early 1996 and relate the changes that have taken place to those outlined in Case study 22.2 and to changes in strategic thinking. You could also make a useful comparison with other holding companies and their level of strategic success over the last few years. Opinions on the strategic value of such companies have changed markedly. Some of the French, Belgian and North American holding companies have had an indifferent record.

FURTHER READING

It is worth examining Peters, T and Waterman, R (1982) *In Search of Excellence*, Harper Collins, New York. The main argument was reprinted in De Wit, R and Meyer, B (1994) *Strategy: Process, content and context*, West Publishing, Minn, pp176–82. Any of Tom Peters's books is also worth examining. Try Peters, T (1992) *Liberation Management*, Macmillan, London.

Richard Pascale's book (1990) *Managing on the Edge*, Viking Penguin, London, is also worth exploring.

To look into the strategic future, it is certainly worth reading: Hamel, G and Prahalad, C K (1994) 'Strategy as a field of study: why search for new paradigms?', *Strategic Management Journal*, Special Issue, Vol 15, pp5–16. The 'Special Issue' of *Long Range Planning*, Apr 1996, also has a most interesting review of this area.

REFERENCES

1 References for Novartis case: *Financial Times*, 8 Mar 1996, pp1, 17 and 28; 19 Mar 1996, p25; 11 Apr 1996, p18 (Dr Håken Mogren's comments). *See also* Lynch, R (1994) *European Business Strategies*, 2nd edn, Kogan Page, London, pp31–2, for a longer exploration of global strategies in the drugs industry.

2 Handy, C (1993) *Understanding Organisations*, 4th edn, Penguin, Harmondsworth, p187. *See also*: Pascale, R and Athos, A (1982) *The Art of Japanese Management*, Allen Lane, London, and Peters, T and Waterman, R (1982) *In Search of Excellence*, HarperCollins, New York.

3 In the original publication by McKinsey & Co, the central 'S' was for 'Superordinate goals'. This was later changed to 'shared values' by Peters and Waterman which they interpreted as meaning culture when they repeated the diagram in their book *In Search of Excellence*. This appears to have been not just a semantic change but to alter the fundamental meaning of the model. In the original publication, the authors coupled the word 'style' with culture and left 'superordinate goals' to mean the mission and purpose of the organisation. To avoid confusion, the original wording has been adopted in this book. *Original reference*: article reprinted in De Wit, R and Meyer, B (1994) *Strategy: Process, content and context*, West Publishing, Minn, pp176–82. *Revised reference*: Peters, T and Waterman, R (1982) *In Search of Excellence*, HarperCollins, New York, p9.

4 Peters, T and Waterman, R (1982) *In Search of Excellence*, HarperCollins, New York.

5 Peters, T and Waterman, R (1982) Ibid, p16.

6 Peters, T and Waterman, R (1982) Ibid, p17.

7 *Source*: Adapted by the author from Peters, T and Waterman, R (1982) Ibid, pp13–15. The last three areas have been summarised from pp308, 103 and 110 respectively.

8 Peters, T (1992) *Liberation Management*, Macmillan, London.

9 Pascale, R (1990) *Managing on the Edge*, Viking Penguin, London, pp16 and 17.

10 Lawrence, P R and Lorsch, J W (1967) *Organisation and Environment*, Harvard University Press, Mass.

11 Adapted by the author from Pascale, R (1990) Ibid, Ch 3.

12 Miller, D and Friesen, P (1982) 'Structural change and performance: Quantum versus Piecemeal-incremental approaches', *Academy of Management Journal*, pp867–92. Quoted in Pascale, R (1990) Ibid, pp113 and 295.

13 Pascale, R (1990) Ibid, p115.

14 Adapted by the author from Pascale, R (1990) Ibid, p24.

15 Hay, M and Williamson, P (1991) *The Strategy Handbook*, Blackwell, Oxford, p249. The authors give no references for this concept (or for all the others that they describe) and it does not appear to be in any of the other major strategy texts, so it is possibly their invention. It is certainly useful where the objective has been agreed.

16 Adapted by the author from *Financial Times*, 6 Mar 1995, p11. Reproduced with permission.

17 Drucker, P (1995) *Managing in a time of great change*, Butterworth-Heinemann, Oxford, pvii.

18 Whitehill, M (1996) 'Introduction to foresight: Exploring and Creating the Future', *Long Range Planning*, Apr, p146. This edition has a range of articles that tackle this subject from a number of perspectives, including those that believe it is a waste of time.

19 Handy, C (1996) 'The White Stone: six choices', *London Business School Alumni News*, Spring, p17.

20 Handy, C (1996) Ibid, p17.

21 *See*, for example, Hamel, G and Prahalad, C K (1994) 'Strategy as a field of study: why search for new paradigms?', *Strategic Management Journal*, Special Issue, 15, pp5–16. *See also Long Range Planning*, Apr 1996.

22 Henkel, A G, *Annual Report and Accounts: 1987*.

23 Adapted from the article by John Plender (1996) 'Predator that lost its habitat', *Financial Times*, 3 Feb, p8. Reprinted with permission.

GLOSSARY

Added value The difference between the market value of the output and the cost of the inputs to the organisation.

Architecture The network of relationships and contracts both within and around the organisation.

Backward integration The process whereby an organisation acquires the activities of its inputs, e.g. manufacturer into raw material supplier.

Benchmarking The comparison of practice in other organisations in order to identify areas for improvement. Note that the comparison does *not* have to be with another organisation within the same industry, simply one whose practices are better at a particular *aspect* of the task or function.

Branding The additional reassurance provided to the customer by the brand name and reputation beyond the intrinsic value of the assets purchased by the customer.

Breakeven The point at which the total costs of undertaking a new strategy are equal to the total revenue from the strategy.

Bretton Woods Agreement System of largely fixed currency exchange rates between the leading industrialised nations of the world. In operation from 1944 to 1973.

Business ethics *See Ethics*

Business process re-engineering The replacement of people in administrative tasks by technology, often accompanied by delayering and other organisational change.

Capability-based resources Covers the resources across the entire value chain and goes beyond key resources and core competences.

Change options matrix This links the areas of human resource activity with the three main areas of strategic change: work, cultural and political change.

Changeability of the environment The degree to which the environment is likely to change.

Competitive advantage The *significant* advantages that an organisation has over its competitors. Such advantages allow the organisation to add more value than its competitors in the same market.

Competitor profiling Explores one or two leading competitors by analysing their resources, past performance, current products and strategies.

Complete competitive formula The business formula that offers both value for money to customers and competitive advantage against competitors.

Concentration ratio The degree to which value added or turnover is concentrated in the hands of a few firms in an industry. Measures the dominance of firms in an industry.

Contend The constructive conflict that some strategists argue is needed by every organisation.

Content of corporate strategy The main actions of the proposed strategy.

Context of corporate strategy The environment within which the strategy operates and is developed.

Controls Employed to ensure that strategic objectives are achieved and financial, human resource and other guidelines are not breached during the implementation process or the ongoing phase of strategic activity.

Controls The process of monitoring the proposed plans as they are implemented and adjusting for any variances where necessary.

Core competences The distinctive group of skills and technologies that enable an organisation to provide particular benefits to customers and deliver competitive advantage. Together, they form key resources of the organisation that assist it in being distinct from its competitors.

Core resources The important strategic resources of the organisation, usually summarised as architecture, reputation and innovation.

Corporate strategy The pattern of major objectives, purposes or goals and the essential policies or plans for achieving those goals. Note that this is not the only definition.

Cost/benefit analysis Evaluates strategic projects especially in the public sector where an element of unquantified public service beyond commercial profit may be involved. It attempts to quantify the broader social benefits to be derived from particular strategic initiatives.

Cost of capital The cost of the capital employed in an organisation, often measured by the cost of investing outside in a risk-free bond coupled with some element for the extra risks, if any, of investing in the organisation itself. *See also Weighted average cost of capital.*

Cost-plus pricing Sets the price of goods and services primarily by totalling the costs and adding a percentage profit margin. *See also Target pricing.*

Cultural web The factors that can be used to characterise the culture of an organisation. Usually summarised as stories, symbols, power structures, organisational structure, control systems, routines and rituals.

Culture: *See Organisational culture and International culture.* It is important to distinguish between these two quite distinct areas of the subject.

Customer–competitor matrix Links together the extent to which customers have common needs and competitors can gain competitive advantage through areas such as differentiation and economies of scale.

Customer-driven strategy The strategy of an organisation where every function is directed towards customer satisfaction. It goes beyond those functions, such as sales and marketing, that have traditionally had direct contact with the customer.

Customer profiling Describes the main characteristics of the customer and how customers make their purchase decisions.

Cyclicality The periodic rise and fall of a mature market.

Delayering The removal of layers of management and administration in an organisation's structure.

Demerger The split of an organisation into its constituent parts with some parts possibly being sold to outside investors.

Derived demand Demand for goods and services that is derived from the economic performance of the customers. *See also Primary demand.*

Differentiation The development of unique benefits or attributes in a product or service that positions it to appeal especially to a part (segment) of the total market.

Dirigiste policy Describes the policies of a government relying on an approach of centrally-directed government actions to manage the economy. *See also Laissez-faire policy.*

Discontinuity Radical, sudden and largely unpredicted change in the environment.

Discounted cash flow (DCF) The sum of the projected cash flows from a future strategy, after revaluing each individual element of the cash flow in terms of its present worth.

Division A separate part of a multi-product company with profit responsibility for its range of products. Each division usually has a complete range of the main functions such as finance, operations and marketing.

Economies of scale The extra cost savings that occur when higher volume production allows unit costs to be reduced.

Economies of scope The extra cost savings that are available as a result of separate products sharing some facilities.

Emergent change The whole process of developing a strategy whose outcome only emerges as the strategy proceeds. There is no defined list of implementation actions in advance of the strategy emerging. *See also Prescriptive change.*

Emergent corporate strategy A strategy whose final objective is unclear and whose elements are developed during the course of its life, as the strategy proceeds. *See also Prescriptive corporate strategy.*

Empowerment The devolution of power and decision-making responsibility to those lower in the organisation.

Environment Everything and everyone outside the organisation: competitors, customers, government, etc. Note that 'green' environmental issues are only one part of the overall definition. *See also Changeability of the environment and Predictability of the environment.*

Ethics The principles that encompass the standards and conduct that an organisation sets itself in its dealings within the organisation and with its external environment.

Expansion method matrix Explores in a structured way the methods by which the market opportunities associated with strategy options might be achieved.

Experience curve The relationship between the unit costs of a product and the total units *ever produced* of that product, plotted in graphical form. Note that the units are cumulative from the first day of production.

Fit The consistencies, coherence and congruence of the organisation.

Floating and fixed exchange rates Currency exchange rates, such as the rate of exchange between the US$ and the German DM, are said to *float* when market forces determine the rate depending on market demand. They are *fixed* when national governments (or their associated national banks) fix the rates by international agreement and intervene in international markets to hold those rates.

Focus strategy *See Niche marketing.*

Formal organisation structures Those structures formally defined by the organisation in terms of reporting relationships, responsibilities and tasks. *See also Informal organisation structures.*

Forward integration When an organisation acquires the activities of its outputs, e.g. manufacturer into distribution and transport.

Functional organisation structure A structure in which the different functions of the organisation, such as finance and operations, report to the chief executive. Used in organisations with a limited product range.

Game theory Structured methods of bargaining with and between customers, suppliers and others, both inside and outside the organisation.

Gearing ratio The ratio of debt finance to the total shareholders' funds.

General Agreement on Tariffs and Trade (GATT) International agreement designed to encourage and support world trade.

Generic strategies The three basic strategies of cost leadership, differentiation and focus (sometimes called niche) which are open to any business.

Global and national responsiveness matrix This links together the extent of the need for global activity with the need for an organisation to be responsive to national and regional variations. These two areas are not mutually exclusive.

Global product company This will often involve the global integration of manufacturing and one common global brand. There is only *limited* national variation. *See also Transnational product company.*

Growth-share matrix *See Portfolio matrix.*

Holding company organisation structure Used for organisations with very diverse product ranges and share relationships. The headquarters acts only as a banker, with strategy largely decided by the individual companies. Sometimes shortened to *H-Form* structure.

Horizontal integration When an organisation moves to acquire its competitors or make some other form of close association.

Human resource audit An examination of the organisation's people and their skills, backgrounds and relationships with each other.

Human resource-based theories of strategy Emphasise the importance of the people element in strategy development. *See also Emergent strategy, Negotiation-based and Learning-based strategic routes forward.*

Implementation The process by which the organisation's chosen strategies are put into operation.

Informal organisation structures Those structures, often unwritten, that have been developed by the history, culture and individuals in an organisation to facilitate the flow of information and allocate power within the structure. *See also Formal organisation structures.*

Innovation The generation and exploitation of new ideas. The process moves products and services, human and capital resources, markets and production processes beyond their current boundaries and capabilities.

Intended rationality The principle that managers reduce tasks, including implementation, to a series of small steps, even though this may grossly over-simplify the situation and may not be the optimal way to proceed.

International culture Collective programming of the mind that distinguishes one human group from another.

International Monetary Fund (IMF) International body designed to lend funds to countries in international difficulty and to promote trade stability through co-operation and discussion.

Just-in-time System that ensures that stock is delivered from suppliers only when it is required, with none being held in reserve.

Kaizen The process of continuous improvement in production and every aspect of value added (Japanese).

Kanban Control system on the factory floor to keep production moving (Japanese).

Key factors for success Those resources, skills and attributes of the organisations in an industry that are essential to deliver success in the market place. Sometimes called *critical success factors*.

Laissez-faire policy Describes the policies of a government relying on an approach of non-interference and free-market forces to manage the economy of a country. *See also Dirigiste policy.*

Leadership The art or process of influencing people so that they will strive willingly and enthusiastically towards the achievement of the group's mission.

Learning The strategic process of developing strategy by crafting, experimentation and feedback. Note that learning in this context does *not* mean rote or memory learning.

Learning-based strategic route forward Emphasises learning and crafting as aspects of the development of successful corporate strategy. *See also Human resource-based theories of strategy*

Life cycle Plots the evolution of industry annual sales over time. Often divided into distinct phases – introduction, growth, maturity and decline – with specific strategies for each phase.

Logical incrementalism The process of developing a strategy by small, incremental and logical steps. The term was first used by Professor J B Quinn.

Logistics The science of stockholding, delivery and customer service.

Loose-tight principle The concept of the need for tight central control by headquarters, while allowing individuals or operating subsidiaries loose autonomy and initiative within defined managerial limits.

Macroeconomic conditions Economic activity at the general level of the national or international economy.

Market equilibrium The state that allows competitors a viable and stable market share accompanied by adequate profits.

Market options matrix Identifies the product and the market options available to the organisation, including the possibility of withdrawal and movement into unrelated markets.

Market segmentation The identification of specific groups (or segments) of customers who respond to competitive strategies differently from other groups.

Market segmentation The identification of specific parts of a market and the development of different market offerings that will be attractive to those segments.

Mass marketing One product is sold to all types of customer.

Matrix organisation structure Instead of the product-based multi-divisional structure, some organisations have chosen to operate with two overlapping structures. One structure might typically be product-based, with another parallel structure being based on some other element such as geographic region. The two elements form a *matrix* of responsibilities. Strategy needs to be agreed by both parts of the matrix. *See also Multi-divisional structure.*

Milestones Interim indicators of progress during the implementation phase of strategy.

Minimum intervention The principle that managers implementing strategy should only make changes where they are absolutely necessary.

Mission statement Defines the business that the organisation is in or should be in against the values and expectations of the stakeholders.

Multi-divisional organisation structure As the product range of the organisation becomes larger and more diverse, similar parts of the product range are grouped together into divisions, each having its own functional management team. Each division has some degree of profit responsibility and reports to the headquarters, which usually retains a signficant role in the development of business strategy. Sometimes this is shortened to *M-Form* structure. *See also Matrix structure*

Multinational enterprise (MNE) One of the global companies that operate in many countries around the world, for example, Ford, McDonald's and Unilever.

Negative-sum game Actions of each party undermine both themselves and their opponents.

Negotiation-based strategic route forward Has both human resource and game theory elements. Human resource aspects emphasise the importance of negotiating with colleagues in order to establish the optimal strategy. Game theory aspects explore the consequences of the balance of power in the negotiation situation.

Net cash flow Approximately, the sum of pre-tax profits plus depreciation, less the capital to be invested in a strategy.

Niche marketing Concentration on a small market segment with the objective of achieving dominance of that segment.

Objectives or goals State more precisely than a mission statement what is to be achieved and when the results are to be accomplished. They may be quantified.

Oligopoly A market dominated by a small number of firms.

Organisational culture The style and learned ways that govern and shape the organisation's people relationships.

Paradigm The recipe or model that links the elements of a theory together and shows, where possible, the nature of the relationships.

Parenting The special relationships and strategies pursued at the headquarters of a diversified group of companies.

PEST analysis Checklist of the political, economic, socio-cultural and technological aspects of the environment.

Plans or programmes The specific actions that follow from the strategies. Often a step-by-step sequence and timetable.

Portfolio matrix analysis Analyses the range of products possessed by an organisation (its portfolio) against two criteria: relative market share and market growth. It is sometimes called the growth–share matrix.

Predictability of the environment The degree to which changes in the environment can be predicted.

Prescriptive change The implementation actions that result from the selected strategy option. A defined list of actions is identified once the strategy has been chosen. *See also Emergent change.*

Prescriptive corporate strategy A strategy whose objective has been defined in advance and whose main elements have been developed before the strategy commences. *See also Emergent corporate strategy,* where such elements are crafted during the development of the strategy and not defined in advance.

Pressure points for influence The groups or individuals that significantly influence the direction of the organisation, especially in the context of strategic change. Note that they may have no *formal* power or responsibility.

Primary demand Demand from customers for themselves or their families. *See also Derived demand*

Process of corporate strategy How the actions of corporate strategy are linked together or interact with each other as strategy unfolds.

Profit-maximising theories of strategy Emphasise the importance of the market place and the generation of profit. *See also Prescriptive strategy*.

Profitability The ratio of profits from a strategy divided by the capital employed in that strategy. It is important to define clearly the elements in the equation, e.g. whether the profits are calculated before or after tax and before or after interest payments. This is often called the *Return on capital employed,* shortened to ROCE.

Quotas A maximum number placed by a nation state on the goods that can be imported into the country in any one period. The quota is defined for a particular product category.

Reputation The strategic standing of the organisation in the eyes of its customers.

Resource allocation The process of allocating the resources of the organisation selectively between competing strategies according to their merit.

Resource-based theories of strategy Stress the resources of the organisation in strategic development. *See also Prescriptive strategy*

Retained profits The profits that are retained in an organisation rather than distributed to shareholders. These can be used to fund new strategies.

Reward The result of successful strategy, adding value to the organisation and the individual.

ROCE *See Profitability*

Scenario Model of a possible future environment for the organisation, whose strategic implications can then be investigated.

Seven S Framework The seven elements of superordinate goals, strategy, structure, systems, skills, style and staff. In some later versions, the first item was replaced by share values.

Share issues New shares in an organisation can be issued to current or new shareholders to raise finance for new strategy initiatives.

Shareholder value added Takes the concept of cash flow generated from each strategy and applies it more broadly to the whole *Division* (or *SBU*), usually coupled with a calculation of the benefits to shareholders from such a procedure.

Socio-cultural theories of strategy Focus on the social and cultural dimensions of the organisation in developing corporate strategy. *See also Prescriptive strategy*

Split The variety of techniques that can be employed to develop and sustain the autonomy and diversity of large organisations.

Stakeholders The individuals and groups who have an interest in the organisation and, therefore, may wish to influence aspects of its mission, objectives and strategies.

Strategic business unit (SBU) The level of a multi-business unit at which the strategy needs to be developed. The unit has the responsibility for determining the strategy of that unit. Not necessarily the same as a Division of the company: there may be more than one SBU within a Division and SBUs may combine elements from more than one Division.

Strategic change The proactive management of change in organisations in order to achieve clearly-defined strategic objectives. *See also Prescriptive change and Emergent change.*

Strategic fit The matching process between strategy and organisational structure.

Strategic groups Groups of firms within an industry that follow the same strategies or ones that have similar dimensions and which compete closely.

Strategic planning A formal planning system for the development and implementation of the strategies related to the mission and objectives of the organisation. It is no substitute for strategic thinking.

Strategic space The identification of gaps in an industry representing strategic marketing opportunities.

Strategic staircase The link between expectations and time while strategy is implemented. It shows the sequential implementation of the organisation's resources competences and assets in order to reach a defined strategic objective.

Strategies The principles that show how an organisation s major objectives or goals are to be achieved over a defined time period. Usually confined only to the *general logic* for achieving the objectives.

Survival-based theories of strategy Regard the survival of the fittest in the market place as being the prime determinant of corporate strategy. *See also Emergent strategy.*

Sustainable competitive advantage An advantage over competitors that cannot be easily imitated. Such advantages will generate more value than competitors have.

SWOT Analysis An analysis of the strengths and weaknesses present internally in the organisation, coupled with the opportunities and threats that the organisation faces externally.

Synergy The combination of parts of a business such that the sum is worth more than the individual parts – often remembered as '2 + 2 = 5'.

Target pricing Sets the price of goods and services primarily on the basis of the competitive position of the organisation, the profit margin required and, therefore, the target costs that need to be achieved. *See also Cost-plus pricing.*

Targeted marketing *See Market segmentation.*

Tariffs Taxes on imported goods imposed by a nation state. They do not stop imports into the country but make them more expensive.

Taylorism Named after F W Taylor (1856–1915). The division of work into measurable parts, such that new standards of work performance could be defined, coupled with a willingness by management and workers to achieve these.

It fell into disrepute when it was used to exploit workers in the early twentieth century. Taylor always denied that this had been his intention.

Tiger economies Countries of south east Asia exhibiting exceptionally strong economic growth over the last twenty years, including Singapore, Malaysia, Hong Kong, Thailand and Korea.

Trade barriers The barriers set up by governments to protect industries in their own countries.

Trade block Agreement between a group (or block) of countries designed to encourage trade between the countries and keep out other countries.

Transcend Given the inevitable complexities of corporate strategy, some strategists argue that every organisation needs an approach to management that *transcends* these problems and copes with such difficulties.

Transfer price The price for which one part of an organisation will sell its goods to another part in a multi-divisional organisation.

Transnational product company This usually involves some global integration of manufacturing coupled with *significant* national responsiveness to national or regional variations in customer demand. *See also Global product company*

Uncertainty-based theories of strategy Regard prediction of the environment as being of little value and therefore long-term planning as having little value. *See also Emergent strategy*

United Nations Conference on Trade and Development (UNCTAD) A trade body set up to highlight the trading concerns of the developing nations of the world and promote their interests.

Value chain Identifies where the value is added in an organisation and links the process with the main functional parts of the organisation. It is used for developing competitive advantage because such chains tend to be unique to an organisation.

Value system The wider routes in an industry that add value to incoming supplies and outgoing distributors and customers. It links the industry value chain to that of other industries. It is used for developing competitive advantage.

Vertical integration The backward acquisition of raw material suppliers and/or the forward purchase of distributors.

Vision A challenging and imaginative picture of the future role and objectives of an organisation, signficantly going beyond its current environment and competitive position. It is often associated with an outstanding leader of the organisation.

Weighted average cost of capital The combination of the costs of debt and equity capital in proportion to the capital structure of the organisation. *See also Cost of capital*

Zero-sum game Has no pay-off because the gains of one player are negated by the losses of another.

NAME INDEX

This index consists of author references in the text.

Aaker, D 107, 110, 113, 128, 165, 182, 197, 199
Abegglen, J C 58
Abernathy, W 253, 255
Adam, E A 376
Adcock, D 115, 223
Adler, N 64
Adonis, A 11
Alchian, A 593
Alexander, M 477
Andrews, K 8
Ansoff, I 7, 42, 44, 47, 59, 60, 91, 442, 502, 738
Argenti, J 22
Argyris, C 608, 729

Baden-Fuller, C 132, 159, 490, 552, 554, 768
Baker, M 107, 129, 159, 207, 404, 405, 501
Banbury, C 640
Bartlett, C 568, 571
Barwise, P 330, 341, 342
Baxter, A 114, 199
Bayliss, B 330
Beer, M 758
Benjamin, R 418, 419
Bennis, W 393, 763
Berle, A A 428
Boston Consulting Group 47, 110
Boyacigiller, N 64
Boydell, T 608
Bradfield, A 115, 223
Brandenberg, R G 20, 516
Brooke, M Z 336
Brown, A 275, 278, 285
Broyles, J E B 320, 342

Bruce, P 447
Buckley, N 536, 544
Bungay, S 693
Burgoyne, J 608
Burnes, B 737, 738, 746, 750, 754, 772
Buzzell, R 110, 411, 500, 555, 556

Campbell, A 415, 438, 439, 446, 452, 477, 630, 679, 680, 689, 699
Cane, A 590
Cannon, T 428, 452
Carnegy, H 372, 522
Carr, C 330
Chakravarthy, B 47
Chambers, S 383, 411, 413
Chandler, A 59, 74, 274, 275, 587, 625, 626, 627, 629, 632, 636, 638, 647, 707, 708
Christopher, M 371, 438, 439, 440
Citron, R 337
Clausewitz, C von 47
Collins, R 372
Contractor, F J 394, 419
Cox, A 438
Cusumano, M 107, 216, 368
Cyert, R 17, 22, 52, 54, 60, 69, 602, 671

Davidson, H 114, 199, 501
Day, G S 113, 406, 462, 519, 543, 666, 668, 679, 685
De Geus, A 275, 606, 686, 699
Dean, J 328
Dhalla, N K 129
Dickel, K 536
Dixit, A 603
Douglas, S 59, 220

Doz, Y 159, 439, 568, 603
Drucker, P 7, 41, 61, 444, 450, 462, 469, 648, 791
Duncan, J 137
Dunning, J 159

Egan, C 116, 292, 304, 608, 687, 699, 750, 754
Eisenhart, R 758
Ellis, J 159, 535, 543
Ergas, J 408
Evans, P 260, 261, 470

Fayol, H 40, 41
Ford, H 41, 42, 61, 253, 293, 626
Franks, J R 320, 342
Freeman, C 416
Freeman, J 61, 594
Friedman, A 447
Friesen, B 607
Friesen, P 67, 784
Furnham, A 611

Galbraith, J R 463, 624, 638, 642, 646, 647, 679, 680, 691, 718, 721
Gale, B 110, 411, 516, 555, 556
Garvin, D 751, 773
Garvin, J 328
Ghoshal, S 568, 571
Gilbert, X 714
Gilmore, F F 20
Ginter, P 137
Gitman, L J 319
Glautier, M W E 537, 543, 565
Gleick, J 67, 597
Gluck, F 406
Glueck, W 22, 519, 543, 586
Goffee, R 765
Gogel, R 315

Goold, M 477, 630, 680, 689, 693, 696, 699
Gourlay, R 358, 370
Granovetter, M 64, 610
Grant, R M 328
Gray, B 523
Green, D 183
Greiner, L 291, 717
Griffiths, J 358
Grundy, A N 543
Gummeson, E 412

Halborg, A 115, 223
Hall, R C 66
Hamel, G 61, 62, 73, 180, 197, 243, 258, 268, 392, 398, 403, 406, 438, 469, 471, 568, 635, 682, 686, 687, 793, 800
Handy, C 275, 281, 282, 285, 194, 433, 452, 641, 648, 738, 754, 757, 761, 772, 778, 792
Hannon, M T 61, 594
Hardy, L 255
Harland, C 383, 411, 413
Harrison, A 383, 411, 413
Harrison, M 382
Hart, S 640, 649
Hartley, J 359
Harvey-Jones, J 107
Haslam, C 62, 330, 357, 358, 443, 535, 626
Hatvany, N 637
Hay, M 787
Hay, R 543
Hayes, R 341, 342
Hayes, W 328
Henderson, B 66
Hendry, J 492, 608, 750
Henry, J 419
Hill, A 12
Hill, T 351, 353, 362, 363, 368, 370, 382
Hitch, C J 66
Hodgetts, R 159
Hofer, C W 593

Hofstede, G 284, 296, 297
Holberton, S 600
Holl, P 429
Homans, G 433
Hooley, G 438
Houle V 764
Hout, T 186, 568
Hrebiniak, L 670, 699
Hu, Y S 610
Hunger, J D 28, 59, 585, 676, 721

Jackson, T 588
Jacobsen, R 110
Jauch, L R 22, 586
Jick, T 742, 745, 773
Johal, S 357, 358
Johanson, J 603
Johnson, G 52, 281, 431, 559, 629, 706, 717, 732, 758
Johnston, R 383, 411, 413
Jones, A 608
Jones, D 359
Jones, G 765
Joyce, W 670, 699

Kanter, R M 602, 636, 637, 716 et seq, 732, 742, 745, 773
Kawaii, T 406
Kay, J 32, 61, 62, 168, 175, 178, 207, 237, 244, 253, 254, 255, 256, 258, 398, 470, 490, 507, 559
Kazanjian, R K 624, 642, 646, 647, 679, 680, 691, 721
Kehoe, L 522, 567
Kennedy, P 41, 133, 143, 159, 352, 355
Kluckhohn, C 296, 611
Kono, T 535, 585
Koontz, H 432
Kotler, P 174, 498, 548
Kuczmarski, T 501

Larreche, J-C 315
Lawrence, P R 704, 782
Lawriwsky, M L 429

Leadbeater, C 191
Lederer, A L 399
Leemhuis, J P 556
Lenz, R T 589, 686
Levitt, T 59, 114, 196, 199, 219, 379
Lewin, K 746 et seq
Liddell-Hart, B H 47, 175
Lindblom, C E 54
Lindemann, M 600
Lloyd, T 598
Loasby, B 686
Lorange, P 47
Lorenz, C 353
Lorsch, J W 704, 782
Lyles, M 589, 686
Lynch, R 27, 51, 104, 146, 150, 171, 183, 372, 448, 502, 506, 507, 521, 522, 523, 567, 568, 710, 761

Machiavelli, N 760, 761
Majaro, S 438, 440
Mansfield, E 405
March, J 17, 22, 52, 54, 60, 69, 602, 671
Marris, R 64
Marsh, P 330, 341, 342, 368
Marx, K 134
Marx, T 588, 686
Maslow, A H 280
Mason, A 536
Mattson, L-G 603
Mayo, E 52
McCauley, R 321, 337
McDonald, M 438, 440
McDonnel, E 91
McGee, J 179, 180
McKiernan, P 111, 159, 552
Meade, R 297
Means, G C 428
Merrett, A J 328, 330
Mesch, J 137
Miles, R E 289
Millar, V E 398, 419
Miller, D 67, 490, 784
Mills, D 607

Mindel, R 764
Mintzberg, H 9, 17, 22, 23, 47,
    48, 52, 61, 69, 70, 75, 294,
    433, 606, 629, 641, 642
    et seq, 687, 699, 706, 715,
    718, 719, 732, 757, 761
Morris, H 416
Mueller, D 559
Mullins, L 624, 629, 630, 729,
    731, 732
Munchau, W 522

Nakanoto, M 611
Nalebuff, B 603
Nanus, B 393, 763
Neale, R 764
Nelson, R 69
Newman, W 667
Nonaka, I 406
Norman, P 522
Nraryan, V K 120, 395, 419

Ohmae, K 9, 60, 205, 237,
    268, 564
Ohno, T 352, 357
Olie, R 299

Pascale, R 67, 584, 780, 782
    et seq, 800
Pedler, M 608
Peters, T 637, 648, 778 *et seq*,
    780, 800
Pettigrew, A 20, 52, 275, 602,
    670, 671, 692, 751
    et seq, 773
Porter, M E 16, 44, 47, 59, 60,
    74, 101–8, 114, 115, 120,
    125, 128, 144, 159, 168,
    174, 179, 183, 186, 188,
    205, 237, 246, 248, 250,
    253, 268, 274, 398, 406,
    419, 476, 486, 513, 548,
    568
Prahalad, C K 61, 62, 73, 180,
    197, 243, 258, 268, 392,
    403, 406, 439, 469, 471,

568, 638 *et seq*, 682, 686,
    687, 793, 800
Pryce-Jones, D 135
Pucik, V 637
Pugh, D 627, 656

Quinn, J B 8, 17, 36, 69, 75,
    405, 446, 638, 671, 715
Quinn, J J 696
Quinn, S 607

Rappaport, A 535
Reve, T 603
Ridding, J 370
Ries, A 174
Roos, D 359
Rosen, R 118, 120
Ross, C 115, 223
Rowe, A 536, 544
Rudden, E 186, 568
Rugman, A 159
Rumelt, R 59, 132, 181, 519,
    543, 555, 564, 595

Sainsbury, D 260
Schein, E H 737
Schendel, D 59, 593, 595, 625
Schmenner, R 372
Scholes, K 559, 629
Segal-Horn, S 179, 180
Senge, P 52, 70, 434, 607, 629,
    637, 640, 647, 671, 750
Sethi, V 399
Shulman, L 260, 261, 470
Silver, S 501
Simmons, K 174
Simon, H 52, 69, 95
Singh, R 174
Skapinker, M 217
Skinner, W 369
Slack, N 383, 411, 413
Sloan, A 41, 42, 46, 59, 74,
    587, 708
Smallwood, J E 129
Smith, A 47, 59, 134
Smith, R J 566
Snow C C 289

Sommer Luchs, K 679
Spector, B 758
Stacey, R 68, 265, 597
Stalk, G 58, 260, 470
Stein, B 742, 745, 773
Stopford, J 132, 159, 490, 552,
    554, 768
Strebel, P 68, 354, 714
Strickland, A 335, 568, 629, 720
Strodtbeck, F 296, 611
Sun Tzu, 46
Swamiglas, P 376
Sykes, A 328, 330

Takeishi, A 107, 216, 368
Tasker, P 448
Taylor, B 566
Taylor, F W 40, 41, 293,
    352, 795
Teece, D 59
Thomas, K 330
Thompson, A 335, 568,
    629, 720
Tichy, N 739, 742, 757
Tiles, S 519, 543
Tomkins, C 330
Tregoe, B B 419
Trompenaars, F 764
Trout, J 174
Tyson, S 275

Underdown, B 537, 543, 565
UNIDO, 141, 147, 149, 150, 159

Vielba, C A 431
Voss, C A 383

Wagstyl, S 150
Walker, D 419
Waterman, R 648, 778 *et seq*,
    800
Wayne, K 253, 255
Weinrich, H 432
Wensley, R 321, 330, 341, 342
Westley, F 433, 453
Wheelan, T 28, 59, 585,
    676, 721

Whipp, R 20, 275, 602, 670,
    671, 692, 751 *et seq*, 773
Whitehill, M 791
Whitley, R 64
Whitney, D 369, 383
Whittington, R 47, 54, 64, 67,
    276, 330, 404, 429, 433,
    610, 755
Wiersma, F 500
Wigand, R 418, 419
Wild, R 362
Wiles, P J D 47

Wilks, S 60
Williams, D 159, 535, 543
Williams, J 62, 330, 357, 358,
    443, 535, 626
Williams, K 62, 330, 357, 358,
    443, 535, 626
Williamson, O 66, 535, 595,
    602, 625, 627 *et seq*
Williamson, P 787
Wind, Y 59, 220
Winter, S 69
Womack, J 359

Wong, P K 355
Woodward, J 719
Woolf, M 147
World Bank, 27, 43, 135, 144,
    159, 355, 637

Yavitz, B 667
Yeung, S 415, 438, 439, 446
Yuspeh, J 129

Zimmer, S 321, 337

SUBJECT INDEX

acquisitions
    and growth strategy 155
    as means of expansion 504,
      506
    at Hanson 694–6
    evidence on 558
    in packaging 155
    in pharmaceuticals 235
added value: *see* value added
AEG 31, 390
aerospace industry 141, 220–3,
    390, 508–11
Aerospatiale 195, 511
Africa 134, 610
Ahold retailing 173
Air France 665
air travel 665
Airbus 195, 201, 209, 215,
    221, 390
Aldi retailing 173, 175, 239
alliances 497, 504, 506, 592
Allied Domecq 326
Alsthom 650
America: *see* USA
analysis 17, 60
Anglo-American 63
architecture 62, 257, 470
Asea Brown Boveri (ABB)
    238, 650–3
ASEAN 146, 149
Asia 39, 154, 610, 651, 791
Asia-Pacific 43, 63, 64, 117,
    134, 141, 142, 326, 622,
    725, 749
Associated British Foods 56
Auchan retailing 173

Bally shoes 171
barriers to entry 74, 101,
    103, 142
barriers to trade 150, 355

Bass brewing 309
Bata shoes 171
BCG Matrix: *see* product
    portfolio analysis
Belgium 51
Ben & Jerry's ice cream 129, 191
benchmarking 301
Benefon Telephones 117, 488
BMW 33, 500
Boeing 141, 210, 220, 508
branding 208, 209
Brazil 98
breakeven 537
breakfast cereals 38
breakpoints 68
brewing industry 309, 316, 342
British Aerospace 195, 508–11
British Airways (BA) 73, 222, 605
British Petroleum (BP) 71,
    286–8
British Steel 150
British Telecom 11, 171,
    590, 614
Bulgaria 310
Bull Computers 15
bureaucracy 630, 635
    see also planning
Business in the Community
    (BITC) 437
business judgement: *see*
    judgement in strategy
business process re-engineering
    292, 301
buyers
    bargaining power 102, 206
    relationships 107
    see also customers

Cadbury Schweppes 164
Canada 42, 151, 153
Canon 9, 238, 300, 673–5, 692

capability-based resources 260,
    470, 473
capacity utilisation 256
capital asset pricing model
    320–2
capital investment 558
capital structure 324, 326, 628
car market 142, 357, 401, 626,
    633, 725
Carlsberg breweries 309, 327
Carrefour retailing 173
Casa aerospace 195
cash flow 110, 330
Casino retailing 173
CBS Television 73
central heating market 538
centralisation 630, 631, 689,
    705, 719, 781, 782, 792
Cereal Partners 38, 45
Change Options Matrix 757
change: *see* strategic change
chaos theory 67
charities: *see* non-profit
    organisations
China 41, 98, 99, 133, 134,
    150, 310, 354, 622, 791
Ciba pharmaceuticals and
    chemicals 777
CNN 73, 466
Coca-Cola 150, 238
communications 207–12
Companhia Siderurgica
    Nacional 98
comparative advantage 144
competition 59, 64, 74
competition analysis 108–12,
    161 *et seq*, 224
competition
    and company relationship
    223
    and customer matrix 217

competition (*continued*)
  and good competitors 188
  and home market 143
  and key success factors
      237, 238
  and life cycle 127
  and operations 362
  extent of 105
  intensity 169
  international 186
  objectives of 175
  perfect 169
  profiling 109
  reactions to 522
  rivalry 195
  size of 106
  strategies 174–8
competitive advantage 16, 47,
      61, 66, 165–9, 521
  and culture 284
  and customers 206, 217
  and human resources 275
  and industry solutions 554
  and information
      technology 398
  and operations 361
  and resource options 463
  and stability 168
  and technology 394, 416
  importance of 165
  in public services 166
  of nations 144
  prescriptive and
      emergent 166
  purpose of 415
  sources of 166–7
  tests for 168
      see also competition
computer industry 35
concentration ratio 170
content: *see* strategy content
context: *see* strategy context
control systems 778, 786
controls 691–3
      see also financial controls
controls
  and budgeting 684, 693

and implementation 666
and planning 689
and strategic control 397
definition 19
elements of 692
core competences 62, 256–61,
      778, 781
  and architecture 257
  and innovation 257
  and link with vision 259
  and options 471, 472
  and reputation 257
  and resource allocation 681
  and skills 258
  definition 258
  guidelines for 473
  in aerospace industry 509
  limits of 260
Corning glass 400
corporate planning: *see* strategic
      planning
corporate strategy
  and core competences 261
  and objectives 58
      see also strategy
  and operations 351, 381, 367
  and world trade 148–50
  capability resources 261
  conclusions 793
  contradictions 782
  definition 5, 7, 8–10
  importance of 16
  in low-growth markets 156
  information technology 397
  innovation 402
  overcoming problems in 154
  parenting 476
  quality 411
  technology 394–6
  theories 38 *et seq*
  uncertainty 265
  core areas 17–18, 23
corporation 223, 237, 239
cost
  focus strategy 489
  leadership 486, 487, 492
  of finance 320–5

profiles 241
reduction 252–5, 472, 474
structures 182
costs
  and operations 362
  global 187
  low 167, 369
  of competitors 189
Cultural Web 281–2
culture
  organisational 167, 278,
      281, 302, 587
  and change options 757, 798
  and feasibility 521
  and ideas generation 589
  and mission 431
  and strategic change 762
  and structures 706, 777
  elements of 278
  environmental influences 279
  guidelines for analysing 285
  identification of 282
  strategy implications of
      283, 302
  values and style 792
cultures international 29, 63,
      64, 284, 296 *et seq*, 610,
      641, 648, 763–5
currency 137, 391
customer-driven organisation
      197, 792
customer switching 206
customers
  analysis of 114, 193 *et seq*
  and company relationship
      223, 781
  and competitor matrix 217
  and growth 127
  and key factors for success
      237, 238
  and segmentation 115, 204,
      206
  and service 115
  characteristics 199
  communicating with 207,
      208, 209
  demand 195, 196

international 219
types of 200
unmet needs of 197
see also buyers
CWS 56
cyclicality 130, 139, 153

Daimler–Benz 33, 238, 390, 419, 510, 522
Dalgety foods 70–2, 78
Danone foods 78, 309, 410
DASA aerospace 195, 510
Dassault aerospace 510
debt finance: *see* long-term debt *and* short-term debt
DEC computers 15
decentralisation: *see* centralisation
declining markets 553
delayering 292, 795
Delhaize retailing 173
Dell computers 14
demerger 499, 798
designing-in cost reduction 252, 357, 369
Deutsche Bank 390
Deutsche Telekom 10, 172, 590
differentiation 66, 74, 106, 167, 168, 169, 486, 488, 493
differentiation focus strategy 489
dirigiste policy 135, 147
discounted cash flow (DCF) 329, 330, 534, 535
distribution analysis 183–4
distribution
  in ice cream 185
  in pharmaceuticals 234
distribution strength 155
diversification 501, 559, 627
dividend payout 319
divisional structures 627
Dornier aircraft 390

Eastern Europe 43, 117, 134, 150, 651, 791
Eastman Kodak 478

economic analysis 137
economies of scale 28, 41, 148, 154, 178, 186, 252, 626, 777
  benefits of 253
  definition of 253
Electrolux electrical appliances 29–32
emergent strategy 22, 26, 48, 60, 75, 87, 90, 93, 116, 166, 198, 235, 274, 284, 352, 426, 446, 624, 671, 672, 685, 738, 754, 756, 782, 793, 795
  advantages 55
  and managing change 750–6
  concept of 52–4
  difficulties 55
  theories of 65–70
emerging industries 551
empowerment 637, 651, 781
entrants to an industry
  and barriers 74
  and threats 103
  early entrants 128
  strategies for 132
environment 8, 9, 32, 40, 45, 67, 69, 83
  analysis 101
  and culture 279
  and history 636
  and operations 352–6
  and organisation structure 635, 718
  and prescriptive process 587
  and strategic change 742
  and strategy 91
  definition 87
  dynamics of 92, 266
  exploration of 90
  importance of 118
  prediction of 790–1, 795
  stages of 87
environmental influences 90
environmental turbulence 92, 93, 118, 265, 746
Ericsson telecommunications 117, 186

ethics 435–6
European Bank for Reconstruction and Development (EBRD) 134, 147
European Commission 11, 89, 98, 146, 410
European Union 11, 31, 88, 135, 142, 146
evaluation criteria 519–28
  attractiveness to shareholders 522
  business risk 522
  commercial organisations 526
  consistency 519
  feasibility 521
  international variations 523
  non-profit 527
  perspectives 528
  suitability 521
  validity 521
evaluation process 529–37
excellent organisations 780, 795
exchange controls 142
Exchange Rate Mechanism 89
exit from an industry
  strategies for 132
  the expense of 106, 189
exit from paper industry 154
Expansion Method Matrix 503–6
experience curve 254–5
exports 141, 143, 507

feasibility 521, 561–4
Fila sports shoes 354
financial appraisal of strategy 327–30
  and risk 522, 565
  assessment 329
  assumptions 328
  country approaches 330
  general concepts 327
  prediction 328
  ratios 345
financial controls 795

financial objectives 332–4
financial objectives and
    corporate objectives 335
financial planning 689, 694–6
financial resources
    analysis of 307–40
    and appraisal of strategy
        327–33
    constraints 318–20
    cost of capital 323
    cost of equity 320, 322
    cost of funds 320–5
    cost of long-term debt 323
    international issues 337
    optimal capital structure 324
    relationship with corporation
        332, 333–5
    sources of finance 312–15
Five Forces model 101–8, 180
focus strategy 486, 489, 493
Fokker aircraft 390
food industry 78
footwear industry 171
Ford Motor Company 41, 424,
    633, 725–8
forecasting 45, 68, 265
fragmentation of market share
    128, 171, 218
fragmented industries 549
France 51, 60, 89, 792
France Telecom 10, 172, 591
franchising 505, 506
free market 43, 135
functional organisation
    structure 707

game theory 603
gearing 318
GEC (UK) 509, 523, 650
General Agreement on Tariffs
    and Trade (GATT) 28,
    142, 145, 355
Générale des Eaux 240, 244, 259
General Electric (US) 502, 588,
    650, 797
General Mills food products 38
General Motors 41, 73,

632–4, 725
generic strategies 168, 486–94
Germany 41, 51, 98, 99, 792
glass industry 155, 400
Glaxo Wellcome 224, 240,
    244, 259, 501
global institutions 145–6
global organisation structure
    723 et seq
global strategy 40, 43, 59, 64,
    97, 99, 568–71
    and competition 186
    and cost reduction 354
    and customers 219
    and growth 150
    and international trade
        141–3, 146
    and market forces 141–50
    and operations 380, 507
    and politics 146–8
    and stakeholders 447
    in biscuits 749
    in brewing 309
    in cars 424, 634, 725
    in paper and pulp market
        151–5
    in pharmaceuticals 268, 777
    in television 466, 492, 499
    selection 568
    theories of 143–4
government
    and influence on strategy
        143, 144
    and strategy 133–40
    taxes 139
    trade issues 144
Grand Metropolitan 500
grocery retailers 78
growth
    and cyclicality 130–2
    and lifecycle 126–30
    low rates of 156
    markets 123
    in national economies 137
    rate of 125–6
    strategy issues 123–37

through acquisition 155
Guinness 309, 327

Häagen-Dazs 129, 210
Hachette media 460
Hanson group 502, 694–6,
    796–8
headquarters' role 626, 628,
    632, 636
    see also parenting
Heineken 309–11, 312,
    319, 343
Hewlett–Packard 6, 9, 673
Hoesch steel 736
holding companies 707,
    709–10, 796
Honda cars and motorcycles
    33, 186, 584
Hong Kong 135, 298
hospitals 201, 209, 215, 377
human resource audit
    276–8, 781
human resource-based theories
    68–70
human resources
    and competitive advantage
        275
    and international culture
        296–7, 763–5
    and morale 720–2, 768, 777
    and operations 363, 365, 372
    and organisational culture
        278–86
    and strategic change 288–92,
        734–68
    and strategic issues 274–6,
        751–3, 781, 783
    change programme 756, 758
    culture and style 762
    power and politics 293–5,
        760–2
    analysis of 270–302
        see also culture; motivation;
        politics of organisation
Hutchison Mobilfunk 600
Hutchison Whampoa group 600

IBM computers 12–15, 21, 62
ice cream market 128, 163, 180, 185, 187, 191, 203, 238, 491, 682
ICI chemicals 499, 797
Ilva steel 97
Imperial Tobacco 695
implementation 17, 22, 23, 26, 45, 46, 48, 53, 627
  and strategic staircase 787
  and strategy development 670
  guidelines 786
  elements of 666
  types of 667
India 41, 61, 98, 150, 623
Indonesia 310, 354, 623
industry characteristics 74, 101
  and cyclicality 131
  and government 138–9
  and life cycle 126–30
  concentration 170
information technology strategy 397–9
innovation 11, 177, 223, 257, 470, 781
  and corporate strategy 402–8
  and mission 792
  and organisation structure 712, 714–17
  controlled chaos 406
  definition 403
  guidelines for 406
  international 408
  market pull 404
  planning 684–7, 691
  technology push 404
  role of 403
  routes to 405
Intel computer chips 14
intended rationality 670
Interbrew brewing 309, 326, 342
Intermarché retailing 173
International Monetary Fund (IMF) 134, 145
international strategy development

and brewing industry 342
and corporate strategy 148–50
and finance 28
and innovation 408
and operations 372
and organisation 723
and trade theories 144
cost of capital 337
dimensions 28–9
evaluation of 523, 568–71
finance 336
investment appraisal 330
strategic routes to 609–11
Iran 41, 64
Iraq 41
Ireland 12
ISS office cleaning services 375
Italy 99, 298

Japan 42, 58, 61, 63, 99, 135, 222, 298, 355, 623, 723
joint ventures 38, 497, 505, 506, 592
judgement in strategy 20, 589
  and generic industry 548
  and life cycle matrix 459
  by types of industry 550–5
just-in-time 358

Kaizen 358
Kanban 358
Kelloggs breakfast cereals 38
key factors for success 236–40, 603
  and government 138
  and mission 237
  and planning 693
  and value system 249
  definition 100, 268
  examples 100
  importance of 239
  in global TV 467
  in paper industry 152
  in telecommunications 591
Kodak: *see* Eastman Kodak
Komatsu construction

equipment 186
Korea 41, 63, 64, 99, 135, 298, 622
KPN telecommunications and post 591, 592
Kronenburg beer 309
Kvaerner 350
Kwiksave retailing 239

labour markets 148, 280
Lagardère group 460
laissez-faire policy 135, 147
Latin America 142
layout of plant 358, 370
leadership 167, 179, 281, 393, 433, 434, 641
learning-based strategy 70, 606–8, 769
  and change 746, 750, 792
  and leadership 640
  and organisation structure 635, 637
leasing 314
Leclerc 173
life cycle 126–30, 213, 549
loans 313, 316
logistics 371
long-term debt 313, 316, 318
loose-tight principle: *see* centralisation
low-cost production 74
Lufthansa airline 665

macroeconomic analysis 137–8
Maerz beer 309
mail order 51
make-or-buy decision 367
Malaysia 41, 43, 61, 64, 135, 143, 149, 623, 723
manufacturing 368, 369
  see also operations
market analysis 122 *et seq*
market growth and product portfolio 110
market intelligence 174
Market Options Matrix 498–501

market penetration 500
market share
    and competitors 182
    fragmentation 128
    and relative share 110
    evidence on 557
    strength 154
marketing 224, 234, 363, 557
markets
    and global issues 141–51
    and government 133–8
    and organisation structures
        718, 719
    and segmentation 201
    and vision 393
    centrally directed policy 135
    cyclicality 130
    definition 112
    development of 500
    free market policy 135
    growth 125–8
    maturity 132, 156
    pull for innovation 404
    rules of operation 177
        see also market share;
        Market Options Matrix;
        Expansion Method Matrix
Mars confectionery and
    ice cream 129, 163, 183,
    185, 488
Matra aerospace 460
matrix organisation structure
    711, 727
Matsushita 355
maturing industries 552
MBB aerospace 390
McDonald's restaurants 201,
    209, 215, 239, 500
McDonnell Douglas aircraft
    141, 222, 508
MCI telecommunications 11,
    519, 612–14
media companies 481, 460,
    466–8
Merck pharmaceuticals 268
mergers 235, 505, 506, 558, 777

Microsoft computer software
    14, 522
Middle East 43, 65, 117
milestones 786
minimum intervention 670
mission
    and competitive advantage
        415
    and culture 431
    and key factors for success
        237
    and leadership 432
    and organisation structure
        705
    at Rank Xerox 300
    criteria 440
    definition 19, 425
    in non-profit organisations
        437
    selection of 532
    statement and values
        790, 792
    statement at Ford Motors 441
    statement clarity 440, 781
    statement development 426,
        438, 710
Mitsubishi 650
Mitsui 650
mobile telephones 117, 394,
    600, 613
monitoring: see controls
monopolies 169, 171, 175, 591
MorphoSys pharmaceuticals
    338
motivation 721–2, 738, 739,
    742, 744, 745, 747, 750,
    751, 757, 768
motorcycle industry 584
Motorola telecommunications
    equipment 117, 394, 407
multidivisional organisation
    structure 708
multinational companies 147
    and growth 150
    and operations 507
    and parenting 476

Muzak piped music 485

Nabisco foods 749
Nederlandse Spoorwegen:
    Dutch Railways 240,
    244, 259
negotiating 214, 601
negotiation-based strategy
    601–6
Nestlé foods 38, 163, 185, 187,
    238, 410, 682–4, 686, 692
Netherlands, The 51, 60
News International 239,
    466–8, 491, 500, 613
niche strategy 74, 167
        see also segmentation;
        focus strategy
Nigeria 41
Nippon steel 89
Nokia 117, 407, 560
Nolan motorcycle helmets 264
non-profit organisations 28, 166,
    200, 201, 209, 215, 290,
    415, 437, 476, 690, 705
North American Free Trade
    Association 28
Novartis pharmaceuticals and
    chemicals 777, 788

objectives
    and coherence 751, 784–5
    and competitors 175, 182,
        189
    and evaluation 532
    and fast-changing markets
        678
    and key factors for success
        237
    balancing 450, 784
    communicating 679
    corporate 58
    definition 19
    development 45–6, 442–4
    implementation 666,
        676–9, 787

setting 72, 677
strategic and financial 335
Oetker foods 309
oil companies 272, 286, 305
Oki printers 9
Olivetti electronics 15
operations 61, 62
and corporate strategy
351, 380
and environment 352–6
and technology 366–73
and value added 360–3
definition 349
guidelines for 374
in service industries 376–80
see also manufacturing
options 45, 46, 53, 611
and constraints 469
and core competences 472
and value added 463
in special types of
organisation 475
prioritising 461
organisation change:
see strategic change
Organisation for Economic
Co-operation and
Development
(OECD) 97
and centralisation 630–1
organisation structure 182, 717
and age 290, 704
and behavioural aspects 729
and co-ordination 644
and environment 718
and innovation 714–17
and leadership 640
and learning 637
and motivation 721
and politics 293–5
and purpose 705
and size 290, 704
and strategy 624–6, 629,
635, 637, 642–6, 777,
783, 785
basics 717

definition 624, 715
elements of 643
in international companies
722–5, 726
types of 645, 707–12
Otto Versand mail order 48, 49
Owens-Corning 743, 747, 753

Pan Am airline 73
paper and pulp market 124,
151, 158, 239
parenting 476
partnerships 178
payback 534
PepsiCo 72
Perrier water 409
persuasion 207
PEST analysis 94, 522
pharmaceuticals 183, 234, 777
Philippines 41
Philips electronics 72, 239
Pilkington glass 502
PIMS Databank 556–8
Pink Elephant Company 449
planning 19, 60, 587, 589, 666
see also strategic planning
plant capacity 153
Poland 41, 60, 310
politics of nation 97, 98, 133
and industry analysis 138
and macroeconomic
analysis 137
and role of state 134, 136
politics of organisation 293–5
and change 742, 757, 760–2
and implementation 672
portfolio matrices 50
Posco steel 89
prediction 90, 92, 95, 109
prescriptive strategy 22, 24, 75,
87, 90, 108, 166, 198, 235,
274, 284, 352, 425, 624,
685, 737, 754, 756, 782,
793, 795
advantages 47, 48
and change 744–8

and learning 609
and negotiation 605
and survival 596
and uncertainty 599
concept of 44–6
problems with 585–8
solutions 589
theories of 58–65
pricing 127
and indices 137
in pulp and paper 153
strategy 212–17
Prisoner's dilemma 604
privatisation 500
process: see strategy process
product development 235, 501
product portfolio analysis 110–12
and lifecycle 549
and resources 681
and technology 395
profit-maximising theories
59–61
profitability 59, 533
see also return on capital
employed
promotions (advertising) 208–9
PTT Schweiz
telecommunications
services 591, 592
public organisations 27, 109,
166, 200, 201, 209, 215,
290, 415, 690, 705
public relations 208
purpose: see mission

Quaker foods 72
quality 115, 167, 370, 409, 527
and profit 412
and total quality
management 413
strategy 556
quotas 142

Rank Xerox 300–2
Rank Hovis McDougall 56

RCA electronics 74
research and development
    strategy 127, 155, 234, 777
recruitment 291
reputation 62, 257, 470
resource-based options 458–82
    see also human resources;
    financial resources;
    operations
resource-based theories of
    strategy 61–3
resources 8, 19, 32, 40, 73, 182
    adding value 243–5
    allocation of 666, 680–2
    analysis of 232–63
    organisation structures 719
    special circumstances 681
retailers 78, 173, 175
retained profits 312, 316
return on capital employed
    (ROCE) 533
return on investment 189
reward 19, 281, 721
risk
    and financial issues 336, 338
    and resource allocation 681
    evaluation 522, 564–7
    in global TV 496
Rolls-Royce cars 703
Royal Dutch/Shell 140, 239,
    272–4, 510, 686, 791
rules of the market 177, 188
Russia 99

Saes Getters 72–3
Sainsbury retailing 173
sale of assets 315
Sandoz pharmaceuticals and
    chemicals 777
satellite TV 466
Saudi Arabia 41, 64, 509
SCA pulp and paper 154, 332
Scandinavia 60, 117, 151
scenarios 95, 96–9, 566
Schoeller foods 185
segmentation 115, 128, 201–5

selling 208, 209
sensitivity analysis 565
service operations 376–9
service strategy 115, 165,
    178, 379
Seven S Framework 778, 783
share exchange 777
share issues 313, 316
shareholder value added 535
shareholders 319, 522, 793, 797
    see also stakeholders
Sharp electronics 407
Shell: see Royal Dutch/Shell
short-term debt 314, 316
Siemens 523, 650
simulation modelling 566
Singapore 14, 41, 43, 61, 135,
    141, 143, 149, 623
SKF engineering 364–6, 383
skills 778, 783
    see also human resources
Sloan, Alfred 41, 42, 74
small business
    and communications 209
    and competition 109, 165,
    200, 201
    and competitive advantage
    415
    and implementation 669
    and organisation 290, 705,
    707
    and planning 691
    and pricing 215
    and resources 475
    objectives of 445, 679
SmithKline Beecham
    pharmaceuticals 268
socio-cultural theories of
    strategy 63–5
Sony electronics 67, 72, 74,
    355, 622–4
South Africa 39, 41, 140
Spain 713
Spillers foods 49–50, 56–7,
    70–2

sponsorship 208, 209
Sprint telecommunications
    services 10, 592
St Gobain 502
staff 778, 783
    see also human resources
stakeholder evaluation 567
stakeholders 10, 207, 208, 325,
    334, 427–30
    and co-operatives 447
    international 447
steel industry 88–9, 97–9, 106
Stella Artois lager 326
STET telecommunications
    services 172
stock control 364
Stora paper and packaging
    124, 132, 152, 212
strategic business units (SBUs)
    445, 628, 682
strategic change 276, 284,
    289–91
    and multicultural teams
    763–5
    and politics 760
    concepts of 737
    emergent 750–6
    in British Petroleum 286
    in merchant banking 766–8
    managing the process 638,
    734–8
    prescriptive 744–8
    pressure points for 738, 739
    programme 756
    resistance to 739, 759
    time costs of 740
strategic decisions 10, 611
strategic fit 646
strategic groups 108, 179–80
strategic planning 50, 60, 61,
    683, 699
    and bureaucracy 696
    approaches 684–6
    in small companies 691
    reasons for failure 688
    status of 686–7

styles of 688–90
strategic staircase 787–9
strategy
    analysis of 24
    and bureaucracy 630
    and chaotic systems 68
    and communications 210
    and competition 74, 127
    and culture 284, 302, 611
    and customer types 218
    and financial objectives 335
    and implementation 670
    and innovation 177
    and operations 380
    and organisation 624–6,
        629, 635, 637, 642–6
    and role of HQ 627, 628
    and warfare 174
    attack 176–7
    content 21
    context 21
    core areas 17, 23
    customer-driven 197, 198
    definition of 19, 33, 74
    generic strategies 486
    historical foundations 39–44
    issues 392–6
    process 21
    relationship of elements 778
        see also competition;
        corporate strategy;
        emergent strategy;
        prescriptive strategy;
        and strategic change
stuck-in-the-middle 490
style of organisation 167, 648,
    690, 698, 778, 783, 792
substitutes 105
suitability 521
Sun Microsystems computers 14
superordinate goals: see vision
supplier relationships 358, 368
suppliers 107, 201
    and cost reduction 252
survival-based theories of
    strategy 65–7, 595, 596

Swatch 547
SWOT analysis 262, 263, 521
synergy 167, 502, 679, 680
systems 778, 783

Taiwan 14, 141, 622
tariffs 142
tax 337
team-working 763–5
technology strategy 167, 177
    and change 738, 742, 757
    and competitive
        advantage 394
    and corporate strategy 416
    and culture 281
    and innovation 404
    and new technologies 396,
        401
    and operations 352,
        366–73, 380
    and organisation structure
        706, 719
    development 395–8
    discontinuities 353
Telecom Italia 12, 591
telecommunications 11, 12,
    171, 590–3, 612, 614, 617
TeleDanmark 592
Telefonica de Espagna 172, 591
Telenor 592
Telepizza fast food 712
Televerket 591
Tesco retailing 173
Thailand 135, 355
tiger economies 135, 149, 355
TomTec imaging 790
total quality management
    (TQM) 411–13
Toyota cars 73, 238, 357–60,
    500, 633, 725
trade blocks 146
transport industry 199
turbulence of environment: see
    environment
Turkey 98
TV companies 466–8, 481

UK 99, 610, 748, 792, 797
uncertainty-based theories of
    strategy 67–8, 597–9
Unilever 129, 163, 185, 201,
    209, 215
Unisource telecommunications
    592
United Airlines 222
United Biscuits 72, 78,
    748–9, 755
United Nations Commission on
    Trade and Development
    (UNCTAD) 145
UPM/Kymmene paper and
    pulp 125, 149
USA 31, 40, 42, 58, 60, 99,
    135, 142, 151, 411, 500,
    610, 612, 624, 626, 633,
    725, 749, 792, 796
Usinor–Sacilor steel 88–9, 95,
    97, 102–4, 239

validity 521
value added 9, 11 16, 141, 155
    and operations 360–3
    and resource analysis 243
    and resource options 463
    and uncertainty 265
    evaluation 243, 245, 533
    strategic implications 245
value chain
    and operations 360, 361, 378
    and organisation 636, 638
    and resources 681
    definition 246–8
    linkages 250–1, 680
value system 249–51
values 790, 792
        see also mission
vertical integration 167, 495
Viag engineering 592
Vickers engineering 703
Vietnam 310, 623
vision 179, 391, 392, 792
    and change 758, 784
    and core competences
        259, 393

vision (*continued*)
   and finance 331
   and link with market
     opportunities 393
   and superordinate goals
     778
   criteria for 393

wage levels 139

Warburg merchant bank
   766–8
warfare strategies 174–8
watch and clock industry
   547, 579
weighted average cost of capital
   (WACC) 323
Westinghouse engineering
   650

Whitbread brewing and
   catering 309
World Bank 144, 145
world trade 148

Xerox 300, 673

Zantac 501
Zeneca 797